Essentials of
Life-Span Development

FIFTH EDITION

John W. Santrock

University of Texas at Dallas

McGraw Hill Education

ESSENTIALS OF LIFE-SPAN DEVELOPMENT, FIFTH EDITION

Published by McGraw-Hill Education, 2 Penn Plaza, New York, NY 10121. Copyright © 2018 by McGraw-Hill Education. All rights reserved. Printed in the United States of America. Previous editions © 2016, 2014, and 2012. No part of this publication may be reproduced or distributed in any form or by any means, or stored in a database or retrieval system, without the prior written consent of McGraw-Hill Education, including, but not limited to, in any network or other electronic storage or transmission, or broadcast for distance learning.

Some ancillaries, including electronic and print components, may not be available to customers outside the United States.

This book is printed on acid-free paper.

1 2 3 4 5 6 7 8 9 LMN 21 20 19 18 17

ISBN 978-1-259-70879-4
MHID 1-259-70879-9

Chief Product Officer, SVP Products & Markets: *G. Scott Virkler*
Vice President, General Manager, Products & Markets: *Michael Ryan*
Managing Director: *William R. Glass*
Executive Director: *Krista Bettino*
Brand Manager: *Ryan Treat*
Lead Product Developer: *Dawn Groundwater*
Product Developer: *Vicki Malinee, Van Brien & Associates*
Senior Marketing Manager: *Ann Helgerson*
Market Development Manager: *Sheryl Adams*
Digital Product Developer: *Betty Chen*
Digital Product Analyst: *Neil Kahn*
Editorial Coordinator: *Carly Britton*
Director, Content Design & Delivery: *Terri Schiesl*
Program Manager: *Debra Hash*
Content Project Managers: *Sheila Frank (Core), Jodi Banowetz (Assessment)*
Buyer: *Sandy Ludovissy*
Design: *Matt Backhaus*
Content Licensing Specialists: *Carrie Burger (Image), Lori Slattery (Text)*
Cover Image: *© Peopleimages/Getty Images (baby girl); ulkas/Getty Images Plus (little girl and dandelion); Todor Tsvetkov/Getty Images (friends texting); Sam Edwards/Getty Images (smiling senior couple); PeopleImages.com/Getty Images (little girl and umbrella); Jon Ragel/Getty Images (sisters taking a selfie); Georgijevic/Getty Images (young man listening to music); Geber86/Getty Images (father and son); wundervisuals/Getty Images (boy eating popsicle); Lisa Gagne/Getty Images (Group of senior friends singing)*
Compositor: *Aptara®, Inc.*
Printer: *LSC Communications*

All credits appearing on page are considered to be an extension of the copyright page.

Library of Congress Cataloging-in-Publication Data

Santrock, John W., author.
  Essentials of life-span development / John W. Santrock, University of
Texas at Dallas.
Fifth Edition. | New York : McGraw-Hill Education, 2018. |
  Revised edition of the author's Essentials of life-span development, [2016]
LCCN 2016038147 | ISBN 9781259708794 (alk. paper) | ISBN
  1259708799 (alk. paper)
LCSH: Developmental psychology.
LCC BF713 .S256 2016b | DDC 155—dc23 LC record available at https://lccn.loc.gov/2016038147

The Internet addresses listed in the text were accurate at the time of publication. The inclusion of a website does not indicate an endorsement by the authors or McGraw-Hill Education, and McGraw-Hill Education does not guarantee the accuracy of the information presented at these sites.

Brief Contents

McGraw-Hill Education Psychology's APA Documentation Style Guide

© Image Source/Getty Images RF

© Stockbyte/Veer RF

© Blue Moon Stock/PunchStock RF

© Image Source/Getty Images RF

Contents

© Stockbyte/Getty Images RF

© Randy Faris/Getty Images RF

© Creatas/PunchStock RF

© Peeter Viisimaa/Getty RF

© Corbis RF

How Would You?

About the Author

John W. Santrock

John Santrock received his Ph.D. from the University of Minnesota in 1973. He taught at the University of Charleston and the University of Georgia before joining the Program in Psychology and Human Development at the University of Texas at Dallas, where he currently teaches a number of undergraduate courses and recently was given the University's Effective Teaching Award. In 2010, he created the UT-Dallas Santrock undergraduate scholarship, an annual award that is given to outstanding undergraduate students majoring in developmental psychology to enable them to attend research conventions.

John has been a member of the editorial boards of *Child Development* and *Developmental Psychology*. His research on the multiple factors involved in how divorce affects children's development is widely cited and used in expert witness testimony to promote flexibility and alternative considerations in custody disputes.

John also has authored these exceptional McGraw-Hill texts: *Children* (13th edition), *Adolescence* (16th edition), *Life-Span Development* (16th edition), *A Topical Approach to Life-Span Development* (8th edition), and *Educational Psychology* (6th edition).

John Santrock (back row middle) with the 2015 recipients of the Santrock Travel Scholarship Award in developmental psychology. Created by Dr. Santrock, this annual award provides undergraduate students with the opportunity to attend a professional meeting. A number of the students shown here attended the Society for Research in Child Development conference.
© Jessica Serna

For many years, John was involved in tennis as a player, teaching professional, and coach of professional tennis players. At the University of Miami (FL), the tennis team on which he played still holds the NCAA Division I record for most consecutive wins (137) in any sport. His wife, Mary Jo, has a master's degree in special education and has worked as a teacher and a realtor. He has two daughters, Tracy and Jennifer, who are both realtors. Tracy has run the Boston and New York marathons. Jennifer is a former professional tennis player and NCAA tennis player of the year. John has one granddaughter, Jordan, age 25, who works at Ernst & Young accounting firm, and two grandsons, Alex, age 12, and Luke, age 10. In the last two decades, John also has spent time painting expressionist art.

Dedication:

With special appreciation to my wife, Mary Jo.

Connecting *research* and *results*

As a master teacher, John Santrock connects current research and real-world applications. Through an integrated, personalized digital learning program, students gain the insight they need to study smarter and improve performance.

McGraw-Hill Education Connect is a digital assignment and assessment platform that strengthens the link between faculty, students, and course work, helping everyone accomplish more in less time. Connect Psychology includes assignable and assessable videos, quizzes, exercises, and interactivities, all associated with learning objectives. Interactive assignments and videos allow students to experience and apply their understanding of psychology to the world with fun and stimulating activities.

Learn, Apply, Reflect

At the higher end of Bloom's taxonomy (analyze, evaluate, create), students can learn, apply, and reflect through McGraw-Hill Education's *Quest: Psychology* now available for lifespan development, which takes them on an engaging journey through the lifespan where they are in the center of the action. Using a game-like learning environment based on real-life situations and points of view, including those of guidance counselors, health-care professionals, and parents, students collect clues and make decisions to see how their choices affect outcomes. The purpose-driven approach not only helps students build their critical thinking skills using core concepts and related research, but also answers the age-old question of "why does this matter for me?" These modules are assignable and assessable within Connect Psychology, to track student performance.

Real People, Real World, Real Life

Also at the higher end of Bloom's taxonomy, the McGraw-Hill Education Milestones video series is an observational tool that allows students to experience life as it unfolds, from infancy to late adulthood. This ground-breaking, longitudinal video series tracks the development of real children as they progress through the early stages of physical, social, and emotional development in their first few weeks, months, and years of life. Assignable and assessable within Connect Psychology, Milestones also includes interviews with adolescents and adults to reflect development throughout the entire lifespan.

Inform and Engage on Psychological Concepts

At the lower end of Bloom's taxonomy, students are introduced to Concept Clips—the dynamic, colorful graphics and stimulating animations that break down some of psychology's most difficult concepts in a step-by-step manner, engaging students and aiding in retention. They are assignable and assessable in Connect or can be used as a jumping-off point in class. Now with audio narration, the Fifth Edition also includes new Concept Clips on topics such as object permanence and conservation, as well as theories and theorists like Bandura's social cognitive theory, Vygotsky's sociocultural theory, Buss's evolutionary theory, and Kuhl's language development theory.

Better Data, Smarter Revision, Improved Results

Students helped inform the revision strategy of *Essentials of Life-Span Development.*

McGraw-Hill Education's Smartbook is the first and only adaptive reading and learning experience! SmartBook helps students distinguish

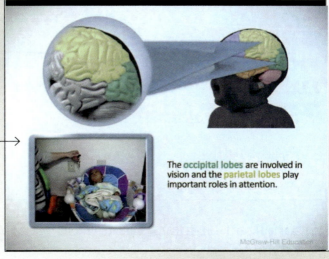
Developing Brain: Infant

Developing Brain: Infant

The occipital lobes are involved in vision and the parietal lobes play important roles in attention.

McGraw-Hill Education

SMARTBOOK®

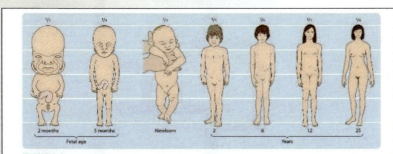

FIGURE 3.1

CHANGES IN PROPORTIONS OF THE HUMAN BODY DURING GROWTH. As individuals develop from infancy through adulthood, one of the most noticeable physical changes is that the head becomes smaller in relation to the rest of the body. The fractions listed refer to head size as a proportion of total body length at different ages.

Infancy The average North American newborn is 20 inches long and weighs 7½ pounds. Ninety-five percent of full-term newborns are 18 to 22 inches long and weigh between 5½ and 10 pounds.

In the first several days of life, most newborns lose 5 to 7 percent of their body weight. Once infants adjust to sucking, swallowing, and digesting, they grow rapidly, gaining an average of 5 to 6 ounces per week during the first month. Typically they have doubled their birth weight by the age of 4 months and have nearly tripled it by their first birthday. Infants grow about ¾ inch per month during the first year, increasing their birth length by about 40 percent by their first birthday.

Infants' rate of growth slows considerably in the second year of life (Burns & others, 2013). By 2 years of age, infants weigh approximately 26 to 32 pounds, having gained a quarter to half a pound per month during the second year; at age 2 they have reached about one fifth of their adult weight. The average 2-year-old is 32 to 35 inches tall, which is nearly one-half of adult height.

Early Childhood As the preschool child grows older, the percentage of increase in height and weight decreases with each additional year (Leifer, 2011). Girls are only slightly smaller and lighter than boys during these years. Both boys and girls slim down as the trunks of their bodies lengthen. Although their heads are still somewhat large for their bodies, by the end of the preschool years most children have lost their top-heavy look. Body fat also shows a slow, steady decline during the preschool years. Girls have more fatty tissue than boys; boys have more muscle tissue (McMahon & Stryjewski, 2012).

Growth patterns vary individually (Wilson & Hockenberry, 2012). Think back to your preschool years. This was probably the first time you noticed that some children were taller than you, some shorter; some were fatter, some thinner; some were stronger, some weaker. Much of the variation is due to heredity, but environmental experiences are also involved. A review of the height and weight of children around the world concluded that two important contributors to height differences are ethnic origin and nutrition (Meredith, 1978).

Why are some children unusually short? The culprits for unusual shortness include prenatal problems, growth hormone deficiency, a physical problem that develops in childhood, maternal smoking during pregnancy, or an emotional difficulty (Wit, Kiess, & Mullis, 2011).

Middle and Late Childhood The period of middle and late childhood involves slow, consistent growth. This is a period of calm before the rapid growth spurt of adolescence.

The bodies of 5-year-olds and 2-year-olds are different from one another. The 5-year-old not only is taller and heavier, but also has a longer trunk and legs than the 2-year-old. *What might be some other physical differences between 2- and 5-year-olds?*

the concepts they know from the concepts they don't, while pinpointing the concepts they are about to forget. SmartBook continuously adapts to create a truly personalized learning path. SmartBook's real-time reports help both students and instructors identify the concepts that require more attention, making study sessions and class time more efficient.

Informed by Students

Content revisions are informed by data collected anonymously through McGraw-Hill Education's SmartBook.

STEP 1. Over the course of three years, data points showing concepts that caused students the most difficulty were anonymously collected from Connect for *Essentials of Life-Span Development* SmartBook®.

STEP 2. The data from LearnSmart was provided to the author in the form of a *Heat Map*, which graphically illustrates "hot spots" in the content that affect student learning (see image at left).

STEP 3. The author used the *Heat Map* data to refine the content and reinforce student comprehension in the new edition. Additional quiz questions and assignable activities were created for use in Connect to further support student success.

RESULT: Because the *Heat Map* gave the author empirically based feedback at the paragraph and even sentence level, he was able to develop the new edition using precise student data that pinpointed concepts that gave students the most difficulty.

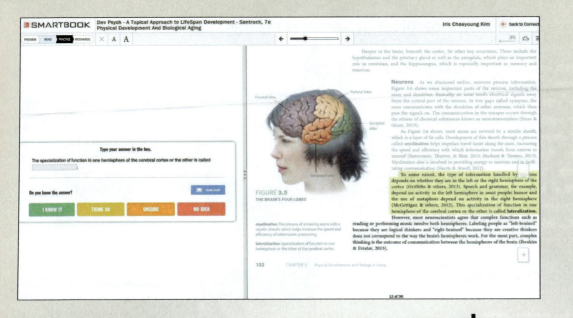

SMARTBOOK   Dev Psych - A Topical Approach to LifeSpan Development - Santrock, 7e   Physical Development And Biological Aging   Iris Chaeyoung Kim   ← back to Connect

PREVIEW   READ   PRACTICE   RECHARGE   X   A   A

FIGURE 3.5
THE BRAIN'S FOUR LOBES

Personalized Grading, On the Go, At a Glance

McGraw Hill Education — **connect** INSIGHT

Connect Insight™ is a one-of-kind visual analytics dashboard—now available for both instructors and students—that provides at-a-glance information regarding student performance. The immediate analysis from Connect Insight empowers students and helps instructors improve class performance efficiently and effectively.

- **Make It Intuitive.** Instructors and students receive instant, at-a-glance views of performance matched with student activity.
- **Make It Dynamic.** Connect Insight puts real-time analytics in the user's hands for a just-in-time approach to teaching and learning.
- **Make It Mobile.** Connect Insight is available on demand wherever and whenever needed.

The Essential Approach to Life-Span Development

In the view of many instructors who teach the lifespan development course, the biggest challenge they face is covering all periods of human development within one academic term. My own teaching experience bears this out. I have had to skip over much of the material in a comprehensive lifespan development text in order to focus on key topics and concepts that students find difficult and to fit in applications that are relevant to students' lives. I wrote *Essentials of Life-Span Development* to respond to the need for a shorter text that covers core content in a way that is meaningful to diverse students.

This fifth edition continues my commitment to provide a brief introduction to lifespan development—with an exciting difference. Recognizing that most of today's students have grown up in a digital world, I take very seriously the need for communicating content in different ways, online as well as in print. Consequently, I'm enthusiastic about McGraw-Hill's online assignment and assessment platform, **Connect for Life-Span Development,** which incorporates this text, the captivating **Milestones** video modules, and the brand new game-based learning assignment, *Quest: Psychology.* Together, these resources give students and instructors the essential coverage, applications, and course tools they need to tailor the lifespan course to meet their specific needs.

The Essential Teaching and Learning Environment

Research shows that students today learn in multiple modalities. Not only do their work preferences tend to be more visual and more interactive, but also their reading and study sessions often occur in short bursts. With shorter chapters and innovative interactive study modules, *Essentials of Life-Span Development* allows students to study whenever, wherever, and however they choose. Regardless of individual study habits, preparation, and approaches to the course, *Essentials* connects with students on a personal, individual basis and provides a road map for success in the course.

Essential Coverage

The challenge in writing *Essentials of Life-Span Development* was determining what comprises the core content of the course. With the help of consultants and instructors who have responded to surveys and reviewed the content at different stages of development, I am able to present all of the core topics, key ideas, and most important research in lifespan development that students need to know in a brief format that stands on its own merits.

The 17 brief chapters of *Essentials* are organized chronologically and cover all periods of the human lifespan, from the prenatal period through late adulthood and death. Providing a broad overview of lifespan development, this text especially gives attention to the theories and concepts that students seem to have difficulty mastering.

Essential Applications

Applied examples give students a sense that the field of lifespan development has personal meaning for them. In this edition of *Essentials* are numerous real-life applications as well as research applications for each period of the lifespan.

In addition to applied examples, *Essentials of Life-Span Development* offers applications for students in a variety of majors and career paths.

- *How Would You . . . ?* questions. Given that students enrolled in the lifespan course have diverse majors, *Essentials* includes applications that appeal to different interests. The most prevalent areas of specialization are education, human development and family studies, health professions, psychology, and social work. To engage these students and ensure that *Essentials* orients them to concepts that are key to their understanding of lifespan development, instructors specializing in these fields contributed *How Would You . . . ?* questions for each chapter. Strategically placed in the margin next to relevant topics, these questions highlight the essential takeaway ideas for these students.
- *Careers in Life-Span Development.* This feature personalizes lifespan development by describing an individual working in a career related to the chapter's focus. One example is Holly Ishmael, a genetic counselor. The feature describes Ms. Ishmael's education and work setting, includes a direct quote from Ms. Ishmael, discusses various employment options for genetic counselors, and provides resources for students who want to find out more about careers in genetic counseling.

Essential Resources

The following resources accompany *Essentials of Life-Span Development*, 5th edition. Please contact your McGraw-Hill representative for details concerning the availability of these and other valuable materials that can help you design and enhance your course.

- Instructor's Manual
- Test Bank
- PowerPoint Slides

Content Revisions

As an indication of the up-to-date nature of this new edition, the text has more than 1,500 citations from 2014, 2015, and 2016. Following are many of the chapter-by-chapter changes that were made in this new edition of *Essentials of Life-Span Development*.

Chapter 1: Introduction

- Update on life expectancy in the United States (U.S. Census Bureau, 2015)
- Expanded coverage of the effects of the rapid and dramatic increase in life expectancy on society and on the quality of life for older adults, with commentary about how society has essentially been built for young people rather than older adults and what is needed to improve the lives of older people (Carstensen, 2015, 2016)
- Updated statistics on the percentage of U.S. children and adolescents under 18 years of age living in poverty, including data reported separately for African American and Latino families (DeNavas-Walt & Proctor, 2015)
- Description of recent research that found a higher level of conscientiousness was protective of older adults' cognitive functioning (Wilson & others, 2015)
- Inclusion of recent research on individuals from 22 to 93 years of age that found older adults reported having more positive emotional experiences than did young adults (English & Carstensen, 2014)
- Inclusion of recent information from studies on variations in age and well-being, including variations involving middle age and health (OECD, 2014; Steptoe, Deaton, & Stone, 2015)
- New section, "Three Developmental Patterns of Aging," that describes the pathways of normal aging, pathological aging, and successful aging (Schaie, 2016)
- New coverage of the distinction between the evaluative and hedonic aspects of well-being, and how these different aspects produce different life course trajectories (Lachman, Teshale, & Agrigoroaei, 2015)
- Expanded discussion of physiological measures to include cortisol and its use by researchers to assess stress (Jacoby & others, 2016)
- Coverage of a recent study in which older adults assessed in 2013–2014 engaged in a higher level of abstract reasoning than their counterparts who were assessed two decades earlier (Gerstorf & others, 2015)
- Inclusion of findings that cross-sectional studies indicate that 90 percent of cognitive aging decline is due to a slowing of processing speed while longitudinal studies reveal that 20 percent or less of cognitive aging decline is due to processing speed (MacDonald & Stawski, 2015, 2016)

Chapter 2: Biological Beginnings

- Editing and updating of chapter based on comments by leading expert David Moore

- Updated and expanded discussion of genome-wide association studies, including research on suicide (Sokolowski, Wasserman, & Wasserman, 2016) and glaucoma (Bailey & others, 2016)
- New description of recent research on how exercise and nutrition can modify the behavior of genes (Lindholm & others, 2014; Ma & others, 2015)
- New content on how sleep deprivation can influence gene expression in negative ways such as increased inflammation, expression of stress-related genes, and impairment of protein functioning (Da Costa Souza & Ribeiro, 2015)
- Update on the percentage of individuals who have Klinefelter syndrome (1 in 1000 males)
- New content on fertility drugs being more likely to produce multiple births than in vitro fertilization (March of Dimes, 2016)
- Coverage of a recent large-scale study in Brazil in which flour that was fortified with folic acid produced a significant reduction in neural tube defects (Santos & others, 2016)
- Description of a recent research review that concluded many aspects of the developing prenatal brain can be detected in the first trimester using ultrasound, which also can help to identify spina bifida early (Engels & others, 2016)
- Inclusion of information from a recent review that concluded fetal MRI does not provide good results in the first trimester of pregnancy because of small fetal structures and movement artifacts (Watanagara & others, 2016). In this review, it also was argued that fetal MRI can especially be beneficial in assessing central nervous system abnormalities in the third trimester of pregnancy.
- Discussion of recent research that found isotretinoin (used to treat acne) is one of the most commonly prescribed drugs for adolescent girls seeking contraceptive advice, yet girls do not receive adequate information about its harmful effects on offspring if they become pregnant (Eltonsy & others, 2016; Stancil & others, 2016)
- Coverage of recent research on negative outcomes for fetal alcohol spectrum disorders (FASD) that include a lower level of executive function (Kingdon, Cardoso, & McGrath, 2016), externalized and internalized behavior problems (Tsang & others, 2016), and a significantly lower life expectancy (Thanh & Johnsson, 2016)
- Inclusion of recent research indicating that maternal cigarette smoking during pregnancy was linked to increased risk of smoking by offspring at 16 years of age (De Genna & others, 2016)
- Discussion of a recent study that found simultaneous exposure to environmental tobacco smoke and alcohol

during pregnancy increased the offspring's risk of having ADHD (Suter & others, 2015)

- Description of a recent study that revealed maternal smoking during pregnancy was associated with increased risk of asthma and wheezing in adolescence (Hollams & others, 2014)
- Discussion of recent research indicating that cocaine use by pregnant women is linked to attention deficit hyperactivity disorder, oppositional defiant disorder, and posttraumatic stress disorder (PTSD) in offspring (Richardson & others, 2016)
- Coverage of a recent meta-analysis that found marijuana use during pregnancy was associated with low birth weight in offspring and an increased likelihood of being placed in a neonatal intensive care unit (Gunn & others, 2016)
- Inclusion of two recent research reviews that concluded maternal obesity during pregnancy is associated with an increased likelihood of offspring becoming obese in childhood and adulthood (Pinto Pereira & others, 2016; Santangeli, Sattar, & Huda, 2015)
- Coverage of the recent increase in e-cigarette use, including a survey that found pregnant women hold misconceptions about e-cigarettes (Mark & others, 2015)
- Description of a recent study in which at 14 weeks following conception fetuses of obese pregnant women had less efficient cardiovascular functioning (Ingul & others, 2016)
- Inclusion of a recent research review indicating that pregestational diabetes increases the risk of fetal heart disease (Pauliks, 2015)
- Coverage of a recent study that found maternal pregnancy diabetes was linked to an increased risk of fatty liver disease in offspring at 18 years of age (Patel & others, 2016)
- Description of recent research in which maternal pregnancy diabetes was associated with an increased risk of autism in offspring (Xiang & others, 2015)
- Discussion of a recent study in China that revealed folic acid supplementation during pregnancy decreased the risk of preterm birth (Liu & others, 2015)
- Revised content on fish consumption by pregnant women, who are now being advised to increase their fish consumption, especially low-mercury fish such as salmon, shrimp, tilapia, and cod (American Pregnancy Association, 2016; Federal Drug Administration, 2016)
- Coverage of two recent studies that found very advanced maternal age (40 years and older) was linked to negative perinatal outcomes, including spontaneous abortion, preterm birth, stillbirth, and fetal growth restriction (Traisrislip & Tongsong, 2015; Waldenstrom & others, 2015)
- Inclusion of a recent research review that found antidepressant use by pregnant women is linked to small increased risks of cardiac malfunctions in the fetus and persistent pulmonary hypertension in the newborn (Pearlstein, 2015), increased risk of miscarriage (Almeida & others, 2016), and increased risk of autism spectrum disorders in children (Boukhris & others, 2016)
- Coverage of recent research that has found increasing paternal age decreases the success rate of in vitro fertilization and increases the risk of preterm birth (Sharma & others, 2015)
- New discussion of how the father's relationship with the mother might influence the mother's health and well-being and contribute to positive or negative prenatal development and birth
- Inclusion of a recent study that found intimate partner violence increased the mother's stress level (Fonseca-Machado Mde & others, 2015)
- Description of recent research in which CenteringPregnancy participation was linked to reduced incidence of low birth weight and reduced likelihood of placement in a neonatal intensive care unit (Gareau & others, 2016)
- Coverage of a recent study of adolescent mothers in which the CenteringPregnancy program was successful in getting participants to attend meetings, have appropriate weight gain, increase the use of highly effective contraceptive methods, and increase breast feeding (Trotman & others, 2015)
- Discussion of a recent research review in which waterbirth neonates experienced fewer negative outcomes than non-waterbirth neonates (Bovbjerg, Cheyney, & Everson, 2016)
- Description of a recent research review that concluded waterbirth is associated with high levels of maternal satisfaction with pain relief and the experience of childbirth (Nutter & others, 2015)
- Discussion of a recent study in which acupuncture reduced labor pain 30 minutes after the intervention (Allameh, Tehrani, & Ghasemi, 2015)
- Coverage of recent studies that have found low Apgar scores are linked to long-term additional educational support needs and decreased educational attainment (Tweed & others, 2016), risk of developmental vulnerability at 5 years of age (Razaz & others, 2016), and risk of developing ADHD (Hanc & others, 2016)
- Update on the percentage of U.S. births that take place in hospitals, at home, and in birthing centers and the percentage of babies born through caesarean delivery (Martin & others, 2015)
- Updated statistics on the percentage of babies born preterm and low birth weight in the United States, including ethnic variations (Martin & others, 2015)
- Inclusion of information about a recent study in which kangaroo care and massage therapy were equally effective in improving body weight and reducing hospital stay for low birth weight infants (Rangey & Sheth, 2015)
- Description of a recent study that found kangaroo care significantly reduced the amount of crying and increased heart rate stability in preterm infants (Choudhary & others, 2016)

- Coverage of a recent study in Great Britain in which the use of kangaroo care in neonatal units resulted in substantial cost savings mainly because of its reductions in diseases such as gastroenteritis and colitis (Lowson & others, 2016)
- Inclusion of a recent study in which massage therapy improved the scores of HIV-exposed infants on both physical and mental scales, as well as improving their hearing and speech (Perez & others, 2015)
- Discussion of a recent study in which depressive symptoms in both the mother and father were associated with impaired bonding with their infant in the postpartum period (Kerstis & others, 2016)

Chapter 3: Physical and Cognitive Development in Infancy

- New description indicating that neuronal connections number in the trillions (de Haan, 2015)
- Coverage of a recent study that found higher-quality mother-infant interaction predicted a higher level of frontal lobe functioning when assessed by EEG later in infancy (Bernier, Calkins, & Bell, 2016)
- New discussion of the recent increase in the use of functional near-infrared spectroscopy to assess infants' brain activity through a device that is portable and allows researchers to monitor infants' brain activity while they are exploring the world around them (Brigadoi & Cooper, 2015; de Haan & Johnson, 2016; Ravicz & others, 2015). Also, inclusion of new Figure 3 that shows an infant in an experiment using near-infrared spectroscopy.
- New commentary that after prone sleeping position, the two most critical factors in predicting SIDS are (1) maternal smoking, and (2) bed sharing (Mitchell & Krous, 2015)
- Coverage of three recent studies that found sleep difficulties in infancy were linked to later developmental problems in attention (Geva, Yaron, & Kuint, 2016; Sadeh & others, 2015) and emotional dysfunction (Geva, Yaron, & Kuint, 2016)
- Updated data on the continuing increase in breast feeding by U.S. mothers (Centers for Disease Control and Prevention, 2014)
- Description of a recent Danish study that found breast feeding did not protect against allergic sensitization in early childhood and allergy-related diseases at 7 years of age (Jelding-Dannemand, Malby Schoos, & Bisgaard, 2015)
- Coverage of a recent large-scale study of more than 500,000 Scottish children in which those who were exclusively breast fed at 6 to 8 weeks were less likely to ever have been hospitalized through early childhood than their formula-fed counterparts (Ajetunmobi & others, 2015)
- Inclusion of recent research that found breast feeding was associated with a small increase in intelligence in children (Kanazawa, 2015)

- New discussion of how walking skills might produce a developmental cascade of changes in infancy, including increases in language skills (Adolph & Robinson, 2015; He, Walle, & Campo, 2015)
- Description of recent studies that indicated short-term training involving practice of reaching movements increased both preterm and full-term infants' reaching for and touching objects (Cunha & others, 2015; Guimaraes & Tudelia, 2015)
- Coverage of a recent study in which 3-month-olds who had regular gentle tactile stimulation when they were fetuses were more likely to have an easy temperament than their counterparts who experienced irregular gentle or no gentle tactile stimulation as fetuses (Wang, Hua, & Xu, 2015)
- Inclusion of recent research in which kangaroo care was effective in reducing neonatal pain (Seo, Lee, & Ahn, 2016)
- Coverage of recent research that revealed problems in joint attention as early as 8 months of age were linked to diagnosis of autism by 7 years of age (Veness & others, 2014)
- A recent study that found infants who initiated joint attention at 14 months of age had higher executive function at 18 months of age (Miller & Marcovitch, 2015)
- Discussion of recent research on when infantile amnesia begins to occur by Patricia Bauer and her colleagues (Bauer, 2015; Bauer & Larkina, 2015; Pathman, Doydum, & Bauer, 2015). In a recent study, by 8 to 9 years of age, children's memory of events that occurred at 3 years of age began to significantly fade away (Bauer & Larkina, 2014).
- New discussion of Patricia Kuhl's (2015) findings that a baby's brain is most open to learning the sounds of a native language beginning at 6 months for vowels and at 9 months for consonants
- Description of recent research in which vocabulary development from 16 to 24 months of age was linked to vocabulary, phonological awareness, reading accuracy, and reading comprehension five years later (Duff & others, 2015)
- Discussion of a recent study of toddlers in which frequent TV exposure increased the risk of delayed language development (Lin & others, 2015)
- Coverage of a recent study that found Skype provides some improvement in children's language learning over television and videos (Roseberry & others, 2014)

Chapter 4: Socioemotional Development in Infancy

- Revisions in chapter based on feedback from leading experts John Bates and Ross Thompson
- Coverage of recent research indicating that smiling and laughter at 7 months of age was associated with self-regulation at 7 years of age (Posner & others, 2014)

- Inclusion of a recent study in which mothers were more likely than fathers to use soothing techniques to reduce infant crying (Dayton & others, 2015)
- New discussion of describing infant temperament in terms of reactivity and self-regulation (Bates & Pettit, 2015)
- Revised description of the temperament category of extraversion/surgency
- Description of recent research that found an inhibited temperament at 2 to 3 years of age was related to social-phobia-related symptoms at 7 years of age (Lahat & others, 2014)
- Inclusion of recent findings indicating that an inhibited temperament in infants and young children is linked to the development of social anxiety disorder in adolescence and adulthood (Rapee, 2014; Perez-Edgar & Guyer, 2014)
- New research that revealed effortful control was a strong predictor of academic success skills in kindergarten children from low-income families (Morris & others, 2014)
- New discussion of the recent interest in the *differential susceptibility* and *biological sensitivity to context* models that emphasize certain characteristics—such as a difficult temperament—may render children more vulnerable to difficulty in adverse contexts but also make them more likely to experience optimal growth in very supportive conditions (Belsky & others, 2015; Belsky & Pluess, 2016; Simpson & Belsky, 2016)
- New commentary about recent advances in infants' understanding of others (Rhodes & others, 2015), including research indicating that infants as young as 13 months of age seem to consider another's perspective when predicting their actions (Choi & Luo, 2015)
- Inclusion of recent research in which infant attachment insecurity (especially insecure resistant attachment) and early childhood behavioral inhibition predicted adolescent social anxiety symptoms (Lewis-Morrarty & others, 2015)
- Discussion of a recent study in dual-earner couples that found women did more than 2 hours of additional work compared with 40 minutes more for men after the birth of their child (Yavorsky & others, 2015)
- Description of a recent national poll that estimated there are 2 million stay-at-home dads in the United States, a significant increase from 1.6 million in 2004 and 1.1 million in 1989 (Livingston, 2014)
- Coverage of a recent study in which both paternal and maternal sensitivity assessed when the infant was 10 to 12 months old were linked to the child's cognitive development at 18 months of age and the child's language development at 36 months (Malmburg & others, 2016)
- Added commentary that infants and toddlers are more likely to be found in family child care and informal care settings while older children are more likely to be in child care centers and preschool and early education programs

- Description of a recent Australian study in which higher-quality child care at 2 to 3 years of age was linked to children's better self-regulation of attention and emotion at 4 to 5 and 6 to 7 years of age (Gialamas & others, 2014)

Chapter 5: Physical and Cognitive Development in Early Childhood

- Coverage of a recent study in which young children with higher cognitive ability showed increased myelination by 3 years of age (Deoni & others, 2016)
- Inclusion of recent research on how poverty is linked to maturational lags in children's frontal and temporal lobes that in turn were associated with lower school readiness skills (Meyer & others, 2015)
- Description of a recent study that revealed higher levels of maternal sensitivity in early childhood were related to higher total brain volume in children (Kok & others, 2015)
- Discussion of a recent study in which viewing as little as one hour of television daily was associated with an increase in body mass index (BMI) between kindergarten and the first grade (Peck & others, 2015)
- Coverage of recent research indicating that in longitudinal studies, when mothers participated in prenatal and early childhood WIC programs, young children showed short-term cognitive benefits and longer-term reading and math benefits (Jackson, 2015)
- Recent description by expert panels from Australia, Canada, the United Kingdom, and the United States that were remarkably similar in recommending that young children get an average of 15 or more minutes of physical activity per hour over a 12-hour period, or about 3 hours total activity per day (Pate & others, 2015)
- Coverage of recent research in which 60 minutes of physical activity per day in preschool academic contexts improved young children's early literacy (Kirk & Kirk, 2016)
- Inclusion of recent research in which myelination in a number of brain areas was linked to young children's processing speed (Chevalier & others, 2015)
- Discussion of recent research that found preschool sustained attention was linked to a greater likelihood of completing college by 25 years of age (McClelland & others, 2013)
- Coverage of a recent study of young children that found executive function was associated with emergent literacy and vocabulary development (Becker & others, 2014)
- Description of recent research in which executive function at 3 years of age predicted theory of mind at 4 years of age and executive function at 4 years of age predicted theory of mind at 5 years of age, but the reverse did not occur—theory of mind at earlier ages did not predict executive function at later ages (Marcovitch & others, 2015)

- New coverage of developmental changes in executive function in early childhood, including recent research on executive function and school readiness (Willoughby & others, 2016)
- Inclusion of research in which secure attachment to mothers during the toddler years was linked to a higher level of executive function at 5 to 6 years of age (Bernier & others, 2015)
- Discussion of a recent observational study that found a higher level of control by fathers predicted a lower level of executive function in 3-year-olds (Meuwissen & Carlson, 2016)
- Coverage of recent research in which experiencing peer problems in early childhood was linked to lower executive function later in childhood (Holmes, Kim-Spoon, & Deater-Deckard, 2016)
- Expanded and updated coverage of factors that influence children's theory of mind development: prefrontal cortex functioning (Powers, Chavez, & Hetherington, 2016) and various aspects of social interaction (Hughes & Devine, 2015), including secure attachment and mental state talk, and having older siblings and friends who engage in mental state talk
- Description of two recent studies that confirmed the importance of improved parenting engagement and skills in the success of Head Start programs (Ansari & Gershoff, 2016; Roggman & others, 2016)

Chapter 6: Socioemotional Development in Early Childhood

- Some changes made in chapter based on feedback from leading expert Jennifer Lansford
- Expanded coverage of the importance of emotion regulation in childhood and links between emotion regulation and executive function (Calkins & Perry, 2016; Durlak, Comitrovich, & Gullotta, 2015; Griffin, Freund, & McCardle, 2015)
- Description of recent research in which young children with authoritative parents were less likely to be obese than their counterparts with authoritarian parents (Kakinami & others, 2015)
- Inclusion of new information that physical punishment is outlawed in 41 countries (Committee on Rights of the Child, 2014)
- New content on the correlational nature of research on punishment, as well as bidirectional, reciprocal socialization influences that take into account child characteristics and problems (Laible, Thompson, & Froimson, 2015; Sheehan & Watson, 2008)
- Coverage of a recent study in which unmarried African American parents who were instructed in coparenting techniques during the prenatal period and also one month after the baby was born had better rapport, communication, and problem-solving skills when the baby was 3 months old (McHale, Salman-Engin, & Covert, 2015)

- Updated data on the number of U.S. children who were victims of child maltreatment in 2013 (U.S. Department of Health and Human Services, 2015)
- Discussion of a recent study in which individuals who had experienced their parents' divorce were more at risk for engaging in a lifetime suicide attempt (Alonzo & others, 2015)
- Inclusion of a 30-year longitudinal study that found offspring of parents who engaged in child maltreatment and neglect are at increased risk for engaging in child neglect and sexual maltreatment themselves (Widom, Czaja, & Dumont, 2015)
- Description of recent research on almost 3,000 adolescents that revealed a negative association of the father's, but not the mother's, unemployment on the adolescents' health (Bacikov-Sleskova, Benka, & Orosova, 2015)
- Coverage of recent research indicating that enriched work-family experiences were positively linked to better parenting quality, which in turn was associated with better child outcomes; by contrast, conflicting work-family experiences were related to poorer parenting quality, which in turn was linked to more negative child outcomes (Viera & others, 2016)
- Inclusion of recent research in which children were more likely to have behavior problems if their post-divorce environment was less supportive and stimulating, their mother was less sensitive and more depressed, and their household income was lower (Weaver & Schofield, 2015). Also in this study, higher levels of predivorce maternal sensitivity and child IQ served as protective factors in reducing child problems after the divorce.
- Inclusion of recent research in which maladaptive marital conflict when children were 2 years old was associated with an increase in internalizing problems eight years later due to an undermining of attachment security in girls, while negative emotional aftermath of conflict increased both boys' and girls' internalizing problems (Brock & Kochanska, 2016)
- Coverage of a longitudinal study that revealed parental divorce experienced prior to 7 years of age was linked to a lower level of the children's health through 50 years of age (Thomas & Hognas, 2015)
- Description of recent research on non-residential fathers in divorced families that linked high father-child involvement and low interparental conflict to positive child outcomes (Flam & others, 2016)
- Discussion of a recent study that found co-parenting following divorce was positively associated with better mental health and higher self-esteem and academic achievement (Lamela & Figueiredo, 2016)
- Inclusion of a recent research review that concluded higher screen time was associated with a lower level of cognitive development in early childhood (Carson & others, 2015)
- Description of a study that found parental reduction in their own screen time was associated with a decrease in child screen time (Xu, Wen, & Rissel, 2014)

- Inclusion of recent research on children in which higher viewing of TV violence, video game violence, and music video violence was independently associated with a higher level of physical aggression (Coker & others, 2015)
- New coverage of recommendations by Kathy Hirsh-Pasek and her colleagues (2015) that the best educational applications (apps) for young children are characterized by active involvement, engagement, meaningfulness, and social interaction

Chapter 7: Physical and Cognitive Development in Middle and Late Childhood

- Inclusion of a recent Chinese study that found higher blood pressure in 23 percent of boys and 15 percent of girls was attributable to being overweight or obese (Dong & others, 2015)
- Description of a 14-year longitudinal study in which parental weight gain predicted children's weight change (Andriani, Liao, & Kuo, 2015)
- Coverage of a study that found both a larger waist circumference and a higher body mass index (BMI) combined to place children at higher risk for developing cardiovascular disease (de Koning & others, 2015)
- Discussion of a recent study of elementary school children that revealed 55 minutes or more of daily moderate-to-vigorous physical activity was associated with a lower incidence of obesity (Nemet, 2016)
- Updated statistics on the percentage of U.S. children who have ever been diagnosed with ADHD (American Psychiatric Association, 2013; Centers for Disease Control and Prevention, 2016)
- New research that revealed the dopamine transporter gene DAT 1 was involved in decreased cortical thickness in the prefrontal cortex of children with ADHD (Fernandez-Jaen & others, 2015)
- Inclusion of recent research in which a higher physical activity level in adolescence was linked to a lower level of ADHD in emerging adulthood (Rommel & others, 2015)
- Description of a recent meta-analysis that concluded short-term aerobic exercise is effective in reducing symptoms such as inattention, hyperactivity, and impulsivity (Cerillo-Urbina & others, 2015)
- Coverage of a recent meta-analysis in which exercise was associated with better executive function in children with ADHD (Vysniauske & others, 2016)
- Discussion of a recent meta-analysis in which mindfulness training significantly improved the attention of children with ADHD (Cairncross & Miller, 2016)
- Updated data on the increasing percentage of children diagnosed with autism spectrum disorder (Centers for Disease Control and Prevention, 2016)

- Update on the percentage of children with a disability who spend time in a regular classroom (*Condition of Education*, 2015)
- Expanded and updated coverage of Alan Baddeley's important concept of working memory, including coverage of its link to improving many aspects of children's cognitive and academic development (Gerst & others, 2016; Peng & Fuchs, 2016)
- Discussion of a recent study in which a social and emotional learning program focused on mindfulness and caring for others was effective in improving a number of cognitive processes in fourth- and fifth-grade students, including mindfulness and cognitive control (Schonert-Reichl & others, 2015)
- Expansion of the activities that improve executive function to include scaffolding of self-regulation (Bodrova & Leong, 2015)
- Coverage of recent research in which mindfulness training improved children's attention and self-regulation (Poehlmann-Tynan & others, 2016), achievement (Singh & others, 2016), and coping strategies in stressful situations (Dariotis & others, 2016)
- Updated description of the most recent editions of the various Wechsler intelligence scales
- Description of a recent meta-analysis that revealed a correlation of +.54 between intelligence and school grades (Roth & others, 2015)
- Description of a recent study using Stanford-Binet intelligence scales that found no differences between non-Latino White and African American preschool children when they were matched for age, gender, and level of parent education (Dale & others, 2014)
- Coverage of a recent analysis that concluded the underrepresentation of African Americans in STEM subjects and careers is linked to practitioners' expectations that they have less innate talent than non-Latino Whites (Leslie & others, 2015)
- New description of how children who are gifted excel in various aspects of processing information (Ambrose & Sternberg, 2016a)
- Discussion of a recent study that revealed parents and teachers rated elementary school children who are not gifted as having more emotional and behavioral problems than children who are gifted (Eklund & others, 2015)
- Inclusion of some changes in the coverage of language development based on recommendations by leading expert Mandy McGuire
- Revised and updated content on bilingualism, including information about whether parents of infants and young children should teach them two languages simultaneously (Bialystok, 2014, 2015)
- New description of the rate at which bilingual and monolingual children learn language(s) (Hoff, 2016) and inclusion of a recent study that found by 4 years of age children who continued to learn both Spanish and English had a total vocabulary growth that was greater than that of monolingual children (Hoff & others, 2014)

Chapter 8: Socioemotional Development in Middle and Late Childhood

- Description of a recent study that found narcissistic parents especially overvalue their children's talents (Brummelman & others, 2015)
- Inclusion of recent research in which higher levels of self-control at 4 years of age were linked to improvements in math and reading achievement in the early elementary school years for children living predominantly in rural and low-income contexts (Blair & others, 2015)
- New content on how during middle and late childhood, as part of their understanding of emotions, children can engage in "mental time travel," in which they anticipate and recall the cognitive and emotional aspects of events (Lagattuta, 2014a, b; Lagattuta & others, 2015)
- New commentary on how children who have developed a number of coping techniques have the best chance of adapting and functioning competently after disasters and traumas (Ungar, 2015)
- New section on Jonathan Haidt's (2013) criticism of Kohlberg's view of moral reasoning as always conscious and deliberate, and his lack of attention to the automatic, intuitive precursors of moral reasoning
- New commentary about the multiple factors that may contribute to gender differences in academic achievement in areas such as reading and math (Wentzel & Miele, 2016)
- Inclusion of information from a meta-analysis that found females are better than males at recognizing non-verbal displays of emotion (Thompson & Voyer, 2014)
- New content on peer rejection being consistently linked to the development and maintenance of conduct problems (Chen, Drabick, & Burgers, 2015)
- Discussion of a recent analysis that concluded bullying can have long-term effects, including problems at work and difficulty in establishing long-term relationships (Wolke & Lereya, 2015)
- New research review that found antibullying interventions that focused on the whole school, such as Olweus', were more effective than interventions involving classroom curricula or social skills training (Cantone & others, 2015)
- New content on the *Every Student Succeeds Act (ESSA)* that became U.S. law in December 2015 (Rothman, 2016). This law replaces *No Child Left Behind* and while not totally eliminating state standards for testing students, reduces their influence. The new law also allows states to opt out of *Common Core* standards.
- New discussion of recent research in which underachieving high school students who read online modules about how the brain changes when people learn and study improved their grade point averages (Paunesku & others, 2015)

- Description of a longitudinal study of university students in which a nonlimited mindset predicted better self-regulation and higher grades (Job & others, 2015)
- Discussion of a recent study that found young Chinese adolescents have a greater sense of responsibility to parents than do their U.S. counterparts and that the U.S. students' sense of responsibility, but not the Chinese students', declined across two years (Qu & Pomerantz, 2015)

Chapter 9: Physical and Cognitive Development in Adolescence

- Description of a recent research review that concluded there is insufficient quality research to confirm that changing testosterone levels in puberty are linked to adolescent males' mood and behavior (Duke, Glazer, & Steinbeck, 2014)
- Inclusion of a recent study of Chinese girls that confirmed childhood obesity contributed to an earlier onset of puberty (Zhai & others, 2015)
- Coverage of a recent Korean study in which early menarche was associated with risky sexual behavior in females (Cheong & others, 2015)
- Coverage of a recent study that found early maturation predicted a stable higher level of depression for adolescent girls (Rudolph & others, 2015)
- Discussion of a recent study that revealed early-maturing Chinese boys and girls engaged in delinquency more than their on-time or late-maturing counterparts (Chen & others, 2015)
- New discussion of neurotransmitter changes in adolescence, particularly increased dopamine production (Monahan & others, 2016)
- Updated national data on the percentages of adolescents at different age levels who have engaged in sexual intercourse, including gender and ethnic variations, as well as updates in Figure 3 (Kann & others, 2014)
- Description of a recent Swedish study of more than 3,000 adolescents indicating that sexual intercourse prior to age 14 was linked to a number of risky sexual behaviors at age 18 (Kastbom & others, 2015)
- Discussion of a recent study of a number of parenting practices that found the factor that best predicted a lower level of risky sexual behavior by adolescents was supportive parenting (Simons & others, 2016)
- New research indicating that adolescent males who play sports engage in more risky sexual behavior while adolescent females who play sports engage in less risky sexual behavior (Lipowski & others, 2016)
- Updated data on the percentage of adolescents who use contraceptives when they have sexual intercourse (Kann & others, 2014)
- Inclusion of a recent cross-cultural study of adolescent pregnancy rates in 21 countries (Sedgh & others, 2015)
- Updated statistics on the continuing decline in overall adolescent pregnancy rates in the United States and the

- decline in all ethnic groups, including updates in Figure 4 (Martin & others, 2015)
- Coverage of a recent study of African American teen versus nonteen mothers' and fathers' long-term life outcomes in a number of areas (Assini-Meytim & Green, 2015)
- Description of a recent study in which family meals during adolescence protected against being overweight or obese in adulthood (Berge & others, 2015)
- Updated national data on adolescents' exercise patterns, including gender and ethnic variations (Kann & others, 2014)
- Inclusion of recent research in which an exercise program of 180 minutes per week improved the sleep patterns of obese adolescents (Mendelson & others, 2016)
- Discussion of a recent study in which a high-intensity exercise program decreased the depressive symptoms and improved the moods of depressed adolescents (Carter & others, 2016)
- Updated national data on adolescents' sleep patterns, including developmental changes (Kann & others, 2014)
- Coverage of a large-scale study of more than 270,000 adolescents from 1991 to 2012 that found adolescents have been decreasing the amount of sleep they get in recent years (Keyes & others, 2015)
- Description of recent Swedish studies of 16- to 19-year-olds in which shorter sleep duration was associated with a greater likelihood of school absence and shorter sleep duration and sleep deficit were the best sleep predictors of having a low grade point average (Hysing & others, 2015, 2016)
- Discussion of a recent study that revealed early school start times were linked to a higher vehicle crash rate by adolescent drivers (Vorona & others, 2014)
- Inclusion of the recent recommendation by the American Academy of Pediatrics that schools institute start times from 8:30 to 9:30 a.m. to improve students' academic performance and quality of life (Adolescent Sleep Working Group, AAP, 2014)
- Updated coverage of the Monitoring the Future study's assessment of drug use by secondary school students with 2014 data on U.S. eighth-, tenth-, and twelfth-graders (Johnston & others, 2016)
- Description of a longitudinal study in which earlier age at first use of alcohol was linked to risk of heavy alcohol use in early adulthood (Liang & Chikritzhs, 2015)
- New research that revealed early- and rapid-onset trajectories of alcohol, marijuana, and substance use were associated with substance use in early adulthood (Nelson, Van Ryzin, & Dishion, 2015)
- New content on why the transition to high school may produce problems for students (Eccles & Roeser, 2016)
- Updated data on school dropouts with a continuing decline in dropout rates for various ethnic groups (Child Trends, 2014; National Center for Education Statistics, 2014)
- Discussion of a recent study in which adolescents took greater risks when they were with three same-aged peers than when they were alone (Silva, Chein, & Steinberg, 2016)

Chapter 10: Socioemotional Development in Adolescence

- Changes made based on leading expert Kate McLean's recommendations
- New coverage of the narrative approach to identity, which involves examining identity by having individuals tell their life stories and then evaluating the extent to which the stories are meaningful and integrated (McAdams & Zapata-Gietl, 2015; Singer & Kasmark, 2015)
- Inclusion of a recent study that examined identity domains using both identity status and narrative approaches with the interpersonal domain (especially dating and friendship aspects) frequently mentioned (McLean & others, 2016). In the narrative approach, family stories were common.
- Coverage of two recent studies that found a strong and positive ethnic identity was linked to a lower incidence of substance abuse and psychiatric problems (Anglin & others, 2016; Grindal & Nieri, 2016)
- Description of recent research in which higher parental monitoring reduced negative peer influence on adolescent risk-taking (Wang & others, 2016)
- Coverage of a recent meta-analysis that found a higher level of parental monitoring and rule enforcement were linked to later initiation of sexual intercourse and greater use of condoms by adolescents (Dittus & others, 2016)
- New research in which lower disclosure to parents was linked to antisocial behavior in 10- to 18-year-olds (Chriss & others, 2015)
- Discussion of recent research that found snooping was a relatively infrequent parental monitoring technique (compared with solicitation and control) but was a better indicator of problems in adolescent and family functioning (Hawk, Becht, & Branje, 2016)
- Coverage of a recent study that revealed insecure attachment to mothers was linked to becoming depressed and remaining depressed from 15 to 20 years of age (Agerup & others, 2015)
- Description of a study in which high parent-adolescent conflict was associated with a lower level of empathy across a six-year period (Van Lissa & others, 2015)
- Inclusion of a recent study that found a higher level of parent-adolescent conflict was linked to higher anxiety, depression, and aggression, and lower self-esteem (Smokowski & others, 2015a)
- New research on Chinese American families that revealed parent-adolescent conflict was linked to a sense of alienation between parents and adolescents, which in turn was related to more depressive

- symptoms, delinquent behavior, and lower academic achievement (Hou, Kim, & Wang, 2016)
- Discussion of a recent study that found boys were more likely to be influenced by peer pressure involving sexual behavior than were girls (Widman & others, 2016)
- Description of recent research in which adolescents adapted their smoking and drinking behavior to that of their best friends (Wang & others, 2016b)
- Inclusion of recent research that revealed mother-daughter conflict in Mexican American families was linked to an increase in daughters' romantic involvement (Tyrell & others, 2016)
- Description of a recent research review in which a higher level of media multitasking was linked to lower levels of school achievement, executive function, and growth mindset in adolescents (Cain & others, 2016)
- New information from a research review with details about the complexities of why media multitasking can interfere with learning and driving (Courage & others, 2015)
- Updated data on the percentage of adolescents who use social networking sites and engage in text messaging daily (Lenhart, 2015a, b)
- Coverage of a recent study in which having friends who engage in delinquency is associated with early onset and more persistent delinquency (Evans, Simons, & Simons, 2015)
- New content on the link between low academic success and delinquency (Mercer & others, 2015) and the association of cognitive factors, such as low self-control, with delinquency (Fine & others, 2016)
- New coverage of the roles of stress and loss in adolescent depression and inclusion of a recent study that found adolescents who became depressed were characterized by a sense of hopelessness (Weersing & others, 2016)
- New description of a recent study that found adolescent girls' greater experience of interpersonal dependent stress was linked to their higher level of rumination, which accounted for their higher level of depressive symptoms than boys (Hamilton & others, 2015)
- Description of a recent study in which family therapy improved juvenile court outcomes beyond what was achieved in nonfamily-based treatment (Dakof & others, 2015)
- Inclusion of recent research that revealed positive parenting characteristics were associated with less depression in adolescents (Smokowski & others, 2015)
- New information from a research review that concluded SSRIs show clinical benefits for adolescents at risk for moderate and severe depression (Cousins & Goodyer, 2015)
- Updated data on the percentage of U.S. adolescents who seriously consider suicide each year (Kann & others, 2014)
- Inclusion of recent research in which both depression and hopelessness were predictors of whether adolescents would repeat a suicide attempt across a six-month period (Consoli & others, 2015)
- Coverage of a recent study that found child maltreatment was linked to adolescent suicide attempts (Hadland & others, 2015)
- New research in which a lower level of school connectedness was associated with increased suicidal ideation in female and male adolescents, and with suicide attempts by female adolescents (Langille & others, 2015)

Chapter 11: Physical and Cognitive Development in Early Adulthood

- Description of a recent Danish study focused on the most widely described markers of emerging adulthood (Arnett & Padilla-Walker, 2015)
- New commentary that 70 percent of college students do not get adequate sleep and 50 percent report daytime sleepiness (Hershner & Chervin, 2015)
- Inclusion of information from a recent national survey indicating that 29.5 percent of U.S. 20- to 39-year-olds are overweight and 31.5 percent are obese (Dietary Guidelines Advisory Committee, 2015)
- Discussion of recent international comparisons of 33 countries in which the United States had the highest percentage of obese adults (35.3 percent) and Japan the lowest percentage (3.7); the average of the countries was 23.2 percent of the population being obese
- Coverage of recent research on binge drinking by U.S. college students, including recent trends (Johnston & others, 2015)
- Recent research on the atypical features of depression in overweight/obese adults (Lojko & others, 2015)
- Coverage of a recent meta-analysis in which moderate and vigorous aerobic exercise resulted in a lower incidence of major depressive disorder (Schuch & others, 2016b)
- Description of a recent study in which adults who regularly exercise had lower levels of anxiety and depression (Khanzada, Soomro, & Khan, 2015)
- Discussion of recent research that found a one-year exercise intervention decreased stress symptoms in working adults (Kettunen, Vuorimaa, & Vasankari, 2015)
- Coverage of recent research indicating that 40 percent of 22-year-olds reported recently having had a casual sex partner (Lyons & others, 2015)
- Description of a recent study that revealed when emerging adults drink alcohol, they are more likely to have casual sex and less likely to discuss possible risks (Johnson & Chen, 2015)
- Inclusion of recent research of more than 3,900 18- to 25-year-olds that found having casual sex was negatively linked to well-being and positively related to psychological distress (Bersamin & others, 2014)
- Updated data on the percentage of individuals who have AIDS globally (UNAIDS, 2015)
- New description of a recent study in which the personality trait of openness to experience predicted creativity

in the arts while intellect predicted creativity in the sciences (Kaufman & others, 2016)

- Inclusion of two recent studies indicating the importance of purpose in life in predicting well-being in emerging adulthood (Hill & others, 2016) and a lower incidence of cardiovascular disease and likelihood of living a longer life (Cohen, Bavishi, & Rozanski, 2016)
- Updated discussion of the job categories most likely to have an increase in openings through 2024 (Occupational Outlook Handbook, 2016/2017)
- New coverage of the unemployment rate of recent college graduates and the high percentage who have to take jobs that do not require a college degree (Center for Economic and Policy Research, 2014; Gabor, 2014)
- Discussion of a recent study in which unemployment was associated with higher mortality but the link was higher among those who were unmarried (Van Hedel & others, 2015)
- Inclusion of a longitudinal study that found low self-control in childhood was linked to the emergence and persistence of unemployment from 21 to 50 years of age (Daly & others, 2015)
- Description of recent research in which women reported more family interference from work than did men (Allen & Finkelstein, 2014)
- Inclusion of recent research in which partner coping, having a positive attitude about multiple roles, using planning and management skills, and not having to cut back on professional responsibilities were linked to better relationships between dual earners (Matias & Fontaine, 2015)

Chapter 12: Socioemotional Development in Early Adulthood

- Discussion of a longitudinal study in which insecure avoidant attachment at 8 years of age was linked to negative social outcomes at 21 years of age (Fransson & others, 2016)
- Description of a recent study of adoptees that found higher maternal sensitivity in infancy and middle and late childhood predicted more secure attachment representations in emerging adulthood (Schoenmaker & others, 2015)
- Discussion of recent research that revealed young adults with an anxious attachment style were more likely to be characterized by higher negative affect, stress, and perceived social rejection; those with an avoidant attachment style were more likely to be characterized by less desire to be with others when alone (Sheinbaum & others, 2015)
- New research in which adults with a secure attachment style had fewer sleep disruptions than their counterparts with an insecure avoidant or insecure anxious attachment (Adams & McWilliams, 2015)
- Coverage of a recent study in which insecurely attached adults had a higher level of social anxiety than their securely attached counterparts (Notzon & others, 2016)

- New content on the potential positive and negative aspects of cross-gender friendships (Hart, Adams, & Tullet, 2016)
- Updated coverage of the continued dramatic rise in the number of never married, single adults in the United States, including specific data on the 18- to 29-year age bracket (Gallup Poll, 2015; U.S. Census Bureau, 2015a)
- Inclusion of a recent U.S. survey on the percentage of adults in different age brackets who had used online dating sites or apps (Pew Research Center, 2015)
- Discussion of a recent study that confirmed declaring a relationship status on Facebook was associated with both romantic love and jealousy (Orosz & others, 2015)
- Updated information about the continuing sharp increase in cohabitation in the United States
- Updated data on the continuing decline of U.S. marriage rates (Centers for Disease Control and Prevention, 2014)
- Updated data on the continuing rise in the age at which U.S. men and women get married (U.S. Census Bureau, 2015b)
- Description of recent research indicating that an increasing number of children are growing up in homes in which their parents never got married and that this is far more likely to occur when the mother has a low level of education (Pew Research, 2015)
- Coverage of a recent study that explored what U.S. never-married men and women are looking for in a potential spouse (Wang, 2014)
- Updated data on the continuing decline in the percentage of U.S. adults who are getting divorced (Centers for Disease Control and Prevention, 2015)
- Inclusion of a recent research review that concluded the experience of divorce or separation confers risk for poor health outcomes, including a 23 percent higher mortality rate (Sbarra, 2015)
- Description of a recent large-scale study in the United States and six European countries that explored the buffering effect of marriage on mortality for individuals who are not in the labor force (Van Hedel & others, 2015)
- Coverage of a recent research review that concluded divorced men and women are more likely to commit suicide than their married counterparts (Yip & others, 2015)
- Discussion of a recent study on the increased risk of heart attack for divorced adults, especially female divorced adults (Dupre & others, 2015)
- Updated data on the percentage of U.S. adults who get remarried and the gender remarriage gap in which men were almost twice as likely to get remarried in a recent year than women were (Payne, 2015)
- Discussion of a recent study that found remarried adults had less frequent sex than those in their first marriage (Stroope, McFarland, & Uecker, 2015)
- Inclusion of content from a recent study that found greater sharing of responsibilities in same-sex couples than in different-sex couples (Matos & others, 2015)
- New coverage of the increasing interest in individuals who describe themselves as transgender (Scelfo, 2015)

- Updated data on the average age at which U.S. women have their first child (Martin & others, 2015)
- Inclusion of content from a recent Pew Research (2015) poll on the influence of educational attainment on the age when U.S. women first became mothers

Chapter 13: Physical and Cognitive Development in Middle Adulthood

- Changes based on input from leading experts K. Warner Schaie, George Rebok, and David Almeida
- New commentary about middle adulthood not getting nearly as much research attention as late adulthood
- Description of recent data from the U.S. Census Bureau (2012) that indicate more than 102,000,000 U.S. adults are 40 to 64 years of age, which accounts for 33 percent of the U.S. population
- Inclusion of Margie Lachman and her colleagues' (2015) recent comments about why middle age is a pivotal period in life
- Coverage of recent research that has shown a combination of adaptive biological and social factors can buffer physical and cognitive declines in middle adulthood (Agrigoroaei & Lachman, 2010; Lachman, Teshale, & Agrigoroaei, 2015; Puteman & others, 2013)
- Discussion of a recent study in which sarcopenic obesity was associated with a 24 percent increase in risk for all-cause mortality, with men having a higher risk than women (Tian & Xu, 2016)
- Description of a recent study that found middle-aged individuals who exercised regularly in adolescence were less likely to develop cardiovascular disease (Nechuta & others, 2015)
- Coverage of a recent study in which a high level of physical activity was associated with a lower risk of cardiovascular disease in all three weight categories studied (normal, overweight, and obese) (Carlsson & others, 2016)
- Inclusion of a recent national study that confirmed moderate-to-vigorous exercise on a regular basis was linked to reduced all-cause mortality, especially for men (Loprinzi, 2015)
- Coverage of a recent study in which having an unhealthy diet was a strong predictor of cardiovascular disease (Menotti & others, 2015)
- Inclusion of a recent Korean study that linked a number of lifestyle factors to sleep problems in middle age (Yoon & others, 2015)
- Description of recent research in which poor sleep quality in middle adulthood was linked to cognitive decline (Waller & others, 2016)
- New commentary that chronic disorders account for 86 percent of all health care expenditures in the United States (Qin & others, 2015)
- Discussion of recent research indicating that how individuals react to daily stressors is linked to future health

outcomes and longevity (Mroczek & others, 2015; Sin & others, 2015)
- New coverage of recent research on the influence of yoga, relaxation, and hypnosis on immune system functioning (Derry & others, 2015; Kiecolt-Glazer & others, 2014)
- Updated data on deaths in middle age due to cancer and cardiovascular disease (Centers for Disease Control and Prevention, 2015)
- New discussion of testosterone replacement therapy (TRT), including a recent large-scale study of more than 80,000 men that linked testosterone replacement therapy with a reduction in cardiovascular disease and all-cause mortality (Sharma & others, 2015)
- Description of a recent study in which TRT was associated with increased longevity in men with a low level of testosterone (Comhaire, 2016)
- Updated data on the percentage of men 40 to 70 years of age and over 70 years of age who have erectile dysfunction (Mola, 2015)
- Discussion of Timothy Salthouse's (2015) recent emphasis on the main reason for different age trends in longitudinal and cross-sectional comparisons of cognitive functioning being prior experience, with test scores improving the next time a test is taken
- Coverage of a recent study in which a smaller decline in processing speed was one of the key predictors of living longer (Aichele, Rabbitt, & Ghisletta, 2016)
- Updated and expanded information about the percentage of U.S. 45- to 54- and 55- to 65-year-olds in the workforce, including trends from 2000 to 2015 (Short, 2015)
- Description of recent research that found engaging in physical and cognitive leisure activities after retirement decreased cognitive decline for individuals who worked in less cognitively challenging jobs prior to retirement (Andel, Finkel, & Pedersen, 2015)
- Inclusion of recent research in which middle-aged individuals who engaged in active leisure pursuits had a higher level of cognitive performance in late adulthood (Ihle & others, 2015)
- Coverage of a recent study that revealed individuals who engaged in a greater amount of sedentary screen-based leisure activity had shorter telomere lengths (Loprinzi, 2015)

Chapter 14: Socioemotional Development in Middle Adulthood

- Discussion of a recent meta-analysis that revealed stressful life events were related to increased risk of autoimmune diseases such as arthritis and psoriasis (Porcelli & others, 2016)
- Coverage of a recent study that found stressful daily hassles were linked to increased anxiety and lower physical well-being (Falconier & others, 2015)
- New discussion of Margie Lachman and her colleagues' (2015) recent views on how personal control

changes when individuals move into middle age, including comparison of the factors involved in personal control for young people and middle-aged adults

- Revised organization of the discussion of the Big Five factors of personality describing research on each of the five factors
- Description of recent research that found individuals high in openness to experience have superior cognitive functioning across the lifespan (Briley, Domiteaux, & Tucker-Drob, 2014) and experience less negative affect to stressors (Leger & others, 2016)
- Inclusion of recent research that found conscientiousness was linked to superior problem-focused coping (Sesker & others, 2016), greater success in accomplishing goals (McCabe & Fleeson, 2016), and better cognitive status and less cognitive decline in older adults (Luchetti & others, 2016)
- Coverage of recent research indicating that individuals high in extraversion are more satisfied with their relationships (Toy, Nai, & Lee, 2016), show less negative affect to stressors (Leger & others, 2016), and have a more positive outlook on their future well-being (Soto & others, 2015)
- Discussion of recent research indicating that people high in agreeableness engage in more positive affect to stressors (Leger & others, 2016)
- Description of recent research documenting that individuals high in neuroticism have a lower sense of well-being 40 years later (Gale & others, 2014)
- New section on the personality-trait-like characteristic of optimism and recent research on its link to better health and physical functioning in middle age (Boelen, 2015)
- Inclusion of a recent study in which a higher level of optimism increased the likelihood that individuals who had just experienced an acute coronary event would engage in more physical activity and have fewer cardiac readmissions (Huffman & others, 2016)
- Description of a recent research review of the influence of optimism on positive outcomes for individuals with chronic diseases through direct and indirect pathways (Avvenuti, Baiardini, & Giardini, 2016)
- Discussion of a recent study indicating that middle-aged married individuals have a lower likelihood of work-related health limitations than their counterparts who are not married (Lo, Cheng, & Simpson, 2016)
- Inclusion of recent research with middle-aged adults that indicated positive marital quality was linked to better health for both spouses (Choi, Yorgason, & Johnson, 2016)
- New discussion of the increasing divorce rate in middle-aged adults and the reasons for the increase (Brown & Lin, 2013)
- Coverage of a recent study that found the life satisfaction of middle-aged women in low-quality marriages increased after divorce (Bourassa, Sbarra, & Whisman, 2015)
- Updated information about the percentage of children who are living with at least one grandparent in the United States (U.S. Census Bureau, 2015)

Chapter 15: Physical and Cognitive Development in Late Adulthood

- Changes based on feedback from leading experts K. Warner Schaie, Kristen Kennedy, George Rebok, and William Hoyer
- Update on the increasing life expectancy at birth in the United States (78.8 years in 2013) and at age 65 (19.3 additional years) (Yu & others, 2016)
- Updated data on international comparisons of the countries where life expectations are highest and lowest (Central Intelligence Agency, 2015)
- Update on gender and ethnic differences in life expectancies in the United States (U.S. Department of Health and Human Services, 2015)
- Updated data on the increasing number of U.S. centenarians, which reached 72,000 in 2014 (Xu, 2016)
- Description of a recent list (2015) of the oldest people who have ever lived, with the list having only two men (number 11 and number 17) in the top 25
- New criticisms of the evolutionary theory of aging (Singer, 2016)
- Coverage of a recent study in which greater leisure time screen-based sedentary behavior was linked to shorter telomere length (Loprinzi, 2015)
- Inclusion of recent interest in energy sensing and apoptosis as key aspects of the mitochondrial theory of aging (Gonzalez-Freire & others, 2015)
- Reorganization of the discussion of biological theories of aging to include a new heading, "Cellular Processes," with new content on the increasing interest in sirtuins (Covington & Bajpeyi, 2016; Giblin & Lombard, 2016) and the mTOR pathway (Chen & others, 2016; Cheng & others, 2016; Schreiber, O'Leary, & Kennedy, 2016) as key cellular processes in aging and longevity
- Description of a recent study in which the percentage of T cells decreased in adults in their seventies, eighties, and nineties (Valiathan, Ashman, & Asthana, 2016)
- New section, "Conclusions," that describes the current belief that although there are some individual aging triggers, such as telomere shortening, a full understanding of biological aging involves multiple processes operating at different biological levels (de Magalhaes & Tacutu, 2016)
- Inclusion of research indicating that global brain volume predicted mortality in adults (Van Elderen & others, 2016)
- Discussion of a recent study in which mice in an enriched environment learned more flexibly because of adult hippocampal neurogenesis (Garthe, Roeder, & Kempermann, 2016)
- New discussion of the increasing risk of falls in older adults and a recent meta-analysis that concluded exercise reduces the risk of falls in adults 60 years of age and older (Stubbs, Brefka, & Denkginer, 2015) and another study that found walking was more effective

- than balance training in reducing older adults' falls (Okubo & others, 2016)
- New discussion of researchers' conclusions that older adults' sleep is lighter and more disrupted than young adults' sleep (McRae & others, 2016)
- New content on the increasing consensus that short (less than seven hours) and long (nine hours or more) sleep duration per night is detrimental to older adults' cognitive functioning (DeVore, Grodstein, & Schemhammer, 2016; Lo & others, 2016)
- Description of a recent study in which engaging in regular aerobic exercise improved the sleep profiles of older men (Melancon, Lorrain, & Dionne, 2015)
- Description of a recent study of older adults indicating that regular walking at or above 150 minutes per week predicted a lower likelihood of sleep onset and sleep maintenance problems four years later (Hartescu, Morgan, & Stevinson, 2015)
- Coverage of a recent study of older adults in which a faster walking pace, not smoking, modest alcohol intake, and avoiding obesity were associated with a lower risk of heart failure (Del Gobbo & others, 2015)
- Inclusion of a national study of the percentage of community-dwelling older adults with touch, taste, and smell impairment (Correia & others, 2016)
- Inclusion of recent research with sarcopenic older adults that found those who were physically active had a 25 percent probability of greater longevity than their sedentary counterparts (Brown, Harhay, & Harhay, 2016)
- Discussion of a recent research review that concluded more physically fit and active older adults have greater prefrontal cortex and hippocampal volume, a higher level of brain connectivity, more efficient brain activity, better memory, and a higher level of executive function (Erickson, Hillman, & Kramer, 2015)
- New research on women that indicated leisure-time physical inactivity was a risk factor for subsequent development of arthritis (Di Giuseppe & others, 2016)
- Discussion of recent research indicating that calorie restriction slows RNA decline during the aging process (Hou & others, 2016)
- Description of research on joggers in Denmark that revealed engaging in light or moderate jogging on a regular basis was linked to increased longevity (Schnohr & others, 2015)
- Discussion of a recent study in which core resistance and balance training improved older adult women's balance, muscle strength, leg power, and body composition better than Pilates training (Markovic & others, 2015)
- Inclusion of new information about the benefits of exercise for cellular functioning, including recent research that found aerobic exercise was linked to greater telomere length in older adults (Loprinzi & Loenneke, 2015)
- Description of recent research in which calorie restriction maintained more youthful functioning of the hippocampus, which is an important brain structure in memory (Schafer & others, 2015)
- New research involving a 20-year longitudinal study of 42- to 97-year-olds that revealed a greater processing speed decline was associated with mortality risk (Aichele, Rabbitt, & Ghisletta, 2015)
- Coverage of research in which episodic memory performance predicted which individuals would develop dementia 10 years prior to the clinical diagnosis of the disease (Boraxbekk & others, 2015)
- Inclusion of a recent study that found executive function but not memory predicted a higher risk of coronary disease and stroke three years later (Rostamian & others, 2015)
- New research that indicated executive function predicted higher levels of self-rated health in community-dwelling older adults (McHugh & Lawlor, 2015)
- Discussion of a recent study in which executive dysfunction was a strong predictor of stroke in cognitively normal aging adults (Oveisgharan & Hachinski, 2015)
- Coverage of a recent study in which older adults assessed in 2013–2014 engaged in a higher level of abstract reasoning than their counterparts who had been assessed two decades earlier (Gerstorf & others, 2015)
- Discussion of recent research on 60- to 90-year-olds in which iPad training 15 hours a week for 3 months improved their episodic memory and processing speed relative to engaging in social or non-challenging activities (Chan & others, 2015)
- Discussion of a recent research review in which Exergaming was linked to improved cognitive functioning in older adults (Ogawa, You, & Leveille, 2016)
- New research indicating that use of fish oil supplements was linked to higher cognitive scores and less atrophy in one or more brain regions (Daiello & others, 2015)
- Updated information on brain training games based on the consensus of leading experts (Stanford Center for Longevity and Max Planck Institute for Human Development, 2014)
- Updated data on the dramatically increased percentage of older adults who are in the work force and projections of work force participation to 2020, including gender differences (Short, 2015)
- Coverage of recent research in which cortical thickness in frontoparietal networks predicts executive function in older adults (Schmidt & others, 2016)
- Expanded content on the diverse mix of pathways of work and retirement that individuals now pursue (Kojola & Moen, 2016)
- New description of how new neuroimaging techniques have been developed that can detect the presence of plaques and tangles, providing scientists with an opportunity to identify the transition from healthy cognitive functioning to the earliest indication of Alzheimer disease (Park & Farrell, 2016)
- New commentary noting that more than 60 percent of individuals with Alzheimer disease have at least one ApoE4 allele (Riedel, Thompson, & Brinton, 2016)

- New coverage of a recent meta-analysis of modifiable risk factors for Alzheimer disease, including some medical exposures, dietary factors, preexisting diseases, cognitive activity, and alcohol consumption (Xu & others, 2015)

Chapter 16: Socioemotional Development in Late Adulthood

- Discussion of a recent study of older adults with dementia revealing that reminiscence therapy reduced their depressive symptoms and improved their self-acceptance and positive relationships with others (Gonzales & others, 2015)
- Coverage of a recent study in which *attachment-focused* reminiscence therapy reduced the depressive symptoms, perceived stress, and emergency room visits of older African Americans (Sabir & others, 2016)
- Inclusion of recent research in which aging adults who were more physically active were more satisfied with their lives (Maher & others, 2015)
- Description of a recent study that revealed older adults who increased their leisure-time activity were three times more likely to have a slower progression to functional disability (Chen & others, 2016)
- New content on how individuals with a positive affect, upbeat outlook on life, and optimism live longer (Carstensen & others, 2015; Reed & Carstensen, 2015)
- Inclusion of new content about a recent large-scale examination of healthy living in different age groups by the Stanford Center on Longevity that found social engagement with individuals and communities appeared to be weaker today than it was 15 years ago for 55- to 64-year-olds (Parker, 2016)
- Discussion of a recent study of 22- to 94-year-olds that found older adults showed selective optimization with compensation if they had a high level of cognitive resources (Robinson, Rickenbach, & Lachman, 2015)
- Inclusion of research that revealed processing speed was slower for older adults living in poverty (Zhang & others, 2015)
- Updates on the percentage of U.S. older adults living in poverty, including gender and ethnicity differences (Cubanski, Casillas, & Damice, 2015; Gabe, 2015)
- Inclusion of recent research on 65-and-older adults that found having an iPad increased their family ties and sense of having a greater overall connection to society (Delello & McWhorter, 2016)
- Updated information about the percentage of older adults who are married (U.S. Census Bureau, 2015)
- Description of a recent study of married and cohabiting older adults that indicated negative relationship quality predicted a higher level of blood pressure when both members of the couple reported having negative relationship quality (Birditt & others, 2016)
- Discussion of recent research of 40- to 60-year-olds who reported that their relationships with their children were more important than those with their parents but that their relationships with their children were more negative than with their parents (Birditt & others, 2015)
- Description of a recent study in which more frequent negative (but not positive) marital experiences were linked to a slower increase in older adults' cognitive limitations over time (Xu, Thomas, & Umbersom, 2016)
- Coverage of a recent study that found spousal support was more strongly linked to an important biomarker of biological aging, telomere length, than were other sources of social support (Barger & Cribbet, 2016)
- Discussion of a recent study in which a higher level of social support was associated with older adults' increased life satisfaction (Dumitrache, Rubio, & Rubio-Herrera, 2016)
- Description of recent research in which older adults involved in volunteering showed a strong link to lower incidence of cardiovascular disease and living longer (Han & others, 2016)
- New research that revealed having multiple chronic diseases was linked to a lower level of successful aging (Hsu, 2015)
- Inclusion of recent research on 90- to 91-year-olds that found living circumstances, independence, health, and a good death were associated with successful aging (Nosraty & others, 2015)
- Coverage of Laura Carstensen's (2015) recent commentary about the challenges and opportunities involved in the dramatic increase in life expectancy that has been occurring and continues to occur

Chapter 17: Death, Dying, and Grieving

- Some changes made in chapter based on feedback from leading expert Crystal Park
- Updated information that two additional states (New Mexico and Vermont) are among the five that allow assisted suicide
- New inclusion of Canada on the list of countries that allow assisted suicide, a change that occurred in 2016
- New content on why euthanasia is so controversial
- Discussion of recent research that found 61 percent of dying patients were in pain in their last year of life and almost one-third had symptoms of depression and confusion prior to death (Singer & others, 2015)
- Description of a recent research review that concluded the three most frequent themes in articles on a good death involved (1) preference for dying process, (2) pain-free status, and (3) emotional well-being (Meier & others, 2016)
- Discussion of recent research that found college students who lost someone close to them in college shootings and had severe posttraumatic stress symptoms four

- months later were more likely to have severe grief one year after the shootings (Smith & others, 2015)
- Among individuals diagnosed with complicated grief, 40 percent reported at least one full or limited-symptom grief-related panic attack in the past week (Bui & others, 2015)
- Coverage of recent research that identified four meaning-making processes (sense making, benefit finding, continuing bonds, and identity reconstruction) in parent-physician bereavement meetings following a child's death (Meert & others, 2015)
- Updated data on the percentages of U.S. women and men 65 years and older who are widowed (Administration on Aging, 2014)

- Discussion of a recent study that found Mexican American older adults experienced a signficant increase in depressive symptoms during the transition to widowhood (Monserud & Markides, 2016). In this study, frequent church attendance served as a protective buffer against increases in depressive symptoms.
- New commentary noting that becoming widowed is especially difficult when individuals have been happily married for a number of decades
- Updated data on the dramatic increase in the percentage of people in the United States who choose cremation (45 percent in 2013, compared with 27 percent in 2000 and 14 percent in 1985) (Cremation Association of America, 2015)

Acknowledgments

The development and writing of *Essentials of Life-Span Development* has been strongly influenced by a remarkable group of consultants, reviewers, and adopters.

Expert Consultants

In writing the fifth edition of *Essentials of Life-Span Development,* I benefitted considerably from the following leading experts who provided detailed feedback in their areas of expertise for *Life-Span Development,* Sixteenth Edition:

K. Warner Schaie, *Pennsylvania State University*

Elena Grigorenko, *Yale University*

Ross Thompson, *University of California–Davis*

Michelle de Haan, *University College-London*

Scott Johnson, *University of California–Los Angeles*

Megan McClelland, *Oregon State University*

David Almeida, *Pennsylvania State University*

George Rebok, *Johns Hopkins University*

Applications Contributors

I especially thank the contributors who helped develop the *How Would You . . . ?* questions for students in various majors who are taking the life-span development course:

Michael E. Barber, *Santa Fe Community College*

Maida Berenblatt, *Suffolk Community College*

Susan A. Greimel, *Santa Fe Community College*

Russell Isabella, *University of Utah*

Jean Mandernach, *University of Nebraska–Kearney*

General Reviewers

I gratefully acknowledge the comments and feedback from instructors around the nation who have reviewed *Essentials of Life-Span Development.*

Eileen Achorn, *University of Texas–San Antonio*

Michael E. Barber, *Santa Fe Community College*

Gabriel Batarseh, *Francis Marion University*

Troy E. Beckert, *Utah State University*

Stefanie Bell, *Pikes Peak Community College*

Maida Berenblatt, *Suffolk Community College*

Kathi Bivens, *Asheville Buncombe Technical Community College*

Alda Blakeney, *Kennesaw State University*

Candice L. Branson, *Kapiolani Community College*

Ken Brewer, *Northeast State Technical Community College*

Margaret M. Bushong, *Liberty University*

Krista Carter, *Colby Community College*

Stewart Cohen, *University of Rhode Island*

Rock Doddridge, *Asheville Buncombe Technical Community College*

Laura Duvall, *Heartland Community College*

Jenni Fauchier, *Metro Community College–Omaha*

Richard Ferraro, *University of North Dakota*

Terri Flowerday, *University of New Mexico–Albuquerque*

Laura Garofoli, *Fitchburg State College*

Sharon Ghazarian, *University of North Carolina–Greensboro*

Dan Grangaard, *Austin Community College*

Rodney J. Grisham, *Indian River Community College*

Rea Gubler, *Southern Utah University*

Myra M. Harville, *Holmes Community College*

Brett Heintz, *Delgado Community College*

Sandra Hellyer, *Butler University*

Randy Holley, *Liberty University*

Debra L. Hollister, *Valencia Community College*

Rosemary T. Hornack, *Meredith College*

Alycia Hund, *Illinois State University*

Rebecca Inkrott, *Sinclair Community College–Dayton*

Russell Isabella, *University of Utah*

Alisha Janowsky, *Florida Atlantic University*

Lisa Judd, *Western Technical College*

Tim Killian, *University of Arkansas–Fayetteville*

Shenan Kroupa, *Indiana University–Purdue University Indianapolis*

Pat Lefler, *Bluegrass Community and Technical College*

Jean Mandernach, *University of Nebraska–Kearney*

Carrie Margolin, *Evergreen State College*

Michael Jason McCoy, *Cape Fear Community College*

Carol Miller, *Anne Arundel Community College*

Gwynn Morris, *Meredith College*

Ron Mossler, *Los Angeles Community College*

Bob Pasnak, *George Mason University*

Curtis D. Proctor-Artz, *Wichita State University*

Janet Reis, *University of Illinois–Urbana*

Kimberly Renk, *University of Central Florida*

Vicki Ritts, *St. Louis Community College–Meramec*

Jeffrey Sargent, *Lee University*

James Schork, *Elizabethtown Community and Technical College*

Jason Scofield, *University of Alabama*

Christin E. Seifert, *Montana State University*

Elizabeth Sheehan, *Georgia State University*

Peggy Skinner, *South Plains College*

Christopher Stanley, *Winston-Salem State University*

Wayne Stein, *Brevard Community College–Melbourne*

Rose Suggett, *Southeast Community College*

Kevin Sumrall, *Montgomery College*

Joan Test, *Missouri State University*

Barbara VanHorn, *Indian River Community College*

John Wakefield, *University of North Alabama*

Laura Wasielewski, *St. Anselm College*

Lois Willoughby, *Miami Dade College–Kendall*

Paul Wills, *Kilgore College*

A. Claire Zaborowski, *San Jacinto College*

Pauline Davey Zeece, *University of Nebraska–Lincoln*

Design Reviewers

Cheryl Almeida, *Johnson and Wales University*

Candice L. Branson, *Kapiolani Community College*

Debra Hollister, *Valencia Community College*

Alycia Hund, *Illinois State University*

Jean Mandernach, *University of Nebraska–Kearney*

Michael Jason Scofield, *University of Alabama*

Christin Seifert, *Montana State University*

The McGraw-Hill Education Team

A large number of outstanding professionals at McGraw-Hill Education helped me to produce this edition of *Essentials of Life-Span Development*. I especially want to thank Krista Bettino, Dawn Groundwater, Sheryl Adams, Ann Helgerson, and A.J. Laferrera for their extensive efforts in developing, publishing, and marketing this book. Sheila Frank, Vicki Malinee, Janet Tilden, and Jennifer Blankenship were superb in the production and copyediting phases of the text.

1 Introduction

© Jay Reilly/Upper Cut Images/Getty Images

CHAPTER OUTLINE

Stories of Life-Span Development: How Did Ted Kaczynski Become Ted Kaczynski and Alice Walker Become Alice Walker?

Ted Kaczynski sprinted through high school, not bothering with his junior year and making only passing efforts at social contact. Off to Harvard at age 16, Kaczynski was a loner during his college years. One of his roommates at Harvard said that he avoided people by quickly shuffling by them and slamming the door behind him. After obtaining his Ph.D. in mathematics at the University of Michigan, Kaczynski became a professor at the University of California at Berkeley. His colleagues there remember him as hiding from social interaction—no friends, no allies, no networking.

After several years at Berkeley, Kaczynski resigned and moved to a rural area of Montana, where he lived as a hermit in a crude shack for 25 years. Town residents described him as a bearded eccentric. Kaczynski traced his own difficulties to growing up as a genius in a kid's body and sticking out like a sore thumb in his surroundings as a child. In 1996, he was arrested and charged as the notorious Unabomber, America's most wanted killer. Over the course of 17 years, Kaczynski had sent 16 mail bombs that left 23 people wounded or maimed and 3 people dead. In 1998, he pleaded guilty to the offenses and was sentenced to life in prison.

A decade before Kaczynski mailed his first bomb, Alice Walker spent her days battling racism in Mississippi. She had recently won her first writing fellowship, but rather than use the money to follow her dream of moving to Senegal, Africa, she put herself into the heart and heat of the civil rights movement. Walker had grown up knowing the brutal effects of poverty and racism. Born in 1944, she was the eighth child of Georgia sharecroppers who earned $300 a year. When Walker was 8, her brother accidentally shot her in the left eye with a BB gun. Since her parents had no car, it took them a week to get her to a hospital. By the time she received medical care, she was blind in that eye, and it had developed a disfiguring layer of scar tissue. Despite the counts against her, Walker overcame pain and anger and went on to win a Pulitzer Prize for her book *The Color Purple*. She became not only a novelist but also an essayist, a poet, a short-story writer, and a social activist.

What leads one individual, so full of promise, to commit brutal acts of violence and another to turn poverty and trauma into a rich literary harvest? If you have ever wondered why people turn out the way they do, you have asked yourself the central question we will explore in this book.

Essentials of Life-Span Development is a window into the journey of human development—your own and that of every other member of the human species. Every life is distinct, a new biography in the world. Examining the shape of life-span development helps us to understand it better. In this chapter, we explore what it means to take a life-span perspective on development, examine the nature of development, and outline how science helps us to understand it. ■

Ted Kaczynski, the convicted Unabomber, traced his difficulties to growing up as a genius in a kid's body and not fitting in when he was a child.

(Top) © Seanna O'Sullivan; (bottom) © WBBM-TV/ AFP/Getty Images

Alice Walker won the Pulitzer Prize for her book *The Color Purple*. Like the characters in her book, Walker overcame pain and anger to triumph and celebrate the human spirit.

(Top) © AP Images; (bottom) © Alice Walker

The Life-Span Perspective

Each of us develops partly like all other individuals, partly like some other individuals, and partly like no other individual. Most of the time we notice the qualities in an individual that make that person unique. But as humans, we have all traveled some common paths. Each of us—Leonardo da Vinci, Joan of Arc, George Washington, Martin Luther King, Jr., and you—walked at about 1 year, engaged in fantasy play as a young child, and became more independent as a youth. Each of us, if we live long enough, will experience hearing problems and the death of family members and friends. This is the general course of our **development,** the pattern of movement or change that begins at conception and continues through the human life span.

In this section we explore what is meant by the concept of development and why the study of life-span development is important. We outline the main characteristics of the life-span perspective and discuss various influences on development. In addition, we examine some contemporary concerns related to life-span development.

development The pattern of movement or change that starts at conception and continues through the life span.

The Importance of Studying Life-Span Development

How might you benefit from studying life-span development? Perhaps you are, or will be, a parent or teacher. If so, responsibility for children is, or will be, a part of your everyday life. The more you learn about them, the better you can raise them or teach them. Perhaps you hope to gain some insight about your own history—as an infant, a child, an adolescent, or a young adult. Perhaps you want to know more about what your life will be like as you grow through the adult years—as a middle-aged adult, or as an adult in old age, for example. Or perhaps you just stumbled across this course, thinking that it sounded intriguing. Whatever your reasons, you will discover that the study of life-span development addresses some provocative questions about who we are, how we came to be this way, and where our future will take us.

In our exploration of development, we will examine the life span from the point of conception until the time when life (at least, life as we know it) ends. You will see yourself as an infant, as a child, and as an adolescent, and you will learn about how those years influenced the kind of individual you are today. And you will see yourself as a young adult, as a middle-aged adult, and as an adult in old age, and you may be motivated to consider how your experiences will affect your development through the remainder of your adult years.

Characteristics of the Life-Span Perspective

Growth and development are dramatic during the first two decades of life, but development is not something that happens only to children and adolescents. The traditional approach to the study of development emphasizes extensive change from birth to adolescence (especially during infancy), little or no change in adulthood, and decline in old age. Yet a great deal of change does occur in the decades after adolescence. The life-span approach emphasizes developmental change throughout adulthood as well as childhood (Schaie & Willis, 2016).

Recent increases in human life expectancy have contributed to greater interest in the life-span approach to development. The upper boundary of the human life span (based on the oldest age documented) is 122 years. The maximum life span of humans has not changed since the beginning of recorded history. What has changed is life expectancy, the average number of years that a person born in a particular year can expect to live. In the twentieth century alone, life expectancy increased by 30 years, thanks to improvements in sanitation, nutrition, and medicine (see Figure 1). In the middle of the second decade of the twenty-first century, the life expectancy in the United States was 79 years of age (U.S. Census Bureau, 2015). Today, for most individuals in developed countries, childhood and adolescence represent only about one-fourth of their lives.

Laura Carstensen (2015, 2016) recently described the challenges and opportunities involved in this dramatic increase in life expectancy. In her view, the remarkable increase in the number of people living to old age has taken place so quickly that science, technology, and behavioral challenges have not kept pace. She proposes that the challenge is to transform a world constructed mainly for young people into a world that is more compatible and supportive for the increasing number of people living to 100 and older.

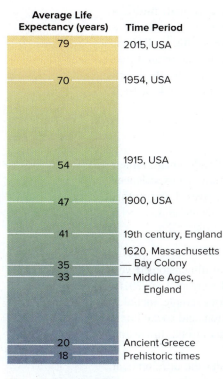

Average Life Expectancy (years)	Time Period
79	2015, USA
70	1954, USA
54	1915, USA
47	1900, USA
41	19th century, England
35	1620, Massachusetts Bay Colony
33	Middle Ages, England
20	Ancient Greece
18	Prehistoric times

Figure 1 Human Life Expectancy at Birth from Prehistoric Times to Contemporary Times
It took 5,000 years to extend human life expectancy from 18 to 41 years of age.

In further commentary, Carstensen (2015, p. 70) remarked that making this transformation would be no small feat:

> . . . parks, transportation systems, staircases, and even hospitals presume that the users have both strength and stamina; suburbs across the country are built for two parents and their young children, not single people, multiple generations or elderly people who are not able to drive. Our education system serves the needs of young children and young adults and offers little more than recreation for experienced people.
>
> Indeed, the very conception of work as a full-time endeavor ending in the early 60s is ill suited for long lives. Arguably the most troubling is that we fret about ways the older people lack the qualities of younger people rather than exploit a growing new resource right before our eyes: citizens who have deep expertise, emotional balance, and the motivation to make a difference.

Certainly recent progress has been made in improving the lives of older adults. In our discussion of late adulthood, you will read about researchers who are exploring ways to modify the activity of genes related to aging, methods for improving brain functioning in older people, medical discoveries for slowing or even reversing the effects of various chronic diseases, and ways to prepare for a better quality of life when we get old, including strategies for staying cognitively sharp, maintaining our physical fitness, and becoming more satisfied with our lives as older adults. But much more remains to be accomplished, as described earlier by Laura Carstensen (2015, 2016) and others (Antonucci & others, 2016; Hudson, 2016).

The belief that development occurs throughout life is central to the life-span perspective on human development, but this perspective has other characteristics as well. According to life-span development expert Paul Baltes (1939–2006), the **life-span perspective** views development as lifelong, multidimensional, multidirectional, plastic, multidisciplinary, and contextual, and as a process that involves growth, maintenance, and regulation of loss (Baltes, 1987, 2003; Baltes, Lindenberger, & Staudinger, 2006). In this view, it is important to understand that development is constructed through biological, sociocultural, and individual factors working together (Baltes, Reuter-Lorenz, & Rösler, 2006). Let's look at each of these characteristics.

Development Is Lifelong

In the life-span perspective, early adulthood is not the endpoint of development; rather, no age period dominates development. Researchers increasingly study the experiences and psychological orientations of adults at different points in their lives. Later in this chapter we describe the age periods of development and their characteristics.

Development Is Multidimensional

Development consists of biological, cognitive, and socioemotional dimensions. Even within each of those dimensions, there are many components (Lustig & Lin, 2016; Reuter-Lorenz, Festini, & Jantz, 2016). The cognitive dimension, for example, includes attention, memory, abstract thinking, speed of processing information, and social intelligence. At every age, changes occur in every dimension. Changes in one dimension also affect development in the other dimensions.

life-span perspective The perspective that development is lifelong, multidimensional, multidirectional, plastic, multidisciplinary, and contextual; that it involves growth, maintenance, and regulation; and that it is constructed through biological, sociocultural, and individual factors working together.

To get an idea of how interactions occur, consider the development of Ted Kaczynski, the so-called Unabomber discussed at the opening of the chapter. When he was 6 months old, he was hospitalized with a severe allergic reaction, and his parents were rarely allowed to visit him. According to his mother, the previously happy baby was never the same after his hospital stay. He became withdrawn and unresponsive. As Ted grew up, he had periodic "shutdowns" accompanied by rage. In his mother's view, a biological event in infancy warped the development of her son's mind and emotions.

Development Is Multidirectional

Throughout life, some dimensions or components of a dimension expand and others shrink. For example, when one language (such as English) is acquired early in development, the capacity for acquiring second and third languages (such as Spanish and Chinese) decreases later in development, especially after early childhood (Levelt, 1989). During adolescence, as individuals establish romantic relationships, their relationships with friends might decrease. During late adulthood, older adults might become wiser by being able to call on experience to guide their intellectual decision making (Lim & Yu, 2015), but they perform more poorly on tasks that require speed in processing information (Hedden & others, 2016; Salthouse, 2014).

Development Is Plastic

Even at 10 years old, Ted Kaczynski was extraordinarily shy. Was he destined to remain forever uncomfortable with people? Developmentalists debate how much plasticity people have in various dimensions at different points in their development (Kuhn & Lindenberger, 2016). Plasticity means the capacity for change. For example, can you still improve your intellectual skills when you are in your seventies or eighties? Or might these intellectual skills be fixed by the time you are in your thirties so that further improvement is impossible? Researchers have found that the cognitive skills of older adults can be improved through training and developing better strategies (Willis & Belleville, 2016). However, possibly we possess less capacity for change when we become old (Salthouse, 2012). The exploration of plasticity and its constraints is a key element on the contemporary agenda for developmental research (Kuhn & Lindenberger, 2016; Schaie, 2016).

Developmental Science Is Multidisciplinary

Psychologists, sociologists, anthropologists, neuroscientists, and medical researchers all share an interest in unlocking the mysteries of development through the life span (George & Ferraro, 2016; Kaeberlein & Martin, 2016; Schaie & Willis, 2016). How do your heredity and health limit your intelligence? Do intelligence and social relationships change with age in the same way around the world? How do families and schools influence intellectual development? These are examples of research questions that cut across disciplines.

Development Is Contextual

All development occurs within a **context,** or setting. Contexts include families, schools, peer groups, churches, cities, neighborhoods, university laboratories, countries, and so on. Each of these settings is influenced by historical, economic, social, and cultural factors (Eccles & Roeser, 2016; Kerig, 2016).

Contexts, like individuals, change (Gauvain & Perez, 2015). Thus, individuals are changing beings in a changing world. As a result of these changes, contexts exert three types of influences (Baltes, 2003): (1) normative age-graded influences, (2) normative history-graded influences, and (3) nonnormative or highly individualized life events. Each of these types can have a biological or environmental impact on development.

Normative age-graded influences are similar for individuals in a particular age group. These influences include biological processes such as puberty and menopause. They also include sociocultural, environmental processes such as beginning formal education (usually at about age 6 in most cultures) and retirement (which takes place during the fifties and sixties in most cultures).

Normative history-graded influences are common to people of a particular generation because of historical circumstances. For example, in their youth American baby boomers shared the experience of the Cuban missile crisis, the assassination of John F. Kennedy, and the Beatles invasion. Other examples of normative history-graded influences

context The setting in which development occurs, which is influenced by historical, economic, social, and cultural factors.

normative age-graded influences Biological and environmental influences that are similar for individuals in a particular age group.

normative history-graded influences Biological and environmental influences that are associated with history. These influences are common to people of a particular generation.

Nonnormative life events, such as Hurricane Sandy, are unusual circumstances that can have a major influence on a person's development.

© Adam Hunger/Reuters

include economic, political, and social upheavals such as the Great Depression in the 1930s, World War II in the 1940s, the civil rights and women's rights movements of the 1960s and 1970s, the terrorist attacks of 9/11/2001, as well as the integration of computers and cell phones into everyday life during the 1990s (Schaie, 2013). Long-term changes in the genetic and cultural makeup of a population (due to immigration or changes in fertility rates) are also part of normative historical change.

Nonnormative life events are unusual occurrences that have a major impact on the individual's life. These events do not happen to all people, and when they do occur they can influence people in different ways. Examples include the death of a parent when a child is young, pregnancy in early adolescence, a fire that destroys a home, winning the lottery, or getting an unexpected career opportunity.

How Would You...?

As a **social worker,** how would you explain the importance of considering nonnormative life events when working with a new client?

Development Involves Growth, Maintenance, and Regulation of Loss

Baltes and his colleagues (2006) assert that the mastery of life often involves conflicts and competition among three goals of human development: growth, maintenance, and regulation of loss. As individuals age into middle and late adulthood, maintenance and regulation of loss in their capacities takes center stage away from growth. Thus, a 75-year-old man might aim not to improve his memory or his golf swing but to maintain his independence and to continue playing golf. In other chapters, we will discuss these ideas about maintenance and regulation of loss in greater depth.

Development Is a Co-Construction of Biology, Culture, and the Individual

Development comes from biological, cultural, and individual factors influencing each other (Baltes, Reuter-Lorenz, & Rösler, 2006). For example, the brain shapes culture, but it is also shaped by culture and the experiences that individuals have or pursue. In terms of individual factors, we can go beyond what our genetic inheritance and environment give us. We can create a unique developmental path by actively choosing from the environment the things that optimize our lives (Rathunde & Csikszentmihalyi, 2006).

Contemporary Concerns in Life-Span Development

Pick up a newspaper or magazine and you might see headlines like these: "Political Leanings May Be Written in the Genes," "Mother Accused of Tossing Children into Bay," "Gender Gap Widens," "FDA Warns About ADHD Drug," "Heart Attack Deaths Higher in African American Patients," "Test May Predict Alzheimer Disease."

nonnormative life events Unusual occurrences that have a major impact on a person's life. The occurrence, pattern, and sequence of these events are not applicable to many individuals.

Researchers using the life-span perspective explore these and many other topics of contemporary concern. The roles that health and well-being, parenting, education, and sociocultural contexts play in life-span development, as well as how social policy is related to these issues, are a particular focus of this textbook.

Health and Well-Being

Health professionals today recognize the power of lifestyles and psychological states in health and well-being (Donatelle, 2017; Insel & Roth, 2016). Clinical psychologists are among the health professionals who help people improve their well-being. Read about one clinical psychologist who helps adolescents who have become juvenile delinquents or substance abusers in the *Careers in Life-Span Development* profile.

Careers in life-span development

Luis Vargas, Child Clinical Psychologist

Luis Vargas is Director of the Clinical Child Psychology Internship Program and a professor in the Department of Psychiatry at the University of New Mexico Health Sciences Center. He also is Director of Psychology at the University of New Mexico Children's Psychiatric Hospital.

Luis obtained an undergraduate degree in psychology from St. Edward's University in Texas, a master's degree in psychology from Trinity University in Texas, and a Ph.D. in clinical psychology from the University of Nebraska–Lincoln.

Luis' main areas of interest are cultural issues and the assessment and treatment of children, adolescents, and families. He is motivated to find better ways to provide culturally responsive mental health services. One of his special interests is the treatment of Latino youth for delinquency and substance abuse.

Clinical psychologists like Luis Vargas seek to help people with psychological problems. They work in a variety of settings, including colleges and universities, clinics, medical schools, and private practice. Some clinical psychologists only conduct psychotherapy; others do psychological assessment and psychotherapy; some also do research. Clinical psychologists may specialize in a particular age group, such as children (child clinical psychologist) or older adults (geropsychologist).

Luis Vargas (*left*) conducts a child therapy session.
© Dr. Luis A. Vargas

Clinical psychologists like Dr. Vargas have either a Ph.D. (which involves clinical and research training) or a Psy.D. degree (which only involves clinical training). This graduate training usually takes five to seven years and includes courses in clinical psychology and a one-year supervised internship in an accredited setting toward the end of the training. Most states require clinical psychologists to pass a test to become state licensed and to call themselves clinical psychologists.

Parenting and Education

Can two gay men raise a healthy family? Do children suffer if they grow up in a divorced family? Are U.S. schools failing to teach children how to read and write and calculate adequately? We hear many questions like these related to pressures on the contemporary family and the problems of U.S. schools (Bullard, 2017; Lamb & Lewis, 2015). In later chapters, we analyze child care, the effects of divorce, parenting styles, intergenerational relationships, early childhood education, relationships between childhood poverty and education, bilingual education, new educational efforts to improve lifelong learning, and many other issues related to parenting and education (Feeney, Moravcik, & Nolte, 2016; Pianta, 2016; Wadsworth & others, 2016).

Sociocultural Contexts and Diversity

Health, parenting, and education—like development itself—are all shaped by their sociocultural context. To analyze this context, four concepts are especially useful: culture, ethnicity, socioeconomic status, and gender.

Culture encompasses the behavior patterns, beliefs, and all other products of a particular group of people that are passed on from generation to

culture The behavior patterns, beliefs, and all other products of a group that are passed on from generation to generation.

Two Korean-born children on the day they became United States citizens. Asian American and Latino children are the fastest-growing immigrant groups in the United States. *How diverse are the students in your life-span development class? Are their experiences in growing up likely to have been similar to or different from yours?*

© Nancy Agostini

generation. Culture results from the interaction of people over many years (Cole & Tan, 2015). A cultural group can be as large as the United States or as small as an isolated Appalachian town. Whatever its size, the group's culture influences the behavior of its members (Masumoto & Juang, 2017). **Cross-cultural studies** compare aspects of two or more cultures. The comparison provides information about the degree to which development is similar, or universal, across cultures, or is instead culture-specific (Chen & Liu, 2016).

Ethnicity (the word *ethnic* comes from the Greek word for "nation") is rooted in cultural heritage, nationality, race, religion, and language. African Americans, Latinos, Asian Americans, Native Americans, European Americans, and Arab Americans are a few examples of broad ethnic groups in the United States. Diversity exists within each ethnic group (Gonzales & others, 2016). In recent years, there has been a growing realization that research on children's development needs to include more children from diverse ethnic groups (Schaefer, 2015). A special concern is the discrimination and prejudice experienced by ethnic minority children (Spencer & Swanson, 2016).

Socioeconomic status (SES) refers to a person's position within society based on occupational, educational, and economic characteristics. Socioeconomic status implies certain inequalities. Differences in the ability to control resources and to participate in society's rewards produce unequal opportunities (George & Ferraro, 2016; Wadsworth & others, 2016).

Gender, the characteristics of people as females and males, is another important aspect of sociocultural contexts. Few aspects of our development are more central to our identity and social relationships than gender (Leaper, 2015). We discuss sociocultural contexts and diversity in each chapter.

The conditions in which many of the world's women live are a serious concern (UNICEF, 2016). Inadequate educational opportunities, violence, and lack of political access are just some of the problems faced by many women.

Social Policy

Social policy is a government's course of action designed to promote the welfare of its citizens. Values, economics, and politics all shape a nation's social policy. Out of concern that policy makers are doing too little to protect the well-being of children and older adults, life-span researchers are increasingly undertaking studies that they hope will lead to effective social policy (Hudson, 2016; Sommer & others, 2016; Yeung & Mui-Teng, 2015).

How Would You...?

As a **health-care professional**, how would you explain the importance of examining cross-cultural research when searching for developmental trends in health and wellness?

How Would You...?

As a **psychologist,** how would you explain the importance of examining sociocultural factors in developmental research?

Doly Akter, age 17, lives in a slum in Dhaka, Bangladesh, where sewers overflow, garbage rots in the streets, and children are undernourished. Nearly two-thirds of the women in Bangladesh marry before they are 18. Doly organized a club supported by UNICEF in which girls go door-to-door to monitor the hygiene habits of households in their neighborhood, which has led to improved hygiene and health in the families. Also, her group has managed to stop several child marriages by meeting with parents and convincing them that it is not in their daughter's best interests. They emphasize the importance of staying in school and how this will improve their daughter's future. Doly says that the girls in her UNICEF group are far more aware of their rights than their mothers ever were (UNICEF, 2007).

© Naser Siddique/UNICEF Bangladesh

cross-cultural studies Comparisons of one culture with one or more other cultures. These provide information about the degree to which children's development is similar, or universal, across cultures, and the degree to which it is culture-specific.

ethnicity A range of characteristics rooted in cultural heritage, including nationality, race, religion, and language.

socioeconomic status (SES) Refers to the conceptual grouping of people with similar occupational, educational, and economic characteristics.

gender The characteristics of people as females and males.

social policy A national government's course of action designed to promote the welfare of its citizens.

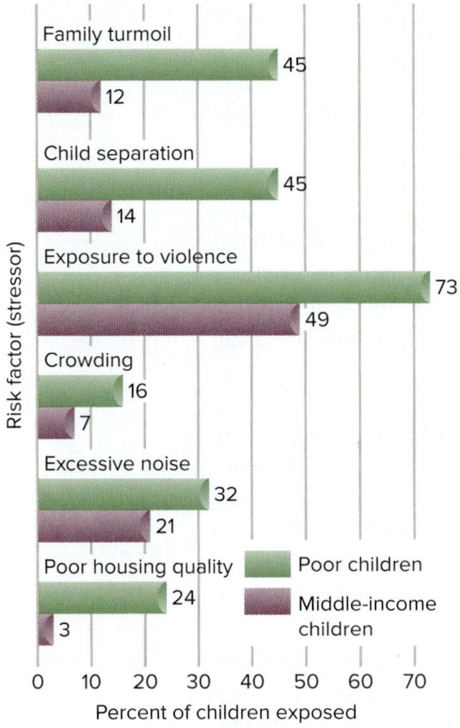
Family turmoil
45
12
Child separation
45
14
Exposure to violence
73
49
Crowding
16
7
Excessive noise
32
21
Poor housing quality
24
3
Poor children
Middle-income children
Risk factor (stressor)
0
10
20
30
40
50
60
70
Percent of children exposed

Figure 2 Exposure to Six Stressors Among Poor and Middle-Income Children
One study analyzed the exposure to six stressors among poor children and middle-income children (Evans & English, 2002). Poor children were much more likely to face each of these stressors.

Children who grow up in poverty represent a special concern (Duncan, Magnuson, & Votruba-Drzal, 2015; Wadsworth & others, 2016). In 2014, 21.1 percent of U.S. children under 18 years of age were living in families with incomes below the poverty line, with African American and Latino families with children having especially high rates of poverty (more than 30 percent) (DeNavas-Walt & Proctor, 2015). This is an increase from 2001 (16 percent) but slightly down from a peak of 23 percent in 1993. As indicated in Figure 2, one study found that a higher percentage of children in poor families than in middle-income families were exposed to family turmoil, separation from a parent, violence, crowding, excessive noise, and poor housing (Evans & English, 2002).

Developmental psychologists are seeking ways to help families living in poverty improve their well-being, and they have offered many suggestions for improving government policies (Gonzales & others, 2016; McCartney & Yoshikawa, 2015; Yoshikawa & others, 2016). For example, the Minnesota Family Investment Program (MFIP) was designed in the 1990s primarily to influence the behavior of adults—specifically, to move adults off welfare rolls and into paid employment. A key element of the program was its guarantee that adults participating in the program would receive more income if they worked than if they did not. How did the increase in income affect their children? A study of the effects of MFIP found that higher incomes of working poor parents were linked with benefits for their children (Gennetian & Miller, 2002). The children's achievement in school improved, and their behavior problems decreased. A current MFIP study is examining the influence of specific services on low-income families at risk for child maltreatment and other negative outcomes for children (Minnesota Family Investment Program, 2009).

There is increasing interest in developing two-generation educational interventions to improve the academic success of children living in poverty (Gardner, Brooks-Gunn, & Chase-Lansdale, 2016; Sabol & others, 2016; Sommer & others, 2016). For example, a recent large-scale effort to help children escape from poverty is the Ascend two-generation educational intervention being conducted by the Aspen Institute (2013; King, Chase-Lansdale, & Small, 2015). The focus of the intervention emphasizes education (increasing postsecondary education for mothers and improving the quality of their children's early childhood education), economic support (housing, transportation, financial education, health insurance, and food assistance), and social capital (peer support including friends and neighbors; participation in community and faith-based organizations; school and work contacts).

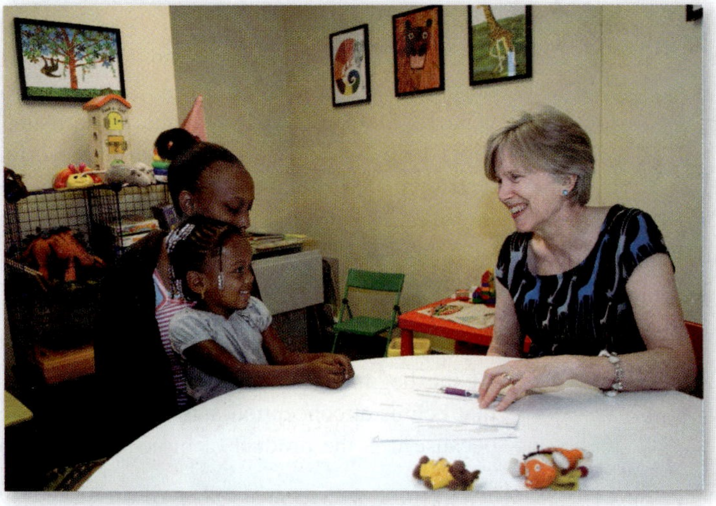

Ann Masten (*far right*) with a homeless mother and her child who are participating in her research on resilience. She and her colleagues have found that good parenting skills and good cognitive skills (especially attention and self-control) improve the likelihood that children in challenging circumstances will do well when they enter elementary school.
© Dawn Villella Photography

Some children triumph over poverty or other adversities. They show *resilience* (Masten & Cicchetti, 2016). Think back to the chapter-opening story about Alice Walker. In spite of racism, poverty, her low socioeconomic status, and a disfiguring eye injury, she went on to become a successful author and champion for equality.

Are there certain characteristics that make children like Alice Walker resilient? Are there other characteristics that influence children like Ted Kaczynski, who despite his intelligence and education, became a killer? After analyzing research on this topic, Ann Masten and her colleagues (Masten, 2006, 2014, 2015; Masten, Burt, & Coatsworth, 2006; Masten & Cicchetti, 2016; Masten & Monn, 2015; Masten & others, 2015, 2016) concluded that a number of individual factors, such as good intellectual functioning, influence resiliency. In addition, family and extrafamilial contexts of resilient individuals tend to share certain features. For example, resilient children are likely to have a close relationship to a caring parent figure and bonds to caring adults outside the family.

At the other end of the life span, older adults have health issues that social policy can address (Hooyman, Kiyak, & Kawamoto, 2015; Hudson, 2016). Key concerns are escalating health-care costs and the access of older adults to adequate health care (Gaugler, 2016; Moon, 2016). One study found that the health-care system fails older adults in many ways (Wenger & others, 2003). For example, older adults received the recommended care for general medical conditions such as heart disease only 52 percent of the time; they received appropriate care for undernutrition and Alzheimer disease only 31 percent of the time.

Concerns about the well-being of older adults are heightened by two facts. First, the number of older adults in the United States is growing rapidly. Second, many of these older Americans are likely to need society's help (Williamson & Beland, 2016). Compared with earlier decades, U.S. adults today are less likely to be married, more likely to be childless, and more likely to live alone (Machielse, 2015). As the older population continues to expand during the twenty-first century, an increasing number of older adults will be without either a spouse or children—traditionally the main sources of support for older adults. These individuals will need social relationships, networks, and other supports (Antonucci & others, 2016; LaMantia & others, 2015).

The Nature of Development

In this section we explore what is meant by developmental processes and periods, as well as variations in the way age is conceptualized. We examine some key developmental issues.

If you wanted to describe how and why Alice Walker or Ted Kaczynski developed during their lifetimes, how would you go about it? A chronicle of the events in any person's life can quickly become a confusing and tedious array of details. Two concepts help provide a framework for describing and understanding an individual's development: developmental processes and periods.

Biological, Cognitive, and Socioemotional Processes

At the beginning of this chapter, we defined development as the pattern of change that begins at conception and continues through the life span. The pattern is complex because it is the product of biological, cognitive, and socioemotional processes.

Biological Processes

Biological processes produce changes in an individual's physical nature. Genes inherited from parents, the development of the brain, height and weight gains, changes in motor skills, nutrition, exercise, the hormonal changes of puberty, and cardiovascular decline are all examples of biological processes that affect development.

biological processes Changes in an individual's physical nature.

Cognitive Processes

Cognitive processes refer to changes in an individual's thinking, intelligence, and language. Watching a colorful mobile swinging above the crib, putting together a two-word sentence, memorizing a poem, imagining what it would be like to be a movie star, and solving a crossword puzzle all involve cognitive processes.

Socioemotional Processes

Socioemotional processes involve changes in the individual's relationships with other people, changes in emotions, and changes in personality. An infant's smile in response to a parent's touch, a toddler's aggressive attack on a playmate, a school-age child's development of assertiveness, an adolescent's joy at the senior prom, and the affection of an elderly couple all reflect the role of socioemotional processes in development.

Connecting Biological, Cognitive, and Socioemotional Processes

Biological, cognitive, and socioemotional processes are inextricably intertwined (Diamond, 2013). Consider a baby smiling in response to a parent's touch. This response depends on biological processes (the physical nature of touch and responsiveness to it), cognitive processes (the ability to understand intentional acts), and socioemotional processes (the act of smiling often reflects a positive emotional feeling, and smiling helps to connect us in positive ways with other human beings). Nowhere is the connection across biological, cognitive, and socioemotional processes more obvious than in two rapidly emerging fields:

- *developmental cognitive neuroscience,* which explores links between development, cognitive processes, and the brain (de Haan & Johnson, 2016; Johnson, 2016)
- *developmental social neuroscience,* which examines connections between socioemotional processes, development, and the brain (Decety & Cowell, 2016; Monahan & others, 2016).

In many instances, biological, cognitive, and socioemotional processes are bidirectional. For example, biological processes can influence cognitive processes and vice versa. For the most part, we will study the different processes of development (biological, cognitive, and socioemotional) in separate chapters, but the human being is an integrated individual with a mind and body that are interdependent. Thus, in many places throughout the book we will call attention to the connections between these processes.

Periods of Development

The interplay of biological, cognitive, and socioemotional processes (see Figure 3) over time gives rise to the developmental periods of the human life span. A developmental period is a time frame in a person's life that is characterized by certain features. The most widely used classification of developmental periods involves an eight-period sequence. For the purposes of organization and understanding, this book is structured according to these developmental periods.

The *prenatal period* is the time from conception to birth. It involves tremendous growth—from a single cell to a complete organism with a brain and behavioral capabilities— and takes place in approximately a nine-month period.

Infancy is the developmental period from birth to 18 or 24 months when humans are extremely dependent on adults. During this period,

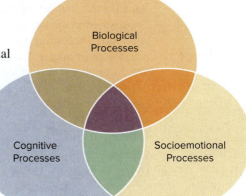

Figure 3 Processes Involved in Developmental Changes Biological, cognitive, and socioemotional processes interact as individuals develop.

"This is the path to adulthood. You're here."

© Robert Weber/The New Yorker
Collection/www.cartoonbank.com

many psychological activities—language, symbolic thought, sensorimotor coordination, and social learning, for example—are just beginning.

Early childhood is the developmental period from the end of infancy to age 5 or 6. This period is sometimes called the "preschool years." During this time, young children learn to become more self-sufficient and to care for themselves. They also develop school readiness skills, such as the ability to follow instructions and identify letters, and they spend many hours playing with peers. First grade typically marks the end of early childhood.

Middle and late childhood is the developmental period from about 6 to 11 years of age, approximately corresponding to the elementary school years. During this period, children master the fundamental skills of reading, writing, and arithmetic. They are formally exposed to the world outside the family and to the prevailing culture. Achievement becomes a more central theme of the child's world, and self-control increases.

Adolescence encompasses the transition from childhood to early adulthood, entered at approximately 10 to 12 years of age and ending at 18 to 22 years of age. Adolescence begins with rapid physical changes—dramatic gains in height and weight, changes in body contour, and the development of sexual characteristics such as enlargement of the breasts, growth of pubic and facial hair, and deepening of the voice. At this point in development, the pursuit of independence and an identity are prominent themes. Thought is more logical, abstract, and idealistic. More time is spent outside the family.

Early adulthood is the developmental period that begins in the late teens or early twenties and lasts through the thirties. For young adults, this is a time for establishing personal and economic independence, becoming proficient in a career, and for many, selecting a mate, learning to live with that person in an intimate way, starting a family, and rearing children.

Middle adulthood is the developmental period from approximately 40 years of age to about 60. It is a time of expanding personal and social involvement and responsibility; of assisting the next generation in becoming competent, mature individuals; and of achieving and maintaining satisfaction in a career.

Late adulthood is the developmental period that begins in the sixties or seventies and lasts until death. It is a time of life review, retirement from the workforce, and adjustment to new social roles involving decreasing strength and health.

Late adulthood potentially lasts longer than any other period of development. Because the number of people in this age group has been increasing dramatically, life-span developmentalists have been paying more attention to differences within late adulthood. According to Paul Baltes and Jacqui Smith (2003), a major change takes place in older adults' lives as they become the "oldest-old," at about 85 years of age. The "young-old" (classified as 65 through 84 in this analysis) have substantial potential for physical and cognitive fitness, retain much of their cognitive capacity, and can develop strategies to cope with the gains and losses of aging. In contrast, the oldest-old (85 and older) show considerable loss in cognitive skills, experience an increase in chronic stress, and are more frail (Baltes & Smith, 2003). Nonetheless, considerable variation exists in how much of their capabilities the oldest-old retain (Rowe & Kahn, 2016).

Conceptions of Age

In our description of developmental periods, we attached an approximate age range to each period. But we also have noted that there are variations in the capabilities of individuals of the same age, and we have seen how age-related changes can be exaggerated. How important is age when we try to understand an individual?

(a)   (b)

(*a*) Dawn Russel, competing in a Senior Olympics competition in Oregon. (*b*) A sedentary, overweight middle-aged man. *Even if Dawn Russel's chronological age is older, might her biological age be younger than the middle-aged man's?*

(*a*) © Jay Syverson/Corbis; (*b*) © Owaki-Kulla Corbis

According to some life-span experts, chronological age is not very relevant to understanding a person's psychological development (Hoyer & Roodin, 2009). Chronological age is the number of years that have elapsed since birth. But time is a crude index of experience, and it does not cause development. Chronological age, moreover, is not the only way of measuring age (MacDonald & Stawski, 2016). Just as there are different domains of development, there are different ways of thinking about age.

Four Types of Age

Age has been conceptualized not just as chronological age but also as biological age, psychological age, and social age (Hoyer & Roodin, 2009). *Biological age* is a person's age in terms of biological health. Determining biological age involves knowing the functional capacities of a person's vital organs. One person's vital capacities may be better or worse than those of others of comparable chronological age. The younger the person's biological age, the longer the person is expected to live, regardless of chronological age.

Psychological age is an individual's adaptive capacities compared with those of other individuals of the same chronological age. Thus, older adults who continue to learn, remain flexible, are motivated, think clearly, and have positive personality traits are engaging in more adaptive behaviors than their chronological age-mates who do not do these things (Schaie, 2016). And a recent study found that a higher level of conscientiousness was protective of cognitive functioning in older adults (Wilson & others, 2015).

Social age refers to connectedness with others and the social roles individuals adopt. Individuals who have better social relationships with others are happier and tend to live longer than individuals who are lonely (Antonucci & others, 2016; Carstensen, 2015).

From a life-span perspective, an overall age profile of an individual involves not just chronological age but also biological age, psychological age, and social age. For example, a 70-year-old man (chronological age) might be in good physical health (biological age), but might be experiencing memory problems and having trouble coping with the demands placed on him by his wife's recent hospitalization (psychological age) and dealing with a lack of social support (social age).

Three Developmental Patterns of Aging

K. Warner Schaie (2016) recently described three different developmental patterns that provide a portrait of how aging can involve individual variations:

- *Normal aging* characterizes most individuals, for whom psychological functioning often peaks in early middle age, remains relatively stable until the late fifties to early sixties, and then shows a modest decline through the early eighties. However, marked decline can occur as individuals near death.

- *Pathological aging* characterizes individuals who show greater than average decline as they age through the adult years. In early old age, they may have mild cognitive impairment, develop Alzheimer disease later on, or have a chronic disease that impairs their daily functioning.

- *Successful aging* characterizes individuals whose positive physical, cognitive, and socioemotional development is maintained longer, declining later in old age than is the case for most people. For too long, only the declines that occur in late adulthood were highlighted but recently there has been increased interest in the concept of successful aging (Araujo & others, 2016; Carstensen, Smith, & Jaworski, 2015; Rowe & Kahn, 2015).

Age and Happiness

Is there a best age to be? An increasing number of studies indicate that at least in the United States adults are happier as they age (Stone & others, 2010). Consider also a U.S. study of approximately 28,000 individuals from 18 to 88 that revealed happiness increased with age (Yang, 2008). For example, about 33 percent were very happy at 88 years of age compared with only about 24 percent in their late teens and early twenties. In a recent study of individuals from 22 to 93 years of age, older adults reported having more positive emotional experiences than did young adults (English & Carstensen, 2014).

Why might older people report being happier and more satisfied with their lives than younger people? Despite the increase in physical problems and losses older adults experience, they are more content with what they have in their lives, have better relationships with the people who matter to them, are less pressured to achieve, have more time for leisurely pursuits, and have many years of experience that may help them adapt to their circumstances with greater wisdom than younger adults do (Carstensen, 2015, 2016; Sims, Hogan, & Carstensen, 2015).

Not all studies, though, have found an increase in life satisfaction with age (Steptoe, Deaton, & Stone, 2015). Some studies indicate that the lowest levels of life-satisfaction are in middle age, especially from 45 to 54 years of age (OECD, 2014). Other studies have found that life satisfaction varies across some countries. For example, research with respondents from the former Soviet Union and Eastern Europe, as well as those from South American countries, report a decrease in life satisfaction with advancing age (Deaton, 2008). Further, older adults in poor health, such as those with cardiovascular disease, chronic lung disease, and depression, are less satisfied with their lives than are their healthier older adult counterparts (Wikman, Wardle, & Steptoe, 2011).

Researchers also have distinguished between the evaluative and hedonic aspects of life-course trajectories (Lachman, Teshale, & Agrigoroaei, 2015). In some studies, it is only the *evaluative* dimension (life satisfaction) that reaches a low point in middle adulthood (Stone & others, 2010). In contrast, the *hedonic* aspects (happiness and positive affect) take an upward trajectory from early adulthood through late adulthood, which is sometimes referred to as a *positivity effect* (Carstensen, 2015; Sims, Hogan, & Carstensen, 2015).

Now that you have read about age variations in life satisfaction, think about how satisfied you are with your life. To help you answer this question, complete the items in Figure 4, which presents the most widely used measure in research on life satisfaction (Diener, 2016).

Developmental Issues

Was Ted Kaczynski born a killer, or did his life turn him into one? Kaczynski himself thought that his childhood was the root of his troubles. He said he grew up as a genius in a boy's body and never fit in with other children. Did his early experiences determine his later life? Is your own journey through life marked out ahead of time, or can your

Below are five statements that you may agree or disagree with. Using the 1–7 scale below, indicate your agreement with each item by placing the appropriate number on the line preceding that item. Please be open and honest in your responding.

Scale

7 Strongly agree
6 Agree
5 Slightly agree
4 Neither agree nor disagree
3 Slightly disagree
2 Disagree
1 Strongly disagree

Response	Statement
_____	In most ways my life is close to my ideal.
_____	The conditions of my life are excellent.
_____	I am satisfied with my life.
_____	So far I have gotten the important things I want in life.
_____	If I could live my life over, I would change almost nothing.
_____	Total score

Scoring

31–35 Extremely satisfied
26–30 Satisfied
21–25 Slightly satisfied
20 Neutral
15–19 Slightly dissatisfied
10–14 Dissatisfied
5–9 Extremely dissatisfied

Figure 4 How Satisfied Am I With My Life?
Source: Diener, E., Emmons, R.A., Larson, R.J., & Griffin, S. (1985). The Satisfaction with Life Scale. *Journal of Personality Assessment, 49,* 71–75.

experiences change your path? Are the experiences you have early in your journey more important than later ones? Is your journey more like taking an elevator up a skyscraper with distinct stops along the way or more like a cruise down a river with smoother ebbs and flows? These questions point to three issues about the nature of development: the roles played by nature and nurture, stability and change, and continuity and discontinuity.

Nature and Nurture

The **nature-nurture issue** concerns the extent to which development is influenced by nature and by nurture. *Nature* refers to an organism's biological inheritance, *nurture* to its environmental experiences.

According to those who emphasize the role of nature, just as a sunflower grows in an orderly way—unless flattened by an unfriendly environment—so too the human grows in an orderly way. An evolutionary and genetic foundation produces commonalities in growth and development (Belsky & Pluess, 2016; Buss, 2015; Del Giudice & Ellis, 2016; Sutphin & Korstanje, 2016). We walk before we talk, speak one word before two words, grow rapidly in infancy and less so in early childhood, experience a rush of sex hormones in puberty, reach the peak of our physical strength in late adolescence and early adulthood, and then physically decline. Proponents of the importance of nature acknowledge that extreme environments—those that are psychologically barren or hostile—can depress development. However, they believe that basic growth tendencies are genetically programmed into humans (Yang, Song, & Johnson, 2016).

By contrast, other psychologists emphasize the importance of nurture, or environmental experiences, in development (Burt, Coatsworth, & Masten, 2016). Experiences run the gamut from the individual's biological environment (nutrition, exercise, medical care, drugs, and physical accidents) to the social environment (family, peers, schools, community, media, and culture) (Gonzales & others, 2016; Pianta, 2016).

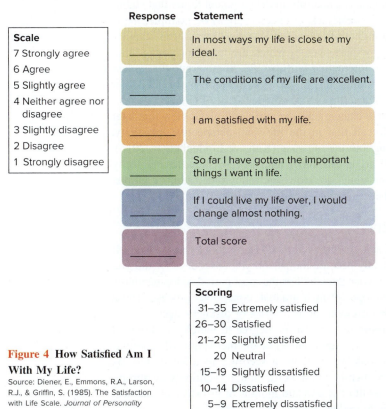

nature-nurture issue The debate about the extent to which development is influenced by nature and by nurture. Nature refers to an organism's biological inheritance, nurture to its environmental experiences.

Stability and Change

Is the shy child who hides behind the sofa when visitors arrive destined to become a wallflower at college dances, or might the child become a sociable, talkative individual? Is the fun-loving, carefree adolescent

What are some key developmental issues?
© Rubberball/PictureQuest RF

bound to have difficulty holding down a 9-to-5 job as an adult? These questions reflect the **stability-change issue,** involving the degree to which early traits and characteristics persist or change over time.

Many developmentalists who emphasize stability in development argue that stability is the result of heredity and possibly early experiences in life. For example, many argue that if an individual is shy throughout life (as Ted Kaczynski was), this stability is due to heredity and possibly early experiences in which the infant or young child encountered considerable stress when interacting with people. Some argue that unless infants experience warm, nurturant caregiving in the first year or so of life, their development will never be optimal (Easterbrooks & others, 2013; O'Connor, 2016).

Developmentalists who emphasize change take the more optimistic view that later experiences can produce change. Recall that in the life-span perspective, plasticity, the potential for change, exists throughout the life span (Kuhn & Lindenberger, 2016). Experts such as Paul Baltes (2003) argue that older adults often show less capacity for learning new things than younger adults do. However, many older adults continue to be good at applying what they have learned in earlier times.

Continuity and Discontinuity

When developmental change occurs, is it gradual or abrupt? Think about your own development for a moment. Did you gradually become the person you are today? Or did you experience sudden, distinct changes in your growth? For the most part, developmentalists who emphasize nurture describe development as a gradual, continuous process. Those who emphasize nature often describe development as a series of distinct stages.

The **continuity-discontinuity issue** focuses on the degree to which development involves either gradual, cumulative change (continuity) or distinct stages (discontinuity). In terms of continuity, as the oak grows from a seedling to a giant tree, its development is continuous. Similarly, a child's first word, though seemingly an abrupt, discontinuous event, is actually the result of weeks and months of growth and practice. Puberty might seem abrupt, but it is a gradual process that occurs over several years.

In terms of discontinuity, as an insect grows from a caterpillar to a chrysalis to a butterfly, it passes through a sequence of stages in which change is qualitatively rather than quantitatively different. Similarly, at some point a child moves from not being able to think abstractly about the world to being able to do so. This is a qualitative, discontinuous change in development rather than a quantitative, continuous change.

Evaluating the Developmental Issues

Developmentalists generally acknowledge that development is not all nature or all nurture, not all stability or all change, and not all continuity or all discontinuity. Nature and nurture, stability and change, continuity and discontinuity characterize development throughout the life span.

Although most developmentalists do not take extreme positions on these three important issues, there is spirited debate regarding how strongly development is influenced by each of these factors (Grigorenko & others, 2016; Hill & Roth, 2016; Sroufe, 2016; Thompson & Goodvin, 2016).

Theories of Development

stability-change issue The debate about the degree to which early traits and characteristics persist through life or change.

continuity-discontinuity issue The debate about the extent to which development involves gradual, cumulative change (continuity) or distinct stages (discontinuity).

How can we answer questions about the roles of nature and nurture, stability and change, and continuity and discontinuity in development? How can we determine, for example, whether memory loss in older adults can be prevented or whether special care can repair the harm inflicted by child neglect? The scientific method is the best tool we have to answer such questions (Smith & Davis, 2016).

The scientific method is essentially a four-step process: (1) conceptualize a process or problem to be studied, (2) collect research information (data), (3) analyze data, and (4) draw conclusions.

In step 1, when researchers are formulating a problem to study, they often draw on theories and develop hypotheses. A **theory** is an interrelated, coherent set of ideas that helps to explain phenomena and make predictions. It may suggest **hypotheses,** which are specific assertions and predictions that can be tested. For example, a theory on mentoring might state that sustained support and guidance from an adult makes a difference in the lives of children from impoverished backgrounds because the mentor gives the children opportunities to observe and imitate the behavior and strategies of the mentor.

This section outlines five theoretical orientations to development: psychoanalytic, cognitive, behavioral and social cognitive, ethological, and ecological. These theories look at development from different perspectives, and they disagree about certain aspects of development. But many of their ideas are complementary, and each contributes an important piece to the life-span development puzzle. Although the theories disagree about certain aspects of development, many of their ideas are complementary rather than contradictory. Together they let us see the total landscape of life-span development in all its richness.

theory A coherent set of ideas that helps to explain data and to make predictions.

hypotheses Assertions or predictions, often derived from theories, that can be tested.

psychoanalytic theories Theories holding that development depends primarily on the unconscious mind and is heavily couched in emotion, that behavior is merely a surface characteristic, that it is important to analyze the symbolic meanings of behavior, and that early experiences are important in development.

Psychoanalytic Theories

Psychoanalytic theories describe development primarily in terms of unconscious (beyond awareness) processes that are heavily colored by emotion. Psychoanalytic theorists emphasize that behavior is merely a surface characteristic and that a true understanding of development requires analyzing the symbolic meanings of behavior and the deep inner workings of the mind. Psychoanalytic theorists also stress that early experiences with parents extensively shape development. These characteristics are highlighted in the main psychoanalytic theory, that of Sigmund Freud (1856–1939).

Freud's Theory

Freud was a pioneer in the treatment of psychological problems. Based on his belief that patients who talked about their problems could be restored to psychological health, Freud developed a technique called psychoanalysis. As he listened to, probed, and analyzed his patients, he became convinced that their problems were the result of experiences early in life. He thought that as children grow up, their focus of pleasure and sexual impulses shifts from the mouth to the anus and eventually to the genitals. Consequently, he determined, we pass through five stages of psychosexual development: oral, anal, phallic, latency, and genital (see Figure 5). Our adult personality, Freud (1917) claimed, is determined by the way we resolve conflicts between sources of pleasure at each stage and the demands of reality.

Freud's followers significantly revised his psychoanalytic theory. Many of today's psychoanalytic theorists believe that Freud overemphasized sexual instincts; they place more emphasis on cultural experiences as determinants of an individual's development. Unconscious thought remains a central theme, but conscious thought plays a

Figure 5 Freudian Stages
Because Freud emphasized sexual motivation, his stages of development are known as psychosexual stages. In his view, if the need for pleasure at any stage is either undergratified or overgratified, an individual may become fixated, or locked in, at that stage of development.

Oral Stage	Anal Stage	Phallic Stage	Latency Stage	Genital Stage
Infant's pleasure centers on the mouth.	Child's pleasure focuses on the anus.	Child's pleasure focuses on the genitals.	Child represses sexual interest and develops social and intellectual skills.	A time of sexual reawakening; source of sexual pleasure becomes someone outside the family.
Birth to 1½ Years	**1½ to 3 Years**	**3 to 6 Years**	**6 Years to Puberty**	**Puberty Onward**

Erikson's Stages	Developmental Period
Integrity versus despair	Late adulthood (60s onward)
Generativity versus stagnation	Middle adulthood (40s, 50s)
Intimacy versus isolation	Early adulthood (20s, 30s)
Identity versus identity confusion	Adolescence (10 to 20 years)
Industry versus inferiority	Middle and late childhood (elementary school years, 6 years to puberty)
Initiative versus guilt	Early childhood (preschool years, 3 to 5 years)
Autonomy versus shame and doubt	Infancy (1 to 3 years)
Trust versus mistrust	Infancy (first year)

Figure 6 **Erikson's Eight Life-Span Stages**

Like Freud, Erikson proposed that individuals go through distinct, universal stages of development. In terms of the continuity-discontinuity issue, both favor the discontinuity side of the debate. Notice that the timing of Erikson's first four stages is similar to that of Freud's stages. *What are the implications of saying that people go through stages of development?*

Erikson's theory A psychoanalytic theory in which eight stages of psychosocial development unfold throughout the life span. Each stage consists of a unique developmental task that confronts individuals with a crisis that must be faced.

greater role than Freud envisioned. Next, we will outline the ideas of an important revisionist of Freud's theory—Erik Erikson.

Erikson's Psychosocial Theory

Erik Erikson recognized Freud's contributions but believed that Freud misjudged some important dimensions of human development. For one thing, Erikson (1950, 1968) said we develop in psychosocial stages, rather than the psychosexual stages that Freud described. According to Freud, the primary motivation for human behavior is sexual in nature; according to Erikson, motivation is social and reflects a desire to affiliate with other people. According to Freud, our basic personality is shaped in the first five years of life; according to Erikson, developmental change occurs throughout the life span. Thus, Freud viewed early experiences as far more important than later experiences, whereas Erikson emphasized the importance of both early and later experiences.

In **Erikson's theory,** eight stages of development unfold as we go through life (see Figure 6). At each stage, a unique developmental task confronts individuals with a crisis that must be resolved. According to Erikson, this crisis is not a catastrophe but a turning point marked by both increased vulnerability and enhanced potential. The more successfully an individual resolves these crises, the healthier his or her development will be.

Trust versus mistrust is Erikson's first psychosocial stage, which is experienced in the first year of life. Trust during infancy sets the stage for a lifelong expectation that the world will be a good and pleasant place to live.

Autonomy versus shame and doubt is Erikson's second stage. This stage occurs in late infancy and toddlerhood (1 to 3 years). After gaining trust in their caregivers, infants begin to discover that their behavior is their own. They start to assert their sense of independence or autonomy. They realize their will. If infants and toddlers are restrained too much or punished too harshly, they are likely to develop a sense of shame and doubt.

Initiative versus guilt, Erikson's third stage of development, occurs during the preschool years. As preschool children encounter a widening social world, they face new challenges that require active, purposeful, responsible behavior. Feelings of guilt may arise, though, if the child is irresponsible and is made to feel too anxious.

Industry versus inferiority is Erikson's fourth developmental stage, occurring approximately in the elementary school years. Children now need to direct their energy toward mastering knowledge and intellectual skills. The negative outcome is that the child may develop a sense of inferiority—feeling incompetent and unproductive.

During the adolescent years individuals face finding out who they are, what they are all about, and where they are going in life. This is Erikson's fifth developmental stage, *identity versus identity confusion*. If

Erik Erikson with his wife, Joan, an artist. Erikson generated one of the most important developmental theories of the twentieth century. *Which stage of Erikson's theory are you in? Does Erikson's description of this stage characterize you?*

© Jon Erikson/The Image Works

adolescents explore roles in a healthy manner and arrive at a positive path to follow in life, then they achieve a positive identity; if not, then identity confusion reigns.

Intimacy versus isolation is Erikson's sixth developmental stage, which individuals experience during early adulthood. At this time, individuals face the developmental task of forming intimate relationships. If young adults form healthy friendships and an intimate relationship with a partner, intimacy will be achieved; if not, isolation will result.

Generativity versus stagnation, Erikson's seventh developmental stage, occurs during middle adulthood. By generativity, Erikson means primarily a concern for helping the younger generation to develop and lead useful lives. The feeling of having done nothing to help the next generation is stagnation.

Integrity versus despair is Erikson's eighth and final stage of development, which individuals experience in late adulthood. During this stage, a person reflects on the past. If the person's life review reveals a life well spent, integrity will be achieved; if not, the retrospective glances likely will yield doubt or gloom—the despair Erikson described.

Evaluating Psychoanalytic Theories

Contributions of psychoanalytic theories like Freud's and Erikson's to life-span development include an emphasis on a developmental framework, family relationships, and unconscious aspects of the mind. These theories have been criticized for a lack of scientific support, too much emphasis on sexual underpinnings, and an image of people that is too negative.

Cognitive Theories

Whereas psychoanalytic theories stress the unconscious, cognitive theories emphasize conscious thoughts. Three important cognitive theories are Piaget's cognitive developmental theory, Vygotsky's sociocultural cognitive theory, and information-processing theory. All three focus on the development of complex thinking skills.

Piaget's Cognitive Developmental Theory

Piaget's theory states that children go through four stages of cognitive development as they actively construct their understanding of the world. Two processes underlie this cognitive construction of the world: organization and adaptation. To make sense of our world, we organize our experiences. For example, we separate important ideas from less important ideas, and we connect one idea to another. In addition to organizing our observations and experiences, we must adjust to changing environmental demands (Miller, 2015).

Piaget (1954) described four stages in understanding the world (see Figure 7). Each stage is age-related and consists of a distinct way of thinking, a different way of understanding the world. Thus, according to Piaget, the child's cognition is *qualitatively* different in one stage compared with another. What are Piaget's four stages of cognitive development?

The *sensorimotor stage,* which lasts from birth to about 2 years of age, is the first Piagetian stage. In this stage, infants construct an understanding of the world by coordinating sensory experiences (such as seeing and hearing) with physical, motor actions—hence the term *sensorimotor.*

The *preoperational stage,* which lasts from approximately 2 to 7 years of age, is Piaget's second stage. In this stage, children begin to go beyond simply connecting sensory information with physical action and are now able to represent the world with words, images, and drawings. However, according to Piaget, preschool children still lack the ability to perform what he calls *operations,* which are internalized mental actions that allow children to do mentally what they previously could only do physically. For example, if you imagine putting two sticks together to see whether they would be as long as another stick, without actually moving the sticks, you are performing a concrete operation.

Piaget's theory The theory that children construct their understanding of the world and go through four stages of cognitive development.

Jean Piaget, the famous Swiss developmental psychologist, changed the way we think about the development of children's minds. *What are some key ideas in Piaget's theory?*

© Yves DeBraine/BlackStar/Stock Photo

Sensorimotor Stage	**Preoperational Stage**	**Concrete Operational Stage**	**Formal Operational Stage**
The infant constructs an understanding of the world by coordinating sensory experiences with physical actions. An infant progresses from reflexive, instinctual action at birth to the beginning of symbolic thought toward the end of the stage.	The child begins to represent the world with words and images. These words and images reflect increased symbolic thinking and go beyond the connection of sensory information and physical action.	The child can now reason logically about concrete events and classify objects into different sets.	The adolescent reasons in more abstract, idealistic, and logical ways.
Birth to 2 Years of Age	**2 to 7 Years of Age**	**7 to 11 Years of Age**	**11 Years of Age Through Adulthood**

Figure 7 **Piaget's Four Stages of Cognitive Development**
According to Piaget, how a child thinks—not how much the child knows—determines the child's stage of cognitive development.
Left to right © Stockbyte/Getty Images RF; © BananaStock/PunchStock RF; © image100/Corbis RF; © Purestock/Getty Images RF

Lev Vygotsky was born the same year as Piaget, but he died much earlier, at the age of 37. There is considerable interest today in Vygotsky's sociocultural cognitive theory of child development. *What are some key characteristics of Vygotsky's theory?*
© A.R. Lauria/Dr. Michael Cole, Laboratory of Human Cognition, University of California, San Diego

The *concrete operational stage,* which lasts from approximately 7 to 11 years of age, is the third Piagetian stage. In this stage, children can perform operations that involve objects, and they can reason logically about specific or concrete examples. Concrete operational thinkers, however, cannot imagine the steps necessary to complete an algebraic equation because doing so would require a level of thinking that is too abstract for this stage of development.

The *formal operational stage,* which appears between the ages of 11 and 15 and continues through adulthood, is Piaget's fourth and final stage. In this stage, individuals move beyond concrete experiences and think in abstract and more logical terms. As part of thinking more abstractly, adolescents develop images of ideal circumstances. They might think about what an ideal parent is like and compare their parents to this ideal standard. They begin to entertain possibilities for the future and are fascinated with what they can become. In solving problems, they become more systematic, developing hypotheses about why something is happening the way it is and then testing these hypotheses. We will examine Piaget's cognitive developmental theory further.

Vygotsky's Sociocultural Cognitive Theory

Like Piaget, the Russian developmentalist Lev Vygotsky (1896–1934) reasoned that children actively construct their knowledge. However, Vygotsky (1962) gave social interaction and culture far more important roles in cognitive development than Piaget did.

Vygotsky's theory is a sociocultural cognitive theory that emphasizes how culture and social interaction guide cognitive development. Vygotsky portrayed the child's development as inseparable from social and cultural activities (Gauvain & Perez, 2015). He stressed that cognitive development involves learning to use the inventions of society, such as language, mathematical systems, and memory strategies. Thus, in one culture children might learn to count with the help of a computer; in another they might learn by using beads. According to Vygotsky, children's social interaction with more-skilled adults and peers is indispensable to their cognitive development (Rogoff & others, 2015). Through this interaction, they learn to use the tools that will help them adapt and be successful in their culture. Later we will examine ideas about learning and teaching that are based on Vygotsky's theory.

Information-Processing Theory

Information-processing theory emphasizes that individuals manipulate information, monitor it, and strategize about it. Unlike Piaget's theory but like Vygotsky's theory, information-processing theory does not describe development as stage-like. Instead, according to this theory individuals develop a gradually increasing capacity for processing information, which allows them to acquire increasingly complex knowledge and skills (Muller & Kerns, 2015).

Robert Siegler (2006, 2013), a leading expert on children's information processing, states that thinking is information processing. In other words, when individuals perceive, encode, represent, store, and retrieve information, they are thinking. Siegler emphasizes that an important aspect of development is learning good strategies for processing information (Siegler, 2016a, b). For example, becoming a better reader might involve learning to monitor the key themes of the material being read.

Siegler (2006) also argues that the best way to understand how children learn is to observe them while they are learning. He emphasizes the importance of using the *microgenetic method* to obtain detailed information about processing mechanisms as they are occurring moment to moment. Siegler concludes that most research methods indirectly assess cognitive change, being more like snapshots than movies. The microgenetic method seeks to discover not just what children know but the cognitive processes involved in how they acquired the knowledge (Miller, 2015). A number of microgenetic studies have focused on a specific aspect of academic learning, such as how children learn whole number arithmetic, fractions, and other areas of math (Siegler, 2016a, b).

Evaluating Cognitive Theories

Contributions of cognitive theories include a positive view of development and an emphasis on the active construction of understanding. Criticisms include skepticism about the pureness of Piaget's stages and a belief that too little attention is paid to individual variations.

Behavioral and Social Cognitive Theories

Behavioral and social cognitive theories hold that development can be described in terms of behaviors learned through interactions with our surroundings. Behaviorism essentially holds that we can study scientifically only what can be directly observed and measured. Out of the behavioral tradition grew the belief that development is observable behavior that can be learned through experience with the environment (Spiegler, 2016). In terms of the continuity-discontinuity issue discussed earlier in this chapter, the behavioral and social cognitive theories emphasize continuity in development and argue that development does not occur in stage-like fashion. Let's explore two versions of behaviorism: Skinner's operant conditioning and Bandura's social cognitive theory.

Vygotsky's theory A sociocultural cognitive theory that emphasizes how culture and social interaction guide cognitive development.

information-processing theory A theory emphasizing that individuals manipulate information, monitor it, and strategize about it. The processes of memory and thinking are central.

behavioral and social cognitive theories Theories holding that development can be described in terms of the behaviors learned through interactions with the environment.

Skinner's Operant Conditioning

According to B. F. Skinner (1904–1990), through *operant conditioning* the consequences of a behavior produce changes in the probability of the behavior's recurrence. A behavior followed by a rewarding stimulus is more likely to recur, whereas a behavior followed by a punishing stimulus is less likely to recur. For example, when an adult smiles at a child after the child has done something, the child is more likely to engage in that behavior again than if the adult gives the child a disapproving look.

In Skinner's (1938) view, such rewards and punishments shape development. For Skinner the key aspect of development is behavior, not thoughts and feelings. He emphasized that development consists of the pattern of behavioral changes that are brought about by rewards and punishments. For example, Skinner would say that shy people learned to be shy as a result of experiences they had while growing up. It follows that modifications to an environment can help a shy person become more socially oriented.

Albert Bandura is a leading architect of social cognitive theory. *How does Bandura's theory differ from Skinner's?*
© Dr. Albert Bandura

Bandura's Social Cognitive Theory

Some psychologists agree with the behaviorists' notion that development is learned and is influenced strongly by environmental interactions. However, unlike Skinner, they also see cognition as important in understanding development. **Social cognitive theory** holds that behavior, environment, and person/cognitive factors are the key factors in development.

American psychologist Albert Bandura (1925) is the leading architect of social cognitive theory. Bandura (1986, 2004, 2010a, b, 2012, 2015) emphasizes that cognitive processes have important links with the environment and behavior. His early research program focused heavily on *observational learning* (also called *imitation* or *modeling*), which is learning that occurs through observing what others do. For example, a young boy might observe his father yelling in anger and treating other people with hostility; and then later with his peers, the young boy acts very aggressively, showing the same behavioral characteristics as his father. Social cognitive theorists stress that people acquire a wide range of behaviors, thoughts, and feelings through observing others' behavior and that these observations form an important part of life-span development.

What is *cognitive* about observational learning in Bandura's view? He proposes that people cognitively represent the behavior of others and then sometimes adopt this behavior themselves.

Bandura's (2004, 2010a, b, 2012, 2015) most recent model of learning and development includes three elements: behavior, the person/cognition, and the environment. An individual's confidence that he or she can control his or her success is an example of a person factor; strategies for achieving success are an example of a cognitive factor. As shown in Figure 8, influences from behavior, person/cognition, and environment operate interactively.

Evaluating Behavioral and Social Cognitive Theories

Contributions of the behavioral and social cognitive theories include an emphasis on scientific research and environmental determinants of behavior. These theories have been criticized for placing too little emphasis on cognition (Skinner) and giving inadequate attention to developmental changes.

social cognitive theory The theory that behavior, environment, and person/cognitive factors are important in understanding development.

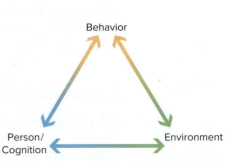

Figure 8 Bandura's Social Cognitive Model
The arrows illustrate how relations between behavior, person/cognition, and environment are reciprocal rather than one-way. Person/cognition refers to cognitive processes (for example, thinking and planning) and personal characteristics (for example, believing that you can control your experiences).

Ethological Theory

ethology An approach stressing that behavior is strongly influenced by biology, tied to evolution, and characterized by critical or sensitive periods.

Ethology is the study of the behavior of animals in their natural habitat. Ethological theory stresses that behavior is strongly influenced by biology, is tied to evolution, and is characterized by critical or sensitive periods (Bateson, 2015). These are specific time frames during which, according to ethologists, the presence or absence of certain experiences has a long-lasting influence on individuals.

Lorenz's Research with Greylag Geese

European zoologist Konrad Lorenz (1903–1989) helped bring ethology to prominence. In his best-known research, Lorenz (1965) studied the behavior of greylag geese, which follow their mothers as soon as they hatch. Lorenz separated the eggs laid by one goose into two groups. One group he returned to the goose to be hatched by her. The other group was hatched in an incubator. The goslings in the first group performed as predicted. They followed their mother as soon as they hatched. However, those in the second group, which saw Lorenz when they first hatched, followed him everywhere as though he were their mother. Lorenz marked the goslings and then placed both groups under a box. Mother goose and "mother" Lorenz stood aside as the box was lifted. Each group of goslings went directly to its "mother." Lorenz called this process *imprinting*—the rapid, innate learning that involves attachment to the first moving object seen.

John Bowlby (1969, 1989) illustrated an important application of ethological theory to human development. Bowlby stressed that attachment to a caregiver over the first year of life has important consequences throughout the life span. In his view, if this attachment is positive and secure, the individual will likely develop positively in childhood and adulthood. If the attachment is negative and insecure, development will likely not be optimal. Later we will explore the concept of infant attachment in much greater detail.

In Lorenz's view, imprinting needs to take place at a specific, very early time in the life of the animal, or else it will not take place. This point in time is called a critical period. A related concept is that of a sensitive period, and an example is the time during infancy when, according to Bowlby, attachment should occur in order to promote optimal development of social relationships.

Another theory that emphasizes biological foundations of development—evolutionary psychology—will be presented in another chapter, along with views on the role of heredity in development. In addition, we will examine a number of biological theories of aging.

Evaluating Ethological Theory

Contributions of ethological theory include a focus on the biological and evolutionary basis of development, and the use of careful observations in naturalistic settings. Criticisms include a belief that it places too much emphasis on biological foundations and that the concept of a critical and sensitive period might be too rigid.

Ecological Theory

While ethological theory stresses biological factors, ecological theory emphasizes environmental factors. One ecological theory that has important implications for understanding life-span development was created by Urie Bronfenbrenner (1917–2005).

Konrad Lorenz, a pioneering student of animal behavior, is followed through the water by three imprinted greylag geese. Describe Lorenz's experiment with the geese. *Do you think his experiment would have the same results with human babies? Explain.*

© Nina Leen/Time & Life Pictures/Getty Images

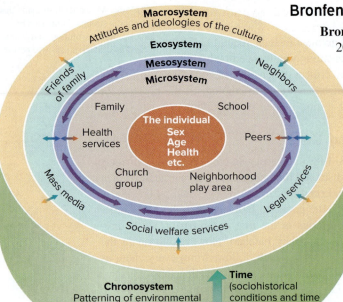

Bronfenbrenner's Ecological Theory

Bronfenbrenner's ecological theory (1986, 2004; Bronfenbrenner & Morris, 2006) holds that development reflects the influence of several environmental systems. The theory identifies five environmental systems: microsystem, mesosystem, exosystem, macrosystem, and chronosystem (see Figure 9).

The *microsystem* is the setting in which the individual lives. These contexts include the person's family, peers, school, and neighborhood. It is in the microsystem that the most direct interactions with social agents take place—with parents, peers, and teachers, for example. The individual is not a passive recipient of experiences in these settings, but someone who helps to construct the settings.

The *mesosystem* involves relations between microsystems or connections between contexts. Examples are the relation of family experiences to school experiences, school experiences to church experiences, and family experiences to peer experiences. For example, children whose parents have rejected them may have difficulty developing positive relations with teachers.

The *exosystem* consists of links between a social setting in which the individual does not have an active role and the individual's immediate context. For example, a husband's or child's experience at home may be influenced by a mother's experiences at work. The mother might receive a promotion that requires more travel, which might increase conflict with the husband and change patterns of interaction with the child.

Figure 9 Bronfenbrenner's Ecological Theory of Development
Bronfenbrenner's ecological theory consists of five environmental systems: microsystem, mesosystem, exosystem, macrosystem, and chronosystem.

How Would You...?
If you were an **educator,** how might you explain a student's chronic failure to complete homework from the mesosystem level? From the exosystem level?

The *macrosystem* involves the culture in which individuals live. Remember from earlier in the chapter that *culture* refers to the behavior patterns, beliefs, and all other products of a group of people that are passed on from generation to generation. Remember also that cross-cultural studies—the comparison of one culture with one or more other cultures—provide information about the generality of development.

The *chronosystem* consists of the patterning of environmental events and transitions over the life course, as well as sociohistorical circumstances. For example, divorce is one transition. Researchers have found that the negative effects of divorce on children often peak in the first year after the divorce (Hetherington, 2006). By two years after the divorce, family interaction has become more stable. As an example of sociohistorical circumstances, consider how the opportunities for women to pursue a career have increased since the 1960s.

Bronfenbrenner's ecological theory Bronfenbrenner's environmental systems theory, which focuses on five environmental systems: microsystem, mesosystem, exosystem, macrosystem, and chronosystem.

Urie Bronfenbrenner developed ecological theory, a perspective that is receiving increased attention today. His theory emphasizes the importance of both micro and macro dimensions of the environment in which the child lives.
© Cornell University

Responding to growing interest in biological contributions to development, Bronfenbrenner (2004) added biological influences to his theory and relabeled it as a bioecological theory. Nonetheless, it is still dominated by ecological, environmental contexts (Gauvain & Perez, 2015).

Evaluating Ecological Theory

Contributions of ecological theory include its systematic examination of macro and micro dimensions of environmental systems and its attention to connections between environmental systems. A further contribution of Bronfenbrenner's theory is an emphasis on a range of social contexts beyond the family, such as neighborhood, religious, school, and workplace environments, as influential in children's development (Gauvain & Perez, 2015). The theory has been criticized for giving inadequate attention to biological factors, as well as placing too little emphasis on cognitive factors.

An Eclectic Theoretical Orientation

No single theory described in this chapter can explain entirely the rich complexity of life-span development, but each has contributed to our understanding of development. Psychoanalytic theory highlights the importance of the unconscious mind. Erikson's theory best describes the changes that occur in adult development. Piaget's, Vygotsky's, and the information-processing views provide the most complete description of cognitive development. The behavioral and social cognitive and ecological theories have been the most adept at examining the environmental determinants of development. The ethological theories have drawn attention to biology's role and the importance of sensitive periods in development.

In short, although theories are helpful guides, relying on a single theory to explain development is probably a mistake. This book instead takes an **eclectic theoretical orientation,** which does not follow any one theoretical approach but rather presents what are considered the best features of each theory. In this way, it represents the study of development as it actually exists—with different theorists making different assumptions, stressing different problems, and using different strategies to discover information. Figure 10 compares the main theoretical perspectives in terms of how they view important issues in life-span development.

eclectic theoretical orientation An approach that selects and uses whatever is considered the best in many theories.

THEORY	ISSUES	
	Continuity/discontinuity, early versus later experiences	**Biological and environmental factors**
Psychoanalytic	Discontinuity between stages—continuity between early experiences and later development; early experiences very important; later changes in development emphasized in Erikson's theory	Freud's biological determination interacting with early family experiences; Erikson's more balanced biological-cultural interaction perspective
Cognitive	Discontinuity between stages in Piaget's theory; continuity between early experiences and later development in Piaget's and Vygotsky's theories; no stages in Vygotsky's theory or information-processing theory	Piaget's emphasis on interaction and adaptation; environment provides the setting for cognitive structures to develop; information-processing view has not addressed this issue extensively but mainly emphasizes biological-environmental interaction
Behavioral and social cognitive	Continuity (no stages); experience at all points of development important	Environment viewed as the cause of behavior in both views
Ethological	Discontinuity but no stages; critical or sensitive periods emphasized; early experiences very important	Strong biological view
Ecological	Little attention to continuity/discontinuity; change emphasized more than stability	Strong environmental view

Figure 10 Summary of Theories and Issues in Life-Span Development

Research in Life-Span Development

How do scholars and researchers with an eclectic orientation determine that one theory is somehow better than a different theory? The scientific method discussed earlier in this chapter provides a guide. Through scientific research, theories are tested and refined (Christensen, Johnson, & Turner, 2015).

Generally, research in life-span development is designed to test hypotheses, which may be derived from the theories just described. Through research, theories are modified to reflect new data, and occasionally new theories arise. How are data about life-span development collected? What types of research designs are used to study life-span development? And what are some ethical considerations in conducting research on life-span development?

Methods for Collecting Data

Whether we are interested in studying attachment in infants, the cognitive skills of children, or social relationships in older adults, we can choose from several ways of collecting data (Salkind, 2017; Trochim, Donnelly, & Arora, 2016). Here we outline the measures most often used, beginning with observation.

Observation

Scientific observation requires an important set of skills. For observations to be effective, they must be systematic (Jackson, 2016). We need to have some idea of what we are looking for. We have to know whom we are observing, when and where we will observe, how the observations will be made, and how they will be recorded.

Where should we make our observations? We have two choices: the laboratory and the everyday world.

When we observe scientifically, we often need to control certain factors that determine behavior but are not the focus of our inquiry (Stangor, 2015). For this reason, some research in life-span development is conducted in a **laboratory,** a controlled setting where many of the complex factors of the "real world" are absent. For example, suppose you want to observe how children react when they see other people behaving aggressively. If you observe children in their homes or schools, you have no control over how much aggression the children observe, what kind of aggression they see, which people they see acting aggressively, or how other people treat the children. In contrast, if you observe the children in a laboratory, you can control these and other factors and therefore have more confidence about how to interpret your observations.

Laboratory research does have some drawbacks, however, including the following concerns: (1) it is almost impossible to conduct research without the participants' knowing they are being studied; (2) the laboratory setting is unnatural and therefore can cause the participants to behave unnaturally; (3) people who are willing to come to a university laboratory may not fairly represent groups from diverse cultural backgrounds; (4) people who are unfamiliar with university settings, and with the idea of "helping science," may be intimidated by the laboratory setting.

Naturalistic observation provides insights that we sometimes cannot attain in the laboratory (Leedy & Ormrod, 2016). **Naturalistic observation** means observing behavior in real-world settings and making no effort to manipulate or control the situation. Life-span researchers

What are some important strategies in conducting observational research with children?
© Charles Fox/Philadelphia Inquirer/MCT/Landov

laboratory A controlled setting in which research can take place.

naturalistic observation Observation that occurs in a real-world setting without any attempt to manipulate the situation.

conduct naturalistic observations at sporting events, child-care centers, work settings, malls, and other places people live in and frequent.

Naturalistic observation was used in one study that focused on conversations in a children's science museum (Crowley & others, 2001). When visiting exhibits at the museum with their children, parents were more than three times as likely to engage boys than girls in explanatory talk. The gender difference occurred regardless of whether the father, the mother, or both parents were with the child, although the gender difference was greatest for fathers' science explanations to sons and daughters. This finding suggests a gender bias that encourages boys more than girls to be interested in science.

Survey and Interview

Sometimes the best and quickest way to get information about people is to ask them for it. One technique is to interview them directly. A related method is administering a survey (sometimes referred to as a questionnaire) consisting of a standard set of questions designed to obtain people's self-reported attitudes or beliefs about a particular topic. Surveys are especially useful when information from many people is needed (Madill, 2012). In a good survey, the questions are clear and unbiased, allowing respondents to answer unambiguously.

Surveys and interviews can be used to study topics ranging from religious beliefs to sexual habits to attitudes about gun control to beliefs about how to improve schools. Surveys and interviews may be conducted in person, over the telephone, by mail, and over the Internet.

One problem with surveys and interviews is the tendency of participants to answer questions in a way that they think is socially acceptable or desirable rather than to say what they truly think or feel. For example, on a survey or in an interview some individuals might say that they do not take drugs even though they do.

Standardized Test

A **standardized test** has uniform procedures for administration and scoring. Many standardized tests allow performance comparisons; they provide information about individual differences among people (Gregory, 2014). One example is the Stanford-Binet intelligence test, which is discussed in detail later. Your score on the Stanford-Binet test tells you how your performance compares with that of thousands of other people who have taken the test.

One criticism of standardized tests is that they assume a person's behavior is consistent and stable, yet personality and intelligence—two primary targets of standardized testing—can vary with the situation. For example, a person may perform poorly on a standardized intelligence test in an office setting but score much higher at home, where he or she is less anxious.

Mahatma Gandhi was the spiritual leader of India in the mid-twentieth century. Erik Erikson conducted an extensive case study of Gandhi's life to determine what contributed to his identity development. *What are some limitations of the case study approach?*
© Bettmann/Corbis

Case Study

A **case study** is an in-depth look at a single individual. Case studies are performed mainly by mental health professionals when, for either practical or ethical reasons, the unique aspects of an individual's life cannot be duplicated and tested in other individuals. A case study provides information about one person's experiences; it may focus on

standardized test A test that is given with uniform procedures for administration and scoring.

case study An in-depth examination of an individual.

nearly any aspect of the subject's life that helps the researcher understand the person's mind, behavior, or other attributes. A researcher may gather information for a case study from interviews and medical records. In later chapters we discuss vivid case studies, such as that of Michael Rehbein, who had much of the left side of his brain removed at 7 years of age to end severe epileptic seizures.

A case study can provide a dramatic, in-depth portrayal of an individual's life, but we must be cautious when generalizing from this information. The subject of a case study is unique, with a genetic makeup and personal history that no one else shares. In addition, case studies involve judgments of unknown reliability. Researchers who conduct case studies rarely check to see whether other professionals agree with their observations or findings (Yin, 2012).

Physiological Measures

Researchers are increasingly using physiological measures when they study development at different points in the life span (Johnson, 2016; Kennedy & others, 2015; Zisner & Beauchaine, 2016). A physiological measure that is increasingly being used is neuroimaging, especially *functional magnetic resonance imaging* (fMRI), in which electromagnetic waves are used to construct images of a person's brain tissue and biochemical activity (de Haan & Johnson, 2016; Galvan & Tottenham, 2016; Park & Farrell, 2016). Heart rate has been used as an indicator of infants' and children's development of perception, attention, and memory (Kim, Yang, & Lee, 2015). Further, heart rate has been used as an index of different aspects of emotional development, such as inhibition, anxiety, and depression (Blood & others, 2015).

Cortisol is a hormone produced by the adrenal gland that is linked to the body's stress level and has been measured in studies of temperament, emotional reactivity, peer relations, and child psychopathology (Jacoby & others, 2016). As puberty unfolds, the blood levels of certain hormones increase. To determine the nature of these hormonal changes, researchers analyze blood samples from adolescent volunteers (Susman & Dorn, 2013).

Yet another dramatic change in physiological methods is the advancement in methods to assess the actual units of hereditary information—genes—in studies of biological influences on development (Cho & Suh, 2016; Grigorenko & others, 2016). For example, in the chapter on physical and cognitive development in late adulthood you will read about the role of the ApoE4 gene in Alzheimer disease (Park & Farrell, 2016).

Research Designs

In addition to a method for collecting data, you also need a research design to study life-span development. There are three main types of research designs: descriptive, correlational, and experimental.

Descriptive Research

All of the data-collection methods that we have discussed can be used in **descriptive research,** which aims to observe and record behavior. For example, a researcher might observe the extent to which people are altruistic or aggressive toward each other. By itself, descriptive research cannot prove what causes some phenomenon, but it can reveal important information about people's behavior and provide a basis for more scientific studies (Leedy & Ormrod, 2016).

descriptive research Type of research that aims to observe and record behavior.

correlational research A type of research that focuses on describing the strength of the relation between two or more events or characteristics.

Correlational Research

In contrast with descriptive research, correlational research goes beyond describing phenomena by providing information that helps to predict how people will behave. In **correlational research,** the goal is to describe the strength of the relationship between two or more events or characteristics. The more strongly the two events are correlated

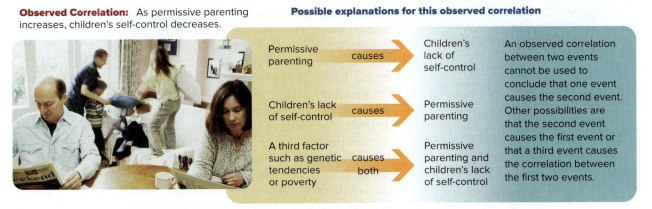

Observed Correlation: As permissive parenting increases, children's self-control decreases.

Possible explanations for this observed correlation

Permissive parenting	causes →	Children's lack of self-control
Children's lack of self-control	causes →	Permissive parenting
A third factor such as genetic tendencies or poverty	causes both →	Permissive parenting and children's lack of self-control

An observed correlation between two events cannot be used to conclude that one event causes the second event. Other possibilities are that the second event causes the first event or that a third event causes the correlation between the first two events.

Figure 11 Possible Explanations for Correlational Data

© Digital Vision/PunchStock RF

(or related or associated), the more effectively we can predict one event from the other (Aron, Aron, & Coups, 2017).

For example, to determine whether children of permissive parents have less self-control than other children, you would need to carefully record observations of parents' permissiveness and their children's self-control. You might observe that the higher a parent was in permissiveness, the lower the child was in self-control. You would then analyze these data statistically to yield a **correlation coefficient,** a number based on a statistical analysis that is used to describe the degree of association between two variables. Correlation coefficients range from –1.00 to +1.00. A negative number means an inverse relation. In the above example, you might find an inverse correlation between permissive parenting and children's self-control, with a coefficient of, say, –.30 meaning that parents who are permissive with their children are likely to have children who have low self-control. By contrast, you might find a positive correlation of +.30 between parental monitoring of children and children's self-control, meaning that parents who monitor their children effectively have children with good self-control.

The higher the correlation coefficient (whether positive or negative), the stronger the association between the two variables. A correlation of 0 means that there is no association between the variables. A correlation of –.40 is stronger than a correlation of +.20 because we disregard whether the correlation is positive or negative in determining the strength of the correlation.

A word of caution is in order, however. Correlation does not equal causation (Heiman, 2014, 2015). The correlational finding just mentioned does not mean that permissive parenting necessarily causes low self-control in children. It could have that meaning, but it also could mean that a child's lack of self-control caused the parents to throw up their arms in despair and give up trying to control the child. It also could mean that other factors, such as heredity or poverty, caused the correlation between permissive parenting and low self-control in children. Figure 11 illustrates these possible interpretations of correlational data.

Experimental Research

To study causality, researchers turn to experimental research. An **experiment** is a carefully regulated procedure in which one or more factors believed to influence the behavior being studied are manipulated while all other factors are held constant. If the behavior under study changes when a factor is manipulated, we say that the manipulated factor has caused the behavior to change. In other words, the experiment has demonstrated cause and effect. The cause is the factor that was manipulated. The effect is the behavior that changed because of the manipulation. Nonexperimental research methods (descriptive and correlational research) cannot establish cause and effect because they do not involve manipulating factors in a controlled way (Kantowitz, Roediger, & Elmes, 2015).

correlation coefficient A number based on statistical analysis that is used to describe the degree of association between two variables.

experiment A carefully regulated procedure in which one or more of the factors believed to influence the behavior being studied is manipulated and all other factors are held constant. Experimental research permits the determination of cause.

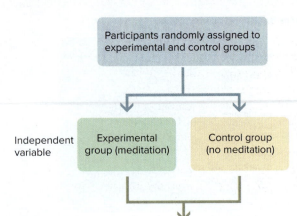

Independent variable — Experimental group (meditation)

Control group (no meditation)

Participants randomly assigned to experimental and control groups

Dependent variable — Newborns' breathing and sleeping patterns

Figure 12 Principles of Experimental Research
Imagine that you decide to conduct an experimental study of the effects of meditation by pregnant women on their newborns' breathing and sleeping patterns. You randomly assign pregnant women to experimental and control groups. The experimental-group women engage in meditation over a specified number of sessions and weeks. The control group does not. Then, when the infants are born, you assess their breathing and sleeping patterns. If the breathing and sleeping patterns of newborns whose mothers were in the experimental group are more positive than those of the control group, you conclude that meditation caused the positive effects.

Independent and Dependent Variables Experiments include two types of changeable factors: independent and dependent variables. An *independent variable* is a manipulated, influential experimental factor. It is a potential cause. The label "independent" is used because this variable can be manipulated independently of other factors to determine its effect. An experiment may include one independent variable or several of them.

A *dependent variable* is a factor that can change in an experiment, in response to changes in the independent variable. As researchers manipulate the independent variable, they measure the dependent variable for any resulting effect (Gravetter & Forzano, 2016).

For example, suppose that you wanted to study whether pregnant women could change the breathing and sleeping patterns of their newborn babies by meditating during pregnancy. You might require one group of pregnant women to engage in a certain amount and type of meditation each day, while another group would not meditate; the meditation is thus the independent variable. When the infants are born, you would observe and measure their breathing and sleeping patterns. These patterns are the dependent variable, the factor that changes as the result of your manipulation.

Experimental and Control Groups Experiments can involve one or more experimental groups and one or more control groups. An experimental group is a group whose experience is manipulated. A control group is a comparison group that is as much like the experimental group as possible and that is treated in every way like the experimental group except for the manipulated factor (independent variable). The control group serves as a baseline against which the effects of the manipulated condition can be compared.

Random assignment is an important principle for deciding whether each participant will be placed in the experimental group or in the control group. Random assignment means that researchers assign participants to experimental and control groups by chance. It reduces the likelihood that the experiment's results will be due to any preexisting differences between groups (Gravetter & Forzano, 2016). In the example of the effects of meditation by pregnant women on the breathing and sleeping patterns of their newborns, you would randomly assign half of the pregnant women to engage in meditation over a period of weeks (the experimental group) and the other half to not meditate over the same number of weeks (the control group). Figure 12 illustrates the nature of experimental research.

Time Span of Research

Researchers in life-span development have a special concern with the relation between age and some other variable. To explore these relations, researchers can study different individuals of different ages and compare them, or they can study the same individuals as they age over time.

Cross-Sectional Approach

cross-sectional approach A research strategy in which individuals of different ages are compared at one time.

The **cross-sectional approach** is a research strategy that simultaneously compares individuals of different ages. A typical cross-sectional study might include three groups of children: 5-year-olds, 8-year-olds, and

11-year-olds. Another study might include groups of 15-year-olds, 25-year-olds, and 45-year-olds. The groups can be compared with respect to a variety of dependent variables, such as IQ, memory, peer relations, attachment to parents, hormonal changes, and so on. All of this can be accomplished in a short time. In some studies data are collected in a single day. Even in large-scale cross-sectional studies with hundreds of subjects, data collection does not usually take longer than several months to complete.

The main advantage of the cross-sectional study is that the researcher does not have to wait for the individuals to grow up or become older. Despite its efficiency, though, the cross-sectional approach has its drawbacks. It gives no information about how individuals change or about the stability of their characteristics. It can obscure the hills and valleys of growth and development. For example, a cross-sectional study of life satisfaction might reveal average increases and decreases, but it would not show how the life satisfaction of individual adults waxed and waned over the years. It also would not tell us whether the same adults who had positive or negative perceptions of life satisfaction in early adulthood maintained their relative degree of life satisfaction as they became middle-aged or older adults.

Longitudinal Approach

The **longitudinal approach** is a research strategy in which the same individuals are studied over a period of time, usually several years or more. For example, in a longitudinal study of life satisfaction, the same adults might be assessed periodically over a 70-year time span—at the ages of 20, 35, 45, 65, and 90, for example.

Longitudinal studies provide a wealth of information about vital issues such as stability and change in development and the importance of early experience for later development, but they do have drawbacks (Cicchetti & Toth, 2015, 2016). They are expensive and time-consuming. The longer the study lasts, the more participants drop out—they move, get sick, lose interest, and so forth. The participants who remain may be dissimilar to those who drop out, biasing the outcome of the study. Those individuals who remain in a longitudinal study over a number of years may be more responsible and conformity-oriented than the ones who dropped out, for example, or they might have more stable lives.

Cohort Effects

A *cohort* is a group of people who are born at a similar point in history and share similar experiences as a result, such as living through the Vietnam war or growing up in the same city around the same time. These shared experiences may produce a range of differences among cohorts (Kadlecova & others, 2015; MacDonald & Stawski, 2016). For example, people who were teenagers during the Great Depression are likely to differ from people who were teenagers during the booming 1990s in their educational opportunities and economic status, in how they were raised, and in their attitudes toward sex and religion. In life-span development research, **cohort effects** are due to a person's time of birth, era, or generation but not to actual age.

Cohort effects are important because they can powerfully affect the dependent measures in a study ostensibly concerned with age (Carstensen & others, 2015; George & Ferraro, 2016). Researchers have shown it is especially important to be aware of cohort effects when assessing adult intelligence (Schaie, 2013, 2016). Individuals born at different points in time—such as 1920, 1940, and 1960—have had varying opportunities for education. Individuals born in earlier years had less access to education, and this fact may have a significant effect on how this cohort performs on intelligence tests. Some researchers have found that cross-sectional studies indicate more than 90 percent of cognitive decline in aging is due to a slowing of processing speed, whereas longitudinal studies reveal that 20 percent or less of cognitive decline is due to processing speed (MacDonald & others, 2003; MacDonald & Stawski, 2015, 2016; Stawski, Sliwinski, & Hofer, 2013). Another recent example of a cohort effect occurred in a study in which older adults assessed in 2013–2014 engaged in a higher

longitudinal approach A research strategy in which the same individuals are studied over a period of time, usually several years or more.

cohort effects Effects that are due to a subject's time of birth or generation but not age.

Generation	Historical Period	Reasons for Label
Millennials	Individuals born in 1980 and later	First generation to come of age and enter emerging adulthood (18 to 25 years of age) in the twenty-first century (the new millennium). Two main characteristics: (1) connection to technology, and (2) ethnic diversity.
Generation X	Individuals born between 1965 and 1980	Described as lacking an identity and savvy loners.
Baby Boomers	Individuals born between 1946 and 1964	Label used because this generation represents the spike in the number of babies born after World War II; the largest generation ever to enter late adulthood in the United States.
Silent Generation	Individuals born between 1928 and 1945	Children of the Great Depression and World War II; described as conformists and civic minded.

Figure 13 Generations, Their Historical Periods, and Characteristics

level of abstract reasoning than their counterparts assessed two decades earlier in 1990–1993 (Gerstorf & others, 2015).

Cross-sectional studies can show how different cohorts respond, but they can confuse age changes and cohort effects. Longitudinal studies are effective in studying age changes, but only within one cohort.

Various generations have been given labels by the popular culture. Figure 13 describes the labels of various generations, the historical period for each one, and the reasons for their labels. Consider the following description of the current generation of youth and think about how they differ from earlier youth generations:

They are history's first "always connected" generation. Steeped in digital technology and social media, they treat their multi-tasking hand-held gadgets almost like a body part—for better or worse. More than 8-in-10 say they sleep with a cell phone glowing by the bed, poised to disgorge texts, phone calls, e-mails, songs, news, videos, games, and wake-up jingles. But sometimes convenience yields to temptation. Nearly two-thirds admit to texting while driving (Pew Research Center, 2010, p. 1).

How does the youth experienced by today's millennials differ from that of earlier generations?
© Hero Images/Alamy RF

Conducting Ethical Research

Researchers who study human development and behavior confront many ethical issues. For example, a developmentalist who wanted to study aggression in children would have to design the study in such a way that no child would be harmed physically or psychologically, and the researcher would need to get permission from the university to carry out the study. Then the researcher would have to explain the study to the children's parents and obtain consent for the children to participate. Ethics in research may affect you personally if you ever serve as a participant in a study. In that event, you need to know your rights as a participant and the responsibilities of researchers to ensure that these rights are safeguarded.

Today, proposed research at colleges and universities must pass the scrutiny of a research ethics committee before the research can begin. In addition, the American Psychological Association (APA) has developed ethics guidelines for its members. This code of ethics instructs psychologists to protect their research participants from mental and physical harm. The participants' best interests need to be kept foremost in the researcher's mind (Jackson, 2016).

APA's guidelines address four important issues:

1. *Informed consent*—All participants must know what their research participation will involve and what risks might develop. Even after informed consent is given, participants must retain the right to withdraw from the study at any time and for any reason.

2. *Confidentiality*—Researchers are responsible for keeping all of the data they gather on individuals completely confidential and, when possible, completely anonymous.

3. *Debriefing*—After the study has been completed, participants should be informed of its purpose and the methods that were used. In most cases, the experimenter also can inform participants in a general manner beforehand about the purpose of the research without leading participants to behave in a way they think that the experimenter is expecting.

4. *Deception*—In some circumstances, telling the participants beforehand what the research study is about substantially alters the participants' behavior and invalidates the researcher's data. In all cases of deception, however, the psychologist must ensure that the deception will not harm the participants and that the participants will be *debriefed* (told the complete nature of the study) as soon as possible after the study is completed.

Summary

The Life-Span Perspective
- Development is the pattern of change that begins at conception and continues through the life span. It includes both growth and decline.
- The life-span perspective includes these basic ideas: development is lifelong, multidimensional, multidirectional, and plastic; its study is multidisciplinary; it is embedded in contexts; it involves growth, maintenance, and regulation; and it is a co-construction of biological, sociocultural, and individual factors.
- Health and well-being, parenting, education, sociocultural contexts and diversity, and social policy are all areas of contemporary concern for those who study life-span development.

The Nature of Development
- Three key developmental processes are biological, cognitive, and socioemotional. Development is influenced by an interplay of these processes.
- The life span is commonly divided into the prenatal period, infancy, early childhood, middle and late childhood, adolescence, early adulthood, middle adulthood, and late adulthood.
- We often think of age only in chronological terms, but a full evaluation of age requires the consideration of biological age, psychological age, and social age as well.
- Three pathways of aging are pathological aging, normal aging, and successful aging.
- In research covering adolescence through late adulthood, many but not all studies find that older adults report the highest level of life satisfaction.
- Three important issues in the study of development are the nature-nurture issue, the continuity-discontinuity issue, and the stability-change issue.

Theories of Development
- According to psychoanalytic theories, including those of Freud and Erikson, development primarily depends on the unconscious mind and is heavily couched in emotion.
- Cognitive theories emphasize thinking, reasoning, language, and other cognitive processes. Three main cognitive theories are Piaget's, Vygotsky's, and information processing.
- Behavioral and social cognitive theories emphasize the environment's role in development. Two key behavioral and social cognitive theories are Skinner's operant conditioning and Bandura's social cognitive theory.
- Lorenz's ethological theory stresses the biological and evolutionary bases of development.
- According to Bronfenbrenner's ecological theory, development predominantly reflects the influence of five environmental systems—the microsystem, mesosystem, exosystem, macrosystem, and chronosystem.
- An eclectic orientation incorporates the best features of different theoretical approaches.

Research in Life-Span Development
- The main methods for collecting data about life-span development are observation, survey (questionnaire) or interview, standardized test, case study, and physiological measures.
- Three basic research designs are descriptive, correlational, and experimental.
- To examine the effects of time and age, researchers can conduct cross-sectional or longitudinal studies. Life-span researchers are especially concerned about cohort effects.
- Researchers have an ethical responsibility to safeguard the well-being of research participants.

Key Terms

behavioral and social
  cognitive theories
biological processes
Bronfenbrenner's ecological
  theory
case study
cognitive processes
cohort effects
context
continuity-discontinuity issue
correlational research
correlation coefficient

cross-cultural studies
cross-sectional approach
culture
descriptive research
development
eclectic theoretical orientation
Erikson's theory
ethnicity
ethology
experiment
gender
hypotheses

information-processing
  theory
laboratory
life-span perspective
longitudinal approach
naturalistic observation
nature-nurture issue
nonnormative life events
normative age-graded
  influences
normative history-graded
  influences

Piaget's theory
psychoanalytic theories
social cognitive theory
social policy
socioeconomic status (SES)
socioemotional processes
stability-change issue
standardized test
theory
Vygotsky's theory

2 Biological Beginnings

© MedicalRF.com/Getty Images RF

CHAPTER OUTLINE

Stories of Life-Span Development: The Jim and Jim Twins

Jim Springer and Jim Lewis are identical twins. They were separated at 4 weeks of age and did not see each other again until they were 39 years old. Both worked as part-time deputy sheriffs, vacationed in Florida, drove Chevrolets, had dogs named Toy, and married and divorced women named Betty. One twin named his son James Allan, and the other named his son James Alan. Both liked math but not spelling, enjoyed carpentry and mechanical drawing, chewed their fingernails down to the nubs, had almost identical drinking and smoking habits, had hemorrhoids, put on 10 pounds at about the same point in development, first suffered headaches at the age of 18, and had similar sleep patterns.

Jim and Jim do have some differences. One wears his hair over his forehead, the other slicks it back and has sideburns. One expresses himself best orally; the other is more proficient in writing. But, for the most part, their profiles are remarkably similar.

Another pair of identical twins, Daphne and Barbara, were called the "giggle sisters" by researchers because after being reunited they were always making each other laugh. A thorough search of their adoptive families' histories revealed no gigglers. The giggle sisters ignored stress, avoided conflict and controversy whenever possible, and showed no interest in politics.

Jim and Jim and the giggle sisters were part of the Minnesota Study of Twins Reared Apart, directed by Thomas Bouchard and his colleagues. The study brings identical twins (who are identical genetically because they come from the same fertilized egg) and fraternal twins (who come from different fertilized eggs) from all over the world to Minneapolis to investigate their lives. There the twins complete personality and intelligence tests, and provide detailed medical histories, including information about diet and smoking, exercise habits, chest X-rays, heart stress tests, and EEGs. The twins are asked more than 15,000 questions about their family and childhood, personal interests, vocational orientation, values, and aesthetic judgments (Bouchard & others, 1990).

When genetically identical twins who were separated as infants show such striking similarities in their tastes and habits and choices, can we conclude that their genes must have caused these similarities? Although genes play a role, we also need to consider other possible causes. The twins shared not only the same genes but also some similar experiences. Some of the separated twins lived together for several months prior to their adoption; some had been reunited prior to testing (in some cases, many years earlier); adoption agencies often place twins in similar homes; and even strangers who spend several hours together and start comparing their lives are likely to come up with some coincidental similarities (Joseph, 2006).

The Minnesota study of identical twins points to both the importance of the genetic basis of human development and the need for further research on genetic and environmental factors.

The examples of Jim and Jim and the giggle sisters stimulate us to think about our genetic heritage and the biological foundations of our existence. Organisms are not like billiard balls, moved by simple, external forces to predictable positions on life's pool table. Environmental experiences and biological foundations work together to make us who we are. Our coverage of life's biological beginnings and experiences will emphasize the evolutionary perspective; genetic foundations; the interaction of heredity and environment; and charting growth from conception through the prenatal period, the birth process itself, and the postpartum period that follows birth. ■

The Evolutionary Perspective

From the perspective of evolutionary time, humans are relative newcomers to Earth. As our earliest ancestors left the forest to feed on the savannahs and then to form hunting societies on the open plains, their minds and behaviors changed, and humans eventually became the dominant species on Earth. How did this evolution come about?

Natural Selection and Adaptive Behavior

Charles Darwin (1859) described *natural selection* as the evolutionary process by which those individuals of a species that are best *adapted* to their environment are the ones that are most likely to survive and reproduce. He reasoned that an intense, constant struggle for food, water, and resources must occur among the young of each generation, because many of them do not survive. Those that do survive and reproduce pass on their characteristics to the next generation (Audesirk, Audesirk, & Byers, 2017; Johnson, 2017). Darwin concluded that these survivors are better adapted to their world than are the nonsurvivors. The best-adapted individuals survive and leave the most offspring. Over the course of many generations, organisms with the characteristics needed for survival make up an increased percentage of the population (Mader & Windelspecht, 2016; Simon, 2017).

How Would You...?
As a **health-care professional,** how would you explain technology and medicine working against natural selection?

Evolutionary Psychology

evolutionary psychology Emphasizes the importance of adaptation, reproduction, and "survival of the fittest" in shaping behavior.

Although Darwin introduced the theory of evolution by natural selection in 1859, his ideas have only recently become a popular framework for explaining behavior. Psychology's newest approach, **evolutionary psychology,** emphasizes the importance of adaptation, reproduction, and "survival of the fittest" in shaping behavior. ("Fit" in this sense refers to the ability to bear offspring that survive long enough to bear offspring of their own.) In this view, natural selection favors behaviors that increase reproductive success—that is, the ability to pass your genes to the next generation (Del Giudice & Ellis, 2016; Grinde, 2016).

David Buss (2008, 2012, 2015) argues that just as evolution has contributed to our physical features, such as body shape and height, it also pervasively influences how we make decisions, how aggressive we are, our fears, and our mating patterns. For example, assume that our ancestors were hunters and gatherers on the plains and that men did most of the hunting and women stayed close to home, gathering seeds and plants for food. If you have to travel some distance from your home to track and slay a fleeing animal, you need certain physical traits along with the capacity for certain types of spatial thinking. Men with these traits would be more likely than men without them to survive, to bring home lots of food, and to be considered attractive mates—and thus to reproduce and pass on these characteristics to their children. In other words, if their assumptions were correct, potentially these traits would provide a reproductive advantage for males, and over many generations, men with good spatial thinking skills might become more numerous in the population. Critics point out that this scenario might or might not have actually happened.

Evolutionary Developmental Psychology

There is growing interest in using the concepts of evolutionary psychology to understand human development (Bjorklund, 2012; Bugental, Corpuz, & Beaulieu, 2015). Following are some ideas proposed by evolutionary developmental psychologists (Bjorklund & Pellegrini, 2002).

One important concept is that an extended childhood period might have evolved because humans require time to develop a large brain and learn the complexity of human societies. Humans take longer to become reproductively mature than any other primate (see Figure 1). During this extended childhood period, they develop a large brain and have the experiences needed to become competent adults in a complex society.

Another key idea is that many of our evolved psychological mechanisms are *domain-specific*. That is, the mechanisms apply only to a specific aspect of a person's psychological makeup. According to evolutionary psychology, the mind is not a general-purpose device that can be applied equally to a vast array of problems. Instead, as our ancestors dealt with certain recurring problems such as hunting and finding shelter, specialized modules evolved that process information related to those problems: for example, such specialized modules might include a module for physical knowledge for tracking animals, a module for mathematical knowledge for trading, and a module for language.

How Would You...?

As an **educator,** how would you apply the concept of domain-specific psychological mechanisms to explain how a student with a learning disability in reading may perform exceptionally well in math?

Evolved mechanisms are not always adaptive in contemporary society. Some behaviors that were adaptive for our prehistoric ancestors may not serve us well today. For example, the food-scarce environment of our ancestors likely led to humans' propensity to gorge when food is available and to crave high-caloric foods, a trait that might lead to an epidemic of obesity when food is plentiful.

Evaluating Evolutionary Psychology

Although the popular press gives a lot of attention to the ideas of evolutionary psychology, it remains just one theoretical approach. Like the theories described earlier, it has limitations, weaknesses, and critics (Hyde, 2014). One criticism comes from

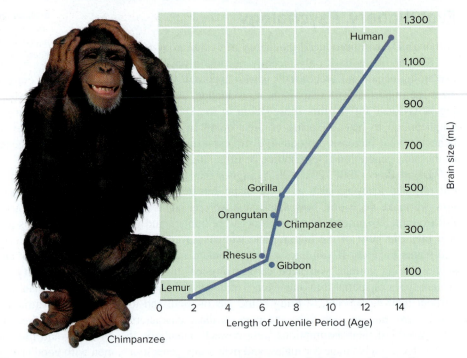

Figure 1 **The Brain Sizes of Various Primates and Humans in Relation to the Length of the Juvenile Period**
Compared with other primates, humans have both a larger brain and a longer childhood period. *What conclusions can you draw from the relationship indicated by this graph?*
© 1996 PhotoDisc, Inc./Getty Images RF

Children in all cultures are interested in the tools used by adults in their cultures. This 11-month-old boy from the Efe culture in the Democratic Republic of the Congo in Africa is trying to cut a papaya with an apopau (a smaller version of a machete). *Might the infant's behavior be evolutionary-based or be due to both biological and environmental conditions?*
© Dr. Gilda Morelli

Albert Bandura (1998), whose social cognitive theory was described earlier. Bandura acknowledges the important influence of evolution on human adaptation. However, he rejects what he calls "one-sided evolutionism," which sees social behavior as the product of evolved biological characteristics. An alternative is a *bidirectional view* in which environmental and biological conditions influence each other. In this view, evolutionary pressures created changes in biological structures that allowed the use of tools, which enabled our ancestors to manipulate the environment, constructing new environmental conditions. In turn, environmental innovations produced new selection pressures that led to the evolution of specialized biological systems for consciousness, thought, and language.

In other words, evolution gave us bodily structures and biological potentialities, but it does not dictate behavior. People have used their biological capacities to produce diverse cultures—aggressive and peace-loving, egalitarian and autocratic. As American scientist Stephen Jay Gould (1981) concluded, in most domains of human functioning, biology allows a broad range of cultural possibilities.

The "big picture" idea of natural selection leading to the development of human traits and behaviors is difficult to refute or test because evolution occurs on a time scale that does not lend itself to empirical study. Thus, studying specific genes in humans and other species—and their links to traits and behaviors—may be the best approach for testing ideas coming out of the evolutionary psychology perspective.

Genetic Foundations of Development

Genetic influences on behavior evolved over time and across many species. Our many traits and characteristics that are genetically influenced have a long evolutionary history that is retained in our DNA. In other words, our DNA is not just inherited from our parents; it's also what we've inherited as a species from the species that came before our own. Let's take a closer look at DNA and its role in human development.

How are characteristics that suit a species for survival transmitted from one generation to the next? Darwin did not know the answer to this question because genes and the principles of genetics had not yet been discovered. Each of us carries a human "genetic code" that we inherited from our parents. Because a fertilized egg carries this human code, a fertilized human egg cannot grow into an egret, eagle, or elephant.

Each of us began life as a single cell weighing about one twenty-millionth of an ounce. This tiny piece of matter housed our entire genetic code—instructions that orchestrated growth from that single cell to a person made of trillions of cells, each containing a replica of the original code. That code is carried by our genes. What are genes and what do they do? For the answer, we need to look into our cells.

The nucleus of each human cell contains **chromosomes,** which are threadlike structures made up of deoxyribonucleic acid, or DNA. **DNA** is a complex molecule that has a double helix shape, like a spiral staircase, and contains genetic information. **Genes,** the units of hereditary information, are short segments of DNA, as you can see in Figure 2. They help cells to reproduce themselves and to assemble proteins. Proteins, in turn, are the building blocks of cells as well as the regulators that direct the body's processes (Cowan, 2015; Goodenough & McGuire, 2017).

Each gene has its own designated place on a particular chromosome. Today, there is a great deal of enthusiasm about efforts to discover the specific locations of genes that are linked to certain functions and developmental outcomes (Johnson, 2017; Sutphin & Korstanje, 2016). An important step in this direction was taken when the Human Genome Project and the Celera Corporation completed a preliminary map of the human *genome*—the complete set of developmental instructions for creating proteins that initiate the making of a human organism (Brooker, 2015).

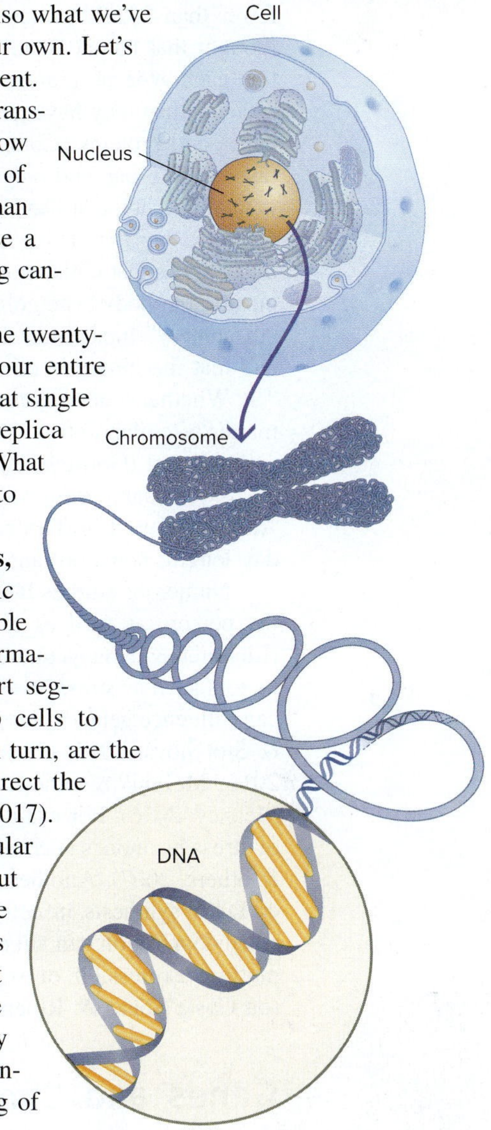

Completion of the Human Genome Project has led to use of the *genome-wide association method* to identify genetic variations linked to a particular disease, such as cancer, cardiovascular disease, or Alzheimer disease (Cho & Suh, 2016; Hou & others, 2016). To conduct a genome-wide association study, researchers obtain DNA from individuals who have the disease and those who don't have it. Then, each participant's complete set of DNA, or genome, is purified from the blood or other cells and scanned on machines to determine markers of genetic variation. If the genetic variations occur more frequently in people who have the disease than in those who don't have it, the variations point to the region in the human genome where the disease-causing problem exists. Genome-wide association studies have recently been conducted for childhood obesity (Zandona & others, 2016); cancer (Johnson & others, 2016); cardiovascular disease (Schick & others, 2016); depression (Knowles & others, 2016; Nho & others, 2015); suicide (Sokolowski, Wasserman, & Wasserman, 2016); glaucoma (Bailey & others, 2016); and Alzheimer disease (Chauhan & others, 2015; Ramos Dos Santos & others, 2016).

One of the big surprises of the Human Genome Project was a report indicating that humans have only about 30,000 genes (U.S. Department of Energy, 2001). More recently, the number of human genes has been revised further downward, to approximately 20,700 (Flicek & others, 2013). Further recent analysis proposes that humans may actually have

Cell

Nucleus

Chromosome

DNA

Figure 2 Cells, Chromosomes, DNA, and Genes
(Top) The body contains trillions of cells. Each cell contains a central structure, the nucleus. *(Middle)* Chromosomes are threadlike structures located in the nucleus of the cell. Chromosomes are composed of DNA. *(Bottom)* DNA has the structure of a spiral staircase. A gene is a segment of DNA.

chromosomes Threadlike structures made up of deoxyribonucleic acid, or DNA.

DNA A complex molecule with a double helix shape that contains genetic information.

genes Units of hereditary information composed of DNA. Genes direct cells to reproduce themselves and manufacture the proteins that maintain life.

fewer than 20,000 protein-producing genes (Ezkurida & others, 2014). Scientists had thought that humans had as many as 100,000 or more genes. They had also believed that each gene programmed just one protein. In fact, humans appear to have far more proteins than they have genes, so there cannot be a one-to-one correspondence between genes and proteins (Commoner, 2002). Each gene is not translated, in automaton-like fashion, into one and only one protein. A gene does not act independently, as developmental psychologist David Moore (2001) emphasized by titling his book *The Dependent Gene*. Rather than being a group of independent genes, the human genome consists of many genes that collaborate both with each other and with nongenetic factors inside and outside the body. The collaboration operates at many points. For example, the cellular "machinery" mixes, matches, and links small pieces of DNA to reproduce the genes, and that machinery is influenced by what is going on around it (Moore, 2015).

Whether a gene is turned "on"—that is, working to assemble proteins—is also a matter of collaboration. The activity of genes (*genetic expression*) is affected by their environment (Gottlieb, 2007; Moore, 2015). For example, hormones that circulate in the blood make their way into the cell, where they can turn genes "on" and "off." And the flow of hormones can be affected by environmental conditions such as light, day length, nutrition, and behavior.

Numerous studies have shown that external events outside of the original cell and the person, as well as events inside the cell, can excite or inhibit gene expression (Lickliter & Honeycutt, 2015; Moore, 2015). Recent research has documented that factors such as stress, exercise, nutrition, respiration, radiation, temperature, and sleep can influence gene expression (Craft & others, 2014; Dedon & Begley, 2014; Donnelly & Storchova, 2015; Giles & others, 2016; Lindholm & others, 2014; Ma & others, 2015; McInnis & others, 2015; Mychasiuk, Muhammad, & Kolb, 2016; Turecki & Meaney, 2016). For example, one study revealed that an increase in the concentration of stress hormones such as cortisol produced a fivefold increase in DNA damage (Flint & others, 2007). Another study also found that exposure to radiation changed the rate of DNA synthesis in cells (Lee & others, 2011). And recent research indicates that sleep deprivation can affect gene expression in negative ways such as increased inflammation, expression of stress-related genes, and impairment of protein functioning (da Costa Souza & Ribeiro, 2015).

Genes and Chromosomes

Genes are not only collaborative; they are enduring. How do they get passed from generation to generation and end up in all of the trillion cells in the body? Three processes are central to this story: mitosis, meiosis, and fertilization.

Mitosis, Meiosis, and Fertilization

All cells in your body, except the sperm and egg, have 46 chromosomes arranged in 23 pairs. These cells reproduce through a process called **mitosis.** During mitosis, the cell's nucleus—including the chromosomes—duplicates itself and the cell divides. Two new cells are formed, each containing the same DNA as the original cell, arranged in the same 23 pairs of chromosomes.

However, a different type of cell division—**meiosis**—forms eggs and sperm (which also are called *gametes*). During meiosis, a cell of the testes (in men) or ovaries (in women) duplicates its chromosomes but then divides *twice*, thus forming four cells, each of which has only half of the genetic material of the parent cell (Johnson, 2017). By the end of meiosis, each egg or sperm has 23 *unpaired* chromosomes.

During *fertilization*, an egg and a sperm fuse to create a single cell, called a *zygote*. In the zygote, the 23 unpaired chromosomes from the egg and the 23 unpaired chromosomes from the sperm combine to form one set of 23 paired chromosomes—one chromosome of each pair from the mother's egg and the other from the father's sperm. In this manner, each parent contributes half of the offspring's genetic material.

mitosis Cellular reproduction in which the cell's nucleus duplicates itself with two new cells being formed, each containing the same DNA as the parent cell, arranged in the same 23 pairs of chromosomes.

meiosis A specialized form of cell division that occurs to form eggs and sperm (or gametes).

Figure 3 shows 23 paired chromosomes of a male and a female. The members of each pair of chromosomes are both similar and different: Each chromosome in the pair contains varying forms of the same genes, at the same location on the chromosome. A gene that influences hair color, for example, is located on both members of one pair of chromosomes, at the same location on each. However, one of those chromosomes might carry the gene associated with blond hair; the other might carry the gene associated with brown hair.

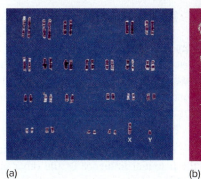

(a)   (b)

Do you notice any obvious differences between the chromosomes of the male and those of the female in Figure 3? The difference lies in the 23rd pair. Ordinarily, in females this pair consists of two chromosomes called *X chromosomes*; in males the 23rd pair consists of an X chromosome and a *Y chromosome*. The presence of a Y chromosome is one factor that makes a person male rather than female.

Sources of Variability

Combining the genes of two parents in their offspring increases genetic variability in the population, which is valuable for a species because it provides more characteristics on which natural selection can operate (Belk & Borden Maier, 2016; Simon, 2017). In fact, the human genetic process creates several important sources of variability.

First, the chromosomes in the zygote are not exact copies of those in the mother's ovaries and the father's testes. During the formation of the sperm and egg in meiosis, the members of each pair of chromosomes are separated, but which chromosome in the pair goes to the gamete is a matter of chance. In addition, before the pairs separate, pieces of the two chromosomes in each pair are exchanged, creating a new combination of genes on each chromosome. Thus, when chromosomes from the mother's egg and the father's sperm are brought together in the zygote, the result is a truly unique combination of genes.

Another source of variability comes from DNA. Chance events, a mistake by the cellular machinery, or damage caused by an environmental agent such as radiation may produce a *mutated gene*, a permanently altered segment of DNA (Bauman, 2015; Freeman & others, 2017).

Even when their genes are identical, however, as for the identical twins described at the beginning of the chapter, people vary. The difference between *genotypes* and *phenotypes* helps us understand this source of variability. All of a person's genetic material makes up his or her **genotype**. There is increasing interest in studying *susceptibility genes*, those that make the individual more vulnerable to specific diseases or accelerated aging, and *longevity genes*, those that make the individual less vulnerable to certain diseases and more likely to live to an older age (Cho & Suh, 2016; Dong & others, 2015; Sutphin & Korstanje, 2016). These are aspects of the individual's genotype.

However, not all of the genetic material is apparent in an individual's observed and measurable characteristics. A **phenotype** consists of observable characteristics, including physical characteristics (such as height, weight, and hair color) and psychological characteristics (such as personality and intelligence).

For each genotype, a range of phenotypes can be expressed, providing another source of variability (Klug & others, 2016; Solomon & others, 2015). An individual can inherit the genetic potential to grow very large, for example, but good nutrition, among other things, will be essential to achieving that potential.

genotype A person's genetic heritage; the actual genetic material.

phenotype The way an individual's genotype is expressed in observed and measurable characteristics.

Genetic Principles

What determines how a genotype is expressed to create a particular phenotype? This question has not yet been fully answered (Moore, 2015). However, a number of genetic principles have been discovered, among them those of dominant and recessive genes, sex-linked genes, and polygenically determined characteristics.

Dominant and Recessive Genes

In some cases, one gene of a pair always exerts its effects; in other words, it is *dominant*, overriding the potential influence of the other gene, which is called the *recessive* gene. This is the *dominant-and-recessive genes principle.* A recessive gene exerts its influence only if the two genes of a pair are both recessive. If you inherit a recessive gene for a trait from each of your parents, you will show the trait. If you inherit a recessive gene from only one parent, you may never know that you carry the gene. Brown hair, farsightedness, and dimples override blond hair, nearsightedness, and freckles in the world of dominant and recessive genes. Can two brown-haired parents have a blond-haired child? Yes, they can. Suppose that each parent has a dominant gene for brown hair and a recessive gene for blond hair. Since dominant genes override recessive genes, the parents have brown hair, but both are *carriers* of blondness and pass on their recessive genes for blond hair. With no dominant gene to override them, the recessive genes can make the child's hair blond.

Sex-Linked Genes

Most mutated genes are recessive. When a mutated gene is carried on the X chromosome, the result is called *X-linked inheritance*. It may have implications for males that differ greatly from those for females (Simon & others, 2016). Remember that males have only one X chromosome. Thus, if there is an absent or altered, disease-relevant gene on the X chromosome, males have no "backup" copy to counter the harmful gene and therefore may develop an X-linked disease. However, females have a second X chromosome, which is likely to be unchanged. As a result, they are not likely to have the X-linked disease. Thus, most individuals who have X-linked diseases are males. Females who have one abnormal copy of the gene on the X chromosome are known as carriers, and they usually do not show any signs of the X-linked disease. Fragile X syndrome, which we will discuss later in the chapter, is an example of X-linked inheritance (Karmiloff-Smith & others, 2016).

Polygenic Inheritance

Genetic transmission is usually more complex than the simple examples we have examined thus far (Moore, 2015). Few characteristics reflect the influence of only a single gene or pair of genes. Most are determined by the interaction of many different genes; they are said to be *polygenically* determined. Even a simple characteristic such as height reflects the interaction of many genes as well as the influence of the environment. Most diseases, such as cancer and diabetes, develop as a consequence of complex gene interactions and environmental factors.

The term *gene-gene interaction* is increasingly used to describe studies that focus on the interdependent process by which two or more genes influence characteristics, behavior, diseases, and development (Cho & Suh, 2016; Hodge, Hager, & Greenberg, 2016). For example, recent studies have documented gene-gene interaction in immune system functioning (Heinonen & others, 2015), asthma (Hua & others, 2016), alcoholism (Yokoyama & others, 2013), cancer (Wu & others, 2016), cardiovascular disease (Musameh & others, 2015), arthritis (Hohman & others, 2016), and Alzheimer disease (Ebbert & others, 2016).

Chromosome and Gene-Linked Abnormalities

In some (relatively rare) cases, genetic inheritance involves an abnormality. Some of these abnormalities come from whole chromosomes that do not separate properly during meiosis. Others are produced by defective genes.

Name	Description	Treatment	Incidence
Down syndrome	An extra chromosome causes mild to severe intellectual disabilities and physical abnormalities.	Surgery, early intervention, infant stimulation, and special learning programs	1 in 1,900 births at age 20 1 in 300 births at age 35 1 in 30 births at age 45
Klinefelter syndrome (XXY)	An extra X chromosome causes physical abnormalities.	Hormone therapy can be effective	1 in 1,000 male births
Fragile X syndrome	An abnormality in the X chromosome can cause intellectual disabilities, learning disabilities, or short attention span.	Special education, speech and language therapy	More common in males than in females
Turner syndrome (XO)	A missing X chromosome in females can cause intellectual disabilities and sexual underdevelopment.	Hormone therapy in childhood and puberty	1 in 2,500 female births
XYY syndrome	An extra Y chromosome can cause above-average height.	No special treatment required	1 in 1,000 male births

Figure 4 Some Chromosome Abnormalities
The treatments for these abnormalities do not necessarily erase the problem but may improve the individual's adaptive behavior and quality of life.

Chromosome Abnormalities

Sometimes a gamete is formed in which the combined sperm and ovum do not have their normal set of 23 chromosomes. The most notable examples involve Down syndrome and abnormalities of the sex chromosomes. Figure 4 describes some chromosome abnormalities, along with their treatment and incidence.

Down Syndrome Down syndrome is one of the most common genetically linked causes of intellectual disability; it is also characterized by certain physical features (Lewanda & others, 2016). An individual with Down syndrome has a round face, a flattened skull, an extra fold of skin over the eyelids, a thickened tongue, short limbs, and retardation of motor and mental abilities. The syndrome is caused by the presence of an extra copy of chromosome 21. It is not known why the extra chromosome is present, but the health of the male sperm or female ovum may be involved.

Down syndrome appears approximately once in every 700 live births. Women between the ages of 16 and 34 are less likely to give birth to a child with Down syndrome than are younger or older women. African American children are rarely born with Down syndrome.

Sex-Linked Chromosome Abnormalities Recall that a newborn normally has either an X and a Y chromosome, or two X chromosomes. Human embryos must possess at least one X chromosome to be viable. The most common sex-linked chromosome abnormalities involve the presence of an extra chromosome (either an X or a Y) or the absence of one X chromosome in females.

Klinefelter syndrome is a chromosomal disorder in which males have an extra X chromosome, making them XXY instead of XY. Males with this disorder have undeveloped testes, and they usually have enlarged breasts and become tall (Lunenfeld & others, 2015). Klinefelter syndrome occurs approximately once in every 1,000 live male births. Only 10 percent of individuals with Klinefelter syndrome are diagnosed before puberty, with the majority not identified until adulthood (Aksglaede & others, 2013).

These athletes, several of whom have Down syndrome, are participating in a Special Olympics competition. Notice the distinctive facial features of the individuals with Down syndrome, such as a round face and a flattened skull. *What causes Down syndrome?*
© James Shaffer/PhotoEdit

Down syndrome A chromosomally transmitted form of intellectual disability, caused by the presence of an extra copy of chromosome 21.

How Would You...?
As a **social worker,** how would you respond to a 33-year-old pregnant woman who is concerned about the risk of giving birth to a baby with Down syndrome?

Fragile X syndrome is a genetic disorder that results from an abnormality in the X chromosome, which becomes constricted and often breaks (Karmiloff-Smith & others, 2016). The outcome frequently takes the form of an intellectual disability, autism, a learning disability, or a short attention span (Hall & others, 2014). This disorder occurs more frequently in males than in females, possibly because the second X chromosome in females negates the effects of the other, abnormal X chromosome (McDuffie & others, 2015; Rocca & others, 2016).

Turner syndrome is a chromosomal disorder in females in which either an X chromosome is missing, making the person XO instead of XX, or part of one X chromosome is deleted. Females with Turner syndrome are short in stature and have a webbed neck (Miguel-Neto & others, 2016; Vlatkovic & others, 2014). In some cases, they are infertile. They have difficulty in mathematics, but their verbal ability is often quite good. Turner syndrome occurs in approximately 1 of every 2,500 live female births.

XYY syndrome is a chromosomal disorder in which the male has an extra Y chromosome (Lepage & others, 2014). Early interest in this syndrome focused on the belief that the extra Y chromosome found in some males contributed to aggression and violence. However, researchers subsequently found that XYY males are no more likely to commit crimes than are XY males (Witkin & others, 1976).

Gene-Linked Abnormalities

Abnormalities can be produced not only by an abnormal number of chromosomes, but also by defective genes. Figure 5 describes some gene-linked abnormalities and outlines their treatment and incidence.

Phenylketonuria (PKU) is a genetic disorder in which the individual cannot properly metabolize phenylalanine, an amino acid that naturally occurs in many food sources. It results from a recessive gene and occurs about once in every 10,000 to 20,000 live births. Today, phenylketonuria is easily detected in infancy, and it is treated by a diet that prevents an excess accumulation of phenylalanine (Rohde & others, 2014). If phenylketonuria is left untreated, however, excess phenylalanine

Name	Description	Treatment	Incidence
Cystic fibrosis	Glandular dysfunction that interferes with mucus production; breathing and digestion are hampered, resulting in a shortened life span.	Physical and oxygen therapy, synthetic enzymes, and antibiotics; most individuals live to middle age.	1 in 2,000 births
Diabetes	Body does not produce enough insulin, which causes abnormal metabolism of sugar.	Early onset can be fatal unless treated with insulin.	1 in 2,500 births
Hemophilia	Delayed blood clotting causes internal and external bleeding.	Blood transfusions/injections can reduce or prevent damage due to internal bleeding.	1 in 10,000 males
Huntington disease	Central nervous system deteriorates, producing problems in muscle coordination and mental deterioration.	Does not usually appear until age 35 or older; death likely 10 to 20 years after symptoms appear.	1 in 20,000 births
Phenylketonuria (PKU)	Metabolic disorder that, left untreated, causes intellectual disability.	Special diet can result in average intelligence and normal life span.	1 in 10,000 to 1 in 20,000 births
Sickle-cell anemia	Blood disorder that limits the body's oxygen supply; it can cause joint swelling, as well as heart and kidney failure.	Penicillin, medication for pain, antibiotics, and blood transfusions.	1 in 400 African American children (lower among other groups)
Spina bifida	Neural tube disorder that causes brain and spine abnormalities.	Corrective surgery at birth, orthopedic devices, and physical/medical therapy.	2 in 1,000 births
Tay-Sachs disease	Deceleration of mental and physical development caused by an accumulation of lipids in the nervous system.	Medication and special diet are used, but death is likely by 5 years of age.	1 in 30 American Jews is a carrier.

Figure 5 Some Gene-Linked Abnormalities

builds up in the child, producing intellectual disability and hyperactivity. Phenylketonuria accounts for approximately 1 percent of individuals who are institutionalized for intellectual disabilities, and it occurs primarily in Whites.

Sickle-cell anemia, which occurs most often in African Americans, is a genetic disorder that impairs functioning of the body's red blood cells. Red blood cells, which carry oxygen to the body's other cells, are usually shaped like a disk. In sickle-cell anemia, a recessive gene causes the red blood cell to become a hook-shaped "sickle" that cannot carry oxygen properly and dies quickly. As a result, the body's cells do not receive adequate oxygen, causing anemia and early death (Derebail & others, 2014). About 1 in 400 African American babies is affected by sickle-cell anemia. One in 10 African Americans is a carrier, as is 1 in 20 Latin Americans. Recent research strongly supports the use of hydroxyurea therapy for infants with sickle-cell anemia beginning at 9 months of age (Yawn & John-Sowah, 2015).

Other diseases that result from genetic abnormalities include cystic fibrosis, some forms of diabetes, hemophilia, Huntington disease, Alzheimer disease, spina bifida, and Tay-Sachs disease. Someday, scientists may be able to determine why these and other genetic abnormalities occur and discover how to cure them (Capurro & others, 2015; Tai & others, 2015; Wang & others, 2016; Williams & others, 2016).

Genetic counselors, usually physicians or biologists who are well-versed in the field of medical genetics, may specialize in providing information to individuals who are at risk of giving birth to children with the kinds of genetic abnormalities just described (Stilwell, 2016). They can evaluate the degree of risk involved and offer helpful strategies for offsetting some of the effects of these diseases (Paneque, Sequeiros, & Skirton, 2015; Redlinger-Grosse & others, 2016). To read about the career and work of a genetic counselor, see *Careers in Life-Span Development.*

How Would You...?

As a **health-care professional,** how would you explain the heredity-environment interaction to new parents who are upset when they discover that their child has a treatable genetic defect?

Careers in life-span development

Holly Ishmael, Genetic Counselor

Holly Ishmael is a genetic counselor at Children's Mercy Hospital in Kansas City. She obtained an undergraduate degree in psychology and then a master's degree in genetic counseling from Sarah Lawrence College.

Genetic counselors work as members of a health-care team, providing information and support to families with birth defects or genetic disorders. They identify families at risk by analyzing inheritance patterns and explore options with the family. Some genetic counselors, like Holly, become specialists in prenatal and pediatric genetics; others might specialize in cancer genetics or psychiatric genetic disorders.

Holly says, "Genetic counseling is a perfect combination for people who want to do something science-oriented, but need human contact and don't want to spend all of their time in a lab or have their nose in a book" (Rizzo, 1999, p. 3).

Genetic counselors hold specialized graduate degrees in the areas of medical genetics and counseling. They enter graduate school with undergraduate backgrounds from a variety of

Holly Ishmael (left) in a genetic counseling session.
© Holly Ishmael Welsh

disciplines, including biology, genetics, psychology, public health, and social work. There are approximately 30 graduate genetic counseling programs in the United States. If you are interested in this profession, you can obtain further information from the National Society of Genetic Counselors at www.nsgc.org.

The Interaction of Heredity and Environment: The Nature-Nurture Debate

Is it possible to untangle the influence of heredity from that of environment and discover the role of each in producing individual differences in development? When heredity and environment interact, how does heredity influence the environment, and vice versa?

Behavior Genetics

Behavior genetics is the field that seeks to discover the influence of heredity and environment on individual differences in human traits and development. Behavior geneticists often study either twins or adoption situations (Jaffee, 2016; Lickliter & Honeycutt, 2015; Nes & Roysamb, 2016; South & Jarnecke, 2016).

In a **twin study,** the behavioral similarities between identical twins (who are genetically identical) are compared with the behavioral similarities between fraternal twins. Recall that although fraternal twins share the same womb, they are no more genetically alike than are non-twin siblings. By comparing groups of identical and fraternal twins, behavior geneticists capitalize on this basic knowledge that identical twins are more similar genetically than are fraternal twins: If they observe that a behavioral trait is more often shared by identical twins than by fraternal twins, they can infer that the trait has a genetic basis (Jansen & others, 2015; Tan & others, 2015). For example, one study revealed a higher incidence of conduct problems shared by identical twins than by fraternal twins, and the researchers discerned an important role for heredity in conduct problems (Scourfield & others, 2004).

However, several issues complicate the interpretation of twin studies. For example, perhaps the environments of identical twins are more similar than those of fraternal twins. Parents and caregivers might stress the similarities of identical twins more than those of fraternal twins, and identical twins might perceive themselves as a "set" and play together more than fraternal twins do. If so, the observed similarities between identical twins might have a significant environmental basis.

In an **adoption study,** investigators seek to discover whether the behavior and psychological characteristics of adopted children are more like those of their adoptive parents, who have provided a home environment, or more like those of their biological parents, who have contributed their heredity (McAdams & others, 2015). Another form of the adoption study compares adoptees with their adoptive siblings and their biological siblings (Kendler & others, 2016).

Heredity-Environment Correlations

The difficulties that researchers encounter in interpreting the results of twin and adoption studies reflect the complexities of heredity-environment interactions. Some of these interactions are heredity-environment correlations, which means that individuals' genes may influence the types of environments to which they are exposed. In a sense, individuals "inherit" environments that may be related or linked to genetic "propensities" (Klahr & Burt, 2014; Jaffee, 2016). Behavior geneticist Sandra Scarr (1993) described three ways in which heredity and environment are correlated:

- *Passive genotype-environment correlations* occur because biological parents, who are genetically related to the child, provide a rearing environment for the child. For example, the parents might have a genetic predisposition to be intelligent and read skillfully. Because they read well and enjoy reading, they provide their children with books to read. The likely outcome is that their children, given their own inherited predispositions from their parents and their book-filled environment, will become skilled readers.

behavior genetics The field that seeks to discover the influence of heredity and environment on individual differences in human traits and development.

twin study A study in which the behavioral similarity of identical twins is compared with the behavioral similarity of fraternal twins.

adoption study A study in which investigators seek to discover whether, in behavior and psychological characteristics, adopted children are more like their adoptive parents, who provided a home environment, or more like their biological parents, who contributed their heredity. Another form of the adoption study compares adoptive and biological siblings.

- *Evocative genotype-environment correlations* occur because a child's characteristics elicit certain types of environments. For example, active, smiling children receive more social stimulation than passive, quiet children do. Cooperative, attentive children evoke more pleasant and instructional responses from the adults around them than uncooperative, distractible children do.

- *Active (niche-picking) genotype-environment correlations* occur when children seek out environments that they find compatible and stimulating. *Niche-picking* refers to finding a setting that is suited to one's abilities. Children select from their surrounding environment specific aspects that they respond to, learn about, or ignore. Their active selections of environments are related to their particular genotype. For example, outgoing children tend to seek out social contexts in which to interact with people, whereas shy children don't. Children who are musically inclined are likely to select musical environments in which they can successfully perform their skills.

The Epigenetic View and Gene × Environment (G × E) Interaction

Notice that Scarr's view gives the preeminent role in development to heredity: her analysis describes how heredity may influence the types of environments that children experience. Critics argue that the concept of heredity-environment correlation gives heredity too great an influence in determining development because it does not consider the role of prior environmental influences in shaping the correlation itself (Gottlieb, 2007; Moore, 2015). In this section we look at some approaches that place greater emphasis on the role of the environment.

The Epigenetic View

In line with the concept of a collaborative gene, Gilbert Gottlieb (2007) proposed an **epigenetic view,** which states that development is the result of an ongoing, bidirectional interchange between heredity and the environment. Figure 6 compares the heredity-environment correlation and epigenetic views of development.

Heredity-Environment Correlation View

Heredity ⟶ Environment

Epigenetic View

Heredity ⟷ Environment

Figure 6 Comparison of the Heredity-Environment Correlation and Epigenetic Views

How Would You...?

As a **human development and family studies professional,** how would you apply the epigenetic view to explain why one identical twin can develop alcoholism while the other twin does not?

Let's look at an example that reflects the epigenetic view. A baby inherits genes from both parents at conception. During prenatal development, toxins, nutrition, and stress can influence some genes to stop functioning while others become stronger or weaker. During infancy, additional environmental experiences, such as exposure to toxins, nutrition, stress, learning, and encouragement, continue to modify genetic activity and the activity of the nervous system that directly underlies behavior. Heredity and environment thus operate together—or collaborate—to produce a person's well-being, intelligence, temperament, health, ability to pitch a baseball, ability to read, and so on (Gottlieb, 2007; Moore, 2015; Szyf & Pluess, 2016).

Gene × Environment (G × E) Interaction

epigenetic view Emphasizes that development is the result of an ongoing, bidirectional interchange between heredity and environment.

An increasing number of studies are exploring how the interaction between heredity and environment influences development, including interactions that involve specific DNA sequences (Grigorenko & others, 2016;

To what extent are this young girl's piano skills likely due to heredity, environment, or both?
© Francisco Romero/E+/Getty Images RF

Hill & Roth, 2016; Pluess & Meaney, 2016). The epigenetic mechanisms involve the actual molecular modification of the DNA strand as a result of environmental inputs in ways that alter gene functioning (Moore, 2015).

One study found that individuals who have a short version of a gene labeled 5-HTTLPR (a gene involving the neurotransmitter serotonin) have an elevated risk of developing depression only if they *also* lead stressful lives (Caspi & others, 2003). Thus, the specific gene did not directly cause the development of depression; rather the gene interacted with a stressful environment in a way that allowed the researchers to predict whether individuals would develop depression. A recent meta-analysis indicated that the short version of 5-HTTLPR was linked with higher cortisol stress reactivity (Miller & others, 2013). Recent studies also have found support for the interaction between the 5-HTTLPR gene and stress levels in predicting depression in adolescents and older adults (Petersen & others, 2012; Zannas & others, 2012).

Other research involving interaction between genes and environmental experiences has focused on attachment, parenting, and supportive child-rearing environments (Brody & others, 2016; Hostinar, Cicchetti, & Rogosch, 2014; Mileva-Seitz, Bakermans-Kranenburg, & van IJzendoom, 2016; Naumova & others, 2016). In one study, adults who experienced parental loss as young children were more likely to have unresolved attachment issues as adults only when they had the short version of the 5-HTTLPR gene (Caspers & others, 2009). The long version of the serotonin transporter gene apparently provided some protection and ability to cope better with parental loss. Other recent research has found that variations in dopamine-related genes interact with supportive or unsupportive rearing environments to influence children's development (Bakermans-Kranenburg & van IJzendoorn, 2011). The type of research just described is referred to as studies of **gene × environment (G × E) interaction**—the interaction of a specific measured variation in DNA and a specific measured aspect of the environment (Grigorenko & others, 2016; Hill & Roth, 2016; Moore, 2015).

Although there is considerable enthusiasm about the concept of gene x environment interaction (G × E), a recent research review concluded that this approach is plagued by difficulties in replicating results, inflated claims, and other weaknesses (Manuck & McCaffery, 2014). The science of G × E interaction is very young, and in the next several decades it will likely produce more precise findings.

Conclusions About Heredity-Environment Interaction

If an attractive, popular, intelligent girl is elected president of her high school senior class, is her success due to heredity or to environment? Of course, the answer is "both."

The relative contributions of heredity and environment are not additive. That is, we can't say that such-and-such a percentage of nature and such-and-such a percentage of experience make us who we are. Nor is it accurate to say that full genetic expression happens once, at the time of conception or birth, after which we carry our genetic legacy into the world to see how far it takes us. Genes produce proteins throughout the life span, in many different environments. Or they don't produce these proteins, depending in part on how harsh or nourishing those environments are.

The emerging view is that complex behaviors are influenced by genes in ways that give people a propensity for a particular developmental trajectory (Reiss, 2016). However, the individual's actual development requires more: a particular environment. And that environment is complex, just like the mixture of genes we inherit (O'Connor, 2016; Toth & others, 2016). Environmental influences range from the things we lump together under "nurture" (such as culture, parenting, family dynamics, schooling, and neighborhood quality) to biological encounters (such as viruses, birth complications, and even biological events in cells).

In developmental psychologist David Moore's (2013, 2015) view, the biological systems that generate behaviors are extremely complex but too often these systems have been described in overly simplified ways that can

gene × environment (G × E) interaction The interaction of a specified measured variation in DNA and a specific measured aspect of the environment.

be misleading. Thus, although genetic factors clearly contribute to behavior and psychological processes, they don't determine these phenotypes independently from the contexts in which they develop. From Moore's (2013, 2015) perspective, it is misleading to talk about "genes for" eye color, intelligence, personality, or other characteristics. Moore commented that in retrospect we should not have expected to be able to make the giant leap from DNA's molecules to a complete understanding of human behavior any more than we should anticipate being able to easily link air molecules in a concert hall with a full-blown appreciation of a symphony's wondrous experience.

Imagine for a moment that there is a cluster of genes that are somehow associated with youth violence. (This example is hypothetical because we don't know of any such combination.) The adolescent who carries this genetic mixture might experience a world of loving parents, regular nutritious meals, lots of books, and a series of competent teachers. Or the adolescent's world might include parental neglect, a neighborhood in which gunshots and crime are everyday occurrences, and inadequate schooling. In which of these environments are the adolescent's genes likely to manufacture the biological underpinnings of criminality?

If heredity and environment interact to determine the course of development, is that all there is to answering the question of what causes development? Are humans completely at the mercy of their genes and their environment as they develop through the life span? Genetic heritage and environmental experiences are pervasive influences on development. But in thinking about what causes development, recall our discussion of development as the co-construction of biology, culture, *and* the individual. Not only are we the outcomes of our heredity and the environment we experience, but we also can author a unique developmental path by changing our environment. As one psychologist recently concluded:

> In reality, we are both the creatures and creators of our worlds. We are . . . the products of our genes and environments. Nevertheless, . . . the stream of causation that shapes the future runs through our present choices . . . Mind matters . . . Our hopes, goals, and expectations influence our future. (Myers, 2010, p. 168)

Prenatal Development

We turn now to a description of how the process of development unfolds from its earliest moment—the moment of conception—when two parental cells, with their unique genetic contributions, merge to create a new individual.

Conception occurs when a single sperm cell from a male unites with an ovum (egg) in a female's fallopian tube in a process called fertilization. Over the next few months the genetic code discussed earlier directs a series of changes in the fertilized egg, but many events and hazards will influence how that egg develops and becomes a person.

The Course of Prenatal Development

Prenatal development lasts approximately 266 days, beginning with fertilization and ending with birth. Pregnancy can be divided into three periods: germinal, embryonic, and fetal.

The Germinal Period

The **germinal period** is the period of prenatal development that takes place in the first two weeks after conception. It includes the creation of the fertilized egg (the zygote), cell division, and the attachment of the multicellular organism to the uterine wall.

Rapid cell division by the zygote begins the germinal period. (Recall from earlier in the chapter that this cell division occurs through a process called mitosis.) Within one week after conception, the differentiation of

germinal period The period of prenatal development that takes place during the first two weeks after conception. It includes the creation of the zygote, continued cell division, and the attachment of the zygote to the uterine wall.

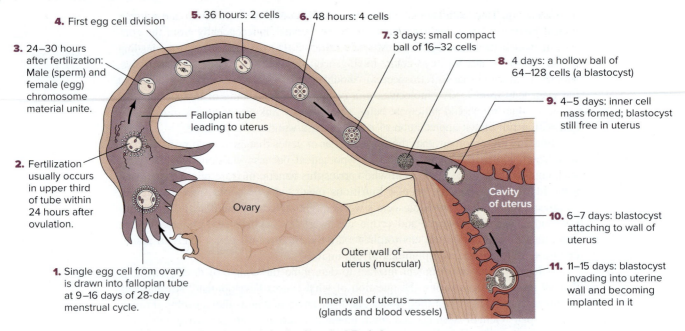

4. First egg cell division

5. 36 hours: 2 cells

6. 48 hours: 4 cells

7. 3 days: small compact ball of 16–32 cells

3. 24–30 hours after fertilization: Male (sperm) and female (egg) chromosome material unite.

8. 4 days: a hollow ball of 64–128 cells (a blastocyst)

9. 4–5 days: inner cell mass formed; blastocyst still free in uterus

Fallopian tube leading to uterus

2. Fertilization usually occurs in upper third of tube within 24 hours after ovulation.

Cavity of uterus

Ovary

10. 6–7 days: blastocyst attaching to wall of uterus

Outer wall of uterus (muscular)

11. 11–15 days: blastocyst invading into uterine wall and becoming implanted in it

1. Single egg cell from ovary is drawn into fallopian tube at 9–16 days of 28-day menstrual cycle.

Inner wall of uterus (glands and blood vessels)

Figure 7 Major Developments in the Germinal Period

these cells—their specialization for different tasks—has already begun. At this stage the organism, now called the blastocyst, consists of a hollow ball of cells that will eventually develop into the embryo, and the trophoblast, an outer layer of cells that later provides nutrition and support for the embryo. Implantation, the embedding of the blastocyst in the uterine wall, takes place during the second week after conception. Figure 7 summarizes these significant developments in the germinal period.

The Embryonic Period

The **embryonic period** is the period of prenatal development that occurs from two to eight weeks after conception. During the embryonic period, the rate of cell differentiation intensifies, support systems for cells form, and organs develop.

The mass of cells is now called an *embryo*, and three layers of cells form. The embryo's *endoderm* is the inner layer of cells, which will develop into the digestive and respiratory systems. The *ectoderm* is the outermost layer, which will become the nervous system, sensory receptors (ears, nose, and eyes, for example), and skin parts (hair and nails, for example). The *mesoderm* is the middle layer, which will become the circulatory system, bones, muscles, excretory system, and reproductive system. Every body part eventually develops from these three layers. The endoderm primarily produces internal body parts, the mesoderm primarily produces parts that surround the internal areas, and the ectoderm primarily produces surface parts. **Organogenesis** is the name given to the process of organ formation during the first two months of prenatal development. While they are being formed, the organs are especially vulnerable to environmental influences.

As the embryo's three layers form, life-support systems for the embryo develop rapidly. These systems include the amnion, the umbilical cord (both of which develop from the fertilized egg, not the mother's body), and the placenta. The amnion is like a bag or an envelope; it contains a clear fluid in which the developing embryo floats. The amniotic fluid provides an environment that is temperature- and humidity-controlled, as well as shockproof. The *umbilical cord*, which typically contains two arteries and one vein, connects the baby to the placenta. The *placenta* consists of a disk-shaped group of tissues in which small blood vessels from the mother and the offspring intertwine but do not join.

embryonic period The period of prenatal development that occurs two to eight weeks after conception. During the embryonic period, the rate of cell differentiation intensifies, support systems for the cells form, and organs appear.

organogenesis Organ formation that takes place during the first two months of prenatal development.

How Would You...?

As a **human development and family studies professional,** how would you characterize the greatest risks at each period of prenatal development?

Very small molecules—oxygen, water, salt, and nutrients from the mother's blood, as well as carbon dioxide and digestive wastes from the baby's blood—pass back and forth between the mother and the embryo or fetus. Large molecules cannot pass through the placental wall; these include red blood cells and some harmful substances, such as most bacteria, maternal wastes, and hormones (Holme & others, 2015; Pfeifer & Bunders, 2016). Virtually any drug or chemical substance a pregnant woman ingests can cross the placenta to some degree, unless it is metabolized or altered during passage, or is too large (Burton & Jauniaux, 2015).

A recent study confirmed that ethanol crosses the human placenta and primarily reflects maternal alcohol use (Matlow & others, 2013). Another study revealed that cigarette smoke weakened and increased the oxidative stress of fetal membranes from which the placenta develops (Menon & others, 2011). The stress hormone cortisol also can cross the placenta (Parrott & others, 2014). The mechanisms that govern the transfer of substances across the placental barrier are complex and not yet entirely understood (Kohan-Ghadr & others, 2016; Lecarpentier & others, 2016; Mandelbrot & others, 2015).

The Fetal Period

The **fetal period,** which lasts about seven months, is the prenatal period that extends from two months after conception until birth in typical pregnancies. Growth and development continue their dramatic course during this time.

Three months after conception, the fetus is about 3 inches long and weighs about 1 ounce. It has become active, moving its arms and legs, opening and closing its mouth, and moving its head. The face, forehead, eyelids, nose, and chin are distinguishable, as are the upper arms, lower arms, hands, and lower limbs. In most cases, the genitals can be identified as male or female. By the end of the fourth month of pregnancy, the fetus has grown to 6 inches in length and weighs 4 to 7 ounces. At this time, a growth spurt occurs in the body's lower parts. For the first time, the mother can feel arm and leg movements.

By the end of the fifth month, the fetus is about 12 inches long and weighs close to a pound. Structures of the skin have formed—including toenails and fingernails. The fetus is more active, showing a preference for a particular position in the womb. By the end of the sixth month, the fetus is about 14 inches long and has gained another 6 to 12 ounces. The eyes and eyelids are completely formed, and a fine layer of hair covers the head. A grasping reflex is present and irregular breathing movements occur.

As early as six months of pregnancy (about 24 to 25 weeks after conception), the fetus for the first time has a chance of surviving outside the womb—that is, it is *viable.* Infants that are born early, or between 24 and 37 weeks of pregnancy, usually need help breathing because their lungs are not yet fully mature. By the end of the seventh month, the fetus is about 16 inches long and weighs about 3 pounds.

During the last two months of prenatal development, fatty tissues develop and the functioning of various organ systems—heart and kidneys, for example—steps up. During the eighth and ninth months, the fetus grows longer and gains substantial weight—about 4 more pounds. At birth, the average American baby weighs 7½ pounds and is about 20 inches long.

In addition to describing prenatal development in terms of germinal, embryonic, and fetal periods, prenatal development also can be divided into equal three-month periods called *trimesters.* Figure 8 gives an overview of the main events during each trimester. Remember that the three trimesters are not the same as the three prenatal periods we have discussed. The germinal and embryonic periods occur in the first trimester. The fetal period begins toward the end of the first trimester and continues through the second and third trimesters.

The Brain

One of the most remarkable aspects of the prenatal period is the development of the brain (Bale, 2015; Stiles & others, 2015). By the time babies are born, they have approximately 100 billion **neurons,** or nerve cells, which handle information processing at the cellular level in the brain.

fetal period The prenatal period of development that begins two months after conception and usually lasts for seven months.

neurons Nerve cells that handle information processing at the cellular level in the brain.

First trimester (first 3 months)

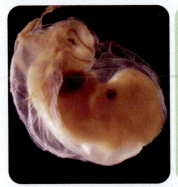

Conception to 4 weeks

- Is less than $\frac{1}{10}$ inch long
- Beginning development of spinal cord, nervous system, gastrointestinal system, heart, and lungs
- Amniotic sac envelops the preliminary tissues of entire body
- Is called a "zygote," then a "blastocyst"

8 weeks

- Is just over 1 inch long
- Face is forming with rudimentary eyes, ears, mouth, and tooth buds
- Arms and legs are moving
- Brain is forming
- Fetal heartbeat is detectable with ultrasound
- Is called an "embryo"

12 weeks

- Is about 3 inches long and weighs about 1 ounce
- Can move arms, legs, fingers, and toes
- Fingerprints are present
- Can smile, frown, suck, and swallow
- Sex is distinguishable
- Can urinate
- Is called a "fetus"

Second trimester (middle 3 months)

16 weeks

- Is about 6 inches long and weighs about 4 to 7 ounces
- Heartbeat is strong
- Skin is thin, transparent
- Downy hair (lanugo) covers body
- Fingernails and toenails are forming
- Has coordinated movements; is able to roll over in amniotic fluid

20 weeks

- Is about 12 inches long and weighs close to 1 pound
- Heartbeat is audible with ordinary stethoscope
- Sucks thumb
- Hiccups
- Hair, eyelashes, eyebrows are present

24 weeks

- Is about 14 inches long and weighs about 1 to $1\frac{1}{2}$ pounds
- Skin is wrinkled and covered with protective coating (vernix caseosa)
- Eyes are open
- Waste matter is collected in bowel
- Has strong grip

Third trimester (last 3 months)

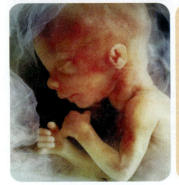

28 weeks

- Is about 16 inches long and weighs about 3 pounds
- Is adding body fat
- Is very active
- Rudimentary breathing movements are present

32 weeks

- Is $16\frac{1}{2}$ to 18 inches long and weighs 4 to 5 pounds
- Has periods of sleep and wakefulness
- Responds to sounds
- May assume the birth position
- Bones of head are soft and flexible
- Iron is being stored in liver

36 to 38 weeks

- Is 19 to 20 inches long and weighs 6 to $7\frac{1}{2}$ pounds
- Skin is less wrinkled
- Vernix caseosa is thick
- Lanugo is mostly gone
- Is less active
- Is gaining immunities from mother

Figure 8 Growth and Development in the Three Trimesters of Prenatal Development

(*Top*) © David Spears/PhotoTake, Inc.; (*middle*) © Neil Bromhall/Science Source; (*bottom*) © Brand X Pictures/PunchStock RF

During prenatal development, neurons move to specific locations and start to become connected. The basic architecture of the human brain is assembled during the first two trimesters of prenatal development. In typical development, the third trimester of prenatal development and the first two years of postnatal life are characterized by connectivity and functioning of neurons (Nelson, 2012).

Four important phases of the brain's development during the prenatal period involve (1) formation of the neural tube; (2) neurogenesis; (3) neural migration, and (4) neural connectivity.

As the human embryo develops inside its mother's womb, the nervous system begins forming as a long, hollow tube located on the embryo's back. This pear-shaped *neural tube*, which forms at about 18 to 24 days after conception, develops out of the ectoderm. The tube closes at the top and bottom ends at about 24 days after conception. Figure 9 shows that the nervous system still has a tubular appearance 6 weeks after conception.

Two birth defects related to a failure of the neural tube to close are anencephaly and spina bifida. When a fetus has anencephaly (that is, when the head end of the neural tube fails to close), the highest regions of the brain fail to develop and the baby dies in the womb, during childbirth, or shortly after birth (Steric & others, 2015). Spina bifida, an incomplete development of the spinal cord, results in varying degrees of paralysis of the lower limbs. Individuals with spina bifida usually need assistive devices such as crutches, braces, or wheelchairs. Both maternal diabetes and obesity also place the fetus at risk for developing neural tube defects (McMahon & others, 2013; Yu, Wu, & Yang, 2016). Further, a recent study revealed that a high level of maternal stress during pregnancy was associated with neural tube defects in offspring (Li & others, 2013). A strategy that can help to prevent neural tube defects is for women to take adequate amounts of the B vitamin folic acid (Bergman & others, 2016). A recent large-scale study in Brazil found that when flour was fortified with folic acid it produced a significant reduction in neural tube defects (Santos & others, 2016).

In a normal pregnancy, once the neural tube has closed, a massive proliferation of new immature neurons begins to take place about the fifth prenatal week and continues throughout the remainder of the prenatal period. The production of new neurons is called *neurogenesis.* At the peak of neurogenesis, it is estimated that as many as 200,000 neurons are being generated every minute.

At approximately 6 to 24 weeks after conception, *neuronal migration* occurs (Nelson, 2012). Cells begin moving outward from their point of origin to their appropriate locations and creating the different levels, structures, and regions of the brain (Miyazaki, Song, & Takahashi, 2016; Zeisel, 2011). Once a cell has migrated to its target destination, it must mature and develop a more complex structure.

At about the 23rd prenatal week, connections between neurons begin to form, a process that continues postnatally (Kostovic, Judas, & Sedmak, 2011; Miller, Huppi, & Mallard, 2016). We will have much more to say about the structure of neurons, their connectivity, and the development of the infant brain.

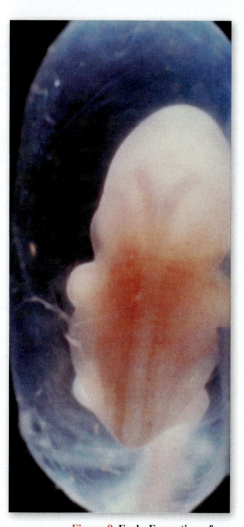

Figure 9 Early Formation of the Nervous System
The photograph shows the primitive, tubular appearance of the nervous system at six weeks in the human embryo.
© Claude Edelmann/Science Source

Prenatal Tests

Together with her doctor, a pregnant woman will decide the extent to which she should undergo prenatal testing. A number of tests can indicate whether a fetus is developing normally; these include ultrasound sonography, fetal MRI, chorionic villus sampling, amniocentesis, maternal blood screening, and noninvasive prenatal diagnosis. The decision to have a given test depends on several criteria, such as the mother's age, medical history, and genetic risk factors.

Ultrasound Sonography

An ultrasound test is generally performed 7 weeks into a pregnancy and at various times later in pregnancy. *Ultrasound sonography* is a noninvasive prenatal medical procedure in which high-frequency sound waves are directed into the pregnant woman's abdomen (Goncalves, 2016; Li & others, 2015). The echo from the sounds is transformed into a visual representation of the fetus's inner structures. This technique can detect many structural abnormalities in the fetus, including microencephaly, a form of intellectual disability involving an abnormally small brain; it can also give clues to the baby's sex and indicate whether there is more than one fetus (Calvo-Garcia, 2016; Rink & Norton, 2016). A recent research review concluded that many aspects of the developing prenatal brain can be detected by ultrasound in the first trimester and that about 50 percent of spina bifida cases can be identified at this time, most of these being severe cases (Engels & others, 2016). There is virtually no risk to the woman or fetus in using ultrasound.

Chorionic Villus Sampling

At some point between the 10th and 12th weeks of pregnancy, chorionic villus sampling may be used to screen for genetic defects and chromosome abnormalities. *Chorionic villus sampling (CVS)* is a prenatal medical procedure in which a tiny tissue sample from the placenta is removed and analyzed (Lankford & others, 2015; Monni & others, 2016). The results are available in about 10 days.

Amniocentesis

Between the 15th and 18th weeks of pregnancy, *amniocentesis* may be performed. In this procedure, a sample of amniotic fluid is withdrawn by syringe and tested for chromosomal or metabolic disorders (Ekblad & others, 2015; Lehmann, 2016). The later in the pregnancy amniocentesis is performed, the better its diagnostic potential. However, the earlier it is performed, the more useful it is in deciding how to handle a pregnancy when the fetus is found to have a disorder. It may take two weeks for enough cells to grow so that amniocentesis test results can be obtained. Amniocentesis brings a small risk of miscarriage: about 1 woman in every 200 to 300 miscarries after amniocentesis.

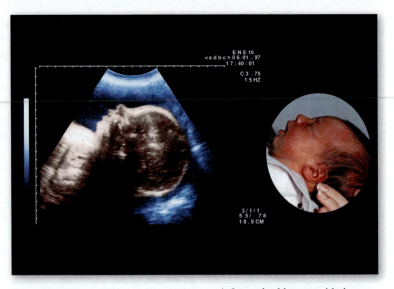

A 6-month-old poses with the ultrasound image taken four months into the baby's prenatal development. *What is ultrasound sonography and what can it detect?*

© AJ Photo/BSIP/age fotostock

Maternal Blood Screening

During the 16th to 18th weeks of pregnancy, maternal blood screening may be performed. *Maternal blood screening* identifies pregnancies that have an elevated risk for birth defects such as spina bifida and Down syndrome (Charkiewicz & others, 2016; Cuckle & Maymon, 2016), as well as congenital heart disease risk for children (Sun & others, 2016). The current blood test is called the *triple screen* because it measures three substances in the mother's blood. After an abnormal triple screen result, the next step is usually an ultrasound examination. If an ultrasound does not explain the abnormal triple screen results, amniocentesis typically is used.

Fetal MRI

The development of brain-imaging techniques has led to increasing use of *fetal MRI* to diagnose fetal malformations (Gat & others, 2016; Sanz-Cortes & others, 2015; You & others, 2016) (see Figure 10). MRI, which stands for magnetic resonance imaging, uses a powerful magnet and radio images to generate detailed images of the body's organs and structures. Currently, high-quality ultrasound is still the first choice in fetal screening, but fetal MRI can provide more detailed images than ultrasound (Wataganara & others, 2016). In many instances, ultrasound will indicate a possible abnormality and fetal MRI will then be used to obtain a clearer, more detailed image

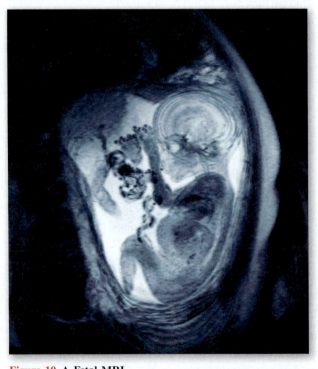

Figure 10 A Fetal MRI
Increasingly, MRI is being used to diagnose fetal malformations.
© Du Cane Medical Imaging Ltd/Science Source

(Milani & others, 2015; Tee & others, 2016). Among the fetal malformations that fetal MRI may be able to detect better than ultrasound sonography are certain abnormalities of the central nervous system, chest, gastrointestinal tract, genital/urinary organs, and placenta (Malinger & Lerman-Sagie, 2015). In a recent research review, it was concluded that fetal MRI often does not provide good results in the first trimester of pregnancy because of small fetal structures and movement artifacts (Wataganara & others, 2016). Also, in this review, it was argued that fetal MRI can be especially beneficial in assessing central nervous system abnormalities in the third trimester of pregnancy.

Fetal Sex Determination

Chorionic villus sampling has often been used to determine the sex of the fetus at some point between 11 and 13 weeks of gestation. Also, in a recent study, ultrasound accurately identified the sex of the fetus between 11 and 13 weeks of gestation (Manzanares & others, 2016). Recently, though, some noninvasive techniques, such as cell-free DNA analysis in blood plasma, have been able to detect the sex of the fetus at an earlier point (Breveglieri & others, 2016; Koumbaris & others, 2016; Moise & others, 2013). A meta-analysis of studies confirmed that a baby's sex can be detected as early as 7 weeks into pregnancy (Devaney & others, 2011). Being able to detect an offspring's sex as well as the presence of various diseases and defects at such an early stage raises ethical concerns about couples' motivation to terminate a pregnancy (Browne, 2016; Lewis & others, 2012).

Infertility and Reproductive Technology

Recent advances in biological knowledge have also opened up many choices for infertile people (Asero & others, 2014). Approximately 10 to 15 percent of couples in the United States experience infertility, which is defined as the inability to conceive a child after 12 months of regular intercourse without contraception. The cause of infertility can rest with either the woman or the man, or both (Brazdova & others, 2016; Zhou & others, 2016). The woman may not be ovulating (releasing eggs to be fertilized); she may be producing abnormal ova; her fallopian tubes (by which ova normally reach the womb) may be blocked; or she may have a condition that prevents implantation of the embryo into the uterus. The man may produce too few sperm; the sperm may lack motility (the ability to move adequately); or he may have a blocked passageway (Takasaki & others, 2014).

Surgery can correct some causes of infertility; for others, hormone-based drugs may be effective. Of the 2 million U.S. couples who seek help for infertility every year, about 40,000 try assisted reproduction technologies. *In vitro fertilization (IVF)*, the technique that produced the world's first "test tube baby" in 1978, involves eggs and sperm being combined in a laboratory dish. If any eggs are successfully fertilized, one or more of the resulting fertilized eggs is transferred into the woman's uterus.

How Would You...?
As a **psychologist,** how would you advise a 25-year-old mother who is concerned about the possibility of birth defects but has no genetic history of these types of problems?

The creation of families by means of assisted reproduction techniques raises important questions about the physical and psychological consequences for children (March of Dimes, 2016). For example, one result of fertility treatments is an increase in multiple births (De Neubourg & others, 2016). Twenty-five to 30 percent of pregnancies achieved by fertility treatments—including in vitro fertilization—result in multiple births. Fertility drugs are more likely to produce multiple births than in vitro fertilization (March of Dimes, 2016). Any multiple birth increases the likelihood that the babies will have life-threatening and costly problems, such as extremely low birth weight (March of Dimes, 2016).

Hazards to Prenatal Development

For most babies, the course of prenatal development goes smoothly. Their mother's womb protects them as they develop. Despite this protection, however, the environment can affect the embryo or fetus in many well-documented ways.

General Principles

A **teratogen** is any agent that can potentially cause a birth defect or negatively alter cognitive and behavioral outcomes. The field of study that investigates the causes of birth defects is called *teratology* (Eltonsy & others, 2016; Kaushik & others, 2016; Stancil & others, 2016). Teratogens include drugs, incompatible blood types, environmental pollutants, infectious diseases, nutritional deficiencies, maternal stress, advanced maternal and paternal age, and environmental pollutants.

The dose, genetic susceptibility, and time of exposure to a particular teratogen influence both the severity of the damage to an embryo or fetus and the type of defect: (1) *Dose*—The dose effect is rather obvious—the greater the dose of an agent, such as a drug, the greater the effect. (2) *Genetic susceptibility*—The type or severity of abnormalities caused by a teratogen is linked to the genotype of the pregnant woman and the genotype of the embryo or fetus (de Planell-Saguer, Lovinsky-Desir, & Miller, 2014). (3) *Time of exposure*—Teratogens do more damage when they occur at some points in development than at others. The probability of a structural defect is greatest early in the embryonic period, when organs are being formed (Holmes, 2011). After organogenesis is complete, teratogens are less likely to cause anatomical defects. Instead, exposure during the fetal period is more likely to stunt growth or create problems in the way organs function. To examine some key teratogens and their effects, let's begin with drugs.

Prescription and Nonprescription Drugs

Prescription drugs that can function as teratogens include antibiotics, such as streptomycin and tetracycline; some antidepressants; certain hormones, such as progestin and synthetic estrogen; and isotretinoin (often prescribed for acne) (Gonzalez-Echavarri & others, 2015). In a recent study, isotretinoin was the fourth most common drug given to female adolescents who were seeking contraception advice from a physician (Stancil & others, 2016). However, physicians did not give the adolescent girls adequate information about the negative effects of isotretinoin on offspring if the girls become pregnant. In a recent review of teratogens that should never be taken during the first trimester of pregnancy, isotreninoin was on the prohibited list (Eltonsy & others, 2016). Nonprescription drugs that can be harmful include diet pills and high doses of aspirin.

Psychoactive Drugs

Psychoactive drugs act on the nervous system to alter states of consciousness, modify perceptions, and change moods. Examples include caffeine, alcohol, and nicotine, as well as illegal drugs such as cocaine, marijuana, and heroin.

Caffeine People often consume caffeine by drinking coffee, tea, or colas, or by eating chocolate. Research has been mixed on the effects of caffeine intake by pregnant women on the fetus (Chen & others, 2016; Hahn & others, 2015; Sengpiel & others, 2013). However, the influence of increased consumption of energy drinks that typically have extremely high levels of caffeine on the development of offspring has not yet been studied. The U.S. Food and Drug Administration recommends that pregnant women either not consume caffeine or consume it only sparingly.

Alcohol Heavy drinking by pregnant women can be devastating to offspring (Alexander, Dasinger, & Intapad, 2015; Valenzuela & others, 2016). **Fetal alcohol spectrum disorders (FASD)** are a cluster of abnormalities and problems that appear in the offspring of mothers who drink alcohol heavily during pregnancy (Coles & others, 2016; Roozen & others, 2016). The abnormalities include facial deformities and defective limbs, face, and heart (Arnold & others, 2013; Cook & others, 2016). Most children with FASD have learning problems, and many are below average in intelligence; some have an intellectual disability (Harper & others, 2014; Khoury & Milligan, 2016). A recent study revealed that children with FASD have deficiencies in the brain pathways involved in working memory (Diwadkar & others, 2012). A recent research review concluded that FASD is linked

teratogen Any agent that can potentially cause a birth defect or negatively alter cognitive and behavioral outcomes.

fetal alcohol spectrum disorders (FASD) A cluster of abnormalities that appears in the offspring of mothers who drink alcohol heavily during pregnancy.

to a lower level of executive function in children, especially in planning (Kingdon, Cardoso, & McGrath, 2016). And in a recent study, FASD was associated with both externalized and internalized behavior problems in childhood (Tsang & others, 2016). Also, in a recent study in the United Kingdom, the life expectancy of individuals with FASD was only 34 years of age, about 42 percent of the life expectancy of the general population (Thanh & Jonsson, 2016). In this study, the most common causes of death among individuals with FASD were suicide (15 percent), accidents (14 percent), and poisoning by illegal drugs or alcohol (7 percent). Although mothers of FASD infants are heavy drinkers, many mothers who are heavy drinkers may not have children with FASD or may have one child with FASD and other children who do not have it.

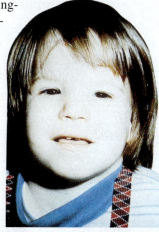

Fetal alcohol spectrum disorders (FASD) are characterized by a number of physical abnormalities and learning problems. Notice the wide-set eyes, flat cheekbones, and thin upper lip in this child with FASD.

© Streissguth, AP, Landesman-Dwyer S, Martin, JC, & Smith, DW (1980). Teratogenic effects of alcohol in humans and laboratory animals. *Science, 209,* 353–361.

What are some guidelines for alcohol use during pregnancy? Even drinking just one or two servings of beer or wine or one serving of hard liquor a few days a week can have negative effects on the fetus, although it is generally agreed that this level of alcohol use will not cause fetal alcohol spectrum disorders (Valenzeula & others, 2012). The U.S. Surgeon General recommends that no alcohol be consumed during pregnancy, as does the French Alcohol Society (Rolland & others, 2016). And research suggests that it may not be wise to consume alcohol at the time of conception. One study revealed that intakes of alcohol by both men and women during the weeks of conception increased the risk of early pregnancy loss (Henriksen & others, 2004).

However, in Great Britain, the National Institutes of Care and Health Excellence have concluded that consuming one to two drinks not more than twice a week is safe during pregnancy (O'Keeffe, Greene, & Kearney, 2014). Also, a recent study of more than 7,000 7-year-olds found that children born to mothers who were light drinkers during pregnancy (up to two drinks per week) did not show more developmental problems than children born to non-drinking mothers (Kelly & others, 2013).

Nicotine Cigarette smoking by pregnant women can also adversely influence prenatal development, birth, and postnatal development (Ekblad, Korkeila, & Lehtonen, 2015; Palmer & others, 2016). Preterm births and low birth weights, fetal and neonatal deaths, respiratory problems, sudden infant death syndrome (SIDS, also known as crib death), and cardiovascular problems are all more common among the offspring of mothers who smoked during pregnancy (Grabenhenrich & others, 2014; Zhang & others, 2016). Prenatal smoking has been implicated in as many as 25 percent of infants being born with a low birth weight (Brown & Graves, 2013).

Researchers also have found that maternal smoking during pregnancy is a risk factor for the development of attention deficit hyperactivity disorder in children (Knopik & others, 2016). And in a recent study, maternal cigarette smoking during pregnancy was linked with offspring being more likely to smoke cigarettes at 16 years of age (De Genna & others, 2016). Further, a recent study found that maternal smoking during pregnancy was associated with increased risk of asthma and wheezing of offspring during adolescence (Hollams & others, 2014). And in a recent research review, it was concluded that maternal cigarette use during pregnancy is linked to alterations in a number of neurotransmitters in offspring, including serotonin and dopamine, as well as elevated blood pressure in offspring when they are adults (Suter & others, 2015).

Researchers have documented that environmental tobacco smoke is linked to negative outcomes for offspring (Vardavas & others, 2016). In one study, environmental tobacco smoke led to an increased risk of low birth weight in offspring (Salama & others, 2013) and to diminished ovarian functioning in female offspring (Kilic & others, 2012). Also, one study revealed that environmental tobacco smoke was associated with 114 deregulations, especially those involving immune functioning, in the fetal cells of offspring (Votavova & others, 2012). Another recent study found that maternal exposure to environmental tobacco smoke during prenatal development increased the risk of stillbirth (Varner & others, 2014).

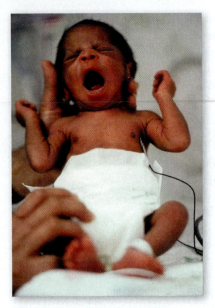

This baby was exposed to cocaine prenatally. *What are some of the possible effects on development of being exposed to cocaine prenatally?*

© Chuck Nacke/Alamy

A final point about nicotine use during pregnancy involves the recent dramatic increase in the use of e-cigarettes (Spindel & McEvoy, 2016). A recent study found that misconceptions about e-cigarettes were common among pregnant women (Mark & others, 2015). The most common reasons pregnant women gave for using e-cigarettes were the perceptions that they are less harmful than regular cigarettes (74 percent) and that they promote smoking cessation (72 percent).

Cocaine Does cocaine use during pregnancy harm the developing embryo and fetus? A recent research study found that cocaine quickly crossed the placenta to reach the fetus (De Giovanni & Marchetti, 2012). The most consistent finding is that cocaine exposure during prenatal development is associated with reduced birth weight, length, and head circumference (Gouin & others, 2011). In other studies, prenatal cocaine exposure has been linked to lower arousal, less effective self-regulation, higher excitability, and lower quality of reflexes at 1 month of age (Ackerman, Riggins, & Black, 2010); impaired motor development at 2 years of age and a slower rate of growth through 10 years of age (Richardson, Goldschmidt, & Willford, 2008); impaired language development and information processing, including attention deficits (especially impulsivity) (Accornero & others, 2006; Richardson & others, 2011); attention deficit hyperactivity disorder (Richardson & others, 2016); increased behavioral problems, especially externalizing problems such as high rates of aggression, oppositional defiant disorder, and delinquency (Minnes & others, 2010; Richardson & others, 2011, 2016); posttraumatic stress disorder (PTSD) (Richardson & others, 2016), and increased likelihood of being in a special education program that involves support services (Levine & others, 2008).

Some researchers argue that these findings should be interpreted cautiously (Accornero & others, 2006). Why? Because other factors in the lives of pregnant women who use cocaine (such as poverty, malnutrition, and other substance abuse) often cannot be ruled out as possible contributors to the problems found in their children (Hurt & others, 2005; Messiah & others, 2011). For example, cocaine users are more likely than nonusers to smoke cigarettes, use marijuana, drink alcohol, and take amphetamines.

Despite these cautions, the weight of research evidence indicates that children born to mothers who use cocaine are likely to have neurological, medical, and cognitive deficits (Cain, Bornick, & Whiteman, 2013; Field, 2007; Mayer & Zhang, 2009; Richardson & others, 2011, 2016). Cocaine use by pregnant women is never recommended.

How Would You...?

As a **social worker,** what advice would you offer to women in their childbearing years who frequently abuse drugs and other psychoactive substances?

Marijuana An increasing number of studies find that marijuana use by pregnant women has negative outcomes for offspring. In a recent meta-analysis, marijuana use during pregnancy was linked to offsprings' low birth weight and a greater likelihood of being placed in a neonatal intensive care unit (NICU) (Gunn & others, 2016). A recent study also revealed that marijuana use by pregnant women was associated with stillbirth (Varner & others, 2014). Another study found that prenatal marijuana exposure was related to lower intelligence in children (Goldschmidt & others, 2008). And one study indicated that prenatal exposure to marijuana was linked to marijuana use at 14 years of age (Day, Goldschmidt, & Thomas, 2006). In sum, marijuana use is not recommended for pregnant women.

Heroin It is well documented that infants whose mothers are addicted to heroin show several behavioral difficulties at birth (Lindsay & Burnett, 2013). The difficulties include withdrawal symptoms, such as tremors, irritability, abnormal crying, disturbed sleep, and impaired motor control. Many still show behavioral problems at their first birthday, and attention deficits may appear later in development. The most common treatment for heroin addiction, methadone, is associated with very severe withdrawal symptoms in newborns (Blandthorn, Forster, & Love, 2011). Increasingly, buprenorphine is being used to treat heroin use during pregnancy (Krans & others, 2016).

Environmental Hazards

Many aspects of our modern industrial world can endanger the embryo or fetus. Some specific hazards to the embryo or fetus include radiation, toxic wastes, and other environmental pollutants (Dursun & others, 2016; Ornoy, Weinstein-Fudim, & Ergaz, 2015).

X-ray radiation can affect the developing embryo or fetus, especially in the first several weeks after conception, when women do not yet know they are pregnant. Women and their physicians should weigh the risk of an X-ray when the woman is or might be pregnant (Rajaraman & others, 2011). However, a routine diagnostic X-ray of a body area other than the abdomen, with the woman's abdomen protected by a lead apron, is generally considered safe (Brent, 2009, 2011).

Maternal Diseases

Maternal diseases and infections can produce defects in offspring by crossing the placental barrier, or they can cause damage during birth (Brunell, 2014). Rubella (German measles) is one disease that can cause prenatal defects. In a recent research review, rubella exposure during pregnancy is most likely to cause impairments involving the cardiovascular system, the pulmonary system, and microcephaly (Yazigi & others, 2016). Women who plan to have children should have a blood test before they become pregnant to determine whether they are immune to the disease (Ogbuanu & others, 2014).

Syphilis (a sexually transmitted infection) is more damaging later in prenatal development—four months or more after conception. Damage includes eye lesions, which can cause blindness, and skin lesions (Braccio, Sharland, & Ladhani, 2016). Penicillin is the only known treatment for syphilis during pregnancy (Moline & Smith, 2016).

Another infection that has received widespread attention is genital herpes. Newborns contract this virus when they are delivered through the birth canal of a mother with genital herpes (Sampath, Maduro, & Schillinger, 2016). About one-third of babies delivered through an infected birth canal die; another one-fourth suffer brain damage. If an active case of genital herpes is detected in a pregnant woman close to her delivery date, a cesarean section can be performed (in which the infant is delivered through an incision in the mother's abdomen) to keep the virus from infecting the newborn (Pinninti & Kimberlin, 2013).

AIDS is a sexually transmitted infection that is caused by the human immunodeficiency virus (HIV), which destroys the body's immune system. A mother can infect her offspring with HIV/AIDS in three ways: (1) across the placenta during gestation, (2) through contact with maternal blood or fluids during delivery, and (3) through breast feeding. The transmission of AIDS through breast feeding is a particular problem in many developing countries. Babies born to HIV-infected mothers can be (1) infected and symptomatic (show HIV symptoms), (2) infected but asymptomatic (not show HIV symptoms), or (3) not infected at all. An infant who is infected and asymptomatic may still develop HIV symptoms up to 15 months of age.

The more widespread disease of diabetes, characterized by high levels of sugar in the blood, also affects offspring (Bider-Canfield & others, 2016; Eriksson, 2016). Women who have gestational diabetes (a condition in which women without previously diagnosed diabetes develop high blood glucose levels during pregnancy) have an increased risk of having very large infants (weighing 10 pounds or more), and the infants themselves are at risk for diabetes (Mitanchez & others, 2015). Also, a recent research review concluded that pregestational diabetes increases the risk of fetal heart disease (Pauliks, 2015). Further, a recent study found that maternal pregnancy diabetes was linked to offspring having an increased risk for fatty liver disease at 18 years of age (Patel & others, 2016). And another recent study revealed that maternal pregnancy diabetes was associated with an increased risk of autism in offspring (Xiang & others, 2015).

Other Parental Factors

So far we have discussed a number of drugs, environmental hazards, maternal diseases, and incompatible blood types that can harm the embryo or fetus. Now we will explore other characteristics of the mother and father that can affect prenatal and child development, including nutrition, age, and emotional states and stress.

Maternal Diet and Nutrition A developing embryo or fetus depends completely on its mother for nutrition, which comes from the mother's blood. The nutritional status of the embryo or fetus is determined by the mother's total caloric intake as well as her intake of proteins, vitamins, and minerals. Children born to malnourished mothers are more likely than other children to be malformed.

Maternal obesity adversely affects pregnancy outcomes through increased rates of hypertension, diabetes, respiratory complications, and infections in the mother (Kominiarek & Chauhan, 2016; Ojha & others, 2015; Stang & Huffman, 2016). Research studies have found that maternal obesity is linked to an increase in stillbirth (Gardosi & others, 2013), preterm birth (Cnattingius & others, 2013), and increased likelihood that the newborn will be placed in a neonatal intensive care unit (Minsart & others, 2013). A recent study revealed that at 14 weeks following conception fetuses of obese pregnant women had less efficient cardiovascular functioning (Ingul & others, 2016). Further, a longitudinal study revealed that obesity during pregnancy was associated with long-term cardiovascular morbidity in adults (Yaniv-Salem & others, 2016). Further, two recent research reviews concluded that maternal obesity during pregnancy is associated with an increased likelihood of offspring being obese in childhood and adulthood (Pinto Pereira & others, 2016; Santangeli, Sattar, & Huda, 2015). Management of obesity that includes weight loss and increased exercise prior to pregnancy is likely to benefit both the mother and the baby (Ingul & others, 2016).

Because the fetus depends entirely on its mother for nutrition, it is important for the pregnant woman to have good nutritional habits. In Kenya, this government clinic provides pregnant women with information about how their diet can influence the health of their fetus and offspring. *What might the information about diet be like?*
© Betty Press

One aspect of maternal nutrition that is important for normal prenatal development is folic acid, a B-complex vitamin (Atta & others, 2016). A study of more than 34,000 women found that taking folic acid either alone or as part of a multivitamin for at least one year prior to conceiving was linked with a 70 percent lower risk of delivering at 20 to 28 weeks and a 50 percent lower risk of delivering at 28 to 32 weeks (Bukowski & others, 2008). Another study revealed that toddlers of mothers who did not use folic acid supplements in the first trimester of pregnancy had more behavioral problems (Roza & others, 2010). Also, as indicated earlier in the chapter, lack of folic acid is related to neural tube defects in offspring (Chitayat & others, 2016; Kondo & others, 2015). The U.S. Department of Health and Human Services (2016) recommends that pregnant women consume a minimum of 400 micrograms of folic acid per day (about twice the amount the average woman gets in one day). Orange juice and spinach are examples of foods that are rich in folic acid. Also, a recent research study in China found that folic acid supplementation during pregnancy reduced the risk of preterm birth (Liu & others, 2015).

Fish is often recommended as part of a healthy diet and in general fish consumption during pregnancy has positive benefits for children's development (Golding & others, 2016; Julvez & others, 2016). The Federal Drug Administration (FDA) (2016) recommends that pregnant women increase their consumption of fish especially because they contain vital nutrients such as omega-3 fatty acids, protein, vitamins, and minerals such as iron. However, pollution has made some kinds of fish a risky choice for pregnant women. Some fish contain high levels of mercury, which is released into the air both naturally and by industrial processes (Wells & others, 2011). Mercury that falls into the water can accumulate in large fish, such as shark, swordfish, king mackerel, and some species of large tuna (American Pregnancy Association, 2016; Mayo Clinic, 2016). Researchers have found that prenatal mercury exposure is linked to adverse outcomes, including miscarriage, preterm birth, and lower intelligence (Xue & others, 2007).

Recently, the American Pregnancy Association (2016) revised its conclusions about fish consumption during pregnancy, although still recommending avoidance of high-mercury-content fish such as tilefish from the Gulf of Mexico, swordfish, shark, and king mackerel. The association and the FDA now recommend that pregnant women increase their consumption of low-mercury-content fish such as salmon, shrimp, tilapia, and cod.

Maternal Age When possible harmful effects on the fetus and infant are considered, two maternal age categories are of special interest: adolescence and 35 years and older (Ben David & others, 2016; de Jongh & others, 2015; Gockley & others, 2016; Kawakita & others, 2016; Tearne & others, 2016). The mortality rate of infants born to adolescent mothers is double that of infants born to mothers in their twenties. Adequate prenatal care decreases the probability that a child born to an adolescent girl will have physical problems. However, adolescents are the least likely of women in all age groups to obtain prenatal assistance from clinics and health services.

Maternal age is also linked to the risk that a child will have Down syndrome (Ghosh & others, 2010; Rumi Kataguiri & others, 2014). A baby with Down syndrome rarely is born to a mother 16 to 34 years of age. However, when the mother reaches 40 years of age, the probability is slightly higher than 1 in 100 that a baby born to her will have Down syndrome, and by age 50 it is almost 1 in 10. When mothers are 35 years and older, risks also increase for low birth weight, preterm delivery, and fetal death (Koo & others, 2012). A recent Norwegian study found that maternal age of 30 years or older was linked to the same level of increased risk for fetal deaths as 25- to 29-year-old pregnant women who were overweight/obese or were smokers (Waldenstrom & others, 2014). Also, in two recent studies, very advanced maternal age (40 years and older) was linked to adverse perinatal outcomes, including spontaneous abortion, preterm birth, stillbirth, and fetal growth restriction (Traisrislip & Tongsong, 2015; Waldenstrom & others, 2015).

We still have much to learn about the role of the mother's age in pregnancy and childbirth. As women remain active, exercise regularly, and are careful about their nutrition, their reproductive systems may remain healthier at older ages than was thought possible in the past.

Emotional States and Stress When a pregnant woman experiences intense fears, anxieties, and other emotions or negative mood states, physiological changes occur that may affect her fetus. A mother's stress may also influence the fetus indirectly by increasing the likelihood that the mother will engage in unhealthy behaviors such as taking drugs and receiving poor prenatal care.

High maternal anxiety and stress during pregnancy can have long-term consequences for the offspring (Bauer, Knapp, & Parsonage, 2016; Brunton, 2015; Dalke, Wentzel, & Kim, 2016; Fan & others, 2016). A recent study found that high levels of depression, anxiety, and stress during pregnancy were linked to internalizing problems in adolescence (Betts & others, 2014). A research review indicated that pregnant women with high levels of stress are at increased risk for having a child with emotional or cognitive problems, attention deficit hyperactivity disorder (ADHD), and language delay (Taige & others, 2007). Also, a large-scale study found that a higher level of maternal stress in the period immediately prior to conception posed a risk for infant mortality (Class & others, 2013). Another study revealed that maternal stressful life events prior to conception increased the risk of having a very low birth weight infant (Witt & others, 2014).

How Would You...?

As a **health-care professional,** what advice would you give to an expectant mother who is experiencing extreme psychological stress?

Might maternal depression also have an adverse effect on birth outcomes? A research review concluded that maternal depression is linked to preterm birth (Mparmpakas & others, 2013). And a recent study discovered that maternal depression during pregnancy was associated with low birth weight in full-term offspring (Chang & others, 2014). There is some concern about pregnant women taking antidepressant medication. For example, a recent research review concluded that antidepressant medication use during pregnancy is linked to slightly increased risks of cardiac malfunctions in the fetus and persistent pulmonary hypertension in the newborn (Pearlstein, 2015). Also, a recent study found that taking antidepressants early in pregnancy was linked to an increased risk of miscarriage (Almeida & others, 2016). Further, a recent study revealed that taking antidepressants in the second or third trimester of pregnancy was linked to an increased risk of autism spectrum disorders in children (Boukhris & others, 2016).

In one study, in China, the longer fathers smoked, the higher the risk that their children would develop cancer (Ji & others, 1997). *What are some other paternal factors that can influence the development of the fetus and the child?*

© Ryan Pyle/Ryan Pyle/Corbis

Paternal Factors So far, we have discussed how characteristics of the mother—such as drug use, disease, diet and nutrition, age, and emotional states—can influence prenatal development and the development of the child. Might there also be some paternal risk factors? Indeed, there are several. Men's exposure to lead, radiation, certain pesticides, and petrochemicals may cause abnormalities in sperm that lead to miscarriage or diseases such as childhood cancer (Cordier, 2008). The father's smoking during the mother's pregnancy also can cause problems for the offspring (Agricola & others, 2016; Han & others, 2015). In one study, heavy paternal smoking was associated with an increased risk of early miscarriage (Venners & others, 2005). This negative outcome may be related to the mother's exposure to secondhand smoke. And in a recent study, paternal smoking around the time of the child's conception was linked to an increased risk of the child developing leukemia (Milne & others, 2012). Researchers have found that increasing paternal age decreases the success rate of in vitro fertilization and increases the risk of preterm birth (Sharma & others, 2015). Also, a research review concluded that there is an increased risk of spontaneous abortion, autism, and schizophrenic disorders when the father is 40 years of age and older (Reproductive Endocrinology and Infertility Committee & others, 2012).

Another way that the father can influence prenatal and birth outcomes is through his relationship with the mother. By being supportive, helping with chores, and having a positive attitude toward the pregnancy, the father can improve the physical and psychological well-being of the mother. Negative behavior by the father also affects the mother: a recent study found that intimate partner violence increased the mother's stress level (Fonseca-Machado Mde & others, 2015).

Much of our discussion on prenatal development has focused on what can go wrong. Prospective parents should take steps to avoid the vulnerabilities to fetal development that we have described. But it is important to keep in mind that most of the time, prenatal development does not go awry and development occurs along a positive path.

Prenatal Care

Although prenatal care varies enormously from one woman to another, it usually involves a defined schedule of visits for medical care, which typically includes screening for manageable conditions and treatable diseases that can affect the baby or the mother. In addition to medical care, prenatal programs often include comprehensive educational, social, and nutritional services (Kroll-Desrosiers & others, 2016).

Information about pregnancy, labor, delivery, and caring for the newborn can be especially valuable for first-time mothers (McDonald & others, 2015). Prenatal care is also very important for women in poverty and immigrant women because it links them with other social services (Mazul, Salm Ward, & Ngui, 2016). A recent study found that adequacy of prenatal care was associated with very low birth weight (Xaverius & others, 2016).

An innovative program that is rapidly expanding in the United States is CenteringPregnancy (Barger, Faucher, & Murphy, 2015; DeCesare & Jackson, 2015; Liu & others, 2016). This program is relationship-centered and provides complete prenatal care in a group setting (Heberlein & others, 2016). It replaces traditional 15-minute physician visits with 90-minute peer group support sessions and self-examination led by a physician or certified nurse-midwife. Groups of up to 10 women (and often their partners) meet regularly beginning at 12 to 16 weeks of pregnancy. The sessions emphasize empowering women to play an active role in experiencing a positive pregnancy. Research has revealed that CenteringPregnancy group prenatal care is associated with a reduction in preterm birth (Novick & others, 2013), as well as reductions in low birth weight and placement in a neonatal intensive care unit (Gareau & others, 2016). In another recent study with adolescent mothers, CenteringPregnancy was successful in getting participants to attend meetings, have appropriate weight gain, increase the use of highly effective contraceptive methods, and increase breast feeding (Trotman & others, 2015).

The increasingly widespread CenteringPregnancy program alters routine prenatal care by bringing women out of exam rooms and into relationship-oriented groups.
© MBI/Stockbroker/Alamy Stock Photo RF

Some prenatal programs for parents focus on home visitation (Issel & others, 2011). A recent study found that use of home visiting services was associated with reduced risk of low birth weight (Shah & Austin, 2014). Research evaluations indicate that the Nurse-Family Partnership created by David Olds and his colleagues (2004, 2007, 2014) is successful. The Nurse-Family Partnership involves home visits by trained nurses beginning in the second or third trimester of prenatal development. The extensive program consists of approximately 50 home visits beginning during the prenatal period and extending through the child's first two years. Research has revealed that the Nurse-Family Partnership has numerous positive outcomes, including fewer pregnancies, better work circumstances, and stability in relationship partners for the mother, and improved academic success and social development for the child (Olds & others, 2004, 2007, 2014).

Exercise increasingly is recommended as part of a comprehensive prenatal care program (Barakat & others, 2015; Perales & others, 2016; Schmidt, Chari, & Davenport, 2016). Exercise during pregnancy helps prevent constipation, conditions the body, reduces excessive weight gain, and is associated with a more positive mental state, including a reduced level of depression (Marques & others, 2015; Shirazian & others, 2016). One study found that exercise during pregnancy improved mothers' perception of their health (Barakat & others, 2011). Further, a recent study indicated that pregnant women who did not exercise three or more times a week were more likely to develop hypertension (Barakat & others, 2016). And in one study, following 12 weeks of twice-weekly yoga or massage therapy, both therapy groups had a greater decrease in depression, anxiety, and back and leg pain than a control group (Field & others, 2013). Also, a recent study revealed that yoga participation provided immediate stress reduction for pregnant women (Kusaka & others, 2016). And a recent study revealed that physical exercise during pregnancy reduced the risk of cesarean delivery (Domenjoz, Kayser, & Boulvain, 2014).

Birth and the Postpartum Period

The long wait for the moment of birth is over, and the infant is about to appear. What happens during childbirth, and what can be done to make the experience a positive one?

Nature writes the basic script for how birth occurs, but parents make important choices about the conditions surrounding birth. We look first at the sequence of physical steps through which a child is born.

The Birth Process

The birth process occurs in three stages. It may take place in different contexts and in most cases involves one or more attendants.

Stages of Birth

The first stage of the birth process is the longest. Uterine contractions are 15 to 20 minutes apart at the beginning and last up to a minute each. These contractions cause the woman's cervix to stretch and open. As the first stage progresses, the contractions come closer together, occurring every two to five minutes. Their intensity increases. By the end of the first stage, contractions dilate the cervix to an opening of about 10 centimeters (4 inches) so that the baby can move from the uterus to the birth canal. For a woman having her first child, the first stage lasts an average of 6 to 12 hours; for subsequent children, this stage typically is much shorter.

The second birth stage begins when the baby's head starts to move through the cervix and the birth canal. It terminates when the baby completely emerges from the mother's body. With each contraction, the mother bears down hard to push the baby out of her body. By the time the baby's head is out of the mother's body, the contractions come almost every minute and last for about a minute. This stage typically lasts approximately 45 minutes to an hour.

Afterbirth is the third stage, during which the placenta, umbilical cord, and other membranes are detached and expelled. This final stage is the shortest of the three birth stages, lasting only minutes.

After the long journey of prenatal development, birth takes place. During birth the baby is on a threshold between two worlds. *What are the characteristics of the three stages of birth?*
© Jonathan Nourok/Getty Images

Childbirth Setting and Attendants

In 2013 in the United States, 98.6 percent of births took place in hospitals (Martin & others, 2015). Of the 1.4 percent of births occurring outside of a hospital, approximately two-thirds took place in homes and almost 30 percent in free-standing birthing centers. The percentage of U.S. births at home is the highest since reporting of this context began in 1989. An increase in home births has occurred mainly among non-Latino White women, especially those who are older and married. For these non-Latino White women, two-thirds of their home births are attended by a midwife.

The person who helps a mother during birth varies across cultures. In U.S. hospitals, it has become the norm for fathers or birth coaches to be with the mother throughout labor and delivery. In the East African Nigoni culture, by contrast, men are completely excluded from the childbirth process. When a woman is ready to give birth, female relatives move into the woman's hut and the husband leaves, taking his belongings (clothes, tools, weapons, and so on) with him. He is not permitted to return until after the baby is born. In some cultures, childbirth is an open, community affair. For example, in the Pukapukan culture in the Pacific Islands, women give birth in a shelter that is open to villagers, who may observe the birth.

Midwives *Midwifery* is a profession that provides health care to women during pregnancy, birth, and the postpartum period (Ekelin, Kvist, & Persson, 2016; Feijen-de Jong & others, 2015a, b; Reed, Rowe, & Barnes, 2016). Midwives also may give women information about reproductive health and annual gynecological examinations. They may refer women to general practitioners or obstetricians if a pregnant woman needs medical care beyond a midwife's expertise and skill.

Midwifery is practiced in most countries throughout the world (ten Hoope-Bender & others, 2016). In Holland, more than 40 percent of babies are delivered by midwives rather than by doctors. However, in 2013 in the United States only 7.8 percent of women who delivered a baby were attended by a midwife, a figure that was unchanged since 2000 (Martin & others, 2015). Nevertheless, the 7.8 percent figure for 2013 represents a substantial increase from less than 1 percent in 1975. A research review concluded that for low-risk women, midwife-led care was characterized by a reduction in procedures during labor and increased satisfaction with care (Sutcliffe & others, 2012). Also, in this study no adverse outcomes were found for midwife-led care compared with physician-led care.

Doulas In some countries, a doula attends a childbearing woman. *Doula* is a Greek word that means "a woman who helps." A *doula* is a caregiver who provides continuous physical, emotional, and educational support for the mother before, during, and after childbirth (Kozhimannil & others, 2016). Doulas remain with the parents throughout labor, assessing and responding to their needs. Researchers have found positive effects when a doula is present at the birth of a child (Ahlemeyer & Mahon, 2015; Zielinski, Brody, & Low, 2016). A recent study also revealed that for Medicaid recipients the odds of having a cesarean delivery were 41 percent lower for doula-supported births in the United States (Kozhimmanil & others, 2013). Thus, increasing doula-supported births could substantially lower the cost of a birth by reducing cesarean rates.

In the United States, most doulas work as independent providers hired by the expectant parents. Doulas typically function as part of a "birthing team," serving as an adjunct to the midwife or the hospital's obstetric staff.

Methods of Childbirth

U.S. hospitals often allow the mother and her obstetrician a range of options regarding their method of delivery. Key choices involve the use of medication, whether to use any of a number of nonmedicated techniques to reduce pain, and when to have a cesarean delivery.

Medication Three basic kinds of drugs that are used for labor are analgesia, anesthesia, and oxytocin/Pitocin.

Analgesia is used to relieve pain. Analgesics include tranquilizers, barbiturates, and narcotics such as Demerol.

Anesthesia is used in late first-stage labor and during delivery to block sensation in an area of the body or to block consciousness. There is a trend toward not using general anesthesia, which blocks consciousness, in normal births because general anesthesia can be transmitted through the placenta to the fetus (Pennell & others, 2011). An *epidural block* is regional anesthesia that numbs the woman's body from the waist down.

Oxytocin is a hormone that promotes uterine contractions; a synthetic form called Pitocin™ is widely used to decrease the duration of the first stage of labor. The relative benefits and risks of administering synthetic forms of oxytocin during childbirth continue to be debated (Bell, Erickson, & Carter, 2014; Shiner, Many, & Maslovitz, 2016).

Predicting how a drug will affect an individual woman and her fetus is difficult (Ansari & others, 2016). A particular drug might have only a minimal effect on one fetus yet have a much stronger effect on another. The drug's dosage is also a factor. Stronger doses of tranquilizers and narcotics given to decrease the mother's pain potentially have a more negative effect on the fetus than do mild doses. It is important for the mother to assess her level of pain and have a voice in deciding whether she should receive medication.

How Would You...?

As a **health-care provider,** how would you advise a woman in her first trimester about the options available for her baby's birth and for her own comfort during the process?

Natural and Prepared Childbirth For a brief time not long ago, the idea of avoiding all medication during childbirth gained favor in the United States. Instead, many women chose to reduce the pain of childbirth through techniques known as natural childbirth and prepared childbirth. Today, at least some medication is used in the typical childbirth, but elements of natural childbirth and prepared childbirth remain popular (Podgurski, 2016).

natural childbirth A childbirth method in which no drugs are given to relieve pain or assist in the birth process. The mother and her partner are taught to use breathing methods and relaxation techniques during delivery.

Natural childbirth is a childbirth method in which no drugs are given to relieve pain or assist in the birth process. The mother and her partner are taught to use breathing methods and relaxation techniques during delivery. French obstetrician Ferdinand Lamaze developed a method similar to natural childbirth that is known as **prepared childbirth,** or the Lamaze method. It includes a special breathing technique to control pushing in the final stages of labor, as well as more detailed education about anatomy and physiology. The Lamaze method has become very popular in the United States. The pregnant woman's partner usually serves as a coach; the partner attends childbirth classes with her and helps her with her breathing and relaxation during delivery. In sum, proponents of current prepared childbirth methods conclude that when information and support are provided, women *know* how to give birth.

prepared childbirth Developed by French obstetrician Ferdinand Lamaze, this childbirth strategy is similar to natural childbirth but includes a special breathing technique to control pushing in the final stages of labor and more detailed anatomy and physiology instruction.

Other Nonmedicated Techniques to Reduce Pain The effort to reduce stress and control pain during labor has recently led to an increase in the use of some older and some newer nonmedicated techniques (Henderson & others, 2014). These include waterbirth, massage, and acupuncture.

What characterizes the use of waterbirth in delivering a baby?
© Daisy Smith/Alamy

Waterbirth involves giving birth in a tub of warm water. Some women go through labor in the water and get out for delivery; others remain in the water for delivery. The rationale for waterbirth is that the baby has been in an amniotic sac for many months and that delivery in a similar environment is likely to be less stressful for the baby and the mother (Kavosi & others, 2015; Taylor & others, 2016). An increasing number of studies are either showing no differences in neonatal and maternal outcomes for waterbirth and non-waterbirth deliveries or positive outcomes (Davies & others, 2015; Taylor & others, 2016). For example, a recent large-scale study of more than 16,000 waterbirth and non-waterbirth deliveries found fewer negative outcomes for the waterbirth newborns (Bovbjerg, Cheyney, & Everson, 2016). Further, a recent research review concluded that waterbirth is associated with high levels of maternal satisfaction with pain relief and the experience of childbirth (Nutter & others, 2015). Waterbirth has been practiced more often in European countries such as Switzerland and Sweden in recent decades than in the United States, but is increasingly being included in U.S. birth plans.

Massage is increasingly used during pregnancy, labor, and delivery (Frawley & others, 2016; Vargens, Silva, & Progianti, 2013). Two research reviews concluded that massage therapy reduced pain during labor (Jones & others, 2012; Smith & others, 2012).

Acupuncture, the insertion of very fine needles into specific locations in the body, is used as a standard procedure to reduce the pain of childbirth in China, although it only recently has begun to be used for this purpose in the United States (Moleti, 2009; Smith, Armour, & Ee, 2016). Research indicates that acupuncture can have positive effects on labor and delivery (Akbarzadeh & others, 2015; Smith & others, 2011). For example, in a recent study acupuncture was successful in reducing labor pain 30 minutes after the intervention (Allameh, Tehrani, & Ghasemi, 2015).

Cesarean Delivery

Normally, the baby's head comes through the vagina first. But if the baby is in a *breech position*, its buttocks are the first part to emerge from the vagina. In 1 of every 25 deliveries, the baby's head is still in the uterus when the rest of the body is out. Because breech births can cause respiratory problems, if the baby is in a breech position a surgical procedure known as a cesarean delivery is usually performed. In a *cesarean delivery* (or cesarean section), the baby is removed from the uterus through an incision made in the mother's abdomen. The benefits and risks of cesarean deliveries continue to be debated (Furukawa, Sameshima, & Ikenoue, 2014). Some critics argue that far too many babies are delivered by cesarean section in the United States and around the world (Gibbons & others, 2012). The U.S. cesarean birth rate (38.7 percent) was essentially unchanged from 2010 through 2013 (Martin & others, 2015).

The Transition from Fetus to Newborn

Much of our discussion of birth so far has focused on the mother. However, birth also involves considerable stress for the baby. If the delivery takes too long, the baby can develop anoxia, a condition in which the fetus or newborn has an insufficient supply of oxygen. Anoxia can cause brain damage.

The baby has considerable capacity to withstand the stress of birth. Large quantities of adrenaline and noradrenaline, hormones that protect the fetus in the event of oxygen deficiency, are secreted in the newborn's body during the birth process.

Immediately after birth, the umbilical cord is cut and the baby is on its own. Before birth, oxygen came from the mother via the umbilical cord, but now the baby can breathe independently.

Almost immediately after birth, a newborn is taken to be weighed, cleaned up, and tested for signs of developmental problems that might require urgent attention. The **Apgar Scale** is widely used to assess the health of newborns at one and five minutes after birth. The Apgar Scale evaluates infants' heart rate, respiratory effort, muscle tone, body color, and reflex irritability. An obstetrician or nurse does the evaluation and gives the newborn a score, or reading, of 0, 1, or 2 on each of these five health signs. A total score of 7 to 10 indicates that the newborn's condition is good. A score of 5 indicates that there may be developmental difficulties. A score of 3 or below signals an emergency and warns that the baby might not survive. The Apgar Scale is especially good at assessing the newborn's ability to respond to the stress of delivery and its new environment (Miyakoshi & others, 2013). It also identifies high-risk infants who need resuscitation. Recent studies have found that low Apgar scores are associated with long-term additional support needs in education and educational attainment (Tweed & others, 2016), risk of developmental vulnerability at 5 years of age (Razaz & others, 2016), and risk of developing ADHD (Hanc & others, 2016).

Nurses often play important roles in the birth of a baby. To read about the work of a nurse who specializes in the care of women during labor and delivery, see *Careers in Life-Span Development.*

Apgar Scale A widely used assessment of the newborn's health at 1 and 5 minutes after birth.

Careers in life-span development

Linda Pugh, Perinatal Nurse

Perinatal nurses work with childbearing women to support health and growth during the childbearing experience. Linda Pugh, Ph.D., R.N.C., is a perinatal nurse on the faculty at The Johns Hopkins University School of Nursing. She is certified as an inpatient obstetric nurse and specializes in the care of women during labor and delivery. She teaches undergraduate and graduate students, educates professional nurses, and conducts research. In addition, Pugh consults with hospitals and organizations about women's health issues and many of the topics we discuss in this chapter.

Her research interests include nursing interventions with low-income breast-feeding women, discovering ways to prevent and ameliorate fatigue during childbearing, and using breathing exercises during labor.

Linda Pugh (right) with a mother and her newborn.
© Dr. Linda Pugh

Low Birth Weight and Preterm Infants

Three related conditions pose threats to many newborns: low birth weight, preterm birth, and being small for date. *Low birth weight* infants weigh less than 5 pounds at birth. *Very low birth weight* newborns weigh under 3 pounds, and *extremely low birth weight* newborns weigh under 2 pounds. Preterm infants are born three weeks or more before the pregnancy has reached its full term—in other words, 35 or fewer weeks after conception. Small for date infants (also called *small for gestational age infants*) have a birth weight that is below normal when the length of the pregnancy is considered. They weigh less than 90 percent of all babies of the same gestational age. Small for date infants may be preterm or full term. One study found that small for date infants have a 400 percent greater risk of death (Regev & others, 2003).

In 2013, 11.4 percent of U.S. infants were born preterm—a 34 percent increase since the 1980s but a decrease of 1.4 percent since 2008 (Martin & others, 2015). The increase in preterm birth is likely due to such factors as the increasing number of births to women 35 years and older, increasing rates of multiple births, increased management of maternal and fetal conditions (for example, inducing labor preterm if medical technology indicates it will increase the likelihood of survival), increased substance abuse (tobacco, alcohol), and increased stress (Goldenberg & Culhane, 2007). Ethnic variations characterize preterm birth (Raglan & others, 2016; Sorbye, Wanigaratne, & Urgula, 2016). For example, in 2013, the likelihood of being born preterm was 11.4 percent for all U.S. infants and 10.4 percent for non-Latino White infants, but the rate was 16.8 percent for African American infants and 11.7 for Latino infants (Martin & others, 2015).

Incidence and Causes of Low Birth Weight

Most, but not all, preterm babies are also low birth weight babies. The incidence of low birth weight varies considerably from country to country. In some countries, such as India and Sudan, where poverty is rampant and the health and nutrition of mothers are poor, the percentage of low birth weight babies reaches as high as 31 percent. In the United States, there has been an increase in low birth weight infants in the last two decades, and the U.S. low birth weight rate of 8.02 percent in 2013 was considerably higher than that of many other developed countries (Martin & others, 2015). For example, only 4 percent of the infants born in Sweden, Finland, Norway, and Korea are low birth weight, and only 5 percent of those born in New Zealand, Australia, and France are low birth weight.

Consequences of Low Birth Weight

Many preterm and low birth weight infants are healthy, but as a group they have more health and developmental problems than do normal birth weight infants (Webb & others, 2014). The number and severity of these problems increase when infants are born very early and as their birth weight decreases (Griffin & others, 2015; Tchamo, Prista, & Leandro, 2016). Survival rates for infants who are born very early and very small have risen, but with this improved survival rate have come increased rates of severe brain damage (McNicholas & others, 2014).

For preterm birth, the terms *extremely preterm* and *very preterm* are increasingly used (Kato & others, 2016; Ohlin & others, 2015). *Extremely preterm infants* are those born less than 28 weeks preterm, and *very preterm infants* are those born at less than 33 weeks of gestational age.

Low birth weight children are more likely than their normal birth weight counterparts to develop a learning disability, attention deficit

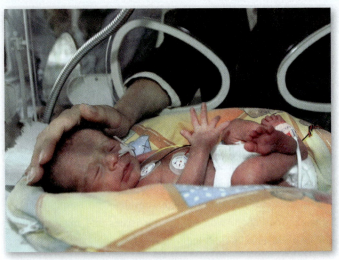

A "kilogram kid," weighing less than 2.3 pounds at birth. *What are some long-term outcomes of weighing so little at birth?*
© Diether Endlicher/AP Images

hyperactivity disorder, autism spectrum disorders, or breathing problems such as asthma (Leung & others, 2016; Schieve & others, 2016). Also, one study revealed that very preterm, low birth weight infants had abnormal axon development in their brain and impaired cognitive development at 9 years of age (Iwata & others, 2012). Approximately 50 percent of all low birth weight children are enrolled in special education programs.

Nurturing Low Birth Weight and Preterm Infants

Two increasingly used interventions in the neonatal intensive care unit (NICU) are kangaroo care and massage therapy. *Kangaroo care* involves skin-to-skin contact in which the baby, wearing only a diaper, is held upright against the parent's bare chest, much as a baby kangaroo is carried by its mother. Kangaroo care is typically practiced for two to three hours per day over an extended time in early infancy.

Why use kangaroo care with preterm infants? Preterm infants often have difficulty coordinating their breathing and heart rate, and the close physical contact with the parent provided by kangaroo care can help stabilize the preterm infant's heartbeat, temperature, and breathing (Boundy & others, 2016; Cho & others, 2016; Park & others, 2014). Preterm infants who experience kangaroo care also gain more weight than their counterparts who are not given this care (Faye & others, 2016). Also, a recent study

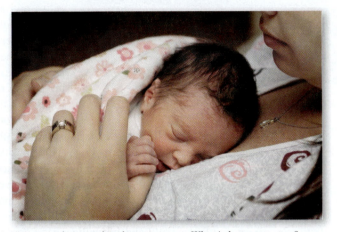

A new mother practices kangaroo care. *What is kangaroo care? What are some outcomes of kangaroo care?*
© iStockphoto.com/casenbina RF

discovered that preterm infants who experienced kangaroo care for 16 weeks had more complex electroencephalogram (EEG) patterns, which reflects neurological maturation) at 40 weeks of age than preterm infants who did not receive kangaroo care (Kaffashi & others, 2013).

And a recent study demonstrated the positive long-term benefits of kangaroo care (Feldman, Rosenthal, & Eidelman, 2014). In this study, maternal-newborn kangaroo care with preterm infants was linked to better respiratory and cardiovascular functioning, sleep patterns, and cognitive functioning from 6 months to 10 years of age. Further, a recent study in the United Kingdom found that the use of kangaroo care in neonatal units resulted in substantial cost savings mainly because of its reduction in diseases such as gastroenteritis and colitis (Lowson & others, 2016). And in another recent study, kangaroo care significantly reduced the amount of crying and improved heart rate stability in preterm infants (Choudhary & others, 2016).

A recent U.S. survey found that mothers had a much more positive view of kangaroo care than did neonatal intensive care nurses and that mothers were more likely to say that it should be provided daily (Hendricks-Munoz & others, 2013). There is concern that kangaroo care is not used more often in neonatal intensive care units (Kymre, 2014; Penn, 2015). Increasingly, kangaroo care is recommended as standard practice for all newborns (Seidman & others, 2015).

Many adults will attest to the therapeutic effects of receiving a massage. In fact, many will pay a premium to receive one at a spa on a regular basis. But can massage play a role in improving the developmental outcomes for preterm infants? A recent study found that both kangaroo care and massage therapy were equally effective in improving body weight and reducing length of hospital stay for low birth weight infants (Rangey & Sheth, 2015).

Many preterm infants experience less touch than full-term infants do because they are isolated in temperature-controlled incubators. Research by Tiffany Field and her colleagues (2001, 2007, 2010a; Diego, Field, & Hernandez-Reif, 2008, 2014; Field, Diego, & Hernandez-Reif, 2008, 2011) has led to a surge of interest in the role that massage might play in improving developmental outcomes for preterm infants. In Field's first study

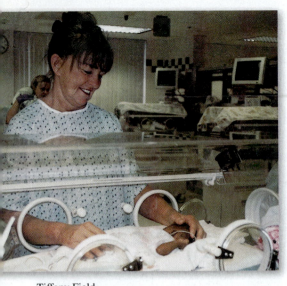

Tiffany Field massages a newborn infant. *What types of infants has massage therapy been shown to help?*
© Dr. Tiffany Field

in this area, massage therapy consisting of firm stroking with the palms of the hands was given three times per day for 15-minute periods to pre-term infants (Field & others, 1986). The massage therapy led to 47 percent greater weight gain than did standard medical treatment. The massaged infants also were more active and alert than preterm infants who were not massaged, and they performed better on developmental tests.

How Would You...?

As a **health-care professional,** how would you advise hospital administrators about implementing kangaroo care or massage therapy in the newborn intensive care unit?

In later studies, Field demonstrated the benefits of massage therapy for infants who faced a variety of problems. For example, preterm infants exposed to cocaine in utero who received massage therapy gained weight and improved their scores on developmental tests (Field, 2001). In other research, massage therapy improved the scores of HIV-exposed infants on both physical and mental scales, while also improving their hearing and speech (Perez & others, 2015). Also, one study investigated 1- to 3-month-old infants born to depressed adolescent mothers (Field & others, 1996). The infants of depressed mothers who received massage therapy had lower stress—as well as improved emotionality, sociability, and soothability—compared with non-massaged infants of depressed mothers. In a review of the use of massage therapy with preterm infants, Field and her colleagues (2004) concluded that the most consistent findings involve two positive results: (1) increased weight gain and (2) discharge from the hospital three to six days earlier. One study revealed that the mechanisms responsible for increased weight gain as a result of massage therapy were stimulation of the vagus nerve (one of 12 cranial nerves leading to the brain) and in turn the release of insulin (a food absorption hormone) (Field, Diego, & Hernandez-Reif, 2011). Another recent study found that both massage therapy (moderate-pressure stroking) and exercise (flexion and extension of the limbs) led to weight gain in preterm infants (Diego, Field, & Hernandez-Reif, 2014). In this study, massage was linked to increased vagal activity while exercise was associated with increased calorie consumption.

Bonding

A special component of the parent-infant relationship is *bonding*, the formation of a connection, especially a physical bond between parents and the newborn in the period shortly after birth. In the mid-twentieth century, U.S. hospitals seemed almost determined to deter bonding. Anesthesia given to the mother during delivery would make the mother drowsy, interfering with her ability to respond to and stimulate the newborn. Mothers and newborns were often separated shortly after delivery, and preterm infants were isolated from their mothers even more than full-term infants were separated from their mothers. In recent decades these practices have changed, but to some extent they are still followed in many hospitals.

Do these practices do any harm? Some physicians believe that during the "critical period" shortly after birth the parents and newborn need to form an emotional attachment as a foundation for optimal development in years to come (Kennell, 2006; Kennell & McGrath, 1999). Although some research supports this bonding hypothesis (Klaus & Kennell, 1976), a body of research challenges the significance of the first few days of life as a critical period (Bakeman & Brown, 1980; Rode & others, 1981). Indeed, the extreme form of the bonding hypothesis—the idea that the newborn *must* have close contact with the mother in the first few days of life to develop optimally—simply is not true.

Nevertheless, the weakness of the bonding hypothesis should not be used as an excuse to keep motivated mothers from interacting with their newborns. Such contact brings pleasure to many mothers and may dispel maternal anxiety about the baby's health and safety. In some cases—including preterm infants, adolescent mothers, and mothers from disadvantaged circumstances—early close contact is key to establishing a climate for improved interaction after the mother and infant leave the hospital.

Many hospitals now offer a *rooming-in* arrangement in which the baby remains in the mother's room most of the time during its hospital stay. However, if parents choose not to use this rooming-in arrangement, the weight of the research suggests that this decision will not harm the infant emotionally (Lamb, 1994).

The Postpartum Period

The weeks after childbirth present challenges for many new parents and their offspring. This is the **postpartum period,** the period after childbirth or delivery that lasts for about six weeks or until the mother's body has completed its adjustment and has returned to a nearly prepregnant state. It is a time when the woman adjusts, both physically and psychologically, to the process of childbearing.

Physical Adjustments

A woman's body makes numerous physical adjustments in the first days and weeks after childbirth (Durham & Chapman, 2014). She may have a great deal of energy or feel exhausted and let down. Though these changes are normal, the fatigue can undermine the new mother's sense of well-being and confidence in her ability to cope with a new baby and a new family life (Runquist, 2007).

A concern is the loss of sleep that the primary caregiver experiences in the postpartum period (Bei, Coo, & Trinder, 2015; Thomas & Spieker, 2016). In the 2007 Sleep in America survey, a substantial percentage of women reported loss of sleep during pregnancy and in the postpartum period (National Sleep Foundation, 2007). The loss of sleep can contribute to stress, marital conflict, and impaired decision making (Meerlo, Sgoifo, & Suchecki, 2008). A recent study, though, linked postpartum depression to poor-quality sleep (such as disrupted, fragmented sleep) rather than to lesser amounts of sleep (Park, Meltzer-Brody, & Stickgold, 2013).

After delivery, the mother's body undergoes sudden and dramatic changes in hormone production. When the placenta is delivered, estrogen and progesterone levels drop steeply and remain low until the ovaries start producing hormones again.

Involution is the process by which the uterus returns to its prepregnant size five or six weeks after birth. Immediately following birth, the uterus weighs 2 to 3 pounds. By the end of five or six weeks, the uterus weighs 2 to 3½ ounces. Nursing the baby helps contract the uterus at a more rapid rate.

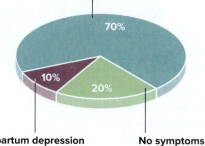

Postpartum blues
Symptoms appear 2 to 3 days after delivery and usually subside within 1 to 2 weeks.

70%

10%

20%

Postpartum depression
Symptoms linger for weeks or months and interfere with daily functioning.

No symptoms

Figure 11 **Postpartum Blues and Postpartum Depression Among U.S. Women.**
Some health professionals refer to the postpartum period as the "fourth trimester." Though the time span of the postpartum period does not necessarily cover three months, the term "fourth trimester" suggests continuity and emphasizes the importance of the first several months after birth for the mother.

Emotional and Psychological Adjustments

Emotional fluctuations are common for mothers in the postpartum period (Haran & others, 2014). For some women, emotional fluctuations decrease within several weeks after the delivery, but other women experience more long-lasting emotional swings.

As shown in Figure 11, about 70 percent of new mothers in the United States have what are called the postpartum blues. About two to three days after birth, they begin to feel depressed, anxious, and upset. These feelings may come and go for several months after the birth, often peaking about three to five days after birth. Even without treatment, these feelings usually go away after one or two weeks.

However, some women develop postpartum depression, which involves a major depressive episode that typically occurs about four weeks after delivery (Brummelte & Galea, 2016). In other words, women with postpartum depression have such strong feelings of sadness, anxiety, or despair that

postpartum period The period after childbirth when the mother adjusts, both physically and psychologically, to the process of childbearing. This period lasts for about six weeks or until her body has completed its adjustment and returned to a nearly prepregnant state.

for at least a two-week period they have trouble coping with their daily tasks. Without treatment, postpartum depression may become worse and last for many months (Di Florio & others, 2014). And many women with postpartum depression don't seek help. For example, one study found that 15 percent of the women reported postpartum depression symptoms but less than half sought help (McGarry & others, 2009). Estimates indicate that 10 to 14 percent of new mothers experience postpartum depression.

A recent research review identified the following risk factors for developing postpartum depression: a history of depression, depression and anxiety during pregnancy, neuroticism, low self-esteem, postpartum blues, poor marital relationship, and a low level of social support (O'Hara & McCabe, 2013). Also, in this research review, a number of perinatal-related stressors such as perinatal complications, infant health and temperament, and type of delivery (cesarean section, for example) were found to be potential risk factors for postpartum depression. A subset of women likely develop postpartum depression in the context of hormonal changes associated with late pregnancy and childbirth (O'Hara & McCabe, 2013). Also, a recent study found that depression during pregnancy, a history of physical abuse, migrant status, and postpartum physical complications were major risk factors for postpartum depression (Gaillard & others, 2014).

Several antidepressant drugs are effective in treating postpartum depression and appear to be safe for breast feeding women (Molyneaux, Trevillion, & Howard, 2015). Psychotherapy, especially cognitive therapy, also is effective in treating postpartum depression for many women (Carta & others, 2015; Sockol, 2015). In addition, engaging in regular exercise may help to relieve postpartum depression (Ko & others, 2013).

The postpartum period is a time of considerable adjustment and adaptation for both the mother and the father. Fathers can provide an important support system for mothers, especially in helping mothers care for young infants. *What kinds of tasks might the father of a newborn do to support the mother?*

© Howard Grey/Getty Images RF

A mother's postpartum depression can affect the way she interacts with her infant (Giallo & others, 2015; Kerstis & others, 2016). A research review concluded that the interaction difficulties of depressed mothers and their infants occur across cultures and socioeconomic status groups, and encompass less sensitivity of the mothers and less responsiveness on the part of infants (Field, 2010b). Several caregiving activities also are compromised, including feeding, sleep routines, and safety practices.

How Would You...?

As a **human development and family studies professional,** how would you talk with mothers and fathers about vulnerabilities in mental health and relationships in the postpartum period?

Fathers also undergo considerable adjustment in the postpartum period, even when they work away from home all day (Gawlik & others, 2014; Nishimura & others, 2015; Paulson & others, 2016). Many fathers feel that the baby comes first and gets all of the mother's attention; some feel that they have been replaced by the baby.

The father's support and caring can play a role in whether the mother develops postpartum depression. One study revealed that higher support by fathers was related to lower incidence of postpartum depression in women (Smith & Howard, 2008).

Summary

The Evolutionary Perspective

- Darwin proposed that natural selection fuels evolution. In evolutionary theory, adaptive behavior is behavior that promotes the organism's survival in a natural habitat.

- Evolutionary psychology holds that adaptation, reproduction, and "survival of the fittest" are important in shaping behavior. Evolutionary developmental psychology emphasizes that humans need an extended "juvenile" period to develop a large brain and learn the complexity of social communities.

Genetic Foundations of Development

- Except in the sperm and egg, the nucleus of each human cell contains 46 chromosomes, which are composed of DNA. Short segments of DNA constitute genes, the units of hereditary information that direct cells to reproduce and manufacture proteins. Genes act collaboratively, not independently.
- Genes are passed on to new cells when chromosomes are duplicated during the processes of mitosis and meiosis.
- Genetic principles include those involving dominant-recessive genes, sex-linked genes, and polygenic inheritance.
- Chromosome abnormalities can produce Down syndrome and other problems; gene-linked disorders, such as PKU, involve defective genes.

The Interaction of Heredity and Environment:
The Nature-Nurture Debate

- Behavior geneticists use twin studies and adoption studies to determine the strength of heredity's influence on development.
- In Scarr's heredity-environment correlation view, heredity directs the types of environments that children experience. Scarr identified three types of genotype-environment interactions: passive, evocative, and active (niche-picking).
- The epigenetic view emphasizes that development is the result of an ongoing, bidirectional interchange between heredity and environment. Recently, interest has developed regarding how gene interaction influences development.
- The interaction of heredity and environment is complex, but we can create a unique developmental path by changing our environment.

Prenatal Development

- Prenatal development can be divided into three periods: germinal, embryonic, and fetal. The growth of the brain during prenatal development is remarkable.
- A number of prenatal tests, including ultrasound sonography, chorionic villus sampling, amniocentesis,

maternal blood screening, and fetal MRI, can reveal whether a fetus is developing normally.
- Approximately 10 to 15 percent of U.S. couples have infertility problems. Assisted reproduction techniques, such as in vitro fertilization, are increasingly being used by infertile couples.
- Some prescription drugs and nonprescription drugs can harm the unborn child. In particular, the psychoactive drugs caffeine, alcohol, nicotine, cocaine, marijuana, and heroin can endanger developing offspring. Other potential sources of harmful effects on the fetus include environmental hazards, maternal diseases, maternal diet and nutrition, age, emotional states and stress, and paternal factors.
- Prenatal care usually involves medical care services with a defined schedule of visits and often encompasses educational, social, and nutritional services as well. Inadequate prenatal care may increase the risk of infant mortality and result in low birth weight.

Birth and the Postpartum Period

- Childbirth occurs in three stages. Childbirth strategies involve the childbirth setting and attendants. In many countries, a midwife attends a childbearing woman. In some countries, a doula helps with the birth. Methods of delivery include medicated, natural and prepared, and cesarean.
- Being born involves considerable stress for the baby, but the baby is well prepared and adapted to handle the stress. Low birth weight, preterm, and small for date infants are at risk for developmental problems, although most of these infants are normal and healthy. Kangaroo care and massage therapy have been shown to produce benefits for preterm infants.
- Early bonding has not been found to be critical in the development of a competent infant, but close contact during the first few days after birth may reduce the mother's anxiety and lead to better interaction later.
- The postpartum period lasts for about six weeks after childbirth or until the body has returned to a nearly pre-pregnant state; postpartum depression is a serious condition that may become worse if not treated.

Key Terms

adoption study
Apgar Scale
behavior genetics
chromosomes
DNA
Down syndrome
embryonic period

epigenetic view
evolutionary psychology
fetal alcohol spectrum
   disorders (FASD)
fetal period
gene × environment (G × E)
   interaction

genes
genotype
germinal period
meiosis
mitosis
natural childbirth
neurons

organogenesis
phenotype
postpartum period
prepared childbirth
teratogen
twin study

3 Physical and Cognitive Development in Infancy

© Rob Hainer/Shutterstock RF

CHAPTER OUTLINE

PHYSICAL GROWTH AND DEVELOPMENT IN INFANCY
Patterns of Growth
Height and Weight
The Brain
Sleep
Nutrition

MOTOR DEVELOPMENT
Dynamic Systems Theory
Reflexes
Gross Motor Skills
Fine Motor Skills

SENSORY AND PERCEPTUAL DEVELOPMENT
Exploring Sensory and Perceptual Development
Visual Perception
Other Senses
Intermodal Perception
Nature, Nurture, and Perceptual Development
Perceptual Motor Coupling

COGNITIVE DEVELOPMENT
Piaget's Theory
Learning, Remembering, and Conceptualizing

LANGUAGE DEVELOPMENT
Defining Language
How Language Develops
Biological and Environmental Influences

Stories of Life-Span Development: Newborn Babies in Ghana and Nigeria

Latonya is a newborn baby in Ghana. During her first days of life she has been kept apart from her mother and bottle fed. Manufacturers of infant formula provide free or subsidized milk powder to the hospital where she was born. Latonya's mother has been persuaded to bottle feed rather than breast feed her. When her mother bottle feeds Latonya, she overdilutes the milk formula with unclean water and puts it in bottles that have not been sterilized. Latonya becomes very sick, and she dies before her first birthday.

Ramona was born in Nigeria in a "baby-friendly" program. In this program, babies are not separated from their mothers when they are born, and the mothers are encouraged to breast feed them. The mothers are told of the perils that bottle feeding can cause because of unsafe water and unsterilized bottles. They also are informed about the advantages of breast milk, which include its nutritious and hygienic qualities, its ability to immunize babies against common illnesses, and its role in reducing the mother's risk of breast and ovarian cancer. Ramona's mother is breast feeding her. At 1 year of age, Ramona is very healthy.

For many years, maternity units in hospitals favored bottle feeding and did not give mothers adequate information about the benefits of breast feeding. In recent years, the World Health Organization and UNICEF have tried to reverse the trend toward bottle feeding of infants in many impoverished countries. They instituted the "baby-friendly" program in many countries. They also persuaded the International Association of Infant Formula Manufacturers to stop marketing their baby formulas to hospitals in countries where governments support the baby-friendly initiatives (Grant, 1993). For the hospitals themselves, costs actually were reduced as infant formula, feeding bottles, and separate nurseries became unnecessary. For example, baby-friendly Jose Fabella Memorial Hospital in the Philippines reported saving 8 percent of its annual budget. Still, there are many places in the world where the baby-friendly initiatives have not been implemented.

(*Left*) An HIV-infected mother breast feeding her baby in Nairobi, Africa; (*Right*) A Rwandan mother bottle feeding her baby. *What are some concerns about breast versus bottle feeding in impoverished African countries?*

(Left) © Wendy Stone/Corbis; (right) © Dave Bartruff/Corbis

The advantages of breast feeding in impoverished countries are substantial (UNICEF, 2016; Williams & others, 2016; Woods, 2015). However, these advantages must be balanced against the risk of passing HIV to the baby through breast milk if the mother has the virus (Coovadia & Moodley, 2016; Fowler & others, 2014). The majority of mothers with HIV don't know that they are infected. In some areas of Africa more than 30 percent of mothers have the virus.

In the first two years of life, an infant's body and brain undergo remarkable growth and development. In this chapter we explore how this takes place: through physical growth, motor development, sensory and perceptual development, cognitive development, and language development. ■

Physical Growth and Development in Infancy

At birth, an infant has few of the physical abilities we associate with being human. Its head, which is huge relative to the rest of the body, flops around uncontrollably. Apart from some basic reflexes and the ability to cry, the newborn is unable to perform many actions. Over the next 12 months, however, the infant becomes capable of sitting, standing, stooping, climbing, and usually walking. During the second year, while growth slows, rapid increases in activities such as running and climbing take place. Let's now examine in greater detail the sequence of physical development in infancy.

Patterns of Growth

During prenatal development and early infancy, the head occupies an extraordinary proportion of the total body (see Figure 1). The **cephalocaudal pattern** is the sequence in which the earliest growth always occurs at the top—the head—with physical growth and differentiation of features gradually working their way down from top to bottom (shoulders, middle trunk, and so on). This same pattern occurs in the head area, as the top parts of the head—the eyes and brain—grow faster than the lower parts, such as the jaw.

cephalocaudal pattern The sequence in which the earliest growth always occurs at the top—the head—with physical growth in size, weight, and feature differentiation gradually working from top to bottom.

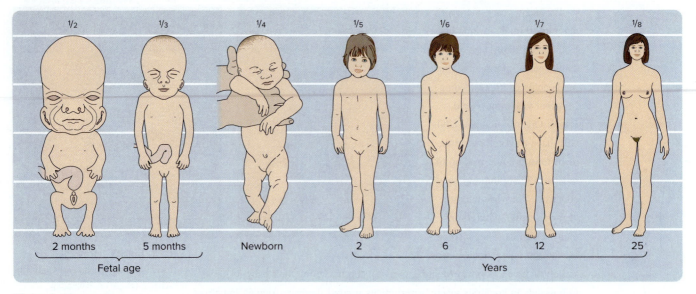

| 1/2 | 1/3 | 1/4 | 1/5 | 1/6 | 1/7 | 1/8 |

| 2 months | 5 months | Newborn | 2 | 6 | 12 | 25 |
| Fetal age | | | Years | | | |

Figure 1 Changes in Proportions of the Human Body During Growth

As individuals develop from infancy through adulthood, one of the most noticeable physical changes is that the head becomes smaller in relation to the rest of the body. The fractions listed refer to head size as a proportion of total body length at different stages.

Sensory and motor development generally proceed according to the cephalocaudal pattern. For example, infants see objects before they can control their torso, and they can use their hands long before they can crawl or walk. However, development does not follow a rigid blueprint. One study found that infants reached for toys with their feet four weeks earlier, on average, than they reached for them with their hands (Galloway & Thelen, 2004).

Growth also follows the **proximodistal pattern,** a sequence in which growth starts at the center of the body and moves toward the extremities. For example, infants control the muscles of their trunk and arms before they control their hands, and they use their whole hands before they can control several fingers.

Height and Weight

The average North American newborn is 20 inches long and weighs 7½ pounds. Ninety-five percent of full-term newborns are 18 to 22 inches long and weigh between 5½ and 10 pounds.

In the first several days of life, most newborns lose 5 to 7 percent of their body weight before they adjust to feeding by sucking, swallowing, and digesting. They then grow rapidly, gaining an average of 5 to 6 ounces per week during the first month. They double their birth weight by the age of 4 months and nearly triple it by their first birthday. Infants grow about 3/4 inch per month during the first year, increasing their birth length by about 40 percent by their first birthday.

Growth slows considerably in the second year of life (Marcdante & Kliegman, 2015). By 2 years of age, children weigh approximately 26 to 32 pounds, having gained a quarter to half a pound per month during the second year; now they have reached about one-fifth of their adult weight. At 2 years of age, the average child is 32 to 35 inches tall, nearly half of his or her eventual adult height.

The Brain

At birth, the infant that began as a single cell has a brain that contains tens of billions of nerve cells, or neurons. Extensive brain development continues after birth, through infancy, and later (de Haan & Johnson, 2016; Denes, 2016; Monahan & others, 2016). Because the brain is developing so rapidly in infancy, the infant's head should be protected from falls or other injuries and the baby should never be shaken. *Shaken baby syndrome,* which includes brain swelling and hemorrhaging, affects hundreds of babies in the United States each year

proximodistal pattern The sequence in which growth starts at the center of the body and moves toward the extremities.

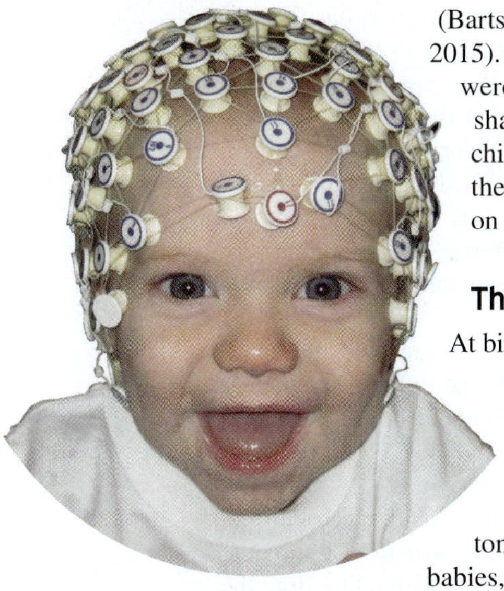

(Bartschat & others, 2016; Mian & others, 2015). A recent analysis found that fathers were most often the perpetrators of shaken baby syndrome, followed by child-care providers and boyfriends of the victims' mothers (National Center on Shaken Baby Syndrome, 2012).

The Brain's Development

At birth, the brain weighs about 25 percent of its adult weight. By the second birthday, it is about 75 percent of its adult weight. However, the brain's areas do not mature uniformly.

Assessing the infant's brain activity is not as easy as it might seem. Positron-emission tomography (PET) scans pose a radiation risk to babies, and sometimes infants wriggle too much to allow the technician to capture accurate brain images with magnetic resonance imaging (MRI). However, researchers have been successful in using the electroencephalogram (EEG), a measure of the brain's electrical activity, to learn about the brain's development in infancy (Kuhn-Popp & others, 2016; Perry & others, 2016) (see Figure 2). For example, a recent study found that higher-quality mother-infant interaction early in infancy predicted higher-quality frontal lobe functioning that was assessed with EEG later in infancy (Bernier, Calkins, & Bell, 2016).

Researchers also are increasingly studying infants' brain activity by using functional near-infrared spectroscopy (fNIRS), which uses very low levels of near-infrared light to monitor changes in blood oxygen (see Figure 3) (Brigadoi & Cooper, 2015; de Haan & Johnson, 2016; Ravicz & others, 2015). Unlike fMRI, which uses magnetic fields or electrical activity, fNIRS is portable and allows the infants to be assessed as they explore the world around them.

Figure 2 Measuring the Activity of the Infant's Brain
As shown here, a large number of electrodes are attached to a baby's scalp to measure the brain's activity as part of an EEG assessment.

Figure 3 Functional Near-Infrared Spectroscopy (fNRIS)
This brain-imaging technology is increasingly being used to assess infants' brain activity as they move about their environment.

Mapping the Brain Scientists analyze and categorize areas of the brain in numerous ways (de Haan & Johnson, 2016; Hensch, 2016; Richards & others, 2015). Of greatest interest is the portion farthest from the spinal cord, known as the *forebrain,* which includes the cerebral cortex and several structures beneath it. The *cerebral cortex* covers the forebrain like a wrinkled cap. It has two halves, or hemispheres. Based on ridges and valleys in the cortex, scientists distinguish four main areas, called lobes, in each hemisphere: the *frontal lobes,* the *occipital lobes,* the *temporal lobes,* and the *parietal lobes* (see Figure 4).

Although these areas are found in the cerebral cortex of each hemisphere, the two hemispheres are not identical in anatomy or function. **Lateralization** is the specialization of function in one hemisphere or the other. Researchers continue to explore the degree to which each is involved in various aspects of thinking, feeling, and behavior (Steri & de Hevia, 2015). At birth, the hemispheres of the cerebral cortex have already started to specialize: Newborns show greater electrical brain activity in the left hemisphere than in the right hemisphere when listening to speech sounds (Hahn, 1987).

lateralization Specialization of function in one hemisphere of the cerebral cortex or the other.

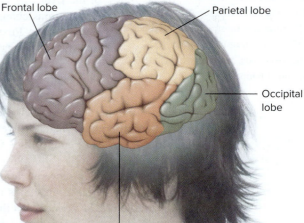

Frontal lobe

Parietal lobe

Occipital lobe

Temporal lobe

Figure 4 The Brain's Four Lobes
Shown here are the locations of the brain's four lobes: frontal, occipital, temporal, and parietal.

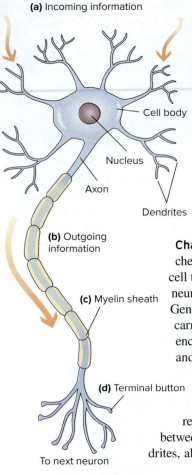

(a) Incoming information

Cell body

Nucleus

Axon

Dendrites

(b) Outgoing information

(c) Myelin sheath

(d) Terminal button

To next neuron

Figure 5 The Neuron
(*a*) The dendrites of the cell body receive information from other neurons, muscles, or glands through the axon. (*b*) Axons transmit information away from the cell body. (*c*) A myelin sheath covers most axons and speeds information transmission. (*d*) As the axon ends, it branches out into terminal buttons.

The most extensive research on brain lateralization has focused on language. Speech and grammar are localized in the left hemisphere in most people, but some aspects of language, such as appropriate language use in different contexts and the use of metaphor and humor, involve the right hemisphere (Moore, Brendel, & Fiez, 2014). Thus, language is not controlled exclusively by the brain's left hemisphere. Further, most neuroscientists agree that complex functions—such as reading, performing music, and creating art—are the outcome of communication between the two sides of the brain (Ries, Dronkers, & Knight, 2016).

How do the areas of the brain in the newborn and the infant differ from those of an adult, and why do the differences matter? Important differences have been documented at both the cellular and the structural levels.

Changes in Neurons Within the brain, neurons send electrical and chemical signals, communicating with each other. A *neuron* is a nerve cell that handles information processing (see Figure 5). Extending from the neuron's cell body are two types of fibers, known as *axons* and *dendrites*. Generally, the axon carries signals away from the cell body and dendrites carry signals toward it. A *myelin sheath,* which is a layer of fat cells, encases many axons (see Figure 5). The myelin sheath provides insulation and helps electrical signals travel faster down the axon (Tomassy, Dershowitz, & Arlotta, 2016). Myelination also is involved in providing energy to neurons and in facilitating communication (Kiray & others, 2016). At the end of the axon are terminal buttons, which release chemicals called *neurotransmitters* into *synapses,* tiny gaps between neurons. Chemical interactions in synapses connect axons and dendrites, allowing information to pass from one neuron to another (Beart, 2016).

Think of the synapse as a river that blocks a road. A grocery truck arrives at one bank of the river, crosses by ferry, and continues its journey to market. Similarly, a message in the brain is "ferried" across the synapse by a neurotransmitter, which pours out information contained in chemicals when it reaches the other side of the river.

Neurons change in two very significant ways during the first years of life. First, *myelination,* the process of encasing axons with fat cells, begins prenatally and continues throughout childhood, even into adolescence (Galvan & Tottenham, 2016; Monahan & others, 2016). Second, connectivity among neurons increases, creating new neural pathways. New dendrites grow, connections among dendrites increase, and synaptic connections between axons and dendrites proliferate. Whereas myelination speeds up neural transmissions, the expansion of dendritic connections facilitates the spreading of neural pathways in infant development.

Researchers have discovered an intriguing aspect of synaptic connections: Nearly twice as many of these connections are made as will ever be used (Huttenlocher & Dabholkar, 1997). The connections that are used become stronger and survive, while the unused ones are replaced by other pathways or disappear. In the language of neuroscience, these connections will be "pruned" (Selemon, 2016).

How complex are these neural connections? In a recent analysis, it was estimated that each of the billions of neurons is connected to as many as 1,000 other neurons, producing neural networks with trillions of connections (de Haan, 2015).

Changes in Regions of the Brain Figure 6 vividly illustrates the dramatic growth and later pruning of synapses in the visual, auditory, and prefrontal cortex (Huttenlocher & Dabholkar, 1997). Notice that "blooming and pruning" vary considerably by brain region. In the prefrontal cortex, the area of the brain where higher-level thinking and

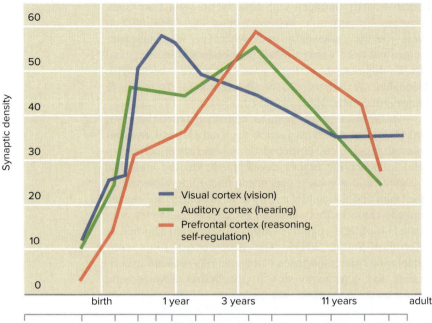

Figure 6 Synaptic Density in the Human Brain from Infancy to Adulthood
The graph shows the dramatic increase and then pruning in synaptic density for three regions of the brain: visual cortex, auditory cortex, and prefrontal cortex. Synaptic density is believed to be an important indication of the extent of connectivity between neurons.

self-regulation occur, the peak of overproduction occurs at just over 3 years of age; it is not until middle to late adolescence that the adult density of synapses is achieved (Monahan & others, 2016). Both heredity and environment are thought to influence the timing and course of synaptic overproduction and subsequent retraction.

Meanwhile, the pace of myelination also varies in different areas of the brain (Croteau-Chonka & others, 2016; Gogtay & Thompson, 2010). Myelination for visual pathways occurs rapidly after birth and is completed in the first six months. Auditory myelination is not completed until 4 or 5 years of age.

Early Experience and the Brain

What determines how these changes in the brain occur? The infant's brain is literally waiting for experiences to determine how connections are made. Before birth, it appears that genes mainly direct how the brain establishes basic wiring patterns; after birth, environmental experiences guide the brain's development. The inflowing stream of sights, sounds, smells, touches, language, and eye contact help shape neural connections (Gao & others, 2016; Nelson, 2013). It may not surprise us, then, that depressed brain activity has been found in children who grow up in a deprived environment (Berens & Nelson, 2015; Nelson, Fox, & Zeanah, 2014). Infants whose caregivers expose them to a variety of stimuli—talking, touching, playing—are most likely to develop to their full potential.

The profusion of neural connections described earlier provides the growing brain with flexibility and resilience (de Haan & Johnson, 2016). As an extreme example, consider 16-year-old Michael Rehbein. When Michael was 4½, he began to experience uncontrollable seizures—from 60 to 400 a day. Doctors said that the only solution was to remove the left hemisphere of his brain, where the seizures were occurring. Michael had his first major surgery at age 7 and another at age 10. Although recovery was slow, his right hemisphere began to reorganize and eventually took over functions, such as speech, that normally occur in the brain's left hemisphere (see Figure 7). Individuals like Michael are living proof of the growing brain's remarkable ability to adapt and recover from a loss of brain tissue.

The Neuroconstructivist View

Not long ago, scientists thought that our genes determined how our brains were "wired" and that the cells in the brain responsible for processing information just

(a)

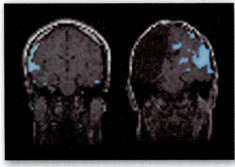

(b)

Figure 7 Plasticity in the Brain's Hemispheres.
(*a*) Michael Rehbein at 14 years of age.
(*b*) Brain scans of an intact brain (left) and Michael Rehbein's brain (right). Michael's right hemisphere has reorganized to take over the language functions normally carried out by corresponding areas in the left hemisphere of an intact brain. However, the right hemisphere is not as efficient as the left, and more areas of the brain are recruited to process speech.

© The Rehbein Family

maturationally unfolded with little or no input from environmental experiences. Whatever brain your heredity dealt you, you were essentially stuck with. This view, however, turned out to be wrong. Instead, the brain has plasticity and its development depends on context (Gao & others, 2016; Monahan & others, 2016; Westermann, Thomas, & Karmiloff-Smith, 2011).

In the increasingly popular **neuroconstructivist view,** (a) biological processes (genes, for example) and environmental experiences (enriched or impoverished, for example) influence the brain's development; (b) the brain has plasticity and is context dependent; and (c) development of the brain and the child's cognitive development are closely linked. These factors constrain or advance children's construction of their cognitive skills (Westermann, Thomas, & Karmiloff-Smith, 2011). The neuroconstructivist view emphasizes the importance of interactions between experiences and gene expression in the brain's development, much as the epigenetic view proposes.

Sleep

When we were infants, sleep consumed more of our time than it does now (Lushington & others, 2014). The typical newborn sleeps 16 to 17 hours a day, but there is considerable individual variation in how much infants sleep. For newborns, the range is from about 10 hours to about 21 hours per day. A recent research review concluded that infants 0 to 2 years of age slept an average of 12.8 hours out of the 24, within a range of 9.7 to 15.9 hours (Galland & others, 2012). A recent study also revealed that by 6 months of age the majority of infants slept through the night, awakening their parents only once or twice a week (Weinraub & others, 2012).

The most common infant sleep-related problem reported by parents is nighttime waking (Hospital for Sick Children & others, 2010). Surveys indicate that 20 to 30 percent of infants have difficulty going to sleep at night and staying asleep until morning (Sadeh, 2008). A recent study found that nighttime wakings at 1 year of age predicted lower sleep efficiency at 4 years of age (Tikotzky & Shaashua, 2012). Infant nighttime waking problems have consistently been linked to excessive parental involvement in sleep-related interactions with their infant (Sadeh, 2008).

REM Sleep

A much greater amount of time is taken up by *REM (rapid eye movement)* sleep in infancy than at any other point in the life span (Funk & others, 2016). Unlike adults, who spend about one-fifth of their night in REM sleep, infants spend about half of their sleep time in REM sleep, and they often begin their sleep cycle with REM sleep rather than non-REM sleep. By the time infants reach 3 months of age, the percentage of time they spend in REM sleep decreases to about 40 percent, and REM sleep no longer begins their sleep cycle.

Why do infants spend so much time in REM sleep? Researchers are not certain. The large amount of REM sleep may provide infants with

neuroconstructivist view Developmental perspective in which biological processes and environmental conditions influence the brain's development; the brain has plasticity and is context dependent; and cognitive development is closely linked with brain development.

added self-stimulation, since they spend less time awake than do older children. REM sleep also might promote the brain's development in infancy (Graven, 2006).

SIDS

Sudden infant death syndrome (SIDS) is a condition that occurs when an infant stops breathing, usually during the night, and dies suddenly without an apparent cause. SIDS remains one of the main causes of infant death in the United States, with more than 2,000 infant deaths annually attributed to SIDS (Heron, 2016). Risk of SIDS is highest at 2 to 4 months of age (NICHD, 2016). In 1992, the American Academy of Pediatrics (AAP) began recommending that infants be placed to sleep on their backs to reduce the risk of SIDS, and since then far fewer infants have been placed on their stomachs to sleep (AAP, 2000). Researchers have found that SIDS does indeed decrease when infants sleep on their backs rather than on their stomachs or sides (Elder, 2015; Moon, Hauck, & Colson, 2016). Why? Because sleeping on their backs increases their access to fresh air and reduces their chances of getting overheated.

Is this a good sleep position for infants? Why or why not?
© Maria Teijeiro/Cultura/Getty Images RF

How Would You...?

As a **health-care provider,** what advice would you provide to parents about preventing SIDS?

SIDS also occurs more often in infants with abnormal brain stem functioning involving the neurotransmitter serotonin (Rognum & others, 2014). Also, heart arrhythmias are estimated to occur in as many as 10 to 15 percent of SIDS cases and research indicates that gene mutations are linked to the occurrence of these arrhythmias in SIDS cases (Sarquella-Brugada & others, 2016). SIDS also is less common in infants who are breast fed (Wennergren & others, 2015). SIDS occurs more in infants whose mothers smoke and infants who are exposed to secondhand smoke in general (Salm Ward & Balfour, 2016). Further, SIDS is more likely to occur in low birth weight infants, African American and Eskimo infants, infants who are passively exposed to cigarette smoke, infants who sleep with their parents in the same bed, infants who don't use a pacifier when they go to sleep, and infants who sleep in a bedroom without a fan (Adams, Ward, & Garcia, 2015; Alm & others, 2016; Jarosinska & others, 2014; Mollborg & others, 2015). In a recent analysis, it was concluded that after prone sleeping, the two factors that best predict SIDS are (1) maternal smoking, and (2) bed sharing (Mitchell & Krous, 2015).

Sleep and Cognitive Development

Might infant sleep be linked to children's cognitive development? A recent study revealed that children who had done most of their sleeping at night during infancy engaged in a higher level of executive function at age 4 (Bernier & others, 2013). The link between infant sleep and children's cognitive functioning likely occurs because of sleep's role in brain maturation and memory consolidation, which may improve daytime alertness and learning (Sadeh, 2007). Another study found that poor sleep consolidation in infancy was associated with language delays in early childhood (Dionne & others, 2011). And in recent research, infant sleep difficulties were linked to negative outcomes later in development. For example, in one study lower quality of sleep at 1 year of age was linked to lower attention regulation and more behavior problems at 3 to 4 years of age (Sadeh & others, 2015). In another study, newborns who showed poorer sleep patterns were more likely to have attention orienting difficulties at 4 months of age and attention distractibility problems at 18 months of age (Geva, Yaron, & Kuint, 2016). And in a longitudinal study, infants who had more sleep problems were more likely to have emotional dysregulation at 2 to 3 years of age, which in turn was related to poor attention functioning in elementary school (Williams & Sciberras, 2016).

sudden infant death syndrome (SIDS) A condition that occurs when an infant stops breathing, usually during the night, and suddenly dies without an apparent cause.

Nutrition

From birth to 1 year of age, human infants nearly triple their weight and increase their length by 40 percent. What kind of nourishment do they need to sustain this rapid growth?

Breast Feeding Versus Bottle Feeding

For the first four to six months of life, human milk or an alternative formula is the baby's source of nutrients and energy. For years, debate has focused on whether breast feeding is better for the infant than bottle feeding. The growing consensus is that breast feeding is better for the baby's health (Gertosio & others, 2017). Since the 1970s, breast feeding by U.S. mothers has become widespread. In 2011 more than 79 percent of U.S. mothers breast fed their newborns, and 49 percent breast fed their 6-month-olds (Centers for Disease Control and Prevention, 2014).

What are some of the benefits of breast feeding? During the first two years of life and beyond, benefits include appropriate weight gain and reduced risk of child and adult obesity (Carling & others, 2015); reduced risk of SIDS (Wennergen & others, 2015); fewer gastrointestinal infections (Le Doare & Kampmann, 2014); and fewer lower respiratory tract infections (Prameela, 2011). Further, a recent study of more than 500,000 Scottish children found that those who were breast fed exclusively at 6 to 8 weeks of age were less likely to have ever been hospitalized through early childhood than their formula-fed counterparts (Ajetunmobi & others, 2015). However, a recent Danish study found that breast feeding did not protect against allergic sensitization in early childhood and allergy-related diseases at 7 years of age (Jelding-Dannemand, Malby Schoos, & Bisgaard, 2015). And in a large-scale review, no evidence for the benefits of breast feeding was found for children's cognitive development and cardiovascular functioning (Agency for Healthcare Research and Quality, 2007). However, a recent study did find that breast feeding resulted in a small increase in children's intelligence (Kanazawa, 2015). Benefits of breast feeding for the mother include a lower incidence of breast cancer (Akbari & others, 2011) and a reduction in ovarian cancer (Stuebe & Schwartz, 2010).

Many health professionals have argued that breast feeding facilitates the development of an attachment bond between mother and infant (Wittig & Spatz, 2008). However, a recent research review found that the positive effect of breast feeding on the mother-infant relationship is not supported by research (Jansen, de Weerth, & Riksen-Walraven, 2008). The review concluded that recommending breast feeding should not be based on its role in improving the mother-infant relationship but rather on its positive effects on infant and maternal health.

The American Academy of Pediatrics Section on Breastfeeding (2012) reconfirmed its recommendation of exclusive breast feeding in the first six months followed by continued breast feeding as complementary foods are introduced, and further breast feeding for one year or longer as mutually desired by the mother and infant.

Are there circumstances when mothers should not breast feed? Yes. A mother should not breast feed if she (1) is infected with AIDS or any other infectious disease that can be transmitted through her milk, (2) has active tuberculosis, or (3) is taking any drug that may not be safe for the infant (Fowler & others, 2014).

Some women cannot breast feed their infants because of physical difficulties; others feel guilty if they terminate breast feeding early. Mothers also may worry that they are depriving their infants of important emotional and psychological benefits if they bottle feed rather than breast feed. Some researchers have found, however, that there are few, if any,

Human milk or an alternative formula is a baby's source of nutrients for the first four to six months. The growing consensus is that breast feeding is better for the baby's health, although controversy still swirls about breast versus bottle feeding. *What do research studies indicate are the outcomes of breast feeding for children and mothers?*
© Blend Images/Getty Images RF

long-term physical and psychological differences between breast fed and bottle fed infants (Colen & Ramey, 2014; Ferguson, Harwood, & Shannon, 1987; Young, 1990).

A further issue in interpreting the benefits of breast feeding was underscored in a recent large-scale research review (Agency for Healthcare Research and Quality, 2007). While highlighting a number of benefits of breast feeding for children and mothers, the report issued a caution about research on breast feeding: None of the findings imply causality. Breast feeding versus bottle feeding studies are correlational, not experimental, and women who breast feed tend to be wealthier, older, and better educated, and are likely to be more health-conscious than those who bottle feed, which could explain why breast fed children are healthier.

Nutritional Needs

Individual differences among infants in terms of their nutrient reserves, body composition, growth rates, and activity patterns make it difficult to define actual nutrient needs (Blake, Munoz, & Volpe, 2016; Schiff, 2016). However, because parents need guidelines, nutritionists recommend that infants consume approximately 50 calories per day for each pound they weigh—more than twice an adult's requirement per pound.

A national study of more than 3,000 randomly selected 4- to 24-month-olds documented that many U.S. parents are feeding their babies too few fruits and vegetables and too much junk food (Fox & others, 2004). Up to one-third of the babies ate no vegetables and fruit; almost half of the 7- to 8-month-old babies were fed desserts, sweets, or sweetened drinks. By 15 months, French fries were the most common vegetables the babies ate.

Caregivers play very important roles in infants' early development of eating patterns (Christian & others, 2015; Kitsantas & others, 2016; Montano & others, 2015). Caregivers who are not sensitive to developmental changes in infants' nutritional needs, neglectful caregivers, and conditions of poverty can contribute to the development of eating problems in infants (Black & Lozoff, 2008; Robinson, 2015; Virudachalam & others, 2016). One study found that low maternal sensitivity when infants were 15 and 24 months of age was linked to a higher risk of obesity in adolescence (Anderson & others, 2012).

In sum, adequate early nutrition is an important aspect of healthy development (Ejlerskov & others, 2015). To be healthy, children need a nurturant, supportive environment. One individual who has stood out as an advocate of caring for children is T. Berry Brazelton, who is featured in *Careers in Life-Span Development*.

Careers in life-span development

T. Berry Brazelton, Pediatrician

T. Berry Brazelton is America's best-known pediatrician as a result of his numerous books, television appearances, and newspaper and magazine articles about parenting and children's health. He takes a family-centered approach to child development issues and communicates with parents in easy-to-understand ways.

Dr. Brazelton founded the Child Development Unit at Boston Children's Hospital and created the Brazelton Neonatal Behavioral Assessment Scale, a widely used measure of the newborn's health and well-being. He also has conducted a number of research studies on infants and children and has been president of the Society for Research in Child Development, a leading research organization.

T. Berry Brazelton with a young child.
© Brazelton Touchpoints Center

Motor Development

Meeting infants' nutritional needs helps them to develop the strength and coordination required for motor development. How do infants develop their motor skills, and which skills do they develop when?

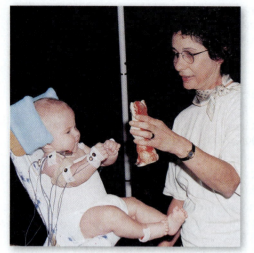

Esther Thelen conducts an experiment to discover how infants learn to control their arms to reach and grasp for objects. A computer device monitors the infant's arm movements and tracks muscle patterns. Thelen's research is conducted from a dynamic systems perspective. *What is the nature of this perspective?*
© Dr. David Thelen

Dynamic Systems Theory

Developmentalist Arnold Gesell (1934) thought his painstaking observations had revealed how people develop their motor skills. He had discovered that infants and children develop rolling, sitting, standing, and other motor skills in a fixed order and within specific time frames. These observations, said Gesell, show that motor development comes about through the unfolding of a genetic plan, or maturation.

Later studies, however, demonstrated that the sequence of developmental milestones is not as fixed as Gesell indicated and not due as much to heredity as Gesell argued (Adolph & Berger, 2016; Adolph & Robinson, 2015). In the last two decades, the study of motor development underwent a renaissance as psychologists developed new insights about *how* motor skills develop (Kretch & Adolph, 2016). One increasingly influential perspective is dynamic systems theory, proposed by Esther Thelen (Thelen & Smith, 1998, 2006).

According to **dynamic systems theory,** infants assemble motor skills for perceiving and acting. In other words, perception and action are coupled (Thelen & Smith, 2006). In order to develop motor skills, infants must perceive something in the environment that motivates them to act, then use their perceptions to fine-tune their movements. Motor skills thus represent pathways to the infant's goals (Adolph & Robinson, 2015).

How is a motor skill developed, according to this theory? When infants are motivated to do something, they might create a new motor behavior. The new behavior is the result of many converging factors: the development of the nervous system, the body's physical properties and its possibilities for movement, the goal the child is motivated to reach, and environmental support for the skill. For example, babies will learn to walk only when their nervous system has matured sufficiently to allow them to control certain leg muscles, their legs have grown enough to support their weight, and they have decided they want to walk (Adolph & Berger, 2016).

Mastering a motor skill requires the infant's active efforts to coordinate several components of the skill (Chen, Jeka, & Clark, 2016). Infants explore and select possible solutions to the demands of a new task, and they assemble adaptive patterns by modifying their current movement patterns. The first step, for example, occurs when the infant is motivated by a new challenge—such as the desire to cross a room—and initiates this task by taking a few stumbling steps. The infant then "tunes" these movements to make them smoother and more effective. The tuning is achieved through repeated cycles of action and perception of the consequences of that action. According to the dynamic systems view, even universal milestones such as crawling, reaching, and walking are learned through this process of adaptation: Infants modulate their movement patterns to fit a new task by exploring and selecting possible configurations (Adolph & Robinson, 2015).

Thus, according to dynamic systems theory, motor development is not a passive process in which genes dictate the unfolding of a sequence of skills. Rather, the infant actively puts together a skill in order to achieve a goal within the constraints set by the infant's body and environment. Nature and nurture, the infant and the environment, are all working together as part of an ever-changing system.

As we examine the course of motor development, we will describe how dynamic systems theory applies to some specific skills. First, though, let's examine how the story of motor development begins with reflexes.

dynamic systems theory The perspective on motor development that seeks to explain how motor behaviors are assembled for perceiving and acting.

Reflexes

The newborn is not completely helpless. Among other things, the newborn has some basic reflexes. Reflexes are built-in reactions to stimuli, and they govern the newborn's movements. Reflexes are genetically carried survival mechanisms that are automatic and involuntary. They allow infants to respond adaptively to their environment before they have had the opportunity to learn. For example, if immersed in water, the newborn automatically holds its breath and contracts its throat to keep water out.

Other important examples are the rooting and sucking reflexes. Both have survival value for newborn mammals, who must find a mother's breast to obtain nourishment. The *rooting reflex* occurs when the infant's cheek is stroked or the side of the mouth is touched. In response, the infant turns its head toward the side that was touched in an apparent effort to find something to suck. The *sucking reflex* occurs when newborns automatically suck an object placed in their mouth. This reflex enables newborns to get nourishment before they have associated a nipple with food.

Another example is the *Moro reflex,* which occurs in response to a sudden, intense noise or movement. When startled, the newborn arches its back, throws back its head, and flings out its arms and legs. Then the newborn rapidly closes its arms and legs. The Moro reflex is believed to be a way of grabbing for support while falling; it would have had survival value for our primate ancestors. An overview of the reflexes we have discussed, along with others, is presented in Figure 8.

Some reflexes—coughing, sneezing, blinking, shivering, and yawning, for example—persist throughout life. They are as important for the adult as they are for the infant. Other reflexes, though, disappear several months after birth, as the infant's brain matures and voluntary control over many behaviors develops. The rooting, sucking, and Moro reflexes, for example, all tend to disappear when the infant is 3 to 4 months old.

The movements of some reflexes eventually become incorporated into more complex, voluntary actions. One important example is the *grasping reflex,* which occurs when something touches the infant's palm. The infant responds by grasping tightly.

Reflex	Stimulation	Infant's Response	Developmental Pattern
Blinking	Flash of light, puff of air	Closes both eyes	Permanent
Babinski	Sole of foot stroked	Fans out toes, twists foot in	Disappears after 9 months to 1 year
Grasping	Palms touched	Grasps tightly	Weakens after 3 months, disappears after 1 year
Moro (startle)	Sudden stimulation, such as hearing loud noise or being dropped	Startles, arches back, throws head back, flings out arms and legs and then rapidly closes them to center of body	Disappears after 3 to 4 months
Rooting	Cheek stroked or side of mouth touched	Turns head, opens mouth, begins sucking	Disappears after 3 to 4 months
Stepping	Infant held above surface and feet lowered to touch surface	Moves feet as if to walk	Disappears after 3 to 4 months
Sucking	Object touching mouth	Sucks automatically	Disappears after 3 to 4 months
Swimming	Infant put face down in water	Makes coordinated swimming movements	Disappears after 6 to 7 months
Tonic neck	Infant placed on back	Forms fists with both hands and usually turns head to the right (sometimes called the "fencer's pose" because the infant looks like it is assuming a fencer's position)	Disappears after 2 months

Figure 8 Infant Reflexes

By the end of the third month, the grasping reflex diminishes, and the infant shows a more voluntary grasp. For example, when an infant sees a mobile turning slowly above a crib, it may reach out and try to grasp it. As its motor development becomes smoother, the infant will grasp objects, carefully manipulate them, and explore their qualities.

The old view of reflexes is that they were exclusively genetic, built-in mechanisms that govern the infant's movements. The new perspective on infant reflexes is that they are not automatic or completely beyond the infant's control. For example, infants can control such movements as alternating their legs to make a mobile jiggle or changing their sucking rate to listen to a recording (Adolph & Robinson, 2015).

Gross Motor Skills

Gross motor skills are skills that involve large-muscle activities, such as moving one's arms and walking. Newborn infants cannot voluntarily control their posture. Within a few weeks, though, they can hold their heads erect, and soon they can lift their heads while prone. By 2 months of age, babies can sit while supported on a lap or an infant seat, but they cannot sit independently until they are 6 or 7 months of age. Standing also develops gradually during the first year of life. By about 8 months of age, infants usually learn to pull themselves up and hold on to a chair, and by about 10 to 12 months of age they can often stand alone.

Locomotion and postural control are closely linked, especially in walking upright (Soska & Adolph, 2014). To walk upright, the baby must be able both to balance on one leg as the other is swung forward and to shift its weight from one leg to the other (Thelen & Smith, 2006).

Infants must also learn what kinds of places and surfaces are safe for crawling or walking (Adolph & Robinson, 2015; Ishak, Franchak, & Adolph, 2014). Karen Adolph (1997) investigated how experienced and inexperienced crawling and walking infants go down steep slopes (see Figure 9). Newly crawling infants, who averaged about 8 months in age, rather indiscriminately went down the steep slopes, often falling in the process (with their mothers standing next to the slope to catch them). After weeks of practice, the crawling babies became more adept at judging which slopes were too steep to crawl down and which ones they could navigate safely.

You might expect that babies who learned that a slope was too steep for crawling would know when they began walking whether a slope was safe. But Adolph's research indicated that newly walking infants could not judge the safety of the slopes. Only when infants became experienced walkers were they able to accurately match their skills with the steepness of the slopes. They rarely fell downhill, either refusing to go down the steep slopes or going down backward in a cautious manner. Experienced walkers

Figure 9 The Role of Experience in Crawling and Walking Infants' Judgments of Whether to Go Down a Slope

Karen Adolph (1997) found that locomotor experience rather than age was the primary predictor of adaptive responding on slopes of varying steepness. Newly crawling and walking infants could not judge the safety of the various slopes. With experience, they learned to avoid slopes where they would fall. When expert crawlers began to walk, they again made mistakes and fell, even though they had judged the same slope accurately when crawling. Adolph referred to this as the specificity of learning because it does not transfer across crawling and walking.

© Dr. Karen Adolph, New York University

Newly crawling infant

Experienced walker

assessed the situation perceptually—looking, swaying, touching, and thinking before they moved down the slope. With experience, both crawlers and walkers learned to avoid the risky slopes where they would fall, integrating perceptual information with the development of a new motor behavior. In this research, we again see the importance of perceptual-motor coupling in the development of motor skills.

Practice is especially important in learning to walk (Adolph & Berger, 2016). Infants and toddlers accumulate an immense number of experiences with balance and locomotion (Cole, Robinson, & Adolph, 2016). For example, the average toddler traverses almost 40 football fields a day and has 15 falls an hour (Adolph, 2010).

Might the development of walking be linked to advances in other aspects of development? Walking experience leads to being able to gain contact with objects that were previously out of reach and to initiate interaction with parents and other adults, thereby promoting language development (Adolph & Robinson, 2015; He, Walle, & Campos, 2015). Thus, just as with advances in postural skills, walking skills can produce a cascade of changes in the infant's development.

The First Year: Milestones and Variations

Figure 10 summarizes important accomplishments in gross motor skills during the first year, culminating in the ability to walk easily. The timing of these milestones, especially the later ones, may vary by as much as two to four months, and experiences can modify the onset of these accomplishments. For example, since 1992, when pediatricians began recommending that parents put their infants to sleep on their backs, there has been an increase in the number of babies who skip the stage of crawling (Davis & others, 1998). In the African Mali tribe, most infants do not crawl (Bril, 1999).

According to Karen Adolph and Sarah Berger (2005), "The old-fashioned view that growth and motor development reflect merely the age-related output of maturation is, at best, incomplete. Rather, infants acquire new skills with the help of their caregivers in a real-world environment of objects, surfaces, and planes" (p. 273).

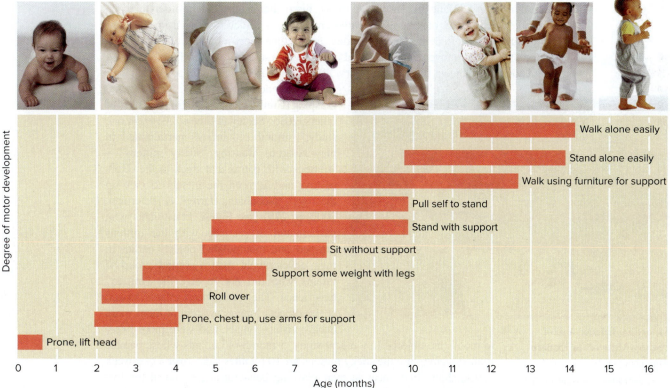

Figure 10 Milestones in Gross Motor Development.

The horizontal red bars indicate the range in which most infants reach various milestones in gross motor development.

fine motor skills Motor skills that involve more finely tuned movements, such as finger dexterity.

How Would You...?

As a **human development and family studies professional,** how would you advise parents who are concerned that their infant is one or two months behind the average gross motor milestones?

Development in the Second Year

The motor accomplishments of the first year bring increasing independence, allowing infants to explore their environment more extensively and to initiate interaction with others more readily. In the second year of life, toddlers become more mobile as their motor skills are honed. Child development experts believe that motor activity during the second year is vital to the child's competent development and that few restrictions, except those having to do with safety, should be placed on their adventures (Fraiberg, 1959).

By 13 to 18 months, toddlers can pull a toy attached to a string and use their hands and legs to climb up steps. By 18 to 24 months, toddlers can walk quickly or run stiffly for a short distance, balance on their feet in a squatting position while playing with objects on the floor, walk backward without losing their balance, stand and kick a ball without falling, stand and throw a ball, and jump in place.

Fine Motor Skills

Whereas gross motor skills involve large-muscle activity, **fine motor skills** involve finely tuned movements. Grasping a toy, using a spoon, buttoning a shirt, or anything that requires finger dexterity demonstrates fine motor skills. At birth, infants have very little control over fine motor skills, but they do have many components of what will become finely coordinated arm, hand, and finger movements (McCormack, Hoerl, & Butterfill, 2012).

The onset of reaching and grasping marks a significant achievement in infants' ability to interact with their surroundings (Greif & Needham, 2012). During the first two years of life, infants refine how they reach and grasp. Initially, they reach by moving the shoulder and elbow crudely, swinging toward an object. Later, when they reach for an object they move the wrist, rotate the hand, and coordinate the thumb and forefinger. An infant does not have to see his or her own hand in order to reach for an object (Clifton & others, 1993); rather, reaching is guided by cues from muscles, tendons, and joints. Recent research studies found that short-term training involving practice of reaching movements increased both preterm and full-term infants' reaching for and touching objects (Cunha & others, 2016; Guimaraes & Tudellia, 2015).

Experience plays a role in reaching and grasping (Cunha & others, 2016; Rachwani & others, 2015; Sacrey & others, 2014). In one study, 3-month-old infants participated in play sessions wearing "sticky mittens"— "mittens with palms that stuck to the edges of toys and allowed the infants to pick up the toys" (Needham, Barrett, & Peterman, 2002, p. 279) (see Figure 11). Infants who participated in sessions with the mittens grasped and manipulated objects earlier in their development than a control group of infants who did not receive the "mitten" experience. The experienced infants looked at the objects longer, swatted at them more during visual contact, and were more likely to mouth the objects. In a recent study, 5-month-old infants whose parents trained them to use the sticky mittens for 10 minutes a day over a two-week period showed advances in their reaching behavior at the end of the two weeks (Libertus & Needham, 2010).

Rachel Keen (2011; Keen, Lee, & Adolph, 2014) emphasizes that tool use is an excellent context for studying problem solving in infants because tool use provides information about how infants plan to reach a goal. Researchers in this area have studied infants' intentional actions,

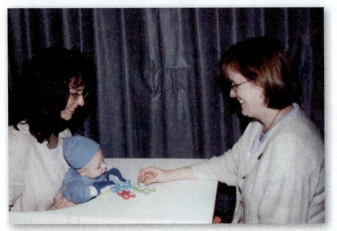

Figure 11 Infants' Use of "Sticky Mittens" to Explore Objects

Amy Needham (at right in this photo) and her colleagues (2002) found that "sticky mittens" enhanced young infants' object exploration skills.

© Dr. Amy Needham

which range from picking up a spoon in different orientations to retrieving rakes from inside tubes. A recent study explored motor origins of tool use by assessing developmental changes in banging movements in 6- to 15-month-olds (Kahrs, Jung, & Lockman, 2013). In this study, younger infants were inefficient and variable when banging an object but by 1 year of age infants showed consistent straight up-and-down hand movements that resulted in precise aiming and consistent levels of force.

Just as infants need to exercise their gross motor skills, they also need to exercise their fine motor skills (Cunha & others, 2016; Loucks & Sommerville, 2012). Especially when they can manage a pincer grip, infants delight in picking up small objects. Many develop the pincer grip and begin to crawl at about the same time, and infants at this time pick up virtually everything in sight, especially on the floor, and put the objects in their mouth. Thus, parents need to be vigilant in monitoring objects within the infant's reach.

Sensory and Perceptual Development

Can a newborn see? If so, what can it perceive? How do sensations and perceptions develop? Can an infant put together information from two modalities, such as sight and sound? These are among the intriguing questions that we explore in this section.

Exploring Sensory and Perceptual Development

How does a newborn know that her mother's skin is soft rather than rough? How does a 5-year-old know what color his hair is? Infants and children "know" these things as a result of information that comes through the senses.

Sensation occurs when information interacts with sensory *receptors*—the eyes, ears, tongue, nostrils, and skin. The sensation of hearing occurs when waves of pulsating air are collected by the outer ear and transmitted through the bones of the inner ear to the auditory nerve. The sensation of vision occurs as rays of light contact the eyes, become focused on the retina, and are transmitted by the optic nerve to the visual centers of the brain.

Perception is the interpretation of what is sensed. The air waves that contact the ears might be interpreted as noise or as musical sounds, for example. The physical energy transmitted to the retina of the eye might be interpreted as a particular color, pattern, or shape, depending on how it is perceived.

The Ecological View

In recent decades, much of the research on perceptual development in infancy has been guided by the ecological view proposed by Eleanor and James J. Gibson (E. Gibson, 1969, 1989, 2001; J. Gibson, 1966, 1979). They argue that we do not have to take bits and pieces of data from sensations and build up representations of the world in our minds. Instead, our perceptual system can select from the rich information that the environment itself provides.

According to the Gibsons' **ecological view,** we directly perceive information that exists in the world around us. Perception brings us into contact with the environment in order to interact with and adapt to it. Perception is designed for action. It gives people information such as when to duck, when to turn their bodies as they move through a narrow passageway, and when to put their hands up to catch something (Adolph & Kretch, 2015; Kretch & Adolph, 2016).

Studying the Infant's Perception

Studying the infant's perception is not an easy task. Unlike most research participants, infants cannot write, type on a computer keyboard, or speak well enough to explain to an experimenter what their responses are to a given stimulus or condition. Yet scientists have developed several ingenious research methods to examine infants' sensory and perceptual development (Bendersky & Sullivan, 2007).

sensation The product of the interaction between information and the sensory receptors—the eyes, ears, tongue, nostrils, and skin.

perception The interpretation of what is sensed.

ecological view The view that perception functions to bring organisms in contact with the environment and to increase adaptation.

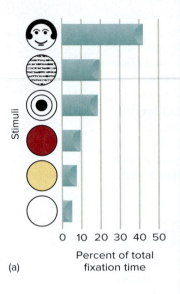

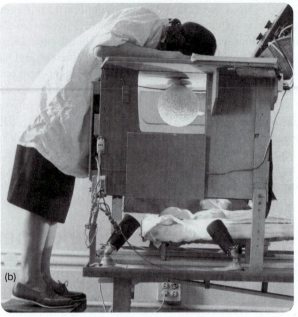

Figure 12 Fantz's Experiment on Infants' Visual Perception
(*a*) Infants 2 to 3 weeks old preferred to look at some stimuli more than others. In Fantz's experiment, infants preferred to look at patterns rather than at color or brightness. For example, they looked longer at a face, a piece of printed matter, or a bull's-eye than at red, yellow, or white discs. (*b*) Fantz used a "looking chamber" to study infants' perception of stimuli.
© David Linton

The Visual Preference Method Robert Fantz (1963), a pioneer in this effort, made an important discovery: Infants look at different things for different lengths of time. Fantz placed infants in a "looking chamber," which had two visual displays on the ceiling above the infant's head. An experimenter viewed the infant's eyes by looking through a peephole. If the infant was gazing at one of the displays, the experimenter could see the display's reflection in the infant's eyes. This allowed the experimenter to determine how long the infant looked at each display. Fantz (1963) found that infants only 2 days old would gaze longer at patterned stimuli (such as faces or concentric circles) than at red, white, or yellow discs. Similar results were found with infants 2 to 3 weeks old (see Figure 12). Fantz's research method—studying whether infants can distinguish one stimulus from another by measuring the length of time they attend to different stimuli—is referred to as the **visual preference method.**

Habituation and Dishabituation Another way in which researchers study infant perception is to present a stimulus (such as a sight or a sound) a number of times. If the infant decreases its response to the stimulus after several presentations, this indicates that the infant is no longer interested in the stimulus. If the researcher now presents a new stimulus, the infant's response will recover—indicating the infant could discriminate between the old and new stimuli (Baker, Pettigrew, & Poulin-Dubois, 2014).

Habituation is the name given to decreased responsiveness to a stimulus after repeated presentations of the stimulus. **Dishabituation** is the recovery of a habituated response after a change in stimulation. Newborn infants can habituate to repeated sights, sounds, smells, or touches (Bendersky & Sullivan, 2007). Among the measures researchers use in habituation studies are sucking behavior (sucking behavior stops when the infant attends to a novel object), heart and respiration rates, and the length of time the infant looks at an object.

visual preference method A method developed by Fantz to determine whether infants can distinguish one stimulus from another by measuring the length of time they attend to different stimuli.

habituation Decreased responsiveness to a stimulus after repeated presentations of the stimulus.

dishabituation Recovery of a habituated response after a change in stimulation.

Equipment Technology can facilitate the use of most methods for investigating the infant's perceptual abilities. Videotape equipment allows researchers to investigate elusive behaviors. High-speed computers make it possible to perform complex data analysis in minutes. Other equipment records respiration, heart rate, body movement, visual fixation, and sucking behavior, which provide clues to what the infant is perceiving.

Eye Tracking The most important recent advance in measuring infant perception is the development of sophisticated eye-tracking equipment (Eisner & others, 2013; Franchak & others, 2016; Kretch, Franchak, &

Adolph, 2014). Eye tracking consists of measuring eye movements that follow (track) a moving object and can be used to evaluate an infant's early visual ability (Bendersky & Sullivan, 2007).

Figure 13 shows an infant wearing eye-tracking headgear in a recent study on visually guided motor behavior and social interaction.

One of the main reasons that infant perception researchers are so enthusiastic about the recent availability of sophisticated eye-tracking equipment is that looking time is among the most important measures of infant perceptual and cognitive development (Aslin, 2012). The new eye-tracking equipment allows for far greater precision in assessing various aspects of infant looking and gaze than is possible with human observation (Franchak & others, 2016; Liu & others, 2015; Richmond, Zhao, & Burns, 2015). Among the areas of infant perception in which eye-tracking equipment is being used are attention (Schmitow & Stenberg, 2015; Yu & Smith, 2016), memory (Kingo & Krojgaard, 2015), and face processing (Jakobsen, Umstead, & Simpson, 2016; Xiao & others, 2015). Further, eye-tracking equipment is improving our understanding of atypically developing infants, such as those with autism (Chita-Tegmark, 2016; Elsabbagh & Johnson, 2016; Thorup & others, 2016).

Figure 13 **An Infant Wearing Eye-Tracking Headgear**
Photo from Karen Adolph's laboratory at New York University.
© Dr. Karen Adolph, New York University

One eye-tracking study shed light on the effectiveness of TV programs and DVDs that claim to educate infants (Kirkorian, Anderson, & Keen, 2012). In this study, 1-year-olds, 4-year-olds, and adults watched *Sesame Street* and the eye-tracking equipment recorded precisely what they looked at on the screen. The 1-year-olds were far less likely to consistently look at the same part of the screen as their older counterparts, suggesting that the 1-year-olds showed little understanding of the Sesame Street video but instead were more likely to be attracted by what was salient than by what was relevant.

Visual Perception

Psychologist William James (1890/1950) called the newborn's perceptual world a "blooming, buzzing confusion." A century later, we can safely say that he was wrong (De Heering & others, 2016; Johnson & Hannon, 2015). Even the newborn perceives a world with some order.

Visual Acuity and Color

Just how well can infants see? The newborn's vision is estimated to be 20/600 on the well-known Snellen eye examination chart (Banks & Salapatek, 1983). This means that an object 20 feet away is only as clear to the newborn's eyes as it would be if it were viewed from a distance of 600 feet by an adult with normal vision (20/20). By 6 months of age, though, an average infant's vision is 20/40 (Aslin & Lathrop, 2008). Figure 14 shows a computer estimation of what a picture of a face looks like to an infant at different ages from a distance of about 6 inches.

Faces are possibly the most important visual stimuli in children's social environment, and it is important that they extract key information from others' faces (Cashon & Holt, 2015; Jakobsen, Umstead, & Simpson, 2016; Otte & others, 2015). Infants show an interest in human faces soon after birth (Johnson & Hannon, 2015; Liu & others, 2015). Within hours after they are born, research shows that infants prefer to look at faces rather than other objects and to look at attractive faces more than at unattractive ones (Lee & others, 2013).

The infant's color vision also improves. By 8 weeks, and possibly even by 4 weeks, infants can discriminate among some colors (Kelly, Borchert, & Teller, 1997).

Figure 14 Visual Acuity During the First Months of Life
The four photographs represent a computer estimation of what a picture of a face looks like to a 1-month-old, 2-month-old, 3-month-old, and 1-year-old (which approximates the visual acuity of an adult).
© Kevin Peterson/Getty Images/Simulation by Vischeck RF

Perceiving Occluded Objects

Take a moment to look at your surroundings. You will likely see that some objects are partly occluded by other objects that are in front of them—possibly a desk behind a chair, some books behind a computer, or a car parked behind a tree. Do infants perceive an object as complete when it is occluded by an object in front of it?

In the first two months of postnatal development, infants do not perceive occluded objects as complete, instead only perceiving what is visible. Beginning at about 2 months of age, infants develop the ability to perceive that occluded objects are whole (Slater, Field, & Hernandez-Reif, 2007). How does perceptual completion develop? In Scott Johnson's (2010, 2011, 2013; Johnson & Hannon, 2015) research, learning, experience, and self-directed exploration via eye movements play key roles in the development of perceptual completion in young infants.

Many objects that are occluded appear and disappear behind closer objects, as when you are walking down the street and see cars appear and disappear behind buildings. Infants develop the ability to track briefly occluded moving objects at about 3 to 5 months (Bertenthal, 2008). A recent study explored the ability of 5- to 9-month-old infants to track moving objects that disappeared gradually behind an occluded partition, disappeared abruptly, or imploded (shrank quickly) (Bertenthal, Longo, & Kenny, 2007) (see Figure 15). In this study, the infants were more likely to accurately track the moving object when it disappeared gradually rather than vanishing abruptly or imploding.

Depth Perception

To investigate whether infants have depth perception, Eleanor Gibson and Richard Walk (1960) constructed a miniature cliff with a drop-off covered by glass. They placed 6- to 12-month-old infants on the edge of this visual cliff and had their mothers coax them to crawl onto the glass (see Figure 16). Most infants would not crawl out on the glass, choosing instead to remain on the shallow side, an indication that they could perceive depth, according to Gibson and Walk. Although researchers do not know exactly how early in life infants can perceive depth, they have found that infants develop the ability to use binocular (two-eyed) cues to depth by about 3 to 4 months of age.

Other Senses

Other sensory systems besides vision also develop during infancy. In this section, we explore development in hearing, touch and pain, smell, and taste.

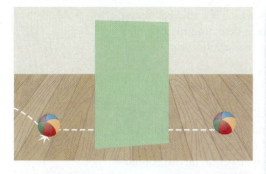

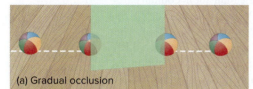

(a) Gradual occlusion

(b) Abrupt occlusion

(c) Implosion

Figure 15 Infants' Predictive Tracking of a Briefly Occluded Moving Ball
The top drawing shows the visual scene that infants experienced. At the beginning of each event, a multicolored ball bounced up and down with an accompanying bouncing sound, and then rolled across the floor until it disappeared behind the partition. The bottom drawings show the three stimulus events that the 5- to 9-month-old infants experienced: (*a*) gradual occlusion—the ball gradually disappears behind the right side of the occluding partition located in the center of the display; (*b*) abrupt occlusion—the ball abruptly disappears when it reaches the location of the white circle and then abruptly reappears 2 seconds later at the location of the second white circle on the other side of the occluding partition; (*c*) implosion—the rolling ball quickly decreases in size as it approaches the occluding partition and rapidly increases in size as it reappears on the other side of the occluding partition.

Figure 16 Examining Infants' Depth Perception on the Visual Cliff
Eleanor Gibson and Richard Walk (1960) found that most infants would not crawl out on the glass, which, according to Gibson and Walk, indicated that they had depth perception. However, critics point out that the visual cliff is a better indication of the infant's social referencing and fear of heights than of the infant's perception of depth.
© Mark Richards/PhotoEdit

Hearing

During the last two months of pregnancy, as the fetus nestles in its mother's womb, it can hear sounds such as the mother's voice (Kisilevsky & others, 2009). In one study, researchers had 16 women read *The Cat in the Hat* aloud to their fetuses during the last months of pregnancy (DeCasper & Spence, 1986). Then, shortly after their babies were born, the mothers read aloud either *The Cat in the Hat* or a story with a different rhyme and pace, *The King, the Mice and the Cheese* (which had not been read during prenatal development). The infants sucked on a nipple in a different way when the mothers read the two stories, suggesting that the infants recognized the pattern and tone of *The Cat in the Hat*. A recent fMRI study confirmed that the fetus can hear at 33 to 34 weeks into the prenatal period by assessing fetal brain response to auditory stimuli (Jardri & others, 2012).

Newborns are especially sensitive to human speech sounds (Saffran, Werker, & Werner, 2006). Just a few days after birth, newborns will turn toward the sound of a familiar caregiver's voice.

What changes in hearing take place during infancy? They involve perception of a sound's loudness, pitch, and localization. Immediately after birth, infants cannot hear soft sounds quite as well as adults can; a stimulus must be louder for the newborn to hear it (Trehub & others, 1991). By 3 months of age, infants' perception of sounds improves, although some aspects of loudness perception do not reach adult levels until 5 to 10 years of age (Trainor & He, 2013). Infants are also less sensitive to the pitch of a sound than adults are. *Pitch* is the frequency of a sound; a soprano voice sounds high-pitched, a bass voice low-pitched. Infants are less sensitive to low-pitched sounds and are more likely to hear high-pitched sounds (Aslin, Jusczyk, & Pisoni, 1998). By 2 years of age, infants have considerably improved their ability to distinguish sounds with different pitches.

Even newborns can determine the general location from which a sound is coming, but by 6 months they are more proficient at localizing sounds, detecting their origins. The ability to localize sounds continues to improve during the second year (Saffran, Werker, & Werner, 2006).

Touch and Pain

Newborns respond to touch. A touch to the cheek produces a turning of the head; a touch to the lips produces sucking movements. Regular gentle tactile stimulation during prenatal development may have positive developmental outcomes. For example, a recent study found that 3-month-olds who had received regular gentle tactile stimulation as fetuses were more likely to have an easy temperament than their counterparts who had irregular gentle or no tactile stimulation as fetuses (Wang, Hua, & Xu, 2015).

Newborns can also feel pain (Bellini & others, 2016; Witt & others, 2016). The issue of an infant's pain perception often becomes important to parents who give birth to a son and need to consider whether he should be circumcised. An investigation by Megan Gunnar and her colleagues (1987) found that although newborn infant males cry intensely during circumcision, they also display amazing resiliency. Many newly circumcised infants go into a deep sleep not long after the procedure, probably as a coping mechanism. Also, once researchers discovered that newborns feel pain, the practice of operating on newborns without anesthesia began to be reconsidered. Anesthesia is now used in some circumcisions (Morris & others, 2012). And in a recent study, kangaroo care was very effective in reducing neonatal pain, especially indicated by the significantly lower level of crying when the care was instituted after the newborn's blood had been drawn by a heel stick (Seo, Lee, & Ahn, 2016).

Smell

Newborns can differentiate among odors (Doty & Shah, 2008). For example, the expressions on their faces indicate that they like the scents of vanilla and strawberry but do not like the scent of rotten eggs or fish (Steiner, 1979).

It may take time to develop other odor preferences, however. By the time they were 6 days old, breast-fed infants in one study showed a clear preference for smelling their mother's breast pad rather than a clean breast pad (MacFarlane, 1975). When they were 2 days old they did not show this preference, indicating that they require several days of experience to recognize this scent.

Taste

Sensitivity to taste might be present even before birth (Doty & Shah, 2008). In one very early experiment, when saccharin was added to the amniotic fluid of a near-term fetus, swallowing increased (Windle, 1940). In another study, even at only 2 hours of age, babies made different facial expressions when they tasted sweet, sour, and bitter solutions (Rosenstein & Oster, 1988). At about 4 months, infants begin to prefer salty tastes, which as newborns they had found to be aversive (Harris, Thomas, & Booth, 1990).

Intermodal Perception

How do infants put all these stimuli together? Imagine yourself playing basketball or tennis. You are experiencing many visual inputs: the ball coming and going, other players moving around, and so on. However, you are experiencing many auditory inputs as well: the sound of the ball bouncing or being hit, the grunts and groans of the participants, and so on. There is good correspondence between much of the visual and auditory information: When you see the ball bounce, you hear a bouncing sound; when a player stretches to hit a ball, you hear a groan. When you look at and listen to what is going on, you do not experience just the sounds or just the sights; you put all these things together. You experience a unitary episode. This is **intermodal perception,** which involves integrating information from two or more sensory modalities, such as vision and hearing (Bremner & others, 2012). Most perception is intermodal (Bahrick, 2010).

intermodal perception The ability to relate and integrate information from two or more sensory modalities, such as vision and hearing.

Early, exploratory forms of intermodal perception exist even in newborns (Bahrick & Hollich, 2008). For example, newborns turn their eyes and their head toward the sound of a voice or rattle when the sound is maintained for several seconds (Clifton & others, 1981). Intermodal perception becomes sharper with experience in the first year of life (Kirkham & others, 2012). In the first six months, infants have difficulty connecting sensory input from different modes (such as vision and sound), but in the second half of the first year they show an increased ability to make this connection mentally.

Nature, Nurture, and Perceptual Development

Now that we have discussed many aspects of perceptual development, let's explore one of developmental psychology's key issues as it relates to perceptual development: the nature-nurture issue. There has been a longstanding interest in how strongly infants' perception is influenced by nature or nurture (Johnson & Hannon, 2015; Slater & others, 2011). In the field of perceptual development, those who emphasize nature are referred to as *nativists* and those who emphasize learning and experience are called *empiricists*.

In the nativist view, the ability to perceive the world in a competent, organized way is inborn or innate. At the beginning of our discussion of perceptual development, we examined the Gibsons' ecological view because it has played such a pivotal role in guiding research in perceptual development. This approach leans toward a nativist explanation of perceptual development because it holds that perception is direct and evolved over time to allow the detection of size and shape constancy, a three-dimensional world, intermodal perception, and so on early in infancy. However, the Gibsons' view is not entirely nativist because they emphasized that perceptual development involves distinctive features that are detected at different ages (Slater & others, 2011).

The Gibsons' ecological view is quite different from Piaget's constructivist view, which reflects an empiricist approach to explaining perceptual development. According to Piaget, much of perceptual development in infancy must await the development of a sequence of cognitive stages in which infants become able to construct more complex perceptual tasks. Thus, in Piaget's view the ability to perceive size and shape constancy, a three-dimensional world, intermodal perception, and so on develops later in infancy than the Gibsons envision.

What roles do nature and nurture play in the infant's perceptual development?
© altrendo/Getty Images

The longitudinal research of Daphne Maurer and her colleagues (Lewis & Maurer, 2005, 2009; Maurer & Lewis, 2013; Maurer & others, 1999) has focused on infants born with cataracts—a thickening of the lens of the eye that causes vision to become cloudy, opaque, and distorted and thus severely restricts these infants' ability to experience their visual world. Studying infants whose cataracts were removed at different points in development, they discovered that those whose cataracts were removed and new lenses placed in their eyes in the first several months after birth showed a normal pattern of visual development. However, the longer the delay in removing the cataracts, the more their visual development was impaired. In their research, Maurer and her colleagues (2007) have found that experiencing patterned visual input early in infancy is important for holistic and detailed face processing after infancy. Maurer's research program illustrates how deprivation and experience influence visual development, including an early sensitive period in which visual input is necessary for normal visual development (Maurer & Lewis, 2013).

Today it is clear that an extreme empiricist position on perceptual development is unwarranted. Much of early perception develops from innate (nature) capabilities, and the basic foundation of many perceptual abilities can be detected in newborns, whereas others unfold through maturation (Bornstein, Arterberry, & Mash, 2011). However, as infants develop, environmental experiences (nurture) refine or calibrate many perceptual functions, and they may be the driving force behind some functions (Johnson & Hannon, 2015). The accumulation of experience with and knowledge about their perceptual world contributes to infants' ability to perceive coherent impressions of people and things (Slater & others, 2011). Thus, a full portrait of perceptual development includes the influence of nature, nurture, and a developing sensitivity to information (Arterberry, 2008).

Perceptual Motor Coupling

A central theme of the ecological approach is the interplay between perception and action. Action can guide perception, and perception can guide action. Only by moving one's eyes, head, hands, and arms and by moving from one location to another can an individual fully experience his or her environment and learn how to adapt to it. Thus, perception and action are coupled (Adolph & Robinson, 2015).

Babies, for example, continually coordinate their movements with perceptual information to learn how to maintain balance, reach for objects in space, and move across various surfaces and terrains (Thelen & Smith, 2006). They are motivated to move by what they perceive. Consider the sight of an attractive toy across the room. In this situation, infants must perceive the current state of their bodies and learn how to use their limbs to reach the toy. Although their movements at first are awkward and uncoordinated, babies soon learn to select patterns that are appropriate for reaching their goals.

Equally important is the other part of the perception-action coupling. That is, action educates perception (Adolph & Berger, 2016). For example, watching an object while exploring it manually helps infants discover its texture, size, and hardness. Moving around in their environment teaches babies about how objects and people look from different perspectives, or whether surfaces will support their weight. In short, infants perceive in order to move and move in order to perceive. Perceptual and motor development do not occur in isolation from each other but instead are coupled.

Cognitive Development

The competent infant not only develops motor and perceptual skills, but also develops cognitive skills. Our coverage of cognitive development in infancy focuses on Piaget's theory and sensorimotor stages as well as on how infants learn, remember, and conceptualize.

Piaget's Theory

Piaget's theory is a general, unifying story of how biology and experience sculpt cognitive development. The Swiss child psychologist Jean Piaget thought that, just as our physical bodies have structures that enable us to adapt to the world, we build mental structures that help us to adapt to the world. *Adaptation* involves adjusting to new environmental demands. Piaget stressed that children actively construct their own cognitive worlds; information is not just poured into their minds from the environment. He sought to discover how children at different points in their development think about the world and how systematic changes in their thinking occur.

Processes of Development

What processes do children use as they construct their knowledge of the world? Piaget developed several concepts to answer this question.

Schemes According to Piaget (1954), as the infant or child seeks to construct an understanding of the world, the developing brain creates **schemes.**

schemes In Piaget's theory, actions or mental representations that organize knowledge.

These are actions or mental representations that organize knowledge. In Piaget's theory, infants create behavioral schemes (physical activities), whereas toddlers and older children create mental schemes (cognitive activities) (Lamb, Bornstein, & Teti, 2002). A baby's schemes are structured by simple actions that can be performed on objects, such as sucking, looking, and grasping. Older children's schemes include strategies and plans for solving problems.

In Piaget's view, what is a scheme? What schemes might this young infant be displaying?
© CSP_NikolayK/age fotostock RF

Assimilation and Accommodation To explain how children use and adapt their schemes, Piaget offered two concepts: assimilation and accommodation. **Assimilation** occurs when children use their existing schemes to deal with new information or experiences. **Accommodation** occurs when children adjust their schemes to account for new information and experiences.

Think about a toddler who has learned the word *car* to identify the family's automobile. The toddler might call all moving vehicles on roads "cars," including motorcycles and trucks; the child has assimilated these objects to his or her existing scheme. But the child soon learns that motorcycles and trucks are not cars and fine-tunes the category to exclude those vehicles. The child has accommodated the scheme.

Organization To make sense out of their world, said Piaget, children cognitively organize their experiences. **Organization,** in Piaget's theory, is the grouping of isolated behaviors and thoughts into a higher-order system. Continual refinement of this organization is an inherent part of development. A child who has only a vague idea about how to use a hammer may also have a vague idea about how to use other tools. After learning how to use each one, she relates these uses to one another, thereby organizing her knowledge.

Equilibration and Stages of Development Assimilation and accommodation always take the child to a higher level, according to Piaget. In trying to understand the world, the child inevitably experiences cognitive conflict, or *disequilibrium*. That is, the child is constantly faced with inconsistencies and counterexamples to his or her existing schemes. For example, if a child believes that pouring water from a short, wide container into a tall, narrow container changes the amount of water in the container, the child might wonder where the "extra" water came from and whether there is actually more water to drink. This puzzle creates disequilibrium; and in Piaget's view the resulting search for equilibrium creates motivation for change. The child assimilates and accommodates, adjusting old schemes, developing new schemes, and organizing and reorganizing the old and new schemes. Eventually the organization is fundamentally different from the old organization; it becomes a new way of thinking.

Equilibration is the name Piaget gave to this mechanism by which children shift from one stage of thought to the next. Equilibration does not, however, happen all at once. There is considerable movement between states of cognitive equilibrium and disequilibrium as assimilation and accommodation work in concert to produce cognitive change.

A result of these processes, according to Piaget, is that individuals go through four stages of development. A different way of understanding the world makes one stage more advanced than another. Cognition is *qualitatively* different in one stage compared with another. In other words, the way children reason at one stage is different from the way they reason at another stage. Here our focus is on Piaget's stage of infant cognitive development.

The Sensorimotor Stage

The **sensorimotor stage** lasts from birth to about age 2. In this stage, infants construct an understanding of the world by coordinating sensory

assimilation Piagetian concept of using existing schemes to deal with new information or experiences.

accommodation Piagetian concept of adjusting schemes to fit new information and experiences.

organization Piaget's concept of grouping isolated behaviors and thoughts into a higher-order, more smoothly functioning cognitive system.

equilibration A mechanism that Piaget proposed to explain how children shift from one stage of thought to the next.

sensorimotor stage The first of Piaget's stages, which lasts from birth to about 2 years of age; during this stage, infants construct an understanding of the world by coordinating sensory experiences with motoric actions.

experiences (such as seeing and hearing) with physical, motor actions—hence the term *sensorimotor*. At the beginning of this stage, newborns have little more than reflexes to work with. At the end of the sensorimotor stage, 2-year-olds can produce complex sensorimotor patterns and use primitive symbols. We first summarize Piaget's descriptions of how infants develop. Later we consider criticisms of his view.

Object Permanence **Object permanence** is the understanding that objects continue to exist even when they cannot be seen, heard, or touched. Acquiring the sense of object permanence is one of the infant's most important accomplishments, according to Piaget.

How could anyone know whether or not an infant had a sense of object permanence? The principal way in which object permanence is studied is by watching an infant's reaction when an interesting object disappears (see Figure 17). If infants search for the object, it is inferred that they know it continues to exist.

Evaluating Piaget's Sensorimotor Stage Piaget opened up a new way of looking at infants with his view that their main task is to coordinate their sensory impressions with their motor activity. However, the infant's cognitive world is not as neatly packaged as Piaget portrayed it, and some of Piaget's explanations for the cause of change are debated. In the past several decades, there have been many research studies on infant development using sophisticated experimental techniques (Gerson & others, 2015; Huang & Spelke, 2015). Much of the new research suggests that Piaget's view of sensorimotor development needs to be modified (Adolph & Berger, 2016; Johnson & Hannon, 2015; Stiles & others, 2015).

A-not-B error is the term used to describe the tendency of infants to reach where an object was located earlier rather than where the object was last hidden. Older infants are less likely to make the A-not-B error because their concept of object permanence is more complete.

Researchers have found, however, that the A-not-B error does not show up consistently (Sophian, 1985). The evidence indicates that A-not-B errors are sensitive to the delay between hiding the object at B and the infant's attempt to find it (Diamond, 1985). Thus, the A-not-B error might be due to a failure in memory. Another explanation is that infants tend to repeat a previous motor behavior (Clearfield & others, 2006).

A number of theorists, such as Eleanor Gibson (1989) and Elizabeth Spelke (2004, 2011, 2013), have concluded that infants' perceptual abilities are highly developed very early in life. For example, intermodal perception—the ability to coordinate information from two or more sensory modalities, such as vision and hearing—develops much earlier than Piaget would have predicted (Spelke & Owsley, 1979).

Object permanence also develops earlier than Piaget thought. In his view, object permanence does not develop until approximately 8 to 9 months. However, research by Renée Baillargeon and her colleagues (2004, 2014; Baillargeon & others, 2012) documents that infants as young as 3 to 4 months expect objects to be *substantial* (in the sense that other objects cannot move through them) and *permanent* (in the sense that they continue to exist when they are hidden).

Today researchers believe that infants see objects as bounded, unitary, solid, and separate from their background, possibly at birth or shortly thereafter, but definitely by 3 to 4 months, much earlier than Piaget envisioned. Young infants still have much to learn about objects, but the world appears both stable and orderly to them.

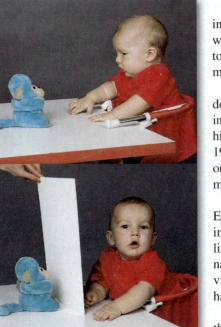

Figure 17 Object Permanence
Piaget argued that object permanence is one of infancy's landmark cognitive accomplishments. For this 5-month-old boy, "out of sight" is literally out of mind. The infant looks at the toy monkey (top), but when his view of the toy is blocked (bottom), he does not search for it. Several months later, he will search for the hidden toy monkey, an action reflecting the presence of object permanence.

© Doug Goodman/Science Source

object permanence The Piagetian term for understanding that objects and events continue to exist, even when they cannot directly be seen, heard, or touched.

A-not-B error This term is used to describe the tendency of infants to reach where an object was located earlier rather than where the object was last hidden.

core knowledge approach States that infants are born with domain-specific innate knowledge systems.

In considering the big issue of whether nature or nature plays a more important role in infant development, Elizabeth Spelke (2011, 2013; Huang & Spelke, 2015; Spelke, Bernier, & Snedeker, 2013) comes down clearly on the side of nature. Spelke endorses a **core knowledge approach,** which states that infants are born with domain-specific innate knowledge systems. Among these knowledge systems are those involving space, number sense, object permanence, and language (which we will discuss later in this chapter). Strongly influenced by evolution, the core knowledge domains are theorized to be "prewired" to allow infants to make sense of their world (Coubart & others, 2014). After all, Spelke concludes, how could infants possibly grasp the complex world in which they live if they did not come into the world equipped with core sets of knowledge? In this approach, the innate core knowledge domains form a foundation around which more mature cognitive functioning and learning develop. The core knowledge approach argues that Piaget greatly underestimated the cognitive abilities of infants, especially young infants (Huang & Spelke, 2015).

Recently, researchers also have explored whether preverbal infants might have a built-in, innate sense of morality (Steckler & Hamlin, 2016; Van de Vondervoort & Hamlin, 2016a, b). In this research, infants as young as 4 months of age are more likely to make visually guided reaches toward a puppet who has acted as a helper (such as helping someone get up a hill, assisting in opening a box, or giving a ball back) rather than toward a puppet who has hindered others' efforts to achieve such goals (Hamlin, 2013, 2014).

In criticizing the core knowledge approach, British developmental psychologist Mark Johnson (2008) says that the infants Spelke assesses in her research have already accumulated hundreds, and in some cases even thousands, of hours of experience in grasping what the world is about, which gives considerable room for the environment's role in the development of infant cognition (Highfield, 2008). According to Johnson (2008), infants likely come into the world with "soft biases to perceive and attend to different aspects of the environment, and to learn about the world in particular ways." A major criticism is that nativists completely neglect the infant's social immersion in the world and instead focus only on what happens inside the infant's head apart from the environment (Nelson, 2013).

In sum, many researchers conclude that Piaget wasn't specific enough about how infants learn about their world and that infants, especially young infants, are more competent than Piaget thought (Adolph & Berger, 2016; Johnson & Hannon, 2015; Needham, 2016). As these researchers have examined the specific ways that infants learn, the field of infant cognition has become very specialized. There are many researchers working on different questions, with no general theory emerging that can connect all of the different findings. Their theories often are local theories, focused on specific research questions, rather than grand theories like Piaget's (Kuhn, 1998). Among the unifying themes in the study of infant cognition are seeking to understand more precisely how developmental changes in cognition take place, considering the big issue of nature and nurture, and examining the brain's role in cognitive development (Aslin, 2012; Gliga & others, 2016; Perry & others, 2016). Recall that exploring connections between brain, cognition, and development is the focus of the recently emerging field of *developmental cognitive neuroscience* (Anzures & others, 2016; Berens & Nelson, 2015; de Haan & Johnson, 2016; Smith & others, 2016).

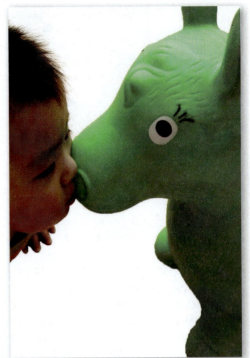

What are some conclusions that can be reached about infant learning and cognition?
© baobao ou/Flickr/Getty Images RF

Learning, Remembering, and Conceptualizing

Earlier we described the behavioral and social cognitive theories, as well as information-processing theory. These theories emphasize that cognitive development

Figure 18 The Technique Used in Rovee-Collier's Investigation of Infant Memory
In Rovee-Collier's experiment, operant conditioning was used to demonstrate that infants as young as 2½ months of age can retain information from the experience of being conditioned. *What did infants recall in Rovee-Collier's experiment?*
© Dr. Carolyn Rovee-Collier

does not unfold in a stage-like process as Piaget proposed, but rather advances more gradually (Diamond, 2013). In this section we explore what researchers using these approaches can tell us about how infants learn, remember, and conceptualize.

Conditioning

We have discussed Skinner's theory of operant conditioning, in which the consequences of a behavior influence the probability of the behavior's recurrence. Infants can learn through operant conditioning: If an infant's behavior is followed by a rewarding stimulus, the behavior is likely to recur.

Operant conditioning has been especially helpful to researchers in their efforts to determine what infants perceive (Rovee-Collier & Barr, 2010). For example, infants will suck faster on a nipple when the sucking behavior is followed by a visual display, music, or a human voice (Rovee-Collier, 2008).

Carolyn Rovee-Collier (1987) has demonstrated that infants can retain information from the experience of being conditioned. In a characteristic experiment, Rovee-Collier places a 2½-month-old baby in a crib under an elaborate mobile (see Figure 18). She then ties one end of a ribbon to the baby's ankle and the other end to the mobile. Subsequently, she observes that the baby kicks and makes the mobile move. The movement of the mobile is the reinforcing stimulus (which increases the baby's kicking behavior) in this experiment. Weeks later, the baby is returned to the crib, but its foot is not tied to the mobile. The baby kicks, suggesting that it has retained the information that if it kicks a leg, the mobile will move.

Attention

Attention, the focusing of mental resources on select information, improves cognitive processing on many tasks (Ristic & Enns, 2015; Reynolds & Romano, 2016; Rothbart & Posner, 2015). Even newborns can detect a contour and fix their attention on it. Older infants scan patterns more thoroughly. By 4 months, infants can selectively attend to an object. A longitudinal study found that 5-month-olds who were more efficient in processing information quickly had better higher-level cognitive functioning in the preschool years (Cuevas & Bell, 2014). Another recent study examined 7- and 8-month-old infants' visual attention to sequences of events that varied in complexity (Kidd, Piantadosi, & Aslin, 2012). The infants tended to look away from events that were overly simple or complex, preferring instead to attend to events of intermediate complexity.

Closely linked with attention are the processes of habituation and dishabituation, which we discussed earlier in this chapter (Columbo & Salley, 2015). Infants' attention is strongly governed by novelty and habituation. When an object becomes familiar, attention becomes shorter, making infants more vulnerable to distraction (Kavsek, 2013).

Another aspect of attention that plays an important role in infant development is **joint attention,** in which individuals focus on the same object or event (Hoehl & Striano, 2015; Yu & Smith, 2016). Joint attention requires (1) the ability to track each other's behavior, such as following someone's gaze; (2) one person directing another's attention; and (3) reciprocal interaction. Early in infancy, joint attention usually involves a caregiver pointing or using words to direct an infant's attention. Emerging forms of joint attention occur at about 7 to 8 months, but it is not until 10 to 11 months that joint attention skills are frequently observed (Meltzoff & Brooks, 2009). By their first birthday, infants have begun to direct adults' attention to objects that capture their interest (Heimann & others, 2006). And a

attention The focusing of mental resources on select information.

joint attention Process that occurs when (1) individuals focus on the same object and track each other's behavior, (2) one individual directs another's attention, and (3) reciprocal interaction takes place.

recent study found that problems in joint attention as early as 8 months of age were linked to a child having been diagnosed with autism by 7 years of age (Veness & others, 2014).

How Would You...?

As a **human development and family studies professional,** what strategies would you recommend to parents who are want to foster their infant's development of attention?

Joint attention plays important roles in many aspects of infant development and considerably increases infants' ability to learn from other people (Abels & Hutman, 2015; Brooks & Meltzoff, 2014; Yu & Smith, 2016). Nowhere is this more apparent than in observations of interchanges between caregivers and infants as infants are learning language (Igualada, Bosch, & Prieto, 2015; Tomasello, 2011, 2014). When caregivers and infants frequently engage in joint attention, infants say their first word earlier and develop a larger vocabulary (Beuker & others, 2013; Flom & Pick, 2003; Mastin & Vogt, 2016). Joint attention skills in infancy also are associated with the development of self-regulation later in childhood. For example, one study revealed that responding to joint attention at 12 months of age was linked to self-regulation skills at 3 years of age that involved delaying gratification for an attractive object (Van Hecke & others, 2012). In another study, infants who initiated joint attention at 14 months of age had higher executive function at 18 months of age (Miller & Marcovitch, 2015).

Imitation

Infant development researcher Andrew Meltzoff (2004, 2007, 2011) has conducted numerous studies of infants' imitative abilities. He sees infants' imitative abilities as biologically based, because infants can imitate a facial expression within the first few days after birth. He also emphasizes that the infant's imitative abilities do not resemble a hardwired response but rather involve flexibility and adaptability. In Meltzoff's observations of infants during the first 72 hours of life, the infants gradually displayed more complete imitation of an adult's facial expression, such as protruding the tongue or opening the mouth wide (see Figure 19).

Meltzoff (2007, 2011) concludes that infants don't blindly imitate everything they see and often make creative errors. He also argues that beginning at birth there is an interplay between learning by observing and learning by doing (Piaget emphasized learning by doing).

Not all experts on infant development accept Meltzoff's conclusion that newborns are capable of imitation. Some say that these babies were engaging in little more than automatic responses to a stimulus.

Meltzoff (2005, 2011; Meltzoff & Williamson, 2013) has also studied **deferred imitation,** which occurs after a time delay of hours or days. Piaget held that deferred imitation does not occur until about 18 months. Meltzoff's research suggested that it occurs much earlier. In one study, Meltzoff (1988) demonstrated that 9-month-old infants could imitate actions—such as pushing a recessed button in a box, which produced a beeping sound—that they had seen performed 24 hours earlier.

Figure 19 Infant Imitation
Infant development researcher Andrew Meltzoff protrudes his tongue in an attempt to get the infant to imitate his behavior. *How do Meltzoff's findings about imitation compare with Piaget's descriptions of infants' abilities?*
© Dr. Andrew Meltzoff

Memory

Meltzoff's studies of deferred imitation suggest that infants have another important cognitive ability: **memory,** which involves the retention of information over time. Sometimes information is retained only for a few seconds, and at other times it is retained for a lifetime. What can infants remember, and when?

Some researchers, such as Rovee-Collier (2008), have concluded that infants as young as 2 to 6 months can remember some experiences through 1½ to 2 years of age.

deferred imitation Imitation that occurs after a delay of hours or days.

memory A central feature of cognitive development, pertaining to all situations in which an individual retains information over time.

However, critics such as Jean Mandler (2000), a leading expert on infant cognition, argue that the infants in Rovee-Collier's experiments are displaying only implicit memory.

Implicit memory refers to memory without conscious recollection—memories of skills and routine procedures that are performed automatically. In contrast, **explicit memory** refers to conscious memory of facts and experiences.

When people think about memory, they are usually referring to explicit memory. Most researchers find that babies do not show explicit memory until the second half of the first year (Bauer, 2013; Bauer & Larkina, 2016). Explicit memory improves substantially during the second year of life (Bauer, 2013; Bauer & Leventon, 2015). In one longitudinal study, infants were assessed several times during their second year (Bauer & others, 2000). The older infants showed more accurate memory and required fewer prompts to demonstrate their memory than did younger infants. Figure 20 summarizes how long infants of different ages can remember information (Bauer, 2009). As indicated, researchers have documented that 6-month-olds can remember information for 24 hours but 20-month-old infants can remember information they encountered 12 months earlier.

Let's examine another aspect of memory. Do you remember your third birthday party? Probably not. Most adults can remember little, if anything, from the first 3 years of their life. This is called *infantile* or *childhood amnesia*. The few memories that adults are able to report of their life at age 2 or 3 are at best very sketchy (Fivush, 2011; Riggins, 2012).

Patricia Bauer and her colleagues (Bauer, 2015; Bauer & Larkina, 2016; Pathman, Doydum, & Bauer, 2013) have been recently studying when infantile amnesia begins to occur. In one study, children's memory for events that occurred at 3 years of age were periodically assessed through age 9 (Bauer & Larkina, 2014). By 8 to 9 years of age, children's memory of events that occurred at 3 years of age began to significantly fade away. In Bauer's (2015) view, the processes that account for these developmental changes are early, gradual development of the ability to form, retain, and later retrieve memories of personally relevant past events followed by an accelerated rate of forgetting in childhood.

What is the cause of infantile amnesia? One reason older children and adults have difficulty recalling events from their infant and early childhood years is that during these years the prefrontal lobes of the brain are immature, and this area of the brain is believed to play an important role in storing memories of events (Bauer, 2015).

In sum, most of young infants' conscious memories appear to be rather fragile and short-lived, although their implicit memory of perceptual-motor actions can be substantial (Bauer, 2015; Bauer & Fivush, 2014). By the end of the second year, long-term memory is more substantial and reliable (Bauer, 2015).

implicit memory Memory without conscious recollection; involves skills and routine procedures that are automatically performed.

explicit memory Memory of facts and experiences that individuals consciously know and can state.

concepts Cognitive groupings of similar objects, events, people, or ideas.

Age Group	Length of Delay
6-month-olds	24 hours
9-month-olds	1 month
10–11-month-olds	3 months
13–14-month-olds	4–6 months
20-month-olds	12 months

Figure 20 Age-Related Changes in the Length of Time Over Which Memory Occurs

Concept Formation and Categorization

Along with attention, imitation, and memory, concepts are a key aspect of infants' cognitive development (Quinn, 2016). **Concepts** are cognitive groupings of similar objects, events, people, or ideas. Without concepts, you would see each object and event as unique; you would not be able to make any generalizations.

Do infants have concepts? Yes, they do, although we do not know just how early concept formation begins (Quinn & Bhatt, 2015). Using habituation experiments like those described earlier in the chapter, some researchers have found that infants as young as 3 months of age can group together objects with similar appearances (Quinn & others, 2013). This research capitalizes on the knowledge that infants are more likely to look at a novel object than at a familiar one.

Jean Mandler (2009) argues that these early categorizations are best described as *perceptual categorization.* That is, the categorizations are based on similar perceptual features of objects, such as size, color, and movement, as well as parts of objects, such as legs for animals. Mandler (2004) concludes that it is not until about 7 to 9 months that infants form *conceptual* categories rather than just making perceptual discriminations between different categories. In one study of 9- to 11-month-olds, infants classified birds as animals and airplanes as vehicles even though the objects were perceptually similar—airplanes and birds with their wings spread (Mandler & McDonough, 1993) (see Figure 21).

Figure 21 Categorization in 9- to 11-Month-Olds
These are the stimuli used in the study that indicated 9- to 11-month-old infants categorized birds as animals and airplanes as vehicles even though the objects were perceptually similar (Mandler & McDonough, 1993).

In addition to infants categorizing items on the basis of external, perceptual features such as shape, color, and parts, they also may categorize items on the basis of prototypes, or averages, that they extract from the structural regularities of items (Quinn & Bhatt, 2015).

Further advances in categorization occur in the second year of life (Booth, 2006). Many infants' "first concepts are broad and global in nature, such as 'animal' or 'indoor thing.' Gradually, over the first two years these broad concepts become more differentiated into concepts such as 'land animal,' then 'dog,' or to 'furniture,' then 'chair'" (Mandler, 2009, p. 1).

Learning to put things into the correct categories— what makes something one kind of thing rather than another kind of thing, such as what makes a bird a bird, or a fish a fish—is an important aspect of learning (Quinn, 2016; Rakison & Lawson, 2013). As infant development researcher Alison Gopnik (2010, p. 159) pointed out, "If you can sort the world into the right categories—put things in the right boxes—then you've got a big advance on understanding the world."

How Would You...?
As an **educator,** how would you talk with parents about the importance of concept development in their infants?

In sum, the infant's advances in processing information—through attention, imitation, memory, and concept formation—is much richer, more gradual and less stage-like, and occurs earlier than was envisioned by earlier theorists (Bauer, 2015; Quinn, 2016). As leading infant researcher Jean Mandler (2004) concluded, "The human infant shows a remarkable degree of learning power and complexity in what is being learned and in the way it is represented" (p. 304).

Language Development

In 1799, villagers in the French town of Aveyron observed a nude boy running through the woods and captured him. Known as the Wild Boy of Aveyron, he was judged to be about 11 years old and believed to have lived in the woods alone for six years (Lane, 1976). When found, he made no effort to communicate, and he never did learn to communicate effectively.

Sadly, a modern-day wild child was discovered in Los Angeles in 1970. Despite intensive intervention, the child, named Genie by researchers, never acquired more than a primitive form of language. Both of these cases—the Wild Boy of Aveyron and Genie— raise questions about the biological and environmental determinants of language, topics that we also examine later in the chapter. First, though, we need to define language.

Defining Language

Language is a form of communication—whether spoken, written, or signed—that is based on a system of symbols. Language consists of the words used by a community and the rules for varying and combining them. All human languages have some common characteristics, such as organizational rules and infinite generativity (Hoff, 2015; MacWhinney, 2015). Rules describe the way the language works. **Infinite generativity** is the ability to produce an endless number of meaningful sentences using a finite set of words and rules.

language A form of communication, whether spoken, written, or signed, that is based on a system of symbols. Language consists of the words used by a community and the rules for varying and combining them.

infinite generativity The ability to produce an endless number of meaningful sentences using a finite set of words and rules.

How Language Develops

Whatever language they learn, infants all over the world follow a similar path in language development. What are some key milestones in this development?

Babbling and Gestures

Babies actively produce sounds from birth onward. The effect of these early communications is to attract attention (Dimitrova, Moro, & Mohr, 2015; Masapolio, Polka, & Menard, 2016). Babies' sounds and gestures go through the following sequence during the first year:

- *Crying.* Babies cry even at birth. Crying can signal distress, but as we will discuss later, there are different types of cries that signal different things.

- *Cooing.* Babies first coo at about 2 to 4 months. Coos are gurgling sounds that are made in the back of the throat and usually express pleasure during interaction with the caregiver.

- *Babbling.* In the middle of the first year, babies babble—that is, they produce strings of consonant-vowel combinations such as "ba, ba, ba, ba."

- *Gestures.* Infants start using gestures, such as showing and pointing, at about 8 to 12 months (Goldin-Meadow, 2015, 2017). They may wave bye-bye, nod to mean "yes," and show an empty cup to ask for more milk. Lack of pointing is a significant indicator of problems in the infant's communication system (Cartmill & Goldin-Meadow, 2015; Cooperrider & Goldin-Meadow, 2017; Demir & Goldin-Meadow, 2015).

Recognizing Language Sounds

Long before they begin to learn words, infants can make fine distinctions among the sounds of a language (Kuhl & Damasio, 2012). In Patricia Kuhl's (2000, 2009, 2011, 2012, 2015) research, *phonemes* (the basic sound units of a language) from languages all over the world are piped through a speaker for infants to hear (see Figure 22). A box with a toy bear in it is placed where the infant can see it. A string of identical syllables is played; then the syllables are changed (for example, *ba ba ba ba,* and then *pa pa pa pa*). If the infant turns its head when the syllables change, the box lights up and the bear dances and drums, rewarding the infant for noticing the change.

Kuhl's research has demonstrated that from birth up to about 6 months, infants are "citizens of the world": They can tell when sounds change most of the time no matter what language the syllables come from. But over the next six months, infants get even better at perceiving

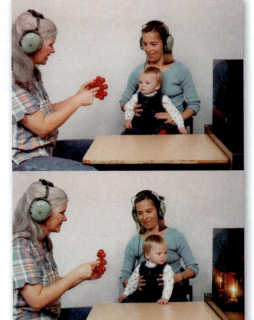

Figure 22 From Universal Linguist to Language-Specific Listener

In Patricia Kuhl's research laboratory babies listen to tape-recorded voices that repeat syllables. When the sounds of the syllables change, the babies quickly learn to look at the bear. Using this technique, Kuhl has demonstrated that babies are universal linguists until about 6 months of age, but in the next six months they become language-specific listeners. *Does Kuhl's research give support to the view that either "nature" or "nurture" is the source of language acquisition?*

© Dr. Patricia Kuhl, Institute for Learning and Brain Sciences, University of Washington

changes in sounds from their "own" language, the one their parents speak, and gradually lose the ability to recognize differences that are not important in their own language (Kuhl, 2009, 2011, 2012, 2015). Recently, Kuhl (2015) has found that the age at which a baby's brain is most open to learning the sounds of a native language begins at 6 months for vowels and at 9 months for consonants.

Also, in the second half of their first year, infants begin to segment the continuous stream of speech they encounter into words (Stahl & others, 2014). Initially, they likely rely on statistical information such as the co-occurrence patterns of phonemes and syllables, which allows them to extract potential word forms. For example, discovering that the sequence *br* occurs more often at the beginning of words while *nt* is more common at the end of words helps infants detect word boundaries. And as infants extract an increasing number of potential word forms from the speech stream they hear, they begin to associate these with concrete, perceptually available objects in their world (Zamuner, Fais, & Werker, 2014).

First Words

Infants understand words before they can produce or speak them (Tamis-LeMonda & Bornstein, 2015). For example, as early as 5 months many infants recognize their name. However, the infant's first spoken word, a milestone eagerly anticipated by every parent, usually doesn't occur until 10 to 15 months of age and happens at an average of about 13 months. Yet long before babies say their first words, they have been communicating with their parents, often by gesturing and using their own special sounds. The appearance of first words is a continuation of this communication process.

A child's first words include those that name important people (*dada*), familiar animals (*kitty*), vehicles (*car*), toys (*ball*), food (*milk*), body parts (*eye*), clothes (*hat*), household items (*clock*), and greeting terms (*bye*). Children often express various intentions with their single words, so that "cookie" might mean, "That's a cookie" or "I want a cookie." Nouns are easier to learn because the majority of words in this class are more perceptually accessible than other types of words (Parish-Morris, Golinkoff, & Hirsh-Pasek, 2013). Think how the noun "car" is so much more concrete and imaginable than the verb "goes," making the word "car" much easier to acquire than the word "goes."

As indicated earlier, children understand their first words earlier than they speak them. On average, infants understand about 50 words at the age of 13 months, but they can't say that many words until about 18 months. Thus, in infancy *receptive vocabulary* (words the child understands) considerably exceeds *spoken vocabulary* (words the child uses). A recent study revealed that 6-month-olds understand words that refer to body parts, such as "hand" and "feet," but of course, they cannot yet speak these words (Tincoff & Jusczyk, 2012).

The infant's spoken vocabulary rapidly increases once the first word is spoken (Waxman & Goswami, 2012). Whereas the average 18-month-old can speak about 50 words, a 2-year-old can speak about 200 words. This rapid increase in vocabulary that begins at approximately 18 months is called the *vocabulary spurt* (Bloom, Lifter, & Broughton, 1985).

Like the timing of a child's first word, the timing of the vocabulary spurt varies (Dale & Goodman, 2004). Figure 23 shows the range for these two language milestones in 14 children. On average, these children said their first word at 13 months and had a vocabulary spurt at 19 months. However, the ages for the first word of individual children varied from 10 to 17 months and, for their vocabulary spurt, from 13 to 25 months.

Does early vocabulary development predict later language development? A recent study found that infant vocabulary development at 16 to 24 months of age was linked to vocabulary, phonological awareness, reading accuracy, and reading comprehension five years later (Duff & others, 2015).

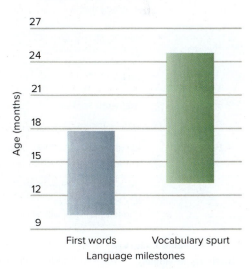

Figure 23 **Variation in Language Milestones.**
What are some possible explanations for variations in the timing of these milestones?

Two-Word Utterances

By the time children are 18 to 24 months of age, they usually produce two-word utterances. To convey meaning with just two words, the child relies heavily on gesture, tone, and context. The wealth of meaning children can communicate with a two-word utterance includes the following (Slobin, 1972): identification—"See doggie"; location—"Book there"; repetition—"More milk"; negation—"Not wolf"; possession—"My candy"; attribution—"Big car"; and question—"Where ball?" These examples are from children whose first language is English, German, Russian, Finnish, Turkish, or Samoan.

Notice that two-word utterances omit many parts of speech and are remarkably succinct. In fact, in every language a child's first combinations of words have this economical quality; they are telegraphic. **Telegraphic speech** is the use of short, precise words without grammatical markers such as articles, auxiliary verbs, and other connectives. Telegraphic speech is not limited to two words; "Mommy give ice cream" and "Mommy give Tommy ice cream" are also examples of telegraphic speech.

Around the world, most young children learn to speak in two-word utterances at about 18 to 24 months of age. *What are some examples of these two-word utterances?*
© McPhoto/age fotostock

Biological and Environmental Influences

We have discussed a number of language milestones in infancy; Figure 24 summarizes the ages at which infants typically reach these milestones. But what makes this amazing development possible? Everyone who uses language in some way "knows" its rules and has the ability to create an infinite number of words and sentences. Where does this knowledge come from? Is it the product of biology, or is language learned and influenced by experiences?

Biological Influences

The ability to speak and understand language requires a certain vocal apparatus as well as a nervous system with specific capabilities. The nervous system and vocal apparatus of humans' predecessors changed over hundreds of thousands, or millions, of years. With advances in the nervous system and vocal structures, *Homo sapiens* went beyond the grunting and shrieking of other animals to develop speech (Lieberman, 2016). Although estimates vary, many experts believe that humans acquired language about 100,000 years ago, which in evolutionary time represents a very recent acquisition. It gave humans an enormous edge over other animals and increased the chances of human survival (McMurray, 2016; Pinker, 2015).

Some language scholars view the remarkable similarities in how children acquire language all over the world as strong evidence that language has a biological basis. There is evidence that particular regions of the brain are

Typical Age	Language Milestones
Birth	Crying
2 to 4 months	Cooing begins
5 months	Understands first word
6 months	Babbling begins
7 to 11 months	Change from universal linguist to language-specific listener
8 to 12 months	Uses gestures, such as showing and pointing Comprehension of words appears
13 months	First word spoken
18 months	Vocabulary spurt starts
18 to 24 months	Uses two-word utterances Rapid expansion of understanding of words

Figure 24 Some Language Milestones in Infancy
Despite substantial variations in the language input received by infants, around the world they follow a similar path in learning to speak.

telegraphic speech The use of short and precise words without grammatical markers such as articles, auxiliary verbs, and other connectives.

predisposed to be used for language (Dubois & others, 2016; Roehrich-Gascon, Small, & Tremblay, 2015). Two regions involved in language were first discovered in studies of brain-damaged individuals: *Broca's area,* an area in the left frontal lobe of the brain that is involved in producing words; and *Wernicke's area,* a region of the brain's left hemisphere that is involved in language comprehension (see Figure 25). Damage to either of these areas produces types of *aphasia,* a loss or impairment of language processing. Individuals with damage to Broca's area have difficulty producing speech but can comprehend what others say; those with damage to Wernicke's area have poor comprehension and often produce fluent but nonsensical speech.

Linguist Noam Chomsky (1957) proposed that humans are biologically "prewired" to learn language at a certain time and in a certain way. He said that children are born into the world with a **language acquisition device (LAD),** a biological endowment that enables the child to detect the various features and rules of language. Children are prepared by nature with the ability to detect the sounds of language, for example, and follow linguistic rules such as those governing how to form plurals and ask questions.

Chomsky's LAD is a theoretical construct, not a physical part of the brain. Is there evidence for the existence of a LAD? Supporters of the LAD concept cite the uniformity of language milestones across languages and cultures, evidence that children create language even in the absence of well-formed input, and the importance of language's biological underpinnings. But as we will see, critics argue that even if infants have something like a LAD, it cannot explain the whole process of language acquisition.

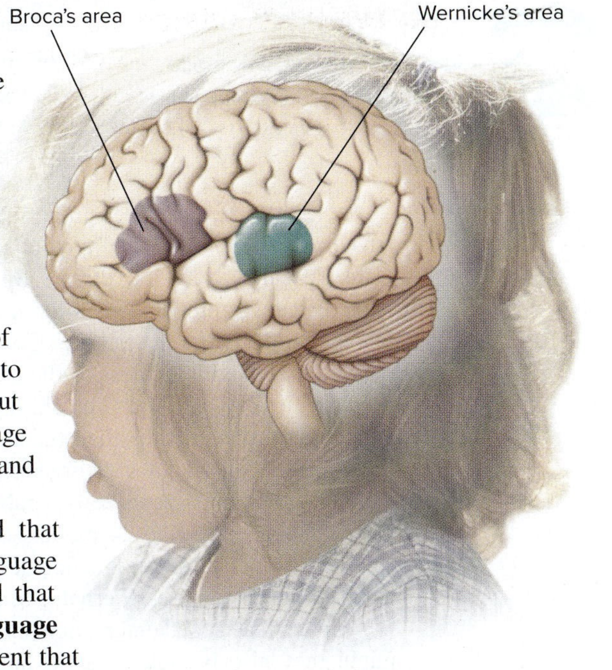

Broca's area

Wernicke's area

Figure 25 Broca's Area and Wernicke's Area
Broca's area is located in the frontal lobe of the brain's left hemisphere, and it is involved in the control of speech. Wernicke's area is a portion of the left hemisphere's temporal lobe that is involved in understanding language. *How does the role of these areas of the brain relate to lateralization?*

Environmental Influences

Decades ago, behaviorists opposed Chomsky's hypothesis and argued that language represents nothing more than chains of responses acquired through reinforcement (Skinner, 1957). A baby happens to babble "Ma-ma"; Mama rewards the baby with hugs and smiles; the baby says "Mama" more and more frequently. Bit by bit, said the behaviorists, the baby's language is built up in this way. According to behaviorists, language is a complex, learned skill, much like playing the piano or dancing.

The behavioral view of language learning has problems. First, it does not explain how people create novel sentences—sentences they have never heard or spoken before. Second, it does not account for how children learn the syntax of their native language even if they are not reinforced for doing so. Social psychologist Roger Brown (1973) spent long hours observing parents and their young children. He found that parents did not directly or explicitly reward or correct the syntax of most children's utterances. That is, parents did not say "good," "correct," "right," "wrong," and so on. Parents also did not offer direct corrections such as "You should say 'two shoes,' not 'two shoe.'" However, as we will see shortly, many parents do expand on their young children's grammatically incorrect utterances and recast many of those that contain grammatical errors.

The behavioral view is no longer considered a viable explanation of how children acquire language. But a great deal of research describes ways in which children's environmental experiences influence their language skills (Houston & others, 2016). Many language experts argue that a child's experiences, the particular language to be learned, and the context in which learning takes place can strongly influence language acquisition (Bornstein & others, 2015; Pace & others, 2016).

language acquisition device (LAD) Chomsky's term that describes a biological endowment enabling the child to detect the features and rules of language, including phonology, syntax, and semantics.

How Would You...?

As a **social worker,** how would you intervene in a family in which a child has lived in social isolation for years?

Language is not learned in a social vacuum. Most children are bathed in language from a very early age. The support and involvement of caregivers and teachers greatly facilitate a child's language learning (Houston & others, 2016; Pace & others, 2016).

In particular, researchers have documented the important effect that early speech input and poverty can have on the development of a child's language skills (Hoff, 2015; NICHD Early Child Care Research Network, 2005). Betty Hart and Todd Risley (1995) observed the language environments of children whose parents were professionals and children whose parents were on welfare. Compared with the professional parents, the parents on welfare talked much less to their young children, talked less about past events, and provided less elaboration. The children of the professional parents had a much larger vocabulary at 36 months than the children of the welfare parents did. Keep in mind, though, that individual variations characterize language development and that some welfare parents do spend considerable time talking to their children. A recent study also found that at 18 to 24 months of age, infants in low-SES families already had a smaller vocabulary and less efficient language processing than their infant counterparts in middle-SES families (Fernald, Marchman, & Weisleder, 2013).

Given that social interaction is critical for infants to learn language effectively, might they also be able to learn language effectively through television and videos? Researchers have found that infants and young children cannot effectively learn language (phonology or words) from television or videos (Kuhl, 2007; Roseberry & others, 2009). A recent study of toddlers found that frequent viewing of television increased the risk of delayed language development (Lin & others, 2015). Thus, just hearing language is not enough even when infants seemingly are fully engaged in the experience. However, a recent study revealed that Skype provides some improvement in child language learning over videos and TV (Roseberry & others, 2014), and older children can use information provided from television in their language development.

One intriguing component of the young child's linguistic environment is **child-directed speech** (also referred to as "parentese"), which is language spoken in a higher-than-usual pitch, slower tempo, and exaggerated intonation, with simple words and sentences (Golinkoff & others, 2015; Houston & others, 2016). It is hard for most adults to use child-directed speech when not in the presence of a baby. As soon as adults start talking to a baby, though, they often shift into child-directed speech. Much of this is automatic and something most parents are not aware they are doing. Even 4-year-olds speak in simpler ways to 2-year-olds than to their 4-year-old friends. Child-directed speech has the important function of capturing the infant's attention and maintaining communication (Ratner, 2013). A recent study found that child-directed speech in a one-to-one social context at 11 to 14 months of age was linked to greater word production at 2 years of age than standard speech and speech in a group setting (Ramirez-Esparza, Garcia-Sierra, & Kuhl, 2014). Another recent study of low-SES Spanish-speaking families revealed that infants who experienced more child-directed speech were better at processing words in real time and had larger vocabularies at 2 years of age (Weisleder & Fernald, 2013).

Adults often use strategies other than child-directed speech to enhance the child's acquisition of language, including recasting, expanding, and labeling. *Recasting* is rephrasing something the child has said, perhaps turning it into a question or restating the child's immature utterance in the form of a fully grammatical sentence. For example, if the child says, "The dog was barking," the adult can respond by asking, "When was the dog barking?" Effective recasting lets the child indicate an interest and then elaborates on that interest. *Expanding* is restating, in a linguistically sophisticated form, what a child has said. For example, a child says, "Doggie eat," and the parent replies, "Yes, the doggie is eating." *Labeling* is identifying the names of objects. Young children are forever being asked to identify the names of objects. Roger Brown (1958) called this "the original word game" and claimed that much of a child's early vocabulary learning is motivated by this adult pressure to identify the words associated with objects.

child-directed speech Also called parentese, language spoken in a higher pitch, slower tempo, and exaggerated intonation than normal with simple words and sentences.

Parents should begin talking to their babies at the start. The best language teaching occurs when the talking is begun before the infant becomes capable of intelligible speech. *What are some other guidelines for parents to follow to help their infants and toddlers develop their language skills?*

© John Carter/Science Source

Parents use these strategies naturally and in meaningful conversations. Parents do not (and should not) use any deliberate method to teach their children to talk, even with children who are slow in learning language. Children usually benefit when parents guide their discovery of language rather than over-loading them; "following in order to lead" helps a child learn language. If children are not ready to take in some information, they are likely to indicate this, perhaps by turning away. Thus, giving the child more information is not always better.

Infants, toddlers, and young children benefit when adults read books to and with them, a process called shared reading (Hirsh-Pasek & Golinkoff, 2014). In one study, reading daily to children at 14 to 24 months was positively related to the children's language and cognitive development at 36 months (Raikes & others, 2006).

How Would You...?

As a **human development and family studies professional,** how would you encourage parents to talk with their infants and toddlers?

Michael Tomasello (2003, 2006, 2011, 2014) stresses that young children are intensely interested in their social world and that early in their development they can understand the intentions of other people. He emphasizes that children learn language in specific contexts. For example, when a toddler and a father are jointly focused on a book, the father might say, "See the birdie." In this case, even a toddler understands that the father intends to name something and knows to look in the direction of the pointing. Through this kind of joint attention, early in their development children are able to use their social skills to acquire language (Mastin & Vogt, 2016; Tomasello, 2014). One study revealed that joint attention at 12 and 18 months predicted language skills at 24 months of age (Mundy & others, 2007).

What are some effective ways that parents can facilitate their children's language development? They include the following strategies (Baron, 1992; Galinsky, 2010):

- *Be an active conversational partner.* Initiate conversation with the baby.

- *Talk in a slowed-down pace and don't worry about how you sound to other adults when you talk to your baby.* Talking in a slowed-down pace will help your baby detect words in the sea of sounds they experience.

- *Use parent-look and parent-gesture, and name what you are looking at.* When you want your child to pay attention to something, look at it and point to it. Then name it—for example, by saying "Look, Alex, it's an airplane."

- *When you talk with infants and toddlers, be simple, concrete, and repetitive.* Don't try to talk to them in abstract, high-level ways and think you have to say something new or different all of the time. Using familiar words often will help them remember the words.

- *Play games.* Use word games like peek-a-boo and pat-a-cake to help infants learn words.

- *Remember to listen.* Since toddlers' speech is often slow and laborious, parents are often tempted to supply words and thoughts for them. Be patient and let toddlers express themselves.

- *Expand and elaborate language abilities and horizons with infants and toddlers.* Ask questions that encourage answers other than "Yes" and "No." Actively repeat, expand, and recast the utterances. Your toddler might say, "Dada." You could follow with, "Where's Dada?," and then you might continue, "Let's go find him."

An Interactionist View

If language acquisition depended only on biology, Genie and the Wild Boy of Aveyron (discussed earlier in the chapter) should have talked without difficulty. A child's experiences do influence language acquisition (Houston & others, 2016; Pace & others, 2016). But we have seen that language also has strong biological foundations (Dubois & others, 2016); no matter how much you converse with a dog, it won't learn to talk. Unlike dogs, children are biologically equipped to learn language (McMurray, 2016; Pinker, 2015). Children all over the world acquire language milestones at about the same time and in about the same order. An interactionist view emphasizes that both biology and experience contribute to language development (Hoff, 2015; Tomasello, 2014).

This interaction of biology and experience can be seen in variations in the acquisition of language. Children vary in their ability to acquire language, and this variation cannot be completely explained by differences in environmental input alone. However, virtually every child benefits enormously from opportunities to talk and be talked with. Children whose parents and teachers provide them with a rich verbal environment show many positive outcomes (Beaty & Pratt, 2015). Parents and teachers who pay attention to what children are trying to say, expand their children's utterances, read to them, and label things in the environment, are providing valuable, if unintentional, benefits (Hirsh-Pasek & Golinkoff, 2014).

Summary

Physical Growth and Development in Infancy

- Most development follows cephalocaudal and proximodistal patterns.
- Physical growth is rapid in the first year, but the rate of growth slows in the second year.
- Dramatic changes characterize the brain's development in the first two years. The neuroconstructivist view is an increasingly popular view of the brain's development.
- Newborns usually sleep 16 to 17 hours a day, but by 4 months many American infants approach adult-like sleeping patterns. Sudden infant death syndrome (SIDS) is a condition that occurs when a sleeping infant suddenly stops breathing and dies without an apparent cause.
- Infants need to consume about 50 calories per day for each pound they weigh. The growing consensus is that breast feeding is more beneficial than bottle feeding.

Motor Development

- Dynamic systems theory seeks to explain how motor behaviors are assembled for perceiving and acting. This theory emphasizes that experience plays an important role in motor development, and that perception and action are coupled.
- Reflexes—automatic movements—govern the newborn's behavior.
- Key gross motor skills, which involve large-muscle activities, developed during infancy include control of posture and walking.
- Fine motor skills involve finely tuned movements. The onset of reaching and grasping marks a significant accomplishment, and this becomes more refined during the first two years of life.

Sensory and Perceptual Development

- Sensation occurs when information interacts with sensory receptors. Perception is the interpretation of sensation.
- Created by the Gibsons, the ecological view states that perception brings people into contact with the environment to interact with and adapt to it.
- The infant's visual acuity increases dramatically in the first year of life. By 3 months of age, infants show size and shape constancy. In Gibson and Walk's classic study, infants had depth perception as young as 6 months of age.
- The fetus can hear several weeks prior to birth. Just after being born, infants can hear but their sensory threshold is higher than that of adults. Newborns can respond to touch, feel pain, differentiate among odors, and may be sensitive to taste at birth.
- A basic form of intermodal perception is present in newborns and sharpens over the first year of life.
- In perception, nature advocates are referred to as nativists and nurture proponents are called empiricists. A strong empiricist approach is unwarranted. A full account of perceptual development includes the roles of nature, nurture, and the infant's developing sensitivity to information.

Cognitive Development

- In Piaget's theory, children construct their own cognitive worlds, building mental structures to adapt to their world. Schemes, assimilation and accommodation, organization, and equilibration are key processes in Piaget's theory. According to Piaget, there are four qualitatively different stages of thought. In sensorimotor thought, the first of Piaget's four stages, the infant organizes and coordinates sensations with physical movements. The stage lasts from birth to about 2 years of age. One key accomplishment of this stage is object permanence. In the past several decades, revisions of Piaget's view have been proposed based on research.

- An approach different from Piaget's focuses on infants' operant conditioning, attention, imitation, memory, and concept formation.

Language Development

- Rules describe the way language works. Language is characterized by infinite generativity.

- Infants reach a number of milestones in development, including first words and two-word utterances.
- Chomsky argues that children are born with the ability to detect basic features and rules of language. The behavioral view has not been supported by research. How much of language is biologically determined, and how much depends on interaction with others, is a subject of debate among linguists and psychologists. However, all agree that both biological capacity and relevant experience are necessary. Parents should talk extensively with an infant, especially about what the baby is attending to.

Key Terms

A-not-B error
accommodation
assimilation
attention
cephalocaudal pattern
child-directed speech
concepts
core knowledge approach
deferred imitation
dishabituation

dynamic systems theory
ecological view
equilibration
explicit memory
fine motor skills
gross motor skills
habituation
implicit memory
infinite generativity
intermodal perception

joint attention
language
language acquisition device
  (LAD)
lateralization
memory
neuroconstructivist view
object permanence
organization
perception

proximodistal pattern
schemes
sensation
sensorimotor stage
sudden infant death syndrome
  (SIDS)
telegraphic speech
visual preference method

4 Socioemotional Development in Infancy

© SelectStock/Getty Images RF

CHAPTER OUTLINE

EMOTIONAL AND PERSON-ALITY DEVELOPMENT

Emotional Development

Temperament

Personality Development

SOCIAL ORIENTATION AND ATTACHMENT

Social Orientation and Understanding

Attachment

SOCIAL CONTEXTS

The Family

Child Care

Stories of Life-Span Development: Darius and His Father

An increasing number of fathers are staying home to care for their children (Brott, 2015; Dette-Hagenmeyer, Erzinger, & Reichle, 2016; Lamb, 2013). Consider 17-month-old Darius. On weekdays, Darius' father, a writer, cares for him during the day while his mother works full-time as a landscape architect. Darius' father is doing a great job of caring for him. He keeps Darius nearby while he is writing and spends lots of time talking to him and playing with him. From their interactions, it is clear that they genuinely enjoy each other's company.

Last month, Darius began spending one day a week at a child-care center. His parents selected the center after observing a number of centers and interviewing teachers and center directors. His parents placed him in the center because they wanted him to get some experience with peers and his father to have some time out from caregiving.

Darius' father looks to the future and imagines the Little League games Darius will play in and the many other activities he can enjoy with his son. Remembering how little time his own father spent with him, he is dedicated to making sure that Darius has an involved, nurturing relationship with his father.

When Darius' mother comes home in the evening, she spends considerable time with him. Darius is securely attached to both his mother and his father.

How might fathers influence their infants' and children's development?
© Rick Gomez/Corbis

You have read about how infants perceive, learn, and remember. Infants also are socio-emotional beings, capable of displaying emotions and initiating social interaction with people close to them. The main topics that we explore in this chapter are emotional and personality development, attachment, and the social contexts of the family and child care. ■

Emotional and Personality Development

Anyone who has been around infants for even a brief time can tell that they are emotional beings. Not only do infants express emotions, but they also vary in temperament. Some are shy and others are outgoing. Some are active and others much less so. Let's explore these and other aspects of emotional and personality development in infants.

Emotional Development

Imagine what your life would be like without emotion. Emotion is the color and music of life, as well as the tie that binds people together. How do psychologists define and classify emotions, and why are they important to development? How do emotions develop during the first two years of life?

What Are Emotions?

For our purposes, we will define **emotion** as feeling, or affect, that occurs when a person is in a state or an interaction that is important to him or her, especially to his or her well-being. Especially in infancy, emotions have important roles in (1) communication with others and (2) behavioral organization. Through emotions, infants communicate such important aspects of their lives as joy, sadness, interest, and fear (Witherington & others, 2010). In terms of behavioral organization, emotions influence infants' social responses and adaptive behavior as they interact with others in their world (Cole, 2016; Denham & Zinsser, 2014; Goodvin, Thompson, & Winer, 2015; Thompson, 2015, 2016).

Psychologists classify the broad range of emotions in many ways, but almost all classifications designate an emotion as either positive (pleasant) or negative (unpleasant) (Shuman & Scherer, 2014). Positive emotions include happiness, joy, love, and enthusiasm. Negative emotions include anxiety, anger, guilt, and sadness.

Biological and Environmental Influences

Emotions are influenced both by biological foundations and by a person's experiences (Calkins, 2015; Frenkel & Fox, 2015; Thompson & Goodvin, 2016). For example, children who are blind from birth and have never observed the smile or frown on another person's face smile and frown in the same way that children with normal vision do. Moreover, facial expressions of basic emotions such as happiness, surprise, anger, and fear are the same across cultures.

Cultural experiences and relationships influence emotional development (Cole, 2016). Emotion-linked interchanges provide the foundation for the infant's attachment to the parent (Goodvin, Thompson, & Winer, 2015). When toddlers hear their parents quarreling, they often react with distress and inhibit their play. Well-functioning families make each other laugh and may develop a light mood to defuse conflicts. A recent study of 18- to 24-month-olds found that parents' elicitation of talk about emotions was associated with their toddlers' sharing and helping behaviors (Brownell & others, 2013).

Emotional development and coping with stress are influenced by whether caregivers have maltreated or neglected children and whether children's caregivers are depressed or not (Cicchetti & Toth, 2016). When infants become stressed, they show better biological recovery from the stressors when their caregivers engage in sensitive caregiving with them (Thompson & Goodvin, 2016).

A recent study documented how babies pick up on their mothers' stress (Waters, West, & Mendes, 2014). In this study, mothers were

emotion Feeling, or affect, that occurs when a person is in a state or interaction that is important to them. Emotion is characterized by behavior that reflects (expresses) the pleasantness or unpleasantness of the state a person is in or the transactions being experienced.

separated from their babies and required to give a 5-minute speech, with half of the mothers receiving a positive evaluation and the other half a negative evaluation. Mothers who received negative feedback reported an increase in negative emotion and cardiac stress, while those who were given positive feedback reported an increase in positive emotion. The babies quickly detected their mothers' stress as reflected in an increased heart rate when reunited with them. And the greater the mother's stress response, the more her baby's heart rate increased.

Display rules—rules governing when, where, and how emotions should be expressed—are not universal. For example, researchers have found that East Asian infants display less frequent and less intense positive and negative emotions than do non-Latino White infants (Cole & Tan, 2007). Throughout childhood, East Asian parents encourage their children to show emotional reserve rather than to be emotionally expressive (Cole, 2016).

How do East Asian mothers handle their infants' and children's emotional development differently from non-Latina White mothers?
© ICHIRO/Getty Images RF

Early Emotions

Emotions that infants express in the first six months of life include surprise, interest, joy, anger, sadness, fear, and disgust (see Figure 1). Other emotions that appear in infancy include jealousy, empathy, embarrassment, pride, shame, and guilt; most of these occur for the first time at some point in the second half of the first year or during the second year. These later-developing emotions have been called self-conscious or other-conscious emotions because they involve the emotional reactions of others (Lewis, 2007, 2010, 2015).

Some experts on infant socioemotional development, such as Jerome Kagan (2010, 2013), conclude that the structural immaturity of the infant brain makes it unlikely that emotions that require thought—such as guilt, pride, despair, shame, empathy, and jealousy—can be experienced in the first year. Thus, both Kagan (2010) and Joseph Campos (2009) argue that so-called "self-conscious" emotions don't occur until after the first year, a view that increasingly is shared by most developmental psychologists.

Emotional Expressions and Relationships

Emotional expressions are involved in infants' first relationships. The ability of infants to communicate emotions permits coordinated interactions with their caregivers and the beginning of an emotional bond between them (Goodvin, Thompson, & Winer, 2015; Thompson, 2015, 2016). Not only do parents change their emotional expressions in

| Joy | Sadness | Fear | Surprise |

Figure 1 Expression of Different Emotions in Infants

(Left to right) © BananaStock/PictureQuest RF; © The McGraw-Hill Companies, Inc./Jill Braaten, photographer; © David Sacks/Getty Images; © Stockbyte/Getty Images RF

response to those of their infants (and each other), but infants also modify their emotional expressions in response to those of their parents. In other words, these interactions are mutually regulated. Because of this coordination, the interactions between parents and infants are described as *reciprocal,* or *synchronous,* when all is going well. Sensitive, responsive parents help their infants grow emotionally, whether the infants respond in distressed or happy ways (Wilson, Havighurst, & Harley, 2012).

Crying Cries and smiles are two emotional expressions that infants display when interacting with parents. These are babies' first forms of emotional communication. Crying is the most important mechanism newborns have for communicating with their world. Cries may also provide information about the health of the newborn's central nervous system. Newborns even tend to respond with cries and negative facial expressions when they hear other newborns cry (Dondi, Simion, & Caltran, 1999). However, a recent study revealed that newborns of depressed mothers showed less vocal distress when another infant cried, reflecting emotional and physiological dysregulation (Jones, 2012).

Babies have at least three types of cries:

- **Basic cry:** A rhythmic pattern that usually consists of a cry, followed by a briefer silence, then a shorter whistle that is somewhat higher in pitch than the main cry, then another brief rest before the next cry. Some experts believe that hunger is one of the conditions that incite the basic cry.

- **Anger cry:** A variation of the basic cry, with more excess air forced through the vocal cords.

- **Pain cry:** A sudden long, initial loud cry followed by the holding of the breath; no preliminary moaning is present. The pain cry may be stimulated by physical pain or by any high-intensity stimulus.

basic cry A rhythmic pattern usually consisting of a cry, a briefer silence, a shorter inspiratory whistle that is higher-pitched than the main cry, and a brief rest before the next cry.

anger cry A cry similar to the basic cry, with more excess air forced through the vocal cords.

pain cry A sudden outburst of loud crying without preliminary moaning, followed by breath holding.

reflexive smile A smile that does not occur in response to external stimuli. It appears during the first month after birth, usually during sleep.

What are some different types of cries?
© Andy Cox/The Image Bank/Getty Images

Most adults can determine whether an infant's cries signify anger or pain (Zeskind, Klein, & Marshall, 1992). Parents can distinguish among the various cries of their own baby better than among those of another baby.

Should parents respond to an infant's cries? Many developmental psychologists recommend that parents soothe a crying infant, especially in the first year. This reaction should help infants develop a sense of trust and secure attachment to the caregiver. One study revealed that mothers' negative emotional reactions (anger and anxiety) to crying increased the risk of subsequent attachment insecurity (Leerkes, Parade, & Gudmundson, 2011). Also, another study found that problems in infant soothability at 6 months of age were linked to insecure attachment at 12 months of age (Mills-Koonce, Propper, & Barnett, 2012). And a recent study found that mothers were more likely than fathers to use soothing techniques to reduce infant crying (Dayton & others, 2015).

How Would You...?

As a **human development and family studies professional,** how would you respond to the parents of a 13-month-old baby who are concerned because their son has suddenly started crying every morning when they drop him off at child care despite the fact that he has been going to the same child care provider for over six months?

Smiling Smiling is a critical social skill and a key social signal (Sauter & others, 2014). Two types of smiling can be distinguished in infants:

- **Reflexive smile:** A smile that does not occur in response to external stimuli and appears during the first month after birth, usually during sleep.

- **Social smile:** A smile that occurs in response to an external stimulus, typically a face in the case of the young infant. Social smiling occurs as early as 2 months of age.

Recent research found that smiling and laughter at 7 months of age were associated with self-regulation at 7 years of age (Posner & others, 2014). And one study found that higher maternal effortful control and positive emotionality predicted more initial infant smiling and laughter, while a higher level of parenting stress predicted a lower trajectory of infant smiling and laughter (Bridgett & others, 2013).

Fear One of a baby's earliest emotions is fear, which typically first appears at about 6 months and peaks at about 18 months. However, abused and neglected infants can show fear as early as 3 months (Witherington & others, 2010). The most frequent expression of an infant's fear involves **stranger anxiety,** in which an infant shows fear and wariness of strangers.

Stranger anxiety usually emerges gradually. It first appears at about 6 months in the form of wary reactions. By 9 months, fear of strangers is often more intense, and it continues to escalate through the infant's first birthday (Emde, Gaensbauer, & Harmon, 1976).

Not all infants show distress when they encounter a stranger. Besides individual variations, whether an infant shows stranger anxiety also depends on the social context and the characteristics of the stranger. Infants show less stranger anxiety when they are in familiar settings. For example, in one study, 10-month-olds showed little stranger anxiety when they met a stranger in their own home but much greater fear when they encountered a stranger in a research laboratory (Sroufe, Waters, & Matas, 1974). Also, infants show less stranger anxiety when they are sitting on their mothers' laps than when they are in an infant seat several feet away from their mothers (Bohlin & Hagekull, 1993). Thus, it appears that when infants feel secure they are less likely to show stranger anxiety.

Who the stranger is and how the stranger behaves also influence stranger anxiety in infants. Infants are less fearful of child strangers than of adult strangers. They also are less fearful of friendly, outgoing, smiling strangers than of passive, unsmiling strangers (Bretherton, Stolberg, & Kreye, 1981).

In addition to stranger anxiety, infants experience fear of being separated from their caregivers. The result is **separation protest**—crying when the caregiver leaves. Separation protest tends to peak at about 15 months among U.S. infants. A study of four different cultures found, similarly, that separation protest peaked at about 13 to 15 months (Kagan, Kearsley, & Zelazo, 1978). As indicated in Figure 2, the percentage of infants who engaged in separation protest varied across cultures, but the infants reached a peak of protest at about the same age—just before the middle of the second year.

Social Referencing Infants not only express emotions like fear but also "read" the emotions of other people (Cornew & others, 2012). **Social referencing** involves "reading" emotional cues in others to help determine how to act in a particular situation. The development of social referencing helps infants interpret ambiguous situations more accurately, as when they encounter a stranger (Pelaez, Virues-Ortega, & Gewirtz, 2012). By the end of the first year, a parent's facial expression—either smiling or fearful—influences whether an infant will explore an unfamiliar environment.

social smile A smile in response to an external stimulus, which, early in development, typically is a face.

stranger anxiety An infant's fear and wariness of strangers that typically appears in the second half of the first year of life.

separation protest An infant's distressed crying when the caregiver leaves.

social referencing "Reading" emotional cues in others to help determine how to act in a particular situation.

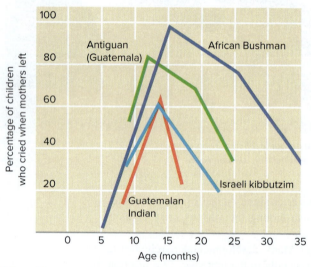

Figure 2 Separation Protest in Four Cultures

Note that separation protest peaked at about the same age in all four cultures in this study (13 to 15 months) (Kagan, Kearsley, & Zelazo, 1978). However, 100 percent of infants in an African Bushman culture engaged in separation protest compared with only about 60 percent of infants in Guatemalan Indian and Israeli kibbutzim cultures. *What might explain the fact that separation protest peaks at about the same age in different cultures?*

Infants become better at social referencing in the second year of life. At this age, they tend to "check" with their mother before they act; they look at her to see if she is happy, angry, or fearful.

temperament An individual's behavioral style and characteristic way of responding emotionally.

easy child A child who is generally in a positive mood, who quickly establishes regular routines in infancy, and who adapts easily to new experiences.

Emotion Regulation and Coping

During the first year, the infant gradually develops an ability to inhibit, or minimize, the intensity and duration of emotional reactions (Calkins & Perry, 2016). From early in infancy, babies put their thumbs in their mouths to soothe themselves. In their second year, they may say things to help soothe themselves. When placed in his bed for the night, after a little crying and whimpering, a 20-month-old was overheard saying, "Go sleep, Alex. Okay." But at first, infants depend mainly on caregivers to help them soothe their emotions, as when a caregiver rocks an infant to sleep, sings lullabies, gently strokes the infant, and so on.

Caregivers' actions influence the infant's neurobiological regulation of emotions (Goodvin, Thompson, & Winer, 2015). By soothing the infant, caregivers help infants modulate their emotions and reduce the level of stress hormones (de Haan & Gunnar, 2009). Many developmental psychologists believe it is a good strategy for a caregiver to soothe an infant before the infant gets into an intense, agitated, uncontrolled state (Calkins & Perry, 2016).

Later in infancy, when they become aroused, infants sometimes redirect their attention or distract themselves in order to reduce their arousal. By age 2, children can use language to define their feeling states and identify the context that is upsetting them (Calkins & Markovitch, 2010). A 2-year-old might say, "Doggy scary." This type of communication may cue caregivers to help the child regulate emotion.

Contexts can influence emotion regulation (Groh & others, 2016; Thompson, 2015, 2016). Infants are often affected by fatigue, hunger, time of day, which people are around them, and where they are. Infants must learn to adapt to different contexts that require emotion regulation. Further, new demands appear as the infant becomes older and parents modify their expectations. For example, a parent may take it in stride if a 6-month-old infant screams in a restaurant but may react very differently if a 1½-year-old starts screaming.

Temperament

Do you get upset easily? Does it take much to get you angry or to make you laugh? Even at birth, babies seem to have different emotional styles. One infant is cheerful and happy much of the time; another seems to cry constantly. These tendencies reflect **temperament, or individual differences in behavioral styles, emotions, and characteristic ways of responding.** With regard to its link to emotion, temperament refers to individual differences in how quickly the emotion is shown, how strong it is, how long it lasts, and how quickly it fades away (Campos, 2009).

Another way of describing temperament is in terms of predispositions toward emotional reactivity and self-regulation (Bates & Pettit, 2015). *Reactivity* involves variations in the speed and intensity with which an individual responds to situations with positive or negative emotions. *Self-regulation* involves variations in the extent or effectiveness of an individual's control over emotions.

Describing and Classifying Temperament

How would you describe your temperament or the temperament of a friend? Researchers have described and classified the temperaments of individuals in different ways (Gartstein, Putnam, & Kliewer, 2016; Stifter & Dollar, 2016). Here we examine three of those ways.

Chess and Thomas' Classification Psychiatrists Alexander Chess and Stella Thomas (Chess & Thomas, 1977; Thomas & Chess, 1991) identified three basic types, or clusters, of temperament:

- **Easy child:** This child is generally in a positive mood, quickly establishes regular routines in infancy, and adapts easily to new experiences.

- **Difficult child:** This child reacts negatively and cries frequently, engages in irregular daily routines, and is slow to accept change.
- **Slow-to-warm-up child:** This child has a low activity level, is somewhat negative, and displays a low intensity of mood.

In their longitudinal investigation, Chess and Thomas found that 40 percent of the children they studied could be classified as easy, 10 percent as difficult, and 15 percent as slow to warm up. Notice that 35 percent did not fit any of the three patterns. Researchers have found that these three basic clusters of temperament are moderately stable across the childhood years.

One study revealed that young children with a difficult temperament showed more problems when they experienced low-quality child care and fewer problems when they experienced high-quality child care than did young children with an easy temperament (Pluess & Belsky, 2009).

Kagan's Concept of Behavioral Inhibition Another way of classifying temperament focuses on the differences between a shy, subdued, timid child and a sociable, extraverted, bold child. Jerome Kagan (2002, 2010, 2013) regards shyness with strangers (peers or adults) as one feature of a broad temperament category called *inhibition to the unfamiliar*. Inhibited children react to many aspects of unfamiliarity with initial avoidance, distress, or subdued affect, beginning around 7 to 9 months. In recent research, having an inhibited temperament at 2 to 3 years of age was related to having social phobia symptoms at 7 years of age (Lahat & others, 2014). And recent findings also indicate that infants and young children who have an inhibited temperament are at risk for developing social anxiety disorder in adolescence and adulthood (Perez-Edgar & Guyer, 2014; Rapee, 2014).

Effortful Control (Self-Regulation) Mary Rothbart and John Bates (2006) stress that effortful control (self-regulation) is an important dimension of temperament. Infants who are high in effortful control show an ability to keep their arousal from getting too intense and have strategies for soothing themselves. By contrast, children who are low in effortful control are often unable to control their arousal; they are easily agitated and become intensely emotional. One study found that young children higher in effortful control were more likely to wait longer to express anger and were more likely to use a self-regulatory strategy, distraction (Tan, Armstrong, & Cole, 2013). Another study revealed effortful control was a strong predictor of academic success skills in kindergarten children from low-income families (Morris & others, 2013).

An important point about temperament classifications such as Chess and Thomas' and Rothbart and Bates' is that children should not be pigeonholed as having only one temperament

What are some ways that developmentalists have classified infants' temperaments? Which classification makes the most sense to you, based on your observations of infants?

© Tom Merton/Getty Images RF

dimension, such as "difficult" or "negative." A good strategy when attempting to classify a child's temperament is to think of temperament as consisting of multiple dimensions (Bates, 2012a, b). For example, a child might be extraverted, show little emotional negativity, and have good self-regulation. Another child might be introverted, show little emotional negativity, and have a low level of self-regulation.

The development of temperament capabilities such as effortful control allows individual differences to emerge (Bates & Pettit, 2015). For example, although maturation of the brain's prefrontal lobes must occur for any child's attention to improve and the child to achieve effortful control, some children develop effortful control while others do not. And it is these individual differences in children that are at the heart of what temperament is (Bates, 2012a, b).

Biological Foundations and Experience

How does a child acquire a certain temperament? Kagan (2010, 2013) argues that children inherit a physiology that predisposes them to have a particular type of temperament. However, through experience they may learn to modify their temperament to some degree. For example, children may inherit a physiology that predisposes them to be fearful and inhibited but then learn to reduce their fear and inhibition to some degree.

How might caregivers help a child become less fearful and inhibited? An important first step is to find out what frightens the child. Comforting and reassuring the child, and addressing their specific fears, are good strategies.

Biological Influences Physiological characteristics have been linked with different temperaments (Clauss, Avery, & Blackford, 2015). In particular, an inhibited temperament is associated with a unique physiological pattern that includes a high and stable heart rate, high levels of the hormone cortisol, and high activity in the right frontal lobe of the brain (Kagan, 2013). This pattern may be tied to the excitability of the amygdala, a structure in the brain that plays an important role in fear and inhibition. Twin and adoption studies also suggest that heredity has a moderate influence on differences in temperament within a group of people (Plomin & others, 2009).

Too often the biological foundations of temperament are interpreted as meaning that temperament cannot develop or change. However, important self-regulatory dimensions of temperament such as adaptability, soothability, and persistence look very different in a 1-year-old and a 5-year-old (Thompson, 2015). These temperament dimensions develop and change with the growth of the neurobiological foundations of self-regulation (Calkins & Perry, 2016).

Gender, Culture, and Temperament Gender may be an important factor shaping the context that influences temperament. Parents might react differently to an infant's temperament based on whether the baby is a boy or a girl (Gaias & others, 2012). For example, in one study, mothers were more responsive to the crying of irritable girls than to that of irritable boys (Crockenberg, 1986).

Similarly, the reaction to an infant's temperament may depend in part on culture (Chen, Fu, & Zhao, 2015; Chen & Schmidt, 2015). For example, an active temperament might be valued in some cultures (such as the United States) but not in others (such as China). Indeed, children's temperament can vary across cultures. For example, behavioral inhibition is valued more highly in China than in North America (Cole, 2016).

In short, many aspects of a child's environment can encourage or discourage the persistence of temperament characteristics (Goodvin, Thompson, & Winer, 2015). One useful way of thinking about these relationships applies the concept of goodness of fit, which we examine next.

Goodness of Fit and Parenting

Goodness of fit refers to the match between a child's temperament and the environmental demands the child must cope with. Suppose Jason is an active toddler who is made to sit still for long periods and Jack is a slow-to-warm-up toddler who is abruptly pushed into new situations on a regular basis. Both Jason and Jack face a lack of fit between their temperament and environmental demands. Lack of fit can produce adjustment problems (Rothbart, 2011). Researchers have found that decreases in infants' negative emotionality are linked to higher levels of parental sensitivity, involvement, and responsivity (Wachs & Bates, 2010).

How Would You...?

As a **social worker,** how would you apply information about an infant's temperament to maximize the goodness of fit in a clinical setting?

Many parents don't come to believe in the importance of temperament until the birth of their second child. They viewed their first child's behavior as stemming from how they treated the child. But then they find that some strategies that worked with their first child are not as effective with the second child. Some problems experienced with the first child (such as those associated with feeding, sleeping, and coping with strangers) may not arise with the second child, but new problems arise. Such experiences strongly suggest that children differ from each other very early in life and that these differences have important implications for parent-child interaction (Rothbart, 2011).

What are the implications of temperamental variations for parenting? Decreases in infants' negative emotionality occur when parents are more involved, responsive, and sensitive when interacting with their children (Goodvin, Thompson, & Winer, 2015). Temperament experts Ann Sanson and Mary Rothbart (1995) also recommend the following strategies for temperament-sensitive parenting:

- *Attention to and respect for individuality.* One implication is that it is difficult to generate general prescriptions for "good parenting." A goal might be accomplished in one way with one child and in another way with another child, depending on each child's temperament. Parents need to be flexible and sensitive to the infant's signals and needs.

- *Structuring the child's environment.* Crowded, noisy environments can pose greater problems for some children (such as a "difficult child") than for others (such as an "easy child"). We might also expect that a fearful, withdrawing child would benefit from slower entry into new contexts.

goodness of fit Refers to the match between a child's temperament and the environmental demands with which the child must cope.

- *Avoid applying negative labels to the child.* Acknowledging that some children are harder to parent than others is often helpful, and

What are some good strategies for parents to adopt when responding to their infant's temperament?

© Corbis/age fotostock RF

advice on how to handle particular kinds of difficult circumstances can be helpful. However, labeling a child "difficult" runs the risk of becoming a self-fulfilling prophecy. That is, if a child is identified as "difficult," people may treat him or her in a way that elicits "difficult" behavior.

A final comment about temperament is that recently the *differential susceptibility model* and the *biological sensitivity to context model* have been proposed and studied (Belsky, 2016; Belsky & others, 2015; Belsky & Pluess, 2016; Simpson & Belsky, 2016). These models emphasize that certain characteristics—such as a difficult temperament—that render children more vulnerable to difficulty in adverse contexts also make them more susceptible to optimal growth in very supportive conditions. These models may help us see "negative" temperament characteristics in a new light.

Personality Development

Emotions and temperament are key aspects of personality, the enduring personal characteristics of individuals. Let's now examine characteristics that are often thought of as central to personality development during infancy: trust, the development of a sense of self, and progress toward independence.

Trust

According to Erik Erikson (1968), the first year of life is characterized by the trust-versus-mistrust stage of development. Upon emerging from a life of regularity, warmth, and protection in the mother's womb, the infant faces a world that is less secure. Erikson proposed that infants learn trust when they are cared for in a consistently nurturant manner. If the infant is not well fed and kept warm on a consistent basis, a sense of mistrust is likely to develop.

In Erikson's view, the issue of trust versus mistrust is not resolved once and for all in the first year of life. It arises again at each successive stage of development, and the outcomes can be positive or negative. For example, children who leave infancy with a sense of trust can still have their sense of mistrust activated at a later stage, perhaps if their parents become separated or divorced.

The Developing Sense of Self

It is difficult to study the self in infancy mainly because infants cannot tell us how they experience themselves. Infants cannot verbally express their views of the self. They also cannot understand complex instructions from researchers.

A rudimentary form of self-recognition—being attentive and positive toward one's image in a mirror—appears as early as 3 months (Mascolo & Fischer, 2007; Pipp, Fischer, & Jennings, 1987). However, a central, more complete index of self-recognition—the ability to recognize one's physical features—does not emerge until the second year (Thompson, 2006).

One ingenious strategy to test infants' visual self-recognition is the use of a mirror technique in which an infant's mother first puts a dot of rouge on the infant's nose. Then, an observer watches to see how often the infant touches its nose. Next, the infant is placed in front of a mirror and observers detect whether nose touching increases. Why does this matter? The idea is that increased nose touching indicates that the infant recognizes itself in the mirror and is trying to touch or rub off the rouge because the rouge violates the infant's view of itself; that is, the infant thinks something is not right, since it believes its real self does not have a dot of rouge on it.

Figure 3 displays the results of two investigations that used the mirror technique. The researchers found that before they were 1 year old, infants did not recognize themselves in the mirror (Amsterdam, 1968; Lewis & Brooks-Gunn, 1979). Signs of self-recognition began to appear among some infants when they were 15 to 18 months old. By the time they were 2 years old, most children recognized themselves in the mirror.

In sum, infants begin to develop a self-understanding, called self-recognition, at approximately 18 months of age (Hart & Karmel, 1996; Lewis, 2005).

In one study, biweekly assessments of infants from 15 to 23 months of age were conducted (Courage, Edison, & Howe, 2004). Self-recognition emerged gradually over this period, first appearing in the form of mirror recognition, followed by use of the personal pronoun "me" and then by recognizing a photo of themselves. These aspects of self-recognition are often referred to as the first indications of toddlers' understanding of the mental state of "me," "that they are objects in their own mental representation of the world" (Lewis, 2005, p. 363).

Late in the second year and early in the third year, toddlers show other emerging forms of self-awareness that reflect a sense of "me" (Goodvin, Thompson, & Winer, 2015). For example, they refer to themselves by saying "Me big"; they label internal experiences such as emotions; they monitor themselves, as when a toddler says, "Do it myself"; and they announce that things are theirs (Bullock & Lutkenhaus, 1990; Fasig, 2000).

Also, researchers recently have found that the capacity to understand others may begin to develop during infancy (Carpendale & Lewis, 2015; Rhodes & others, 2015). Research indicates that as early as 13 months of age, infants seem to consider another's perspective when predicting their actions (Choi & Luo, 2015).

Independence

Not only does the infant develop a sense of self in the second year of life, but independence also becomes a more central theme in the infant's life. Erikson (1968) stressed that independence is an important issue in the second year of life. Erikson's second stage of development is identified as autonomy versus shame and doubt. Autonomy builds as the infant's mental and motor abilities develop. At this point, not only can infants walk, but they can also climb, open and close, drop, push and pull, and hold and let go. Infants feel pride in these new accomplishments and want to do everything themselves, whether the activity is flushing a toilet, pulling the wrapping off a package, or deciding what to eat. It is important to recognize toddlers' motivation to do what they are capable of doing at their own pace. Then they can learn to control their muscles and their impulses themselves. Conversely, when caregivers are impatient and do for toddlers what they are capable of doing themselves, shame and doubt develop. To be sure, every parent has rushed a child from time to time, and one instance of rushing is unlikely to result in impaired development. It is only when parents consistently overprotect toddlers or criticize accidents (wetting, soiling, spilling, or breaking, for example) that children are likely to develop an excessive sense of shame and doubt about their ability to control themselves and their world.

Erikson also argued that the stage of autonomy versus shame and doubt has important implications for the development of independence and identity during adolescence. The development of autonomy during the toddler years gives adolescents the courage to be independent individuals who can choose and guide their own future.

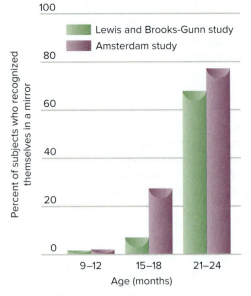

Figure 3 **The Development of Self-Recognition in Infancy**
The graph shows the findings of two studies in which infants less than 1 year of age did not recognize themselves in the mirror. A slight increase in the percentage of infant self-recognition occurred around 15 to 18 months of age. By 2 years of age, a majority of children recognized themselves. *Why do researchers study whether infants recognize themselves in a mirror?*
© Digital Vision/Getty Images RF

How Would You...?
As a **human development and family studies professional,** how would you work with parents who showed signs of being overly protective or critical to the point of impairing their toddler's autonomy?

Social Orientation and Attachment

So far, we have discussed how emotions and emotional competence change as children develop. We have also examined the role of emotional style; in effect, we have seen how emotions set the tone of our experiences in life. But emotions also write the lyrics because they are at the core of our interest in the social world and our relationships with others.

Social Orientation and Understanding

In Ross Thompson's (2006, 2014, 2015, 2016) view, infants are socioemotional beings who show a strong interest in their social world and are motivated to orient themselves toward it and to understand it. In earlier chapters we described many of the biological and cognitive foundations that contribute to the infant's development of social orientation and understanding. We will call attention to relevant biological and cognitive factors as we explore social orientation; locomotion; intention, goal-directed behavior and cooperation; and social referencing. Discussing biological, cognitive, and social processes together reminds us of an important aspect of development that was pointed out earlier—that these processes are intricately intertwined (Denham & Howarth, 2016).

Social Orientation

From early in their development, infants are captivated by the social world. Young infants are attuned to the sounds of human voices and stare intently at faces, especially their caregiver's face (Jakobsen, Umstead, & Simpson, 2016; Montirosso & others, 2015). As infants develop, they become adept at interpreting the meaning of facial expressions (Otte & others, 2015). Face-to-face play often begins to characterize caregiver-infant interactions when the infant is about 2 to 3 months of age. Such play reflects many mothers' motivation to create a positive emotional state in their infants (Laible, Thompson, & Froimson, 2015).

Infants also learn about the social world through contexts other than face-to-face play with a caregiver. Even though infants as young as 6 months show an interest in each other, their interaction with peers increases considerably in the latter half of the second year. Between 18 and 24 months, children markedly increase their imitative and reciprocal play—for example, imitating nonverbal actions like jumping and running (Eckerman & Whitehead, 1999). One study involved presenting 1- and 2-year-olds with a simple cooperative task that consisted of pulling a lever to get an attractive toy (Brownell, Ramani, & Zerwas, 2006) (see Figure 4). Any coordinated actions of the 1-year-olds appeared to be coincidental rather than cooperative, whereas the 2-year-olds' behavior was characterized as active cooperation to reach a goal.

Locomotion

Recall from earlier in the chapter how important independence is for infants, especially in the second year of life. As infants develop the ability to crawl, walk, and run, they are able to explore and expand their social world. These newly developed self-produced locomotor skills allow the infant to independently initiate social interchanges on a more frequent basis.

Figure 4 **The Cooperation Task**
The cooperation task consisted of two handles on a box, atop which was an animated musical toy, surreptitiously activated by remote control when both handles were pulled. The handles were placed far enough apart that one child could not pull both handles. The experimenter demonstrated the task, saying, "Watch! If you pull the handles, the doggie will sing" (Brownell, Ramani, & Zerwas, 2006).
© Celia A. Brownell, University of Pittsburgh

Locomotion is also important for its motivational implications (Adolph & Berger, 2015; Adolph & Robinson, 2015; Cole, Robinson, & Adolph, 2016). Once infants have the ability to move in goal-directed pursuits, the rewards gained from these pursuits lead to further efforts to explore and develop skills.

Intention, Goal-Directed Behavior, and Cooperation

The ability to perceive people as engaging in intentional and goal-directed behavior is an important social-cognitive accomplishment, and this initially occurs toward the end of the first year (Thompson, 2015, 2016). Joint attention and gaze-following help the infant understand that other people have intentions (Hoehl & Striano, 2015; Yu & Smith, 2016). By their first birthday, infants have begun to direct their caregiver's attention to objects that capture their interest (Heimann & others, 2006).

Infants' Social Sophistication and Insight

In sum, researchers are discovering that infants are more socially sophisticated and insightful at younger ages than was previously envisioned (Thompson, 2015, 2016). This sophistication and insight is reflected in infants' perceptions of others' actions as intentionally motivated and goal-directed and their motivation to share and participate in that intentionality by their first birthday (Tomasello, 2014). The more advanced social-cognitive skills of infants could be expected to influence their understanding and awareness of attachment to a caregiver.

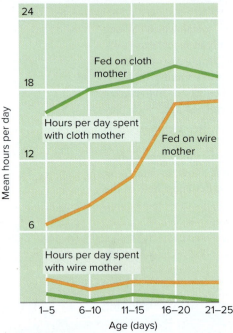

Figure 5 Contact Time with Wire and Cloth Surrogate Mothers
Regardless of whether the infant monkeys were fed by a wire or a cloth mother, they overwhelmingly preferred to spend contact time with the cloth mother. *How do these results compare with what Freud's theory and Erikson's theory would predict about human infants?*

© Martin Rogers/Getty Images

Attachment

Attachment is a close emotional bond between two people. There is no shortage of theories about infant attachment. Three theorists—Freud, Erikson, and Bowlby—proposed influential views of attachment.

Freud theorized that infants become attached to the person or object that provides them with oral satisfaction. For most infants, this is the mother, since she is most likely to feed the infant. Is feeding as important as Freud thought? A classic study by Harry Harlow (1958) indicates that the answer is no (see Figure 5).

Harlow removed infant monkeys from their mothers at birth; for six months they were fed by two surrogate (substitute) "mothers." One surrogate mother was made of wire, the other of cloth. Half of the infant monkeys were fed by the wire mother, half by the cloth mother. Periodically, the amount of time the infant monkeys spent with either the wire or the cloth mother was computed. Regardless of which mother fed them, the infant monkeys spent far more time with the cloth mother. Even if the wire mother, but not the cloth mother, provided nourishment, the infant monkeys spent more time with the cloth mother. And when Harlow frightened the monkeys, those who were "raised" by the cloth mother ran to that mother and clung to it; those who were raised by the wire mother did not. Whether the mother provided comfort seemed to determine whether the monkeys associated

attachment A close emotional bond between two people.

that mother with security. This study clearly demonstrated that feeding is not the crucial element in the attachment process and that contact comfort is important.

Physical comfort also plays a role in Erik Erikson's (1968) view of the infant's development. Recall Erikson's proposal that during the first year of life infants are in the stage of trust versus mistrust. Physical comfort and sensitive care, according to Erikson (1968), are key to establishing a basic level of trust during infancy. The infant's sense of trust, in turn, is the foundation for attachment and sets the stage for a lifelong expectation that the world will be a good and pleasant place.

The ethological perspective of British psychiatrist John Bowlby (1969, 1989) also stresses the importance of attachment in the first year of life and the responsiveness of the caregiver. Bowlby believed that both the infant and its primary caregivers are biologically predisposed to form attachments. He argued that the newborn is biologically equipped to elicit attachment behavior. The baby cries, clings, coos, and smiles. Later, the infant crawls, walks, and follows the mother. The immediate result is to keep the primary caregiver nearby; the long-term effect is to increase the infant's chances of survival (Thompson, 2006, 2015).

Attachment does not emerge suddenly but rather develops in a series of phases, moving from a baby's general preference for human figures to a partnership with primary caregivers. Following are four such phases based on Bowlby's conceptualization of attachment (Schaffer, 1996):

- *Phase 1: From birth to 2 months.* Infants instinctively direct their attachment to human figures. Strangers, siblings, and parents are equally likely to elicit smiling or crying from the infant.

- *Phase 2: From 2 to 7 months.* Attachment becomes focused on one figure, usually the primary caregiver, as the baby gradually learns to distinguish between familiar and unfamiliar people.

- *Phase 3: From 7 to 24 months.* Specific attachments develop. With increased locomotor skills, babies actively seek contact with regular caregivers, such as the mother or father.

- *Phase 4: From 24 months on.* Children become aware of other people's feelings, goals, and plans and begin to take these into account in directing their own actions.

Bowlby argued that infants develop an *internal working model* of attachment, a simple mental model of the caregiver, their relationship to him or her, and the self as deserving of nurturant care. The infant's internal working model of attachment with the caregiver influences the infant's, and later the child's, subsequent responses to other people (Cassidy, 2016; Roisman & Groh, 2011). The internal model of attachment also has played a pivotal role in the discovery of links between attachment and subsequent emotional understanding, conscious development, and self-concept (Bretherton & Munholland, 2016; Thompson, 2015, 2016).

Individual Differences in Attachment

Although attachment to a caregiver intensifies midway through the first year, isn't it likely that the quality of a baby's attachment varies? Mary Ainsworth (1979) thought so. Ainsworth created the **Strange Situation,** an observational measure of infant attachment in which the infant experiences a series of introductions, separations, and reunions with the caregiver and an adult stranger in a prescribed order. In using the Strange Situation, researchers hope that their observations will provide information about the infant's motivation to be near the caregiver and the degree to which the caregiver's presence provides the infant with security and confidence (Brownell & others, 2015; Solomon & George, 2016).

Based on how babies respond in the Strange Situation, they are described as being securely attached or insecurely attached (in one of three ways) to the caregiver:

- **Securely attached babies** use the caregiver as a secure base from which to explore the environment. When they are in the presence of

Strange Situation An observational measure of infant attachment that requires the infant to move through a series of introductions, separations, and reunions with the caregiver and an adult stranger in a prescribed order.

securely attached babies Babies that use the caregiver as a secure base from which to explore their environment.

their caregiver, securely attached infants explore the room and examine toys that have been placed in it. When the caregiver departs, securely attached infants might protest mildly; when the caregiver returns, these infants reestablish positive interaction with her, perhaps by smiling or climbing onto her lap. Subsequently, they often resume playing with the toys in the room.

- **Insecure avoidant babies** show insecurity by avoiding the caregiver. In the Strange Situation, these babies engage in little interaction with the caregiver, are not distressed when she leaves the room, usually do not reestablish contact with her upon her return, and may even turn their back on her. If contact is established, the infant usually leans away or looks away.

- **Insecure resistant babies** often cling to the caregiver and then resist her by fighting against the closeness, perhaps by kicking or pushing away. In the Strange Situation, these babies often cling anxiously to the caregiver and don't explore the playroom. When the caregiver leaves, they often cry loudly and then push away if she tries to comfort them upon her return.

- **Insecure disorganized babies** are disorganized and disoriented. In the Strange Situation, these babies might appear dazed, confused, and fearful. To be classified as disorganized, babies must show strong patterns of avoidance and resistance or display certain specified behaviors, such as extreme fearfulness around the caregiver.

What is the nature of secure and insecure attachment?

© George Doyle/
Stockbyte/Getty
Images RF

How Would You...?

As a **psychologist,** how would you identify an insecurely attached toddler? How would you encourage a parent to strengthen the attachment bond?

Do individual differences in attachment matter? Ainsworth proposed that secure attachment in the first year of life provides an important foundation for psychological development later in life. The securely attached infant moves freely away from the caregiver but keeps track of where she is through periodic glances. The securely attached infant responds positively to being picked up by others and, when put back down, freely moves away to play. An insecurely attached infant, by contrast, avoids the caregiver or is ambivalent toward her, fears strangers, and is upset by minor, everyday separations.

If early attachment to a caregiver is important, it should relate to a child's social behavior later in development. For some children, early attachments seem to foreshadow later functioning (Frazier & Scharf, 2015; Gander & Buchheim, 2015; Marvin, Britner, & Russell, 2016; Mesman, van IJzendoorn, & Sagi-Schwartz, 2016; Sroufe, 2016). In an extensive longitudinal study conducted by Alan Sroufe and his colleagues (2005), early secure attachment (assessed by the behavior during the Strange Situation at 12 and 18 months) was linked with positive emotional health, high self-esteem, self-confidence, and socially competent interaction with peers, teachers, camp counselors, and romantic partners through adolescence. Also, a recent meta-analysis found that secure attachment in infancy was linked to social competence with peers in childhood (Groh & others, 2014). Further, a recent study revealed that infant attachment

insecure avoidant babies Babies that show insecurity by avoiding their mothers.

insecure resistant babies Babies that often cling to the caregiver, then resist her by fighting against the closeness, perhaps by kicking or pushing away.

insecure disorganized babies Babies that show insecurity by being disorganized and disoriented.

To what extent might this adolescent girl's development be linked to how securely or insecurely attached she was during infancy?

(Top) © Westend61/Getty Images RF; (bottom) © iStockphoto.com/
Andrew Rich RF

insecurity (especially insecure resistant attachment) and early childhood behavioral inhibition predicted adolescent social anxiety symptoms (Lewis-Morrarty & others, 2015).

Few studies have assessed infants' attachment security to the mother and the father separately. However, a recent study revealed that infants who were insecurely attached to their mother and father ("double-insecure") at 15 months of age had more externalizing problems (out-of-control behavior, for example) in the elementary school years than their counterparts who were securely attached to at least one parent (Kochanska & Kim, 2013).

An important issue regarding attachment is whether infancy is a critical or sensitive period for development. The studies just described show continuity, with secure attachment in infancy predicting subsequent positive development in childhood and adolescence. For some children, though, there is little continuity. Not all research reveals the power of infant attachment to predict subsequent development (Hudson & others, 2016; Lamb & Lewis, 2015; Roisman & others, 2016; Thompson, 2015, 2016). In one longitudinal study, attachment classification in infancy did not predict attachment classification at 18 years of age (Lewis, Feiring, & Rosenthal, 2000). In this study, the best predictor of an insecure attachment classification at 18 was the occurrence of parental divorce in the intervening years. Consistently positive caregiving over a number of years is likely to be an important factor in connecting early attachment with the child's functioning later in development. Indeed, researchers have found that early secure attachment and subsequent experiences, especially maternal care and life stresses, are linked with children's later behavior and adjustment (Thompson, 2015, 2016). For example, a longitudinal study revealed that changes in attachment security/insecurity from infancy to adulthood were linked to stresses and supports in socioemotional contexts (Van Ryzin, Carlson, & Sroufe, 2011). These results suggest that attachment continuity may be a reflection of stable social contexts as much as early working models. The study just described (Van Ryzin, Carlson, & Sroufe, 2011) reflects an increasingly accepted view of the development of attachment and its influence on development. That is, it is important to recognize that attachment security in infancy does not always by itself produce long-term positive outcomes, but rather is linked to later outcomes through connections with the way children and adolescents subsequently experience various social contexts as they develop.

The Van Ryzin, Carlson, and Sroufe (2011) study reflects a **developmental cascade model,** which involves connections across domains over time that influence developmental pathways and outcomes (Cicchetti & Toth, 2015, 2016; Pasco-Fearon & others, 2016). Developmental cascades can include connections between a wide range of biological, cognitive, and socioemotional processes (attachment, for example), and also can involve social contexts such as families, peers, schools, and culture. Further, links can produce positive or negative outcomes at different points in development, such as infancy, early childhood, middle and late childhood, adolescence, and adulthood.

A recent meta-analysis supported the views just described (Pinquart, Feubner, & Ahnert, 2013). In this analysis of 127 research reports, the following conclusions were reached: (1) moderate stability of attachment security occurred from early infancy to adulthood; (2) no significant stability occurred for time intervals of more than 15 years; (3) attachment stability was greater when the time span was less than 2 years than when it was more than 5 years; and (4) securely attached children at risk were less likely to maintain attachment security while insecurely attached children at risk were likely to continue to be insecurely attached.

In addition to challenging whether secure attachment in infancy serves as a critical or sensitive period, some developmentalists argue that the secure attachment concept does not adequately consider certain biological factors in development, such as genes and temperament (Bakermans-Kranenburg & van IJzendoorn, 2016; Raby, Roisman, & Booth-Laforce, 2016; Simpson & Belsky, 2016; Vaughn & Bost, 2016). For example, Jerome Kagan (1987, 2002) points out that infants are highly resilient and adaptive; he argues that they are evolutionarily equipped to stay on a positive developmental course, even in the face of wide variations in parenting. Kagan and others stress that genetic characteristics and temperament play more important roles in a child's social competence than the attachment

developmental cascade model Involves connections across domains over time that influence developmental pathways and outcomes.

In the Hausa culture, siblings and grand-mothers provide a significant amount of care for infants. *How might these variations in care affect attachment?*

© Penny Tweedie/The Image Bank/Getty Images

theorists, such as Bowlby and Ainsworth, are willing to acknowl-edge (Bakermans-Kranenburg & van IJzendoorn, 2011). For example, if some infants inherit a low tolerance for stress, this, rather than an insecure attachment bond, may be responsible for an inability to get along with peers. One study found links between disorganized attachment in infancy, a specific gene, and levels of maternal responsiveness (Spangler & others, 2009). In this study, infants with the short version of the gene—serotonin transporter gene 5-HTTLPR—developed a disorganized attach-ment style only when mothers were slow or inconsistent in responding to them. However, some researchers have not found support for gene-environment interactions related to infant attach-ment (Fraley & others, 2013; Roisman & Fraley, 2013).

Another criticism of attachment theory is that it ignores the diversity of socializing agents and contexts that exists in an infant's world. A culture's value system can influence the nature of attachment (Mistry, Contreras, & Dutta, 2013). In northern Germany, for example, expectations for an infant's independence may be responsible for infants showing little distress upon a brief separation from the mother, whereas the Japanese mother's moti-vation for extremely close proximity to her infant may explain why Japanese infants become upset when they are separated from the mother. Also, in some cultures infants show attachments to many people. Among the Hausa (who live in Nigeria), both grandmothers and siblings provide a significant amount of care for infants (Harkness & Super, 1995). Infants in agricultural societies tend to form attachments to older siblings, who have major responsibility for their younger siblings' care. Researchers recognize the importance of competent, nurturant caregivers in an infant's development (Cicchetti & Toth, 2015, 2016; Grusec & Davidov, 2015). At issue, though, is whether or not secure attachment, especially to a single caregiver, is essential (Lamb & Lewis, 2015; Roisman & others, 2016; Thompson, 2015, 2016).

Despite such criticisms, there is ample evidence that security of attachment is important to development (Cassidy, 2016; Groh & others, 2014; Powell & others, 2014; Marvin, Britner, & Russell, 2016; Sroufe, 2016; Thompson, 2014, 2015, 2016). Secure attachment in infancy is important because it reflects a positive parent-infant relationship and provides a foundation that supports healthy socioemotional develop-ment in the years that follow.

Caregiving Styles and Attachment

Is the style of caregiving linked with the quality of the infant's attachment? Securely attached babies have caregivers who are sensitive to their signals and are consistently available to respond to the infant's needs (Pasco-Fearon & Belsky, 2016; Powell & oth-ers, 2014). These caregivers often let their babies take an active part in determining the onset and pacing of interactions in the first year of life. A recent study of 130 mother-infant dyads when infants were 7 months to 2 years of age found that maternal sensitivity and autonomy support predicted secure attachment (Bernier & others, 2014).

How do the caregivers of insecurely attached babies interact with them? Caregivers of avoidant babies tend to be unavailable or rejecting. They often don't respond to their babies' signals and have little physical contact with them. When they do interact with their babies, they may behave in an angry and irritable way. Caregivers of resis-tant babies tend to be inconsistent; sometimes they respond to their babies' needs, and sometimes they don't. In general, they tend not to be very affectionate with their babies and show little synchrony when interacting with them. Caregivers of disorganized babies often neglect or physically abuse them (Cicchetti & Toth, 2016).

How Would You...?

As a **health-care professional,** how would you use an infant's at-tachment style and/or a parent's caregiving style to determine whether an infant may be at risk for neglect or abuse?

Social Contexts

Now that we have explored the infant's emotional and personality development and attachment, let's examine the social contexts in which these occur. We begin by studying a number of aspects of the family and then turn to a social context in which infants increasingly spend time: child care.

The Family

The family can be thought of as a constellation of subsystems—a complex whole made up of interrelated, interacting parts—defined in terms of generation, gender, and role. Each family member participates in several subsystems (Parfitt, Pike, & Ayers, 2014). The father and child represent one subsystem, the mother and father another; the mother, father, and child represent yet another; and so on.

These subsystems have reciprocal influences on each other, as Figure 6 highlights (Maccoby, 2015). For example, Jay Belsky (1981) stresses that marital relations, parenting, and infant behavior and development can have both direct and indirect effects on each other. An example of a direct effect is the influence of the parents' behavior on the child. An indirect effect is how the relationship between the spouses mediates the way a parent acts toward the child. For example, marital conflict might reduce the efficiency of parenting, in which case marital conflict would indirectly affect the child's behavior (Cummings, Koss, & Cheung, 2015). The simple fact that two people are becoming parents may have profound effects on their relationship.

The Transition to Parenthood

Whether people become parents through pregnancy, adoption, or stepparenting, they face disequilibrium and must adapt to it. Parents want to develop a strong attachment with their infant, but they also want to maintain strong attachments to their spouse and friends, and possibly to continue their careers. Parents ask themselves how this new being will change their lives. A baby places new restrictions on partners; no longer will they be able to rush out to a movie at a moment's notice, and money may not be readily available for vacations and other luxuries. Dual-career parents ask, "Will it harm the baby to place her in child care? Will we be able to find responsible baby-sitters?"

In a longitudinal investigation of couples from late pregnancy until 3 years after the baby was born, couples enjoyed more positive marital relations before the baby was born than afterward (Cowan & Cowan, 2000; Cowan & others, 2005). Still, almost one-third reported an increase in marital satisfaction. Some couples said that the baby had both brought them closer together and moved them farther apart; being parents enhanced their sense of themselves and gave them a new, more stable identity as a couple. Babies opened men up to greater concern with intimate relationships, and the demands of juggling work and family roles stimulated women to manage family tasks more efficiently and pay attention to their own personal growth. The Bringing Home Baby project is a workshop for new parents that emphasizes strengthening their relationship with each other, understanding and becoming acquainted with their baby, resolving conflict, and developing parenting skills (Gottman, 2016). Evaluations of the project revealed that parents who participated became better able to work together as parents; fathers were more involved with their baby and sensitive to the baby's

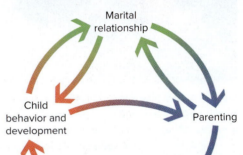

Figure 6

Interaction Between Children and Their Parents: Direct and Indirect Effects

© Katrina Wittkamp/ Photodisc/Getty Images RF

Marital relationship

Child behavior and development

Parenting

behavior; mothers had fewer symptoms of postpartum depression; and babies showed better overall development than was the case among parents and babies in a control group (Gottman, Gottman, & Shapiro, 2009).

Other recent studies have explored the transition to parenthood (Ferriby & others, 2015). One study revealed that mothers experienced unmet expectations in the transition to parenting, with fathers doing less than their partners had anticipated (Biehle & Mickelson, 2012). And in a recent study of dual-earner couples, a gender gap was not present prior to the transition to parenthood, but after a child was born, women did more than 2 hours of additional work per day compared with an additional 40 minutes for men (Yavorksy, Dush, & Schoppe-Sullivan, 2015).

Reciprocal Socialization

For many years, socialization was viewed as a one-way process: Children were considered to be the products of their parents' socialization techniques. According to more recent research, however, parent-child interaction is reciprocal (Nishamura, Kanakogi, & Myowa-Yamakoshi, 2016). **Reciprocal socialization** is socialization that is bidirectional. That is, children socialize their parents just as parents socialize their children (Maccoby, 2015). The types of behaviors involved in reciprocal socialization in infancy are temporally connected, mutually contingent behaviors such as one partner imitating the sound of another or the mother responding with a vocalization to the baby's arm

Caregivers often play games with infants such as peek-a-boo and pat-a-cake. *How is scaffolding involved in these games?*

(Left) © BrandXPictures/PunchStock RF; (right) © Stephanie Rausser/The Image Bank/Getty Images

movements. These reciprocal interchanges and mutual influence processes are sometimes referred to as *transactional* (Sameroff, 2009, 2012).

An important form of reciprocal socialization is **scaffolding,** in which parents time interactions in such a way that the infant experiences turn-taking with the parents. Scaffolding can be used to support children's efforts at any age.

The game peek-a-boo, in which parents initially cover their babies, then remove the covering, and finally register "surprise" at the babies' reappearance, reflects the concept of scaffolding. As infants become more skilled at this game, they gradually do some of the covering and uncovering themselves. Parents try to time their actions in such a way that the infant takes turns with the parent.

Increasingly, genetic and epigenetic factors are being studied to discover not only parental influences on children but also children's influence on parents (Avinun & Knafo-Noam, 2015; Bakermans-Kranenburg & van IJzendoorn, 2016). Recall that the *epigenetic view* emphasizes that development is the result of an ongoing, bidirectional interchange between heredity and the environment (Moore, 2015). For example, harsh, hostile parenting is associated with negative outcomes for children, such as being defiant and oppositional (Deater-Deckard, 2013). This likely reflects bidirectional influences rather than a unidirectional parenting effect. That is, the parents' harsh, hostile parenting and the children's defiant, oppositional behavior may mutually influence each other. In this bidirectional influence, the parents' and children's behavior may have genetic linkages as well as experiential connections.

reciprocal socialization Socialization that is bidirectional, meaning that children socialize parents, just as parents socialize children.

scaffolding Process in which parents time interactions so that infants experience turn-taking with their parents.

Managing and Guiding Infants' Behavior

In addition to sensitive parenting involving warmth and caring that can result in infants being securely attached to their parents, other important aspects of parenting infants involve managing and guiding their behavior in an attempt to reduce or eliminate undesirable behaviors (Holden, Vittrup, & Rosen, 2011). This management process includes (1) being proactive and childproofing the environment so infants won't encounter potentially dangerous objects or situations, and (2) engaging in corrective methods when infants engage in undesirable behaviors, such as excessive fussing and crying, throwing objects, and so on.

One study assessed discipline and corrective methods that parents had used by the time their infants were 12 and 24 months old (Vittrup, Holden, & Buck, 2006) (see Figure 7). Notice in Figure 7 that the main method parents used by the time infants were 12 months old was diverting the infants' attention, followed by reasoning, ignoring, and negotiating. Also note in Figure 7 that more than one-third of parents had yelled at their infant, about one-fifth had slapped the infant's hands or threatened the infant, and approximately one-sixth had spanked the infant by their first birthday.

As infants move into the second year of life and become more mobile and capable of exploring a wider range of environments, parental management of the toddler's behavior often triggers increased corrective feedback and discipline (Holden, Vittrup, & Rosen, 2011). As indicated in Figure 7, in the study just described, yelling increased from 36 percent at 1 year of age to 81 percent by 2 years of age, slapping the infant's hands increased from 21 percent at 1 year to 31 percent by age 2, and spanking increased from 14 percent at age 1 to 45 percent by age 2 (Vittrup, Holden, & Buck, 2006).

A special concern is that such corrective discipline tactics not become abusive. Too often what starts out as mild to moderately intense discipline on the part of parents can move into highly intense anger. Later, you will read more extensively about the use of punishment with children and child maltreatment.

Maternal and Paternal Caregiving

Much of our discussion of attachment has focused on mothers as caregivers. Do mothers and fathers differ in their caregiving roles? In general, mothers on average still spend considerably more time in caregiving with infants and children than do fathers (Blakemore, Berenbaum, & Liben, 2009). Mothers especially are more likely to engage in the managerial role with their children, coordinating their activities, making sure their health-care needs are met, and so on (Clarke-Stewart & Parke, 2014).

However, an increasing number of U.S. fathers stay home full-time with their children (Dette-Hagenmeyer, Erzinger, & Reichle, 2016; Lamb & Lewis, 2016). The number of stay-at-home dads in the United States was estimated to be two million in 2012 (Livingston, 2014). This figure represents a significant increase from 1.6 million in 2004 and 1.1 million in 1989.

A large portion of these full-time fathers have career-focused wives who are the primary providers of family income (O'Brien & Moss, 2010). One study revealed that the stay-at-home fathers were as satisfied with their marriage as traditional parents, although they indicated that they missed their daily life in the workplace (Rochlen & others, 2008). In this study, the stay-at-home fathers reported that they tended to be ostracized when they took their children to playgrounds and often were excluded from parent groups.

Method	12 Months	24 Months
Spank with hand	14	45
Slap infant's hand	21	31
Yell in anger	36	81
Threaten	19	63
Withdraw privileges	18	52
Time-out	12	60
Reason	85	100
Divert attention	100	100
Negotiate	50	90
Ignore	64	90

Figure 7 Parents' Methods for Managing and Correcting Infants' Undesirable Behavior

Shown here are the percentages of parents who had used various corrective methods by the time the infants were 12 and 24 months old.

Source: Vittrup, Holden, & Buck (2006).

An Aka pygmy father with his infant son. In the Aka culture, fathers were observed to be holding or near their infants 47 percent of the time (Hewlett, 1991).

© Barry S. Hewlett

Observations of fathers and their infants suggest that fathers have the ability to act as sensitively and responsively with their infants as mothers do (Lamb & Lewis, 2016). Consider the Aka pygmy culture in Africa, in which fathers spend as much time interacting with their infants as mothers do (Hewlett, 1991, 2000; Hewlett & MacFarlan, 2010). A recent study also found that marital intimacy and partner support during prenatal development were linked to father-infant attachment following childbirth (Yu & others, 2012). Remember, however, that although fathers can be active, nurturant, involved caregivers, as in the case of Aka pygmies, in many cultures men have not chosen to follow this pattern.

Do fathers interact with their infants differently from the way mothers do? Maternal interactions usually center on child-care activities—feeding, changing diapers, and bathing. Paternal interactions are more likely to include play, especially rough-and-tumble play (Lamb & Lewis, 2016). Fathers bounce infants, throw them up in the air, tickle them, and so on. Mothers also play with their infants, but their play is less physical and exciting than that of fathers.

Do children benefit when fathers are positively involved in their caregiving? A study of more than 7,000 children who were assessed from infancy to adulthood revealed that those whose fathers were extensively involved in their lives (such as engaging in various activities with them and showing a strong interest in their education) were more successful in school (Flouri & Buchanan, 2004). However, if fathers have mental health problems, they may not interact as effectively with their infants. A recent study revealed that depressed fathers focused more on their own needs than their infants' needs, and directed more negative and critical speech toward their infants (Sethna, Murray, & Ramchandani, 2012). Further, a recent study found that infants who showed a higher level of externalizing, disruptive problems at 1 year of age had fathers who displayed a low level of engagement with them as early as the third month of life (Ramchandani & others, 2013). And a recent study revealed that both fathers' and mothers' sensitivity assessed when infants were 10 to 12 months old were linked to children's cognitive development at 18 months and language development at 36 months (Malmberg & others, 2016).

Child Care

Many U.S. children today experience multiple caregivers. Most do not have a parent staying home to care for them; instead, the children receive "child care"—that is, some type of care provided by others. Many parents worry that child care will have adverse effects such as reducing their infants' emotional attachment to them, constraining their cognitive development, failing to teach them how to control anger, or allowing them to be unduly influenced by their peers. Are these concerns justified?

In the United States, approximately 15 percent of children age 5 and younger experience more than one child-care arrangement. One study of 2- and 3-year-old children revealed that an increase in the number of child-care arrangements the children experienced was linked to an increase in behavioral problems and a decrease in prosocial behavior (Morrissey, 2009).

Parental Leave

Today far more young children are in child care than at any other time in U.S. history. About 2 million children in the United States currently receive formal, licensed child care, and uncounted millions of children are cared for by unlicensed baby-sitters.

In part, these numbers reflect the fact that many U.S. adults do not receive paid leave from their jobs to care for their young children. Child-care policies around the world vary (Burchinal & others, 2015). Europe has led the way in creating new standards of parental leave: In 1992, the European Union (EU) mandated a paid 14-week maternity leave. In most European countries today, working parents on leave receive 70 to 100 percent of the worker's prior wage, and paid leave averages about 16 weeks (Tolani & Brooks-Gunn, 2008). The United States currently allows up to 12 weeks of unpaid leave for parents who are caring for a newborn.

Most countries restrict eligible benefits to women who have been employed for a minimum length of time prior to childbirth. In Denmark, however, even unemployed mothers are eligible for extended parental leave related to childbirth. In Germany, child-rearing leave is available to almost all parents. The Nordic countries (Denmark, Norway, and Sweden) have extensive gender-equity family leave policies for childbirth that emphasize the contributions of both women and men. For example, in Sweden parents can take an 18-month, job-protected parental leave with benefits to be shared by parents and applied to full-time or part-time work.

How are child-care policies in many European countries, such as Sweden, different from those in the United States?
© Matilda Lindeblad/Johner Images/Getty Images

Variations in Child Care

Because the United States does not have a policy of paid leave for child care, child care in the United States has become a major national concern (Lamb & Lewis, 2015). Many factors influence the effects of child care, including the age of the child, the type of child care, and the quality of the program.

The type of child care varies extensively (Burchinal & others, 2015; Hasbrouck & Pianta, 2016; Shivers & Farago, 2016). Child care is provided in large centers with elaborate facilities and in private homes. Some child-care centers are commercial operations; others are nonprofit centers run by churches, civic groups, and employers. Some child-care providers are professionals; others are untrained adults who want to earn extra money. Infants and toddlers are more likely to be found in family child care and informal care settings, while older children are more likely to be in child-care centers and preschool and early education programs. Figure 8 presents the primary care arrangements for U.S. children under age 5 with employed mothers (Clarke-Stewart & Miner, 2008).

Child-care quality makes a difference (Howes, 2016; Sanders & Guerra, 2016; Vu, 2016). A recent Australian study revealed that higher-quality child care that included positive child-caregiver relationships at 2 to 3 years of age was linked to children's better self-regulation of attention and emotion at 4 to 5 and 6 to 7 years of age (Gialamas & others, 2014). What constitutes a high-quality child-care program for infants? In high-quality child care (Clarke-Stewart & Miner, 2008, p. 273):

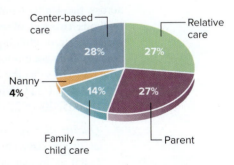

Figure 8 **Primary Care Arrangements in the United States for Children Under 5 Years of Age with Employed Mothers**

Caregivers encourage the children to be actively engaged in a variety of activities, have frequent, positive interactions that include smiling, touching, holding, and speaking at the child's eye level, respond properly to the child's questions or requests, and encourage children to talk about their experiences, feelings, and ideas.

High-quality child care also involves providing children with a safe environment, access to age-appropriate toys and participation in age-appropriate activities, and a low caregiver-child ratio that allows caregivers to spend considerable time with children on an individual basis.

Children are more likely to experience poor-quality child care if they come from families with few resources (psychological, social, and economic) (Carta & others, 2012). Many researchers have examined the role of poverty in quality of child care. One study found that extensive child care was harmful to low-income children only when the care was of low quality (Votruba-Drzal, Coley, & Chase-Lansdale, 2004). Even if the child was in child care more than 45 hours a week, high-quality care was associated with fewer internalizing problems (anxiety, for example) and externalizing problems (aggressive and destructive behaviors, for example). A recent study revealed that children from low-income families benefited in terms of school readiness and language development when their parents selected higher-quality child care (McCartney & others, 2007).

To read about one individual who provides quality child care to individuals from impoverished backgrounds, see *Careers in Life-Span Development*.

Careers in life-span development

Wanda Mitchell, Child-Care Director

Wanda Mitchell is the Center Director at the Hattie Daniels Day Care Center in Wilson, North Carolina. Her responsibilities include directing the operation of the center, which involves creating and maintaining an environment in which young children can learn effectively, and ensuring that the center meets state licensing requirements. Wanda obtained her undergraduate degree from North Carolina A&T University, majoring in Child Development. Prior to her current position, she had been an education coordinator for Head Start and an instructor at Wilson Technical Community College. Describing her chosen career, Wanda says, "I really enjoy working in my field. This is my passion. After graduating from college, my goal was to advance in my field."

Wanda Mitchell, child-care director, works with some of the children at her center.

© Wanda Mitchell

The National Longitudinal Study of Child Care

In 1991, the National Institute of Child Health and Human Development (NICHD) began a comprehensive longitudinal study of child-care experiences. Data were collected from a diverse sample of almost 1,400 children and their families at 10 locations across the United States over a period of seven years. Researchers used multiple methods (trained observers, interviews, questionnaires, and testing) and measured many facets of children's development, including physical health, cognitive development, and socioemotional development. Following are some of the results of what is now referred to as the NICHD Study of Early Child Care and Youth Development or NICHD SECCYD (NICHD Early Child Care Research Network, 2001, 2002, 2003, 2004, 2005, 2006, 2010).

- *Quality of care.* Evaluations of quality of care were based on characteristics such as group size, child–adult ratio, physical environment, caregiver characteristics (such as formal education, specialized training, and child-care experience), and caregiver behavior (such as sensitivity to children). An alarming conclusion is that a majority of the child care in the first three years of life was of unacceptably low quality. Positive caregiving by nonparents in child-care settings was infrequent—only 12 percent of the children in the study experienced positive nonparental child care (such as positive talk and language stimulation). Further, infants from low-income families experienced lower-quality child care than did infants from higher-income families. When quality of caregivers' care was high, children performed better on cognitive and language tasks, were more cooperative with their mothers during play, showed more positive and skilled interaction with peers, and had fewer behavior problems. Caregiver training and favorable child–staff ratios were linked with higher cognitive and social competence when children

What are some important findings from the national longitudinal study of child care conducted by the National Institute of Child Health and Human Development?
© Reena Rose Sibayan/The Jersey Journal/ Landov Images

were 54 months of age. In research involving the NICHD sample, links were found between nonrelative child care from birth to 4 years of age and adolescent development at 15 years of age (Vandell & others, 2010). In this analysis, better quality of early care was related to a higher level of academic achievement and a lower level of externalizing problems at age 15. In a recent study, high-quality infant-toddler child care was linked to better memory skills at the end of the preschool years (Li & others, 2013).

- *Amount of child care.* The quantity of child care predicted some outcomes (Vandell & others, 2010). When children spent extensive amounts of time in child care beginning in infancy, they experienced fewer sensitive interactions with their mothers, showed more behavior problems, and had higher rates of illness. In general, when children spent 30 hours or more per week in child care, their development was less than optimal. However, a recent study in Norway (a country that meets or exceeds 8 of 10 UNICEF benchmarks for quality child care) revealed that a high quantity of child care there was not linked to children's externalizing problems (Zachrisson & others, 2013).

- *Family and parenting influences.* The influence of families and parenting was not weakened by extensive child care. Parents played a significant role in helping children regulate their emotions. Especially important parenting influences were being sensitive to children's needs, being involved with children, and providing cognitive stimulation. Indeed, parental sensitivity has been the most consistent predictor of secure attachment (Friedman, Melhuish, & Hill, 2010). An important final point about the extensive NICHD SECCYD research is that findings have consistently shown that family factors are considerably stronger and more consistent predictors of a wide variety of child outcomes than are child-care experiences (quality, quantity, type). The worst outcomes for children occur when both home and child-care settings are of poor quality. For example, a recent study involving the NICHD SECCYD data revealed that worse socioemotional outcomes (more problem behavior, lower levels of prosocial behavior) for children occurred when they experienced both home and child-care environments that conferred risk (Watamura & others, 2011).

What are some strategies parents can follow in regard to child care? Child-care expert Kathleen McCartney (2003, p. 4) offers this advice:

- *Recognize that the quality of your parenting is a key factor in your child's development.*

- *Make decisions that will improve the likelihood that you will be good parents.* "For some this will mean

How Would You...?

As a **psychologist,** based on the findings from the NICHD study, how would you advise parents about their role in their child's development versus the role of non-parental child care?

working full-time"—for personal fulfillment, income, or both. "For others, this will mean working part-time or not working outside the home."

- *Monitor your child's development.* "Parents should observe for themselves whether their children seem to be having behavior problems." They should also talk with child-care providers and their pediatrician about their child's behavior.

- *Take some time to find the best child care.* Observe different child-care facilities and be certain that you like the one you choose. "Quality child care costs money, and not all parents can afford the child care they want."

Summary

Emotional and Personality Development

- Emotion is feeling, or affect, that occurs when a person is in a state or an interaction that is important to them. Infants display a number of emotions early in their development, such as by crying, smiling, and showing fear. Two fears that infants develop are stranger anxiety and fear of separation from a caregiver. As infants develop, it is important for them to increase their ability to regulate their emotions.

- Temperament is an individual's behavioral style and characteristic way of responding emotionally. Chess and Thomas classified infants as (1) easy, (2) difficult, or (3) slow to warm up. Kagan proposed that inhibition to the unfamiliar is an important temperament category. Rothbart and Bates emphasized that effortful control (self-regulation) is an important temperament dimension. Goodness of fit can be an important aspect of a child's adjustment.

- Erikson argued that an infant's first year is characterized by the stage of trust versus mistrust. Independence becomes a central theme in the second year of life, which is characterized by the stage of autonomy versus shame and doubt.

Social Orientation and Attachment

- Infants show a strong interest in the social world and are motivated to understand it. Infants are more socially sophisticated and insightful at an earlier age than was previously thought.

- Attachment is a close emotional bond between two people. In infancy, contact comfort and trust are important in the development of attachment. Securely attached babies use the caregiver, usually the mother, as a secure base from which to explore their environment. Three types of insecure attachment are avoidant, resistant, and disorganized. Caregivers of securely attached babies are more sensitive to the babies' signals and are consistently available to meet their needs.

Social Contexts

- The transition to parenthood requires considerable adaptation and adjustment on the part of parents. Children socialize parents just as parents socialize children. Parents use a wide range of methods to manage and guide infants' behavior. In general, mothers spend more time in caregiving than fathers do; fathers tend to engage in more physical, playful interaction with infants than mothers do.

- The quality of child care is uneven, and child care remains a controversial topic. Quality child care can be achieved and seems to have few adverse effects on children.

Key Terms

anger cry	emotion	reciprocal socialization	social referencing
attachment	goodness of fit	reflexive smile	social smile
basic cry	insecure avoidant babies	scaffolding	Strange Situation
developmental cascade model	insecure disorganized babies	securely attached babies	stranger anxiety
difficult child	insecure resistant babies	separation protest	temperament
easy child	pain cry	slow-to-warm-up child	

5 Physical and Cognitive Development in Early Childhood

© Christopher Futcher/E+/Getty Images RF

CHAPTER OUTLINE

PHYSICAL CHANGES
Body Growth and Change
The Brain
Motor Development
Nutrition and Exercise
Illness and Death

COGNITIVE CHANGES
Piaget's Preoperational Stage
Vygotsky's Theory
Information Processing

LANGUAGE DEVELOPMENT
Understanding Phonology and Morphology
Changes in Syntax and Semantics
Advances in Pragmatics
Young Children's Literacy

EARLY CHILDHOOD EDUCATION
Variations in Early Childhood Education
Education for Young Children Who Are Disadvantaged
Controversies in Early Childhood Education

Stories of Life-Span Development: Reggio Emilia's Children

The Reggio Emilia approach is an educational program for young children that was developed in the northern Italian city of Reggio Emilia. Children of single parents and children with disabilities have priority in admission; other children are admitted according to a scale of needs. Parents pay on a sliding scale based on income.

The children are encouraged to learn by investigating and exploring topics that interest them (Bredekamp, 2017). A wide range of stimulating media and materials are available for children to use as they learn music, movement, drawing, painting, sculpting, collage, puppetry, and photography, among other things (Bond, 2015).

In this program, children often explore topics in a group, which fosters a sense of community, respect for diversity, and a collaborative approach to problem solving (Jones & Reynolds, 2011). In this group setting, two co-teachers guide the children in their exploration. The Reggio Emilia teachers treat each project as an adventure. It can start from an adult's suggestion, from a child's idea, or from an unexpected event such as a snowfall. Every project is based on what the children say and do. The teachers allow children enough time to plan and craft a project.

At the core of the Reggio Emilia approach is an image of children who are competent and have rights, especially the right to outstanding care and education. Parent participation

137

is considered essential, and cooperation is a major theme in the schools. Many experts on early childhood education believe that the Reggio Emilia approach provides a supportive, stimulating context in which children are motivated to explore their world in a competent and confident manner (Morrison, 2017; Vatalaro, Szente, & Levin, 2015).

Parents and educators who clearly understand how young children develop can play an active role in creating programs that foster their natural interest in learning, rather than stifling it. In this chapter, the first of two chapters on early childhood (ages 3 to 5), we explore the physical, cognitive, and language changes that typically occur as the toddler develops into the preschooler, and then we look at early childhood education. ■

In a Reggio Emilia classroom, young children explore topics that interest them.
© Ruby Washington/The New York Times/Redux Pictures

Physical Changes

Earlier, we described a child's growth in infancy as rapid and following cephalocaudal and proximodistal patterns. Fortunately, the growth rate slows in early childhood; otherwise, we would be a species of giants.

Body Growth and Change

Despite the slowing of growth in height and weight that characterizes early childhood, this growth is still the most obvious physical change during this period of development. Yet unseen changes in the brain and nervous system are no less significant in preparing children for advances in cognition and language.

The average child grows 2½ inches in height and gains between 5 and 7 pounds a year during early childhood. As the preschool child grows older, the percentage of increase in height and weight decreases with each additional year (Goldstone & Reynolds, 2014; Marcdante & Kliegman, 2015). Girls are only slightly smaller and lighter than boys during these years, a difference that continues until puberty. In addition, girls have more fatty tissue than boys, and boys have more muscle tissue than girls.

During the preschool years, both boys and girls slim down as the trunk of the body lengthens (Kliegman & others, 2016). Although the head is still somewhat large for the body, by the end of the preschool years most children have lost the top-heavy look they had as toddlers. Body fat also shows a slow, steady decline during the preschool years. The chubby baby often looks much leaner by the end of early childhood.

Growth patterns vary from one individual to another (Ball, Bindler, & Cowen, 2014). Think back to your preschool years. That was probably the first time you noticed that some children were taller than you, some shorter; some were fatter, some thinner; some were stronger, some weaker. Much of the variation was due to heredity, but environmental experiences were also involved (Barstow & Rerucha, 2015). A review of the height and weight of children around the world concluded that the two most important contributors to height differences are ethnic origin and nutrition (Meredith, 1978). Urban, middle-socioeconomic status, and firstborn children were taller than rural, lower-socioeconomic status, and later-born children. In the United States, African American children are also taller than White children.

The bodies of 5-year-olds and 2-year-olds are different. Notice that the 5-year-old not only is taller and weighs more, but also has a longer trunk and legs than the 2-year-old. *Can you think of some other physical differences between 2- and 5-year-olds?*
© Michael H/Digital Vision/Getty Images RF

The Brain

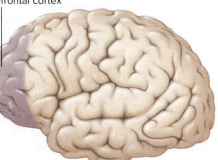

Prefrontal cortex

One of the most important physical developments during early childhood is the continuing development of the brain and other parts of the nervous system (Bell & Cuevas, 2015). The increasing maturation of the brain, combined with opportunities to experience a widening world, contribute to children's emerging cognitive abilities. In particular, changes in the brain during early childhood enable children to plan their actions, attend to stimuli more effectively, and make considerable strides in language development.

Although the brain does not grow as rapidly during early childhood as in infancy, it does undergo remarkable changes. By repeatedly obtaining brain scans of the same children for up to four years, researchers have found that children's brains experience rapid, distinct spurts of growth (Gogtay & Thompson, 2010). The overall size of the brain does not increase dramatically from ages 3 to 5; what does change dramatically are local patterns within the brain. The amount of brain material in some areas can nearly double in as little as a year, followed by a dramatic loss of tissue as unneeded cells are pruned and the brain continues to reorganize itself. From 3 to 6 years of age the most rapid growth in the brain takes place in the part of the frontal lobes known as the *prefrontal cortex* (see Figure 1)*,* which plays a key role in planning and organizing new actions and maintaining attention to tasks (Gogtay & Thompson, 2010).

The continuation of two changes that began before birth contributes to the brain's growth during early childhood. First, the number and size of dendrites increase, and second, myelination continues. Recall that **myelination** is the process through which axons (nerve fibers that carry signals away from the cell body) are covered with a layer of fat cells, which increases the speed and efficiency of information traveling through the nervous system. Myelination is important in the development of a number of abilities (Croteau-Chonka & others, 2016). For example, myelination in the areas of the brain related to hand-eye coordination is not complete until about age 4. Myelination in the areas of the brain related to focusing attention is not complete until the end of middle or late childhood. And myelination of many aspects of the prefrontal cortex, especially those involving higher-level thinking skills, is not completed until late adolescence or emerging adulthood (Casey, 2015; de Haan & Johnson, 2016; Galvan & Tottenham, 2016; Monahan & others, 2016). In a recent study, young children with higher cognitive ability showed increased myelination by 3 years of age (Deoni & others, 2016).

Recently, researchers have found that contextual factors such as poverty and parenting quality are linked to the development of the brain (Meyer & others, 2015). In one study, children from the poorest homes had significant maturational lags in their frontal and temporal lobes at 4 years of age, and these lags were associated with lower school readiness skills (Hair & others, 2015). In another study, higher levels of maternal sensitivity in early childhood were associated with higher total brain volume (Kok & others, 2015).

Figure 1 The Prefrontal Cortex The brain pathways and circuitry involving the prefrontal cortex (shaded in purple) show significant advances in development during middle and late childhood. *What cognitive processes are linked with these changes in the prefrontal cortex?*

Motor Development

Running as fast as you can, falling down, getting right back up and running just as fast as you can . . . building towers with blocks . . . scribbling, scribbling, and scribbling some more . . . cutting paper with scissors . . . During your preschool years, you probably developed the ability to perform all these activities. What physical changes made this possible?

Gross Motor Skills

myelination The process by which axons are covered and insulated with a layer of fat cells, which increases the speed at which information travels through the nervous system.

The preschool child no longer has to make an effort simply to stay upright and move around. As children move their legs with more confidence and carry themselves more purposefully, moving around in the environment becomes more automatic (Ball, Bindler, & Cowen, 2014).

Around age 3, children enjoy simple movements such as hopping, jumping, and running back and forth, just for the sheer delight of performing them. They delight in showing how they can run across a room and jump all of 6 inches. The run-and-jump will win no Olympic medals, but for the 3-year-old it brings considerable pride and a sense of accomplishment.

At age 4, children are still enjoying the same kinds of activities, but they have become more adventurous. They scramble over low jungle gyms as they display their athletic prowess. Although they have been able to climb stairs with one foot on each step for some time, they are just beginning to be able to come down the same way.

By age 5, children are even more adventuresome than when they were 4. It is not unusual for self-assured 5-year-olds to perform hair-raising stunts on playground equipment. Five-year-olds also run hard and enjoy races with each other and their parents.

Fine Motor Skills

By the time they turn 3, children have had the ability to pick up the tiniest objects between their thumb and forefinger for some time, but they are still somewhat clumsy at it. Three-year-olds can build surprisingly high block towers, each block placed with intense concentration but often not in a completely straight line. When 3-year-olds play with a simple jigsaw puzzle, they are rather rough in placing the pieces. Even when they recognize the hole a piece fits into, they are not very precise in positioning the piece. They often try to force the piece into the hole or pat it vigorously.

By age 4, children's fine motor coordination has improved substantially and is much more precise. Sometimes 4-year-olds have trouble building high towers with blocks because, in their desire to place each of the blocks perfectly, they may upset those already in the stack. Fine motor coordination continues to improve so that by age 5, hand, arm, and body all move together under better command of the eye. Mere towers no longer interest the 5-year-old, who now wants to build a house or a church, complete with steeple, though adults might still need to be told what each finished project is meant to be.

Nutrition and Exercise

Eating habits are important aspects of development during early childhood (Blake, 2017; Sorte, Daeschel, & Amador, 2017). What children eat affects their skeletal growth, body shape, and susceptibility to disease. Exercise and physical activity are also very important aspects of young children's lives (Powers & Dodd, 2017; Wuest & Fisette, 2015).

Overweight Young Children

What are some trends in the eating habits and weight of young children?
© Lilian Perez/Corbis

Being overweight has become a serious health problem in early childhood (Hutchinson, Emerick, & Saxena, 2016; Xue & Xue, 2016). A national study revealed that 45 percent of children's meals exceed recommendations for saturated and trans fat, which can raise cholesterol levels and increase the risk of heart disease (Center for Science in the Public Interest, 2008). This study also found that one-third of children's daily caloric intake comes from restaurants, twice the percentage consumed away from home in the 1980s. Further, 93 percent of almost 1,500 possible choices at 13 major fast-food chains exceeded 430 calories—one-third of what the National Institute of Medicine recommends that 4- to 8-year-old children consume in a day. Nearly all of the children's meal offerings at KFC, Taco Bell, Sonic, Jack in the Box, and Chick-fil-A were too high in calories. Also, a study of U.S. 2- and 3-year-olds found that French fries and other fried potatoes were the vegetable they were most likely to consume (Fox & others, 2010).

How Would You...?

As a **health-care professional,** how would you work with parents to increase the nutritional value of meals and snacks they provide to their young children?

Young children's eating behavior is strongly influenced by their caregivers' behavior (Jarman & others, 2015; Sorte, Daeschel, & Amador, 2017; Tan & Holub, 2015). Children's eating behavior improves when caregivers eat with children on a predictable schedule, model eating healthy food, make mealtimes pleasant occasions, and engage in certain feeding styles (Silva Garcia & others, 2016; Steinsbekk, Belsky, & Wichstrom, 2016). Distractions created by television, family arguments, and competing activities should be minimized so that children can focus on eating. Experts recommend a sensitive, responsive caregiver feeding style, in which the caregiver is nurturant, provides clear information about what is expected, and responds appropriately to children's cues (Black & Lozoff, 2008). Forceful and restrictive caregiver behaviors are not recommended, as they can lead to excessive weight gain (Micaly & others, 2016; Rollins & others, 2016).

The Centers for Disease Control and Prevention (2016) has categories for obesity, overweight, and at risk for being overweight. These categories are determined by body mass index (BMI), which is computed using a formula that takes into account height and weight. Children and adolescents at or above the 97th percentile are classified as obese; those at the 95th or 96th percentile as overweight; and those from the 85th to the 94th percentile as at risk of being overweight.

The percentages of young children who are overweight or at risk of being overweight in the United States have increased dramatically in recent decades, but in the last several years there are indications that fewer preschool children are obese (Wardlaw, Smith, & Collene, 2015). In 2009–2010, 12.1 percent of U.S. 2- to 5-year-olds were classified as obese, compared with 5 percent in 1976–1980 and 10.4 percent in 2007–2008 (Ogden & others, 2012). However, in 2011–2012, a substantial drop (43 percent) in the obesity rate of 2- to 5-year-old children occurred in comparison with their counterparts in 2003–2004 (Ogden & others, 2014). In 2011–2012, 8 percent of 2- to 5-year-olds were obese compared with 14 percent in 2004. It is not clear why this drop occurred, but among the possible explanations are families buying lower-calorie foods and being influenced by the Special Supplementation Program for Women, Infants, and Children (which subsidizes food for women and children in low-income families) that emphasizes consuming less fruit juice, cheese, and eggs and more whole fruits and vegetables.

The risk that overweight children will continue to be overweight when they are older was documented in a recent U.S. study of nearly 8,000 children (Cunningham, Kramer, & Narayan, 2014). In this study, overweight 5-year-olds were four times more likely to be obese at 14 years of age than their 5-year-old counterparts who began kindergarten at a normal weight. Also, in the recent study described earlier in which obesity was reduced in preschool children, the children who were obese were five times more likely to be overweight or obese in adulthood (Ogden & others, 2014).

A comparison of 34 countries revealed that the United States had the second highest rate of childhood obesity (Janssen & others, 2005). Childhood obesity contributes to a number of health problems in young children (Faguy, 2016; Small & Aplasca, 2016). For example, physicians are now seeing type 2 (adult-onset) diabetes (a condition directly linked with obesity and a low level of fitness) in children as young as age 5 (Chaturvedi & others, 2014). We will have much more to consider about children's eating behavior and weight status later.

Many aspects of children's lives can contribute to becoming overweight or obese. Prevention of obesity in children includes helping children, parents, and teachers see food as a way to satisfy hunger and meet nutritional needs, not as proof of love or as a reward for good behavior (Fedewa, 2015; Steinsbekk, Belsky, & Wichstrom, 2016). Routine physical activity should be a daily occurrence (Street, Wells, & Hills, 2015). A recent research study also found that viewing as little as one hour of television daily was associated with an increase in body mass index (BMI) between kindergarten and first grade (Peck & others, 2015).

Malnutrition

Poor nutrition affects many young children from low-income families. Many of these children do not obtain essential amounts of iron, vitamins, or protein. Poor nutrition is a particular concern in the lives of infants from low-income families.

To address this problem in the United States, the WIC (Women, Infants, and Children) program provides federal grants to states for healthy supplemental foods, health-care referrals, and nutrition education for women from low-income families beginning in pregnancy, and to infants and young children up to 5 years of age who are at nutritional risk (Kennedy & Guthrie, 2016). WIC serves approximately 7,500,000 participants in the United States. Positive influences on infants' and young children's nutrition and health, as well as mothers' health, have been found for participants in WIC (Chiasson & others, 2016; Reat & others, 2015). For example, a multiple-year literacy intervention with Spanish-speaking families in the WIC program in Los Angeles increased literacy resources and activities at home, which in turn led to a higher level of school readiness in children (Whaley & others, 2011). And in recent longitudinal studies, when mothers participated prenatally and in early childhood in WIC programs, young children showed short-term cognitive benefits and longer-term reading and math benefits (Jackson, 2015).

Exercise

Young children should engage in physical activity every day (Cruz & others, 2016; Innella & others, 2016; Wuest & Fisette, 2015). Recently, four expert panels from Australia, Canada, the United Kingdom, and the United States issued physical activity guidelines for young children that were quite similar (Pate & others, 2015). The guidelines recommend that young children get an average of 15 or more minutes of physical activity per hour over a 12-hour period, or about 3 hours per day total. These guidelines reflect an increase from earlier guidelines (National Association for Sport and Physical Education, 2002). The child's life should center on activities, not meals (Janssen, 2014; Rowland, 2016). Following are some recent research studies that examine young children's exercise and activities:

- In preschoolers, more time spent in vigorous physical activity was strongly linked to a lower probability of being overweight or obese (Collings & others, 2013).

- Observations of 3- to 5-year-old children during outdoor play at preschools revealed that the preschool children were mainly sedentary even when participating in outdoor play (Brown & others, 2009). In this study, throughout the day the preschoolers were sedentary 89 percent of the time, engaged in light activity 8 percent of the time, and participated in moderate to vigorous physical activity only 3 percent of the time.

- A research review of 17 studies concluded that exercise was an effective strategy for reducing body fat in overweight and obese children (Kelley & Kelley, 2013).

- Preschool children's physical activity was enhanced by family members engaging in sports together and by parents' perception that it was safe for their children to play outside (Beets & Foley, 2008).

- Incorporation of a "move and learn" physical activity curriculum increased the activity level of 3- to 5-year-old children in a half-day preschool program (Trost, Fees, & Dzewaltowski, 2008).

- Sixty minutes of physical activity per day in preschool academic contexts improved early literacy (Kirk & Kirk, 2016).

How Would You...?

As a **health-care professional,** how would you advise parents who want to get their talented 4-year-old child into a soccer league for preschool children?

How much physical activity should preschool children engage in per day?
© RubberBall Productions/ Getty Images RF

Illness and Death

The vast majority of children in the United States go through the physical changes just described and reach adulthood without serious illness or death. However, some do not. In the United States accidents are the leading cause of death in young children, followed by cancer and cardiovascular disease (National Center for Health Statistics, 2015). In addition to motor vehicle accidents, other accidental deaths in children involve drowning, falls, and poisoning.

Children's safety is influenced not only by their own skills and safety-related behaviors but also by characteristics of their family and home, school and peers, and community (Shah & others, 2015; Sharma & Ford-Jones, 2015). Figure 2 describes steps that can be taken in each of these contexts to enhance children's safety and prevent injury (Sleet & Mercy, 2003).

One major danger to children is parental smoking (Mason, Wheeler, & Brown, 2015; Mbulo & others, 2016). An estimated 22 percent of children and adolescents in the United States are exposed to tobacco smoke in the home. A recent study found that children living in low-income families are more likely to be exposed to environmental tobacco smoke than their counterparts in middle-income families (Kit & others, 2013). An increasing number of studies indicate that children are at risk for health problems when they live in homes in which a parent smokes (Sheehan & Phipatanakul, 2015). Children exposed to tobacco smoke in the home are more likely to develop wheezing and asthma than are children in homes where no one smokes (Hur, Liang, & Lin, 2014). Another study revealed that exposure to secondhand smoke was related to young children's sleep problems, including sleep-disordered breathing (Yolton & others, 2010). Researchers have also found that maternal cigarette smoking and alcohol consumption when children were 5 years of age were linked to children subsequently engaging in early onset of smoking in adolescence (Hayatbakhsh & others, 2013).

Although accidents and serious illnesses such as cancer are the leading causes of death among children in the United States, this is not the case in a number of other countries in the world, where many children die of preventable infectious diseases. Many of the deaths of young children around the world could be prevented by a reduction in poverty and improvements in nutrition, sanitation, education, and health services (UNICEF, 2016). High poverty rates have devastating effects on the health of a country's young children, as they often experience lives of hunger, malnutrition, illness, inadequate access to health care, unsafe water, and a lack of protection from harm (Mace, 2016; UNICEF, 2016). In the last decade, there has been a dramatic increase in the number of young children who have died because of HIV/AIDS transmitted to them by their parents. Deaths of young children due to HIV/AIDS especially occur in countries with high rates of poverty and low levels of education (UNICEF, 2016).

How Would You...?

As a **health-care professional,** how would you talk with parents about the impact of secondhand smoke on children's health to encourage parents to stop smoking?

Many children in impoverished countries die before reaching the age of 5 from dehydration and malnutrition brought about by diarrhea. *What are some of the other main causes of death in young children around the world?*
© Kent Page/AP Images

Individual

Development of social skills and ability to regulate emotions

Impulse control (such as not darting out into a street to retrieve a ball)

Frequent use of personal protection (such as bike helmets and safety seats)

Family/Home

High awareness and knowledge of child management and parenting skills

Frequent parent protective behaviors (such as use of child safety seats)

Presence of home safety equipment (such as smoke alarms and cabinet locks)

School/Peers

Promotion of home/school partnerships

Absence of playground hazards

Injury prevention and safety promotion policies and programs

Community

Availability of positive activities for children and their parents

Active surveillance of environmental hazards

Effective prevention policies in place (such as pool fencing)

Figure 2
Characteristics That Enhance Young Children's Safety
In each context of a child's life, steps can be taken to create conditions that enhance the child's safety and reduce the likelihood of injury. *How are the contexts listed in the figure related to Bronfenbrenner's theory?*

Cognitive Changes

The cognitive world of the preschool child is creative, free, and fanciful. Preschool children's imaginations work overtime, and their mental grasp of the world improves. Our coverage of cognitive development in early childhood focuses on three theories: Piaget's, Vygotsky's, and information processing.

Piaget's Preoperational Stage

Remember that during Piaget's first stage of development, the sensorimotor stage, the infant becomes increasingly able to organize and coordinate sensations and perceptions with physical movements and actions. The **preoperational stage,** which lasts from approximately age 2 to 7, is the second stage in Piaget's theory. In this stage, children begin to represent the world with words, images, and drawings. They form stable concepts and begin to reason. At the same time, the young child's cognitive world is dominated by egocentrism and magical beliefs.

Because Piaget called this stage "preoperational," it might sound like an unimportant waiting period. Not so. However, the label *preoperational* emphasizes that the child does not yet perform **operations,** which are reversible mental actions that allow children to do mentally what before they could do only physically. Mentally adding and subtracting numbers are examples of operations. *Preoperational thought* is the beginning of the ability to reconstruct in thought what has been established in behavior. It can be divided into two substages: the symbolic function substage and the intuitive thought substage.

The Symbolic Function Substage

The **symbolic function substage** is the first substage of preoperational thought, occurring roughly between the ages of 2 and 4. In this substage, the young child gains the ability to mentally represent an object that is not present. This ability vastly expands the child's mental world (Lillard & Kavanaugh, 2014; Mandler & DeLoache, 2012). In this substage, children use scribble designs to represent people, houses, cars, clouds, and so on; they begin to use language more effectively and engage in pretend play. However, although young children make distinct progress during this substage, their thinking still has important limitations, two of which are egocentrism and animism.

Egocentrism is the inability to distinguish between one's own perspective and someone else's perspective. The following telephone conversation between 4-year-old Marie, who is at home, and her father, who is at work, typifies Marie's egocentric thought:

Father: Marie, is Mommy there?
Marie silently nods.

Father: Marie, may I speak to Mommy?
Marie nods again, silently.

Marie's response is egocentric in that she fails to consider her father's perspective before replying. A nonegocentric thinker would have responded verbally.

Piaget and Barbel Inhelder (1969) initially studied young children's egocentrism by devising the three mountains task (see Figure 3). The child walks around the model of the mountains and becomes familiar with what the mountains look like from different perspectives, and she can see that there are different objects on the mountains. The child is then seated on one side of the table on which the mountains are placed. The experimenter moves a doll to different locations around the table, and at each location asks the child to select from a series of photos the one that most accurately reflects the view that the doll is seeing. Children in the preoperational stage often pick their own view rather than the doll's view. Preschool children frequently show the ability to take another's perspective on some tasks but not others.

preoperational stage Piaget's second stage, lasting from about 2 to 7 years of age, during which children begin to represent the world with words, images, and drawings, and symbolic thought goes beyond simple connections of sensory information and physical action; stable concepts are formed, mental reasoning emerges, egocentrism is present, and magical beliefs are constructed.

operations In Piaget's theory, these are internalized, reversible sets of actions that allow children to do mentally what they formerly did physically.

symbolic function substage Piaget's first substage of preoperational thought, in which the child gains the ability to mentally represent an object that is not present (between about 2 and 4 years of age).

egocentrism The inability to distinguish between one's own perspective and someone else's (salient feature of the first substage of preoperational thought).

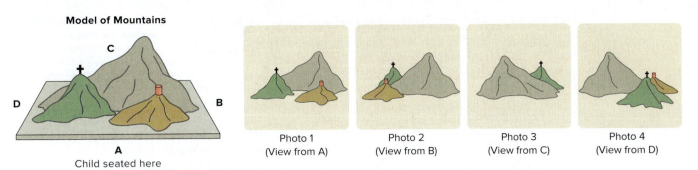

Model of Mountains

C

D · B

A
Child seated here

Photo 1
(View from A)

Photo 2
(View from B)

Photo 3
(View from C)

Photo 4
(View from D)

Figure 3 The Three Mountains Task

Photo 1 shows the child's perspective from where he or she is sitting (location A). Photos 2, 3, and 4 show what the mountains would look like to a person sitting at locations B, C, and D, respectively. When asked to choose the photograph that shows what the mountains looks like from position B, the preoperational child selects a photograph taken from location A, the child's view at the time. A child who thinks in a preoperational way cannot take the perspective of a person sitting at another spot.

Animism, another limitation of preoperational thought, is the belief that inanimate objects have lifelike qualities and are capable of action. A young child might show animism by saying, "That tree pushed the leaf off, and it fell down," or "The sidewalk made me mad; it made me fall down." A young child who shows animism fails to distinguish among appropriate and inappropriate occasions for using human perspectives.

The Intuitive Thought Substage

The **intuitive thought substage** is the second substage of preoperational thought, occurring between ages 4 and 7. In this substage, children begin to use primitive reasoning and want to know the answers to all sorts of questions. Consider 4-year-old Terrell, who is at the beginning of the intuitive thought substage. Although he is starting to develop his own ideas about the world he lives in, his ideas are still simple, and he is not very good at thinking things out. He has difficulty understanding events that he knows are taking place but that he cannot see. His fantasized thoughts bear little resemblance to reality. He cannot yet answer the question "What if?" in any reliable way. For example, he has only a vague idea of why he needs to avoid getting hit by a car. He also has difficulty negotiating traffic because he cannot do the mental calculations necessary to estimate whether an approaching car will hit him when he crosses the road.

By age 5 children have just about exhausted the adults around them with "why" questions. The child's questions signal the emergence of interest in reasoning and in figuring out why things are the way they are. Following are some samples of the questions children ask during the intuitive thought substage (Elkind, 1976): "What makes you grow up?" "Why does a woman have to be married to have a baby?" "Who was the mother when everybody was a baby?" "Why do leaves fall?" "Why does the sun shine?"

Piaget called this substage *intuitive* because young children seem so sure about their knowledge and understanding, yet are unaware of how they know what they know. That is, they know something but know it without the use of rational thinking and are sometimes wrong as a result.

Centration and the Limits of Preoperational Thought

Another limitation of preoperational thought is **centration,** a centering of attention on one characteristic to the exclusion of all others. Centration is most clearly evidenced in young children's lack of **conservation;** that is, they lack the awareness that altering an object or substance's appearance does not change its basic properties. For example, to adults it is obvious that a certain amount of liquid remains the same when it is poured from one container to another, regardless of the containers' shapes. But this is not at all obvious to young children.

The situation that Piaget devised to study conservation is his most famous task. In the conservation task, children are presented with two

animism The belief that inanimate objects have lifelike qualities and are capable of action.

intuitive thought substage Piaget's second substage of preoperational thought, in which children begin to use primitive reasoning and want to know the answers to all sorts of questions (between about 4 and 7 years of age).

centration The focusing of attention on one characteristic to the exclusion of all others.

conservation In Piaget's theory, awareness that altering an object's or a substance's appearance does not change its basic properties.

identical beakers, each filled to the same level with liquid (see Figure 4). They are asked if these beakers contain the same amount of liquid, and they usually say yes. Then the liquid from one beaker is poured into a third beaker, which is taller and thinner than the first two. The children are then asked if the amount of liquid in the tall, thin beaker is equal to that which remains in one of the original beakers. Children who are less than 7 or 8 years old usually say no and justify their answers in terms of the differing height or width of the two beakers. They are typically struck by the height of the liquid in a tall, narrow container and focus on that characteristic to the exclusion of others. Older children usually answer yes and justify their answers appropriately ("If you poured the water back, the amount would still be the same").

In Piaget's theory, failing the conservation of liquid task is a sign that children are at the preoperational stage of cognitive development. The failure demonstrates not only centration but also inability to mentally reverse actions. For example, in the conservation of matter example shown in Figure 5, preoperational children say that the longer shape contains more clay because they assume that "longer is more." Preoperational children cannot mentally reverse the clay-rolling process to see that the amount of clay is the same in both the shorter ball shape and the longer stick shape.

In addition to failing to conserve volume, preoperational children fail to conserve number, matter, length, and area. However, children often vary in their performance on different conservation tasks. Thus, a child might be able to conserve volume but not number.

Some developmental psychologists do not believe that Piaget was entirely correct in his estimate of when children's conservation skills emerge. For example, Rochel Gelman (1969) showed that when children's attention to relevant aspects of the conservation task is improved, they are more likely to conserve. Gelman has also demonstrated that attentional training on one dimension, such as number, improves preschool children's performance on another dimension, such as mass. Thus, Gelman believes that conservation appears earlier than Piaget thought and that attention is especially important in explaining conservation.

How Would You...?

As a **human development and family studies professional,** how would you explain the child's response in the following scenario: A parent gives a 3-year-old a cookie. The child says, "I want two cookies." The parent breaks the cookie in half and hands the two pieces to the child, who happily accepts them.

Vygotsky's Theory

Like Piaget, Vygotsky was a constructivist, but Vygotsky's theory is a **social constructivist approach,** and it emphasizes the social contexts of learning and the construction of knowledge through social interaction. In Vygotsky's view, children's cognitive

Figure 4 Piaget's Conservation Task
The beaker test is a well-known Piagetian test to determine whether a child can think operationally—that is, can mentally reverse actions and show conservation of the substance. (a) Two identical beakers, A and B, are presented to the child. Then the experimenter pours the liquid from B into C, which is taller and thinner than A or B. (b) The child is asked if these beakers (A and C) have the same amount of liquid. The preoperational child says "no." When asked to point to the beaker that has more liquid, the preoperational child points to the tall, thin beaker.
© Tony Freeman/PhotoEdit

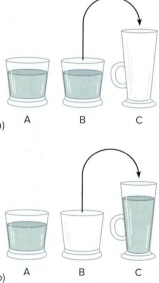

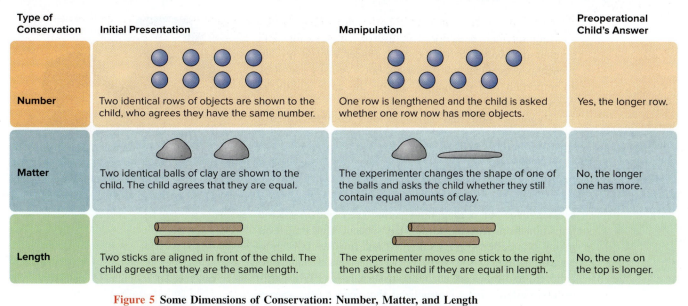

Type of Conservation	Initial Presentation	Manipulation	Preoperational Child's Answer
Number	Two identical rows of objects are shown to the child, who agrees they have the same number.	One row is lengthened and the child is asked whether one row now has more objects.	Yes, the longer row.
Matter	Two identical balls of clay are shown to the child. The child agrees that they are equal.	The experimenter changes the shape of one of the balls and asks the child whether they still contain equal amounts of clay.	No, the longer one has more.
Length	Two sticks are aligned in front of the child. The child agrees that they are the same length.	The experimenter moves one stick to the right, then asks the child if they are equal in length.	No, the one on the top is longer.

Figure 5 Some Dimensions of Conservation: Number, Matter, and Length

What characteristics of preoperational thought do children demonstrate when they fail these conservation tasks?

development depends on the tools provided by society and their minds are shaped by the cultural context in which they live (Gauvain & Perez, 2015; Roth, 2016; Yasnitsky & Van der Veer, 2016). Earlier, we described some basic elements of Vygotsky's theory. Here we expand on his theory, exploring his ideas about the zone of proximal development, scaffolding, and the young child's use of language.

The Zone of Proximal Development and Scaffolding

Vygotsky's belief in the importance of social influences, especially instruction, on children's cognitive development is reflected in his concept of the zone of proximal development. **Zone of proximal development (ZPD)** is Vygotsky's term for the range of tasks that are too difficult for the child to master alone but can be learned with the guidance and assistance of adults or more-skilled children. Thus, the lower limit of the ZPD is the level of skill reached by the child working independently. The upper limit is the level of additional responsibility the child can accept with the assistance of an able instructor (see Figure 6). The ZPD captures the child's cognitive skills that are in the process of maturing and can be accomplished only with the assistance of a more-skilled person (Holzman, 2016). Vygotsky (1962) called these the "buds" or "flowers" of development, to distinguish them from the "fruits" of development, which the child can already accomplish independently.

What are some factors that can influence the effectiveness of the ZPD in children's learning and development? Researchers have found that the ZPD's effectiveness can be enhanced by factors such as the following (Gauvain, 2013): better emotion regulation, secure attachment, absence of maternal depression, and child compliance.

Closely linked to the idea of the ZPD is the concept of scaffolding, introduced earlier in the context of parent-infant interaction. *Scaffolding* means changing the level of support. Over the course of a teaching session, a more-skilled person (a teacher or advanced peer) adjusts the amount of guidance to fit the child's current performance (Holzman, 2016). When the student is learning a new task, the skilled person may use direct instruction. As the student's competence increases, less guidance is given. A recent study found that scaffolding techniques that heightened engagement, encouraged direct exploration, and facilitated "sense-making," such as guided play, improved 4- to 5-year-old children's acquisition of geometric knowledge (Fisher & others, 2013).

Language and Thought

According to Vygotsky, children use speech not only for social communication but also to help them solve tasks. Vygotsky (1962) further

zone of proximal development (ZPD) Vygotsky's term for tasks that are too difficult for children to master alone but can be mastered with assistance.

believed that young children use language to plan, guide, and monitor their behavior. This use of language for self-regulation is called *private speech.* Piaget viewed private speech as egocentric and immature, but Vygotsky saw it as an important tool of thought during the early-childhood years (Alderson-Day & Fernyhough, 2014).

Vygotsky said that language and thought initially develop independently of each other and then merge. He emphasized that all mental functions have external, or social, origins. Children must use language to communicate with others before they can focus inward on their own thoughts. Children also must communicate externally and use language for a long time before they can make the transition from external to internal speech. This transition period occurs between ages 3 and 7 and involves talking to oneself. After a while, self-talk becomes second nature to children, and they can act without verbalizing. When this occurs, children have internalized their egocentric speech in the form of *inner speech,* which becomes their thoughts.

Vygotsky saw children who use a lot of private speech as more socially competent than those who don't. He argued that private speech represents an early transition toward becoming more socially communicative. For Vygotsky, when young children talk to themselves they are using language to govern their behavior and guide themselves. For example, a child working on a puzzle might say to herself, "Which pieces should I put together first? I'll try those green ones first. Now I need some blue ones. No, that blue one doesn't fit there. I'll try it over here." Researchers have found support for Vygotsky's view that private speech plays a positive role in children's development (Winsler, Carlton, & Barry, 2000). Children use private speech more often when tasks are difficult, when they have made errors, and when they are not sure how to proceed (Berk, 1994). Researchers have also found that children who use private speech are more attentive and improve their performance more than do children who do not use private speech (Berk & Spuhl, 1995).

Upper limit

Level of additional responsibility child can accept with assistance of an able instructor

Zone of proximal development (ZPD)

Lower limit

Level of problem solving reached on these tasks by child working alone

Figure 6 Vygotsky's Zone of Proximal Development
Vygotsky's zone of proximal development has a lower limit and an upper limit. Tasks in the ZPD are too difficult for the child to perform alone. They require assistance from an adult or a more-skilled child. As children experience the verbal instruction or demonstration, they organize the information in their existing mental structures so they can eventually perform the skill or task alone.

© Jose Luis Pelaez, Inc./Blend Images/ Getty Images RF

How Would You...?

As an **educator,** how would you apply Vygotsky's ZPD theory and the concept of scaffolding to help a young child complete a puzzle?

Teaching Strategies Based on Vygotsky's Theory

Vygotsky's theory has been embraced by many teachers and has been successfully applied to education (Adams, 2015). Here are some ways in which educators can apply Vygotsky's theory:

1. *Assess the child's ZPD.* Like Piaget, Vygotsky did not believe that formal, standardized tests are the best way to assess children's learning. Rather, Vygotsky argued that assessment should focus on determining the child's zone of proximal development. The skilled helper presents the child with tasks of varying difficulty to determine the best level at which to begin instruction.

2. *Use the child's zone of proximal development in teaching.* Teaching should begin near the zone's upper limit, so that the child can reach the goal with help and move to a higher level of skill and knowledge. Offer just enough assistance. You might ask, "What can I do to help you?" Or simply observe the child's intentions and attempts, providing support only when it is needed.

3. *Use more-skilled peers as teachers.* Remember that it is not just adults who are important in helping children learn. Children also benefit from the support and guidance of more-skilled children.

4. *Monitor and encourage children's use of private speech.* Be aware of the developmental change from talking to oneself externally when solving a problem during the preschool years to talking to oneself privately in the early elementary school years. In the elementary school years, encourage children to internalize and self-regulate their talk to themselves.

5. *Place instruction in a meaningful context.* Educators today are moving away from abstract presentations of material, instead providing students with opportunities to experience learning in real-world settings. For example, instead of just memorizing math formulas, students work on math problems that have real-world implications.

With Vygotsky's theory in mind, let's examine an early childhood program that reflects these concepts. Tools of the Mind is an early-childhood education curriculum that emphasizes children's development of self-regulation and the cognitive foundations of literacy. The curriculum was created by Elena Bodrova and Deborah Leong (2007, 2015) and has been implemented in more than 200 classrooms. Most of the children in the Tools of the Mind programs are considered at risk of academic failure because of their living circumstances, which in many instances are characterized by poverty and other difficult conditions such as being homeless and having parents with drug problems.

Tools of the Mind is grounded in Vygotsky's (1962) theory, with special attention to cultural tools and the development of self-regulation, the zone of proximal development, scaffolding, private speech, shared activity, and play as important activity. In a Tools of the Mind classroom, dramatic play has a central role. Teachers guide children in creating themes that are based on the children's interests, such as treasure hunt, store, hospital, and restaurant. Teachers also incorporate field trips, visitor presentations, videos, and books in the development of children's play. They help children develop a play plan, which increases the maturity of their play. Play plans describe what the children expect to do in the play period, including the imaginary context, roles, and props to be used. The play plans increase the quality of their play and self-regulation.

Scaffolding children's writing is another important theme in the Tools of the Mind classroom. Teachers guide children in planning their own message by drawing a line to stand for each word the child says. Children then repeat the message, pointing to each line as they say the word. Then the child writes on the lines, trying to represent each word with some letters or symbols.

Research assessments of children's writing in Tools of the Mind classrooms revealed that they have more advanced writing skills than do children in other early childhood programs (Bodrova & Leong, 2007, 2015). For example, they write more complex messages, use more words, spell more accurately, show better letter recognition, and have a better understanding of the concept of a sentence. Also, one study assessed the effects of the Tools of the Mind curriculum on at-risk preschool children (Diamond & others, 2007). The results indicated that the Tools of the Mind curriculum improved the self-regulatory and cognitive control skills (such as resisting distractions and temptations) of such children. Other research on the Tools of the Mind curriculum has found that it improves young children's cognitive skills (Barnett & others, 2006; Saifer, 2007).

Evaluating Vygotsky's Theory

How does Vygotsky's theory compare with Piaget's? We already have mentioned several comparisons, such as Vygotsky's emphasis on the importance of inner speech in cognitive development and Piaget's view that such speech is immature. Figure 7 compares the two theories. The implication of Piaget's theory for teaching is that children need support to explore their world and discover knowledge. The main implication of Vygotsky's theory is that students need many opportunities to learn with a teacher and more-skilled peers (Gauvain, 2016). In both theories, teachers serve as facilitators and guides rather than as directors and molders (Borich, 2014).

	Vygotsky	Piaget
Sociocultural Context	Strong emphasis	Little emphasis
Constructivism	Social constructivist	Cognitive constructivist
Stages	No general stages of development proposed	Strong emphasis on stages (sensorimotor, preoperational, concrete operational, and formal operational)
Key Processes	Zone of proximal development, language, dialogue, tools of the culture	Schema, assimilation, accommodation, operations, conservation, classification
Role of Language	A major role; language plays a powerful role in shaping thought	Language has a minimal role; cognition primarily directs language
View on Education	Education plays a central role, helping children learn the tools of the culture	Education merely refines the child's cognitive skills that have already emerged
Teaching Implications	Teacher is a facilitator and guide, not a director; establish many opportunities for children to learn with the teacher and more-skilled peers	Also views teacher as a facilitator and guide, not a director; provide support for children to explore their world and discover knowledge

Figure 7 **Comparison of Vygotsky's and Piaget's Theories**

(Left) © A.R. Lauria / Dr. Michael Cole, Laboratory of Human Cognition, University of California, San Diego; (right) © Bettmann/Corbis

Even though their theories were proposed at about the same time, most of the world learned about Vygotsky's theory later than they did about Piaget's, so Vygotsky's theory has not yet been evaluated as thoroughly. Vygotsky's view of the importance of sociocultural influences on children's development fits with the current belief that it is important to evaluate contextual factors in learning (Muller Mirza, 2016; Yasnitsky & Van der Veer, 2016).

Some critics say that Vygotsky was not specific enough about age-related changes (Gauvain & Perez, 2015). Another criticism is that he overemphasized the role of language in thinking. His emphasis on collaboration and guidance also has potential pitfalls. Might facilitators be too helpful in some cases, as when a parent becomes overbearing and controlling? Further, some children might become lazy and expect help when they could have done something on their own.

Information Processing

Piaget's and Vygotsky's theories provided important ideas about how young children think and how their thinking changes. More recently, the information-processing approach has generated research that illuminates how children process information during the preschool years (Siegler, 2016a, b; Siegler & others, 2015). What are the limitations and advances in young children's ability to pay attention to their environment, to remember, to develop strategies and solve problems, and to understand their own mental processes and those of others?

Attention

Recall that we defined *attention* as the focusing of mental resources on select information. The child's ability to pay attention improves significantly during the preschool years (Rothbart & Posner, 2015). Toddlers wander around, shift attention from one activity to another, and seem to spend little time focused on any one object or event. By comparison, the preschool child might be observed watching television for half an hour. However, one study revealed that television watching and video game playing were both linked to attention problems in children (Swing & others, 2010).

Young children especially make advances in two aspects of attention: executive attention and sustained attention (Bell & Cuevas, 2015). **Executive attention** involves planning actions, allocating attention to goals, detecting and compensating for errors, monitoring progress on tasks, and dealing with novel or difficult circumstances. **Sustained attention,** also referred to as *vigilance,* is focused and extended engagement with an object, task, event, or other aspect of the environment. Research indicates that although older children and adolescents show increases in vigilance, it is during the preschool years that individuals show the greatest increase in vigilance (Rothbart & Posner, 2015). A recent study found that preschool sustained attention was linked to a greater likelihood of completing college at 25 years of age (McClelland & others, 2013).

In at least two ways, however, the preschool child's control of attention is still deficient:

What are some advances in children's attention in early childhood?
© BananaStock/PunchStock RF

1. *Salient versus relevant dimensions.* Preschool children are likely to pay attention to stimuli that stand out, or are *salient,* even when those stimuli are not relevant to solving a problem or performing a task. For example, if a flashy, attractive clown presents the directions for solving a problem, preschool children are likely to pay more attention to the clown than to the directions. After age 6 or 7, children attend more efficiently to the dimensions of the task that are relevant, such as the directions for solving a problem. This change reflects a shift to cognitive control of attention, so that children act less impulsively and reflect more.

2. *Planfulness.* When experimenters ask children to judge whether two complex pictures are the same, preschool children tend to use a haphazard comparison strategy, not examining all the details before making a judgment. By comparison, elementary-school-age children are more likely to systematically compare the details across the pictures, one detail at a time (Vurpillot, 1968).

In central European countries such as Hungary, kindergarten children participate in exercises designed to improve their attention (Posner & Rothbart, 2007). For example, in one eye-contact exercise, the teacher sits in the center of a circle of children and each child is required to catch the teacher's eye before being permitted to leave the group. In other exercises created to improve attention, teachers have children participate in stop-go activities during which they have to listen for a specific signal, such as a drumbeat or an exact number of rhythmic beats, before stopping the activity.

Computer exercises recently have been developed to improve children's attention (Rothbart & Posner, 2015; Stevens & Bavelier, 2012). For example, one study revealed that five days of computer exercises that involved learning how to use a joystick, relying on working memory, and resolving conflict improved the attention of 4- to 6-year-old children (Rueda, Posner, & Rothbart, 2005). Although not commercially available, further information about computer exercises for improving children's attention can be downloaded from www.teach-the-brain.org/learn/attention/index.

executive attention Involves planning actions, allocating attention to goals, detecting and compensating for errors, monitoring progress on tasks, and dealing with novel or difficult circumstances.

sustained attention Also referred to as vigilance; involves focused and extended engagement with an object, task, event, or other aspect of the environment.

The ability of preschool children to control and sustain their attention is related to school readiness (Rothbart & Posner, 2015). For example, a study of more than 1,000 children revealed that their ability to sustain their attention at 54 months of age was linked to their school readiness (which included achievement and language skills) (NICHD Early Child Care Research Network, 2005). A later study showed that children whose parents and teachers rated them higher on a scale of having attention problems at 54 months of age had a lower level of social skills in peer relations in the first and third grades than their counterparts who were rated lower on the attention problems scale (NICHD Early Child Care Research Network, 2009).

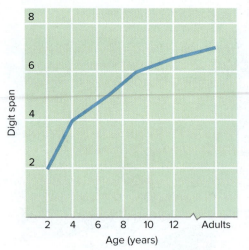

And in yet another study, the ability to focus attention better at age 5 was linked to a higher level of school achievement at age 9 (Razza, Martin, & Brooks-Gunn, 2012).

Memory

Memory—the retention of information over time—is a central process in children's cognitive development. Most of an infant's memories are fragile and, for the most part, short-lived—except for the memory of perceptual-motor actions, which can be substantial (Bauer & Leventon, 2015). Thus, to understand the infant's capacity to remember, we need to distinguish *implicit memory* from *explicit memory*. Explicit memory itself, however, comes in many forms. One distinction is between relatively permanent or *long-term memory* and short-term memory.

Figure 8 Developmental Changes in Memory Span In one study, from 2 to 7 years of age children's memory span increased from 2 digits to about 5 digits (Dempster, 1981). Between 7 and 13 years of age, memory span had increased on average only another 1½ digits, to about 7 digits. *What factors might contribute to the increase in memory span during childhood?*

Short-Term Memory In **short-term memory,** individuals retain information for up to 30 seconds if there is no rehearsal of the information. Using *rehearsal* (repeating information after it has been presented), we can keep information in short-term memory for a much longer period. One method of assessing short-term memory is the memory-span task. You hear a short list of stimuli—usually digits—presented at a rapid pace (one per second, for example). Then you are asked to repeat the digits.

Research with the memory-span task suggests that short-term memory increases during early childhood. For example, in one investigation memory span increased from about 2 digits in 2- to 3-year-old children to about 5 digits in 7-year-old children, yet between ages 7 and 13 memory span increased by only 1½ digits (Dempster, 1981) (see Figure 8). Keep in mind, though, that memory span varies from one individual to another.

Why does memory span change with age? Rehearsal of information is important; older children rehearse the digits more than younger children do. Also important are efficiency of processing and speed, especially the speed with which memory items can be identified (Schneider, 2011).

The speed-of-processing explanation highlights a key point in the information-processing perspective: The speed with which a child processes information is an important aspect of the child's cognitive abilities, and there is abundant evidence that the speed with which many cognitive tasks are completed improves dramatically during the childhood years (Rose, Feldman, & Jankowski, 2015). A recent study found that myelination (the process by which the sheath that encases axons helps electrical signals travel faster down the axon) in a number of brain areas was linked to young children's processing speed (Chevalier & others, 2015).

How Accurate Are Young Children's Long-Term Memories? Just as toddlers' short-term memory span increases during the early childhood years, their memory also becomes more accurate. Young children can remember a great deal of information if they are given appropriate cues and prompts (Bruck & Ceci, 2012). Increasingly, young children are even being allowed to testify in court, especially if they are the only witnesses to abuse or a crime (Lamb & others, 2015). Several factors can influence the accuracy of a young child's memory, however (Bruck & Ceci, 1999):

- *There are age differences in children's susceptibility to suggestion.* Preschoolers are the most suggestible age group (Lehman & others, 2010). For example, preschool children are more susceptible to believing misleading or incorrect information given after an event (Ghetti & Alexander, 2004). Despite these age differences, there is still concern about the reaction of older children when they are subjected to suggestive interviews (Brown & Lamb, 2016).

- *There are individual differences in susceptibility.* Some preschoolers are highly resistant to interviewers' suggestions, whereas others immediately succumb to the slightest suggestion (Ceci, Hritz, & Royer, 2016).

short-term memory The memory component in which individuals retain information for up to 30 seconds, assuming there is no rehearsal of the information.

- *Interviewing techniques can produce substantial distortions in children's reports about highly salient events.* Children are suggestible not just about peripheral details but also about the central aspects of an event. In some cases, children's false reports can be tinged with sexual connotations. In laboratory studies, young children have made false claims about "silly events" that involved body contact (such as "Did the nurse lick your knee?" or "Did she blow in your ear?"). A significant number of preschool children have falsely reported that someone touched their private parts, kissed them, or hugged them, when these events clearly did not happen. Nevertheless, young children are capable of recalling much that is relevant about an event (Lamb & others, 2015). When young children do recall information accurately, the interviewer often has a neutral tone and avoids asking misleading questions, and there is no reason for the child to make a false report.

In sum, the accuracy of a young child's eyewitness testimony may depend on a number of factors, such as the type, number, and intensity of the suggestive techniques the child has experienced (Andrews, Lamb, & Lyon, 2016; Lamb & others, 2015). It appears that the reliability of young children's reports has as much to do with the skills and motivation of the interviewer as with any natural limitations on young children's memory (Bruck & Ceci, 2012; Ceci, Hritz, & Royer, 2016).

Autobiographical Memory Another aspect of long-term memory that has been extensively studied in children's development is autobiographical memory (Pathman, Doydum, & Bauer, 2013; Valentino & others, 2014). *Autobiographical memory* involves memory of significant events and experiences in one's life. You are engaging in autobiographical memory when you answer questions such as: Who was your first-grade teacher and what was s/he like? What is the most traumatic event that happened to you as a child?

During the preschool years, young children's memories increasingly take on more autobiographical characteristics (Bauer, 2015; Bauer & Larkina, 2016). In some areas, such as remembering a story, a movie, a song, or an interesting event or experience, young children have been shown to have reasonably good memories. From 3 to 5 years of age, they (1) increasingly remember events as occurring at a specific time and location, such as "on my birthday at Chuck E. Cheese's last year" and (2) include more elements that are rich in detail in their narratives (Bauer, 2013). In one study, children went from using 4 descriptive items per event at 3½ years of age to 12 such items at 6 years of age (Fivush & Haden, 1997).

Executive Function

Recently, increased interest has been directed toward the development of children's **executive function,** an umbrella-like concept that encompasses a number of higher-level cognitive processes linked to the development of the brain's prefrontal cortex (Cassidy, 2016; Groppe & Elsner, 2016; Moriguchi, Chevalier, & Zelazo, 2016). Executive function involves managing one's thoughts to engage in goal-directed behavior and exercise self-control. Earlier in this chapter, we described the recent interest in *executive attention*, which comes under the umbrella of executive function.

In early childhood, executive function especially involves developmental advances in cognitive inhibition (such as inhibiting a strong tendency that is incorrect), cognitive flexibility (such as shifting attention to another item or topic), goal-setting (such as sharing a toy or mastering a skill like catching a ball), and delay of gratification (the ability to forego an immediate pleasure or reward for a more desirable one later) (Griffin, Freund, & McCardle, 2015; Muller & Kerns, 2015). During early childhood, the relatively stimulus-driven toddler is transformed into a child capable of flexible, goal-directed problem solving that characterizes executive function (Zelazo & Muller, 2011). Figure 9 describes a research study on young children's executive function (Carlson & White, 2011).

Walter Mischel and his colleagues (Berman & others, 2013; Mischel, 2014; Mischel, Cantor, & Feldman, 1996; Mischel & Moore, 1980; Mischel & others, 2011; Schlam & others, 2013) have conducted a number of studies of delay of gratification with young children. One way they assess delay of

executive function An umbrella-like concept that consists of a number of higher-level cognitive processes linked to the development of the brain's prefrontal cortex. Executive function involves managing one's thoughts to engage in goal-directed behavior and to use self-control.

Figure 9 Studying Executive Function in Young Children

Researcher Stephanie Carlson has conducted a number of research studies on young children's executive function. In one study, young children were read either *Planet Opposite*—a fantasy book in which everything is turned upside down—or *Fun Town*—a reality-oriented fiction book (Carlson & White, 2011). After being read one of the books, the young children completed the Less Is More Task, in which they were shown two trays of candy—one with 5 pieces, the other with 2—and told that the tray they pick will be given to the stuffed animal seated at the table. Sixty percent of the 3-year-olds who heard the *Planet Opposite* story gave away the five pieces of candy compared with only 20 percent of their counterparts who heard the more straightforward story. The results indicated that learning about a topsy-turvy imaginary world likely helped the young children become more flexible in their thinking.

© Dawn Villella Photography

gratification is to place a young child alone in a room with an alluring cookie that is within their reach. The children are told that they either can ring a bell at any time and eat the cookie or they can wait until the experimenter returns and then receive two cookies. For the young children who waited for the experimenter to return, what did they do to help them wait? They engaged in a number of strategies to distract their attention from the cookie, including singing songs, picking their noses—anything to keep from looking at the cookie. Mischel and his colleagues labeled these strategies "cool thoughts" (that is, doing non-cookie-related thoughts and activities), whereas they said the young children who looked at the cookie were engaging in "hot thoughts." The young children who engaged in cool thoughts were more likely to eat the cookie later or wait until the experimenter returned to the room. In one study using the delay of gratification task just described, longer delay of gratification at 4 years of age was linked to a lower body mass index (BMI) three decades later (Schlam & others, 2013).

Researchers have found that advances in executive function in the preschool years are linked with math skills, language development, and school readiness (Ursache, Blair, & Raver, 2012). A recent study revealed that executive function skills predicted mathematical gains in kindergarten (Fuhs & others, 2014). Another recent study of young children also revealed that executive function was associated with their emergent literacy and vocabulary development (Becker & others, 2014). And a recent study found that young children who showed delayed development of executive function had a lower level of school readiness (Willoughby & others, 2016).

Parents and teachers play important roles in the development of executive function (Cuevas & others, 2014). Ann Masten and her colleagues (Herbers & others, 2011; Masten, 2013; Masten & others, 2008) have found that executive function and parenting skills are linked to homeless children's success in school. Masten believes that executive function and good parenting skills are related. In her words, "When we see kids with good executive function, we often see adults around them that are good self-regulators. . . . Parents model, they support, and they scaffold these skills" (Masten, 2012, p. 11). A recent study revealed that secure attachment to mothers during the toddler years was linked to a higher level of executive function at 5 to 6 years of age (Bernier & others, 2015). Another recent observational study found that a higher level of control by fathers was linked to 3-year-olds' lower executive function (Meuwissen & Carlson, 2016). And a recent study revealed that experiencing peer problems (such as victimization and rejection) beginning in early childhood is linked to lower executive function later in childhood (Holmes, Kim-Spoon, & Deater-Deckard, 2016). Also in this study, better executive function reduced the likelihood of experiencing peer problems later in childhood.

Significant advances in the development of executive function occur in middle and late childhood (Diamond, 2013). Adult-level

How did Walter Mischel and his colleagues study young children's delay of gratification? In their research, what later developmental outcomes were linked to the preschoolers' ability to delay gratification?
© Amy Kiley Photography

executive function emerges in early adolescence on many tasks, but on some tasks executive function continues to improve during adulthood (Zelazo & Muller, 2011).

Some developmental psychologists use their training in areas such as cognitive development to pursue careers in applied areas. To read about the work of Helen Hadani, an individual who followed this path, see the *Careers in Life-Span Development* profile.

Careers in life-span development

Helen Hadani, Developmental Psychologist, Toy Designer, and Associate Director of Research for the Center for Childhood Creativity

Helen Hadani obtained a Ph.D. from Stanford University in developmental psychology. As a graduate student at Stanford, she worked part-time for Hasbro Toys and Apple testing children's software and computer products for young children. Her first job after graduate school was with Zowie Intertainment, which was subsequently bought by LEGO. In her work as a toy designer there, Helen conducted experiments and focus groups at different stages of a toy's development and also studied the age-effectiveness of the toy. In Helen's words, "Even in a toy's most primitive stage of development . . . you see children's creativity in responding to challenges, their satisfaction when a problem is solved or simply their delight in having fun" (Schlegel, 2000, p. 50).

More recently, she began working with the Bay Area Discovery Museum's Center for Childhood Creativity (CCC) in Sausalito, California, an education-focused think tank that pioneers new research, thought-leadership, and teacher training programs that advance creative thinking in all children. Helen is currently the Associate Director of Research for the CCC.

Helen Hadani, a developmental psychologist, has worked as a toy designer and is currently directing research on creativity at a children's museum.

© Dr. Helen Hadani

The Child's Theory of Mind

Even young children are curious about the nature of the human mind (Hughes & Devine, 2015; Lane & others, 2016; Sodian & others, 2016; Wellman, 2011, 2015). They have a **theory of mind,** a term that refers to awareness of one's own mental processes and those of others. Studies of theory of mind view the child as "a thinker who is trying to explain, predict, and understand people's thoughts, feelings, and utterances" (Harris, 2006). Children's theory of mind changes as they develop through childhood (Gelman, 2013; Wellman, 2011, 2015). However, whether infants have a theory of mind continues to be questioned by some (Rakoczy, 2012). The consensus is that some changes occur quite early in development, as we see next. The main changes occur at ages 2 to 3, 4 to 5, and beyond age 5.

Ages 2 to 3 In this time frame, children begin to understand the following three mental states:

1. *Perceptions:* The child realizes that other people see what is in front of their eyes and not necessarily what is in front of the child's eyes.

2. *Emotions:* The child can distinguish between positive and negative emotions. A child might say, "Vic feels bad."

3. *Desires*: The child understands that if someone wants something, he or she will try to get it. A child might say, "I want my mommy."

theory of mind Refers to the awareness of one's own mental processes and the mental processes of others.

Children refer to desires earlier and more frequently than they refer to cognitive states such as thinking and knowing (Harris, 2006). Two- to 3-year-olds understand the way desires are related to actions and to simple emotions (Harris, 2006). For example, they understand that people will search for what they want and that if they obtain it, they are likely to feel happy, but if they don't, they will keep searching for it and are likely to feel sad or angry.

Ages 4 to 5 Children come to understand that the mind can represent objects and events accurately or inaccurately (Rhodes & Brandone, 2014). The realization that people can have *false beliefs*—beliefs that are not true—develops in a majority of children by the time they are 5 years old (Wellman, Cross, & Watson, 2001) (see Figure 10).

In a classic false-belief task, children are told a story about Sally and Anne. In the story, Sally places a toy in a basket and then leaves the room. In her absence, Anne takes the toy from the basket and places it in a box. Children are asked where Sally will look for the toy when she returns. The major finding is that 3-year-olds tend to fail false-belief tasks, saying that Sally will look in the box (even though Sally could not know that the toy has been moved to this new location). Four-year-olds and older children tend to pass the task, correctly saying that Sally will have a "false belief"—she will think the object is in the basket, even though that belief is now false. The conclusion from these studies is that children younger than age 4 do not understand that it is possible to have a false belief.

Young children's understanding of thinking has some limitations (Wellman, 2011). They often underestimate when mental activity is likely occurring. For example, they fail to attribute mental activity to someone who is sitting quietly, reading, or talking (Flavell, Green, & Flavell, 1995). Their understanding of their own thinking is also limited.

Beyond Age 5 It is only beyond the preschool years that children have a deepening appreciation of the mind itself rather than just an understanding of mental states (Wellman, 2011, 2015). Not until middle and late childhood do children see the mind as an active constructor of knowledge or a processing center (Flavell, Green, & Flavell, 2000). It is only then that they move from understanding that beliefs can be false to realizing that the same event can be open to multiple interpretations (Carpendale & Chandler, 1996).

Individual Differences As in other developmental research, there are individual differences in the ages when children reach certain milestones in their theory of mind (Hughes & Devine, 2015; Wellman, 2015). For example, children who talk with their parents about feelings frequently as 2-year-olds show better performance on theory of mind tasks (Ruffman, Slade, & Crowe, 2002), as do children who frequently engage in pretend play (Harris, 2000).

Executive function, which involves goal-directed behavior and self-control, and which was discussed earlier in the chapter, is linked to the development of a theory of mind (Devine & others, 2016; Fizke & others, 2014). For example, in one executive function task, children are asked to say the word "night" when they see a picture of a sun and the word "day" when they see a picture of a moon and stars.

Children who perform better at such executive function tasks show a better understanding of theory of mind (Muller & Kerns, 2015). In recent research, executive function at 3 years of age predicted theory of mind at 4 years of age, and likewise executive function at 4 years of age predicted theory of mind at 5 years of age (Marcovitch & others, 2015). In this research, the reverse did not occur—that is, theory of mind at earlier ages did not predict executive function at later ages.

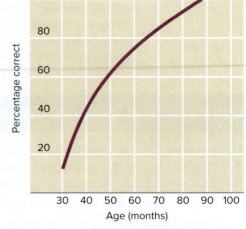

Figure 10 Developmental Changes in False-Belief Performance
False-belief performance—the child's understanding that a person has a false belief that contradicts reality—dramatically increases from 2½ years of age through the middle of the elementary school years. In a summary of the results of many studies, 2½-year-olds gave incorrect responses about 80 percent of the time (Wellman, Cross, & Watson, 2001). At 3 years, 8 months, they were correct about 50 percent of the time, and after that, gave increasingly correct responses.

Language development also likely plays a prominent role in the increasingly reflective nature of theory of mind as children go through the early childhood and middle and late childhood years (Meins & others, 2013). Researchers have found that differences in children's language skills predict performance on theory of mind tasks (Hughes & Devine, 2015).

Among other factors that influence children's theory of mind development are advances in prefrontal cortex functioning (Powers, Chavez, & Heatherton, 2016), engaging in make-believe play (Kavanaugh, 2006), and various aspects of social interaction (Hughes & Devine, 2015). Among the social interaction factors that advance children's theory of mind are being securely attached to parents who engage children in mental state talk ("That's a good thought you have" or "Can you tell what he's thinking?") (Laranjo & others, 2010) and having older siblings and friends who engage in mental state talk (Hughes & others, 2010).

Another individual difference in understanding the mind involves autism (Fletcher-Watson & others, 2014; Leung & others, 2016). Children with autism show a number of behaviors that differ from those of most children their age, including deficits in social interaction and communication as well as repetitive behaviors or interests. Researchers have found that autistic children have difficulty developing a theory of mind, especially when it comes to understanding other people's beliefs and emotions (Broekhof & others, 2015; Luiselli, 2014). However, children with autism might have difficulty in understanding others' beliefs and emotions not solely due to theory of mind deficits but to other aspects of cognition such as problems in focusing attention, eye gaze, face recognition, memory, language impairment, or some general intellectual impairment (Mutreja, Craig, & O'Boyle, 2016; Richard & Lajiness-O'Neill, 2015; Stephanie & Julie, 2015).

Young children's symbolic skills also contribute to the development of theory of mind. A recent study found that young children's symbolic understanding provided a foundation for their theory of mind and also for language, pretend play, and representational understanding (Lillard & Kavanaugh, 2014).

Language Development

Toddlers move rather quickly from producing two-word utterances to creating three-, four-, and five-word combinations. Between ages 2 and 3, they begin the transition from saying simple sentences that express a single proposition to saying complex sentences.

As young children learn the special features of their own language, there are extensive regularities in how they acquire that particular language (Berko Gleason, 2009; Clark, 2017; Hoff, 2014; Litz, Snyder, & Pater, 2016). For example, all children learn the prepositions *on* and *in* before other prepositions. Children learning other languages, such as Russian or Chinese, also acquire the particular features of those languages in a consistent order.

Understanding Phonology and Morphology

Phonology refers to the sound system of a language, including the sounds used and how they may be combined. During the preschool years, most children gradually become more sensitive to the sounds of spoken words and increasingly capable of producing all the sounds of their language (Bailey, Osipova, & Kelly, 2016; Goad, 2016). By their third birthday they can produce all the vowel sounds and most of the consonant sounds (Menn & Stoel-Gammon, 2009).

By the time children move beyond two-word utterances, they demonstrate a knowledge of morphology rules (Snyder, 2016). **Morphology** refers to the units of meaning involved in word formation. Children begin using the plural and possessive forms of nouns (such as *dogs* and *dog's*). They put appropriate endings on verbs (such as -*s* when the subject is third-person singular and -*ed* for the past tense). They use prepositions (such as *in* and *on*), articles (such as *a* and *the*), and various forms of the verb *to be* (such as "I *was* going to the store"). Some of the best evidence for changes in children's use of morphological rules occurs in their overgeneralization of the rules, as when a preschool child says "foots" instead of "feet," or "goed" instead of "went."

phonology The sound system of a language, including the sounds used and how they may be combined.

morphology Units of meaning involved in word formation.

In a classic experiment that was designed to study children's knowledge of morphological rules, such as how to make a plural, Jean Berko (1958) presented preschool and first-grade children with cards such as the one shown in Figure 11. The children were asked to look at the card while the experimenter read aloud the words on the card. Then the children were asked to supply the missing word. This might sound easy, but Berko was interested in the children's ability to apply the appropriate morphological rule—in this case, to say "wugs" with the *z* sound that indicates the plural.

Although the children's answers were not perfect, they were much better than chance. What makes Berko's study impressive is that most of the words were made up for the experiment. Thus, the children could not base their responses on remembering past instances of hearing the words. That they could make the plurals or past tenses of words they had never heard before was proof that they knew the morphological rules.

This is a wug.

Now there is another one.
There are two of them.
There are two _____.

Changes in Syntax and Semantics

Preschool children also learn and apply rules of **syntax,** which involves the way words are combined to form acceptable phrases and sentences (Clark, 2017; de Villiers & de Villiers, 2013). They show a growing mastery of complex rules for how words should be ordered. Consider *wh-* questions, such as "Where is Daddy going?" or "What is that boy doing?" To ask these questions properly, the child must know two important differences between *wh-* questions and affirmative statements (for instance, "Daddy is going to work" and "That boy is waiting for the school bus"). First, a *wh-* word must be added at the beginning of the sentence. Second, the auxiliary verb must be inverted—that is, exchanged with the subject of the sentence. Young children learn quite early where to put the *wh-*word, but they take much longer to learn the auxiliary-inversion rule. Thus, preschool children might ask, "Where Daddy is going?" and "What that boy is doing?"

Gains in **semantics,** the aspect of language that refers to the meaning of words and sentences, also characterize early childhood. Vocabulary development is dramatic (Bailey, Osipova, & Kelly, 2016; Thornton, 2016; Parish-Morris, Golinkoff, & Hirsh-Pasek, 2013). Some experts have concluded that between 18 months and 6 years, young children learn an average of about one new word every waking hour (Gelman & Kalish, 2006)! By the time they enter first grade, it is estimated that children know about 14,000 words (Clark, 1993).

How can children learn so many new words so quickly? One possible explanation is **fast mapping,** which involves children's ability to make an initial connection between a word and its referent after only limited exposure to the word (Bailey, Osipova, & Kelly, 2016; Kan, 2014). Researchers have found that exposure to words on multiple occasions over several days results in more successful word learning than the same number of exposures in a single day (Childers & Tomasello, 2002). Recent research using eye-tracking found that even 15-month-old infants fast map words (Puccini & Liszkowski, 2012).

What are some important aspects of how word learning optimally occurs? Kathy Hirsh-Pasek and Roberta Golinkoff (Harris, Golinkoff, & Hirsh-Pasek, 2011; Hirsh-Pasek & Golinkoff, 2014) emphasize six key principles in young children's vocabulary development:

1. *Children learn the words they hear most often.* They learn the words they encounter when interacting with parents, teachers, siblings, and peers, and also from books. They especially benefit from encountering words that they do not know.

Figure 11 Stimuli in Berko's Study of Young Children's Understanding of Morphological Rules
In Jean Berko's (1958) study, young children were presented with cards such as this one with a "wug" on it. Then the children were asked to supply the missing word; in supplying the missing word, they also had to say it correctly. "Wugs" is the correct response here.

syntax The ways words are combined to form acceptable phrases and sentences.

semantics The meaning of words and sentences.

fast mapping A process that helps to explain how young children learn the connection between a word and its referent so quickly.

2. *Children learn words for things and events that interest them.* Parents and teachers can direct young children to experience words in contexts that interest the children; playful peer interactions are especially helpful in this regard.

3. *Children learn words best in responsive and interactive contexts rather than passive contexts.* Children who experience turn-taking opportunities, joint focusing experiences, and positive, sensitive socializing contexts with adults encounter the scaffolding necessary for optimal word learning. They learn words less effectively when they are passive learners.

4. *Children learn words best in contexts that are meaningful.* Young children learn new words more effectively when new words are encountered in integrated contexts rather than as isolated facts.

5. *Children learn words best when they access clear information about word meaning.* Children whose parents and teachers are sensitive to words the children might not understand and provide support and elaboration with hints about word meaning learn words better than children whose parents and teachers quickly state a new word and don't monitor whether the child understands its meaning.

6. *Children learn words best when grammar and vocabulary are considered.* Children who experience a large number of words and diversity in verbal stimulation develop a richer vocabulary and better understanding of grammar. In many cases, vocabulary and grammar development are connected.

Advances in Pragmatics

Changes in **pragmatics,** the appropriate use of language in different contexts, also characterize young children's language development (Waxman, 2013). A 6-year-old is simply a much better conversationalist than a 2-year-old. What are some of the improvements in pragmatics during the preschool years?

Young children begin to engage in extended discourse (Akhtar & Herold, 2008). For example, they learn culturally specific rules of conversation and politeness, and they become sensitive to the need to adapt their speech to different settings. Their developing linguistic skills and increasing ability to take the perspective of others contribute to their generation of more competent narratives.

As children grow older, they become increasingly able to talk about things that are not here (Grandma's house, for example) and not now (what happened to them yesterday or might happen tomorrow, for example). A preschool child can tell you what she wants for lunch tomorrow, something that would not have been possible at the two-word stage of language development.

Around age 4 or 5, children learn to change their speech style to suit the situation. For example, even 4-year-old children speak to a 2-year-old differently from the way they talk to a same-aged peer; they use shorter sentences with the 2-year-old. They also speak to an adult differently from a same-aged peer, using more polite and formal language with the adult (Shatz & Gelman, 1973).

Young Children's Literacy

Concern about U.S. children's ability to read and write has led to a careful examination of preschool and kindergarten children's experiences, with the hope that a positive orientation toward reading and writing can be developed early in life (Beaty & Pratt, 2015). Parents and teachers need to provide young children with a supportive environment for the development of literacy skills (Vukelich & others, 2016). Children should be active participants in a wide range of interesting listening, talking, writing, and reading experiences (Lonigan, 2015; Tompkins, 2015).

Instruction should be built on what children already know about oral language, reading, and writing. Further, early precursors of literacy and academic success include language skills, phonological and syntactic knowledge, letter identification, and enjoyment of books (McGhee & Richgels, 2012).

pragmatics The appropriate use of language in different contexts.

What are some strategies for using books effectively with preschool children? Ellen Galinsky (2010) recently emphasized these strategies:

- *Use books to initiate conversation with young children.* Ask them to put themselves in the book characters' places and imagine what they might be thinking or feeling.

- *Use what and why questions.* Ask young children to tell you what they think is going to happen next in a story and then to see if it occurs.

- *Encourage children to ask questions about stories.*

- *Choose some books that play with language.* Creative books on the alphabet, including those with rhymes, often interest young children.

Early Childhood Education

How do early education programs treat children, and how do the children fare? Our exploration of early childhood education focuses on variations in programs, education for children who are disadvantaged, and some controversies in early childhood education.

Variations in Early Childhood Education

There are many variations in the way young children are educated (Bredekamp, 2017; Burchinal & others, 2015; Feeney, Moravcik, & Nolte, 2016). The foundation of early childhood education is the child-centered kindergarten.

The Child-Centered Kindergarten

Nurturing is a key aspect of the **child-centered kindergarten,** which emphasizes educating the whole child and promoting his or her physical, cognitive, and socioemotional development (Morrison, 2015, 2017). Instruction is organized around the child's needs, interests, and learning styles. Emphasis is on the process of learning, rather than what is learned (Kostelnik & others, 2015). The child-centered kindergarten honors three principles: (1) each child follows a unique developmental pattern; (2) young children learn best through firsthand experiences with people and materials; and (3) play is extremely important in the child's total development. *Experimenting, exploring, discovering, trying out, restructuring, speaking,* and *listening* are frequent activities in excellent kindergarten programs. Such programs are closely attuned to the developmental status of 4- and 5-year-old children.

The Montessori Approach

Montessori schools are patterned on the educational philosophy of Maria Montessori (1870–1952), an Italian physician-turned-educator who at the beginning of the twentieth century crafted a revolutionary approach to young children's education. The **Montessori approach** is a philosophy of education in which children are given considerable freedom and spontaneity in choosing activities. They are allowed to move from one activity to another as they desire, and the teacher acts as a facilitator rather than a director. The teacher shows the child how to perform intellectual activities, demonstrates interesting ways to explore curriculum materials, and offers help when the child requests it (Isaacs, 2012). "By encouraging children to make decisions from an early age, Montessori programs seek to develop self-regulated problem solvers who can make choices and manage their time effectively" (Hyson, Copple, & Jones, 2006, p. 14). The number of Montessori schools in the United States has expanded dramatically in recent years, from one school in 1959 to 355 schools in 1970 to more than 4,000 today.

Some developmental psychologists favor the Montessori approach, but others believe that it neglects children's socioemotional development. For example, although the Montessori approach fosters independence and the development of cognitive skills, it deemphasizes verbal interaction between

child-centered kindergarten Education that involves the whole child by considering both the child's physical, cognitive, and socioemotional development and the child's needs, interests, and learning styles.

Montessori approach An educational philosophy in which children are given considerable freedom and spontaneity in choosing activities and are allowed to move from one activity to another as they desire.

the teacher and child and between peers. Montessori's critics also argue that it restricts imaginative play and that its heavy reliance on self-corrective materials may not adequately allow for creativity and for a variety of learning styles.

Developmentally Appropriate Education

Many educators and psychologists conclude that preschool and young elementary school children learn best through active, hands-on teaching methods such as games and dramatic play. They believe that schools need to accommodate individual differences in children's development. They also argue that schools should focus on promoting children's socioemotional development as well as their cognitive development. Educators refer to this type of schooling as **developmentally appropriate practice (DAP),** which is based on knowledge of the typical development of children within a particular age span (age-appropriateness), as well as on the uniqueness of the individual child (individual-appropriateness). DAP emphasizes the importance of creating settings that encourage children to be active learners and reflect children's interests and capabilities (Bredekamp, 2017; Follari, 2015). Desired outcomes for DAP include thinking critically, working cooperatively, solving problems, developing self-regulatory skills, and enjoying learning. The emphasis in DAP is on the process of learning rather than on its content.

*As an **educator,** how would you design a developmentally appropriate lesson to teach kindergartners the concept of gravity?*

Larry Page and Sergey Brin, founders of Google, say their years at Montessori schools were a major factor in their success (International Montessori Council, 2006). They taught them to be self-directed and self-starters (ABC News, 2005) and their Montessori experiences encouraged them to think for themselves and to develop their own interests.

© James Leynse/Corbis Images

Do developmentally appropriate educational practices improve young children's development? Some researchers have found that young children in developmentally appropriate classrooms are likely to feel less stress, be more motivated, be more socially skilled, have better work habits, be more creative, have better language skills, and demonstrate better math skills than children in developmentally inappropriate classrooms (Hart & others, 2003). However, not all studies find DAP to have significant positive effects (Hyson, Copple, & Jones, 2006). Among the reasons that it is difficult to generalize about research on developmentally appropriate education is that individual programs often vary, and developmentally appropriate education is an evolving concept. Recent changes in the concept have given more attention to sociocultural factors and the teacher's active involvement and implementation of systematic intentions, as well as how strongly academic skills should be emphasized and how they should be taught.

Education for Young Children Who Are Disadvantaged

For many years, U.S. children from low-income families did not receive any education before they entered the first grade. Often when they began first grade they were already several steps behind their classmates in readiness to learn. In the summer of 1965, the federal government began striving to break the cycle of poverty and poor education for young children through **Project Head Start.** Head Start is a compensatory program designed to give children from low-income families the opportunity to acquire skills and experiences that are important for success in school (Hustedt, Friedman, & Barnett, 2012; Miller, Farkas, & Duncan, 2016; Zigler & Styfco, 2010). After almost half a century, Head Start continues to be the largest federally funded

developmentally appropriate practice (DAP) Education that focuses on the typical developmental patterns of children (age appropriateness) and the uniqueness of each child (individual appropriateness).

Project Head Start A government-funded program that is designed to provide children from low-income families the opportunity to acquire the skills and experiences important for school success.

program for U.S. children, with almost 1 million children enrolled in it annually (Hagen & Lamb-Parker, 2008). In 2007, 3 percent of Head Start children were 5 years old, 51 percent were 4 years old, 36 percent were 3 years old, and 10 percent were under age 3 (Administration for Children & Families, 2008).

Mixed results have been found for Head Start. A recent study found that one year of Head Start was linked to higher performance in early math, early reading, and receptive vocabulary (Miller, Farkas, & Duncan, 2016). In another recent study, the best results occurred for Head Start children who had low initial cognitive ability, whose parents had low levels of education, and who attended Head Start more than 20 hours a week (Lee & others, 2014). It is not unusual to find early gains, then see them go away in elementary school. For example, a national evaluation of Head Start revealed that the program had a positive influence on the language and cognitive development of 3- and 4-year-olds (Puma & others, 2010). However, by the end of the first grade, there were few lasting outcomes.

Early Head Start was established in 1995 to serve children from birth to 3 years of age. In 2007, half of all new funds appropriated for Head Start programs were used for the expansion of Early Head Start. One study revealed that Early Head Start had a protective effect on risks young children might experience in parenting stress, language development, and self-control (Ayoub, Vallotton, & Mastergeorge, 2011). However, some studies have revealed mixed effects for Early Head Start (Love & others, 2013).

Two recent studies confirmed the role of parenting in the success of Head Start programs. In a national study, when Head Start centers promoted greater parental involvement and the parents got more involved, the parents engaged in increased cognitive stimulation of their children (Ansari & Gershoff, 2016). In turn, these parental behaviors were linked to children's gains in academic skills. In a second study, home visit quality variation (greater emphasis on children's development in early Head Start programs) was associated with improved parenting quality (more parental engagement and collaboration) and positive child outcomes (vocabulary development gains) (Roggman & others, 2016).

More attention needs to be given to developing consistently high-quality Head Start programs (Hillemeier & others, 2013). One person who is strongly motivated to make Head Start a valuable learning experience for young children from disadvantaged backgrounds is Yolanda Garcia. To read about her work, see *Careers in Life-Span Development*.

How Would You...?

As a **health-care professional,** how would you explain the importance of including health services as part of an effective Head Start program?

Careers in life-span development

Yolanda Garcia, Director of Children's Services, Head Start

Yolanda Garcia has been the director of the Children's Services Department of the Santa Clara, California, County Office of Education since 1980. As director, she is responsible for managing child development programs for 2,500 3- to 5-year-old children in 127 classrooms. Her training includes two master's degrees: one in public policy and child welfare from the University of Chicago and another in education administration from San Jose State University.

Garcia has served on many national advisory committees that have produced improvements in the staffing of Head Start programs. Most notably, she served on the Head Start Quality Committee that recommended the development of Early Head Start and revised performance standards for Head Start programs. Garcia currently is a member of the American Academy of Science Committee on the Integration of Science and Early Childhood Education.

Yolanda Garcia, Director of WestEd's E3 Institute, works with a child.
© Yolanda Garcia

One high-quality early childhood education program (although not a Head Start program) is the Perry Preschool program in Ypsilanti, Michigan, a two-year preschool program that includes weekly home visits from program personnel. In analyses of the long-term effects of the program, adults who had been in the Perry Preschool program were compared with a control group of adults from the same background who had not received the enriched early childhood education (Schweinhart & others, 2005; Weikert, 1993). Those who had been in the Perry Preschool program had fewer teen pregnancies and better high school graduation rates, and at age 40 they were more likely to be in the workforce, to own a home, and to have a savings account, and they also had fewer arrests.

Controversies in Early Childhood Education

Two current controversies in early childhood education involve (1) what the curriculum for early childhood education should be (Feeney, Moravcik, & Nolte, 2016) and (2) whether preschool education should be universal in the United States (Zigler, Gilliam, & Barnett, 2011).

Controversy Over Curriculum

A current controversy in early childhood education involves what the curriculum for early childhood education should be (Bredekamp, 2017; Morrison, 2015, 2017). On one side are those who advocate a child-centered, constructivist approach much like that emphasized by the National Association for the Education of Young Children (NAEYC), along the lines of developmentally appropriate practice. On the other side are those who advocate an academic, direct-instruction approach.

In practice, many high-quality early-childhood education programs include both academic and constructivist approaches. Many education experts, such as Lilian Katz (1999), though, worry about academic approaches that place too much pressure on young children to achieve and don't provide opportunities to actively construct knowledge. Competent early childhood programs also should focus on both cognitive development *and* socioemotional development, not exclusively on cognitive development (Bredekamp, 2017; NAEYC, 2009).

How Would You...?
As a **psychologist,** how would you advise preschool teachers to balance the development of young children's skills for academic achievement with opportunities for healthy social interaction?

Universal Preschool Education

Another controversy in early childhood education focuses on whether preschool education should be instituted for all U.S. 4-year-old children. Edward Zigler and his colleagues (2006, 2011) argue that the United States should have universal preschool education. They emphasize that quality preschools prepare children for later academic success. Zigler and his colleagues (2006) cite research showing that quality preschool programs decrease the likelihood that children will be retained in a grade or drop out before graduating from high school. They also point to analyses indicating that universal preschool would bring cost savings on the order of billions of dollars because of a diminished need for remedial and justice services (Karoly & Bigelow, 2005).

Critics of universal preschool education argue that the gains attributed to preschool and kindergarten education are often overstated. They especially stress that research has not proven that nondisadvantaged children benefit from attending a preschool. Thus, the critics say it is more important to improve preschool education for young children who are disadvantaged than to fund preschool education for all 4-year-old children. Some critics, especially homeschooling advocates, emphasize that young children should be educated by their parents, not by schools. Thus, universal preschool education remains a subject of controversy.

Summary

Physical Changes

- The average child grows 2½ inches in height and gains between 5 and 7 pounds a year during early childhood, although growth patterns vary from one child to another.
- Some of the brain's growth in early childhood is due to increases in the number and size of dendrites, some to myelination. From ages 3 to 6, the most rapid growth in the brain occurs in the frontal lobes.
- Gross and fine motor skills improve dramatically during early childhood.
- Too many young children in the United States are being raised on diets that are too high in fat. Other nutritional concerns include malnutrition in early childhood and the inadequate diets of many children living in poverty. The child's life should be centered on activities, not meals. Regular exercise should be a part of young children's lives.
- Accidents are the leading cause of death in young children. A special concern is the poor health status of many young children in low-income families. There has been a dramatic increase in HIV/AIDS in young children in developing countries in recent decades.

Cognitive Changes

- According to Piaget, in the preoperational stage children cannot yet perform operations, but they begin to represent the world with symbols, to form stable concepts, and to reason. Preoperational thought is characterized by two substages: symbolic function (2 to 4 years) and intuitive thought (4 to 7 years). Centration and a lack of conservation also characterize the preoperational stage.
- Vygotsky's theory represents a social constructivist approach to development. Vygotsky argues that it is important to discover the child's zone of proximal development to improve the child's learning.
- Young children make substantial strides in executive and sustained attention. Significant improvement in short-term memory occurs during early childhood. Advances in executive function, an umbrella-like concept that consists of a number of higher-level cognitive processes linked to the development of the prefrontal cortex, occur in early childhood. Theory of mind is the awareness of one's own mental processes and the mental processes of others. Children begin to understand mental states involving perceptions, emotions, and desires at 2 to 3 years of age and at 4 to 5 years of age realize that people can have false beliefs.

Language Development

- Young children increase their grasp of language's rule systems. In terms of phonology, children become more sensitive to the sounds of spoken language. Berko's classic study demonstrated that young children understand morphological rules.
- Preschool children learn and apply rules of syntax, which involves how words should be ordered. In terms of semantics, vocabulary development increases dramatically in early childhood.
- Young children's conversational skills improve in early childhood.
- Early precursors of literacy and academic success develop in early childhood.

Early Childhood Education

- The child-centered kindergarten emphasizes the education of the whole child. The Montessori approach has become increasingly popular. Developmentally appropriate practice focuses on the typical patterns of children (age appropriateness) and the uniqueness of each child (individual appropriateness).
- The U.S. government has tried to break the poverty cycle with programs such as Head Start. Model programs have had positive effects on young children's education.
- Controversy over early childhood education involves what the curriculum should be and whether universal preschool education should be implemented.

Key Terms

animism	executive attention	operations	social constructivist approach
centration	executive function	phonology	sustained attention
child-centered kindergarten	fast mapping	pragmatics	symbolic function substage
conservation	intuitive thought substage	preoperational stage	syntax
developmentally appropriate practice (DAP)	Montessori approach	Project Head Start	theory of mind
egocentrism	morphology	semantics	zone of proximal development (ZPD)
	myelination	short-term memory	

6 Socioemotional Development in Early Childhood

© Ariel Skelley/Blend Images/Getty Images RF

CHAPTER OUTLINE

EMOTIONAL AND PERSONALITY DEVELOPMENT
The Self
Emotional Development
Moral Development
Gender

FAMILIES
Parenting
Child Maltreatment
Sibling Relationships and Birth Order
The Changing Family in a Changing Society

PEER RELATIONS, PLAY, AND MEDIA/SCREEN TIME
Peer Relations
Play
Media and Screen Time

Stories of Life-Span Development: Nurturing Socioemotional Development

Like many children, Sarah Newland loves animals. During a trip to the zoo when she was 4 years old, Sarah learned about an animal that was a member of an endangered species, and she became motivated to help. With her mother's guidance, she baked lots of cakes and cookies, then sold them on the sidewalk outside her home. She was excited about making $35 from the cake and cookie sales, and she mailed the money to the World Wildlife Fund. Several weeks later, the fund wrote back to Sarah requesting more money. Sarah was devastated because she thought she had taken care of the animal problem. Her mother consoled her and told her that the endangered animal problem and many others are so big that it takes ongoing help from many people to solve them. Her mother's guidance when Sarah was a young child must have worked because by the end of elementary school, Sarah had begun helping out at a child-care center and working with her mother to provide meals to the homeless.

Sensitive parents like Sarah's mother can encourage young children's sense of morality. Just as parents support and guide their children to become good readers, musicians, or athletes, they also play key roles in promoting young children's socioemotional development. (*Source:* Kantrowitz & Namuth, 1991). ∎

Emotional and Personality Development

Many changes characterize young children's socioemotional development in early childhood. Children's developing minds and social experiences produce remarkable advances in the development of the self, emotional maturity, moral understanding, and gender awareness.

The Self

During the second year of life, children make considerable progress in self-recognition. In the early childhood years, young children develop in many ways that enable them to enhance their self-understanding.

Initiative Versus Guilt

Erik Erikson's (1968) eight developmental stages are encountered during certain time periods in the human life span. Erikson's first stage, trust versus mistrust, describes what he considers to be the main developmental task of infancy. According to Erikson, the psychosocial stage associated with early childhood is *initiative versus guilt*. At this point in development, children have become convinced that they are persons of their own; during early childhood, they begin to discover what kind of person they will become. They identify intensely with their parents, who most of the time appear to them to be powerful and beautiful, though often unreasonable, disagreeable, and sometimes even dangerous. During early childhood, children use their perceptual, motor, cognitive, and language skills to make things happen. They have a surplus of energy that permits them to forget failures quickly and to approach new areas that seem desirable—even if dangerous—with undiminished zest and an increased sense of direction. On their own initiative, then, children at this stage exuberantly move out into a wider social world.

The great governor of initiative is conscience. Children's initiative and enthusiasm may bring them not only rewards but also guilt, which lowers self-esteem.

Self-Understanding and Understanding Others

Recent research studies have revealed that young children are more psychologically aware—of themselves and others—than was formerly thought (Thompson, 2015). This increased awareness reflects young children's expanding psychological sophistication.

Self-Understanding In Erikson's portrait of early childhood, the young child clearly has begun to develop **self-understanding,** which is the representation of self, the substance and content of self-conceptions (Harter, 2012, 2016). Though not the whole of personal identity, self-understanding provides its rational underpinnings. Mainly through interviews, researchers have probed children's conceptions of many aspects of self-understanding (Harter, 2016).

Early self-understanding involves self-recognition. In early childhood, young children think the self can be described by material characteristics such as size, shape, and color. They distinguish themselves from others through physical and material attributes. Says 4-year-old Sandra,

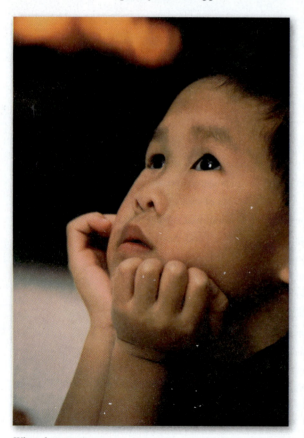

What characterizes young children's self-understanding?
© Roger Allyn Lee/ SuperStock

self-understanding The child's cognitive representation of self, the substance and content of the child's self-conceptions.

"I'm different from Jennifer because I have brown hair and she has blond hair." Says 4-year-old Ralph, "I am different from Hank because I am taller, and I am different from my sister because I have a bicycle." Physical activities are also a central component of the self in early childhood (Keller, Ford, & Meacham, 1978). For example, preschool children often describe themselves in terms of activities such as play. In sum, in early childhood, children often provide self-descriptions that involve body attributes, material possessions, and physical activities.

Although young children mainly describe themselves in terms of concrete, observable features and activities, at age 4 to 5, as they hear others use psychological trait and emotion terms, they begin to include these in their self-descriptions (Marsh, Ellis, & Craven, 2002). Thus, in a self-description a 4-year-old might say, "I'm not scared. I'm always happy."

Young children's self-descriptions are typically unrealistically positive, as reflected in the comment of the 4-year-old who says he is always happy, which he is not (Harter, 2012, 2016). They express this optimism because they don't yet distinguish between their desired competence and their actual competence, tend to confuse ability and effort (thinking that differences in ability can be changed as easily as can differences in effort), don't engage in spontaneous social comparison of their abilities with those of others, and tend to compare their present abilities with what they could do at an earlier age (which usually makes them look quite good).

Understanding Others Children also make advances in their understanding of others (Harter, 2012, 2016; Mills & Elashi, 2014; Thompson, 2015). Young children's theory of mind includes understanding that other people have emotions and desires. And at age 4 to 5 children not only start describing themselves in terms of psychological traits but also begin to perceive others in terms of psychological traits. Thus, a 4-year-old might say, "My teacher is nice."

Young children are more psychologically aware of themselves and others than used to be thought. Some children are better than others at understanding people's feelings and desires—and, to some degree, these individual differences are influenced by conversations caregivers have with young children about feelings and desires.
© Don Hammond/Deisgn Pics/Corbis RF

An important part of children's socioemotional development is gaining an understanding that people don't always give accurate reports of their beliefs (Mills, 2013; Mills & Elashi, 2014). Researchers have found that even 4-year-olds understand that people may make statements that aren't true to obtain what they want or to avoid trouble (Lee & others, 2002). A recent study compared preschool children's trust in the accuracy of an expert's comments (Landrum, Mills, & Johnston, 2013). In this study, in one condition, 5-year-olds trusted the expert's claim more than did 3-year-olds. However, in other conditions, preschoolers tended to trust a nice non-expert more than a mean expert, indicating that young children often are more likely to believe someone who is nice to them than someone who is an expert.

Another important aspect of understanding others involves understanding joint commitments. As children approach their third birthday, their collaborative interactions with others increasingly involve obligations to the partner (Tomasello, 2014). One study revealed that 3-year-olds, but not 2-year-olds, recognized when an adult is committed and when they themselves are committed to joint activity that involves obligation to a partner (Grafenhain & others, 2009).

Both the extensive theory of mind research and the recent research on young children's social understanding underscore that young children are not as egocentric as Piaget envisioned (Thompson, 2012). Piaget's concept of egocentrism has become so ingrained in people's thinking about young children that too often the current research on social awareness in infancy and early childhood has been overlooked. Research increasingly shows that young children are more socially sensitive and perceptive than previously envisioned, suggesting that parents and teachers can help them to better understand and interact in the social world by how they interact with them

(Thompson, 2015). If young children are seeking to better understand various mental and emotional states (intentions, goals, feelings, desires) that they know underlie people's actions, then talking with them about these internal states can improve young children's understanding of them (Thompson, 2011, 2015).

However, there is ongoing debate about whether young children are socially sensitive or basically egocentric. Ross Thompson (2012, 2015) comes down on the side of viewing young children as socially sensitive while Susan Harter (2012, 2016) argues that there is still evidence to support the conclusion that young children are essentially egocentric.

Emotional Development

The young child's growing awareness of self is linked to the ability to feel an expanding range of emotions. Young children, like adults, experience many emotions during the course of a day. Their emotional development allows them to try to make sense of other people's emotional reactions and to begin to control their own emotions (Rogers & others, 2016; Thompson, 2015).

Expressing Emotions

Recall that even young infants experience emotions such as joy and fear, but to experience *self-conscious emotions* children must be able to refer to themselves and be aware of themselves as distinct from others (Lewis, 2010, 2014, 2015, 2016). Pride, shame, embarrassment, and guilt are examples of self-conscious emotions. These emotions do not appear to develop until self-awareness appears around 18 months of age.

During the early childhood years, emotions such as pride and guilt become more common. They are especially influenced by parents' responses to children's behavior. For example, a young child may experience shame when a parent says, "You should feel bad about biting your sister." One study revealed that young children's emotional expression was linked to their parents' own expressive behavior (Nelson & others, 2012). In this study, mothers who expressed a high incidence of positive emotions and a low incidence of negative emotions at home had children who were observed to use more positive emotion words during mother-child interactions than did the children of mothers who expressed few positive emotions at home.

Understanding Emotions

Among the most important changes in emotional development in early childhood is an increased understanding of emotions (Calkins & Perry, 2016; Denham, Bassett, & Wyatt, 2015; Karstad & others, 2015). Young children increasingly understand that certain situations are likely to evoke particular emotions, facial expressions indicate specific emotions, and emotions affect behavior and can be used to influence others. One study also found that young children's emotional understanding was linked to an increase in prosocial behavior (Ensor, Spencer, & Hughes, 2011). Also, in a recent study of 5- to 7-year-olds, understanding others' emotions was linked to the children's emotion regulation (Hudson & Jacques, 2014).

Between ages 2 and 4, children considerably increase the number of terms they use to describe emotions. During this time, they are also learning about the causes and consequences of feelings (Denham & others, 2012).

When they are 4 to 5 years old, children show an increased ability to reflect on emotions. They also begin to understand that the same event can elicit different feelings in different people. Moreover, they show growing awareness that they need to manage their emotions to meet social standards. And by age 5 most children can accurately determine emotions that are produced by challenging circumstances and describe strategies they might call on to cope with everyday stress (Cole & others, 2009).

Regulating Emotions

Emotion regulation is an important aspect of development. In particular, it plays a key role in children's ability to manage the demands and conflicts they face in interacting with others (Durlak, Domitrovich, & Gullotta, 2015; Eisenberg, Spinrad, & Valiente, 2016; Thompson, 2015).

Many researchers consider the growth of emotion regulation in children as fundamental to the development of social competence (Calkins & Perry, 2016; Cole, 2016; Denham, Bassett, & Wyatt, 2015; Thompson, 2015). Emotion regulation can be conceptualized as an important component of self-regulation or of executive function. Recall that executive function is increasingly thought to be a key concept in describing the young child's higher-level cognitive functioning (Carlson, Zelazo, & Faja, 2013; Griffin, Freund, & McCardle, 2015). Cybelle Raver and her colleagues (Blair & Raver, 2012, 2015; Blair, Raver, & Finegood, 2016; McCoy & Raver, 2011; Raver & others, 2011, 2012, 2013; Zhai, Raver, & Jones, 2012) are using interventions, such as increasing caregiver emotional expressiveness, to improve young children's emotion regulation and reduce behavior problems in Head Start families.

Emotion-Coaching and Emotion-Dismissing Parents Parents can play an important role in helping young children regulate their emotions (Cole & Tan, 2015). Depending on how they talk with their children about emotion, parents can be described as taking an *emotion-coaching* or an *emotion-dismissing* approach (Gottman, 2016). The distinction between these approaches is most evident in the way the parent deals with the child's negative emotions (anger, frustration, sadness, and so on). *Emotion-coaching parents* monitor their children's emotions, view their children's negative emotions as opportunities for teaching, assist them in labeling emotions, and coach them in how to deal effectively with emotions. In contrast, *emotion-dismissing parents* view their role as to deny, ignore, or change negative emotions. Emotion-coaching

What are some differences between emotion-coaching and emotion-dismissing parents?
© LWA-Dann Tardif/Corbis

parents interact with their children in a less rejecting manner, use more scaffolding and praise, and are more nurturant than are emotion-dismissing parents. Moreover, children of emotion-coaching parents are better at soothing themselves when they get upset, are more effective in regulating their negative affect, focus their attention better, and have fewer behavior problems than do children of emotion-dismissing parents. Recent studies found that fathers' emotion coaching was related to children's social competence (Baker, Fenning, & Crnic, 2011) and that mothers' emotion coaching was linked to less oppositional behavior (Dunsmore, Booker, & Ollendick, 2013).

Parents' knowledge of their children's emotional world can help them to guide their children's emotional development and teach them how to cope effectively with problems (Denham, Bassett, & Wyatt, 2015). For example, one study found that mothers' knowledge about what distresses and comforts their children predicts the children's coping, empathy, and prosocial behavior (Vinik, Almas, & Grusec, 2011).

Regulation of Emotion and Peer Relations Emotions play a strong role in determining the success of a child's peer relationships (Denham, Bassett, & Wyatt, 2015). Specifically, the ability to modulate one's emotions is an important skill that benefits children in their relationships with peers. Moody and emotionally negative children are more likely to experience rejection by peers, whereas emotionally positive children are more popular.

Moral Development

Unlike a crying infant, a screaming 5-year-old is likely to be considered responsible for making a fuss. The parents may worry about whether the 5-year-old is a "bad" child. Although there are some who view children as innately good, many developmental psychologists believe that just as parents help their children become good readers, musicians, or athletes, parents must nurture goodness and help their children develop morally.

Moral development involves the development of thoughts, feelings, and behaviors regarding rules and conventions about what people should do in their interactions with other people. Major developmental theories have focused on different aspects of moral development (Vozzola, 2014).

Moral Feelings

Feelings of anxiety and guilt are central to the account of moral development provided by Freud's psychoanalytic theory. According to Freud, children attempt to reduce anxiety, avoid punishment, and maintain parental affection by identifying with their parents and internalizing their standards of right and wrong, thereby developing the *superego,* the moral element of the personality.

Freud's ideas are not backed by research, but guilt certainly can motivate moral behavior. Other emotions, however, also contribute to moral development, including positive feelings. One important example is *empathy,* or responding to another person's feelings with an emotion that echoes those feelings (Denham, Bassett, & Wyatt, 2015).

Infants have the capacity for some purely empathic responses, but empathy often requires the ability to discern another person's emotional states, or what is called *perspective taking.* Learning how to identify a wide range of emotional states in others, and to anticipate what kinds of action will improve another person's emotional state, help to advance children's moral development (Thompson, 2015).

Moral Reasoning

Interest in how children think about moral issues was stimulated by Piaget (1932), who extensively observed and interviewed children from ages 4 through 12. Piaget watched children play marbles to learn how they used and thought about the game's rules. He also asked children about ethical issues—theft, lies, punishment, and justice, for example. He concluded that children go through two distinct stages in how they think about morality:

- From ages 4 to 7, children display **heteronomous morality,** the first stage of moral development in Piaget's theory. Children think of justice and rules as unchangeable properties, beyond the control of people.

- From ages 7 to 10, children are in a period of transition, showing some features of the first stage of moral reasoning and some of the second stage, autonomous morality.

- From about age 10 and older, children show **autonomous morality.** They become aware that rules and laws are created by people, and in judging an action they consider the actor's intentions as well as the action's consequences.

Because young children are heteronomous moralists, they judge the rightness or goodness of behavior by considering its consequences, not the intentions of the actor. For example, to the heteronomous moralist, breaking twelve cups accidentally is worse than breaking one cup intentionally. As children develop into moral autonomists, intentions become more important than consequences.

The heteronomous thinker also believes that rules are unchangeable and are handed down by all-powerful authorities. When Piaget suggested to young children that they use new rules in a game of marbles, they resisted. By contrast, older children—moral autonomists—accept change and recognize that rules are merely conventions that are subject to change.

The heteronomous thinker also believes in **immanent justice,** the concept that if a rule is broken, punishment will be meted out immediately. The young child believes that a violation is connected automatically

Piaget extensively observed and interviewed 4- to 12-year-old children as they played games to learn how they used and thought about the games' rules.

© Yves De Braine/BlackStar/StockPhoto

to its punishment. Thus, young children often look around worriedly after doing something wrong, expecting the inevitable punishment. Immanent justice also implies that if something unfortunate happens to someone, that person must have transgressed earlier. Older children, who are moral autonomists, recognize that punishment occurs only if someone witnesses the wrongdoing and that, even then, punishment is not inevitable.

How Would You...?

As a **health-care professional**, how would you expect a child in the heteronomous stage of moral development to judge the behaviors of a doctor who unintentionally caused pain to a child during a medical procedure?

How do these changes in moral reasoning occur? Piaget argued that as children develop, they become more sophisticated in their thinking about social matters, especially about the possibilities and conditions of cooperation. Piaget stressed that this social understanding comes about through the mutual give-and-take of peer relations. In the peer group, where others have power and status similar to the child's, plans are negotiated and coordinated, and disagreements are reasoned about and eventually settled. Parent-child relations, in which parents have the power and children do not, are less likely to advance moral reasoning, because rules are often handed down in an authoritarian manner.

Earlier you read about Ross Thompson's view that young children are not as egocentric as Piaget envisioned. Thompson (2012) recently further elaborated on this view, arguing that recent research indicates that young children often show a non-egocentric awareness of others' goals, feelings, and desires and how such internal states are influenced by the actions of others. These links between advances in moral understanding and theory of mind research indicate that young children possess cognitive resources that allow them to be aware of others' intentions and to know when someone violates a moral prohibition. One study of 3-year-olds found that they were less likely to offer assistance to an adult they had previously observed being harmful to another person (Vaish, Carpenter, & Tomasello, 2010). However, because of limitations in their self-control skills, social understanding, and cognitive flexibility, young children's moral advancements often are inconsistent and vary across situations. They still have a long way to go before they are able to develop a consistent moral character and make ethical judgments.

How will this child's moral thinking about stealing a cookie differ according to whether he is in Piaget's heteronomous or autonomous stage?
© Tom Grill/Corbis RF

Moral Behavior

The behavioral and social cognitive approach to development focuses on moral behavior rather than moral reasoning. It holds that the processes of reinforcement, punishment, and imitation explain the development of moral behavior. When children are rewarded for behavior that is consistent with laws and social conventions, they are likely to repeat that behavior. When models who behave morally are provided, children are likely to adopt their actions. And when children are punished for immoral behavior, those behaviors are likely to be reduced or eliminated. However, because punishment may have adverse side effects, it needs to be used judiciously and cautiously.

If a mother has rewarded a 4-year-old boy for telling the truth when he broke a glass at home, does this mean he is likely to tell the truth to his preschool teacher when he knocks over a vase and breaks it? Not necessarily; the situation influences behavior. More than half a century ago, a comprehensive study of thousands of children in many situations—at home, at school, and at church, for example—found that a totally honest child is virtually nonexistent; so is a child who cheats in all situations (Hartshorne & May, 1928–1930). Behavioral and social cognitive researchers emphasize that what children do in one situation is often only weakly related to what they do in other situations. A child might cheat in class but not in a game; a child might steal a piece of candy when alone but not when others are present.

Social cognitive theorists also emphasize that the ability to resist temptation is closely tied to the development of self-control (Mischel, 2004), which involves learning to delay gratification. According to social cognitive theorists, cognitive factors are important in the child's development of self-control (Bandura, 2010a).

Gender

Gender refers to the characteristics of people as females and males. **Gender identity** is the sense of being male or female, which most children acquire by the time they are 3 years old. **Gender roles** are sets of expectations that prescribe how females or males should think, act, and feel. During the preschool years, most children increasingly act in ways that match their culture's gender roles.

How do these and other gender differences come about? Biology clearly plays a role. Among the possible biological influences are chromosomes, hormones, and evolution (Buss, 2015; Hines, 2015; Johnson, 2017). However, our focus in this chapter is on the social aspects of gender.

Social Influences

Many social scientists do not locate the cause of psychological gender differences in biological dispositions. Rather, they argue that these differences are due to social experiences (Matlin, 2012). Their explanations include both social and cognitive theories.

Social Theories of Gender Three main social theories of gender have been proposed: social role theory, psychoanalytic theory, and social cognitive theory. Alice Eagly (2001, 2010, 2012) proposed **social role theory,** which states that gender differences result from the contrasting roles of women and men. In most cultures around the world, women have less power and status than men do, and they control fewer resources (Helgeson, 2017). Compared with men, women perform more domestic work, spend fewer hours in paid employment, receive lower pay, and are more thinly represented in the highest levels of organizations. In Eagly's (2010, 2012) view, as women adapted to roles with less power and less status in society, they showed more cooperative, less dominant profiles than men did. Thus, the social hierarchy and division of labor are important causes of gender differences in power, assertiveness, and nurture (Eagly & Wood, 2016).

The **psychoanalytic theory of gender** stems from Freud's view that the preschool child develops a sexual attraction to the opposite-sex parent. This is the process known as the Oedipus (for boys) or Electra (for girls) complex. At age 5 or 6, the child renounces this attraction because of anxious feelings. Subsequently, the child identifies with the same-sex parent, unconsciously adopting that parent's characteristics. However, developmental psychologists have observed that gender development does not proceed in the manner that Freud proposed (Callan, 2001). Children become gender-typed much earlier than age 5 or 6, and they become masculine or feminine even when the same-sex parent is not present in the family.

The social cognitive approach provides an alternative explanation. According to the **social cognitive theory of gender,** children's gender development occurs through observation and imitation of what other people say and do, and through being rewarded and punished for gender-appropriate and gender-inappropriate behavior (Bussey & Bandura, 1999). From birth onward, males and females are treated differently. When infants and toddlers show gender differences, adults tend to reward them. Parents often use rewards and punishments to teach their daughters to be feminine ("Karen, you are being a good girl when you play gently with your doll") and their sons to be masculine ("Keith, a boy as big as you are is not supposed to cry"). Parents, however, are only one of many

First imagine that this is a photograph of a baby girl. *What expectations would you have of her?* Then imagine that this is a photograph of a baby boy. *What expectations would you have of him?*
© Getty Images RF

gender identity The sense of being male or female, which most children acquire by the time they are 3 years old.

gender roles Sets of expectations that prescribe how females or males should think, act, and feel.

social role theory A theory that gender differences result from the contrasting roles of men and women.

psychoanalytic theory of gender A theory deriving from Freud's view that the preschool child develops a sexual attraction to the opposite-sex parent, by approximately 5 or 6 years of age renounces this attraction because of anxious feelings, and subsequently identifies with the same-sex parent, unconsciously adopting the same-sex parent's characteristics.

social cognitive theory of gender A theory emphasizing that children's gender development occurs through the observation and imitation of gender behavior and through the rewards and punishments children experience for gender-appropriate and gender-inappropriate behavior.

sources from which children learn gender roles (Leaper, 2015). Culture, schools, peers, the media, and other family members also provide gender role models (Hyde & Else-Quest, 2013). For example, children learn about gender by observing other adults in the neighborhood and on television. As children grow older, peers become increasingly important. Let's look more closely at the influence of parents and peers.

Parental Influences

Parents influence their children's gender development by action and by example. (Helgeson, 2017; Leaper & Farkas, 2015; Liben, Bigler, & Hilliard, 2014). Both mothers and fathers are psychologically important to their children's gender development (Tenenbaum & May, 2014). Cultures around the world, however, can vary in the roles expected for mother and fathers (Chen & Liu, 2016). A research review provided these conclusions (Bronstein, 2006):

- *Mothers' socialization strategies.* In many cultures, mothers socialize their daughters to be more obedient and responsible than their sons. They also place more restrictions on their daughters' autonomy.

- *Fathers' socialization strategies.* Fathers show more attention to their sons than to their daughters, engage in more activities with their sons, and put forth more effort to promote their sons' intellectual development.

How Would You...?

As a **human development and family studies professional,** how would you describe the ways in which parents influence their children's notions of gender roles?

Thus, according to Bronstein (2006, pp. 269–270), "Despite an increased awareness in the United States and other Western cultures of the detrimental effects of gender stereotyping, many parents continue to foster behaviors and perceptions that are consonant with traditional gender role norms."

Peer Influences

Parents provide the earliest discrimination of gender roles, but before long, peers join the process of responding to and modeling masculine and feminine behavior (Leaper, 2015). In fact, peers become so important to gender development that the playground has been described as "gender school" (Luria & Herzog, 1985).

Peers extensively reward and punish gender behavior (Rubin, Bukowski, & Bowker, 2015). For example, when children play in ways that the culture considers sex-appropriate, their peers tend to reward them. But peers often reject children who act in a manner that is considered more characteristic of the other gender (Handrinos & others, 2012). A little girl who brings a doll to the park may find herself surrounded by new friends; a little boy who does the same thing might be jeered at. However, there is greater pressure for boys to conform to a traditional male role than for girls to conform to a traditional female role (Fagot, Rodgers, & Leinbach, 2000). For example, a preschool girl who wants to wear boys' clothing receives considerably more approval than a boy who wants to wear a dress. The very term "tomboy" implies broad social acceptance of girls' adopting traditional male behaviors.

Gender molds important aspects of peer relations (Rubin, Bukowski, & Bowker, 2015). It influences the composition of children's groups, the size of groups, and interactions within a group (Maccoby, 1998, 2002).

- *Gender composition of children's groups.* Around age 3, children already show a preference for spending time with same-sex playmates. This preference increases until around age 12, and during the elementary school years children spend a large majority of their free time with children of their own sex (see Figure 1). Observations of children show that they are more likely to play in same-sex than mixed-sex groups. This tendency increases between 4 and 6 years of age.

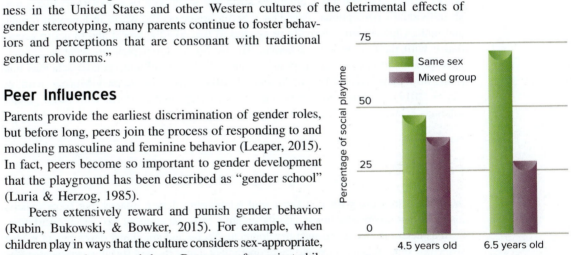

Figure 1

Developmental Changes in Percentage of Time Spent in Same-Sex and Mixed-Group Settings
Observations of children show that they are more likely to play in same-sex than mixed-sex groups. This tendency increases between 4 and 6 years of age.

- *Group size.* From about age 5, boys are more likely to interact socially in larger clusters than girls are. Boys are also more likely to participate in organized group games than girls are. In one study, same-sex groups of six children were permitted to use play materials in any way they wished (Benenson, Apostolaris, & Parnass, 1997). Girls were more likely than boys to play in dyads or triads, while boys were more likely to interact in larger groups and seek to attain a group goal.

- *Interaction in same-sex groups.* Boys are more likely than girls to engage in rough-and-tumble play, competition, conflict, ego displays, risk taking, and seeking dominance. By contrast, girls are more likely to engage in "collaborative discourse," in which they talk and act in a more reciprocal manner.

Cognitive Influences

Observation, imitation, rewards, and punishment—these are the mechanisms by which gender develops, according to social cognitive theory. Interactions between the child and the social environment are the main keys to gender development. Some critics argue that this explanation pays too little attention to the child's own mind and understanding, and portrays the child as passively acquiring gender roles (Martin & Ruble, 2010).

How Would You...?

As an **educator,** how would you create a classroom climate that promotes healthy gender development for both boys and girls?

One influential cognitive theory is **gender schema theory,** which states that gender typing emerges as children gradually develop gender schemas of what is gender-appropriate and gender-inappropriate in their culture (Halim & others, 2016; Martin & others, 2013). A schema is a cognitive structure, a network of associations that guide an individual's perceptions. A gender schema organizes the world in terms of female and male. Children are internally motivated to perceive the world and to act in accordance with their developing schemas. Bit by bit, children pick up what is gender-appropriate and gender-inappropriate in their culture, developing gender schemas that shape how they perceive the world and what they remember (Conry-Murray, Kim, & Turiel, 2012). Children are motivated to act in ways that conform with these gender schemas. Thus, gender schemas fuel gender typing.

Families

Attachment to a caregiver is a key social relationship during infancy, but some experts maintain that secure attachment and the infant's early experiences have been overdramatized as determinants of life-span development. Social and emotional development is also shaped by other relationships and by temperament, contexts, and social experiences in the early childhood years and later (Kerig, 2016; Stifter & Dollar, 2016). In this section, we discuss aspects of social relationships in early childhood that go beyond attachment.

Parenting

Some recent media accounts portray many parents as unhappy, feeling little joy in caring for their children. However, recent research found that parents were more satisfied with their lives than were nonparents, felt relatively better on a daily basis than did nonparents, and had more positive feelings related to caring for their children than to other daily activities (Nelson & others, 2013). Also, a recent research review concluded that parents are unhappy when they experience more negative emotions, financial problems, sleep problems, and troubled marriages, and that parents are happy when they experience meaning in life, satisfaction of basic needs, more positive emotions, and positive social roles (Nelson, Kushley, & Lyubomirsky, 2014).

Good parenting takes time and effort (Bornstein, 2016). You can't do it in a minute here and a minute there. You can't do it with CDs or DVDs. Of course, it's not just the quantity of time parents spend with

gender schema theory The theory that gender typing emerges as children gradually develop gender schemas of what is gender-appropriate and gender-inappropriate in their culture.

children that is important for children's development—the quality of the parenting is clearly important (Wadsworth & others, 2016). For example, a recent study found that maternal scaffolding, sensitivity, and support for autonomy were linked to better executive function in preschool children (Blair, Raver, & Berry, 2014).

Baumrind's Parenting Styles

Diana Baumrind (1971) stresses that parents should be neither punitive nor aloof. Rather, they should develop rules for their children and be affectionate with them. She has described four parenting styles:

- **Authoritarian parenting** is a restrictive, punitive style in which parents exhort the child to follow their directions and respect their work and effort. The authoritarian parent places firm limits and controls on the child and allows little verbal exchange. For example, an authoritarian parent might say, "You do it my way or else." Authoritarian parents also might spank the child frequently, enforce rules rigidly but not explain them, and show anger toward the child. Children of authoritarian parents are often unhappy, fearful, and anxious about comparing themselves with others; they also fail to initiate activity and have weak communication skills.

- **Authoritative parenting** encourages children to be independent but still places limits and controls on their actions. Extensive verbal give-and-take is allowed, and parents are warm and nurturant toward the child. An authoritative parent might put his arm around the child in a comforting way and say, "You know you shouldn't have done that. Let's talk about how you could handle the situation better next time." Authoritative parents show pleasure and support in response to their children's constructive behavior. They also expect independent, age-appropriate behavior. Children whose parents are authoritative are often cheerful, self-controlled and self-reliant, and achievement-oriented; they tend to maintain friendly relations with peers, cooperate with adults, and cope well with stress. A recent study also found that young children with authoritative parents were less likely to be obese than their counterparts with authoritarian parents (Kakinami & others, 2015).

- **Neglectful parenting** is a style in which the parent is uninvolved in the child's life. Children whose parents are neglectful develop the sense that other aspects of the parents' lives are more important than they are. These children tend to be socially incompetent. Many have poor self-control and don't handle independence well. They frequently have low self-esteem, are immature, and may be alienated from the family. In adolescence, they may show patterns of truancy and delinquency.

- **Indulgent parenting** is a style in which parents are highly involved with their children but place few demands or controls on them. Such parents let their children do what they want. Some parents deliberately rear their children in this way because they believe the combination of warm involvement and few restraints will produce a creative, confident child. However, children whose parents are indulgent rarely learn respect for others and have difficulty controlling their behavior. They might be domineering, egocentric, and noncompliant, and have unsatisfactory peer relations.

These four classifications of parenting involve combinations of acceptance and responsiveness on the one hand and demand and control on the other (Maccoby & Martin, 1983). How these dimensions combine to produce authoritarian, authoritative, neglectful, and indulgent parenting is shown in Figure 2.

Keep in mind that research on parenting styles and children's development is correlational, not causal, in nature. Thus, if a study reveals that authoritarian parenting is linked to higher levels of aggression in children, it may be just as likely that aggressive children elicited authoritarian parenting as it is that authoritarian parenting produced aggressive children (Bush & Peterson, 2013). Also recall that a third factor may influence the correlation between two factors. Thus, in the example of the correlation between authoritarian

authoritarian parenting A restrictive, punitive style in which parents exhort the child to follow their directions and to respect work and effort. The authoritarian parent places firm limits and controls on the child and allows little verbal exchange. Authoritarian parenting is associated with children's social incompetence.

authoritative parenting A parenting style in which parents encourage their children to be independent but still place limits and controls on their actions. Extensive verbal give-and-take is allowed, and parents are warm and nurturant toward the child. Authoritative parenting is associated with children's social competence.

neglectful parenting A style of parenting in which the parent is very uninvolved in the child's life; it is associated with children's social incompetence, especially a lack of self-control.

indulgent parenting A style of parenting in which parents are highly involved with their children but place few demands or controls on them. Indulgent parenting is associated with children's social incompetence, especially a lack of self-control.

parenting and aggressive children, possibly authoritarian parents (first factor) and aggressive children (second factor) share genes (third factor) that predispose them to behave in ways that produced the correlation.

Parenting Styles in Context

Among Baumrind's four parenting styles, authoritative parenting clearly conveys the most benefits to the child and to the family as a whole. Do the benefits of authoritative parenting transcend the boundaries of ethnicity, socioeconomic status, and household composition? Although some exceptions have been found, evidence linking authoritative parenting with competence on the part of the child occurs in research across a wide range of ethnic groups, social strata, cultures, and family structures (Steinberg, 2014).

Nevertheless, researchers have found that in some ethnic groups, aspects of the authoritarian style may be associated with more positive outcomes than Baumrind predicts. In the Arab world, many families are very authoritarian, dominated by the father's rule, and children are taught strict codes of conduct and family loyalty (Booth, 2002). As another example, Asian American parents often continue aspects of traditional Asian child-rearing practices that have sometimes been described as authoritarian. The parents exert considerable control over their children's lives. However, Ruth Chao (2001, 2005, 2007; Chao & Otsuki-Clutter, 2011; Chao & Tseng, 2002) argues that the style of parenting used by many Asian American parents is distinct from the domineering control that is characteristic of the authoritarian style. Instead, Chao argues that it reflects concern and involvement in children's lives and is best conceptualized as a type of training. The high academic achievement of Asian American children may be a consequence of their parents' "training" (Stevenson & Zusho, 2002).

	Accepting, responsive	Rejecting unresponsive
Demanding, controlling	Authoritative	Authoritarian
Undemanding, uncontrolling	Indulgent	Neglectful

Figure 2 Classification of Parenting Styles
The four types of parenting styles (authoritative, authoritarian, indulgent, and neglectful) involve the dimensions of acceptance and responsiveness, on the one hand, and demand and control on the other. For example, authoritative parenting involves being both accepting/responsive and demanding/controlling.
© Ariel Skelley/Corbis

How Would You...?

As a **human development and family studies professional,** how would you characterize the parenting style that prevails within your own family?

How Would You...?

As a **psychologist,** how would you use the research on parenting styles to design a parent education class that teaches effective skills for interacting with young children?

Punishment

Use of corporal punishment is legal in every state in the United States. A national survey of U.S. parents with 3- and 4-year-old children found that 26 percent of parents reported spanking their children frequently, and 67 percent reported yelling at their children frequently (Regalado & others, 2004). A recent study of more than 11,000 U.S. parents indicated that 80 percent of the parents reported spanking their children by the time they reached kindergarten (Gershoff & others, 2012). A cross-cultural comparison found that individuals in the United States and Canada were among those who held the most favorable attitudes toward corporal punishment and were most likely to remember it being used by their parents

According to Ruth Chao, which type of parenting style do many Asian American parents use?

© Blend Images/ SuperStock RF

(see Figure 3) (Curran & others, 2001). Physical punishment is outlawed in 41 countries, with a number of countries increasing the ban on physical punishment mainly to promote children's rights to protection from abuse and exploitation (Committee on the Rights of the Child, 2014).

What are some reasons for avoiding spanking or similar punishments? They include the following:

- When adults punish a child by yelling, screaming, or spanking, they are presenting children with out-of-control models for handling stressful situations. Children may imitate this behavior.

- Punishment can instill fear, rage, or avoidance. For example, spanking the child may cause the child to avoid being near the parent and to fear the parent.

- Punishment tells children what not to do rather than what to do. Children should be given constructive feedback, such as "Why don't you try this?"

- Parents might unintentionally become so angry when they are punishing the child that they become abusive.

Most child psychologists recommend handling misbehavior by reasoning with the child, especially explaining the consequences of the child's actions for others. *Time out*, in which the child is removed from a setting that offers positive reinforcement, can also be effective. For example, when the child has misbehaved, a parent might forbid TV viewing for a specified time.

Debate about the effects of punishment on children's development continues (Deater-Deckard, 2013; Ferguson, 2013; Gershoff, 2013; Laible, Thompson, & Froimson, 2015; Theunissen, Vogels, & Reijneveld, 2015). Several recent longitudinal studies also have found that physical punishment of young children is associated with higher levels of aggression later in childhood and adolescence (Gershoff & others, 2012; Lansford & others, 2014; Taylor & others, 2010).

However, a recent meta-analysis that focused on longitudinal studies revealed that the negative outcomes of punishment on children's internalizing and externalizing problems were minimal (Ferguson, 2013). A research review of 26 studies concluded that only severe or predominant use of spanking, not mild spanking, compared unfavorably with alternative discipline practices (Larzelere & Kuhn, 2005). In addition to considering whether physical punishment is mild or out of control, another factor in evaluating effects on children's development involves cultural contexts. Recently researchers have found that in countries such as Kenya in which physical punishment is considered normal and necessary for handling children's transgressions, the effects of physical punishment are less harmful than in countries such as Thailand where physical punishment is perceived as more harmful to children's development (Lansford & others, 2005, 2012).

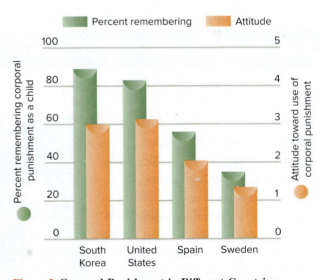

Figure 3 Corporal Punishment in Different Countries
A 5-point scale was used to assess attitudes toward corporal punishment, with scores closer to 1 indicating an attitude against its use and scores closer to 5 suggesting an attitude favoring its use. *Why are studies of corporal punishment correlational studies, and how does that affect their usefulness?*

Thus, in the view of some experts, it is still difficult to determine whether the effects of physical punishment are harmful to children's development, although such a view might be distasteful to some individuals (Ferguson, 2013). Also, as with other research on parenting, research on punishment is correlational in nature, making it difficult to discover causal factors. Also, consider the concept of reciprocal socialization (discussed in the chapter on socioemotional development in infancy), which emphasizes bidirectional child and parent influences. Researchers have found links between children's early behavioral problems and parents' greater use of physical punishment over time (Laible, Thompson, & Froimson, 2015; Sheehan & Watson, 2008). Nonetheless, a large majority of leading experts on parenting conclude that physical punishment has harmful effects on children and should not be used.

In a recent research review, Elizabeth Gershoff (2013) concluded that the defenders of spanking have not produced any evidence that spanking produces positive outcomes for children and that negative outcomes of spanking have been replicated in many studies. Also, physical punishment that involves abuse can be very harmful to children's development, as discussed later in this chapter (Cicchetti & Toth, 2015, 2016).

Coparenting

Coparenting refers to the support that parents give each other in raising a child. Poor coordination between parents, undermining by one parent of the other, lack of cooperation and warmth, and aloofness by one parent are conditions that place children at risk (Galdiolo & Roskam, 2016; Goldberg & Carlson, 2015; Lewin & others, 2015; Parent & others, 2016). In addition, one study revealed that coparenting is more beneficial than either maternal or paternal parenting in terms of children's development of self-control (Karreman & others, 2008). And a recent study found that greater father involvement in young children's play was linked to an increase in supportive coparenting (Jia & Schoppe-Sullivan, 2011). Also, in a recent study, unmarried African American parents who were instructed in coparenting techinques during the prenatal period and also one month after the baby was born improved their rapport, communication, and problem-solving skills when the baby was 3 months old (McHale, Salman-Engin, & Coovert, 2015).

Parents who do not spend enough time with their children or who have problems in child rearing can benefit from counseling and therapy. To read about the work of marriage and family counselor Darla Botkin, see *Careers in Life-Span Development.*

Careers in life-span development

Darla Botkin, Marriage and Family Therapist

Darla Botkin is a marriage and family therapist who teaches, conducts research, and engages in marriage and family therapy. She is on the faculty of the University of Kentucky. Botkin obtained a bachelor's degree in elementary education with a concentration in special education, and she went on to receive a master's degree in early childhood education. She spent the next six years working with children and their families in a variety of settings, including child care, elementary school, and Head Start. These experiences led her to recognize the interdependence of the developmental settings

Darla Botkin (*left*) conducts a family therapy session.
© Dr. Darla Botkin

that children and their parents experience (such as home, school, and work). She returned to graduate school and obtained a Ph.D. in family studies from the University of Tennessee. She then became a faculty member in the Family Studies program at the University of Kentucky. Completing further coursework and clinical training in marriage and family therapy, she became certified as a marriage and family therapist.

Botkin's current interests include working with young children in family therapy, exploring gender and ethnic issues in family therapy, and understanding the role of spirituality in family wellness.

Child Maltreatment

Unfortunately, punishment sometimes leads to the abuse of infants and children (Cicchetti & Toth, 2015, 2016; Jackson & Deye, 2015). In 2013, 679,000 U.S. children were found to be victims of child abuse at least once during that year (U.S. Department of Health and Human Services, 2015). Ninety-one percent of these children were abused by one or both parents. Laws in many states now require physicians and teachers to report suspected cases of child abuse, yet many cases go unreported, especially those involving battered infants.

Eight-year-old Donnique Hein lovingly holds her younger sister, 6-month-old Maria Paschel, after a meal at Laura's Home, a crisis shelter in suburban Cleveland run by the City Mission.
© Joshua Gunter/The Plain Dealer/Landov Images

Types of Child Maltreatment

The four main types of child maltreatment are physical abuse, child neglect, sexual abuse, and emotional abuse (Jackson, Kissoon, & Greene, 2015; National Clearinghouse on Child Abuse and Neglect, 2013):

- *Physical abuse* is characterized by the infliction of physical injury as a result of punching, beating, kicking, biting, burning, shaking, or otherwise harming a child. The parent or other person may not intend to hurt the child; the injury may result from excessive physical punishment (Cicchetti & Toth, 2016; Villodas & others, 2016).

- *Child neglect* is characterized by failure to provide for the child's basic needs. Neglect can be physical (abandonment, for example), educational (allowing chronic truancy, for example), or emotional (marked inattention to the child's needs, for example). Child neglect is by far the most common form of child maltreatment. In every country where relevant data have been collected, neglect occurs up to three times as often as abuse (O'Hara & others, 2016).

- *Sexual abuse* includes fondling of genitals, intercourse, incest, rape, sodomy, exhibitionism, and commercial exploitation through prostitution or production of pornographic materials (Collin-Vezina & others, 2015; Mathews, Lee, & Norman, 2016).

- *Emotional abuse (psychological/verbal abuse/mental injury)* includes acts or omissions by parents or other caregivers that have caused, or could cause, serious behavioral, cognitive, or emotional problems (Shin & others, 2015).

Although any of these forms of child maltreatment may be found separately, they often occur in combination. Emotional abuse is almost always present when other forms are identified.

How Would You...?
As a **health-care professional,** how would you work with parents during infant and early childhood checkups to prevent child maltreatment?

The Context of Abuse

No single factor causes child maltreatment (Cicchetti & Toth, 2016). A combination of factors, including the culture, characteristics of the family, and developmental characteristics of the child, likely contribute to child maltreatment. Among the family and family-associated characteristics that may contribute to child maltreatment are parenting stress, substance abuse, social isolation, single parenting, and socioeconomic difficulties (especially poverty) (Cicchetti & Toth, 2015). The interactions among all family members need to be considered, regardless of who performs violent acts against the child. For example, even though the father may be the one who physically abuses the child, the behavior of the mother, the child, and siblings should also be evaluated.

Were parents who abuse children abused by their own parents? A 30-year longitudinal study found that offspring of parents who engaged in child maltreatment and neglect are at risk for engaging in child neglect and sexual maltreatment themselves (Widom, Czaja, & Dumont, 2015). It is estimated that about one-third of parents who were abused themselves when they were young go on to abuse their own children (Cicchetti & Toth, 2006).

Developmental Consequences of Abuse

Among the consequences of maltreatment in childhood and adolescence are poor emotion regulation, attachment problems, problems in peer relations, difficulty in adapting to school, and other psychological problems, such as depression and delinquency (Cicchetti & Toth, 2015, 2016). Compared with their peers, adolescents who experienced abuse or neglect as children are more likely to engage in violent romantic relationships, delinquency, sexual risk taking, and substance abuse (Trickett & others, 2011). And a recent study revealed that a significant increase in suicide attempts before age 18 occurred with repeated child maltreatment (Jonson-Reid, Kohl, & Drake, 2012).

Later, during the adult years, individuals who were maltreated as children are more likely to experience physical illness, mental illness, and sexual problems (Lacelle & others, 2012). A 30-year longitudinal study found that middle-aged adults who had experienced maltreatment during childhood were at increased risk for diabetes, lung disease, malnutrition, and vision problems (Widom & others, 2012). However, this study also found that 75 percent of parents who had experienced maltreatment during childhood had never abused their own children, and thus it is important to note that the majority of people who were abused in childhood are unlikely to abuse their own children. Another study revealed that young adults who had experienced child maltreatment, especially physical abuse, at any age were more likely to be depressed and to engage in suicidal ideation as adults (Dunn & others, 2013). Further, adults who were maltreated as children often have difficulty in establishing and maintaining healthy intimate relationships (Dozier, Stovall-McClough, & Albus, 2009). As adults, maltreated children are also at higher risk for violent behavior toward other adults—especially dating partners and marital partners—as well as for substance abuse, anxiety, and depression (Miller-Perrin, Perrin, & Kocur, 2009).

An important research agenda is to discover how to prevent child maltreatment or intervene in children's lives when they have been maltreated (Cicchetti & Toth, 2015, 2016). In one study of maltreating mothers and their 1-year-olds, two treatments were effective in reducing child maltreatment: (1) home visitation that emphasized improved parenting, coping with stress, and increasing support for the mother; and (2) parent-infant psychotherapy that focused on improving maternal-infant attachment (Cicchetti, Toth, & Rogosch, 2005).

How Would You...?

As an **educator,** how would you explain the potential impact of maltreatment at home on a child's performance in school?

Sibling Relationships and Birth Order

How do developmental psychologists characterize sibling relationships? And how does birth order influence behavior, if at all?

Sibling Relationships

Approximately 80 percent of American children have one or more siblings—that is, sisters and brothers (Dunn, 2007, 2015). If you grew up with siblings, you probably have rich memories of your relationships with them. Two- to 4-year-old siblings in each other's presence have a conflict once every 10 minutes, on average; the rate of conflict declines somewhat from ages 5 to 7 (Kramer, 2006). What do parents do when they encounter siblings having a verbal or physical confrontation? One study revealed that they do one of three things: (1) intervene and try to help them resolve the conflict, (2) admonish or threaten them, or (3) do nothing at all (Kramer & Perozynski, 1999). Of interest is the fact that in families with two siblings ages 2 to 5 the most frequent parental reaction to sibling conflict is to do nothing at all.

Laurie Kramer (2006), who has conducted a number of research studies on siblings, says that not intervening and letting sibling conflict escalate are not good strategies. She developed a program titled "More Fun with Sisters and Brothers" that teaches 4- to 8-year-old siblings social skills for developing positive interactions (Kramer & Radey, 1997). Among the skills taught in the program are how to appropriately initiate play, how to accept and refuse invitations to play, how to take another person's perspective, how to deal with angry feelings, and how to manage conflict.

However, conflict is only one of the many dimensions of sibling relations (McHale, Updegraff, & Whiteman, 2013). Sibling relations include helping, sharing, teaching, fighting, compromising, and playing, and siblings can act as emotional supports, rivals, and communication partners. A recent review concluded that sibling relationships in adolescence are not as close, are less intense, and are more egalitarian than in childhood (East, 2009).

Do parents usually favor one sibling over others—and if so, does it make a difference in an adolescent's development? One study of 384 sibling pairs revealed that 65 percent of their mothers and 70 percent of their fathers showed favoritism toward one sibling (Shebloski, Conger, & Widaman, 2005). When favoritism of one sibling occurred, it was linked to lower self-esteem and sadness in the less-favored sibling. Indeed, equality and fairness are major concerns in regard to siblings' relationships with each other and how they are treated by their parents (Aldercotte, White, & Hughes, 2016; Campione-Barr, Greer, & Kruse, 2013).

Judy Dunn (2007, 2015), a leading expert on sibling relationships, described three important characteristics of sibling relationships:

1. *The emotional quality of the relationship.* Siblings often express intense emotions—both positive and negative—toward each other. Many children and adolescents have mixed feelings toward their siblings.

2. *The familiarity and intimacy of the relationship.* Siblings typically know each other very well, and this intimacy suggests that they can either provide support or tease and undermine each other, depending on the situation.

3. *The variation in sibling relationships.* Some siblings describe their relationships more positively than others do. Thus, there is considerable variation in sibling relationships. We just noted that many siblings have mixed feelings about each other, but some children and adolescents describe their siblings mainly in warm, affectionate ways, whereas others primarily talk about how irritating and mean a sibling is.

What characterizes children's sibling relationships?
© RubberBall Productions/Getty Images RF

Birth Order

Whether a child has older or younger siblings has been linked to the development of certain personality characteristics. For example, a recent review concluded that "firstborns are the most intelligent, achieving, and conscientious, while later-borns are the most rebellious, liberal, and agreeable" (Paulhus, 2008, p. 210). Compared with later-born children, firstborn children have also been described as more adult-oriented, helpful, conforming, and self-controlled. However, when such birth-order differences are reported, they often are small.

What accounts for differences related to birth order? Proposed explanations usually point to variations in interactions associated with a particular position in the family. In one study, mothers became more negative, coercive, and restraining and played less with the firstborn following the birth of a second child (Dunn & Kendrick, 1982).

What about children who don't have siblings? The popular conception is that an only child is a "spoiled brat" with undesirable characteristics such as dependency, lack of self-control, and self-centered behavior. But researchers present a more positive portrayal, in which only children are often achievement-oriented and display desirable personality characteristics, especially in comparison with later-borns and children from large families (Falbo & Poston, 1993; Jiao, Ji, & Jing, 1996).

So far, our discussion suggests that birth order might be a strong predictor of behavior. However, an increasing number of family researchers stress that, when all the factors that influence behavior are considered, birth order by itself has limited ability to predict behavior. Think about some of the other important factors in children's lives that influence their behavior. They include heredity, models of competency or incompetency that parents present to children on a daily basis, peer and school influences, socioeconomic and sociohistorical factors, and cultural variations. When someone says that firstborns are always like this but last-borns are always like that, he or she is making overly simplistic statements that do not adequately take into account the complexity of influences on a child's development.

The Changing Family in a Changing Society

Beyond variations in number of siblings, the families that children experience differ in many important ways (Grusec & Hastings, 2015; Morrill, Hawrilenko, & Cordova, 2016; Yu, Cheah, & Calvin, 2016). As shown in Figure 4, the United States has one of the highest percentages of single-parent families in the world. Among two-parent families, there are those in which both parents work, those in which parents have found new spouses after divorce, and those in which the parents are gay or lesbian. Differences in culture and socioeconomic status (SES) also influence families. How do these variations in families affect children?

Working Parents

More than half of U.S. mothers with a child under age 5 are in the labor force, as are more than two-thirds with a child 6 to 17 years of age. Maternal employment is a part of modern life, but its effects are still being debated.

Parental employment can have positive and negative effects on parenting (O'Brien & others, 2014). Recent research indicates that what matters for children's development is the nature of the parents' work rather than whether or not both parents work outside the home (Goldberg & Lucas-Thompson, 2008; Clarke-Stewart & Parke, 2014). For example, a recent study of almost 3,000 adolescents found a negative association of the father's, but not the mother's, unemployment on the adolescents' health (Bacikova-Sleskova, Benka, & Orosova, 2015). Also, a recent study of dual-earner couples found that work-family enrichment experiences had positive outcomes on parenting quality, which in turn was linked to positive child outcomes; by contrast, work-family conflict experiences were associated with poorer parenting quality, which in turn was related to negative child outcomes (Vieira & others, 2016).

How does work affect parenting?
© Keith Brofsky/Photodisc/Getty Images RF

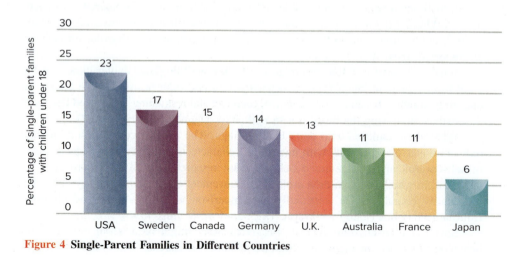

Figure 4 **Single-Parent Families in Different Countries**

Ann Crouter (2006) described how parents bring their experiences at work into their homes. She concluded that parents who experience poor working conditions, such as long hours, overtime work, stressful working conditions, and lack of autonomy at work, are likely to be more irritable at home and engage in less effective parenting than their counterparts who experience better working conditions. A consistent finding is that children (especially girls) whose mothers are employed engage in less gender stereotyping and have more egalitarian views of gender than do children whose mothers do not work outside the home (Goldberg & Lucas-Thompson, 2008).

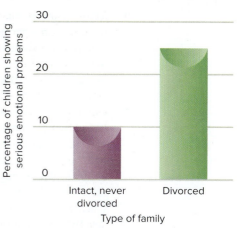

Children in Divorced Families

Divorce rates changed rather dramatically in the United States and many countries around the world in the late twentieth century (Braver & Lamb, 2013). The U.S. divorce rate increased dramatically in the 1960s and 1970s but has declined since the 1980s. However, the divorce rate in the United States is still much higher than in most other countries.

It is estimated that 40 percent of children born to married parents in the United States will experience their parents' divorce (Hetherington & Stanley-Hagan, 2002). Let's examine some important questions about children in divorced families:

● *Are children better adjusted in intact, never-divorced families than in divorced families?* Most researchers agree that children from divorced families show poorer adjustment than their counterparts in never-divorced families (Amato & Anthony, 2014; Arkes, 2015; Hetherington, 2006; Weaver & Schofield, 2015) (see Figure 5). Those who have experienced multiple divorces are at greater risk. Children in divorced families are more likely than those in never-divorced families to have academic problems, to exhibit externalized problems (such as acting out and delinquency) and experience internalized problems (such as anxiety and depression), to be less socially responsible, to have less competent intimate relationships, to drop out of school, to become sexually active at an earlier age, to take drugs, to associate with antisocial peers, to have low self-esteem, and to be less securely attached as young adults (Lansford, 2012, 2013). In a recent study, individuals who had experienced their parents' divorce were more at risk for engaging in a lifetime suicide attempt (Alonzo & others, 2014).

● *Should parents stay together for the sake of the children?* Whether parents should stay in an unhappy or conflicted marriage for the sake of their children is one of the most commonly asked questions about divorce (Hetherington, 2006). If the stresses and disruptions in family relationships associated with an unhappy marriage that erode the well-being of children are reduced by the move to a divorced, single-parent family, divorce can be advantageous. However, if the diminished resources and increased risks associated with divorce are accompanied by inept parenting and sustained or increased conflict, not only between the divorced couple but also among the parents, children, and siblings, the best choice for the children would be for an unhappy marriage to be continued (Hetherington & Stanley-Hagan, 2002). It is difficult to determine how these "ifs" will play out when parents either remain together in an acrimonious marriage or become divorced.

Figure 5 Divorce and Children's Emotional Problems In Hetherington's research, 25 percent of children from divorced families showed serious emotional problems, compared with only 10 percent of children from intact, never-divorced families. However, keep in mind that a substantial majority (75 percent) of the children from divorced families did not show serious emotional problems.

What concerns are involved in whether parents should stay together for the sake of the children or become divorced?

© Image Source/PunchStock RF

- Many of the problems experienced by children of divorced parents begin during the predivorce period, a time when parents often are in active conflict. Thus, when children of divorced parents show problems, the problems may be due not only to the divorce itself but also to the marital conflict that led to it (Davies, Martin & Sturge-Apple, 2016; El-Sheikh & others, 2013; Jouriles, McDonald, & Kouros, 2016). E. Mark Cummings and his colleagues (Cummings & Miller, 2015; Cummings & Valentino, 2015; Koss & others, 2014; McCoy & others, 2013) have proposed emotion security theory, which has its roots in attachment theory and states that children appraise marital conflict in terms of their sense of security and safety in the family. These researchers make a distinction between marital conflict that is negative for children (such as hostile emotional displays and destructive conflict tactics) and marital conflict that can be positive for children (such as marital disagreement that involves calmly discussing each person's perspective and then working together to find a solution). In a recent study, maladaptive marital conflict (destructive strategies, severity of arguments) when children were 2 years old was associated with an increase in internalizing problems eight years later due to an undermining of attachment security for girls, while negative emotional aftermath of conflict (unresolved, lingering tension) increased both boys' and girls' internalizing problems (Brock & Kochanska, 2016).

- *How much do family processes matter after a divorce?* They matter a great deal (Demby, 2016; Elam & others, 2016; Lansford, 2012, 2013; Luecken & others, 2016; Warshak, 2014). When divorced parents' relationship with each other is harmonious and when they use authoritative parenting, children's adjustment improves (Hetherington, 2006). A number of researchers have shown that a disequilibrium, which includes diminished parenting skills, occurs in the year following the divorce—but by two years after the divorce, restabilization has occurred and parenting skills have improved (Hetherington, 1989). When the divorced parents can agree on childrearing strategies and can maintain a cordial relationship with each other, frequent visits by the noncustodial parent usually benefit the child (Fabricius & others, 2010). Following a divorce, father involvement with children drops off more than mother involvement, especially for fathers of girls. Also, a recent study in divorced families revealed that an intervention focused on improving the mother-child relationship was linked to improvements in relationship quality that increased children's coping skills over the short term (six months) and long term (six years) (Velez & others, 2011). And a longitudinal study revealed that parental divorce experienced before age 7 was linked to a lower level of the children's health through 50 years of age (Thomas & Hognas, 2015). Further, a recent study of non-residential fathers in divorced families indicated that high father-child involvement and low interparental conflict were linked to positive child outcomes (Flam & others, 2016). Also, a recent research review concluded that co-parenting (co-parental support, cooperation, and agreement) following divorce was related to positive child outcomes such as lower anxiety and depression, as well as higher self-esteem and academic performance (Lamela & Figueiredo, 2016).

- *What factors influence an individual child's vulnerability to suffering negative consequences as a result of divorce?* Among the factors involved are the parent's and child's adjustment prior to the divorce, as well as the child's personality and temperament, gender, and custody situation (Hetherington, 2006). In a recent study, a higher level of predivorce maternal sensitivity and child IQ served as protective factors in reducing children's problems after the divorce (Weaver & Schofield, 2015). Children whose parents later divorce show poorer adjustment before the breakup (Lansford, 2012, 2013). Children who are socially mature and responsible, who show few behavioral problems, and who have an easy temperament are better able to cope with their parents' divorce. Children with a difficult temperament often have problems coping with their parents' divorce (Hetherington, 2006). Joint custody works best for children when the parents can get along with each other (Clarke-Stewart & Parke, 2014).

- *What role does socioeconomic status play in the lives of children whose parents have divorced?* Mothers who have custody of their children experience the loss of about one-fourth to one-half of their predivorce income, compared with a loss of only one-tenth by fathers who have custody. This income loss for divorced mothers is accompanied by increased workloads, high rates of job instability, and residential moves to less desirable neighborhoods with inferior schools (Lansford, 2009).

Gay and Lesbian Parents

Increasingly, gay and lesbian couples are creating families that include children (Patterson, 2013, 2014; Patterson & Farr, 2014; Patterson, Farr, & Hastings, 2015). Approximately 20 percent of lesbians and 10 percent of gay men are parents. There may be more than 1 million gay and lesbian parents in the United States today.

Like heterosexual couples, gay and lesbian parents vary greatly. They may be single, or they may have same-gender partners. Many lesbian mothers and gay fathers are noncustodial parents because they lost custody of their children to heterosexual spouses after a divorce.

Parenthood among lesbians and gay men is controversial. Opponents claim that being raised by gay or lesbian parents harms the child's development. But researchers have found few differences between children growing up with lesbian mothers or gay fathers on the one hand, and children growing up with heterosexual parents on the other (Golombok, 2011a, b; Patterson, Farr, & Hastings, 2015). For example, children raised by gay or lesbian parents are just as popular with their peers, and no differences are found in the adjustment and mental health of children living in these families in comparison with children raised by heterosexual parents (Patterson, 2013, 2014). Contrary to the once-popular expectation that being raised by a gay or lesbian parent would result in the child's growing up to be gay or lesbian, in reality the overwhelming majority of children from gay or lesbian families have a heterosexual orientation (Golombok, 2011a, b).

Also, a recent study compared the incidence of coparenting in adoptive heterosexual, lesbian, and gay couples with preschool-aged children (Farr & Patterson, 2013). Both self-reports and observations found that lesbian and gay couples shared child care more than heterosexual couples did, with lesbian couples being the most supportive and gay couples the least supportive. Further, a recent study revealed more positive parenting in adoptive gay father families and fewer child externalizing problems in these families than in heterosexual families (Golombok & others, 2014).

What are the research findings regarding the development and psychological well-being of children raised by gay and lesbian couples?
© 2009 JupiterImages Corporation RF

Cultural, Ethnic, and Socioeconomic Variations

Parenting can be influenced by culture, ethnicity, and socioeconomic status. Recall from Bronfenbrenner's ecological theory that a number of social contexts influence the child's development. In Bronfenbrenner's theory, culture, ethnicity, and socioeconomic status are classified as part of the macrosystem because they represent broader societal contexts.

Cross-Cultural Studies Different cultures often give different answers to such basic questions as what the father's role in the family should be, what support systems are available to families, and how children should be disciplined (Chen, Fu, & Zhao, 2015; Gaskins, 2016). There are important cross-cultural variations in parenting (Cole & Tan, 2015; Mistry & Dutta, 2015). In some cultures, such as rural areas of many countries, authoritarian parenting is widespread.

Cultural change, brought about by factors such as increasingly frequent international travel, the Internet and electronic communications, and economic globalization, is affecting families in many countries around the world. There are trends toward greater family

What are some characteristics of families within different ethnic groups?

© Bill Aron/PhotoEdit

mobility, migration to urban areas, and separation as some family members work in cities or countries far from their homes. Other trends include smaller families, fewer extended-family households, and increases in maternal employment (Brown & Larson, 2002). These trends can change the nature of the resources available to children. For example, when several generations no longer live in close proximity, children may lose the support and guidance of grandparents, aunts, and uncles. On the positive side, smaller families may produce more openness and communication between parents and children.

Ethnicity Families within various ethnic groups in the United States differ in their typical size, structure, composition, reliance on kinship networks, and levels of income and education (Gonzales & others, 2016). Large and extended families are more common among minority groups than among the non-Latino White majority. For example, 19 percent of Latino families have three or more children, compared with 14 percent of African American and 10 percent of White families. African American and Latino children interact more with grandparents, aunts, uncles, cousins, and more distant relatives than do non-Latino White children.

Single-parent families are more common among African Americans and Latinos than among non-Latino White Americans. In comparison with two-parent households, single parents often have more limited resources in terms of time, money, and energy (Evans, Li, & Sepanski Whipple, 2013). Ethnic minority parents also tend to be less educated and are more likely to live in low-income circumstances than their non-Latino White counterparts. Still, many impoverished ethnic minority families manage to find ways to raise competent children.

Of course, individual families vary, and how ethnic minority families deal with stress depends on many factors (Yoshikawa & others, 2016). Whether the parents are native-born or immigrants, how long the family has been in this country, its socioeconomic status, and its national origin all make a difference (Berry, 2015; Renzetti & Kennedy-Bergen, 2015). The characteristics of the family's social context also influence its adaptation. What are the attitudes toward the family's ethnic group within its neighborhood or city? Can the family's children attend good schools? Are there community groups that welcome people from the family's ethnic group? Do members of the family's ethnic group form community groups of their own?

A major change in families in the last several decades has been the dramatic increase in the immigration of Latino and Asian families into the United States (Parra-Cardona & others, 2016; Tang, 2015). Immigrant families often experience stressors uncommon to or less prominent among longtime residents, such as language barriers, dislocations and separations from support networks, the dual struggle to preserve identity and to acculturate, and changes in SES status (Gonzales & others, 2016; Suarez-Orozco & Suarez-Orozco, 2015/2016).

What are some of the stressors that immigrant families experience when they come to the United States?

© Emilio J. Flores/Corbis

Many members of families that have recently immigrated to the United States adopt a bicultural orientation, selecting characteristics of the U.S. culture that help them to survive and advance, while still retaining aspects of their culture of origin. In adopting characteristics of the U.S. culture, Latino families are increasingly embracing the importance of education. Although their school dropout rates have remained higher than the rates for other ethnic groups, toward the end of the first decade of the twenty-first century they declined considerably (National Center for Education Statistics, 2015). Also, a recent study of Asian American adolescents found that a bicultural orientation of both adolescents and their parents was associated with higher academic achievement (Kim & others, 2015).

However, while many ethnic/immigrant families adopt a bicultural orientation, parenting in many ethnic minority families also focuses on issues associated with promoting children's ethnic pride, knowledge of their ethnic group, and awareness of discrimination (McLoyd, Purtell, & Hardaway, 2015; Updegraff & Umana-Taylor, 2015).

Socioeconomic Status Low-income families have less access to resources than do higher-income families (Gonzales & others, 2016; McBride Murry & others, 2015). The resources in question include nutrition, health care, protection from danger, and enriching educational and socialization opportunities, such as tutoring and lessons in various activities (Leventhal, Dupere, & Shuey, 2015). These differences are compounded in low-income families characterized by long-term poverty (Wadsworth & others, 2016). In one study, poverty-related adversity in family and school contexts in early childhood were linked to less effective executive function in second- and third-graders (Raver & others, 2013).

In the United States and most Western cultures, researchers have identified differences in child-rearing practices among groups of varying socioeconomic status (SES) (Hoff, Laursen, & Tardif, 2002, p. 246):

- "Lower-SES parents (1) are more concerned that their children conform to society's expectations, (2) create a home atmosphere in which it is clear that parents have authority over children," (3) are more likely to use physical punishment in disciplining their children, and (4) are more directive and less conversational with their children.

- "Higher-SES parents (1) are more concerned with developing children's initiative" and their capacity to delay gratification, (2) "create a home atmosphere in which children are more nearly equal participants and in which rules are discussed as opposed to being laid down" in an authoritarian manner, (3) are less likely to use physical punishment, and (4) "are less directive and more conversational" with their children.

Peer Relations, Play, and Media/Screen Time

The family is an important social context for children's development. However, children's development also is strongly influenced by what goes on in other social contexts, such as in peer groups and when children are playing or using various media.

Peer Relations

As children grow older, they spend an increasing amount of time with their peers—children of about the same age or maturity level.

What are the functions of a child's peer group? One of its most important functions is to provide a source of information and comparison about the world outside the family. Children receive feedback about their abilities from their peer group. They evaluate what they can do in terms of whether it is better than, as good as, or worse than what other children can do. It is hard to make these judgments at home because siblings are usually older or younger.

What are some characteristics of young children's peer relations?

© Fotosearch/PhotoLibrary RF

Good peer relations promote normal socioemotional development (Prinstein & Giletta, 2016; Schneider, 2016). Special concerns in peer relations focus on children who are withdrawn or aggressive (Rubin, Bukowski, & Bowker, 2015; Rubin & others, 2016). Withdrawn children who are rejected by peers or are victimized and feel lonely are at risk for depression. Children who are aggressive with their peers are at risk for developing a number of problems, including delinquency and dropping out of school (Chen, Drabick, & Burgers, 2015).

Good peer relations can be necessary for normal socioemotional development. Recall from our discussion of gender that by about age 3, children already prefer to spend time with same-sex rather than opposite-sex playmates, and this preference increases in early childhood. During these same years, the frequency of peer interactions, both positive and negative, picks up considerably (Cillessen & Bellmore, 2011). Although aggressive interactions and rough-and-tumble play increase, the proportion of aggressive exchanges, compared with friendly exchanges, decreases. Many preschool children spend considerable time in peer interaction just conversing with playmates about such matters as "negotiating roles and rules in play, arguing, and agreeing" (Rubin, Bukowski, & Parker, 2006).

Parents may influence their children's peer relations in many ways, both direct and indirect (Caruthers, Van Ryzin, & Dishion, 2014; Tilton-Weaver & others, 2013). Parents affect their children's peer relations through their interactions with their children, how they manage their children's lives, and the opportunities they provide to their children (Brown & Bakken, 2011). For example, when mothers coached their preschool daughters about the negative aspects of peer conflicts involving relational aggression (harming someone by manipulating relationships), the daughters engaged in lower rates of relational aggression (Werner & others, 2014).

Play

An extensive amount of peer interaction during childhood involves play, but social play is only one type of play. Play is a pleasurable activity that is engaged in for its own sake, and its functions and forms vary.

Functions of Play

Play is an important aspect of children's development (Bergen, 2015; Clark, 2016; Johnson & others, 2015; Lillard, 2015). Theorists have focused on different aspects of play and highlighted a long list of functions (Henricks, 2015a, b).

According to Freud and Erikson, play helps the child master anxieties and conflicts (Demanchick, 2015). Because pent-up tensions are released through play, the child can cope better with life's problems. Therapists use *play therapy* both to allow the child to work off frustrations and to analyze the child's conflicts and ways of coping with them (Clark, 2015, 2016). Children may feel less threatened and be more likely to express their true feelings in the context of play.

Play is also an important context for cognitive development. Both Piaget and Vygotsky concluded that play is the child's work. Piaget (1962) maintained that play advances children's cognitive development. At the same time, he said that children's cognitive development constrains the way they play. Play permits children to practice their competencies and acquired skills in a relaxed, pleasurable way. Piaget thought that cognitive structures need to be exercised, and play provides the perfect setting for this exercise (DeLisi, 2015).

Vygotsky (1962) also considered play to be an excellent setting for cognitive development. He was especially interested in the symbolic and make-believe aspects of play,

sensorimotor play Behavior engaged in by infants to derive pleasure from exercising their existing sensorimotor schemes.

practice play Play that involves repetition of behavior when new skills are being learned or when physical or mental mastery and coordination of skills are required for games or sports.

pretense/symbolic play Play in which the child transforms the physical environment into a symbol.

as when a child substitutes a stick for a horse and rides the stick as if it were a horse. For young children, the imaginary situation is real (Bodrova & Leong, 2015). Parents should encourage such imaginary play because it advances the child's cognitive development, especially creative thought.

Daniel Berlyne (1960) described play as exciting and pleasurable in itself because it satisfies our exploratory drive. This drive involves curiosity and a quest for information about something new or unusual. Play encourages exploratory behavior by offering children the possibilities of novelty, complexity, uncertainty, surprise, and incongruity.

More recently, play has been described as an important context for the development of language and communication skills (Christie & Roskos, 2015; Hirsh-Pasek & Golinkoff, 2014; Zosh, Hirsh-Pasek, & Golinkoff, 2015). Language and communication skills may be enhanced through discussions and negotiations regarding roles and rules in play as young children practice various words and phrases. These types of social interactions during play can benefit young children's literacy skills (Kostelnik & others, 2015). And play is a central focus of the child-centered kindergarten and is thought to be an essential aspect of early childhood education (Feeney, Moravcik, & Nolte, 2016).

Types of Play

The contemporary perspective on play emphasizes both the cognitive and the social aspects of it (Lillard, 2015). Among the most widely studied types of children's play are sensorimotor and practice play, pretense/symbolic play, social play, constructive play, and games (Bergen, 1988).

Sensorimotor and Practice Play Sensorimotor play is behavior that allows infants to derive pleasure from exercising their sensorimotor schemes. The development of sensorimotor play follows Piaget's description of sensorimotor thought. Infants begin to engage in exploratory and playful visual and motor transactions during the second quarter of the first year of life. By the age of 9 months, many infants can select novel objects for exploration and play, especially responsive objects such as toys that make noise or bounce.

Practice play involves the repetition of behavior when new skills are being learned or when physical or mental mastery and coordination of skills are required for games or sports. Sensorimotor play, which often involves practice play, is primarily confined to infancy, whereas practice play can continue to occur throughout life. During the preschool years, children often engage in practice play.

Pretense/Symbolic Play Pretense/symbolic play occurs when the child transforms the physical environment into a symbol. Between 9 and 30 months, children increasingly use objects in symbolic play. They learn to transform objects—substituting them for other objects and acting toward them as if they were these other objects. For example, a preschool child may treat a table as if it were a car and say, "I'm fixing the car" as he grabs a leg of the table.

Many experts on play consider the preschool years the "golden age" of pretense/symbolic play that is dramatic or sociodramatic in nature. This type of make-believe play often appears at about 18 months and reaches a peak at ages 4 to 5, then gradually declines.

Some child psychologists believe that pretend play is an important aspect of young children's development and often reflects advances in their cognitive development, especially as an indication of symbolic understanding. For example, Catherine Garvey (2000) and Angeline Lillard

A preschool "superhero" at play.
© Dann Tardif/LWA/Corbis

(2006, 2015) emphasize that hidden in young children's pretend-play narratives are remarkable capacities for role-taking, balancing of social roles, metacognition (thinking about thinking), testing of the distinction between reality and pretense, and numerous nonegocentric capacities that reveal young children's remarkable cognitive skills.

Social Play **Social play** is play that involves interaction with peers. It increases dramatically during the preschool years. For many children, social play is the main context for their social interactions with peers. Social play includes varied interchanges such as turn taking, conversations about numerous topics, social games and routines, and physical play. It often provides a high degree of pleasure to the participants.

Constructive Play **Constructive play** combines sensorimotor/practice play with symbolic representation. It occurs when children engage in the self-regulated creation of a product or solution. Constructive play increases in the preschool years as symbolic play increases and sensorimotor play decreases. Constructive play is also a frequent form of play in the elementary school years, both in and out of the classroom.

How Would You...?

As an **educator,** how would you integrate play into the learning process?

Games **Games** are activities that are engaged in for pleasure and have rules. Often they involve competition. Preschool children may begin to participate in social games that involve simple rules of reciprocity and turn taking. However, games take on a much stronger role in the lives of elementary school children. In one study, the highest incidence of game playing occurred between ages 10 and 12 (Eiferman, 1971). After age 12, games decline in popularity (Bergen, 1988).

Trends in Play

Kathy Hirsh-Pasek, Roberta Golinkoff, and Dorothy Singer (Hirsh-Pasek & others, 2009; Singer, Golinkoff, & Hirsh-Pasek, 2006) are concerned about the decline in the amount of free play time that young children have, reporting that it has declined considerably in recent decades. They especially are worried about young children's play time being restricted at home and school so they can spend more time on academic subjects. They also point out that many schools have eliminated recess. And it is not just the decline in free play time that bothers them. They underscore that learning in playful contexts captivates children's minds in ways that enhance their cognitive and socioemotional development—Singer, Golinkoff, and Hirsh-Pasek's (2006) first book on play was titled *Play = Learning.* Among the cognitive benefits of play they described are these skills: creative; abstract thinking; imagination; attention, concentration, and persistence; problem-solving; social cognition, empathy, and perspective taking; language; and mastering new concepts. Among the socioemotional experiences and development they believe play promotes are enjoyment, relaxation, and self-expression; cooperation, sharing, and turn-taking; anxiety reduction; and self-confidence. With so many positive cognitive and socioemotional outcomes of play, clearly it is important that we find more time for play in young children's lives.

Kathy Hirsh-Pasek in a play setting with a young child. *What are some concerns of Hirsh-Pasek and her colleagues about trends in children's play?*
© Temple University, photo by Joseph V. Labolito

social play Play that involves social interactions with peers.

constructive play Play that combines sensorimotor and repetitive activity with symbolic representation of ideas. Constructive play occurs when children engage in self-regulated creation or construction of a product or a problem solution.

games Activities engaged in for pleasure that include rules and often involve competition between two or more individuals.

Media and Screen Time

Few developments in society in the second half of the twentieth century had a greater impact on children than television. Television continues to have a strong influence on children's development, but children's use of other

What are some concerns about young children's media and screen time?

© Jekaterina Nikitina/ Flickr/Getty Images

media and information/communication devices has led to the use of the term *screen time,* which includes how much time individuals spend watching/using television, DVDs, computers, playing video games, and using mobile media such as iPhones (Cote-Lussier, Mathieu, & Barnett, 2015; Goh & others, 2016; LeBlanc & others, 2015; Straker & Howie, 2016). Television is still the elephant in young children's media life, with 2- to 4-year-old children watching TV approximately 2 to 4 hours per day (Roberts & Foehr, 2008). However, one study revealed that 12 percent of 2- to 4-year-old U.S. children use computers every day and 22 percent of 5- to 8-year-olds use computers daily (Common Sense Media, 2011). A recent recommendation stated that for children 2 to 4 years of age screen time should be limited to no more than 1 hour per day (Tremblay & others, 2012). Nonetheless, many children spend more time with various screen media than they do interacting with their parents and peers.

Some types of TV shows are linked to positive outcomes for children. For example, a recent meta-analysis of studies in 14 countries found positive outcomes for watching the TV show *Sesame Street* in three areas: cognitive, learning about the world, and social reasoning and attitudes toward outgroups (Mares & Pan, 2013).

However, too much screen time can have a negative influence on children by making them passive learners, distracting them from doing homework, teaching them stereotypes, providing them with violent models of aggression, and presenting them with unrealistic views of the world (Busschaert & others, 2015; Calvert, 2015). Among other concerns about young children engaging in so much screen time are decreased time spent in play, less time interacting with peers, reduced physical activity, increased risk of being overweight or obese, poor sleep habits, and higher rates of aggression. Viewing as little as one hour of television daily was associated with an increase in body fat. And a recent research review concluded that higher levels of screen time (mostly involving TV viewing) were associated with lower levels of cognitive development in early childhood (Carson & others, 2015). Also, a recent study of preschool children found that each additional hour of screen time was linked to less nightly sleep, later bedtime, and reduced likelihood of sleeping 10 or more hours per night (Xu & others, 2016).

The extent to which children are exposed to violence and aggression on television raises special concerns (Calvert, 2015). For example, Saturday morning cartoon shows average more than 25 violent acts per hour. In a recent study of children, greater exposure to TV violence, video game violence, and music video violence was independently associated with a higher level of physical aggression (Coker & others, 2015).

How Would You...?

As a **human development and family studies professional,** how would you talk with parents about strategies for improving television viewing by their children?

Parents play an important role in children's media use. A recent study found that a higher degree of parental monitoring of children's media use was linked to a number of positive outcomes in children's lives (more sleep, better school performance, less aggressive behavior, and more prosocial behavior) (Gentile & others, 2014). And a recent study found that parental reduction in their own screen time was associated with decreased child screen time (Xu, Wen, & Rissel, 2014).

Children also benefit when parents are knowledgeable about the best digital applications (apps) for children. In a recent survey, 72 percent of the best apps for sale in Apple's App store were in the toddler/preschool category! Leading expert Kathy Hirsh-Pasek and her colleagues (2015) recently described criteria for the best types of educational apps parents can purchase for their young children:

- *Active involvement.* It is important that the app require thinking, reflection, and manipulation of information, requiring "minds on" activity rather than just physical tapping and swiping.

- *Engagement.* Children learn the content better when it requires focused attention and is embedded in an app-based story. However, if the app includes distracting side games and noise, children's learning is often harmed.

- *Meaningfulness.* Children's learning benefits when the app is meaningfully linked to past knowledge/experience or if it is personally relevant and purposeful for the children.
- *Social interaction.* Children's learning also is aided when the app encourages quality social interaction with others, as when the app motivates them to discuss its content with parents or teachers.

Summary

Emotional and Personality Development

- In Erikson's theory, early childhood is a period when development involves resolving the conflict of initiative versus guilt. Young children improve their self-understanding and understanding of others.
- Young children's range of emotions expands during early childhood as they increasingly experience self-conscious emotions such as pride, shame, and guilt. Children benefit from having emotion-coaching parents.
- Moral development involves thoughts, feelings, and actions regarding rules and regulations about what people should do in their interactions with others. Piaget proposed cognitive changes in children's moral reasoning. Behavioral and social cognitive theorists argue that there is considerable situational variability in moral behavior.
- Gender refers to the social and psychological dimensions of being male or female. Both psychoanalytic theory and social cognitive theory emphasize the adoption of parents' gender characteristics. Peers are especially adept at rewarding gender-appropriate behavior. Gender schema theory emphasizes the role of cognition in gender development.

Families

- Authoritarian, authoritative, neglectful, and indulgent parenting styles produce different results. Authoritative parenting is the style most often associated with children's social competence. Ethnic variations characterize parenting styles. Physical punishment is widely used by U.S. parents, but there are a number of reasons why it is not a good choice. Coparenting has positive effects on children's development.

- Child maltreatment may take the form of physical abuse, child neglect, sexual abuse, and emotional abuse.
- Siblings interact with each other in positive and negative ways. Birth order is related in certain ways to child characteristics, but by itself it is not a good predictor of behavior.
- In general, having both parents employed full-time outside the home has not been shown to have negative effects on children. If divorced parents develop a harmonious relationship and practice authoritative parenting, children's adjustment improves. Researchers have found few differences between children growing up in gay or lesbian families and children growing up in heterosexual families. Culture, ethnicity, and socioeconomic status are linked to a number of aspects of families and children's development.

Peer Relations, Play, and Media/Screen Time

- Peers are powerful socialization agents. Peers provide a source of information and comparison about the world outside the family.
- Play's functions include affiliation with peers, tension release, advances in cognitive development, exploration, and provision of a safe haven. The contemporary perspective on play emphasizes both the cognitive and the social aspects of play. Among the most widely studied types of children's play are sensorimotor play, practice play, pretense/symbolic play, social play, constructive play, and games.
- There are serious concerns about the extensive amount of time young children are spending with various media. Watching TV violence and playing violent video games have been linked to children's aggressive behavior.

Key Terms

authoritarian parenting
authoritative parenting
autonomous morality
constructive play
games
gender identity

gender roles
gender schema theory
heteronomous morality
immanent justice
indulgent parenting
moral development

neglectful parenting
practice play
pretense/symbolic play
psychoanalytic theory of gender
self-understanding

sensorimotor play
social cognitive theory of gender
social play
social role theory

7 Physical and Cognitive Development in Middle and Late Childhood

© JGI/Jamie Grill/Blend Images/Getty Images RF

CHAPTER OUTLINE

PHYSICAL CHANGES AND HEALTH
Body Growth and Change
The Brain
Motor Development
Exercise
Health, Illness, and Disease

CHILDREN WITH DISABILITIES
The Scope of Disabilities
Educational Issues

COGNITIVE CHANGES
Piaget's Cognitive Developmental Theory
Information Processing
Intelligence

LANGUAGE DEVELOPMENT
Vocabulary, Grammar, and Metalinguistic Awareness
Reading
Second-Language Learning and Bilingualism

Stories of Life-Span Development: Angie and Her Weight

The following comments are by Angie, an elementary-school-age girl:

When I was eight years old, I weighed 125 pounds. My clothes were the size that large teenage girls wear. I hated my body, and my classmates teased me all the time. I was so overweight and out of shape that when I took a P.E. class my face would get red and I had trouble breathing. I was jealous of the kids who played sports and weren't overweight like I was.

I'm nine years old now and I've lost 30 pounds. I'm much happier and proud of myself. How did I lose the weight? My mom said she had finally decided enough was enough. She took me to a pediatrician who specializes in helping children lose weight and keep it off. The pediatrician counseled my mom about my eating and exercise habits, then had us join a group that he had created for overweight children and their parents. My mom and I go to the group once a week, and we've now been participating in the program for six months. I no longer eat fast-food meals, and my mom is cooking more healthy meals. Now that I've lost weight, exercise is not as hard for me, and I don't get teased by the kids at school. My mom's pretty happy, too, because she's lost 15 pounds herself since we've been in the counseling program.

Not all overweight children are as successful as Angie at reducing their weight. Indeed, being overweight in childhood has become a major national health concern in the United States. Later in the chapter, we further explore being overweight in childhood.

During the middle and late childhood years, which last from approximately 6 years of age to 10 or 11 years of age, children grow taller, heavier, and stronger, and become more adept at using their physical skills. During these years, disabilities may emerge that call for special attention and intervention. It is also in this age period that children's cognitive abilities increase dramatically. Their command of grammar becomes proficient, they learn to read, and they may acquire a second language. ■

Physical Changes and Health

Continued growth and change in proportions characterize children's bodies during middle and late childhood. During this time period, some important changes in the brain also take place and motor skills improve. Developing a healthy lifestyle that involves regular exercise and good nutrition is a key aspect of making sure these years are a time of healthy growth and development.

What characterizes physical growth during middle and late childhood?
© Chris Windsor/Digital Vision/Getty Images RF

Body Growth and Change

The period of middle and late childhood involves slow, consistent growth. This is a period of calm before the rapid growth spurt of adolescence. During the elementary school years, children grow an average of 2 to 3 inches a year until, at the age of 11, the average girl is 4 feet, 10¼ inches tall, and the average boy is 4 feet, 9 inches tall. During the middle and late childhood years, children gain about 5 to 7 pounds a year. The weight increase is due mainly to increases in the size of the skeletal and muscular systems, as well as the size of some body organs.

Proportional changes are among the most pronounced physical changes in middle and late childhood (Kliegman & others, 2016). Head and waist circumference decrease in relation to body height. A less noticeable physical change is that bones continue to ossify during middle and late childhood, although they still yield to pressure and pull more than do mature bones.

Muscle mass and strength gradually increase during these years as "baby fat" decreases. The loose movements and knock-knees of early childhood give way to improved muscle tone. Thanks both to heredity and to exercise, children double their strength capabilities during these years. Because of their greater number of muscle cells, boys are usually stronger than girls.

The Brain

Total brain volume stabilizes by the end of late childhood, but significant changes in various structures and regions of the brain continue to occur (de Haan & Johnson, 2016; Wendelken & others, 2016). As children develop, activation in some brain areas increases while it decreases in other areas (Denes, 2016; Deoni & others, 2015). One shift in activation that occurs is from diffuse, larger areas to more focal, smaller areas (Turkeltaub & others, 2003). This shift is characterized by synaptic pruning, in which areas of the brain not being used lose synaptic connections and those areas being used show an increase in connections. In one study, researchers found less diffusion and more focal activation in the prefrontal cortex from 7 to 30 years of age (Durston & others, 2006). This shift in activation was accompanied by increased efficiency in cognitive performance, especially *cognitive control*, which involves effective control and flexibility in a number of areas (Markant & Thomas, 2013).

Leading researchers in developmental cognitive neuroscience have proposed that the prefrontal cortex likely orchestrates the functions of many other brain regions during development (de Haan & Johnson, 2016; Johnson, Grossmann, &

Cohen-Kadosh, 2009). As part of this organizational role, the prefrontal cortex may provide an advantage to neural networks and connections that include the prefrontal cortex. In this view, the prefrontal cortex coordinates which neural connections are the most effective for solving a problem at hand.

Motor Development

During middle and late childhood, children's motor skills become much smoother and more coordinated than they were in early childhood. For example, only one child in a thousand can hit a tennis ball over the net at the age of 3, yet by the age of 10 or 11 most children can learn to play the sport. Running, climbing, skipping rope, swimming, bicycle riding, and skating are just a few of the many physical skills elementary school children can master. In gross motor skills that involve large muscle activity, boys usually outperform girls.

Increased myelination of the central nervous system is reflected in the improvement of fine motor skills during middle and late childhood. Children can more adroitly use their hands as tools. Six-year-olds can hammer, paste, tie shoes, and fasten clothes. By 7 years of age, children's hands have become steadier. At this age, children prefer a pencil to a crayon for printing, and they reverse letters less often. Printing becomes smaller. At 8 to 10 years of age, they can use their hands independently with more ease and precision. Fine motor coordination develops to the point at which children can write rather than print words. Cursive letter size becomes smaller and more even. At 10 to 12 years of age, children begin to show manipulative skills similar to the abilities of adults. They can master the complex, intricate, and rapid movements needed to produce fine-quality crafts or to play a difficult piece on a musical instrument. Girls usually outperform boys in their use of fine motor skills.

Exercise

American children and adolescents are not getting enough exercise. Increasing children's exercise levels has positive outcomes (Nemet, 2016; Wuest & Fisette, 2015).

An increasing number of studies document the importance of exercise in children's physical development (Innella & others, 2016; Pan & others, 2016; Pate & others, 2015). One recent research review concluded that exercise programs with a frequency of three weekly sessions lasting longer than 60 minutes was effective in lowering both systolic and diastolic blood pressure (Garcia-Hermoso, Saavedra, & Escalante, 2013).

Researchers also have found that aerobic exercise benefits children's attention, memory, effortful and goal-directed thinking and behavior, creativity, and academic success (Pan & others, 2016; Tomporowski, 2016). For example, in a recent fMRI study of physically unfit 8- to 11-year-old overweight children, a daily instructor-led aerobic exercise program that lasted eight months was effective in improving the efficiency or flexible modulation of neural circuits that support better cognitive functioning (Krafft & others, 2014). Further, a recent study found that moderately intensive aerobic exercise improved children's cognitive inhibitory control (Drolette & others, 2014).

Parents and schools play important roles in determining children's exercise levels (Aires & others, 2016; Kesten & others, 2016). Growing up with parents who exercise regularly provides positive models of exercise for children (Crawford & others, 2010). In one study, a school-based physical activity was successful in improving children's fitness and lowering their fat content (Kriemler & others, 2010).

Screen time also is linked with low activity levels, obesity, and worse sleep patterns in children (LeBlanc & others, 2015; Shang & others, 2015; Xu & others, 2016). Researchers have found that the total time that children and adolescents spend in front of a television or computer screen places them at risk for reduced activity and being overweight (Taverno Ross & others, 2013).

How Would You...?

As an **educator,** how would you structure the curriculum to ensure that elementary school students are getting adequate physical activity throughout the day?

Health, Illness, and Disease

For the most part, middle and late childhood is a time of excellent health. Disease and death are less prevalent at this time than during other periods in childhood and in adolescence. However, many children in middle and late childhood face health problems that threaten their development (Wardlaw & Smith, 2015).

Overweight Children

Being overweight is an increasingly prevalent health problem in children (Schiff, 2015, 2016; Sorte, Daeschel, & Amador, 2017). Over the last three decades, the overall percentage of U.S. children who are at risk for being overweight has increased dramatically (Orsi, Hale, & Lynch, 2011). Recently, however, the percentage of 2- to 5-year-old children who are obese has decreased from 12.1 percent in 2009–2010 to 8 percent in 2011–2012 (Ogden & others, 2014). In 2011–2012, 17.5 percent of 6- to 11-year-old U.S. children were classified as obese, which is essentially unchanged from 2009–2010 (Ogden & others, 2014).

It is not just in the United States that more children are becoming overweight (Fernandez & others, 2015). For example, a study found that general and abdominal obesity in Chinese children increased significantly from 1993 to 2009 (Liang & others, 2012). Further, a recent Chinese study revealed that high blood pressure in 23 percent of boys and 15 percent of girls could be attributed to being overweight or obese (Dong & others, 2015).

What are some concerns about overweight children?

© Image Source/ PunchStock RF

Causes of Children Being Overweight

Heredity and environmental contexts are related to being overweight in childhood. Recent genetic analysis indicates that heredity is an important factor in children becoming overweight (Llewellyn & others, 2014; Wang & others, 2016). Overweight parents tend to have overweight children (Pufal & others, 2012). Environmental factors that influence whether children become overweight include availability of food (especially food high in fat content), energy-saving devices, declining physical activity, parents' eating habits and monitoring of children's eating habits, the context in which a child eats, and heavy screen time (Nguyen & others, 2016; Parkes & others, 2016). In a 14-year longitudinal study, parental weight change predicted children's weight change (Andriani, Liao, & Kuo, 2015). Another study found that having two overweight/obese parents significantly increased the likelihood that children would be overweight/obese (Xu & others, 2011). Screen time also is linked with low activity levels and obesity in children (Taverno Ross & others, 2013). A recent research study found that a higher level of screen time increased the risk of obesity for low- and high-activity children (Lane, Harrison, & Murphy, 2014). Also, a recent study of more than 6,000 elementary school children revealed that 55 minutes or more of moderate-to-vigorous physical activity daily was associated with a lower incidence of obesity (Nemet, 2016).

How Would You...?

As a **social worker,** how would you use your knowledge of overweight risk factors to design a workshop for parents and children about healthy lifestyle choices?

Consequences of Children Being Overweight The increasing number of overweight children in recent decades is cause for great concern because being overweight raises the risk for many medical and psychological problems (de Koning & others, 2015; Sahoo & others, 2015; Sorte, Daeschel, & Amador, 2017). Diabetes, hypertension (high blood pressure), and elevated blood cholesterol levels are common in children who are overweight (Propst & others, 2015; So & others, 2016). In a recent study, a larger waist circumference and a higher body mass index (BMI) combined to place children at higher risk for cardiovascular disease (de Koning & others, 2015). Also, a research review concluded that obesity was linked with low self-esteem in children (Gomes & others, 2011). And in one study, overweight children reported being teased more by their peers and family members than did normal-weight children (McCormack & others, 2011).

Intervention Programs A combination of diet, exercise, and behavior modification is often recommended to help children lose weight (Street, Wells, & Hills, 2015). Intervention programs that emphasize getting parents to engage in healthier lifestyles themselves, as well as feeding their children healthier food and getting them to exercise more, can produce weight reduction in overweight and obese children (Ling, Robbins, & Wen, 2016; Lumpkin, 2014).

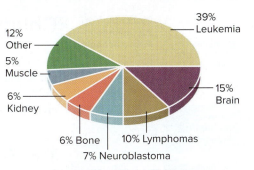

Figure 1 **Types of Cancer in Children**
Cancers in children have a different profile from adult cancers, which attack mainly the lungs, colon, breast, prostate, and pancreas.

Cancer

Cancer is the second leading cause of death in U.S. children 5 to 14 years of age. One in every 330 children in the United States develops cancer before the age of 19. The incidence of cancer in children has increased slightly in recent years (National Cancer Institute, 2016).

Childhood cancers mainly attack the white blood cells (leukemia), brain, bone, lymph system, muscles, kidneys, and nervous system. All are characterized by an uncontrolled proliferation of abnormal cells (Bleeker & others, 2014). As indicated in Figure 1, the most common cancer in children is leukemia, a cancer in which bone marrow manufactures an abundance of abnormal white blood cells that crowd out normal cells, making the child susceptible to bruising and infection (Tomizawa, 2015).

Because of advancements in cancer treatment, children with cancer are surviving longer than in the past (National Cancer Institute, 2016). For example, approximately 80 percent of children with acute lymphoblastic leukemia are cured with chemotherapy (Wayne, 2011).

Child life specialists are among the health professionals who strive to reduce stress in children with diseases. To read about the work of child life specialist Sharon McLeod, see *Careers in Life-Span Development.*

Careers in life-span development

Sharon McLeod, Child Life Specialist

Sharon McLeod is a child life specialist who is clinical director of the Child Life and Recreational Therapy Department at the Children's Hospital Medical Center in Cincinnati. Under McLeod's direction, the goals of the Child Life Department are to promote children's optimal growth and development, reduce the stress of health-care experiences, and provide support to child patients and their families. These goals are accomplished through therapeutic play and developmentally appropriate activities, educating and psychologically preparing children for medical procedures, and serving as a resource for parents and other professionals regarding children's development and health-care issues.

McLeod says that human growth and development provides the foundation for her profession as a child life specialist. She also describes her best times as a student as those when she conducted fieldwork, had an internship, and experienced hands-on applications of theories and concepts she learned in her courses.

Sharon McLeod, child life specialist, works with a child at Children's Hospital Medical Center in Cincinnati.
© Sharon McLeod

Disability	Percentage of All Children in Public Schools
Learning disabilities	4.7
Speech or hearing impairments	2.8
Intellectual disability	0.9
Autism	0.9
Emotional disturbance	0.8

Figure 2 **U.S. Children with a Disability Who Receive Special Education Services**
Figures are for the 2011–2012 school year and represent the four categories with the highest numbers and percentages of children. Both learning disability and attention deficit hyperactivity disorder are combined in the learning disabilities category (Condition of Education, 2015).

Children with Disabilities

The elementary school years are a time when disabilities become prominent for some children. What are some of the disabilities that children have? What characterizes the educational issues facing children with disabilities?

The Scope of Disabilities

Of all children in the United States, 13 percent from 3 to 21 years of age received special education or related services in 2011–2012, an increase of 3 percent since 1980–1981 (Condition of Education, 2015). Figure 2 shows the four largest groups of students with a disability who were served by federal programs during the 2011–2012 school year (Condition of Education, 2015).

As indicated in Figure 2, students with a learning disability were by far the largest group of students with a disability to be given special education, followed by children with speech or language impairments, intellectual disabilities, and emotional disturbance. Note that the U.S. Department of Education includes both students with a learning disability and students with ADHD in the category of learning disability.

Learning Disabilities

The U.S. government uses the following definition to determine whether a child should be classified as having a learning disability: A child with a **learning disability** has difficulty in learning that involves understanding or using spoken or written language, and the difficulty can appear in listening, thinking, reading, writing, and spelling. A learning disability also may involve difficulty in doing mathematics (Kucian & von Aster, 2015). To be classified as a learning disability, the learning problem is not primarily the result of visual, hearing, or motor disabilities; intellectual disability; emotional disorders; or environmental, cultural, or economic disadvantage.

About three times as many boys as girls are classified as having a learning disability. Among the explanations for this gender difference are a greater biological vulnerability among boys and *referral bias*. That is, boys are more likely than girls to be referred by teachers for treatment because of troublesome behavior.

Approximately 80 percent of children with a learning disability have a reading problem (Shaywitz, Gruen, & Shaywitz, 2007). Three types of learning disabilities are dyslexia, dysgraphia, and dyscalculia:

- *Dyslexia* is a category reserved for individuals who have a severe impairment in their ability to read and spell (Thompson & others, 2015).

- *Dysgraphia* is a learning disability that involves difficulty in handwriting (Berninger & others, 2015). Children with dysgraphia may write very slowly, their writing products may be virtually illegible, and they may make numerous spelling errors because of their inability to match up sounds and letters.

- *Dyscalculia*, also known as developmental arithmetic disorder, is a learning disability that involves difficulty in math computation (Kucian & von Aster, 2015).

The precise causes of learning disabilities have not yet been determined (Vaughn & Bos, 2015). To reveal any regions of the brain that

How Would You...?
As an **educator,** how would you explain the nature of learning disabilities to a parent whose child has recently been diagnosed with a learning disability?

learning disability Describes a child who has difficulty understanding or using spoken or written language or doing mathematics. To be classified as a learning disability, the problem is not primarily the result of visual, hearing, or motor disabilities; intellectual disability; emotional disorders; or due to environmental, cultural, or economic disadvantage.

attention deficit hyperactivity disorder (ADHD) A disability in which children consistently show one or more of the following characteristics: (1) inattention, (2) hyperactivity, and (3) impulsivity.

might be involved in learning disabilities, researchers use brain-imaging techniques such as magnetic resonance imaging (Shaywitz, Lyon, & Shaywitz, 2006) (see Figure 3). This research indicates that it is unlikely learning disabilities reside in a single, specific brain location. More likely, learning disabilities are due to problems in integrating information from multiple brain regions or subtle difficulties in brain structures and functions.

Interventions with children who have a learning disability often focus on improving reading ability (Bursuck & Damer, 2015). Intensive instruction over a period of time by a competent teacher can help many children (Del Campo & others, 2015).

Attention Deficit Hyperactivity Disorder (ADHD)

Attention deficit hyperactivity disorder (ADHD) is a disability in which children consistently show one or more of these characteristics over a period of time: (1) inattention, (2) hyperactivity, and (3) impulsivity. Children who are inattentive have such difficulty focusing on any one thing that they may get bored with a task after only a few minutes—or even seconds. Children who are hyperactive show high levels of physical activity, seeming to be almost constantly in motion. Children who are impulsive have difficulty curbing their reactions; they do not do a good job of thinking before they act. Depending on the characteristics that children with ADHD display, they can be diagnosed as (1) ADHD with predominantly inattention, (2) ADHD with predominantly hyperactivity/impulsivity, or (3) ADHD with both inattention and hyperactivity/impulsivity.

Figure 3 Brain Scans and Learning Disabilities
An increasing number of studies are using MRI brain scans to examine the brain pathways involved in learning disabilities. Shown here is 9-year-old Patrick Price, who has dyslexia. Patrick is going through an MRI scanner disguised by drapes to look like a child-friendly castle. Inside the scanner, children must lie virtually motionless as words and symbols flash on a screen, and they are asked to identify them by clicking different buttons.
© Manuel Balce Ceneta/AP Images

Many children with ADHD show impulsive behavior, such as this boy reaching to pull a girl's hair. *How would you handle this situation if you were a teacher?*
© Nicole Hill/Rubberball/Getty Images RF

The number of children diagnosed and treated for ADHD has increased substantially in recent decades, by some estimates doubling in the 1990s. The American Psychiatric Association (2013) reported in the DSM-V Manual that 5 percent of children have ADHD, although estimates are higher in community samples. For example, the Centers for Disease Control and Prevention (2016) estimates that ADHD continues to increase in 4- to 17-year-old children, going from 8 percent in 2003 to 9.5 percent in 2007 and to 11 percent in 2016. According to the Centers for Disease Control and Prevention, 13.2 percent of U.S. boys and 5.6 of U.S. girls have ever been diagnosed with ADHD. The disorder is diagnosed four to nine times more often in boys than in girls.

There is controversy, however, about the reasons for the increased diagnosis of ADHD (Turnbull & others, 2016). Some experts attribute the increase mainly to heightened awareness of the disorder; others are concerned that many children might be incorrectly diagnosed (Watson & others, 2014).

Adjustment and optimal development are difficult for children who have ADHD, so it is important that the diagnosis be accurate. Children diagnosed with ADHD have an increased risk of school dropout, adolescent pregnancy, substance use problems, and antisocial behavior (Chang, Lichtenstein, & Larsson, 2012).

Definitive causes of ADHD have not been found. However, a number of causes have been proposed (Smith & others, 2016). Some children likely inherit a tendency to

How Would You...?

As a **health-care professional,** how would you respond to this comment from a parent? "I do not believe that ADHD is a real disorder. Children are supposed to be active."

develop ADHD from their parents (Lee & Song, 2014). Other children likely develop ADHD because of damage to their brain during prenatal or postnatal development (Lindblad & Hjern, 2010). Among early possible contributors to ADHD are cigarette and alcohol exposure, as well as a high level of maternal stress during prenatal development and low birth weight (Glover, 2014; Obel & others, 2016; Yochum & others, 2014).

As with learning disabilities, the development of brain-imaging techniques is leading to a better understanding of ADHD (Berger & others, 2015; Chiang & others, 2015; Dougherty & others, 2016; Park & others, 2016). One study revealed that peak thickness of the cerebral cortex occurred three years later (10.5 years) in children with ADHD than in children without ADHD (peak at 7.5 years) (Shaw & others, 2007). The delay was more prominent in the prefrontal regions of the brain that are especially important in attention and planning (see Figure 4). Another study also found delayed development in the brain's frontal lobes among children with ADHD, which likely was due to delayed or decreased myelination (Nagel & others, 2011). Researchers also are exploring the roles that various neurotransmitters, such as serotonin and dopamine, might play in ADHD (Gold & others, 2014; Kollins & Adcock, 2014; Zhong, Liu, & Yan, 2016). A recent study found that the dopamine transporter gene DAT 1 was involved in decreased cortical thickness in the prefrontal cortex of children with ADHD (Fernandez-Jaen & others, 2015).

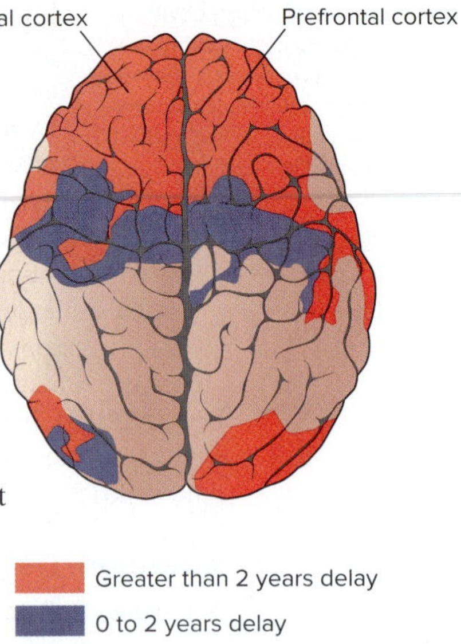

The delays in brain development just described are in areas linked to executive function. An increasing focus of interest in the study of children with ADHD is their difficulty on tasks involving executive function, such as behavioral inhibition when necessary, use of working memory, and effective planning (Dovis & others, 2015). Researchers also have found deficits in theory of mind in children with ADHD (Mary & others, 2016). Children diagnosed with ADHD have an increased risk of school dropout, adolescent pregnancy, substance use problems, and antisocial behavior (Jaber & others, 2015; Miller, Loya, & Hinshaw, 2013; Notzon & others, 2016).

Prefrontal cortex   Prefrontal cortex

■ Greater than 2 years delay
■ 0 to 2 years delay

Figure 4 Regions of the Brain in Which Children with ADHD Had a Delayed Peak in the Thickness of the Cerebral Cortex
Note: The greatest delays occurred in the prefrontal cortex.

How Would You...?

As a **human development and family studies professional,** how would you advise parents who are hesitant about medicating their child who was recently diagnosed with a mild form of ADHD?

Stimulant medication such as Ritalin or Adderall (which has fewer side effects than Ritalin) is effective in improving the attention of many children with ADHD, but it usually does not improve their attention to the same level as in children who do not have ADHD (Sclar & others, 2012). A meta-analysis (statistical analysis that combines the results of many different studies) concluded that behavior management treatments are effective in reducing the effects of ADHD (Fabiano & others, 2009). Researchers have often found that a combination of medication (such as Ritalin) and behavior management improves the behavior of children with ADHD better than medication alone or behavior management alone, although this treatment does not work in all cases (Parens & Johnston, 2009).

Recently, researchers have been exploring the possibility that three types of training exercises might reduce ADHD symptoms. First, *neurofeedback* can improve the attention of children with ADHD (Bluschke, Roessner, & Beste, 2016; Zuberer, Brandeis, & Drechsler, 2015). Neurofeedback trains individuals to become more aware of their physiological responses so they can attain better control over their brain's prefrontal cortex, where executive control primarily occurs. Second, *mindfulness training* also has been found to decrease ADHD symptoms in children (Anderson & Guthery, 2015). For example, a recent meta-analysis concluded that mindfulness training significantly improved the attention of children with ADHD (Cairncross & Miller, 2016). And, third, physical exercise also is being investigated as a possible treatment for children with ADHD (Pan & others, 2016). A recent meta-analysis concluded that short-term aerobic exercise is effective in reducing symptoms such as inattention, hyperactivity, and impulsivity (Cerillo-Urbina & others, 2015). Another recent meta-analysis indicated that exercise is associated with better executive function in children with ADHD (Vysniauske & others, 2016).

Autism Spectrum Disorders

Autism spectrum disorders (ASD), also called pervasive developmental disorders, range from the more severe disorder called *autistic disorder* to the milder disorder called *Asperger syndrome.* Autism spectrum disorders are characterized by problems in social interaction, problems in verbal and nonverbal communication, and repetitive behaviors (Bernier & Dawson, 2016; Wheeler, Mayton, & Carter, 2015). Children with these disorders may also show atypical responses to sensory experiences (National Institute of Mental Health, 2016). Autism spectrum disorders can often be detected in children as young as 1 to 3 years of age.

What characterizes autism spectrum disorders?
© Pixland/PunchStock RF

Recent estimates of autism spectrum disorders indicate that they are dramatically increasing in occurrence or are increasingly being detected. Once thought to affect only 1 in 2,500 children decades ago, they were estimated to be present in about 1 in 150 children in 2002 (Centers for Disease Control and Prevention, 2007) and 1 in 68 children in 2012 (Centers for Disease Control and Prevention, 2016). In the 2012 survey, autism spectrum disorders were identified five times more often in boys than in girls.

Autistic disorder is a severe developmental autism spectrum disorder that has its onset during the first three years of life and includes deficiencies in social relationships; abnormalities in communication; and restricted, repetitive, and stereotyped patterns of behavior.

Asperger syndrome is a relatively mild autism spectrum disorder in which the child has relatively good verbal language skills, milder nonverbal language problems, and a restricted range of interests and relationships (Barahona-Correa & Filipe, 2016; Helles & others, 2015). Children with Asperger syndrome often engage in obsessive, repetitive routines and preoccupations with a particular subject. For example, a child may be obsessed with baseball scores or YouTube videos.

What causes autism spectrum disorders? The current consensus is that autism is a brain dysfunction characterized by abnormalities in brain structure and neurotransmitters (Conti & others, 2015). Recent interest has focused on a lack of connectivity between brain regions as a key factor in autism (Fakhoury, 2015). Genetic factors also likely play a role in the development of autism spectrum disorders (Ning & others, 2015), but there is no evidence that family socialization causes autism. Intellectual disability is present in some children with autism, while others show average or above-average intelligence (Memari & others, 2012).

Children with autism benefit from a well-structured classroom, individualized teaching, and small-group instruction (Simmons, Lanter, & Lyons, 2014). Behavior modification techniques are sometimes effective in helping autistic children learn (Wheeler, Mayton, & Carter, 2015; Zirpoli, 2016).

Educational Issues

Until the 1970s most U.S. public schools either refused enrollment to children with disabilities or inadequately served them. This changed in 1975, when *Public Law 94-142,* the Education for All Handicapped Children Act, required that all students with disabilities be given a free, appropriate public education. In 1990, Public Law 94-142 was recast as the *Individuals with Disabilities Education Act* (IDEA). IDEA was amended in 1997 and then reauthorized in 2004 and renamed the Individuals with Disabilities Education Improvement Act.

IDEA spells out broad mandates for providing educational services to children with disabilities of all kinds (Heward, Alber-Morgan, & Konrad, 2017; Kirk, Gallagher, & Coleman, 2015). These services include evaluation and eligibility determination, appropriate education and an individualized education plan (IEP), and education in the least restrictive environment (LRE) (Hallahan, Kauffman, & Pullen, 2015).

An **individualized education plan (IEP)** is a written statement that spells out a program that is specifically tailored for a student with a disability. The **least restrictive environment (LRE)** is a setting that is as similar as possible to the one in which children who do not have a disability are educated. This provision of the IDEA has given a legal basis to efforts to educate children with a disability in the regular classroom. The term **inclusion** describes educating a child with special educational needs full-time in the regular classroom (Friend & Bursuck, 2015; Lewis, Wheeler, & Carter, 2017). In a recent school year (2014), 61 percent of U.S. students with a disability spent more than 80 percent of their school day in a general classroom (compared with only 33 percent in 1990) (Condition of Education, 2015).

individualized education plan (IEP) A written statement that spells out a program tailored to a child with a disability.

least restrictive environment (LRE) The concept that a child with a disability should be educated in a setting that is as similar as possible to the one in which children who do not have a disability are educated.

inclusion Educating a child who requires special education full-time in the regular classroom.

IDEA mandates free, appropriate education for all children. *What services does IDEA mandate for children with disabilities?*
© Bill Aron/PhotoEdit

Many legal changes regarding children with disabilities have been extremely positive (Smith & others, 2016). Compared with several decades ago, far more children today are receiving competent, specialized services. For many children, inclusion in the regular classroom, with modifications or supplemental services, is appropriate (Turnbull & others, 2016). However, some leading experts on special education argue that some children with disabilities may not benefit from inclusion in the regular classroom. James Kauffman and his colleagues, for example, advocate a more individualized approach that does not necessarily involve full inclusion but allows options such as special education outside the regular classroom with trained professionals and adapted curricula (Kauffman, McGee, & Brigham, 2004). They go on to say, "We sell students with disabilities short when we pretend that they are not different from typical students. We make the same error when we pretend that they must *not* be expected to put forth extra effort if they are to learn to do some things—or learn to do something in a different way" (p. 620). Like general education, special education should challenge students with disabilities "to become all they can be."

Cognitive Changes

It is the wisdom of the human life span that at no time are children more ready to learn than during the period of expansive imagination at the end of early childhood. Do children enter a new stage of cognitive development in middle and late childhood?

Piaget's Cognitive Developmental Theory

According to Piaget (1952), the preschool child's thought is preoperational. Preschool children can form stable concepts, and they have begun to reason, but their thinking is flawed by egocentrism and magical belief systems. As we discussed in the chapter on physical and cognitive development in early childhood, however, Piaget may have underestimated the cognitive skills of preschool children. Some researchers argue that under the right conditions, young children may display abilities that are characteristic of Piaget's next stage of cognitive development, the stage of concrete operational thought (Gelman, 1969). Here we will cover the characteristics of concrete operational thought and evaluate Piaget's portrait of this stage.

The Concrete Operational Stage

Piaget proposed that the *concrete operational stage* lasts from approximately 7 to 11 years of age. In this stage, children can perform concrete operations, and they can reason logically as long as reasoning can be applied to specific or concrete examples. Remember that *operations* are mental actions that are reversible, and *concrete operations* are operations that are applied to real, concrete objects.

The conservation tasks described in the chapter on physical and cognitive development in early childhood indicate whether children are capable of concrete operations. For example, recall that in one task involving conservation of matter, the child is presented with two identical balls of clay. The experimenter rolls one ball into a long, thin shape; the other remains in its original ball shape. The child is then asked if there is more clay in the ball or in the long, thin piece of clay. By the time children reach the age of 7 or 8, most answer that the amount of clay is the same. To answer this problem correctly, children have to imagine the clay rolling back into a ball. This type of imagination involves a reversible mental action applied to a real, concrete object. Concrete operations allow the child to consider several characteristics rather than focus on a single property of an object. In the clay example, the preoperational child is likely to focus on height or width. The concrete operational child coordinates information about both dimensions.

What other abilities are characteristic of children who have reached the concrete operational stage? One important skill is the ability to classify or divide things into different sets or subsets and to consider their interrelationships. Consider the family tree of four generations that is shown in Figure 5 (Furth & Wachs, 1975). This family tree suggests that the grandfather (A) has three children (B, C, and D), each of whom has two children (E through J), and that one of these children (J) has three children (K, L, and M). A child who comprehends the classification system can move up and down a level, across a level, and up and down and across within the system. The concrete operational child understands that person J can at the same time be father, brother, and grandson, for example.

Children who have reached the concrete operational stage are also capable of **seriation,** which is the ability to order stimuli along a quantitative dimension (such as length). To see if students can serialize, a teacher might haphazardly place eight sticks of different lengths on a table. The teacher then asks the students to order the sticks by length. Many young children end up with two or three small groups of "big" sticks or "little" sticks, rather than a correct ordering of all eight sticks. Another ineffective strategy they use is to line up the tops of the sticks evenly but ignore the bottoms. The concrete operational thinker simultaneously understands that each stick must be longer than the one that precedes it and shorter than the one that follows it.

Another aspect of reasoning about the relations between classifications is **transitivity,** which is the ability to logically combine relations to understand certain conclusions. In this case, consider three sticks (A, B, and C) of differing lengths. A is the longest, B is intermediate in length, and C is the shortest. Does the child understand that if A is longer than B and B is longer than C, then A is longer than C? In Piaget's theory, concrete operational thinkers do; preoperational thinkers do not.

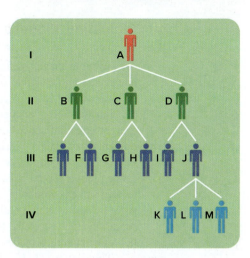

Figure 5 Classification: An Important Ability in Concrete Operational Thought
A family tree of four generations (I to IV): The preoperational child has trouble classifying the members of the four generations; the concrete operational child can classify the members vertically, horizontally, and obliquely (up and down and across). For example, the concrete operational child understands that a family member can be a son, a brother, and a father, all at the same time.

seriation The concrete operation that involves ordering stimuli along a quantitative dimension (such as length).

transitivity The ability to logically combine relations to understand certain conclusions.

How Would You...?
As a **psychologist,** how would you characterize the contribution Piaget made to our current understanding of cognitive development in childhood?

Evaluating Piaget's Concrete Operational Stage

Has Piaget's portrait of the concrete operational child stood the test of research? According to Piaget, various aspects of a stage should emerge at the same time. In fact, however, some concrete operational abilities do not appear in synchrony. For example, children do not learn to conserve at the same time they learn to cross-classify.

Furthermore, education and culture exert stronger influences on children's development than Piaget reasoned (Gauvain & Perez, 2015; Goodnow & Lawrence, 2015). Some preoperational children can be trained to reason at a concrete operational stage. And the age at which children acquire conservation skills is related to how much practice their culture provides in these skills.

Thus, although Piaget was a giant in the field of developmental psychology, his conclusions about the concrete operational stage have been challenged. Later, after examining the final stage in his theory of cognitive development, we will further evaluate Piaget's contributions and the criticisms of his theory.

An outstanding teacher and education in the logic of science and mathematics are important cultural experiences that promote the development of operational thought. *Might Piaget have underestimated the roles of culture and schooling in children's cognitive development?*
© Majority World/Getty Images

Neo-Piagetians argue that Piaget got some things right but that his theory needs considerable revision. They give more emphasis to how children use attention, memory, and strategies to process information (Case & Mueller, 2001). They especially believe that a more accurate portrayal of children's thinking requires attention to children's strategies, the speed at which children process information, the particular task involved, and the division of problems into smaller, more precise steps (Morra & others, 2008). These issues are addressed by the information-processing approach, and we will discuss some of them later in this chapter.

Information Processing

If we examine how children handle information during middle and late childhood instead of analyzing the type of thinking they display, what do we find? During these years, most children dramatically improve their ability to sustain and control attention (Ristic & Enns, 2015). Other changes in information processing during middle and late childhood involve memory, thinking, and metacognition (Casey & others, 2016; Swanson, 2016).

Memory

Short-term memory increases considerably during early childhood but after the age of 7 does not show as much increase. British cognitive psychologist Alan Baddeley (1990, 2001, 2007, 2010, 2012, 2013) defines **working memory** as a kind of mental "workbench" where individuals manipulate and assemble information when they make decisions, solve problems, and comprehend written and spoken language. Working memory is described as being more active and powerful in modifying information than short-term memory. Working memory involves bringing information to mind and mentally working with or updating it, as when you link one idea to another and relate what you are reading now to something you read earlier.

Working memory develops slowly. Even by 8 years of age, children can only hold in memory half the items that adults can remember (Kharitonova, Winter, & Sheridan, 2015). Working memory is linked to many aspects of children's development (Cowan, Saults, & Clark, 2015; Gerst & others, 2016). For example, children who have better working

neo-Piagetians Developmentalists who have elaborated on Piaget's theory, giving more emphasis to how children use attention, memory, and strategies to process information.

working memory A mental "workbench" where individuals manipulate and assemble information when making decisions, solving problems, and comprehending written and spoken language.

memory are more advanced in language comprehension, math skills, and problem solving than their counterparts with less effective working memory (Fuchs & others, 2016; Peng & Fuchs, 2016).

Long-term memory, a relatively permanent and unlimited type of memory, increases with age during middle and late childhood. In part, improvements in memory reflect children's increased knowledge and their increased use of strategies. Keep in mind that it is important not to view memory in terms of how children add something to it but rather to underscore how children actively construct their memory (Bauer, Hattenschwiler, & Larkina, 2016; Howe, 2015).

Knowledge and Expertise Much of the research on the role of knowledge in memory has compared experts and novices. *Experts* have acquired extensive knowledge about a particular content area; this knowledge influences what they notice and how they organize, represent, and interpret information (Ericsson & others, 2016; Gong, Ericsson, & Moxley, 2015). This in turn affects their ability to remember, reason, and solve problems. When individuals have expertise about a particular subject, their memory also tends to be good regarding material related to that subject (Staszewski, 2013).

For example, one study found that 10- and 11-year-olds who were experienced chess players ("experts") were able to remember more information about chess pieces than college students who were not chess players ("novices") (Chi, 1978). In contrast, when the college students were presented with other stimuli, they were able to remember them better than the children were. Thus, the children's expertise in chess gave them superior memories, but only regarding chess.

There are developmental changes in expertise (Blair & Somerville, 2009). Older children usually have more expertise about a subject than younger children do, which can contribute to their better memory for the subject.

Strategies Long-term memory depends on the learning activities individuals engage in when learning and remembering information. **Strategies** consist of deliberate mental activities to improve the processing of information. They do not occur automatically but require effort and work (Miller, McCulloch, & Jarrold, 2015). Following are some effective strategies for adults to use in helping children improve their memory skills:

- *Guide children to elaborate about the information they are to remember.* **Elaboration** involves more extensive processing of the information, such as thinking of examples or relating the information to one's own life. Elaboration makes the information more meaningful.

- *Encourage children to engage in mental imagery.* Mental imagery can help even young school children to remember visuals. However, for remembering verbal information, mental imagery works better for older children than for younger children.

- *Motivate children to remember material by understanding it rather than by memorizing it.* Children will remember information better over the long term if they understand the information rather than just rehearse and memorize it. Rehearsal works well for encoding information into short-term memory, but when children need to retrieve the information from long-term memory, it is much less efficient. For most information, encourage children to understand it, give it meaning, elaborate on it, and personalize it.

- *Repeat and vary instructional information, and link it to other information early and often.* These recommendations improve children's consolidation and reconsolidation of the information they are learning (Bauer, 2009). Varying the themes of a lesson increases the number of associations in memory storage, and linking the information expands the network of associations in memory storage; both strategies expand the routes for retrieving information from storage in the brain.

- *Embed memory-relevant language when instructing children.* Teachers who use mnemonic devices and metacognitive questions that encourage children to think about their thinking can improve student performance.

long-term memory A relatively permanent type of memory that holds huge amounts of information for a long period of time.

strategies Deliberate mental activities designed to improve the processing of information.

elaboration An important strategy that involves engaging in more extensive processing of information.

Fuzzy Trace Theory Might something other than knowledge and strategies be responsible for the improvement in memory during the elementary school years? Charles Brainerd and Valerie Reyna (2014) argue that fuzzy traces account for much of this improvement. Their **fuzzy trace theory** states that memory is best understood by considering two types of memory representations: (1) verbatim memory trace and (2) gist. The *verbatim memory trace* consists of the precise details of the information, whereas *gist* refers to the central idea of the information. When gist is used, fuzzy traces are built up. Although individuals of all ages extract gist, young children tend to store and retrieve verbatim traces. At some point during the early elementary school years, children begin to use gist more, and according to the theory, this contributes to the improved memory and reasoning of older children because fuzzy traces are more enduring and less likely to be forgotten than verbatim traces.

Thinking

Thinking involves manipulating and transforming information in memory. Two important aspects of thinking are being able to think critically and creatively.

Critical Thinking Currently there is considerable interest among psychologists and educators regarding critical thinking (Bonney & Sternberg, 2016; Cooney, 2015). **Critical thinking** involves thinking reflectively and productively, and evaluating evidence. In this book, the "How Would You . . . ?" questions in the margins challenge you to think critically about a topic or an issue related to the discussion.

Jacqueline and Martin Brooks (2001) lament that few schools really teach students to think critically and develop a deep understanding of concepts. Deep understanding occurs when students are stimulated to rethink previously held ideas. In Brooks and Brooks' view, schools spend too much time getting students to give a single correct answer in an imitative way, rather than encouraging them to expand their thinking by coming up with new ideas and rethinking earlier conclusions. They observe that too often teachers ask students to recite, define, describe, state, and list, rather than to analyze, infer, connect, synthesize, criticize, create, evaluate, think, and rethink. Many successful students complete their assignments, do well on tests and get good grades, yet they don't ever learn to think critically and deeply. They think superficially, staying on the surface of problems rather than stretching their minds and becoming deeply engaged in meaningful thinking.

"For God's sake, think! Why is he being so nice to you?"

© Sam Gross/The New Yorker Collection/www.cartoonbank.com

Recently, Robert Roeser and his colleagues (Roeser & Eccles, 2015; Roeser & others, 2014; Roeser & Zelazo, 2012) have emphasized that mindfulness is an important mental process that children can engage in to improve a number of cognitive and socioemotional skills, such as executive function, focused attention, emotion regulation, and empathy. *Mindfulness* involves paying careful attention to your thoughts, feelings, and environment (Britton & others, 2014). It has been proposed that mindfulness training could be implemented in schools through practices such as using age-appropriate activities that increase children's reflection on moment-to-moment experiences and result in improved self-regulation (Roeser & Eccles, 2015). For example, a training program in mindfulness and caring for others was effective in improving the cognitive control of fourth- and fifth-graders (Schonert-Reichl & others, 2015). In other recent research, mindfulness training has been found to improve children's attention and self-regulation (Poehlmann-Tynan & others, 2016); achievement (Singh & others, 2016); and coping strategies in stressful situations (Dariotis & others, 2016). Also, in a recent study, mindfulness-based intervention reduced stress in public school teachers (Taylor & others, 2016).

In addition to mindfulness, activities such as yoga, meditation, and tai chi have been recently suggested as candidates for improving children's cognitive and socioemotional development. Together these activities are

fuzzy trace theory States that memory is best understood by considering two types of memory representations: (1) verbatim memory trace and (2) gist. In this theory, older children's better memory is attributed to the fuzzy traces created by extracting the gist of information.

thinking Manipulating and transforming information in memory.

critical thinking Thinking reflectively and productively, as well as evaluating the evidence.

being grouped under the topic of *contemplative science*, a cross-disciplinary term that involves the study of how various types of mental and physical training might enhance children's development (Roeser & Eccles, 2015).

Creative Thinking Cognitively competent children not only think critically, but also creatively (Sternberg & Sternberg, 2016). **Creative thinking** is the ability to think in novel and unusual ways and to come up with unique solutions to problems. Thus, intelligence and creativity are not the same thing. This difference was recognized by J. P. Guilford (1967), who distinguished between **convergent thinking,** which produces one correct answer and characterizes the kind of thinking that is required on conventional tests of intelligence, and **divergent thinking,** which produces many different answers to the same question and characterizes creativity. For example, a typical item on a conventional intelligence test is "How many quarters will you get in return for 60 dimes?" In contrast, the following question has many possible answers: "What images come to mind when you hear the phrase 'sitting alone in a dark room' or 'some unique uses for a paper clip'?"

It is important to recognize that children will show more creativity in some domains than others (Baer & Kaufman, 2013). A child who shows creative thinking skills in mathematics may not exhibit these skills in art, for example. An important goal is to help children learn to think creatively.

A special concern today is that the creative thinking of children in the United States appears to be declining. A study of approximately 300,000 U.S. children and adults found that creativity scores rose until 1990, but since then have steadily declined (Kim, 2010). Among the likely causes of this decline are the amount of time U.S. children spend watching TV and playing video games instead of engaging in creative activities, as well as the lack of emphasis on creative thinking skills in schools (Gregorson, Kaufman, & Snyder, 2013). In some countries, though, there has been increasing emphasis on creative thinking in schools. For example, historically, creative thinking has typically been discouraged in Chinese schools. However, Chinese educators are now encouraging teachers to spend more classroom time on creative activities (Plucker, 2010).

How Would You...?

As a **psychologist,** how would you talk with teachers and parents about ways to improve children's creative thinking?

Metacognition

Metacognition is cognition about cognition, or knowing about knowing (Flavell, 2004). Many studies classified as "metacognitive" have focused on *metamemory,* or knowledge about memory. This includes general knowledge about memory, such as knowing that recognition tests are easier than recall tests. It also encompasses knowledge about one's own memory, such as a student's ability to monitor whether she has studied enough for a test that is coming up next week (Dimmitt & McCormick, 2012). Conceptualization of metacognition consists of several dimensions of executive function, such as planning (deciding how much time to spend focusing on a task, for example) and self-regulation (modifying strategies as work on a task progresses, for example) (Dimmitt & McCormick, 2012; McCormick, Dimmitt, & Sullivan, 2013). Recent research found that metacognition involved children's confidence in their eyewitness judgments (Buratti, Allwood, & Johansson, 2014).

Young children do have some general knowledge about memory (Lukowski & Bauer, 2014). By 5 or 6 years of age, children usually already know that familiar items are easier to learn than unfamiliar ones, that short lists are easier to memorize than long ones, that recognition is easier than

Cognitive developmentalist John Flavell is a pioneer in providing insights about children's thinking. Among his many contributions are establishing the field of metacognition and conducting numerous studies in this area, including metamemory and theory of mind studies.

© Dr. John Flavell

creative thinking The ability to think in novel and unusual ways and to come up with unique solutions to problems.

convergent thinking The type of thinking that produces one correct answer and is typically assessed by standardized intelligence tests.

divergent thinking Thinking that produces many answers to the same question and is characteristic of creativity.

metacognition Cognition about cognition, or knowing about knowing.

recall, and that forgetting is more likely to occur over time (Lyon & Flavell, 1993). However, in other ways young children's metamemory is limited. They don't understand that related items are easier to remember than unrelated ones and that remembering the gist of a story is easier than remembering information verbatim (Kreutzer, Leonard, & Flavell, 1975). By the fifth grade, children do understand that gist recall is easier than verbatim recall.

Young children also have only limited knowledge about their own memory. They have an inflated opinion of their memory abilities. For example, in one study a majority of young children predicted that they would be able to recall all 10 items on a list of 10 items. When tested for this, however, none of the young children managed this feat (Flavell, Friedrichs, & Hoyt, 1970). As they move through the elementary school years, children can give more realistic evaluations of their memory skills.

In addition to metamemory, metacognition includes knowledge about memory strategies (McCormick, Dimmitt, & Sullivan, 2013). In the view of Michael Pressley (2007), the key to education is helping students learn a rich repertoire of strategies that produce solutions to problems. Good thinkers routinely use strategies and effective planning to solve problems. Good thinkers also know when and where to use strategies. Understanding when and where to use strategies often results from monitoring the learning situation (Dimmitt & McCormick, 2012).

How Would You...?

As an **educator,** how would you advise teachers and parents about ways to improve children's meta-cognitive skills?

Executive Function

Earlier you read about executive function and its characteristics in early childhood (Griffin, Freund, & McCardle, 2015; Müller & Kerns, 2015). Some of the cognitive topics we already have discussed in this chapter—working memory, critical thinking, creative thinking, and metacognition—can be considered under the umbrella of executive function and linked to the development of the brain's prefrontal cortex (Casey & others, 2016; Groppe & Elsner, 2016; Moriguchi, Chevalier, & Zelazo, 2016).

What are some changes in executive function from 4 to 11 years of age?

© Hero Images/Corbis/
Glow Images RF

Also, earlier in the chapter in the coverage of brain development in middle and late childhood, you read about the increase in cognitive control, which involves flexible and effective control in a number of areas such as focusing attention, reducing interfering thoughts, inhibiting motor actions, and exercising flexibility in deciding between competing choices.

Adele Diamond and Kathleen Lee (2011) recently highlighted the following dimensions of executive function that they conclude are the most important for 4- to 11-year-old children's cognitive development and school success:

- *Self-control/inhibition.* Children need to develop self-control that will allow them to concentrate and persist on learning tasks, to inhibit their tendencies to repeat incorrect responses, and to resist the impulse to do something that they later would regret.

- *Working memory.* Children need an effective working memory to mentally work with the masses of information they will encounter as they go through school and beyond.

- *Flexibility.* Children need to be flexible in their thinking so as to consider different strategies and perspectives.

Researchers have found that executive function is a better predictor of school readiness than general IQ (Blair & Razza, 2007). A number of diverse activities have been found to increase children's executive function, such as computerized training that uses games to improve working memory (Cogmed, 2013); aerobic exercise (Hillman & others, 2014); mindfulness (Gallant, 2016); scaffolding of self-regulation (Bodrova & Leong, 2015); and some types of school curricula (the Montessori curriculum, for example) (Diamond, 2013; Diamond & Lee, 2011).

Intelligence

How can intelligence be defined? **Intelligence** is the ability to solve problems and to adapt and learn from experiences. Interest in intelligence has often focused on individual differences and assessment. *Individual differences* are the stable, consistent ways in which people differ from each other. We can talk about individual differences in personality or any other domain, but it is in the domain of intelligence that the most attention has been directed at individual differences. For example, an intelligence test purports to inform us about whether a student can reason better than others who have taken the test. Let's go back in history and see what the first intelligence test was like.

The Binet Tests

In 1904, the French Ministry of Education asked psychologist Alfred Binet to devise a method of identifying children who were unable to learn in school. School officials wanted to reduce crowding by placing students who did not benefit from regular classroom teaching in special schools. Binet and his student Theophile Simon developed an intelligence test to meet this request. The test is called the *1905 Scale*. It consists of 30 questions on topics ranging from the ability to touch one's ear to the ability to draw designs from memory and define abstract concepts.

Binet developed the concept of **mental age (MA),** an individual's level of mental development relative to others. A few years later, in 1912, William Stern created the concept of **intelligence quotient (IQ),** a person's mental age divided by chronological age (CA) and multiplied by 100. That is, IQ = MA/CA × 100. If mental age is the same as chronological age, then the person's IQ is 100. If mental age is above chronological age, then IQ is more than 100. If mental age is below chronological age, then IQ is less than 100.

The Binet test has been revised many times to incorporate advances in the understanding of intelligence and intelligence tests. These revisions are called the *Stanford-Binet tests* (Stanford University is where the revisions have been done). In 2004, the test—now called the *Stanford-Binet 5*—was revised to analyze an individual's response in five content areas: fluid reasoning, knowledge, quantitative reasoning, visual-spatial reasoning, and working memory. A general composite score also is still obtained.

By administering the test to large numbers of people of different ages (from preschool through late adulthood) from different backgrounds, researchers have found that scores on the Stanford-Binet approximate a normal distribution (see Figure 6).

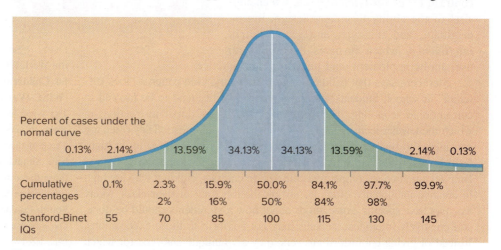

Figure 6 The Normal Curve and Stanford-Binet IQ Scores
The distribution of IQ scores approximates a normal curve. Most of the population falls in the middle range of scores. Notice that extremely high and extremely low scores are very rare. Slightly more than two-thirds of the scores fall between 85 and 115. Only about 1 in 50 individuals has an IQ of more than 130, and only about 1 in 50 individuals has an IQ of less than 70.

A **normal distribution** is symmetrical, with a majority of the scores falling in the middle of the possible range of scores and few scores appearing toward the extremes of the range.

The Wechsler Scales

Another set of tests widely used to assess students' intelligence is called the Wechsler scales, developed by psychologist David Wechsler. They include the Wechsler Preschool and Primary Scale of Intelligence—Fourth Edition (WPPSI-IV) to test children from 2.5 years to 7.25 years of age; the Wechsler Intelligence Scale for Children—Fourth Edition (WISC-IV) for children and adolescents 6 to 16 years of age; and the Wechsler Adult Intelligence Scale—Fourth Edition (WAIS-IV).

The Wechsler subscales not only provide an overall IQ score but also yield several composite indexes, such as the Verbal Comprehension Index, the Working Memory Index, and the Processing Speed Index. These types of indexes allow the examiner to quickly identify the areas in which the child is strong or weak. Three of the Wechsler subscales are shown in Figure 7.

Types of Intelligence

Is it more appropriate to think of a child's intelligence as a general ability or as a number of specific abilities? Robert Sternberg and Howard Gardner have proposed influential theories that reflect this second viewpoint.

Sternberg's Triarchic Theory Robert J. Sternberg (1986, 2004, 2010, 2012, 2013, 2015a, b, 2016a, b, c) developed the **triarchic theory of intelligence,** which states that intelligence comes in three forms: (1) *analytical intelligence,* which refers to the ability to analyze, judge, evaluate, compare, and contrast; (2) *creative intelligence,* which consists of the ability to create, design, invent, originate, and imagine; and (3) *practical intelligence,* which involves the ability to use, apply, implement, and put ideas into practice.

Sternberg says that children with different triarchic patterns "look different" in school. Students with high analytic ability tend to be favored in conventional schooling. They often do well under direct instruction, in which the teacher lectures and gives students objective tests. They often are considered to be "smart" students who get good grades, show up in high-level tracks, do well on traditional tests of intelligence and the SAT, and later get admitted to competitive colleges. In contrast, children who are high in creative intelligence often are not on the top rung of their class. Many teachers have specific expectations about how assignments should be done, and creatively intelligent students may not conform to those expectations. Instead of giving conformist answers, they give unique answers, for which they might get reprimanded or marked down. No teacher wants to discourage creativity, but Sternberg stresses that too often a teacher's desire to increase students' knowledge suppresses creative thinking.

Like children high in creative intelligence, children who are practically intelligent often do not relate well to the demands of school. However,

Verbal Subscales

Similarities

A child must think logically and abstractly to answer a number of questions about how things might be similar.

Example: "In what way are a lion and a tiger alike?"

Comprehension

This subscale is designed to measure an individual's judgment and common sense.

Example: "What is the advantage of keeping money in a bank?"

Nonverbal Subscales

Block Design

A child must assemble a set of multicolored blocks to match designs that the examiner shows.
Visual-motor coordination, perceptual organization, and the ability to visualize spatially are assessed.

Example: "Use the four blocks on the left to make the pattern on the right."

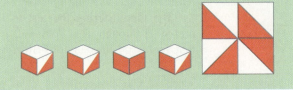

Figure 7 Sample Subscales of the Wechsler Intelligence Scale for Children—Fourth Edition (WISC-IV)

The Wechsler includes 11 subscales, 6 verbal and 5 nonverbal. Three of the subscales are shown here. Simulated items similar to those found in the Wechsler Intelligence Scale for Children—Fourth Edition.

many of these children do well outside of the classroom's walls. They may have excellent social skills and good common sense. As adults, some become successful managers, entrepreneurs, or politicians in spite of having undistinguished school records.

Gardner's Eight Frames of Mind Howard Gardner (1983, 1993, 2002, 2014) suggests there are eight types of intelligence, or "frames of mind." These are described here, with examples of the types of vocations in which they are reflected as strengths (Campbell, Campbell, & Dickinson, 2004):

Verbal: The ability to think in words and use language to express meaning. Occupations: Authors, journalists, speakers.

Mathematical: The ability to carry out mathematical operations. Occupations: Scientists, engineers, accountants.

Spatial: The ability to think three-dimensionally. Occupations: Architects, artists, sailors.

Bodily-kinesthetic: The ability to manipulate objects and be physically adept. Occupations: Surgeons, craftspeople, dancers, athletes.

Musical: A sensitivity to pitch, melody, rhythm, and tone. Occupations: Composers, musicians, and sensitive listeners.

Interpersonal: The ability to understand and interact effectively with others. Occupations: Successful teachers, mental health professionals.

Intrapersonal: The ability to understand oneself. Occupations: Theologians, psychologists.

Naturalist: The ability to observe patterns in nature and understand natural and human-made systems. Occupations: Farmers, botanists, ecologists, landscapers.

Howard Gardner, shown here working with a young child, developed the concept that intelligence comprises eight kinds of skills: verbal, mathematical, spatial, bodily-kinesthetic, musical, intrapersonal, interpersonal, and naturalist.

© Dr. Howard Gardner and Jay Gardner

According to Gardner, everyone has all of these intelligences to varying degrees. As a result, we prefer to learn and process information in specific ways. People learn best when they can do so in a way that uses their stronger intelligences.

Evaluating the Multiple-Intelligences Approaches Sternberg's and Gardner's approaches have much to offer. They have stimulated teachers to think more broadly about what makes up children's competencies. And they have motivated educators to develop programs that instruct students in multiple domains. These approaches have also contributed to interest in assessing intelligence and classroom learning in innovative ways, such as by evaluating student portfolios (Moran & Gardner, 2007).

Still, doubts about multiple-intelligences approaches persist. A number of psychologists think that the multiple-intelligences views have taken the concept of specific intelligences too far (Reeve & Charles, 2008). Some argue that a research base to support the three intelligences of Sternberg or the eight intelligences of Gardner has not yet emerged. One expert on intelligence, Nathan Brody (2007), observes that people who excel at one type of intellectual task are likely to excel in others. Thus, individuals who do well at memorizing lists of digits are also likely to be good at solving verbal problems and spatial layout problems. If musical skill reflects a distinct type of intelligence, ask other critics, why not label the skills of outstanding chess players, prizefighters, painters, and poets as types of intelligence?

How Would You...?

As a **psychologist,** how would you use Gardner's theory of multiple intelligences to respond to children who are distressed by their below-average score on a traditional intelligence test?

Advocates of the concept of general intelligence point to its accuracy in predicting school and job success. For example, scores on tests of general intelligence are substantially correlated with school grades and achievement test performance, both at the time of the test and years later (Cucina & others, 2016; Strenze, 2007). For example, a recent meta-analysis of 240 independent samples and more than 100,000 individuals found a correlation of +.54 between intelligence and school grades (Roth & others, 2015).

The argument between those who support the concept of general intelligence and those who advocate the multiple-intelligences view is ongoing (Gardner, 2014; Traskowski & others, 2014). Sternberg (2015a, b, 2016a, b, c) actually accepts that there is a general intelligence for the kinds of analytical tasks that traditional IQ tests assess but thinks that the range of tasks those tests measure is far too narrow.

Culture and Intelligence

Differing conceptions of intelligence occur not only among psychologists but also among cultures (Zhang & Sternberg, 2012). What is viewed as intelligent in one culture may not be thought of as intelligent in another. For example, people in Western cultures tend to view intelligence in terms of reasoning and thinking skills, whereas people in Eastern cultures see intelligence as a way for members of a community to engage successfully in social roles (Nisbett, 2003).

Interpreting Differences in IQ Scores

The IQ scores that result from tests such as the Stanford-Binet and Wechsler scales provide information about children's mental abilities. However, interpretation of scores on intelligence tests is a controversial topic.

The Influence of Genetics How strong is the effect of genetics on intelligence? Some researchers argue that heredity plays a strong role in intelligence (Zhao, Kong, & Qu, 2014), but this assertion is difficult to prove because teasing apart the influences of heredity and environment is virtually impossible. Also, most research on heredity and environment does not include environments that differ radically. Thus, it is not surprising that many genetic studies show environment to be a fairly weak influence on intelligence.

Have scientists been able to pinpoint specific genes that are linked to intelligence? A recent research review concluded that there may be more than 1,000 genes that affect intelligence, each possibly having a small influence on an individual's intelligence (Davies & others, 2011). However, researchers have not been able to identify the specific genes that contribute to intelligence (Deary, 2012).

One strategy for examining the role of heredity in intelligence is to compare the IQs of identical and fraternal twins. Recall that identical twins have exactly the same genetic makeup but fraternal twins do not. If intelligence is genetically determined, say some investigators, identical twins' IQs should be more similar than those of fraternal twins. A research review of many studies found that the difference in the average correlation of intelligence between identical and fraternal twins was 0.15, suggesting a relatively low correlation between genetics and intelligence (Grigorenko, 2000) (see Figure 8).

Today, most researchers agree that genetics and environment interact to influence intelligence (Grigorenko & others, 2016; Sternberg, 2016a, b, c). For most people, this means that modifications in environment can change their IQ scores considerably. Although genetic endowment may always influence a person's intellectual ability, the environmental

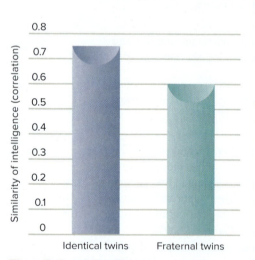

Figure 8 Correlation Between Intelligence Test Scores and Twin Status

The graph represents a summary of research findings that have compared the intelligence test scores of identical and fraternal twins. An approximate .15 difference has been found, with a higher correlation for identical twins (.75) and a lower correlation for fraternal twins (.60).

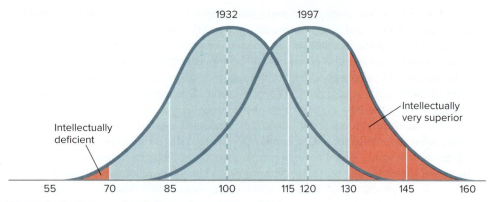

Figure 9 **The Increase in IQ Scores from 1932 to 1997**
As measured by the Stanford-Binet intelligence test, American children seem to be getting smarter. Scores of a group tested in 1932 fell along a bell-shaped curve with half below 100 and half above. Studies show that if children took that same test today, half would score above 120 on the 1932 scale. Very few of them would score in the "intellectually deficient" end on the left side, and about one-fourth would rank in the "very superior" range.

influences and opportunities we provide children and adults do make a difference (Grigorenko & others, 2016; Sternberg, 2016a, b, c).

Environmental Influences The environment's role in intelligence is reflected in the 12- to 18-point increase in IQ when children are adopted from lower-SES to middle-SES homes (Nisbett & others, 2012). Environmental influences on intelligence also involve schooling (Gustafsson, 2007). The biggest effects have been found when large groups of children have been deprived of formal education for an extended period, resulting in lower intelligence (Ceci & Gilstrap, 2000). Another possible effect of education can be seen in rapidly increasing IQ test scores around the world (Flynn, 1999, 2007, 2011, 2013; Flynn & Blair, 2013). IQ scores have been increasing so fast that a high percentage of people regarded as having average intelligence at the turn of the century would be considered below average in intelligence today (see Figure 9). If a representative sample of people today took the Stanford-Binet test version used in 1932, about 25 percent would be defined as having very superior intelligence, a label usually accorded to fewer than 3 percent of the population. Because the increase has taken place in a relatively short time, it can't be due to heredity, but rather may be due to increasing levels of education attained by a much greater percentage of the world's population, or to other environmental factors such as the explosion of information to which people are exposed (Flynn & Blair, 2013). The worldwide increase in intelligence test scores that has occurred over a short time frame has been called the *Flynn effect* after the researcher who discovered it, James Flynn.

Students in an elementary school in South Africa. *How might schooling influence the development of children's intelligence?*
© Owen Franken/Corbis

Researchers are increasingly concerned about improving the early environment of children who are at risk for impoverished intelligence (Currie & Rossin-Slater, 2015; Duncan, Magnuson, & Votruba-Drzal, 2015; O'Connor, 2016). For various reasons, many low-income parents have difficulty providing an intellectually stimulating environment for their children. Programs that educate parents to be more sensitive caregivers and better teachers, as well as access to support services such as quality child-care programs, can make a difference in a child's intellectual development (Burchinal & others, 2015). Thus the efforts to counteract a deprived early environment's effect on intelligence emphasize prevention rather than remediation.

A review of the research on early interventions concluded that (1) high-quality child-care center–based interventions are associated with increases in children's intelligence and school achievement; (2) the interventions are most successful with poor children and children whose parents have little education; (3) the positive benefits continue through adolescence but are not as strong as in early childhood or the beginning of elementary school; and (4) the programs that continue into middle and late childhood have the best long-term results (Brooks-Gunn, 2003).

In sum, there is a consensus among psychologists that both heredity and environment influence intelligence (Grigorenko & others, 2016). This consensus reflects the nature-nurture issue, which focuses on the extent to which development is influenced by nature (heredity) and nurture (environment). Although psychologists agree that intelligence is the product of both nature and nurture, there is still disagreement about how strongly each influences intelligence.

Group Differences On average, African American schoolchildren in the United States score 10 to 15 points lower on standardized intelligence tests than non-Latino White American schoolchildren do (Brody, 2000). Children from Latino families also score lower than non-Latino White children. These are *average scores,* however; there is significant overlap in the distribution of scores. About 15 to 25 percent of African American schoolchildren score higher than half of White schoolchildren do, and many White schoolchildren score lower than most African American schoolchildren. As African Americans have gained social, economic, and educational opportunities, the gap between African Americans and Whites on standardized intelligence tests has begun to narrow. This gap especially narrows in college, where African American and White students often experience more similar environments than in the elementary and high school years (Myerson & others, 1998). Further, a recent study using the Stanford Binet Intelligence Scales found no differences in overall intellectual ability between non-Latino White and African American preschool children when the children were matched on age, gender, and parental education level (Dale & others, 2014). Nonetheless, a recent analysis concluded that the underrepresentation of African Americans in STEM (science, technology, engineering, and math) subjects and careers is linked to practitioners' expectations that they have less innate talent than non-Latino Whites (Leslie & others, 2015).

Creating Culture-Fair Tests Culture-fair tests are tests of intelligence that are intended to be free of cultural bias. Two types of culture-fair tests have been devised. The first includes items that are familiar to children from all socioeconomic and ethnic backgrounds, or items that at least are familiar to the children taking the test. For example, a child might be asked how a bird and a dog are different, on the assumption that all children have been exposed to birds and dogs. The second type of culture-fair test has no verbal questions.

Why is it so hard to create culture-fair tests? Most tests tend to reflect what the dominant culture thinks is important (Zhang & Sternberg, 2012). If tests have time limits, that will bias the test against groups not concerned with time. If languages differ, the same words might have different meanings for different language groups. Even pictures can produce bias because some cultures have less experience with drawings and photographs. Because of such difficulties in creating culture-fair tests, Robert Sternberg (2012) concludes that there are no culture-fair tests, only *culture-reduced tests.*

Extremes of Intelligence

culture-fair tests Tests of intelligence that are designed to be free of cultural bias.

Intelligence tests have been used to discover indications of intellectual disability or giftedness, the extremes of intelligence. At times, they have been misused for this purpose. Keeping in mind the theme that an intelligence test should not be used as the sole indicator of intellectual disability or giftedness, we will explore the nature of these intellectual extremes.

intellectual disability A condition of limited mental ability in which an individual has a low IQ, usually below 70 on a traditional test of intelligence, and has difficulty adapting to the demands of everyday life.

Intellectual Disability Intellectual disability is a condition of limited mental ability in which an individual has a low IQ, usually below 70 on a traditional intelligence test, and has difficulty adapting to the demands of everyday life (Burack & others, 2016). About 5 million Americans fit this definition of intellectual disability.

About 89 percent of the individuals with an intellectual disability fall into the mild intellectual disability category, with IQs of 55 to 70; most of them are able to live independently as adults and work at a variety of jobs. About 6 percent are classified as having a moderate intellectual disability, with IQs of 40 to 54; these people can attain a second-grade level of skills and may be able to support themselves as adults through some types of labor. About 3.5 percent are in the severe category, with IQs of 25 to 39; these individuals learn to talk and accomplish very simple tasks but require extensive supervision. Less than 1 percent have IQs below 25; they fall into the profoundly disabled classification and need constant supervision.

Intelligence disability can have an organic cause, or it can be social and cultural in origin:

- **Organic intellectual disability** is intellectual disability that is caused by a genetic disorder or by brain damage; the word *organic* refers to the tissues or organs of the body, indicating physical damage. Most people who suffer from organic intellectual disability have IQs that range between 0 and 50. However, children with Down syndrome have an average IQ of approximately 50. As discussed earlier, Down syndrome is caused by an extra copy of chromosome 21.

- **Cultural-familial intellectual disability** is a mental deficit in which no evidence of organic brain damage can be found; individuals' IQs generally range from 50 to 70. Psychologists suspect that such mental deficits result from the normal variation that distributes people along the range of intelligence scores combined with growing up in a below-average intellectual environment.

What causes a child to develop Down syndrome?
© Stockbyte/Veer RF

Giftedness There have always been people whose abilities and accomplishments outshine others'—the whiz kid in class, the star athlete, the natural musician. People who are **gifted** have above-average intelligence (an IQ of 130 or higher) or superior talent for something or both. When it comes to programs for the gifted, most school systems select children who have intellectual superiority and academic aptitude, whereas children who are talented in the visual and performing arts (arts, drama, dance, music), athletics, or other special aptitudes tend to be overlooked (Olszewski-Kubilius & Thomson, 2013). There also are increasing calls to further expand the criteria for giftedness to include such factors as creativity and commitment (Ambrose & Steinberg, 2016a, b).

Estimates vary but indicate that approximately 3 to 5 percent of U.S. students are gifted (National Association for Gifted Children, 2009). This percentage is likely conservative because it focuses more on children who are gifted intellectually and academically, often failing to include those who are gifted in creative thinking or the visual and performing arts (Ford, 2012). Also, African American, Latino, and Native American children are underrepresented in gifted programs (Ford, 2012, 2015a, b, 2016). Much of the underrepresentation involves the lower test scores for these children compared with non-Latino White and Asian American children, which may be due to a number of reasons such as test bias and fewer opportunities to develop language skills such as vocabulary and comprehension (Ford, 2012, 2015a, b, 2016).

What are the characteristics of children who are gifted? Despite speculation that giftedness is linked with having a mental disorder, no relation between giftedness and mental disorder has been found. Similarly, the idea that gifted children are maladjusted is a myth, as Lewis Terman (1925) found when he conducted an extensive study of 1,500 children whose Stanford-Binet IQs averaged 150. The children in Terman's study

organic intellectual disability Intellectual disability that involves some physical damage and is caused by a genetic disorder or brain damage.

cultural-familial intellectual disability Intellectual disability in which there is no evidence of organic brain damage, but the individual's IQ generally is between 50 and 70.

gifted Having above-average intelligence (an IQ of 130 or higher) and/or superior talent for something.

were socially well adjusted, and many went on to become successful doctors, lawyers, professors, and scientists. Studies support the conclusion that gifted people tend to be more mature than others, have fewer emotional problems than average, and grow up in a positive family climate (Feldman, 2001). For example, a recent study revealed that parents and teachers identified elementary school children who are not gifted as having more emotional and behavioral risks than children who are gifted (Eklund & others, 2015). In this study, when children who are gifted did have problems, they were more likely to be internalized problems, such as anxiety and depression, than externalized problems, such as acting out and high levels of aggression.

Ellen Winner (1996) described three criteria that characterize gifted children, whether in art, music, or academic domains:

1. *Precocity.* Gifted children are precocious. They begin to master an area earlier than their peers. Learning in their domain is more effortless for them than for ordinary children. In most instances, these gifted children are precocious because they have an inborn high ability in a particular domain or domains.

2. *Marching to a different drummer.* Gifted children learn in a qualitatively different way from ordinary children. One way that they march to a different drummer is that they need minimal help, or scaffolding, from adults to learn. In many instances, they resist any kind of explicit instruction. They often make discoveries on their own and solve problems in unique ways.

3. *A passion to master.* Gifted children are driven to understand the domain in which they have high ability. They display an intense, obsessive interest and an ability to focus. They motivate themselves, says Winner, and do not need to be "pushed" by their parents.

4. *Information-processing skills.* Researchers have found that children who are gifted learn at a faster pace, process information more rapidly, are better at reasoning, use superior strategies, and monitor their understanding better than their nongifted counterparts (Ambrose & Sternberg, 2016a).

At 2 years of age, art prodigy Alexandra Nechita (shown here as a teenager) colored in coloring books for hours and also took up pen and ink. She had no interest in dolls or friends. By age 5 she was using watercolors. Once she started school, she would paint as soon as she got home. At age 8, she saw the first public exhibit of her work. In succeeding years, working quickly and impulsively on canvases as large as 5 feet by 9 feet, she has completed hundreds of paintings, some of which sell for close to $100,000 apiece. Now in her early thirties, she continues to paint—relentlessly and passionately. It is, she says, what she loves to do. *What are some characteristics of children who are gifted?*
© Koichi Kamoshida/Newsmakers/Getty Images

Is giftedness a product of heredity or environment? The answer is likely both (Duggan & Friedman, 2014; Johnson & Bouchard, 2014). Individuals who are gifted recall that they had signs of high ability in a particular area at a very young age, prior to or at the beginning of formal training (Howe & others, 1995). This suggests the importance of innate ability in giftedness. However, researchers have also found that individuals with world-class status in the arts, mathematics, science, and sports all report strong family support and years of training and practice (Bloom, 1985). Deliberate practice is an important characteristic of individuals who become experts in a particular domain. For example, in one study, the best musicians engaged in twice as much deliberate practice over their lives as did the least successful ones (Ericsson, Krampe, & Tesch-Romer, 1993).

Individuals who are highly gifted are typically not gifted in many domains, and research on giftedness is increasingly focused on domain-specific developmental paths (Kell & Lubinski, 2014; Sternberg & Bridges, 2014). During the childhood years, the domain(s) in which individuals are gifted usually emerges. Thus, at some point in the childhood years, the child who will become a gifted artist or the child who will become a gifted mathematician begins to show expertise in that domain. Regarding domain-specific giftedness, software genius Bill Gates (1998), the founder of Microsoft and one of the world's richest people, commented that when you are good at something, you may have to resist the urge to think that you will be good at everything. Because he has been so successful at software

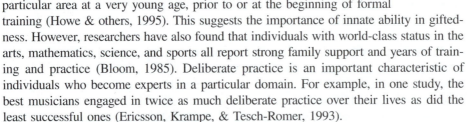

How Would You...?
As an **educator,** how would you structure educational programs for children who are gifted that would challenge and expand their talents?

development, he has found that people also expect him to be brilliant in other domains in which he is far from gifted.

An increasing number of experts argue that the education of children who are gifted in the United States requires a significant overhaul (Reis & Renzulli, 2014). Ellen Winner (1996, 2009) argues that too often children who are gifted are socially isolated and underchallenged in the classroom. It is not unusual for other students to label them "nerds" or "geeks." Many eminent adults report that school was a negative experience for them, that they were bored and sometimes knew more than their teachers (Bloom, 1985). Winner argues that American students will benefit more from their education when standards are raised for all children. She recommends that some underchallenged students be allowed to attend advanced classes in their domain of exceptional ability, such as allowing some precocious middle school students to take college classes in their area of expertise. For example, at age 13, Bill Gates took college math classes and hacked a computer security system; Yo-Yo Ma, famous cellist, graduated from high school at 15 and attended Juilliard School of Music in New York City.

A young Bill Gates, founder of Microsoft and now one of the world's richest people. Like many highly gifted students, Gates was not especially fond of school. He hacked a computer security system when he was 13 and was allowed to take some college math classes during high school. He dropped out of Harvard University and began developing a plan for what was to become Microsoft Corporation. *What are some ways that schools can enrich the education of highly talented students to make it a more challenging and meaningful experience?*

© Doug Wilson/Corbis

Language Development

Children gain new skills as they enter school that make it possible for them to learn to read and write (Bailey, Osipova, & Kelly, 2016). These include increased use of language to talk about things that are not physically present, learning what a word is, and learning how to recognize and talk about sounds (Berko Gleason, 2003). They also learn the *alphabetic principle*—that the letters of the alphabet represent sounds of the language.

Vocabulary, Grammar, and Metalinguistic Awareness

During middle and late childhood, changes occur in the way children's mental vocabulary is organized. When asked to say the first word that comes to mind when they hear a word, preschool children typically provide a word that often follows the word in a sentence. For example, when asked to respond to "dog" the young child may say "barks," or to the word "eat" respond with "lunch." At about 7 years of age, children begin to respond with a word that is the same part of speech as the stimulus word. For example, a child may now respond to the word "dog" with "cat" or "horse." To "eat," they now might say "drink." This is evidence that children of this age have begun to categorize their vocabulary by parts of speech (Berko Gleason, 2003).

The process of categorizing becomes easier as children increase their vocabulary (Clark, 2012, 2017). Children's vocabulary increases from an average of about 14,000 words at age 6 to an average of about 40,000 words by age 11.

Children make similar advances in grammar (Behrens, 2012; Clark, 2017). During the elementary school years, children's improvement in logical reasoning and analytical skills helps them understand such constructions as the appropriate use of comparatives (*shorter, deeper*) and subjectives ("If you were president . . . "). During the elementary school years, children become increasingly able to understand and use complex grammar, such as the following sentence: *The boy who kissed his mother wore a hat.* They also learn to use language in a more connected way, producing connected discourse. They become able to relate sentences to one another to produce descriptions, definitions, and narratives that make sense. Children must be able to do these things orally before they can be expected to deal with them in written assignments.

These advances in vocabulary and grammar during the elementary school years are accompanied by the development of **metalinguistic awareness,** which is knowledge about language, such as knowing what a preposition is or being able to discuss the sounds of a language (Tong, Deacon, & Cain, 2014). Metalinguistic awareness allows children "to think about their language, understand what words are, and even define them" (Berko Gleason, 2009, p. 4). It improves considerably during the elementary school years (Pan & Uccelli, 2009). Defining words becomes a regular part of classroom discourse, and children increase their knowledge of syntax as they study and talk about the components of sentences, such as subjects and verbs (Crain, 2012).

Children also make progress in understanding how to use language in culturally appropriate ways—a process called pragmatics (Bryant, 2012). By the time they enter adolescence, most children know the rules for the use of language in everyday contexts—that is, what is appropriate and inappropriate to say.

Reading

Before learning to read, children learn to use language to talk about things that are not present; they learn what a word is; and they learn how to recognize sounds and talk about them. Children who begin elementary school with a robust vocabulary have an advantage when it comes to learning to read.

How should children be taught to read? Currently, one debate focuses on the whole-language approach versus the phonics approach (Lloyd & others, 2015; Reutzel & Cooter, 2015).

The **whole-language approach** stresses that reading instruction should parallel children's natural language learning. In some whole-language classes, beginning readers are taught to recognize whole words or even entire sentences, and to use the context of what they are reading to guess at the meaning of words. Reading materials that support the whole-language approach are whole and meaningful—that is, children are given material in its complete form, such as stories and poems, so that they learn to understand language's communicative function. Reading is connected with listening and writing skills. Although there are variations in whole-language programs, most share the premise that reading should be integrated with other skills and subjects, such as science and social studies, and that it should focus on real-world material. Thus, a class might read newspapers, magazines, or books, and then write about and discuss what they have read.

A teacher helps a student sound out words. Researchers have found that phonics instruction is a key aspect of teaching students to read, especially beginning readers and students with weak reading skills.

© Gideon Mendel/Corbis

In contrast, the **phonics approach** emphasizes that reading instruction should teach basic rules for translating written symbols into sounds. Early phonics-centered reading instruction should involve simplified materials. Only after children have learned correspondence rules that relate spoken phonemes to the alphabet letters that are used to represent them should they be given complex reading materials, such as books and poems.

Which approach is better? Research suggests that children can benefit from both approaches, but instruction in phonics needs to be emphasized (Del Campo & others, 2015; Tompkins, 2015). An increasing number of experts in the field of reading now conclude that direct instruction in phonics is a key aspect of learning to read (Cunningham, 2013).

Beyond the phonics/whole language issue in learning to read, becoming a good reader includes learning to read fluently (Allington, 2015). Many beginning or poor readers do not recognize words automatically. Their processing capacity is consumed by the demands of word recognition, so they have less comprehension of groupings of words as

metalinguistic awareness Refers to knowledge about language, such as knowing what a preposition is or being able to discuss the sounds of a language.

whole-language approach An approach to reading instruction based on the idea that instruction should parallel children's natural language learning. Reading materials should be whole and meaningful.

phonics approach The idea that reading instruction should teach the basic rules for translating written symbols into sounds.

phrases or sentences. As their processing of words and passages becomes more automatic, it is said that their reading becomes more *fluent*. Metacognitive strategies, such as learning to monitor one's reading progress, getting the gist of what is being read, and summarizing also are important in becoming a good reader (McCormick, Dimmitt, & Sullivan, 2013).

Second-Language Learning and Bilingualism

Are there sensitive periods in learning a second language? That is, if individuals want to learn a second language, how important is the age at which they begin to learn it? What is the best way for U.S. schools to teach children who come from homes in which English is not the primary language?

Second-Language Learning

For many years, it was claimed that if individuals did not learn a second language prior to puberty they would never reach native-language learners' proficiency in the second language (Johnson & Newport, 1991). However, recent research indicates a more complex conclusion: There are sensitive periods for learning a second language. Additionally, these sensitive periods likely vary across different areas of language systems (Thomas & Johnson, 2008). For example, late language learners, such as adolescents and adults, may learn new vocabulary more easily than new sounds or new grammar (Neville, 2006). Also, children's ability to pronounce words with a native-like accent in a second language typically decreases with age, with an especially sharp drop occurring after the age of about 10 to 12. Adults tend to learn a second language faster than children, but their level of second-language mastery is not as high as children's. And the way children and adults learn a second language differs somewhat. Compared with adults, children are less sensitive to feedback, less likely to use explicit strategies, and more likely to learn a second language from large amounts of input (Thomas & Johnson, 2008).

Students in the United States are far behind their counterparts in many developed countries in learning a second language. For example, in Russia, schools have 10 grades, called *forms,* which roughly correspond to the 12 grades in American schools. Russian children begin school at age 7 and begin learning English in the third form. Because of this emphasis on teaching English, most Russian citizens under the age of 40 today are able to speak at least some English. The United States is the only technologically advanced Western nation that does not have a national foreign language requirement at the high school level, even for students in rigorous academic programs.

U.S. students who do not learn a second language may be missing more than the chance to acquire a skill. *Bilingualism*—the ability to speak two languages—has a positive effect on children's cognitive development (Tompkins, 2015). Children who are fluent in two languages perform better than their single-language counterparts on tests of control of attention, concept formation, analytical reasoning, cognitive flexibility, and cognitive complexity (Bialystok, 2001, 2007, 2011, 2014, 2015; Bialystok & Craik, 2010; Sullivan & others, 2014). They also are more conscious of the structure of spoken and written language and better at noticing errors of grammar and meaning, skills that benefit their reading ability (Bialystok, 1997; Kuo & Anderson, 2012).

Research indicates that bilingual children do have a smaller vocabulary in each language than monolingual children (Bialystok, 2011). Most children who learn two languages are not exposed to the same quantity and quality of each language. However, bilingual children do not show delays in the rate at which they acquire language overall (Hoff, 2016). In a recent study, by 4 years of age children who continued to learn Spanish and English languages had a total vocabulary growth that was greater than that of monolingual children (Hoff & others, 2014).

Overall, bilingualism is linked to more positive outcomes for both children's language and cognitive development. An especially important developmental question that many parents of infants and young children have is whether they should teach them two languages simultaneously or whether doing this would confuse them. The answer is that teaching infants and young children two languages simultaneously (as when a mother's native language is English and her husband's is Spanish) has numerous benefits and few drawbacks (Bialystok, 2014, 2015).

In the United States, many immigrant children go from being monolingual in their home language to bilingual in that language and in English, only to end up as monolingual speakers of English. This is called *subtractive bilingualism,* and it can have negative effects on children, who often become ashamed of their home language.

How Would You...?

As a **human development and family studies professional,** how would you describe the advantages of promoting bilingualism in the home for school-age children in the United States who come from families whose first language is not English?

Bilingual Education

A current controversy related to bilingualism involves the millions of U.S. children who come from homes in which English is not the primary language (Echevarria, Vogt, & Short, 2017; Peregoy & Boyle, 2017). What is the best way to teach these English language learners (ELLs)?

ELLs have been taught in one of two main ways: (1) instruction in English only, or (2) a *dual-language* (used to be called *bilingual*) approach that involves instruction in their home language and English. In a dual-language approach, instruction is given in both the ELL child's home language and English for varying amounts of time at certain grade levels. One of the arguments for the dual-language approach is the research discussed earlier demonstrating that bilingual children have more advanced information-processing skills than monolingual children do.

If a dual-language strategy is used, too often it has been thought that immigrant children need only one or two years of this type of instruction. However, in general it takes immigrant children approximately three to five years to develop speaking proficiency and seven years to develop reading proficiency in English (Hakuta, Butler, & Witt, 2000). Also, immigrant children vary in their ability to learn English. Children who come from lower socioeconomic backgrounds have more difficulty than those from higher socioeconomic backgrounds (Hakuta, 2001). Thus, especially for immigrant children from low socioeconomic backgrounds, more years of dual-language instruction may be needed than they currently are receiving.

A first- and second-grade bilingual English-Cantonese teacher instructing students in Chinese in Oakland, California. *What have researchers found about the effectiveness of bilingual education?*
© Elizabeth Crews

What have researchers found regarding outcomes of ELL programs? Drawing conclusions about the effectiveness of ELL programs is difficult because of variations across programs in the number of years they are in effect, type of instruction, quality of schooling other than ELL instruction, teachers, children, and other factors. Further, no effective experiments have been conducted that compare bilingual education with English-only education in the United States (Snow & Kang, 2006). Some experts have concluded that the quality of instruction is more important in determining outcomes than the language in which it is delivered (Lesaux & Siegel, 2003).

Nonetheless, other experts, such as Kenji Hakuta (2001, 2005), support the combined home language and English approach because (1) children have difficulty learning a subject when it is taught in a language they do not understand; and (2) when both languages are integrated in the classroom, children learn the second language more readily and participate more actively. In support of Hakuta's view, most large-scale studies have found that the academic achievement of ELLs is higher in dual-language programs than English-only programs (Genesee & Lindholm-Leary, 2012).

Summary

Physical Changes and Health

- The period of middle and late childhood involves slow, consistent growth.
- Changes in the brain in middle and late childhood include advances in functioning in the prefrontal cortex, which is associated with an increase in cognitive control.
- Motor development becomes much smoother and more coordinated. Boys usually are better at gross motor skills, girls at fine motor skills.
- Most U.S. children do not get nearly enough exercise.
- For the most part, middle and late childhood is a time of excellent health. However, being overweight in childhood poses serious health risks. Cancer is the second leading cause of death in children (after accidents).

Children with Disabilities

- Approximately 13 percent of U.S. children from 3 to 21 years of age receive special education or related services. Approximately 80 percent of children with a learning disability have a reading problem. The number of children diagnosed with ADHD has been increasing. Autism spectrum disorders recently have been estimated to characterize 1 in 88 U.S. children.
- U.S. legislation requires that all children with disabilities be given a free, appropriate public education. Increasingly, this education has involved full inclusion.

Cognitive Changes

- Piaget theorized that the stage of concrete operational thought characterizes children from about 7 to 11 years of age. During this stage children are capable of concrete operations, conservation, classification, seriation, and transitivity. Criticisms of Piaget's theory have been proposed.
- Changes in these aspects of information occur in middle and late childhood: attention, memory, critical thinking, creative thinking, metacognition, and executive function.
- Widely used intelligence tests today include the Stanford-Binet test and Wechsler scales. Sternberg proposed that intelligence comes in three main forms, whereas Gardner said there are eight types of intelligence. Intelligence is influenced by heredity and environment. Extremes of intelligence include intellectual disability and giftedness.

Language Development

- In the elementary school years, improvements in children's language development include vocabulary, grammar, and metalinguistic awareness.
- Both the phonics and whole-language approaches to reading instruction can benefit children, but experts increasingly view phonics instruction as critical in learning to read.
- Recent research indicates a complex conclusion about whether there are sensitive periods in learning a second language. Bilingual education in the United States aims to teach academic subjects to immigrant children in their native language while gradually adding English instruction.

Key Terms

attention deficit hyperactivity disorder (ADHD)
autism spectrum disorders (ASD)
convergent thinking
creative thinking
critical thinking
cultural-familial intellectual disability
culture-fair tests

divergent thinking
long-term memory
working memory
elaboration
fuzzy trace theory
gifted
inclusion
individualized education plan (IEP)
intellectual disability

intelligence
intelligence quotient (IQ)
learning disability
least restrictive environment (LRE)
long-term memory
mental age (MA)
metacognition
metalinguistic awareness
neo-Piagetians

normal distribution
organic intellectual disability
phonics approach
seriation
strategies
thinking
transitivity
triarchic theory of intelligence
whole-language approach

8 Socioemotional Development in Middle and Late Childhood

© damircudic/E+/Getty Images RF

CHAPTER OUTLINE

Stories of Life-Span Development: Learning in Troubled Schools

In *The Shame of the Nation,* Jonathan Kozol (2005) described his visits to 60 U.S. schools in urban low-income areas in 11 states. He saw many schools in which the minority population was 80 to 90 percent. Kozol observed numerous inequities—unkempt classrooms, hallways, and restrooms; inadequate textbooks and supplies; and lack of resources. He also saw teachers mainly instructing students to memorize material by rote, especially as preparation for mandated tests, rather than stimulating them to engage in higher-level thinking. Kozol also frequently observed teachers using threatening disciplinary tactics to control the classroom.

However, some teachers Kozol observed were effective in educating children in these undesirable conditions. At P.S. 30 in the South Bronx, Mr. Bedrock teaches fifth grade. One student in his class, Serafina, recently lost her mother to AIDS. When Kozol visited the class, he was told that two other children had taken the role of "allies in the child's struggle for emotional survival" (Kozol, 2005, p. 291). Textbooks are in short supply for the class, and the social studies text is so out of

What are some of the challenges faced by children growing up in the South Bronx?
© Andy Levin/Science Source

222

date it claims that Ronald Reagan is the country's president. But Mr. Bedrock told Kozol that it's a "wonderful" class this year. About their teacher, 56-year-old Mr. Bedrock, one student said, "He's getting old . . . but we love him anyway" (p. 292). Kozol found the students orderly, interested, and engaged.

The years of middle and late childhood bring many changes to children's social and emotional lives. The development of their self-conceptions, moral reasoning, and gendered behavior is significant. Transformations in their relationships with parents and peers occur, and schooling takes on a more academic flavor. ■

Emotional and Personality Development

In this section, we explore how the self continues to develop during middle and late childhood and the emotional changes that take place during these years. We also discuss children's moral development and many aspects of the role that gender plays in their development in middle and late childhood.

The Self

What is the nature of the child's self-understanding, understanding of others, and self-esteem during the elementary school years? What roles do self-efficacy and self-regulation play in children's achievement?

The Development of Self-Understanding

In middle and late childhood, especially from 8 to 11 years of age, children increasingly describe themselves with psychological characteristics and traits rather than the more concrete self-descriptions of younger children. Older children are more likely to describe themselves as *"popular, nice, helpful, mean, smart,* and *dumb"* (Harter, 2006, p. 526).

In addition, during the elementary school years, children become more likely to recognize social aspects of the self (Harter, 2012, 2013, 2016). They include references to social groups in their self-descriptions, such as referring to themselves as a Girl Scout, a Catholic, or someone who has two close friends (Livesly & Bromley, 1973).

Children's self-understanding in the elementary school years also includes increasing reference to social comparison (Harter, 2012, 2013, 2016). At this point in development, children are more likely to distinguish themselves from others in comparative rather than in absolute terms. That is, elementary-school-age children are no longer as likely to think about what they do or do not do, but are more likely to think about what they can do in comparison with others.

How Would You...?

As a **psychologist,** how would you explain the role of social comparison for the development of a child's sense of self?

Consider a series of studies in which Diane Ruble (1983) investigated children's use of social comparison in their self-evaluations. Children were given a difficult task and then offered feedback on their performance as well as information about the performances of other children their age. The children were then asked for self-evaluations. Children younger than 7 made virtually no reference to the information about other children's performances. However, many children older than 7 included socially comparative information in their self-descriptions.

Understanding Others

Earlier we described the advances and limitations of young children's social understanding. In middle and late childhood, **perspective taking,** the social cognitive process involved in assuming the perspective of others and understanding their thoughts and feelings, improves. Executive function is at work in perspective taking. Among the executive functions called on when

perspective taking The social cognitive process involved in assuming the perspective of others and understanding their thoughts and feelings.

children engage in perspective taking are cognitive inhibition (controlling one's own thoughts to consider the perspective of others) and cognitive flexibility (seeing situations in different ways).

In middle and late childhood, children also become more skeptical of others' claims (Heyman, Fu, & Lee, 2013). They become increasingly skeptical of some sources of information about psychological traits. A recent study of 6- to 9-year-olds revealed that older children were less trusting and more skeptical of others' distorted claims than were younger children (Mills & Elashi, 2014).

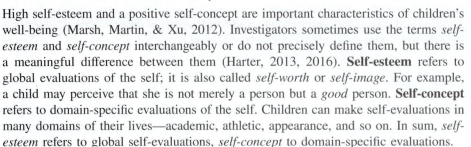

What are some changes in children's understanding of others in middle and late childhood?
© Paul Edmondson/Corbis

Self-Esteem and Self-Concept

High self-esteem and a positive self-concept are important characteristics of children's well-being (Marsh, Martin, & Xu, 2012). Investigators sometimes use the terms *self-esteem* and *self-concept* interchangeably or do not precisely define them, but there is a meaningful difference between them (Harter, 2013, 2016). **Self-esteem** refers to global evaluations of the self; it is also called *self-worth* or *self-image*. For example, a child may perceive that she is not merely a person but a *good* person. **Self-concept** refers to domain-specific evaluations of the self. Children can make self-evaluations in many domains of their lives—academic, athletic, appearance, and so on. In sum, *self-esteem* refers to global self-evaluations, *self-concept* to domain-specific evaluations.

The foundations of self-esteem and self-concept emerge from the quality of parent-child interaction in infancy and early childhood. Thus, if children have low self-esteem in middle and late childhood, they may have experienced neglect or abuse in relationships with their parents earlier in development. Children with high self-esteem are more likely to be securely attached to their parents and have parents who engage in sensitive caregiving (Thompson, 2015, 2016).

Self-esteem reflects perceptions that do not always match reality (Miller & others, 2015). A child's self-esteem might reflect a belief about whether he or she is intelligent and attractive, for example, but that belief is not necessarily accurate. Thus, high self-esteem may refer to accurate, justified perceptions of one's worth as a person and one's successes and accomplishments, but it can also refer to an arrogant, grandiose, unwarranted sense of superiority over others (Lavner & others, 2016). In the same manner, low self-esteem may reflect either an accurate perception of one's shortcomings or a distorted, even pathological insecurity and inferiority.

Variations in self-esteem have been linked with many aspects of children's development. However, much of the research is *correlational* rather than *experimental*. Recall that correlation does not equal causation. Thus, if a correlational study finds an association between children's low self-esteem and low academic achievement, low academic achievement could cause the low self-esteem as much as low self-esteem could cause low academic achievement. A recent longitudinal study explored whether self-esteem is a cause or consequence of social support in youth (Marshall & others, 2014). In this study, self-esteem predicted subsequent changes in social support but social support did not predict subsequent changes in self-esteem.

What are the consequences of low self-esteem? Low self-esteem has been implicated in overweight and obesity, anxiety, depression, suicide, drug use, and delinquency (Blanco & others, 2014; Hill, 2016; Orth & others, 2016; Park & Park, 2015; Rieger & others, 2016; Sanders & others, 2015). One study revealed that youth with low self-esteem had lower life satisfaction at 30 years of age (Birkeland & others, 2012). Another recent study found that low and decreasing self-esteem in adolescence was linked to adult depression two decades later (Steiger & others, 2014).

Researchers have found only moderate correlations between school performance and self-esteem, and these correlations do not suggest that high self-esteem produces better school performance (Baumeister, 2013).

self-esteem The global evaluative dimension of the self. Self-esteem is also referred to as self-worth or self-image.

self-concept Domain-specific evaluations of the self.

How Would You...?

As an **educator,** how would you work with children to improve their self-esteem in relation to their academic ability?

In fact, efforts to increase students' self-esteem have not always led to improved school performance (Davies & Brember, 1999).

Children with high self-esteem have greater initiative, but this can produce positive or negative outcomes. For example, children with high self-esteem are prone to both prosocial and antisocial actions (Krueger, Vohs, & Baumeister, 2008).

In addition, a current concern is that too many of today's children grow up receiving praise for mediocre or even poor performance and as a consequence have inflated self-esteem (Stipek, 2005). They may have difficulty handling competition and criticism. This theme is vividly captured by the title of a book, *Dumbing Down Our Kids: Why American Children Feel Good About Themselves But Can't Read, Write, or Add* (Sykes, 1995). In a series of studies, researchers found that inflated praise, although well intended, may cause children with low self-esteem to avoid important learning experiences such as tackling challenging tasks (Brummelman & others, 2014). And a recent study found that narcissistic parents especially overvalue their children's talents (Brummelman & others, 2015).

Increasing Children's Self-Esteem

Teachers, social workers, health-care professionals, and others are often concerned about low self-esteem in the children they serve. Researchers have suggested several strategies to improve self-esteem in at-risk children (Bednar, Wells, & Peterson, 1995; Harter, 2006, 2012, 2016).

- *Identify the causes of low self-esteem.* Intervention should target the causes of low self-esteem. Children have the highest self-esteem when they perform competently in domains that are important to them. Therefore, it is helpful to encourage children to identify and value their areas of competence, such as academic skills, athletic skills, physical attractiveness, and social acceptance.

- *Provide emotional support and social approval.* Some children with low self-esteem come from conflictual families or conditions of abuse or neglect—situations in which emotional support is unavailable. In some cases, alternative sources of support can be arranged either informally through the encouragement of a teacher, a coach, or another significant adult, or more formally through programs such as Big Brothers and Big Sisters.

- *Help children achieve.* Achievement also can improve children's self-esteem. For example, the straightforward teaching of real skills to children often results in increased achievement and thus in enhanced self-esteem. Children develop higher self-esteem when they know which tasks will achieve their goals and when they have successfully performed them or similar tasks.

How can parents help children develop higher self-esteem?
© Roy Mehta/Taxi/Getty Images

- *Help children cope.* Self-esteem can be built when a child faces a problem and tries to cope with it, rather than avoiding it. If coping rather than avoidance prevails, children often face problems realistically, honestly, and nondefensively. This produces favorable self-evaluative thoughts, which lead to the self-generated approval that raises self-esteem.

Self-Efficacy

Self-efficacy is the belief that one can master a situation and produce favorable outcomes. Albert Bandura (2001, 2006, 2010, 2012, 2016), whose social cognitive theory was described earlier, states that self-efficacy is a critical factor in whether or not students achieve. Self-efficacy is the belief that "I can"; helplessness is the belief that "I cannot." Students with high self-efficacy

self-efficacy The belief that one can master a situation and produce favorable outcomes.

How Would You...?

As an **educator,** how would you encourage enhanced self-efficacy in a student who says, "I can't do this work"?

endorse such statements as "I know that I will be able to learn the material in this class" and "I expect to be able to do well at this activity."

Dale Schunk (2008, 2012, 2016) has applied the concept of self-efficacy to many aspects of students' achievement. In his view, self-efficacy influences a student's choice of activities. Students with low self-efficacy for learning may avoid many learning tasks, especially those that are challenging. By contrast, children with high self-efficacy eagerly work at learning tasks (Schunk, 2012, 2016). Students with high self-efficacy are more likely to expend effort and persist longer at a learning task than students with low self-efficacy.

Self-Regulation

One of the most important aspects of the self in middle and late childhood is the increased capacity for self-regulation (Blair, 2016; Eisenberg, Smith, & Spinrad, 2016; Muller & Kerns, 2015; Wang & Cai, 2016). This increased capacity is characterized by deliberate efforts to manage one's behavior, emotions, and thoughts that lead to increased social competence and achievement (Blair, Raver, & Finegood, 2016; Eisenberg, Spinrad, & Valiente, 2016; Schunk, 2016). In a recent study, higher levels of self-control assessed at 4 years of age were linked to improvements in the math and reading achievement of early elementary school children living in predominantly rural and low-income contexts (Blair & others, 2015). Also, study of almost 17,000 3- to 7-year-old children revealed that self-regulation was a protective factor for children growing up in low-socioeconomic-status (SES) conditions (Flouri, Midouhas, & Joshi, 2014).

The increased capacity for self-regulation is linked to developmental advances in the brain's prefrontal cortex, which was discussed in the chapter on physical and cognitive development in middle and late childhood (Wendelken & others, 2016). In that discussion, increased focal activation in the prefrontal cortex was linked to improved cognitive control. Such cognitive control includes self-regulation.

Industry Versus Inferiority

Earlier we described Erik Erikson's (1968) eight stages of human development. His fourth stage, industry versus inferiority, appears during middle and late childhood. The term *industry* expresses a dominant theme of this period: Children become interested in how things are made and how they work. When children are encouraged in their efforts to make, build, and work—whether building a model airplane, constructing a tree house, fixing a bicycle, solving an addition problem, or cooking—their sense of industry increases. Conversely, parents who see their children's efforts at making things as "mischief" or "making a mess" will tend to foster a sense of inferiority in their children.

Emotional Development

Preschoolers become more adept at talking about their own and others' emotions. They also show a growing awareness of the need to control and manage their emotions to meet social standards. In middle and late childhood, children further develop their understanding and self-regulation of emotion (Calkins & Perry, 2016).

Developmental Changes

Developmental changes in emotions during middle and late childhood include the following (Denham, Bassett, & Wyatt, 2015; Goodvin, Thompson, & Winer, 2015; Kuebli, 1994):

- *Improved emotional understanding.* Children in elementary school develop an increased ability to understand such complex emotions as pride and shame. These emotions become less tied to the reactions of other people; they become more self-generated and integrated with a sense of personal responsibility. Also, during middle and late childhood as part of their understanding of emotions, children can engage in "mental time travel," in which they anticipate and recall the cognitive and emotional aspects of events (Lagattuta, 2014a, b; Lagattuta & others, 2015).

- *Increased understanding that more than one emotion can be experienced in a particular situation.* A third-grader, for example, may realize that achieving something might involve both anxiety and joy.

- *Increased tendency to be aware of the events leading to emotional reactions.* A fourth-grader may become aware that her sadness today is influenced by her friend moving to another town last week.

- *Ability to suppress or conceal negative emotional reactions.* A fifth-grader has learned to tone down his anger better than he used to when one of his classmates irritates him.

- *The use of self-initiated strategies for redirecting feelings.* In the elementary school years, children become more reflective about their emotional lives and increasingly use strategies to control their emotions. They become more effective at cognitively managing their emotions, such as soothing themselves after an upset.

- *A capacity for genuine empathy.* A fourth-grader, for example, feels sympathy for a distressed person and experiences vicariously the sadness the distressed person is feeling.

Coping with Stress

An important aspect of children's emotional lives is learning how to cope with stress. As children get older, they more accurately appraise a stressful situation and determine how much control they have over it (Brenner, 2016; Lieberman & Chu, 2016; Masten, 2015). Older children generate more coping alternatives to stressful conditions and use more cognitive coping strategies (Saarni & others, 2006). They are better than younger children at intentionally shifting their thoughts to something that is less stressful; and at reframing, or changing their perception of a stressful situation. For example, a younger child may be very disappointed that a teacher did not say hello when the child arrived in the classroom. An older child may reframe the situation and think, "My teacher may have been busy with other things and just forgot to say hello."

Children grieve at a memorial near the Sandy Hook Elementary School in Newtown, Connecticut, following the shooting in December 2012 that left 26 people dead, 20 of them young children. *What are some effective strategies that adults can use to help children cope with traumatic events?*

© Justin Lane/EPA/Corbis

By 10 years of age, most children are able to use cognitive strategies to cope with stress (Saarni, 1999). However, in families that have not been supportive and are characterized by turmoil or trauma, children may be so overwhelmed by stress that they do not use such strategies (Klingman, 2006).

Disasters, such as the bombing of the World Trade Center in New York City in September 2001 or Hurricane Sandy in 2012, can especially harm children's development and produce adjustment problems (Scheeringa, Cobham, & McDermott, 2014). Among the outcomes for children who experience disasters are acute stress reactions, depression, panic disorder, and post-traumatic stress disorder (Pfefferbaum, Newman, & Nelson, 2014). The likelihood that a child will face these problems following a disaster depends on factors such as the nature and severity of the disaster and the type of support available to the child (Masten & others, 2015). Also, children who have developed a number of coping techniques have the best chance of adapting and functioning competently in the face of disasters and trauma (Ungar, 2015).

In research on disasters and trauma, the term *dose-response effects* is often used. A widely supported finding in this research area is that the more severe the disaster or trauma (dose), the worse the adaptation and adjustment (response) following the event (Masten, 2015).

Researchers have offered some recommendations for parents, teachers, and other adults caring for children after a disaster (Gurwitch & others, 2001):

- Reassure children (numerous times, if necessary) of their safety and security.
- Allow children to retell events and be patient in listening to them.
- Encourage children to talk about any disturbing or confusing feelings, reassuring them that such feelings are normal after a stressful event.
- Protect children from re-exposure to frightening situations and reminders of the trauma—for example, by limiting discussion of the event in front of the children.
- Help children make sense of what happened, keeping in mind that children may misunderstand what took place. For example, young children "may blame themselves, believe things happened that did not happen, believe that terrorists are in the school, etc. Gently help children develop a realistic understanding of the event" (p. 10).

How Would You...?

As a **social worker,** how would you counsel a child who has been exposed to a traumatic event?

Moral Development

Recall that Piaget proposed that younger children are characterized by heteronomous morality but that by 10 years of age they have moved into a higher stage called autonomous morality. According to Piaget, older children consider the intentions of the individual, believe that rules are subject to change, and are aware that punishment does not always follow wrongdoing.

A second major perspective on moral development was proposed by Lawrence Kohlberg (1958, 1986). Piaget's cognitive stages of development serve as the underpinnings for Kohlberg's theory, but Kohlberg proposed six stages of moral development, which he believed are universal. Development from one stage to another, said Kohlberg, is fostered by opportunities to take the perspective of others and to experience conflict between one's current stage of moral thinking and the reasoning of someone at a higher stage.

The Kohlberg Stages

Kohlberg's stages fall into three levels of moral thinking, each of which is characterized by two stages (see Figure 1).

LEVEL 1	LEVEL 2	LEVEL 3
Preconventional Level	**Conventional Level**	**Postconventional Level**
Stage 1 Heteronomous Morality *Children obey because adults tell them to obey. People base their moral decisions on fear of punishment.*	**Stage 3** Mutual Interpersonal Expectations, Relationships, and Interpersonal Conformity *Individuals value trust, caring, and loyalty to others as a basis for moral judgments.*	**Stage 5** Social Contract or Utility and Individual Rights *Individuals reason that values, rights, and principles undergird or transcend the law.*
Stage 2 Individualism, Instrumental purpose, and Exchange *Individuals pursue their own interests but let others do the same. What is right involves equal exchange.*	**Stage 4** Social System Morality *Moral judgments are based on understanding of the social order, law, justice, and duty.*	**Stage 6** Universal Ethical Principles *The person has developed moral judgments that are based on universal human rights. When faced with a dilemma between law and conscience, a personal, individualized conscience is followed.*

Figure 1 Kohlberg's Three Levels and Six Stages of Moral Development

Kohlberg argued that people everywhere develop their moral reasoning by passing through these age-based stages. *Where does Kohlberg's theory stand on the nature-nurture and continuity-discontinuity issues?*

Preconventional reasoning is Kohlberg's lowest level of moral reasoning. At this level, children interpret good and bad in terms of external rewards and punishments.

- *Stage 1.* **Heteronomous morality** is the first stage in preconventional reasoning. At this stage, moral thinking is tied to punishment. For example, children think that they must obey because they fear punishment for disobedience.

- *Stage 2.* **Individualism, instrumental purpose, and exchange** is the second stage of preconventional reasoning. At this stage, children reason that pursuing their own interests is the right thing to do, but they let others do the same. Thus, they think that what is right involves an equal exchange. They reason that if they are nice to others, others will be nice to them in return.

Conventional reasoning is the second, or intermediate, level in Kohlberg's theory of moral development. At this level, individuals apply certain standards, but they are the standards set by others, such as parents or the government.

- *Stage 3.* **Mutual interpersonal expectations, relationships, and interpersonal conformity** is Kohlberg's third stage of moral development. At this stage, individuals value trust, caring, and loyalty to others as a basis of moral judgments. Children and adolescents often adopt their parents' moral standards at this stage, seeking parental approval as a "good girl" or a "good boy."

- *Stage 4.* **Social systems morality** is the fourth stage in Kohlberg's theory of moral development. At this stage, moral judgments are based on understanding the social order, law, justice, and duty. For example, adolescents may reason that in order for a community to work effectively, it needs to be protected by laws that community members obey.

Postconventional reasoning is the highest level in Kohlberg's theory of moral development. At this level, the individual recognizes alternative moral courses, explores the options, and then decides on a personal moral code.

- *Stage 5.* **Social contract or utility and individual rights** is the fifth Kohlberg stage. At this stage, individuals reason that values, rights, and principles undergird or transcend the law. A person evaluates the validity of actual laws and may examine social systems in terms of the degree to which they preserve and protect fundamental human rights and values.

- *Stage 6.* **Universal ethical principles** is the sixth and highest stage in Kohlberg's theory of moral development. At this stage, the person has developed a moral standard based on universal human rights. When faced with a conflict between law and conscience, the person reasons that conscience should be followed, even though the decision might bring risk.

Kohlberg believed that these levels and stages occur in a sequence and are age related: Before age 9, most children use level 1, preconventional reasoning based on external rewards and punishments. By early adolescence, moral reasoning is increasingly based on level 2, the application of standards set by others. Most adolescents reason at the higher part of level 2 (stage 3), with some signs of stages 2 and 4. Not everyone progresses beyond level 2, even in adulthood, but by early adulthood a small number of individuals reason in postconventional ways (level 3).

What evidence supports this description of development? A 20-year longitudinal investigation found that use of stages 1 and 2 decreased with age (Colby & others, 1983) (see Figure 2). Stage 4, which did not appear at all in the moral reasoning of 10-year-olds, was reflected in the moral thinking of 62 percent of the 36-year-olds. Stage 5 did not appear in any individuals until age 20 to 22, and even later in adulthood it never

preconventional reasoning The lowest level in Kohlberg's theory of moral development. The individual's moral reasoning is controlled primarily by external rewards and punishment.

heteronomous morality Kohlberg's first stage in preconventional reasoning, in which moral thinking is tied to punishment.

individualism, instrumental purpose, and exchange The second Kohlberg stage of moral development. At this stage, individuals pursue their own interests but also let others do the same.

conventional reasoning The second, or intermediate, level in Kohlberg's theory of moral development. At this level, individuals abide by certain standards, but they are the standards of others, such as parents or the laws of society.

mutual interpersonal expectations, relationships, and interpersonal conformity Kohlberg's third stage of moral development. At this stage, individuals value trust, caring, and loyalty to others as a basis of moral judgments.

social systems morality The fourth stage in Kohlberg's theory of moral development. Moral judgments are based on understanding the social order, law, justice, and duty.

postconventional reasoning The highest level in Kohlberg's theory of moral development. At this level, the individual recognizes alternative moral courses, explores the options, and then decides on a personal moral code.

social contract or utility and individual rights The fifth Kohlberg stage. At this stage, individuals reason that values, rights, and principles undergird or transcend the law.

universal ethical principles The sixth and highest stage in Kohlberg's theory of moral development. Individuals develop a moral standard based on universal human rights.

characterized more than 10 percent of the individuals. Thus, this research found that the moral stages appeared somewhat later than Kohlberg initially envisioned, and reasoning at the higher stages, especially stage 6, was rare.

Influences on the Kohlberg Stages

What factors influence movement through Kohlberg's stages? Although moral reasoning at each stage presupposes a certain level of cognitive development, Kohlberg argued that advances in children's cognitive development did not ensure development of moral reasoning. Instead, moral reasoning also reflects children's experiences in dealing with moral questions and moral conflict.

Several investigators have tried to advance individuals' levels of moral development by having a model present arguments that reflect moral thinking one stage above the individuals' established levels. This approach applies Vygotsky's principle of scaffolding; it also applies the concepts of equilibrium and conflict that Piaget used to explain cognitive development. By presenting arguments slightly beyond the children's level of moral reasoning, the researchers created a disequilibrium that motivated the children to restructure their moral thought. The upshot of studies using this approach is that virtually any discussion about the adolescent's current stage seems to promote more advanced moral reasoning (Walker, 1982).

Kohlberg believed that peer interaction is a critical part of the social stimulation that challenges children to change their moral reasoning. Whereas adults characteristically impose rules and regulations on children, the give-and-take among peers gives children an opportunity to take the perspective of another person and to generate rules democratically. Kohlberg stressed that encounters with peers can produce perspective-taking opportunities that may advance a child's moral reasoning.

Kohlberg's Critics

Kohlberg's theory has provoked debate, research, and criticism (Killen & Smetana, 2015; Narváez, 2015, 2016a, b, c; Turiel, 2015). Key criticisms involve the link between moral thought and moral behavior, whether moral reasoning is conscious/deliberative or unconscious/automatic, the roles of culture and the family in moral development, and the significance of concern for others.

Moral Thought and Moral Behavior Kohlberg's theory has been criticized for placing too much emphasis on moral thought and not enough emphasis on moral behavior (Walker, 2004). Moral reasons can sometimes be used as a shelter for immoral behavior (Bandura, 2016). Corrupt CEOs and politicians have usually endorsed the loftiest of moral virtues in public before their own immoral behavior is exposed. Whatever the type of public scandal, you will probably find that the culprits expressed virtuous thoughts but engaged in immoral behavior. No one wants a nation of cheaters and thieves who can reason at the postconventional level and who may know what is right yet still do what is wrong.

Conscious/Deliberate Versus Unconscious/Automatic Social psychologist Jonathan Haidt (2006, 2013) argues that a major flaw in Kohlberg's theory is his view that moral thinking is deliberative and that individuals go around all the time contemplating and reasoning about morality. Haidt believes that moral thinking is more often an

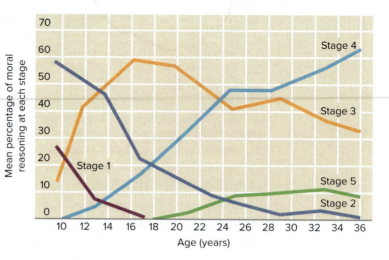

Figure 2 **Age and the Percentage of Individuals at Each Kohlberg Stage**
In one longitudinal study of males from 10 to 36 years of age, at age 10 most moral reasoning was at stage 2 (Colby & others, 1983). At 16 to 18 years of age, stage 3 became the most frequent type of moral reasoning, and it was not until the mid-twenties that stage 4 became the most frequent. Stage 5 did not appear until 20 to 22 years of age, and it never characterized more than 10 percent of the individuals. In this study, the moral stages appeared somewhat later than Kohlberg envisioned and stage 6 was absent. *Do you think it matters that all of the participants in this study were males? Why or why not?*

intuitive gut reaction, with deliberative moral reasoning serving as an after-the-fact justification. Thus, in his view, much of morality begins with rapid evaluative judgments of others rather than with strategic reasoning about moral circumstances.

Culture and Moral Reasoning Kohlberg emphasized that his stages of moral reasoning are universal, but some critics claim his theory is culturally biased (Gibbs, 2014; Mrkva & Narváez, 2015). Both Kohlberg and his critics may be partially correct. One review of 45 studies in 27 cultures around the world, mostly non-European, provided support for the universality of Kohlberg's first four stages (Snarey, 1987). Individuals in diverse cultures developed through these four stages in sequence as Kohlberg predicted. Stages 5 and 6, however, have not been found in all cultures (Gibbs & others, 2007; Snarey, 1987). Furthermore, Kohlberg's scoring system does not recognize the higher-level moral reasoning of certain cultures and thus does not acknowledge that moral reasoning is more culture-specific than Kohlberg envisioned (Snarey, 1987). In sum, although Kohlberg's approach does capture much of the moral reasoning used in various cultures around the world, his approach misses or misconstrues some important moral concepts in particular cultures (Gibbs, 2014).

Families and Moral Development Kohlberg argued that family processes are essentially unimportant in children's moral development. As noted earlier, he argued that parent-child relationships usually provide children with little opportunity for give-and-take or perspective taking. Rather, Kohlberg said that such opportunities are more likely to be provided by children's peer relations.

Did Kohlberg underestimate the contribution of family relationships to moral development? Most experts on children's moral development conclude that parents' moral values and actions influence children's development of moral thoughts (Eisenberg, Spinrad, & Knafo-Noam, 2015; Grusec & others, 2014). Nonetheless, most developmentalists agree with Kohlberg and Piaget that peers play an important role in the development of moral reasoning.

Gender and the Care Perspective The most publicized criticism of Kohlberg's theory has come from Carol Gilligan (1982, 1996), who argues that Kohlberg's theory reflects a gender bias. According to Gilligan, Kohlberg's theory is based on a male norm that puts abstract principles above relationships and concern for others and sees the individual as standing alone and independently making moral decisions. It puts justice at the heart of morality. In contrast with Kohlberg's **justice perspective,** Gilligan argues for a **care perspective,** which is a moral perspective that views people in terms of their connectedness with others and emphasizes interpersonal communication, relationships with others, and concern for others. According to Gilligan, Kohlberg greatly underplayed the care perspective, perhaps because he was a male, because most of his research was with males rather than females, and because he used male responses as a model for his theory.

However, questions have been raised about Gilligan's gender conclusions (Walker & Frimer, 2011). For example, a meta-analysis casts doubt on Gilligan's claim of substantial gender differences in moral judgment (Jaffee & Hyde, 2000). And a review concluded that girls' moral orientations are "somewhat more likely to focus on care for others than on abstract principles of justice, but they can use both moral orientations when needed (as can boys . . .)" (Blakemore, Berenbaum, & Liben, 2009, p. 132).

Domain Theory: Moral, Social Conventional, Personal Reasoning

The **domain theory of moral development** states that there are different domains of social knowledge and reasoning, including moral, social conventional, and personal domains. In domain theory,

justice perspective A moral perspective that focuses on the rights of the individual; individuals independently make moral decisions.

care perspective The moral perspective of Carol Gilligan, which views people in terms of their connectedness with others and emphasizes interpersonal communication, relationships with others, and concern for others.

domain theory of moral development Theory that identifies different domains of social knowledge and reasoning, including moral, social conventional, and personal domains. These domains arise from children's and adolescents' attempts to understand and deal with different forms of social experience.

children's and adolescents' moral, social conventional, and personal knowledge and reasoning emerge from their attempts to understand and deal with different forms of social experience (Killen & Smetana, 2015; Turiel, 2015).

Social conventional reasoning focuses on conventional rules that have been established by social consensus in order to control behavior and maintain the social system. The rules themselves are arbitrary, such as raising your hand in class before speaking, using one staircase at school to go up and the other to go down, not cutting in front of someone standing in line to buy movie tickets, and stopping at a stop sign when driving. There are sanctions if we violate these conventions, although the rules can be changed by consensus.

In contrast, moral reasoning focuses on ethical issues and rules of morality. Unlike conventional rules, moral rules are not arbitrary. They are obligatory, widely accepted, and somewhat impersonal (Turiel, 2015). Rules pertaining to lying, cheating, stealing, and physically harming another person are moral rules because violation of these rules affronts ethical standards that exist apart from social consensus and convention. Moral judgments involve concepts of justice, whereas social conventional judgments are concepts of social organization. Violating moral rules is usually more serious than violating conventional rules.

The social conventional approach is a serious challenge to Kohlberg's approach because Kohlberg argued that social conventions are a stop-over on the road to higher moral sophistication. For social conventional reasoning advocates, social conventional reasoning is not lower than postconventional reasoning but rather something that needs to be disentangled from the moral thread (Killen & Smetana, 2015).

Recently, a distinction also has been made between moral and conventional issues, which are viewed as legitimately subject to adult social regulation, and personal issues, which are more likely subject to the child's or adolescent's independent decision making and personal discretion (Killen & Smetana, 2015). Personal issues include control over one's body, privacy, and choice of friends and activities. Thus, some actions belong to a *personal* domain not governed by moral strictures or social norms.

How does children's sharing change from the preschool to the elementary school years?

© Norbert Schaefer/Corbis

Prosocial Behavior

Whereas Kohlberg's and Gilligan's theories have focused primarily on the development of moral reasoning, the study of prosocial moral behavior has placed more emphasis on the behavioral aspects of moral development (Eisenberg & Spinrad, 2016; Eisenberg, Spinrad, & Knafo-Noam, 2015). Children engage in both immoral antisocial acts, such as lying and cheating, and prosocial moral behavior, such as showing empathy or helping others altruistically. Even during the preschool years, children may care for others or comfort someone in distress, but prosocial behavior is more prevalent in adolescence than in childhood (Eisenberg, Spinrad, & Knafo-Noam, 2015). Parents can be especially helpful in guiding children to engage in prosocial behavior (Laible & Karahuta, 2016).

Sharing is one aspect of prosocial behavior that researchers have studied. Children's sharing comes to reflect a more complex sense of what is just and right during middle and late childhood. By the start of the elementary school years, children begin to express objective ideas about fairness (Eisenberg, Fabes, & Spinrad, 2006). It is common to hear 6-year-old children use the word *fair* as synonymous with *equal* or *same*. By the middle to late elementary school years, children come to believe that equity can also mean that people with special merit or special needs deserve special treatment.

Gender

Gilligan's claim that Kohlberg's theory of moral development reflects gender bias reminds us of the pervasive influence of gender on development. Long before elementary school, boys and girls show preferences for different toys and activities. As we discussed in the chapter on socioemotional development in early childhood, preschool children display a gender identity and gender-typed behavior that reflects biological, cognitive, and social influences. Here we examine gender stereotypes, gender similarities and differences, and gender-role classification.

Gender Stereotypes

In the past, a well-adjusted boy was supposed to be independent, aggressive, and powerful. A well-adjusted girl was supposed to be dependent, nurturing, and uninterested in power. These notions reflect **gender stereotypes,** which are broad categories that reflect general impressions and beliefs about females and males.

Recent research has found that gender stereotypes are, to a great extent, still present in today's world, in the lives of both children and adults (Leaper, 2015; Liben, Bigler, & Hilliard, 2014). Gender stereotyping continues to change during middle and late childhood and adolescence (Blakemore, Berenbaum, & Liben, 2009). During the elementary school years, children have considerable knowledge about which activities are linked with being male or female. For example, a study of 6- to 10-year-olds revealed gender stereotyping in math—both boys and girls indicated math is for boys (Cvencek, Meltzoff, & Greenwald, 2011). Researchers also have found that boys' gender stereotypes are more rigid than girls' (Blakemore, Berenbaum, & Liben, 2009).

Gender Similarities and Differences

What is the reality behind gender stereotypes? Let's examine some of the similarities and differences between boys and girls, keeping in mind that (1) the differences are averages—not characteristics of all boys versus all girls; (2) even when differences are reported, there is considerable gender overlap; and (3) the differences may be due primarily to biological factors, sociocultural factors, or both. First, we examine physical similarities and differences, and then we turn to cognitive and socioemotional similarities and differences.

Physical Development Women have about twice the body fat of men, with most of it concentrated around the breasts and hips. In males, fat is more likely to go to the abdomen. On average, males grow to be 10 percent taller than females. Other physical differences are less obvious. From conception onward, females have a longer life expectancy than males, and females are less likely than males to develop physical or mental disorders. Males have twice the risk of coronary disease that females do.

Does gender matter when it comes to brain structure and function? Human brains are much alike, whether the brain belongs to a male or a female (Halpern & others, 2007). However, researchers have found some differences in the brains of males and females (Hofer & others, 2007). Female brains are approximately 10 percent smaller than male brains (Giedd, 2012). However, female brains have more folds; the larger number of folds (called convolutions) allows more surface brain tissue within the skulls of females than males (Luders & others, 2004). An area of the parietal lobe that functions in visuospatial skills is larger in males than females (Frederikse & others, 2000). And the areas of the brain involved in emotional expression show more metabolic activity in females than males (Gur & others, 1995).

Although some differences in brain structure and function have been found, many of these differences are small and research often is inconsistent regarding the differences. Also, when sex differences in the brain have been revealed, in many cases they have not been directly linked to psychological differences (Blakemore, Berenbaum, & Liben, 2009).

Although research on sex differences in the brain is still in its infancy, it is likely that there are far more similarities than differences

gender stereotypes Broad categories that reflect society's impressions and beliefs about females and males.

"So according to the stereotype, you can put two and two together, but I can read the handwriting on the wall."

in the brains of females and males. A further point is worth noting: Anatomical sex differences in the brain may be due to the biological origins of these differences, behavioral experiences (which underscores the brain's continuing plasticity), or a combination of these factors.

Cognitive Development and Achievement No gender differences in general intelligence have been revealed, but gender differences have been found in some cognitive areas (Blakemore, Berenbaum, & Liben, 2009). Research has shown that in general girls and women have slightly better verbal skills than boys and men, although in some verbal skill areas the differences are substantial (Blakemore, Berenbaum, & Liben, 2009).

There is strong evidence that females outperform males in reading and writing. In national studies, girls have had higher reading achievement than have boys (National Assessment of Educational Progress, 2012). A recent international study in 65 countries found that girls had higher reading achievement than did boys in every country (Reilly, 2012). In this study, the gender difference in reading was stronger in countries with less gender equity and lower economic prosperity. In the United States, girls also have consistently outperformed boys in writing skills in the National Assessment of Educational Progress in fourth-, eighth-, and twelfth-grade assessments.

Are there gender differences in math? A very large-scale study of more than 7 million U.S. students in grades 2 through 11 revealed no differences in math scores for boys and girls (Hyde & others, 2008). And a recent meta-analysis found no gender differences in math scores for adolescents (Lindberg & others, 2010). A recent research review concluded that girls have more negative math attitudes and that parents' and teachers' expectancies for children's math competence are often gender-biased in favor of boys (Gunderson & others, 2012).

One area of math that has been examined for possible gender differences is visuospatial skills, which include being able to rotate objects mentally and determine what they would look like when rotated (Halpern, 2012). These types of skills are important in courses such as plane and solid geometry and geography. A research review revealed that boys have better visuospatial skills than girls (Halpern & others, 2007). For example, despite equal participation in the National Geography Bee, in most years all 10 finalists are boys (Liben, 1995). However, some experts argue that the gender difference in visuospatial skills is small (Hyde & Else-Quest, 2013).

Are there gender differences in school contexts and achievement? With regard to school achievement, girls earn better grades, complete high school at a higher rate, and are more likely to drop out of school than boys (Halpern, 2012). Males are more likely than females to be assigned to special/remedial education classes. Girls are more likely than boys to be engaged with academic material, be attentive in class, put forth more academic effort, and participate more in class (DeZolt & Hull, 2001).

Keep in mind that measures of achievement in school or scores on standardized tests may reflect many factors besides cognitive ability. For example, performance in school may in part reflect attempts to conform to gender roles or differences in motivation, self-regulation, or other socioemotional characteristics (Klug & others, 2016; Martin & others, 2016; Wentzel & Miele, 2016; Wigfield & others, 2015).

Might single-sex education be better for children than coed education? The argument for single-sex education is that it eliminates distraction from the other sex and reduces sexual harassment. Single-sex public education has increased dramatically in recent years. In 2002, only 12 public schools in the U.S. provided single-sex education; in the 2011–2012 school year, 116 public schools were single-sex (NASSPE, 2012).

What are some recent changes in single-sex education in the United States? What does research say about whether single-sex education is beneficial?

The increase in single-sex education has especially been fueled by its inclusion in the No Child Left Behind legislation as a means of improving the educational experiences and academic achievement of low-income students of color. However, two recent research reviews concluded that there have been no documented benefits of single-sex education for low-income students of color (Goodkind, 2013; Halpern & others, 2011). They emphasize that among the many arguments against single-sex education, the strongest is its reduction in the opportunities for boys and girls to work together in a supervised, purposeful environment.

There has been a special call for single-sex public education for one group of adolescents—African American boys—because of their historically poor academic achievement and high dropout rate from school (Mitchell & Stewart, 2013). In 2010, Urban Prep Academy for Young Men became the first all-male, all African American public charter school. One hundred percent of its first graduates enrolled in college, despite the school's location in a section of Chicago where poverty, gangs, and crime predominate. Because so few public schools focus solely on educating African American boys, it is too early to tell whether this type of single-sex education can be effective across a wide range of participants.

Socioemotional Development Three areas of socioemotional development in which gender similarities and differences have been studied extensively are aggression, emotion, and prosocial behavior.

One of the most consistent gender differences is that boys are more physically aggressive than girls are (Leaper, 2015). The difference occurs in all cultures and appears very early in children's development. The physical aggression difference is especially pronounced when children are provoked. Both biological and environmental factors have been proposed to account for gender differences in aggression. Biological factors include heredity and hormones. Environmental factors include cultural expectations, adult and peer models, and social agents that reward aggression in boys and punish aggression in girls.

Although boys are consistently more physically aggressive than girls, might girls show as much or more verbal aggression, such as yelling, than boys? When verbal aggression is examined, gender differences often disappear; sometimes, though, verbal aggression is more pronounced in girls (Eagly & Steffen, 1986).

Recently, increased interest has been shown in *relational aggression*, which involves harming someone by manipulating a relationship (Blakely-McClure & Ostrov, 2016; Cooley & Fife, 2016; Busching & Krahe, 2015). Relational aggression includes such behaviors as trying to make others dislike a certain individual by spreading malicious rumors about the person (Orpinas, McNicholas, & Nahapetyan, 2015). Relational aggression increases in middle and late childhood (Dishion & Piehler, 2009). Mixed findings have characterized research on whether girls show more relational aggression than boys, but one consistency in findings is that relational aggression comprises a greater percentage of girls' overall aggression than it does for boys (Putallaz & others, 2007). One research review revealed that girls engage in more relational aggression than boys in adolescence but not in childhood (Smith, Rose, & Schwartz-Mette, 2010).

Gender differences occur in some aspects of emotion (Leaper, 2015). Females express emotion more than males do, are better than males at decoding emotion, smile more, cry more, and are happier. Males report experiencing and expressing more anger than females do (Kring, 2000). And a recent meta-analysis found that females are better than males at recognizing nonverbal displays of emotion (Thompson & Voyer, 2014). Males usually show less self-regulation of emotion than females do, and this low self-control can translate into behavioral problems. A recent meta-analysis found that overall gender differences in children's emotional expression were small, with girls showing more positive emotions (sympathy, for example) and more internalized emotions (sadness and anxiety, for example) (Chaplin & Aldao, 2013). In this analysis, the gender difference in positive emotions became more pronounced with age as girls more strongly expressed positive emotions than boys in middle and late childhood and in adolescence.

Are there gender differences in prosocial behavior? Across childhood and adolescence, females engage in more prosocial behavior than males do (Hastings, Miller, & Troxel, 2015). Females also view themselves as more empathic than males do (Eisenberg, Spinrad, & Knafo-Noam, 2015). There is a small difference between boys and girls in the extent to which they share, with girls sharing slightly more than boys. However, the greatest gender difference in prosocial behavior occurs with kind and considerate behavior, which females perform more often than males.

How Would You...?

As a **psychologist,** how would you discuss gender similarities and differences with a parent or teacher who is concerned about a child's academic progress and social skills?

Gender-Role Classification

Not long ago, it was accepted that boys should grow up to be masculine and girls to be feminine. In the 1970s, however, as both females and males became dissatisfied with the burdens imposed by their stereotypic roles, alternatives to femininity and masculinity were proposed. Instead of describing masculinity and femininity as a continuum in which more of one means less of the other, it was proposed that individuals could have both masculine and feminine traits.

This thinking led to the development of the concept of **androgyny,** the presence of positive masculine and feminine characteristics in the same person (Bem, 1977; Spence & Helmreich, 1978). The androgynous boy might be assertive (masculine) and nurturing (feminine). The androgynous girl might be powerful (masculine) and sensitive to others' feelings (feminine). Measures have been developed to assess androgyny, such as the Bem Sex Role Inventory (Bem, 1977).

Gender experts such as Sandra Bem argue that androgynous individuals are more flexible, competent, and mentally healthy than their masculine or feminine counterparts. To some degree, though, which gender-role classification is best depends on the context involved. For example, in close relationships, feminine and androgynous orientations might be more desirable. One study found that girls and individuals high in femininity showed a stronger interest in caring than did boys and individuals high in masculinity (Karniol, Grosz, & Schorr, 2003). However, masculine and androgynous orientations might be more desirable in traditional academic and work settings because of the achievement demands in these contexts.

Despite talk about the "sensitive male," William Pollack (1999) argues that little has been done to change traditional ways of raising boys. He says that the "boy code" tells boys that they should show little if any emotion and should act tough. Boys learn the boy code in many contexts—sandboxes, playgrounds, schoolrooms, camps, hangouts. The result, according to Pollack, is a "national crisis of boyhood." Pollack and others suggest that boys would benefit from being socialized to express their anxieties and concerns and to better regulate their aggression.

Gender in Context

Both the concept of androgyny and stereotypes about gender describe people in terms of personality traits such as "aggressive" or "caring." However, which traits people display may vary with the situation (Leaper, 2015). Thus, the nature and extent of gender differences may depend on the context (Liben, Bigler, & Hilliard, 2014).

Consider helping behavior. The stereotype is that females are better than males at helping. But it depends on the situation. Females are more likely than males to volunteer their time to help children with personal problems and to engage in caregiving behavior. However, in situations where males feel a sense of competence and those that involve danger, males are more likely than females to help (Eagly & Crowley, 1986). For example, a male is more likely than a female to stop and help a person stranded by the roadside with a flat tire. Indeed, one study documented that males are more likely to help when the context is masculine in nature (MacGeorge, 2003).

The importance of considering gender in context is nowhere more apparent than when examining what is culturally prescribed behavior for females and males in different countries around the world (Hyde &

androgyny The presence of positive masculine and feminine characteristics in the same individual.

Else-Quest, 2013; UNICEF, 2016). Although there has been greater acceptance of androgyny and similarities in male and female behavior in the United States, in many countries gender roles have remained gender-specific. For example, in many Middle Eastern and some Asian countries, the division of labor between males and females is dramatic. Males are socialized and schooled to work in the public sphere, females in the private world of home and child rearing. In Iran, the dominant view is that the man's duty is to provide for his family and the woman's is to care for her family and household. China also has been a male-dominant culture. Although women have made some strides in China, especially in urban areas, the male role is still dominant. Most males in China do not accept androgynous behavior and gender equity.

In China, females and males are usually socialized to behave, feel, and think differently. The old patriarchal traditions of male supremacy have not been completely uprooted. Chinese women still make considerably less money than Chinese men do. In rural China, male supremacy still governs many women's lives.

© Diego Azubel/EPA/Newscom

Families

Our discussion of parenting and families in this section focuses on how parent-child interactions typically change in middle and late childhood, how parents act as managers, the role of attachment, and how children are affected by living with stepparents.

Developmental Changes in Parent-Child Relationships

As children move into the middle and late childhood years, parents spend considerably less time with them (Grusec & others, 2013). In one study, parents spent less than half as much time with their children aged 5 to 12 in caregiving, instruction, reading, talking, and playing as they did when the children were younger (Hill & Stafford, 1980). However, parents continue to be extremely important in their children's lives. One analysis concluded: "Parents serve as gatekeepers and provide scaffolding as children assume more responsibility for themselves and . . . regulate their own lives" (Huston & Ripke, 2006, p. 422).

Parents especially play an important role in supporting and stimulating children's academic achievement in middle and late childhood (Simpkins, Fredricks, & Eccles, 2015). The value parents place on education can make a difference in whether children do well in school. Parents not only influence children's in-school achievement, but they also make decisions about children's out-of-school activities. Whether children participate in sports, music, and other activities is heavily influenced by the extent to which parents sign up children for such activities and encourage their participation (Simpkins & others, 2006).

Elementary school children tend to receive less physical discipline than preschoolers. Instead of spanking or coercive holding, their parents are more likely to use deprivation of privileges, appeals to the child's self-esteem, comments designed to increase the child's sense of guilt, and statements that the child is responsible for his or her actions. During middle and late childhood, some control is transferred from

What are some changes in the focus of parent-child interaction in middle and late childhood?

© Tim Pannell/Corbis/Getty Images

parent to child. A gradual process, it produces *coregulation* rather than control by either the child or the parent alone (Maccoby, 1984). Parents continue to exercise general supervision and control, while children are allowed to engage in moment-to-moment self-regulation. The major shift to autonomy does not occur until about the age of 12 or later. A key developmental task as children move toward autonomy is learning to relate to adults outside the family on a regular basis—adults such as teachers who interact with the child much differently from the way parents do.

Parents as Managers

Parents can play important roles as managers of children's opportunities, as monitors of their behavior, and as social initiators and arrangers (Clarke-Stewart & Parke, 2014). Mothers are more likely than fathers to engage in a managerial role in parenting.

Family management practices are positively related to students' grades and self-responsibility, and negatively to school-related problems (Eccles, 2007). Among the most important are maintaining a structured and organized family environment, such as establishing routines for homework, chores, bedtime, and so on, and effectively monitoring the child's behavior. A research review of family functioning in African American students' academic achievement found that when parents monitored their son's academic achievement by ensuring that homework was completed, restricted time spent on nonproductive distractions (such as video games and TV), and participated in a consistent, positive dialogue with teachers and school officials, their son's academic achievement benefited (Mandara, 2006).

Attachment

Earlier you read about the importance of secure attachment in infancy and the role of sensitive parenting in attachment (Thompson, 2015, 2016). During middle and late childhood, attachment becomes more sophisticated. As children's social worlds expand to include peers, teachers, and others, they typically spend less time with parents. Kathryn Kerns and her colleagues (Kerns & Brumariu, 2016; Kerns & Seibert, 2012) have studied links between attachment to parents and various child outcomes in the middle and late childhood years and found that secure attachment is associated with a lower level of internalized symptoms, anxiety, and depression in children. One study revealed that children who were less securely attached to their mothers reported having more anxiety (Brumariu, Kerns, & Seibert, 2012). Also in this study, secure attachment was linked to a higher level of children's emotion regulation and less difficulty in identifying emotions.

Stepfamilies

Not only has divorce become commonplace in the United States, so has getting remarried (Ganong, Coleman, & Russell, 2015). It takes time to marry, have children, get divorced, and then remarry. Consequently, there are far more elementary and secondary school children than infants or preschool children living in stepfamilies. The number of remarriages involving children has grown steadily in recent years. Also, divorces occur at a 10 percent higher rate in remarriages than in first marriages (Cherlin & Furstenberg, 1994). About half of all children whose parents divorce will have a stepparent within four years after the separation.

Remarried parents face unique tasks. The couple must define and strengthen their marriage while renegotiating the biological parent-child relationships and establishing stepparent-stepchild and stepsibling relationships (Ganong, Coleman, & Russell, 2015). The complex histories and multiple relationships make adjustment difficult (Dodson & Davies, 2014). Only one-third of stepfamily couples stay remarried.

Most stepfamilies are preceded by divorce rather than death of a spouse (Pasley & Moorefield, 2004). Three common types of stepfamily structure are (1) stepfather,

(2) stepmother, and (3) blended or complex. In stepfather families, the mother typically had custody of the children and remarried, introducing a stepfather into her children's lives. In stepmother families, the father usually had custody and remarried, introducing a stepmother into his children's lives. In a blended or complex stepfamily, both parents bring children from previous marriages.

In Hetherington's (2006) longitudinal analyses, children and adolescents who had been in a simple stepfamily (stepfather or stepmother) for a number of years were adjusting better than in the early years of the remarried family and were functioning well in comparison with children and adolescents in conflictual families that had not gone through a divorce, and children and adolescents in complex (blended) stepfamilies. More than 75 percent of the adolescents in long-established simple stepfamilies described their relationships with their stepparents as "close" or "very close." Hetherington (2006) concluded that in long-established simple stepfamilies adolescents seem to eventually benefit from the presence of a stepparent and the resources provided by the stepparent.

Children often have better relationships with their custodial parents (mothers in stepfather families, fathers in stepmother families) than with stepparents (Santrock, Sitterle, & Warshak, 1988). Also, children in simple families (stepmother, stepfather) often show better adjustment than their counterparts in complex (blended) families (Hetherington, 2006).

As in divorced families, children in stepfamilies show more adjustment problems than children in never-divorced families (Hetherington, 2006)—academic problems and lower self-esteem, for example (Anderson & others, 1999). However, it is important to recognize that a majority of children in stepfamilies do not have problems. In one analysis, 25 percent of children from stepfamilies showed adjustment problems, compared with 10 percent in intact, never-divorced families (Hetherington & Kelly, 2002).

How Would You…?

As a **human development and family studies professional,** what advice would you offer to divorced parents who want to ease their children's adjustment to remarriage?

Peers

Having positive relationships with peers is especially important in middle and late childhood (Rubin & others, 2016; Wentzel & Ramani, 2016). Engaging in positive interactions with peers, resolving conflicts in nonaggressive ways, and having quality friendships not only bring positive outcomes at this time in children's lives, but also are linked to more positive relationships in adolescence and adulthood (Huston & Ripke, 2006). In one longitudinal study, being popular with peers and engaging in low levels of aggression at 8 years of age were related to higher levels of occupational status at 48 years of age (Huesmann & others, 2006). Another study found that peer competence (a composite measure that included social contact with peers, popularity with peers, friendship, and social skills) in middle and late childhood was linked to having better relationships with coworkers in early adulthood (Collins & van Dulmen, 2006). And a recent study indicated that low peer status in childhood (low acceptance/likeability) was linked to increased probability of being unemployed and having mental health problems in adulthood (Almquist & Brannstrom, 2014).

What are some key aspects of peer relationships in middle and late childhood?

© KidStock/Blend Images/ Getty Images RF

popular children Children who are frequently nominated as a best friend and are rarely disliked by their peers.

average children Children who receive an average number of both positive and negative nominations from their peers.

neglected children Children who are infrequently nominated as a best friend but are not disliked by their peers.

rejected children Children who are infrequently nominated as a best friend and are actively disliked by their peers.

controversial children Children who are frequently nominated both as someone's best friend and as being disliked.

Developmental Changes

As children enter the elementary school years, reciprocity becomes especially important in peer interchanges. Researchers estimate that the percentage of time spent in social interaction with peers increases from approximately 10 percent at 2 years of age to more than 30 percent in middle and late childhood (Rubin, Bukowski, & Parker, 2006). In an early classic study, a typical day in elementary school included approximately 300 episodes with peers (Barker & Wright, 1951). As children move through middle and late childhood, the size of their peer group increases, and peer interaction is less closely supervised by adults (Rubin & others, 2016). Until about 12 years of age, children's preference for same-sex peer groups increases.

Peer Status

Which children are likely to be popular with their peers and which ones tend to be disliked? Developmentalists address this and similar questions by examining *sociometric status,* a term that describes the extent to which children are liked or disliked by their peer group (Rubin, Bukowski, & Bowker, 2015). Sociometric status is typically assessed by asking children to rate how much they like or dislike each of their classmates. Status may also be assessed by asking children to nominate the children they like the most and those they like the least.

Developmentalists have distinguished five peer statuses:

- **Popular children** are frequently nominated as a best friend and are rarely disliked by their peers.

- **Average children** receive an average number of both positive and negative nominations from their peers.

- **Neglected children** are infrequently nominated as a best friend but are not disliked by their peers.

- **Rejected children** are infrequently nominated as someone's best friend and are actively disliked by their peers.

- **Controversial children** are frequently nominated both as someone's best friend and as being disliked.

Popular children have many social skills that contribute to their being well liked. They give out reinforcements, listen carefully, maintain open lines of communication with peers, are happy, control their negative emotions, show enthusiasm and concern for others, and are self-confident without being conceited (Hartup, 1983; Rubin, Bukowski, & Bowker, 2015).

Rejected children often have significant adjustment problems (Rubin & others, 2016). For example, a recent study revealed a link between peer rejection and depression in adolescence (Platt, Kadosh, & Lau, 2013). Researchers also have found that peer rejection consistently is linked to the development and maintenance of conduct problems (Chen, Drabick, & Burgers, 2015). John Coie (2004, pp. 252–253) provided three reasons why aggressive, peer-rejected boys have problems in social relationships:

- "First, the rejected, aggressive boys are more impulsive and have problems sustaining attention. As a result, they are more likely to be disruptive of ongoing activities in the classroom and in focused group play.

- Second, rejected, aggressive boys are more emotionally reactive. They are aroused to anger more easily and probably have more difficulty calming down once aroused. Because of this they are more prone to become angry at peers and attack them verbally and physically. . . .

- Third, rejected children have fewer social skills in making friends and maintaining positive relationships with peers."

How Would You...?

As a **social worker,** how would you help a rejected child develop more positive relationships with peers?

Social Cognition

Social cognition involves thoughts about social matters, such as an aggressive boy's interpretation of an encounter as hostile and his classmates' perception of his behavior as inappropriate (Carpendale & Lewis, 2015). Children's social cognition about their peers becomes increasingly important for understanding peer relationships in middle and late childhood. Of special interest are the ways in which children process information about peer relations and their social knowledge (Dodge, 2011).

Kenneth Dodge (1983) argues that children go through six steps in processing information about their social world. They selectively attend to social cues, attribute intent, generate goals, access behavioral scripts from memory, make decisions, and enact behavior. Dodge has found that aggressive boys are more likely to perceive another child's actions as hostile when the child's intention is ambiguous. Furthermore, when aggressive boys search for cues to determine a peer's intention, they respond more rapidly, less efficiently, and less reflectively than do nonaggressive children. These are among the social cognitive factors believed to be involved in children's conflicts.

Social knowledge also is involved in children's ability to get along with peers. They need to know what goals to pursue in poorly defined or ambiguous situations, how to initiate and maintain a social bond, and what scripts to follow to get other children to be their friends. For example, as part of the script for getting friends, it helps to know that saying nice things, regardless of what the peer does or says, will make the peer like the child more.

How Would You...?

As a **psychologist,** how would you characterize differences in the social cognition of aggressive children compared with children who behave in less hostile ways?

Bullying

Significant numbers of students are victimized by bullies (Connell, Morris, & Piquero, 2016; Espelage & Colbert, 2016). In a survey of 15,000 students in grades 6 through 10, nearly one-third said that they had experienced occasional or frequent involvement as a victim or perpetrator in bullying (Nansel & others, 2001). Bullying was defined as verbal or physical behavior intended to disturb someone less powerful (see Figure 3). Boys are more likely to be bullies than girls, but gender differences regarding victims of bullies are less clear (Peets, Hodges, & Salmivalli, 2011). In the study, boys and younger middle school students were most likely to be bullied (Nansel & others, 2001). Bullied children reported more loneliness and difficulty in making friends, while those who did the bullying were more likely to have low grades and to smoke and drink alcohol.

Anxious, socially withdrawn, and aggressive children are often the victims of bullying. Anxious and socially withdrawn children may be victimized because they are nonthreatening and unlikely to retaliate if bullied, whereas aggressive children may be the targets of bullying because their behavior is irritating to bullies (Rubin & others, 2016). A recent study revealed that having supportive friends was linked to a lower level of bullying and victimization (Kendrick, Jutengren, & Stattin, 2012).

Social contexts also influence bullying (Prinstein & Giletta, 2016; Troop-Gordon & Ladd, 2015). Seventy to 80 percent of victims and their bullies are in the same classroom (Salmivalli, Peets, & Hodges, 2011). Classmates are often aware of and may witness bullying. The larger

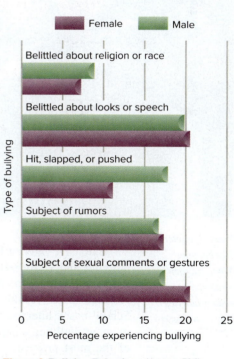

Figure 3 Bullying Behaviors Among U.S. Youth

This graph shows the types of bullying most often experienced by U.S. youth. The percentages reflect the extent to which bullied students said that they had experienced a particular type of bullying. In terms of gender, note that when they were bullied, boys were more likely to be hit, slapped, or pushed than girls were.

social context of the peer group plays an important role in bullying. Bullies often torment victims to gain higher status in the peer group and need others to witness their power displays. Many bullies are not rejected by the peer group.

What are the outcomes of bullying? Children who are bullied are more likely to experience depression, engage in suicidal ideation, and attempt suicide than their counterparts who have not been the victims of bullying (Yen & others, 2014). Peer victimization during the elementary school years was a leading indicator of internalizing problems (depression, for example) in adolescence (Schwartz & others, 2015). Also, a recent longitudinal study of 6,000 children found that children who were the victims of peer bullying from 4 to 10 years of age were more likely to engage in suicidal ideation at 11½ years of age (Winsper & others, 2012). Further, a recent analysis concluded that bullying can have long-term effects, including difficulty in forming lasting relationships and getting along with coworkers (Wolke & Lereya, 2015).

An increasing concern is peer bullying and harassment on the Internet (called *cyberbullying*) (Vollink, Dehue, & McGuckin, 2016; Wolke, Lereya, & Tippett, 2016). One study involving third- to sixth-graders revealed that engaging in cyber aggression was related to loneliness, lower self-esteem, fewer mutual friendships, and lower peer popularity (Schoffstall & Cohen, 2011). Another recent study revealed that cyberbullying contributed to depression and suicidal ideation above and beyond the contribution of involvement in traditional types of bullying (physical and verbal bullying in school and in neighborhood contexts, for example) (Bonanno & Hymel, 2013). And a recent meta-analysis concluded that being the victim of cyberbullying was linked to stress and suicidal ideation (Kowalski & others, 2014). Further, a longitudinal study found that adolescents experiencing social and emotional difficulties were more likely to be both cyberbullied and traditionally bullied than traditionally bullied only (Cross, Lester, & Barnes, 2015). In this study, adolescents targeted in both ways stayed away from school more than their counterparts who were traditionally bullied only. Information about preventing cyber bullying can be found at www.stopcyberbullying.org/.

What characterizes bullying? What are some strategies to reduce bullying?
© SW Productions/Getty Images RF

Extensive interest has been directed toward finding ways to prevent and treat bullying and victimization (Cantone & others, 2015; Espelage & Colbert, 2016; Menesini, Palladino, & Nocentini, 2016; Olweus, 2013). A research review revealed mixed results for school-based intervention (Vreeman & Carroll, 2007). School-based interventions vary greatly, ranging from involving the whole school in an antibullying campaign to providing individualized social skills training. One of the most promising bullying intervention programs has been created by Dan Olweus. This program focuses on 6- to 15-year-olds with the goal of decreasing opportunities and rewards for bullying. School staff is instructed in ways to improve peer relations and make schools safer. When properly implemented, the program reduces bullying by 30 to 70 percent (Olweus, 2003). A recent research review concluded that interventions focused on the whole school, such as Olweus', are more effective than interventions involving classroom curricula or social skills training (Cantone & others, 2015).

Friends

Friendship is an important aspect of children's lives in middle and late childhood (Rubin & others, 2016). Like adult friendships, children's friendships are typically characterized by similarity (Prinstein & Giletta, 2016). Throughout childhood, friends are more similar than dissimilar in terms of age, sex, race, and many other factors. Friends often have similar attitudes toward school, similar educational aspirations, and closely aligned achievement orientations.

Willard Hartup (1983, 1996, 2009) has studied peer relations and friendship for more than three decades and has concluded that friends can be cognitive and emotional resources from childhood through old age, fostering self-esteem and a sense of well-being. More specifically, children's friendships can serve six functions (Gottman & Parker, 1987):

- *Companionship.* Friendship provides children with a familiar partner and playmate, someone who is willing to spend time with them and join in collaborative activities.

- *Stimulation.* Friendship provides children with interesting information, excitement, and amusement.

- *Physical support.* Friendship provides time, resources, and assistance.

- *Ego support.* Friendship provides the expectation of support, encouragement, and feedback, which helps children maintain an impression of themselves as competent, attractive, and worthwhile individuals.

- *Social comparison.* Friendship provides information about where the child stands vis-ã-vis others and whether the child is doing okay.

- *Affection and intimacy.* Friendship provides children with a warm, close, trusting relationship with another individual. Intimacy in friendships is characterized by self-disclosure and the sharing of private thoughts. Research reveals that intimate friendships may not appear until early adolescence (Berndt & Perry, 1990).

Although having friends can bring developmental advantages, not all friendships are alike (Choukas-Bradley & Prinstein, 2016; Deutsch & others, 2015; Furman & Rose, 2015). People differ in the company they keep—that is, who their friends are. Developmental advantages occur when children have friends who are socially skilled and supportive (Chow, Tan, & Buhrmester, 2015; Kindermann, 2016; Schneider, 2016). However, it is not developmentally advantageous to have coercive and conflict-ridden friendships (Schneider, 2016).

Friendship also plays an important role in children's emotional well-being and academic success. Students with friends who are academically oriented are more likely to achieve success in school themselves (Wentzel, 2015; Wentzel & Ramani, 2016). In one study, sixth-grade students who did not have any friends engaged in less prosocial behavior (cooperation, sharing, helping others), had lower grades, and were more emotionally distressed (depression, lower levels of well-being) than their counterparts who had one or more friends (Wentzel, Barry, & Caldwell, 2004). In this study, two years later as eighth graders, the students who did not have a friend in the sixth grade continued to be more emotionally distressed.

Schools

For most children, entering the first grade signals new obligations. They form new relationships and develop new standards by which to judge themselves. School provides children with a rich source of new ideas to shape their sense of self. They will spend many years in schools as members of small societies in which there are tasks to be accomplished, people to socialize with and be socialized by, and rules that define and limit behavior, feelings, and attitudes. By the time students graduate from high school, they will have spent 12,000 hours in the classroom.

Contemporary Approaches to Student Learning

Because there are so many different educational approaches, controversy swirls about the best way to teach children (Borich, 2017; Lynch, 2015; Powell, 2015). There also is considerable interest in finding the best way to hold schools and teachers accountable for whether children are learning (McMillan, 2014).

Constructivist and Direct Instruction Approaches

The **constructivist approach** is learner centered and emphasizes the importance of individuals actively constructing their knowledge and understanding with guidance from the teacher. In the constructivist view, teachers should not attempt to simply pour information into children's minds. Rather, children should be encouraged to explore their world, discover knowledge, reflect, and think critically with careful monitoring and meaningful guidance from the teacher (Burden & Byrd, 2016; Robinson-Zanartu, Doerr, & Portman, 2015). The constructivist belief is that for too long in American education children have been required to sit still, be passive learners, and rotely memorize irrelevant as well as relevant information (Sadker & Zittleman, 2016). Today, constructivism may include an emphasis on collaboration—children working with each other in their efforts to know and understand. A teacher with a constructivist instructional philosophy would not have children memorize information rotely but would guide their learning while giving them opportunities to meaningfully construct their knowledge and deepen their understanding of the material.

By contrast, the **direct instruction approach** is structured and teacher centered. It is characterized by teacher direction and control, high teacher expectations for students' progress, maximum time spent by students on academic tasks, and efforts by the teacher to keep negative affect to a minimum. An important goal in the direct instruction approach is maximizing student learning time (Parkay, 2016).

Advocates of the constructivist approach argue that the direct instruction approach turns children into passive learners and does not adequately challenge them to think in critical and creative ways (Robinson-Zanartu, Doerr, & Portman, 2015). The direct instruction enthusiasts say that the constructivist approaches do not give enough attention to the content of a discipline, such as history or science. They also believe that the constructivist approaches are too relativistic and vague.

Some experts believe that many effective teachers use both a constructivist *and* a direct instruction approach rather than relying on either approach exclusively (Bransford & others, 2006). Some circumstances may call more for a constructivist approach, others for direct instruction. For example, experts increasingly recommend an explicit, intellectually engaging direct instruction approach when teaching students who have a learning disability involving reading or writing (Berninger & others, 2015).

Is this classroom more likely to be constructivist or direct instruction? Explain.
© Elizabeth Crews

constructivist approach
A learner-centered approach that emphasizes the importance of individuals actively constructing their knowledge and understanding with guidance from the teacher.

direct instruction approach A structured, teacher-centered approach that is characterized by teacher direction and control, high teacher expectations for students' progress, maximum time spent by students on learning tasks, and efforts by the teacher to keep negative affect to a minimum.

Accountability

Since the 1990s, the U.S. public and governments at every level have demanded increased accountability from schools. One result has been the spread of state-mandated tests to measure what students have or have not learned (Brookhart & Nitko, 2015; Popham, 2017). Many states have identified objectives for students in their state and created tests to measure whether students were meeting those objectives. This approach became national policy in 2002 when the No Child Left Behind (NCLB) legislation was signed into law.

Advocates argue that statewide standardized testing will have a number of positive effects. These include improved student performance; more time teaching the subjects that are tested; high expectations for all students; identification of poorly performing schools, teachers, and administrators; and improved confidence in schools as test scores rise.

Critics argue that the NCLB legislation is doing more harm than good (Sadker & Zittleman, 2012). One criticism stresses that using a single test as the sole indicator of students' progress and competence presents a very narrow view of students' skills (Lewis, 2007). This criticism is similar to the one leveled at IQ tests. To assess student progress and achievement, many psychologists and educators emphasize that a number of measures should be used, including tests, quizzes, projects, portfolios, classroom observations, and so on. Also, the tests used as part of NCLB don't measure creativity, motivation, persistence, flexible thinking, and social skills (Stiggins, 2008). Teachers may end up spending far too much class time "teaching to the test" by drilling students and having them memorize isolated facts rather than focusing on thinking skills needed for success in life (Brookhart & Nitko, 2015). Also, some individuals are concerned that gifted students are neglected as schools focus on raising the achievement level of students who are not doing well (Clark, 2008).

Each state is allowed to have different criteria for what constitutes passing or failing grades on tests designated for NCLB inclusion. An analysis of NCLB data indicated that almost every fourth-grade student in Mississippi knows how to read but only half of Massachusetts' students do (Birman & others, 2007). Clearly, Mississippi's standards for passing the reading test are far below those of Massachusetts. Many states have taken the safe route and kept the standard for passing low. Thus, while one of NCLB's goals was to raise standards for achievement in U.S. schools, apparently allowing states to set their own standards likely has lowered achievement standards.

In 2009, the Common Core State Standards Initiative was endorsed by the National Governors Association in an effort to implement more rigorous state guidelines for educating students. The Common Core Standards specify what students should know and the skills they should develop at each grade level in various content areas (Common Core State Standards Initiative, 2016). A large majority of states have agreed to implement the Standards but they have generated considerable controversy, with some critics arguing that they are simply a further effort by the federal government to control education and that they emphasize a "one-size-fits-all" approach that pays little attention to individual variations in students. Supporters say that the Standards provide much-needed detailed guidelines and important milestones for students to achieve.

Every Student Succeeds Act (ESSA)

The most recent accountability initiative is the *Every Student Succeeds Act (ESSA),* which was passed into law in December 2015 and will be fully implemented during the 2017–2018 school year (Rothman, 2016). The law replaced *No Child Left Behind*, in the process modifying but not completely eliminating standardized testing. ESSA retains annual testing for reading and writing in grades 3 to 8, then once more in high school. The new law also allows states to scale back the role that tests have in holding schools accountable for student achievement. And schools must use at least one nonacademic factor—such as student engagement—when tracking schools' success.

The new law continues to require states and districts to improve their lowest-performing schools and to increase their effectiveness in teaching historically underperforming students, such as English-language learners, ethnic minority students, and students with a disability. Also, states and districts are required to put in place challenging academic standards, although they can opt out of state standards involving Common Core.

Socioeconomic Status, Ethnicity, and Culture

Children from low-income, ethnic minority backgrounds have more difficulties in school than do their middle-socioeconomic-status, White counterparts. Why? Critics argue that schools have not done a good job of assisting low-income, ethnic minority students to overcome the barriers to their achievement (Crosnoe & Benner, 2015; Duncan, Magnuson, & Vtroba-Drzal, 2015). And recent comparisons of student achievement indicate that U.S. students have lower achievement in math and science than students in a number of other countries, especially those in eastern Asia (National Center for Education Statistics, 2009).

The Education of Students from Low-Income Backgrounds

Many children in poverty face problems that present barriers to their learning (Bradley, 2015; Leventhal, Dupere, & Shuey, 2015; Wadsworth & others, 2016). They might have parents who don't set high educational standards for them, who are incapable of reading to them, or who can't afford educational materials and experiences such as books and trips to zoos and museums. They might be malnourished or live in areas with more crime and violence. One study revealed that neighborhood disadvantage (involving such characteristics as low neighborhood income and high unemployment) was linked to less consistent, less stimulating, and more punitive parenting, and ultimately to negative child outcomes such as behavioral problems and low verbal ability (Kohen & others, 2008). Another study revealed that the longer children experienced poverty, the more detrimental the poverty was to their cognitive development (Najman & others, 2009).

How Would You...?

As a **health-care professional,** how would you advise school administrators about health and nutrition challenges faced by low-income students that may influence their performance on achievement tests?

The schools that children from impoverished backgrounds attend often have fewer resources than schools in higher-income neighborhoods. Compared with schools in higher-income areas, schools in low-income areas are more likely to have more students with low achievement test scores, low graduation rates, and small percentages of students going to college; they are more likely to have young teachers with less experience; and they are more likely to encourage rote learning than to work with children to improve their thinking skills (Banks, 2015; Bennett, 2015). Many of the school buildings and classrooms are old and crumbling. These are the types of undesirable conditions Jonathan Kozol

In *The Shame of the Nation*, Jonathan Kozol (2005) criticized the inadequate quality and lack of resources in many U.S. schools, especially those in the poverty areas of inner cities that have high concentrations of ethnic minority children. Kozol praises teachers like Angela Lively (*above*), who keeps a box of shoes in her Indianapolis classroom for students in need.

© Michael Conroy/AP Images

(2005) observed in many inner-city schools. In sum, far too many schools in low-income neighborhoods provide students with environments that are not conducive to effective learning (Bradley, 2015; Gardner, Brooks-Gunn, & Chase-Lansdale, 2016; Leventhal, Dupere, & Shuey, 2015).

Much of the focus on the lives of children living in poverty has emphasized improving their future prospects in educational and economic development. A recent analysis concluded that their social and emotional functioning has often been ignored and should be given more attention (Crosnoe & Leventhal, 2014). Further, efforts to intervene in the lives of children living in poverty need to jointly focus on schools and neighborhoods (Gershoff & Benner, 2014).

Ethnicity in Schools

More than one-third of African American and almost one-third of Latino students attend schools in the 47 largest city school districts, compared with only 5 percent of White and 22 percent of Asian American students. Many of these inner-city schools are still segregated, are grossly underfunded, and do not provide adequate opportunities for children to learn effectively. Thus, the effects of low socioeconomic status (SES) and of ethnicity are often intertwined (Banks, 2015).

The school experiences of students from different ethnic groups vary considerably (Bennett, 2015). African American and Latino students are much less likely than non-Latino White or Asian American students to be enrolled in college preparatory programs and more likely to be enrolled in remedial and special education programs. Asian American students are far more likely to take advanced math and science courses in high school. African American students are twice as likely as Latinos, Native Americans, or Whites to be suspended from school. However, diversity characterizes every ethnic group (Cushner, McClelland, & Safford, 2015). For example, the higher percentage of Asian American students in advanced classes mainly applies to students from Chinese, Taiwanese, Japanese, Korean, and East Indian cultural backgrounds; students with Hmong and Vietnamese cultural backgrounds have had less academic success. Following are some strategies for improving relationships among ethnically diverse students:

- *Turn the class into a jigsaw classroom.* When Eliot Aronson was a professor at the University of Texas at Austin, the school system contacted him for ideas on how to reduce the increasing racial tension in classrooms. Aronson (1986) developed the concept of a "jigsaw classroom" in which students from different cultural backgrounds are placed in a cooperative group in which they have to construct different parts of a project to reach a common goal. Aronson used the term *jigsaw* because he saw the technique as much like a group of students cooperating to put different pieces together to complete a jigsaw puzzle.

  How might this work? Team sports, drama productions, and music performances are examples of contexts in which students participate cooperatively to reach a common goal; however, the jigsaw technique also lends itself to group science projects, history reports, and other learning experiences involving a variety of subject matter.

How Would You...?

As an **educator,** how would you structure a lesson plan using the jigsaw strategy?

- *Encourage students to have positive personal contact with diverse other students.* Mere contact does not do the job of improving relationships with diverse others. For example, busing ethnic minority students to predominantly White schools, or vice versa, has not reduced prejudice or improved interethnic relations. What matters is what happens after children get to school. Especially beneficial in improving interethnic relations is sharing one's worries, successes, failures, coping strategies, interests, and other personal information with people of other ethnicities. When this happens, people tend to look at others as individuals rather than as members of a homogeneous group.

- *Reduce bias.* Teachers can reduce bias by displaying images of children from diverse ethnic and cultural groups, selecting play materials and classroom activities that encourage cultural understanding, helping students resist stereotyping, and working with parents to reduce children's exposure to bias and prejudice at home.

- *Be a competent cultural mediator.* Teachers can play a powerful role as cultural mediators by being sensitive to biased content in materials and classroom interactions, learning more about different ethnic groups, being sensitive to children's ethnic attitudes, viewing students of color positively, and thinking of positive ways to get parents of color more involved as partners with teachers in educating children.

- *View the school and community as a team.* James Comer (1988, 2004, 2006, 2010) advocates a community, team approach as the best way to educate children. Three important aspects of the Comer Project for Change are (1) a governance and management team that develops a comprehensive school plan, assessment strategy, and staff development plan; (2) a mental health or school support team; and (3) a parents' program. Comer believes that the entire school community should have a cooperative rather than an adversarial attitude. The Comer program is currently operating in more than 600 schools in 26 states. Read further about James Comer's work in the *Careers in Life-Span Development* profile.

Careers in life-span development

James Comer, Child Psychiatrist

James Comer grew up in a low-income neighborhood in East Chicago, Indiana, and credits his parents with leaving no doubt about the importance of education. He obtained a B.A. degree from Indiana University. He went on to obtain a medical degree from Howard University College of Medicine, a Master of Public Health degree from the University of Michigan School of Public Health, and psychiatry training at the Yale University School of Medicine's Child Study Center. He currently is the Maurice Falk Professor of Child Psychiatry at the Yale University Child Study Center and an associate dean at the Yale University Medical School. During his years at Yale, Comer has concentrated his career on promoting a focus on child development as a way of improving schools. His efforts in support of healthy development of young people are known internationally.

Comer is, perhaps, best known for founding the School Development Program in 1968, which promotes the collaboration

James Comer is shown with some of the inner-city children who attend a school that became a better learning environment because of Comer's intervention.

© Chris Volpe

of parents, educators, and community to improve social, emotional, and academic outcomes for children.

Cross-Cultural Comparisons

In the past three decades, the poor performance of American children in math and science has become well publicized (Educational Testing Service, 1992). In a large-scale comparison of math and science achievement in fourth-grade students in 2007, the average U.S. fourth-grade math score was higher than 23 of the 35 countries and lower than 8 countries (all in Asia and Europe) (National Center for Education Statistics, 2009). Fourth-graders from Hong Kong had the highest math score. The average U.S. fourth-grade math score did improve slightly (11 points) from the same assessment in 1995, but some Asian countries improved their scores considerably more—the Hong Kong score was 50 points higher and the Slovenia score 40 points higher in 2007 than in 1995, for example.

In 2007, the U.S. fourth-grade science score was higher than those in 25 countries and lower than those in 4 countries (all in Asia). However, the average U.S. fourth-grade science score decreased 3 points from 1995 to 2007 while the science scores for some countries increased dramatically—63 points in Singapore, 56 points in Latvia, and 55 points in Iran, for example.

Harold Stevenson's (1995, 2000; Stevenson, Hofer, & Randel, 1999; Stevenson & others, 1990) research explores reasons for the poor performance of U.S. students compared with students in selected Asian countries. Stevenson and his colleagues have completed five cross-cultural comparisons of students in the United States, China, Taiwan, and Japan. In these studies, Asian students consistently outperform American students. And the longer the students are in school, the wider the gap becomes between Asian and American students—the lowest difference is in the first grade, the highest in the eleventh grade (the highest grade studied). Stevenson and his colleagues spent thousands

How do U.S. students fare against Asian students in math and science achievement? What were some findings in Stevenson's research that might explain the results of those international comparisons?

© amana Images, Inc./Alamy RF

of hours observing in classrooms, as well as interviewing and surveying teachers, students, and parents. They found that the Asian teachers spent more of their time teaching math than did the U.S. teachers. More than one-fourth of total classroom time in the first grade was spent on math instruction in Japan, compared with only one-tenth of the time in the U.S. first-grade classrooms. Also, the Asian students were in school an average of 240 days a year, compared with 178 days in the United States.

Differences were also found between the Asian and American parents. The U.S. parents had much lower expectations for their children's education and achievement than did the Asian parents. Also, the U.S. parents were more likely to believe that their children's math achievement was due to innate ability; the Asian parents were more likely to say that their children's math achievement was the consequence of effort and training (see Figure 4). The Asian students were more likely to do math homework than were the U.S. students, and the Asian parents were far more likely to help their children with their math homework than were the U.S. parents (Chen & Stevenson, 1989). A recent study examined factors that might account for the superior academic performance of Asian American children (Hsin & Xie, 2014). In this study, the Asian American advantage was mainly due to children exerting greater academic effort and not to advantages in tested cognitive abilities or sociodemographic factors.

There is rising concern that U.S. children are not reaching their full potential, which ultimately will reduce the success of the United States to compete globally (Pomerantz, 2016). Interested in determining how parents can maximize their children's motivation and achievement in school while also maintaining positive emotional adjustment. To this end, Eva Pomerantz and her colleagues are conducting research with children and their parents in the United States and China, where children often attain higher levels of achievement than their U.S. counterparts (Pomerantz, Cheung, & Qin, 2012; Pomerantz & Kempner, 2013; Pomerantz, Kim, & Cheung, 2012; Qu & others, 2016).

East Asian parents spend considerably more time helping their children with homework than U.S. parents do (Chen & Stevenson, 1989). Pomerantz's research indicates that East Asian parental involvement in children's learning is present as early as the preschool years and continues during the elementary school years (Cheung & Pomerantz, 2012; Ng, Pomerantz, & Deng, 2014; Ng, Pomerantz, & Lam, 2013). In East Asia, children's learning is considered to be a far greater responsibility of parents than it is in the United States (Ng, Pomerantz, & Lam, 2013; Pomerantz, Kim, & Cheung, 2012). However, a recent study revealed that when U.S. parents are more involved in their children's learning, the children's achievement benefits (Cheung & Pomerantz, 2012). In this study, more than 800 U.S. and Chinese children (average age = 12.73 years) reported on their parents' involvement in their learning and their motivation in school every six months from the fall of seventh grade to the end of eighth grade. The researchers also collected data on children's self-regulated learning strategies and grades. Over time, the greater the extent to which parents were involved in their children's learning, the more strongly motivated children were to do well academically for

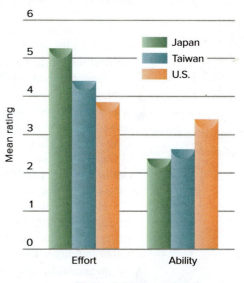

Figure 4 Mothers' Beliefs About the Factors Responsible for Children's Math Achievement in Three Countries

In one study, mothers in Japan and Taiwan were more likely to believe that their children's math achievement was due to effort rather than innate ability, while U.S. mothers were more likely to believe their children's math achievement was due to innate ability (Stevenson, Lee, & Stigler, 1986). If parents believe that their children's math achievement is due to innate ability and their children are not doing well in math, the implication is that they are less likely to think their children will benefit from putting forth more effort.

parent-oriented reasons, which improved children's self-regulated learning and grades. In a recent study, a decline in U.S. young adolescents' but not Chinese young adolescents' sense of responsibility to parents occurred (Qu & Pomerantz, 2015). The U.S. adolescents' decline in sense of responsibility to parents was linked to the lower value they placed on school and their lower engagement in school as they went from the beginning of the seventh to the end of the eighth grade (Qu & Pomerantz, 2015).

Pomerantz and her colleagues also are conducting research on the role of parental control in children's achievement. In a recent study in which the title of the resulting article included the phrase "My Child Is My Report Card," Chinese mothers exerted more control (especially psychological control) over their children than did U.S. mothers (Ng, Pomerantz, & Deng, 2014). Chinese mothers' self-worth was more contingent on their children's achievement than was the case for U.S. mothers. Pomerantz's research reflects a variation of authoritarian parenting in which the parenting strategy of many Asian parents is to train their children to achieve high levels of academic success. Amy Chua's 2011 book, *Battle Hymn of the Tiger Mom,* sparked considerable interest in the role of parenting in children's achievement. Chua uses the term "Tiger Mom" to mean a mother who engages in strict disciplinary practices. In another recent book, *Tiger Babies Strike Back*, Kim Wong Keltner (2013) argues that the Tiger Mom parenting style can be so demanding and confining that being an Asian American child is like being in an "emotional jail." She says that the Tiger Mom authoritarian style does provide some advantages for children, such as emphasizing the value of going for what you want and not taking no for an answer, but that too often the outcome is not worth the emotional costs that accompany it.

Recent research on Chinese-American immigrant families with first- and second-grade children has found that children with authoritarian (highly controlling) parents are more aggressive, are more depressed, have a higher anxiety level, and show poorer social skills than children whose parents engage in non-authoritarian styles (Zhou & others, 2013). Qing Zhou (2013), lead author on the study just described and the director of the University of California's Culture and Family Laboratory, is conducting workshops to teach Chinese mothers positive parenting strategies such as using listening skills, praising their children for good behavior, and spending more time with their children in fun activities.

In sum, while an authoritarian, psychologically controlling style of parenting may be associated with higher levels of achievement, especially in Asian children, there are concerns that an authoritarian, highly controlling style also may produce more emotional difficulties in children.

Related to the differences in the attitudes of Asian and U.S. parents involving explanations of effort and ability, Carol Dweck (2006, 2015, 2016) described the importance of children's **mindset,** which she defines as the cognitive view individuals develop for themselves. She concludes that individuals have one of two mindsets: (1) *fixed mindset,* in which they believe that their qualities are carved in stone and cannot change; or (2) *growth mindset,* in which they believe their qualities can change and improve through their effort. Dweck (2006, 2015, 2016) argued that individuals' mindsets influence whether they will be optimistic or pessimistic, what their goals will be and how hard they will strive to reach those goals, and their achievement. Dweck says that mindsets begin to be shaped in childhood as children interact with parents, teachers, and coaches, who themselves have either a fixed mindset or a growth mindset.

Dweck and her colleagues (Blackwell & Dweck, 2008; Blackwell, Trzesniewski, & Dweck, 2007; Dweck, 2015, 2016; Dweck & Master, 2009) have incorporated information about the brain's plasticity into their efforts to improve students' motivation to achieve and succeed. In one study, they assigned two groups of students to eight sessions of either (1) study skills instruction, or (2) study skills instruction plus information about the importance of developing a growth mindset (Blackwell, Trzesniewski, & Dweck, 2007). One of the exercises in the growth-mindset group, titled "You Can Grow Your Brain," emphasized that the brain is like a muscle that can get stronger as it is exercised and develops new connections. Students were informed that the more you challenge your brain to learn, the more your brain cells grow. Both groups had a pattern of declining math scores prior to the intervention. Following the intervention, scores for the group that received only the study skills

mindset The cognitive view that individuals develop for themselves.

Figure 5 A Screen from Carol Dweck's Brainology Program, Which is Designed to Cultivate Children's Growth Mindset
© Dr. Carol S. Dweck

instruction continued to decline, but the group that received the combination of study skills instruction plus the growth-mindset emphasis improved their math achievement. In a recent study conducted by Dweck and her colleagues (Paunesku & others, 2015), underachieving high school students read online modules about how the brain changes when people learn and study hard. Following the online exposure about the brain and learning, the underachieving students improved their grade point averages.

Dweck has also created a computer-based workshop, "Brainology," to teach students that their intelligence can change (Blackwell & Dweck, 2008) (see Figure 5). The workshop includes six modules about how the brain works and discussion about how students can make their brain improve. After the workshop was tested in 20 New York City schools, students strongly endorsed the value of the computer-based brain modules. Said one student, "I will try harder because I know that the more you try, the more your brain knows" (Dweck & Master, 2009, p. 137).

Other research indicates that willpower is a virtually nonlimited mindset that predicts how long people will work and resist temptations during stressful circumstances (Dweck, 2012, 2015, 2016; Job, Dweck, & Walton, 2010; Job & others, 2015; Miller & others, 2012). In a longitudinal study of university students, a nonlimited theory of mind predicted better self-regulation (improvements in time management and less procrastination, unhealthy eating, and impulsive spending) (Job & others, 2015). Among students taking a heavy course load, those who had a nonlimited theory of mind got higher grades.

Summary

Emotional and Personality Development

- Self-descriptions increasingly involve psychological and social characteristics in middle and late childhood. Perspective taking increases in middle and late childhood. Self-concept refers to domain-specific evaluations of the self. Self-esteem refers to global evaluations of the self and is also referred to as self-worth or self-image. Self-efficacy and self-regulation are linked to children's competence and achievement. Erikson's fourth stage of development, industry versus inferiority, characterizes the middle and late childhood years.

- Emotional development occurs in middle and late childhood. As children get older, they use a greater variety of coping strategies and more cognitive strategies.

- Kohlberg argued that moral development consists of three levels—preconventional, conventional, and post-conventional—and six stages (two at each level). Criticisms of Kohlberg's theory have been made, especially by Gilligan. The domain theory of moral development states that there are different domains of social knowledge and reasoning, including moral, social conventional, and personal. Prosocial behavior involves positive moral behaviors such as sharing.

- Gender stereotyping is present in children's lives, and research indicates it increases during middle and late childhood. A number of physical differences exist between males and females. Some experts argue that cognitive differences between males and females have been exaggerated. In terms of socioemotional differences, males are more physically aggressive than females, whereas females regulate their emotions better and engage in more prosocial behavior than males do. Gender-role classification focuses on masculinity, femininity, and androgyny.

Families

- Parents spend less time with children during middle and late childhood than in early childhood. New parent-child issues emerge and discipline changes. Control is more coregulatory.
- Parents can play important roles as managers of children's opportunities.
- Secure attachment to parents is linked to lower levels of internalized symptoms, anxiety, and depression in children during middle and late childhood.
- Children living in stepparent families have more adjustment problems than their counterparts in never-divorced families.

Peers

- A number of developmental changes in peer relations occur in middle and late childhood.

- Peer statuses—popular children, neglected children, rejected children, controversial children, and average children—are important in middle and late childhood.
- Social information processing and social knowledge are two important dimensions of social cognition.
- Significant numbers of children are bullied, and this can result in negative developmental outcomes for victims as well as bullies.
- Children who are friends tend to be similar to each other. Children's friendships serve a number of functions.

Schools

- Contemporary approaches to student learning include constructivism and direct instruction. In the United States, standardized testing of elementary school students has been mandated to improve accountability of schools.
- Children in poverty face many barriers to learning at school as well as at home. Low expectations for ethnic minority children represent one of the barriers to their learning.
- U.S. children are more achievement-oriented than children in many countries but perform more poorly in math and science than many children in Asian countries. Fixed or growth mindset is the cognitive view that individuals develop for themselves.

Key Terms

androgyny
average children
care perspective
constructivist approach
controversial children
conventional reasoning
direct instruction
   approach
domain theory of moral
   development

gender stereotypes
heteronomous morality
individualism, instrumental
   purpose, and exchange
justice perspective
mindset
mutual interpersonal
   expectations, relationships,
   and interpersonal
   conformity

neglected children
perspective taking
popular children
postconventional
   reasoning
preconventional
   reasoning
rejected children
self-concept
self-efficacy

self-esteem
social contract or utility and
   individual rights
social conventional
   reasoning
social systems morality
universal ethical principles

9 Physical and Cognitive Development in Adolescence

© Rolf Bruderer/Blend Images/Getty Images RF

Stories of Life-Span Development: Annie, Arnie, and Katie

Fifteen-year-old Annie developed a drinking problem, and recently she was kicked off the cheerleading squad at her school for missing practice so often—but that didn't stop her drinking. She and her friends began skipping school regularly so they could drink.

Fourteen-year-old Arnie is a juvenile delinquent. Last week he stole a TV set, struck his mother and bloodied her face, broke some streetlights in the neighborhood, and threatened a boy with a wrench and hammer.

Twelve-year-old Katie, more than just about anything else, wanted a playground in her town. She knew that other kids also wanted one, so she put together a group that generated funding ideas for the playground. They presented their ideas to the town council. Her group got more youth involved, and they raised money by selling candy and sandwiches door-to-door. The playground became a reality, a place where, as Katie says, "People can have picnics and make friends." Katie's advice: "You won't get anywhere if you don't try."

Adolescents like Annie and Arnie are the ones we hear about the most. But there are many adolescents like Katie who contribute in positive ways to their community, and competently make the transition through adolescence. Indeed, for most young people, adolescence is not a time of rebellion, crisis, pathology, and deviance. A far more accurate vision of adolescence is of a time of evaluation, of decision making, of commitment, of carving out a

253

place in the world. Most of the problems of today's youth are not with the youth themselves. What adolescents need is access to a range of legitimate opportunities and to long-term support from adults who care deeply about them (Spencer & Swanson, 2016).

Adolescence is a transitional period in the human life span, entered at approximately 10 to 12 years of age and exited at about 18 to 22 years of age. We begin this chapter by examining some general characteristics of adolescence, then turn our attention to major physical changes and health issues of adolescence. Next, we describe the significant cognitive changes that take place during adolescence. Last, we consider various aspects of schools for adolescents. ∎

The Nature of Adolescence

There is a long history of worrying about how adolescents will "turn out." In 1904, G. Stanley Hall proposed the "storm-and-stress" view that adolescence is a turbulent time charged with conflict and mood swings. However, when Daniel Offer and his colleagues (1988) studied the self-images of adolescents in a number of countries, at least 73 percent of the adolescents displayed a healthy self-image rather than attitudes of storm-and-stress.

In matters of taste and manners, the young people of every generation have seemed unnervingly radical and different from adults—different in how they look, in how they behave, in the music they enjoy, in their hairstyles, and in the clothing they choose. It would be an enormous error, though, to confuse adolescents' enthusiasm for trying on new identities and enjoying moderate amounts of outrageous behavior with hostility toward parental and societal standards. Acting out and boundary testing are time-honored ways in which adolescents move toward accepting, rather than rejecting, parental values.

Katie (*front*) and some of her volunteers.
© Ronald Cortes

Most adolescents negotiate the lengthy path to adult maturity successfully, but too large a group does not. Ethnic, cultural, gender, socioeconomic, age, and lifestyle differences influence the actual life trajectory of each adolescent (Juster & others, 2016; Spencer & Swanson, 2016; Wadsworth & others, 2016). Different portrayals of adolescence emerge, depending on the particular group of adolescents being described. Today's adolescents are exposed to a complex menu of lifestyle options through the media, and many face the temptations of drug use and sexual activity at increasingly young ages. Too many adolescents are not provided with adequate opportunities and support to become competent adults (Crosnoe & Benner, 2015; Gonzales & others, 2016; Lerner & others, 2015; Masten & Cicchetti, 2016).

Peter Benson and his colleagues (Benson, 2010; Benson, Roehlkepartain, & Scales, 2012; Benson & Scales, 2009, 2011) argue that the United States has a fragmented social policy for youth that too often has focused only on the negative developmental deficits of adolescents, especially health-compromising behaviors such as drug use and delinquency, and not enough on positive, strength-based approaches. According to Benson and his colleagues (2004, p. 783), a strength-based approach to social policy for youth

> adopts more of a wellness perspective, places particular emphasis on the existence of healthy conditions, and expands the concept of health to include the skills and competencies needed to succeed in employment, education, and life. It moves beyond the eradication of risk and deliberately argues for the promotion of well-being.

Growing up has never been easy. However, adolescence is not best viewed as a time of rebellion, crisis, pathology, and deviance. A far more accurate vision of adolescence describes it as a time of evaluation, decision making, commitment, and carving out a place in the world. Most of the problems of today's youth are not with the youth themselves. What adolescents need is access to a range of legitimate opportunities and long-term support from adults who care deeply about them. *What might be some examples of such support and caring?*
© BananaStock/PunchStock RF

Physical Changes

One father remarked that the problem with his teenage son was not that he grew, but that he did not know when to stop growing. In addition to pubertal changes, other physical changes we will explore involve sexuality and the brain.

Puberty

Puberty is not the same as adolescence. For most of us, puberty ends long before adolescence does, although puberty is the most important marker of the beginning of adolescence.

Puberty is a brain-neuroendocrine process occurring primarily in early adolescence that provides stimulation for the rapid physical changes that take place during this period of development (Berenbaum, Beltz, & Corley, 2015; Susman & Dorn, 2013). Puberty is not a single, sudden event. We know whether a young boy or girl is going through puberty, but pinpointing puberty's beginning and end is difficult. Among the most noticeable changes are signs of sexual maturation and increases in height and weight.

Sexual Maturation, Height, and Weight

Think back to the onset of your puberty. Of the striking changes that were taking place in your body, what was the first to occur? Researchers have found that male pubertal characteristics typically develop in this order: increase in penis and testicle size, appearance of straight pubic hair, minor voice change, first ejaculation (which usually occurs through masturbation or a wet dream), appearance of kinky pubic hair, onset of maximum growth in height and weight, growth of hair in armpits, more detectable voice changes, and, finally, growth of facial hair.

What is the order of appearance of physical changes in females? First, either the breasts enlarge or pubic hair appears. Later, hair appears in the armpits. As these changes occur, the female grows in height and her hips become wider than her shoulders. **Menarche**—a girl's first menstruation—comes rather late in the pubertal cycle.

Marked weight gains coincide with the onset of puberty. During early adolescence, girls tend to outweigh boys, but by about age 14 boys begin to surpass girls. Similarly, at the beginning of the adolescent period, girls tend to be as tall as or taller than boys of their age, but by the end of the middle school years most boys have caught up, or, in many cases, surpassed girls in height.

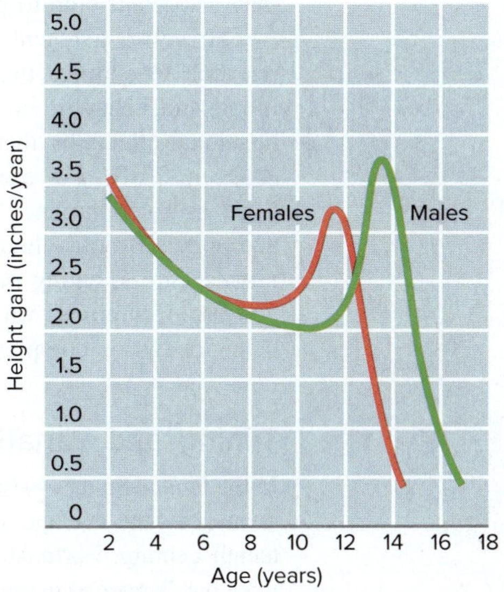

As indicated in Figure 1, the growth spurt occurs approximately two years earlier for girls than for boys. The mean age at the beginning of the growth spurt in girls is 9; for boys, it is 11. The peak rate of pubertal change occurs at 11½ years for girls and 13½ years for boys. During their growth spurt, girls increase in height about 3½ inches per year, boys about 4 inches. Boys and girls who are shorter or taller than their peers before adolescence are likely to remain so during adolescence.

Hormonal Changes

Behind the first whisker in boys and the widening of hips in girls is a flood of **hormones,** powerful chemical substances secreted by the endocrine glands and carried through the body by the bloodstream. The endocrine system's role in puberty involves the interaction of the hypothalamus, the pituitary gland, and the gonads. The **hypothalamus** is a structure in the brain that monitors eating and sex. The **pituitary gland** is an

Figure 1

Pubertal Growth Spurt

On average, the peak of the growth spurt during puberty occurs two years earlier for girls (11½) than for boys (13½). *How are hormones related to the growth spurt and to the difference between the average height of adolescent boys and that of girls?*

puberty A brain-neuroendocrine process occurring primarily in early adolescence that provides stimulation for the rapid physical changes that occur in this period of development.

menarche A girl's first menstruation.

hormones Powerful chemical substances secreted by the endocrine glands and carried through the body by the bloodstream.

hypothalamus A structure in the higher portion of the brain that monitors eating and sex.

pituitary gland An important endocrine gland that controls growth and regulates other glands, including the gonads.

gonads The sex glands—the testes in males and the ovaries in females.

important endocrine gland that controls growth and regulates other glands; among these, the **gonads**—the testes in males, the ovaries in females—are particularly important in giving rise to pubertal changes in the body.

The concentrations of certain hormones increase dramatically during adolescence (Berenbaum, Beltz, & Corley, 2015; Koolschijn, Peper, & Crone, 2014). *Testosterone* is a hormone associated in boys with the development of genitals, an increase in height, and a change in voice. *Estradiol* is a type of estrogen; in girls it is associated with breast, uterine, and skeletal development. In one study, testosterone levels increased eighteenfold in boys but only twofold in girls during puberty; estradiol increased eightfold in girls but only twofold in boys (Nottelmann & others, 1987). Thus, both testosterone and estradiol are present in the hormonal makeup of both boys and girls, but testosterone dominates in male pubertal development, estradiol in female pubertal development. The same influx of hormones that grows hair on a male's chest and increases the fatty tissue in a female's breasts may also contribute to psychological development in adolescence.

However, a recent research review concluded that there is insufficient quality research to confirm that changing testosterone levels during puberty are linked to mood and behavior in adolescent males (Duke, Balzer, & Steinbeck, 2014). Thus, hormonal effects by themselves do not account for adolescent development (Susman & Dorn, 2013). For example, in one study, social factors accounted for two to four times as much variance as did hormonal factors in young adolescent girls' depression and anger (Brooks-Gunn & Warren, 1989). Behavior and moods also can affect hormones. Stress, eating patterns, exercise, sexual activity, tension, and depression can activate or suppress various aspects of the hormonal system. In sum, the hormone-behavior link is complex (Susman & Dorn, 2013).

Timing and Variations in Puberty

In the United States—where children mature up to a year earlier than children in European countries—the average age of menarche has declined significantly since the mid-nineteenth century. Fortunately, however, we are unlikely to see pubescent toddlers, since what has happened in the past century is likely the result of improved nutrition and health (Herman-Giddens, 2007).

Why do the changes of puberty occur when they do, and how can variations in their timing be explained? The basic genetic program for puberty is wired into the species (Dvornyk & Waqar-ul-Haq, 2012), but nutrition, health, family stress, and other environmental factors also affect puberty's timing and makeup (James & others, 2012; Villamor & Jansen, 2016). A recent cross-cultural study in 29 countries found that childhood obesity was linked to early puberty in girls (Currie & others, 2012). Also, a recent study of Chinese girls confirmed that childhood obesity contributed to an earlier onset of puberty (Zhai & others, 2015). Another study of more than 15,000 girls in China revealed that girls living in an urban environment started puberty earlier than their counterparts who lived in a rural environment (Sun & others, 2012). For most boys, the pubertal sequence may begin as early as age 10 or as late as 13½ and may end as early as age 13 or as late as 17. Thus, the normal range is wide enough that, given two boys of the same chronological age, one might complete the pubertal sequence before the other one has begun it. For girls, menarche is considered within the normal range if it appears between the ages of 9 and 15.

What are some of the differences in the ways girls and boys experience pubertal growth?
© Colorblind/Corbis RF

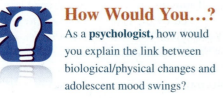

How Would You...?

As a **psychologist,** how would you explain the link between biological/physical changes and adolescent mood swings?

How Would You...?

As a **human development and family studies professional,** how would you counsel parents about communicating with their adolescent daughter regarding changes in her behavior that likely reflect a downward turn in her body image?

Body Image

One psychological aspect of physical change in puberty is certain: Adolescents are preoccupied with their bodies and develop images of what their bodies are like (Leone & others, 2014; Voelker, Reel, & Greenleaf, 2015). One study revealed that adolescents with the most positive body images engaged in health-enhancing behaviors, especially regular exercise (Frisen & Holmqvist, 2010).

Gender differences characterize adolescents' perceptions of their bodies. In general, girls are less happy with their bodies and have more negative body images than boys throughout puberty (Bearman & others, 2006). Girls' more negative body images may be due to media portrayals of the attractiveness of being thin and the increase in body fat in girls during puberty (Benowitz-Fredericks & others, 2012). A recent study found that both boys' and girls' body images became more positive as they moved from the beginning to the end of adolescence (Holsen, Carlson Jones, & Skogbrott Birkeland, 2012). Also, a recent study found that in the early high school years, late-maturing boys had a more negative body image than early-maturing boys did (de Guzman & Nishina, 2014).

Early and Late Maturation

You may have entered puberty earlier or later than average, or perhaps you were right on time. Adolescents who mature earlier or later than their peers perceive themselves differently (Susman & Dorn, 2013). In the Berkeley Longitudinal Study some years ago, early-maturing boys perceived themselves more positively and had more successful peer relations than did their late-maturing counterparts (Jones, 1965). When the late-maturing boys were in their thirties, however, they had developed a stronger sense of identity than the early-maturing boys had (Peskin, 1967). This may have occurred because the late-maturing boys had more time to explore life's options, or because the early-maturing boys continued to focus on their advantageous physical status instead of on career development and achievement. More recent research confirms, though, that at least during adolescence it is advantageous to be an early-maturing rather than a late-maturing boy (Graber, Brooks-Gunn, & Warren, 2006).

An increasing number of researchers have found that early maturation increases girls' vulnerability to a number of problems (Cheong & others, 2015; Graber, 2013; Hamilton & others, 2014). Early-maturing girls are more likely to smoke, drink, be depressed, have an eating disorder, struggle for earlier independence from their parents, and have older friends; and their bodies are likely to elicit responses from males that lead to earlier dating and earlier sexual experiences (Baker & others, 2012; Negriff, Susman, & Trickett, 2011; Rudolph & others, 2014; Wang & others, 2016). For example, in a recent Korean study, early menarche was associated with risky sexual behavior in females (Cheong & others, 2015). Researchers also have found that early-maturing girls tend to engage in sexual intercourse earlier and have more unstable sexual relationships (Moore, Harden, & Mendle, 2014). Further, a recent study revealed that early-maturing Chinese girls and boys engaged in delinquency more than their on-time or late-maturing counterparts (Chen & others, 2015). A recent study found that early maturation predicted a stable higher level of depression for adolescent girls (Rudolph & others, 2014). Also, early-maturing girls are less likely to graduate from high school, and they tend to cohabit and marry earlier (Cavanagh, 2009).

The Brain

Along with the rest of the body, the brain is changing during adolescence, but the study of adolescent brain development is in its infancy. As advances in technology take place, significant strides will also likely be made in charting developmental changes in the adolescent brain

How Would You...?

As a **health-care professional,** how would you use your knowledge of puberty to reassure adolescents who are concerned that they are maturing slower than their friends?

(Casey, 2015; Galvan & Tottenham, 2016; Monahan & others, 2016; Steinberg, 2015a, b). What do we know now?

The dogma of the unchanging brain has been discarded and researchers are mainly focused on context-induced plasticity of the brain over time (Zelazo, 2013). The development of the brain mainly changes in a bottom-up, top-down sequence, with sensory, appetitive (eating, drinking), sexual, sensation-seeking, and risk-taking brain linkages maturing first and higher-level brain linkages such as self-control, planning, and reasoning maturing later (Zelazo, 2013).

Recall that researchers have discovered that nearly twice as many synaptic connections are made as we will ever use (Huttenlocher & Dabholkar, 1997). The connections that we do use are strengthened and survive, while the unused ones are replaced by other pathways or disappear. That is, in the language of neuroscience, these connections will be "pruned." As a result of this pruning, by the end of adolescence individuals have "fewer, more selective, more effective neuronal connections than they did as children" (Kuhn, 2009, p. 153). And this pruning indicates that the activities adolescents choose to engage in and not to engage in influence which neural connections will be strengthened and which will disappear.

Using fMRI brain scans, scientists have discovered that adolescents' brains undergo significant structural changes (Casey, 2015; Casey, Galvan, & Somerville, 2016; Cohen & others, 2016; de Haan & Johnson, 2016; Galvan & Tottenham, 2016; Monahan & others, 2016). The **corpus callosum,** where nerve fibers connect the brain's left and right hemispheres, thickens in adolescence, and this improves adolescents' ability to process information (Chavarria & others, 2014). Earlier we described advances in the development of the prefrontal cortex—the highest level of the frontal lobes involved in reasoning, decision making, and self-control. However, the prefrontal cortex doesn't finish maturing until the emerging adult years—approximately 18 to 25 years of age—or later (Shulman & others, 2016; Steinberg, 2015a, b).

corpus callosum The location where nerve fibers connect the brain's left and right hemispheres.

limbic system A lower, subcortical system in the brain that is the seat of emotions and experience of rewards.

amygdala The region of the brain that is the seat of emotions.

At a lower, subcortical level, the **limbic system,** which is the seat of emotions and where rewards are experienced, matures much earlier than the prefrontal cortex and is almost completely developed by early adolescence (Casey, Galvan, & Somerville, 2016; Monahan & others, 2016; Shulman & others, 2016; Somerville, 2016; Steinberg, 2015a, b). The limbic system structure that is especially involved in emotion is the **amygdala.** Figure 2 shows the locations of the corpus callosum, prefrontal cortex, and the limbic system.

With the onset of puberty, the levels of neurotransmitters change (Monahan & others, 2016). For example, an increase in the neurotransmitter dopamine occurs in both the prefrontal cortex and the limbic system during adolescence (Casey, 2015). Increases in dopamine have been linked to increased risk taking and the use of addictive drugs (Steinberg, 2015a, b). Researchers have found that dopamine plays an important role in reward seeking during adolescence (Leyton & Vezina, 2014).

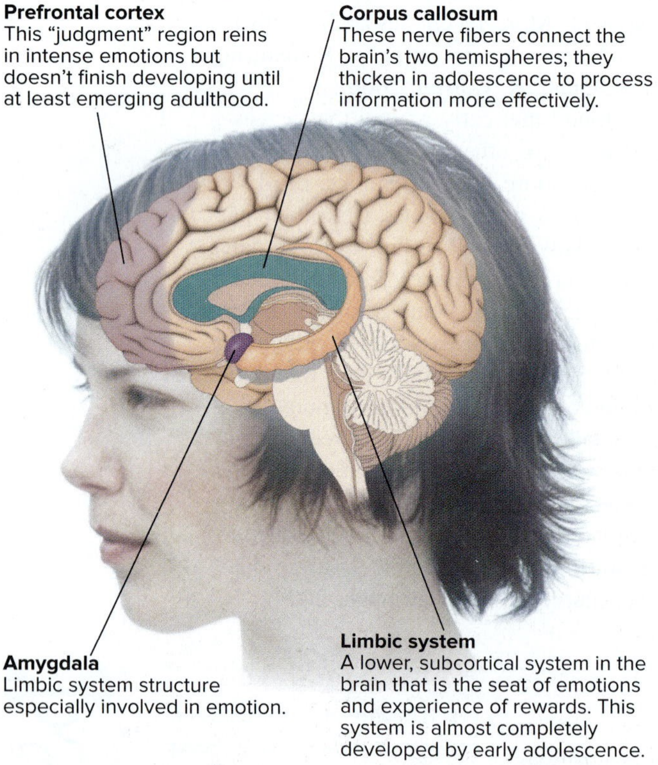

Prefrontal cortex
This "judgment" region reins in intense emotions but doesn't finish developing until at least emerging adulthood.

Corpus callosum
These nerve fibers connect the brain's two hemispheres; they thicken in adolescence to process information more effectively.

Amygdala
Limbic system structure especially involved in emotion.

Limbic system
A lower, subcortical system in the brain that is the seat of emotions and experience of rewards. This system is almost completely developed by early adolescence.

Figure 2 The Changing Adolescent Brain: Prefrontal Cortex, Limbic System, and Corpus Callosum

Earlier we described the increased focal activation that is linked to synaptic pruning in a specific region, such as the prefrontal cortex. In middle and late childhood, while there is increased focal activation within a specific brain region, such as the prefrontal cortex, there also are only limited connections across distant brain regions. By the time individuals reach emerging adulthood, there is an increase in connections across brain areas (Casey, Galvan, & Somerville, 2016; Galvan & Tottenham, 2016). The increased connectedness (referred to as brain networks) is especially prevalent across more distant brain regions. Thus, as children and adolescents develop, greater efficiency and focal activation occurs in local areas of the brain, and simultaneously there is an increase in brain networks across different brain regions (de Haan & Johnson, 2016).

Many of the changes in the adolescent brain that have been described involve the rapidly emerging field of *developmental social neuroscience,* which involves connections between development, the brain, and socioemotional processes (Decety & Cowell, 2016; Johnson, 2015; Monahan & others, 2016). For example, consider leading researcher Charles Nelson's (2003) view that, although adolescents are capable of very strong emotions, their prefrontal cortex hasn't adequately developed to the point at which they can control these passions. It is as if their brain doesn't have the brakes to slow down their emotions. Or consider this interpretation of the development of emotion and cognition in adolescents: "early activation of strong 'turbo-charged' feelings with a relatively un-skilled set of 'driving skills' or cognitive abilities to modulate strong emotions and motivations" (Dahl, 2004, p. 18).

Of course, a major issue is which comes first, biological changes in the brain or experiences that stimulate these changes (Lerner, Boyd, & Du, 2008)? Consider a study in which the prefrontal cortex thickened and more brain connections formed when adolescents resisted peer pressure (Paus & others, 2007). Scientists have yet to determine whether the brain changes come first or whether the brain changes are the result of experiences with peers, parents, and others (Monahan & others, 2016). Once again, we encounter the nature/nurture issue that is so prominent in an examination of development through the life span.

In closing this section on the development of the brain in adolescence, a further caution is in order. Much of the research on neuroscience and the development of the brain in adolescence is correlational in nature, and thus causal statements need to be scrutinized (de Haan, 2015). This caution, of course, applies to any period in the human life span.

Adolescent Sexuality

Not only are adolescents characterized by substantial changes in physical growth and the development of the brain, but adolescence also is a bridge between the asexual child and the sexual adult. Adolescence is a time of sexual exploration and experimentation, of sexual fantasies and realities, of incorporating sexuality into one's identity.

Developing a Sexual Identity

Mastering emerging sexual feelings and forming a sense of sexual identity is a multifaceted and lengthy process (Diamond & Savin-Williams, 2015). It involves learning to manage sexual feelings (such as sexual arousal and attraction), developing new forms of intimacy, and learning the skills to regulate sexual behavior to avoid undesirable consequences.

An adolescent's sexual identity involves activities, interests, styles of behavior, and an indication of sexual orientation (whether an individual has same-sex or other-sex attractions) (Buzwell & Rosenthal, 1996). For example, some adolescents have a high anxiety level about sex, others a low level. Some adolescents are strongly aroused sexually, others less so. Some adolescents are very active sexually, others not at all (Haydon & others, 2012). Some adolescents are sexually inactive in response to their strong religious upbringing; others go to church regularly, yet their religious training does not inhibit their sexual activity (Thornton & Camburn, 1989).

It is commonly believed that most gay and lesbian individuals quietly struggle with same-sex attractions in childhood, do not engage in heterosexual dating, and gradually recognize that they are gay or lesbian in middle to late adolescence. Many youth do follow this developmental pathway, but others do not (Savin-Williams & Cohen, 2015). For example, many youth have no recollection of early same-sex attractions and experience a more abrupt sense of their same-sex attraction in late adolescence. Researchers also have found that the majority of adolescents with same-sex attractions also experience some degree of other-sex attractions. Even though some adolescents who are attracted to individuals of their own sex fall in love with these individuals, others claim that their same-sex attractions are purely physical (Diamond & Savin-Williams, 2015; Savin-Williams, 2015).

In sum, gay and lesbian youth have diverse patterns of initial attraction, often have bisexual attractions, and may have physical or emotional attraction to same-sex individuals but do not always fall in love with them (Diamond & Savin-Williams, 2015). (Later we will further explore same-sex and heterosexual attraction.)

The Timing of Adolescent Sexual Behaviors

What is the current profile of sexual activity of adolescents? In a U.S. national survey conducted in 2013, 64 percent of twelfth-graders reported having experienced sexual intercourse, compared with 30 percent of ninth-graders (Kann & others, 2014). By age 20, 77 percent of U.S. youth report having engaged in sexual intercourse (Dworkin & Santelli, 2007). Nationally, in 2013, 49 percent of twelfth-graders, 40 percent of eleventh-graders, 29 percent of tenth-graders, and 20 percent of ninth-graders reported that they were currently sexually active (Kann & others, 2014).

What trends in adolescent sexual activity have occurred in recent decades? From 1991 to 2013, fewer adolescents reported any of the following: ever having had sexual intercourse, currently being sexually active, having had sexual intercourse before the age of 13, and having had sexual intercourse with four or more persons during their lifetime (Kann & others, 2014).

Sexual initiation varies by ethnic group in the United States (Kann & others, 2014). African Americans are likely to engage in sexual behaviors earlier than other ethnic groups, whereas Asian Americans are likely to engage in them later (Feldman, Turner, & Araujo, 1999). In a more recent national U.S. survey (2014) of ninth- to twelfth-graders, 61 percent of African Americans, 49 percent of Latinos, and 44 percent of non-Latino Whites said they had experienced sexual intercourse (Kann & others, 2014). In this study, 14 percent of African Americans (compared with 6 percent of Latinos and 3 percent of non-Latino Whites) said they had their first sexual experience before 13 years of age.

Recent research indicates that oral sex is now a common occurrence among U.S. adolescents (Fava & Bay-Cheng, 2012; Holway, 2015). In a national survey, 55 percent of U.S. 15- to 19-year-old boys and 54 percent of girls said they had engaged in oral sex (National Center for Health Statistics, 2002). A recent study also found that among female adolescents who reported having vaginal sex first, 31 percent reported having a teen pregnancy, whereas among those who initiated oral-genital sex first, only 8 percent reported having a teen pregnancy (Reese & others, 2013). Thus, how adolescents initiate their sex lives may have positive or negative consequences for their sexual health.

Many adolescents are not emotionally prepared to handle sexual experiences, especially in early adolescence (Chan & others, 2015; Skinner & others, 2015). A recent study of more than 3,000 Swedish adolescents revealed that sexual intercourse before age 14 was linked to risky behaviors such as an increased number of sexual partners, experience of oral and anal sex, negative health behaviors (smoking, drug and alcohol use), and antisocial behavior (being violent, stealing, running away from home) at 18 years of age (Kastbom & others, 2015).

A number of family factors are associated with sexual risk taking (de Looze & others, 2015; Simons & others, 2016). For example, a recent study found that difficulties and disagreements between Latino adolescents and their parents were linked to the adolescents' early sex initiation (Cordova & others, 2014). And a recent study revealed that of a number of parenting practices, the factor that best predicted a lower level of risky sexual behavior by adolescents was supportive parenting (Simons & others, 2016).

What are some risk factors for adolescent sexual problems?
© Masterfile RF

Socioeconomic, peer, school, and sport contexts provide further information about sexual risk taking in adolescents (Choukas-Bradley & Prinstein, 2016; Widman & others, 2016). The percentage of sexually active young adolescents is higher in low-income areas of inner cities (Morrison-Beedy & others, 2013). Also, one study found that adolescents who associated with more deviant peers in early adolescence were likely to have more sexual partners at age 16 (Lansford & others, 2010). And a recent research review found that school connectedness was linked to positive sexuality outcomes (Markham & others, 2010). Also, a study of middle school students revealed that better academic achievement was a protective factor in keeping boys and girls from engaging in early initiation of sexual intercourse (Laflin, Wang, & Barry, 2008). And a recent study found that adolescent males who play sports engage in a higher level of sexual risk taking, while adolescent females who play sports engage in a lower level of sexual risk taking (Lipowski & others, 2016).

Contraceptive Use

Sexual activity brings considerable risks if appropriate safeguards are not taken (Liddon & others, 2016). Youth encounter two kinds of risks: unintended, unwanted pregnancy and sexually transmitted infections. Both of these risks can be reduced significantly if condoms are used.

Many sexually active adolescents still do not use contraceptives, or they use them inconsistently (Amialchuk & Gerhardinger, 2015). In 2013, 34 percent of sexually active adolescents had not used a condom the last time they had sexual intercourse (Kann & others, 2014). In the recent national U.S. survey (2014), among sexually active adolescents, ninth-graders (63 percent), tenth-graders (62 percent), and eleventh-graders (62 percent) reported that they had used a condom during their last sexual intercourse more often than did twelfth-graders (53 percent) (Kann & others, 2014). Researchers have found that U.S. adolescents are less likely to use condoms than their European counterparts (Jorgensen & others, 2015).

Sexually Transmitted Infections

Some forms of contraception, such as birth control pills or implants, do not protect against sexually transmitted infections, or STIs. **Sexually transmitted infections (STIs)** are contracted primarily through sexual contact, including oral-genital and anal-genital contact. Every year more than 3 million American adolescents (about one-fourth of those who are sexually experienced) acquire an STI (Centers for Disease Control and Prevention, 2016). In a single act of unprotected sex with an infected partner, a teenage girl has a 1 percent risk of getting HIV, a 30 percent risk of acquiring genital herpes, and a 50 percent chance of contracting gonorrhea (Glei, 1999). Other very widespread STIs are chlamydia and human papillomavirus (HPV). Later we will consider these and other sexually transmitted infections.

Adolescent Pregnancy

In cross-cultural comparisons, the United States continues to have some of the highest rates of adolescent pregnancy and childbearing in the industrialized world, despite a considerable decline in the 1990s. The U.S. adolescent pregnancy rate is eight times as high as that in the Netherlands. Although U.S. adolescents are no more sexually active than their counterparts in the Netherlands, their adolescent pregnancy rate is dramatically higher. In the United States, 82 percent of pregnancies to mothers 15 to 19 years of age are unintended (Koh, 2014). A recent cross-cultural comparison found that among 21 countries, the United States had the highest adolescent pregnancy rate among 15- to 19-year-olds and Switzerland the lowest (Sedgh & others, 2015).

Despite the negative comparisons of the United States with many other developed countries, there have been some encouraging trends in U.S. adolescent pregnancy rates. In 2013, the U.S. birth rate for 15- to 19-year-olds was 26.5 births per 1,000 females, the lowest rate ever recorded, which represents a dramatic decrease from the 61.8 births for the same age range

sexually transmitted infections (STIs) Infections contracted primarily through sexual contact, including oral-genital and anal-genital contact.

in 1991 (Martin & others, 2015) (see Figure 3). There also has been a substantial decrease in adolescent pregnancies across ethnic groups in recent years. Reasons for the decline include school/community health classes, increased contraceptive use, and fear of sexually transmitted infections such as AIDS.

Ethnic variations characterize birth rates for U.S. adolescents. Latina adolescents are more likely than African American and non-Latina White adolescents to have a child (Martin & others, 2015). Latina and African American adolescent girls who have a child are also more likely to have a second child than are non-Latina White adolescent girls (Rosengard, 2009). And daughters of teenage mothers are at increased risk for teenage childbearing, thus perpetuating an intergenerational cycle (Meade, Kershaw, & Ickovics, 2008).

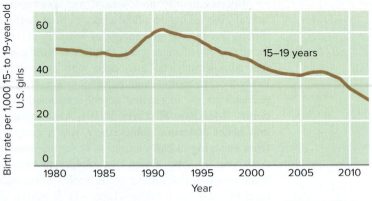

Figure 3 Birth Rates for U.S. 15- to 19-Year-Old Girls from 1980 to 2013

Source: Martin, J.A. & others, 2015.

Outcomes Adolescent pregnancy creates health risks for both the baby and the mother (Lau, Lin, & Flores, 2015). Infants born to adolescent mothers are more likely to have low birth weights—a prominent factor in infant mortality—as well as neurological problems and childhood illness (Khashan, Baker, & Kenny, 2010). Adolescent mothers are more likely to be depressed and to drop out of school than their peers (Siegel & Brandon, 2014). Although many adolescent mothers resume their education later in life, they generally never catch up economically with women who postpone childbearing until their twenties. Also, a recent study of African American urban youth found that at 32 years of age, women who had been teenage mothers were more likely to be unemployed, live in poverty, depend on welfare, and not have completed college than were women who had not been teenage mothers (Assini-Meytin & Green, 2015). In this study, at 32 years of age, men who had been teenage fathers were more likely to not have a job than were men who had not been teenage fathers.

What are some consequences of adolescent pregnancy?

© Geoff Manasse/Getty Images RF

Though the consequences of America's high adolescent pregnancy rate are cause for great concern, it often is not pregnancy alone that leads to negative consequences for an adolescent mother and her offspring. Adolescent mothers are more likely to come from low-SES backgrounds (Molina & others, 2010). Many adolescent mothers also were not good students before they became pregnant (Malamitsi-Puchner & Boutsikou, 2006). However, not every adolescent female who bears a child lives a life of poverty and low achievement. Thus, although adolescent pregnancy is a high-risk circumstance and adolescents who do not become pregnant generally fare better than those who do, some adolescent mothers do well in school and have positive outcomes (Schaffer & others, 2012).

Serious, extensive efforts are needed to help pregnant adolescents and young mothers enhance their educational and occupational opportunities (Asheer & others, 2014; Tang & others, 2016). Adolescent mothers also need help in obtaining competent child care and in planning for the future.

Adolescents can benefit from age-appropriate family life education. Family and consumer science educators teach life skills, such as effective decision making, to adolescents. *Careers in Life-Span Development* describes the work of one family and consumer science educator.

Lynn Blankinship, Family and Consumer Science Educator

Lynn Blankinship is a family and consumer science educator. She has an undergraduate degree in this area from the University of Arizona and has taught for more than 20 years, the last 14 at Tucson High Magnet School.

Lynn received the Tucson Federation of Teachers Educator of the Year Award for 1999–2000 and was honored as the Arizona Teacher of the Year in 1999.

Lynn especially enjoys teaching life skills to adolescents. One of her favorite activities is having students care for an automated baby that imitates the needs of real babies. She says that this program has a profound impact on students because the baby must be cared for around the clock for the duration of the assignment. Lynn also coordinates real-world work experiences and training for students in several child-care facilities in the Tucson area.

Family and consumer science educators like Lynn Blankinship may specialize in early childhood education or instruct middle and high school students about such matters as nutrition, interpersonal relationships, human sexuality, parenting, and human development.

Lynn Blankinship (*center*) teaching life skills to students.
© Lynn Blankinship

Hundreds of colleges and universities throughout the United States offer two- and four-year degree programs in family and consumer science. These programs usually require an internship. Additional education courses may be needed to obtain a teaching certificate. Some family and consumer science educators go on to graduate school for further training, which provides a background for possible jobs in college teaching or research.

Reducing Adolescent Pregnancy Girls Inc. offers four programs that are intended to increase adolescent girls' motivation to avoid pregnancy until they are mature enough to make responsible decisions about motherhood (Roth & others, 1998). Growing Together, a series of five two-hour workshops for adolescent girls and their mothers, and Will Power/Won't Power, a series of six two-hour sessions that focus on assertiveness training, are designed for 12- to 14-year-old girls. For older adolescent girls, Taking Care of Business provides nine sessions that emphasize career planning and provide information about sexuality, reproduction, and contraception. The program Health Bridge coordinates health and educational services—girls can participate in this program as one of their Girls Inc. club activities. Girls who participated in these programs were less likely to get pregnant than girls who did not participate (Girls Inc., 1991).

Currently, a major controversy in sex education is whether schools should have an abstinence-only program or a program that emphasizes contraceptive knowledge (Erkut & others, 2013; Manlove, Fish, & Moore, 2015). A number of leading experts on adolescent sexuality now conclude that sex education programs that emphasize contraceptive knowledge do not increase the incidence of sexual intercourse and are more likely to reduce the risk of adolescent pregnancy and sexually transmitted infections than abstinence-only programs (Crooks & Baur, 2016; Hyde & DeLamater, 2014; Yarber, Sayad, & Strong, 2016).

Some sex-education programs are starting to include abstinence-plus sexuality by promoting abstinence as well as providing instructions for contraceptive use (Barr & others, 2014; Nixon & others, 2011). Also, in 2010, the U.S. government launched the Teen Pregnancy Prevention (TPP) Program under the direction of the newly created Office of Adolescent Health (Koh, 2014). Currently, a number of studies are being funded by the program in an effort to find ways to reduce the rate of adolescent pregnancy.

How Would You...?

As an **educator,** how would you incorporate sex education throughout the curriculum to encourage adolescents' healthy, responsible sexual development?

Adolescent Health

Adolescence is a critical juncture in the adoption of behaviors that are relevant to health (Griesler, Hu, & Kandel, 2016; Latt & others, 2015). Many of the behaviors that are linked to poor health habits and early death in adults begin during adolescence (Blackstone & Herrmann, 2016). Conversely, the early formation of healthy behavior patterns, such as regular exercise and a preference for foods low in fat and cholesterol, not only has immediate health benefits but helps in adulthood to delay or prevent disability and mortality from heart disease, stroke, diabetes, and cancer (Blake, 2017; Donatelle, 2017; Schiff, 2015).

Nutrition and Exercise

Concerns are growing about adolescents' nutrition and exercise habits (Donatelle, 2016; Finistrella & others, 2015; Powers & Dodd, 2017; Stephenson & Schiff, 2016). National data indicate that the percentage of overweight U.S. 12- to 19-year-olds increased from 11 percent in the early 1990s to nearly 21 percent in 2011–2012 (Ogden & others, 2014). In another recent study, 12.4 percent of U.S. kindergarten children were obese and by 14 years of age, 20.8 percent were obese (Cunningham, Kramer, & Narayan, 2014).

Being obese in adolescence predicts obesity in emerging adulthood. For example, a longitudinal study of more than 8,000 adolescents found that obese adolescents were more likely to develop severe obesity in emerging adulthood than were overweight or normal-weight adolescents (The & others, 2010). In another longitudinal study, the percentage of overweight individuals increased from 20 percent at 14 years of age to 33 percent at 24 years of age (Patton & others, 2011).

Researchers have found that individuals become less active as they reach and progress through adolescence (Alberga & others, 2012). A national study revealed that only 48.7 percent of U.S. adolescents met the federal government's exercise recommendations (a minimum of 60 minutes of moderate to vigorous exercise per day) (Kann & others, 2014). This national study also found that adolescent boys were much more likely to engage in 60 minutes or more of vigorous exercise per day than were girls (57.3 percent versus 37.3 percent) (Kann & others, 2014). Ethnic differences in exercise participation rates of U.S. adolescents also occur, and these rates vary by gender. In the national study just mentioned, non-Latino White boys exercised the most, African American and Latino girls the least (Kann & others, 2014).

Exercise is linked to a number of positive physical outcomes in adolescence (Ten Hoor & others, 2016; Todd & others, 2015). Regular exercise has a positive effect on adolescents' weight status. Other positive outcomes of exercise in adolescence are reduced triglyceride levels, lower blood pressure, and a lower incidence of type II diabetes (Anyaegbu & Dharnidharka, 2014). Also, a recent study found that highly fit adolescents had better connectivity between brain regions than did adolescents with low physical fitness (Herting & others, 2014). And in a recent study, an exercise program of 180 minutes per week improved the sleep patterns of obese adolescents (Mendelson & others, 2016). In further research, a high-intensity exercise program reduced depressive symptoms and improved the moods of depressed adolescents (Carter & others, 2016).

Adolescents' exercise levels are increasingly being found to be associated with parenting, peer relationships, and screen-based activity. A recent study revealed that

What are some characteristics of adolescents' exercise patterns?
© Tom Stewart/Corbis

How Would You…?

As a **health-care professional,** how would you explain the benefits of physical fitness in adolescence to adolescents, parents, and teachers?

family meals during adolescence protected against the development of being overweight or obese in adulthood (Berge & others, 2015). Also, a recent study revealed that female adolescents' physical activity was linked to their male and female friends' physical activity, while male adolescents' physical activity was associated with their female friends' physical activity (Sirard & others, 2013).

A recent research review concluded that screen-based activity is linked to a number of adolescent health problems (Costigan & others, 2013). In this review, a higher level of screen-based sedentary behavior was associated with being overweight, having sleep problems, being depressed, and having lower levels of physical activity/fitness and psychological well-being (higher stress levels, for example).

Sleep Patterns

Like nutrition and exercise, sleep is an important influence on well-being. Might changing sleep patterns in adolescence contribute to adolescents' health-compromising behaviors? Recently there has been a surge of interest in adolescent sleep patterns (Doane & Thurston, 2014; Fuligni & others, 2015; Hysing & others, 2015, 2016). A longitudinal study in which adolescents completed daily diaries every 14 days in ninth, tenth, and twelfth grades found that regardless of how much students studied each day, when the students sacrificed sleep time to study more than usual, they had difficulty understanding what was taught in class and were more likely to struggle with class assignments the next day (Gillen-O'Neel, Huynh, & Fuligni, 2013). Further, a recent study found that adolescents who got less than 7.7 hours of sleep per night on average had more emotional and peer-related problems, higher anxiety, and a higher level of suicidal ideation (Sarchiapone & others, 2014).

In a national survey of youth, only 32 percent of U.S. adolescents got eight or more hours of sleep on an average school night (Kann & others, 2014). In this study, the percentage of adolescents getting this much sleep on an average school night decreased as they got older. Also, another study of more than 270,000 U.S. adolescents from 1991–2012 found that they have gotten decreasing amounts of sleep in recent years (Keyes & others, 2015).

The National Sleep Foundation (2006) conducted a U.S. survey of 1,602 caregivers and their 11- to 17-year-olds. Forty-five percent of the adolescents got inadequate sleep on school nights (less than eight hours). Older adolescents (ninth- to twelfth-graders) got markedly less sleep on school nights than younger adolescents (sixth- to eighth-graders)—62 percent of the older adolescents got inadequate sleep compared with 21 percent of the younger adolescents. Adolescents who got inadequate sleep (less than eight hours) on school nights were more likely to feel tired, cranky, and irritable; to fall asleep in school; to be in a depressed mood; and to drink caffeinated beverages than their counterparts who got optimal sleep (nine or more hours).

Mary Carskadon and her colleagues (2006, 2011a, b; Jenni & Carskadon, 2007; Tarokh & Carskadon, 2010) have conducted a number of research studies on adolescent sleep patterns. They found that when given the opportunity, adolescents will sleep an average of 9 hours and 25 minutes a night. Most get considerably less than 9 hours of sleep, however, especially during the week. This shortfall creates a sleep deficit,

In Mary Carskadon's sleep laboratory at Brown University, an adolescent girl's brain activity is being monitored. Carskadon (2006) says that in the morning, sleep-deprived adolescents' "brains are telling them it's night time . . . and the rest of the world is saying it's time to go to school" (p. 19).

© Jim LoScalzo

which adolescents often attempt to make up on the weekend. The researchers also found that older adolescents tend to be sleepier during the day than younger adolescents are. They theorized that this sleepiness was not due to academic work or social pressures. Rather, their research suggests that adolescents' biological clocks undergo a shift as they get older, delaying their period of wakefulness by about one hour. A delay in the nightly release of the sleep-inducing hormone melatonin, which is produced in the brain's pineal gland, seems to underlie this shift. Melatonin is secreted at about 9:30 p.m. in younger adolescents and approximately an hour later in older adolescents.

How Would You...?

As an **educator,** how would you use developmental research to convince your school board to change the starting time of high school?

Carskadon concludes that early school starting times may cause grogginess, inattention in class, and poor performance on tests. Based on her research, school officials in Edina, Minnesota, decided to start classes at 8:30 a.m. rather than the usual 7:25 a.m. Since then, there have been fewer referrals for discipline problems, and the number of students who report being ill or depressed has decreased. The school system reports that test scores have improved for high school students but not for middle school students. This finding supports Carskadon's suspicion that early start times are likely to be more stressful for older than for younger adolescents.

One study found that just a 30-minute delay in school start time was linked to improvements in adolescents' sleep, alertness, mood, and health (Owens, Belon, & Moss, 2010). In another study, early school start times were linked to a higher vehicle crash rate in adolescent drivers (Vorona & others, 2014). Recently, the American Academy of Pediatrics recommended that schools institute start times from 8:30 to 9:30 a.m. to improve adolescents' academic performance and quality of life (Adolescent Sleep Working Group, AAP, 2014).

Do sleep patterns change in emerging adulthood? Research indicates that they do (Galambos, Howard, & Maggs, 2011). A recent study revealed that more than 60 percent of college students were categorized as poor-quality sleepers (Lund & others, 2010). In this study, the weekday bedtimes and rise times of first-year college students were approximately 1 hour and 15 minutes later than those of seniors in high school (Lund & others, 2010). However, the first-year college students had later bedtimes and rise times than third- and fourth-year college students, indicating that at about 20 to 22 years of age, a reverse shift in the timing of bedtimes and rise times occurs.

Leading Causes of Death in Adolescence

The three leading causes of death in adolescence are unintentional injuries, homicide, and suicide (National Center for Health Statistics, 2016). Almost half of all deaths occurring from 15 to 24 years of age are due to unintentional injuries, the majority of them involving motor vehicle accidents.

Risky driving habits, such as speeding, tailgating, and driving under the influence of alcohol or other drugs, may be more important contributors to these accidents than lack of driving experience (Curry & others, 2015). In about 50 percent of motor vehicle fatalities involving adolescents, the driver has a blood alcohol level of 0.10 percent—twice the level needed to be designated as "under the influence" in some states. A high rate of intoxication is also found in adolescents who die as pedestrians or while using recreational vehicles.

Homicide is the second-leading cause of death in adolescence (National Center for Health Statistics, 2014), especially among African American male adolescents. The rate of the third-leading cause, adolescent suicide, has tripled since the 1950s. Suicide accounts for 6 percent of deaths in the 10-to-14 age group and 12 percent of deaths in the 15-to-19 age group.

Substance Use and Abuse

Each year since 1975, Lloyd Johnston and his colleagues at the Institute of Social Research at the University of Michigan have monitored the drug use of America's

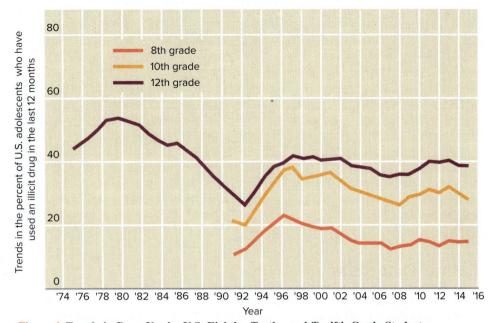

Figure 4 Trends in Drug Use by U.S. Eighth-, Tenth-, and Twelfth-Grade Students

This graph shows the percentage of U.S. eighth-, tenth-, and twelfth-grade students who reported having taken an illicit drug in the last 12 months in surveys conducted from 1991 to 2015 (for eighth- and tenth-graders), and from 1975 to 2015 (for twelfth-graders) (Johnston & others, 2016).

high school seniors in a wide range of public and private high schools. Since 1991, they also have surveyed drug use by eighth- and tenth-graders. In 2015, the study surveyed more than 44,900 secondary school students in 382 public and private schools (Johnston & others, 2016).

According to this study, the proportions of eighth-, tenth-, and twelfth-grade U.S. students who used any illicit drug declined in the late 1990s and the first decade and a half of the twenty-first century (Johnston & others, 2016) (see Figure 4). Marijuana is the illicit drug most widely used in the United States, and its use by adolescents increased from 2008 to 2015 (Johnston & others, 2016). As shown in Figure 4, in which marijuana is included, an increase in illicit drug use by U.S. adolescents occurred from 2008 to 2015. However, when marijuana use is subtracted from the illicit drug index, no increase in illicit drug use by adolescents occurred in this time frame (Johnston & others, 2016). The United States still has one of the highest rates of adolescent drug use of any industrialized nation.

A special concern involves adolescents who begin to use drugs early in adolescence or even in childhood. A longitudinal study of individuals from 8 to 42 years of age found that early onset of drinking was linked to increased risk of heavy drinking in middle age (Pitkänen, Lyrra, & Pulkkinen, 2005). A recent study revealed that the onset of alcohol use before age 11 was linked to a higher risk for alcohol dependence in early adulthood (Guttmannova & others, 2012). Further, a longitudinal study found that earlier age at first use of alcohol was linked to risk of heavy alcohol use in early adulthood (Liang & Chikritzhs, 2015). And another recent study indicated that early- and rapid-onset trajectories of alcohol, marijuana, and substance use were associated with substance abuse in early adulthood (Nelson, Van Ryzin, & Dishion, 2015).

How Would You...?

As a **human development and family studies professional,** how would you explain to parents the importance of parental monitoring in preventing adolescent substance abuse?

Parents play an important role in preventing adolescent drug abuse (Chassin & others, 2016; Zucker, Hicks, & Heitzeg, 2016). Researchers have found that parental monitoring is linked with a lower incidence of problem behavior by adolescents, including substance abuse (Wang & others, 2014). A research review found that when adolescents ate dinner more often with their families they were less likely to have problems such as substance abuse (Sen, 2010). And recent research revealed that authoritative parenting was linked to lower adolescent alcohol consumption

(Piko & Balazs, 2012) while parent-adolescent conflict was related to a higher level of adolescent alcohol use (Chaplin & others, 2012).

Along with parents, peers play a very important role in adolescent substance use (Choukas-Bradley & Prinstein, 2016; Prinstein & Giletta, 2016). A large-scale study of eighth- and tenth-graders found that of various risk factors the strongest predictors of substance use involved peer relations (Patrick & Schulenberg, 2010). In this study, spending more evenings out with peers, having friends who get drunk, feeling pressure to drink, and perceived availability of alcohol were linked to heavy episodic drinking.

Educational success is also a strong buffer for the emergence of drug problems in adolescence (Balsa, Giuliano, & French, 2011). An analysis by Jerald Bachman and his colleagues (2008) revealed that early educational achievement considerably reduced the likelihood that adolescents would develop drug problems, including alcohol abuse, smoking, and abuse of various illicit drugs.

Eating Disorders

Earlier in the chapter under the topic of nutrition and exercise, we described the increasing numbers of adolescents who are overweight. Let's now examine two different eating problems—anorexia nervosa and bulimia nervosa—that are far more common in adolescent girls than boys.

Anorexia Nervosa

Although most U.S. girls have been on a diet at some point, slightly less than 1 percent ever develop anorexia nervosa. **Anorexia nervosa** is an eating disorder that involves the relentless pursuit of thinness through starvation. It is a serious disorder that can lead to death (Westmoreland, Krantz, & Mehler, 2016). Four main characteristics apply to people suffering from anorexia nervosa: (1) weight less than 85 percent of what is considered normal for their age and height; (2) an intense fear of gaining weight that does not decrease with weight loss; (3) a distorted image of their body shape (Reville, O'Connor, & Frampton, 2016), and (4) amenorrhea (lack of menstruation) in girls who have reached puberty. Obsessive thinking about weight and compulsive exercise also are linked to anorexia nervosa (Simpson & others, 2013). Even when they are extremely thin, they see themselves as too fat (Cornelissen & others, 2015). They never think they are thin enough, especially in the abdomen, buttocks, and thighs. They usually weigh themselves frequently, often take their body measurements, and gaze critically at themselves in mirrors.

Anorexia nervosa typically begins in the early to middle adolescent years, often following an episode of dieting and some type of life stress (Fitzpatrick, 2012). It is about 10 times more likely to occur in females than males. When anorexia nervosa does occur in males, the symptoms and other characteristics (such as a distorted body image and family conflict) are usually similar to those reported by females who have the disorder (Ariceli & others, 2005).

Most individuals with anorexia are non-Latina White adolescent or young adult females from well-educated, middle- and upper-income families and are competitive and high achieving (Darcy, 2012). They set high standards, become stressed about not being able to reach these standards, and are intensely concerned about how others perceive them (Woelders & others, 2011). Unable to meet these high expectations, they turn to something they can control—their weight. Offspring of mothers with anorexia nervosa are at risk for becoming anorexic themselves (Machado & others, 2014). Problems in family functioning are increasingly being found to be linked to the appearance of anorexia nervosa in adolescent girls (Espie & Eisler, 2015), and a research review indicated that family therapy is often the most effective treatment for adolescent girls with anorexia nervosa (Bulik & others, 2007).

Biology and culture are involved in anorexia nervosa. Genes play an important role in anorexia nervosa (Boraska & others, 2014). Also, the physical effects of dieting may change neural networks and thus

Anorexia nervosa has become an increasing problem for adolescent girls and young adult women. *What are some possible causes of anorexia nervosa?*
© Ian Thraves/Alamy

anorexia nervosa An eating disorder that involves the relentless pursuit of thinness through starvation.

sustain the disordered pattern (Fuglset & others, 2015). The fashion image in U.S. culture likely contributes to the incidence of anorexia nervosa (Carr & Peebles, 2012). The media portray thin as beautiful in their choice of fashion models, whom many adolescent girls strive to emulate (Carr & Peebles, 2012; Cazzato & others, 2016). And many adolescent girls who strive to be thin hang out together.

Bulimia Nervosa

Whereas people with anorexia control their eating by restricting it, most individuals with bulimia cannot. **Bulimia nervosa** is an eating disorder in which the individual consistently follows a binge-and-purge pattern, self-inducing vomiting or using a laxative. Although many people binge and purge occasionally, a person is considered to have a serious bulimic disorder only if the episodes occur at least twice a week for three months (Cuzzolaro, 2014).

Most people with bulimia are preoccupied with food, have a strong fear of becoming overweight, are depressed or anxious, and have a distorted body image. Bulimics may have difficulty controlling their emotions (Lavender & others, 2014). Unlike people who have anorexia, people who binge and purge typically fall within a normal weight range, which makes bulimia more difficult to detect.

How Would You...?

As a **health-care professional,** how would you educate parents to identify the signs and symptoms that may signal an eating disorder?

One to 2 percent of U.S. women develop bulimia nervosa, and about 90 percent of people with bulimia are women. Bulimia nervosa typically begins in late adolescence or early adulthood. Many women who develop bulimia nervosa were somewhat overweight before the onset of the disorder, and the binge eating often began during an episode of dieting. About 70 percent of individuals who develop bulimia nervosa eventually recover from the disorder (Agras & others, 2004). Like anorexics, bulimics are highly perfectionistic (Lampard & others, 2012). Drug therapy and psychotherapy have been effective in treating bulimia nervosa (Harrington & others, 2015) and cognitive behavior therapy has especially been helpful (Dalle Grave & others, 2016; Hay, 2013).

Adolescent Cognition

Adolescents' developing power of thought opens up new cognitive and social horizons. Let's examine what their developing power of thought is like, beginning with the perspective provided by Piaget's theory (1952).

Piaget's Theory

Piaget proposed that around 7 years of age children enter the concrete operational stage of cognitive development. They can reason logically about concrete events and objects, and they make gains in their ability to classify objects and to reason about the relationships between classes of objects. Around age 11, according to Piaget, the fourth and final stage of cognitive development—the formal operational stage—begins.

The Formal Operational Stage

Formal operational thought is more abstract than concrete operational thought. Adolescents are no longer limited to actual, concrete experiences as anchors for thought. They can conjure up make-believe situations, abstract propositions, and events that are purely hypothetical, and can try to reason logically about them. The abstract quality of thinking during the formal operational stage is evident in the adolescent's verbal problem-solving ability. The concrete operational thinker needs to see the concrete elements A, B, and C to be able to make the logical inference that if A = B and B = C, then A = C, whereas the formal operational thinker can solve this problem merely through verbal presentation.

Another indication of the abstract quality of adolescents' thought is their increased tendency to think about thought itself. One adolescent commented, "I began thinking about why I was thinking what I was. Then I began thinking about why I was thinking about what I was thinking about what I was." If this sounds abstract, it is, and it characterizes the adolescent's enhanced focus on thought and its abstract qualities.

Accompanying the abstract nature of formal operational thought is thought full of idealism and possibilities, especially during the beginning of the formal operational stage. Adolescents engage in extended speculation about ideal characteristics—qualities they desire in themselves and in others. Such thoughts often lead adolescents to compare themselves with others in regard to such ideal standards. And their thoughts are often fantasy flights into future possibilities.

Might adolescents' ability to reason hypothetically and to evaluate what is ideal versus what is real lead them to engage in demonstrations such as this one promoting public education? What other causes might be attractive to adolescents' newfound cognitive abilities of hypothetical-deductive reasoning and idealistic thinking?
© Jim West/Alamy

Adolescents also think more logically. Children are likely to solve problems through trial and error; adolescents begin to think more as a scientist thinks, devising plans to solve problems and systematically testing solutions. This type of problem solving requires **hypothetical-deductive reasoning,** which involves creating a hypothesis and deducing its implications, which provides ways to test the hypothesis. Thus, formal operational thinkers develop hypotheses about ways to solve problems and then systematically deduce the best path to follow to solve the problem.

Evaluating Piaget's Theory

Researchers have challenged some of Piaget's ideas on the formal operational stage (Reyna & Zayas, 2014). Among their findings is that there is much more individual variation than Piaget envisioned: Only about one in three young adolescents is a formal operational thinker, and many American adults never become formal operational thinkers; neither do many adults in other cultures.

Furthermore, education in the logic of science and mathematics promotes the development of formal operational thinking. This point recalls a criticism of Piaget's theory: Culture and education exert stronger influences on cognitive development than Piaget argued (Gauvain & Perez, 2015).

Piaget's theory of cognitive development has been challenged on other points as well (Kuhn, 2013). Piaget conceived of stages as unitary structures of thought, with various aspects of a stage emerging at the same time. However, most contemporary developmentalists agree that cognitive development is not as stage-like as Piaget thought (Muller & Kerns, 2015; Ricco, 2015). Furthermore, children can be trained to reason at a higher cognitive stage, and some cognitive abilities emerge earlier than Piaget thought (Johnson & Hannon, 2015). Some understanding of the conservation of number has been demonstrated as early as age 3, although Piaget did not think it emerged until age 7. Other cognitive abilities can emerge later than Piaget thought (Kuhn, 2013).

hypothetical-deductive reasoning
Piaget's formal operational concept that adolescents have the cognitive ability to develop hypotheses, or best guesses, about ways to solve problems.

Despite these challenges to Piaget's ideas, we owe him a tremendous debt (Miller, 2011). Piaget was the founder of the present field of cognitive development, and he developed a long list of masterful concepts of enduring power and fascination: assimilation, accommodation, object permanence, egocentrism, conservation, and others. Psychologists also owe him the current vision of children as active, constructive thinkers. And they are indebted to him for creating a theory that has generated a huge volume of research on children's cognitive development.

Piaget was a genius when it came to observing children. His careful observations demonstrated inventive ways to discover how children act on, and adapt to, their world. Children need to make their experiences fit their schemes yet simultaneously adapt their schemes to reflect their experience. Piaget revealed how cognitive change is likely to occur if the context is structured to allow gradual movement to the next higher level. Concepts do not emerge suddenly, full-blown, but instead develop through a series of partial accomplishments that lead to increasingly comprehensive understanding (Sloutsky, 2015).

Adolescent Egocentrism

Adolescent egocentrism is the heightened self-consciousness of adolescents. David Elkind (1976) maintains that adolescent egocentrism has two key components—the imaginary audience and personal fable. The **imaginary audience** is adolescents' belief that others are as interested in them as they themselves are, as well as attention-getting behavior—attempts to be noticed, visible, and "on stage." For example, an eighth-grade boy might walk into the classroom thinking that all eyes are riveted on his spotty complexion. Adolescents sense that they are "on stage" in early adolescence, believing they are the main actors and all others are the audience.

The **personal fable** is the part of adolescent egocentrism involving a sense of uniqueness and invincibility (or invulnerability). For example, a 13-year-old says about herself: "No one understands me, particularly my parents. They have no idea of what I am feeling." Adolescents' sense of personal uniqueness makes them believe that no one can understand how they really feel. As part of their effort to retain a sense of personal uniqueness, they might craft a story about the self that is filled with fantasy in a world that is far removed from reality. Personal fables frequently show up in adolescent diaries.

Adolescents also often show a sense of invincibility or invulnerability. For example, during a conversation with another girl, 14-year-old Margaret says, "Are you kidding? I won't get pregnant." This sense of invincibility may lead adolescents to believe that they are invulnerable to dangers and catastrophes (such as deadly car wrecks) that happen to other people. As a result, some adolescents engage in risky behaviors such as drag racing, drug use, and having sexual intercourse without using contraceptives or barriers against STIs (Alberts, Elkind, & Ginsberg, 2007). However, some research studies suggest that rather than perceiving themselves to be invulnerable, adolescents tend to portray themselves as vulnerable to experiencing a premature death (Fischhoff & others, 2010; Reyna & Rivers, 2008).

Might social media such as Facebook serve as an amplification tool for adolescent egocentrism? A recent study found that Facebook usage does indeed increase self-interest (Chiou, Chen, & Liao, 2014).

Many adolescent girls spend long hours in front of the mirror. *How might this behavior be related to changes in adolescent cognitive and physical development?*

© Image Source/Jupiter Images RF

Information Processing

Deanna Kuhn (2009) discussed some important characteristics of adolescents' information processing and thinking. In her view, in the later years of childhood and continuing in adolescence, individuals approach cognitive levels that may or may not be achieved, in contrast with the largely universal cognitive levels that young children attain. By adolescence, considerable variation in cognitive functioning is

adolescent egocentrism The heightened self-consciousness of adolescents.

imaginary audience Involves adolescents' belief that others are as interested in them as they themselves are; attention-getting behavior motivated by a desire to be noticed, visible, and "on stage."

personal fable The part of adolescent egocentrism that involves an adolescent's sense of uniqueness and invincibility (or invulnerability).

present across individuals. This variability supports the argument that adolescents are producers of their own development to a greater extent than are children. That is, adolescents are more likely than children to initiate changes in thinking rather than depend on others, such as parents and teachers, to direct their thinking.

Executive Function

Kuhn (2009) argues that the most important cognitive change in adolescence is improvement in *executive function,* an umbrella-like concept that consists of a number of higher-level cognitive processes linked to the development of the prefrontal cortex. Executive function involves managing one's thoughts to engage in goal-directed behavior and to exercise self-control (Muller & Kerns, 2015). Our further coverage of executive function in adolescence focuses on cognitive control and decision making.

Cognitive Control Cognitive control involves effective control in a number of areas, including controlling attention, reducing interfering thoughts, and being cognitively flexible. Cognitive control continues to increase in adolescence and emerging adulthood (Casey, 2015; Luna & others, 2015; Somerville, 2016). Think about all the times adolescents need to engage in cognitive control, such as the following situations (Galinsky, 2010):

- making a real effort to stick with a task, avoiding interfering thoughts or environmental events, and instead doing what is most effective;

- stopping and thinking before acting to avoid blurting out something that a minute or two later they will wish they hadn't said;

- continuing to work on something that is important but boring when there is something a lot more fun to do, inhibiting their behavior and doing the boring but important task, saying to themselves, "I have to show the self-discipline to finish this."

Controlling attention is a key aspect of learning and thinking in adolescence and emerging adulthood. Distractions that can interfere with attention come from the external environment (other students talking while the student is trying to listen to a lecture, or the student turning on a laptop or phone during a lecture to look at Facebook, for example) or intrusive distractions from competing thoughts in the individual's mind. Self-oriented thoughts, such as worrying, self-doubt, and intense emotionally laden thoughts may interfere with focusing attention on thinking tasks (Walsh, 2011).

Decision Making Adolescence is a time of increased decision making—which friends to choose; which person to date; whether to have sex, buy a car, go to college, and so on (Reyna & others, 2015; Reyna & Zayas, 2014; Steinberg, 2015a, b: Monahan & others, 2016). How competent are adolescents at making decisions? Older adolescents are described as more competent than younger adolescents, who in turn are more competent than children (Keating, 1990). Compared with children, young adolescents are more likely to generate different options, examine a situation from a variety of perspectives, anticipate the consequences of decisions, and consider the credibility of sources. In risky situations it is important for an adolescent to quickly get the *gist,* or meaning, of what is happening and glean that the situation is a dangerous context, which can cue personal values that will protect the adolescent from making a risky decision (Reyna & Zayas, 2014).

How Would You...?

As an **educator,** how would you incorporate decision-making exercises into the school curriculum for adolescents?

Most people make better decisions when they are calm than when they are emotionally aroused. That may especially be true for adolescents, who have a tendency to be emotionally intense. The same adolescent who makes a wise decision when calm may make an unwise decision when emotionally aroused (Steinberg, 2015a, b).

The social context plays a key role in adolescent decision making (Cauffman & others, 2015; Monahan & others, 2016; Steinberg, 2015a, b). Adolescents' willingness to make risky decisions is more likely to occur in contexts where substances and other temptations are readily available (Reyna & Zayas, 2014). And the presence of peers in risk-taking situations increases the likelihood that adolescents will make risky decisions (Albert & Steinberg, 2011a, b). In a recent study, adolescents took greater risks and showed stronger preference for immediate rewards when they were with three same-aged peers than when alone (Silva, Chein, & Steinberg, 2016).

Adolescents need more opportunities to practice and discuss realistic decision making. Many real-world decisions on matters such as sex, drugs, and daredevil driving occur in an atmosphere of stress that includes time constraints and emotional involvement. One strategy for improving adolescent decision making is to provide more opportunities for them to engage in role playing and peer-group problem solving.

Schools

Our discussion of adolescents' schooling will focus on the transition from elementary to middle or junior high school, the characteristics of effective schools for adolescents, aspects of high school life that interfere with learning, and how adolescents can benefit from engaging in service learning.

The Transition to Middle or Junior High School

The first year of middle school or junior high school can be difficult for many students (Wigfield & others, 2015). In one study of the transition from sixth grade in an elementary school to seventh grade in a junior high school, adolescents' perceptions of the quality of their school life plunged in the seventh grade (Hirsch & Rapkin, 1987). Compared with their earlier feelings as sixth-graders, the seventh-graders were less satisfied with school, were less committed to school, and liked their teachers less. This occurred regardless of how academically successful the students were.

How Would You…?

As an **educator,** how would you design school programs to enhance students' smooth transition into middle school?

The transition to middle or junior high school takes place at a time when many changes—in the individual, the family, school—are occurring simultaneously (Simpkins, Fredricks, & Eccles, 2015; Wigfield, Tonks, & Klauda, 2016). These changes include puberty and concerns about body image; the emergence of at least some aspects of formal operational thought, including changes in social cognition; increased responsibility and decreased dependency on parents; change to a larger, more impersonal school structure; change from one teacher to many teachers and from a small, homogeneous set of peers to a larger, more heterogeneous set; and an increased focus on achievement and performance. Moreover, when students make the transition to middle or junior high school, they experience the **top-dog phenomenon,** moving from being the oldest, biggest, and most powerful students in the elementary school to being the youngest, smallest, and least powerful students.

There can also be positive aspects to this transition. Students are more likely to feel grown up, have more subjects from which to select and may be more challenged intellectually by academic work, have more opportunities to spend time with peers and locate compatible friends, and enjoy increased independence from direct parental monitoring.

Effective Schools for Young Adolescents

Educators and psychologists worry that junior high and middle schools have become watered-down versions of high schools, mimicking their curricular and extracurricular schedules. Critics argue that these schools should offer activities that reflect a wide range of individual differences in biological and psychological development among young adolescents. The Carnegie Foundation (1989) issued an extremely negative evaluation of U.S. middle schools. It concluded that most young adolescents attended massive, impersonal schools; were taught from irrelevant curricula; trusted few adults in school; and lacked access to health care and counseling. It recommended that the nation develop smaller "communities" or "houses" to lessen the impersonal nature of large middle schools, maintain lower

top-dog phenomenon The circumstance of moving from the top position in elementary school to the lowest position in middle or junior high school.

student-to-counselor ratios (10 to 1 instead of several hundred to 1), involve parents and community leaders in schools, develop new curricula, have teachers team teach in more flexibly designed curriculum blocks that integrate several disciplines, boost students' health and fitness with more in-school programs, and help students who need public health care to get it. Twenty-five years later, experts are still finding that middle schools throughout the nation need a major redesign if they are to be effective in educating adolescents (Roeser, 2016; Wigfield & others, 2015).

High School

Just as there are concerns about U.S. middle school education, so are there concerns about U.S. high school education (Eccles & Roeser, 2016; Kitsantas & Cleary, 2016). Critics stress that many high schools have low expectations for success and inadequate standards for learning. Critics also argue that too often high schools foster passivity instead of creating a variety of pathways for students to achieve an identity. Many students graduate from high school with inadequate reading, writing, and mathematical skills—including many who go on to college and have to enroll in remediation classes there. Other students drop out of high school and do not have skills that will allow them to obtain decent jobs, much less to be informed citizens.

The transition to high school can have problems just as the transition to middle school has. These problems may include the following (Eccles & Roeser, 2016): High schools are often even larger, more bureaucratic, and more impersonal than middle schools are; there isn't much opportunity for students and teachers to get to know each other, which can lead to distrust; and teachers too infrequently make content relevant to students' interests. Such experiences likely undermine the motivation of students.

Robert Crosnoe's (2011) book, *Fitting In, Standing Out,* highlighted another major problem with U.S. high schools: How the negative social aspects of adolescents' lives undermine their academic achievement. Adolescents become immersed in complex peer group cultures that demand conformity. High school is supposed to be about getting an education, but in reality for many youth it is more about navigating the social worlds of peer relations that may or may not value education and academic achievement. The adolescents who fail to fit in, especially those who are obese or gay, become stigmatized. Crosnoe recommends increased school counseling services, expanded extracurricular activities, and improved parental monitoring to reduce such problems. A recent study revealed that immigrant adolescents who participated in extracurricular activities improved their academic achievement and increased their school engagement (Camacho & Fuligni, 2015).

In the last half of the twentieth century and the first decade of the twenty-first century, U.S. high school dropout rates declined (National Center for Education Statistics, 2014). In the 1940s, more than half of U.S. 16- to 24-year-olds had dropped out of school; by 2012, this figure had decreased to 6.6 percent. The dropout rate of Latino adolescents remains high, although it has been decreasing considerably in the twenty-first century (from 28 percent in 2000 to 15.1 percent in 2010 to 12.7 percent in 2012). The lowest dropout rate in 2013 occurred for Asian American adolescents (3.4 percent), followed by non-Latino White adolescents (5.1 percent), African American adolescents (7.9 percent), and Latino adolescents (11.7 percent) (Child Trends, 2014).

Gender differences characterize U.S. dropout rates, with males more likely to drop out than females in 2012 (7.3 versus 5.9 percent) (National Center for Education Statistics, 2014). The gender gap in dropout rates for Latino adolescents still favors females—11.3 for females, 12.7 for males, but that gender gap has come down considerably in recent years.

National data on Native American adolescents are inadequate because statistics have been collected sporadically and/or from small samples. However, there are some indications that they may have the highest dropout rate. Also, the average U.S. high school dropout rates mask some very high dropout rates in low-income areas of inner cities. For example, in Detroit, Cleveland, and Chicago, dropout rates are higher than 50 percent. Also, the percentages cited earlier are for 16- to 24-year-olds. When dropout rates are

Students use the technology training center at Wellpinit Elementary/High School located on the Spokane Indian Reservation in the state of Washington. An important educational goal is to increase the high school graduation rate of Native American adolescents.

© Ed Kashi/VII Photo

calculated in terms of students who do not graduate from high school within four years, the percentages are much higher. Thus, in considering high school dropout rates, it is important to examine age, the number of years it takes to complete high school, and various contexts including ethnicity, gender, and location.

Students drop out of school for many reasons (Dupere & others, 2015; Schoeneberger, 2012). In one study, almost 50 percent of the dropouts cited school-related reasons for leaving school, such as not liking school or being expelled or suspended (Rumberger, 1983). Twenty percent of the dropouts (but 40 percent of the Latino students) cited economic reasons for leaving school. One-third of the female students dropped out for personal reasons such as pregnancy or marriage.

According to a research review, the most effective programs to discourage dropping out of high school provide early reading support, tutoring, counseling, and mentoring (Lehr & others, 2003). Clearly, then, early detection of children's school-related difficulties and getting children engaged with school in positive ways are important strategies for reducing the dropout rate (Crosnoe, Bonazzo, & Wu, 2015; Fall & Roberts, 2012).

Service Learning

Service learning is a form of education that promotes social responsibility and service to the community. Adolescents engage in activities such as tutoring, helping older adults, working in a hospital, assisting at a child-care center, or cleaning up a vacant lot to make it into a play area. An important goal of service learning is to encourage adolescents to become less self-centered and more strongly motivated to help others (Kackar-Cam & Schmidt, 2014). Service learning is often more effective when two conditions are met (Nucci, 2006): (1) giving students some degree of choice in the service activities in which they participate, and (2) providing students with opportunities to reflect about their participation.

What are some of the positive effects of service learning?

© Ariel Skelley/Blend Images/Getty Images RF

How Would You…?

As an **educator,** how would you devise a program to increase adolescents' motivation to participate in service learning?

A key feature of service learning is that it benefits not only adolescents but also the recipients of their help. One eleventh-grade student worked as a reading tutor for students from low-income backgrounds with reading skills well below their grade levels. Until she did the tutoring, she had not realized how many students had not experienced the same opportunities that she had when she was growing up. An especially rewarding moment was when one young girl told her, "I want to learn to read like you so I can go to college when I grow up."

Researchers have found that service learning also benefits adolescent development in other ways (Kielsmeier, 2011), including higher grades in school, increased goal setting, higher self-esteem, an improved sense of being able to make a difference for others, and an increased likelihood that the adolescents will serve as volunteers in the future (Hart, Matsuba, & Atkins, 2008). One study found that adolescent girls participated in service learning more than did adolescent boys (Webster & Worrell, 2008).

service learning A form of education that promotes social responsibility and service to the community.

Summary

The Nature of Adolescence

- Many stereotypes of adolescents are too negative. Most adolescents today successfully negotiate the path from childhood to adulthood. However, too many of today's adolescents are not provided with adequate opportunities and support to become competent adults. It is important to view adolescents as a heterogeneous group because different portraits of adolescents emerge, depending on the particular set of adolescents being described.

Physical Changes

- Puberty's determinants include nutrition, health, and heredity. Hormonal changes occurring in puberty are substantial. Puberty occurs approximately two years earlier for girls than for boys. Individual variation in pubertal changes is substantial. Adolescents show considerable interest in their body image, with girls having more negative body images than boys. Early-maturing girls are vulnerable to a number of risks.
- Changes in the brain during adolescence involve the thickening of the corpus callosum and a gap in maturation between the limbic system, which is the seat of emotions, and the prefrontal cortex, which functions in reasoning and self-regulation.
- Adolescence is a time of sexual exploration and sexual experimentation. About one in four sexually experienced adolescents acquires a sexually transmitted infection (STI). America's adolescent pregnancy rate has declined since the 1990s but is still higher than that of other industrialized nations.

Adolescent Health

- Adolescence is a critical juncture in health. Poor nutrition and lack of exercise are special concerns.
- Many adolescents stay up later than when they were children and are getting less sleep than they need.

- Accidents are the leading cause of death in adolescence.
- Although drug use in adolescence has declined in recent years, it still is a major concern.
- Eating disorders have increased in adolescence, with a substantial increase in the percentage of adolescents who are overweight. Two eating disorders that may emerge in adolescence are anorexia nervosa and bulimia nervosa.

Adolescent Cognition

- In Piaget's formal operational stage, thought is more abstract, idealistic, and logical than during the concrete operational stage. However, many adolescents are not formal operational thinkers.
- Adolescent egocentrism, which involves a heightened self-consciousness, reflects another cognitive change in adolescence in addition to Piaget's description of three cognitive stages.
- Changes in information processing in adolescence are mainly reflected in improved executive function, which includes advances in cognitive control and decision making.

Schools

- The transition to middle or junior high school is often stressful. One source of stress is the move from the top-dog to the lowest position in school.
- Some critics argue that a major redesign of U.S. middle schools is needed.
- The overall U.S. high school dropout rate declined considerably in the last half of the twentieth century, but the dropout rates for Native American and Latino adolescents remain very high.
- Service learning is linked to a number of positive benefits for adolescents.

Key Terms

adolescent egocentrism
amygdala
anorexia nervosa
bulimia nervosa
corpus callosum

gonads
hormones
hypothalamus
hypothetical-deductive
    reasoning

imaginary audience
limbic system
menarche
personal fable
pituitary gland

puberty
service learning
sexually transmitted infections
    (STIs)
top-dog phenomenon

10 Socioemotional Development in Adolescence

CHAPTER OUTLINE

IDENTITY
What Is Identity?
Erikson's View
Developmental Changes
Ethnic Identity

FAMILIES
Parental Management and Monitoring
Autonomy and Attachment
Parent-Adolescent Conflict

PEERS
Friendships
Peer Groups
Dating and Romantic Relationships

CULTURE AND ADOLESCENT DEVELOPMENT
Cross-Cultural Comparisons
Ethnicity
The Media

ADOLESCENT PROBLEMS
Juvenile Delinquency
Depression and Suicide
The Interrelation of Problems and Successful Prevention/Intervention Programs

© Huntstock, Inc./Alamy Stock Photo RF

Stories of Life-Span Development: Jewel Cash, Teen Dynamo

The mayor of the city says she is "everywhere." She persuaded the city's school committee to consider ending the practice of locking tardy students out of their classrooms. She also swayed a

neighborhood group to support her proposal for a winter jobs program. According to one city councilman, "People are just impressed with the power of her arguments and the sophistication of the argument" (Silva, 2005, pp. B1, B4). She is Jewel E. Cash, and she did all these things while she was a teenager attending the prestigious Boston Latin Academy.

Jewel was raised in one of Boston's housing projects by her mother, a single parent. During high school she was a member of the Boston Student Advisory Council, mentored children, volunteered at a women's shelter, managed and danced in two troupes, and participated in a neighborhood watch group—among other

Jewel Cash, seated next to her mother, participates in a crime watch meeting at a community center.

© Matthew J. Lee/The Boston Globe/Getty Images

277

activities. Jewel is far from typical, but her activities illustrate that cognitive and socioemotional development allows adolescents—even those from disadvantaged backgrounds—to be capable, effective individuals.

Significant changes characterize socioemotional development in adolescence. These changes include searching for identity. Changes also take place in the social contexts of adolescents' lives, with transformations occurring in relationships with families and peers in cultural contexts. Adolescents also may develop socioemotional problems such as delinquency and depression. ■

Identity

Jewel Cash told an interviewer from the *Boston Globe,* "I see a problem and I say, 'How can I make a difference?'. . . I can't take on the world, even though I can try. . . . I'm moving forward but I want to make sure I'm bringing people with me" (Silva, 2005, pp. B1, B4). Jewel's confidence and positive identity sound at least as impressive as her activities. This section examines how adolescents develop characteristics like these. How well did you understand yourself during adolescence, and how did you acquire the stamp of your identity? Is your identity still developing?

What Is Identity?

Questions about identity surface as common, virtually universal, concerns during adolescence. Some decisions made during adolescence might seem trivial: whom to date, whether or not to break up, which major to study, whether to study or play, whether or not to be politically active, and so on. Over the years of adolescence, however, such decisions begin to form the core of what the individual is all about as a human being—what is called his or her identity.

Identity is a self-portrait composed of many pieces, including these:

What are some important dimensions of identity?
© Art Grafts/The Image Bank/Getty Images

- The career and work path the person wants to follow (vocational/career identity)
- Whether the person is conservative, liberal, or middle-of-the-road (political identity)
- The person's spiritual beliefs (religious identity)
- Whether the person is single, married, divorced, and so on (relationship identity)
- The extent to which the person is motivated to achieve and is intellectually oriented (achievement, intellectual identity)
- Whether the person is heterosexual, homosexual, bisexual, or transgendered (sexual identity)
- Which part of the world or country a person is from and how intensely the person identifies with his or her cultural heritage (cultural/ethnic identity)
- The kind of things a person likes to do, which can include sports, music, hobbies, and so on (interests)
- The individual's personality characteristics, such as being introverted or extraverted, anxious or calm, friendly or hostile, and so on (personality)
- The individual's body image (physical identity)

Synthesizing the identity components can be a long-drawn-out process, with many negations and affirmations of various roles and faces (Kroger, 2015; McLean & Syed, 2015). Identity development takes place in bits and pieces. Decisions are not made once and for all, but have to be made again and again. Identity development does not happen neatly, and it does not happen cataclysmically (Beyers & Luyckx, 2016; Cote, 2015; Schwartz & others, 2015a, b, c; Waterman, 2015).

crisis Marcia's term for a period of identity development during which the adolescent is exploring alternatives.

Erikson's View

It was Erik Erikson (1950, 1968) who first understood that questions about identity are central to understanding adolescent development. Today, as a result of Erikson's masterful thinking and analysis, identity is considered a key aspect of adolescent development.

Recall that in Erikson's theory, his fifth developmental stage, which individuals experience during adolescence, is *identity versus identity confusion*. During this time, said Erikson, adolescents are faced with deciding who they are, what they are all about, and where they are going in life.

The search for an identity during adolescence is aided by a *psychosocial moratorium*, which is Erikson's term for the gap between childhood security and adult autonomy. During this period, society leaves adolescents relatively free of responsibilities and able to try out different identities. Adolescents in effect search their culture's identity files, experimenting with different roles and personalities. They may want to pursue one career one month (lawyer, for example) and another career the next month (doctor, actor, teacher, social worker, or astronaut, for example). They may dress neatly one day, sloppily the next. This experimentation is a deliberate effort on the part of adolescents to find out where they fit into the world. Most adolescents eventually discard undesirable roles.

Developmental Changes

Although questions about identity may be especially important during adolescence, identity formation neither begins nor ends during these years (Kroger, 2015). It begins with the appearance of attachment, the development of the sense of self, and the emergence of independence in infancy; the process reaches its final phase with a life review and integration in old age. What is important about identity development in adolescence, especially late adolescence, is that for the first time, physical development, cognitive development, and socioemotional development advance to the point at which the individual can begin to sort through and synthesize childhood identities and identifications to construct a viable path toward adult maturity.

How do individual adolescents go about the process of forming an identity? Eriksonian researcher James Marcia (1980, 1994) believes that Erikson's theory of identity development encompasses four *statuses* of identity, or ways of resolving the identity crisis: identity diffusion, identity foreclosure, identity moratorium, and identity achievement. What determines an individual's identity status? Marcia classifies individuals based on the existence or extent of their crisis or commitment (see Figure 1). **Crisis** is defined as a period of identity development during which the individual is

	Identity Status			
Position on Occupation and Ideology	**Identity Diffusion**	**Identity Foreclosure**	**Identity Moratorium**	**Identity Achievement**
Crisis	Absent	Absent	Present	Present
Commitment	Absent	Present	Absent	Present

Figure 1 Marcia's Four Statuses of Identity
According to Marcia, an individual's status in developing an identity can be described as identity diffusion, identity foreclosure, identity moratorium, or identity achievement. The status depends on the presence or absence of (1) a crisis or exploration of alternatives and (2) a commitment to an identity. *What is the identity status of most young adolescents?*

exploring alternatives. Most researchers use the term *exploration* rather than crisis. **Commitment** is personal investment in identity.

The four statuses of identity are described as follows:

- **Identity diffusion** is the status of individuals who have not yet experienced a crisis or made any commitments. Not only are they undecided about occupational and ideological choices, they are also likely to show little interest in such matters.

- **Identity foreclosure** is the status of individuals who have made a commitment but have not experienced a crisis. This occurs most often when parents hand down commitments to their adolescents, usually in an authoritarian way, before adolescents have had a chance to explore different approaches, ideologies, and vocations on their own.

- **Identity moratorium** is the status of individuals who are in the midst of a crisis but whose commitments are either absent or are only vaguely defined.

- **Identity achievement** is the status of individuals who have undergone a crisis and have made a commitment.

commitment Marcia's term for the part of identity development in which adolescents show a personal investment in forming an identity.

identity diffusion Marcia's term for adolescents who have not yet experienced a crisis (explored meaningful alternatives) or made any commitments.

identity foreclosure Marcia's term for adolescents who have made a commitment but have not experienced a crisis.

identity moratorium Marcia's term for adolescents who are in the midst of a crisis, but their commitments are either absent or vaguely defined.

identity achievement Marcia's term for adolescents who have undergone a crisis and have made a commitment.

How Would You...?

As a **psychologist,** how would you apply Marcia's theory of identity formation to describe your current identity status or that of adolescents you know?

Some critics argue that the identity status approach does not produce enough depth in understanding identity development (Cote, 2015). One way that researchers are now examining identity changes in depth is to use a *narrative approach*. This involves asking individuals to tell their life stories and evaluate the extent to which their stories are meaningful and integrated (McAdams & Zapata-Gietl, 2015; Singer & Kasmark, 2015). The term *narrative identity* "refers to the stories people construct and tell about themselves to define who they are for themselves and others. Beginning in adolescence and young adulthood, our narrative identities are the stories we live by" (McAdams, Josselson, & Lieblich, 2006, p. 4).

A recent study used both identity status and narrative approaches to examine college students' identity domains. In both approaches, the interpersonal domain was most frequently described (McLean & others, 2016). In the interpersonal domain, dating and friendships were frequently mentioned, although there was no mention of gender roles. In the narrative domain, family stories were common.

Researchers are developing a consensus that the key changes in identity are more likely to take place in emerging adulthood, the period from about 18 to 25 years of age (Arnett, 2015; Kroger, 2015; Schwartz & others, 2015a, b). For example, Alan Waterman (1985, 1992) has found that from the years preceding high school through the last few years of college, the number of individuals who are identity achieved increases, whereas the number of individuals who are identity diffused decreases. Many young adolescents are identity diffused. College upperclassmen are more likely than high school students or college freshmen to be identity achieved.

Why might college produce some key changes in identity? Increased complexity in the reasoning skills of college students combined with a wide range of new experiences that highlight contrasts between home and college and between themselves and others stimulate them to reach a higher level of integrating various dimensions of their identity (Phinney, 2008). College contexts serve as a virtual "laboratory" for identity development through such experiences as diverse coursework and exposure to peers from diverse backgrounds. Also, one of emerging adulthood's key themes is not having many social commitments, which gives individuals considerable independence in developing a life path (Arnett, 2015).

Resolution of the identity issue during adolescence and emerging adulthood does not mean that identity will be stable through the remainder of life (McAdams & Zapata-Gietl, 2015). Many individuals who develop positive identities follow what are called "MAMA" cycles; that is, their identity status changes from *moratorium* to *a*chievement to *m*oratorium to *a*chievement (Marcia, 1994). These cycles may be repeated throughout life (Francis, Fraser, & Marcia, 1989). Marcia (2002) points out that the first identity is just that—it is not, and should not be regarded as, the final product.

Ethnic Identity

Throughout the world, ethnic minority groups have struggled to maintain their ethnic identities while blending in with the dominant culture (Erikson, 1968). **Ethnic identity** is an enduring aspect of the self that includes a sense of membership in an ethnic group, along with the attitudes and feelings related to that membership (Syed & Juang, 2014; Tang, McLoyd, & Hallman, 2016). Most adolescents from ethnic minorities develop a *bicultural identity.* That is, they identify in some ways with their ethnic group and in other ways with the majority culture (Cooper, Gonzales, & Wilson, 2015; Fleischmann & Verkuyten, 2016).

For ethnic minority individuals, adolescence and emerging adulthood are often special junctures in their development (Azmitia, 2015; Gonzalez-Bracken, Bamaca-Colbert, & Allen, 2016). Although children are aware of some ethnic and cultural differences, individuals consciously confront their ethnicity for the first time in adolescence or emerging adulthood. Unlike children, adolescents and emerging adults have the ability to interpret ethnic and cultural information, to reflect on the past, and to speculate about the future. With their advancing cognitive skills of abstract thinking and self-reflection, adolescents (especially older adolescents) increasingly consider the meaning of their ethnicity and also have more ethnic-related experiences (O'Hara & others, 2012).

Researchers are also increasingly finding that a positive ethnic identity is related to positive outcomes for ethnic minority adolescents (Ikram & others, 2016; Williams & others, 2014). In a recent study, having pride in one's ethnic group and a strong ethnic identity were linked to lower substance use in adolescents (Grindal & Nieri, 2016). And in another recent study, strong ethnic group affiliation and connection were associated with reduced risk of psychiatric problems (Anglin & others, 2016).

The indicators of identity change often differ for each succeeding generation (Phinney & Vedder, 2013). First-generation immigrants are likely to be secure in their identities and unlikely to change much; they may or may not develop a new identity. The degree to which they begin to feel "American" appears to be related to whether or not they learn English, develop social networks beyond their ethnic group, and become culturally competent in their new country. Second-generation immigrants are more likely to think of themselves as "American," possibly because citizenship is granted at birth. Their ethnic identity is likely to be linked to retention of their ethnic language and social networks. In the third and later generations, the issues become more complex. Historical, contextual, and political factors that are unrelated to acculturation may affect the extent to which members of this generation retain their ethnic identities. For non-European ethnic groups, racism and discrimination influence whether ethnic identity is retained.

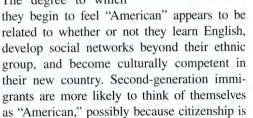

How Would You...?

As a **human development and family studies professional,** how would you design a community program that assists ethnic minority adolescents to develop a healthy bicultural identity?

One adolescent girl, 16-year-old Michelle Chinn, made these comments about ethnic identity development: "My parents do not understand that teenagers need to find out who they are, which means a lot of experimenting, a lot of mood swings, a lot of emotions and awkwardness. Like any teenager, I am facing an identity crisis. I am still trying to figure out whether I am a Chinese American or an American with Asian eyes."

© Red Chopsticks/Getty Images RF

ethnic identity An enduring, basic aspect of the self that includes a sense of membership in an ethnic group and the attitudes and feelings related to that membership.

Families

Adolescence typically alters the relationship between parents and their children. Among the most important aspects of family relationships in adolescence are those that involve parental management and monitoring, autonomy and attachment, and parent-adolescent conflict.

Parental Management and Monitoring

A key aspect of the managerial role of parenting is effective monitoring, which is especially important as children move into the adolescent years (Chu & others, 2015; Clark & others, 2015; Donaldson, Handren, & Crano, 2016; Kuntsche & Kuntsche, 2016; Low & Shortt, 2016; Sajber & others, 2016). Monitoring includes supervising adolescents' choice of social settings, activities, and friends, as well as their academic efforts. One study found that a high level of parental monitoring within the context of parental warmth was linked to positive academic outcomes for ethnic minority youth (Lowe & Dotterer, 2013). In further research, low parental monitoring was a key factor in predicting a developmental trajectory of delinquency and substance use in adolescence (Wang & others, 2014). In another recent study, higher parental monitoring reduced negative peer influence on adolescent risk taking (Wang & others, 2016a). And a recent meta-analysis revealed that a higher level of parental monitoring and rule enforcement were linked to later initiation of sexual intercourse and a greater use of condoms by adolescents (Dittus & others, 2015).

A current interest involving parental monitoring focuses on adolescents' management of their parents' access to information, especially strategies for disclosing or concealing information about their activities (Smetana, Robinson, & Rote, 2015). When parents engage in positive parenting practices, adolescents are more likely to disclose information. For example, disclosure increases when parents ask adolescents questions and when adolescents' relationship with parents is characterized by a high level of trust, acceptance, and quality (McElvaney, Greene, & Hogan, 2014). Researchers have found that adolescents' disclosure to parents about their whereabouts, activities, and friends is linked to positive adolescent adjustment (Smetana & Rote, 2015). A recent study of 10- to 18-year-olds found that lower adolescent disclosure to parents was linked to antisocial behavior (Criss & others, 2015).

Three ways that parents can engage in parental monitoring are (1) solicitation (asking questions), (2) control (enforcing disclosure rules), and (3) when youth don't comply, snooping. In a recent study, snooping was perceived by both adolescents and parents as the most likely of these three strategies to violate youths' privacy rights (Hawk, Becht, & Branje, 2016). Also, in this study, snooping was a relatively infrequent parental monitoring tactic but was a better indicator of problems in adolescent and family functioning than were solicitation and control.

Autonomy and Attachment

With most adolescents, parents are likely to find themselves engaged in a delicate balancing act, weighing competing needs for autonomy and control, for independence and connection.

The Push for Autonomy

The typical adolescent's push for autonomy and responsibility puzzles and angers many parents. As parents see their teenager slipping from their grasp, they may have an urge to take stronger control. Heated emotional exchanges may ensue, with either side calling names, making threats, and doing whatever seems necessary to gain control. Parents may feel frustrated because they *expect* their teenager to heed their advice, to want to spend time with the family, and to grow up to do what is right. Most parents anticipate that their teenager will have some difficulty adjusting to the changes that adolescence brings, but few parents imagine and predict just how strong an adolescent's desires will be to spend time with peers or how intensely adolescents will want to show that it is they—not their parents—who are responsible for their successes and failures.

Adolescents' ability to attain autonomy and gain control over their behavior is facilitated by appropriate adult reactions to their desire for control (McElhaney & Allen, 2012). At the onset of adolescence, the average individual does not have the knowledge to make appropriate or mature decisions in all areas of life. As the adolescent pushes for autonomy, the wise adult relinquishes control in those areas where the adolescent can make reasonable decisions, but continues to guide the adolescent to make reasonable decisions in areas in which the adolescent's knowledge is more limited. Gradually, adolescents acquire the ability to make mature decisions on their own.

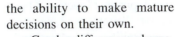

Gender differences characterize autonomy-granting in adolescence. Boys are given more independence than girls. In one study, this was especially true in U.S. families with a traditional gender-role orientation (Bumpus, Crouter, & McHale, 2001). Also, Latino parents protect and monitor their daughters more closely than is the case for non-Latino parents (Romo, Mireles-Rios, & Lopez-Tello, 2014). Although Latino cultures may place a stronger emphasis on parental authority and restrict adolescent autonomy, a recent study revealed that regardless of where they were born, Mexican-origin adolescent girls living in the United States expected autonomy at an earlier age than their mothers preferred (Bamaca-Colbert & others, 2012).

What kinds of strategies can parents use to guide adolescents in effectively handling their increased motivation for autonomy?
© Myrleen Pearson/ PhotoEdit

According to one adolescent girl, Stacey Christensen, age 16: "I am lucky enough to have open communication with my parents. Whenever I am in need or just need to talk, my parents are there for me. My advice to parents is to let your teens grow at their own pace, be open with them so that you can be there for them. We need guidance; our parents need to help but not be too overwhelming."
© Stockbyte/Getty Images RF

The Role of Attachment

Recall that one of the most widely discussed aspects of socioemotional development in infancy is secure attachment to caregivers (Pasco-Fearon & others, 2016; Thompson, 2015, 2016). In the past decade, researchers have explored whether secure attachment also might be an important concept in adolescents' relationships with their parents (Kobak & Kerig, 2015). Researchers have found that securely attached adolescents are less likely than those who are insecurely attached to have emotional difficulties and to engage in problem behaviors such as juvenile delinquency and drug abuse (Allen & Tan, 2016; de Vries & others, 2016; Hoeve & others, 2012). A recent study involving adolescents and emerging adults from 15 to 20 years of age found that insecure attachment to mothers was linked to becoming depressed and remaining depressed (Agerup & others, 2015). In a longitudinal study, Joseph Allen and colleagues (2009) found that secure attachment at 14 years of age was linked to a number of positive outcomes at 21 years of age, including relationship competence, financial/career competence, and fewer problematic behaviors. And in a research review, the most consistent outcomes of secure attachment in adolescence involved positive peer relations and development of the adolescent's capacity to regulate emotions (Allen & Miga, 2010).

Parent-Adolescent Conflict

Although parent-adolescent conflict increases in early adolescence, it does not reach the tumultuous proportions G. Stanley Hall envisioned at the beginning of the twentieth century (Bornstein, Jager, & Steinberg, 2013). Rather, much of the conflict involves the everyday events of family life, such as keeping a bedroom clean, dressing neatly, getting home by a certain time, and not talking endlessly on the phone. The conflicts rarely involve major dilemmas such as drugs or delinquency.

Conflict with parents often escalates during early adolescence, remains somewhat stable during the high school years, and then lessens as the adolescent reaches 17 to 20 years of age. Parent-adolescent relationships become more positive if adolescents go away to college than if they attend college while living at home (Sullivan & Sullivan, 1980).

The everyday conflicts that characterize parent-adolescent relationships may actually serve a positive developmental function. These minor disputes and negotiations facilitate the adolescent's transition from being dependent on parents to becoming an autonomous individual. Recognizing that conflict and negotiation can serve a positive developmental function can tone down parental hostility.

The old model of parent-adolescent relationships suggested that as adolescents mature they detach themselves from parents and move into a world of autonomy apart from parents. The old model also suggested that parent-adolescent conflict is intense and stressful throughout adolescence. The new model emphasizes that parents serve as important attachment figures and support systems while adolescents explore a wider, more complex social world. The new model also emphasizes that in most families, parent-adolescent conflict is moderate rather than severe and that the everyday negotiations and minor disputes not only are normal but also can serve the positive developmental function of helping the adolescent make the transition from childhood dependency to adult independence (see Figure 2).

Still, a high degree of conflict characterizes some parent-adolescent relationships (Moed & others, 2015; Skinner & McHale, 2016). And this prolonged, intense conflict is associated with various adolescent problems: movement out of the home, juvenile delinquency, school dropout, pregnancy and early marriage, membership in religious cults, and drug abuse (Brook & others, 1990). For example, a recent study found that a higher level of parent-adolescent conflict was associated with higher adolescent anxiety, depression, and aggression, and lower self-esteem (Smokowski & others, 2016). Also, a recent study found that high parent-adolescent conflict was associated with a lower level of empathy in adolescents throughout the six years of the study from 13 to 18 years of age (Van Lissa & others, 2015).

When families emigrate to another country, adolescents typically acculturate more quickly to the norms and values of their new country than do their parents (Fuligni, 2012).

Old Model

Autonomy, detachment from parents; parent and peer worlds are isolated

Intense, stressful conflict throughout adolescence; parent-adolescent relationships are filled with storm and stress on virtually a daily basis

New Model

Attachment and autonomy; parents are important support systems and attachment figures; adolescent-parent and adolescent-peer worlds have some important connections

Moderate parent-adolescent conflict is common and can serve a positive developmental function; conflict greater in early adolescence

Figure 2 Old and New Models of Parent-Adolescent Relationships
© BananaStock/PunchStock RF

This likely occurs because of immigrant adolescents' exposure in school to the language and culture of the host country. The norms and values immigrant adolescents experience are especially likely to diverge from those of their parents in areas such as autonomy and romantic relationships. Such divergences are likely to increase parent-adolescent conflict in immigrant families. Andrew Fuligni (2012) argues that these conflicts aren't always expressed openly but are often present in underlying feelings. For example, immigrant adolescents may feel that their parents want them to give up their personal interests for the sake of the family, and the adolescents don't think this is fair. Such acculturation-based conflict focuses on issues related to core cultural values and is likely to occur in immigrant families, such as Latino and Asian American families, who come to the United States to live (Juang & Umana-Taylor, 2012). In a recent study of Chinese American families, parent-adolescent conflict was linked to a sense of alienation between parents and adolescents, which in turn was related to more depressive symptoms, delinquent behavior, and lower academic achievement (Hou, Kim, & Wang, 2016).

Peers

Peers play powerful roles in the lives of adolescents (Wentzel, 2015; Wentzel & Ramani, 2016). When you think back to your own adolescent years, you probably recall many of your most enjoyable moments as experiences shared with peers. Peer relations undergo important changes in adolescence, including changes in friendships, peer groups, and the beginning of romantic relationships.

Friendships

For most children, being popular with their peers is a strong motivator. Beginning in early adolescence, however, teenagers typically prefer to have a smaller number of friendships that are more intense and intimate than those of young children.

Harry Stack Sullivan (1953) was the most influential theorist to discuss the importance of adolescent friendships. In contrast with other psychoanalytic theorists who focused almost exclusively on parent-child relationships, Sullivan argued that friends are also important in shaping the development of children and adolescents. Everyone, said Sullivan, has basic social needs, such as the need for tenderness (secure attachment), playful companionship, social acceptance, intimacy, and sexual relations. Whether or not these needs are fulfilled largely determines our emotional well-being. For example, if the need for playful companionship goes unmet, then we become bored and depressed; if the need for social acceptance is not met, we suffer a diminished sense of self-worth.

During adolescence, said Sullivan, friends become increasingly important in meeting social needs. In particular, Sullivan argued that the need for intimacy intensifies during early adolescence, motivating teenagers to seek out close friends. If adolescents fail to forge such close friendships, they experience loneliness and a reduced sense of self-worth. The nature of relationships with friends during adolescence can foreshadow the quality of romantic relationships in emerging adulthood. For example, a longitudinal study revealed that having more secure relationships with close friends at age 16 was linked with more positive romantic relationships at age 20 to 23 (Simpson & others, 2007).

Many of Sullivan's ideas have withstood the test of time. For example, adolescents report disclosing intimate and personal information to their friends more often than

What changes take place in friendship during the adolescent years?
© SW Productions/ Getty Images RF

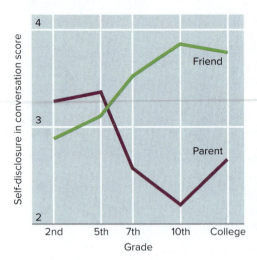

Figure 3 Developmental Changes in Self-Disclosing Conversations

Self-disclosing conversations with friends increased dramatically in adolescence while declining in an equally dramatic fashion with parents. However, self-disclosing conversations with parents began to pick up somewhat during the college years. The measure of self-disclosure involved a 5-point rating scale completed by the children and youth, with a higher score representing greater self-disclosure. The data shown represent the means for each age group.

do younger children (Buhrmester, 1998) (see Figure 3). Adolescents also say they depend more on friends than on parents to satisfy their needs for companionship, reassurance of worth, and intimacy. The ups and downs of experiences with friends shape adolescents' well-being (Prinstein & Giletta, 2016). Adolescent girls are more likely to disclose information about problems to a friend than are adolescent boys (Rose & others, 2012).

Although having friends can be a developmental advantage, not all friendships are alike and the quality of friendship matters (Choukas-Bradley & Prinstein, 2016; Rubin & others, 2016; Wentzel & Muenks, 2016). People differ in the company they keep—that is, who their friends are. It is a developmental disadvantage to have coercive, conflict-ridden, and poor-quality friendships (Chen, Drabick, & Burgers, 2015; Graber, Turner, & Madill, 2016; Rubin, Bukowski, & Bowker, 2015). A recent study revealed that having friends who engage in delinquent behavior is associated with early onset and more persistent delinquency (Evans, Simons, & Simons, 2015). Another recent study found that adolescents adapted their smoking and drinking behavior to that of their best friends (Wang & others, 2016b).

Although most adolescents develop friendships with individuals who are close to their own age, some adolescents become best friends with younger or older individuals. Adolescents who interact with older youth engage in deviant behavior more frequently, but it is not known whether the older youth guide younger adolescents toward deviant behavior or whether the younger adolescents were already prone to deviant behavior before they developed friendships with older youth.

Peer Groups

How extensive is peer pressure in adolescence? What roles do cliques and crowds play in adolescents' lives? As we see next, researchers have found that the standards of peer groups and the influence of crowds and cliques become increasingly important during adolescence.

Peer Pressure

Young adolescents conform more to peer standards than children do (Choukas-Bradley & Prinstein, 2016). Around the eighth and ninth grades, conformity to peers—especially to their antisocial standards—peaks (Brown & Larson, 2009). At this point, adolescents are most likely to go along with a peer to steal hubcaps off a car, paint graffiti on a wall, or steal cosmetics from a store counter. One study found that U.S. adolescents are more likely than Japanese adolescents to put pressure on their peers to resist parental influence (Rothbaum & others, 2000). Adolescents are more likely to conform to their peers when they are uncertain about their social identity and when they are in the presence of someone they perceive to have higher status than they do (Prinstein & Giletta, 2016). Also, a recent study found that boys were more likely to be influenced by peer pressure involving sexual behavior than were girls (Widman & others, 2016).

What characterizes peer pressure in adolescence?

© Christin Rose/Getty Images RF

Cliques and Crowds

Cliques and crowds assume more important roles during adolescence than during childhood (Brown, 2011). **Cliques** are small groups that range from 2 to about 12 individuals and average about 5 or 6 individuals. The clique members are usually of the same sex and about the same age.

Cliques can form because adolescents engage in similar activities, such as being in a club or on a sports team. Some cliques also form because of friendship. Several adolescents may form a clique because they have spent time with each other, share mutual interests, and enjoy each other's company. Not necessarily friends to start with, they often develop a friendship if they stay in the clique. What do adolescents do in cliques? They share ideas and hang out together. Often they develop an in-group identity in which they believe that their clique is better than other cliques.

Crowds are larger than cliques and less personal. Adolescents are usually members of a crowd based on reputation, and they may or may not spend much time together. Many crowds are defined by the activities adolescents engage in (such as "jocks" who are good at sports or "druggies" who take drugs).

clique A small group that ranges from 2 to about 12 individuals, averaging about 5 or 6 individuals, and often consists of adolescents who engage in similar activities.

crowd A larger group structure than a clique, a crowd is usually formed based on reputation, and members may or may not spend much time together.

Dating and Romantic Relationships

Adolescents spend considerable time either dating or thinking about dating (Davila, Capaldi, & La Greca, 2016; Furman & Rose, 2015). Dating can be a form of recreation, a source of status, a setting for learning about close relationships, and a way to find a mate.

Developmental Changes in Dating and Romantic Relationships

Three stages characterize the development of romantic relationships in adolescence (Connolly & McIsaac, 2009):

1. *Entering into romantic attractions and affiliations at about age 11 to 13.* This initial stage is triggered by puberty. From age 11 to 13, adolescents become intensely interested in romance and it dominates many conversations with same-sex friends. Developing a crush on someone is common, and the crush often is shared with a same-sex friend. Young adolescents may or may not interact with the individual who is the object of their infatuation. When dating occurs, it usually takes place in a group setting.

2. *Exploring romantic relationships at approximately age 14 to 16.* At this point in adolescence, two types of romantic involvement occur: (a) *Casual dating* emerges between individuals who are mutually attracted. These dating experiences are often short-lived, last a few months at best, and usually endure no longer than a few weeks. (b) *Dating in groups* is common and reflects the importance of peers in adolescents' lives. A friend often acts as a third-party facilitator of a potential dating relationship by communicating their friend's romantic interest and determining whether the other person feels a similar attraction.

3. *Consolidating dyadic romantic bonds at about age 17 to 19.* At the end of the high school years, more serious romantic relationships develop. This stage is characterized by the formation of strong emotional bonds more closely resembling those in adult romantic relationships. These bonds often are more stable and enduring than earlier bonds, typically lasting one year or more.

What are some developmental changes in dating and romantic relationships in adolescence?

© Digital Vision/Getty Images RF

Two variations on these stages in the development of romantic relationships in adolescence involve early and late bloomers (Connolly & McIsaac, 2009). *Early bloomers* include 15 to 20 percent of 11- to 13-year-olds who say that they currently are in a romantic relationship and 35 percent who indicate that they have had some prior experience in romantic relationships. *Late bloomers* comprise approximately 10 percent of 17- to 19-year-olds who say that they have had no experience with romantic relationships and another 15 percent who report that they have not engaged in any romantic relationships that lasted more than four months. A recent study found that early bloomers externalized problem behaviors through adolescence more than their on-time and late-bloomer counterparts (Connolly & others, 2013).

Dating in Gay and Lesbian Youth

Recently, researchers have begun to study romantic relationships among gay and lesbian youth (Savin-Williams, 2015). Many sexual minority youth date other-sex peers, which can help them to clarify their sexual orientation or disguise it from others (Savin-Williams & Cohen, 2015). Most gay and lesbian youth have had some same-sex sexual experience, often with peers who are "experimenting," and then go on to a primarily heterosexual orientation (Diamond & Savin-Williams, 2015).

Sociocultural Contexts and Dating

The sociocultural context exerts a powerful influence on adolescents' dating patterns (Moosmann & Roosa, 2015). This influence may be seen in differences in dating patterns among ethnic groups within the United States. Values, religious beliefs, and traditions often dictate the age at which dating begins, how much freedom in dating is allowed, whether dates must be chaperoned by adults or parents, and the roles of males and females in dating. For example, Latino and Asian American cultures have more conservative standards regarding adolescent dating than does the Anglo-American culture. Dating may become a source of conflict within a family if the parents have immigrated from cultures in which dating begins at a late age, little freedom in dating is allowed, dates are chaperoned, and dating is especially restricted for adolescent girls. A recent study found that mother-daughter conflict in Mexican American families was linked to an increase in daughters' romantic involvement (Tyrell & others, 2016). When immigrant adolescents choose to adopt the ways of the dominant U.S. culture (such as unchaperoned dating), they often clash with parents and extended-family members who have more traditional values.

Dating and Adjustment

Researchers have linked dating and romantic relationships with various measures of how well adjusted adolescents are (Davila, Capaldi, & La Greca, 2016). For example, one study of 200 tenth-graders revealed that the more romantic experiences they had had, the more likely they were to report high levels of social acceptance, friendship competence, and romantic competence; however, having more romantic experience also was linked to a higher level of substance use, delinquency, and sexual behavior (Furman, Low, & Ho, 2009).

Dating and romantic relationships at an early age can be especially problematic (Furman & Rose, 2015). One study found that romantic activity was linked to depression in early adolescent girls (Starr & others, 2012). Researchers also have found that early dating and "going with" someone are linked with adolescent pregnancy and problems at home and school (Florsheim, Moore, & Edgington, 2003).

How Would You...?

As a **psychologist,** how would you explain the risks of dating and romantic relationships during early adolescence?

Culture and Adolescent Development

We live in an increasingly diverse world, one that includes more extensive contact between adolescents from different cultures and ethnic groups. In this section, we explore these differences as they relate to adolescents. We explore how adolescents in various cultures spend their time, and some of the rites of passage they undergo. We also examine how ethnicity and the media affect U.S. adolescents and influence their development.

Asian Indian adolescents in a marriage ceremony.
© Prakash Hatvalne/AP Images

Cross-Cultural Comparisons

What traditions remain for adolescents around the globe? What circumstances are changing adolescents' lives?

Traditions and Changes in Adolescence Around the Globe

Depending on the culture being observed, adolescence may involve many different experiences (Arnett, 2015).

Health Adolescent health and well-being have improved in some respects but not in others. Overall, fewer adolescents around the world die from infectious diseases and malnutrition now than in the past (UNICEF, 2016). However, a number of adolescent health-compromising behaviors (especially illicit drug use and unprotected sex) are increasing in frequency. Extensive increases in the rates of HIV in adolescents have occurred in many sub-Saharan countries (UNICEF, 2016).

How Would You…?

As a **health-care professional**, how would you explain to policy makers and insurance providers the importance of cultural context when creating guidelines for adolescent health coverage?

Muslim school in Middle East with boys only.
© AFP/Getty Images

Gender Around the world, the experiences of male and female adolescents continue to be quite different (Larson, Wilson, & Rickman, 2009). Except in a few regions such as Japan, the Philippines, and Western countries, males have far greater access to educational opportunities than females do (UNICEF, 2016). In many countries, adolescent females have less freedom than males to pursue a variety of careers and engage in various leisure activities. Gender differences in sexual expression are widespread, especially in India, Southeast Asia, Latin America, and Arab countries where there are far more restrictions on the sexual activity of adolescent females than on that of males. These gender differences do appear to be narrowing over time, however. In some countries, educational and career opportunities for women are expanding, and control over adolescent girls' romantic and sexual relationships is weakening.

Street youth in Rio de Janeiro.
© Tom Stoddart/Getty Images

Family In some countries, adolescents grow up in closely knit families with extensive extended-kin networks that retain a traditional way of life. For example, in Arab countries, "adolescents are taught strict codes of conduct and loyalty" (Brown & Larson, 2002, p. 6). However, in Western countries such as the United States, parenting is less authoritarian than in the past, and much larger numbers of adolescents are growing up in divorced families and stepfamilies.

In many countries around the world, current trends "include greater family mobility, migration to urban areas, family members working in distant cities or countries, smaller families, fewer extended-family households, and increases in mothers' employment" (Brown & Larson, 2002, p. 7). Unfortunately, many of these changes may reduce the ability of families to spend time with their adolescents.

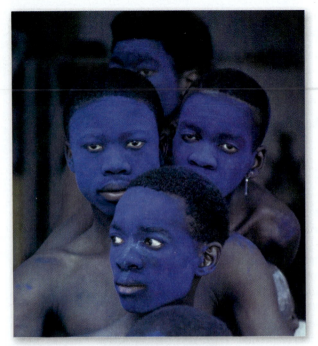

These Congolese Kota boys painted their faces as part of a rite of passage to adulthood. *What rites of passage do American adolescents have?*

© Daniel Laine/Gamma Rapho

Peers Some cultures give peers a stronger role in adolescence than other cultures do (Brown & Larson, 2002). In most Western nations, peers figure prominently in adolescents' lives, in some cases taking on roles that would otherwise be assumed by parents. Among street youth in South America, the peer network serves as a surrogate family that supports survival in dangerous and stressful settings. In other regions of the world, such as in Arab countries, peer relations are restricted, especially for girls (Booth, 2002).

Adolescents' lives, then, are shaped by a combination of change and tradition. Researchers have found both similarities and differences in the experiences of adolescents in different countries (Larson & Dawes, 2015).

Rites of Passage

Another variation in the experiences of adolescents in different cultures is whether the adolescents go through a rite of passage. Some societies have elaborate ceremonies that signal the adolescent's move to maturity and achievement of adult status (Ember, Ember, & Peregrine, 2015). A **rite of passage** is a ceremony or ritual that marks an individual's transition from one status to another. Most rites of passage focus on the transition to adult status. In many primitive cultures, rites of passage are the avenue through which adolescents gain access to sacred adult practices, to knowledge, and to sexuality. These rites often involve dramatic practices intended to facilitate the adolescent's separation from the immediate family, especially the mother. The transformation is usually characterized by some form of ritual death and rebirth, or by means of contact with the spiritual world. Bonds are forged between the adolescent and the adult instructors through shared rituals, hazards, and secrets to allow the adolescent to enter the adult world. This kind of ritual provides a forceful and discontinuous entry into the adult world at a time when the adolescent is perceived to be ready for the change.

An especially rich tradition of rites of passage for adolescents has prevailed in African cultures, especially sub-Saharan Africa. Under the influence of Western industrialized culture, many of these rites are disappearing today, although they are still prevalent in locations where formal education is not readily available.

Do we have such rites of passage for American adolescents? We certainly do not have universal formal ceremonies that mark the passage from adolescence to adulthood. Certain religious and social groups do, however, have initiation ceremonies that indicate that an advance in maturity has been reached: the Jewish bar and bat mitzvah, the Catholic confirmation, and social debuts, for example. School graduation ceremonies come the closest to being culture-wide rites of passage in the United States. The high school graduation ceremony has become nearly universal for middle-class adolescents and increasing numbers of adolescents from low-income backgrounds.

How Would You…?

As an **educator,** how would you modify high school graduation to make it a more meaningful rite of passage for adolescents in the United States?

Ethnicity

Earlier in this chapter we explored the identity development of ethnic minority adolescents. Here, we further examine immigration and the relationship between ethnicity and socioeconomic status.

rite of passage A ceremony or ritual that marks an individual's transition from one status to another. Most rites of passage focus on the transition to adult status.

Immigration

Relatively high rates of immigration are contributing to the growing proportion of ethnic minority adolescents and emerging adults in the United States (Fuligni & Tsai, 2015; Kane & others, 2016). Immigrant families are those in which at least one of the parents is born outside of the country of residence. Variations in immigrant families involve whether one or both parents are foreign born, whether the child was born in the host country, and the ages at which immigration took place for both the parents and the children (Kim & others, 2015).

What are some cultural adaptations these Mexican American girls likely have made as immigrants to the United States?

© Caroline Woodham/Photographer's Choice RF/ Getty Images RF

Different models have been proposed as to whether children and adolescents in immigrant families are more vulnerable or more successful in relation to the general population of children and adolescents (Crosnoe & Fuligni, 2012). Historically, *an immigrant risk model* was emphasized, concluding that youth of immigrants had a lower level of well-being and were at risk for more problems. More recently, an *immigrant paradox model* has been proposed, emphasizing that despite the many cultural, socioeconomic, language, and other obstacles that immigrant families face, their youth show a high level of well-being and fewer problems than native-born youth (Garcia Coll & others, 2012). Based on current research, some support exists for each model. Robert Crosnoe and Andrew Fuligni (2012, p. 1473) reached the following conclusion:

> Some children from immigrant families are doing quite well, some less so, depending on the characteristics of migration itself (including the nation of origin) and their families' circumstances in their new country (including their position in socioeconomic and race-ethnic stratification systems).

What are some of the circumstances immigrants face that challenge their adjustment? Immigrants often experience stressors uncommon to or less prominent among longtime residents, such as language barriers, dislocations and separations from support networks, the dual struggle to preserve identity and to acculturate, and changes in SES status (Kao & Huang, 2015; Schwartz & others, 2015c). Many individuals in immigrant families are dealing with the problem of being undocumented. Living in an undocumented family can affect children's and adolescents' developmental outcomes through parents being unwilling to sign up for services for which they are eligible, through conditions linked to low-wage work and lack of benefits, through stress, and through a lack of cognitive stimulation in the home. Consequently, when working with adolescents and their immigrant families, counselors need to adapt intervention programs to optimize cultural sensitivity (Gonzales & others, 2016; Sue & others, 2015).

The ways in which ethnic minority families deal with stress depend on many factors (Slopen & others, 2015; Spencer & Swanson, 2016). Whether the parents are native-born or immigrants, how long the family has been in the United States, its socioeconomic status, and its national origin all make a difference. A recent study revealed that parents' education before migrating was strongly linked to their children's academic achievement (Pong & Landale, 2012). Another recent study found that first-generation immigrant adolescents had more internalizing problems (anxiety and depression, for example) than second-generation immigrants (Katsiaficas & others, 2013).

Ethnicity and Socioeconomic Status

Much of the research on ethnic minority adolescents has failed to tease apart the influences of ethnicity and socioeconomic status (SES). These factors can interact in ways that exaggerate the influence of ethnicity because ethnic minority individuals are overrepresented in the lower socioeconomic levels of American society (Cushner, McClelland, & Safford, 2015). Consequently, researchers too often have given ethnic explanations for aspects of adolescent development that were largely attributable to SES.

Not all ethnic minority families are poor. However, poverty contributes to the stressful life experiences of many ethnic minority adolescents (Duncan, Magnuson, & Votruba-Drzal, 2015; Wadsworth & others, 2016). Thus, many ethnic minority adolescents experience a double disadvantage: (1) prejudice, discrimination, and bias because of their ethnic minority status; and (2) the stressful effects of poverty (McCartney & Yoshikawa, 2015).

Although some ethnic minority youth come from middle-income backgrounds, economic advantage does not entirely enable them to escape the prejudice, discrimination, and bias associated with being a member of an ethnic minority group (Golnick & Chinn, 2017; Marks & others, 2015). Even Japanese Americans, who are often characterized as a "model minority" because of their strong achievement orientation and family cohesiveness, still experience stress associated with ethnic minority status.

The Media

The culture adolescents experience involves not only cultural values, SES, and ethnicity, but also media influences (Calvert, 2015; Maloy & others, 2017; Roblyer, 2016). To better understand various aspects of U.S. adolescents' media use, the Kaiser Family Foundation funded national surveys in 1999, 2004, and 2009. The 2009 survey documented that adolescent media use had increased dramatically in the past decade (Rideout, Foehr, & Roberts, 2010). Today's youth live in a world in which they are encapsulated by media. In this 2009 survey, 8- to 11-year-olds used media 5 hours and 29 minutes a day, but 11- to 14-year-olds used media an average of 8 hours and 40 minutes a day, and 15- to 18-year-olds an average of 7 hours and 58 minutes a day. Thus, media use jumps more than 3 hours in early adolescence! Adding up the daily media use figures to obtain weekly media use leads to the staggering levels of more than 60 hours a week of media use by 11- to 14-year-olds and almost 56 hours a week by 15- to 18-year-olds!

A major trend in the use of technology is the dramatic increase in media multitasking (Courage & others, 2015). In the 2009 survey, when the amount of time spent multitasking was included in computing media use, 11- to 14-year-olds spent nearly 12 hours a day (compared with almost 9 hours a day when multitasking was not included) exposed to media (Rideout, Foehr, & Roberts, 2010)! A recent study of 8- to 12-year-old girls also found that a higher level of media multitasking was linked to negative social well-being while a higher level of face-to-face communication was associated with positive social well-being indicators, such as greater social success, feeling more normal, and having fewer friends whom parents thought were a bad influence (Pea & others, 2012). In another study, heavy media multitaskers were more likely to be depressed and have social anxiety than their counterparts who engaged in a lower incidence of media multitasking (Becker, Alzahabi, & Hopwood, 2013). And in a recent research review, a higher level of media multitasking was linked to lower levels of school achievement, executive function, and growth mindset in adolescents (Cain & others, 2016).

In some cases, media multitasking—such as text messaging, listening to an iPod, and updating a YouTube site simultaneously—is engaged in while doing homework. It is hard to imagine that this allows a student to do homework efficiently, although there is little research on media multitasking. A recent research review concluded that at a general level, using digital technologies (surfing the Internet, texting someone) while engaging in a learning task (reading, listening to a lecture) distracts learners and impairs performance on many tasks (Courage & others, 2015). Also in this research, it was concluded that when driving subtasks such as various perceptual-motor activities (steering control, changing lanes, maneuvering through traffic, braking, and acceleration) and ongoing cognitive tasks (planning, decision making, or maintaining a conversation with a passenger) are combined with interactive in-vehicle devices (phones, navigation aids, portable music devices), the task of driving becomes more complex and the potential for distraction high.

Mobile media, such as cell phones and iPods, are mainly driving the increased media use by adolescents. For example, in the 2004 survey, only 18 percent of youth owned an iPod or MP3 player but in 2009, 76 percent owned them; in 2004, 39 percent owned a cell phone, a figure that jumped to 66 percent in 2009 (Rideout, Foehr, & Roberts, 2010),

The digitally mediated social environment of adolescents and emerging adults includes e-mail, instant messaging, social networking sites such as Facebook, chat rooms, videosharing and photosharing, multiplayer online computer games, and virtual worlds (Lever-Duffy & McDonald, 2015; Smaldino & others, 2015). Most of these digitally mediated social interactions began on computers but more recently have also shifted to cell phones, especially smartphones.

A national survey revealed dramatic increases in adolescents' use of social media and text messaging (Lenhart, 2015a). In 2015, 92 percent of U.S. 13- to 17-year-olds reported using social networking sites daily. Twenty-four percent of the adolescents said they go online almost constantly. Much of this increase in going online has been fueled by smartphones and mobile devices. Facebook is the most popular and frequently used social networking site—71 percent reported using Facebook and half reported using Instagram.

Text messaging has become the main way that adolescents connect with their friends, surpassing face-to-face contact, e-mail, instant messaging, and voice calling (Lenhart, 2015b). In the national survey and a further update (Lenhart, 2012, 2015b), daily text messaging increased from 38 percent who texted friends daily in 2008 to 55 percent in 2015. However, voice mail is the primary way that most adolescents prefer to connect with parents.

Adolescent Problems

Earlier we described several adolescent problems: substance abuse, sexually transmitted infections, and eating disorders. In this chapter, we examine the problems of juvenile delinquency, depression, and suicide. We also explore interrelationships among adolescent problems and how such problems can be prevented or remedied.

Juvenile Delinquency

The label **juvenile delinquent** is applied to an adolescent who breaks the law or engages in behavior that is considered illegal. Like other categories of disorders, juvenile delinquency is a broad concept; legal infractions range from littering to murder. Because the adolescent technically becomes a juvenile delinquent only after being judged guilty of a crime by a court of law, official records do not accurately reflect the number of illegal acts juvenile delinquents commit (Puzzanchera & Robson, 2014).

Males are more likely to engage in delinquency than females are. However, delinquency caseloads involving females increased from 19 percent in 1985 to 27 percent in 2005 (Puzzanchera & Sickmund, 2008).

Delinquency rates among minority groups and lower-socioeconomic-status youth are especially high in proportion to the overall population of these groups. However, such groups have less influence over the judicial decision-making process in the United States and therefore may be judged delinquent more readily than their non-Latino White, middle-socioeconomic-status counterparts.

juvenile delinquent An adolescent who breaks the law or engages in behavior that is considered illegal.

What are some factors that are linked to whether adolescents will engage in delinquent acts?
© Bill Aron/PhotoEdit

One issue in juvenile justice is whether an adolescent who commits a crime should be tried as an adult (Cauffman & others, 2015). Some psychologists have proposed that individuals 12 and under should not be evaluated under adult criminal laws and that those 17 and older should be (Cauffman & others, 2015). They also recommend that individuals 13 to 16 years of age be given some type of individualized assessment to determine whether they will be tried in a juvenile court or an adult criminal court.

Causes of Delinquency

What causes delinquency? Many causes have been proposed, including heredity, identity problems, community influences, and family experiences. Erik Erikson (1968), for example, argues that adolescents whose development has restricted them from acceptable social roles, or made them feel that they cannot measure up to the demands placed on them, may choose a negative identity. Adolescents with a negative identity may find support for their delinquent image among peers, reinforcing the negative identity. For Erikson, delinquency is an attempt to establish an identity, even if it is a negative one.

Although delinquency is less exclusively a phenomenon of lower socioeconomic status (SES) than it was in the past, some characteristics of lower-SES culture might promote delinquency (Dawson-McClure & others, 2015). The norms of many lower-SES peer groups and gangs are antisocial, or counterproductive to the goals and norms of society at large. Getting into or staying out of trouble are prominent features of life for some adolescents in low-income neighborhoods. One study found that youth whose families had experienced repeated poverty were more than twice as likely to be delinquent at 14 and 21 years of age (Najman & others, 2010).

Certain characteristics of family support systems are also associated with delinquency (Burke & Loeber, 2015; Dishion & Patternson, 2016). Parental monitoring of adolescents is especially important in determining whether an adolescent becomes a delinquent (Fosco & others, 2012). And one study found that low rates of delinquency from 14 to 23 years of age were associated with an authoritative parenting style (Mann & others, 2015). Further, recent research indicates that family therapy is often effective in reducing delinquency (Darnell & Schuler, 2015). A recent meta-analysis found that of five program types (case management, individual treatment, youth court, restorative justice, and family treatment), family treatment was the only one that was linked to a reduction in recidivism for juvenile offenders (Schwalbe & others, 2012). Also, in a recent study, family therapy improved juvenile court outcomes beyond what was achieved in non-family-based treatment, especially in reducing criminal behavior and rearrests (Dakof & others, 2015).

How Would You...?

As a **social worker,** how would you apply your knowledge of juvenile delinquency and adolescent development to improve the juvenile justice system?

An increasing number of studies have found that siblings can influence whether an adolescent becomes a delinquent (Bank, Burraston, & Snyder, 2004). Peer relations also can influence delinquency (Dong & Krohn, 2016; Trucco & others, 2014). A recent study revealed that having friends who engage in delinquency was associated with early onset and more persistent delinquency (Evans, Simons, & Simons, 2016).

Lack of academic success is associated with delinquency (Mercer & others, 2016). And a number of cognitive factors such as low self-control, low intelligence, and lack of sustained attention are linked to delinquency (Fine & others, 2016).

Rodney Hammond is an individual whose goal is to help at-risk adolescents, such as juvenile delinquents, cope more effectively with their lives. Read about his work in *Careers in Life-Span Development.*

Rodney Hammond, Health Psychologist

In describing his college experiences, Rodney Hammond said:

> When I started as an undergraduate at the University of Illinois, Champaign-Urbana, I hadn't decided on my major. But to help finance my education, I took a part-time job in a child development research program sponsored by the psychology department. There, I observed inner-city children in settings designed to enhance their learning. I saw firsthand the contribution psychology can make, and I knew I wanted to be a psychologist. (American Psychological Association, 2003, p. 26)

Rodney Hammond went on to obtain a doctorate in school and community psychology with a focus on children's development. For a number of years, he trained clinical psychologists at Wright State University in Ohio and directed a program to reduce violence in ethnic minority youth. There, he and his associates taught at-risk youth how to use social skills to effectively manage conflict and to recognize situations that could lead to violence. Today, Rodney is Director of Violence Prevention at the Centers for Disease Control and Prevention in Atlanta, Georgia. Rodney says that if you are interested in people and problem solving, psychology is a wonderful way to put these subjects together.

School psychology was one of Rodney Hammond's doctoral concentrations. School psychologists focus on improving the psychological and intellectual well-being of elementary, middle/junior, and high school students. They give psychological tests, interview students and their parents, consult with teachers, and

Rodney Hammond counsels an adolescent girl about the risks of adolescence and how to effectively cope with them.
© Dr. Rodney Hammond

may provide counseling to students and their families. They may work in a centralized office in a school district or in one or more schools. School psychologists usually have a master's or doctoral degree in school psychology. In graduate school, they take courses in counseling, assessment, learning, and other areas of education and psychology.

Depression and Suicide

What is the nature of depression in adolescence? What causes an adolescent to commit suicide?

Depression

Rates of ever experiencing major depressive disorder range from 15 to 20 percent for adolescents (Graber & Sontag, 2009). Adolescents who are experiencing a high level of stress and/or a loss of some type are at risk for developing depression (Hamilton & others, 2015). Also, a recent study found that adolescents who became depressed were characterized by a sense of hopelessness (Weersing & others, 2016).

By about age 15, adolescent females have a rate of depression that is twice that of adolescent males. Reasons for this include that females tend to ruminate in their depressed mood and amplify it; females' self-images, especially their body images, are more negative than males'; females face more discrimination; and puberty occurs earlier for girls (Chen & others, 2015; Kouros, Morris, & Garber, 2016).

Although these gender differences in adolescent depression hold true for many cultures, a recent study of more than 17,000 Chinese 11- to 22-year-olds revealed that the male adolescents and emerging adults experienced more depression than their female counterparts did (Sun & others, 2010). Explanation of the higher rate of depression among males in China focused on stressful life events and a less positive coping style.

Is adolescent depression linked to problems in emerging and early adulthood? A recent study initially assessed U.S. adolescents when they were 16 to 17 years of age and then again every two years until they were 26 to 27 years of age (Naicker & others, 2013). In this study, significant effects that persisted after 10 years were depression recurrence, stronger depressive symptoms, migraine headaches, poor self-rated health, and low levels of social support. Adolescent depression was not associated with employment status, personal income, marital status, and educational attainment a decade later.

Genes are linked to adolescent depression (Hansell & others, 2012). A recent study found that certain dopamine-related genes were associated with depressive symptoms in adolescents (Adkins & others, 2012). And another recent study revealed that the link between adolescent girls' perceived stress and depression occurred only when the girls had the short version of the serotonin-related gene—5HTTLPR (Beaver & others, 2012).

Certain family factors place adolescents at risk for developing depression (Kelly & others, 2016; Olino & others, 2016). These include having a depressed parent, emotionally unavailable parents, parents who have high marital conflict, and parents with financial problems. A recent study also revealed that mother-adolescent co-rumination, especially when focused on the mother's problems, were linked to adolescents' depression (Waller & Rose, 2010). Also, another recent study found that positive parenting characteristics such as emotional and educational support were associated with less depression in adolescents (Smokowski & others, 2015).

Poor peer relationships also are associated with adolescent depression (Vanhalst & others, 2012). Not having a close relationship with a best friend, having less contact with friends, having friends who are depressed, and experiencing peer rejection all increase depressive tendencies in adolescents (Platt & others, 2013). One study found that relational aggression was linked to depression for girls (Spieker & others, 2012). And as indicated earlier in this chapter, problems in adolescent romantic relationships can also trigger depression (Davila, Capaldi, & La Greca, 2016).

A recent research review concluded that drug therapy using serotonin reuptake inhibitors, cognitive behavior therapy, and interpersonal therapy are effective in treating adolescent depression (Maalouf & Brent, 2012). However, the most effective treatment was a combination of drug therapy and cognitive behavior therapy. Another research review concluded that Prozac and other SSRIs (selective serotonin reuptake inhibitors) show clinical benefits for adolescents at risk for moderate and severe depression (Cousins & Goodyear, 2015).

What are some characteristics of adolescents who become depressed? What are some factors that are linked with suicide attempts by adolescents?

Suicide

Suicide behavior is rare in childhood but escalates in adolescence and then increases further in emerging adulthood (Park & others, 2006). Suicide is the third-leading cause of death in 10- to 19-year-olds today in the United States. Approximately 4,600 adolescents commit suicide each year (Centers for Disease Control and Prevention, 2015).

Although a suicide threat should always be taken seriously, far more adolescents contemplate or attempt it unsuccessfully than actually commit it. A recent national study found that in the last two decades there has been a considerable decline in the percentage of adolescents who think seriously about committing suicide, although from 2009 to 2013 this percentage increased from 14 to 17 percent (Kann & others, 2014). In this study, in 2013, 8 percent attempted suicide and 3 percent engaged in suicide attempts that required medical attention.

Females are more likely to attempt suicide than males, but males are more likely to succeed in committing suicide (Hamilton & Klimes-Dougan, 2015). Males use more lethal means, such as guns, in their suicide attempts, whereas adolescent females are more likely to cut their wrists or take an overdose of sleeping pills—methods less likely to result in death.

Suicidal adolescents often have depressive symptoms. Although not all depressed adolescents are suicidal, depression is the most frequently cited factor associated with adolescent suicide (du Roscoat & others, 2016; Mirkovic & others, 2015). A recent study also found that both depression and hopelessness were predictors of whether adolescents repeated a suicide attempt over a six-month period (Consoli & others, 2015). Further, a study indicated that adolescents who used alcohol while they were sad or depressed were at risk for attempting suicide (Schilling & others, 2009).

Family and peer relationships also are linked to suicide attempts. One study found that family discord and negative relationships with parents were associated with increased suicide attempts by depressed adolescents (Consoli & others, 2013). In a recent study, child maltreatment was linked to adolescent suicide attempts (Hadland & others, 2015). Further, being victimized by bullying is associated with suicide-related thoughts and behavior (McMahon & others, 2012). Peer victimization has been linked to suicidal ideation and suicide attempts, with cyberbullying more strongly associated with suicidal ideation than traditional bullying (van Geel, Vedder, & Tanilon, 2014).

How Would You...?

As a **psychologist,** how would you talk with an adolescent who has just threatened suicide?

Recent and current stressful circumstances, such as getting poor grades in school or experiencing the breakup of a romantic relationship, may trigger suicide attempts (Soller, 2014). In a recent study, a lower level of school connectedness was associated with decreased suicidal ideation in female and male adolescents, and with suicide attempts in female adolescents (Langille & others, 2015).

The Interrelation of Problems and Successful Prevention/Intervention Programs

The four problems that affect the most adolescents are (1) drug abuse, (2) juvenile delinquency, (3) sexual problems, and (4) school-related problems (Dryfoos, 1990; Dryfoos & Barkin, 2006). The adolescents most at risk have more than one of these problems.

Researchers are increasingly finding that problem behaviors in adolescence are interrelated (Feldstein Ewing & others, 2016; Nakawaki & Crano, 2015). For example, heavy substance abuse is related to early sexual activity, lower grades, dropping out of school, and delinquency (Swartzendruber & others, 2015). Early initiation of sexual activity is associated with the use of cigarettes and alcohol, the use of marijuana and other illicit drugs, lower grades, dropping out of school, and delinquency (Chan & others, 2015). Delinquency is related to early sexual activity, early pregnancy, substance abuse, and dropping out of school (Dudovitz, McCoy, & Chung, 2015; Liddon & others, 2016). As many as 10 percent of adolescents in the United States have been estimated to engage in all four of these problem behaviors (for example, adolescents who have dropped out of school are behind in their grade level, are users of heavy drugs, regularly use cigarettes and marijuana, and are sexually active but do not use contraception). In 1990, it was estimated that another 15 percent of high-risk youth engaged in two or three of the four main problem behaviors (Dryfoos, 1990). More recently, this estimate was increased from the 15 percent figure in 1990 to 20 percent of all adolescents in 2006 (Dryfoos & Barkin, 2006).

A review of the programs that have been successful in preventing or reducing adolescent problems found these common components (Dryfoos, 1990; Dryfoos & Barkin, 2006):

1. *Intensive individualized attention.* In successful programs, high-risk adolescents are attached to a responsible adult who gives the adolescent attention and deals with the adolescent's specific needs. This theme occurs in a number of programs. In a successful substance-abuse program, for example, a student assistance counselor is available full-time for individual counseling and referral for treatment.

2. *Community-wide multiagency collaborative approaches.* The basic philosophy of community-wide programs is that a number of different programs and services have to be in place. In one successful substance-abuse program, a community-wide health promotion campaign has been implemented that uses local media and community education in concert with a substance-abuse curriculum in the schools.

3. *Early identification and intervention.* Reaching younger children and their families before children develop problems, or at the onset of their problems, is a successful strategy (Cichetti & Toth, 2015, 2016; Masten, 2015; O'Connor, 2016). One preschool program serves as an excellent model for the prevention of delinquency, pregnancy, substance abuse, and dropping out of school. Operated by the High/Scope Foundation in Ypsilanti, Michigan from 1962 to 1967, the Perry Preschool has had a long-term positive impact on its students. This enrichment program, directed by David Weikart, served disadvantaged African American children. They attended a high-quality, two-year preschool program and received weekly home visits from program personnel. Based on official police records, by age 19, individuals who had attended the Perry Preschool program were less likely to have been arrested and reported fewer adult offenses than a control group did. The Perry Preschool students also were less likely to drop out of school, and teachers rated their social behavior as more competent than that of a control group who had not received the enriched preschool experience (High/Scope Resource, 2005).

Summary

Identity

- Identity is a self-portrait composed of many pieces.
- Identity versus identity confusion is Erikson's fifth stage of the human life span, which individuals experience during adolescence.
- James Marcia proposed four identity statuses—identity diffusion, foreclosure, moratorium, and achievement—that are based on crisis (exploration) and commitment. Increasingly, experts argue that the main changes in identity occur in emerging adulthood rather than adolescence.
- Ethnicity is an important influence on identity.

Families

- A key aspect of the managerial role of parenting in adolescence is effectively monitoring the adolescent's development. Adolescents' disclosure to parents about their whereabouts is linked to positive adolescent adjustment.
- The adolescent's push for autonomy is one of the hallmarks of adolescence. Attachment to parents increases the probability that an adolescent will be socially competent.
- Parent-adolescent conflict increases in adolescence. The conflict is usually moderate rather than severe.

Peers

- Harry Stack Sullivan argued that there is a dramatic increase in the psychological importance and intimacy of close friends in early adolescence. Peer conformity and cliques and crowds assume more importance in adolescence.

- Three stages characterize adolescent dating and romantic relationships. Many gay and lesbian youth date other-sex peers. Culture can exert a powerful influence on adolescent dating. Some aspects of dating and romantic relationships are linked to adjustment difficulties.

Culture and Adolescent Development

- Adolescent development varies across cultures, and rites of passage still characterize adolescents in some cultures.
- Immigration is an important aspect of many ethnic adolescents' lives. Although not all ethnic minority families are poor, poverty contributes to the stress experienced by many ethnic minority adolescents.
- There has been a dramatic increase in adolescents' media multitasking and use of the Internet for social connections.

Adolescent Problems

- Juvenile delinquency is a major problem in adolescence. Numerous causes have been proposed to explain delinquency.
- Adolescents have a higher rate of depression than children, and females have a much higher rate of depression than males do. Adolescent suicide is the third leading cause of death in U.S. adolescents, and numerous factors are linked to suicide.
- Researchers are increasingly finding that problem behaviors in adolescence are interrelated, and common components characterize successful programs designed to prevent or reduce adolescent problems.

Key Terms

clique	crowd	identity diffusion	juvenile delinquent
commitment	ethnic identity	identity foreclosure	rite of passage
crisis	identity achievement	identity moratorium	

11 Physical and Cognitive Development in Early Adulthood

© Sam Edwards/Caiaimage/Getty Images RF

CHAPTER OUTLINE

Stories of Life-Span Development: Dave Eggers, Pursuing a Career in the Face of Stress

He was a senior in college when both of his parents died of cancer within five weeks of each other. What would he do? He and his 8-year-old brother left Chicago to live in California, where his older sister was entering law school. Dave would take care of his younger brother, but he needed a job. That first summer, he took a class in furniture painting; then he worked for a geological surveying company, re-creating maps on a computer. Soon, though, he did something very different: With friends from high school, Dave Eggers started *Might*, a satirical magazine for twenty-somethings. It was an edgy, highly acclaimed publication, but not a moneymaker. After a few years, Eggers had to shut down the magazine, and he abandoned California for New York.

This does not sound like a promising start for a career. But within a decade after his parents' death, Eggers had not only raised his young brother but had also founded a quarterly

Dave Eggers, talented and insightful author.
© Cosima Scavolini/LaPresse/Zumapress.com/Newscom

journal and Web site, *McSweeney's,* and had written a best-seller, *A Heartbreaking Work of Staggering Genius,* which received the National Book Critics Circle Award and was nominated for a Pulitzer Prize. It is a slightly fictionalized account of Eggers' life as he helped care for his dying mother, raised his brother, and searched for his own place in the world. Despite the pain of his loss and the responsibility for his brother, Eggers quickly built a record of achievement as a young adult. ■

The Transition from Adolescence to Adulthood

When does an adolescent become an adult? It is not easy to tell when a girl or a boy enters adolescence. The task of determining when an individual becomes an adult is even more difficult.

Becoming an Adult

For most individuals, becoming an adult involves a lengthy transition period. The transition from adolescence to adulthood has been referred to as **emerging adulthood,** which occurs from approximately 18 to 25 years of age (Arnett, 2006, 2010, 2012, 2015). Experimentation and exploration characterize the emerging adult. At this point in their development, many individuals are still exploring which career path they want to follow, what they want their identity to be, and which lifestyle they want to adopt (for example, being single, cohabiting, or getting married).

Key Features of Emerging Adulthood

Jeffrey Arnett (2006) has concluded that five key features characterize emerging adulthood:

- *Identity exploration, especially in love and work.* Emerging adulthood is the time during which key changes in identity take place for many individuals (Kroger, 2015; Schwartz & others, 2013, 2015a, b, c).
- *Instability.* Residential changes peak during early adulthood, a time during which there also is often instability in love, work, and education.
- *Self-focused.* According to Arnett (2006, p. 10), emerging adults "are self-focused in the sense that they have little in the way of social obligations, little in the way of duties and commitments to others, which leaves them with a great deal of autonomy in running their own lives."
- *Feeling in-between.* Many emerging adults don't consider themselves adolescents or full-fledged adults.
- *The age of possibilities, a time when individuals have an opportunity to transform their lives.* Arnett (2006) describes two ways in which emerging adulthood is the age of possibilities: (1) many emerging adults are optimistic about their future; and (2) for emerging adults who have experienced difficult times while growing up, emerging adulthood presents an opportunity to reorient their lives in a more positive direction.

Recent research indicates that these five aspects characterize not only individuals in the United States as they make the transition from adolescence to early adulthood, but also their counterparts in European countries and Australia (Arnett, 2012, 2015; Buhl & Lanz, 2007; Sirsch & others, 2009). Although emerging adulthood does not characterize development in all cultures, it does appear to occur in those where assuming adult roles and responsibilities is postponed (Kins & Beyers, 2010). Critics of the concept of emerging adulthood argue that it applies mainly to privileged adolescents and is not always a self-determined choice for many young people, especially those in limiting

emerging adulthood The transition from adolescence to adulthood (approximately 18 to 25 years of age), which involves experimentation and exploration.

socioeconomic conditions (Cote & Bynner, 2008). A recent study revealed that U.S. at-risk youth entered emerging adulthood slightly earlier than the general population of youth (Lisha & others, 2012).

Markers of Becoming an Adult

In the United States, the most widely recognized marker of entry into adulthood is holding a more or less permanent, full-time job, which usually happens when an individual finishes school—high school for some, college for others, graduate or professional school for still others. However, other criteria are far from clear. Economic independence is one marker of adult status, but achieving it is often a long process. College graduates are increasingly returning to live with their parents as they attempt to establish themselves economically. A longitudinal study found that at age 25 only slightly more than half of the participants were fully financially independent of their family of origin (Cohen & others, 2003). The most dramatic findings in this study, though, involved the extensive variability in the individual trajectories of adult roles across ten years from 17 to 27 years of age; many of the participants moved back and forth between increasing and decreasing economic dependency. A recent study revealed that continued co-residence with parents during emerging adulthood slowed down the process of becoming a self-sufficient and independent adult (Kins & Beyers, 2010).

Other studies show that taking responsibility for oneself is likely an important marker of adult status for many individuals. In one study, both parents and college students agreed that taking responsibility for one's actions and developing emotional control are important aspects of becoming an adult (Nelson & others, 2007). And in a recent study of Danish emerging adults, the most widely described markers of emerging adulthood were accepting self-responsibility, making independent decisions, and becoming financially independent (Arnett & Padilla-Walker, 2015). In this study the least-described markers were the traditional transition events of becoming married and avoiding getting drunk.

What we have discussed about the markers of adult status mainly characterizes individuals in industrialized societies, especially Americans. In developing countries, marriage is more often a significant marker for entry into adulthood, and this usually occurs much earlier than the adulthood markers in the United States (Arnett, 2015). In one study, the majority of 18- to 26-year-olds in India felt that they had achieved adulthood (Seiter & Nelson, 2010).

The Transition from High School to College

For many individuals in developed countries, going from high school to college is an important aspect of the transition to adulthood (Bowman, 2010). Just as the transition from elementary school to middle or junior high school involves change and possible stress, so does the transition

The transition from high school to college often involves positive as well as negative features. In college, students are likely to feel grown up, to be able to spend more time with peers, to have more opportunities to explore different lifestyles and values, and to enjoy greater freedom from parental monitoring. However, college involves a larger, more impersonal school structure and an increased focus on achievement and its assessment. *What was your transition to college like?*
© Stockbyte/PunchStock RF

How Would You...?

As an **educator,** how would you prepare high school students to ease the transition to college?

from high school to college. The two transitions have many parallels. Going from being a senior in high school to being a freshman in college replays the top-dog phenomenon of transferring from the oldest and most powerful group of students to the youngest and least powerful group of students that occurred earlier as adolescence began. For many students, the transition from high school to college involves movement to a larger, more impersonal school structure; interaction with peers from more diverse geographical and sometimes more diverse ethnic backgrounds; and increased focus on achievement and its assessment. And like the transition from elementary to middle or junior high school, the transition from high school to college can involve positive features. Students are more likely to feel grown up, have more subjects from which to select, have more time to spend with peers, have more opportunities to explore different lifestyles and values, enjoy greater independence from parental monitoring, and be challenged intellectually by academic work (Halonen & Santrock, 2013).

College counselors can provide good information about coping with stress and academic matters. To read about the work of college counselor Grace Leaf, see *Careers in Life-Span Development.*

Careers in life-span development

Grace Leaf, College/Career Counselor and College Administrator

For many years, Grace Leaf was a counselor at Spokane Community College in Washington. In 2014, she became Vice President of Instruction at Lower Columbia College in Spokane. She has a master's degree in educational leadership and is working toward a doctoral degree in educational leadership at Gonzaga University in Washington. In her job as a college counselor, she provided orientation sessions for international students, individual and group advising, and individual and group career planning. Grace tries to connect students with their goals and values and helps them design an educational program that fits their needs and visions.

College counselors help students to cope with adjustment problems, identify their abilities and interests, develop academic plans, and explore career options. Some have an undergraduate degree, others a master's degree like Grace Leaf. Some college

Grace Leaf counsels college students at Spokane Community College about careers.

© Grace Leaf

counselors have a graduate degree in counseling; others may have an undergraduate degree in psychology or another discipline.

Physical Development

As emerging and young adults learn more about healthy lifestyles and how they contribute to a longer life span, they are increasingly interested in monitoring their physical performance, health, nutrition, exercise, and substance use.

Physical Performance and Development

Most of us reach our peak physical performance before the age of 30, often between the ages of 19 and 26. This peak of physical performance occurs not only for the average young adult, but for outstanding athletes as well. Even though athletes as a group keep getting better than their predecessors—running faster, jumping higher, and lifting more weight— the age at which they reach their peak performance has remained virtually unchanged.

Different types of athletes, however, reach their peak performances at different ages. Most swimmers and gymnasts peak in their late teens. Golfers and marathon runners tend to peak in their late twenties. In other areas of athletics, peak performance often occurs in the early to mid-twenties.

Not only do we reach our peak in physical performance during early adulthood, it is also during this age period that we begin to decline in physical performance. Muscle tone and strength usually begin to show signs of decline around the age of 30. Sagging chins and protruding abdomens also may begin to appear for the first time. The lessening of physical abilities is a common complaint among the just-turned thirties. Sensory systems show little change in early adulthood, but the lens of the eye loses some of its elasticity and becomes less able to change shape and focus on near objects. Hearing peaks in adolescence, remains constant in the first part of early adulthood, and then begins to decline in the last part of early adulthood. And in the middle to late twenties, the body's fatty tissue increases.

Health

Emerging adults have more than twice the mortality rate of adolescents (Park & others, 2006). As indicated in Figure 1, males are mainly responsible for the higher mortality rate of emerging adults.

Although emerging adults have a higher death rate than adolescents, emerging adults have few chronic health problems, and they have fewer colds and respiratory problems than they did when they were children (Rimsza & Kirk, 2005). Although most college students know how to prevent illness and promote health, they don't fare very well when it comes to applying this information to themselves (Murphy-Hoefer, Alder, & Higbee, 2004; Lau & others, 2013). In many cases, emerging adults are not as healthy as they seem (Fatusi & Hindin, 2010).

A longitudinal study revealed that most bad health habits that were engaged in during adolescence increased in emerging adulthood (Harris & others, 2006). Inactivity, diet, obesity, substance use, reproductive health care, and health-care access worsened in emerging adulthood. For example, when they were 12 to 18 years of age, only 5 percent reported no weekly exercise, but when they became 19 to 26 years of age, 46 percent said they did not exercise during a week. And a recent study found that rates of being over-weight or obese increased from 25.6 percent for college freshmen to 32 percent for college seniors (Nicoteri & Miskovsky, 2014).

In emerging and early adulthood, few individuals stop to think about how their personal lifestyles will affect their health later in their adult lives. As emerging adults, many of us develop a pattern of not eating breakfast, not eating regular meals, relying on snacks as our main food source during the day, eating excessively to the point where we exceed the normal weight for our age, smoking moderately or excessively, drinking moderately or excessively, failing to exercise, and getting only a few hours of sleep at night (Cousineau, Goldstein, & Franco, 2005; Waldron & Dieser, 2010).

Recent research indicates that 70 percent of college students do not get adequate sleep and that 50 percent report daytime sleepiness (Herhsner & Chervin, 2015). Emerging adults are not the only ones who are getting inadequate sleep. Many adults in their late twenties and thirties don't get enough either (Brimah & others, 2013). A recent statement by the

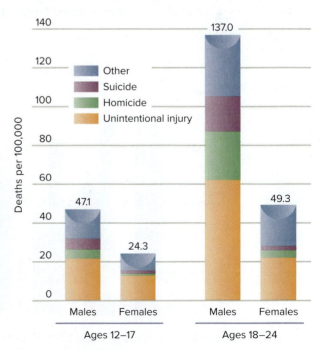

Figure 1 Mortality Rates of U.S. Adolescents and Emerging Adults

American Academy of Sleep Medicine and Sleep Research Society (Luyster & others, 2012) emphasized that chronic sleep deprivation may contribute to cardiovascular disease and a shortened life span, and also result in cognitive and motor impairment that increase the risk of motor vehicle crashes and work-related accidents.

The lifestyles just described are associated with poor health, which in turn reduces life satisfaction (Donatelle & Ketcham, 2016; Fahey, Insel, & Roth, 2017; Insel & Roth, 2016). In the Berkeley Longitudinal Study—in which individuals were evaluated over a period of 40 years—physical health at age 30 predicted life satisfaction at age 70, more so for men than for women (Mussen, Honzik, & Eichorn, 1982). Another study explored links between health behavior and life satisfaction of more than 17,000 individuals who were 17 to 30 years old in 21 countries (Grant, Wardle, & Steptoe, 2009). The young adults' life satisfaction was positively related to not smoking, exercising regularly, using sun protection, eating fruit, and limiting fat intake, but it was not related to alcohol consumption and fiber intake.

Why might it be easy to develop bad health habits in emerging and early adulthood?
© BananaStock/Jupiter Images RF

Eating and Weight

We have discussed aspects of overweight children's lives and have examined the eating disorders of anorexia nervosa and bulimia nervosa in adolescence. Now, we turn our attention to obesity and the extensive preoccupation that many young adults have with dieting.

Obesity Obesity is a serious and pervasive health problem for many individuals (Blake, 2017; Thompson, Manore, & Vaughan, 2017). A national survey found that 29.5 percent of U.S. 20- to 39-year-olds were overweight and 31.5 percent were obese (Dietary Guidelines Advisory Committee, 2015). Also, a recent analysis predicted that by 2030, 42 percent of U.S. adults will be obese (Finkelstein & others, 2012).

An international comparison of 33 developed countries revealed that the United States had the highest percentage of obese adults (OECD, 2010). Figure 2 shows the developed countries with the highest and lowest percentages of obese adults.

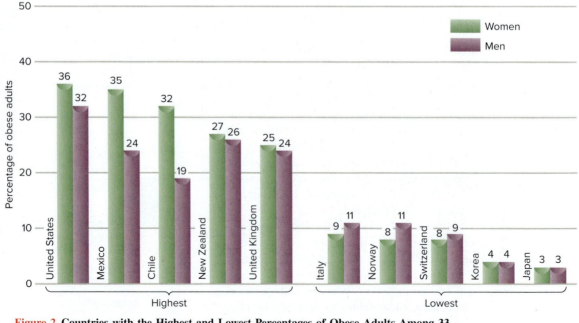

Figure 2 Countries with the Highest and Lowest Percentages of Obese Adults Among 33 Developed Countries

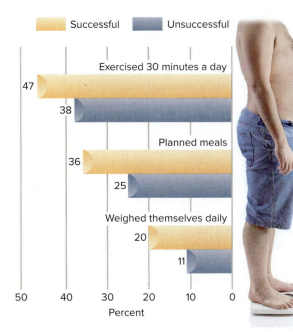

Successful █ Unsuccessful █

Exercised 30 minutes a day
47
38

Planned meals
36
25

Weighed themselves daily
20
11

50 40 30 20 10 0
Percent

Figure 3
Comparison of Strategies Used by Successful and Unsuccessful Dieters
© iStockphoto.com/Ljupco

Being overweight or obese is linked to increased risk of hypertension, diabetes, and cardiovascular disease (Donatelle & Ketcham, 2016; Goh & others, 2016). Overweight and obesity also are associated with mental health problems (Garcia-Toro & others, 2016). For example, in a recent study overweight/obese adults who were depressed were more likely to be characterized by atypical features of depression such as rejection sensitivity and leaden paralysis (a sense of heaviness in arms and legs) than normal-weight depressed adults (Lojko & others, 2015).

One thing we know about losing weight is that the most effective programs include exercise (Ryan & others, 2014). A research review concluded that adults who engaged in diet-plus-exercise programs lost more weight than those who followed diet-only programs (Wu & others, 2009). A study of approximately 2,000 U.S. adults found that exercising 30 minutes a day, planning meals, and weighing themselves daily were the strategies used more often by successful dieters than by unsuccessful dieters (Kruger, Blanck, & Gillespie, 2006) (see Figure 3).

Regular Exercise

One of the main reasons that health experts want people to exercise is that it helps to prevent diseases, such as heart disease and diabetes (Fahey, Insel, & Roth, 2017; Thompson & Manore, 2016). Many health experts recommend that young adults engage in 30 minutes or more of aerobic exercise daily. **Aerobic exercise** is sustained exercise—jogging, swimming, or cycling, for example—that stimulates heart and lung activity. Most health experts recommend exercising vigorously enough to raise your heart rate to at least 60 percent of your maximum heart rate. Only about one-fifth of adults, however, meet these recommended levels of physical activity.

A national poll in the United States found that 51.6 percent of individuals 18 years and older exercised for 30 or more minutes 3 or more days a week (Gallup, 2013). In this survey, young adults 18 to 29 years of age (56.8 percent) were the most likely to exercise of all adult age groups. Also in this survey, men were more likely to exercise than women.

Researchers have found that exercise benefits not only physical health, but mental health as well (Donatelle, 2015; Schuch & others, 2016a). For example, in a recent meta-analysis, moderate and vigorous aerobic exercise was effective in reducing major depressive disorder (Schuch & others, 2016b). Also, in recent research, adults who exercised regularly had lower levels of anxiety and depression (Khanzada, Soomro, & Kahn, 2015). Also, in a recent daily diary study on days when emerging adult (18 to 25 years of age) college students engaged in more physical activity they reported greater satisfaction with life (Maher & others, 2013). Also, a one-year exercise intervention decreased stress symptoms in working adults (Kettunen, Vuorimaa, & Vasankari, 2015).

How Would You…?
As a **health-care professional**, how would you design a community education program to emphasize the importance of regular exercise for young adults?

Substance Abuse

Earlier we explored substance abuse in adolescence. Fortunately, by the time individuals reach their mid-twenties, many have reduced their use of alcohol and drugs

What kinds of problems are associated with binge drinking in college?

© Joe Raedle/Newsmakers/Getty Images

(Bachman & others, 2002). As in adolescence, male college students and young adults are more likely to take drugs than their female counterparts (Johnston & others, 2015). One study revealed that only 20 percent of college students reported abstaining from drinking alcohol (Huang & others, 2009).

Heavy binge drinking often occurs in college, and it can take its toll on students (Fairlie, Maggs, & Lanza, 2016; Marino & Fromme, 2016). In 2014, 35 percent of U.S. college students reported having had five or more drinks in a row at least once in the last two weeks (Johnston & others, 2015). The term *extreme binge drinking* describes individuals who had 10 or more drinks in a row. In 2010 approximately 13 percent of college students reported drinking this heavily (Johnston & others, 2011). While drinking rates among college students have remained high, drinking, including binge drinking, has declined in recent years. For example, binge drinking declined by 6 percent from 2007 to 2014 (Johnston & others, 2015).

In a national survey of drinking patterns on 140 campuses (Wechsler & others, 1994), almost half of the binge drinkers reported problems that included missing classes, sustaining physical injuries, experiencing troubles with police, and having unprotected sex. For example, binge-drinking college students were 11 times more likely to fall behind in school, 10 times more likely to drive after drinking, and twice as likely to have unprotected sex in comparison with college students who did not binge drink.

When does binge drinking peak during development? A longitudinal study revealed that binge drinking peaks at about 21 to 22 years of age and then declines through the remainder of the twenties (Bachman & others, 2002) (see Figure 4). Recent data from the Monitoring the Future study at the University of Michigan also indicate that binge drinking peaks at 21 to 22 years of age, with 39 percent reporting that they had engaged in binge drinking at least once in the last 2 weeks (Johnston & others, 2015).

How Would You...?

As a **social worker,** how would you apply your understanding of binge drinking to develop a program to encourage responsible alcohol use on college campuses?

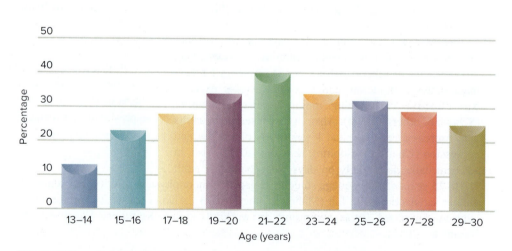

Figure 4 **Binge Drinking in the Adolescence–Early Adulthood Transition**
Note that the percentage of individuals engaging in binge drinking peaked at 21 or 22 years of age and then gradually declined through the remainder of the twenties. Binge drinking was defined as having five or more alcoholic drinks in a row in the previous two weeks.

Sexuality

We have explored how adolescents develop a sexual identity and become sexually active. What happens to their sexuality in adulthood?

Sexual Activity in Emerging Adulthood

At the beginning of emerging adulthood (age 18), surveys indicate that slightly more than 60 percent of individuals have experienced sexual intercourse, but by the end of emerging adulthood (age 25), most individuals have had sexual intercourse (Lefkowitz & Gillen, 2006). Also, the average age of marriage in the United States is currently 29 for males and 27 for females (U.S. Census Bureau, 2015). Thus, emerging adulthood is a time during which most individuals are "both sexually active and unmarried" (Lefkowitz & Gillen, 2006, p. 235).

Casual sex is more common in emerging adulthood than it is during the late twenties (Roberson, Olmstead, & Fincham, 2016). A recent trend has involved "hooking up" to have non-relationship sex (from kissing to intercourse) (Kettrey, 2016; Napper & others, 2016; Vrangalova, 2015a, b). One study revealed that 20 percent of first-year college women on one large university campus had engaged in at least one hook-up over the course of the school year (Fielder & others, 2013). In this study, impulsivity, sensation seeking, and alcohol use were among the predictors of a higher likelihood of hooking up. Further, another recent study indicated that 40 percent of 22-year-olds reporting having had a recent casual sexual partner (Lyons & others, 2015). And a recent study of more than 3,900 18- to 25-year-olds indicated that having casual sex was negatively linked to well-being and positively related to psychological distress (Bersamin & others, 2014). Also, recent research indicated that when emerging adults drank alcohol, they were more likely to have casual sex and less likely to discuss possible risks (Johnson & Chen, 2015). In addition to hooking up, another type of casual sex that has recently increased among emerging adults is "friends with benefits," which involves a relationship formed by the integration of friendship and sexual intimacy without an explicit commitment characteristic of an exclusive romantic relationship (Owen, Fincham, & Manthos, 2013).

Sexual Orientation and Behavior

A national study of sexual behavior in the United States among adults 25 to 44 years of age found that 98 percent of the women and 97 percent of the men said that they had ever engaged in vaginal intercourse (Chandra & others, 2011). Also in this study, 89 percent of the women and 90 percent of the men reported that they had ever had oral sex with an opposite-sex partner, and 36 percent of the women and 44 percent of the men stated that they had ever had anal sex with an opposite-sex partner.

Detailed information about various aspects of sexual activity in adults of different ages comes from the 1994 Sex in America survey. In this study Robert Michael and his colleagues (1994) interviewed more than 3,000 people from 18 to 59 years of age who were randomly selected, in sharp contrast with earlier samples that were based on unrepresentative groups of volunteers.

Heterosexual Attitudes and Behavior

Here are some of the key findings from the 1994 Sex in America survey:

- Americans tend to fall into three categories: One-third have sex twice a week or more, one-third a few times a month, and one-third a few times a year or not at all.
- Married (and cohabiting) couples have sex more often than noncohabiting couples (see Figure 5).
- Most Americans do not engage in kinky sexual acts. When asked about their favorite sexual acts, the vast majority (96 percent) said that vaginal sex was "very"

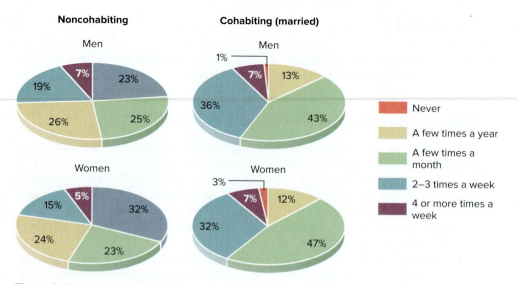

Figure 5 **The Sex in America Survey**

The percentages show noncohabiting and cohabiting (married) males' and females' responses to the question "How often have you had sex in the past year?" in a 1994 survey (Michael & others, 1994). *What was one feature of the Sex in America survey that made it superior to most surveys of sexual behavior?*

or "somewhat" appealing. Oral sex was in third place, after an activity that many have not labeled a sexual act—watching a partner undress.

- Adultery is clearly the exception rather than the rule. Nearly 75 percent of the married men and 85 percent of the married women in the survey indicated that they had never been unfaithful.

- Men think about sex far more often than women do—54 percent of the men said they thought about it every day or several times a day, whereas 67 percent of the women said they thought about it only a few times a week or a few times a month.

In sum, one of the most powerful messages in the 1994 survey was that Americans' sexual lives are more conservative than was previously believed. Although 17 percent of the men and 3 percent of the women said they had had sex with at least 21 partners, the overall impression from the survey was that sexual behavior is ruled by marriage and monogamy for most Americans.

How extensive are gender differences in sexuality? A recent analysis of almost 8,000 emerging adults found that males had stronger permissive attitudes, especially about sex in casual relationships, than did females (Sprecher, Treger, & Sakaluk, 2013). A meta-analysis revealed that men reported having slightly more sexual experiences and more permissive attitudes than women for most aspects of sexuality (Petersen & Hyde, 2010). For the following factors, stronger differences were found: Men said that they engaged more often in masturbation, pornography use, and casual sex, and had more permissive attitudes about casual sex than their female counterparts did.

Given all the media and public attention focusing on the negative aspects of sexuality—such as adolescent pregnancy, sexually transmitted infections, rape, and so on—it is important to underscore that research strongly supports the role of sexuality in well-being (King, 2014, 2016). For example, in a Swedish study frequency of sexual intercourse was strongly linked to life satisfaction for both women and men (Brody & Costa, 2009).

How Would You...?

As a **human development and family studies professional,** what information would you include in a program designed to educate young adults about healthy sexuality and sexual relationships?

Sources of Sexual Orientation

Until the end of the nineteenth century, it was generally believed that people were either heterosexual or homosexual. Today, the more accepted view of sexual orientation depicts it not as an either/or proposition but as a continuum from exclusive male-female relations to exclusive same-sex relations (King, 2016, 2017). Some individuals are bisexual, being sexually attracted to people of both sexes.

People sometimes think that bisexuality is simply a stepping stone to homosexuality, while others view it as a sexual orientation itself or as an indicator of sexual fluidity (King, 2014, 2016, 2017). Evidence supports the notion that bisexuality is a stable orientation that involves attraction to both sexes (Lippa, 2013).

Compared with men, women are more likely to change their sexual patterns and desires (Knight & Hope, 2012). Women are more likely than men to have sexual experiences with same- and opposite-sex partners, even if they identify themselves strongly as being heterosexual or lesbian (King, 2017). Also, women are more likely than men to identify themselves as bisexual (Gates, 2011).

In the Sex in America survey, 2.7 percent of the men and 1.3 percent of the women reported having had same-sex relations in the past year (Michael & others, 1994). Why are some individuals lesbian, gay, or bisexual (LGB) and others heterosexual? Speculation surrounding this question has been extensive (Diamond & Savin-Williams, 2015).

All people, regardless of their sexual orientation, have similar physiological responses during sexual arousal and seem to be aroused by the same types of tactile stimulation. Investigators typically find no differences between LGBs and heterosexuals in a wide range of attitudes, behaviors, and adjustments (Fingerhut & Peplau, 2013).

Recently, researchers have explored the possible biological basis of same-sex relations. The results of hormone studies have been inconsistent. If gay males are given male sex hormones (androgens), their sexual orientation doesn't change. Their sexual desire merely increases. A very early prenatal critical period might influence sexual orientation (Berenbaum & Beltz, 2011). If this critical-period hypothesis turns out to be correct, it would explain why clinicians have found that sexual orientation is difficult, if not impossible, to modify.

Researchers have also examined genetic influences on sexual orientation by studying twins. A recent Swedish study of almost 4,000 twins found that only about 35 percent of the variation in homosexual behavior in men and 19 percent in women were explained by genetic differences (Langstrom & others, 2010). This result suggests that although genes likely play a role in sexual orientation, they are not the only factor involved (King, 2016. 2017).

An individual's sexual orientation—same-sex, heterosexual, or bisexual—is most likely determined by a combination of genetic, hormonal, cognitive, and environmental factors (King, 2016, 2017; Yarber, Sayad, & Strong, 2015). Most experts on same-sex relations believe that no one factor alone causes sexual orientation and that the relative weight of each factor can vary from one individual to the next.

What likely determines an individual's sexual orientation?

(Top) © PhotoAlto/ PunchStock RF; (middle & bottom) © 2009 JupiterImages Corporation RF

Attitudes and Behavior of Lesbians and Gay Males

Many gender differences that appear in heterosexual relationships occur in same-sex relationships (Diamond & Savin-Williams, 2015; Savin-Williams, 2015; Savin-Williams & Cohen, 2015). For example, like heterosexual women, lesbians have fewer sexual partners than gays, and lesbians have less permissive attitudes about casual sex outside a primary relationship than gays do (Fingerhut & Peplau, 2013).

Sexually Transmitted Infections

sexually transmitted infections (STIs) Diseases that are contracted primarily through sex.

Sexually transmitted infections (STIs) are diseases that are primarily contracted through sex—intercourse as well as oral-genital and anal-genital sex. STIs affect about one of every six U.S. adults (National Center for Health Statistics, 2016). Among the most prevalent STIs are bacterial infections—such as gonorrhea, syphilis, and chlamydia—and STIs caused by viruses—such as AIDS (acquired immune deficiency syndrome), genital herpes, and genital warts. Figure 6 describes these sexually transmitted infections.

No single disease has had a greater impact on sexual behavior, or created more public fear in the last several decades, than infection with the human immunodeficiency virus (HIV) (Crooks & Baur, 2016). HIV is a virus that destroys the body's immune system. Once a person is infected with HIV, the virus breaks down and overpowers the immune system, which leads to AIDS. An individual sick with AIDS has such a weakened immune system that a common cold can be life-threatening.

In 2012, more than 1 million people in the United States were living with an HIV infection (National Center for Health Statistics, 2014). In 2012, male-male sexual contact continued to be the most frequent AIDS transmission category. Because of education and the development of more effective drug treatments, deaths due to HIV/AIDS have begun to decline in the United States (National Center for Health Statistics, 2014). Globally, the total number of individuals living with

How Would You...?

As a **health-care professional,** what advice would you give to a patient who is sexually active, does not use condoms, and does not want to be tested for any sexually transmitted infections?

STI	Description/cause	Incidence	Treatment
Gonorrhea	Commonly called the "drip" or "clap." Caused by the bacterium *Neisseria gonorrhoeae*. Spread by contact between infected moist membranes (genital, oral-genital, or anal-genital) of two individuals. Characterized by discharge from penis or vagina and painful urination. Can lead to infertility.	500,000 cases annually in U.S.	Penicillin, other antibiotics
Syphilis	Caused by the bacterium *Treponema pallidum*. Characterized by the appearance of a sore where syphilis entered the body. The sore can be on the external genitals, vagina, or anus. Later, a skin rash breaks out on palms of hands and bottom of feet. If not treated, can eventually lead to paralysis or even death.	100,000 cases annually in U.S.	Penicillin
Chlamydia	A common STI named for the bacterium *Chlamydia trachomatis*, an organism that spreads by sexual contact and infects the genital organs of both sexes. A special concern is that females with chlamydia may become infertile. It is recommended that adolescent and young adult females have an annual screening for this STI.	About 3 million people in U.S. annually	Antibiotics
Genital herpes	Caused by a family of viruses with different strains. Involves an eruption of sores and blisters. Spread by sexual contact.	One of five U.S. adults	No known cure but antiviral medications can shorten outbreaks
AIDS	Caused by a virus, the human immunodeficiency virus (HIV), which destroys the body's immune system. Semen and blood are the main vehicles of transmission. Common symptoms include fevers, night sweats, weight loss, chronic fatigue, and swollen lymph nodes.	More than 300,000 cumulative cases of HIV virus in U.S. 25–34-year-olds; epidemic incidence in sub-Saharan countries	New treatments have slowed the progression from HIV to AIDS; no cure
Genital warts	Caused by the human papillomavirus, which does not always produce symptoms. Usually appear as small, hard painless bumps in the vaginal area, or around the anus. Very contagious. Certain high-risk types of this virus cause cervical cancer and other genital cancers. May recur despite treatment. A new HPV preventive vaccine, Gardasil, has been approved for girls and women 9–26 years of age.	About 5.5 million new cases annually; considered the most common STI in the U.S.	A topical drug, freezing, or surgery

Figure 6 Sexually Transmitted Infections

HIV was 37 million in 2014, with 26 million of these individuals with HIV living in sub-Saharan Africa. Approximately half of all new HIV infections around the world occur in the 15- to 24-year-old age category. In one study, only 49 percent of 15- to 24-year-old females in low- and middle-income countries knew that using a condom helps to prevent HIV infection, compared with 74 percent of young males (UNAIDS, 2011). The good news is that global rates of HIV infection fell by 35 percent from 2000 to 2014 (UNAIDS, 2015).

What are some good strategies for protecting against HIV and other sexually transmitted infections? They include the following:

- *Knowing your own and your partner's risk status.* Anyone who has had previous sexual activity with another person might have contracted an STI without being aware of it. Spend time getting to know a prospective partner before you have sex. Use this time to inform the other person of your STI status and inquire about your partner's. Remember that many people lie about their STI status.

- *Obtaining medical examinations.* Many experts recommend that couples who want to begin a sexual relationship have a medical checkup to rule out STIs before engaging in sex. If cost is an issue, contact your campus health service or a public health clinic.

- *Having protected, not unprotected, sex.* When correctly used, latex condoms help to prevent many STIs from being transmitted. Condoms are most effective in preventing gonorrhea, syphilis, chlamydia, and HIV. They are less effective against the spread of herpes.

- *Not having sex with multiple partners.* One of the best predictors of getting an STI is having sex with multiple partners. Having more than one sex partner elevates the likelihood of encountering an infected partner.

Cognitive Development

Are there changes in cognitive performance during these years? To explore the nature of cognition in early adulthood, we focus on issues related to cognitive stages and creative thinking.

Cognitive Stages

Are young adults more advanced in their thinking than adolescents are? Let's examine how Piaget and others have answered this intriguing question.

Piaget's View

Piaget concluded that an adolescent and an adult think qualitatively in the same way. That is, Piaget argued that at approximately 11 to 15 years of age, adolescents enter the formal operational stage, which is characterized by more logical, abstract, and idealistic thinking than the concrete operational thinking of 7- to 11-year-olds. Piaget did believe that young adults are more quantitatively advanced in their thinking in the sense that they have more knowledge than adolescents possess. He also believed, as do information-processing psychologists, that adults especially increase their knowledge in a specific area, such as a physicist's understanding of physics or a financial analyst's knowledge about finance. According to Piaget, however, formal operational thought is the final stage in cognitive development, and it characterizes adults as well as adolescents.

Some developmentalists theorize it is not until adulthood that many individuals consolidate their formal operational thinking. That is, they may begin to plan and hypothesize about intellectual problems in adolescence, but they become more systematic and sophisticated at this as young adults. Nonetheless, even many adults do not think in formal operational ways at all (Kuhn, 2009).

Postformal Thought

It has been proposed that the idealism of Piaget's formal operational stage declines in young adults and is replaced by more realistic, pragmatic thinking. It also has been proposed that young adults move into a new qualitative stage of cognitive development called postformal thought (Sinnott, 2003). **Postformal thought** is:

What are some ways that young adults might think differently from adolescents?
© Yuri Arcurs/Alamy RF

- *Reflective, relativistic, and contextual.* As young adults engage in solving problems, they might think deeply about many aspects of work, politics, relationships, and other areas of life (Labouvie-Vief, 1986). They find that what might be the best solution to a problem at work (with a boss or co-worker) might not be the best solution at home (with a romantic partner). Thus, postformal thought holds that the correct answer to a problem requires reflective thinking and may vary from one situation to another. Some psychologists argue that reflective thinking continues to increase and becomes more internal and less contextual in middle age (Mascalo & Fischer, 2010; Labouvie-Vief, Gruhn, & Studer, 2010).

- *Provisional.* Many young adults also become more skeptical about the truth and seem unwilling to accept an answer as final. Thus, they come to see the search for truth as an ongoing and perhaps never-ending process.

- *Realistic.* Young adults understand that thinking can't always be abstract. In many instances, it must be realistic and pragmatic.

- *Recognized as being influenced by emotion.* Emerging and young adults are more likely than adolescents to understand that their thinking is influenced by emotions (Labouvie-Vief, 2009; Labouvie-Vief, Gruhn, & Studer, 2010). However, too often negative emotions produce thinking that is distorted and self-serving at this point in development.

How Would You...?

As an **educator,** how would you characterize the differences in the cognitive development of adolescents and adults? How would this distinction influence your approach to teaching these different populations?

Creativity

Early adulthood is a time of great creativity for some people. At the age of 30, Thomas Edison invented the phonograph, Hans Christian Andersen wrote his first volume of fairy tales, and Mozart composed *The Marriage of Figaro*. One early study of creativity found that individuals' most creative products were generated in their thirties, and that 80 percent of the most important creative contributions were completed by age 50 (Lehman, 1960). Even though a decline in creative contributions is often found in the fifties and later, the decline is not as great as was commonly thought.

Any consideration of decline in creativity with age must take into account the field of creativity involved (Jones, Reedy, & Weinberg, 2014; Kandler & others, 2016; McKay & Kaufman, 2014). In fields such as philosophy and history, older adults often show as much creativity as they did when they were in their thirties and forties. By contrast, in fields such as lyric poetry, abstract math, and theoretical physics, the peak of creativity is often reached in the twenties or thirties.

Researchers have found that personality traits are linked to creativity (Kandler & others, 2016). In one recent study, the personality trait of

How Would You...?

As an **educator,** how would you use your understanding of creativity to become a more effective teacher?

postformal thought Thinking that is reflective, relativistic, and contextual; provisional; realistic; and influenced by emotions.

openness to experience predicted creativity in the arts, while intellectual capacity predicted creativity in the sciences (Kaufman & others, 2016).

Can you make yourself more creative? Mihaly Csikszentmihalyi (1995) interviewed 90 leading figures in art, business, government, education, and science to learn how creativity works. He discovered that creative people regularly experience a state he calls *flow,* a heightened state of pleasure experienced when we are engaged in mental and physical challenges that absorb us. Csikszentmihalyi (2000) believes everyone is capable of achieving flow. Based on his interviews with some of the most creative people in the world, the first step toward a more creative life is cultivating your curiosity and interest. How can you do this?

- *Try to be surprised by something every day.* Maybe it is something you see, hear, or read about. Become absorbed in a lecture or a book. Be open to what the world is telling you. Life is a stream of experiences. Swim widely and deeply in it, and your life will be richer.

- *Try to surprise at least one person every day.* In a lot of things you do, you have to be predictable and patterned. Do something different for a change. Ask a question you normally would not ask. Invite someone to go to a show you haven't seen or a museum you never have visited.

- Write down each day what surprised you and how you surprised others. Most creative people keep a diary, notes, or lab records to ensure that their experience is not fleeting or forgotten. Start with a specific task. Each evening, record the most surprising event that occurred that day and your most surprising action. After a few days, reread your notes and reflect on your past experiences. After a few weeks, you might see a pattern of interest emerging in your notes, one that might suggest an area you can explore in greater depth.

Mihaly Csikszentmihalyi, in the setting where he gets his most creative ideas. *When and where do you get your most creative thoughts?*
© Dr. Mihaly Csikszentmihalyi

- When something sparks your interest, follow it. Usually when something captures your attention, it is short-lived—an idea, a song, a flower. Too often we are too busy to explore the idea, song, or flower further. Or we think these areas are none of our business because we are not experts about them. Yet the world is our business. We can't know which part of it is best suited to our interests until we make a serious effort to learn as much about as many aspects of it as possible.

- Wake up in the morning with a specific goal to look forward to. Creative people wake up eager to start the day. Why? Not necessarily because they are cheerful, enthusiastic types but because they know that there is something meaningful to accomplish each day, and they can't wait to get started.

- Spend time in settings that stimulate your creativity. In Csikszentmihalyi's (1995) research, he gave people an electronic pager and beeped them randomly at different times of the day. When he asked them how they felt, they reported the highest levels of creativity when walking, driving, or swimming. I (your author) do my most creative thinking when I'm jogging. These activities are semiautomatic in that they take a certain amount of attention while leaving some time free to make connections among ideas. Another setting in which highly creative people report coming up with novel ideas is the sort of half-asleep, half-awake state we are in when we are deeply relaxed or barely awake.

Careers and Work

Earning a living, choosing an occupation, establishing a career, and developing in a career—these are important themes of early adulthood. Let's consider some of the factors that go into choosing a career and a job, and examine how work typically affects the lives of young adults.

Careers

What are some developmental changes young adults experience as they choose a career? How effectively are individuals finding a path to purpose today?

Developmental Changes

Many children have idealistic fantasies about what they want to be when they grow up. For example, many young children want to be superheroes, sports stars, or movie stars. In the high school years, they often have begun to think about careers on a somewhat less idealistic basis. In their late teens and early twenties, their career decision making has usually turned more serious as they explore different career possibilities and zero in on the career they want to enter. In college, this often means choosing a major or specialization that is designed to lead to work in a particular field. By their early and mid-twenties, many individuals have completed their education or training and started to enter a full-time occupation. From the mid-twenties through the remainder of early adulthood, individuals often seek to establish their emerging career in a particular field. They may work hard to move up the career ladder and improve their financial standing.

"Did you think the ladder of success would be straight up?"

© Joseph Farris/The New Yorker Collection/www.cartoonbank.com.

Phyllis Moen (2009a) described the career mystique, which includes ingrained cultural beliefs that engaging in hard work for long hours through adulthood will produce a path to status, security, and happiness. That is, many individuals have an idealized concept of a career path toward achieving the American dream of upward mobility by climbing occupational ladders. However, the lockstep career mystique has never been a reality for many individuals, especially ethnic minority individuals, women, and poorly educated adults. Further, the career mystique has increasingly become a myth for many individuals in middle-income occupations as global outsourcing of jobs and widespread layoffs during the 2007–2009 recession have led to reduced job security for millions of Americans.

Finding a Path to Purpose

In his book *The Path to Purpose: Helping Our Children Find Their Calling in Life*, William Damon (2008) suggested that purpose is a missing ingredient in many adolescents' and emerging adults' achievement and career development. Too many youth drift aimlessly through their high school and college years, Damon says, engaging in behavior that places them at risk for not fulfilling their potential and not finding a life pursuit that energizes them.

In interviews with 12- to 22-year-olds, Damon found that only about 20 percent had a clear vision of where they wanted to go in life, what they wanted to achieve, and why. The largest percentage—about 60 percent—had engaged in some potentially purposeful

Hari Prabhakar (*in rear*) at a screening camp in India that he created as part of his Tribal India Health Foundation. Hari reflects William Damon's concept of finding a path to purpose. His ambition is to become an international health expert. A 2006 graduate from Johns Hopkins University (with a double major in public health and writing and a 3.9 GPA), he pursued many activities outside the classroom, in the health field. As he transitioned from high school to college, Hari created the Tribal India Health Foundation (www. tihf.org), which provides assistance in bringing low-cost health care to rural areas in India. Juggling roles as a student and as the foundation's director, Hari spent 15 hours a week leading Tribal India Health during his undergraduate years. Hari said (Johns Hopkins University, 2006): "I have found it very challenging to coordinate the international operation. . . . It takes a lot of work, and there's not a lot of free time. But it's worth it when I visit our patients and see how they and the community are getting better."

© Hari Prabhakar

activities, such as service learning or fruitful discussions with a career counselor—but they still did not have a real commitment or any reasonable plans for reaching their goals. And slightly more than 20 percent expressed no aspirations and in some instances said they didn't see any reason to have aspirations.

Damon concludes that most teachers and parents communicate the importance of such goals as studying hard and getting good grades, but rarely discuss the purpose of these goals and where they might lead young adults. Damon emphasizes that too often students focus only on short-term goals and don't explore the big, long-term picture of what they want to do with their life. The following interview questions that Damon (2008, p. 135) has used in his research are good springboards for getting individuals to reflect on their purpose:

- What's most important to you in your life?
- Why do you care about those things?
- Do you have any long-term goals?
- Why are these goals important to you?
- What does it mean to have a good life?
- What does it mean to be a good person?
- If you were looking back on your life now, how would you like to be remembered?

Recent research has provided support for the importance of purpose in people's lives. In one study, purpose predicted emerging adults' well-being (Hill & others, 2016). In another study, a high sense of purpose in life was associated with a lower incidence of cardiovascular disease and a longer life (Cohen, Bavishi, & Rozanski, 2016).

Work

In this final section, we'll examine how work affects people's lives, the role of work in college, the occupational outlook, unemployment, dual-earner couples, and diversity in the workplace.

The Impact of Work

Work defines people in fundamental ways (Parker, 2014). It is an important influence on their financial standing, housing, the way they spend their time, where they live, their friendships, and their health. Some people define their identity through their work. Work also creates a structure and rhythm to life that is often missed when individuals do not work for an extended period. When they are unable to work, many individuals experience emotional distress and low self-esteem.

Most individuals spend about one-third of their lives at work. In one survey, 35 percent of Americans worked 40 hours a week, but 18 percent worked 51 hours or more per week (Center for Survey Research at the University of Connecticut, 2000). Only 10 percent worked less than 30 hours a week.

Special concerns about the work lives of emerging adults are the unemployment rate of college graduates as well as the high percentage of recent college graduates who have had to take jobs that do not require a college degree. In 2015, the unemployment rate for college graduates was 7.2 percent, an increase from 6.4 percent at the peak of the 2009 recession (Davis, Kimball, & Gould, 2015; Gabor, 2014). Also, among college graduates who found jobs in 2014, 46 percent were in jobs that did not require a college degree (Davis, Kimball, & Gould, 2015).

A trend in the U.S. workforce is the disappearing long-term career for an increasing number of adults, especially men in private-sector jobs (Hollister, 2011). Among the reasons for this disappearance of many long-term jobs is the dramatic increase in technology and cheaper labor in other countries.

Many young and older adults are working at a series of jobs, and many work in short-term jobs (Greenhaus, 2013). Early careers are especially unstable as some young workers move from "survival jobs" to "career jobs" in the process of finding a job that matches their personal interests and goals (Mortimer, 2012; Staff,

Mont'Alvao, & Mortimer, 2015). A study of more than 1,100 individuals from 18 to 31 years of age revealed that maintaining a high aspiration and certainty over career goals better insulated individuals against unemployment during the severe economic recession that began in 2007 (Vuolo & others, 2012).

An important consideration regarding work is how stressful it is (Demsky, Ellis, & Fritz, 2014; Lamb & Kwok, 2016). A national survey of U.S. adults revealed that 55 percent indicated they were less productive because of stress (American Psychological Association, 2007). In this study, 52 percent reported that they considered or made a career decision, such as looking for a new job, declining a promotion, or quitting a job, because of stress in the workplace. In this survey, main sources of stress included low salaries (44 percent), lack of advancement opportunities (42 percent), uncertain job expectations (40 percent), and long hours (39 percent). A recent study revealed that stressors at work were linked to arterial hypertension in employees (Lamy & others, 2014).

Many adults hold changing expectations about work, yet employers often aren't meeting their expectations (Hall & Mirvis, 2013). For example, current policies and practices were designed for a single-breadwinner (male) workforce and an industrial economy, making these policies and practices out of step with a service-oriented workforce of women and men, and of single parents and dual earners. Many workers today want flexibility and greater control over the time and timing of their work, and yet most employers offer little flexibility, even if policies like flextime are "on the books."

Work During College

The percentage of full-time U.S. college students who also held jobs increased from 34 percent in 1970 to 47 percent in 2008, then declined to 41 percent in 2011 (down from a peak of 52 percent in 2000) (National Center for Education Statistics, 2013). In this recent survey, 74 percent of part-time U.S. college students were employed, down from 81 percent in 2008.

Working can pay for schooling or help offset some of its costs, but working also can restrict students' opportunities to learn. For those who identified themselves primarily as students, one national study found that as the number of hours worked per week increased, their grades suffered (National Center for Education Statistics, 2002) (see Figure 7). Thus, college students need to carefully examine whether the number of hours they work is having a negative impact on their college success.

Monitoring the Occupational Outlook

As you explore the type of work you are likely to enjoy and in which you can succeed, it is important to be knowledgeable about different fields and companies. Occupations may have many job openings one year but few in another year as economic conditions change. Thus, it is critical to keep up with the occupational outlook in various fields. An excellent resource for doing this is the U.S. government's *Occupational Outlook Handbook,* which is revised every two years.

According to the 2016–2017 handbook, the job categories of wind turbine service technicians, occupational therapy assistants, physical therapist assistants, physical therapist aides, home health aides, commercial drivers, nurse practitioners, physical therapists, and

How Would You...?
As an **educator,** what advice would you give to a student who has a full-time job while taking college classes?

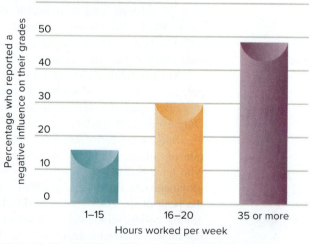

Figure 7 **The Relation of Hours Worked Per Week in College to Grades**
Among college students working to pay for school expenses, 16 percent of those working 1 to 15 hours per week reported that working had a negative impact on their grades (National Center for Education Statistics, 2002). Thirty percent of college students who worked 16 to 20 hours a week said the same, as did 48 percent who worked 35 hours or more per week.

statisticians are projected to be the fastest-growing through 2024. Projected job growth varies widely by educational requirements. Jobs that require a college degree are expected to grow the fastest. Most of the highest-paying occupations require a college degree.

Unemployment

Unemployment produces stress regardless of whether the job loss is temporary, cyclical, or permanent (Frasquilho & others, 2016; Jalles & Andresen, 2014). Banking problems and the recession toward the end of the first decade of the twenty-first century have produced very high unemployment rates, especially in

The economic recession that hit in 2007 resulted in millions of Americans losing their jobs, such as these individuals who are waiting to apply for unemployment benefits in Chicago. *What are some of the potential negative outcomes of the stress caused by job loss?*
© Scott Olson/Getty Images

the United States. Researchers have linked unemployment to physical problems (such as heart attack and stroke), emotional problems (such as depression and anxiety), marital difficulties, and homicide (Rizvi & others, 2015; Yoo & others, 2016). A recent study revealed that 90 or more days of unemployment was associated with subsequent cardiovascular disease across an 8-year follow-up period (Lundin & others, 2014). A 15-year longitudinal study of more than 24,000 adults found that their life satisfaction dropped considerably during unemployment and increased after they were reemployed but did not completely return to the same level of life satisfaction they had experienced prior to being unemployed (Lucas & others, 2004). Another study also revealed that immune system functioning declined with unemployment and increased with new employment (Cohen & others, 2007). A research review concluded that unemployment was associated with an increased mortality risk for individuals in the early and middle stages of their careers, but the link was weaker for those in the later years of their career (Roelfs & others, 2011). And a recent study found that involuntary job loss was linked to an increase in attempted suicide and suicide (Milner & others, 2014). Also, in a recent study, unemployment was associated with higher mortality and the link was higher for those who were unmarried (Van Hedel & others, 2015).

Might unemployment be linked to certain characteristics in childhood? Longitudinal data revealed that low self-control in childhood was linked to the emergence and persistence of unemployment from 21 to 50 years of age (Daly & others, 2015).

Stress from unemployment comes not only from a loss of income and the resulting financial hardships but also from decreased self-esteem (Howe & others, 2012). Individuals who cope best with unemployment have financial resources to rely on, often savings or the earnings of other family members. Emotional support from understanding, adaptable family members also helps individuals to cope with unemployment. Job counseling and self-help groups can provide practical advice on job searching, résumé writing, and interviewing skills, and also can lend emotional support (van Hooft, 2014).

Dual-Earner Couples

Dual-earner couples may have special problems finding a balance between work and the rest of life (Aazami, Shamsuddin, & Akmal, 2015; Schooreel & Verbruggen, 2016). If both partners are working, who cleans the house or calls the repairman or takes care of the other endless details involved in maintaining a home? If the couple has children, who is responsible for being sure that the children get to school or to piano lessons, and who writes the notes to approve field trips or meets the teacher or makes the dental appointments?

Many dual-earner couples engage in a range of adaptive strategies to coordinate their work and manage the family side of the work-family equation (Flood & Genadek, 2016; Moen, 2009b). Researchers have found that even though couples may strive for gender equality in dual-earner families, gender inequalities persist (Cunningham, 2009). For example, women still do not earn as much as men in the same jobs, and this inequity contributes to gender divisions in how much time each partner spends in paid work, homemaking, and caring for children. Thus, the decisions that dual-earner couples often make are in favor of men's greater earning power and women spending more time than men in homemaking and caring for children (Moen, 2009b). A recent study indicated that women reported more family interference from work than did men (Allen & Finkelstein, 2014). Another recent study found that partner coping, having a positive attitude toward multiple roles, using planning and management skills, and not having to cut back on professional responsibilities were linked to better relationships between dual earners (Matias & Fontaine, 2015).

Summary

The Transition from Adolescence to Adulthood

- Emerging adulthood, the time of transition from adolescence to adulthood, is characterized by experimentation and exploration.
- The transition from high school to college can involve both positive and negative features.

Physical Development

- Peak physical performance is often reached between 19 and 26 years of age. Then, toward the latter part of early adulthood, a detectable slowdown in physical performance is apparent for most individuals.
- Health problems in emerging and young adults may include obesity, a serious problem throughout the United States. Binge drinking is a special problem among U.S. college students, but by the mid-twenties alcohol and drug use often decreases.

Sexuality

- Patterns of sexual activity change during emerging adulthood.
- An individual's sexual preference likely stems from a combination of genetic, hormonal, cognitive, and environmental factors.
- Sexually transmitted infections, also called STIs, are contracted primarily through sexual contact.

Cognitive Development

- It has been proposed that the idealism of Piaget's formal operational stage declines in young adults and is replaced by more realistic, pragmatic thinking. A qualitatively different, fifth cognitive stage called postformal thought also has been proposed.
- Creativity peaks in adulthood, often in the forties, and then declines. Csikszentmihalyi proposed that the first step toward living a creative life is to cultivate curiosity and interest.

Careers and Work

- Thoughts about career choice for adolescents and young adults reflect developmental changes. Damon argues that too many individuals have difficulty finding a path to purpose today.
- Work defines people in fundamental ways and is a key aspect of their identity. Working during college can have a positive outcome, but it may also have a negative impact on grades. Jobs that require a college education will be the fastest-growing and highest-paying careers in the United States during the next decade.
- As the number of women working outside the home has increased, new issues involving work and family have arisen.

Key Terms

aerobic exercise

emerging adulthood

postformal thought

sexually transmitted infections (STIs)

12 Socioemotional Development in Early Adulthood

© Ariel Skelley/Blend Images/Corbis RF

CHAPTER OUTLINE

STABILITY AND CHANGE FROM CHILDHOOD TO ADULTHOOD

LOVE AND CLOSE RELATIONSHIPS

Intimacy

Friendship

Romantic and Affectionate Love

Consummate Love

ADULT LIFESTYLES

Single Adults

Cohabiting Adults

Married Adults

Divorced Adults

Remarried Adults

Gay and Lesbian Adults

CHALLENGES IN MARRIAGE, PARENTING, AND DIVORCE

Making Marriage Work

Becoming a Parent

Dealing with Divorce

Stories of Life-Span Development: Gwenna's Pursuit and Greg's Lack of Commitment

Commitment is an important issue in a romantic relationship for most individuals. Consider Gwenna, who decides that it is time to have a talk with Greg about his commitment to their relationship (Lerner, 1989, pp. 44–45):

> She shared her perspective on both the strengths and weaknesses of their relationship and what her hopes were for the future. She asked Greg to do the same. Unlike earlier conversations, this one was conducted without her pursuing him, pressuring him, or diagnosing his problems with women. At the same time, she asked Greg some clear questions, which exposed his vagueness.
>
> "How will you know when you are ready to make a commitment? What specifically would you need to change or be different than it is today?"
>
> "I don't know," was Greg's response. When questioned further, the best he could come up with was that he'd just feel it.
>
> "How much more time do you need to make a decision one way or another?"
>
> "I'm not sure," Greg replied. "Maybe a couple of years, but I really can't answer a question like that. I can't predict my feelings."
>
> And so it went.
>
> Gwenna really loved this man, but two years (and maybe longer) was longer than she could comfortably wait. So, after much thought, she told Greg that she would wait till fall (about ten months), but that she would move on if he couldn't commit himself to marriage by then.

She was open about her wish to marry and have a family with him, but she was equally clear that her first priority was a mutually committed relationship. If Greg had not reached that point by fall, then she would end the relationship—painful though it would be.

During the waiting period, Gwenna was able to not pursue him and not get distant or otherwise reactive to his expressions of ambivalence and doubt. In this way she gave Greg emotional space to struggle with his dilemma, and the relationship had its best chance of succeeding. Her bottom-line position ("a decision by fall") was not a threat or an attempt to rope Greg in, but rather a clear statement of what was acceptable to her.

When fall arrived, Greg told Gwenna he needed another six months to make up his mind. Gwenna deliberated a while and decided she could live with that. But when the six months were up, Greg was uncertain and asked for more time. It was then that Gwenna took the painful but ultimately empowering step of ending their relationship.

Love is of central importance in each of our lives, as it is in Gwenna's and Greg's lives. Shortly, we discuss the many faces of love, as well as the diversity of adult lifestyles, aspects of marriage and the family, and the role of gender in relationships. To begin, though, we will return to an issue we initially raised in the introductory chapter of this text: stability and change. ∎

Stability and Change from Childhood to Adulthood

For adults, socioemotional development revolves around adaptively integrating our emotional experiences into enjoyable relationships with others on a daily basis. Young adults like Gwenna and Greg face choices and challenges in adopting lifestyles that will be emotionally satisfying, predictable, and manageable for them. Clearly they do not come to these tasks as blank slates, but do their decisions and actions simply reflect the persons they had already become when they were 5 years old or 10 years old or 20 years old?

Current research shows that the first 20 years of life lay the foundation for an adult's socioemotional development (Cassidy, 2016; Cicchetti & Toth, 2015, 2016; Fraley & Shaver, 2016; Thompson, 2015, 2016). And there is also every reason to believe that experiences in the early adult years are important in determining what the individual will be like later in adulthood. A common finding is that the smaller the time intervals over which we measure socioemotional characteristics, the more similar an individual will look from one measurement to the next. Thus, if we measure an individual's self-concept at the age of 20, and then again at the age of 30, we will probably find more stability than if we measured the individual's self-concept at the age of 10 and then again at the age of 30.

In trying to understand the young adult's socioemotional development, it would be misleading to look at an adult's life only in the present, ignoring the unfolding of social relationships and emotions. So, too, it would be a mistake to search only through a 30-year-old's first five to ten years of life in trying to understand why he or she is having difficulty in a close relationship. To further explore stability and change, let's examine attachment.

Attachment appears during infancy and plays an important part in socioemotional development (Pasco-Fearon & others, 2016; Thompson, 2015, 2016). We've discussed its role in infancy and adolescence. How do these earlier patterns of attachment and adults' attachment styles influence the lives of adults?

Although relationships with romantic partners differ from those with parents, romantic partners fulfill some of the same needs for adults as parents do for their children (Mikulincer & Shaver, 2016; Zayas & Hazan, 2014).

Recall that *securely attached* infants are defined as those who use the caregiver as a secure base from which to explore the environment. Similarly, adults may count on their romantic partner to be a secure base to which they can return and obtain comfort and security during stressful times (Mikulincer & Shaver, 2016).

How Would You...?

As a **human development and family studies professional,** how would you help individuals understand how early relationship experiences might influence their close relationships in adulthood?

secure attachment style An attachment style that describes adults who have positive views of relationships, find it easy to get close to others, and are not overly concerned or stressed out about their romantic relationships.

avoidant attachment style An attachment style that describes adults who are hesitant about getting involved in romantic relationships and once they are in a relationship tend to distance themselves from their partner.

Do adult attachment patterns with partners reflect childhood attachment patterns with parents and parental sensitivity in infancy? In a retrospective study, Cindy Hazan and Phillip Shaver (1987) revealed that young adults who were securely attached in their romantic relationships were more likely to describe their early relationship with their parents as securely attached. In a longitudinal study, infants who were securely attached at age 1 were securely attached 20 years later in their adult romantic relationships (Steele & others, 1998). Also, a longitudinal study revealed that securely attached infants were in more stable romantic relationships in adulthood than their insecurely attached counterparts (Salvatore & others, 2011). A longitudinal study found that insecure avoidant attachment at 8 years of age was linked to a lower level of social initiative and prosocial behavior and a higher level of social anxiety and loneliness at 21 years of age (Fransson & others, 2016). Further, a recent study of adoptees found that higher maternal sensitivity in infancy and middle and late childhood predicted more secure attachment to partners in emerging adulthood (Schoenmaker & others, 2015). However, in another longitudinal study, links between early attachment styles and later attachment styles were lessened by stressful and disruptive experiences such as the death of a parent or instability of caregiving (Lewis, Feiring, & Rosenthal, 2000).

Adults' attachment can be categorized as secure, avoidant, or anxious:

- **Secure attachment style.** Securely attached adults have positive views of relationships, find it easy to get close to others, and are not overly concerned with or stressed out about their romantic relationships. These adults tend to enjoy sexuality in the context of a committed relationship and are less likely than others to have one-night stands.

- **Avoidant attachment style.** Avoidant individuals are hesitant about getting involved in romantic relationships, and once they are in a relationship, they tend to distance themselves from their partner.

What are some key dimensions of attachment in adulthood, and how are they related to relationship patterns and well-being?

© MM Productions/Corbis RF

● **Anxious attachment style.** These individuals demand closeness, are less trusting, and are more emotional, jealous, and possessive.

The majority of adults (about 60 to 80 percent) describe themselves as securely attached, and not surprisingly adults prefer having a securely attached partner (Zeifman & Hazan, 2008). Researchers are studying links between adults' current attachment styles and various aspects of their lives (Birnbaum, 2015; Mikulincer & Shaver, 2016; Reiner & others, 2016; Zayas, Merrill, & Hazan, 2015). For example, securely attached adults are more satisfied with their close relationships than insecurely attached adults, and the relationships of securely attached adults are more likely to be characterized by trust, commitment, and longevity. In a recent study, young adults with an anxious attachment style were more likely to be characterized by higher negative affect, stress, and perceived social rejection; those with an avoidant attachment style were more likely to be characterized by less desire to be with others when alone (Sheinbaum & others, 2015). In another recent study, secure attachment in adults was linked to fewer sleep disruptions than insecure avoidant and anxious attachment (Adams & McWilliams, 2015). Also, in one study, insecurely attached adults had a higher level of social anxiety than their securely attached counterparts (Notzon & others, 2016). And a recent meta-analysis of 94 samples of U.S. college students from 1988 to 2011 found that the percentage of students with a secure attachment style had decreased in recent years while the percentage of students with insecure attachment styles had increased (Konrath & others, 2014).

If you have an insecure attachment style, are you stuck with it and does it doom you to have problematic relationships? Attachment categories are somewhat stable in adulthood, but adults do have the capacity to change their attachment thinking and behavior (Mikulincer & Shaver, 2016). Although attachment insecurities are linked to relationship problems, attachment style is only one factor that contributes to relationship functioning; other factors also contribute to relationship satisfaction and success. Later in the chapter, we will discuss some of these factors in our coverage of marital relationships.

Love and Close Relationships

Love refers to a vast and complex territory of human behavior, spanning a range of relationships that includes friendship, romantic love, affectionate love, and consummate love (Berscheid, 2010; Sternberg & Sternberg, 2013). In most of these types of love, one recurring theme is intimacy.

Intimacy

Self-disclosure and the sharing of private thoughts are hallmarks of intimacy (Prager, 2013). Adolescents have an increased need for intimacy. At the same time, they are engaged in the essential tasks of developing an identity and establishing their independence from their parents. Juggling the competing demands of intimacy, identity, and independence also becomes a central task of adulthood.

Recall that Erik Erikson (1968) argues that identity versus identity confusion—pursuing who we are, what we are all about, and where we are going in life—is the most important issue to be negotiated in adolescence. In early adulthood, according to Erikson, after individuals are well on their way to establishing stable and successful identities, they enter the sixth developmental stage, which is intimacy versus isolation. Erikson describes intimacy as finding oneself while losing oneself in another person, and it requires a commitment to another person.

Why is intimacy an important aspect of early adulthood?
© Peeter Viisimaa/Getty RF

Development in early adulthood often involves balancing intimacy and commitment on the one hand, and independence and freedom on the other. At the same time that individuals are trying to establish an identity, they face the challenges of increasing their independence from their parents, developing an intimate relationship with another individual, and continuing their friendship commitments. They also face the task of making decisions for themselves without always relying on what others say or do.

Friendship

Increasingly, researchers are finding that friendship plays an important role in development throughout the life span (Blieszner & Roberto, 2012a, b). Most U.S. men and women have a best friend. Ninety-two percent of women and 88 percent of men have a best friend of the same sex (Blieszner, 2009). Many friendships are long-lasting, as 65 percent of U.S. adults have known their best friend for at least 10 years and only 15 percent have known their best friend for less than 5 years. Adulthood brings opportunities for new friendships; when individuals move to new locations, they may establish new friendships in their neighborhood or at work (Blieszner, 2009).

How is adult friendship different among female friends, male friends, and cross-gender friends?
© PhotoAlto RF

As in the childhood years, there are gender differences in adult friendship (Blieszner & Roberto, 2012b). Compared with men, women have more close friends and their friendships involve more self-disclosure and mutual support (Wood, 2012). Women are more likely to listen at length to what a friend has to say and be sympathetic, and women have been labeled "talking companions" because talk is so central to their relationships (Gouldner & Strong, 1987). Women's friendships tend to be characterized not only by depth but also by breadth: Women share many aspects of their experiences, thoughts, and feelings (Helgeson, 2012). One study revealed that in their early twenties, women showed more emotional intimacy with their closest friend than did men (Boden, Fischer, & Niehuis, 2010).

Cross-gender friendships can provide both opportunities and problems (Helgeson, 2012). The opportunities involve learning more about common feelings and interests and shared characteristics, as well as acquiring knowledge and understanding of beliefs and activities that historically have been typical of the other gender. Problems can arise in cross-gender friendships because of different expectations. One problem that can plague an adult cross-gender friendship is unclear sexual boundaries, which can produce tension and confusion (Hart, Adams, & Tullett, 2016).

Romantic and Affectionate Love

Although friendship is included in some conceptualizations of love, when we think about what love is, other types of love typically come to mind. In this section we explore two widely recognized types of love: romantic love and affectionate love.

Romantic Love

How Would You...?

As a **health-care professional,** how would you advise individuals who are concerned about their sexual functioning because their romantic relationship seems to be losing its spark?

Some friendships evolve into **romantic love,** which is also called passionate love, or *eros.* Romantic love has strong components of sexuality and infatuation, and as well-known love researcher Ellen Berscheid (2010) has found, it often predominates in the early part of a love relationship. A meta-analysis found that males show higher avoidance and lower anxiety about romantic love than females do (Del Giudice, 2011).

romantic love Also called passionate love, or *eros;* romantic love has strong sexual and infatuation components and often predominates in the early period of a love relationship.

affectionate love In this type of love, also called companionate love, an individual desires to have the other person near and has a deep, caring affection for the other person.

A complex intermingling of different emotions goes into romantic love—including passion, fear, anger, sexual desire, joy, and jealousy. Sexual desire is the most important ingredient of romantic love (Berscheid, 2010). Obviously, some of these emotions are a source of anguish, which can lead to other issues such as depression. One study found that a relationship between romantic lovers was more likely than a relationship between friends to be a cause of depression (Berscheid & Fei, 1977). Also, a recent study revealed that a heightened state of romantic love in young adults was linked to stronger depression and anxiety symptoms but better sleep quality (Bajoghli & others, 2014). And a recent study confirmed that declaring a relationship status on Facebook was associated with both romantic love and jealousy (Orosz & others, 2015).

Affectionate Love

Love is more than just passion. **Affectionate love,** also called companionate love, is the type of love that occurs when someone desires to have the other person near and has a deep, caring affection for the person.

The early stages of love have more romantic love ingredients—but as love matures, passion tends to give way to affection (Berscheid, 2010). Phillip Shaver (1986) proposed a developmental model of love in which the initial phase of romantic love is fueled by a mixture of sexual attraction and gratification, a reduced sense of loneliness, uncertainty about the security of developing another attachment, and excitement from exploring the novelty of another human being. With time, he says, sexual attraction wanes, attachment anxieties either lessen or produce conflict and withdrawal, novelty is replaced with familiarity, and lovers find themselves either securely attached in a deeply caring relationship or distressed—feeling bored, disappointed, lonely, or hostile, for example. In the latter case, one or both partners may eventually end the relationship and then move on to another relationship.

Consummate Love

So far we have discussed two forms of love: romantic (or passionate) and affectionate (or companionate). According to Robert J. Sternberg (1988; Sternberg & Sternberg, 2013), these are not the only forms of love. Sternberg proposed a triarchic theory of love in which love can be thought of as a triangle with three main dimensions—passion, intimacy, and commitment. Passion involves physical and sexual attraction to another. Intimacy relates to the emotional feelings of warmth, closeness, and sharing in a relationship. Commitment is the cognitive appraisal of the relationship and the intent to maintain the relationship even in the face of problems.

In Sternberg's theory, the strongest, fullest form of love is *consummate love,* which involves all three dimensions (see Figure 1). If passion is the only ingredient in a relationship (with intimacy and commitment low or absent), we are merely *infatuated.* An affair or a fling in which there is little intimacy and even less commitment is an example. A relationship marked by intimacy and commitment but low or lacking in passion is called *affectionate love,* a pattern often found among couples who have been married for many years. If passion and commitment are present but intimacy is not, Sternberg calls the relationship *fatuous love,* as when one person worships another from a distance. But if couples share all three dimensions—passion, intimacy, and commitment— they experience consummate love (Sternberg & Sternberg, 2013).

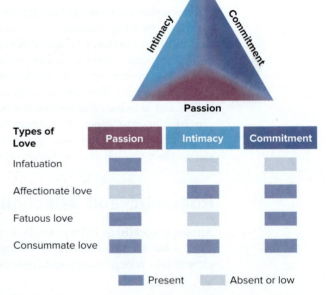

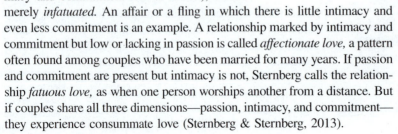

Types of Love	Passion	Intimacy	Commitment
Infatuation	Present	Absent or low	Absent or low
Affectionate love	Absent or low	Present	Present
Fatuous love	Present	Absent or low	Present
Consummate love	Present	Present	Present

Figure 1 Sternberg's Triangle of Love

Sternberg identified three dimensions of love: passion, intimacy, and commitment. Various combinations of these dimensions result in infatuation, affectionate love, fatuous love, and consummate love.

Adult Lifestyles

A striking social change in recent decades has been the decreased stigma attached to individuals who do not maintain what were long considered conventional families. Adults today choose many lifestyles and form many types of families (Hiekel, Liefbroer, & Poortman, 2015). They live alone, cohabit, marry, divorce, or live with someone of the same sex.

In his book *The Marriage-Go-Round* sociologist Andrew Cherlin (2009) concluded that the United States has more marriages and remarriages, more divorces, and more short-term cohabiting (living together) relationships than most countries. Combined, these lifestyles create more turnover and movement in and out of relationships in the United States than in virtually any other country. Let's explore these varying relationship lifestyles.

Single Adults

Recent decades have seen a dramatic rise in the percentage of single adults. In 2014, 45 percent of U.S. adults 18 years of age and older had never been married (U.S. Census Bureau, 2015a). In the 18- to 29-year-old age bracket, the percentage of individuals who are single and never been married increased from 48 percent in 2005 to 64 percent in 2014 (Gallup Poll, 2015). The increasing number of single adults reflects rising rates of cohabitation and a trend toward postponing marriage. The United States has a lower percentage of single adults than many other countries such as Great Britain, Germany, and Japan. The fastest growth in adopting a single adult lifestyle is occurring in rapidly developing countries such as China, India, and Brazil (Klinenberg, 2013).

Common challenges faced by single adults may include forming intimate relationships with other adults, confronting loneliness, and finding a niche in a society that is marriage-oriented. Bella DePaulo (2006, 2011) argues that society has a widespread bias against unmarried adults that is seen in everything from missed perks in jobs to deep social and financial prejudices.

Advantages of being single include having time to make decisions about one's life course, time to develop personal resources to meet goals, freedom to make autonomous decisions and pursue one's own schedule and interests, opportunities to explore new places and try out new experiences, and privacy.

Cohabiting Adults

Cohabitation refers to living together in a sexual relationship without being married. Cohabitation has undergone considerable changes in recent years (Barr, Simons, & Simons, 2015; Hognas & Thomas, 2016; Tach & Eads, 2015; Willoughby & Belt, 2016). There has been a dramatic increase in the number of cohabiting U.S. couples since 1970, with more than 60 percent cohabiting prior to getting married (National Marriage Project, 2011). As shown in Figure 2, the upward trend shows no sign of letting up—from 3.8 million cohabiting couples in 2000 to 7.8 million cohabiting couples in 2012 (Vespa, Lewis, & Kreider, 2013). Cohabitation rates are even higher in some countries—in Sweden, for example, cohabitation before marriage is virtually universal (Stokes & Raley, 2009).

A number of couples view their cohabitation not as a precursor to marriage but as an ongoing lifestyle (Klinenberg, 2013). These couples do not want the official aspects of marriage. In the United States, cohabiting arrangements tend to be short-lived, with

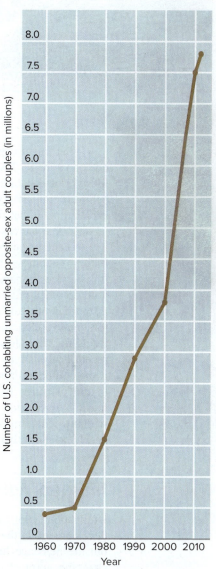

Figure 2 **The Increase in Cohabitation in the United States** Since 1970, there has been a dramatic increase in the number of unmarried adults living together in the United States.

What are some potential advantages and disadvantages of cohabitation?

© Image Source/Corbis RF

one-third lasting less than a year (Hyde & DeLamater, 2014). Fewer than 1 out of 10 lasts five years. Of course, it is easier to dissolve a cohabitation relationship than a marriage.

Couples who cohabit face certain problems (Blumberg, Vahratian, & Blumberg, 2014; Willoughby & Belt, 2015). Disapproval by parents and other family members can place emotional strain on the cohabiting couple. Some cohabiting couples have difficulty owning property jointly. Legal rights on the dissolution of the relationship are less certain than in a divorce.

If a couple live together before they marry, does cohabiting help or harm their chances of later having a stable and happy marriage? The majority of studies have found lower rates of marital satisfaction and higher rates of divorce in couples who lived together before getting married (Copen, Daniels, & Mosher, 2013; Whitehead & Popenoe, 2003). However, recent research indicates that the link between marital cohabitation and marital instability in first marriages has weakened in recent cohorts (Smock & Gupta, 2013).

What might explain the finding that cohabiting is linked with divorce more than not cohabiting? The most frequently given explanation is that the less traditional lifestyle of cohabitation may attract less conventional individuals who are not great believers in marriage in the first place (Whitehead & Popenoe, 2003). An alternative explanation is that the experience of cohabiting changes people's attitudes and habits in ways that increase their likelihood of divorce.

Recent research has provided clarification of cohabitation outcomes. One meta-analysis found the negative link between cohabitation and marital instability did not hold up when only cohabitation with the eventual marital partner was examined, indicating that these cohabitors may attach more long-term positive meaning to living together (Jose, O'Leary, & Moyer, 2010). Also, a recent analysis indicated that cohabiting does not have a negative effect on marriage if the couple did not have any previous live-in lovers and did not have children prior to the marriage (Cherlin, 2009). And a recent study concluded that the risk of marital dissolution between cohabitors (compared with individuals who married without cohabiting) was much smaller when they cohabited in their mid-twenties and later (Kuperberg, 2014).

How Would You...?

As a **psychologist,** how would you counsel a couple deciding whether to cohabit before marriage?

Married Adults

Until about 1930, stable marriage was widely accepted as the endpoint of adult development. In the last 70 to 80 years, however, personal fulfillment both inside and outside marriage has emerged as a goal that competes with marital stability. The changing norm of male-female equality in marriage and increasingly high expectations for what a marital relationship should be have produced marital relationships that are more fragile and intense than they were for earlier generations (Seccombe, 2015). A study of 502 newlyweds found that nearly all couples had optimistic forecasts of how their marriage would change over the next four years (Lavner & Bradbury, 2013). Despite their optimistic forecasts, their marital satisfaction declined across this time frame. Wives with the most optimistic forecasts showed the steepest declines in marital satisfaction.

Some characteristics of marital partners predict whether the marriage will last longer. Two such characteristics are education and ethnicity. A recent interview study involving more than 22,000 women found that both women and men with a bachelor's degree were more likely to delay marriage but were also more likely to eventually get married and stay married for more than 20 years (Copen, Daniels, & Mosher, 2013). Also in this study, Asian American women were the most likely of all ethnic groups to be in a first marriage that lasted at least 20 years—70 percent were in a first marriage that lasted this long, compared with 54 percent for non-Latino White women, 53 percent for Latino women, and 37 percent for African American women.

Marital Trends

In recent years, marriage rates in the United States have declined. Recently, the marriage rate continued to drop to 6.7 per 1,000 individuals, down from 8.2 in 2000 (Centers for Disease Control and Prevention, 2014). In 2012, 48.6 percent of Americans were married, down from 72 percent in 1960 (U.S. Census Bureau, 2013).

More adults are remaining single longer, with 27 percent of U.S. adults currently having never married (Pew Research Center, 2010). By 2014, the U.S. average age for a first marriage had climbed to 29.3 years for men and 27 years for women, higher than at any other point in history (U.S. Census Bureau, 2015b). In 1960, the average age for a first marriage in the United States was 23 years for men and 20 years for women. In addition, the increase in cohabitation and a slight decline in the percentage of divorced individuals who remarry contribute to declining marriage rates in the United States (Copen & others, 2012).

An increasing number of children are growing up in families with unmarried parents not because of divorce but because their parents have never married, a circumstance that is far more likely to occur when the mother has a low level of education (Pew Research Center, 2015b). In a recent study, women with lower levels of education were more likely to have a birth in a cohabiting relationship that was established prior to conception (Gibson-Davis & Rackin, 2014). In this study, the probability that a low-educated mother would have a conventional married birth was only 11.5 percent compared with 78.4 percent for highly educated mothers.

A recent study explored what U.S. never-married men and women are looking for in a potential spouse (Wang, 2014). Following are the percentages who reported that various factors would be very important for them:

Factor	Men	Women
Similar ideas about having and raising children	62	70
A steady job	46	78
Same moral and religious beliefs	31	38
At least as much education	26	28
Same racial or ethnic background	7	10

Thus, in this study, never-married men said that the most important factor for a potential spouse was similar ideas about having and raising children, but never-married women placed greater importance on having a partner with a steady job.

Despite the decline in marriage rates, the United States is still a marrying society (Welch, 2015). In 2010, by 40 years of age, 77 percent of individuals had ever been married, although this figure is substantially below the figure of 93 percent in the 1960s (Pew Research Center, 2011). In a national poll, more than 40 percent of Americans under 30 expressed a belief that marriage was headed for extinction, yet only 5 percent of those young adults said they didn't want to get married (Pew Research Center, 2010). These findings may reflect marriage's role as a way to show friends and family that you have a successful social life (Cherlin, 2009).

Recently, romantic attraction has not only taken place in person but also over the Internet (Khan & Chaudhry, 2015; Kmietowicz, 2015; Reed, Tolman, & Ward, 2016). In a recent U.S. survey, 10 percent of 18- to 24-year-olds, 22 percent of 25- to 34-year-olds, and 17 percent of 35- to 44-year-olds reported that they had used online dating sites or apps (Pew Research Center, 2015a). In their twenties, women have more online pursuers than men, but in their forties men have more online pursuers. When online dating began in 2005 it was viewed by most people as not being a good way to meet people, but in a recent national survey a majority

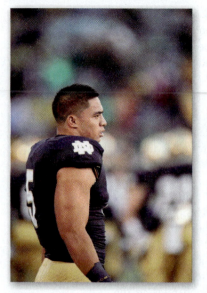

Manti Te'o.
© John Biever/Sports
Illustrated/Getty Images

of Americans said that online dating is a good way to meet people (Pew Research Center, 2015a).

Is looking for love and a marital partner online likely to work out? It didn't work out well in 2012 for Notre Dame linebacker Manti Te'o, whose online girlfriend turned out to be a "catfish," someone who fakes an identity online. However, online dating sites claim that their sites often have positive outcomes. A poll commissioned by Match.com in 2009 reported that twice as many marriages occurred between individuals who met through an online dating site as between people who met at bars, clubs, and other social events.

One problem with online matchmaking is that many individuals misrepresent their characteristics, such as how old they are, how attractive they are, and their occupation. Despite such dishonesty, some researchers have found that romantic relationships initiated on the Internet are more likely than relationships established in person to last for more than two years (Bargh & McKenna, 2004). And a national study of more than 19,000 individuals found that more than one-third of marriages now begin online (Cacioppo & others, 2013). Also in this study, marriages that began online were slightly less likely to break up and were characterized by slightly higher marital satisfaction than those that started in traditional offline contexts.

Is there a best age to get married? Marriages in adolescence are more likely to end in divorce than marriages in adulthood (Copen & others, 2012). However, researchers have not been able to pin down a specific age range for getting married that is most likely to result in a successful marriage (Furstenberg, 2007).

How happy are people who do marry? The average duration of a marriage in the United States is currently just over nine years. As indicated in Figure 3, the percentage of married individuals in the United States who said their marriages were "very happy" declined from the 1970s through the early 1990s, but recently the decline has begun to flatten out (Popenoe, 2009). Notice in Figure 3 that men consistently report being happier in their marriages than women do.

The Benefits of a Good Marriage

Are there any benefits to having a good marriage? Individuals who are happily married live longer, healthier lives than either divorced individuals or those who are unhappily married (Kilpi & others, 2015; Lo, Cheng, & Simpson, 2015). In a recent research review, it was concluded that the experience of divorce or separation confers risk for poor health outcomes, including a 23 percent higher mortality rate (Sbarra, 2015). A survey of U.S. adults 50 years and older also revealed that a lower portion

Figure 3 Percentage of Married Persons Age 18 and Older with "Very Happy" Marriages

of adult life spent in marriage was linked to an increased likelihood of dying at an earlier age (Henretta, 2010). Also, in a recent large-scale study in the United States and six European countries, not being in the labor force was associated with higher mortality but marriage attenuated the increased mortality risk linked to labor force inactivity (Van Hedel & others, 2015). Further, an unhappy marriage can shorten a person's life by an average of four years (Gove, Style, & Hughes, 1990).

What are the reasons for the benefits of a happy marriage? People in happy marriages are likely to feel less physically and emotionally stressed, which puts less wear and tear on a person's body. Such wear and tear can lead to numerous physical ailments, such as high blood pressure and heart disease, as well as psychological problems such as anxiety, depression, and substance abuse.

Divorced Adults

In the 1980s divorce reached epidemic proportions in the United States (Braver & Lamb, 2013). However, the divorce rate declined in recent decades, peaking at 5.1 divorces per 1,000 people in 1981 and declining to 3.2 divorces per 1,000 people in 2014 (Centers for Disease Control and Prevention, 2015). The 2014 divorce rate of 3.2 compares with a marriage rate of 6.9 per 1,000 people in 2014.

Although the divorce rate has dropped, the United States still has one of the highest divorce rates in the world. Russia has the highest divorce rate (4.7 divorces per 1,000 people) (UNSTAT, 2011). In the United States, nearly half of first marriages will break up within 20 years (Copen, Daniels, & Mosher, 2013).

Individuals in some groups have higher rates of divorce (Repetti, Flook, & Sperling, 2011). Youthful marriage, low educational level, low income, not having a religious affiliation, having parents who are divorced, and having a baby before marriage are factors that are associated with increases in divorce (Hoelter, 2009). And certain characteristics of one's partner increase the likelihood of divorce: alcoholism, psychological problems, domestic violence, infidelity, and inadequate division of household labor (Hoelter, 2009).

Earlier, we indicated that researchers have not been able to pin down a specific age that is the best time to marry so that the marriage will be less likely to end in a divorce. However, if a divorce is going to occur, it usually takes place early in a marriage, most often between the fifth and tenth years of marriage (National Center for Health Statistics, 2000) (see Figure 4). For example, a recent study found that divorce peaked in Finland at approximately 5 to 7 years after a marriage, then the rate of divorce gradually declined (Kulu, 2014). This timing may reflect an effort by partners in troubled marriages to stay in the marriage and try to work things out.

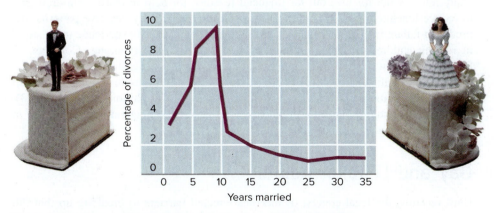

Figure 4 The Divorce Rate in Relation to Number of Years Married
Shown here is the percentage of divorces as a function of how long couples have been married. Notice that most divorces occur in the early years of marriage, peaking in the fifth to tenth years of marriage.

© Digital Vision/Getty Images RF

If after several years these efforts have not improved the relationship, the couple may then seek a divorce.

Both partners experience challenges after a marriage dissolves (Sbarra, Hasselamo, & Bourassa, 2015). Divorced adults have higher rates of depression, anxiety, physical illnesses, suicide, motor vehicle accidents, alcoholism, and mortality (Braver & Lamb, 2013). Both divorced women and divorced men complain of loneliness, diminished self-esteem, anxiety about the unknowns in their lives, and difficulty in forming satisfactory new intimate relationships (Hetherington, 2006). A recent research review concluded that both divorced men and women are more likely to commit suicide than their married counterparts (Yip & others, 2015). And in a recent study, both divorced men and women had a higher risk for having a heart attack than those who were married, but the risk for this cardiovascular disease was higher for divorced women than for divorced men (Dupre & others, 2015).

There are gender differences in the process and outcomes of divorce (Braver & Lamb, 2013). Women are more likely to sense that something is wrong with the marriage and are more likely to seek a divorce than are men. Women also show better emotional adjustment and are more likely to perceive divorce as a "second chance" to increase their happiness, improve their social lives, and seek better work opportunities. However, divorce typically has a more negative economic impact on women than it does on men.

Remarried Adults

Adults who remarry usually do so rather quickly, with approximately 50 percent remarrying within three years after they initially divorce (Sweeney, 2009, 2010). Men remarry sooner than women. Men with higher incomes are more likely to remarry than their counterparts with lower incomes. Remarriage occurs sooner for partners who initiate a divorce (especially in the first several years after divorce and for older women) than for those who do not initiate it (Sweeney, 2009, 2010). And some remarried individuals are more adult-focused, responding more to the concerns of their partner, while others are more child-focused, responding more to the concerns of their children (Anderson & Greene, 2011).

Recent data indicate that the remarriage rate in the United States has declined, going from 50 of every 1,000 divorced or widowed Americans in 1990 to 28 of every 1,000 in 2013 (Payne, 2015). One reason for the decline is the dramatic increase in cohabitation in recent years. Men are more likely to get remarried than women; in 2013, the remarriage rate was almost twice as high for men as women (40 per 1,000 for men and 21 per 1,000 for women in that year) (Payne, 2015). Thus, men are either more eager or more able to find new spouses than are women.

Remarried adults often find it difficult to stay remarried. Why? For one thing, many remarry not for love but for financial reasons, for help in rearing children, and to reduce loneliness. They also might carry into the stepfamily negative patterns that produced failure in an earlier marriage. Remarried couples also experience more stress in rearing children than parents in never-divorced families (Ganong, Coleman, & Russell, 2015; Sierra, 2015). One study revealed that positive attitudes about divorce, low marital quality, and divorce proneness were more common among remarried persons than among their counterparts in first marriages (Whitton & others, 2013). Another recent study found that remarried adults had less frequent sex than those in their first marriage (Stroope, McFarland, & Uecker, 2015).

Gay and Lesbian Adults

Until recently, the legal context of marriage created barriers to breaking up that did not exist for same-sex partners. However, the legalization of same-sex marriage in all 50 states in 2015 also created this barrier for same-sex partners. In many additional ways, researchers have found that gay and lesbian relationships are similar—in their satisfactions, loves, joys, and conflicts—to heterosexual relationships (Fingerhut & Peplau, 2013). For example, like heterosexual couples, gay and lesbian couples need to find a balance of romantic love, affection, autonomy, and equality that is acceptable to both partners (Hope, 2009). An increasing number of gay and lesbian couples are creating families that include children.

to find a balance of romantic love, affection, autonomy, and equality that is acceptable to both partners (Hope, 2009). An increasing number of gay and lesbian couples are creating families that include children.

transgender A broad term that refers to individuals whose gender identity or behavior is either completely or partially at odds with the sex into which they were born.

Data from the American Community Survey conducted in 2006–2010 indicate that among same-sex couples in the United States, lesbian couples are approximately five times more likely to be raising children than are gay couples (Miller & Price, 2013). An increasing number of same-sex couples are adopting children (Farr & Patterson, 2013). The percentage of same-sex couples who had adopted children nearly doubled from 10 percent in 2000 to 19 percent in 2009 (DiBennardo & Gates, 2014). Recall that recent research indicated lesbian and gay couples shared child care more than heterosexual couples did, with lesbian couples being the most supportive and gay couples the least supportive (Farr & Patterson, 2013). Also, a recent survey found that a greater percentage of same-sex, dual-earner couples than different sex couples said they share laundry (44 versus 31 percent), household repairs (33 versus 15 percent), and routine (74 versus 38 percent) and sick (62 versus 32 percent) child care responsibilities (Matos, 2015).

There are a number of misconceptions about gay and lesbian couples. Contrary to stereotypes, one partner is masculine and the other feminine in only a small percentage of gay and lesbian couples. Only a small segment of the gay population has a large number of sexual partners, and this is uncommon among lesbians. Furthermore, researchers have found that gay and lesbian couples prefer long-term, committed relationships (Fingerhut & Peplau, 2013). About half of committed gay couples do have an open relationship that allows the possibility of sex (but not affectionate love) outside of the relationship. Lesbian couples usually do not have an open relationship.

A special concern is the stigma, prejudice, and discrimination that lesbian, gay, and bisexual individuals experience because of widespread social devaluation of same-sex relationships (van der Star & Branstrom, 2015). However, researchers have found that many individuals in these relationships saw stigma as bringing them closer together and strengthening their relationship (Frost, 2011).

Recently, considerable interest has been shown in the term **transgender,** a broad term that refers to individuals whose gender identity or behavior is either completely or partially at odds with the sex into which they were born. For example, an individual may have a female body but identify more strongly with being masculine than being feminine. Transgender persons also may not want to be labeled "he" or "she" but prefer a more neutral label such as "they" or "ze" (Scelfo, 2015). Transgender individuals can be straight, gay, lesbian, or bisexual.

Challenges in Marriage, Parenting, and Divorce

No matter what lifestyles young adults choose, their choices will bring certain challenges. Because many choose the lifestyle of marriage, we'll consider some of the challenges in marriage and how to make it work. We also examine some challenges in parenting and trends in childbearing. Given the statistics about divorce rates in the previous section, we'll then consider how to deal with divorce.

Making Marriage Work

John Gottman (1994, 2006, 2011; Gottman & Gottman, 2009; Gottman & Silver, 2000) uses many methods to analyze what makes marriages work. He interviews couples about the history of their marriage, their philosophy about marriage, and how they view their parents' marriages. He videotapes them talking to each other about how their day went and evaluates what they say about the good and bad times of their marriages. Gottman also uses physiological measures to chart their heart rate, blood flow, blood pressure, and immune functioning moment by moment. In addition, he checks back with the couples every year to see how their marriage is faring. Gottman's research represents the most extensive assessment of marital relationships available. Currently, he and his colleagues are following 700 couples in seven studies.

What makes marriages work? What are the benefits of having a good marriage?
© Image Source Pink/ Alamy RF

Among the principles Gottman has found that determine whether a marriage will work are the following:

- *Establishing love maps.* Individuals in successful marriages have personal insights and detailed maps of each other's life and world. They aren't psychological strangers. In good marriages, partners are willing to share their feelings with each other. They use these "love maps" to express not only their understanding of each other but also their fondness and admiration.

- *Nurturing fondness and admiration.* In successful marriages, partners sing each other's praises. More than 90 percent of the time, when couples put a positive spin on their marriage's history, the marriage is likely to have a positive future.

- *Turning toward each other instead of away.* In good marriages, spouses are adept at turning toward each other regularly. They see each other as friends. This friendship doesn't keep arguments from occurring, but it can prevent differences from overwhelming the relationship. In these good marriages, spouses respect each other and appreciate each other's point of view despite disagreements.

- *Letting your partner influence you.* Bad marriages often involve one spouse who is unwilling to share power with the other. Although power-mongering is more common in husbands, some wives also show this trait. A willingness to share power and to respect the other person's view is a prerequisite to compromising.

- *Creating shared meaning.* The more partners can speak candidly and respectfully with each other, the more likely they are to create shared meaning in their marriage. This also includes sharing goals with one's spouse and working together to achieve each other's goals.

How Would You...?

As a **human development and family studies professional,** how would you counsel a newly married couple seeking advice on how to make their marriage work?

In a provocative book titled *Marriage, a History: How Love Conquered Marriage,* Stephanie Coontz (2005) concluded that marriages in America today are fragile not because Americans have become self-centered and career-minded but because expectations for marriage have become unrealistically high compared with previous generations. To make a marriage work, Coontz emphasizes like Gottman that partners need to develop a deep friendship, show respect for each other, and embrace commitment.

Becoming a Parent

For many young adults, parental roles are well planned, coordinated with other roles in life, and developed with the individual's economic situation in mind. For others, the discovery that they are about to become parents is a startling surprise. In either event, the prospective parents may have mixed emotions and romantic illusions about having a child (Florsheim, 2014).

Janis Keyser, Parent Educator

Janis Keyser is a parent educator who teaches in the Department of Early Childhood Education at Cabrillo College in California. In addition to teaching college classes and conducting parenting workshops, she has co-authored a book with Laura Davis (1997): *Becoming the Parent You Want to Be: A Sourcebook of Strategies for the First Five Years.*

Janis co-authors a nationally syndicated parenting column, "Growing Up, Growing Together." She is the mother of three, step-mother of five, grandmother of twelve, and great-grandmother of six.

Parent educators may have different educational backgrounds and occupational profiles. Janis Keyser has a background in early childhood education and, as just indicated, teaches at a college. Many parent educators have majored in areas such as child development as an undergraduate and/or taken a specialization of parenting and family courses in a master's or doctoral degree program in human development and family studies, clinical psychology, counseling psychology, or social work. As part of, or

Janis Keyser (*right*) conducts a parenting workshop.
© Janis Keyser

in addition to, their work in colleges and clinical settings, they may conduct parent education groups and workshops.

Parenting requires a number of interpersonal skills and imposes emotional demands, yet there is little in the way of formal education for this task. Most parents learn parenting practices from their own parents—some they accept, some they discard. Unfortunately, when parenting practices are passed on from one generation to the next, both desirable and undesirable practices are perpetuated. Adding to the challenges of the task of parenting, husbands and wives may bring different parenting practices to the marriage (Huston & Holmes, 2004). The parents, then, may disagree about which is a better way to interact with a child.

Parent educators seek to help individuals become better parents. To read about the work of one parent educator, see *Careers in Life-Span Development.*

Like the age when individuals first marry, the age at which individuals have children has been increasing (Baca Zinn, Eitzen, & Wells, 2016; Benokraitis, 2015). In 2014, the average age of U.S. women who gave birth for the first time was 26, up from 21 in 2001 (Martin & others, 2015). A recent national poll of 40- to 50-year-old U.S. women found that those with a master's degree or more first became mothers at 30; in comparison, the average age for women with a high school diploma was just 24 (Pew Research Center, 2015b).

As birth control has become common practice, many individuals consciously choose when they will have children and how many children they will rear. The

What are some trends in having children?
© Ryan McVay/Getty Images RF

CHALLENGES IN MARRIAGE, PARENTING, AND DIVORCE   **333**

number of one-child families is increasing, for example, and U.S. women overall are having fewer children. These childbearing results are creating several trends:

- By giving birth to fewer children, and reducing the demands of child care, women free up a significant portion of their life spans for other endeavors.

- As working women increase in number, they invest less actual time in the child's development.

- Men are apt to invest a greater amount of time in fathering.

- Parental care is often supplemented by institutional care (child care, for example).

As more women show an increased interest in developing a career, they are not only marrying later, but also having fewer children and having them later in life. What are some of the advantages of having children early or late? Some of the advantages of having children early (in the twenties) are that the parents are likely to have more physical energy (for example, they can cope better with such matters as getting up in the middle of the night with infants and waiting up until adolescents come home at night); the mother is likely to have fewer medical problems with pregnancy and childbirth; and the parents may be less likely to build up expectations for their children, as do many couples who have waited many years to have children.

How Would You...?

As a **human development and family studies professional,** how would you advise a young woman who is inquiring about the best age to have children?

There are also advantages to having children later (in the thirties). These parents have had more time to consider and achieve some of their goals in life and to determine what they want from their family and career roles. Older parents also are more mature and able to benefit from their life experiences to engage in more competent parenting, and they are more securely established in their careers and tend to have more income for child-rearing expenses than younger parents do.

Dealing with Divorce

If a marriage doesn't work, what happens after divorce? Psychologically, one of the most common characteristics of divorced adults is difficulty trusting someone else in a romantic relationship. Following a divorce, though, people's lives can take diverse turns (Hatemi, McDermott, & Eaves, 2015; Sbarra, Hasselmo, & Bourasssa, 2015). For example, in one research study 20 percent of the divorced group became more competent and better adjusted following their divorce (Hetherington & Kelly, 2002).

Strategies for divorced adults include the following (Hetherington & Kelly, 2002):

- Think of divorce as a chance to grow personally and to develop more positive relationships.

- Make decisions carefully, realizing that the consequences of your decisions regarding work, lovers, and children may last a lifetime.

- Focus more on the future than the past. Think about what is most important for you going forward in your life, set some challenging goals, and plan how to reach them.

- Use your strengths and resources to cope with difficulties.

- Don't expect to be successful and happy in everything you do. The path to a more enjoyable life will likely have a number of twists and turns, and moving forward will require considerable effort and resilience.

What are some strategies for coping with divorce?

© Image Source/Getty Images RF

Summary

Stability and Change from Childhood to Adulthood

- The first 20 years are important in predicting an adult's personality, but so are ongoing experiences in the adult years. Attachment styles, for example, reflect childhood patterns and continue to influence relationships in adulthood. Adult attachments are categorized as secure, avoidant, or anxious. A secure attachment style is linked with positive aspects of relationships.

Love and Close Relationships

- Erikson theorized that intimacy versus isolation is the key developmental issue in early adulthood.
- Friendship plays an important role in adult development, especially in terms of emotional support.
- Romantic love, also called passionate love, includes passion, sexuality, and a mixture of emotions, not all of which are positive. Affectionate love, also called companionate love, usually becomes more important as relationships mature.
- Sternberg proposed a triarchic model of love: passion, intimacy, and commitment. If all three qualities are present, the result is consummate love.

Adult Lifestyles

- Being single has become an increasingly prominent lifestyle. Autonomy is one of its advantages. Challenges faced by single adults include achieving intimacy, coping with loneliness, and finding a positive identity in a marriage-oriented society.
- Cohabitation, an increasingly popular lifestyle, does not lead to greater marital happiness but sometimes is linked to possible negative consequences if a cohabiting couple marries.
- The age at which individuals marry in the United States is increasing. Though marriage rates have declined, a large percentage of Americans still marry. The benefits of marriage include better physical and mental health and a longer life.
- The U.S. divorce rate increased dramatically in the middle of the twentieth century but began to decline in the 1980s.
- Divorce is a complex and emotional experience.
- Stepfamilies are complex, and adjustment is difficult. Evidence on the benefits of remarriage after divorce is mixed.
- One of the most striking research findings about gay and lesbian couples is how similar their relationships are to heterosexual couples' relationships. Considerable interest has recently been shown in the term *transgender*.

Challenges in Marriage, Parenting, and Divorce

- Gottman's research indicates that couples in successful marriages establish love maps, nurture fondness and admiration, turn toward each other, accept the influence of the partner, and create shared meaning.
- Families are becoming smaller, and many women are delaying childbirth until they have become well established in a career.
- Divorced adults often have difficulty trusting someone else in a romantic relationship. Certain strategies are effective in dealing with divorce.

Key Terms

affectionate love	avoidant attachment style	secure attachment style	transgender
anxious attachment style	romantic love		

13 Physical and Cognitive Development in Middle Adulthood

© Tomas Rodriguez/Corbis RF

CHAPTER OUTLINE

Stories of Life-Span Development: Changing Perceptions of Time

Our perception of time depends on where we are in the life span. We are more concerned about time at some points in life than others (Hoppmann & others, 2016; MacDonald, DeCarlo, & Dixon, 2011). Pink Floyd, in their song "Time," described how when people are young life seems longer and time passes more slowly, but when we get older, time seems to pass much more quickly.

In middle adulthood, individuals increasingly think about time-left-to-live instead of time-since-birth (Brothers & others, 2016; Kotter-Gruhn & Smith, 2011; Setterson, 2009; Strough & others, 2016). Middle-aged adults begin to look back to where they have been, reflecting on what they have done with the time they have had. They look toward the future in terms of how much time remains to accomplish what they hope to do with their lives. Older adults look backward even more than middle-aged adults, which is not surprising given the shorter future that awaits them. Also not surprisingly, given the many years they still have to live, emerging adults and young adults are more likely to look forward in time than backward in time.

In this first chapter on middle adulthood, we discuss physical changes; cognitive changes; changes in careers, work, and leisure. We also discuss the importance of religion and meaning in life. To begin, though, we explore how middle age is changing. ■

The Nature of Middle Adulthood

Is midlife experienced the same way today as it was 100 years ago? How can middle adulthood be defined, and what are some of its main characteristics?

Changing Midlife

Many of today's 50-year-olds are in better shape, more alert, and more productive than their 40-year-old counterparts from a generation or two earlier. As more people lead healthier lifestyles and medical discoveries help to slow down the aging process, the boundaries of middle age are being pushed upward. It seems that middle age is starting later and lasting longer for increasing numbers of active, healthy, and productive people. A current saying is "60 is the new 40," implying that many 60-year-olds today are living a life that is as active, productive, and healthy as earlier generations did in their forties.

Questions such as, "To which age group do you belong?" and "How old do you feel?" reflect the concept of *age identity*. A consistent finding is that as adults become older their age identity is younger than their chronological age (Setterson & Trauten, 2009; Westerhof, 2009). One study found that almost half of the individuals 65 to 69 years of age considered themselves middle-aged (National Council on Aging, 2000), and another study found a similar pattern: Half of the 60- to 75-year-olds viewed themselves as middle-aged (Lachman, Maier, & Budner, 2000). And a recent British survey of people over 50 years of age revealed that they perceived middle age to begin at 53 (Beneden Health, 2013). In this study, respondents said that being middle aged is characterized by enjoying afternoon naps, groaning when you bend down, and preferring a quiet night in rather than a night out. Also, some individuals consider the upper boundary of midlife as the age when they make the transition from work to retirement.

How is midlife changing?

© Zigy Kaluzny-Charles Thatcher/The Image Bank/ Getty Images

When Carl Jung studied midlife transitions early in the twentieth century, he referred to midlife as "the afternoon of life" (Jung, 1933). Midlife serves as an important preparation for late adulthood, "the evening of life" (Lachman, 2004, p. 306). But "midlife" came much earlier in Jung's time. In 1900 the average life expectancy was only 47 years of age; only 3 percent of the population lived past 65. Today, the average life expectancy is 79, and 12 percent of the U.S. population is older than 65 (U.S. Census Bureau, 2015). As a much greater percentage of the population lives to older ages, the midpoint of life and what constitutes middle age or middle adulthood are getting harder to pin down (Cohen, 2012). Statistically, the middle of life today is about 39.5 years of age, but most 39-year-olds don't want to be called "middle-aged." What we think of as middle age comes later—anywhere from 40 or 45 to about 60 or 65 years of age. And as more people live longer, the upper boundary of middle age will likely be nudged higher still.

In comparison with previous decades and centuries, an increasing percentage of today's population is made up of middle-aged and older adults. In the past, the age structure of the population could be represented by a pyramid, with the largest percentage of the population in the childhood years. Today, the percentages of people at different ages in the life span are more similar, creating what is called the "rectangularization" of the age distribution (a vertical rectangle) (Himes, 2009).

Compared to late adulthood, far less research attention has been given to middle adulthood (Lachman, Teshale, & Agrigoroaei, 2015). In a recent U.S. Census Bureau (2012) assessment, more than 102,713,000 people in the U.S. were 40 to 64 years of age, which accounts for 33.2 percent of the U.S. population. Given the large percentage of people in middle adulthood and the key roles that individuals in midlife play in families, the workplace, and the community, researchers need to give greater attention to this age period.

middle adulthood The developmental period beginning at approximately 40 years of age and extending to about 60 to 65 years of age.

Defining Middle Adulthood

Although the age boundaries are not set in stone, we will consider **middle adulthood** to be the developmental period that begins at approximately 40 years of age and extends to about 60 to 65 years of age. For many people, middle adulthood is a time of declining physical skills and expanding responsibility; a period in which people become more conscious of the young-old polarity and the shrinking amount of time left in life; a point when individuals seek to transmit something meaningful to the next generation; and a time when people reach and maintain satisfaction in their careers. In sum, middle adulthood involves "balancing work and relationship responsibilities in the midst of the physical and psychological changes associated with aging" (Lachman, 2004, p. 305).

What are the main characteristics of middle adulthood? What differentiates early and late midlife?

© Paul Barton/Corbis

In midlife, as in other age periods, individuals make choices, selecting what to do, deciding how to invest time and resources, and evaluating what aspects of their lives they need to change (Hahn & Lachman, 2015; Robinson, Rickenbach, & Lachman, 2015). In midlife, "a serious accident, loss, or illness" may be a "wake-up call" that produces "a major restructuring of time and a reassessment" of life's priorities (Lachman, 2004, p. 310).

For many increasingly healthy adults, middle age is lasting longer. Indeed, a growing number of experts on middle adulthood describe the age period of 55 to 65 as *late midlife* (Deeg, 2005). Compared with earlier midlife, late midlife is more likely to be characterized by the death of a parent, the last child leaving the parental home, becoming a grandparent, preparing for retirement, and in most cases actual retirement. Many people in this age range experience their first confrontation with health problems. Overall, then, although gains and losses may balance each other in early midlife, losses may begin to outweigh gains for many individuals in late midlife (Baltes, Lindenberger, & Staudinger, 2006). Margie Lachman and her colleagues (2015) recently described middle age as a pivotal period because it is a time of balancing growth and decline, linking earlier and later periods of development, and connecting younger and older generations.

Keep in mind, though, that midlife is characterized by individual variations (Hayslip, Pruett, & Caballero, 2015; Lachman, Agrigoroaei, & Hahn, 2016; List & others, 2015). As life-span expert Gilbert Brim (1992) commented, middle adulthood is full of changes, twists, and turns; the path is not fixed. People move in and out of states of success and failure.

Physical Development

What physical changes accompany the change to middle adulthood? How healthy are middle-aged adults? How sexually active are they?

Physical Changes

Although everyone experiences some physical changes due to aging in the middle adulthood years, the rates of this aging vary considerably from one individual to another. Genetic makeup and lifestyle factors play important roles in whether chronic disease will appear and when (Simons & others, 2016; Theendakara & others, 2016; Zhu & others, 2016). Middle age is a window through which we can glimpse later life while there is still time to engage in prevention and to influence some of the course of aging (Bertrand, Graham, & Lachman, 2013; Lachman, Teshale, & Agrigoroaei, 2015).

How Would You...?

As a **human development and family studies professional,** how would you characterize the impact of the media in shaping middle-aged adults' expectations about their changing physical appearance?

Visible Signs

One of the most visible signs of change in middle adulthood is physical appearance. The first outwardly noticeable signs of aging usually are apparent by the forties or fifties. The skin begins to wrinkle and sag because of a loss of fat and collagen in underlying tissues (Miyawaki & others, 2016; Pageon & others, 2014). Small, localized areas of pigmentation in the skin produce age spots, especially in areas that are exposed to sunlight, such as the hands and face. For most people, their hair becomes thinner and grayer. Fingernails and toenails develop ridges and become thicker and more brittle. A recent twin study found that twins who had been smoking longer were more likely to have more sagging facial skin and wrinkles, especially in the middle and lower portion of the face (Okada & others, 2013).

Since a youthful appearance is valued in our culture, many individuals whose hair is graying, whose skin is wrinkling, whose bodies are sagging, and whose teeth are yellowing strive to make themselves look younger. Undergoing cosmetic surgery, dyeing hair, wearing wigs, enrolling in weight-reduction programs, participating in exercise regimens, and taking heavy doses of vitamins are common in middle age. Many baby boomers have shown a strong interest in plastic surgery and Botox, which may reflect their desire to take control of the aging process (Carruthers & others, 2015; Solish & others, 2016).

Height and Weight

Individuals lose height in middle age, and many gain weight (Haftenberger & others, 2016; Winett & others, 2014). On average, from 30 to 50 years of age, men lose about half an inch in height; they may lose another 3/4 inch from 50 to 70 years of age (Hoyer & Roodin, 2009). The height loss for women can be as much as 2 inches over a 50-year span from 25 to 75 years of age. Note that there are large variations in the extent to which individuals become shorter with aging. The decrease in height is due to bone loss in the vertebrae.

Although people in middle age may lose height, many gain weight (Wang & others, 2016). On average, body fat accounts for about 10 percent of body weight in adolescence; it makes up 20 percent or more in middle age. Obesity increases from early to middle adulthood. In a recent national U.S. survey, in 2011–2012 39.5 percent of U.S. adults 40 to 59 years of age were classified as obese compared with 30.3 percent of younger adults (Ogden & others, 2013). Being overweight is a critical health problem in middle adulthood and increases the risk that individuals will develop a number of other health problems such as hypertension and diabetes (Kawakami & others, 2015; Xie & others, 2016).

Strength, Joints, and Bones

Maximum physical strength often is attained in the twenties. The term *sarcopenia* refers to age-related loss of muscle mass and strength (Bianchi & others, 2016; Spira & others, 2015). Muscle loss with age occurs at a rate of approximately 1 to 2 percent per year past the age of 50 (Marcell, 2003).

Famous actor Sean Connery as a young adult in his twenties (*top*) and as a middle-aged adult in his fifties (*bottom*). *What are some of the most outwardly noticeable signs of aging in middle adulthood?*

(Top) © Bettmann/Corbis; (bottom) © Matthew Mendelsohn/Corbis

How Would You...?

As a **social worker,** how would you apply information on weight and health to promote healthier lifestyles for middle-aged adults?

A loss of strength especially occurs in the back and legs. Obesity is a risk factor for sarcopenia (Cauley, 2015). Recently, researchers have increasingly used the term "sarcopenic obesity" to describe individuals who have sarcopenia and are obese (Lee & others, 2016; Ma & others, 2016). In a recent study sarcopenic obesity was associated with a 24 percent increase in risk for all-cause mortality, with a higher risk of mortality for men than for women (Tian & Xu, 2016).

Peak functioning of the body's joints also usually occurs in the twenties. The cartilage that cushions the movement of bones and other connective tissues, such as tendons and ligaments, become less efficient in the middle-adult years, a time when many individuals experience joint stiffness and greater difficulty in movement.

Maximum bone density occurs by the mid- to late thirties, from which point there is a progressive loss of bone. The rate of this bone loss begins slowly but accelerates during the fifties (Baron, 2012). Women lose bone mass about twice as quickly as men. By the end of midlife, bones break more easily and heal more slowly (Gulsahi, 2015).

Vision and Hearing

Accommodation of the eye—the ability to focus and maintain an image on the retina—declines sharply between 40 and 59 years of age. In particular, middle-aged individuals begin to have difficulty viewing close objects, which means that many individuals have to wear glasses with bifocal lenses—lenses with two sections that enable the wearer to see items at different distances (Schieber, 2006). Also, there is some evidence that the retina becomes less sensitive to low levels of illumination. Laser surgery and implantation of intraocular lenses have become routine procedures for correcting vision in middle-aged adults (Fang, Wang, & He, 2013).

Hearing also can start to decline by the age of 40 (Roring, Hines, & Charness, 2007). Sensitivity to high pitches usually declines first. The ability to hear low-pitched sounds does not seem to decline much in middle adulthood, though. Men usually lose their sensitivity to high-pitched sounds sooner than women do. However, this gender difference might be due to men's greater exposure to noise in occupations such as mining, automobile work, and so on (Scialfa & Kline, 2007). Also, recent advances in the effectiveness of hearing aids are dramatically improving the hearing of many aging adults (Banerjee, 2011). However, even with the advent of technologically sophisticated hearing devices, many people don't always wear them, or wear them inappropriately.

Cardiovascular System

Midlife is the time when high blood pressure and high cholesterol take many individuals by surprise (Wu & others, 2016). Cardiovascular disease increases considerably in middle age (Hulsegge & others, 2016; Wu & others, 2016).

The level of cholesterol in the blood increases through the adult years and in midlife begins to accumulate on the artery walls, increasing the risk of cardiovascular disease (Choi & Lee, 2016; Hasvold & others, 2016). High blood pressure (hypertension), too, often occurs in the forties and fifties (Kitaoka & others, 2016). One study found that uncontrolled hypertension can damage the brain's structure and function as early as the late thirties and early forties (Maillard & others, 2012). Another study revealed that hypertension in middle age was linked to risk of cognitive impairment in late adulthood (23 years later) (Virta & others, 2013).

Exercise, weight control, and a diet rich in fruits, vegetables, and whole grains can often help to stave off many cardiovascular problems in middle

Members of the Masai tribe in Kenya, Africa, can walk on a treadmill for long periods of time because of their high activity levels. Incidence of heart disease is extremely low in the Masai tribe, which also can be attributed to their energetic lifestyle.
© The Family of Dr. George V. Mann

age (Atashak, Stannard, & Azizheigi, 2016; Niu & others, 2016; Sallam & Laher, 2016). In a recent study, a high level of physical activity was associated with a lower risk of cardiovascular disease in the three weight categories studied (normal, overweight, and obese) (Carlsson & others, 2016). Also, in a recent study, middle-aged adults who had exercised regularly during adolescence were less likely to develop cardiovascular disease (Nechuta & others, 2015). A recent national study confirmed that moderate-to-vigorous physical activity (such as running, swimming, bicycling) on a regular basis was linked to reduced rates of all-cause mortality, especially for men (Loprinzi, 2015). Another recent study found that having an unhealthy diet was a strong predictor of cardiovascular disease (Menotti & others, 2015). Also, although heredity influences cholesterol levels, LDL (the bad cholesterol) can be reduced and HDL (the good cholesterol) increased by eating food that is very low in saturated fat and cholesterol and by exercising regularly (Koba & others, 2016). Further, the health benefits of cholesterol-lowering and hypertension-lowering drugs are a major factor in improving the health of many middle-aged adults and increasing their life expectancy (Wenger & others, 2014; Yusuf & others, 2016).

Lungs

There is little change in lung capacity through most of middle adulthood. However, at about the age of 55, the proteins in lung tissue become less elastic. This change, combined with a gradual stiffening of connective tissues in the chest wall, decreases the lungs' capacity to shuttle oxygen from the air people breathe to the blood in their veins. The lung capacity of individuals who are smokers drops precipitously in middle age, but if the individuals quit smoking their lung capacity improves, although not to the level of individuals who have never smoked. Recent research also has found that low cognitive ability in early adulthood is linked to reduced lung functioning in middle age (Carroll & others, 2011).

Exercise is linked to better lung functioning and a lower risk of developing lung cancer (Strookappe & others, 2015). In a recent study, more than 17,000 men were given a cardiovascular fitness assessment at 50 years of age (Lakoski & others, 2013). Subsequent analysis of Medicare claims and deaths found that the risk of being diagnosed with lung cancer was reduced by 68 percent for men who were the most fit compared with those who were the least fit.

Sleep

Some aspects of sleep become more problematic in middle age (Green & others, 2012; Prairie & others, 2015). The total number of hours slept usually remains the same as in early adulthood, but beginning in the forties, wakeful periods are more frequent and there is less of the deepest type of sleep (stage 4). The amount of time spent lying awake in bed at night begins to increase in middle age, and this can produce a feeling of being less rested in the morning (Abbott, 2003). Sleep-disordered breathing and restless legs syndrome become more prevalent in middle age (Polo-Kantola, 2011). One study found that middle-aged adults who sleep less than six hours a night on average had an increased risk of developing stroke symptoms (Ruiter & others, 2012). Another study revealed that sleep deprivation was associated with less effective immune system functioning (Wilder-Smith & others, 2013). Also, a recent study revealed that poor sleep quality in middle adulthood was linked to cognitive decline (Waller & others, 2016), and a research review concluded that sleep deprivation is linked to problems with long-term memory consolidation (Abel & others, 2013). And a recent Korean study found that these factors were linked to sleep problems in middle age: unemployment, being unmarried, currently being a smoker, lack of exercise, having irregular meals, and frequently experiencing stressful events (Yoon & others, 2015).

Health and Disease

In middle adulthood, the frequency of accidents declines, and individuals are less susceptible to colds and allergies than in childhood, adolescence, or early adulthood.

Indeed, many individuals live through middle adulthood without having a disease or persistent health problem. For others, however, disease and persistent health problems become more common in middle adulthood than in earlier life stages.

Stress is increasingly being identified as a factor in disease (Jansen & others, 2016; Lagraauw, Kuiper, & Bot, 2015; Sin & others, 2016). The cumulative effect of chronic stress often takes a toll on the health of individuals by the time they reach middle age. A recent study of middle-aged adults found that when they had a high level of allostatic load (wearing down of the body's systems in response to high stress levels), their episodic memory and executive function were harmed (Karlamangia & others, 2013). And a recent study of occupationally active 44- to 58-year-olds revealed that perceived stress symptoms in midlife were linked to self-care disability and mobility limitations 28 years later (Kulmala & others, 2013).

Chronic stressors have been linked to a downturn in immune system functioning in a number of contexts, including worries about living next to a damaged nuclear reactor, failures in close relationships (divorce, separation, and marital distress), depression, loneliness, and burdensome caregiving for a family member with progressive illness (Bennett, Fagundes, & Kiecolt-Glaser, 2016; Fagundes & others, 2016; Jaremka, Derry, & Kiecolt-Glaser, 2016). A recent study discovered that chronic stress accelerated pancreatic cancer growth (Kim-Fuchs & others, 2014). Recent research indicates that stress-reducing activities such as yoga, relaxation, and hypnosis have positive influences on immune system functioning (Derry & others, 2015; Kiecolt-Glaser & others, 2014).

How individuals react to stressors is linked to health outcomes. In one study, how people reacted to daily stressors in their lives was linked to future chronic health problems (Piazza & others, 2013). Also, in a recent study, adults who did not maintain positive affect when confronted with minor stressors in everyday life had elevated levels of IL-6, an inflammation marker (Sin & others, 2015). And in another recent study, a greater decrease in positive affect in response to daily stressors was associated with earlier death (Mroczek & others, 2015).

Mortality Rates

Infectious disease was the main cause of death until the middle of the twentieth century. As infectious disease rates declined and more individuals lived through middle age, chronic disorders increased. These are characterized by a slow onset and a long duration (Kelley-Moore, 2009). Chronic disorders account for 86 percent of total health-care spending in the United States (Qin & others, 2015).

In middle age, many deaths are caused by a single, readily identifiable condition, whereas in old age, death is more likely to result from the combined effects of several chronic conditions. For many years heart disease was the leading cause of death in middle adulthood, followed by cancer; however, since 2005 more individuals 45 to 64 years of age in the United States died of cancer, followed by cardiovascular disease (Centers for Disease Control and Prevention, 2015). The gap between cancer and the second leading cause of death widens as individuals age from 45 to 54 and from 55 to 64 years of age. In 2013, about 46,000 45- to 54-year-olds died of cancer and about 35,000 died of cardiovascular disease; about 113,000 55- to 64-year-olds died of cancer and about 73,000 died of cardiovascular disease (Centers for Disease Control and Prevention, 2015). Men have higher mortality rates than women for all of the leading causes of death (Kochanek & others, 2011).

Sexuality

What kinds of changes characterize the sexuality of women and men as they go through middle age? **Climacteric** is a term used to describe the midlife transition during which fertility declines. Let's explore the substantial differences in the climacteric of women and men during middle adulthood.

climacteric The midlife transition in which fertility declines.

Menopause

Menopause is the time in middle age, usually in the late forties or early fifties, when a woman's menstrual periods cease completely. The average age at which women have their last period is 51 (Wise, 2006). However, there is large variation in the age at which menopause occurs—from 39 to 59 years of age. Later menopause is linked with increased risk of breast cancer (Mishra & others, 2009).

In menopause, production of estrogen by the ovaries declines dramatically, and this decline produces uncomfortable symptoms in some women—"hot flashes," nausea, fatigue, and rapid heartbeat, for example (Mitchell & Woods, 2015). However, cross-cultural studies reveal wide variations in the menopause experience (Sievert, 2014). For example, hot flashes are uncommon in Mayan women (Beyene, 1986). Asian women report fewer hot flashes than women in Western societies (Payer, 1991). It is difficult to determine the extent to which these cross-cultural variations are due to genetic, dietary, reproductive, or cultural factors.

Menopause overall is not the negative experience for most women that it was once thought to be (Henderson, 2011). Most women do not have severe physical or psychological problems related to menopause. For example, a recent research review concluded that there is no clear evidence that depressive disorders occur more often during menopause than at other times in a woman's reproductive life (Judd, Hickey, & Bryant, 2011).

Hormone replacement therapy (HRT) augments the declining levels of reproductive hormone production by the ovaries (Baber & others, 2016; Gambacciani & Levancini, 2015; Thorley, 2016). HRT can consist of various forms of estrogen, usually in combination with a progestin.

The National Institutes of Health recommends that women who have not had a hysterectomy and who are currently taking hormones consult with their doctor to determine whether they should continue the treatment. If they are taking HRT for short-term relief of menopausal symptoms, the benefits may outweigh the risks. Many middle-aged women are seeking alternatives to HRT such as regular exercise, dietary supplements, herbal remedies, relaxation therapy, acupuncture, and nonsteroidal medications (Asghari & others, 2016; Goldstein & others, 2016; Mansikkamaki & others, 2016; Nasiri, 2015; Yazdkhasti, Simbar, & Abdi, 2015). A recent study revealed that in sedentary women, aerobic training for six months decreased menopausal symptoms, especially night sweats, mood swings, and irritability (Moilanen & others, 2012). Another recent study found that yoga improved the quality of life of menopausal women (Reed & others, 2014).

Researchers have found that almost 50 percent of Canadian and American women have occasional hot flashes, but only one in seven Japanese women do (Lock, 1998). *What factors might account for these variations?*

Hormonal Changes in Middle-Aged Men

Do men go through anything like the menopause that women experience? In other words, is there a male menopause? During middle adulthood, most men do not lose their capacity to father children, although there usually is a modest decline in their sexual hormone level and activity (Blumel & others, 2014). They experience hormonal changes in their fifties and sixties, but nothing like the dramatic drop in estrogen that women experience. Testosterone production begins to decline about 1 percent a year during middle adulthood, and sperm count usually shows a slow decline, but men do not lose their fertility in middle age. The term *male hypogonadism* is used to describe a condition in which the body does not produce enough testosterone (Mayo Clinic, 2016).

Recently, there has been a dramatic surge of interest in *testosterone replacement therapy (TRT)* (Hisasue, 2015). Recent research indicates that TRT can improve sexual functioning, muscle strength, and

menopause The complete cessation of a woman's menstrual cycles, which usually occurs in the late forties or early fifties.

How Would You...?

As a **human development and family studies professional,** how would you counsel middle-aged women who voice the belief that hormone replacement therapy will help them to "stay young"?

bone health (Almehmadi & others, 2016; Hassan & Barkin, 2016; Mayo Clinic, 2016; Seftel, Kathrins, & Niederberger, 2015; Snyder & others, 2016). A recent study found that TRT was associated with increased longevity in men with a low level of testosterone (Comhaire, 2016). Also, a recent large-scale study of more than 80,000 men revealed that testosterone replacement therapy was associated with a reduced incidence of heart attack or a stroke, as well as a reduction in all-cause mortality (Sharma & others, 2015). Men who have prostate cancer or breast cancer should not take TRT, and men who are at risk for blood clotting (those who have atrial fibrillation, for example) also should not use TRT (Osterberg, Bernie, & Ramasamy, 2014).

The gradual decline in men's testosterone levels in middle age can reduce their sexual drive (O'Connor & others, 2011). Their erections are less full and less frequent, and men require more stimulation to achieve them. Researchers once attributed these changes to psychological factors, but increasingly they find that as many as 75 percent of the erectile dysfunctions in middle-aged men stem from physiological problems. Smoking, diabetes, hypertension, elevated cholesterol levels, and obesity are at fault in many erectile problems in middle-aged men (Corona & others, 2015).

Erectile dysfunction (ED), difficulty in attaining or maintaining an erection, is present in approximately 50 percent of men 40 to 70 years of age (Mola, 2015). The main treatment for erectile dysfunction has not focused on TRT but on the drug Viagra and on similar drugs such as Levitra and Cialis (Hosny, El-Say, & Ahmed, 2016; Sheu & others, 2016). Viagra works by allowing increased blood flow into the penis, which produces an erection. Its success rate is in the 60 to 85 percent range (Claes & others, 2010).

Sexual Attitudes and Behavior

Although the ability of men and women to function sexually shows little biological decline in middle adulthood, sexual activity usually occurs less frequently than in early adulthood (Huhtaniemi, 2014). Career interests, family matters, diminishing energy levels, and routine may contribute to this decline (Avis & others, 2009).

In the Sex in America survey, the frequency of sexual activity was greatest for individuals 25 to 29 years old (47 percent had sex twice a week or more) and dropped off for individuals in their fifties (23 percent of 50- to 59-year-old males said they had sex twice a week or more, while only 14 percent of the females in this age group reported this frequency) (Michael & others, 1994). Note, though, that the Sex in America survey may underestimate the frequency of sexual activity of middle-aged adults because the data were collected prior to the widespread use of erectile dysfunction drugs such as Viagra.

Living with a spouse or partner makes all the difference in whether people engage in sexual activity, especially for women over 40 years of age. In one study conducted as part of the Midlife in the United States Study (MIDUS), 95 percent of women in their forties with partners said that they had been sexually active in the last six months, compared with only 53 percent of those without partners (Brim, 1999). By their fifties, 88 percent of women living with a partner have been sexually active in the last six months, but only 37 percent of those who are neither married nor living with someone say they have had sex in the last six months.

A large-scale study of U.S. adults 40 to 80 years of age found that early ejaculation (26 percent) and erectile difficulties (22 percent) were the most common sexual problems

How does the pattern of sexual activity change when individuals become middle-aged?
© Image Source/PunchStock RF

How Would You...?
As a **psychologist,** how would you counsel a couple about the ways that the transition to middle adulthood might affect their sexual relationship?

of older men (Laumann & others, 2009). In this study, the most common sexual problems of women were lack of sexual interest (33 percent) and lubrication difficulties (21 percent).

A person's health in middle age is a key factor in sexual activity in middle age (Field & others, 2013). A recent study of aging adults 55 years and older revealed that their level of sexual activity was associated with their physical and mental health (Bach & others, 2013).

Cognitive Development

We have seen that middle-aged adults may not see as well, run as fast, or be as healthy as they were in their twenties and thirties. We've also seen a decline in their sexual activity. What about their cognitive skills? Do these skills decline as we enter and move through middle adulthood? To answer this question, we will explore the possibility of age-related changes in intelligence and information processing.

Intelligence

Our exploration of possible changes in intelligence in middle adulthood focuses on the concepts of fluid and crystallized intelligence, cohort effects, and the Seattle Longitudinal Study.

How Would You...?
As an **educator,** how would you explain how changes in fluid and crystallized intelligence might influence the way middle-aged adults learn?

Fluid and Crystallized Intelligence

John Horn argues that some abilities begin to decline in middle age, whereas others increase (Horn & Donaldson, 1980). He argues that **crystallized intelligence,** an individual's accumulated information and verbal skills, continues to increase in middle adulthood, whereas **fluid intelligence,** one's ability to reason abstractly, begins to decline during middle adulthood (see Figure 1).

Horn's data were collected in a cross-sectional manner. Recall that a cross-sectional study assesses individuals of different ages at the same point in time. For example, a cross-sectional study might assess the intelligence of different groups of 40-, 50-, and 60-year-olds in a single evaluation, such as in 1980. The 40-year-olds in the study would have been born in 1940 and the 60-year-olds in 1920—different eras that offered different economic and educational opportunities. The 60-year-olds likely had fewer educational opportunities as they grew up. Thus, if we find differences between 40- and 60-year-olds on intelligence tests when they are assessed cross-sectionally, these differences might be due to cohort effects related to educational differences rather than to age.

By contrast, recall that in a longitudinal study, the same individuals are studied over a period of time. Thus, a longitudinal study of intelligence in middle adulthood might consist of giving the same intelligence test to the same individuals when they are 40, then 50, and then 60 years of age. As we see next, whether data on intelligence are

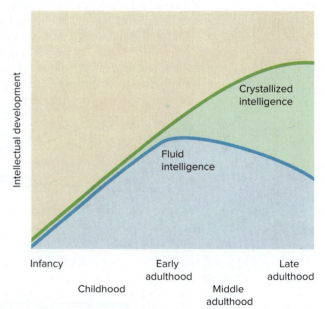

Figure 1 Fluid and Crystallized Intelligence Across the Life Span
According to Horn, crystallized intelligence (based on cumulative learning experiences) increases throughout the life span, but fluid intelligence (the ability to perceive and manipulate information) steadily declines from middle adulthood onward.

crystallized intelligence Accumulated information and verbal skills, which increase in middle age, according to Horn.

fluid intelligence The ability to reason abstractly, which steadily declines from middle adulthood on, according to Horn.

collected cross-sectionally or longitudinally can make a difference in what is found about changes in crystallized and fluid intelligence and about intellectual decline.

The Seattle Longitudinal Study

K. Warner Schaie (1996, 2005, 2010, 2011, 2013) is conducting an extensive study of intellectual abilities in adulthood. Five hundred individuals initially were tested in 1956. New waves of participants are added periodically. The main focus in the Seattle Longitudinal Study has been on individual change and stability in intelligence. The main mental abilities tested are *verbal comprehension* (ability to understand ideas expressed in words); *verbal memory* (ability to encode and recall meaningful language units, such as a list of words); *numeric ability* (ability to perform simple mathematical computations such as addition, subtraction, and multiplication); *spatial orientation* (ability to visualize and mentally rotate stimuli in two- and three-dimensional space); *inductive reasoning* (ability to recognize and understand patterns and relationships in a problem and use this understanding to solve other instances of the problem); and *perceptual speed* (ability to quickly and accurately make simple discriminations in visual stimuli).

The highest level of functioning for four of the six intellectual abilities occurred during middle adulthood (Schaie, 2013) (see Figure 2). For both women and men, peak performance on verbal ability, verbal memory, inductive reasoning, and spatial orientation was attained in middle age. Only two of the six abilities—numeric ability and perceptual speed—showed a decline in middle age. Perceptual speed showed the earliest decline, actually beginning in early adulthood. Interestingly, in terms of John Horn's ideas that were discussed earlier, for the participants in the Seattle Longitudinal Study, middle age was a time of peak performance for some aspects of both crystallized intelligence (verbal ability) and fluid intelligence (spatial orientation and inductive reasoning).

Notice in Figure 2 that declines in functioning for most cognitive abilities began in the sixties, although verbal ability did not drop until the mid-seventies. From the mid-seventies through the mid-nineties, all cognitive abilities showed considerable decline.

When Schaie (1994) assessed intellectual abilities both cross-sectionally and longitudinally, he found declines more often in the cross-sectional than in the

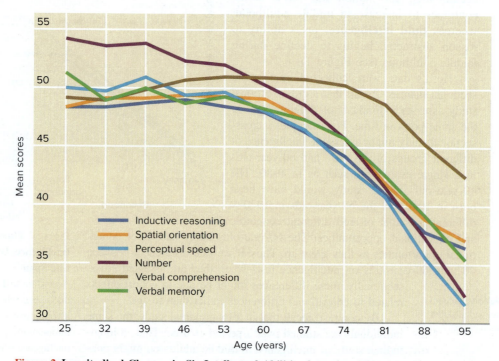

Figure 2 **Longitudinal Changes in Six Intellectual Abilities from Age 25 to Age 95**
Source: Adapted from Schaie, K.W. Figure 5.7a in *Developmental Influences on Intelligence: The Seattle Longitudinal Study* (2nd rev ed.), 2013, p. 162. New York: Oxford University Press.

longitudinal assessments. For example, as shown in Figure 3, when assessed cross-sectionally, inductive reasoning showed a consistent decline during middle adulthood. In contrast, when assessed longitudinally, inductive reasoning increased until toward the end of middle adulthood, when it began to show a slight decline. In Schaie's (2009, 2010, 2011, 2013, 2016) view, it is during middle adulthood, not early adulthood, that people reach a peak in their cognitive functioning for many intellectual skills.

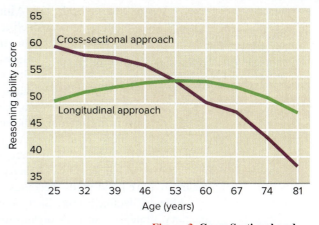

Figure 3 **Cross-Sectional and Longitudinal Comparisons of Intellectual Change in Middle Adulthood**
Why do you think reasoning ability peaks during middle adulthood?

Such differences across generations involve *cohort effects*. In a recent analysis, Schaie (2013, 2016) concluded that the advances in cognitive functioning in middle age that have occurred in recent decades are likely due to a combination of factors: educational attainment, occupational structures (increasing numbers of workers in professional occupations with greater work complexity), changes in health care and lifestyles, immigration, and social interventions in poverty. The impressive gains in cognitive functioning in recent cohorts have been documented more clearly for fluid intelligence than for crystallized intelligence (Schaie, 2013).

Some researchers disagree with Schaie that middle adulthood is the time when the level of functioning in a number of cognitive domains is maintained or even increases (Finch, 2009). For example, Timothy Salthouse (2009, 2012) has emphasized that a lower level of cognitive functioning in middle adulthood is likely due to age-related neurobiological decline. Salthouse (2014, 2016) also recently argued that a main reason for different trends in longitudinal and cross-sectional comparisons of cognitive functioning is that prior experience with tests increases scores the next time a test is taken.

Information Processing

As we saw in the coverage of theories of development and of cognitive development from infancy through adolescence, the information-processing approach provides another way to examine cognitive abilities. Among the information-processing changes that take place in middle adulthood are those involved in speed of processing information, memory, and expertise.

Speed of Information Processing

As we just discussed, in Schaie's (1996, 2013) Seattle Longitudinal Study, perceptual speed begins declining in early adulthood and continues to decline in middle adulthood. A common way to assess speed of information processing is through a reaction-time task, in which individuals simply press a button as soon as they see a light appear. Middle-aged adults are slower to push the button when the light appears than young adults are (Dirk & Schmiedek, 2012; Salthouse, 2009, 2012). However, keep in mind that the decline is not dramatic—less than 1 second in most investigations. Also, in a longitudinal study, a smaller decline in processing speed in middle and late adulthood was one of the key predictors of living longer (Aichele, Rabbitt, & Ghisletta, 2016).

Memory

In Schaie's (1994, 1996, 2013) Seattle Longitudinal Study, verbal memory peaked in the fifties. However, in some other studies, verbal memory has shown a decline in middle age, especially when assessed in cross-sectional studies (Salthouse, 2009). For example, when asked to remember lists of words, numbers, or meaningful prose, younger adults outperformed middle-aged adults (Salthouse &

Skovronek, 1992). Although there still is some controversy about whether memory declines during middle adulthood, most experts conclude that it does decline, at least in late middle age (Ferreira & others, 2015; Salthouse, 2014).

Aging and cognition expert Denise Park (2001) argues that starting in late middle age, more time is needed to learn new information. The slowdown in learning new information has been linked to changes in **working memory,** the mental "workbench" where individuals manipulate and assemble information when making decisions, solving problems, and comprehending written and spoken language (Baddeley, 2007, 2012). In this view, in late middle age, working memory capacity—the amount of information that can be immediately retrieved and used—becomes more limited.

Memory decline is more likely to occur among individuals who don't use effective memory strategies, such as organization and imagery (Hoyer & Roodin, 2009). By organizing lists of phone numbers into different categories or imagining the phone numbers as representing different objects around the house, many people can improve their memory in middle adulthood.

Expertise

Because it takes so long to attain, expertise often shows up more in middle adulthood than in early adulthood (Charness & Krampe, 2008). Recall that *expertise* involves having extensive, highly organized knowledge and understanding of a particular domain. Developing expertise and becoming an "expert" in a field usually is the result of many years of experience, learning, and effort (Ericsson & others, 2016).

Adults in middle age who have become experts in their fields are likely to do the following: rely on their accumulated experience to solve problems; process information automatically and analyze it more efficiently when solving a problem; devise better strategies and shortcuts to solving problems; and be more creative and flexible in solving problems.

Careers, Work, and Leisure

What are some issues that workers face in midlife? What role does leisure play in the lives of middle-aged adults?

Work in Midlife

The role of work, whether one works in a full-time career, at a part-time job, as a volunteer, or as a homemaker, is central during the middle years (Cahill, Giandrea, & Quinn, 2016; Wang & Shi, 2016). Middle-aged adults may reach their peak in position and earnings. They may also be saddled with multiple financial burdens including rent or mortgage payment, medical bills, home repairs, college tuition, loans to family members, or bills from nursing homes for aging parents. A recent study found that difficulty managing different job demands was associated with poor health in middle-aged adults (Nabe-Nielsen & others, 2014).

In 2015 in the United States, 79.4 percent of 45- to 54-year-olds were in the workforce (a decrease of 3.4 percent since 2000) and 64.1 percent of 55- to 64-year-olds were in the workforce (an increase of 8 percent since 2000) (Short, 2015). Later we will describe various aspects of workforce participation among individuals age 65 and over in the United States, which has increased by a remarkable 50 percent since 2000 (Short, 2015).

What characterizes work in middle adulthood?

© BrandXPictures/Punch-Stock RF

How Would You...?

As a **social worker**, what advice would you offer to middle-aged adults who are dissatisfied with their careers?

Do middle-aged workers perform their work as competently as younger adults? Age-related declines occur in some occupations, such as air traffic controllers and professional athletes, but for most jobs, no differences have been found in the work performance of young adults and middle-aged adults (Salthouse, 2012). However, leading Finnish researcher Clas-Hakan Nygard (2013) concludes from his longitudinal research that the ability to work effectively peaks during middle age because of increased motivation, work experience, employer loyalty, and better strategic thinking. Nygard also has found that the quality of work done by middle-aged employees is linked to how much their work is appreciated and how well they get along with their immediate supervisors. And Nygard and his colleagues discovered that work ability in middle age was linked to mortality and disability 28 years later (von Bonsdorff & others, 2011, 2012).

For many people, midlife is a time of evaluation, assessment, and reflection in terms of the work they are doing and want to do in the future (Cahill, Giandrea, & Quinn, 2016). Among the work issues that some people face in midlife are recognizing limitations in career progress, deciding whether to change jobs or careers, deciding whether to rebalance family and work, and planning for retirement (Sterns & Huyck, 2001).

Career Challenges and Changes

The current middle-aged worker faces several important challenges in the twenty-first century (Brand, 2014). These include the globalization of work, rapid developments in information technologies, downsizing of organizations, pressure to choose early retirement, and concerns about pensions and health care.

Globalization has replaced what was once a primarily non-Latino White male workforce in the United States with employees of different ethnic and national backgrounds who have emigrated from different parts of the world. To improve profits, many companies are restructuring, downsizing, and outsourcing jobs. One of the outcomes of this change has been for companies to offer incentives to middle-aged employees who choose to retire early—in their fifties, or in some cases even forties, rather than their sixties.

The decline in defined-benefit pensions and increased uncertainty about the fate of health insurance are eroding the sense of personal control among middle-aged workers. As a consequence, many are delaying their retirement from work.

Some midlife career changes are self-motivated, while others are the consequence of losing one's job (Moen, 2009a, b). Some individuals in middle age decide that they don't want to continue doing the same work for the rest of their working lives (Hoyer & Roodin, 2009). One aspect of middle adulthood involves adjusting idealistic hopes to reflect realistic possibilities in light of how much time individuals have before they retire and how fast they are reaching their occupational goals (Levinson, 1978). Individuals could become motivated to change jobs if they perceive that they are behind schedule, if their goals are unrealistic, if they don't like the work they are doing, or if their job has become too stressful.

HAGAR © 1987 King Features Syndicate, Inc. World Rights Reserved.

Sigmund Freud once commented that the two things adults need to do well to adapt to society's demands are to work and to love. To his list we add "to play." In our fast-paced society, it is all too easy to get caught up in the frenzied, hectic pace of our achievement-oriented work world and ignore leisure and play. Imagine your life as a middle-aged adult. *What would be the ideal mix of work and leisure? What leisure activities do you want to enjoy as a middle-aged adult?*

© Digital Vision/Getty Images RF

A final point to make about career development in middle adulthood is that cognitive factors earlier in development are linked to occupational attainment in middle age. In one study, task persistence at 13 years of age was related to occupational success in middle age (Andersson & Bergman, 2011).

Leisure

As adults, not only must we learn how to work well, but we also need to learn how to relax and enjoy leisure (Eriksson Sorman & others, 2014). **Leisure** refers to the pleasant times after work when individuals are free to pursue activities and interests of their own choosing—hobbies, sports, or reading, for example. In one analysis of research on what U.S. adults regret the most, not engaging in more leisure-time pursuits was one of the top six regrets (Roese & Summerville, 2005). A recent Finnish study found that engaging in little leisure-time activity in middle age was linked to risk of cognitive impairment in late adulthood (23 years later) (Virta & others, 2013). Another recent study revealed that middle-aged individuals who engaged in high levels of leisure-time physical activity were less likely to have Alzheimer disease 28 years later (Tolppanen & others, 2015).

Also, the type of leisure activity may be linked to different outcomes. A recent study found that engaging in higher complexity of work before retirement was associated with less cognitive decline during retirement (Andel, Finkel, & Pedersen, 2016). However, when those who had worked in occupations with fewer cognitive challenges prior to retirement engaged in physical (sports, walking) and cognitive (reading books, doing puzzles, and playing chess) leisure activities during retirement, they showed less cognitive decline. Further, a study revealed that middle-aged adults who engaged in active leisure-time pursuits had a higher-level cognitive performance in late adulthood (Ihle & others, 2015). And in another recent study, individuals who engaged in a greater amount of sedentary screen-based leisure time activity (TV, video games, computer use) had shorter telomere length (telomeres cover the end of chromosomes and as people age their telomeres become shorter and this shorter telomere length is linked to earlier mortality) (Loprinzi, 2015).

Leisure can be an especially important aspect of middle adulthood (Parkes, 2006). By middle adulthood, more money may be available to many individuals, and there may be more free time and paid vacations. In short, midlife changes may produce expanded opportunities for leisure. For many individuals, middle adulthood is the first time in their lives when they have the opportunity to explore their leisure-time interests.

Adults in midlife need to begin preparing psychologically for retirement. Developing constructive and fulfilling leisure-time activities in middle adulthood is an important part of this preparation (Gibson, 2009). If an adult chooses activities that can be continued into retirement, the transition from work to retirement can be less stressful.

How Would You...?

As a **psychologist,** how would you explain the link between leisure and stress reduction to a middle-aged individual?

Religion and Meaning in Life

What role does religion play in our development as adults? Is discovering the meaning of life an important theme for many middle-aged adults?

leisure The pleasant times after work when individuals are free to pursue activities and interests of their own choosing.

Religion and Adult Lives

In research that was part of the Midlife in the United States Study (MIDUS), more than 70 percent of U.S. middle-aged adults said that they are religious and that they consider spirituality a major part of their lives (Brim, 1999). In thinking about religion and adult development, it is important to consider the role of individual differences. Religion is a powerful influence in some adults' lives, whereas it plays little or no role in others' lives (Krause & Hayward, 2016). In a longitudinal study of individuals from their early thirties through their late sixties and early seventies, a significant increase in spirituality occurred between late middle (mid-fifties/early sixties) and late adulthood (Wink & Dillon, 2002) (see Figure 4). And a recent survey found that 77 percent of 30- to 49-year-olds and 84 percent of 50- to 64-year-olds reported having a religious affiliation (compared with 67 percent of 18- to 29-year-olds and 90 percent of adults 90 years of age and older) (Pew Research Center, 2012).

Females have consistently shown a stronger interest in religion than males have (Bijur & others, 1993). Compared with men, they participate more in both organized and personal forms of religion, are more likely to believe in a higher power or presence, and are more likely to feel that religion is an important dimension of their lives. In the longitudinal study just described, the spirituality of women increased more than that of men during the second half of life (Wink & Dillon, 2002).

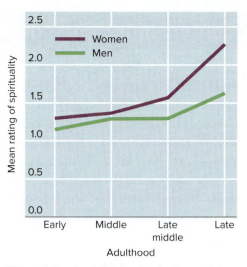

Figure 4 Levels of Spirituality in Four Adult Age Periods
In a longitudinal study, the spirituality of individuals in four different adult age periods—early (thirties), middle (forties), late middle (mid-fifties/early sixties), and late (late sixties/early seventies) adulthood—was assessed (Wink & Dillon, 2002). Based on responses to open-ended questions in interviews, the spirituality of the individuals was coded on a five-point scale with 5 being the highest level of spirituality and 1 the lowest.

Religion and Health

What might be some of the effects of religion on physical health? Some cults and religious sects encourage behaviors that are damaging to health, such as ignoring sound medical advice. For individuals in the religious mainstream, however, researchers are increasingly finding positive links between religion and physical health (Krause & Hayward, 2016). Researchers have found that religious attendance is linked to a reduction in hypertension (Gillum & Ingram, 2007). And in a recent analysis of a number of studies, adults with a higher level of spirituality/religion had an 18 percent increase in longevity (Lucchetti, Lucchetti, & Koenig, 2011). In this analysis, a high level of spirituality/religion was more closely tied to longevity than 60 percent of 25 other health interventions (such as eating fruits and vegetables and taking statin drugs for cardiovascular disease).

What roles do religion and spirituality play in the lives of middle-aged adults? Why might religion promote health?
© Erik S. Lesser/epa/Corbis

Why might religion promote physical health? There are several possible answers (Park, 2013). First, there are *lifestyle issues*—for example, religious individuals have lower rates of drug use than their nonreligious counterparts (Gartner, Larson, & Allen, 1991). Second are *social networks*—the degree to which

Gabriel Dy-Liacco, University Professor and Pastoral Counselor

Gabriel Dy-Liacco currently is a professor in religious and pastoral counseling at Regent University in the Virginia Beach, Virginia, area. He obtained his Ph.D. in pastoral counseling from Loyola College in Maryland and also has experience as a psychotherapist in mental health settings such as a substance-abuse program, military family center, psychiatric clinic, and community mental health center. Earlier in his career he was a pastoral counselor at the Pastoral Counseling and Consultation Centers of Greater Washington, DC, and taught at Loyola University in Maryland. As a pastoral counselor, he works with adolescents and adults in the aspects of their lives that they show the most concern about—psychological, spiritual, or the interface of both. Having lived in Peru, Japan, and the Philippines, he brings considerable multicultural experience to teaching and counseling settings.

individuals are connected to others affects their health. Well-connected individuals have fewer health problems (Hill & Pargament, 2003). Religious groups, meetings, and activities provide social connectedness for individuals. A third answer involves *coping with stress*—religion offers a source of comfort and support when individuals are confronted with stressful events. A recent study revealed that highly religious individuals were less likely than their moderately religious, somewhat religious, and non-religious counterparts to be psychologically distressed (Park, 2013).

Religious counselors often advise people about mental health and coping. To read about the work of one religious counselor, see *Careers in Life-Span Development.*

Meaning in Life

Austrian psychiatrist Viktor Frankl's mother, father, brother, and wife died in the concentration camps and gas chambers in Auschwitz, Poland, during World War II. Frankl survived the concentration camp and went on to write about the search for meaning in life. In his book, *Man's Search for Meaning,* Frankl (1984) emphasized each person's uniqueness and the finiteness of life. He believed that examining the finiteness of our existence and the certainty of death adds meaning to life. If life were not finite, said Frankl, we could spend our life doing just about whatever we pleased because our time would be unlimited.

Frankl said that the three most distinctly human qualities are spirituality, freedom, and responsibility. Spirituality, in his view, does not have a religious underpinning. Rather, it refers to a human being's uniqueness of spirit, philosophy, and mind. Frankl proposed that people ask themselves questions about why they exist, what they want from life, and what their lives mean.

It is in middle adulthood that individuals begin to face death more often, especially the deaths of parents and other older relatives. As they become increasingly aware of the diminishing number of years ahead of them, many individuals in middle age begin to ask and evaluate the questions that Frankl proposed. And meaning-making coping is especially helpful in times of chronic stress and loss.

Researchers are increasingly studying the factors involved in a person's exploration of meaning in life and exploring whether developing a sense of meaning in life is linked to positive developmental outcomes (Park, 2010, 2012). In research studies, many individuals state that religion played an important role in increasing their exploration of meaning in life (Krause, 2008, 2009; Krause & Hayward, 2016). Studies also suggest that individuals who have found a sense of meaning in life are physically healthier and happier, and

What characterizes the search for meaning in life?
© Michael Prince/Corbis

experience less depression, than their counterparts who report that they have not discovered meaning in life (Krause, 2009).

Having a sense of meaning in life can lead to clearer guidelines for living one's life and enhanced motivation to take care of oneself and reach goals. A higher level of meaning in life also is linked to a higher level of psychological well-being and physical health (Park, 2012).

Summary

The Nature of Middle Adulthood

- As more people live to older ages, what we think of as middle age is starting later and lasting longer.
- Middle age involves extensive individual variation. For most people, middle adulthood involves declining physical skills, expanding responsibility, awareness of the young-old polarity, motivation to transmit something meaningful to the next generation, and reaching and maintaining career satisfaction. Increasingly, researchers are distinguishing between early and late midlife.

Physical Development

- The physical changes of midlife are usually gradual. Decline occurs in a number of aspects of physical development.
- In middle adulthood, the frequency of accidents declines and individuals are less susceptible to colds. Stress can be a factor in disease.
- Until recently, cardiovascular disease was the leading cause of death in middle age, but now cancer is the leading cause of death in this age group.
- Most women do not have serious physical or psychological problems related to menopause. Sexual behavior occurs less frequently in middle adulthood than early adulthood.

Cognitive Development

- Horn argued that crystallized intelligence continues to increase in middle adulthood, whereas fluid

intelligence declines. Schaie found that declines in cognitive development are less likely to occur when longitudinal rather than cross-sectional studies are conducted. He also discovered that the highest levels of a number of intellectual abilities occur in middle age.
- Working memory declines in late middle age. Memory is more likely to decline in middle age when individuals don't use effective memory strategies. Expertise often increases in middle adulthood.

Careers, Work, and Leisure

- Midlife is often a time to reflect on career progress and prepare for retirement.
- Today's middle-aged workers face a number of challenges.
- In preparing for late adulthood, adults in midlife not only need to learn to work well, but also discover how to enjoy leisure.

Religion and Meaning in Life

- The majority of middle-aged adults say that spirituality is a major part of their lives.
- In mainstream religions, religion is positively linked to physical health. Religion can play an important role in coping for some individuals.
- Many middle-aged individuals reflect on life's meaning.

Key Terms

climacteric	fluid intelligence	menopause	working memory
crystallized intelligence	leisure	middle adulthood	

14 Socioemotional Development in Middle Adulthood

© Yellow Dog Productions/Getty Images RF

CHAPTER OUTLINE

PERSONALITY THEORIES AND DEVELOPMENT

Adult Stage Theories

The Life-Events Approach

Stress and Personal Control in Midlife

STABILITY AND CHANGE

Longitudinal Studies

Conclusions

CLOSE RELATIONSHIPS

Love and Marriage at Midlife

The Empty Nest and Its Refilling

Sibling Relationships and Friendships

Grandparenting

Intergenerational Relationships

Stories of Life-Span Development: Sarah and Wanda, Middle-Age Variations

Forty-five-year-old Sarah feels tired, depressed, and angry when she looks back on the way her life has gone. She became pregnant when she was 17 and married Ben, the baby's father. They stayed together for three years after their son was born, and then Ben left her for another woman. Sarah went to work as a salesclerk to make ends meet. Eight years later, she married Alan, who had two children of his own from a previous marriage. Sarah stopped working for several years to care for the children. Then, like Ben, Alan started cheating on her. She found out about it from a friend. Nevertheless, Sarah stayed with Alan for another year. Finally, he was gone so much that she could not take it anymore and decided to divorce him. Sarah went back to work again as a salesclerk; she has been in the same position for 16 years now. During those 16 years, she has dated a number of men, but the relationships never seemed to work out. Her son never finished high school and has drug problems. Her father died last year, and Sarah is trying to help her mother financially, although she can barely pay her own bills. Sarah looks in the mirror and does not like what she sees. She sees her past as a shambles, and the future does not look rosy, either.

Forty-five-year-old Wanda feels energetic, happy, and satisfied. As a young woman, she graduated from college and worked for three years as a high school math teacher. She married Andy, who had just finished law school. One year later, they had their first child, Josh. Wanda stayed home with Josh for two years and then returned to her job as a math teacher. Even during her pregnancy, Wanda stayed active and exercised regularly, playing tennis almost every day. After her pregnancy, she kept up her exercise habits. Wanda and Andy had another child, Wendy. Now, as they move into their middle-age years, their children are both in college, and Wanda and Andy are enjoying spending more time with each other. Last weekend they visited Josh at his college, and the weekend before they visited Wendy at her college. Wanda continued working as a high school math teacher until six years ago. She had developed computer skills as part of her job and taken some computer courses at a nearby college, doubling up during the summer months. She resigned her math teaching job and took a job with a computer company, where she has already worked her way into management. Wanda looks in the mirror and likes what she sees. She sees her past as enjoyable, although not without hills and valleys, and she looks to the future with zest and enthusiasm.

As with Sarah and Wanda, there are individual variations in the way people experience middle age. To begin the chapter, we examine personality theories and development in middle age, including ideas about individual variation. Then we turn our attention to how much individuals change or stay the same as they go through the adult years, and finally we explore a number of aspects of close relationships during middle adulthood. ■

Personality Theories and Development

What is the best way to conceptualize middle age? Is it a stage or a crisis? How extensively is middle age influenced by life events? Do middle-aged adults experience stress differently from younger and older adults? Is personality linked with contexts such as the point in history in which individuals go through midlife, their culture, and their gender?

Adult Stage Theories

A number of adult stage theories have been proposed and have contributed to the view that midlife brings a crisis in development. Two prominent theories that define stages of adult development are Erik Erikson's life-span view and Daniel Levinson's seasons of a man's life.

Erikson's Stage of Generativity Versus Stagnation

Erikson (1968) proposed that middle-aged adults face a significant issue—generativity versus stagnation, which is the name Erikson gave to the seventh stage in his life-span theory. **Generativity** encompasses adults' desire to leave legacies of themselves to the next generation. Through these legacies adults achieve a kind of immortality. By contrast, **stagnation** (sometimes called "self-absorption") develops when individuals sense that they have done little or nothing for the next generation.

Generative adults commit themselves to the continuation and improvement of society as a whole through their connection to the next generation. Generative adults develop a positive legacy of the self and then offer it as a gift to the next generation (Hofer & others, 2016; Tabuchi & others, 2015). Middle-aged adults can achieve generativity in a number of ways (Kotre, 1984). Through biological generativity, adults have offspring. Through parental generativity, adults nurture and guide children. Through work generativity, adults develop skills that are passed down to others. And through cultural generativity, adults create, renovate, or conserve some aspect of culture that ultimately survives.

generativity Adults' desire to leave legacies of themselves to the next generation; the positive side of Erikson's generativity versus stagnation middle adulthood stage.

stagnation Sometimes called "self-absorption," this state of mind develops when individuals sense that they have done little or nothing for the next generation; this is the negative side of Erikson's generativity versus stagnation middle adulthood stage.

Through generativity, adults promote and guide the next generation by parenting, teaching, leading, and doing things that benefit the community (Pratt & others, 2008). One of the participants in a study of aging said: "From twenty to thirty I learned how to get along with my wife. From thirty to forty I learned how to be a success at my job, and at forty to fifty I worried less about myself and more about the children" (Vaillant, 2002, p. 114).

Does research support Erikson's theory that generativity is an important dimension of middle age? Yes, it does (Newton & Stewart, 2012). In one study, Carol Ryff (1984) examined the views of women and men at different ages and found that middle-aged adults especially were concerned about generativity. In a longitudinal study of Smith College women, the desire for generativity increased as the participants aged from their thirties to their fifties (Stewart, Ostrove, & Helson, 2001). In another study, generativity was strongly linked to middle-aged adults' positive social engagement in contexts such as family life and community activities (Cox & others, 2010). And in a recent study of males, achievement of generativity in middle age was related to better health in late adulthood (Landes & others, 2014).

How Would You...?

As a **human development and family studies professional,** how would you advise a middle-aged woman who never had children and now fears she has little opportunity to leave a legacy to the next generation?

Era of late adulthood: 60 to ?

Late adult transition: Age 60 to 65

Culminating life structure for middle adulthood: 55 to 60

Age 50 transition: 50 to 55

Entry life structure for middle adulthood: 45 to 50

Middle adult transition: Age 40 to 45

Culminating life structure for early adulthood: 33 to 40

Age 30 transition: 28 to 33

Entry life structure for early adulthood: 22 to 28

Early adult transition: Age 17 to 22

Figure 1 Levinson's Periods of Adult Development

According to Levinson, adulthood for men has three main stages, which are surrounded by transition periods. Specific tasks and challenges are associated with each stage.

(Top) © Amos Morgan/Getty Images RF; (middle) © Stockbyte/Getty Images RF; (bottom) © image100 Ltd RF

Levinson's Seasons of a Man's Life

In *The Seasons of a Man's Life*, clinical psychologist Daniel Levinson (1978) reported the results of extensive interviews with 40 middle-aged men. The interviews were conducted with hourly workers, business executives, academic biologists, and novelists. Levinson bolstered his conclusions with information from the biographies of famous men and the development of memorable characters in literature. Although Levinson's major interest focused on midlife change in men, he described a number of stages and transitions during the period from 17 to 65 years of age, as shown in Figure 1. Levinson emphasizes that developmental tasks must be mastered at each stage.

At the end of one's teens, according to Levinson, a transition from dependence to independence should occur. This transition is marked by the formation of a dream—an image of the kind of life the youth wants to have, especially in terms of a career and marriage. Levinson sees the twenties as a *novice phase* of adult development. It is a time of reasonably free experimentation and of testing the dream in the real world. In early adulthood, the two major tasks to be mastered are exploring the possibilities for adult living and developing a stable life structure.

From about age 28 to 33, the man goes through a transition period in which he must face the more serious question of determining his goals. During his thirties, he usually focuses on family and career development. In the later years of this period, he enters a phase of *Becoming*

One's Own Man (or BOOM, as Levinson calls it). By age 40, he has reached a stable point in his career, has outgrown his earlier, more tenuous attempts at learning to become an adult, and now must look forward to the kind of life he will lead as a middle-aged adult.

According to Levinson, the transition to middle adulthood lasts about five years (ages 40 to 45) and requires the adult male to come to grips with four major conflicts that have existed in his life since adolescence: (1) being young versus being old, (2) being destructive versus being constructive, (3) being masculine versus being feminine, and (4) being attached to others versus being separated from them. Seventy to 80 percent of the men Levinson interviewed found the midlife transition tumultuous and psychologically painful, as many aspects of their lives came into question. According to Levinson, the success of the midlife transition rests on how effectively the individual reduces the polarities and accepts each of them as an integral part of his being.

Because Levinson interviewed middle-aged males, we can consider the data about middle adulthood more valid than the data about early adulthood. When individuals are asked to remember information about earlier parts of their lives, they may distort and forget things. The original Levinson data included no females, although Levinson (1996) reported that his stages, transitions, and the crisis of middle age apply to females as well as males. Levinson's work included no statistical analysis. However, the quality and quantity of the Levinson biographies make them outstanding examples of the clinical tradition.

How Pervasive Are Midlife Crises?

Levinson (1978) views midlife as a crisis, believing that the middle-aged adult is suspended between the past and the future, trying to cope with this gap that threatens life's continuity. George Vaillant (1977) has a different view. Vaillant's study—called the "Grant Study"—involved men who were in their early thirties and in their late forties who initially had been interviewed as undergraduates at Harvard University. He concludes that just as adolescence is a time for detecting parental flaws and discovering the truth about childhood, the forties are a decade of reassessing and recording the truth about adolescence and adulthood. However, whereas Levinson sees midlife as a crisis, Vaillant maintains that only a minority of adults experience a midlife crisis.

© John Simmons/
Alamy RF

Today, adult development experts are virtually unanimous in their belief that midlife crises have been exaggerated (Lachman, Teshale, & Agrigoroaei, 2015). Further, happiness and positive affect have an upward trajectory from early adulthood to late adulthood (Carstensen, 2015; Sims, Hogan, & Carstensen, 2015).

The Life-Events Approach

Age-related stages represent one major way to examine adult personality development. A second major way to conceptualize adult personality development is to focus on life events (Blonski & others, 2016; Leggett, Burgard, & Zivin, 2016; Schwarzer & Luszczynska, 2013). In the early version of the life-events approach, life events were viewed as taxing circumstances for individuals, forcing them to change their personality (Holmes & Rahe, 1967). Such events as the death of a spouse, divorce, marriage, and so on were believed to involve varying degrees of stress and therefore likely to influence the individual's development. A recent study found that stressful life events were associated with cardiovascular disease in middle-aged women (Kershaw & others, 2014). And a recent meta-analysis found an association between stressful life events and autoimmune diseases such as arthritis and psoriasis (Porcelli & others, 2016).

Today's life-events approach is more sophisticated. The **contemporary life-events approach** emphasizes that how life events influence the

contemporary life-events approach An approach emphasizing that how a life event influences the individual's development depends not only on the life event itself but also on mediating factors, the individual's adaptation to the life event, the life-stage context, and the sociohistorical context.

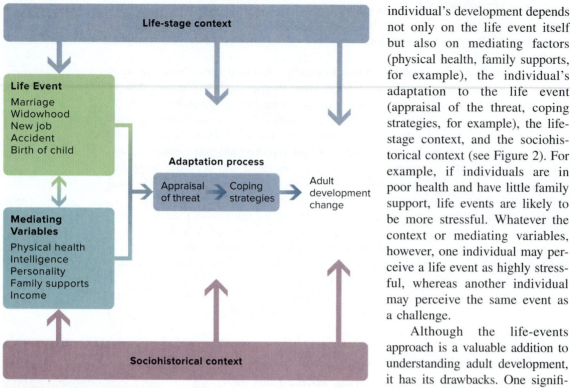

individual's development depends not only on the life event itself but also on mediating factors (physical health, family supports, for example), the individual's adaptation to the life event (appraisal of the threat, coping strategies, for example), the life-stage context, and the sociohistorical context (see Figure 2). For example, if individuals are in poor health and have little family support, life events are likely to be more stressful. Whatever the context or mediating variables, however, one individual may perceive a life event as highly stressful, whereas another individual may perceive the same event as a challenge.

Although the life-events approach is a valuable addition to understanding adult development, it has its drawbacks. One significant drawback is that the life-events approach places too much emphasis on change. Another drawback is its failure to recognize that our daily experiences may be the primary sources of stress in our lives (Hamilton & Julian, 2014; Keles & others, 2016). Enduring a boring but tense job, staying in an unsatisfying marriage, or living in poverty do not show up on scales of major life events. Yet the everyday pounding we take from these living conditions can add up to a highly stressful life and eventually lead to illness (McIntosh, Gillanders, & Rodgers, 2010). A recent study found that stressful daily hassles were linked to increased anxiety and decreased physical well-being (Falconier & others, 2015).

Figure 2 A Contemporary Life-Events Framework for Interpreting Adult Developmental Change

According to the contemporary life-events approach, the influence of a life event depends on the event itself, on mediating variables, on the life-stage and sociohistorical context, and on the individual's appraisal of the event and coping strategies.

Stress and Personal Control in Midlife

Margie Lachman and her colleagues (2015) recently described how personal control changes when individuals move into middle age. In their view, middle age is a time when a person's sense of control is frequently challenged by many demands and responsibilities, as well as physical and cognitive aging. By contrast, young people are more likely to have a sense of invulnerability, an unrealistic view of their personal control, and a lack of awareness regarding the aging process. Many young people focus primarily on self-pursuits and don't need to worry much about taking responsibility for others. But in middle age, less attention is given to self-pursuits and more to responsibility for others, including family members who are younger and older than they are. According to Lachman and her colleagues (2015), how middle adulthood plays out is largely in one's own hands, which can be stressful as individuals are faced with taking on and juggling responsibilities in different areas of their lives.

How Would You...?

As a **health-care professional,** how would you convince a company that it should sponsor a stress-reduction program for its middle-aged employees?

One study in which participants kept daily diaries over a one-week period found that both young and middle-aged adults had more stressful days than older adults (Almeida & Horn, 2004). In this study, although young adults experienced daily stressors more frequently than middle-aged adults did, middle-aged adults experienced more "overload" stressors that involved juggling too many activities at once. In a recent study, healthy older adult women 63 to 93 years of age reported their daily experiences over the course of one week (Charles & others, 2010). In this study, the older the women were, the fewer stressors and less frequent negative emotions they reported. Also, in recent research, greater emotional reactivity to daily stressors was linked to increased risk of reporting a chronic physical health condition and anxiety/mood disorders 10 years later (Charles & others, 2013; Piazza & others, 2013).

Developmental Changes in Perceived Personal Control

To what extent do middle-aged adults perceive that they can control what happens to them? Researchers have found that on average a sense of personal control peaks in midlife and then declines (Lachman, 2006; Lachman, Agrigoroaei, & Hahn, 2016; Lachman, Teshale, & Agrigoroaei, 2015). Some aspects of personal control increase with age while others decrease (Lachman, Neupert, & Agrigoroaei, 2011). For example, middle-aged adults have a greater sense of control over their finances, work, and marriage than younger adults but less control over their sex life and their children (Lachman & Firth, 2004). And having a sense of control in middle age is one of the most important modifiable factors in delaying the onset of diseases in middle adulthood and reducing the frequency of diseases in late adulthood (Lachman, Neupert, & Agrigoroaei, 2011; Robinson & Lachman, 2017).

Stress and Gender

Women and men differ in the way they experience and respond to stressors (Taylor, 2015). Women are more vulnerable to social stressors such as those involving romance, family, and work. For example, women experience higher levels of stress when things go wrong in romantic and marital relationships. Women also are more likely than men to become depressed when they encounter stressful life events such as a divorce or the death of a friend. In one study of more than 2,800 adults 50 years and older in Taiwan, women were more susceptible to depressive symptoms when they felt constant stress from finances, increasing stress from jobs, and fluctuating stress in family relationships (Lin, Hsu, & Chang, 2011).

How do women and men differ in the way they experience and respond to stressors?
© Altrendo images/Getty Images

When men face stress, they are likely to respond in a **fight-or-flight** manner—become aggressive, withdraw from social contact, or drink alcohol. By contrast, according to Shelley Taylor (2011a, b, c, 2015), when women experience stress, they are more likely to engage in a **tend-and-befriend** pattern, seeking social alliances with others, especially friends. Taylor argues that when women experience stress, their bodies produce elevated levels of the hormone *oxytocin*, which is linked to nurturing in animals.

Stability and Change

Questions about stability and change are an important issue in life-span development. One of the main ways that stability and change are assessed is through longitudinal studies that assess the same individuals at different points in their lives.

Longitudinal Studies

We examine three longitudinal studies to help us understand the extent to which there is stability or change in adult personality development: Costa and McCrae's Baltimore Study, the Berkeley Longitudinal Studies, and Vaillant's studies.

fight-or-flight The view that when men experience stress, they are more likely to become aggressive, withdraw from social contact, or drink alcohol.

tend-and-befriend Taylor's view that when women experience stress, they are more likely to seek social alliances with others, especially female friends.

Openness	**C**onscientiousness	**E**xtraversion	**A**greeableness	**N**euroticism (emotional stability)
• Imaginative or practical	• Organized or disorganized	• Sociable or retiring	• Softhearted or ruthless	• Calm or anxious
• Interested in variety or routine	• Careful or careless	• Fun-loving or somber	• Trusting or suspicious	• Secure or insecure
• Independent or conforming	• Disciplined or impulsive	• Affectionate or reserved	• Helpful or uncooperative	• Self-satisfied or self-pitying

Figure 3 The Big Five Factors of Personality
Each of the broad supertraits encompasses more narrow traits and characteristics. Use the acronym OCEAN to remember the Big Five personality factors (openness, conscientiousness, extraversion, agreeableness, neuroticism).

Costa and McCrae's Baltimore Study

A major study of adult personality development continues to be conducted by Paul Costa and Robert McCrae (1998; McCrae & Costa, 2006). They focus on what are called the **Big Five factors of personality,** which are openness to experience, conscientiousness, extraversion, agreeableness, and neuroticism (emotional stability); these factors are described in Figure 3. (Notice that if you create an acronym from these factor names, you will get the word OCEAN.) A number of research studies point to these factors as important dimensions of personality (Hill & Roberts, 2016; McCrae, Gaines, & Wellington, 2013; Roberts & others, 2014).

Using their five-factor personality test, Costa and McCrae (1998, 2000) studied approximately one thousand college-educated men and women aged 20 to 96, assessing the same individuals over many years. Data collection began in the 1950s to mid-1960s and is ongoing. Costa and McCrae concluded that considerable stability exists across the adult years for the five personality factors.

However, more recent research indicates greater developmental changes in the five personality factors in adulthood (Graham & Lachman, 2013). For example, a recent study found that emotional stability, extraversion, openness, and agreeableness were lower in early adulthood, peaked between 40 and 60 years of age, and decreased in late adulthood, while conscientiousness showed a continuous increase from early adulthood to late adulthood (Specht, Egloff, & Schukle, 2011). Most research studies find that the greatest changes in personality occur in early adulthood (Hill, Allemand, & Roberts, 2014; Hill & Roberts, 2016).

Further evidence supporting the importance of the Big Five factors indicates that they are related to major aspects of a person's life such as health, intelligence, achievement, and relationships (Hampson & others, 2015; Hill & Roberts, 2016; McCrae, Gaines, & Wellington, 2013; Mike & others, 2015). The following research supports these links:

- *Openness to experience.* Individuals high on openness to experience are more likely have superior cognitive functioning, achievement, and IQ across the life span (Briley, Domiteaux, & Tucker-Drob, 2014), show creative achievement in the arts (Kaufman & others, 2016), and experience less negative affect to stressors (Leger & others, 2016).

- *Conscientiousness.* Individuals high in conscientiousness have better health and less stress (Gartland & others, 2014), engage in superior problem-focused coping (Sesker & others, 2016), are more successful at accomplishing goals (McCabe & Fleeson, 2016), and have less cognitive decline as aging adults (Luchetti & others, 2016).

- *Extraversion.* Individuals high in *extraversion* are more likely than others to be satisfied in relationships (Toy, Nai, & Lee, 2016), show less negative affect to stressors (Leger & others, 2016), and have a more positive sense of well-being in the future (Soto, 2015).

Big Five factors of personality Emotional stability (neuroticism), extraversion, openness to experience, agreeableness, and conscientiousness.

- *Agreeableness.* People who are high in agreeableness are more likely to be generous and altruistic (Caprara & others, 2010), have more satisfying romantic relationships (Donnellan, Larsen-Rife, & Conger, 2005), and engage in more positive affect to stressors (Leger & others, 2016).

- *Neuroticism.* People high in neuroticism are more likely to be more drug dependent (Valero & others, 2014), have a higher coronary heart disease risk (Lee & others, 2014), and have a lower sense of well-being 40 years later (Gale & others, 2013).

Researchers increasingly are finding that optimism is linked to being healthier and living longer (Anthony, Kritz-Silverstein, & Barrett-Connor, 2016; Boelen, 2015). A recent study involving adults 50 years of age and older revealed that being optimistic and having an optimistic spouse were both associated with better health and physical functioning (Kim, Chopik, & Smith, 2014). Also, in a recent study of 40- to 85-year-olds, individuals who were prepared for physical losses but also had an optimistic outlook on the future had better physical functioning and a lower level of depressive symptoms than those who were unprepared and pessimistic (Wurm & Benyamini, 2014). In another recent study, a higher level of optimism following an acute coronary event was linked to engaging in more physical activity and having fewer cardiac readmissions (Huffman & others, 2016). And a recent research review concluded that the positive influence of optimism on outcomes for people with chronic diseases (such as cancer, cardiovascular disease, and respiratory disease) may reflect either or both of the following factors: (a) a direct effect on the neuroendocrine system and on immune system function; and (b) an indirect effect on health outcomes as a result of protective health behaviors, adaptive coping strategies, and enhanced positive mood (Avvenuti, Baiardini, & Giardini, 2016).

Berkeley Longitudinal Studies

In the Berkeley Longitudinal Studies, more than 500 children and their parents were initially studied in the late 1920s and early 1930s. The book *Present and Past in Middle Life* (Eichorn & others, 1981) profiles these individuals as they became middle-aged. The results from early adolescence through a portion of midlife did not support either extreme in the debate over whether personality is characterized by stability or change. Some characteristics were more stable than others, however. The most stable characteristics were the degree to which individuals were intellectually oriented, self-confident, and open to new experiences. The characteristics that changed the most included the extent to which the individuals were nurturant or hostile and whether they had strong or weak self-control.

George Vaillant's Studies

Longitudinal studies by George Vaillant explore a question that differs somewhat from the studies described so far: Does personality at middle age predict what a person's life will be like in late adulthood? Vaillant (2002) has conducted three longitudinal studies of adult development and aging: (1) a sample of 268 socially advantaged Harvard graduates born about 1920 (called the Grant Study); (2) a sample of 456 socially disadvantaged inner-city men born about 1930; and (3) a sample of 90 middle-SES, intellectually gifted women born about 1910. These individuals have been assessed numerous times (in most cases, every two years), beginning in the 1920s to 1940s and continuing today for those still living. The main assessments involve extensive interviews with the participants, their parents, and teachers.

Vaillant categorized 75- to 80-year-olds as "happy-well," "sad-sick," or "dead." He used data collected from these individuals when they were 50 years of age to predict which categories they were likely to end up in at 75 to 80 years of age. Alcohol abuse and smoking at age 50 were the best predictors of which individuals would be dead at 75 to 80 years of age. Other factors at age 50 were linked with being in the "happy-well" category at 75 to 80 years of age: getting regular exercise, avoiding being overweight, being well-educated, having a stable marriage, being future-oriented, being thankful and forgiving, empathizing with others, being active with other people, and having good coping skills.

Wealth and income at age 50 were not linked with being in the "happy-well" category at 75 to 80 years of age. Generativity in middle age (defined in this study as "taking care of the next generation") was more strongly related than intimacy to whether individuals would have an enduring and happy marriage at 75 to 80 years of age (Vaillant, 2002).

The results for one of Vaillant's studies, the Grant Study of Harvard men, indicated that when individuals at 50 years of age were not heavy smokers, did not abuse alcohol, had a stable marriage, exercised, maintained a normal weight, and had good coping skills, they were more likely to be alive and happy at 75 to 80 years of age.

How Would You...?

As a **health-care professional,** how would you use the results of Vaillant's research to advise a middle-aged adult patient who abuses alcohol and smokes?

Conclusions

What can be concluded about stability and change in personality development during the adult years? Avshalom Caspi and Brent Roberts (2001) concluded that the evidence does not support the view that personality traits become completely fixed at a certain age in adulthood. However, they argue that change is typically limited, and in some cases the changes in personality are small. They also say that age is positively related to stability and that stability peaks in the fifties and sixties. That is, people show greater stability in their personality when they reach midlife than when they were younger adults (Hill & Roberts, 2016; Nye & others, 2016). These findings support what is called a **cumulative personality model** of development, which states that with time and age, people become more adept at interacting with their environment in ways that promote stability of personality.

This does not mean that change is absent throughout midlife. Ample evidence shows that social contexts, new experiences, and sociohistorical changes can affect personality development (Lachman, Teshale, & Agrigoroaei, 2015; Mroczek, Spiro, & Griffin, 2006). However, Caspi and Roberts (2001) concluded that as people get older, stability increasingly outweighs change.

In general, changes in personality traits across adulthood also occur in a positive direction. Over time, "people become more confident, warm, responsible, and calm" (Roberts & Mroczek, 2008, p. 33). Such positive changes equate with becoming more socially mature.

In sum, recent research contradicts the old view that stability in personality begins to set in at about 30 years of age (Donnellan, Hill, & Roberts, 2015; Hill & Roberts, 2016). Although there are some consistent developmental changes in the personality traits of large numbers of people, at the individual level people can show unique patterns of personality traits—and these patterns often reflect life experiences related to themes of their particular developmental period (Roberts & Mroczek, 2008). For example, researchers have found that individuals who are in a stable marriage and on a solid career track become more socially dominant, conscientious, and emotionally stable as they go through early adulthood (Roberts & Wood, 2006). And, for some of these individuals, there is greater change in their personality traits than for other individuals (McAdams & Olson, 2010).

Close Relationships

There is a consensus among middle-aged Americans that a major component of well-being involves positive relationships with others, especially parents, spouse, and offspring (Lachman, Teshale, & Agrigoroaei, 2015). To begin our examination of midlife relationships, let's explore love and marriage in middle-aged adults.

cumulative personality model The principle that with time and age, people become more adept at interacting with their environment in ways that promote stability of personality.

Love and Marriage at Midlife

Two major forms of love are romantic love and affectionate love. The fires of romantic love burn strongly in early adulthood. Affectionate, or companionate, love increases during middle adulthood. That is, physical attraction, romance, and passion are more important in new relationships, especially those begun in early adulthood. Security, loyalty, and mutual emotional interest become more important as relationships mature, especially in middle adulthood.

One study revealed that marital satisfaction increased in middle age (Gorchoff, John, & Helson, 2008). Even some marriages that were difficult and rocky during early adulthood become more stable during middle adulthood. Although the partners may have lived through a great deal of turmoil, they eventually discover a deep and solid foundation on which to anchor their relationship. In middle adulthood, the partners may have fewer financial worries, less housework and chores, and more time with each other. Middle-aged partners are more likely to view their marriage as positive if they engage in mutual activities. Also, a recent study found that middle-aged married individuals had a lower likelihood of work-related health limitations (Lo, Cheng, & Simpson, 2016). And another recent study of middle-aged adults revealed that positive marital quality was linked to better health for both spouses (Choi, Yorgason, & Johnson, 2016).

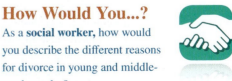

What characterizes marriage in middle adulthood?
© Digital Vision/Getty Images RF

Most individuals in midlife who are married voice considerable satisfaction with being married. In a large-scale study of individuals in middle adulthood, 72 percent of those who were married said their marriage was either "excellent" or "very good" (Brim, 1999). Possibly by middle age, many of the worst marriages already have dissolved. A longitudinal study of African American and non-Latino White men who were initially assessed when they were 51 to 62 years of age and then followed for 18 years found that the longevity gap that favors non-Latino White men was linked to their higher rate of marriage (Su, Stimpson, & Wilson, 2015).

What trends characterize divorce in U.S. middle-aged adults? In 2014, individuals 50 to 64 years of age were twice as likely to become divorced as their counterparts in 1990 (Brown & Lin, 2013). What accounts for this increase? One explanation is the changing view of women, who initiate approximately 60 percent of the divorces after 40 years of age. Compared with earlier decades, divorce has less stigma for women and they are more likely to leave an unhappy marriage. Also compared with earlier decades, more women are employed and are less dependent on their husband's income. Another explanation involves the increase in remarriages, in which the divorce rate is 2½ times as high as it is for those in first marriages.

Divorce in middle adulthood may be a more positive experience in some ways, more negative in others, than divorce in early adulthood (Pudrovska, 2009). On the one hand, for mature individuals, the perils of divorce can be

What are some ways that divorce might be more positive or more negative in middle adulthood than in early adulthood?
© Stock4B/Getty Images

fewer and less intense than for younger individuals. They have more resources, and they can use this time as an opportunity to simplify their lives by disposing of possessions, such as a large home, which they no longer need. Their children are adults and may be able to cope with their parents' divorce more effectively than they would have been able to do in childhood or adolescence. The partners

How Would You...?

As a **social worker,** how would you describe the different reasons for divorce in young and middle-aged couples?

may have gained a better understanding of themselves and may be searching for changes that could include the end to an unhappy marriage.

On the other hand, the emotional and time commitment to marriage that has existed for so many years may not be lightly given up. Many midlife individuals perceive a divorce as failing in the best years of their lives. The divorcer might see the situation as an escape from an untenable relationship, but the divorced partner usually sees it as betrayal, the ending of a relationship that had been built up over many years and that involved a great deal of commitment and trust.

In sum, divorce in midlife may have positive outcomes for some individuals and negative outcomes for others (Pudrovska, 2009). A recent study found that women who became divorced at 40 to 59 years of age reported being more lonely following the divorce than men who became divorced during this age period (Nicolaisen & Thorsen, 2014). A recent study, though, revealed that the life satisfaction of middle-aged women in low-quality marriages increased after they became divorced (Bourassa, Sbarra, & Whisman, 2015).

A survey by AARP (2004) of 1,148 40- to 79-year-olds who were divorced at least once in their forties, fifties, or sixties found that staying married because of their children was by far the main reason many people took a long time to become divorced. Despite the worry and stress involved in going through a divorce, three in four of the divorcees said they had made the right decision to dissolve their marriage and reported a positive outlook on life. Sixty-six percent of the divorced women said they had initiated the divorce, compared with only 41 percent of the divorced men. The divorced women were much more afraid of having financial problems (44 percent) than the divorced men were (11 percent).

Following are the main reasons that middle-aged and older adults cited for their divorce:

Main Causes for Women	Main Causes for Men
1. Verbal, physical, or emotional abuse (23 percent)	1. No obvious problems, just fell out of love (17 percent)
2. Alcohol or drug abuse (18 percent)	2. Cheating (14 percent)
3. Cheating (17 percent)	3. Different values, lifestyles (14 percent)

The Empty Nest and Its Refilling

An important event in a family is the launching of a child into adult life. Parents face new adjustments as a result of the child's absence. College students usually think that their parents suffer from their absence. In fact, parents who live vicariously through their children might experience the **empty nest syndrome,** which includes a decline in marital satisfaction after children leave the home. For most parents, however, marital satisfaction does not decline after children have left home. Rather, for most parents marital satisfaction increases during the years after child rearing has ended (Fingerman & Baker, 2006). With their children gone, marital partners have more time to pursue careers and other interests and more time for each other. One study revealed that the transition to an empty nest increased marital satisfaction and that this improvement was linked to an increase in the quality of time—but not the quantity of time—spent with partners (Gorchoff, John, & Helson, 2008).

In today's uncertain economic climate, the refilling of the empty nest is becoming a common occurrence as adult children return to the family home after several years of college, after graduating from college, or to save money after taking a full-time job (Merrill, 2009). Young adults also may move back in with their parents after an unsuccessful career or a divorce. And some individuals don't leave home at all until their middle to late twenties because they cannot financially support themselves. Numerous labels have been applied to these young adults who return to their parents' homes to live, including "boomerang kids" and "B2B" (or Back-to-Bedroom) (Furman, 2005).

The middle generation has always provided support for the younger generation, even after the nest is bare. Through loans and monetary gifts for education, and through emotional support, the middle generation has helped the younger generation. Adult children appreciate the financial and emotional support their parents provide at a time when they often feel considerable stress about their career, work, and lifestyle. And parents feel good that they can provide this support.

What are some strategies that can help parents and their young adult children get along better?
© Tom Grill/Corbis RF

However, as with most family living arrangements, there are both pluses and minuses when adult children live with their parents. One of the most common complaints voiced by both adult children and their parents is a loss of privacy. The adult children complain that their parents restrict their independence, cramp their sex lives, reduce their rock music listening, and treat them as children rather than adults. Parents often complain that their quiet home has become noisy, that they stay up late worrying until their adult children come home, that meals are difficult to plan because of conflicting schedules, that their relationship as a married couple has been invaded, and that they have to shoulder too much responsibility for their adult children. In sum, when adult children return home to live, it causes a disequilibrium in family life that requires considerable adaptation on the part of parents and their adult children.

When adult children ask to return home to live, parents and their adult children should agree on the conditions and expectations beforehand. For example, they might discuss and agree on whether the young adults will pay rent, wash their own clothes, cook their own meals, do any household chores, pay their phone bills, come and go as they please, be sexually active or drink alcohol at home, and so on. If these conditions aren't negotiated at the beginning, conflict often results because the expectations of parents and young adult children will likely be violated.

How Would You...?

As a **psychologist,** how would you counsel parents of adult children who return to the family home for a few years following their college graduation?

Sibling Relationships and Friendships

Sibling relationships persist over the entire life span for most adults (Whiteman, McHale, & Soli, 2011). Eighty-five percent of today's adults have at least one living sibling. Sibling relationships in adulthood may be extremely close, apathetic, or highly rivalrous (Bedford, 2009). The majority of sibling relationships in adulthood are close (Cicirelli, 2009). Those siblings who are psychologically close to each other in adulthood tended to be that way in childhood. It is rare for sibling closeness to develop for the first time in adulthood (Dunn, 1984). A recent study revealed that adult siblings often provide practical and emotional support to each other (Voorpostel & Blieszner, 2008). Another study revealed that men who had poor sibling relationships in childhood were more likely to develop depression by age 50 than men who had more positive sibling relationships as children (Waldinger, Vaillant, & Orav, 2007).

Friendships continue to be important in middle adulthood just as they were in early adulthood. It takes time to develop intimate friendships, so friendships that have endured over the adult years are often deeper than those that have just been formed in middle adulthood.

Grandparenting

The increase in longevity is influencing the nature of grandparenting (Monserud, 2011). In 1900 only 4 percent of 10-year-old children had four living grandparents, but by 2000 that figure had risen to more than 40 percent. And in 1990 only about

20 percent of people 30 years of age had living grandparents, a figure that is projected to increase to 80 percent in 2020 (Hagestad & Uhlenberg, 2007). Further increases in longevity are likely to support this trend in the future, although the current trend toward delayed childbearing is likely to undermine it.

Grandparent Roles

Grandparents play important roles in the lives of many grandchildren (Bol & Kalmijn, 2016; Choi, Sprang, & Eslinger, 2016; Di Gessa, Glaser, & Tinker, 2016). Many adults become grandparents for the first time during middle age. Researchers have consistently found that grandmothers have more contact with grandchildren than do grandfathers (Watson, Randolph, & Lyons, 2005). Perhaps women tend to define their role as grandmothers as part of their responsibility for maintaining ties between family members across generations. Men may have fewer expectations about the grandfather role and see it as more voluntary.

In 2014, 10 percent (7.4 million) of children in the United States lived with at least one grandparent, a dramatic increase since

What are some changes that are occurring in grandparents' roles?
© KidStock/Getty Images RF

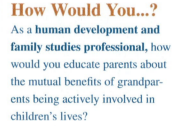

How Would You...?

As a **human development and family studies professional,** how would you educate parents about the mutual benefits of grandparents being actively involved in children's lives?

1981 when 4.7 million children were living with at least one grandparent (U.S. Census Bureau, 2015). Divorce, adolescent pregnancies, and drug use by parents are the main reasons that grandparents are thrust back into the "parenting" role they thought they had shed. One study revealed that grandparent involvement was linked with better adjustment when it occurred in single-parent and stepparent families than in two-parent biological families (Attar-Schwartz & others, 2009).

Grandparents who are full-time caregivers for grandchildren are at elevated risk for health problems, depression, and stress (Silverstein, 2009). A recent review concluded that grandparents raising grandchildren are especially at risk for developing depression (Hadfield, 2014). Caring for grandchildren is linked with these problems in part because full-time grandparent caregivers are often characterized by low-income, minority status and by not being married (Minkler & Fuller-Thompson, 2005). Grandparents who are part-time caregivers are less likely to have the negative health portrait that full-time grandparent caregivers have. In a recent study of part-time grandparent caregivers, few negative effects on grandparents were found (Hughes & others, 2007).

As divorce and remarriage have become more common, a special concern of grandparents is visitation privileges with their grandchildren. In the last 10 to 15 years, more states have passed laws giving grandparents the right to petition a court for visitation privileges with their grandchildren, even if a parent objects. Whether such forced visitation rights for grandparents are in the child's best interest is still being debated.

Intergenerational Relationships

Family is important to most people. When 21,000 adults aged 40 to 79 in 21 countries were asked, "When you think of who you are, you think mainly of _____," 63 percent said "family," 9 percent said "religion," and 8 percent said "work" (HSBC Insurance, 2007). In this study, in all 21 countries, middle-aged and older adults expressed a strong feeling of responsibility between generations in their family, with the strongest intergenerational ties indicated in Saudi Arabia, India, and Turkey. More than

80 percent of the middle-aged and older adults reported that adults have a duty to care for their parents (and parents-in-law) in time of need later in life.

Adults in midlife play important roles in the lives of the young and the old (Antonucci & others, 2016; Birditt & others, 2016; Fingerman & others, 2014; Luong, Rauers, & Fingerman, 2015). Middle-aged adults share their experience and transmit values to the younger generation. They may be launching children and experiencing the empty nest, adjusting to having grown children return home, or becoming grandparents. They also may be giving or receiving financial assistance, caring for a widowed or sick parent, or adapting to being the oldest generation after both parents have died.

Middle-aged and older adults around the world show a strong sense of family responsibility. One study of middle-aged and older adults in 21 countries found that the strongest intergenerational ties were in Saudi Arabia.

© Reza/National Geographic/Getty Images

Middle-aged adults have been described as the "sandwich," "squeezed," or "overload" generation because of the responsibilities they have for their adolescent and young adult children on the one hand and their aging parents on the other (Etaugh & Bridges, 2010). However, an alternative view is that in the United States, a "sandwich" generation, in which the middle generation cares for both grown children and aging parents simultaneously, occurs less often than a "pivot" generation, in which the middle generation alternates attention between the demands of grown children and aging parents (Antonucci & others, 2016; Luong, Rauers, & Fingerman, 2015). By middle age, more than 40 percent of adult children (most of them daughters) provide care for aging parents or parents-in-law (National Alliance for Caregiving, 2009). However, two studies revealed that middle-aged parents are more likely to provide support to their grown children than to their parents (Fingerman & others, 2011a, 2012). When middle-aged adults have a parent with a disability, their support for that parent increases (Fingerman & others, 2011b). This support might involve locating a nursing home and monitoring its quality, procuring medical services, arranging public service assistance, and handling finances. In some cases, adult children provide direct assistance with daily living, including such activities as eating, bathing, and dressing. Even less severely impaired older adults may need help with shopping, housework, transportation, home maintenance, and bill paying.

Some researchers have found that relationships between aging parents and their children are often characterized by ambivalence (Antonucci & others, 2016; Fingerman & others, 2012; Pitzer, Fingerman, & Lefkowitz, 2014). Perceptions include love, reciprocal help, and shared values on the positive side and isolation, family conflicts and problems, abuse, neglect, and caregiver stress on the negative side. A recent study found that middle-aged adults positively supported family responsibility to emerging adult children but were more ambivalent about providing care for aging parents, viewing it as both a joy and a burden (Igarashi & others, 2013).

How Would You...?

As a **health-care professional,** how would you advise a family contemplating the potential challenges of having a middle-aged family member take on primary responsibility for the daily care of a chronically ill parent?

With each new generation, personality characteristics, attitudes, and values are replicated or changed (Antonucci & others, 2016). As older family members die, their biological, intellectual, emotional, and personal legacies are carried on in the next generation. Their children become the oldest generation and their grandchildren the second generation. As adult children become middle-aged, they often develop more positive perceptions of their parents (Field, 1999). Both similarity and dissimilarity across generations are found. For example, similarity between parents and an adult child is most noticeable in religion and politics, least in gender roles, lifestyle, and work orientation.

What is the nature of intergenerational relationships?
© Steve Casimiro/The Image Bank/Getty Images

Gender differences also characterize intergenerational relationships (Antonucci & others, 2016; Luong, Rauers, & Fingerman, 2015). Women play an especially important role in maintaining family relationships across generations. Women's relationships across generations are typically closer than other family bonds (Merrill, 2009). In one study, mothers and their adult daughters had much closer relationships than mothers and sons, fathers and daughters, and fathers and sons (Rossi, 1989). Also in this study, married men were more involved with their wives' kin than with their own. And maternal grandmothers and maternal aunts were cited twice as often as their counterparts on the paternal side of the family as the most important or loved relative. Another study revealed that mothers' intergenerational ties were more influential for grandparent-grandchild relationships than fathers' were (Monserud, 2008).

Summary

Personality Theories and Development

- Erikson says that the seventh stage of the human life span, generativity versus stagnation, occurs in middle adulthood. Levinson concluded that a majority of Americans, especially men, experience a midlife crisis. Research, though, indicates that midlife crises are not pervasive.
- In the contemporary version of the life-events approach, how life events influence the individual's development depends not only on the life event but also on mediating factors, adaptation to the event, the life-stage context, and the sociohistorical context.
- Young and middle-aged adults experience more stress than do older adults, and as adults become older, they report less control over some areas of their lives and more control over other areas.

Stability and Change

- In Costa and McCrae's Baltimore Study, the Big Five personality factors showed considerable stability. In the Berkeley Longitudinal Studies, the extremes in the stability-change argument were not supported. George Vaillant's research revealed links between a number of

characteristics at age 50 and health and well-being at 75 to 80 years of age.
- Some researchers suggest that personality stability peaks in the fifties and sixties, others say that it begins to stabilize at about age 30, and still others argue that limited personality changes continue during midlife.

Close Relationships

- Affectionate love increases in midlife for many individuals.
- Rather than reducing marital satisfaction as was once thought, the empty nest increases it for most parents. Growing numbers of young adults are returning home to live with their middle-aged parents.
- Sibling relationships continue throughout life, and friendships continue to be important in middle age.
- Depending on the family's culture and situation, grandparents assume different roles. The profile of grandparents is changing.
- Family members usually maintain contact across generations. The middle-aged generation plays an important role in linking generations.

Key Terms

Big Five factors of personality
contemporary life-events approach
cumulative personality model
empty nest syndrome
fight-or-flight
generativity
stagnation
tend-and-befriend

15 Physical and Cognitive Development in Late Adulthood

© Rod Porteous/Robert Harding World Imagery/Corbis

CHAPTER OUTLINE

Stories of Life-Span Development: Learning to Age Successfully

In 2010, 90-year-old Helen Small completed her master's degree at the University of Texas at Dallas. The topic of her master's degree research project was romantic relationships in late adulthood. Helen said that she had interviewed only one individual who was older than she was—a 92-year-old man.

I (your author, John Santrock) first met Helen when she took my undergraduate course in life-span development in 2006. After the first test, Helen stopped showing up and I wondered what had happened to her. It turns out that she had broken her shoulder when she tripped over a curb while hurrying to class. The next semester, she took my class again and did a great job in it, even though the first several months she had to take notes with her left hand (she's right-handed) because of her lingering shoulder problem.

Helen grew up in the Great Depression and first went to college in 1938 at the University of Akron, which she attended for only one year. She got married and her marriage lasted 62 years. After her husband's death, Helen went back to college in 2002, first at Brookhaven Community College and then at UT-Dallas. When I interviewed her recently, she told me that she had promised her mother that she would finish college. Her most important advice for college students is "Finish college and be persistent. When you make a commitment, always see it through. Don't quit. Go after what you want in life."

© Helen Small

Helen not only is cognitively fit, she also is physically fit. She works out three times a week for about an hour each time—aerobically on a treadmill for about 30 minutes and then on six different weight machines.

What struck me most about Helen when she took my undergraduate course in life-span development was how appreciative she was of the opportunity to learn and how passionately she pursued studying and doing well in the course. Helen was quite popular with the younger students in the course and she was a terrific role model for them.

After her graduation, I asked her what she planned to do during the next few years and she responded, "I've got to figure out what I'm going to do with the rest of my life." Helen now comes each semester to my course in life-span development when we are discussing cognitive aging. She wows the class and has been an inspiration to all who come in contact with her.

What has Helen done recently to stay cognitively fit? She has worked as a public ambassador for Dr. Denise Park's Center for Vital Longevity at UT-Dallas, regularly served as volunteer guide for Dallas' new Perot Science Museum, and is working on archival materials for the UT-Dallas library. Also, in 2015, she began teaching English to immigrant bilingual adults. Helen also published her first book: *Why Not? My Seventy Year Plan for a College Degree* (Small, 2011). It's a wonderful, motivating invitation to live your life fully and reach your potential no matter what your age.

The story of Helen Small's physical and cognitive well-being in late adulthood raises some truly fascinating questions about life-span development, which we explore in this chapter. They include: Why do we age, and what, if anything, can we do to delay the aging process? What chance do you have of living to be 100? How does the body change in old age? How well do older adults function cognitively? What roles do work and retirement play in older adults' lives? ∎

Helen Small with the author of your text, John Santrock, in his undergraduate course on life-span development at the University of Texas at Dallas in spring 2012. Helen now returns each semester to talk with students in the class about cognitive aging.
© John Santrock

Longevity, Biological Aging, and Physical Development

What do we really know about longevity? What are the current biological theories about why we age? How does our brain change during this part of our life span? What happens to us physically? Does our sexuality change?

Longevity

The United States is no longer a youthful society. As more individuals are living past age 65, the proportion of individuals at different ages has become increasingly similar. Indeed, the concept of a period called "late adulthood," beginning in the sixties or seventies and lasting until death, is a recent one. Before the twentieth century, most individuals died before they reached 65.

life span The upper boundary of life, which is the maximum number of years an individual can live. The maximum life span of human beings is about 120 to 125 years of age.

life expectancy The number of years that will probably be lived by the average person born in a particular year.

Life Span and Life Expectancy

Since the beginning of recorded history, **life span,** the maximum number of years an individual can live, has remained steady at approximately 120 to 125 years of age. But since 1900 improvements in medicine, nutrition, exercise, and lifestyle have increased our life expectancy by an average of 31 years.

Recall that **life expectancy** is the number of years that the average person born in a particular year will probably live. The average life expectancy of individuals born in 2013 in the United States was 78.8 years (Xu, 2016). Sixty-five-year-olds in the United States today can expect to live an average of 19.3 more years (20.5 for females, 17.9 for males) (Xu, 2016). People who are 100 years of age can only expect to live an average of 2.3 years longer (U.S. Census Bureau, 2011).

Differences in Life Expectancy

How does the United States fare in life expectancy, compared with other countries around the world? We do considerably better than some and somewhat worse than others. In 2015, Monaco had the highest estimated life expectancy at birth (90 years), followed by Japan, Singapore, and Macau (a region of China near Hong Kong) (85 years) (Central Intelligence Agency, 2015). Of 224 countries, the United States ranked 43rd at 80 years. The lowest estimated life expectancy in 2015 occurred in the African countries of Chad and Guinea-Bissau (50) and Swaziland and Afghanistan (51 years). Differences in life expectancies across countries are due to factors such as health conditions and medical care throughout the life span.

© Comstock/PunchStock RF

In 2013, the overall life expectancy for women was 81.2 years of age, and for men it was 76.4 years of age (Xu & others, 2016). The gender gap in longevity has come down from 7.8 years in 1979 to 4.8 years in 2013. Beginning in the mid-thirties, women outnumber men; this gap widens during the remainder of the adult years. By the time adults are 75 years of age, more than 61 percent are female; for those 85 and over, the figure is almost 70 percent female. Why can women expect to live longer than men? Social factors such as health attitudes, habits, lifestyles, and occupation are probably important (Saint-Onge, 2009). Men are more likely than women to die from most of the leading causes of death in the United States, including cancer of the respiratory system, motor vehicle accidents, cirrhosis of the liver, emphysema, and coronary heart disease (Dao-Fu & others, 2016; Pedersen & others, 2016). These causes of death are associated with lifestyle. For example, the sex difference in deaths due to lung cancer and emphysema occurs because men are heavier smokers than women.

The sex difference in longevity also is influenced by biological factors (Beltran-Sanchez, Finch, & Crimmins, 2015; Crimmins & Levine, 2016). In virtually all species, females outlive males. Women have more resistance to infections and degenerative diseases (Pan & Chang, 2012). For example, the female's estrogen production helps to protect her from arteriosclerosis (hardening of the arteries) (Valera & others, 2015). And the additional X chromosome that women carry in comparison with men may be associated with the production of more antibodies to fight off disease. The sex difference in mortality is still present in late adulthood but less pronounced than earlier in adulthood, and it is especially linked to the higher level of cardiovascular disease in men than women (Yang & Kozloski, 2011).

Centenarians

In the United States, there were only 15,000 centenarians in 1980, but that number rose to 50,000 in 2000 and to 72,000 in 2014 (Xu, 2016). The number of U.S. centenarians is projected to reach 600,000 by 2050 (U.S. Census Bureau, 2011).

Many people expect that "the older you get, the sicker you get." However, researchers are finding that this is not true for some centenarians (Willcox, Scapagnini, & Willcox, 2014). A study of 93 centenarians revealed that despite some physical limitations, they had a low rate of age-associated diseases and most had good mental

Jeanne Louise Calment, celebrating her 117th birthday. She was the world's oldest living person, dying at age 122. She said reasons for living so long included not worrying about things you can't do anything about; an occasional glass of Port wine; a diet rich in olive oil; and laughter. Regarding her longevity, she once said that God must have forgotten about her. On her 120th birthday, she was asked her what kind of future she anticipated. Calment replied, "A very short one." Becoming accustomed to the media attention she got, at 117 she stated, "I wait for death . . . and journalists." Calment walked, biked, and began taking fencing lessons at age 85 and rode a bicycle until she was 100.

© Jean Pierre Fizet/Sygma/Corbis

health (Selim & others, 2005). And a recent study of centenarians from 100 to 119 years of age found that the older the age group (110 to 119—referred to as *supercentenarians*—compared with 100 to 104, for example), the later the onset of diseases such as cancer and cardiovascular disease, as well as functional decline (Andersen & others, 2012). The research just described was carried out as part of the New England Centenarian Study (NECS) conducted by Thomas Perls and his colleagues. Perls has a term for this process of staving off high-mortality chronic diseases until much later ages than is usually the case in the general population: he calls it the *compression of morbidity* (Sebastiani & Perls, 2012). Further, there are far more female supercentenarians than males—a recent list (2015) of the oldest people who have ever lived had only two men (number 11 and number 17) in the top 25.

Among the factors in the NECS that are associated with living to be 100 are longevity genes and the ability to cope effectively with stress. The researchers also have discovered a strong genetic component to living to be 100 that consists of many genetic links, each with modest effects but collectively having a strong influence (Sebastiani & others, 2013). Other characteristics of centenarians in the NECS study include the following: few of the centenarians are obese, habitual smoking is rare, and only a small percentage (less than 15 percent) have had significant changes in their thinking skills (disproving the belief that most centenarians likely would develop Alzheimer disease).

Biological Theories of Aging

Even if we stay remarkably healthy, we begin to age at some point. Four biological theories provide intriguing explanations of why we age: evolutionary, cellular clock, free-radical, and hormonal stress.

Evolutionary Theory

In the **evolutionary theory of aging,** natural selection has not eliminated many harmful conditions and nonadaptive characteristics in older adults (Metcalf & Jones, 2015; Vanhaelen, 2015). Why? Because natural selection is linked to reproductive fitness, which is present only in the earlier part of adulthood. For example, consider Alzheimer disease, an irreversible brain disorder, which does not appear until late middle adulthood or late adulthood. According to evolutionary theory, possibly if Alzheimer disease occurred earlier in development, it might have been eliminated many centuries ago. Evolutionary theory has its critics (Cohen, 2015). One criticism is that the "big picture" idea of natural selection leading to the development of human traits and behaviors is difficult to refute or test because evolution occurs on a time scale that does not lend itself to empirical study. Another criticism is the failure of evolutionary theory to account for cultural influences (Singer, 2016).

Genetic/Cellular Process Theories

One recent view stated that aging is best explained by cellular maintenance requirements and evolutionary constraints (Vanhaelen, 2015). In recent decades, there has been a significant increase in research on genetic and cellular processes involved in aging (Cho & Suh, 2016; Leiser, Miller, & Kaeberlein, 2016; Sutphin & Korstanje, 2016). Five

evolutionary theory of aging The view that natural selection has not eliminated many harmful conditions and nonadaptive characteristics in older adults.

such advances involve telomeres, free radicals, mitochondria, sirtuins, and the mTOR pathway.

Cellular Clock Theory **Cellular clock theory** is Leonard Hayflick's (1977) theory that cells can divide a maximum of about 75 to 80 times and that as we age our cells become less capable of dividing. Hayflick found that cells extracted from adults in their fifties to seventies divided fewer than 75 to 80 times. Based on the ways cells divide, Hayflick places the upper limit of human life-span potential at about 120 to 125 years of age.

In the last decade, scientists have tried to fill in a gap in cellular clock theory (Ishikawa & others, 2016; Reynolds & Finkel, 2016). Hayflick did not know why cells die. The answer may lie at the tips of chromosomes (Silva & others, 2016; Yang, Song, & Johnson, 2016; Zhang & others, 2016).

Each time a cell divides, *telomeres,* which are DNA sequences that cap chromosomes, become shorter and shorter (see Figure 1). After about 70 or 80 replications, the telomeres are dramatically reduced, and the cell no longer can reproduce. One study revealed that healthy centenarians had longer telomeres than unhealthy centenarians (Terry & others, 2008). And in a recent study, greater leisure time screen-based sedentary behavior was linked to shorter telomere length (Loprinzi, 2015).

Injecting the enzyme *telomerase* into human cells grown in the laboratory can substantially extend the life of the cells beyond the approximately 70 to 80 normal cell divisions (Harrison, 2012). However, telomerase is present in approximately 85 to 90 percent of cancerous cells and thus may not produce healthy life extension of cells (Bertorelle & others, 2014; Fakhoury, Nimmo, & Autexier, 2007). To capitalize on the high presence of telomerase in cancerous cells, researchers currently are investigating gene therapies that inhibit telomerase and lead to the death of cancerous cells while keeping healthy cells alive (Akincilar, Unal, & Tergaonkar, 2016; Sutphin & Korstanje, 2016; Terali & Yilmazer, 2016). A recent focus of these gene therapies is on stem cells and their renewal (Okada & others, 2016). Telomeres and telomerase are increasingly thought to be key components of the stem cell regeneration process, providing a possible avenue to restrain cancer and delay aging (Naxerova & Elledge, 2016; Ozturk, 2015).

Free-Radical Theory A third theory of aging is **free-radical theory,** which states that people age because when cells metabolize energy, the by-products include unstable oxygen molecules known as *free radicals*. The free radicals ricochet around the cells, damaging DNA and other cellular structures (Pinto & Moraes, 2015). The damage can lead to a range of disorders, including cancer and arthritis (Phaniendra, Jestadi, & Periyasamy, 2015). Overeating is linked with an increase in free radicals, and researchers recently have found that calorie restriction—a diet low in calories but adequate in proteins, vitamins, and minerals—reduces the oxidative damage created by free radicals (Kalsi, 2015). A recent study of obese men found that endurance exercise reduced their oxidative damage (Samjoo & others, 2013).

Mitochrondrial Theory **Mitochondrial theory** is a theory of aging that emphasizes the decay of *mitochondria*—tiny bodies within cells that supply essential energy for function, growth, and repair—that is primarily due to oxidative damage and loss of critical micronutrients supplied by the cell (Min-Wen, Jun-Hao, & Shyh-Chang, 2016; Ziegler, Wiley, & Velarde, 2016). More recently, energy sensing and apoptosis (programmed cell death) also have been emphasized as key aspects of the mitochondrial theory of aging (Gonzalez-Freire & others, 2015).

The mitochondrial damage may lead to a range of disorders, including cancer, arthritis, and Alzheimer disease (Benek & others, 2016;

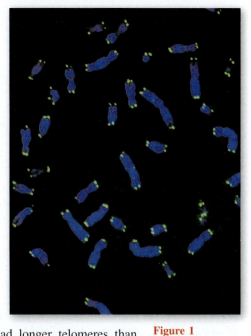

Figure 1

Telomeres and Aging

The photograph shows actual telomeres lighting up the tips of chromosomes.

© Dr. Jerry Shay

cellular clock theory Leonard Hayflick's theory that the maximum number of times human cells can divide is about 75 to 80. As we age, our cells become increasingly less capable of dividing.

free-radical theory A theory of aging proposing that people age because normal cell metabolism produces unstable oxygen molecules known as free radicals. These molecules ricochet around inside cells, damaging DNA and other cellular structures.

mitochondrial theory The theory that aging is caused by the decay of mitochondria, tiny cellular bodies that supply energy for function, growth, and repair.

Mastroeni & others, 2015). However, it is not known whether the defects in mitochondria cause aging or merely accompany the aging process (Brand, 2011).

Sirtuin Theory **Sirtuins** are a family of proteins that have been linked to longevity, regulation of mitochondria functioning in energy, possible benefits of calorie restriction, stress resistance, and a lower incidence of cardiovascular disease (Covington & Bajpeyi, 2016; Giblin & Lombard, 2016; Matsushima & Sadoshima, 2015). One of the sirtuins, SIRT 1, has been connected to DNA repair and aging (Kida & Goligorsky, 2016).

mTOR Pathway Theory The **mTOR pathway** is a cellular pathway that involves the regulation of growth and metabolism. TOR stands for "target of rapamycin," and in mammals it is called mTOR. Rapamycin is a naturally derived antibiotic and immune system suppressant/modulator, first discovered in the 1960s on Easter Island. It has been commonly used and is FDA approved for preventing organ rejection and in bone-marrow transplants. Recently, proposals have been made that the mTOR pathway has a central role in the life of cells, acting as a cellular router for growth, protein production/metabolism, and stem cell functioning (Dai & others, 2016; Maiese, 2015; Nadon & others, 2016; Schreiber, O'Leary, & Kennedy, 2016). Some scientists also argue that the pathway is linked to longevity, the successful outcomes of calorie restriction, reducing cognitive decline, and plays a role in a number of diseases, including cancer, cardiovascular disease, and Alzheimer disease (Chen & others, 2016; Cheng & others, 2016). Rapamycin has not been approved as an anti-aging drug and has some serious side effects, including increased risk of infection and lymphoma, a deadly cancer.

Some critics argue that scientific support for sirtuins and the mTOR pathway as key causes of aging in humans has not been found and that research has not adequately documented the effectiveness of using drugs such as rapamycin to slow the aging process or extend the human life span (Ehninger, Neff, & Xie, 2014; Park, Mori, & Shimokawa, 2013).

Hormonal Stress Theory

Cellular clock and free radical theories attempt to explain aging at the cellular level. In contrast, **hormonal stress theory** argues that aging in the body's hormonal system can lower resistance to stress and increase the likelihood of disease. Normally, when people experience stressors, the body responds by releasing certain hormones. As people age, the hormones stimulated by stress remain at elevated levels longer than when people were younger (Simm & others, 2008). These prolonged, elevated levels of stress-related hormones are associated with increased risks for many diseases, including cardiovascular disease, cancer, diabetes, and hypertension (Steptoe & Kivimaki, 2012). Researchers are exploring stress-buffering strategies, including exercise, in an effort to find ways to attenuate some of the negative effects of stress on the aging process (Bauer & others, 2013).

Recently, a variation of hormonal stress theory has emphasized the contribution of a decline in immune system functioning with aging (Muller & Pawelec, 2015, 2016; Qin & others, 2016; Silva & others, 2016). In a recent study, the percentage of T cells (a type of white blood cell essential for immunity) decreased in older adults in their seventies, eighties, and nineties (Valiathan, Ashman, & Asthana, 2016). Aging contributes to immune system deficits that give rise to infectious diseases in older adults (Chalan & others, 2015). The extended duration of stress and diminished restorative processes in older adults may accelerate the effects of aging on immunity.

sirtuins A family of proteins that have been proposed as having important influences on longevity, mitochondrial functioning in energy, calorie restriction benefits, stress resistance, and a lower incidence of cardiovascular functioning

mTOR pathway A cellular pathway involving the regulation of growth and metabolism that has been proposed as a key aspect of longevity

hormonal stress theory The theory that aging in the body's hormonal system can lower resilience under stress and increase the likelihood of disease.

Conclusions

Which of these biological theories best explains aging? That question has not yet been answered. It likely will turn out that more than one—or perhaps all—of these biological processes contribute to aging. In a recent analysis, it was concluded that aging is a very complex process involving multiple degenerative factors, including interacting cell- and organ level communications (de Magalhaes & Tacutu, 2016). Although there are some individual aging triggers such as telomere shortening, a full understanding of biological aging involves multiple processes operating at different biological levels.

The Aging Brain

How does the brain change during late adulthood? Does it retain plasticity? As we will see, the brain shrinks and slows but still has considerable adaptive ability.

The Shrinking, Slowing Brain

On average, the brain loses 5 to 10 percent of its weight between the ages of 20 and 90. Brain volume also decreases (Liu & others, 2016; Peng & others, 2016). A recent study found a decrease in total brain volume and volume in key brain structures such as the frontal lobes and hippocampus from 22 to 88 years of age (Sherwood & others, 2011). Also, recent analyses concluded that in healthy aging the decrease in brain volume is due mainly to shrinkage of neurons, lower numbers of synapses, reduced length and complexity of axons, and reduced tree-like branching in dendrites, but only to a minor extent attributable to neuron loss (Fjell & Walhovd, 2010; Penazzi, Bakota, & Brandt, 2016). Of course, for individuals with disorders such as Alzheimer disease, neuron loss occurs (Moore & Murphy, 2016). Further, in a recent study, global brain volume predicted mortality in a large population of stroke-free community-dwelling adults (Van Elderen & others, 2016).

Some brain areas shrink more than others with aging (Moore & Murphy, 2016). The prefrontal cortex is one area that shrinks, and recent research has linked this shrinkage with a decrease in working memory and other cognitive activities in older adults (Hoyer, 2015). The sensory regions of the brain—such as the primary visual cortex, primary motor cortex, and somatosensory cortex—are less vulnerable to the aging process (Rodrique & Kennedy, 2011). A general slowing of function in the brain and spinal cord begins in middle adulthood and accelerates in late adulthood (Rosano & others, 2012). Both physical coordination and intellectual performance are affected. For example, after age 70 many adults no longer show a knee-jerk reflex, and by age 90 most reflexes are much slower (Spence, 1989). Slowing of the brain can impair the performance of older adults on intelligence tests, especially timed tests (Lu & others, 2011).

Aging also has been linked to a decline in the production of some neurotransmitters. Reduction in acetylcholine is linked to memory loss, especially in people with Alzheimer disease (Jensen & others, 2015). Severe reductions in dopamine are involved in a reduction in motor control in Parkinson disease (Ruitenberg & others, 2015).

Historically, as in the research just discussed, much of the focus on links between brain functioning and aging has been on volume of brain structures and regions. Currently, however, increased emphasis is being given to changes in myelination and neural networks. Recent research indicates that demyelination (deterioration in the myelin sheath that encases axons, which is associated with information processing) occurs with aging in the brains of older adults (Callaghan & others, 2014; Rodrique & Kennedy, 2011).

The Adaptive Brain

The human brain has remarkable repair capability (Cai & others, 2014; Garcia-Mesa & others, 2016). Even in late adulthood, the brain loses only a portion of its ability to function, and the activities older adults engage in can still influence the brain's development (Espeland & others, 2016; Jackson & others, 2016; Moore & Murphy, 2016). For example, in an fMRI study, higher levels of aerobic fitness were linked with greater volume in the hippocampus, which translates into better memory (Erickson & others, 2011).

Can adults, even aging adults, generate new neurons? Researchers have found that *neurogenesis*, the generation of new neurons, does occur in lower mammalian species, such as mice (Kask & others, 2015). Also, research indicates that exercise and an enriched, complex environment can generate new brain cells in rats and mice, and that stress reduces their survival rate (Garthe, Roeder, & Kempermann, 2016; Lucassen & others, 2015). For example, in a recent study, mice in an enriched environment learned more flexibly because of adult hippocampal neurogenesis (Garthe, Roeder, & Kempermann, 2016). One study revealed that coping with stress stimulated hippocampal neurogenesis in adult monkeys (Lyons & others, 2010). And researchers have discovered that if rats are cognitively challenged to learn something, new brain cells survive longer (Shors, 2009).

It also is now accepted that neurogenesis can occur in human adults (Horgusluoglu & others, 2016; Kempermann, Song, & Gage, 2015; Moore & Murphy, 2016; Wang & others, 2016). However, researchers have documented neurogenesis in only two brain regions: the hippocampus, which is involved in memory (Bowers & Jessberger, 2016; Stolp & Molnar, 2015), and the olfactory bulb, which is involved in smell (Mobley & others, 2014). It also is not known what functions these new brain cells perform, and at this point researchers have documented that they last for only several weeks (Nelson, 2008).

Researchers currently are studying factors that might inhibit and promote neurogenesis, including various drugs, stress, and exercise (Choi, Lee, & Lee, 2016; Hoeijmakers, Lucassen, & Korosi, 2015; Yang & others, 2015). They also are examining how the grafting of neural stem cells to various regions of the brain, such as the hippocampus, might increase neurogenesis (Noguchi & others, 2015). And increasing attention is being given to the possible role neurogenesis might play in neurodegenerative diseases, such as Alzheimer disease, Parkinson disease, and Huntington disease (Choi, Lee, & Lee, 2016; Foltynie, 2015; Sarlak & Vincent, 2016; Wang & Jin, 2015).

How Would You...?

As an **educator,** how would you use a biological perspective to explain changes in learning as people age?

Dendritic growth can occur in human adults, possibly even in older adults (Eliasieh, Liets, & Chalupa, 2007). Recall that dendrites are the receiving portion of the neuron. One study compared the brains of adults at various ages (Coleman, 1986). From the forties through the seventies, the growth of dendrites increased. However, in people in their nineties, dendritic growth no longer occurred.

Changes in lateralization may provide one type of adaptation in aging adults (Hong & others, 2015). Recall that lateralization is the specialization of function in one hemisphere of the brain or the other. Using neuroimaging techniques, researchers found that brain activity in the prefrontal cortex is lateralized less in older adults than in younger adults when they are engaging in cognitive tasks (Cabeza, 2002; Cabeza & Dennis, 2013; Park & Farrell, 2016; Sugiura, 2016). For example, Figure 2 shows that when younger adults are given the task of recognizing words they have previously seen, they process the information primarily in the right hemisphere; older adults are more likely to use both hemispheres (Madden & others, 1999). The decrease in lateralization in older adults might play a compensatory role in the aging brain. That is, using both hemispheres may improve the cognitive functioning of older adults.

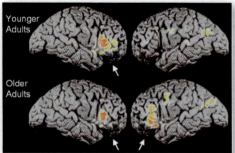

Figure 2 **The Decrease in Brain Lateralization in Older Adults**

Younger adults primarily used the right prefrontal region of the brain (*top left photo*) during a recall memory task, whereas older adults used both the left and right prefrontal regions (*bottom two photos*).

© Dr. Roberto Cabeza

The Nun Study

The Nun Study, directed by David Snowdon, is an intriguing ongoing investigation of aging in 678 nuns, many of whom are from the convent of the Sisters of Notre Dame in Mankato, Minnesota (Pakhomov & Hemmy, 2014; Snowdon, 2003; Tyas & others, 2007). They lead an intellectually challenging life, and brain researchers conclude that this contributes to their quality of life as older adults and possibly to their longevity. All of the 678 nuns agreed to participate in annual assessments of their cognitive and physical functioning. They also agreed to donate their brains for scientific research when they die, and they are the largest group of brain donors in the world. Examination of the nuns' donated brains, as well as others', has led neuroscientists to believe that the brain has a remarkable capacity to change and grow, even in old age.

Physical Development

Physical decline is inevitable if we manage to live to an old age, but the timing of physical problems related to aging is not uniform. Let's examine some physical changes that occur as we age, including changes in physical appearance and movement, some of the senses, and our circulation and lungs.

Physical Appearance and Movement

In late adulthood, the changes in physical appearance that began occurring during middle age become more pronounced. Wrinkles and age spots are the most noticeable changes. We also get shorter as we get older. Both men and women become shorter in late adulthood because of bone loss in their vertebrae (Hoyer & Roodin, 2009).

Our weight usually drops after we reach 60 years of age. This likely occurs because we lose muscle, which also gives our bodies a "sagging" look (Evans, 2010). A recent study found that long-term aerobic exercise was linked with greater muscle strength in 65- to 86-year-olds (Crane, Macneil, & Tarnopolsky, 2013).

Older adults move more slowly than young adults, and this slowing occurs for many types of movement with a wide range of difficulty (Davis & others, 2013). Adequate mobility is an important aspect of maintaining an independent and active lifestyle in late adulthood (Huseth-Zosel & others, 2016; Stubbs, Schofield, & Patchay, 2016). Recent research indicates that obesity is linked to mobility limitation in older adults (Jung & others, 2016; Murphy & others, 2014).

The risk of falling in older adults increases with age and is greater for women than for men. Falls are the leading cause of injury deaths among adults who are 65 years and older (National Center for Health Statistics, 2016). Each year, approximately 200,000 adults over the age of 65 (many of them women) fracture a hip in a fall. Half of these older adults die within 12 months, frequently from pneumonia. A recent meta-analysis found that exercise reduces falls in adults 60 years of age and older (Stubbs, Brefka, & Denkinger, 2015). In one study, walking was more effective than balance training in reducing falls in older adults (Okubo & others, 2016).

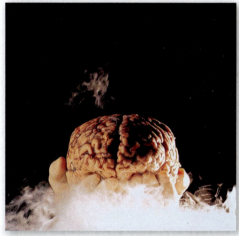

Top: Sister Marcella Zachman (*left*) finally stopped teaching at age 97. She helped ailing nuns exercise their brains by quizzing them on vocabulary or playing a card game called Skip–Bo, which she deliberately lost. Sister Mary Esther Boor (*right*), shown at 99 years of age, was a former teacher who kept alert by doing puzzles and volunteering to work the front desk. *Bottom:* A technician holds the brain of a deceased Mankato nun. The nuns donate their brains for research that explores the effects of stimulation on brain growth.
© James Balog

Sensory Development

Seeing, hearing, and other aspects of sensory functioning are linked with our ability to perform everyday activities, and sensory functioning declines in older adults (Hochberg & others, 2012).

Vision In late adulthood, the decline in vision that began for most adults in early or middle adulthood becomes more pronounced (Polat & others, 2012). The eye does not adapt as quickly when moving from a well-lighted place to one of semidarkness. The tolerance for glare also diminishes. The area of the visual field becomes smaller, and events that occur away from the center of the visual

How Would You...?

As a **health-care professional,** how would you respond to an older adult who shows signs of impaired vision but denies, or is unaware of, the problem?

field sometimes are not detected (Scialfa & Kline, 2007). All of these changes can make night driving especially difficult (West & others, 2010).

Depth perception typically declines in late adulthood, which can make it difficult for older adults to determine how close or far away or how high or low something is (Bian & Anderson, 2008). A decline in depth perception can make steps or street curbs difficult to navigate.

Three diseases that can impair the vision of older adults are cataracts, glaucoma, and macular degeneration:

- **Cataracts** involve a thickening of the lens of the eye that causes vision to become cloudy and distorted (Marra & others, 2016). By age 70, approximately 30 percent of individuals experience a partial loss of vision due to cataracts. Initially, cataracts can be treated by glasses; if they worsen, a simple surgical procedure can replace the natural lenses with artificial ones (Grewal & others, 2016).

- **Glaucoma** involves damage to the optic nerve because of the pressure created by a buildup of fluid in the eye (Kostanyan & others, 2016). Approximately 1 percent of individuals in their seventies and 10 percent of those in their nineties have glaucoma, which can be treated with eye drops. If left untreated, glaucoma can ultimately destroy a person's vision.

- **Macular degeneration** is a disease that involves deterioration of the *macula* of the retina, which corresponds to the focal center of the visual field. Individuals with macular degeneration may have relatively normal peripheral vision but be unable to see clearly what is right in front of them (Owsley & others, 2016) (see Figure 3). This condition affects 1 in 25 individuals from age 66 to 74 and 1 in 6 of those age 75 and older. There is increased interest in using stem-cell based therapy to treat macular degeneration (Hanus, Zhao, & Wang, 2016; Klassen, 2016).

cataracts Involve a thickening of the lens of the eye that causes vision to become cloudy and distorted.

glaucoma Damage to the optic nerve because of the pressure created by a buildup of fluid in the eye.

macular degeneration A disease that involves deterioration of the macula of the retina, which corresponds to the focal center of the visual field.

Figure 3 Macular Degeneration
This simulation of the effect of macular degeneration shows how individuals with this eye disease can see their peripheral field of vision but can't clearly see what is in their central visual field.
© Cordelia Molloy/Science Source

Hearing For hearing as for vision, it is important to determine the degree of decline in the aging adult (Wingfield & Lash, 2016). A national survey revealed that 63 percent of adults 70 years and older had a hearing loss, defined as an inability to hear sounds softer than 25 dB with their better ear (Lin & others, 2011). In this study, hearing aids were used by 40 percent of those with moderate hearing loss. Recent research has found that older adults' hearing problems are associated with less time spent out of home and in leisure activities (Mikkola & others, 2016), an increase in falls (Gopinath & others, 2016), reduction in cognitive functioning (Lin, 2011), and loneliness (Mick & Pichora-Fuller, 2016).

Smell and Taste Most older adults lose some of their sense of smell or taste, or both (Correia & others, 2016). A recent national study of community-dwelling older adults revealed that 74 percent had impaired taste and 22 percent had impaired smell (Correia & others, 2016). These losses often begin around 60 years of age (Hawkes, 2006). A majority of individuals 80 years of age and older experience a significant reduction in

How Would You...?

As an **educator,** how would you structure your classroom and plan class activities to accommodate the sensory decline of older adult students?

smell (Lafreniere & Mann, 2009). Researchers have found that older adults show a greater decline in their sense of smell than in their taste (Schiffman, 2007). Smell and taste decline less in healthy older adults than in their less healthy counterparts.

Touch and Pain Changes in touch and pain are also associated with aging (Kemp & others, 2014). A recent national study of community-dwelling older adults revealed that 70 percent of older adults had impaired touch (Correia & others, 2016). For most older adults, a decline in touch sensitivity is not problematic (Hoyer & Roodin, 2009).

An estimated 60 to 75 percent of older adults report at least some persistent pain (Molton & Terrill, 2014). The most frequent pain complaints of older adults involve back pain (40 percent), peripheral neuropathic pain (35 percent), and chronic joint pain (15 to 25 percent) (Denard & others, 2010). The presence of pain increases with age in older adults, and women are more likely to report having pain than are men (Tsang & others, 2008). Older adults are less sensitive to pain than are younger adults (Harkins, Price, & Martinelli, 1986). However, once older adults experience pain they may be less tolerant of it than are younger adults (Farrell, 2012).

The Circulatory System and Lungs

Cardiovascular disorders increase in late adulthood (Jansen & others, 2015; Wang, Monticone, & Lakatta, 2016). Consistent blood pressures above 120/80 should be treated to reduce the risk of heart attack, stroke, or kidney disease. Various drugs, a healthy diet, and exercise can reduce the risk of cardiovascular disease in older adults (Endes & others, 2016; Kramer, 2015; Wang, Monticone, & Lakatta, 2016). In a recent study of older adults, a faster exercise walking pace, not smoking, modest alcohol intake, and avoiding obesity were associated with a lower risk of heart failure (Del Gobbo & others, 2015).

Lung capacity drops 40 percent between the ages of 20 and 80, even without disease (Fozard, 1992). Lungs lose elasticity, the chest shrinks, and the diaphragm weakens (Lalley, 2013). The good news, though, is that older adults can improve lung functioning with diaphragm-strengthening exercises.

Sleep

Approximately 50 percent of older adults complain of having difficulty sleeping (Farajinia & others, 2014). Researchers have found that older adults' sleep is lighter and more disruptive (takes longer to fall asleep and also involves more awakenings and greater difficulty in going back to sleep) (McRae & others, 2016). Poor sleep is a risk factor for falls, obesity, lower cognitive functioning, and earlier death and is linked to a lower level of cognitive functioning (Xiao & others, 2013). Many of the sleep problems of older adults are associated with health problems (Mantua, Baran, & Spencer, 2016; McRae & others, 2016). Recent research indicates that when older adults sleep less than seven hours and more than nine hours a night, their cognitive functioning is harmed (Devore, Grodstein, & Schemhammer, 2016; Lo & others, 2016). Another recent study revealed that engaging in regular aerobic exercise improved the sleep profiles of older men (Melancon, Lorrain, & Dionne, 2015). In addition, one study of older adults indicated that walking at or above the internationally recommended level of 150 minutes per week predicted a lower likelihood of problems with sleep onset or sleep maintenance four years later (Hartescu, Morgan, & Stevinson, 2015).

Sexuality

In the absence of two circumstances—disease and the belief that old people are or should be asexual—sexuality can be lifelong (Corona & others, 2013). Aging, however, does induce some changes in human sexual performance, more so in the male than in the female (Gray & Garcia, 2012). Orgasm becomes less frequent in males with age, occurring in every second to third attempt rather than every time. More direct stimulation usually is needed to produce an erection.

Many older adults are sexually active as long as they are healthy (Thomas, Hess, & Thurston, 2015). However, in one study, sexual activity did decline through the later years of life: 73 percent of 57- to 64-year-olds, 53 percent of 65- to 74-year-olds, and 26 percent of 75- to 85-year-olds reported that they were sexually active (Lindau & others, 2007). Nonetheless, with recent advances in erectile dysfunction medications, such as Viagra, an increasing number of older men, especially the young-old, are able to have an erection (Hosny, El-Say, & Ahmed, 2016; Sheu & others, 2016). Also, recent research suggests that declining levels of serum testosterone, which is linked to erectile dysfunction, can be treated with testosterone replacement therapy to improve sexual functioning in males (Almehmadi & others, 2016; Hassan & Barkin, 2016; Mayo Clinic, 2016). However, the benefit-risk ratio of testosterone replacement therapy is uncertain for older males (Isidori & others, 2014).

What are some characteristics of sexuality in older adults? How does sexuality change as older adults go through the late adulthood period?

© Image Source/Getty Images RF

Health

What types of health problems do people have in late adulthood, and what can be done to maintain or improve their health and ability to function in everyday life?

Health Problems

As we age, we are more likely to have some disease or illness (Desveaux & others, 2016). The majority of adults still alive at 80 years of age or older have some type of impairment. Chronic diseases (those with a slow onset and a long duration) are rare in early adulthood, increase in middle adulthood, and become more common in late adulthood (Hirsch & Sirois, 2016).

Arthritis is the most common chronic disorder in late adulthood, followed by hypertension. Older women have a higher incidence of arthritis, hypertension, and visual problems but a lower incidence of hearing problems than older men do.

Low income is also strongly related to health problems in late adulthood (Vart & others, 2015). Approximately three times as many poor as non-poor older adults report that chronic disorders limit their activities.

Causes of Death in Older Adults

Nearly 60 percent of U.S. adults 65 to 74 years old die of cancer or cardiovascular disease. Cancer recently replaced cardiovascular disease as the leading cause of death in U.S. middle-aged adults. However, cardiovascular disease is the leading cause of death in U.S. 65- to 74-year-olds (Centers for Disease Control and Prevention, 2015). And in the 75 to 84 and 85 and over age groups, cardiovascular disease also is the leading cause of death (Centers for Disease Control and Prevention, 2015). As individuals age through the late adult years, they become more and more likely to die from cardiovascular disease than from cancer.

Arthritis

Arthritis is an inflammation of the joints accompanied by pain, stiffness, and movement problems. This incurable disorder can affect hips, knees, ankles, fingers, and vertebrae. Individuals with arthritis often experience difficulty moving about and performing routine daily activities. Arthritis is especially prevalent in older adults (Chalan & others, 2015). Recent research documents the benefits of exercise in older adults with arthritis

arthritis Inflammation of the joints that is accompanied by pain, stiffness, and movement problems; especially common in older adults.

(White & others, 2015; Wood & others, 2016). A recent study of women found that leisure-time physical inactivity was found to be a risk factor for subsequent development of arthritis (Di Giuseppe & others, 2016). In this study, women engaging in the most vigorous category of leisure-time activities were the least likely to develop arthritis.

Osteoporosis

Normal aging brings some loss of bone tissue, but for some individuals loss of bone tissue becomes severe. **Osteoporosis** involves an extensive loss of bone tissue and is the main reason many older adults walk with a marked stoop (Black & Rosen, 2016; Rothman & others, 2014). Women are especially vulnerable to osteoporosis, which is the leading cause of broken bones in women (Davis & others, 2013). Approximately 80 percent of osteoporosis cases in the United States occur in females, 20 percent in males. Almost two-thirds of women over the age of 60 are affected by osteoporosis. It is more common in non-Latina White, thin, and small-framed women.

Osteoporosis is related to deficiencies in calcium, vitamin D, and estrogen, and to lack of exercise (Kemmler, Engelke, & von Stengel, 2015). To prevent osteoporosis, young and middle-aged women should eat foods rich in calcium, exercise regularly, and avoid smoking (Lupsa & Insogna, 2015; Motorwala & others, 2016). Drugs such as Fosamax can be used to reduce the risk of osteoporosis (Black & Rosen, 2016; Zhang & others, 2016).

How Would You...?
As a **health-care professional,** how would you educate older adults on the range of chronic diseases that are common for this age group?

Exercise, Nutrition, and Weight

Although we may be in the evening of our lives in late adulthood, we are not meant to live out our remaining years passively. Everything we know about older adults suggests they are healthier and happier the more active they are. Can regular exercise lead to a healthier late adulthood and increase longevity? How does eating a calorie-restricted diet and controlling weight also contribute to living longer?

Exercise

In one study, exercise literally made the difference between life and death for middle-aged and older adults (Blair, 1990). More than 10,000 men and women were divided into categories of low fitness, medium fitness, and high fitness (Blair & others, 1989). Then they were studied over a period of eight years. As shown in Figure 4, sedentary participants (low fitness) were more than twice as likely to die during the eight-year time span of the study as those who were moderately fit and more than three times as likely to die as those who were highly fit. The positive effects of being physically fit occurred for both men and women in this study. Also, a study of joggers in Copenhagen, Denmark, revealed that engaging in light or moderate jogging on a regular basis was linked to increased longevity (Schnohr & others, 2015).

Gerontologists increasingly recommend strength training in addition to aerobic activity and stretching for older adults (Harada & others, 2016; Oesen & others, 2015). Resistance exercise can preserve and possibly increase muscle mass in older adults. A recent study found that core resistance and balance training improved older adult women's balance, trunk muscle strength, leg power, and body composition better than Pilates training (Markovic & others, 2015).

Exercise is an excellent way to maintain physical and mental health (Erickson & Liu-Ambrose, 2016; Gill & others, 2016; Raji & others, 2016; Rhyner & Watts, 2016). The current recommendations for older

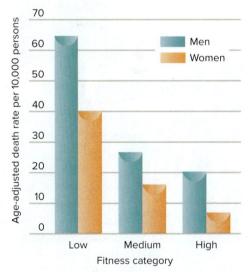

Figure 4 **Physical Fitness and Mortality**

In this study of middle-aged and older adults, being moderately fit or highly fit meant that individuals were less likely to die over a period of eight years than their less fit (more sedentary) counterparts (Blair & others, 1989).

adults' physical activity are 2 hours and 30 minutes of moderate-intensity aerobic activity (brisk walking, for example) per week and muscle strengthening activities on 2 or more days a week (Centers for Disease Control and Prevention, 2016). In the recent recommendations, even greater benefits can be attained with 5 hours of moderate-intensity aerobic activity per week.

Exercise helps people to live independent lives with dignity in late adulthood (Ballesteros & others, 2015; Nagamatsu & others, 2016). At age 80, 90, and even 100, exercise can help prevent older adults from falling down or even being institutionalized (Lupsa & Insogna, 2015; Witard & others, 2016). A recent study found that an exercise program reduced the number of falls in older adults with dementia (Burton & others, 2015). And a recent study of sarcopenic older adults found that those who were physically active had a 25 percent higher probability of greater longevity than their sedentary counterparts (Brown, Harhay, & Harhay, 2016).

Exercise also is linked to the prevention or delayed onset of chronic diseases, such as cardiovascular disease, type 2 diabetes, and obesity, as well as improvement in the treatment of these diseases (Endes & others, 2016; Grace & others, 2016; Roh & others, 2016). Researchers also increasingly are finding that exercise improves cellular functioning in older adults (Broskey & others, 2016). For example, researchers recently have discovered that aerobic exercise is linked to greater telomere length in older adults (Denham, O'Brien, & Charchar, 2016; Loprinzi & Loenneke, 2016).

Exercise improves older adults' brain and cognitive functioning. For example, a recent research review concluded that more physically fit and active older adults have greater prefrontal cortex and hippocampal volume, a higher level of brain connectivity, and more efficient brain activity (Erickson, Hillman, & Kramer, 2015). Older adults who exercise regularly not only show better brain functioning, they also process information more effectively than older adults who are more sedentary (Barnes, 2015; Erickson & Liu-Ambrose, 2016; Johnson & others, 2016). In the recent research review on brain functioning, the researchers also found that more physically fit and active older adults show have superior memory functioning and a higher level of executive function (Erickson, Hillman, & Kramer, 2015).

Exercise also is linked to increased longevity. Energy expenditure during exercise of at least 1,000 kcal/week reduces mortality by about 30 percent, while 2,000 kcal/week reduces mortality by about 50 percent (Lee & Skerrett, 2001). One study of older adults found that total daily physical activity was linked to increased longevity across a four-year period (Buchman & others, 2012).

Nutrition and Weight

Scientists have accumulated considerable evidence that calorie restriction (CR) in laboratory animals (in most cases rats) can increase the animals' life span (Schreiber, O'Leary, & Kennedy, 2016; Xu & others, 2015). Research indicates that calorie restriction slows RNA decline during the aging process (Hou & others, 2016). Animals that are fed diets restricted in calories, although adequate in protein, vitamins, and minerals, live as much as 40 percent longer than animals that have unlimited access to food (Jolly, 2005). And chronic problems such as cardiovascular, kidney, and liver disease appear at a later age (Yan & others, 2013). Also, research indicates that CR may provide neuroprotection for an aging central nervous system (Willette & others, 2012). A recent study found that calorie restriction maintained more youthful functioning in the hippocampus, which is an important brain structure for memory (Schafer & others, 2015).

No one knows for certain how CR works to increase the life span of animals. Some scientists suggest that CR might lower the level of free radicals and reduce oxidative stress in

In 1991, Johnny Kelley ran his sixtieth Boston Marathon and, in 2000, he was named "Runner of the Century" by *Runner's World* magazine. At 70 years of age, Kelley was still running 50 miles a week. At that point in his life, Kelley said, "I'm afraid to stop running. I feel so good. I want to stay alive." He lived 27 more years and died at age 97 in 2004.

© Charles Krupa/AP Images

cells (Kalsi, 2015; Klotz & others, 2015). Others argue that CR might trigger a state of emergency called "survival mode" in which the body eliminates all unnecessary functions to focus only on staying alive (Schreiber, O'Leary, & Kennedy, 2016).

Whether similar very low-calorie diets can stretch the human life span is not known (Locher & others, 2016; Stein & others, 2012). In some instances the animals in these studies received 40 percent less calories than normal. In humans, a typical level of calorie restriction involves a 30 percent decrease, which translates to about 1,120 calories a day for the average woman and 1,540 for the average man.

Health Treatment

About 3 percent of adults age 65 and older in the United States reside in a nursing home at some point in their lives. As older adults age, however, their probability of being in a nursing home or other extended-care facility increases. Twenty-three percent of adults aged 85 and older live in nursing homes or other extended-care facilities.

The quality of nursing homes and other extended-care facilities for older adults varies enormously and is a source of national concern (Kim, 2016). More than one-third are seriously deficient. They fail federally mandated inspections because they do not meet the minimum standards for physicians, pharmacists, and various rehabilitation specialists (occupational and physical therapists). Further concerns focus on the patient's right to privacy, access to medical information, safety, and lifestyle freedom within the individual's range of mental and physical capabilities.

Because of the inadequate quality and the escalating costs of many nursing homes, many specialists in the health problems of the aged stress that home health care, elder-care centers, and preventive medicine clinics are good alternatives (Hunt, Corazzini, & Anderson, 2014; Kim, 2016). They are potentially less expensive than hospitals and nursing homes (Moon & others, 2015). They also are less likely to engender the feelings of depersonalization and dependency that occur so often in residents of institutions. Currently, there is an increased demand for, and a shortage of, home care workers because of the increasing number of older adults and their preference to stay out of nursing homes (Hewko & others, 2015).

How Would You...?

As a **health-care professional,** how would you use your understanding of development in late adulthood to advocate for improved access to quality medical care for older adults?

In a classic study, Judith Rodin and Ellen Langer (1977) found that an important factor related to health, and even survival, in a nursing home is the patient's feelings of control and self-determination. One group was encouraged to make more day-to-day choices and thus to feel they had more control over their lives. They began to decide such matters as what they ate, when their visitors could come, what movies they saw, and who could come to their rooms. Another group in the same nursing home was told by the administrator how caring the nursing home staff was and how much they wanted to help, but these residents were given no added responsibility over their lives. Eighteen months later, the residents who had been given extra responsibility were healthier, happier, and more alert and active than the residents who had not received added responsibility. Even more important was the finding that after 18 months only half as many nursing home residents in the "responsibility" group had died as in the "dependent" group (see Figure 5). Perceived control over one's environment, then, can literally be a matter of life and death.

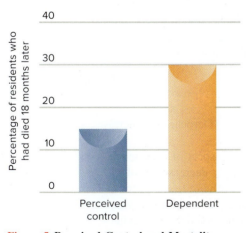

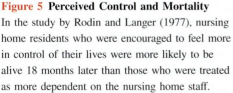

Figure 5 Perceived Control and Mortality
In the study by Rodin and Langer (1977), nursing home residents who were encouraged to feel more in control of their lives were more likely to be alive 18 months later than those who were treated as more dependent on the nursing home staff.

How Would You...?

As a **psychologist,** how would you structure the environment of a nursing home to produce maximum health and psychological benefits for the residents?

Sarah Kagan, Geriatric Nurse

Sarah Kagan is a professor of nursing at the University of Pennsylvania School of Nursing. She provides nursing consultation to patients, their families, nurses, and physicians regarding the complex needs of older adults related to their hospitalization. She also consults on research and the management of patients who have head and neck cancers. Sarah teaches in the undergraduate nursing program, where she directs a course on "Nursing Care in the Older Adult." In 2003, she was awarded a MacArthur Fellowship for her work in the field of nursing.

Geriatric nurses like Sarah Kagan seek to prevent or intervene in the chronic or acute health problems of older adults. They may work in hospitals, nursing homes, schools of nursing, or with geriatric medical specialists or psychiatrists in a medical clinic or in private practice. Like pediatric nurses, geriatric nurses take courses in a school of nursing and obtain a degree in nursing, which takes from two to five years. They complete courses in

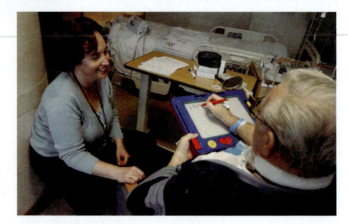

Sarah Kagan with a patient.
© Jacqueline Larma/AP Images

biological sciences, nursing care, and mental health as well as supervised clinical training in geriatric settings. They also may obtain a master's or doctoral degree in their specialty.

Geriatric nurses can be especially helpful in improving health treatment. To read about the work of one geriatric nurse, see *Careers in Life-Span Development.*

Cognitive Functioning

At age 89, the great pianist Arthur Rubinstein gave one of his best performances at New York's Carnegie Hall. When Pablo Casals was 95, a reporter asked him, "Mr. Casals, you are the greatest cellist who ever lived. Why do you still practice six hours a day?" Mr. Casals replied, "Because I feel like I am making progress" (Canfield & Hansen, 1995).

Multidimensionality and Multidirectionality

In thinking about the nature of cognitive change in adulthood, it is important to consider that cognition is a multidimensional concept (Willis & Belleville, 2016). It is also important to consider that, although some dimensions of cognition might decline as we age, others might remain stable or even improve.

Attention

Changes in attention are important aspects of cognitive aging (Deroche & others, 2016; Hoyer, 2015).

Selective attention, which consists of focusing on a specific aspect of experience that is relevant while ignoring others that are irrelevant, generally decreases in older adults (Quigley & Muller, 2014). However, on simple tasks involving a search for a feature, such as determining whether a target item is present on a computer screen, age differences are minimal when individuals are given sufficient practice. In a recent study, 10 weeks of speed of processing training improved the selective attention of older adults (O'Brien & others, 2013). And a recent study revealed that older adults who participated in 20 one-hour video game training sessions with a commercially available program (Lumosity) showed a significant reduction in distraction and increased alertness (Mayas & others, 2014). The Lumosity program sessions focus on problem solving, mental calculation, working memory, and attention.

Sustained attention is the ability to focus attention on a selected stimulus for a prolonged period of time. Researchers have found that older adults often perform as well as middle-aged and younger adults on measures of sustained attention (Berardi, Parasuraman, & Haxby, 2001). However, a recent study of older adults found that the greater the variability in their sustained attention (vigilance), the more likely they were to experience falls (O'Halloran & others, 2011).

Memory

Memory does change during aging, but not all types of memory change with age in the same way. We will begin by exploring possible changes in explicit and implicit memory.

What are some developmental changes in attention in late adulthood?
© Digital Vision/Getty Images RF

Explicit and Implicit Memory Researchers have found that aging is linked with a decline in explicit memory (Lustig & Lin, 2016). **Explicit memory** is memory of facts and experiences that individuals consciously know and can state. Explicit memory also is sometimes called *declarative memory*. Examples of explicit memory include recounting the plot of a movie you have seen or being at a grocery store and remembering what you wanted to buy. **Implicit memory** is memory without conscious recollection; it involves skills and routine procedures, such as driving a car or typing on a computer keyboard, that you perform without having to consciously think about what you are doing. Implicit memory is less likely to be adversely affected by aging than explicit memory is (Norman, Holmin, & Bartholomew, 2011).

Episodic and Semantic Memory Episodic and semantic memory are viewed as forms of explicit memory. **Episodic memory** is the retention of information about the where and when of life's happenings. For example, what was the color of the walls in your bedroom when you were a child? What did you eat for breakfast this morning?

Younger adults have better episodic memory than older adults have (Sandrini & others, 2016; Tromp & others, 2015). Also, older adults think that they can remember long-ago events better than more recent events. However, researchers consistently have found that the older the memory is, the less accurate it is in older adults (Smith, 1996). And a recent study found that episodic memory performance predicted which individuals would develop dementia 10 years prior to the clinical diagnosis of the disease (Boraxbekk & others, 2015).

Semantic memory is a person's knowledge about the world. It includes a person's fields of expertise, general academic knowledge of the sort learned in school, and "everyday knowledge" about the meanings of words, important places, and common things. Older adults often take longer to retrieve semantic information, but usually they can ultimately retrieve it. However, the ability to retrieve very specific information (such as names) usually declines in older adults (Luo & Craik, 2008). For the most part, episodic memory declines more than semantic memory in older adults (Lacombe & others, 2015; Lustig & Lin, 2016).

Cognitive Resources: Working Memory and Perceptual Speed Two important cognitive resource mechanisms are working memory and perceptual speed (McInerney & Suhr, 2016; Salthouse, 2012, 2013). Recall that *working memory* is closely linked to short-term memory but places more emphasis on memory as a place for mental work (Baddeley, 2007, 2012). Researchers have found declines in working memory during late adulthood (Hara & Naveh-Benjamin, 2016; Kilic, Sayali, & Oztekin, 2016). A recent study revealed that working memory continued to decline from 65 to 89 years of age (Elliott & others, 2011). Explanation of the decline in working memory in older adults focuses on their less efficient

explicit memory Memory of facts and experiences that individuals consciously know and can state.

implicit memory Memory without conscious recollection; involves skills and routine procedures that are automatically performed.

episodic memory The retention of information about the where and when of life's happenings.

semantic memory A person's knowledge about the world—including a person's fields of expertise, general academic knowledge of the sort learned in school, and "everyday knowledge."

inhibition in preventing irrelevant information from entering working memory and their increased distractibility (Lustig & Linn, 2016).

Is there plasticity in the working memory of older adults? Researchers have found that older adults' working memory can be improved through training (Cantarella & others, 2016). For example, in a recent study strategy training improved the working memory of older adults (Bailey, Dunlosky, & Hertzog, 2014). Also, an experimental study revealed that moderate exercise resulted in faster reaction time on a working memory task in older adults (Hogan, Mata, & Carstensen, 2013). Thus, there appears to be some plasticity in the working memory of older adults.

Perceptual speed is another cognitive resource that has been studied by researchers on aging. Perceptual speed is the amount of time it takes to perform simple perceptual-motor tasks such as deciding whether pairs of two-digit or two-letter strings are the same, or how long it takes someone to step on the brakes when the car directly ahead stops. Perceptual speed shows considerable decline in late adulthood, and it is strongly linked with decline in working memory (Ross & others, 2016; Salthouse, 2013). Also, in a 20-year longitudinal study of 42- to 97-year-olds, greater declines in processing speed were linked to increased mortality risk (Aichele, Rabbitt, & Ghisletta, 2015).

Executive Function

We discussed executive function in a number of chapters earlier in the text. Recall that *executive function* is an umbrella-like concept that consists of a number of higher-level cognitive processes linked to the development of the brain's prefrontal cortex. Executive function involves managing one's thoughts to engage in goal-directed behavior and to exercise self-control (Reuter-Lorenz, Festini, & Jantz, 2016).

How does executive function change in late adulthood? Earlier in this chapter, you read that the prefrontal cortex is one area of the brain that shrinks with aging, and recent research has linked this shrinkage with a decrease in working memory and other cognitive activities in older adults (Lustig & Lin, 2016; Reuter-Lorenz, Festini, & Jantz, 2016). Older adults also are less effective at engaging in cognitive control than when they were younger (Campbell & others, 2012). For example, in terms of cognitive flexibility, older adults don't perform as well as younger adults at switching back and forth between tasks or mental sets (Luszcz, 2011). And in terms of cognitive inhibition, older adults are less effective than younger adults at inhibiting dominant or automatic responses (Reuter-Lorenz, Festini, & Jantz, 2016).

Although in general aspects of executive function decline in late adulthood, there is considerable variability in executive function among older adults. For example, some older adults have a better working memory and are more cognitively flexible than other older adults (Peltz, Gratton, & Fabiani, 2011). And there is increasing research evidence that aerobic exercise improves executive function in older adults (Eggenberger & others, 2015). For example, a recent study found that more physically fit older adults were more cognitively flexible than their less physically fit counterparts (Berryman & others, 2013).

Executive function increasingly is thought to be involved not only in cognitive performance but also in health, emotion regulation, adaptation to life's challenges, motivation, and social functioning. In a recent study, executive function but not memory predicted a higher risk of coronary heart disease and stroke three years later in older adults (Rostamian & others, 2015). Another recent study found that executive function predicted improvement in self-rated health in community-dwelling older adults (McHugh & Lawlor, 2016). And in yet another recent study, executive dysfunction was a strong predictor of having a stroke in cognitively normal aging adults (Oveisgharan & Hachinski, 2015).

Wisdom

Does wisdom, like good wine, improve with age? What is this thing we call "wisdom"? **Wisdom** is expert knowledge about the practical aspects of life that permits excellent judgment about important matters. This

wisdom Expert knowledge about the practical aspects of life that permits excellent judgment about important matters.

practical knowledge involves exceptional insight into human development and interactions, good judgment, and an understanding of how to cope with difficult life problems. Thus, wisdom, more than standard conceptions of intelligence, focuses on life's pragmatic concerns and human conditions (Ferrari & Weststrate, 2013).

In regard to wisdom, Paul Baltes and his colleagues (2006) have reached the following conclusions: (1) *High levels of wisdom are rare.* Few people, including older adults, attain a high level of wisdom. That only a small percentage of adults show wisdom supports the contention that it requires experience, practice, or complex skills. (2) *Factors other than age are critical for wisdom to develop to a high level.* For example, certain life experiences, such as being trained and working in a field involving difficult life problems and having wisdom-enhancing mentors, contribute to higher levels of wisdom. Also, people higher in wisdom have values that are more likely to consider the welfare of others than their own happiness. (3) *Personality-related factors, such as openness to experience, generativity, and creativity, are better predictors of wisdom than cognitive factors such as intelligence.*

Education, Work, and Health

Education, work, and health are three important influences on the cognitive functioning of older adults. They are also three of the most important factors involved in understanding why cohort effects need to be taken into account in studying the cognitive functioning of older adults. Indeed, cohort effects are very important considerations in the study of cognitive aging (Schaie, 2013, 2016). A recent study found that older adults assessed in 2013–2014 engaged in a higher level of abstract reasoning than their counterparts who were assessed two decades earlier (Gerstorf & others, 2015).

Education Successive generations in America's twentieth century were better educated, and this trend continues in the twenty-first century (Schaie, 2013, 2016). Educational experiences are positively correlated with scores on intelligence tests and information-processing tasks, such as memory exercises (Steffener & others, 2014). Also, a recent study found that older adults with a higher level of education had better cognitive functioning (Rapp & others, 2013).

Work Successive generations have also had work experiences that included a stronger emphasis on cognitively oriented labor. Our great-grandfathers and grandfathers were more likely to be manual laborers than were our fathers, who are more likely to be involved in cognitively oriented occupations.

Researchers have found that when older adults engage in complex working tasks and challenging daily work activities their cognitive functioning shows less age-related decrease (Wang & Shi, 2016). For example, in one study, substantive complex work was linked with higher intellectual functioning in older adults (Schooler, Mulatu, & Oates, 1999). Further, a recent study found that working in an occupation with a high level of mental demands was linked to higher levels of cognitive functioning before retirement and a slower rate of cognitive decline after retirement (Fisher & others, 2014).

How are education, work, and health linked to cognitive functioning in older adults?

(Top) © Silverstock/Getty Images RF; (middle) © Blend Images/Getty Images RF; (bottom) © Tom Grill/Corbis RF

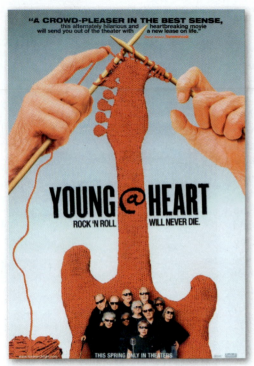

Members of the Young@Heart chorus have an average age of 80. Young@Heart became a hit documentary in 2008. The documentary displays the singing talents, energy, and optimism of a remarkable group of older adults, who clearly are on the "use it" side of "use it or lose it."

© Fox Searchlight/Photofest

Health Successive generations have also been healthier in late adulthood as more effective treatments for a variety of illnesses (such as hypertension) have been developed. Many of these illnesses, such as stroke and heart disease, have a negative impact on intellectual performance (Chuang & others, 2014; Hagenaars & others, 2016; Kherada, Heimowitz, & Rosendorff, 2015). Researchers also have found age-related cognitive decline in adults with mood disorders such as depression (Knight, Rastegar, & Kim, 2016; Mackin & others, 2014). Thus, some of the decline in intellectual performance found for older adults is likely due to health-related factors rather than to age per se (Korten & others, 2014).

K. Warner Schaie (1994) concluded that although some diseases—such as hypertension and diabetes—are linked to cognitive drop-offs, they do not directly cause mental decline. Rather, the lifestyles of the individuals with the diseases might be the culprits. For example, poor eating habits, inactivity, and stress are related to both physical and mental decline (Kraft, 2012). For example, a recent study of older adults found that a higher level of stress was linked to an accelerated decline of cognitive functioning (Aggarwal & others, 2014). And a number of research studies have found that exercise is linked to improved cognitive functioning in older adults (Gill & others, 2016; Leon & others, 2015). And in a recent research review, Exergaming (video games that involve exercising) was linked to improved cognitive function in older adults (Ogawa, You, & Leveille, 2016).

Use It or Lose It

Changes in cognitive activity patterns might result in disuse and consequent atrophy of cognitive skills (de Frias & Dixon, 2014; Park & Farrell, 2016). This concept is captured in the phrase "Use it or lose it." The mental activities that are likely to benefit the maintenance of cognitive skills in older adults include activities such as reading books, doing crossword puzzles, and going to lectures and concerts. In one study, reading daily was linked to reduced mortality in men in their seventies (Jacobs & others, 2008). In another study, 75- to 85-year-olds were assessed for an average of five years (Hall & others, 2009). At the beginning of the research, the older adults indicated how often they participated in six activities on a daily basis: reading, writing, doing crossword puzzles, playing cards or board games, having group discussions, and playing music. For each additional activity the older adult engaged in, the onset of rapid memory loss was delayed by 0.18 year. For older adults who participated in 11 activities per week compared with their counterparts who engaged in only 4 activities per week, the point at which accelerated memory decline occurred was delayed by 1.29 years. And in a recent analysis of older adults over a 12-year period, those who reduced their cognitive lifestyle activities (such as using a computer or playing bridge) subsequently showed declines in verbal speed, episodic memory, and semantic memory (Small & others, 2012). These declines in cognitive functioning were linked to subsequent lower engagement in social activities.

Training Cognitive Skills

If older adults are losing cognitive skills, can these skills be regained through training? An increasing number of research studies indicate that they can be restored to a degree (Cantarella & others, 2016; Mayas & others, 2014; Reuter-Lorenz, Festini, & Jantz, 2016; Willis & Belleville, 2016).

Consider a recent study of 60- to 90-year-olds which found that sustained engagement in cognitively demanding, novel activities improved the older adults' episodic memory (Park & others, 2014). To produce this result, the older adults spent an average of 16.5 hours a week for three months learning how to quilt or use digital photography. Consider also a recent study of 60- to 90-year-olds in which iPad training 15 hours a week for 3 months improved their episodic memory and processing speed relative to engaging in social or non-challenging activities (Chan & others, 2015).

Two key conclusions can be derived from research in this area: (1) training can improve the cognitive skills of many older adults, but (2) there is some loss in plasticity in late adulthood, especially in those who are 85 and older (Baltes, Lindenberger, & Staudinger, 2006).

How Would You...?

As a **psychologist,** how would you design activities and interventions to elicit and maintain cognitive vitality in older adults?

Recent meta-examinations of four longitudinal observational studies (Long Beach Longitudinal Study; Origins of Variance in the Oldest-old [Octo-Twin] Study in Sweden; Seattle Longitudinal Study; and Victoria Longitudinal Study in Canada) of older adults' naturalistic cognitive activities found that changes in cognitive activity predicted cognitive outcomes as long as two decades later (Brown & others, 2012; Lindwall & others, 2012; Mitchell & others, 2012; Rebok & others, 2014). However, the concept that engaging in cognitive activity at an earlier point in development would improve older adults' ability to later withstand cognitive decline was not supported. On a positive note, when older adults continued to increase their engagement in cognitive and physical activities, they were better able to maintain their cognitive functioning in late adulthood.

The Stanford Center for Longevity (2011) and together the Stanford Center for Longevity and the Max Planck Institute for Human Development (2014) reported information based on a consensus of leading scientists in the field of aging on how successfully the cognitive skills of older adults can be improved. One of their concerns is the misinformation given to the public touting products to improve the functioning of the mind for which there is no scientific evidence. Nutritional supplements have been advertised as "magic bullets" to slow the decline of mental functioning and improve the mental ability of older adults. Some of the claims are reasonable but not scientifically tested, while others are unrealistic and implausible (Willis & Bellevue, 2016).

A research review of dietary supplements and cognitive aging did indicate that ginkgo biloba was linked with improvements in some aspects of attention in older adults and that omega-3 polyunsaturated fatty acids (fish oil) was related to reduced risk of age-related cognitive decline (Gorby, Brownawell, & Falk, 2010). In this research review, there was no evidence of cognitive improvements in aging adults who took supplements containing ginseng and glucose. Also, a recent experimental study with 50- to 75-year-old females found that those who took fish oil for 26 weeks had improved executive function and beneficial effects on a number of areas of brain functioning compared with their female counterparts who took a placebo pill (Witte & others, 2014). In another recent study, fish oil supplement use was linked to higher cognitive scores and less atrophy in one or more brain regions (Daiello & others, 2015). Overall, though, research has not provided consistent plausible evidence that dietary supplements can accomplish major cognitive goals in aging adults over a number of years.

However, some software-based cognitive training games have been found to improve older adults' cognitive functioning (Charness & Boot, 2016; Lampit & others, 2015). For example, a recent study of 60- to 85-year-olds found that a multitasking video game that simulates day-to-day driving experiences (NeuroRacer) improved cognitive control skills, such as sustained attention and working memory, immediately after training on the video game and six months later (Anguera & others, 2013). In another recent study, computerized cognitive training slowed the decline in older adults' overall memory performance, an outcome that was linked to enhanced connectivity between the hippocampus and prefrontal cortex (Suo & others, 2016). Nonetheless, it is possible that the training games may improve cognitive skills in a laboratory setting but not generalize to gains in the real world.

In sum, some improvements in the cognitive vitality of older adults can be accomplished through some types of cognitive and fitness training (Erickson & Liu-Ambrose,

2016; Prakash & others, 2015; Rebok & others, 2014; Reuter-Lorenz, Festini, & Jantz, 2016; Willis & Belleville, 2016). However, benefits have not been observed in all studies (Salthouse, 2013). An important finding in the recent meta-analysis of four longitudinal studies was that older adults were better able to maintain their cognitive functioning over a prolonged period of time when increasing their engagement in cognitive and physical activities (Rebok & others, 2014). Further research is needed to determine more precisely which cognitive improvements occur in older adults as a result of training (Salthouse, 2013).

Cognitive Neuroscience and Aging

On several occasions in this chapter, we have noted that certain regions of the brain are involved in links between aging and cognitive functioning. In this section, we further explore the brain's role in aging and cognitive functioning. The field of *cognitive neuroscience* has emerged as the major discipline that studies links between brain activity and cognitive functioning (Ferreira & others, 2015; Lustig & Lin, 2016; Park & Farrell, 2016; Reuter-Lorenz, Festini, & Jantz, 2016). This field especially relies on brain-imaging techniques, such as fMRI, PET, and DTI (diffusion tensor imaging) to reveal the areas of the brain that are activated when individuals engage in certain cognitive activities (Coxon & others, 2016; Fjell & others, 2016). For example, as an older adult is asked to encode and then retrieve verbal materials or images of scenes, the older adult's brain activity will be monitored by an fMRI brain scan.

Changes in the brain can influence cognitive functioning, and changes in cognitive functioning can influence the brain. For example, aging of the brain's prefrontal cortex may produce a decline in working memory (Reuter-Lorenz, Festini, & Jantz, 2016). And, when older adults do not regularly use their working memory (recall the section "Use It or Lose It"), neural connections in the prefrontal lobe may atrophy. Further, cognitive interventions that activate older adults' working memory may increase these neural connections.

Although in its infancy as a field, the cognitive neuroscience of aging is beginning to uncover some important links between aging, the brain, and cognitive functioning (Lustig & Lin, 2016; Park & Farrell, 2016). These include the following:

- Neural circuits in specific regions of the brain's prefrontal cortex decline, and this decline is linked to poorer performance by older adults on tasks involving complex reasoning, working memory, and episodic memory (Grady & others, 2006; Reuter-Lorenz, Festini, & Jantz, 2016). (See Figure 6.)

- Recall from earlier in the chapter that older adults are more likely than younger adults to use both hemispheres of the brain to compensate for age-related declines in attention, memory, and language (Davis & others, 2012; Dennis & Cabeza, 2008; Reuter-Lorenz, Festini, & Jantz, 2016). Two neuroimaging studies revealed that better memory performance in older adults was linked to higher levels of activity in both hemispheres of the brain during information processing (Angel & others, 2011; Manenti, Cotelli, & Miniussi, 2011).

- Functioning of the hippocampus declines but to a lesser degree than the functioning of the frontal lobes in older adults (Antonenko & Floel, 2014). In K. Warner Schaie's (2013) recent research,

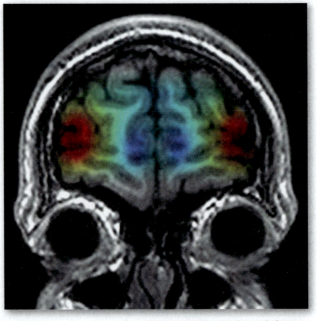

Figure 6 The Prefrontal Cortex Advances in neuroimaging are allowing researchers to make significant progress in connecting changes in the brain with cognitive development. Shown here is an fMRI of the brain's prefrontal cortex. *What links have been found between the prefrontal cortex, aging, and cognitive development?*
© Dr. Sam Gilbert, Institute of Cognitive Neuroscience, UK

individuals whose memory and executive function declined in middle age had more hippocampal atrophy in late adulthood, but those whose memory and executive function improved in middle age did not show a decline in hippocampal functioning in late adulthood.

- Patterns of neural decline with aging are more noticeable for retrieval than for encoding (Gutchess & others, 2005).

- Compared with younger adults, older adults often show greater activity in the frontal and parietal lobes of the brain on simple tasks, but as attentional demands increase, older adults display less effective functioning in the frontal and parietal lobes of the brain that involve cognitive control (Campbell & others, 2012).

- Cortical thickness in the frontoparietal network predicts executive function in older adults (Schmidt & others, 2016).

- Younger adults have better connectivity between brain regions than older adults (Archer & others, 2016; Li & others, 2015).

- An increasing number of cognitive and fitness training studies include brain imaging techniques such as fMRI to assess the results of such training on brain functioning (Erickson & Liu-Ambrose, 2016; Erickson, Hillman, & Kramer, 2015). In one study, older adults who walked one hour a day three days a week for six months showed increased volume in the frontal and temporal lobes of the brain (Colcombe & others, 2006).

Work and Retirement

What percentage of older adults continue to work? How productive are they? Who adjusts best to retirement? These are some of the questions we will examine in this section.

Work

In 2000, 23 percent of U.S. 65- to 69-year-olds were in the work force; in 2015, this percentage had jumped to 32 percent (Short, 2015). For 70- to 74-year-olds, in 2000, 13 percent were in the workforce, but this percentage had increased to 19 percent in 2015. The increases were higher for women than men. For example, the labor force participation for 75-and-over women has risen 78 percent since 2000, while this participation in the work force for 75-and-over men has increased 37 percent (Short, 2015). These increases likely are mainly driven by the need to have adequate money to meet living expenses in old age (Cahill, Giandrea, & Quinn, 2016). The U.S. Labor Department projects that by 2020, 35 percent of men and 28 percent of women ages 65 to 74 will be in the work force (Hayutin, Beals, & Borges, 2013).

Since the mid-1990s, a significant shift has occurred in the percentage of older adults working part-time or full-time (U.S. Bureau of Labor Statistics, 2008). After 1995, of the adults 65 and older in the workforce, those engaging in full-time work rose substantially and those working part-time decreased considerably. This significant rise in full-time employment likely reflects the increasing number of older adults who realize that they may not have adequate money to fund their retirement (Rix, 2011). One survey revealed that 47 percent of Americans 50 years and older now expect to retire later than they previously envisioned (Associated Press–NORC Center for Public Affairs Research, 2013). Seventy-eight percent of the workers cited financial reasons, with many responding that they had less money available for retirement than they had before the recent recession.

Older workers have lower rates of absenteeism, fewer accidents, and increased job satisfaction in comparison with their younger counterparts (Warr, 2004). This means that older workers can be of considerable value to a company, above and beyond their cognitive competence. Changes in federal law now allow individuals over the age of 65 to continue working in most jobs.

An increasing number of middle-aged and older adults are embarking on a second or a third career. In some cases, this is an entirely different type of work or a continuation of previous work but at a reduced level. Many older adults also participate in unpaid work as volunteers or as active participants in a voluntary association. These options afford older adults opportunities for productive activity, social interaction, and a positive identity.

Several recent studies have found that older adults who continue to work have better physical profiles that those who retire. For example, a recent study found that physical functioning declined faster in retirement than in full-time work for employees 65 years of age and older, with the difference not explained by absence of chronic diseases and lifestyle risks (Stenholm & others, 2014). Another study revealed that retirement increased the risk of having a heart attack in older adults (Olesen & others, 2014).

Adjustment to Retirement

In the past, when most people reached an accepted retirement age, usually in their sixties, retirement meant a one-way exit from full-time work to full-time leisure (Higo & Williamson, 2009; Wang & Shi, 2016). Increasingly, individuals are delaying retirement and moving into and out of work (Kojola & Moen, 2016). Currently, there is no single dominant pattern to retirement but rather a diverse mix of pathways involving occupational identities, finances, health, and expectations and perceptions of retirement (Kojola & Moen, 2016). Leading expert Phyllis Moen (2007) described how today, when people reach their sixties, the life path they follow is less clear: (1) some individuals don't retire from their careers, (2) some retire from their career work and then take up a new and different job, (3) some retire from career jobs but do volunteer work, (4) some retire from a post-retirement job and go on to yet another job, (5) some move in and out of the workforce, so they never really have a "career" job from which they retire, (6) some individuals who are in poor health move to a disability status and eventually into retirement, and (7) some who are laid off define it as "retirement."

What are some keys to adjusting effectively in retirement?

© Bronwyn Kidd/Getty Images RF

How Would You...?

As a **psychologist,** how would you assist older adults in making appropriate adjustments and preparations for a psychologically satisfying retirement?

Older adults who adjust best to retirement are healthy, have adequate income, are active, are educated, have an extended social network including both friends and family, and usually were satisfied with their lives before they retired (Damman, Henkens, & Kalmijn, 2014). Older adults who have inadequate income and are in poor health, and who must adjust to other stress that occurs at the same time as retirement, such as the death of a spouse, have the most difficult time adjusting to retirement (Reichstadt & others, 2007).

Mental Health

Although a substantial portion of the population can now look forward to a longer life, that life may be hampered by a mental disorder in old age (Barry & Byers, 2016)—a troubling prospect to individuals and their families and costly to society. Mental disorders make individuals increasingly dependent on the help and care of others. The cost of disorders such as dementia in older adults is estimated at more than $40 billion per year in the United States. More important, though, is the loss of human potential and the suffering involved. Although mental disorders in older adults are a major concern, however, older adults do not have a higher overall incidence of mental disorders than younger adults do (Busse & Blazer, 1996).

Dementia and Alzheimer Disease

Among the most debilitating of mental disorders in older adults are the dementias. In recent years, extensive attention has been focused on the most common dementia, Alzheimer disease.

Dementia

Dementia is a global term for any neurological disorder in which the primary symptoms involve a deterioration of mental functioning. Individuals with dementia often lose the ability to care for themselves and may become unable to recognize familiar surroundings and people—including family members (Teri, McKenzie, & Coulter, 2016). It is estimated that 23 percent of women and 17 percent of men 85 years and older are at risk for developing dementia (Alzheimer's Association, 2014). However, these estimates may be high because of the Alzheimer's Association's lobbying efforts to increase funding for research and treatment facilities. Dementia is a broad category, and it is important that every effort is made to narrow the older adult's disorder and determine a specific cause of the deteriorating mental functioning (Hagenaars & others, 2016; Velayudhan & others, 2014).

Alzheimer Disease

One form of dementia is **Alzheimer disease**—a progressive, irreversible brain disorder that is characterized by a gradual deterioration of memory, reasoning, language, and eventually, physical function. In 2012, an estimated 5.4 million adults in the United States had Alzheimer disease, and it is projected that 10 million baby boomers will develop Alzheimer disease (Alzheimer's Association, 2014). Figure 7 shows the estimated risks for developing Alzheimer disease at different ages for women and men (Alzheimer's Association, 2010). Women are more likely to develop the disease because they live longer than men, increasing the number of years during which they can develop it. Alzheimer disease triples the health-care costs of Americans 65 years of age and older (Alzheimer's Association, 2014).

Causes and Risk Factors Once destruction of brain tissue occurs from Alzheimer disease, it is unlikely that treatment of the disease will reverse the damage, at least based on the state of research now and in the foreseeable future (Teri, McKenzie, & Coulter, 2016). Alzheimer disease involves a deficiency in the brain messenger chemical *acetylcholine,* which plays an important role in memory (Godyn & others, 2016; Thomsen & others, 2016). Also, as Alzheimer disease progresses, the brain shrinks and deteriorates (see Figure 8). This deterioration is characterized by the formation of *amyloid plaques* (dense deposits of protein that accumulate in the blood vessels) and *neurofibrillary tangles* (twisted fibers that build up in neurons) (Ringman & others, 2016). Neurofibrillary tangles consist mainly of a protein called *tau* (Simic & others, 2016; Song & others, 2015). Currently, there is considerable research interest in the roles that amyloid and tau play in Alzheimer disease (Castrillo & Oliver, 2016; Ossenkoppele & others, 2016; Park & Farrell, 2016).

Until recently, neuroimaging of plaques and tangles had not been developed. However, new neuroimaging techniques have been developed that can detect these key indicators of Alzheimer disease in the brain (Park & Farrell, 2016; Villemagne & others, 2015). This imaging breakthrough is providing scientists with an improved opportunity to identify the

dementia A global term for any neurological disorder in which the primary symptoms involve a deterioration of mental functioning.

Alzheimer disease A progressive, irreversible brain disorder characterized by a gradual deterioration of memory, reasoning, language, and eventually physical function.

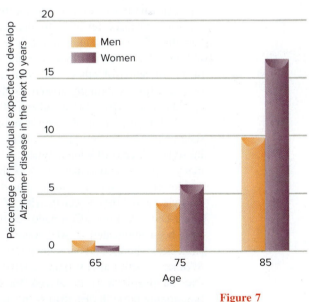

Figure 7

Estimated Risks for Developing Alzheimer Disease at Different Ages for Women and Men

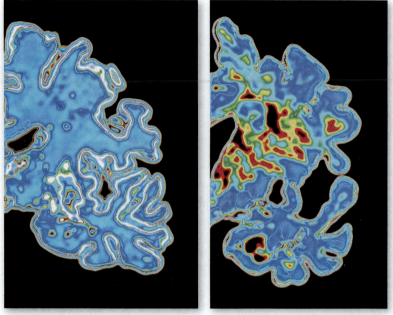

Figure 8 Two Brains: Normal Aging and Alzheimer Disease
The photograph on the left shows a slice of a normal aging brain, while the photograph on the right shows a slice of a brain ravaged by Alzheimer disease. Notice the deterioration and shrinking in the Alzheimer disease brain.

© Alfred Pasieka/Science Source

transition from healthy cognitive functioning to the earliest indication of Alzheimer disease (Chiotis & others, 2016; Park & Farrell, 2016).

There is increasing interest in the role that oxidative stress might play in Alzheimer disease (Conway & Lee, 2015; Kamat & others, 2016). Oxidative stress occurs when the body fails to defend itself against free-radical attacks and oxidation (Serini & Calviello, 2016). Recall from earlier in the chapter that free-radical theory is a major theory of aging.

Although scientists are not certain what causes Alzheimer disease, age is an important risk factor and genes also are likely to play an important role (Hu, Lin, & Chen, 2015; Park & Farrell, 2016). The number of individuals with Alzheimer disease doubles for every five years after the age of 65. A gene called *apolipoprotein E* (*ApoE*) is linked to an increasing presence of plaques and tangles in the brain. Special attention has focused on an allele (an alternative form of a gene) labeled ApoE4 that is a strong risk factor for Alzheimer disease (Das & Gursky, 2015; Theendakara & others, 2016). More than 60 percent of individuals with Alzheimer disease have at least one ApoE4 allele (Riedel, Thompson, & Brinton, 2016). In K. Warner Schaie's (2013) recent research, individuals who had the ApoE4 allele showed more cognitive decline beginning in middle age. A recent study found that the ApoE4 gene creates a cascade of molecular signaling that causes blood vessels to become more porous, allowing toxic substances to leak into the brain and damage neurons (Bell & others, 2012).

Despite links between the presence of the ApoE4 gene and Alzheimer disease, less than 50 percent of individuals who carry the ApoE4 gene develop dementia in old age. Advances as a result of the Human Genome Project have recently resulted in identification of other genes that are risk factors for Alzheimer disease, although they are not as strongly linked to the disease as the ApoE4 gene is (Harrison & Bookheimer, 2016; Mun & others, 2016).

Although individuals with a family history of Alzheimer disease are at greater risk, the disease is complex and likely to be caused by a number of factors, including lifestyles (Arenaza-Urquijo, Wirth, & Chetelat, 2015; Carnevale & others, 2016). For many years, scientists have known that a healthy diet, exercise, and weight control can lower the risk of cardiovascular disease. Now, they are finding that these healthy lifestyle factors may lower the risk of Alzheimer disease as well (Mendez-Sanz, de la Torre-Diez, & Lopez-Coronado, 2016). Recently, a number of cardiac risk factors have been implicated in Alzheimer disease—obesity, smoking, arteriosclerosis, high cholesterol, lipids, and permanent atrial fibrillation (Baumgart & others, 2015; Giudetti & others, 2016; Saito & Ihara, 2016). One of the best strategies for intervening in the lives of people who are at risk for Alzheimer disease is to improve their cardiac functioning through diet, drugs, and exercise (Di Marco & others, 2015; Isla, Vazquez-Cuevas, & Pena-Ortega, 2016).

A recent meta-analysis of modifiable risk factors in Alzheimer disease found that some medical exposures (estrogen, statins, and nonsteroidal anti-inflammatory drugs) and some dietary factors (folate, vitamin E/C, and coffee) were linked to a reduced incidence of Alzheimer disease (Xu & others, 2015). Also in this meta-analysis, some preexisting diseases (arteriosclerosis and hypertension) as well as depression increased the risk of developing Alzheimer disease. Further, cognitive activity and low-to-moderate alcohol use decreased the risk of developing Alzheimer disease.

Mild Cognitive Impairment *Mild cognitive impairment* (*MCI*) represents a transitional state between the cognitive changes of normal aging and very early Alzheimer disease and other dementias (David & others, 2016; Forrester & others, 2016). MCI is increasingly recognized as a risk factor for Alzheimer disease. Estimates indicate that as many as 10 to 20 percent of individuals age 65 and older have MCI (Alzheimer's Association, 2014). Some individuals with MCI do not go on to develop Alzheimer disease, but MCI is a risk factor for Alzheimer disease. A recent study revealed that individuals with mild cognitive impairment who developed Alzheimer disease had at least one copy of the ApoE4 gene (Alegret & others, 2014). In this study, the extent of memory impairment was the key factor that was linked to the speed of decline from mild cognitive impairment to Alzheimer disease. Distinguishing between individuals who merely have age-associated declines in memory and those with MCI is difficult, as is predicting which individuals with MCI will subsequently develop Alzheimer disease (Bruce & others, 2016; O'Caoimh, Timmons, & Molloy, 2016).

How Would You...?

As a **health-care professional,** how would you respond to an older adult who is concerned that her declining short-term memory is an early symptom of dementia?

Drug Treatment of Alzheimer Disease Several drugs called cholinerase inhibitors have been approved by the U.S. Food and Drug Administration to treat Alzheimer disease. They are designed to improve memory and other cognitive functions by increasing the level of acetylcholine in the brain (Godyn & others, 2016; Reale & others, 2014). Keep in mind, though, that the drugs used to treat Alzheimer disease only slow the downward progression of the disease; they do not treat its cause (Stella & others, 2015). These drugs slow the worsening of Alzheimer symptoms for approximately 6 to 12 months for about 50 percent of the individuals who take them (Alzheimer's Association, 2014). Also, no drugs have yet been approved by the Federal Drug Administration for the treatment of MCI (Alzheimer's Association, 2014).

Caring for Individuals with Alzheimer Disease A special concern is caring for Alzheimer patients (Kamiya & others, 2014; Lethin & others, 2016). Health-care professionals believe that the family can be an important support system for the Alzheimer patient, but this support can have costs for family members, who can become emotionally and physically drained by the extensive care required for a person with Alzheimer disease (Ornstein & others, 2014; Svendsboe & others, 2016). A recent study confirmed that family caregivers' health-related quality of life in the first three years after they began caring for a family member with Alzheimer disease deteriorated more than that of their age and gender counterparts who were not caring for an Alzheimer patient (Valimaki & others, 2016). A recent study compared family members' perceptions of caring for someone with Alzheimer disease, cancer, or schizophrenia (Papastavrou & others, 2012). In this study, the highest perceived burden was reported for Alzheimer disease.

Respite care (services that provide temporary relief to those who are caring for individuals with disabilities, illnesses, or the elderly) has been developed to help people who have to meet the day-to-day needs of Alzheimer patients. This type of care provides an important break from the burden of providing chronic care (de la Cuesta-Benjumea, 2011).

Parkinson Disease

Another type of dementia is **Parkinson disease,** a chronic, progressive disorder characterized by muscle tremors, slowing of movement, and partial facial paralysis. Parkinson disease is triggered by degeneration of dopamine-producing neurons in the brain (Hassan & others, 2016). Dopamine is a neurotransmitter that is necessary for normal brain functioning. Why these neurons degenerate is not known.

The main treatment for Parkinson disease involves administering drugs that enhance the effect of dopamine (dopamine agonists) in the disease's earlier stages and later administering the drug L-dopa, which is

Parkinson disease A chronic, progressive disease characterized by muscle tremors, slowing of movement, and partial facial paralysis.

converted by the brain into dopamine (Hernandez, Redgrave, & Obeso, 2015; Simms, Huettner, & Kortagere, 2016). However, it is difficult to determine the correct level of dosage of L-dopa, and the medication loses its efficacy over time (Nomoto & others, 2009). Another treatment for advanced Parkinson disease is deep brain stimulation (DBS), which involves implantation of electrodes within the brain (Cui & others, 2016). The electrodes are then stimulated by a pacemaker-like device. Stem cell transplantation and gene therapy offer hope for treating Parkinson disease (Lindvall, 2016).

Summary

Longevity, Biological Aging, and Physical Development

- Life expectancy has increased dramatically, but life span has not. In the United States, the number of people living to age 100 or older is increasing.
- Biological theories of aging include evolutionary theory, cellular clock theory, free-radical theory, mitochondrial theory, sirtuin theory, the mTOR pathway theory, and hormonal stress theory.
- The aging brain retains considerable plasticity and adaptability.
- Among physical changes that accompany aging are slower movement and the appearance of wrinkled skin and age spots on the skin. There are also declines in perceptual abilities, cardiovascular functioning, and lung capacity. Many older adults' sleep difficulties are linked to health problems.
- Although sexual activity declines in late adulthood, many individuals continue to be sexually active as long as they are healthy.

Health

- The probability of disease or illness increases with age. Chronic disorders, such as arthritis and osteoporosis, become more common in late adulthood. Cancer and cardiovascular disease are the leading causes of death in late adulthood.
- The physical benefits of exercise have been clearly demonstrated in older adults. Leaner adults, especially women, live longer, healthier lives.
- The quality of nursing homes varies enormously. Alternatives include home health care, elder-care centers, and preventive medicine clinics.

Cognitive Functioning

- Although older adults are not as adept as middle-aged and younger adults at complicated tasks that involve

selective and divided attention, they perform just as well on measures of sustained attention. Some aspects of memory, such as episodic memory, decline in older adults. Components of executive function—such as cognitive control and working memory—decline in late adulthood, although there is individual variation in older adults' executive function. Wisdom has been theorized to increase in older adults, but researchers have not consistently documented this increase.
- Older adults who engage in cognitive activities, especially challenging ones, have higher cognitive functioning than those who don't use their cognitive skills.
- Cognitive and fitness training can improve some cognitive skills of older adults, but there is some loss of plasticity in late adulthood.
- There is considerable interest in the cognitive neuroscience of aging. A consistent finding is a decline in the functioning of the prefrontal cortex in late adulthood, which is linked to poorer performance in complex reasoning and aspects of memory.

Work and Retirement

- Increasing numbers of older adults engage in part-time work or volunteer work and continue being productive throughout late adulthood.
- Healthy, economically stable, educated, satisfied individuals with an extended social network adjust best to retirement.

Mental Health

- Individuals with dementias, such as Alzheimer disease, often lose the ability to care for themselves. Alzheimer disease is by far the most common dementia.
- Parkinson disease is a chronic, progressive disease characterized by muscle tremors, slowing of movement, and facial tremors.

Key Terms

Alzheimer disease	evolutionary theory	implicit memory	osteoporosis
arthritis	of aging	life expectancy	Parkinson disease
cataracts	explicit memory	life span	semantic memory
cellular clock theory	free-radical theory	macular degeneration	sirtuins
dementia	glaucoma	mitochondrial theory	wisdom
episodic memory	hormonal stress theory	mTOR pathway	

16 Socioemotional Development in Late Adulthood

Stories of Life-Span Development: Bob Cousy, Adapting to Life as an Older Adult

Bob Cousy was a star player on Boston Celtics teams that won numerous National Basketball Association championships. In recognition of his athletic accomplishments, Cousy was honored by ESPN as one of the top 100 athletes of the twentieth century. After he retired from basketball, he became a college basketball coach and then into his seventies was a broadcaster of Boston Celtics basketball games. Now in his eighties, Cousy has retired from broadcasting but continues to play golf and tennis on a regular basis. He has enjoyed a number of positive social relationships, including his marriage, children and grandchildren, and many friends. In 2013, after 63 years of marriage, Cousy said a last goodbye to his wife, who had dementia and died. After she developed dementia, he cared for her in their home on a daily basis as she slowly succumbed to the deterioration of her mind and body. Since her death, when he goes to bed each night, he tells her he loves her (Williamson, 2013).

As is the case with many famous people, Cousy's awards reveal little about his personal life and contributions. In addition to his extensive provision of care for his wife in her last years, two other examples illustrate his humanitarian efforts to help others (McClellan, 2004). First, when Cousy played for the Boston Celtics, his African

Bob Cousy, as a Boston Celtics star when he was a young adult (*left*) and as an older adult (*right*). *What are some changes he has made in his life as an older adult?*

(Left) © Hy Peskin/Sports Illustrated/Getty Images (right) © Jesse D. Garrabrant/NBAE/Getty Images

American teammate, Chuck Cooper, was refused a hotel room on a road trip because of his race. Cousy expressed anger to his coach about the situation and then accompanied an appreciative Cooper on a train back to Boston. Second, the Bob Cousy Humanitarian Fund "honors individuals who have given their lives to using the game of basketball as a medium to help others" (p. 4). The Humanitarian Fund reflects Cousy's motivation to care for others, be appreciative and give something back, and make the world less self-centered.

Bob Cousy's active, involved life as an older adult reflects some of the themes of socioemotional development in older adults, including the important role that being active plays in life satisfaction, how people adapt to changing skills, and the positive role of close relationships with friends and family in an emotionally fulfilling life. Our coverage of socioemotional development in late adulthood describes a number of theories about the socioemotional lives of older adults; the older adult's personality and roles in society; the importance of family ties and social relationships; the social contexts of ethnicity, gender, and culture; and the increasing attention on elements of successful aging. ■

Theories of Socioemotional Development

In this section, we explore four main theories of socioemotional development that focus on late adulthood: Erikson's theory, activity theory, socioemotional selectivity theory, and selective optimization with compensation theory.

Erikson's Theory

Earlier we described Erik Erikson's (1968) eight stages of the human life span and, as we explored different periods of development, we examined the stages in more detail. **Integrity versus despair** is Erikson's eighth and final stage of development, which individuals experience during late adulthood. This stage involves reflecting on the past and either piecing together a positive review or concluding that one's life has not been well spent. Through many different routes, the older adult may have developed a positive outlook in each of the preceding periods. If so, retrospective glances and reminiscences will reveal a picture of a life well spent, and the older adult will be satisfied (integrity). But if the older adult resolved one or more of the earlier stages in a negative way (being socially isolated in early adulthood or stagnating in middle adulthood, for example), retrospective glances about the total worth of his or her life might be negative (despair).

Life review is prominent in this final stage. It involves looking back at one's life experiences and evaluating, interpreting, and often reinterpreting them (Ros & others, 2016; Thorgrimsdottir & Bjornsdottir, 2016). Distinguished aging researcher Robert Butler (2007) argues that the life review is set in motion by looking forward to death. Sometimes the life review proceeds quietly; at other times it is intense, requiring considerable work to achieve some sense of personality integration. The life review may be observed initially in stray and insignificant thoughts about oneself and

integrity versus despair Erikson's eighth and final stage of development, which individuals experience in late adulthood. This involves reflecting on the past and either piecing together a positive review or concluding that one's life has not been well spent.

one's life history. These thoughts may continue to emerge in brief intermittent spurts or become essentially continuous.

One aspect of life review involves identifying and reflecting on not only the positive aspects of one's life but also regrets as part of developing a mature wisdom and self-understanding (Korte & others, 2014; Randall, 2013). The hope is that by examining both the positive aspects and what an individual has regretted doing, a more accurate vision of the complexity of one's life and possibly increased life satisfaction will be attained (King & Hicks, 2007).

Although thinking about regrets can be helpful as part of a life review, research indicates that older adults should not dwell on regrets, especially since opportunities to undo regrettable actions decline with age (Suri & Gross, 2012). One study revealed that an important factor in the outlook of older adults who showed a higher level of emotion regulation and successful aging was reduced responsiveness to regrets (Brassen & others, 2012).

In working with older clients, some clinicians use *reminiscence therapy*, which involves discussing past activities and experiences with another individual or group (Allen & others, 2016; Djukanovic, Carlsson, & Peterson, 2016). Therapy may include the use of photographs, familiar items, and video/audio recordings. Reminiscence therapy can improve the mood of older adults, including those with dementia (Subramaniam & Woods, 2012). In a recent study with older adults who had dementia, reminiscence therapy reduced their depressive symptoms and improved their self-acceptance and positive relations with others (Gonzalez & others, 2015). Further, in a version of reminiscence therapy, *attach-*

What characterizes a life review in late adulthood?
© Owen Franken/Corbis

ment-focused reminiscence therapy reduced depressive symptoms, perceived stress, and emergency room visits in older African Americans (Sabir & others, 2016).

How Would You...?

As a **psychologist,** how would you explain to an older adult the benefits of engaging in a life review?

Activity Theory

Activity theory states that the more active and involved older adults are, the more likely they are to be satisfied with their lives. Researchers have found that when older adults are active, energetic, and productive, they age more successfully and are happier than they are if they disengage from society (Bielak & others, 2014; Jones & others, 2016; Neugarten, Havighurst, & Tobin, 1968; Soares-Miranda & others, 2016). A recent study found that older adults who increased their leisure-time activity levels were three times more likely to have a slower progression to having a functional disability (Chen & others, 2016). Also, a study of Canadian older adults revealed that those who were more physically active had higher life satisfaction and greater social interaction than their physically inactive counterparts (Azagba & Sharaf, 2014). Another study in which individuals kept daily diaries of their activities found that middle-aged and older adults who were more physically active were more satisfied with their lives than their less physically active counterparts (Maher & others, 2015). On days when the aging adults were physically active they reported higher life satisfaction than on the days when they were not active.

Should adults stay active or become more disengaged as they become older? Explain.
© Chuck Savage/Getty Images

activity theory Theory that the more active and involved older adults are, the more likely they are to be satisfied with their lives.

Activity theory suggests that many individuals will achieve greater life satisfaction if they continue their middle-adulthood roles into late adulthood. If these roles are stripped from them (as in early retirement), it is important for them to find substitute roles that keep them active and involved.

Socioemotional Selectivity Theory

Socioemotional selectivity theory states that older adults become more selective about their social networks. Because they place a high value on emotional satisfaction, older adults spend more time with familiar individuals with whom they have had rewarding relationships. Developed by Laura Carstensen (1998, 2006, 2008, 2010, 2014, 2015; Carstensen & others, 2015), this theory argues that older adults deliberately withdraw from social contact with individuals peripheral to their lives while they maintain or increase contact with close friends and family members with whom they have had enjoyable relationships. This selective narrowing of social interaction maximizes positive emotional experiences and minimizes emotional risks as individuals become older.

Laura Carstensen (*right*), in a caring relationship with an older woman. Her theory of socioemotional selectivity is gaining recognition as an explanation for changes in social networks as people age.
© Dr. Laura Carstensen

Socioemotional selectivity theory challenges the stereotype that the majority of older adults are in emotional despair because of their social isolation (Carstensen, 2014, 2015; Carstensen & others, 2015). Rather, older adults consciously choose to decrease the total number of their social contacts in favor of spending increased time in emotionally rewarding moments with friends and family. That is, they systematically prune their social networks so that available social partners satisfy their emotional needs (Carstensen & others, 2015; Sims, Hogan, & Carstensen, 2015). Not surprising, older adults have far smaller social networks than younger adults do (Carstensen & Fried, 2012). In a recent study of individuals from 18 to 94 years of age, as they grew older they had fewer peripheral social contacts but retained close relationships with people who provided them with emotional support (English & Carstensen, 2014).

However, in a recent large-scale examination of healthy living in different age groups by the Stanford Center on Longevity called the Sightlines Project, social engagement with individuals and communities appeared to be weaker today than it was 15 years ago for 55- to 64-year-olds (Parker, 2016). Many of these individuals, who are about to reach retirement age, had weaker relationships with spouses, partners, family, friends, and neighbors than their counterparts of 15 years ago.

Socioemotional selectivity theory also focuses on the types of goals that individuals are motivated to achieve (Sims, Hogan, & Carstensen, 2015). Two important classes of goals are (1) knowledge-related and (2) emotion-related. The trajectory of motivation for knowledge-related goals starts relatively high in the early years of life, peaks in adolescence and early adulthood, and then declines in middle and late adulthood. The emotion-related trajectory is high during infancy and early childhood, declines from middle childhood through early adulthood, and increases in middle and late adulthood.

In general, compared with younger adults, the feelings of older adults mellow. Emotional life is on a more even keel, with fewer highs and lows.

socioemotional selectivity theory The theory that older adults become more selective about their social networks. Because they place a high value on emotional satisfaction, older adults often prefer to spend time with familiar individuals with whom they have had rewarding relationships.

It may be that although older adults have less extreme joy, they have more contentment, especially when they are connected in positive ways with friends and family. Older adults react less strongly to negative circumstances, are better at ignoring irrelevant negative information, and remember more positive than negative information (Mather, 2012).

A study revealed that positive emotion increased and negative emotion (except for sadness) decreased from 50 years of age through the mid-eighties

How Would You...?

As a **health-care professional,** how would you assess whether an older adult's limited social contacts signal unhealthy social isolation or healthy socioemotional selectivity?

(Stone & others, 2010). A pronounced decline in anger occurred from the early twenties and sadness was essentially unchanged from the early twenties through the mid-eighties. Older adults reported experiencing more positive emotions than younger adults did. Other research also indicates that happier people live longer (Frey, 2011). In sum, the emotional life of older adults is more positive than stereotypes suggest (Sims, Hogan, & Carstensen, 2015).

Selective Optimization with Compensation Theory

Selective optimization with compensation theory states that successful aging is linked with three main factors: selection, optimization, and compensation (SOC). The theory describes how people can produce new resources and allocate them effectively to the tasks they want to master (Baltes, Lindenberger, & Staudinger, 2006; Freund & Hennecke, 2015; Freund, Nikitin, & Riediger, 2013). *Selection* is based on the concept that older adults have a reduced capacity and loss of functioning, which require a reduction in performance in most life domains. *Optimization* suggests that it is possible to maintain performance in some areas through continued practice and the use of new technologies. *Compensation* becomes relevant when life tasks require a level of capacity beyond the current level of the older adult's performance potential. In a recent study of 22- to 94-year-olds, middle-aged adults had the highest daily use of SOC, although older adults also showed high SOC use if they had a high level of cognitive resources (Robinson, Rickenbach, & Lachman, 2016). Older adults especially need to compensate in circumstances involving high mental or physical demands, such as when thinking about and memorizing new material in a very short period of time, reacting quickly when driving a car, or running fast. When older adults develop an illness, the need for compensation is obvious.

In the view of Paul Baltes and his colleagues (2006), the selection of domains and life priorities is an important aspect of development. Life goals and personal life investments likely vary across the life course for most people. For many individuals, it is not just the sheer attainment of goals, but rather the attainment of *meaningful* goals, that makes life satisfying. In one cross-sectional study, the personal life investments of 25- to 105-year-olds were assessed (Staudinger, 1996) (see Figure 1). From

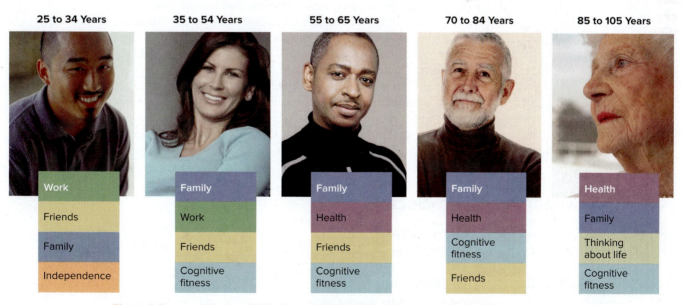

Figure 1 **Degree of Personal Life Investment at Different Points in Life**
Shown here are the top four domains of personal life investment at different points in life. The highest degree of investment is listed at the top (for example, work was the highest personal investment from 25 to 34 years of age, family from 35 to 84, and health from 85 to 105).

Left to right © Ryan McVay/Getty Images RF; © image100/PunchStock RF; © Image Source/Getty Images RF; © Corbis RF; © Image Source/ Getty Images RF

25 to 34 years of age, participants said that they personally invested more time in work, friends, family, and independence, in that order. From 35 to 54 and 55 to 65 years of age, family became more important than friends in terms of their personal investment. Little changed in the rank ordering of persons 70 to 84 years old, but for participants 85 to 105 years old, health became the most important personal investment. Thinking about life showed up for the first time on the most important list for those who were 85 to 105 years old.

Personality and Society

Is personality linked to mortality in older adults? How are older adults perceived and treated by society?

Personality

In the Socioemotional Development in Middle Adulthood chapter, we described the Big Five factors of personality. (Recall that the first letter of each factor spells OCEAN.) Several of the Big Five factors of personality continue to change in late adulthood (Donnellan, Hill, & Roberts, 2015; Hill & Roberts, 2016; Jackson & Roberts, 2016; Roberts, Donnellan, & Hill, 2013). For example, in one study, older adults were more conscientious and agreeable than middle-aged and younger adults (Allemand, Zimprich, & Hendriks, 2008). Another study examined developmental changes in the components of conscientiousness (Jackson & others, 2009). In this study, the transition into late adulthood was characterized by increases in the following aspects of conscientiousness: impulse control, reliability, and conventionality. In another study, perceived social support predicted increased conscientiousness in older adults (Hill & others, 2014). And in another study, more severe depression in older adults was associated with higher neuroticism and lower extraversion and conscientiousness (Koorevaar & others, 2013).

Some personality traits are associated with the mortality of older adults (Donnellan, Hill, & Roberts, 2015; Hill & Roberts, 2016; Roberts, Donnellan, & Hill, 2013). A longitudinal study of more than 1,200 individuals across seven decades revealed that a higher score on the Big Five personality factor of conscientiousness predicted a lower risk of earlier death from childhood through late adulthood (Martin, Friedman, & Schwartz, 2007). A higher level of conscientiousness has been linked to living a longer life than the other four factors (Donnellan, Hill, & Roberts, 2015; Hill & others, 2011; Jackson & Roberts, 2016; Wilson & others, 2015).

Affect and outlook on life are also linked to mortality in older adults (Carstensen, 2014, 2015; Carstensen & others, 2015). Older adults characterized by negative affect don't live as long as those who display more positive affect, and optimistic older adults who have a positive outlook on life live longer than their pessimistic and negative counterparts (Mosing & others, 2012; Reed & Carstensen, 2015).

Older Adults in Society

Does society negatively stereotype older adults? What are some social policy issues in an aging society? What role does technology play in the lives of older adults?

Stereotyping of Older Adults

Social participation by older adults is often discouraged by **ageism,** which is prejudice against others because of their age, especially prejudice against older adults (Allen, 2016; Lawler & others, 2014; Sims, 2016). They are often perceived as incapable of thinking clearly, learning new

ageism Prejudice against people because of their age, especially prejudice against older adults.

How Would You...?
As a **human development and family studies professional,** how would you design a public awareness campaign to reduce ageism?

things, enjoying sex, contributing to the community, or holding responsible jobs. Many older adults face painful discrimination and might be too polite and timid to attack it. Because of their age, older adults might not be hired for new jobs or might be eased out of old ones; they might be shunned socially; and they might be edged out of their family life.

Ageism is widespread (Band-Winterstein, 2015). One study found that men were more likely to negatively stereotype older adults than were women (Rupp, Vodanovich, & Crede, 2005). The most frequent form of ageism is disrespect for older adults, followed by assumptions about ailments or frailty caused by age (Palmore, 2004).

Policy Issues in an Aging Society

The aging society and older persons' status in this society raise policy issues about the well-being of older adults (George & Farrell, 2016; Moon, 2016; Quesnel-Vallée, Willson, & Reiter-Campeau, 2016). These include the status of the economy and income, provision of health care, and eldercare, each of which we consider in turn.

Status of the Economy and Income Many older adults are concerned about their ability to have enough money to live a good life as older adults (Cahill, Giandrea, & Quinn, 2016; Tse & others, 2014). An important issue is whether our economy can bear the burden of so many older persons, who by reason of their age alone are usually consumers rather than producers. Especially troublesome is the low rate of savings among U.S. adults, which has contributed to the financial problems of older adults in the recent economic downturn (Williamson & Beland, 2016). Surveys indicate that Americans' confidence in their ability to retire comfortably has reached all-time lows in recent years (Helman, Copeland, & VanDerhei, 2012).

Of special concern are older adults who are poor (George & Farrell, 2016; Quesnell-Vallée, Willson, & Reiter-Campeau, 2016). A recent study found that cognitive processing speed was slower in older adults living in poverty (Zhang & others, 2015). Researchers also have found that poverty in late adulthood is linked to an increase in physical and mental health problems (George & Farrell, 2016). Also, one study revealed that low SES increases the risk of earlier death in older adults (Krueger & Chang, 2008).

Census data suggest that the overall number of older people living in poverty has declined since the 1960s, but in 2013, 9.5 percent of older adults in the United States still were living in poverty (Gabe, 2015). In 2013, U.S. women 65 years and older (12 percent; up from 10.5 percent in 2010) were much more likely to live in poverty than their male counterparts (7 percent; up from 6.2 percent in 2010) (Cubanski, Casillas, & Damice, 2015). Nineteen percent of single, divorced, or widowed women 65 years and older lived in poverty. There is a special concern about poverty among older women and considerable discussion about the role of Social Security in providing a broad economic safety net for them (Cahill, Giandrea, & Quinn, 2016; Moon, 2016).

Poverty rates among older adults who belong to ethnic minorities are much higher than the rate for non-Latino Whites. In 2013, 20 percent of Latino White older adults and 18 percent of African American older adults lived in poverty, compared with 7 percent of non-Latino Whites (Cubanski, Casillas, & Damice, 2015).

Health Care An aging society also brings with it various problems involving health care (Gaugler, 2016; Moon, 2016), including escalating costs (Hudson, 2016). Approximately one-third of total health-care expenses in the United States involve the care of adults 65 and over, who comprise only 12 percent of the population. Medicare is the program that provides health-care insurance to adults over 65 under the Social Security system (Moon, 2016; Trivedi, 2016; Trivedi & others, 2016). Until the Affordable Care Act was enacted, the United States was the only developed country that did not have a national health care system.

Technology The Internet plays an increasingly important role in providing access to information and communication for adults as well as youth (Charness & Boot, 2016;

How Would You...?

As a **health-care professional,** how would you recommend addressing the medical community's emphasis on "cure" rather than "care" when treating chronic illness in older adults?

Cook & others, 2015; Shahrokni & others, 2015; Willis & Belleville, 2016). A 2013 national survey conducted by the Pew Research Center found that 59 percent of U.S. older adults reported that they use the Internet (in 2000, only 13 percent of older adults said they use the Internet) (Smith, 2014). Two distinct groups of older adult Internet users were identified: (1) those who are younger, more highly educated, and more affluent; and (2) those who are older, less affluent, and who have significant health or disability challenges. Also in this recent survey, once older adults begin using the Internet, it becomes an integral part of their daily lives. Among those 65 years and older who use the Internet, 71 percent report going online every day or almost every day (compared with 88 percent of 18- to 29-year-olds, 84 percent of 30- to 49-year-olds, and 79 percent of 50- to 64-year-olds). At approximately 75 years of age, Internet use drops off considerably.

Are older adults keeping up with changes in technology?
© Peter Dazeley/ Photographer's Choice/ Getty Images

One study found that frequent computer use was linked to higher performance on cognitive tasks in older adults (Tun & Lachman, 2010). Another study revealed that older adults' increased use of the Internet was associated with greater ease in meeting new people, feeling less isolated, and feeling more connected with friends and family (Cotten, Anderson, & McCullough, 2013). A longitudinal study also revealed that Internet use by older adults was associated with a reduction of one-third in their likelihood of being depressed (Cotten & others, 2014). And in a recent study of older adults, having an iPad increased their family ties and sense of having a greater overall connection to society (Delello & McWhorter, 2016). As with children and younger adults, cautions about the accuracy of information on the Internet—especially in areas such as health care—should always be kept in mind (Miller & Bell, 2012).

Families and Social Relationships

Are the close relationships of older adults different from those of younger adults? What are the lifestyles of older adults like? What characterizes the relationships of older adult parents and their adult children? What do friendships and social networks contribute to the lives of older adults? How might older adults' altruism and volunteerism contribute to positive outcomes?

Lifestyle Diversity

The lifestyles of older adults are changing. Formerly, the later years of life were likely to consist of marriage for men and widowhood for women. With demographic shifts toward marital dissolution characterized by divorce, one-third of adults can now expect to marry, divorce, and remarry during their lifetime.

Married Older Adults

In 2014, 58.6 percent of U.S. adults over 65 years of age were married (U.S. Census Bureau, 2015). Older men were far more likely to be married than older women. In 2014, 24.7 percent of U.S. adults over 65 years of age were widowed (U.S. Census Bureau, 2015). There were more than four times as many widows as widowers.

Individuals who are in a marriage or a partnership in late adulthood are usually happier, feel less distressed, and live longer than those who are single (Piazza & Charles, 2012). The following studies support the view that positive marital relationships are linked to a number of positive outcomes for older adults:

- Marital satisfaction helped to insulate older adults' happiness from the effects of daily fluctuations in perceived health (Waldinger & Schulz, 2010).

- More frequent negative (but not positive) marital experiences were linked to a slower decline in older adults' cognitive abilities over time (Xu, Thomas, & Umberson, 2016).

- Compared with other sources of social support, spousal support was more strongly linked to an important biomarker of cellular aging, telomere length (Barger & Cribbet, 2016).

- A longitudinal study of adults 75 years of age and older revealed that individuals who were married were less likely to die during a seven-year time span (Rasulo, Christensen, & Tomassini, 2005).

- Marital satisfaction in older adults was linked to whether an individual was depressed or not (Walker & others, 2013).

- For both married and cohabiting couples, negative relationship quality predicted a higher level of blood pressure when both members of the couple reported having negative relationship quality (Birditt & others, 2016).

What are some adaptations that many married older adults need to make?
© Thinkstock/Stockbyte/Getty Images RF

In late adulthood, married individuals are more likely to find themselves having to care for a sick partner with a limiting health condition (Blieszner & Roberto, 2012a, b; Suitor, Gilligan, & Pillemer, 2016). The stress of caring for a spouse who has a chronic disease can place demands on intimacy.

Divorced and Remarried Older Adults

An increasing number of older adults are divorced (Suitor, Gilligan, & Pillemer, 2016). In 2012, 14 percent of women and 12 percent of men 65 years and older in the United States were divorced or separated (U.S. Census Bureau, 2012). Many of these individuals were divorced or separated before they entered late adulthood. The majority of divorced older adults are women, due to their greater longevity, and men are more likely to remarry, thus removing themselves from the pool of divorced older adults (Peek, 2009). Divorce is far less common among older adults than younger adults, likely reflecting cohort effects rather than age effects since divorce was somewhat rare when current cohorts of older adults were young (Peek, 2009).

There are social, financial, and physical consequences of divorce for older adults (Butrica & Smith, 2012). Divorce can weaken kinship ties when it occurs in later life, especially in the case of older men. Divorced older women are less likely to have adequate financial resources than married older women, and divorce is linked to higher rates of health problems in older adults (Bennett, 2006).

Rising divorce rates, increased longevity, and better health have led to an increase in remarriage by older adults (Ganong & Coleman, 2006; Koren & others, 2016). What happens when an older adult wants to remarry or does remarry? Researchers have found that some older adults perceive negative social pressure about their decision to remarry (McKain, 1972). These negative sanctions range from raised eyebrows to rejection by adult children (Ganong & Coleman, 2006). However, the majority of adult children support the decision of their older adult parents to remarry.

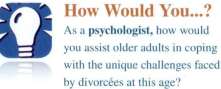

How Would You...?

As a **psychologist,** how would you assist older adults in coping with the unique challenges faced by divorcées at this age?

Adult children can be personally affected by remarriage between older adults. Researchers have found that remarried parents and stepparents provide less support to adult stepchildren than do parents in first marriages (White, 1994).

Cohabiting Older Adults

An increasing number of older adults cohabit (Wu, Schimmele, & Quellet, 2015). In 2010, 3 percent of older adults were cohabiting (U.S. Census Bureau, 2012), which is expected to increase as the large cohort of baby boomers become 65 years of age and older and bring their historically more nontraditional values about love, sex, and relationships to late adulthood. In many cases, the cohabiting is more for companionship than for love. In other cases, such as when one partner faces the potential need for expensive care, a couple may decide to maintain their assets separately and thus not marry. One study found that older adults who cohabited had a more positive, stable relationship than younger adults who cohabited, although cohabiting older adults were less likely to have plans to marry their partner than younger ones were (King & Scott, 2005). Other research also has revealed that middle-aged and older adult cohabiting men and women reported higher levels of depression than their married counterparts (Brown, Bulanda, & Lee, 2005). And one study indicated that cohabiting older adults were less likely to receive partner care than married older adults were (Noel-Miller, 2011).

Attachment

There has been far less research on how attachment affects aging adults than on attachment in children, adolescents, and young adults. A recent research review on attachment in older adults reached the following conclusions (Van Assche & others, 2013):

- Older adults have fewer attachment relationships than younger adults (Cicirelli, 2010).
- With increasing age, attachment anxiety decreases (Chopik, Edelstein, & Fraley, 2013).
- In late adulthood, attachment security is associated with greater psychological and physical well-being than attachment anxiety (Bodner & Cohen-Fridel, 2010).
- Insecure attachment is linked to more perceived negative caregiver burden in caring for patients with Alzheimer disease (Karantzas, Evans, & Foddy, 2010).

A recent large-scale study examined attachment anxiety and avoidance in individuals from 18 to 70 years of age (Chopik, Edelstein, & Fraley, 2013). Attachment anxiety was highest among adults in their mid-twenties and lowest among middle-aged and older adults. Developmental changes in avoidant attachment were not as strong as in anxious attachment, although anxious attachment was highest for middle-aged adults and lowest for young adults and older adults. Also, partnered adults showed lower levels of attachment anxiety and avoidance than single adults.

Older Adult Parents and Their Adult Children

Approximately 80 percent of older adults have living children, many of whom are middle-aged. About 10 percent of older adults have children who are 65 years or older. Adult children are an important part of the aging parent's social network. Older adults with children have more contacts with relatives than do those without children.

Increasingly, diversity characterizes older adult parents and their adult children (Antonucci & others, 2016; Fingerman, Sechrist, & Birditt, 2013). Divorce, cohabitation, and nonmarital childbearing are more common in the history of older adults today than in the past.

Gender plays an important role in relationships involving older adult parents and their children (Antonucci & others, 2016). Adult daughters are more likely than adult sons to be involved in the lives of aging parents. For example, adult daughters are three times more likely than adult sons to give parents assistance with daily living activities (Dwyer & Coward, 1991).

A valuable task that adult children can perform is to coordinate and monitor services for an aging parent (or other relative) who becomes disabled (Jones & others, 2011). This might involve locating a nursing home and monitoring its quality, procuring medical services, arranging public service assistance, and handling finances. In some cases, adult children provide direct assistance with daily living, including such activities as eating, bathing, and dressing. Even less severely impaired older adults may need help with shopping, housework, transportation, home maintenance, and bill paying.

Also, some researchers have found that relationships between aging parents and their children are usually characterized by ambivalence (Antonucci & others, 2016). And in another recent study of 40- to 60-year-old middle-aged adults, they reported that their relationships with their children were more important than those with their parents but that their relationships with their children were more negative than with their parents (Birditt & others, 2015).

Friendship

In early adulthood, friendship networks expand as new social connections are made away from home. In late adulthood, new friendships are less likely to be forged, although some adults do seek out new friendships, especially following the death of a spouse (Zettel-Watson & Rook, 2009). Aging expert Laura Carstensen (2006) concluded that people choose close friends over new friends as they grow older. And as long as they have several close people in their network, they seem content, says Carstensen.

How Would You...?
As a **human development and family studies professional,** how would you characterize the importance of friendships for older adults?

A recent study found that activities with friends increased positive affect and life satisfaction in older adults (Huxhold, Miche, & Schuz, 2014). In another study of married older adults, women were more depressed than men if they did not have a best friend, and women who did have a friend reported lower levels of depression (Antonucci, Lansford, & Akiyama, 2001). Similarly, women who did not have a best friend were less satisfied with life than women who did have a best friend. And a longitudinal study of adults 75 years of age and older revealed that individuals who maintained close ties with friends were less likely to die across a seven-year age span (Rasulo, Christensen, & Tomassini, 2005). These findings were stronger for women than men.

Social Support and Social Integration

Social support and social integration play important roles in the physical and mental health of older adults (Antonucci & others, 2016; Jeon & Lubben, 2016; Lee, Kahana, & Kahana, 2016; Windsor & others, 2016). In the *social convoy* model of social relations, individuals go through life embedded in a personal network of individuals to whom they give, and from whom they receive, social support (Antonucci & others, 2016). Social support can help individuals of all ages cope more effectively with life's challenges. For older adults, social support is related to their physical health, mental health, and life satisfaction (Lee, Kahana, & Kahana, 2016). For example, a recent study found that a higher level of social support was associated with older adults' increased life satisfaction (Dumitrache, Rubio, & Rubio-Herrera, 2016). Social support also decreases the probability that an older adult will be institutionalized and is associated with a lower incidence of depression (Heard & others, 2011). Further, one study revealed that older adults who experienced a higher level of social support showed later cognitive decline than their counterparts with a lower level of social support (Dickinson & others, 2011). In a recent analysis, it was concluded that 80 percent of the supportive care for older adults with some form of limitation was provided by family members or other informal caregivers, which places an enormous burden on the caregiver (Antonucci & others, 2016; Sherman, Webster, & Antonucci, 2016).

Social integration also plays an important role in the lives of many older adults (Antonucci & others, 2016; Li & Zhang, 2015). Remember from our earlier discussion of socioemotional selectivity theory that many older adults choose to have fewer peripheral social contacts and more emotionally positive contacts with friends and family (Carstensen & others, 2011). Thus, a decrease in the overall social activity of many older adults may reflect their greater interest in spending more time in the small circle of friends and family members where they are less likely to have negative emotional experiences. And a recent study found that increased use of the Internet by older adults was associated with making it easier for them to meet new people, feeling less isolated, and feeling more connected with friends and family (Cotten, Anderson, & McCullough, 2013).

Older adults tend to report being less lonely than younger adults and less lonely than would be expected based on their circumstances (Schnittker, 2007). This likely reflects their more selective social networks and greater acceptance of loneliness in their lives (Koropeckyj-Cox, 2009). In one study, the most consistent factor that predicted loneliness in older adults at 70, 78, and 85 years of age was not being married (Stessman & others, 2014). For 60- to 80-year-olds, the partner's death was a stronger indicator of loneliness for men than for women (Nicolaisen & Thorsen, 2014).

Recently, researchers also have explored the extent to which loneliness and social isolation are linked to various outcomes in elderly adults (Skingley, 2013). Both loneliness and social isolation are associated with increased health problems and mortality (Luo & others, 2012). Also, a study of elderly adults revealed that both loneliness and social isolation were associated with decreases in cognitive functioning four years later (Shankar & others, 2013). However, another study found that social isolation was a better predictor of mortality than loneliness (Steptoe & others, 2013).

Altruism and Volunteerism

Are older adults more altruistic than younger adults? In a recent investigation, older adults' strategies were more likely to be aimed at contributing to the public good while younger adults' strategies were more likely to focus on optimizing personal financial gain (Freund & Blanchard-Fields, 2014). Also, a recent national survey found that 24.1 percent of U.S. adults 65 years and older engaged in volunteering in 2013 (U.S. Bureau of Labor Statistics, 2013). In this survey, the highest percentage of volunteering occurred between 35 and 44 years of age (30.6 percent).

Ninety-eight-year-old volunteer Iva Broadus plays cards with 10-year-old DeAngela Williams in Dallas, Texas. Iva was recognized as the oldest volunteer in the Big Sister program in the United States. Iva says that card-playing helps to keep her memory and thinking skills sharp and can help DeAngela's as well.

© Dallas Morning News, photographer Jim Mahoney

A common perception is that older adults need to be given help rather than give help themselves. However, a recent study found that older adults perceived their well-being as better when they provided social support to others than when they received it, except when social support was provided by a spouse or sibling (Thomas, 2010). And a 12-year longitudinal study revealed that older adults who had persistently low or declining feelings of usefulness to others had an increased risk of earlier death (Gruenewald & others, 2009). Further, researchers recently have found that when older adults engage in altruistic behavior and volunteering, they benefit from these activities (Antonucci & others, 2016; Burr, Han, & Tavares, 2016). In one analysis, rates of volunteering did not decline significantly until the mid-seventies, and older adults contributed more hours than younger volunteers (Morrow-Howell, 2010). Older adults are also more likely than any other age group to volunteer more than 100 hours annually (Burr, 2009).

Volunteering is associated with a number of positive outcomes (Kim & Konrath, 2016; Klinedinst & Resnick, 2014). For example, a study of 2,000 older adults in Japan revealed that those who gave more assistance to others had better physical health than their counterparts who gave less assistance (Dulin & others, 2012; Krause & others, 1999). Among the reasons for the positive outcomes of volunteering are its provision of constructive activities and productive roles, social integration, and enhanced meaningfulness. Further, in a recent study exploring four indices (volunteering, informally helping others through a modest time commitment, attending religious services, and going to social group meetings), the strongest predictor of lower risk for cardiovascular disease and living longer was volunteering (Han & others, 2016). In a recent meta-analysis, older adults who engaged in organizational volunteering had a lower mortality risk than those who did not (Okun, Yeung, & Brown, 2013).

How Would You...?

As an **educator,** how would you persuade the school board to sponsor a volunteer program to bring older adults into the school system to work with elementary students?

Ethnicity, Gender, and Culture

How is ethnicity linked to aging? Do gender roles change in late adulthood? What are some of the social aspects of aging in different cultures?

Ethnicity

Ethnic minority older adults, especially African Americans and Latinos, are overrepresented in poverty statistics (Antonucci & others, 2016; Jackson, Govia, & Sellers, 2011). Comparative information about African Americans, Latinos, and non-Latino Whites indicates a possible double jeopardy for elderly ethnic minority individuals, facing problems related to *both* ageism and racism (Allen, 2016; Nadimpalli & others, 2015). They also are more likely to have a history of less education, longer periods of unemployment, worse housing conditions, and shorter life expectancies (Treas & Gubernskaya, 2016). In recent analyses, non-Latino White men and women with 16 years or more of schooling had a life expectancy that was 14 years higher than that of African Americans with fewer than 12 years of education (Antonucci & others, 2016; Olshansky & others, 2012).

Despite the stress and discrimination older ethnic minority individuals face, many of these older adults have developed coping mechanisms that allow them to survive in the dominant non-Latino White world. Extension of family networks helps older minority group individuals cope with the bare essentials of living and gives them a sense of being loved. Churches in African American and Latino communities provide avenues for meaningful social participation, feelings of power, and a sense of internal satisfaction (Hill & others, 2005). To read about one individual who is providing help for aging minorities, see *Careers in Life-Span Development.*

Careers in life-span development

Norma Thomas, Social Work Professor and Administrator

Dr. Norma Thomas has worked for more than three decades in the field of aging. She obtained her undergraduate degree in social work from Pennsylvania State University and her doctoral degree in social work from the University of Pennsylvania. Thomas' activities are varied. Earlier in her career when she was a social work practitioner, she provided services to older adults of color in an effort to improve their lives. She currently is a professor and academic administrator at Widener University in Chester, Pennsylvania, a fellow of the Institute of Aging at the University of Pennsylvania, and the chief executive officer and co-founder of the Center on Ethnic and Minority Aging (CEMA). CEMA was formed to provide research, consultation, training, and services to benefit aging individuals of color, their families, and their communities. Thomas has created numerous community service events that benefit older adults of color, especially African Americans and Latinos. She has also been a consultant to various national, regional, and state agencies in her effort to improve the lives of aging adults of color.

Norma Thomas.
© Dr. Norma Thomas

Gender

Many older women face the burden of both age-ism and sexism (Angel, Mudrazija, & Benson, 2016) and also racism for female ethnic minorities (Hinze, Lin, & Andersson, 2012). The poverty rate for older adult females is almost double that of older adult males.

Culture

Six factors are most likely to predict high status for older adults in a culture (Sangree, 1989):

Cultures vary in the prestige they give to older adults. In the Navajo culture, older adults are especially treated with respect because of their wisdom and extensive life experiences. *What are some other factors that are linked with respect for older adults in a culture?*
© Allison Wright/Corbis

- Older persons have valuable knowledge.
- Older persons control key family/community resources.
- Older persons are permitted to engage in useful and valued functions as long as possible.
- Age-related role changes involve greater responsibility, authority, and advisory capacity.
- The extended family is a common family arrangement in the culture, and the older person is integrated into the extended family.
- In general, respect for older adults is greater in collectivistic cultures (such as China and Japan) than in individualistic cultures (such as the United States). However, some researchers are finding that this collectivistic/individualistic difference in respect for older adults is not as strong as it used to be and that, in some cases, older adults in individualistic cultures receive considerable respect (Antonucci, Vandewater, & Lansford, 2000).

Successful Aging

As we have discussed aging, it should be apparent that there are large individual differences in the patterns of change for older adults. The most common pattern is *normal aging*, which characterizes most individuals (Schaie, 2016). Their psychological functioning often peaks in early midlife, plateaus until the late fifties to early sixties, then modestly declines through the early eighties, although marked decline often occurs prior to death. Another pattern involves *pathological aging*, which characterizes individuals who in late adulthood show greater than average decline. These individuals may have mild cognitive impairment in early old age, develop Alzheimer disease later, or have chronic disease that impairs their daily functioning. A third pattern of change in old age is *successful aging*, which characterizes individuals whose physical, cognitive, and socioemotional development is maintained longer than for most individuals and declines later than for most people.

For too long successful aging has been ignored (Carstensen, 2015, 2016; Carstensen, Smith, & Jaworski, 2015; Rowe & Kahn, 2015; Whitley, Popham, & Benzeval, 2016). Throughout this book, we have called attention to the positive aspects of aging. With a proper diet, an active lifestyle, mental stimulation and flexibility, positive coping skills, good social relationships and support, and the absence of disease, many abilities can be maintained or in some cases even improved as we get older (Antonucci & others, 2016; Erickson & Liu-Ambrose, 2016). Even when individuals develop a disease, improvements in medicine and lifestyle modifications mean that increasing numbers of older adults can continue to lead active, constructive lives. A recent Canadian study found that the predicted self-rated probability of aging successfully was 41 percent for those 65 to 74, 33 percent for those 75 to 84, and 22 percent for those 85+ years of age (Meng & D'Arcy, 2014). In this study, being younger, married, a regular drinker, in better health (self-perceived), and satisfied with life were associated with successful aging. Presence of disease was linked to a significant decline in successful aging. A recent study found that having multiple chronic diseases was linked to a lower level of successful aging (Hsu, 2015).

Being active and engaged are especially important for successful aging (Morrow-Howell & Greenfield, 2016). Older adults who exercise regularly, attend meetings, participate in church activities, and go on trips are more satisfied with their lives than their counterparts who disengage from society (Berchicci & others, 2014). Older adults who engage in challenging cognitive activities are more likely to retain their cognitive skills for a longer period of time (Willis & Belleville, 2016). Older adults who are emotionally selective, optimize their choices, and compensate effectively for losses increase their chances of aging successfully (Carstensen, 2015, 2016). Also, a recent study of 90- to 91-year-olds found that living circumstances, especially owning one's own home and living there as long as possible; independence in various aspects of life; good health; and a good death were described as important themes of successful aging (Nosraty & others, 2015). In this study, social and cognitive aspects were thought to be more important than physical health.

Successful aging also involves perceived control over the environment (Lachman, Agrigoroaei, & Hahn, 2016). In the chapter on physical and cognitive development in late adulthood, we described how perceived control over the environment had a positive effect on nursing home residents' health and longevity. In recent years, the term *self-efficacy* has often been used to describe perceived control over the environment and the ability to produce positive outcomes (Bandura, 2010, 2012, 2015). Researchers have found that many older adults are quite effective in maintaining a sense of control and have a positive view of themselves (Park, Elavsky, & Koo, 2014). For example, a study of centenarians found that many were very happy and that self-efficacy and an optimistic attitude were linked to their happiness (Jopp & Rott, 2006). And one study revealed that maximizing psychological resources (self-efficacy and optimism) was linked to a higher quality of life for older adults (Bowling & Lliffe, 2011). Examining the positive aspects of aging is an important trend in life-span development that is likely to benefit future generations of older adults (Reed & Carstensen, 2015, 2016). And a very important agenda is to continue to improve our understanding of how people can live longer, healthier, more productive and satisfying lives (Carstensen, 2015, 2016; Rowe & Kahn, 2015).

In the "Introduction" chapter, we described Laura Carstensen's (2015) perspective on the challenges and opportunities involved in the dramatic increase in life expectancy that has been occurring and continues to occur. In her view, the remarkable increase in the number of people living to an old age has occurred in such a short time that science, technology, and behavioral adaptations have not kept pace. She proposes that the challenge is to change a world constructed mainly for young people to a world that is more compatible and supportive for the increasing number of people living to 100 and older.

In further commentary, Carstensen (2015, p. 70) remarked that doing so would be no small feat:

> . . . parks, transportation systems, staircases, and even hospitals presume that the users have both strength and stamina; suburbs across the country are built for two parents and their young children, not single people, multiple generations or elderly people who are not able to drive. Our education system serves the needs of young children and young adults and offers little more than recreation for experienced people.
>
> Indeed, the very conception of work as a full-time endeavor ending in the early sixties is ill suited for long lives. Arguably the most troubling is that we fret about ways the older people lack the qualities of younger people rather than exploit a growing new resource right before our eyes: citizens who have deep expertise, emotional balance, and the motivation to make a difference.

Summary

Theories of Socioemotional Development

- Erikson's eighth stage of development is called integrity versus despair. Life review is an important theme during this stage.
- Older adults who are active are more likely to be satisfied with their lives.
- Older adults are more selective about their social networks than are younger adults. Older adults also experience more positive emotions and less negative emotions than younger adults.
- Successful aging involves selection, optimization, and compensation.

Personality and Society

- Some of the Big Five factors of personality, such as conscientiousness, extraversion, and openness, are linked to well-being and mortality in older adults.
- Ageism, which is prejudice against others because of their age, is widespread. Social policy issues in an aging society include the status of the economy and income, as well as provision of health care. Older adults are the fastest-growing segment of Internet users.

Families and Social Relationships

- Married older adults are often happier than single older adults. Divorce and remarriage present challenges to older adults. An increasing number of older adults cohabit.
- Older adults have fewer attachment relationships than younger adults; attachment anxiety decreases with increasing age; attachment security is linked to psychological and physical well-being in older adults.
- Approximately 80 percent of older adults have adult children who are an important part of their social network.
- Older adults tend to choose long-term friends over new friends.
- Social support is linked to improved physical and mental health in older adults. Older adults who participate in more organizations live longer than their counterparts who have low participation rates.
- Altruism and volunteering are associated with positive benefits for older adults.

Ethnicity, Gender, and Culture

- Aging minorities in the United States face the double burden of ageism and racism.
- Many women face the burden of both ageism and gender.
- Factors that predict high status for the elderly across cultures range from value placed on their accumulated knowledge to integration into the extended family.

Successful Aging

- Three patterns of aging are normal, pathological, and successful. Increasingly, the positive aspects of older adulthood are being studied. Factors that are linked with successful aging include an active lifestyle, positive coping skills, good social relationships and support, and the absence of disease.

Key Terms

activity theory
ageism
integrity versus despair
selective optimization with compensation theory
socioemotional selectivity theory

17 Death, Dying, and Grieving

© Fuse/Getty Images RF

CHAPTER OUTLINE

DEFINING DEATH AND LIFE/DEATH ISSUES

Determining Death

Decisions Regarding Life, Death, and Health Care

DEATH AND SOCIOHISTORICAL, CULTURAL CONTEXTS

Changing Historical Circumstances

Death in Different Cultures

FACING ONE'S OWN DEATH

Kübler-Ross' Stages of Dying

Perceived Control and Denial

COPING WITH THE DEATH OF SOMEONE ELSE

Communicating with a Dying Person

Grieving

Making Sense of the World

Losing a Life Partner

Forms of Mourning

Stories of Life-Span Development: Paige Farley-Hackel and Ruth McCourt, 9/11/2001

Paige Farley-Hackel and her best friend Ruth McCourt teamed up to take McCourt's 4-year-old daughter, Juliana, to Disneyland. They were originally booked on the same flight from Boston to Los Angeles, but McCourt decided to use her frequent flyer miles and go on a different airplane. Both their flights exploded 17 minutes apart after terrorists hijacked them, then rammed them into the twin towers of the World Trade Center in New York City on 9/11/2001.

Forty-six-year-old Farley-Hackel was a writer, motivational speaker, and spiritual counselor who lived in Newton, Massachusetts. She was looking forward to the airing of the first few episodes of her new radio program, *Spiritually Speaking,* and wanted to eventually be on *The Oprah Winfrey Show,* said her husband, Allan Hackel. Following 9/11, Oprah televised a memorial tribute to Farley-Hackel, McCourt, and Juliana.

Forty-five-year-old Ruth McCourt was a homemaker from New London, Connecticut, who met Farley-Hackel at a day spa she used to own in Boston. McCourt gave up the business when she got married, but the friendship between the two women lasted. They often traveled together and shared their passion for reading, cooking, and learning.

In this chapter, we explore many aspects of death and dying. Among the questions that we will ask are: How can death be defined? How is death viewed in other cultures? How do people face their own death? How do people cope with the death of someone they love? ■

Defining Death and Life/Death Issues

Is there one point in the process of dying that is *the* point at which death takes place, or is death a more gradual process? What are some decisions individuals can make about life, death, and health care?

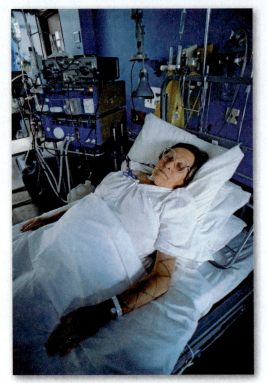

What are some issues in determining death?

© Dario Mitidieri/Getty Images

Determining Death

Twenty-five years ago, determining whether someone was dead was simpler than it is today. The end of certain biological functions—such as breathing and blood pressure—and the rigidity of the body (rigor mortis) were considered to be clear signs of death. Defining death has become more complex (Barron, 2015; Greer & others, 2016; Markert & others, 2016; Pabisiak, 2016).

Brain death is a neurological definition of death which states that a person is brain dead when all electrical activity of the brain has ceased for a specified period of time. A flat EEG (electroencephalogram) recording for a specified period of time is one criterion of brain death. The higher portions of the brain often die sooner than the lower portions. Because the brain's lower portions monitor heartbeat and respiration, individuals whose higher brain areas have died may continue to breathe and have a heartbeat (MacDougall & others, 2014). The definition of brain death currently followed by most physicians includes the death of both the higher cortical functions and the lower brain stem functions (Sung & Greer, 2011).

Some medical experts argue that the criteria for death should include only higher cortical functioning. If the cortical death definition were adopted, then physicians could claim a person is dead who has no cortical functioning, even if the lower brain stem is functioning. Supporters of the cortical death policy argue that the functions we associate with being human, such as intelligence and personality, are located in the higher cortical part of the brain. They believe that when these functions are lost, the "human being" is no longer alive.

How Would You...?

As a **health-care professional,** how would you explain "brain death" to the family of an individual who has suffered a severe head injury in an automobile accident?

Decisions Regarding Life, Death, and Health Care

In cases of catastrophic illness or accidents, patients might not be able to respond adequately to participate in decisions about their medical care. To prepare for this situation, some individuals make choices earlier.

Advance Care Planning

Advance care planning refers to the process of patients thinking about and communicating their preferences regarding end-of-life care (Anderson, 2015; Garmertsfelder & others, 2016; Koss & Baker, 2016). For many patients in a coma, it is not clear what their wishes regarding termination of treatment might be if they still were conscious. A recent study found that advance care planning decreased life-sustaining treatment, increased hospice use, and decreased hospital use (Brinkman-Stoppelenburg, Rietjens, & van der Heide, 2014). Recognizing that some terminally ill patients might prefer to die rather than linger in a painful or vegetative state, the organization "Choice in Dying" created the

brain death A neurological definition of death. A person is brain dead when all electrical activity of the brain has ceased for a specified period of time. A flat EEG recording is one criterion of brain death.

living will, a legal document that reflects the patient's advance care planning. A recent study of older adults found that advance care planning was associated with improved quality of care at the end of life, including less in-hospital death and greater use of hospice care (Bischoff & others, 2013).

Physicians' concerns over malpractice suits and the efforts of people who support the living will concept have produced natural death legislation. Laws in all 50 states now accept an *advance directive,* such as a living will (Mitchell & Dale, 2015; Olsen, 2016). An advance directive states such preferences as whether life-sustaining procedures should or should not be used to prolong the life of an individual when death is imminent. An advance directive must be signed while the individual still is able to think clearly (Lum, Sudore, & Bekelman, 2015; Shin & others, 2016). A study of end-of-life planning revealed that only 15 percent of patients 18 years of age and older had a living will (Clements, 2009). Almost 90 percent of the patients reported that it was important to discuss health-care wishes with their family, but only 60 percent of them had done so. A recent research review concluded that physicians have a positive attitude toward advance directives (Coleman, 2013).

euthanasia The act of painlessly ending the lives of persons who are suffering from incurable diseases or severe disabilities; sometimes called "mercy killing."

passive euthanasia Withholding available treatments, such as life-sustaining devices, and allowing the person to die.

active euthanasia Death induced deliberately, as by injecting a lethal dose of a drug.

How Would You...?

As a **social worker,** how would you explain to individuals the advantages of engaging in advance care planning?

Available or being considered in 34 states, Physician Orders for Life-Sustaining Treatment (POLST) is a more specific document that involves the health-care professional and the patient or surrogate in stating the wishes of the patient (Ibrahim & others, 2016; Sadeghi & others, 2016). POLST translates treatment preferences into medical orders such as those involving cardiopulmonary resuscitation, extent of treatment, and artificial nutrition via a tube (Mirachi & others, 2015; Scotti, 2016).

Euthanasia

Euthanasia ("easy death") is the act of painlessly ending the lives of individuals who are suffering from an incurable disease or severe disability (Macleod, 2015; Pope & Okinski, 2016; Radbruch & others, 2016). Sometimes euthanasia is called "mercy killing." Distinctions are made between two types of euthanasia: passive and active. **Passive euthanasia** occurs when a person is allowed to die by withholding available treatment, such as withdrawing a life-sustaining device. For example, this might involve turning off a respirator or a heart-lung machine. **Active euthanasia** occurs when death is deliberately induced, as when a lethal dose of a drug is injected.

Technological advances in life-support devices raise the issue of quality of life (Bloodworth, Bloodworth, & Ely, 2015). Nowhere was this more apparent than in the highly publicized case of Terri Schiavo, who suffered severe brain damage related to cardiac arrest and a lack of oxygen to the brain. She went into a coma and spent 15 years in a vegetative state. Across the 15 years, the question of whether passive euthanasia should be implemented, or whether she should be kept in the vegetative state with the hope that her condition might change for the better, was debated between family members and eventually at a number of levels in the judicial system. At one point toward the end of her life, a judge ordered that her feeding tube be removed. However, subsequent appeals led to its reinsertion twice. The feeding tube was removed a third and final time on March 18, 2005, and she died 13 days later from passive euthanasia.

Should individuals like Terri Schiavo be kept alive in a vegetative state? The trend is toward acceptance of passive euthanasia in the case of terminally ill patients (Seay, 2011). However, one study revealed that family members were reluctant to have their

Terri Schiavo (*right*) shown with her mother. *What issues did the Terri Schiavo case raise?*

© Handout Courtesy of the Schiavo Family/Corbis

How Would You...?

As a **psychologist**, how would you counsel the family of a brain-dead patient on the topic of euthanasia when there is no living will or advance directive for guidance?

relatives disconnected from a ventilator but rather wanted an escalation of treatment for them (Sviri & others, 2009). In this study, most of the individuals said that in similar circumstances they would not want to be chronically ventilated or resuscitated.

The most widely publicized cases of active euthanasia involve "assisted suicide." Michigan physician Jack Kevorkian assisted terminally ill patients in ending their lives. After a series of trials, Kevorkian was convicted of second-degree murder and served eight years in prison. He was released from prison at age 79 for good behavior in 2007 and promised not to participate in any further assisted suicides. Kevorkian died at the age of 83.

Assisted suicide is legal in Canada, Switzerland, Colombia, The Netherlands, Belgium, and Luxembourg. The U.S. government has no official policy on assisted suicide and leaves the decision up to each of the states. Currently, six states allow assisted suicide—Oregon, Washington, Montana, Vermont, New Mexico, and California. The physician gives the patient an overdose of muscle relaxants or sedatives, which causes a coma and then death. In states where assisted suicide is illegal, the crime is typically considered manslaughter or a felony.

A recent research review also revealed that the percentage of physician-assisted deaths ranged from 0.1 to 0.2 percent in the United States and Luxembourg to 1.8 to 2.9 percent in the Netherlands (Steck & others, 2013). In this review, the percentage of assisted suicide cases reported to authorities has increased in recent years and the individuals who die through assisted suicide are most likely to be males from 60 to 75 years of age.

Why is euthanasia so controversial? Those in favor of euthanasia argue that death should be calm and dignified, not full of agony, pain, and prolonged suffering. Those against euthanasia stress that it is a criminal act of murder in most states in the United States and in most other countries. Many religious individuals, especially Christians, say that taking a life for any reason is against God's will and is an act of murder.

Needed: Better Care for Dying Individuals

Too often, death in America is lonely, prolonged, and painful. Scientific advances sometimes have made dying harder by delaying the inevitable. Also, even though painkillers are available, too many people experience severe pain during their last days and months of life (Meng & others, 2013). A recent study found that 61 percent of dying patients were in pain in the last year of life and that nearly one-third had symptoms of depression and confusion prior to death (Singer & others, 2015).

Care providers are increasingly interested in helping individuals experience a "good death" (Bauchner & Fontanarosa, 2016; Carr & Luth, 2016; Meffert & others, 2015) that involves physical comfort, support from loved ones, acceptance, and appropriate medical care. For some individuals, a good death involves accepting one's impending death and not feeling like a burden to others. Three frequent themes identified in articles on a good death involve (1) preference for dying process (94 percent of reports), (2) pain-free status (81 percent), and (3) emotional well-being (64 percent) (Meier & others, 2016).

Hospice is a program committed to making the end of life as free from pain, anxiety, and depression as possible (Balk, 2016; Odejide, 2016; Ong & others, 2016). Traditionally, a hospital's goals has been to cure illness and prolong life; in contrast, hospice care emphasizes **palliative care,** which involves reducing pain and suffering and helping individuals die with dignity (Cox & Curtis, 2016; Hudson & others, 2016; Moore, 2015). However, U.S. hospitals recently have rapidly expanded their provision of palliative care. More than 85 percent of mid- to large-size U.S. hospitals have a palliative care team (Morrison, 2013). Hospice-care professionals work together to treat the dying person's symptoms, make the individual as comfortable as possible, show interest in the person and the person's family, and help everyone involved cope with death (Levy & others, 2016;

hospice A program committed to making the end of life as free from pain, anxiety, and depression as possible. The goals of hospice care contrast with those of a hospital, which are to cure disease and prolong life.

palliative care Emphasized in hospice care; involves reducing pain and suffering and helping individuals die with dignity.

Kathy McLaughlin, Home Hospice Nurse

Kathy McLaughlin is a home hospice nurse in Alexandria, Virginia. She provides care for individuals with terminal cancer, Alzheimer disease, and other diseases. There currently is a shortage of home hospice nurses in the United States.

Kathy says that she has seen too many people dying in pain, away from home, hooked up to needless machines. In her work as a home hospice nurse, she comments, "I know I'm making a difference. I just feel privileged to get the chance to meet this person who is not going to be around much longer. I want to enjoy the moment with this person. And I want them to enjoy the moment. They have great stories. They are better than novels" (McLaughlin, 2003, p. 1).

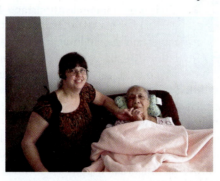

Kathy McLaughlin with her hospice patient.
© The Family of Mary Monteiro

Hospice nurses like Kathy McLaughlin care for terminally ill patients and seek to make their remaining days of life as pain-free and comfortable as possible. They typically spend several hours a day in the terminally ill patient's home, serving not just as a medical caregiver but also as an emotional caregiver. Hospice nurses usually coordinate the patient's care through an advising physician.

Hospice nurses must be registered nurses (RNs) and also be certified for hospice work. Educational requirements are an undergraduate degree in nursing; some hospice nurses also have graduate degrees in nursing. Certification as a hospice nurse requires a current license as an RN, a minimum of two years of experience as an RN in hospice-nursing settings, and passing an exam administered by the National Board for the Certification of Hospice Nurses.

West & others, 2016). Today more hospice programs are home-based, a blend of institutional and home care designed to humanize the end-of-life experience for the dying person. To read about the work of a home hospice nurse, see *Careers in Life-Span Development*.

How Would You...?

As a **human development and family studies professional,** how would you advocate for a terminally ill person's desire for hospice care?

Death and Sociohistorical, Cultural Contexts

Today in the United States, the deaths of older adults account for approximately two-thirds of the 2 million deaths that occur each year. Thus, what we know about death, dying, and grieving mainly is based on information about older adults. Youthful death is far less common. When, where, and how people die have changed historically in the United States. Also, attitudes toward death vary across cultures.

Changing Historical Circumstances

We have already described one of the historical changes involving death—the increasing complexity of determining when someone is truly dead. Another involves the age group in which death most often strikes. Two hundred years ago, almost one of every two children died before the age of 10, and one parent died before children grew up. Today, death occurs most often among older adults. In the United States, life expectancy has increased from 47 years for a person born in 1900 to 79 years for someone born today (U.S. Census Bureau, 2015). In 1900, most people died at home, cared for by their family. As our population has aged and become more mobile, growing numbers of older adults die apart from their families. More than 80 percent of all U.S. deaths occur in institutions or hospitals. The care of a dying older person has shifted away from the family and minimized our exposure to death and its painful surroundings.

Death in Different Cultures

Cultural variations characterize the experience of death and attitudes about death (Bruce, 2007; Miller, 2016). Individuals are more conscious of death in times of war, famine, and plague. Most societies throughout history have had philosophical or religious beliefs about death, and most societies have a ritual that deals with death (see Figure 1). Death may be seen as a punishment for one's sins, an act of atonement, or a judgment of a just God. For some, death means loneliness; for others, death is a quest for happiness. For still others, death represents redemption, a relief from the trials and tribulations of the earthly world. Some embrace death and welcome it; others abhor and fear it. Death may be seen as the fitting end to a fulfilled life. From this perspective, how we depart from earth is influenced by how we have lived.

Figure 1 A Ritual Associated with Death
Family memorial day at the national cemetery in Seoul, South Korea.
© Ahn Young-joon/AP Images

In most societies, death is not viewed as the end of existence—although the biological body has died, the spirit is believed to live on (Hedayat, 2006). This religious perspective is favored by most Americans as well. Cultural variations in attitudes toward death include belief in reincarnation, which is an important aspect of the Hindu and Buddhist religions. In the Gond culture of India, death is believed to be caused by magic and demons.

In many ways, we in the United States are death avoiders and death deniers (Norouzieh, 2005). This denial can take many forms: the tendency of the funeral industry to gloss over death and fashion lifelike qualities in the dead; the persistent search for a "fountain of youth"; the rejection and isolation of the aged, who may remind us of death; and the medical community's emphasis on prolonging biological life rather than on diminishing human suffering.

Facing One's Own Death

Most dying individuals want an opportunity to make some decisions regarding their own life and death (Kastenbaum, 2012). Some individuals want to complete unfinished business; they want time to resolve problems and conflicts and to put their affairs in order (Emanuel, Bennett, & Richardson, 2007). As individuals face death, a majority prefer to be at home when they are near death. A Canadian study found that 71 percent wanted to be at home when they die, 15 percent preferred to be in a hospice/palliative care facility, 7 percent wanted to be in a hospital, and only 2 percent preferred to be in a nursing home (Wilson & others, 2013).

Kübler-Ross' Stages of Dying

Elisabeth Kübler-Ross (1969) divided the behavior and thinking of dying persons into five stages: denial and isolation, anger, bargaining, depression, and acceptance.

Denial and isolation is Kübler-Ross' first stage of dying, in which the person denies that death is really going to take place. The person may say, "No, it can't be me. It's not possible." This is a common reaction to terminal illness. However, denial is usually only a temporary defense. It is eventually replaced with increased awareness when the person is confronted with such matters as financial considerations, unfinished business, and worry about surviving family members.

Anger is the second stage of dying, in which the dying person recognizes that denial can no longer be maintained. Denial often gives way to anger, resentment, rage, and envy. The dying person's question is "Why me?" At this point, the person becomes increasingly difficult to care for as anger may become displaced and projected onto physicians,

denial and isolation Kübler-Ross' first stage of dying, in which the dying person denies that she or he is really going to die.

anger Kübler-Ross' second stage of dying, in which the dying person's denial often gives way to anger, resentment, rage, and envy.

How Would You...?

As a **psychologist**, how would you prepare a dying individual for the emotional and psychological stages they may go through as they approach death?

nurses, family members, and even God. The realization of loss is great, and those who symbolize life, energy, and competent functioning are especially salient targets of the dying person's resentment and jealousy.

Bargaining is the third stage of dying, in which the person develops the hope that death can somehow be postponed or delayed. Some persons enter into a bargaining or negotiation—often with God—as they try to delay their death. Psychologically, the person is saying, "Yes, me, but . . ." In exchange for a few more days, the person promises to lead a reformed life dedicated to God or to the service of others.

Depression is the fourth stage of dying, in which the dying person comes to accept the certainty of death. A period of depression or preparatory grief may appear. The dying person may become silent, refuse visitors, and spend much of the time crying or grieving. This behavior is normal and is an effort to disconnect the self from love objects. Attempts to cheer up the dying person at this stage should be discouraged, says Kübler-Ross, because the dying person has a need to contemplate impending death.

Acceptance is the fifth stage of dying, in which the person develops a sense of peace, an acceptance of his or her fate, and in many cases, a desire to be left alone. Feelings and physical pain may be virtually absent. Kübler-Ross describes this stage as the end of the dying struggle, the final resting stage before death. Figure 2 is a summary of Kübler-Ross' dying stages.

According to Robert Kastenbaum (2009, 2012), there are some problems with Kübler-Ross' approach. For example, the existence of the five-stage sequence has not been demonstrated by either Kübler-Ross or independent research. Also, the stage interpretation neglected the patients' situations, including relationship support, specific effects of illness, family obligations, and the institutional climate in which they were interviewed. However, Kübler-Ross' pioneering efforts were important in calling attention to those who are attempting to cope with life-threatening illnesses. She did much to encourage attention to the quality of life for dying persons and their families.

bargaining Kübler-Ross' third stage of dying, in which the dying person develops the hope that death can somehow be postponed.

depression Kübler-Ross' fourth stage of dying, in which the dying person comes to accept the certainty of her or his death. A period of depression or preparatory grief may appear.

acceptance Kübler-Ross' fifth stage of dying, in which the dying person develops a sense of peace, an acceptance of her or his fate, and in many cases, a desire to be left alone.

Figure 2 Kübler-Ross' Stages of Dying According to Elisabeth Kübler-Ross, we go through five stages of dying: denial and isolation, anger, bargaining, depression, and acceptance. *Does everyone go through these stages, or go through them in the same order?* Explain.
© Science Photo Library/Getty Images RF

Perceived Control and Denial

Perceived control may work as an adaptive strategy for some older adults who face death. When individuals are led to believe they can influence and control events—such as prolonging their lives—they may become more alert and cheerful. Giving nursing home residents options for control improved their attitudes and increased their longevity (Rodin & Langer, 1977).

How Would You...?

As a **human development and family studies professional,** how would you advise family members to empower dying loved ones to feel they have more control over the end of their lives?

Denial also may be a fruitful way for some individuals to approach death. It can be adaptive or maladaptive (Cottrell & Duggleby, 2016). Denial can be used to avoid the destructive impact of shock by delaying the necessity of dealing with one's death. Denial can insulate the individual from having to cope with intense feelings of anger and hurt; however, if denial keeps us from having a life-saving operation, it clearly is maladaptive. Denial is neither good nor bad; its adaptive qualities need to be evaluated on an individual basis.

Coping with the Death of Someone Else

Loss can come in many forms in our lives—divorce, a pet's death, loss of a job, loss of a limb—but no loss is greater than that which comes through the death of someone we love and care for—a parent, sibling, spouse, relative, or friend. In the ratings of life's stresses that require the most adjustment, death of a spouse is given the highest number. How should we communicate with a dying individual? How does grieving help us cope with the death of someone we love? How do we make sense of the world when a loved one has passed away? How are people affected by losing a life partner? And what are some forms of mourning and funeral rites?

Communicating with a Dying Person

Most psychologists believe that dying individuals should know they are dying and significant others know that their loved one is dying, so they can interact and communicate with each other on the basis of this mutual knowledge (Banja, 2005). What are some of the advantages of this open awareness for the dying individual? First, dying individuals can close their lives in accord with their own ideas about proper dying. Second, they

What are some good strategies for communicating with a dying person?
© Monkey Business Images/Getty Images RF

may be able to complete some plans and projects, make arrangements for survivors, and participate in decisions about a funeral and burial. Third, dying individuals have the opportunity to reminisce, to converse with others who have been important to them, and to end life conscious of what life has been like. And fourth, dying individuals have more understanding of what is happening within their bodies and what the medical staff is doing for them (Kalish, 1981).

In addition, some experts believe that conversation should not focus on mental pathology or preparation for death but instead on strengths of the individual and preparation for the remainder of life. Because external accomplishments are not possible, communication should be directed more at internal growth. Important support for a dying individual may come not only from mental health professionals but also from nurses, physicians, a spouse, or intimate friends (DeSpelder & Strickland, 2005). Effective strategies for communicating with a dying person include the following:

1. Establish your presence, be at the same eye level; don't be afraid to touch the dying person—dying individuals are often starved for human touch.

2. Eliminate distractions—for example, ask if it is okay to turn off the TV. Realize that excessive small talk can be a distraction.

3. Dying individuals who are very frail often have little energy. If the dying person you are visiting is very frail, you may want to keep your visit short.

4. Don't insist that the dying person feel acceptance about death if the dying person wants to deny the reality of the situation; on the other hand, don't insist on denial if the dying individual indicates acceptance.

5. Allow the dying person to express guilt or anger; encourage the expression of feelings.

6. Ask the person what the expected outcome for the illness is. Discuss alternatives and unfinished business.

7. Sometimes dying individuals have limited access to other people. Ask the dying person if there is anyone he or she would like to see that you can contact.

8. Encourage the dying individual to reminisce, especially if you have memories in common.

9. Talk with the individual when she or he wishes to talk. If this is impossible, make an appointment for a later time, and keep it.

10. Express your regard for the dying individual. Don't be afraid to express love, and don't be afraid to say good-bye.

Grieving

Grief is a complex emotional state that is an evolving process with multiple dimensions. Our exploration of grief focuses on dimensions of grieving and how coping may vary with the type of death.

Dimensions of Grieving

Grief is the emotional numbness, disbelief, separation anxiety, despair, sadness, and loneliness that accompany the loss of someone we love. An important dimension of grief is pining for the lost person. Pining or yearning reflects an intermittent, recurrent wish or need to recover the lost person. Another important dimension of grief is separation anxiety, which not only includes pining and preoccupation with thoughts of the deceased person but also focuses on places and things associated with the deceased, as well as crying or sighing (Maccallum & others, 2015). Grief may also involve despair and sadness, which include a sense of hopelessness and defeat, depressive symptoms, apathy, loss of meaning for activities that used to involve the person who is gone, and growing desolation (Thomas & others, 2014; Waller & others, 2016). A recent study found that older adults who were bereaved had more dysregulated cortisol patterns, indicative of the intensity of their stress (Holland & others, 2014). And a recent study found that college students who lost someone close to them in campus shootings and had experienced severe posttraumatic stress symptoms four months after the shootings were more likely to have severe grief one year after the shootings (Smith & others, 2015).

These feelings occur repeatedly shortly after a loss. As time passes, pining and protest over the loss tend to diminish, although episodes of depression and apathy may remain or increase. The sense of separation anxiety and loss may continue to the end of one's life, but most of us emerge from grief's tears, turning our attention once again to productive tasks and regaining a more positive view of life (Mendes, 2016).

The grieving process is more like a roller-coaster ride than an orderly progression of stages with clear-cut time frames. The ups and downs of grief often involve rapidly changing emotions, meeting the challenges of learning new skills, detecting personal weaknesses and limitations, creating new patterns of behavior, and forming new friendships and relationships. For most individuals, grief becomes more manageable over time, with fewer abrupt highs and lows. But many grieving spouses report that even though time has brought some healing, they have never gotten over their loss. They have just learned to live with it.

How Would You...?

As a **social worker,** how would you respond to bereaved clients who ask, "What is normal grieving?" as they attempt to cope with the death of a loved one?

However, even six months after their loss, some individuals have difficulty moving on with their life. They feel numb or detached, believe their life is empty without the deceased, and feel that the future has no meaning. This type of grief reaction has been referred to as *prolonged or complicated grief* (Glickman, Shear, & Wall, 2016; Holland & others, 2016; Prigerson & Maciejewski, 2014). Approximately 7 to 10 percent of bereaved individuals have this prolonged or complicated grief (Maccallum & Bryant, 2013). This prolonged grief has been labeled **complicated grief or prolonged grief disorder.** Complicated grief usually has negative consequences for physical and mental health (Li & Prigerson, 2016; Shear, 2015; Tay & others, 2016). In a recent study of individuals diagnosed with complicated grief, 40 percent reported at least one full or limited-symptom grief-related panic attack in the past week (Bui & others, 2015). A person who loses someone on whom he or she was emotionally dependent is often at greatest risk for developing prolonged grief.

grief The emotional numbness, disbelief, separation anxiety, despair, sadness, and loneliness that accompany the loss of someone we love.

complicated grief or prolonged grief disorder Grief that involves enduring despair and is still unresolved over an extended period of time.

Another type of grief is *disenfranchised grief,* which describes an individual's grief over a deceased person that is a socially ambiguous loss that can't be openly mourned or supported (Cavuoti, 2015; Yu & others, 2016). Examples of disenfranchised grief include a relationship that isn't socially recognized such as an ex-spouse, a hidden loss such as an abortion, and circumstances of the death that are stigmatized such as death because of AIDS. Disenfranchised grief may intensify an individual's grief because it cannot be publicly acknowledged. This type of grief may be hidden or repressed for many years, only to be reawakened by later deaths.

Coping and Type of Death

The impact of death on surviving individuals is strongly influenced by the circumstances under which the death occurs. Deaths that are sudden, untimely, violent, or traumatic are likely to have more intense and prolonged effects on surviving individuals and make the coping process more difficult for them (Maercker & Lalor, 2012). Such deaths often are accompanied by post-traumatic stress disorder (PTSD) symptoms, such as intrusive thoughts, flashbacks, nightmares, sleep disturbances, or problems in concentrating (Nakajima & others, 2012). The death of a child can be especially devastating and extremely difficult for parents (Caeymaex & others, 2013; Stevenson & others, 2016).

Making Sense of the World

One beneficial aspect of grieving is that it stimulates many individuals to try to make sense of their world (Balon & Morreale, 2016; Kalanithi, 2016; Meert & others, 2015; Park, 2012, 2013). A common occurrence is to go over again and again all of the events that led up to the death. In the days and weeks after the death, the closest family members share memories with each other, sometimes reminiscing about family experiences. In a recent study, meaning-making following a child's death was examined (Meert & others, 2015). From 8 to 20 weeks following the child's death, the child's intensive care physician conducted a bereavement meeting with 53 parents of 35 children who had died. Four meaning-making processes were identified in the meetings: (1) sense making (seeking biomedical explanations for the death, revisiting parents' prior decisions and roles, and assigning blame); (2) benefit finding (exploring possible positive consequences of the death such as ways to help others, providing feedback to the hospital, and making donations); (3) continuing bonds (reminiscing about the child, sharing photographs, and holding community events to honor the child); and (4) identity reconstruction (changes in the parents' sense of self, including changes in relationships, work, and home).

These restaurant workers, who lost their jobs on 9/11/2001, made a bittersweet return with Colors, their own New York restaurant that is named for the many nationalities and ethnic groups among its owners. World-famous restaurant Windows on the World was destroyed and 73 workers killed when the Twin Towers were demolished by terrorists. The former Windows survivors at the new venture planned to split 60 percent of the profits between themselves and to donate the rest to a fund to open other cooperative restaurants.
© Thomas Hinton/Splash News/Newscom

When a death is caused by an accident or a disaster, the effort to make sense of it is pursued more vigorously. As added pieces of news come trickling in, they are integrated into the puzzle. The bereaved want to put the death into a perspective that they can understand—divine intervention, a curse from a neighboring tribe, a logical sequence of cause and effect, or whatever it may be. A study of more than 1,000 college students found that making sense was an important factor in their grieving of a violent loss by accident, homicide, or suicide (Currier, Holland, & Neimeyer, 2006).

Losing a Life Partner

In 2014 in the United States, 11 percent of men and 35 percent of women age 65 and older were widowed (Administration on Aging, 2014). Those left behind after the death of an intimate partner often suffer profound grief and may endure financial loss, loneliness, increased physical illness, and psychological disorders, including depression (Beam & others, 2016; Lee, 2014; Zhou & Hearst, 2016). In one study, becoming widowed was associated with a 48 percent increase in risk of mortality (Sullivan & Fenelon, 2014). Mortality risk increased for men if their wives' deaths were not expected but for women the unexpected death of a husband mattered less in terms of their mortality risk. In another study, Mexican American older adults experienced a significant increase in depressive symptoms during the transition to widowhood (Monserud & Markides, 2016). Frequent church attendance was a protective factor against increases in depressive symptoms.

How surviving spouses cope varies considerably (Caserta & others, 2014; Hasmanova Marhankova, 2016). Becoming widowed is likely to be especially difficult when individuals have been happily married for a number of decades. In such circumstances, losing your spouse, who may also be your best friend and with whom you have lived a deeply connected life, can be extremely emotional and difficult to cope with. A six-year longitudinal study of individuals aged 80 and older found that the loss of a spouse, especially in men, was related to a lower level of life satisfaction over time (Berg & others, 2009). Another study revealed that widowed persons who did not expect to be reunited with their loved ones in the afterlife reported more depression, anger, and intrusive thoughts at 6 and 18 months after their loss (Carr & Sharp, 2014).

Many widows are lonely. The poorer and less educated they are, the lonelier they tend to be. The bereaved are also at increased risk for many health problems (Ha & Ingersoll-Dayton, 2011). For either widows or widowers, social support helps them adjust to the death of a spouse (Antonucci & others, 2016). The Widow-to-Widow program, begun in the 1960s, provides support for newly widowed women. Volunteer widows reach out to other widows, introducing them to others who may have similar problems, leading group discussions, and organizing social activities. The program has been adopted by the American Association of Retired Persons and disseminated throughout the United States as the Widowed Persons Service. The model has since been adopted by numerous community organizations to provide support for those going through a difficult transition.

How Would You...?

As a **social worker,** how would you help a widow or widower to connect with a support group to deal with the death of a loved one?

Forms of Mourning

One decision facing the bereaved is what to do with the body. In the United States in 2013, 45 percent of deaths were followed by cremation—a significant increase from 14 percent in 1985 and 27 percent in 2000 (Cremation Association of North America, 2015). Cremation is more popular in the Pacific region of the United States and less popular in the South. It is more popular in Canada than in the United States and most popular of all in Japan and other Asian countries.

The funeral industry has been a target of controversy in recent years. Funeral directors and their supporters argue that the funeral provides a form of closure to the relationship with the deceased, especially when there is an open casket. Their critics claim that funeral directors are just trying to make money and that embalming is grotesque. One way to avoid being exploited during bereavement is to purchase funeral arrangements in advance.

The family and the community have important roles in mourning in some cultures. One of

A funeral procession of horse-drawn buggies on their way to the burial of five young Amish girls who were murdered in October 2006. A remarkable aspect of their mourning involved the outpouring of support and forgiveness they gave to the widow of the murderer.

© Glenn Fawcett/Baltimore Sun/MCT/Getty Images

those cultures is the Amish, a conservative group with approximately 80,000 members in the United States, Ontario, and several small settlements in South and Central America. The Amish live in a family-oriented society in which family and community support are essential for survival. At the time of death, close neighbors assume the responsibility of notifying others of the death. The Amish community handles virtually all aspects of the funeral.

The funeral service is held in a barn in warmer months and in a house during colder months. Calm acceptance of death, influenced by a deep religious faith, is an integral part of the Amish culture. Following the funeral, a high level of support is given to the bereaved family for at least a year. Visits to the family, special scrapbooks and handmade items for the family, new work projects started for the widow, and quilting days that combine fellowship and productivity are among the supports given to the bereaved family.

We have arrived at the end of this edition. Our study of the human life span has been long and complex. You have read about many physical, cognitive, and socioemotional changes that take place from conception through death. This is a good time to reflect on what you have learned. Which theories, studies, and ideas were especially interesting to you? What did you learn about your own development?

I hope this edition and course have been a window to the life span of the human species and a window to your own personal journey in life. I wish you all the best in the remaining years of your journey through the human life span.

John W. Santrock

Summary

Defining Death and Life/Death Issues

- Most physicians today agree that the higher and lower portions of the brain must stop functioning in order for an individual to be considered *brain dead.*
- Decisions regarding life, death, and health care can involve a number of circumstances and issues, and individuals can use a living will to make these choices while they can still think clearly. Hospice care emphasizes reducing pain and suffering rather than prolonging life.

Death and Sociohistorical, Cultural Contexts

- Over the years, the circumstances of when, where, and why people die have changed. Throughout history, most societies have had philosophical or religious beliefs about death, and most societies have rituals that deal with death.
- The United States has been described as a death-denying and death-avoiding culture.

Facing One's Own Death

- Kübler-Ross proposed five stages of facing death, and although her view has been criticized, her efforts were important in calling attention to the experience of coping with life-threatening illness.
- Perceived control over events and denial may work together as an adaptive orientation for a dying individual.

Coping with the Death of Someone Else

- Most psychologists recommend an open communication system with someone who is dying and their significant others.
- Grief is multidimensional and in some cases may last for years. Complicated grief or prolonged grief disorder and disenfranchised grief are especially challenging.
- The grieving process may stimulate individuals to strive to make sense out of the world.
- Usually the most difficult loss is the death of a spouse. The bereaved are at increased risk for health problems.
- Forms of mourning vary across cultures.

Key Terms

acceptance	brain death	denial and isolation	hospice
active euthanasia	complicated grief	depression	palliative care
anger	or prolonged grief	euthanasia	passive euthanasia
bargaining	disorder	grief	

A

A-not-B error This term is used to describe the tendency of infants to reach where an object was located earlier rather than where the object was last hidden.

acceptance Kübler-Ross' fifth stage of dying, in which the dying person develops a sense of peace, an acceptance of her or his fate, and in many cases, a desire to be left alone.

accommodation Piagetian concept of adjusting schemes to fit new information and experiences.

active euthanasia Death induced deliberately, as by injecting a lethal dose of a drug.

activity theory Theory that the more active and involved older adults are, the more likely they are to be satisfied with their lives.

adolescent egocentrism The heightened self-consciousness of adolescents.

adoption study A study in which investigators seek to discover whether, in behavior and psychological characteristics, adopted children are more like their adoptive parents, who provided a home environment, or more like their biological parents, who contributed their heredity. Another form of the adoption study compares adoptive and biological siblings.

aerobic exercise Sustained exercise (such as jogging, swimming, or cycling) that stimulates heart and lung activity.

affectionate love In this type of love, also called companionate love, an individual desires to have the other person near and has a deep, caring affection for the other person.

ageism Prejudice against people because of their age, especially prejudice against older adults.

Alzheimer disease A progressive, irreversible brain disorder characterized by a gradual deterioration of memory, reasoning, language, and eventually physical function.

amygdala The region of the brain that is the seat of emotions.

androgyny The presence of positive masculine and feminine characteristics in the same individual.

anger Kübler-Ross' second stage of dying, in which the dying person's denial often gives way to anger, resentment, rage, and envy.

anger cry A cry similar to the basic cry, with more excess air forced through the vocal cords.

animism The belief that inanimate objects have lifelike qualities and are capable of action.

anorexia nervosa An eating disorder that involves the relentless pursuit of thinness through starvation.

anxious attachment style An attachment style that describes adults who demand closeness, are less trusting, and are more emotional, jealous, and possessive.

Apgar Scale A widely used assessment of the newborn's health at 1 and 5 minutes after birth.

arthritis Inflammation of the joints that is accompanied by pain, stiffness, and movement problems; especially common in older adults.

assimilation Piagetian concept of using existing schemes to deal with new information or experiences.

attachment A close emotional bond between two people.

attention The focusing of mental resources on select information.

attention deficit hyperactivity disorder (ADHD) A disability in which children consistently show one or more of the following characteristics: (1) inattention, (2) hyperactivity, and (3) impulsivity.

authoritarian parenting A restrictive, punitive style in which parents exhort the child to follow their directions and to respect work and effort. The authoritarian parent places firm limits and controls on the child and allows little verbal exchange. Authoritarian parenting is associated with children's social incompetence.

authoritative parenting A parenting style in which parents encourage their children to be independent but still place limits and controls on their actions. Extensive verbal give-and-take is allowed, and parents are warm and nurturant toward the child. Authoritative parenting is associated with children's social competence.

autism spectrum disorders (ASD) Also called pervasive developmental disorders, they range from the severe disorder labeled autistic disorder to the milder disorder called Asperger syndrome. These disorders are characterized by problems in social interaction, verbal and nonverbal communication, and repetitive behaviors.

autonomous morality The second stage of moral development in Piaget's theory, displayed by older children (about 10 years of age and older). The child becomes aware that rules and laws are created by people and that in judging an action, one should consider the actor's intentions as well as the consequences.

average children Children who receive an average number of both positive and negative nominations from their peers.

avoidant attachment style An attachment style that describes adults who are hesitant about getting involved in romantic relationships and once they are in a relationship tend to distance themselves from their partner.

B

bargaining Kübler-Ross' third stage of dying, in which the dying person develops the hope that death can somehow be postponed.

basic cry A rhythmic pattern usually consisting of a cry, a briefer silence, a shorter inspiratory whistle that is higher-pitched than the main cry, and a brief rest before the next cry.

behavior genetics The field that seeks to discover the influence of heredity and environment on individual differences in human traits and development.

behavioral and social cognitive theories Theories holding that development can be described in terms of the behaviors learned through interactions with the environment.

Big Five factors of personality Emotional stability (neuroticism), extraversion, openness to experience, agreeableness, and conscientiousness.

biological processes Changes in an individual's physical nature.

brain death A neurological definition of death. A person is brain dead when all electrical activity of the brain has ceased for a specified period of time. A flat EEG recording is one criterion of brain death.

Bronfenbrenner's ecological theory Bronfenbrenner's environmental systems theory, which focuses on five environmental systems: microsystem, mesosystem, exosystem, macrosystem, and chronosystem.

bulimia nervosa An eating disorder in which the individual consistently follows a binge-and-purge pattern.

C

care perspective The moral perspective of Carol Gilligan, which views people in terms of their connectedness with others and emphasizes interpersonal communication, relationships with others, and concern for others.

case study An in-depth examination of an individual.

cataracts Involve a thickening of the lens of the eye that causes vision to become cloudy and distorted.

cellular clock theory Leonard Hayflick's theory that the maximum number of times human cells can divide is about 75 to 80. As we age, our cells become increasingly less capable of dividing.

centration The focusing of attention on one characteristic to the exclusion of all others.

cephalocaudal pattern The sequence in which the earliest growth always occurs at the top—the head—with physical growth in size, weight, and feature differentiation gradually working from top to bottom.

child-centered kindergarten Education that involves the whole child by considering both the child's physical, cognitive, and socioemotional development and the child's needs, interests, and learning styles.

child-directed speech Also called parentese, language spoken in a higher pitch, slower tempo, and exaggerated intonation than normal with simple words and sentences.

chromosomes Threadlike structures made up of deoxyribonucleic acid, or DNA.

climacteric The midlife transition in which fertility declines.

clique A small group that ranges from 2 to about 12 individuals, averaging about 5 or 6 individuals, and often consists of adolescents who engage in similar activities.

cognitive processes Changes in an individual's thought, intelligence, and language.

cohort effects Effects that are due to a subject's time of birth or generation but not age.

commitment Marcia's term for the part of identity development in which adolescents show a personal investment in forming an identity.

complicated grief or prolonged grief disorder Grief that involves enduring despair and is still unresolved over an extended period of time.

concepts Cognitive groupings of similar objects, events, people, or ideas.

conservation In Piaget's theory, awareness that altering an object's or a substance's appearance does not change its basic properties.

constructive play Play that combines sensorimotor and repetitive activity with symbolic representation of ideas.

Constructive play occurs when children engage in self-regulated creation or construction of a product or a problem solution.

constructivist approach A learner-centered approach that emphasizes the importance of individuals actively constructing their knowledge and understanding with guidance from the teacher.

contemporary life-events approach An approach emphasizing that how a life event influences the individual's development depends not only on the life event itself but also on mediating factors, the individual's adaptation to the life event, the life-stage context, and the sociohistorical context.

context The setting in which development occurs, which is influenced by historical, economic, social, and cultural factors.

continuity-discontinuity issue The debate about the extent to which development involves gradual, cumulative change (continuity) or distinct stages (discontinuity).

controversial children Children who are frequently nominated both as someone's best friend and as being disliked.

conventional reasoning The second, or intermediate, level in Kohlberg's theory of moral development. At this level, individuals abide by certain standards, but they are the standards of others, such as parents or the laws of society.

convergent thinking The type of thinking that produces one correct answer and is typically assessed by standardized intelligence tests.

core knowledge approach States that infants are born with domain-specific innate knowledge systems.

corpus callosum The location where nerve fibers connect the brain's left and right hemispheres.

correlation coefficient A number based on statistical analysis that is used to describe the degree of association between two variables.

correlational research A type of research that focuses on describing the strength of the relation between two or more events or characteristics.

creative thinking The ability to think in novel and unusual ways and to come up with unique solutions to problems.

crisis Marcia's term for a period of identity development during which the adolescent is exploring alternatives.

critical thinking Thinking reflectively and productively, as well as evaluating the evidence.

cross-cultural studies Comparisons of one culture with one or more other cultures. These provide information about the

degree to which children's development is similar, or universal, across cultures, and to the degree to which it is culture-specific.

cross-sectional approach A research strategy in which individuals of different ages are compared at one time.

crowd A larger group structure than a clique, a crowd is usually formed based on reputation, and members may or may not spend much time together.

crystallized intelligence Accumulated information and verbal skills, which increase in middle age, according to Horn.

cultural-familial intellectual disability Intellectual disability in which there is no evidence of organic brain damage, but the individual's IQ generally is between 50 and 70.

culture The behavior patterns, beliefs, and all other products of a group that are passed on from generation to generation.

culture-fair tests Tests of intelligence that are designed to be free of cultural bias.

cumulative personality model The principle that with time and age, people become more adept at interacting with their environment in ways that promote stability of personality.

D

deferred imitation Imitation that occurs after a delay of hours or days.

dementia A global term for any neurological disorder in which the primary symptoms involve a deterioration of mental functioning.

denial and isolation Kübler-Ross' first stage of dying, in which the dying person denies that she or he is really going to die.

depression Kübler-Ross' fourth stage of dying, in which the dying person comes to accept the certainty of her or his death. A period of depression or preparatory grief may appear.

descriptive research Type of research that aims to observe and record behavior.

development The pattern of movement or change that starts at conception and continues through the life span.

developmental cascade model Involves connections across domains over time that influence developmental pathways and outcomes.

developmentally appropriate practice (DAP) Education that focuses on the typical developmental patterns of children (age appropriateness) and the uniqueness of each child (individual appropriateness).

difficult child A child who tends to react negatively and cry frequently, who engages in irregular daily routines, and who is slow to accept new experiences.

direct instruction approach   A structured, teacher-centered approach that is characterized by teacher direction and control, high teacher expectations for students' progress, maximum time spent by students on learning tasks, and efforts by the teacher to keep negative affect to a minimum.

dishabituation   Recovery of a habituated response after a change in stimulation.

divergent thinking   Thinking that produces many answers to the same question and is characteristic of creativity.

DNA   A complex molecule with a double helix shape that contains genetic information.

domain theory of moral development   Theory that identifies different domains of social knowledge and reasoning, including moral, social conventional, and personal domains. These domains arise from children's and adolescents' attempts to understand and deal with different forms of social experience.

Down syndrome   A chromosomally transmitted form of intellectual disability, caused by the presence of an extra copy of chromosome 21.

dynamic systems theory   The perspective on motor development that seeks to explain how motor behaviors are assembled for perceiving and acting.

E

easy child   A child who is generally in a positive mood, who quickly establishes regular routines in infancy, and who adapts easily to new experiences.

eclectic theoretical orientation   An approach that selects and uses whatever is considered the best in many theories.

ecological view   The view that perception functions to bring organisms in contact with the environment and to increase adaptation.

egocentrism   The inability to distinguish between one's own perspective and someone else's (salient feature of the first substage of preoperational thought).

elaboration   An important strategy that involves engaging in more extensive processing of information.

embryonic period   The period of prenatal development that occurs two to eight weeks after conception. During the embryonic period, the rate of cell differentiation intensifies, support systems for the cells form, and organs appear.

emerging adulthood   The transition from adolescence to adulthood (approximately 18 to 25 years of age), which involves experimentation and exploration.

emotion   Feeling, or affect, that occurs when a person is in a state or interaction that is important to them. Emotion is characterized by behavior that reflects (expresses) the pleasantness or unpleasantness of the state a person is in or the transactions being experienced.

empty nest syndrome   A term used to indicate a decrease in marital satisfaction after children leave home.

epigenetic view   Emphasizes that development is the result of an ongoing, bidirectional interchange between heredity and environment.

episodic memory   The retention of information about the where and when of life's happenings.

equilibration   A mechanism that Piaget proposed to explain how children shift from one stage of thought to the next.

Erikson's theory   A psychoanalytic theory in which eight stages of psychosocial development unfold throughout the life span. Each stage consists of a unique developmental task that confronts individuals with a crisis that must be faced.

ethnic identity   An enduring, basic aspect of the self that includes a sense of membership in an ethnic group and the attitudes and feelings related to that membership.

ethnicity   A range of characteristics rooted in cultural heritage, including nationality, race, religion, and language.

ethology   An approach stressing that behavior is strongly influenced by biology, tied to evolution, and characterized by critical or sensitive periods.

euthanasia   The act of painlessly ending the lives of persons who are suffering from incurable diseases or severe disabilities; sometimes called "mercy killing."

evolutionary psychology   Emphasizes the importance of adaptation, reproduction, and "survival of the fittest" in shaping behavior.

evolutionary theory of aging   The view that natural selection has not eliminated many harmful conditions and nonadaptive characteristics in older adults.

executive attention   Involves planning actions, allocating attention to goals, detecting and compensating for errors, monitoring progress on tasks, and dealing with novel or difficult circumstances.

executive function   An umbrella-like concept that consists of a number of higher-level cognitive processes linked to the development of the brain's prefrontal cortex. Executive function involves managing one's thoughts to engage in goal-directed behavior and to use self-control.

experiment   A carefully regulated procedure in which one or more of the factors believed to influence the behavior being studied is manipulated and all other factors are held constant. Experimental research permits the determination of cause.

explicit memory   Memory of facts and experiences that individuals consciously know and can state.

F

fast mapping   A process that helps to explain how young children learn the connection between a word and its referent so quickly.

fetal alcohol spectrum disorders (FASD)   A cluster of abnormalities that appears in the offspring of mothers who drink alcohol heavily during pregnancy.

fetal period   The prenatal period of development that begins two months after conception and usually lasts for seven months.

fight-or-flight   The view that when men experience stress, they are more likely to become aggressive, withdraw from social contact, or drink alcohol.

fine motor skills   Motor skills that involve more finely tuned movements, such as finger dexterity.

fluid intelligence   The ability to reason abstractly, which steadily declines from middle adulthood on, according to Horn.

free-radical theory   A theory of aging proposing that people age because normal cell metabolism produces unstable oxygen molecules known as free radicals. These molecules ricochet around inside cells, damaging DNA and other cellular structures.

fuzzy trace theory   States that memory is best understood by considering two types of memory representations: (1) verbatim memory trace and (2) gist. In this theory, older children's better memory is attributed to the fuzzy traces created by extracting the gist of information.

G

games   Activities engaged in for pleasure that include rules and often involve competition between two or more individuals.

gender   The characteristics of people as females and males.

gender identity   The sense of being male or female, which most children acquire by the time they are 3 years old.

gender roles   Sets of expectations that prescribe how females or males should think, act, and feel.

gender schema theory   The theory that gender typing emerges as children gradually develop gender schemas of what is gender-appropriate and gender-inappropriate in their culture.

gender stereotypes Broad categories that reflect society's impressions and beliefs about females and males.

gene × environment (G × E) interaction The interaction of a specified measured variation in DNA and a specific measured aspect of the environment.

generativity Adults' desire to leave legacies of themselves to the next generation; the positive side of Erikson's generativity versus stagnation middle adulthood stage.

genes Units of hereditary information composed of DNA. Genes direct cells to reproduce themselves and manufacture the proteins that maintain life.

genotype A person's genetic heritage; the actual genetic material.

germinal period The period of prenatal development that takes place during the first two weeks after conception. It includes the creation of the zygote, continued cell division, and the attachment of the zygote to the uterine wall.

gifted Having above-average intelligence (an IQ of 130 or higher) and/or superior talent for something.

glaucoma Damage to the optic nerve because of the pressure created by a buildup of fluid in the eye.

gonads The sex glands—the testes in males and the ovaries in females.

goodness of fit Refers to the match between a child's temperament and the environmental demands with which the child must cope.

grief The emotional numbness, disbelief, separation anxiety, despair, sadness, and loneliness that accompany the loss of someone we love.

gross motor skills Motor skills that involve large-muscle activities, such as walking.

H

habituation Decreased responsiveness to a stimulus after repeated presentations of the stimulus.

heteronomous morality Kohlberg's first stage in preconventional reasoning, in which moral thinking is tied to punishment.

heteronomous morality The first stage of moral development in Piaget's theory, occurring from approximately 4 to 7 years of age. Justice and rules are conceived of as unchangeable properties of the world, beyond the control of people.

hormonal stress theory The theory that aging in the body's hormonal system can lower resilience under stress and increase the likelihood of disease.

hormones Powerful chemical substances secreted by the endocrine glands and carried through the body by the bloodstream.

hospice A program committed to making the end of life as free from pain, anxiety, and depression as possible. The goals of hospice care contrast with those of a hospital, which are to cure disease and prolong life.

hypothalamus A structure in the higher portion of the brain that monitors eating and sex.

hypotheses Assertions or predictions, often derived from theories, that can be tested.

hypothetical-deductive reasoning Piaget's formal operational concept that adolescents have the cognitive ability to develop hypotheses, or best guesses, about ways to solve problems.

I

identity achievement Marcia's term for adolescents who have undergone a crisis and have made a commitment.

identity diffusion Marcia's term for adolescents who have not yet experienced a crisis (explored meaningful alternatives) or made any commitments.

identity foreclosure Marcia's term for adolescents who have made a commitment but have not experienced a crisis.

identity moratorium Marcia's term for adolescents who are in the midst of a crisis, but their commitments are either absent or vaguely defined.

imaginary audience Involves adolescents' belief that others are as interested in them as they themselves are; attention-getting behavior motivated by a desire to be noticed, visible, and "on stage."

immanent justice The expectation that, if a rule is broken, punishment will be meted out immediately.

implicit memory Memory without conscious recollection; involves skills and routine procedures that are automatically performed.

inclusion Educating a child who requires special education full-time in the regular classroom.

individualism, instrumental purpose, and exchange The second Kohlberg stage of moral development. At this stage, individuals pursue their own interests but also let others do the same.

individualized education plan (IEP) A written statement that spells out a program tailored to a child with a disability.

indulgent parenting A style of parenting in which parents are highly involved with their children but place few demands or controls on them. Indulgent parenting is

associated with children's social incompetence, especially a lack of self-control.

infinite generativity The ability to produce an endless number of meaningful sentences using a finite set of words and rules.

information-processing theory A theory emphasizing that individuals manipulate information, monitor it, and strategize about it. The processes of memory and thinking are central.

insecure avoidant babies Babies that show insecurity by avoiding their mothers.

insecure disorganized babies Babies that show insecurity by being disorganized and disoriented.

insecure resistant babies Babies that often cling to the caregiver, then resist her by fighting against the closeness, perhaps by kicking or pushing away.

integrity versus despair Erikson's eighth and final stage of development, which individuals experience in late adulthood. This involves reflecting on the past and either piecing together a positive review or concluding that one's life has not been well spent.

intellectual disability A condition of limited mental ability in which an individual has a low IQ, usually below 70 on a traditional test of intelligence, and has difficulty adapting to the demands of everyday life.

intelligence Problem-solving skills and the ability to learn from, and adapt to, the experiences of everyday life.

intelligence quotient (IQ) A person's mental age divided by chronological age and multiplied by 100.

intermodal perception The ability to relate and integrate information from two or more sensory modalities, such as vision and hearing.

intuitive thought substage Piaget's second substage of preoperational thought, in which children begin to use primitive reasoning and want to know the answers to all sorts of questions (between about 4 and 7 years of age).

J

joint attention Process that occurs when (1) individuals focus on the same object and track each other's behavior, (2) one individual directs another's attention, and (3) reciprocal interaction takes place.

justice perspective A moral perspective that focuses on the rights of the individual; individuals independently make moral decisions.

juvenile delinquent An adolescent who breaks the law or engages in behavior that is considered illegal.

L

laboratory A controlled setting in which research can take place.

language A form of communication, whether spoken, written, or signed, that is based on a system of symbols. Language consists of the words used by a community and the rules for varying and combining them.

language acquisition device (LAD) Chomsky's term that describes a biological endowment enabling the child to detect the features and rules of language, including phonology, syntax, and semantics.

lateralization Specialization of function in one hemisphere of the cerebral cortex or the other.

learning disability Describes a child who has difficulty understanding or using spoken or written language or doing mathematics. To be classified as a learning disability, the problem is not primarily the result of visual, hearing, or motor disabilities; intellectual disability; emotional disorders; or due to environmental, cultural, or economic disadvantage.

least restrictive environment (LRE) The concept that a child with a disability should be educated in a setting that is as similar as possible to the one in which children who do not have a disability are educated.

leisure The pleasant times after work when individuals are free to pursue activities and interests of their own choosing.

life expectancy The number of years that will probably be lived by the average person born in a particular year.

life span The upper boundary of life, which is the maximum number of years an individual can live. The maximum life span of human beings is about 120 to 125 years of age.

life-span perspective The perspective that development is lifelong, multidimensional, multidirectional, plastic, multidisciplinary, and contextual; that it involves growth, maintenance, and regulation; and that it is constructed through biological, sociocultural, and individual factors working together.

limbic system A lower, subcortical system in the brain that is the seat of emotions and experience of rewards.

long-term memory A relatively permanent type of memory that holds huge amounts of information for a long period of time.

longitudinal approach A research strategy in which the same individuals are studied over a period of time, usually several years or more.

M

macular degeneration A disease that involves deterioration of the macula of the retina, which corresponds to the focal center of the visual field.

meiosis A specialized form of cell division that occurs to form eggs and sperm (or gametes).

memory A central feature of cognitive development, pertaining to all situations in which an individual retains information over time.

menarche A girl's first menstruation.

menopause The complete cessation of a woman's menstrual cycles, which usually occurs in the late forties or early fifties.

mental age (MA) Binet's measure of an individual's level of mental development, compared with that of others.

metacognition Cognition about cognition, or knowing about knowing.

metalinguistic awareness Refers to knowledge about language, such as knowing what a preposition is or being able to discuss the sounds of a language.

middle adulthood The developmental period beginning at approximately 40 years of age and extending to about 60 to 65 years of age.

mindset The cognitive view that individuals develop for themselves.

mitochondrial theory The theory that aging is caused by the decay of mitochondria, tiny cellular bodies that supply energy for function, growth, and repair.

mitosis Cellular reproduction in which the cell's nucleus duplicates itself with two new cells being formed, each containing the same DNA as the parent cell, arranged in the same 23 pairs of chromosomes.

Montessori approach An educational philosophy in which children are given considerable freedom and spontaneity in choosing activities and are allowed to move from one activity to another as they desire.

moral development Development that involves thoughts, feelings, and actions regarding rules and conventions about what people should do in their interactions with other people.

morphology Units of meaning involved in word formation.

mTOR pathway A cellular pathway involving the regulation of growth and metabolism that has been proposed as a key aspect of longevity

mutual interpersonal expectations, relationships, and interpersonal conformity Kohlberg's third stage of moral development. At this stage, individuals value trust, caring, and loyalty to others as a basis of moral judgments.

myelination The process by which axons are covered and insulated with a layer of fat cells, which increases the speed at which information travels through the nervous system.

N

natural childbirth A childbirth method in which no drugs are given to relieve pain or assist in the birth process. The mother and her partner are taught to use breathing methods and relaxation techniques during delivery.

naturalistic observation Observation that occurs in a real-world setting without any attempt to manipulate the situation.

nature-nurture issue The debate about the extent to which development is influenced by nature and by nurture. Nature refers to an organism's biological inheritance, nurture to its environmental experiences.

neglected children Children who are infrequently nominated as a best friend but are not disliked by their peers.

neglectful parenting A style of parenting in which the parent is very uninvolved in the child's life; it is associated with children's social incompetence, especially a lack of self-control.

neo-Piagetians Developmentalists who have elaborated on Piaget's theory, giving more emphasis to how children use attention, memory, and strategies to process information.

neuroconstructivist view Developmental perspective in which biological processes and environmental conditions influence the brain's development; the brain has plasticity and is context dependent; and cognitive development is closely linked with brain development.

neurons Nerve cells that handle information processing at the cellular level in the brain.

nonnormative life events Unusual occurrences that have a major impact on a person's life. The occurrence, pattern, and sequence of these events are not applicable to many individuals.

normal distribution A symmetrical distribution with most scores falling in the middle of the possible range of scores and few scores appearing toward the extremes of the range.

normative age-graded influences Biological and environmental influences that are similar for individuals in a particular age group.

normative history-graded influences Biological and environmental influences that are associated with history. These influences are common to people of a particular generation.

O

object permanence The Piagetian term for understanding that objects and events continue to exist, even when they cannot directly be seen, heard, or touched.

operations In Piaget's theory, these are internalized, reversible sets of actions that allow children to do mentally what they formerly did physically.

organic intellectual disability Intellectual disability that involves some physical damage and is caused by a genetic disorder or brain damage.

organization Piaget's concept of grouping isolated behaviors and thoughts into a higher-order, more smoothly functioning cognitive system.

organogenesis Organ formation that takes place during the first two months of prenatal development.

osteoporosis A chronic condition that involves an extensive loss of bone tissue and is the main reason many older adults walk with a marked stoop. Women are especially vulnerable to osteoporosis.

P

pain cry A sudden outburst of loud crying without preliminary moaning, followed by breath holding.

palliative care Emphasized in hospice care; involves reducing pain and suffering and helping individuals die with dignity.

Parkinson disease A chronic, progressive disease characterized by muscle tremors, slowing of movement, and partial facial paralysis.

passive euthanasia Withholding available treatments, such as life-sustaining devices, and allowing the person to die.

perception The interpretation of what is sensed.

personal fable The part of adolescent egocentrism that involves an adolescent's sense of uniqueness and invincibility (or invulnerability).

perspective taking The social cognitive process involved in assuming the perspective of others and understanding their thoughts and feelings.

phenotype The way an individual's genotype is expressed in observed and measurable characteristics.

phonics approach The idea that reading instruction should teach the basic rules for translating written symbols into sounds.

phonology The sound system of a language, including the sounds used and how they may be combined.

Piaget's theory The theory that children construct their understanding of the world

and go through four stages of cognitive development.

pituitary gland An important endocrine gland that controls growth and regulates other glands, including the gonads.

popular children Children who are frequently nominated as a best friend and are rarely disliked by their peers.

postconventional reasoning The highest level in Kohlberg's theory of moral development. At this level, the individual recognizes alternative moral courses, explores the options, and then decides on a personal moral code.

postformal thought Thinking that is reflective, relativistic, and contextual; provisional; realistic; and influenced by emotions.

postpartum period The period after childbirth when the mother adjusts, both physically and psychologically, to the process of childbearing. This period lasts for about six weeks or until her body has completed its adjustment and returned to a nearly prepregnant state.

practice play Play that involves repetition of behavior when new skills are being learned or when physical or mental mastery and coordination of skills are required for games or sports.

pragmatics The appropriate use of language in different contexts.

preconventional reasoning The lowest level in Kohlberg's theory of moral development. The individual's moral reasoning is controlled primarily by external rewards and punishment.

preoperational stage Piaget's second stage, lasting from about 2 to 7 years of age, during which children begin to represent the world with words, images, and drawings, and symbolic thought goes beyond simple connections of sensory information and physical action; stable concepts are formed, mental reasoning emerges, egocentrism is present, and magical beliefs are constructed.

prepared childbirth Developed by French obstetrician Ferdinand Lamaze, this childbirth strategy is similar to natural childbirth but includes a special breathing technique to control pushing in the final stages of labor and more detailed anatomy and physiology instruction.

pretense/symbolic play Play in which the child transforms the physical environment into a symbol.

Project Head Start A government-funded program that is designed to provide children from low-income families the opportunity to acquire the skills and experiences important for school success.

proximodistal pattern The sequence in which growth starts at the center of the body and moves toward the extremities.

psychoanalytic theories Theories holding that development depends primarily on the unconscious mind and is heavily couched in emotion, that behavior is merely a surface characteristic, that it is important to analyze the symbolic meanings of behavior, and that early experiences are important in development.

psychoanalytic theory of gender A theory deriving from Freud's view that the preschool child develops a sexual attraction to the opposite-sex parent, by approximately 5 or 6 years of age renounces this attraction because of anxious feelings, and subsequently identifies with the same-sex parent, unconsciously adopting the same-sex parent's characteristics.

puberty A brain-neuroendocrine process occurring primarily in early adolescence that provides stimulation for the rapid physical changes that occur in this period of development.

R

reciprocal socialization Socialization that is bidirectional, meaning that children socialize parents, just as parents socialize children.

reflexive smile A smile that does not occur in response to external stimuli. It appears during the first month after birth, usually during sleep.

rejected children Children who are infrequently nominated as a best friend and are actively disliked by their peers.

rite of passage A ceremony or ritual that marks an individual's transition from one status to another. Most rites of passage focus on the transition to adult status.

romantic love Also called passionate love, or *eros;* romantic love has strong sexual and infatuation components and often predominates in the early period of a love relationship.

S

scaffolding Process in which parents time interactions so that infants experience turn-taking with their parents.

schemes In Piaget's theory, actions or mental representations that organize knowledge.

secure attachment style An attachment style that describes adults who have positive views of relationships, find it easy to get close to others, and are not overly concerned or stressed out about their romantic relationships.

securely attached babies Babies that use the caregiver as a secure base from which to explore their environment.

selective optimization with compensation theory The theory that successful aging involves three main factors: selection, optimization, and compensation.

self-concept   Domain-specific evaluations of the self.

self-efficacy   The belief that one can master a situation and produce favorable outcomes.

self-esteem   The global evaluative dimension of the self. Self-esteem is also referred to as self-worth or self-image.

self-understanding   The child's cognitive representation of self, the substance and content of the child's self-conceptions.

semantic memory   A person's knowledge about the world—including a person's fields of expertise, general academic knowledge of the sort learned in school, and "everyday knowledge."

semantics   The meaning of words and sentences.

sensation   The product of the interaction between information and the sensory receptors—the eyes, ears, tongue, nostrils, and skin.

sensorimotor play   Behavior engaged in by infants to derive pleasure from exercising their existing sensorimotor schemes.

sensorimotor stage   The first of Piaget's stages, which lasts from birth to about 2 years of age; during this stage, infants construct an understanding of the world by coordinating sensory experiences with motoric actions.

separation protest   An infant's distressed crying when the caregiver leaves.

seriation   The concrete operation that involves ordering stimuli along a quantitative dimension (such as length).

service learning   A form of education that promotes social responsibility and service to the community.

sexually transmitted infections (STIs)   Infections contracted primarily through sexual contact, including oral-genital and anal-genital contact.

short-term memory   The memory component in which individuals retain information for up to 30 seconds, assuming there is no rehearsal of the information.

sirtuins   A family of proteins that have been proposed as having important influences on longevity, mitochondrial functioning in energy, calorie restriction benefits, stress resistance, and a lower incidence of cardiovascular functioning.

slow-to-warm-up child   A child who has a low activity level, is somewhat negative, and displays a low intensity of mood.

social cognitive theory of gender   A theory emphasizing that children's gender development occurs through the observation and imitation of gender behavior and through the rewards and punishments children experience for gender-appropriate and gender-inappropriate behavior.

social cognitive theory   The theory that behavior, environment, and person/cognitive factors are important in understanding development.

social constructivist approach   An approach that emphasizes the social contexts of learning and that knowledge is mutually built and constructed. Vygotsky's theory reflects this approach.

social contract or utility and individual rights   The fifth Kohlberg stage. At this stage, individuals reason that values, rights, and principles undergird or transcend the law.

social conventional reasoning   Thoughts about social consensus and convention, in contrast with moral reasoning, which stresses ethical issues.

social play   Play that involves social interactions with peers.

social policy   A national government's course of action designed to promote the welfare of its citizens.

social referencing   "Reading" emotional cues in others to help determine how to act in a particular situation.

social role theory   A theory that gender differences result from the contrasting roles of men and women.

social smile   A smile in response to an external stimulus, which, early in development, typically is a face.

social systems morality   The fourth stage in Kohlberg's theory of moral development. Moral judgments are based on understanding the social order, law, justice, and duty.

socioeconomic status (SES)   Refers to the conceptual grouping of people with similar occupational, educational, and economic characteristics.

socioemotional processes   Changes in an individual's relationships with other people, emotions, and personality.

socioemotional selectivity theory   The theory that older adults become more selective about their social networks. Because they place a high value on emotional satisfaction, older adults often prefer to spend time with familiar individuals with whom they have had rewarding relationships.

stability-change issue   The debate about the degree to which early traits and characteristics persist through life or change.

stagnation   Sometimes called "self-absorption," this state of mind develops when individuals sense that they have done little or nothing for the next generation; this is the negative side of Erikson's generativity versus stagnation middle adulthood stage.

standardized test   A test that is given with uniform procedures for administration and scoring.

Strange Situation   An observational measure of infant attachment that requires the infant to move through a series of introductions, separations, and reunions with the caregiver and an adult stranger in a prescribed order.

stranger anxiety   An infant's fear and wariness of strangers that typically appears in the second half of the first year of life.

strategies   Deliberate mental activities designed to improve the processing of information.

sudden infant death syndrome (SIDS)   A condition that occurs when an infant stops breathing, usually during the night, and suddenly dies without an apparent cause.

sustained attention   Also referred to as vigilance; involves focused and extended engagement with an object, task, event, or other aspect of the environment.

symbolic function substage   Piaget's first substage of preoperational thought, in which the child gains the ability to mentally represent an object that is not present (between about 2 and 4 years of age).

syntax   The ways words are combined to form acceptable phrases and sentences.

T

telegraphic speech   The use of short and precise words without grammatical markers such as articles, auxiliary verbs, and other connectives.

temperament   An individual's behavioral style and characteristic way of responding emotionally.

tend-and-befriend   Taylor's view that when women experience stress, they are more likely to seek social alliances with others, especially female friends.

teratogen   Any agent that can potentially cause a birth defect or negatively alter cognitive and behavioral outcomes.

theory   A coherent set of ideas that helps to explain data and to make predictions.

theory of mind   Refers to the awareness of one's own mental processes and the mental processes of others.

thinking   Manipulating and transforming information in memory.

top-dog phenomenon   The circumstance of moving from the top position in elementary school to the lowest position in middle or junior high school.

transgender   A broad term that refers to individuals whose gender identity or behavior is either completely or partially at odds with the sex into which they were born.

transitivity The ability to logically combine relations to understand certain conclusions.

triarchic theory of intelligence Sternberg's theory that intelligence consists of analytical intelligence, creative intelligence, and practical intelligence.

twin study A study in which the behavioral similarity of identical twins is compared with the behavioral similarity of fraternal twins.

U

universal ethical principles The sixth and highest stage in Kohlberg's theory of moral development. Individuals develop a moral standard based on universal human rights.

V

visual preference method A method developed by Fantz to determine whether infants can distinguish one stimulus from another by measuring the length of time they attend to different stimuli.

Vygotsky's theory A sociocultural cognitive theory that emphasizes how culture and social interaction guide cognitive development.

W

whole-language approach An approach to reading instruction based on the idea that instruction should parallel children's natural language learning. Reading materials should be whole and meaningful.

wisdom Expert knowledge about the practical aspects of life that permits excellent judgment about important matters.

working memory Closely related to short-term memory but places more emphasis on mental work. Working memory is like a mental "workbench" where individuals can manipulate and assemble information when making decisions, solving problems, and deciphering written and spoken language.

Z

zone of proximal development (ZPD) Vygotsky's term for tasks that are too difficult for children to master alone but can be mastered with assistance.

A

AAP (2000). Changing concepts of sudden infant death syndrome. *Pediatrics, 105,* 650–656.

AARP (2004). *The divorce experience: A study of divorce at midlife and beyond.* Washington, DC: AARP.

Aazami, S., Shamsuddin, K., & Akmal, S. (2015). Examining behavioral coping strategies as mediators between work-family conflict and psychological distress. *Scientific World Journal, 2015,* 343075.

Abbott, A. (2003). Restless nights, listless days. *Nature, 425,* 896–898.

ABC News (2005, December 12). Larry Page and Sergey Brin. Available at http://abcnews.go.com?Entertainment/12/8/05.

Abel, T., Havekes, R., Saletin, J.M., & Walker, M.P. (2013). Sleep, plasticity, and memory from molecules to whole-brain networks. *Current Biology, 23,* R774–R788.

Abels, M., & Hutman, T. (2015). Infants' behavioral styles in joint attention situations and parents' socioeconomic status. *Infant Behavior and Development, 40,* 139–150.

Accornero, V.H., Anthony, J.C., Morrow, C.E., Xue, L., & Bandstra, E.S. (2006). Prenatal cocaine exposure: An examination of childhood externalizing and internalizing behavior problems at age 7 years. *Epidemiology, Psychiatry, and Society, 15,* 20–29.

Ackerman, J.P., Riggins, T., & Black, M.M. (2010). A review of the effects of prenatal cocaine exposure among school-aged children. *Pediatrics, 125,* 554–565.

Adams, A. (2015). A cultural historical theoretical perspective of discourse and design in the science classroom. *Cultural Studies of Science Education, 10,* 329–338.

Adams, G.C., & McWilliams, L.A. (2015). Relationships between adult attachment style ratings and sleep disturbances in a nationally representative sample. *Journal of Psychosomatic Research, 79,* 37–42.

Adams, S.M., Ward, C.E., & Garcia, K.L. (2015). Sudden infant death syndrome. *American Family Physician, 91,* 778–783.

Adkins, D.E., Daw, J.K., McClay, J.L., & van den Oord, E.J. (2012). The influence of five monoamine genes on trajectories of depressive symptoms across adolescence and young adulthood. *Development and Psychopathology, 24,* 267–285.

Administration for Children & Families (2008). *Statistical fact sheet fiscal year 2008.* Washington, DC: Author.

Administration on Aging (2014). *A profile of older Americans: 2014.* Washington, DC: U.S. Department of Health and Human Services.

Adolescent Sleep Working Group, AAP (2014). School start times for adolescents. *Pediatrics, 134,* 642–649.

Adolph, K.E. (1997). Learning in the development of infant locomotion. *Monographs of the Society for Research in Child Development, 62*(3, Serial No. 251).

Adolph, K.E. (2010). Perceptual learning. Retrieved January 10, 2010, from http://www.psych.nyu.edu/adolph/research1.php

Adolph, K.E., & Berger, S.E. (2005). Physical and motor development. In M.H. Bornstein &

M.E. Lamb (Eds.), *Developmental psychology* (5th ed.). Mahwah, NJ: Erlbaum.

Adolph, K.E., & Berger, S.E. (2016). Physical and motor development. In M.H. Bornstein & M.E. Lamb (Eds.), *Developmental Science* (7th ed.). New York: Psychology Press.

Adolph, K.E., & Kretch, K.S. (2015). Gibson's theory of perceptual learning. In J.D. Wright (Ed.), *International encyclopedia of the social and behavioral sciences* (2nd ed.). New York: Elsevier.

Adolph, K.E., & Robinson, S.R.R. (2015). Motor development. In R. Lerner (Ed.), *Handbook of child psychology and developmental science* (7th ed.). New York: Wiley.

Agency for Healthcare Research and Quality (2007). *Evidence report/Technology assessment Number 153: Breastfeeding and maternal and health outcomes in developed countries.* Rockville, MD: U.S. Department of Health and Human Services.

Agerup, T., Lydersen, S., Wallander, J., & Sund, A.M. (2015). Associations between parental attachment and course of depression between adolescence and young adulthood. *Child Psychiatry and Human Development, 46,* 632–642.

Aggarwal, N.T., & others (2014). Perceived stress and change in cognitive function among adults 65 years and older. *Psychosomatic Medicine, 76,* 80–85.

Agras, W.S., & others (2004). Report of the National Institutes of Health workshop on overcoming barriers to treatment research in anorexia nervosa. *International Journal of Eating Disorders, 35,* 509–521.

Agricola, E., & others (2016, in press). Investigating paternal preconception risk factors for adverse pregnancy outcomes in a population of Internet users. *Reproductive Health.*

Ahlemeyer, J., & Mahon, S. (2015). Doulas for childbearing women. *MCN: The American Journal of Maternal/Child Nursing, 40,* 122–127.

Aichele, S., Rabbitt, P., & Ghisletta, P. (2015). Life span decrements in fluid intelligence and processing speed predict mortality risk. *Psychology and Aging, 30,* 598–612.

Aichele, S., Rabbitt, P., & Ghisletta, P. (2016). Think fast, feel fine, live long: A 29-year study of cognition, health, and survival in middle-aged and older adults. *Psychological Science, 27,* 518–529.

Ainsworth, M.D.S. (1979). Infant-mother attachment. *American Psychologist, 34,* 932–937.

Aires, L., & others (2016, in press). Exercise intervention and cardiovascular risk factors in obese children. Comparison between obese youngsters taking part in a physical activity school-based program with and without individualized diet counseling: The ACORDA project. *Annals of Human Biology.*

Ajetunmobi, O.M., & others (2015). Breastfeeding is associated with reduced childhood hospitalization: Evidence from a Scottish birth cohort (1997–2009). *Journal of Pediatrics, 166,* 620–625.

Akbari, A., & others (2011). Parity and breastfeeding are preventive measures against breast cancer in Iranian women. *Breast Cancer, 18,* 51–55.

Akbarzadeh, M., Masoudi, Z., Zare, N., & Vazin, F. (2015). Comparison of the effects of doula supportive care and acupressure at the BL32 point on the mother's anxiety level and delivery outcome.

Iranian Journal of Nursing and Midwifery Research, 20, 239–246.

Akhtar, N., & Herold, K. (2008). Pragmatic development. In M.M. Haith & J.B. Benson (Eds.), *Encyclopedia of infant and early childhood development.* Oxford, UK: Elsevier.

Akincilar, S.C., Unal, B., & Tergaonkar, V. (2016). Reactivation of telomerase in cancer. *Cellular and Molecular Life Sciences, 73,* 1659–1670.

Aksglaede, L., & others (2013). 47, XXY Klinefelter syndrome: Clinical characteristics and age-specific recommendations for medical management. *American Journal of Medical Genetics C: Seminars in Medical Genetics, 163,* 55–63.

Alberga, A.S., & others (2012). Healthy eating, aerobic and resistance training in youth (HEARTY): Study rationale, design, and methods. *Contemporary Clinical Trials, 33,* 839–847.

Albert, D., & Steinberg, L. (2011a). Judgment and decision making in adolescence. *Journal of Research on Adolescence, 21,* 211–224.

Albert, D., & Steinberg, L. (2011b). Peer influences on adolescent risk behavior. In M. Bardo, D. Fishbein, & R. Milich (Eds.), *Inhibitory control and drug abuse prevention: From research to translation.* New York: Springer.

Alberts, E., Elkind, D., & Ginsberg, S. (2007). The personal fable and risk taking in early adolescence. *Journal of Youth and Adolescence, 36,* 71–76.

Aldercotte, A., White, N., & Hughes, C. (2016). Sibling and peer relationships in early childhood. In L. Balter & C.S. Tamis-Lemonda (Eds.), *Child psychology* (3rd ed.). New York: Routledge.

Alderson-Day, B., & Fernyhough, C. (2014). More than one voice: Investigating the phenomenological properties of inner speech requires a variety of methods. *Consciousness and Cognition, 24,* 113–114.

Alegret, M., & others (2014). Cognitive, genetic, and brain perfusion factors associated with four-year incidence of Alzheimer's disease from mild cognitive impairment. *Journal of Alzheimer's Disease., 41,*739–748.

Alexander, B.T., Dasinger, J.H., & Intapad, S. (2015). Fetal programming and cardiovascular pathology. *Comprehensive Physiology, 5,* 997–1025.

Allameh, Z., Tehrani, H.G., & Ghasemi, M. (2015). Comparing the impact of acupuncture and pethidine on reducing labor pain. *Advanced Biomedical Research, 4,* 46.

Allemand, M., Zimprich, D., & Hendriks, A.A.J. (2008). Age differences in five personality domains across the life span. *Developmental Psychology, 44,* 758–770.

Allen, J.O. (2016, in press). Ageism as a risk factor for chronic disease. *Gerontologist.*

Allen, J.P., & Miga, E.M. (2010). Attachment in adolescence: A move to the level of emotion regulation. *Journal of Social and Personal Relationships, 27,* 226–234.

Allen, J.P., & others (2009, April). *Portrait of the secure teen as an adult.* Paper presented at the meeting of the Society for Research in Child Development, Denver.

Allen, J.P., & Tan, J. (2016). The multiple facets of attachment in adolescence. In J. Cassidy &

P.R. Shaver (Eds.), *Handbook of attachment* (3rd ed.). New York: Guilford.

Allen, R.S., & others (2016). "It was very rewarding for me . . .": Senior volunteers' experiences with implementing a reminiscence and creativity activity intervention. *Gerontologist, 56,* 357–367.

Allen, T.D., & Finkelstein, L.M. (2014). Work-family conflict among members of full-time dual-earner couples: An examination of family life stage, gender, and age. *Journal of Occupational Health Psychology, 19,* 376–384.

Allington, R.L. (2015). *What really matters for middle school readers.* Upper Saddle River, NJ: Pearson.

Alm, B., Wennergren, G., Mollborg, P., & Lagercrantz, H. (2016). Breastfeeding and dummy use have a protective effect on sudden infant death syndrome. *Acta Pediatrica, 105,* 31–38.

Almehmadi, Y., Yassin, A.A., Nettleship, J.E., & Saad, F. (2016). Testosterone replacement therapy improves the health-related quality of life of men diagnosed with late-onset hypogonadism. *Arab Journal of Urology, 14,* 31–36.

Almeida, D.M., & Horn, M.C. (2004). Is daily life more stressful during middle adulthood? In C.D. Ryff & R.C. Kessler (Eds.), *A portrait of midlife in the United States.* Chicago: University of Chicago Press.

Almeida, N.D., & others (2016, in press). Risk of miscarriage in women receiving antidepressants in early pregnancy, correcting for induced abortions. *Epidemiology.*

Almquist, Y.B., & Brannstrom, L. (2014). Childhood peer status and the clustering of social, economic, and health-related circumstances in adulthood. *Social Science & Medicine, 105,* 67–75.

Alzheimer's Association (2010). 2010 Alzheimer's disease facts and figures. *Alzheimer's Disease & Dementia, 6,* 158–194.

Alzheimer's Association (2014). *2014 Alzheimer's disease facts and figures.* Chicago: Alzheimer's Association.

Amato, P.R., & Anthony, C.J. (2014). Estimating the effects of parental divorce and death with fixed effects models. *Journal of Marriage and the Family, 76,* 370–386.

Ambrose, D., & Sternberg, R.J. (2016a, in press). *Giftedness and talent in the 21st century.* Rotterdam, The Netherlands: Sense Publishers.

Ambrose, D., & Sternberg, R.J. (2016b, in press). Previewing a collaborative exploration of giftedness and talent in the 21st century. In D. Ambrose & R.J. Sternberg (Eds.), *Giftedness and talent in the 21st century.* Rotterdam, The Netherlands: Sense Publishers.

American Academy of Pediatrics Section on Breastfeeding (2012). Breastfeeding and the use of human milk. *Pediatrics, 129,* e827–e841.

American Pregnancy Association (2016). *Promoting pregnancy wellness.* Retrieved April 30, 2016, from www.americanpregnancy.org

American Psychiatric Association (2013). *DSM-V.* Arlington, VA: Author.

American Psychological Association (2003). *Psychology: Scientific problem solvers.* Washington, DC: Author.

American Psychological Association (2007). *Stress in America.* Washington, DC: American Psychological Association.

Amialchuk, A., & Gerhardinger, L. (2015). Contraceptive use and pregnancies in adolescents'

romantic relationships: Role of relationship activities and parental attitudes and communication. *Journal of Developmental and Behavioral Pediatrics, 36,* 86–97.

Amsterdam, B.K. (1968). *Mirror behavior in children under two years of age.* Unpublished doctoral dissertation, University of North Carolina, Chapel Hill.

Andel, R., Finkel, D., & Pedersen, N.L. (2016, in press). Effects of preretirement work complexity and postretirement leisure activity on cognitive aging. *Journals of Gerontology B: Psychological Sciences and Social Sciences.*

Andersen, S.L., Sebastiani, P., Dworkis, D.A., Feldman, L., & Perls, T.T. (2012). Health span approximates life span among many supercentenarians: Compression of morbidity at the approximate limit of life span. *Journals of Gerontology A: Biological Sciences and Medical Sciences, 67A,* 395–405.

Anderson, E., Greene, S.M., Hetherington, E.M., & Clingempeel, W.G. (1999). The dynamics of parental remarriage. In E.M. Hetherington (Ed.), *Coping with divorce, single parenting, and remarriage.* Mahwah, NJ: Erlbaum.

Anderson, E.R., & Greene, S.M. (2011). "My child and I are a package deal": Balancing adult and child concerns in repartnering after divorce. *Journal of Family Psychology, 25,* 741–750.

Anderson, S.B., & Guthery, A.M. (2015). Mindfulness-based psychoeducation for parents of children with attention-deficit/hyperactivity disorder: An applied clinical project. *Journal of Child and Adolescent Psychiatric Nursing, 28,* 43–49.

Anderson, S.E., Gooze, R.A., Lemeshow, S., & Whitaker, R.C. (2012). Quality of early maternal-child relationship and risk of adolescent obesity. *Pediatrics, 129,* 132–140.

Anderson, W.G. (2015). Quantifying the value of palliative care and advance care planning. *Critical Care Medicine, 43,* 1147–1149.

Andersson, H., & Bergman, L.R. (2011). The role of task persistence in young adolescence for successful educational and occupational attainment in middle adulthood. *Developmental Psychology, 47,* 950–960.

Andrews, S.J., Lamb, M.E., & Lyon, T.D. (2016, in press). The effects of question repetition on responses when prosecutors and defense attorneys question children alleging sexual abuse in court. *Law and Human Behavior.*

Andriani, H., Liao, C.Y., & Kuo, H.W. (2015). Parental weight changes as key predictors of child weight changes. *BMC Public Health, 15,* 645.

Angel, J.L., Mudrazija, S., & Benson, R. (2016). Racial and ethnic inequalities in health. In L.K. George & K.F. Ferraro (Eds.), *Handbook of aging and the social sciences* (8th ed.). New York: Elsevier.

Angel, L., Fay, S., Bouazzaoui, B., & Isingrini, M. (2011). Two hemispheres for better memory in old age: Role of executive functioning. *Journal of Cognitive Neuroscience, 23,* 3767–3777.

Anglin, D.M., & others (2016, in press). Ethnic identity, racial discrimination, and attenuated psychotic symptoms in an urban population of emerging adults. *Early Intervention in Psychiatry.*

Anguera, J.A., & others (2013). Video game training enhances cognitive control in older adults. *Nature, 501,* 97–101.

Ansari, A., & Gershoff, E. (2016). Parent involvement in Head Start and children's development:

Indirect effects through parenting. *Journal of Marriage and the Family, 76,* 562–579.

Ansari, J., Carvalho, B., Shafer, S.L., & Flood, P. (2016). Pharmacokinetics and pharmacodynamics of drugs commonly used in pregnancy and parturition. *Anesthesia and Analgesia, 122,* 786–804.

Anthony, E.G., Kritz-Silverstein, D., & Barrett-Connor, E. (2016, in press). Optimism and mortality in older men and women: The Rancho Bernardo Study. *Journal of Aging Research.*

Antonenko, D., & Floel, A. (2014). Healthy aging by staying selectively connected: A mini-review. *Gerontology, 60*(1), 3–9.

Antonucci, T.C., & others (2016). Society and the individual at the dawn of the twenty-first century. In K.W. Schaie & S.L. Willis (Eds.), *Handbook of the psychology of aging* (8th ed.). New York: Elsevier.

Antonucci, T.C., Lansford, J.E., & Akiyama, H. (2001). The impact of positive and negative aspects of marital relationships and friendships on the well-being of older adults. In J.P. Reinhardt (Ed.), *Negative and positive support.* Mahwah, NJ: Erlbaum.

Antonucci, T.C., Vandewater, E.A., & Lansford, J.E. (2000). Adulthood and aging: Social processes and development. In A. Kazdin (Ed.), *Encyclopedia of psychology.* Washington, DC, and New York: American Psychological Association and Oxford University Press.

Anyaegbu, E., & Dharnidharka, V.R. (2014). Hypertension in the teenagers. *Pediatric Clinics of North America, 61,* 131–151.

Anzures, G., Goyet, L., Ganea, N., & Johnson, M.H. (2016). Enhanced ERPs to visual stimuli in unaffected male siblings of ASD children. *Child Neuropsychology, 22,* 220–227.

Araujo, L., Ribeiro, O., Teixeira, L., & Paul, C. (2016). Successful aging at 100 years: The relevance of subjectivity and psychological resources. *International Psychogeriatrics, 28,* 179–188.

Archer, J.A., Lee, A., Qui, A., & Chen, S.H. (2016). A comprehensive analysis of connectivity and aging over the adult lifespan. *Brain Connectivity, 6,* 169–185.

Arenaza-Urquijo, E.M., Wirth, M., & Chetelet, G. (2015). Cognitive reserve and lifestyle: Moving toward preclinical Alzheimer's disease. *Frontiers in Aging Neuroscience, 7,* 134.

Ariceli, G., Castro, J., Cesena, J., & Toro, J. (2005). Anorexia nervosa in male adolescents: Body image, eating attitudes, and psychological traits. *Journal of Adolescent Health, 36,* 221–226.

Arkes, J. (2015). The temporal effects of divorces and separations on children's academic achievement and problem behavior. *Journal of Divorce and Remarriage, 56,* 25–42.

Arnett, J.J. (2006). Emerging adulthood: Understanding the new way of coming of age. In J.J. Arnett & J.L. Tanner (Eds.), *Emerging adults in America.* Washington, DC: American Psychological Association.

Arnett, J.J. (2010). Oh, grow up! Generational grumbling and the new life stage of emerging adulthood—Commentary on Trzesniewski & Donnellan (2010). *Perspectives on Psychological Science, 5,* 89–92.

Arnett, J.J. (Ed.) (2012). *Adolescent psychology around the world.* New York: Psychology Press.

Arnett, J.J. (2015a). *Emerging adulthood* (2nd ed.). New York: Oxford University Press.

Arnett, J.J. (2015b). Identity development from adolescence to emerging adulthood: What we know and (especially) don't know. In K.C. McLean & M. Syed (Eds.), *Oxford handbook of identity development*. New York: Oxford University Press.

Arnett, J.J., & Padilla-Walker, L.M. (2015). Brief report: Danish emerging adults' conceptions of adulthood. *Journal of Adolescence, 38,* 39–44.

Arnold, K., & others (2013). Fetal alcohol spectrum disorders: Knowledge and screening practices of university hospital medical students and residents. *Journal of Population Therapeutics and Clinical Pharmacology, 20,* e18–e25.

Aron, A., Aron, E., & Coups, E. (2017). *REVEL for statistics for psychology* (6th ed.). Upper Saddle River, NJ: Pearson.

Aronson, E. (1986, August). *Teaching students things they think they already know about: The case of prejudice and desegregation.* Paper presented at the meeting of the American Psychological Association, Washington, DC.

Arterberry, M.E. (2008). Perceptual development. In M.E. Haith & J.B. Benson (Eds.), *Encyclopedia of infant and early childhood development*. Oxford, UK: Elsevier.

Asero, P., & others (2014). Relevance of genetic investigation in male infertility. *Journal of Endocrinological Investigation, 37*(5), 415–427.

Asghari, M., & others (2016, in press). Effect of aerobic exercise and nutrition education on quality of life and early menopause symptoms: A randomized controlled trial. *Women and Health.*

Asheer, S., & others (2014). Engaging pregnant and parenting teens: Early challenges and lessons learned from the evaluation of adolescent pregnancy prevention approaches. *Journal of Adolescent health, 54*(3, Suppl.), S84–S91.

Aslin, R.N. (2012). Infant eyes: A window on cognitive development. *Infancy, 17,* 126–140.

Aslin, R.N., Jusczyk, P.W., & Pisoni, D.B. (1998). Speech and auditory processing during infancy: Constraints on and precursors to language. In W. Damon (Ed.), *Handbook of child psychology* (5th ed., Vol. 2). New York: Wiley.

Aslin, R.N., & Lathrop, A.L. (2008). Visual perception. In M. Haith & J. Benson (Eds.), *Handbook of infant and early childhood development*. London: Elsevier.

Aspen Institute (2013). *Two generations, one future.* Washington, DC: Aspen Institute.

Assini-Meytin, L.C., & Green, K.M. (2015). Long-term consequences of adolescent parenthood among African-American youth: A propensity score matching approach. *Journal of Adolescent Health, 56,* 529–535.

Associated Press–NORC Center for Public Affairs Research (2013). *Survey on later-life work.* Chicago: NORC Center for Public Affairs, University of Chicago.

Atashak, S., Stannard, S.R., & Azizbeigi, K. (2016, in press). Cardiovascular risk factors adaptation to concurrent training in overweight sedentary middle-aged men. *Journal of Sports Medicine and Physical Fitness.*

Atta, C.A., & others (2016). Global birth prevalence of spina bifida by folic acid fortification status: A systematic review and meta-analysis. *American Journal of Public Health, 106,* e24–e34.

Attar-Schwartz, S., Tan, J.P., Buchanan, A., Flouri, E., & Griggs, J. (2009). Grandparenting and adolescent development in two-parent biological,

lone-parent, and step-families. *Journal of Family Psychology, 23,* 67–75.

Audesirk, G., Audesirk, T., & Byers, B.E. (2017). *Biology* (11th ed.). Upper Saddle River, NJ: Pearson.

Avinun, R., & Knafo-Noma, A. (2015). Socialization, genetics, and their interplay in development. In J.E. Grusec & P.D. Hastings (Eds.), *Handbook of socialization* (2nd ed.). New York: Guilford.

Avis, N.E., & others (2009). Longitudinal changes in sexual functioning as women transition through menopause: Results from the Study of Women's Health Across the Nation. *Menopause, 16,* 442–452.

Avvenuti, G., Baiardini, I., & Giaradin, A. (2016). Optimism's explicative role for chronic diseases. *Frontiers in Psychology, 7,* 295.

Ayoub, C., Vallotton, C.D., & Mastergeorge, A.M. (2011). Developmental pathways to integrated social skills: The role of parenting and early intervention. *Child Development, 82,* 583–600.

Azagba, S., & Sharaf, M.F. (2014). Physical inactivity among older Canadian adults. *Journal of Physical Activity and Health, 11*(1), 99–108.

Azmitia, M. (2015). Reflections on the cultural lenses of identity development. In K.C. McLean & M. Syed (Eds.), *Oxford handbook of identity development.* New York: Oxford University Press.

B

Baber, R.J., & others (2016). 2016 IMS recommendations on women's midlife health and menopause hormone therapy. *Climacteric, 19,* 109–150.

Baca Zinn, M., Eitzen, D.S., & Wells, B. (2016). *REVEL for diversity in families* (10th ed.). Upper Saddle River, NJ: Pearson.

Bach, L.E., Mortimer, J.A., Vandeweerd, C., & Corvin, J. (2013). The association of physical and mental health with sexual activity in older adults in a retirement community. *Journal of Sexual Medicine, 10*(11), 2671–2678.

Bachman, J.G., & others (2002). *The decline of substance abuse in young adulthood.* Mahwah, NJ: Erlbaum.

Bachman, J.G., & others (2008). *The education-drug use connection.* Clifton, NJ: Psychology Press.

Bacikova-Sleskova, M., Benka, J., & Orosova, O. (2015). Parental employment status and adolescents' health: The role of financial situation, parent-adolescent relationship, and adolescents' resilience. *Psychology and Health, 30,* 400–422.

Baddeley, A.D. (1990). *Human memory: Theory and practice.* Boston: Allyn & Bacon.

Baddeley, A.D. (2001). *Is working memory still working?* Paper presented at the meeting of the American Psychological Association, San Francisco.

Baddeley, A.D. (2007). *Working memory, thought, and action.* New York: Oxford University Press.

Baddeley, A.D. (2010). Working memory. *Current Biology, 20,* 136–140.

Baddeley, A.D. (2012). Working memory: Theories, models, and controversies. *Annual Review of Psychology* (Vol. 63). Palo Alto, CA: Annual Reviews.

Baddeley, A.D. (2013). On applying cognitive psychology. *British Journal of Psychology, 104,* 443–456.

Baer, J., & Kaufman, J.C. (2013). *Being creative inside and outside the classroom.* Rotterdam, The Netherlands: Sense Publishers.

Bahrick, L.E. (2010). Intermodal perception and selective attention to intersensory redundancy:

Implications for social development and autism. In J.G. Bremner & T.D. Wachs (Eds.), *Wiley-Blackwell handbook of infant development* (2nd ed.). New York: Wiley.

Bahrick, L.E., & Hollich, G. (2008). Intermodal perception. In M.M. Haith & J.B. Benson (Eds.), *Encyclopedia of infant and early childhood development.* Oxford, UK: Elsevier.

Bailey, A.L., Osipova, A., & Kelly, K.R. (2016). Language development. In L. Corno & E.M. Anderman (Eds.), *Handbook of educational psychology* (3rd ed.). New York: Routledge.

Bailey, H.R., Dunlosky, J., & Hertzog, C. (2014). Does strategy training reduce age-related deficits in working memory? *Gerontology, 60,* 346–356.

Bailey, J.N., & others (2016, in press). Genome-wide association analysis identifies TXNRD2, ATXN2, and FOXC1 as susceptibility loci for primary open-angle glaucoma. *Nature Genetics.*

Baillargeon, R. (2004). The acquisition of physical knowledge in infancy: A summary in eight lessons. In U. Goswami (Ed.), *Blackwell handbook of childhood cognitive development.* Malden, MA: Blackwell.

Baillargeon, R. (2014). Cognitive development in infancy. *Annual Review of Psychology* (Vol. 65). Palo Alto, CA: Annual Reviews.

Baillargeon, R., & others (2012). Object individuation and physical reasoning in infancy: An integrative account. *Language, Learning, and Development, 8,* 4–46.

Bajoghli, H., & others (2014). "I love you more than I can stand!"—romantic love, symptoms of depression and anxiety, and sleep complaints are related among young adults. *International Journal of Psychiatry in Clinical Practice, 18,* 169–174.

Bakeman, R., & Brown, J.V. (1980). Early interaction: Consequences for social and mental development at three years. *Child Development, 51,* 437–447.

Baker, J.H., Thorton, L.M., Lichtenstein, P., & Bulik, C.M. (2012). Pubertal development predicts eating behaviors in adolescents. *International Journal of Eating Disorders, 45*(7), 819–826.

Baker, J.K., Fenning, R.M., & Crnic, K.A. (2011). Emotion socialization by mothers and fathers: Coherence among behaviors and associations with parent attitudes and children's competence. *Social Development, 20,* 412–430.

Baker, R.K., Pettigrew, T.L., & Poulin-Dubois, D. (2014). Infants' ability to associate motion paths with object kinds. *Infant Behavior and Development, 37,* 119–129.

Bakermans-Kranenburg, M.J., & van IJzendoorn, M.H. (2011). Differential susceptibility to rearing environment depending on dopamine-related genes: New evidence and a meta-analysis. *Development and Psychopathology, 23,* 39–52.

Bakermans-Kranenburg, M.J., & van IJzendoorn, M.H. (2016). Attachment, parenting, and genetics. In J. Cassidy & P.R. Shaver (Eds.), *Handbook of parenting* (3rd ed.). New York: Guilford.

Bale, T.L. (2015). Epigenetic and transgenerational reprogramming of brain development. *Nature Reviews Neuroscience, 16,* 332–344.

Balk, D. (2016). Psychology of death and dying. In K.W. Schaie & S.L. Willis (Eds.), *Handbook of the psychology of aging* (8th ed.). New York: Elsevier.

Ball, J.W., Bindler, R.C., & Cowen, K.J. (2014). *Child health nursing* (3rd ed.). Upper Saddle River, NJ: Pearson.

Ballesteros, S., Kraft, E., Santana, S., & Tziraki, C. (2015). Maintaining older brain functionality: A targeted review. *Neuroscience and Biobehavioral Reviews, 55,* 453–477.

Balon, R., & Morreale, M.K. (2016, in press). In search of meaning: What makes life worth living in the face of death. *Academic Psychiatry.*

Balsa, A.I., Giuliano, L.M., & French, M.T. (2011). The effects of alcohol use on academic achievement in high school. *Economics of Education Review, 30,* 1–15.

Baltes, P.B. (1987). Theoretical propositions of life-span developmental psychology: On the dynamics between growth and decline. *Developmental Psychology, 23,* 611–626.

Baltes, P.B. (2003). On the incomplete architecture of human ontogeny: Selection, optimization, and compensation as foundation of developmental theory. In U.M. Staudinger & U. Lindenberger (Eds.), *Understanding human development.* Boston: Kluwer.

Baltes, P.B., Lindenberger, U., & Staudinger, U. (2006). Life span theory in developmental psychology. In W. Damon & R. Lerner (Eds.), *Handbook of child psychology* (6th ed.). New York: Wiley.

Baltes, P.B., Reuter-Lorene, P., & Rösler, F. (Eds.). (2006). *Lifespan development and the brain.* New York: Cambridge University Press.

Baltes, P.B., & Smith, J. (2003). New frontiers in the future of aging: From successful aging of the young to the dilemmas of the fourth age. *Gerontology, 49,* 123–135.

Bamaca-Colbert, M., Umana-Taylor, A.J., Espinosa-Hernandez, G., & Brown, A.M. (2012). Behavioral autonomy expectations among Mexican-origin mother-daughter dyads: An examination of within-group variability. *Journal of Adolescence, 35,* 691–700.

Bandura, A. (1986). *Social foundations of thought and action: A social cognitive theory.* Englewood Cliffs, NJ: Prentice Hall.

Bandura, A. (1998, August). *Swimming against the mainstream: Accentuating the positive aspects of humanity.* Paper presented at the meeting of the American Psychological Association, San Francisco.

Bandura, A. (2001). Social cognitive theory. *Annual Review of Psychology.* Palo Alto, CA: Annual Reviews.

Bandura, A. (2004, May). *Toward a psychology of human agency.* Paper presented at the meeting of the American Psychological Society, Chicago.

Bandura, A. (2006). Toward a psychology of human agency. *Perspectives on Psychological Science, 1,* 164–180.

Bandura, A. (2010a). Self-efficacy. In D. Matsumoto (Ed.), *Cambridge dictionary of psychology.* New York: Cambridge University Press.

Bandura, A. (2010b). Vicarious learning. In D. Matsumoto (Ed.), *Cambridge dictionary of psychology.* New York: Cambridge University Press.

Bandura, A. (2012). Social cognitive theory. *Annual Review of Clinical Psychology* (Vol. 8). Palo Alto, CA: Annual Reviews.

Bandura, A. (2016). *Moral disengagement.* New York: Worth.

Band-Winterstein, T. (2015). Health care provision for older persons: The interplay between ageism and elder neglect. *Journal of Applied Gerontology, 34,* NP113–NP127.

Banerjee, S. (2011). Hearing aids in the real world: Use of multimemory and multivolume controls. *Journal of the American Academy of Audiology, 22,* 359–374.

Banja, J. (2005). Talking to the dying. *Case Manager, 16,* 37–39.

Bank, L., Burraston, B., & Snyder, J. (2004). Sibling conflict and ineffective parenting as predictors of adolescent boys' antisocial behavior and peer difficulties: Additive and interactive effects. *Journal of Research on Adolescence. 14,* 99–125.

Banks, J.A. (2015). *Cultural diversity and education* (6th ed.). Upper Saddle River, NJ: Pearson.

Banks, M.S., & Salapatek, P. (1983). Infant visual perception. In P.H. Mussen (Ed.), *Handbook of child psychology* (4th ed., Vol. 2). New York: Wiley.

Barahona-Correa, J.B., & Filipe, C.N. (2016). A concise history of Asperger syndrome: The short reign of a troublesome diagnosis. *Frontiers in Psychology, 6,* 2024.

Barakat, R., & others (2011). Exercise during pregnancy improves maternal health perception: A randomized controlled trial. *American Journal of Obstetrics and Gynecology, 204,* e1–e7.

Barakat, R., Perales, M., Garatachea, N., Ruiz, J.R., & Lucia, A. (2015). Exercise during pregnancy. A narrative review asking: What do we know? *British Journal of Sports Medicine, 49,* 1377–1381.

Baraket, R., & others (2016, in press). Exercise during pregnancy protects against hypertension and macrosomia: Randomized clinical trial. *American Journal of Obstetrics and Gynecology.*

Barger, M., Faucher, M.A., & Murphy, P.A. (2015). Part II: The centering pregnancy model of group prenatal care. *Journal of Midwifery and Women's Health, 60,* 211–213.

Barger, S.D., & Cribbet, M.R. (2016). Social support sources matter: Increased cellular aging among adults with unsupportive spouses. *Biological Psychiatry, 115,* 43–49.

Bargh, J.A., & McKenna, K.Y.A. (2004). The Internet and social life. *Annual Review of Psychology* (Vol. 55). Palo Alto, CA: Annual Reviews.

Barker, R., & Wright, H.F. (1951). *One boy's day.* New York: Harper & Row.

Barnes, J.N. (2015). Exercise, cognitive function, and aging. *Advances in Physiology Education, 39,* 55–62.

Barnett, W.S., & others (2006). Educational effectiveness of the Tools of the Mind curriculum: A randomized trial. New Brunswick, NJ: National Institute of Early Education Research, Rutgers University.

Baron, C. (2012). Using the gradient of human cortical bone properties to determine age-related bone changes via ultrasonic guided waves. *Ultrasound in Medicine and Biology, 38,* 972–981.

Baron, N.S. (1992). *Growing up with language.* Reading, MA: Addison-Wesley.

Barr, A.B., Simons, R.L., & Simons, L.G. (2015). Nonmarital relationshps and changing perceptions of marriage among African American young adults. *Journal of Marriage and the Family, 77,* 1202–1216.

Barr, E.M., & others (2014). New evidence: Data documenting parental support for earlier sexuality education. *Journal of School Health, 84,* 10–17.

Barron, R.S. (2015). Death: Past, present, and future. *Journal of Critical Care, 30,* 214–215.

Barry, L.C., & Byers, A.L. (2016). Risk factors and prevention: Strategies for late-life mood and anxiety disorders. In K.W. Schaie & S.L. Willis (Eds.), *Handbook of the psychology of aging* (8th ed.). New York: Elsevier.

Barstow, C., & Rerucha, C. (2015). Evaluation of short and tall stature children. *American Family Physician, 92,* 43–50.

Bartschat, S., Richter, C., Stiller, D., & Banshak, S. (2016). Long-term outcome in a case of shaken baby syndrome. *Medicine, Science, and the Law, 56,* 147–149.

Bates, J.E. (2012a). Temperament as a tool in promoting early childhood development. In S.L. Odom, E.P. Pungello, & N. Gardner-Neblett (Eds.), *Infants, toddlers, and families in poverty.* New York: Guilford University Press.

Bates, J.E. (2012b). Behavioral regulation as a product of temperament and environment. In S.L. Olson & A.J. Sameroff (Eds.), *Biopsychosocial regulatory processes in the development of childhood behavioral problems.* New York: Cambridge University Press.

Bates, J.E., & Pettit, G.S. (2015). Temperament, parenting, and social development. In J.E. Grusec & P.D. Hastings (Eds.), *Handbook of socialization* (2nd ed.). New York: Guilford.

Bateson, P. (2015). Human evolution and development: An ethological perspective. In R.M. Lerner (Ed.), *Handbook of child psychology and developmental science* (7th ed.). New York: Wiley.

Bauchner, H., & Fontanarosa, P.B. (2016). Death, dying, and the end of life. *JAMA, 315,* 270–271.

Bauer, A., Knapp, M., & Parsonage, M. (2016). Lifetime costs of perinatal anxiety and depression. *Journal of Affective Disorders, 192,* 83–90.

Bauer, M.E., & others (2013). Psychoneuroendocrine interventions aimed at attenuating immunosenescence. *Biogerontology, 14*(1), 9–20.

Bauer, P.J. (2009). Learning and memory: Like a horse and carriage. In A. Woodward & A. Needham (Eds.), *Learning and the infant mind.* New York: Oxford University Press.

Bauer, P.J. (2013). Memory. In P.D. Zelazo (Ed.), *Oxford handbook of developmental psychology.* New York: Oxford University Press.

Bauer, P.J. (2015). A complementary processes account of the development of childhood amnesia and a personal past. *Psychological Review, 122,* 204–231.

Bauer, P.J., & Fivush, R. (Eds.) (2014). *Wiley-Blackwell handbook of children's memory.* New York: Wiley.

Bauer, P.J., Hattenschwiler, N., & Larkina, M. (2016). "Owning" the personal past: Adolescents' and adults' autobiographical narratives and ratings of memory of recent and distant events. *Memory, 24,* 165–183.

Bauer, P.J., & Larkina, M. (2014). The onset of childhood amnesia in childhood: A prospective investigation of the course and determinants of forgetting of early-life events. *Memory, 22,* 907–924.

Bauer, P.J., & Larkina, M. (2016, in press). Childhood amnesia in the making: Different distributions of autobiographical memories in children and adolescents. *Journal of Experimental Psychology: General.*

Bauer, P.J., & Leventon, S.J. (2015). The development of declarative memory in infancy and implications for social learning. In S.D. Calkins (Ed.), *Handbook of biopsychosocial development.* New York: Guilford.

Bauer, P.J., Wenner, J.A., Dropik, P.I., & Wewerka, S.S. (2000). Parameters of remembering and forgetting in the transition from infancy to early childhood. *Monographs of the Society for Research in Child Development, 65*(4, Serial No. 263).

Bauman, R.W. (2015). *Microbiology with diseases by body system* (4th ed.). Upper Saddle River, NJ: Pearson.

Baumeister, R.F. (2013). Self-esteem. In E. Anderson (Ed.), *Psychology of classroom learning: An encyclopedia.* Detroit: Macmillan.

Baumgart, M., & others (2015). Summary of the evidence on modifiable risk factors for cognitive decline and dementia: A population-based perspective. *Alzheimer's and Dementia, 11*, 718–726.

Baumrind, D. (1971). Current patterns of parental authority. *Developmental Psychology Monographs, 4* (1, Pt. 2).

Beam, C.R., & others (2016). Widowhood and the stability of late life depressive symptomatology in the Swedish Adoption Twin Study of Aging. *Behavior Genetics, 46*, 100–113.

Bearman, S.K., Presnall, K., Martinez, E., & Stice, E. (2006). The skinny on body dissatisfaction: A longitudinal study of adolescent girls and boys. *Journal of Youth and Adolescence, 35*, 217–229.

Beart, P.M. (2016, in press). Synaptic signaling and its interface with neuropathologies: Snapshots from the past, present, and future. *Journal of Neurochemistry.*

Beaty, J.J., & Pratt, L. (2015). *Early literacy in preschool and kindergarten* (4th ed.). Upper Saddle River, NJ: Pearson.

Beaver, K.M., Vaughn, M.G., Wright, J.P., & Delisi, M. (2012). An interaction between perceived stress and 5HTTLPR genotype in the prediction of stable depressive symptomatology. *American Journal of Orthopsychiatry, 82*, 260–266.

Becker, D.R., Miao, A., Duncan, R., & McClelland, M.M. (2014). Behavioral self-regulation and executive function both predict visuomotor skills and early academic achievement. *Early Childhood Research Quarterly, 29*, 411–424.

Becker, M.W., Alzahabi, R., & Hopwood, C.J. (2013). Media multitasking is associated with symptoms of depression and social anxiety. *Cyberpsychology, Behavior, and Social Networking, 16*, 132–136.

Bedford, V.H. (2009). Sibling relationships: Adulthood. In D. Carr (Ed.), *Encyclopedia of the life course and human development.* Boston: Gale Cengage.

Bednar, R.L., Wells, M.G., & Peterson, S.R. (1995). *Self-esteem* (2nd ed.). Washington, DC: American Psychological Association.

Beets, M.W., & Foley, J.T. (2008). Association of father involvement and neighborhood quality with kindergartners' physical activity: A multilevel structural equation model. *American Journal of Health Promotion, 22*(3), 195–203.

Behrens, H. (2012). Grammatical categories. In E.L. Bavin (Ed.), *Cambridge handbook of child language.* New York: Cambridge University Press.

Bei, B., Coo, S., & Trinder, J. (2015). Sleep and mood during pregnancy and the postpartum period. *Sleep Medicine Clinics, 10*, 25–33.

Belk, C., & Borden Maier, V. (2016). *Biology* (5th ed.). Upper Saddle River, NJ: Pearson.

Bell, A.F., Erickson, E.N., & Carter, C.S. (2014). Beyond labor: The role of natural and synthetic oxytocin in the transition to motherhood. *Journal of Midwifery and Women's Health, 59*, 35–42.

Bell, M.A., & Cuevas, K. (2015). Psychobiology of executive function in early development. In J.A. Griffin, L.S. Freund, & P. McCardle (Eds.), *Executive function in preschool children.* Washington, DC: American Psychological Association.

Bell, R.D., & others (2012). Apolipoprotein E controls cerebrovascular integrity via cyclophillin. *Nature, 485*(7399), 512–516.

Bellini, C.V., & others (2016). How painful is a heel-prick or a venipuncture in a newborn? *Journal of Maternal-Fetal and Neonatal Medicine, 29*, 202–206.

Belsky, J. (1981). Early human experience: A family perspective. *Developmental Psychology, 17*, 3–23.

Belsky, J. (2016). The differential susceptibility hypothesis: Sensitivity to the environment for better or for worse. *JAMA Pediatrics, 170*, 321–322.

Belsky, J., & others (2015). Differential susceptibility to effects of maternal sensitivity? A study of candidate plasticity genes. *Development and Psychopathology, 27*, 725–746.

Belsky, J., & Pluess, M. (2016). Differential susceptibility to context: Implications for developmental psychopathology. In D. Cicchetti (Ed.), *Developmental psychopathology* (3rd ed.). New York: Wiley.

Beltran-Sanchez, H., Finch, C.E., & Crimmins, E.M. (2015). Twentieth-century surge of excess adult male mortality. *Proceedings of the National Academy of Sciences U.S.A., 112*, 8993–8998.

Bem, S.I. (1977). On the utility of alternative procedures for assessing psychological androgyny. *Journal of Consulting and Clinical Psychology, 45*, 196–205.

Ben-David, A., & others (2016). Pregnancy and birth outcomes among primaparae at very advanced maternal age: At what price? *Maternal and Child Health Journal, 20*, 833–842.

Bendersky, M., & Sullivan, M.W. (2007). Basic methods in infant research. In A. Slater & M. Lewis (Eds.), *Introduction to infant development* (2nd ed.). New York: Oxford University Press.

Beneden Health (2013). *Middle age survey.* Unpublished data, Beneden Health, York, ENG.

Benek, O., & others (2016, in press). A direct interaction between mitochondrial proteins and amyloid-B peptide and its significance for the progression and treatment of Alzheimer's disease. *Current Medicinal Chemistry.*

Benenson, J.F., Apostolaris, N.H., & Parnass, J. (1997). Age and sex differences in dyadic and group interaction. *Developmental Psychology, 33*, 538–543.

Bennett, C.I. (2015). *Comprehensive multicultural education* (8th ed.). Upper Saddle River, NJ: Pearson.

Bennett, J.M., Fagundes, C.P., & Kiecolt-Glaser, J.K. (2016). The chronic stress of caregiving accelerates the natural aging of the immune system. In A.C. Phillips, J.M. Lord, & J.A. Bosch (Eds.), *Immunosenescence: Psychological and behavioral determinants.* New York: Springer.

Bennett, K.M. (2006). Does marital status and marital status change predict physical health in older adults? *Psychological Medicine, 36*, 1313–1320.

Benokraitis, N.V. (2015). *Marriages and families* (8th ed.). Upper Saddle River, NJ: Pearson.

Benowitz-Fredericks, C.A., Garcia, K., Massey, M., Vassagar, B., & Borzekowski, D.L. (2012). Body image, eating disorders, and the relationship to adolescent media use. *Pediatric Clinics of North America, 59*, 693–704.

Benson, P.L. (2010). *Parent, teacher, mentor, friend: How every adult can change kids' lives.* Minneapolis: Search Institute Press.

Benson, P.L., Mannes, M., Pittman, K., & Ferber, T. (2004). Youth development, developmental assets, and public policy. In R. Lerner & L. Steinberg (Eds.), *Handbook of adolescent psychology* (2nd ed.). New York: Wiley.

Benson, P.L., Roehlkepartain, E.C., & Scales, P.C. (2012). Spirituality and positive youth development. In L. Miller (Ed.), *Oxford handbook of spirituality and consciousness.* New York: Oxford University Press.

Benson, P.L., & Scales, P.C. (2009). The definition and preliminary measurement of thriving in adolescence. *Journal of Positive Psychology, 4*, 85–104.

Benson, P.L., & Scales, P.C. (2011). Thriving and sparks: Development and emergence of new core concepts in positive youth development. In R.J.R. Levesque (Ed.), *Encyclopedia of adolescence.* Berlin: Springer.

Berardi, A., Parasuraman, R., & Haxby, J.V. (2001). Overall vigilance and sustained attention decrements in healthy aging. *Experimental Aging Research, 27*, 19–39.

Berchicci, M., Lucci, G., Perri, R.L., Spinelli, D., & Di Russo, F. (2014). Benefits of physical exercise on basic visuo-motor functions across age. *Frontiers in Aging Neuroscience, 6*, 48.

Berenbaum, S.A., & Beltz, A.M. (2011). Sexual differentiation of human behavior: Effects of prenatal and pubertal organization hormones. *Frontiers in Neuroscience, 32*, 183–200.

Berenbaum, S.A., Beltz, A.M., & Corley, R. (2015). The importance of puberty for adolescent development: Conceptualization and measurement. *Advances in Child Development and Behavior, 48*, 53–92.

Berens, A.E., & Nelson, C.A. (2015). The science of early adversity: Is there a role for large institutions in the care of vulnerable children? *Lancet, 386*, 388–398.

Berg, A.I., Hoffman, L., Hassing, L.B., McClearn, G.E., & Johansson, B. (2009). What matters, and what matters most, for change in life satisfaction in the oldest old? A study over 6 years among individuals 80+. *Aging and Mental Health, 13*, 191–201.

Berge, J.M., & others (2015). The protective role of family meals for youth obesity: 10-year longitudinal associations. *Journal of Pediatrics, 166*, 296–301.

Bergen, D. (1988). Stages of play development. In D. Bergen (Ed.), *Play as a medium for learning end development.* Portsmouth, NH: Heinemann.

Bergen, D. (2015). Psychological approaches to the study of play. In J.E. Johnson & others (Eds.), *Handbook of the study of play.* Blue Ridge Summit, PA: Rowman & Littlefield.

Berger, I., Remington, A., Leitner, Y., & Leviton, A. (2015). Brain development and the attention spectrum. *Frontiers in Human Neuroscience, 9*, 23.

Bergman, J.E., Olten, E., Verheij, J.B., & de Walle, H.B. (2016). Folic acid supplementation influences the distribution of neural tube defect subtypes: A registry-based study. *Reproductive Toxicology, 59*, 96–100.

Berk, L.E. (1994). Why children talk to themselves. *Scientific American, 271*(5), 78–83.

Berk, L.E., & Spuhl, S.T. (1995). Maternal interaction, private speech, and task performance in preschool children. *Early Childhood Research Quarterly, 10,* 145–169.

Berko Gleason, J. (2003). Unpublished review of J.W. Santrock's *Life-span development* (9th ed.). New York: McGraw-Hill.

Berko Gleason, J. (2009). The development of language: An overview. In J. Berko Gleason & N.B. Ratner (Eds.), *The development of language* (7th ed.). Boston: Allyn & Bacon.

Berko, J. (1958). The child's learning of English morphology. *Word, 14,* 150–177.

Berlyne, D.E. (1960). *Conflict, arousal, and curiosity.* New York: McGraw-Hill.

Berman, M.G., & others (2013). Dimensionality of brain networks linked to life-long individual differences in self-control. *Nature Communications, 4,* 1373.

Berndt, T.J., & Perry, T.B. (1990). Distinctive features and effects of early adolescent friendships. In R. Montemayor (Ed.), *Advances in adolescent research.* Greenwich, CT: JAI Press.

Bernier, A., Beauchamp, M.H., Carlson, S.M., & Lalonde, G. (2015). A secure base from which to regulate: Attachment security in toddlerhood is a predictor of executive functioning at school entry. *Developmental Psychology, 51,* 1177–1189.

Bernier, A., Calkins, S.D., & Bell, M.A. (2016, in press). Longitudinal associations between the quality of mother-infant interactions and brain development across infancy. *Child Development.*

Bernier, A., Matte-Gagne, C., Belanger, M-E., & Whipple, N. (2014). Taking stock of two decades of attachment transmission gap: Broadening the assessment of attachment behavior. *Child Development, 85,* 1852–1865.

Bernier, A., & others (2013). Sleep and cognition in preschool years: Specific links to executive functioning. *Child Development, 84*(5), 1542–1553.

Bernier, R., & Dawson, G. (2016). Autism spectrum disorders. In D. Cicchetti (Ed.), *Developmental psychopathology* (3rd ed.). New York: Wiley.

Berninger, V., Naga, W., Tanimoto, S., Thompson, R., & Abbott, R. (2015). Computer instruction in handwriting, spelling, and composing for students with specific learning disabilities in grades 4 to 9. *Computers and Education, 81,* 154–168.

Berry, J.W. (2015). Acculturation. In J.E. Grusec & P.D. Hastings (Eds.), *Handbook of socialization* (2nd ed.). New York: Guilford.

Berryman, N., & others (2013). Executive functions, physical fitness, and mobility in well-functioning older adults. *Experimental Gerontology, 48,* 1402–1409.

Bersamin, M.M., & others (2014). Risky business: Is there an association between casual sex and mental health among emerging adults? *Journal of Sex Research, 51,* 43–51.

Berscheid, E. (2010). Love in the fourth dimension. *Annual Review of Psychology* (Vol. 61). Palo Alto, CA: Annual Reviews.

Berscheid, E., & Fei, J. (1977). Sexual jealousy and romantic love. In G. Clinton & G. Smith (Eds.), *Sexual jealousy.* Englewood Cliffs, NJ: Prentice Hall.

Bertenthal, B.I. (2008). Perception and action. In M.M. Haith & J.B. Benson (Eds.), *Infant and early childhood development.* Oxford, UK: Elsevier.

Bertenthal, B.I., Longo, M.R., & Kenny, S. (2007). Phenomenal permanence and the development of predictive tracking in infancy. *Child Development, 78,* 350–363.

Bertorelle, R., & others (2014). Telomeres, telomerase, and colorectal cancer. *World Journal of Gastroenterology, 20,* 1940–1950.

Bertrand, R., Graham, E.K., & Lachman, M.E. (2013). Personality development in adulthood and old age. In I.B. Weiner & others (Eds.), *Handbook of psychology* (2nd ed., Vol. 6). New York: Wiley.

Betts, K.S., Williams, G.M., Najman, J.M., & Alati, R. (2014). Maternal depressive, anxious, and stress symptoms during pregnancy predict internalizing problems in adolescence. *Depression and Anxiety, 31,* 9–18.

Beuker, K.T., Rommelse, N.N., Donders, R., & Buitelaar, J.K. (2013). Development of early communication skills in the first two years of life. *Infant Behavior and Development, 36,* 71–83.

Beyene, Y. (1986). Cultural significance and physiological manifestations of menopause: A biocultural analysis. *Culture, Medicine and Psychiatry, 10,* 47–71.

Beyers, W., & Luyckx, K. (2016). Ruminative exploration and reconsideration of commitment as risk factors for suboptimal identity development in adolescence and emerging adulthood. *Journal of Adolescence, 47,* 169–178.

Bialystok, E. (1997). Effects of bilingualism and biliteracy on children's emerging concepts of print. *Developmental Psychology, 33,* 429–440.

Bialystok, E. (2001). *Bilingualism in development: Language, literacy, and cognition.* New York: Cambridge University Press.

Bialystok, E. (2007). Acquisition of literacy in preschool children. A framework for research. *Language Learning, 57,* 45–77.

Bialystok, E. (2011, April). *Becoming bilingual: Emergence of cognitive outcomes of bilingualism in immersion education.* Paper presented at the meeting of the Society for Research in Child Development, Montreal.

Bialystok, E. (2014). Language experience changes language and cognitive ability: Implications for social policy. In B. Spolsky, O. Inbar-Lourie, & M. Tannenbaum (Eds.), *Challenges for language education and policy.* New York: Routledge.

Bialystok, E. (2015). The impact of bilingualism on cognition. In R. Scott & S. Kosslyn (Eds.), *Emerging trends in the social and behavioral sciences.* New York: Wiley.

Bialystok, E., & Craik, F.I.M. (2010). Cognitive and linguistic processing in the bilingual mind. *Current Directions in Psychological Science, 19,* 19–23.

Bian, Z., & Anderson, G.J. (2008). Aging and the perceptual organization of 3-D scenes. *Psychology and Aging, 23,* 342–352.

Bianchi, L., & others (2016). The predictive value of the EWGSOP definition of sarcopenia: Results from the InCHIANTI Study. *Journals of Gerontology A: Biological Sciences and Medical Sciences, 71,* 259–264.

Bider-Canfield, Z., & others (2016, in press). Maternal obesity, gestational diabetes, breastfeeding, and childhood overweight up to age 2 years. *Pediatric Obesity.*

Biehle, S.N., & Mickelson, K.D. (2012). First-time parents' expectations about the division of childcare and play. *Journal of Family Psychology, 26,* 36–45.

Bielak, A.A., Cherbuin, N., Bunce, D., & Anstey, K.J. (2014). Preserved differentiation between physical activity and cognitive performance across young, middle, and older adulthood across eight years.

Journals of Gerontology B: Psychological Sciences and Social Sciences, 69, 523–532.

Bijur, P.E., Wallston, K.A., Smith, C.A., Lifrak, S., & Friedman, S.B. (1993, August). *Gender differences in turning to religion for coping.* Paper presented at the meeting of the American Psychological Association, Toronto.

Birditt, K.S., Hartnett, C.S., Fingerman, K.L., Zarit, S., & Antonucci, T.C. (2015). Extending the intergenerational stake hypothesis: Evidence of an individual stake and implications for well-being. *Journal of Marriage and the Family, 77,* 877–888.

Birditt, K.S., Newton, N.J., Cranford, J.A., & Ryan, L.H. (2016, in press). Stress and negative relationship quality among older couples: Implications for blood pressure. *Journals of Gerontology B: Psychological Sciences and Social Sciences.*

Birditt, K.S., & others (2016). Daily interactions in the parent-adult child tie: Links between children's problems and parents' diurnal cortisol rhythms. *Psychoneuroendocrinology, 63,* 208–216.

Birkeland, M.S., Melkevick, O., Holsen, I., & Wold, B. (2012). Trajectories of global self-esteem development during adolescence. *Journal of Adolescence, 35,* 43–54.

Birman, B.F., & others (2007). *State and local implementation of the "No Child Left Behind" act. Volume II—Teacher Quality under "NCLB": Interim report.* Jessup, MD: U.S. Department of Education.

Birnbaum, G.E. (2015). On the convergence of sexual urges and emotional bonds: The interplay of the sexual and attachment systems during relationship development. In J.A. Simpson & W.S. Rholes (Eds.), *Attachment theory and research.* New York: Guilford.

Bischoff, K.E., Sudore, R., Miao, Y., Boscardin, W.J., & Smith, A.K. (2013). Advance care planning and the quality of end-of-life care in older adults. *Journal of the American Geriatrics Society, 61,* 209–214.

Bjorklund, D.F. (2012). *Children's thinking* (5th ed.). Boston: Cengage.

Bjorklund, D.F., & Pellegrini, A.D. (2002). *The origins of human nature.* New York: Oxford University Press.

Black, D.M., & Rosen, C.J. (2016). Clinical practice. Postmenopausal osteoporosis. *New England Journal of Medicine, 374,* 254–262.

Black, M.M., & Lozoff, B. (2008). Nutrition and diet. In M.M. Haith & J.B. Benson (Eds.), *Encyclopedia of infant and early childhood development.* Oxford, UK: Elsevier.

Blackstone, S.R., & Herrmann, L.K. (2016). Relationships between illicit drug use and body mass index among adolescents. *Health Education and Behavior, 43,* 21–24.

Blackwell, L.S., & Dweck, C.S. (2008). *The motivational impact of a computer-based program that teaches how the brain changes with learning.* Unpublished manuscript, Department of Psychology, Stanford University, Palo Alto, CA.

Blackwell, L.S., Trzesniewski, K.H., & Dweck, C.S. (2007). Implicit theories of intelligence predict achievement across an adolescent transition: A longitudinal study and an intervention. *Child Development, 78,* 246–263.

Blair, C. (2016). The development of executive functions and self-regulation: A bidirectional psychobiological model. In K.D. Vohs & R. Baumeister (Eds.), *Handbook of self-regulation* (3rd ed.). New York: Guilford.

Blair, C., & Raver, C.C. (2012). Child development in the context of poverty: Experiential canalization of brain and behavior. *American Psychologist, 67*, 309–318.

Blair, C., & Raver, C.C. (2015). School readiness and self-regulation: A developmental psychobiological approach. *Annual Review of Psychology* (Vol. 66). Palo Alto, CA: Annual Reviews.

Blair, C., Raver, C.C., & Berry, D.J. (2014). Two approaches estimating the effect of parenting on the development of executive function in early childhood. *Developmental Psychology, 50*, 554–565.

Blair, C., Raver, C.C., & Finegood, E.D. (2016). Self-regulation and developmental psychopathology: Experiential canalization of brain and behavior. In D. Cicchetti (Ed.), *Developmental psychopathology* (3rd ed.). New York: Wiley.

Blair, C., & Razza, R.P. (2007). Relating effortful control, executive functioning, and false belief understanding to emerging math and literacy ability in kindergarten. *Child Development, 78*, 647–663.

Blair, C., & others (2015). Multiple aspects of self-regulation uniquely predict mathematics but not letter-word knowledge in the early elementary grades. *Developmental Psychology, 5*, 459–472.

Blair, M., & Somerville, S.C. (2009). The importance of differentiation in young children's acquisition of expertise. *Cognition, 112*, 259–280.

Blair, S.N. (1990). *Personal communication.* Dallas: Cooper Aerobics Center.

Blair, S.N., & others (1989). Physical fitness and all-cause mortality: A prospective study of healthy men and women. *Journal of the American Medical Association, 262*, 2395–2401.

Blake, J.S. (2017). *Nutrition and you* (4th ed.). Upper Saddle River, NJ: Pearson.

Blake, J.S., Munoz, K.D., & Volpe, S. (2016). *Nutrition: From science to you, plus mastering nutrition with MyDietAnalysis with etext* (3rd ed.). Upper Saddle River, NJ: Pearson.

Blakely-McClure, S.J., & Ostrov, J.M. (2016). Relational aggression, victimization, and self-concept: Testing pathways from middle childhood to adolescence. *Journal of Youth and Adolescence, 45*, 376–390.

Blakemore, J.E.O., Berenbaum, S.A., & Liben, L.S. (2009). *Gender development.* Clifton, NJ: Psychology Press.

Blanco, C., & others (2014). Risk factors for anxiety disorders: Common and specific effects in a national sample. *Depression and Anxiety, 31*, 756–764.

Blandthorn, J., Forster, D.A., & Love, V. (2011). Neonatal and maternal outcomes following maternal use of buprenophine or methadone during pregnancy: Findings of a retrospective audit. *Women and Birth, 24*, 32–39.

Bleeker, F.E., Hopman, S.M., Merks, J.H., Aalfs, C.M., & Hennekam, R.C. (2014). Brain tumors and syndromes in children. *Neuropediatrics, 45*, 137–161.

Blieszner, R. (2009). Friendship, adulthood. In D. Carr (Ed.), *Encyclopedia of the life course and human development.* Boston: Gale Cengage.

Blieszner, R., & Roberto, K.A. (2012a). Intergenerational relationships and aging. In S.K. Whitbourne & M. Sliwinski (Eds.), *Wiley-Blackwell handbook of adult development and aging.* New York: Wiley.

Blieszner, R., & Roberto, K.A. (2012b). Partner and friend relationships in adulthood. In S.K. Whitbourne & M. Sliwinski (Eds.), *Wiley-Blackwell handbook of adult development and aging.* New York: Wiley.

Blonski, S.C., & others (2016). Associations between negative and positive life events and the course of depression: A detailed repeated-assessments study. *Journal of Nervous and Mental Disease, 204*, 175–180.

Blood, J.D., & others (2015). The variable heart: High frequency and very low frequency correlates of depressive symptoms in children and adolescents. *Journal of Affective Disorders, 186*, 119–126.

Bloodworth, M., Bloodworth, N., & Ely, E.W. (2015). A template for non-religious-based discussions about euthanasia. *Lincare Quarterly, 82*, 49–54.

Bloom, B. (1985). *Developing talent in young people.* New York. Ballantine.

Bloom, L., Lifter, K., & Broughton, J. (1985). The convergence of early cognition and language in the second year of life: Problems in conceptualization and measurement. In M. Barrett (Ed.), *Single word speech.* London: Wiley.

Blumberg, S.J., Vahratian, A., & Blumberg, J.H. (2014). Marriage, cohabitation, and men's use of preventive health services. *NCHS Data Brief, 154*, 1–8.

Blumel, J.E., Lavin, P., Vellejo, M.S., & Sarra, S. (2014). Menopause or climacteric, just a semantic discussion or has it clinical implications? *Climacteric, 17*, 235–241.

Bluschke, A., Roessner, V., & Beste, C. (2016). Editorial perspective: How to optimize frequency band neurofeedback for ADHD. *Journal of Child Psychology and Psychiatry, 57*, 457–461.

Boden, J.S., Fischer, J.L., & Niehuis, S. (2010). Predicting marital adjustment from young adults' initial levels of and changes in emotional intimacy over time: A 25-year longitudinal study. *Journal of Adult Development, 17*, 121–134.

Bodner, E., & Cohen-Fridel, S. (2010). Relations between attachment styles, ageism, and quality of life in late life. *International Psychogeriatrics, 22*, 1353–1361.

Bodrova, E., & Leong, D.J. (2007). *Tools of the mind* (2nd ed.). Geneva, Switzerland: International Bureau of Education, UNESCO.

Bodrova, E., & Leong, D.J. (2015). Vygotskian and post-Vygotskian views of children's play. *American Journal of Play, 7*, 371–388.

Boelen, P.A. (2015). Optimism in prolonged grief and depression following loss: A three-wave longitudinal study. *Psychiatry Research, 227*, 313–317.

Bohlin, G., & Hagekull, B. (1993). Stranger wariness and sociability in the early years. *Infant Behavior and Development, 16*, 53–67.

Bol, T., & Kalmijn, M. (2016). Grandparents' resources and grandchildren's schooling: Does grandparental involvement moderate the grandparent effect? *Social Science Research, 55*, 155–170.

Bonanno, R.A., & Hymel, S. (2013). Cyber bullying and internalizing difficulties: Above and beyond the impact of traditional forms of bullying. *Journal of Youth and Adolescence, 42*, 685–697.

Bond, V.L. (2015). Sounds to share: The state of music education in three Reggio Emilia inspired North American preschools. *Journal of Research in Music Education, 62*, 462–484.

Bonney, C.R., & Sternberg, R.J. (2016, in press). Learning to think critically. In R.E. Mayer & P.A. Alexander (Eds.), *Handbook of learning and instruction* (2nd ed.). New York: Routledge.

Booth, A. (2006). Object function and categorization in infancy: Two mechanisms of facilitation. *Infancy, 10*, 145–169.

Booth, M. (2002). Arab adolescents facing the future: Enduring ideals and pressures to change. In B.B. Brown, R.W. Larson, & T.S. Saraswathi (Eds.), *The world's youth.* New York: Cambridge University Press.

Boraska, V., & others (2014). A genome-wide study of anorexia nervosa. *Molecular Psychiatry, 19*, 1085–1094.

Boraxbekk, C.J., & others (2015). Free recall episodic memory performance predicts dementia ten years prior to clinical diagnosis: Findings from the Betula Longitudinal Study. *Dementia and Geriatric Cognitive Disorders Extra, 5*, 191–202.

Borich, G.D. (2014). *Effective teaching methods* (8th ed.). Upper Saddle River, NJ: Pearson.

Borich, G.D. (2017). *Effective teaching methods* (9th ed.). Upper Saddle River, NJ: Pearson.

Bornstein, M.H. (2016). Determinants of parenting. In D. Cicchetti (Ed.), *Developmental psychopathology* (3rd ed.). New York: Wiley.

Bornstein, M.H., Arterberry, M.E., & Mash, C. (2011). Perceptual development. In M.H. Bornstein & M.E. Lamb (Eds.), *Developmental psychology: An advanced textbook* (6th ed.). New York: Psychology Press.

Bornstein, M.H., Jager, J., & Steinberg, L. (2013). Adolescents, parents/friends/peers: A relationship model. In I. Weiner & others (Eds.), *Handbook of psychology* (2nd ed., Vol. 6). New York: Wiley.

Bornstein, M.H., & others (2015). Mother-infant contingent vocalizations in 11 countries. *Psychological Science, 26*, 1272–1284.

Bouchard, T.J., Lykken, D.T., McGue, M., Segl, N.L., & Tellegen, A. (1990). Source of human psychological differences. The Minnesota Study of Twins Reared Apart. *Science, 250*, 223–228.

Boukhris, T., Sheehy, O., Mottron, L., & Berard, A. (2016). Antidepressant use during pregnancy and the risk of autism spectrum disorder in children. *JAMA Pediatrics, 170*, 117–124.

Boundy, E.O., & others (2016, in press). Kangaroo care and neonatal outcomes: A meta-analysis. *Pediatrics.*

Bourassa, K.J., Sbarra, D.A., & Whisman, M.A. (2015). Women in very low quality marriages gain life satisfaction following divorce. *Journal of Family Psychology, 29*, 490–499.

Bovbjerg, M.L., Cheyney, M., & Everson, C. (2016). Maternal and newborn outcomes following waterbirth: The Midwives Alliance of North America Statistics Project, 2004 to 2009 cohort. *Journal of Midwifery and Women's Health, 61*, 11–20.

Bowers, M., & Jessberger, S. (2016, in press). Linking adult hippocampal neurogenesis with human physiology and disease. *Developmental Dynamics.*

Bowlby, J. (1969). *Attachment and loss* (Vol. 1). London: Hogarth Press.

Bowlby, J. (1989). *Secure and insecure attachment.* New York: Basic Books.

Bowling, A., & Iliffe, S. (2011). Psychological approach to successful aging predicts future quality of life in older adults. *Health Quality and Life Outcomes, 9*, 13.

Bowman, N.A. (2010). The development of psychological well-being in first-year college students. *Journal of College Student Development, 51,* 180–200.

Braccio, S., Sharland, M., & Ladhani, S.N. (2016). Prevention and treatment of mother-to-child syphilis. *Current Opinion in Infectious Diseases, 29,* 268–274.

Bradley, R.H. (2015). Children's housing and physical environments. In R.M. Lerner (Ed.), *Handbook of child psychology and developmental science* (7th ed.). New York: Wiley.

Brainerd, C.J., & Reyna, V.E. (2014). Dual processes in memory development: Fuzzy-trace theory. In P. Bauer & R. Fivush (Eds.), *Wiley-Blackwell handbook of children's memory.* New York: Wiley.

Brand, J. (2014). Social consequences of job loss and unemployment. *Annual Review of Sociology* (Vol. 40). Palo Alto, CA: Annual Reviews.

Brand, M. (2011). Mitochondrial functioning and aging. In E. Masoro & S. Austad (Eds.), *Handbook of the biology of aging* (7th ed.). New York: Elsevier.

Bransford, J., & others (2006). Learning theories in education. In P.A. Alexander & P.H. Winne (Eds.), *Handbook of educational psychology* (2nd ed.). Mahwah, NJ: Erlbaum.

Brassen, S., & others (2012). Don't look back in anger! Responsiveness to missed chances in successful and unsuccessful aging. *Science, 336,* 612–614.

Braver, S.L., & Lamb, M.E. (2013). Marital dissolution. In G.W. Peterson & K.R. Bush (Eds.), *Handbook of marriage and the family* (3rd ed.). New York: Springer.

Brazdova, A., Senechal, H., Peltre, G., & Poncet, P. (2016, in press). Immune aspects of female infertility. *International Journal of Fertility and Sterility.*

Bredekamp, S. (2017). *REVEL for effective practices in early childhood* (3rd ed.). Upper Saddle River, NJ: Pearson.

Bremner, J.G., Slater, A.M., Johnson, S.P., Mason, U.C., & Spring, J. (2012). The effects of auditory information on 4-month-old infants' perception of trajectory continuity. *Child Development, 83*(3) 954–984.

Brenner, J.D. (2016). Traumatic stress from a multi-level developmental psychopathology perspective. In D. Cicchetti (Ed.), *Developmental psychopathology* (3rd ed.). New York: Wiley.

Brent, R.L. (2009). Saving lives and changing family histories: Appropriate counseling of pregnant women and men and women of reproductive age concerning the risk of diagnostic radiation exposure during and before pregnancy. *American Journal of Obstetrics and Gynecology, 200,* 4–24.

Brent, R.L. (2011). The pulmonologist's role in caring for pregnant women with regard to reproductive risks of diagnostic radiological studies or radiation therapy. *Clinics in Chest Medicine, 32,* 33–42.

Bretherton, I., & Munholland, K.A. (2016). The internal working model construct in light of contemporary neuroimaging research. In J. Cassidy & P.R. Shaver (Ed.), *Handbook of attachment* (3rd ed.). New York: Guilford.

Bretherton, I., Stolberg, U., & Kreye, M. (1981). Engaging strangers in proximal interaction: Infants' social initiative. *Developmental Psychology, 17,* 746–755.

Breveglieri, G., & others (2016). Y-chromosome identification in circulating cell-free DNA using surface plasmon resonance. *Prenatal Diagnosis, 36,* 353–361.

Bridgett, D.J., Laake, L.M., Gartstein, M.A., & Dorn, D. (2013). Development of infant positive emotionality: The contribution of maternal characteristics and effects on subsequent parenting. *Infant and Child Development, 22*(4), 362–382.

Brigadoi, S., & Cooper, R.J. (2015). How short is short? Optimum source-detector distance for short-separation channels in functional near-infrared spectroscopy. *Neurophotonics, 2*(2), 025005.

Bril, B. (1999). Dires sur l'enfant selon les cultures. Etat des lieux et perspectives. In B. Brill, P.R. Dasen, C. Sabatier, & B. Krewer (Eds.), *Propos sur l'enfant et l'adolescent. Quels enfants pour quelles cultures?* Paris: L'Harmattan.

Briley, D.A., Domiteaux, M., & Tucker-Drob, E.M. (2014). Achievement-relevant personality: Relations with the big five and validation of an efficient instrument. *Learning and Individual Differences, 32,* 26–39.

Brim, G. (1992, December 7). Commentary, *Newsweek,* p. 52.

Brim, O. (1999). *The MacArthur Foundation study of midlife development.* Vero Beach, FL: MacArthur Foundation.

Brimah, P., & others (2013). Sleep duration and reported functional capacity among black and white U.S. adults. *Journal of Sleep Medicine, 9,* 605–609.

Brinkman-Stoppelenburg, A., Rietjens, J.A., & van der Heide, A. (2014). The effects of advance care planning on end-of-life care: A systematic review. *Palliative Medicine, 28,* 1000–1025.

Britton, W.B., & others (2014). A randomized controlled pilot trial of classroom-based mindfulness meditation compared to an active control condition in sixth-grade children. *Journal of School Psychology 52,* 263–278.

Brock, R.L., & Kochanska, G. (2016). Interparental conflict, children's security with parents, and long-term risk of internalizing problems: A longitudinal study from ages 2 to 10. *Development and Psychopathology, 28,* 45–54.

Brody, G.H., & others (2016). Family-centered prevention ameliorates the longitudinal association between risky family processes and epigenetic aging. *Journal of Clinical Psychology and Psychiatry, 57,* 566–574.

Brody, N. (2000). Intelligence. In A. Kazdin (Ed.), *Encyclopedia of psychology.* Washington, DC, & New York: American Psychological Association and Oxford University Press.

Brody, N. (2007). Does education influence intelligence? In P.C. Kyllonen, R.D. Roberts, & L. Stankov (Eds.), *Extending intelligence.* Mahwah, NJ: Erlbaum.

Brody, R.M., & Costa, R.M. (2009). Satisfaction (sexual, life, relationship, and mental health) is associated directly with penile-vaginal intercourse, but inversely related to other sexual behavior frequencies. *Journal of Sexual Medicine, 6,* 1947–1954.

Broekhof, E., & others (2015). The understanding of intentions, desires, and beliefs in young children with autism spectrum disorder. *Journal of Autism and Developmental Disorders, 45,* 2035–2045.

Bronfenbrenner, U. (1986). Ecology of the family as a context for human development: Research perspectives. *Developmental Psychology, 22,* 723–742.

Bronfenbrenner, U. (2004). *Making human beings human.* Thousand Oaks, CA: Sage.

Bronfenbrenner, U., & Morris, P.A. (2006). The ecology of developmental processes. In W. Damon & R. Lerner (Eds.), *Handbook of child psychology* (6th ed.). New York: Wiley.

Bronstein, P. (2006). The family environment: Where gender role socialization begins. In J. Worell & C.D. Goodheart (Eds.), *Handbook of girls' and women's psychological health.* New York: Oxford University Press.

Brook, J.S., Brook, D.W., Gordon, A.S., Whiteman, M., & Cohen, P. (1990). The psychological etiology of adolescent drug use: A family interactional approach. *Genetic Psychology Monographs, 116*(2).

Brooker, R.J. (2015). *Genetics* (5th ed.). New York: McGraw-Hill.

Brookhart, S.M., & Nitko, A.J. (2015). *Educational assessment of students* (7th ed.). Upper Saddle River, NJ: Pearson.

Brooks, J.G., & Brooks, M.G. (2001). *The case for constructivist classrooms* (2nd ed.). Upper Saddle River, NJ: Erlbaum.

Brooks, R., & Meltzoff, A.N. (2014). Gaze following: A mechanism for building social connections between infants and adults. In M. Mikulincer & P.R. Shaver (Eds.), *Mechanisms of social connection.* Washington, DC: American Psychological Association.

Brooks-Gunn, J. (2003). Do you believe in magic?: What we can expect from early childhood programs. *Social Policy Report, Society for Research in Child Development, XVII* (1), 1–13.

Brooks-Gunn, J., & Warren, M.P. (1989). The psychological significance of secondary sexual characteristics in 9- to 11-year-old girls. *Child Development 59,* 161–169.

Broskey, N.T., & others (2016, in press). Exercise efficiency relates with mitochondrial content and function in older adults. *Physiological Reports.*

Brothers, A., Gabrian, M., Wahl, H.W., & Diehl, M. (2016, in press). Future time perspective and awareness of age-related change: Examining their role in predicting psychological well-being. *Psychology and Aging.*

Brott, A.A. (2015). *The new father.* New York: Abbeville Press.

Brown, B.B. (2011). Popularity in peer group perspective: The role of status in adolescent peer systems. In A.H.N. Cillessen, D. Schwartz, & L. Mayeux (Eds.), *Popularity in the peer system.* New York: Guilford.

Brown, B.B., & Bakken, J.P. (2011). Parenting and peer relationships: Reinvigorating research on family-peer linkages in adolescence. *Journal of Research on Adolescence, 21,* 153–165.

Brown, B.B., & Larson, J. (2009). Peer relationships in adolescence. In R.M. Lerner & L. Steinberg (Eds.), *Handbook of adolescent development* (3rd ed.). New York: Wiley.

Brown, B.B., & Larson, R.W. (2002). The kaleidoscope of adolescence: Experiences of the world's youth at the beginning of the 21st century. In B.B. Brown, R.W. Larson, & T.S. Saraswathi (Eds.). *The world's youth.* New York: Cambridge University Press.

Brown, C.L., & others (2012). Social activity and cognitive functioning over time: A coordinated analysis of four longitudinal studies. *Journal of Aging Research, 493–598.*

Brown, D.A., & Lamb, M.E. (2016, in press). Can children be useful witnesses? It depends how they are questioned. *Child Development Perspectives.*

Brown, H.L., & Graves, C.R. (2013). Smoking and marijuana in pregnancy. *Clinical Obstetrics and Gynecology, 56,* 107–113.

Brown, J.C., Harhay, M.O., & Harhay, M.N. (2016, in press). Physical activity, diet quality, and mortality among sarcopenic older adults. *Aging: Clinical, and Experimental Research.*

Brown, R. (1958). *Words and things.* Glencoe, IL: Free-Press.

Brown, R. (1973). *A first language: The early stages.* Cambridge, MA: Harvard University Press.

Brown, S.L., Bulanda, J.R., & Lee, G.R. (2005). The significance of nonmarital cohabitation: Marital status and mental health benefits among middle-aged and older adults. *Journals of Gerontology B: Psychological Sciences and Social Sciences, 60,* S21–S29.

Brown, S.L., & Lin, I-F. (2013, March). *The gray divorce revolution.* Bowling Green, OH; Department of Sociology.

Brown, W.H., & others (2009). Social and environmental factors associated with preschoolers' nonsedentary physical activity. *Child Development, 80,* 45–58.

Browne, T.K. (2016, in press). Why parents should not be told the sex of their fetus. *Journal of Medical Ethics.*

Brownell, C.A., Lemerise, E.A., Pelphrey, K.A., & Roisman, G.I. (2015). Measuring socioemotional behavior and development. In R.M. Lerner (Ed.), *Handbook of child psychology and developmental science* (7th ed.). New York: Wiley.

Brownell, C.A., Ramani, G.B., & Zerwas, S. (2006). Becoming a social partner with peers: Cooperation and social understanding in one- and two-year-olds. *Child Development, 77,* 803–821.

Brownell, C.A., Svetlova, M., Anderson, R., Nichols, S.R., & Drummond, J. (2013). Socialization of early prosocial behavior: Parents' talk about emotions is associated with sharing and helping in toddlers. *Infancy, 18,* 91–119.

Bruce, A. (2007). Time(lessness): Buddhist perspectives and end-of-life. *Nursing Philosophy, 8,* 151–157.

Bruce, I., & others (2016). The clinical utility of naturalistic action test in differentiating mild cognitive impairment from early dementia at a memory clinic. *International Journal of Geriatric Psychiatry, 31,* 309–315.

Bruck, M., & Ceci, S.J. (1999). The suggestibility of children's memory. *Annual Review of Psychology* (Vol. 50). Palo Alto, CA: Annual Reviews.

Bruck, M., & Ceci, S.J. (2012). Forensic developmental psychology in the courtroom. In D. Faust & M. Ziskin (Eds.), *Coping with psychiatric and psychological testimony.* New York: Cambridge University Press.

Brumariu, L.E., Kerns, K.A., & Seibert, A.C. (2012). Mother-child attachment, emotion regulation, and anxiety symptoms in middle childhood. *Personal Relationships, 19*(3), 569–585.

Brummelman, J.E., & others (2014). "That's not beautiful—That's incredibly beautiful!" The adverse impact of inflated praise on children with low self-esteem. *Psychological Science, 25,* 728–735.

Brummelman, J.E., & others (2015). My child is God's gift to humanity: Development and validation of the Parental Overvaluation Scale (POS).

Journal of Personality and Social Psychology, 108, 665–679.

Brummelte, S., & Galea, L.A. (2016). Postpartum depression: Etiology, treatment, and consequences for maternal care. *Hormones and Behavior, 77,* 153–166.

Brunell, P.A. (2014). Measles in pregnancy is not kid's stuff. *Clinical Infectious Diseases, 58,* 1093–1094.

Brunton, P.J. (2015). Programming the brain and behavior by early-life stress: A focus on neuroactive steroids. *Journal of Neuroendocrinology, 27,* 468–480.

Bryant, J.B. (2012). Pragmatic development. In E.L. Bavin (Ed.), *Cambridge handbook of child language.* New York: Cambridge University Press.

Buchman, A.S., Yu, L., Boyle, P.A., Shah, R.C., & Bennett, D.A. (2012). Total daily physical activity and longevity in old age. *Archives of Internal Medicine, 172,* 444–446.

Bugental, D.B., Corpuz, R., & Beaulieu, D.A. (2015). An evolutionary approach to socialization. In J.E. Grusec & P.D. Hastings (Eds.), *Handbook of socialization.* (2nd ed.). New York: Guilford.

Buhl, H.M., & Lanz, M. (2007). Emerging adulthood in Europe: Common traits and variability across five European countries. *Journal of Adolescent Research, 22,* 439–443.

Buhrmester, D. (1998). Need fulfillment, interpersonal competence, and the developmental contexts of early adolescent friendship. In W.M. Bukowski & A.F. Newcomb (Eds.), *The company they keep: Friendship in childhood and adolescence.* New York: Cambridge University Press.

Bui, E., & others (2015). Grief-related panic symptoms in complicated grief. *Journal of Affective Disorders, 170,* 213–216.

Bukowski, R., & others (2008, January). *Folic acid and preterm birth.* Paper presented at the meeting of the Society for Maternal-Fetal Medicine, Dallas.

Bulik, C.M., Berkman, N.D., Brownley, K.A., Sedway, J.A., & Lhor, K.N. (2007). Anorexia nervosa treatment: A systematic review of randomized controlled trials. *International Journal of Eating Disorders, 40,* 310–320.

Bullard, J. (2017). *Creating environments for learning: Birth to eight* (3rd ed.). Upper Saddle River, NJ: Pearson.

Bullock, M., & Lutkenhaus, P. (1990). Who am I? Self-understanding in toddlers. *Merrill-Palmer Quarterly, 36,* 217–238.

Bumpus, M.F., Crouter, A.C., & McHale, S.M. (2001). Parental autonomy granting during adolescence: Gender differences in context. *Developmental Psychology, 37,* 163–173.

Burack, J.A., & others (2016). Developments in the developmental approach to intellectual disability. In D. Cicchetti (Ed.), *Developmental psychopathology* (3rd ed.). New York: Wiley.

Buratti, S., Allwood, C.M., & Johansson, M. (2014). Stability in the metamemory realism of eyewitness confidence judgments. *Cognitive Processing, 15,* 39–53.

Burchinal, M., Magnuson, K., Powell, D., & Hong, S.S. (2015). Early child care and education. In R.M. Lerner (Ed.), *Handbook of child psychology and developmental science* (7th ed.). New York: Wiley.

Burden, P.R., & Byrd, D.M. (2016). *Methods for effective teaching* (7th ed.). Upper Saddle River, NJ: Pearson.

Burke, J.D., & Loeber, R. (2015). The effectiveness of the Stop Now And Plan (SNAP) program for boys at risk for violence and delinquency. *Prevention Science, 16,* 242–253.

Burr, J.A. (2009). Volunteering, later life. In D. Carr (Ed.), *Encyclopedia of the life course and human development.* Boston: Gale Cengage.

Burr, J.A., Han, S.H., & Tavares, J.L. (2016, in press). Volunteering and cardiovascular disease: Does helping others get "under the skin"? *Gerontologist.*

Bursuck, W.D., & Damer, M. (2015). *Teaching reading to students who are at risk or have disabilities* (3rd ed.). Upper Saddle River, NJ: Pearson.

Burt, K.B., Coatsworth, J.D., & Masten, A.S. (2016). Competence and psychopathology in development. In D. Cicchetti (Ed.), *Developmental psychopathology* (3rd ed.). New York: Wiley.

Burton, E., & others (2015). Effectiveness of exercise programs to reduce falls in older people with dementia living in the community: A systematic review and meta-analysis. *Clinical Interventions in Aging, 9,* 421–434.

Burton, G.J., & Jauniaux, E. (2015). What is the placenta? *American Journal of Obstetrics and Gynecology, 213* (Suppl. 4), S6.e1–4.

Busching, R., & Krahe, B. (2015). The girls set the tone: Gendered classroom norms and the development of aggression in adolescence. *Personality and Social Psychology Bulletin, 41,* 659–676.

Bush, K.R., & Peterson, G.W. (2013). Parent-child relationships in diverse contexts. In G.W. Peterson & K.R. Bush (Eds.), *Handbook of marriage and the family* (3rd ed.). New York: Springer.

Buss, D.M. (2008). *Evolutionary psychology* (3rd ed.). Boston: Allyn & Bacon.

Buss, D.M. (2012). *Evolutionary psychology* (4th ed.). Boston: Allyn Bacon.

Buss, D.M. (2015). *Evolutionary psychology* (5th ed.). Upper Saddle River, NJ: Pearson.

Busschaert, C., & others (2015). Tracing and predictors of screen time from early adolescence to early adulthood: A 10-year follow-up study. *Journal of Adolescent Health, 56,* 440–448.

Busse, E.W., & Blazer, D.G. (1996). *The American Psychiatric Press textbook of geriatric psychiatry* (2nd ed.). Washington, DC: American Psychiatric Press.

Bussey, K., & Bandura A. (1999). Social cognitive theory of gender development and differentiation. *Psychological Review, 106,* 676–713.

Butler, R.N. (2007). Life review. In J.E. Birren (Ed.), *Encyclopedia of gerontology* (2nd ed.). San Diego: Academic Press.

Butrica, B.A., & Smith, K.E. (2012). The retirement prospects of divorced women. *Social Security Bulletin, 72,* 11–22.

Buzwell, S., & Rosenthal, D. (1996). Constructing a sexual self: Adolescents' sexual self-perceptions and sexual risk-taking. *Journal of Research on Adolescence, 6,* 489–513.

C

Cabeza, R. (2002). Hemispheric asymmetry reduction in older adults: The HAROLD model. *Psychology and Aging, 17,* 85–100.

Cabeza, R., & Dennis, N.A. (2013). Frontal lobes and aging: Deterioration and compensation.

In D.T. Stuss & R.T. Knight (Eds.), *Principles of frontal lobe function* (2nd ed.). New York: Oxford University Press.

Cacioppo, J.T., Cacioppo, S., Gonzaga, G.C., Ogburn, E.L., & VanderWheele, T.J. (2013). Marital satisfaction and break-ups differ across online and off-line meeting venues. *Proceedings of the National Academy of Sciences, 110* (25), 10135–10140.

Caeymaex, L., & others (2013). Perceived role in end-of-life decision making in the NICU affects long-term parental grief response. *Archives of Disease in Childhood: Fetal and Neonatal Edition, 98*(1), F26–F31.

Cahill, K.E., Giandrea, M.D., & Quinn, J.F. (2016). Evolving patterns of work and retirement. In L.K. George & K.F. Ferraro (Eds.), *Handbook of aging and the social sciences* (8th ed.). New York: Elsevier.

Cai, L., Chan, J.S., Yan, J.H., & Peng, K. (2014). Brain plasticity and motor practice in cognitive aging. *Frontiers in Aging Neuroscience, 6,* 31.

Cain, M.A., Bornick, P., & Whiteman, V. (2013). The maternal, fetal, and neonatal effects of cocaine exposure in pregnancy. *Clinical Obstetrics and Gynecology, 56,* 124–132.

Cain, M.S., Leonard, J.A., Gabriel, J.D., & Finn, A.S. (2016, in press). Media multitasking in adolescence. *Psychonomic Bulletin and Review.*

Cairncross, M., & Miller, C.J. (2016, in press). The effectiveness of mindfulness-based therapies for ADHD: A meta-analytic review. *Journal of Attention Disorders.*

Calkins, S.D. (2015). Introduction to the volume: Seeing infant development through a biopsychosocial lens. In S.D. Calkins (Ed.), *Handbook of infant biopsychosocial development.* New York: Guilford.

Calkins, S.D., & Markovitch, S. (2010). Emotion regulation and executive functioning in early development: Integrating mechanisms of control supporting adaptive functioning. In S.D. Calkins & M.A. Bell (Eds.), *Child development at the intersection of emotion and cognition.* Washington, DC: American Psychological Association.

Calkins, S.D., & Perry, N.B. (2016). The development of emotion regulation. In D. Cicchetti (Ed.), *Developmental psychopathology* (3rd ed.). New York: Wiley.

Callaghan, M.E., & others (2014). Widespread age-related differences in the human brain microstructure revealed by quantitative magnetic resonance imaging. *Neurobiology of Aging, 35,* 1862–1872.

Callan, J.E. (2001). Gender development: Psychoanalytic perspectives. In J. Worrel (Ed.). *Encyclopedia of women and gender.* San Diego: Academic Press.

Calvert, S.L. (2015). Children and digital media. In R.M. Lerner (Ed.), *Handbook of child psychology and developmental science* (7th ed.). New York: Wiley.

Calvo-Garcia, M.A. (2016). Guidelines for scanning twins and triplets with US and MRI. *Pediatric Radiology, 46,* 156–166.

Camacho, D.E., & Fuligni, A.J. (2015). Extracurricular participation among adolescents from immigrant families. *Journal of Youth and Adolescence, 44,* 1251–1262.

Campbell, K.L., Grady, C.L., Ng, C., & Hasher, L. (2012). Age differences in the frontoparietal cognitive control network: Implications for distractibility. *Neuropsychologia., 50*(9), 2212–2223.

Campbell, L., Campbell, B., & Dickinson, D. (2004). *Teaching and learning through multiple intelligences* (3rd ed.). Boston: Allyn & Bacon.

Campione-Barr, N., Greer, K.B., & Kruse, A. (2013). Differential associations between domains of sibling conflict and adolescent emotional adjustment. *Child Development, 84,* 938–954.

Campos, J. (2009). Unpublished review of J.W. Santrock's *Life-span development* (13th ed.). New York: McGraw-Hill.

Canfield, J., & Hansen, M.V. (1995). *A second helping of chicken soup for the soul.* Deerfield Beach, FL: Health Communications.

Cantarella, A., & others (2016, in press). Benefits in tasks related to everyday life competencies after working memory training in older adults. *International Journal of Geriatric Psychiatry.*

Cantone, E., & others (2015). Interventions on bullying and cyberbullying in schools: A systematic review. *Clinical Practice and Epidemiology in Mental Health, 11*(Suppl. 1), S58–S76.

Caprara, G.V., & others (2010). The contributions of agreeableness and self-efficacy beliefs to prosociality. *European Journal of Personality, 24,* 36–55.

Capurro, A., & others (2015). Computational deconvolution of genome wide expression data from Parkinson's and Huntington's disease brain tissues using population-specific expression analysis. *Frontiers of Neuroscience, 8,* 441.

Carling, S.J., Demment, M.M., Kjolhede, C.L., & Olson, C.M. (2015). Breastfeeding duration and weight gain in infancy. *Pediatrics, 135,* 111–119.

Carlson, S.M., & White, R. (2011). Unpublished research. Minneapolis: Institute of Child Development, University of Minnesota.

Carlson, S.M., Zelazo, P.D., & Faja, S. (2013). Executive function. In P.D. Zelazo (Ed.), *Oxford handbook of developmental psychology.* New York: Oxford University Press.

Carlsson, A.C., & others (2016). Physical activity, obesity, and risk of cardiovascular disease in midde-aged men during a median of 30 years of follow-up. *European Journal of Preventive Cardiology, 23,* 359–365.

Carnegie Council on Adolescent Development (1989). *Turning points: Preparing American youth for the twenty-first century.* New York: Carnegie Foundation.

Carnevale, D., Perrotta, M., Lembo, G., & Trimarco, B. (2016). Pathophysiological links among hypertension in Alzheimer's disease. *High Blood Pressure and Cardiovascular Prevention, 23,* 3–7.

Carpendale, J.I., & Chandler, M.J. (1996). On the distinction between false belief understanding and subscribing to an interpretive theory of mind. *Child Development, 67,* 1686–1706.

Carpendale, J.I.M., & Lewis, C. (2015). The development of social understanding. In R.M. Lerner (Ed.), *Handbook of child psychology and developmental science* (7th ed.). New York: Wiley.

Carr, D., & Luth, E. (2016). End-of-life planning and health care. In L.K. George & K.F. Ferraro (Eds.), *Handbook of aging and the social sciences* (8th ed.). New York: Elsevier.

Carr, D., & Sharp, S. (2014). Do afterlife beliefs affect psychological adjustment to late-life spousal loss? *Journals of Gerontology B: Psychological Sciences and Social Sciences, 69B*(1), 103–112.

Carr, R., & Peebles, R. (2012). Developmental considerations of media exposure risk for eating disorders. In J. Lock (Ed.), *Oxford handbook of child and adolescent eating disorders: Developmental perspectives.* New York: Oxford University Press.

Carroll, D., & others (2011). Low cognitive ability in early adulthood is associated with reduced lung function in middle age: The Vietnam Experience Study. *Thorax, 66,* 884–888.

Carruthers, A., & others (2015). Evolution of facial aesthetic treatment over five or more years: A retrospective cross-sectional analysis of continuous onabotulinumtoxinA treatment. *Dermatologic Surgery, 41,* 693–701.

Carskadon, M.A. (2006, March). *Too little, too late: Sleep bioregulatory processes across adolescence.* Paper presented at the meeting of the Society for Research on Adolescence, San Francisco.

Carskadon, M.A. (2011a). Sleep in adolescents: The perfect storm. *Pediatric Clinics of North America, 58,* 637–647.

Carskadon, M.A. (2011b). Sleep's effects on cognition and learning in adolescence. *Progress in Brain Research, 190,* 137–143.

Carson, V., & others (2015). Systematic review of sedentary behavior and cognitive development in early childhood. *Preventive Medicine, 78,* 15–22.

Carstensen, L.L. (1998). A life-span approach to social motivation. In J. Heckhausen & C. Dweck (Eds.), *Motivation and self-regulation across the life span.* New York: Cambridge University Press.

Carstensen, L.L. (2006). The influence of a sense of time on human development. *Science, 312,* 1913–1915.

Carstensen, L.L. (2008, May). *Long life in the 21st century.* Paper presented at the meeting of the Association of Psychological Science, Chicago.

Carstensen, L.L. (2010). Social and emotional aging. *Annual Review of Psychology,* 2009 (Vol. 61). Palo Alto, CA: Annual Reviews.

Carstensen, L.L. (2014). Our aging population may just save us all. In P. Irving (Ed.), *The upside of aging.* New York: Wiley.

Carstensen, L.L. (2015, February). The new age of much older age. *Time Magazine, 185*(6), 68–70.

Carstensen, L.L. (2016, February). The new age of aging. *Time, 186*(2), 22–29.

Carstensen, L.L., & Fried, L.P. (2012). The meaning of old age. *Global population aging: Peril or promise?* Geneva, Switzerland: World Economic Forum.

Carstensen, L.L., Rosenberger, M.E., Smith, K., & Modrek, S. (2015a). Optimizing health in aging societies. *Public Policy and Aging Report, 25,* 38–42.

Carstensen, L.L., Rosenberger, M.E., Smith, K., & Modrek, S. (2015b). Optimizing older workforces. In L.M. Finkelstein & others (Eds.), *Facing the challenges of a multi-age workforce: A use-inspired approach.* New York: Routledge.

Carstensen, L.L., Smith, K., & Jaworski, D. (2015). *The future of aging.* Retrieved September 15, 2015, from www.futureagenda.org/category/topics/aging

Carstensen, L.L., & others (2011). Emotional experience improves with age: Evidence based on over 10 years of sampling. *Psychology and Aging, 26,* 21–33.

Carta, G., & others (2015). How does early cognitive behavioral therapy reduce postpartum depression? *Clinical and Experimental Obstetrics Gynecology, 42,* 49–52.

Carta, J.J., Greenwood, C., Baggett, K., Buzhardt, J., & Walker, D. (2012). Research-based approaches for individualizing caregiving and educational interventions for infants and toddlers in poverty. In S.L. Odom, E.P. Pungello, & N. Gardner-Neblett (Eds.), *Infants, toddlers, and families in poverty.* New York: Guilford.

Carter, T., Morres, I., Repper, J., & Callaghan, P. (2016). Exercise for adolescents with depression: Valued aspects and perceived change. *Journal of Psychiatric and Mental Health Nursing, 23,* 37–44.

Cartmill, E., & Goldin-Meadow, S. (2015). Gesture. In D. Marsumoto, H.C. Hwang, & M.G. Frank (Eds.), *APA handbook of nonverbal communication.* Washington, DC: American Psychological Association.

Caruthers, A.S., Van Ryzin, M.J., & Dishion, T.J. (2014). Preventing high-risk sexual behavior in early adulthood with family interventions in adolescence: Outcomes and developmental processes. *Prevention Science, 15*(Suppl. 1), S59–S69.

Case, R., & Mueller, M.R. (2001). Differentiation, integration, and covariance mapping as fundamental processes in cognitive and neurological growth. In J.L. McClelland & R.S. Slegler (Eds.), *Mechanisms of cognitive development.* Mahwah, NJ: Erlbaum.

Caserta, M., Utz, R., Lund, D., Swenson, K.L., & de Vries, B. (2014). Coping processes among bereaved spouses. *Death Studies, 38,* 145–155.

Casey, B.J. (2015). The adolescent brain and self-control. *Annual Review of Psychology* (Vol. 66). Palo Alto, CA: Annual Reviews.

Casey, B.J., Galvan, A., & Somerville, L.H. (2016). Beyond simple models of adolescence to an integrated circuit-based account: A commentary. *Developmental Cognitive Neuroscience, 17,* 128–130.

Casey, E.C., & others (2016, in press). Promoting resilience through executive function training for homeless and highly mobile preschoolers. In S. Prince-Embury & D. Saklofske (Eds.), *Resilience intervention for diverse populations.* New York: Springer.

Cashon, C.H., & Holt, N.A. (2015). Developmental origins of the face inversion effect. *Advances in Child Development and Behavior, 48,* 117–150.

Caspers, K.M., & others (2009). Association between the serotonin transporter polymorphism (5-HTTLPR) and adult unresolved attachment. *Developmental Psychology, 45,* 64–76.

Caspi, A., & Roberts, B.W. (2001). Personality development across the life course: The argument for change and continuity. *Psychological Inquiry, 12,* 49–66.

Caspi, A., & others (2003). Influence of life stress on depression: Moderation by a polymorphism in the 5-HTT gene. *Science, 301,* 386–389.

Cassidy, A.R. (2016). Executive function and psychosocial adjustment in healthy children and adolescents: A latest variable modeling investigation. *Child Neuropsychology, 22,* 292–317.

Cassidy, J. (2016). The nature of the child's ties. In J. Cassidy & P.R. Shaver (Eds.), *Handbook of attachment* (3rd ed.). New York: Guilford.

Castrillo, J., & Oliver, S.G. (2016). Alzheimer's as a systems-level disease involving the interplay of cellular networks. *Methods in Biological Medicine, 1303,* 3–48.

Cauffman, E., Shulman, E., Bechtold, J., & Steinberg, L. (2015). Children and the law. In R.M. Lerner (Ed.), *Handbook of child psychology* (7th ed.). New York: Wiley.

Cauley, J.A. (2015). An overview of sarcopenic obesity. *Journal of Clinical Densitometry, 18*(4), 499–505.

Cavanagh, S.E. (2009). Puberty. In D. Carr (Ed.), *Encyclopedia of the life course and human development.* Boston: Gale Cengage.

Cavuoti, C. (2015). Giving a voice to the disenfranchised. Book review. *Death Studies, 39,* 663–665.

Cazzato, V., & others (2016). The effects of body exposure on self-body image and esthetic appreciation in anorexia nervosa. *Experimental Brain Research, 234,* 695–709.

Ceci, S.J., & Gilstrap, L.L. (2000). Determinants of intelligence: Schooling and intelligence. In A. Kazdin (Ed.), *Encyclopedia of psychology.* Washington, DC, & New York: American Psychological Association and Oxford University Press.

Ceci, S.J., Hritz, A., & Royer, C.E. (2016). Understanding suggestibility. In W. O'Donohue & M. Fanetti (Eds.), *A guide to evidence-based practice.* New York: Springer.

Center for Science in the Public Interest (2008). *Obesity on the kids' menu at top chains.* Retrieved October 24, 2008, from www.cspinet.org/new/200808041.html

Center for Survey Research at the University of Connecticut (2000). *Hours on the job.* Storrs: University of Connecticut, Center for Survey Research.

Centers for Disease Control and Prevention (2007). *Autism and developmental disabilities monitoring (ADDM) network.* Atlanta: Author.

Centers for Disease Control and Prevention (2014). *Breastfeeding report card. United States 2014.* Atlanta: Author.

Centers for Disease Control and Prevention (2014). *National marriage and divorce rate trends.* Atlanta: Author.

Centers for Disease Control and Prevention (2015). *National marriage and divorce rate trends.* Atlanta: Author.

Centers for Disease Control and Prevention (2015). *Suicide.* Atlanta: Author.

Centers for Disease Control and Prevention (2015, March 31). *Ten leading causes of death and injury.* Atlanta: Author.

Centers for Disease Control and Prevention (2016). *ADHD.* Retrieved January 12, 2016, from www.cdc.gov/ncbddd/adhd/data.html

Centers for Disease Control and Prevention (2016). *Autism spectrum disorders.* Atlanta: Author.

Centers for Disease Control and Prevention (2016). *Body mass index for children and teens.* Atlanta: Author.

Centers for Disease Control and Prevention (2016). *How much physical activity do older adults need?* Atlanta: Author.

Centers for Disease Control and Prevention (2016). *Sexually transmitted disease surveillance.* Atlanta, GA: U.S. Department of Health and Human Services.

Central Intelligence Agency (2015). *The world factbook: Life expectancy at birth.* Washington, DC: CIA.

Cerillo-Urbina, A.J., & others (2015). The effects of physical exercise in children with attention deficit hyperactivity disorder: A systematic review and meta-analysis of randomized controlled trials. *Child Care, Health, and Development, 41,* 779–788.

Chalan, P., & others (2015). Rheumatoid arthritis, immunosenescence, and the hallmarks of aging. *Current Aging Science, 8,* 131–146.

Chan, C.H., & others (2015). Sexual initiation and emotional/behavioral problems in Taiwanese adolescents: A multivariate response profile analysis. *Archives of Sexual Behavior, 44,* 717–727.

Chan, M.Y., Haber, S., Drew, L.M., & Park, D.C. (2014). Training older adults to use tablet computers: Does it enhance cognitive function? *Gerontologist,* doi 10.1093/geront/gnu057

Chandra, A., Mosher, W.D., Copen, C., & Sionean, C. (2011, March 3). Sexual behavior, sexual attraction, and sexual identity in the United States: Data from the 2006–2008 National Survey of Family Growth. *National Health Statistics Reports, 36,* 1–28.

Chang, H.Y., & others (2014). Prenatal maternal depression is associated with low birth weight through shorter gestational age in term infants in Korea. *Early Human Development, 90,*15–20.

Chang, Z., Lichtenstein, P., & Larsson, H. (2012). The effects of childhood ADHD symptoms on early-onset substance use: A Swedish twin study. *Journal of Abnormal Child Psychology, 40,* 425–435.

Chao, R., & Tseng, V. (2002). Parenting of Asians. In M.H. Bornstein, *Handbook of parenting* (2nd ed., Vol. 4). Mahwah: NJ: Erlbaum.

Chao, R. (2001). Extending research on the consequences of parenting style for Chinese Americans and European Americans. *Child Development, 72,* 1832–1843.

Chao, R.K. (2005, April). *The importance of* Guan *in describing control of immigrant Chinese.* Paper presented at the meeting of the Society for Research in Child Development, Atlanta.

Chao, R.K. (2007, March). *Research with Asian Americans: looking back and moving forward.* Paper presented at the meeting of the Society for Research in Child Development, Boston.

Chao, R.K., & Otsuki-Clutter, M. (2011). Racial and ethnic differences: Sociocultural and contextual explanations. *Journal of Research on Adolescence, 21,* 47–60.

Chaplin, T.M., & Aldao, A. (2013). Gender differences in emotion expression in children: A meta-analytic review. *Psychological Bulletin, 139*(4), 735–765.

Chaplin, T.M., & others (2012). Parent-adolescent conflict interactions and adolescent alcohol use. *Addictive Behaviors, 37,* 605–612.

Charkiewicz, K., & others (2016). Brief communication: Maternal plasma autoantibodies screening for fetal Down syndrome. *Journal of Immunology Research, 2016,* 9362169.

Charles, S.T., Piazza, J.R., Mogle, J., Sliwinski, M.J., & Almedia, D.M. (2013). The wear and tear of daily stressors on mental health. *Psychological Science, 24,* 733–741.

Charles, S.T., & others (2010). Fewer ups and downs: Daily stressors mediate age differences in negative affect. *Journals of Gerontology B: Psychological Sciences and Social Sciences, 65B,* 279–286.

Charness, N., & Boot, W.R. (2016). Technology, gaming, and social networking. In L.K. George & K.F. Ferraro (Eds.), *Handbook of aging and the social sciences* (8th ed.). New York: Elsevier.

Charness, N., & Krampe, R.T. (2008). Expertise and knowledge. In D.F. Alwin & S.M. Hofer (Eds.), *Handbook on cognitive aging.* Thousand Oaks, CA: Sage.

Chassin, L., Colder, C.R., Hussong, A., & Sher, K.J. (2016). Substance use and substance use disorders. In D. Cicchetti (Ed.), *Developmental psychopathology* (3rd ed.). New York: Wiley.

Chaturvedi, S., & others (2014). Pharmacological interventions for hypertension in children. *Cochrane Database of Systematic Reviews, 2,* CD008117.

Chauhan, G., & others (2015). Association of Alzheimer's disease GWAS loci with MRI markers of brain aging. *Neurobiology of Aging, 36,* e7–e16.

Chavarria, M.C., & others (2014). Puberty in the corpus callosum. *Neuroscience, 265,* 1–8.

Chen, C., & Stevenson, H.W. (1989). Homework: A cross-cultural comparison. *Child Development, 60,* 551–561.

Chen, D., Drabick, D.A., & Burgers, D.E. (2015). A developmental perspective on peer rejection, deviant peer affiliation, and conduct problems among youth. *Child Psychiatry and Human Development, 46,* 823–838.

Chen, J., Yu, J., Wu, Y., & Zhang, J. (2015). The influence of pubertal timing and stressful life events on depression and delinquency among Chinese adolescents. *Psychology Journal, 4,* 88–97.

Chen, L.C., Jeka, J., & Clark, J.E. (2016). Development of adaptive sensorimotor control in infant sitting posture. *Gait and Posture, 45,* 157–163.

Chen, L.W., & others (2016). Maternal caffeine intake during pregnancy and risk of pregnancy loss: A categorical and dose-response meta-analysis of prospective studies. *Public Health Nutrition, 19,* 1233–1244.

Chen, T.Y., & others (2015). Effects of a selective educational system on fatigue, sleep problems, daytime sleepiness, and depression among senior high school adolescents in Taiwan. *Neuropsychiatric Disease and Treatment, 11,* 741–750.

Chen, X., & Liu, C. (2016). Culture, peer relationships, and developmental psychopathology. In D. Cicchetti (Ed.), *Developmental psychopathology* (3rd ed.). New York: Wiley.

Chen, X., & Schmidt, L.A. (2015). Temperament and personality. In R.M. Lerner (Ed.), *Handbook of child psychology and developmental science* (7th ed.). New York: Wiley.

Chen, X., Fu, R., & Zhao, S. (2015). Culture and socialization. In J.E. Grusec & P.D. Hastings (Eds.), *Handbook of socialization* (2nd ed.). New York: Guilford.

Chen, Y., & others (2016). Rapamycin attenuates splenomegaly in both intrahepatic and prehepatic hypertensive rats by blocking mTOR signaling pathway. *PLoS One, 11*(1), e0141159.

Chen, Y.M., & others (2016, in press). Trajectories of older adults' leisure time activity and functional disability: A 12-year follow-up. *International Journal of Behavioral Medicine.*

Cheng, T.Y., & others (2016). Genetic variants in the mTOR pathway and breast cancer in African American women. *Carcinogenesis, 37,* 49–55.

Cheong, J.I., & others (2015). The effect of early menarche on the sexual behaviors of Korean female adolescents. *Annals of Pediatric Endocrinology and Metabolism, 20,* 130–135.

Cherlin, A.J. (2009). *The marriage-go-round.* New York: Random House.

Cherlin, A.J., & Furstenberg, F.F. (1994). Stepfamilies in the United States: A reconsideration. In J. Blake & J. Hagen (Eds.), *Annual review of sociology.* Palo Alto, CA: Annual Reviews.

Chess, S., & Thomas, A. (1977). Temperamental individuality from childhood to adolescence. *Journal of Child Psychiatry, 16,* 218–226.

Cheung, C., & Pomerantz, E.M. (2012). Why does parents' involvement in children's learning enhance children's achievement? The role of parent-oriented motivation. *Journal of Educational Psychology. 104*(3), 820–832.

Chevalier, N., & others (2015). Myelination is associated with processing speed in early childhood: Preliminary insights. *PLoS One, 10,* e0139897.

Chi, M.T. (1978). Knowledge structures and memory development. In R.S. Siegler (Ed.), *Children's thinking: What develops?* Hillsdale, NJ: Erlbaum.

Chiang, H.L., & others (2015). Altered white matter tract property related to impaired focused attention, sustained attention, cognitive impulsivity, and vigilance in attention-deficit/hyperactivity disorder. *Journal of Psychiatry and Neuroscience, 40,* 140–106.

Chiasson, M.A., & others (2016). Predictors of obesity in a cohort of children enrolled in WIC as infants and retained to 3 years of age. *Journal of Community Health, 41,* 127–133.

Child Trends (2014, October). *High school dropout rates.* Bethesda, MD: Child Trends.

Childers, J.B., & Tomasello, M. (2002). Two-year-olds learn novel nouns, verbs, and conventional actions from massed or distributed exposures. *Developmental Psychology, 38,* 967–978.

Chiotis, K., & others (2016, in press). Imaging in-vivo tau pathology in Alzheimer's disease with THK5317 PET in a multimodal paradigm. *European Journal of Nuclear Medicine and Molecular Imaging.*

Chiou, W.B., Chen, S.W., & Liao, D.C. (2014). Does Facebook promote self-interest? Enactment of indiscriminate one-to-many communication on online social networking sites decreases prosocial behavior. *Cyberpsychology, Behavior, and Social Networking, 17,* 68–73.

Chita-Tegmark, M. (2016). Social attention in ASD: A review and meta-analysis of eye-tracking studies. *Research in Developmental Disabilities, 48,* 79–93.

Chitayat, D., & others (2016). Folic acid supplementation for pregnant women and those planning pregnancy: 2015 update. *Journal of Clinical Pharmacology, 56,* 170–176.

Cho, E.S., & others (2016, in press). The effects of kangaroo care for the neonatal intensive care unit on the physiological functions of preterm infants, maternal-infant attachment, and maternal stress. *Journal of Pediatric Nursing.*

Cho, M., & Suh, Y. (2016). Genetics of human aging. In M.R. Kaeberlein & G.M. Martin (Eds.), *Handbook of the biology of aging* (8th ed.). New York: Elsevier.

Choi, H., Yorgason, J.B., & Johnson, D.R. (2016). Marital quality and health in middle and later adulthood: Dyadic associations. *Journals of Gerontology B: Psychological Sciences and Social Sciences, 7,* 154–164.

Choi, M., Sprang, G., & Eslinger, J.G. (2016). Grandparents raising grandchildren: A synthetic review and theoretical model for interventions. *Family and Community Health, 39,* 120–128.

Choi, S.S., Lee, S.R., & Lee, H.J. (2016). Neurorestorative role of stem cells in Alzheimer's disease: Astrocyte involvement. *Current Alzheimer Research, 13,* 419–427.

Choi, Y., & Lee, H.J. (2016, in press). Do regular cholesterol screenings lead to lower cholesterol levels and better health behaviors for all? Spotlight on middle-aged and older adults in the United States. *Journal of Aging and Health.*

Choi, Y.J., & Luo, Y. (2015). 13-month-olds' understanding of social interaction. *Psychological Science, 26,* 274–283.

Chomsky, N. (1957). *Syntactic structures.* The Hague: Mouton.

Chopik, W.J., Edelstein, R.S., & Fraley, R.C. (2013). From the cradle to the grave: Age differences in attachment from early adulthood to old age. *Journal of Personality, 81,* 171–183.

Choudhary, M., & others (2016). To study the effect of Kangaroo Mother Care on pain response in preterm neonates and to determine the behavioral and physiological responses to painful stimuli in preterm neonates: A study from western Rajasthan. *Journal of Maternal-Fetal and Neonatal Medicine, 29,* 826–831.

Choukas-Bradley, S., & Prinstein, M.J. (2016). Peer relationships and the development of psychopathology. In M. Lewis & D. Rudolph (Eds.), *Handbook of developmental psychopathology* (3rd ed.). New York: Springer.

Chow, C.M., Tan, C.C., & Buhrmester, D. (2015). Interdependence of depressive symptoms, school involvement, and academic performance between adolescent friends: A dyadic analysis. *British Journal of Educational Psycholology, 85,* 316–331.

Christensen, L.B., Johnson, R.B., & Turner, L.A. (2015). *Research methods* (12th ed.). Upper Saddle River, NJ: Pearson.

Christian, P., & others (2015). Nutrition and maternal, neonatal, and child health. *Seminars in Perinatology, 39,* 361–372.

Christie, J.F., & Roskos, K.A. (2015). How does play contribute to literacy? In J.E. Johnson & others (Eds.), *Handbook of the study of play.* Blue Ridge Summit, PA: Rowman & Littlefield.

Chu, J.T., & others (2015). Parent and adolescent effects of a universal group program for the parenting of adolescents. *Prevention Science, 16,* 609–620.

Chuang, Y.F., & others (2014). Cardiovascular risks and brain function: A functional magnetic resonance imaging study of executive function in in older adults. *Neurobiology of Aging, 35,* 1396–1403.

Cicchetti, D., & Toth, S.L. (2006). Developmental psychopathology and preventive intervention. In W. Damon & R. Lerner (Eds.), *Handbook of child psychology* (6th ed.). New York: Wiley.

Cicchetti, D., & Toth, S.L. (2015). A multilevel perspective on child maltreatment. In M. Lamb & C. Garcia Coll (Eds.), *Handbook of child psychology and developmental science* (7th ed., Vol. 3). New York: Wiley.

Cicchetti, D., & Toth, S.L. (2016). Child maltreatment and developmental psychopathology: A multi-level perspective. In D. Cicchetti (Ed.), *Developmental psychopathology* (3rd ed.). New York: Wiley.

Cichetti, D., Toth, S.L., & Rogosch, F.A. (2005). *A prevention program for child maltreatment.* Unpublished manuscript. Rochester, NY: University of Rochester.

Cicirelli, V. (2009). Sibling relationships, later life. In D. Carr (Ed.), *Encyclopedia of the life course and human development.* Boston: Gale Cengage.

Cicirelli, V.G. (2010). Attachment relationships in old age. *Journal of Social and Personal Relationships, 27,* 191–199.

Cillessen, A.H.N., & Bellmore, A.D. (2011). Social skills and social competence in interactions with peers. In P.K. Smith & C.H. Hart (Eds.), *Wiley-Blackwell handbook of childhood social development* (2nd ed.). New York: Wiley.

Claes, H.I., & others (2010). Understanding the effects of sildenafil treatment on erection maintenance and erection hardness. *Journal of Sexual Medicine, 7*(6), 2184–2191.

Clark, B. (2008). *Growing up gifted* (7th ed.). Upper Saddle River, NJ: Prentice Hall.

Clark, C.D. (2015). Play interventions and therapy. In J.E. Johnson & others (Eds.), *Handbook of the study of play.* Blue Ridge Summit, PA: Rowman & Littlefield.

Clark, C.D. (2016). *Play and well-being.* New York: Routledge.

Clark, D.A., Donnellan, M.B., Robins, R.W., & Conger, R.D. (2015). Early adolescent temperament, parental monitoring, and substance use in Mexican-origin adolescents. *Journal of Adolescence, 41,* 121–130.

Clark, E.V. (1993). *The lexicon in acquisition.* New York: Cambridge University Press.

Clark, E.V. (2012). Lexical meaning. In E.L. Bavin (Ed.), *Cambridge handbook of child language.* New York: Cambridge University Press.

Clark, E.V. (2017). *Language in children.* New York: Psychology Press.

Clarke-Stewart, A.K., & Miner, J.L. (2008). Child and day care, effects of. In M.M. Haith & J.B. Benson (Eds.), *Encyclopedia of infant and early childhood development.* Oxford, UK: Elsevier.

Clarke-Stewart, A.K., & Parke, R.D. (2014). *Social development* (2nd ed.). New York: Wiley.

Class, Q.A., & others (2013). Maternal stress and infant mortality: The importance of the preconception period. *Psychological Science, 24*(7), 1309–1316.

Clauss, J.A., Avery, S.N., & Blackford, J.U. (2015). The nature of individual differences in inhibited temperament and risk for psychiatric disease: A review and meta-analysis. *Progress in Neurobiology, 127–128,* 23–45.

Clearfield, M.W., Diedrich, F.J., Smith, L.B., & Thelen, E. (2006). Young infants reach correctly in A-not-B tasks: On the development of stability and perseveration. *Infant Behavior and Development, 29,* 435–444.

Clements, J.M. (2009). Patient perceptions on the use of advance directives and life prolonging technology. *American Journal of Hospice and Palliative Care, 26,* 270–276.

Clifton, R.K., Morrongiello, B.A., Kulig, J.W., & Dowd, J.M. (1981). Developmental changes in auditory localization in infancy. In R.N. Aslin, J.R. Alberts, & M.R. Petersen (Eds.), *Development of perception* (Vol. 1). Orlando, FL: Academic Press.

Clifton, R.K., Muir, D.W., Ashmead, D.H., & Clarkson, M.G. (1993). Is visually guided reaching in early infancy a myth? *Child Development, 64,* 1099–1110.

Cnattingius, S., & others (2013). Maternal obesity and risk of preterm delivery. *Journal of the American Medical Association, 309,* 2362–2370.

Cogmed (2013). *Cogmed: Working memory is the engine of learning.* Upper Saddle River, NJ: Pearson.

Cohen, A.A. (2015). Physiological and comparative evidence fails to confirm an adaptive role for aging in evolution. *Current Aging Science, 8,* 14–23.

Cohen, A.O., & others (2016, in press). When is an adolescent an adult: Assessing cognitive control capacity in emotional and nonemotional contexts. *Psychological Science.*

Cohen, F., & others (2007). Immune function declines with unemployment and recovers after stressor termination. *Psychosomatic Medicine, 69,* 225–234.

Cohen, P. (2012). *In our prime: The invention of middle age.* New York: Scribner.

Cohen, P., Kasen, S., Chen, H., Hartmark, C., & Gordon, K. (2003). Variations in patterns of developmental transitions in the emerging adulthood period. *Developmental Psychology, 39,* 657–669.

Cohen, R., Bavishi, C., & Rozanski, A. (2016). Purpose in life and its relationship to all-cause mortality and cardiovascular events: A meta-analysis. *Psychosomatic Medicine, 78,* 122–133.

Coie, J. (2004). The impact of negative social experiences on the development of antisocial behavior. In J.B. Kupersmidt & K.A. Dodge (Eds.), *Children's peer relations: From development to intervention.* Washington, DC: American Psychological Association.

Coker, T.R., & others (2015). Media violence exposure and physical aggression in fifth-grade children. *Academic Pediatrics, 15,* 82–88.

Colby, A., Kohlberg, L., Gibbs, J., & Lieberman, M. (1983). A longitudinal study of moral judgment. *Monographs of the Society for Research in Child Development* (Serial No. 201).

Colcombe, S.J., & others (2006). Aerobic exercise training increases brain volume in aging humans. *Journals of Gerontology: Medical Sciences, 61A,* 1166–1170.

Cole, P.M. (2016). Emotion and the development of psychopathology. In D. Cicchetti (Ed.), *Developmental psychopathology* (3rd ed.). New York: Wiley.

Cole, P.M., & Tan, P.Z. (2007). Emotion socialization from a cultural perspective. In J.E. Grusec & P.D. Hastings (Eds.), *Handbook of socialization.* New York: Guilford.

Cole, P.M., & Tan, P.Z. (2015). Emotion socialization from a cultural perspective. In J.E. Grusec & P.D. Hastings (Eds.), *Handbook of socialization* (2nd ed.). New York: Wiley.

Cole, P.M., Dennis, T.A., Smith-Simon, K.E., & Cohen, L.H. (2009). Preschoolers' emotion regulation strategy understanding: Relations with maternal socialization and child behavior. *Social Development, 18*(2), 324–352.

Cole, W.G., Robinson, S.R., & Adolph, K.E. (2016). Bouts of steps: The organization of infant exploration. *Developmental Psychobiology, 58,* 341–354.

Coleman, A.M. (2013). Physicians' attitudes toward advance directives: A literature review of variables impacting on physicians' attitudes toward advance directives. *American Journal of Hospice and Palliative Care, 30,* 696–706.

Coleman, P.D. (1986, August). *Regulation of dendritic extent: Human aging brain and Alzheimer's disease.* Paper presented at the meeting of the American Psychological Association, Washington, DC.

Colen, C.G., & Ramey, D.M. (2014). Is breast truly best? Estimating the effects of breastfeeding on long-term health and well-being in the United States using sibling comparisons. *Social Science and Medicine, 109C,* 55–65.

Coles, C.D., & others (2016). A comparison of five methods for the clinical diagnosis of fetal alcohol spectrum disorders. *Alcoholism, Clinical and Experimental Research, 40,* 1000–1009.

Collings, P.J., & others (2013). Physical activity intensity, sedentary time, and body composition in preschoolers. *American Journal of Clinical Nutrition, 97,* 1020–1028.

Collins, W.A., & van Dulmen, M. (2006). The significance of middle childhood peer competence for work and relationships in early childhood. In A.C. Huston & M.N. Ripke (Eds.), *Developmental contexts in middle childhood.* New York: Cambridge University Press.

Collin-Vezina, D., & others (2015). A preliminary mapping of individual, relational, and social factors that impede disclosure of childhood sexual abuse. *Child Abuse and Neglect, 43,* 123–134.

Columbo, J., & Salley, B. (2015). Biopsychosocial perspectives on attention in infancy. In S.D. Calkins (Ed.), *Handbook of infant biopsychosocial development.* New York: Guilford.

Comer, J. (1988). Educating poor minority children. *Scientific American, 259,* 42–48.

Comer, J. (2004). *Leave no child behind.* New Haven, CT: Yale University Press.

Comer, J. (2006). Child development: The underweighted aspect of intelligence. In P.C. Kyllonen, R.D. Roberts, & L. Stankov (Eds.), *Extending intelligence.* Mahwah, NJ: Erlbaum.

Comer, J. (2010). Comer School Development Program. In J. Meece & J. Eccles (Eds.), *Handbook of research on schools, schooling, and human development.* New York: Routledge.

Comhaire, F. (2016). Hormone replacement therapy and longevity. *Andrologia, 48,* 65–68.

Committee on the Rights of the Child (2014). *The Convention on the Rights of the Child and Its Treaty body—The Committee on the Rights of the Child.* Retrieved April 14, 2015, from http://endcorporalpunishment.org/pages/hrlaw/crc_session.html

Common Core State Standards Initiative (2016). *Common Core.* Retrieved January 10, 2015, from www.core standards.org/

Common Sense Media (2011). *Zero to eight: Children's media use in America.* Retrieved June 21, 2012, from www.commonsensemedia.org/research

Commoner, B. (2002). Unraveling the DNA myth: The spurious foundation of genetic engineering. *Harper's Magazine, 304,* 39–47.

Condition of Education (2015). Participation in education. Washington, DC: U.S. Office of Education.

Connell, N.M., Morris, R.G., & Piquero, A.R. (2016). Predicting bullying: Exploring the contribution of negative life experiences in predicting adolescent bullying behavior. *International Journal of Offender Therapy and Comparative Criminology, 60,* 1082–1096.

Connolly, J.A., & McIsaac, C. (2009). Romantic relationships in adolescence. In R.M. Lerner & L. Steinberg (Eds.), *Handbook of adolescent psychology* (3rd ed.). New York: Wiley.

Connolly, J.A., Nguyen, H.N., Pepler, D., Craig, W., & Jiang, D. (2013). Developmental trajectories of romantic stages and associations with problem behaviors during adolescence. *Journal of Adolescence, 36,* 1013–1024.

Conry-Murray, C., Kim, J.M., & Turiel, E. (2012, April). *U.S. and Korean children's judgments of gender norm violations.* Paper presented at the Gender Development Research conference, San Francisco.

Consoli, A., & others (2013). Suicidal behaviors in depressed adolescents: Role of perceived relationships in the family. *Child and Adolescent Psychiatry and Mental Health, 7*(1), 8.

Consoli, A., & others (2015). Risk and protective factors for suicidality at 6-month follow-up in adolescent inpatients who attempted suicide: An exploratory model. *Canadian Journal of Psychiatry, 60*(2, Suppl. 1), S27–S36.

Conti, E., & others (2015). The first 1000 days of the autistic brain: A systematic review of diffusion imaging studies. *Frontiers in Human Neuroscience, 9,* 159.

Conway, M.E., & Lee, C. (2015). The redox switch that regulates molecular chaperones. *Biomedical Concepts, 6,* 269–284.

Cook, J.L., & others (2016). Fetal alcohol spectrum disorder: A guideline for diagnosis across the lifespan. *CMAJ, 168,* 191–197.

Cook, R.F., Hersch, R.K., Schlossberg, D., & Leaf, S.L. (2015). A Web-based health promotion program for older workers: Randomized controlled trial. *Journal of Medical Internet Research, 17,* e82.

Cooley, J.L., & Fife, P.J. (2016). Peer victimization and forms of aggression during middle childhood: The role of emotion regulation. *Journal of Abnormal Child Psychology, 44,* 535–547.

Cooney, C.L. (2015). Critical thinking in its contexts and in itself. *Educational Philosophy and Theory, 47,* 515–528.

Coontz, S. (2005). *Marriage: A history.* New York: Penguin.

Cooper, C.R., Gonzales, E., & Wilson, A.R. (2015). Identities, cultures, and schooling: How students navigate racial-ethnic, indigenous, immigrant, social class, and gender identities on their pathways through school. In K.C. McLean & M. Syed (Eds.), *Oxford handbook of identity development.* New York: Oxford University Press.

Cooperrider, K., & Goldin-Meadow, S. (2017, in press). Gesture, language, and cognition. In B. Dancygier (Ed.), *Cambridge handbook of cognitive linguistics.* New York: Cambridge University Press.

Coovadia, H., & Moodley, D. (2016). Improving HIV pre-exposure prophylaxis for infants. *Lancet, 387,* 513–514.

Copen, C.E., Daniels, C.E., & Mosher, W.D. (2013, April 4). First premarital cohabitation in the United States: 2006–2010. National Survey of Family Growth. *National Health Statistics Reports, 64,* 1–16.

Copen, C.E., Daniels, K., Vespa, J., & Mosher, W.D. (2012). First marriages in the United States: Data from the 2006–2010 National Survey of Family Growth. *National Health Statistics Reports, 49,* 1–22.

Cordier, S. (2008). Evidence for a role of paternal exposure in developmental toxicity. *Basic and Clinical Pharmacology and Toxicology, 102,* 176–181.

Cordova, D., Huang, S., Lally, M., Estrada, Y., & Prado, G. (2014). Do parent-adolescent discrepancies in family functioning increase the risk of Hispanic adolescent HIV risk behaviors? *Family Process, 53,* 348–363.

Cornelissen, K.K., & others (2015). The influence of personal BMI on body size estimations and sensitivity to body size change in anorexia spectrum disorders. *Body Image, 13,* 75–85.

Cornew, L., & others (2012). Atypical social referencing in infant siblings of children with autism spectrum disorders. *Journal of Autism and Developmental Disorders, 42,* 2611–2621.

Corona, G., Rastrelli, G., Maseroli, E., Forti, G., & Maggi, M. (2013). Sexual functioning of the aging male. *Best Practices & Research: Clinical Endocrinology and Metabolism, 27,* 581–601.

Corona, G., & others (2015). Obesity and late-onset hypogonadism. *Molecular and Cellular Endocrinology, 418,* 130–133.

Correia, C., & others (2016). Global sensory impairment in older adults in the United States. *Journal of the American Geriatrics Society, 64,* 306–313.

Costa, P.T., & McCrae, R.R. (1998). Personality assessment. In H.S. Friedman (Ed.), *Encyclopedia of mental health* (Vol. 3). San Diego: Academic Press.

Costa, P.T., & McCrae, R.R. (2000). Contemporary personality psychology. In C.E. Coffey and J.L. Cummings (Eds.), *Textbook of geriatric neuropsychiatry.* Washington, DC: American Psychiatric Press.

Costigan, S.A., Barnett, L., Plotnikoff, R.C., & Lubans, D.R. (2013). The health indicators associated with screen-based sedentary behavior among adolescent girls: A systematic review. *Journal of Adolescent Health, 52*(4), 382–392.

Cote, J.E. (2015). Identity-formation research from a critical perspective: Is a social science developing? In K.C. McLean & M. Syed (Eds.), *Oxford handbook of identity development.* New York: Oxford University Press.

Cote, J., & Bynner, J.M. (2008). Changes in the transition to adulthood in the UK and Canada: The role of structure and aging in emerging adulthood. *Journal of Youth Studies, 11,* 251–258.

Cote-Lussier, C., Mathieu, M.E., & Barnett, T.A. (2015). Independent associations between child and parent perceived neighborhood safety, child screen time, physical activity, and BMI: A structural equation modeling approach. *International Journal of Obesity, 39,* 1475–1481.

Cotten, S.R., Anderson, W.A., & McCullough, B.M. (2013). Impact of Internet use on loneliness and contact with others among older adults: Cross-sectional analysis. *Journal of Medical Internet Research, 15*(2), e39.

Cotten, S.R., Ford, G., Ford, S., & Hale, T.M. (2014). Internet use and depression among retired older adults in the United States: A longitudinal analysis. *Journals of Gerontology B: Psychological Sciences and Social Sciences, 69,* 763–771.

Cottrell, L., & Duggleby, W. (2016, in press). The "good death": An integrative literature review. *Palliative and Supportive Care.*

Coubart, A., & others (2014). Dissociation between small and larger numerosities in newborn infants. *Developmental Science, 17,* 11–22.

Courage, M.L., Bakhtiar, A., Fitzpatrick, C., Kenny, S., & Brandeau, K. (2015). Growing up multitasking: The costs and benefits for cognitive development. *Developmental Review, 35,* 5–41.

Courage, M.L., Edison, S.C., & Howe, M.L. (2004). Variability in the early development of visual self-recognition. *Infant Behavior and Development, 27,* 509–532.

Cousineau, T.M., Goldstein, M., & Franco, D.L. (2005). A collaborative approach to nutrition education for college students. *Journal of American College Health, 53,* 79–84.

Cousins, L., & Goodyer, I.M. (2015). Antidepressants and the adolescent brain. *Journal of Psychopharmacology, 29,* 545–555.

Covington, J.D., & Bajpeyi, S. (2016). The sirtuins: Markers of metabolic health. *Molecular Nutrition and Food Research, 60,* 79–91.

Cowan, C.P., & Cowan, P.A. (2000). *When partners become parents.* Mahwah, NJ: Erlbaum.

Cowan, M.K. (2015). *Microbiology* (4th ed.). New York: McGraw-Hill.

Cowan, N., Saults, J.S., & Clark, K.M. (2015). Exploring age differences in visual working memory capacity: Is there a contribution of memory for configuration? *Journal of Experimental Child Psychology, 135,* 72–85.

Cowan, P., Cowan, C., Ablow, J., Johnson, V.K., & Measelle, J. (2005). *The family context of parenting in children's adaptation to elementary school.* Mahwah, NJ: Lawrence Erlbaum Associates.

Cox, C.E., & Curtis, J.R. (2016). Using technology to create a more humanistic approach to integrating palliative care into the intensive care unit. *American Journal of Respiratory and Critical Care Medicine, 193,* 242–250.

Cox, K.S., Wilt, J., Olson, B., & McAdams, D.P. (2010). Generativity, the Big Five, and psychosocial adaptation in midlife adults. *Journal of Personality, 78,* 1185–1208.

Coxon, J.P., & others (2016). Functional brain activation associated with inhibitory control deficits in older adults. *Cerebral Cortex, 26,* 12–22.

Craft, C.S., & others (2014). The extracellular matrix protein MAGP1 supports thermogenesis and protects against obesity and diabetes through regulation of TGFB. *Diabetes, 63,* 1920–1932.

Crain, S. (2012). Sentence scope. In E.L. Bavin (Ed.), *Cambridge handbook of child language.* New York: Cambridge University Press.

Crane, J.D., Macneil, L.G., & Tarnopolsky, M.A. (2013). Long-term aerobic exercise is associated with greater muscle strength throughout the life span. *Journals of Gerontology A: Biological Sciences and Medical Sciences, 68,* 631–638.

Crawford, D., & others (2010). The longitudinal influence of home and neighborhood environments on children's body mass index and physical activity over 5 years: The CLAN study. *International Journal of Obesity, 34,* 1177–1187.

Cremation Association of North America (2015). *Statistics about cremation trends.* Wheeling, IL: Author.

Crimmins, E.M., & Levine, M.E. (2016). Current status of research on trends in morbidity, health, life expectancy, and the compression of morbidity. In M.R. Kaeberlein & G.M. Martin (Eds.), *Handbook of the biology of aging* (8th ed.). New York: Elsevier.

Criss, M.M., & others (2015). Link between monitoring behavior and adolescent adjustment: An analysis of direct and indirect effects. *Journal of Child and Family Studies, 24,* 668–678.

Crockenberg, S.B. (1986). Are temperamental differences in babies associated with predictable differences in caregiving? In J.V. Lerner & R.M. Lerner (Eds.). *Temperament and social interaction during infancy and childhood.* San Francisco: Jossey-Bass.

Crooks, R.L., & Baur, K. (2016). *Our sexuality* (13th ed.). Boston: Cengage.

Crosnoe, R. (2011). *Fitting in, standing out.* New York: Cambridge University Press.

Crosnoe, R., & Benner, A.D. (2015). Children at school. In R.M. Lerner (Ed.), *Handbook of child psychology and developmental science* (7th ed.). New York: Wiley.

Crosnoe, R., Bonazzo, C., & Wu, N. (2015). *Healthy learners: A whole child approach to disparities in early education.* New York: Teachers College Press.

Crosnoe, R., & Fuligni, A.J. (2012). Children from immigrant families: Introduction to the special section. *Child Development, 83,* 1471–1476.

Crosnoe, R., & Leventhal, T. (2014). School- and neighborhood-based interventions to improve the lives of disadvantaged children. In E.T. Gershoff, R.S. Mistry, & D.A. Crosby (Eds.), *The societal context of child development.* New York: Oxford University Press.

Cross, D., Lester, L., & Barnes, A. (2015). A longitudinal study of the social and emotional predictors and consequences of cyber and traditional bullying victimization. *International Journal of Public Health, 60,* 207–217.

Croteau-Chonka, E.C., & others (2016). Examining the relationships between cortical maturation and white matter myelination throughout early childhood. *Neuroimage, 125,* 413–421.

Crouter, A.C. (2006). Mothers and fathers at work. In A. Clarke-Stewart & J. Dunn (Eds.), *Families count.* New York: Cambridge University Press.

Crowley, K., Callahan, M.A., Tenenbaum, H.R., & Allen, E. (2001). Parents explain more to boys than to girls during shared scientific thinking. *Psychological Science, 12,* 258–261.

Cruz, T.H., & others (2016, in press). Effects of an obesity prevention intervention on physical activity among preschool children: The CHILE study. *Health Promotion and Practice.*

Csikszentmihalyi, M. (1995). *Creativity.* New York: HarperCollins.

Csikszentmihalyi, M. (2000). Creativity: An overview. In A. Kazdin (Ed.), *Encyclopedia of psychology.* Washington, DC, & New York: American Psychological Association and Oxford University Press.

Cubanski, J., Casillas, G., & Damice, A. (2015, June). Poverty among seniors: An updated analysis of national and state level poverty rates under the official and supplemental poverty measures. San Francisco: Kaiser Family Foundation.

Cucina, J.M., Peyton, S.T., Su, C., & Byle, K.A. (2016). Role of mental abilities and mental tests in explaining school grades. *Intelligence, 54,* 90–104.

Cuckle, H., & Maymon, R. (2016). Development of prenatal screening—a historical overview. *Seminars in Perinatology, 40,* 12–22.

Cuevas, K., & Bell, K.A. (2014). Infant attention and early childhood executive function. *Child Development, 85*(2), 397–404.

Cuevas, K., & others (2014). What's mom got to do with it? Contributions of maternal executive function and caregiving to the development of executive function across early childhood. *Developmental Science, 17,* 224–238.

Cui, Z., & others (2016). Intraoperative MRI optimizing electrode placement for deep brain stimulation of the subthalamic nucleus in Parkinson disease. *Journal of Neurosurgery, 124,* 62–69.

Cummings, E.M., Koss, K.J., & Cheung, R.Y.M. (2015). Interparental conflict and children's mental health: Emerging directions in emotional security theory. In C.R. Agnew & S.C. South (Eds.),

Interpersonal relationships and health. New York: Oxford University Press.

Cummings, E.M., & Miller, L.M. (2015). Emotional security theory: An emerging theoretical model for youths' psychological and physiological responses across multiple developmental contexts. *Current Directions in Psychological Science, 24,* 208–213.

Cummings, E.M., & Valentino, K.V. (2015). Developmental psychopathology. In R.M. Lerner (Ed.), *Handbook of child psychology and developmental science* (7th ed.). New York: Wiley.

Cunha, A.B., & others (2016). Effect of short-term training on reaching behavior in infants: A randomized controlled trial. *Journal of Motor Behavior, 48,* 132–142.

Cunningham, M. (2009). Housework. In D. Carr (Ed.), *Encyclopedia of the life course and human development.* Boston: Gale Cengage.

Cunningham, P.M. (2013). *Phonics they use: Words for reading and writing* (6th ed.). Boston: Allyn & Bacon.

Cunningham, S.A., Kramer, M.R., & Narayan, K.M. (2014). Incidence of childhood obesity in the United States. *New England Journal of Medicine, 370,* 403–411.

Curran, K., DuCette, J., Eisenstein, J., & Hyman, I.A. (2001, August). *Statistical analysis of the cross-cultural data: The third year.* Paper presented at the meeting of the American Psychological Association, San Francisco, CA.

Currie, C., & others (2012). Is obesity at individual and national level associated with lower age at menarche? Evidence from 34 countries in the Health Behavior in School-aged Children study. *Journal of Adolescent Health, 50,* 621–626.

Currie, J., & Rossin-Slater, M. (2015). Early-life origins of life-cycle well-being: Research and policy. *Journal of Policy Analysis and Management, 34,* 208–242.

Currier, J.M., Holland, J.M., & Neimeyer, R.A. (2006). Sense-making, grief, and the experience of violent loss: Toward a mediational model. *Death Studies, 30,* 403–428.

Curry, A.E., Peek-Asa, C., Hamann, C.J., & Mirman, J.H. (2015). Effectiveness of parent-focused interventions to increase teen driver safety: A critical review. *Journal of Adolescent Health, 57*(Suppl. 1), S6–S14.

Cushner, K.H., McClelland, A., & Safford, P. (2015). *Human diversity in education* (8th ed.). New York: McGraw-Hill.

Cuzzolaro, M. (2014). Eating and weight disorders: Studies on anorexia, bulimia, and obesity turns 19. *Eating and Weight Disorders, 19,* 1–2.

Cvencek, D., Meltzoff, A.N., & Greenwald, A.G. (2011). Math-gender stereotypes in elementary school children. *Child Development, 82,* 766–779.

D

da Costa Souza, A., & Ribeiro, S. (2015). Sleep deprivation and gene expression. *Current Topics in Behavioral Neurosciences, 25,* 65–90.

Dahl, R.E. (2004). Adolescent brain development: A period of vulnerability and opportunity. *Annals of the New York Academy of Sciences, 1021,* 1–22.

Dai, D.-F., & others (2016). Cardiac aging. In M. Kaeberlein & G.M. Martin (Eds.), *Handbook of the biology of aging* (8th ed.). New York: Elsevier.

Daiello, L.A., & others (2015). Association of fish oil supplement use with preservation of brain volume and cognitive function. *Alzheimer's and Dementia, 11,* 226–235.

Dakof, G.A., & others (2015). A randomized clinical trial of family therapy in juvenile drug court. *Journal of Family Psychology, 29,* 232–241.

Dale, B., & others (2014). Utility of the Stanford-Binet Intelligence Scales, Fifth Edition, with ethnically diverse preschoolers. *Psychology in the Schools, 51,* 581–590.

Dale, P., & Goodman, J. (2004). Commonality and differences in vocabulary growth. In M. Tomasello & D.I. Slobin (Eds.), *Beyond nature-nurture.* Mahwah, NJ: Erlbaum.

Dalke, K.B., Wenzel, A., & Kim, D.R. (2016, in press). Depression and anxiety during pregnancy: Evaluating the literature in support of clinical risk-benefit decision-making. *Current Psychiatry Reports.*

Dalle Grave, R., El Ghoch, M., Sartriana, M., & Calugi, S. (2016). Cognitive behavioral therapy for anorexia nervosa: An update. *Current Psychiatry Reports, 18*(1), 2.

Daly, M., Delaney, L., Egan, M., & Baumeister, R.F. (2015). Childhood self-control and unemployment through the life span: Evidence from two British cohort studies. *Psychological Science, 26,* 709–723.

Damman, M., Henkens, K., & Kalmijn, M. (2015). Missing work after retirement: The role of life histories in the retirement adjustment process. *Gerontologist, 55,* 802–813.

Damon, W. (2008). *The path to purpose.* New York: Free Press.

Dao-Fu, D., & others (2016). Cardiac aging. In M.R. Kaeberlein & G.M. Martin (Eds.), *Handbook of the biology of aging* (8th ed.). New York: Elsevier.

Darcy, E. (2012). Gender issues in child and adolescent eating disorders. In J. Lock (Ed.), *Oxford handbook of child and adolescent eating disorders: Developmental perspectives.* New York: Oxford University Press.

Dariotis, J.K., & others (2016, in press). A qualitative evaluation of student learning and skills use in a school-based mindfulness and yoga program. *Mindfulness.*

Darnell, A.J., & Schuler, M.S. (2015). Quasi-experimental study of functional family therapy effectiveness for juvenile justice aftercare in a racially and ethnically diverse community sample. *Children and Youth Services Review, 50,* 75–82.

Darwin, C. (1859). *On the origin of species.* London: John Murray.

Das, M., & Gursky, O. (2015). Amyloid-forming properties of human apolipoproteins: Sequence analysis and structural insights. *Advances in Experimental Medicine and Biology, 855,* 175–211.

David, N., & others (2016). Trajectories of neuropsychiatric symptoms and cognitive decline in mild cognitive impairment. *American Journal of Geriatric Psychiatry, 24,* 70–80.

Davies, G., & others (2011). Genome-wide association studies establish that human intelligence is highly heritable and polygenic. *Molecular Psychiatry, 16,* 996–1005.

Davies, J., & Brember, I. (1999). Reading and mathematics attainments and self-esteem in years 2 and 6—an eight-year cross-sectional study. *Educational Studies, 25,* 145–157.

Davies, P.T., Martin, M.J., & Sturge-Apple, M.L. (2016). Emotional security theory and developmental psychopathology. In D. Cicchetti (Ed.), *Developmental psychopathology* (3rd ed.). New York: Wiley.

Davies, R., Davies, D., Pearce, M., & Wong, N. (2015). The effect of waterbirth on neonatal mortality and morbidity: A systematic review and meta-analysis. *JBI Database of Systematic Reviews and Implementation Reports, 13,* 180–231.

Davila, J., Capaldi, D.M., & La Greca, A.M. (2016). Adolescent/young adult romantic relationships and psychopathology. In D. Cicchetti (Ed.), *Developmental psychopathology* (3rd ed.). New York: Wiley.

Davis, A., Kimball, W., & Gould, E. (2015, May 27). The class of 2015: Despite an improving economy, young grads still face an uphill climb. Retrieved July 14, 2016, from www.epi.org/publication/the-class-of-2015/

Davis, B.E., Moon, R.Y., Sachs, M.C., & Ottolini, M.C. (1998). Effects of sleep position on infant motor development. *Pediatrics, 102,* 1135–1140.

Davis, L., & Keyser, J. (1997). *Becoming the parent you want to be: A sourcebook of strategies for the first five years.* New York: Broadway.

Davis, M.C., Burke, H.M., Zautra, A.J., & Stark, S. (2013). Arthritis and musculoskeletal conditions. In I.B. Weiner & others (Eds.), *Handbook of psychology* (2nd ed., Vol. 9). New York: Wiley.

Davis, S.W., Kragel, J.E., Madden, D.J., & Cabeza, R. (2012). The architecture of cross-hemispheric communication in the aging brain: Linking behavior to functional and structural connectivity. *Cerebral Cortex, 22,* 232–242.

Dawson-McClure, S., & others (2015). A population-level approach to promoting healthy child development and school success in low-income, urban neighborhoods: Impact on parenting and child conduct problems. *Prevention Science, 16,* 279–290.

Day, N.L., Goldschmidt, L., & Thomas, C.A. (2006). Prenatal marijuana exposure contributes to the prediction of marijuana use at age 14. *Addiction, 101,* 1313–1322.

Dayton, C.J., Walsh, T.B., Oh, W., & Volling, B. (2015). Hush now baby: Mothers' and fathers' strategies for soothing their infants and associated parenting outcomes. *Journal of Pediatric Health Care, 29,* 145–155.

de Frias, C.M., & Dixon, R.A. (2014). Lifestyle engagement affects cognitive status differences and trajectories on executive functions in older adults. *Archives of Clinical Neuropsychology, 29,* 16–25.

De Genna, N.M., Goldschmidt, L., Day N.L., Cornelius, M.D. (2016). Prenatal and postnatal maternal trajectories of cigarette use predict adolescent cigarette use. *Nicotine and Tobacco Research, 18,* 988–992.

De Giovanni, N., & Marchetti, D. (2012). Cocaine and its metabolites in the placenta: A systematic review of the literature. *Reproductive Toxicology, 33,* 1–14.

de Guzman, N.S., & Nishina, A. (2014). A longitudinal study of body dissatisfaction and pubertal timing in an ethnically diverse adolescent sample. *Body Image, 11,* 68–71.

de Haan, M. (2015). Neuroscientific methods with children. In R.M. Lerner (Ed.), *Handbook of child psychology and developmental science* (7th ed.). New York: Wiley.

de Haan, M., & Gunnar, M.R. (Eds.) (2009). *Handbook of developmental social neuroscience.* New York: Guilford.

de Haan, M., & Johnson, M.H. (2016). Typical and atypical human functional brain development. In D. Cicchetti (Ed.), *Developmental psychopathology* (3rd ed.). New York: Wiley.

De Heering, A., & others (2016). Three-month-old infants' sensitivity to horizontal information within faces. *Developmental Psychobiology, 58,* 536–542.

de Jongh, B.E., Mackley, A., Jain, N., Locke, R., & Paul, D.A. (2015). Effects of advanced maternal age and race/ethnicity on placental weight and placental weight/birthweight ratio in very low birthweight infants. *Maternal and Child Health Journal, 19,* 1553–1558.

de Koning, L., Denhoff, E., Kellogg, M.D., & de Ferranti, S.D. (2015). Associations of total and abdominal adiposity with risk marker patterns in children at high risk for cardiovascular disease. *BMC Obesity, 2,* 15.

de la Cuesta-Benjumea, C. (2011). Strategies for the relief of burden in advanced dementia caregiving. *Journal of Advanced Nursing, 67,* 1790–1799.

de Looze, M., & others (2015). Parent-adolescent sexual communication and its association with adolescent sexual behaviors: A nationally representative analysis in the Netherlands. *Journal of Sex Research, 52,* 257–268.

de Magalhaes, J.P., & Tacutu, R. (2016). Integrative genomics and aging. In M.R. Kaeberlein & G.M. Martin (Eds.), *Handbook of the biology of aging* (8th ed.). New York: Elsevier.

De Neubourg, D., & others (2016). How do cumulative live birth rates and summative multiple live birth rates over complete courses of assisted reproductive technology treatment per woman compare among registries? *Human Reproduction, 31,* 93–99.

de Planell-Saguer, M., Lovinsky-Desir, S., & Miller, R.L. (2014). Epigenetic regulation: The interface between prenatal and early-life exposure and asthma susceptibility. *Environmental and Molecular Mutagenesis, 55,* 231–243.

de Villiers, J., & de Villiers, P. (2013). Syntax acquisition. In P.D. Zelazo (Ed.), *Handbook of developmental psychology.* New York: Oxford University Press.

de Vries, S.L., Hoeve, M., Stams, G.J., & Asscher, J.J. (2016). Adolescent-parent attachment and externalizing behavior: The mediating role of individual and social factors. *Journal of Abnormal Child Psychology, 44,* 283–294.

Deary, I.J. (2012). Intelligence. *Annual Review of Intelligence* (Vol. 63). Palo Alto, CA: Annual Reviews.

Deater-Deckard, K. (2013). The social environment and the development of psychopathology. In P.D. Zelazo (Ed.), *Handbook of developmental psychology.* New York: Oxford University Press.

Deaton, A. (2008). Income, health, and well-being around the world: Evidence from the Gallup World Poll. *Journal of Economic Perspectives, 22,* 53–72.

DeCasper, A.J., & Spence, M.J. (1986). Prenatal maternal speech influences newborns' perception of speech sounds. *Infant Behavior and Development, 9,* 133–150.

DeCesare. J.Z., & Jackson, J.R. (2015). Centering Pregnancy: Practical tips for your practice. *Archives of Gynecology and Obstetrics, 29,* 499–507.

Decety, J., & Cowell, J. (2016). Developmental social neuroscience. In D. Cicchetti (Ed.), *Developmental psychopathology* (3rd ed.). New York: Wiley.

Dedon, P.C., & Begley, T.H. (2014). A system of RNA modifications and biased codon use control

cellular stress response at the level of transition. *Chemical Research in Toxicology, 37,* 330–337.

Deeg, D.J.H. (2005). The development of physical and mental health from late midlife to early old age. In S.L. Willis & M. Martin (Eds.), *Middle adulthood: A lifespan perspective.* Thousand Oaks, CA: Sage.

Del Campo, R., Buchanan, W.R., Abbott, R.D., & Berninger, V.W. (2015). Levels of phonology related to reading and writing in middle childhood. *Reading and Writing, 28,* 183–198.

Del Giudice, M. (2011). Sex differences in romantic attachment: A meta-analysis. *Personality and Social Psychology Bulletin, 37,* 193–214.

Del Giudice, M., & Ellis, B.J. (2016). Evolutionary foundations of developmental psychopathology. In D. Cicchetti (Ed.), *Developmental psychopathology* (3rd ed.). New York: Wiley.

Del Gobbo, L.C., & others (2015). Contribution of major lifestyle risk factors for incident heart failure in older adults: The Cardiovascular Health Study. *JACC Heart Failure, 3,* 520–528.

Delello, J.A., & McWhorter, R.R. (2016, in press). Reducing the digital divide: Connecting older adults to iPad technology. *Journal of Applied Gerontology.*

DeLisi, R. (2015). Piaget's sympathetic but unromantic account of children's play. In J.E. Johnson & others (Eds.), *Handbook of the study of play.* Blue Ridge Summit, PA: Rowman & Littlefield.

Demanchick, S.P. (2015). The interpretation of play: Psychoanalysis and beyond. In J.E. Johnson & others (Eds.), *Handbook of the study of play.* Blue Ridge Summit, PA: Rowman & Littlefield.

Demby, S.L. (2016, in press). Parenting coordination: Applying clinical thinking to the management of post-divorce conflict. *Journal of Clinical Psychology.*

Demir, O.E., & Goldin-Meadow, S. (2015). Gesture's role in learning and processing language. In G. Hickok & S. Small (Eds.), *Neurobiology of language.* New York: Elsevier.

Dempster, F.N. (1981). Memory span: Sources of individual and developmental differences. *Psychological Bulletin, 80,* 63–100.

Demsky, C.A., Ellis, M.A., & Fritz, C. (2014). Shrugging it off: Does psychological detachment from work mediate the relationship between workplace aggression and work-family conflict? *Journal of Occupational Health and Psychology, 19,* 195–205.

Denard, P.J., & others (2010). Back pain, neurogenic symptoms, and physical function in relation to spondylolisthesis among elderly men. *Spine Journal, 10,* 865–887.

DeNavas-Walt, C., & Proctor, B.D. (2015). Income and poverty in the United States: 2014. Washington, DC: U.S. Census Bureau.

Denes, G. (2016). *Neural plasticity across the lifespan.* New York: Psychology Press.

Denham, J., O'Brien, B.J., & Charchar, F.J. (2016, in press). Telomere length maintenance and cardio-metabolic disease prevention through exercise training. *Sports Medicine.*

Denham, S.A., Bassett, H.H., & Wyatt, T. (2015). The socialization of emotional competence. In J.E. Grusec & P.D. Hastings (Eds.), *Handbook of socialization* (2nd ed.). New York: Guilford.

Denham, S.A., & Howarth, G.Z. (2016, in press). Emotional competence in early childhood: Construct and measurement considerations. *Journal of Applied Developmental Psychology.*

Denham, S.A., & Zinsser, K.M. (2014). Promoting social and emotional learning in early childhood. In T.P. Gullotta & M. Bloom (Eds.), *Encyclopedia of primary prevention and health promotion* (2nd ed.). New York: Academic/Plenum Publishers.

Denham, S.A., & others (2012). Preschoolers' emotion knowledge: Self-regulatory foundations and predictors of school success. *Cognition and Emotion, 26,* 667–679.

Dennis, N.A., & Cabeza, R. (2008). Neuroimaging of healthy cognitive aging. In F.I.M. Craik & T.A. Salthouse (Eds.). *Handbook of aging and cognition* (3rd ed.). Mahwah, NJ: Erlbaum.

Deoni, S.C., & others (2015). Cortical maturation and myelination in healthy toddlers and young children. *Neuroimage, 115,* 147–161.

Deoni, S.C., & others (2016). White matter maturation profiles through early childhood predict general cognitive ability. *Brain Structure and Function, 22,* 1189–1203.

DePaulo, B. (2006). *Singled out.* New York: St. Martin's Press.

DePaulo, B. (2011). Living single: Lightening up those dark, dopey myths. In W.R. Cupach & B.H. Spitzberg (Eds.), *The dark side of close relationships.* New York: Routledge.

Derebail, V.K., & others (2014). Sickle trait in African-American hemodialysis patients and higher erythropoiesis-stimulating agent dose. *Journal of the American Society of Nephrology, 25,* 819–826.

Deroche, T., Castanier, C., Perrot, A., & Hartley, A. (2016). Joint attention is slowed in older adults. *Experimental Aging Research, 42,* 144–150.

Derry, H.M., & others (2015). Yoga and self-induced cognitive problems in breast cancer survivors: A randomized controlled trial. I *Psycho-Oncology, 24,* 958–966.

DeSpelder, L.A., & Strickland, A.L. (2005). *The last dance: Encountering death and dying* (7th ed.). New York: McGraw-Hill.

Desveaux, L., Goldstein, R., Mathur, S., & Brooks, D. (2016). Barriers to physical activity following rehabilitation: Perspectives of older adults with chronic disease. *Journal of Aging and Physical Activity, 24,* 223–233.

Dette-Hagenmeyer, D.E., Erzinger, A.G., & Reichle, B. (Eds.) (2016). *Fathers in families.* New York: Psychology Press.

Deutsch, A.R., Chernyavskiy, P., Steinley, D., & Slutscke, W.S. (2015). Measuring peer socialization for adolescent substance use: A comparison of perceived and actual friends' substance use effects. *Journal of Studies on Alcohol and Drugs, 76,* 267–277.

Devaney, S.A., Palomaki, G.E., Scott, J.A., & Bianchi, D.W. (2011). Noninvasive fetal sex determination using cell-free fetal DNA: A systematic review and meta-analysis. *Journal of the American Medical Association, 306,* 627–636.

Devine, R.T., White, N., Ersor, R., & Hughes, C. (2016). Theory of mind in middle childhood: Longitudinal associations with executive function. *Developmental Psychology, 52,* 758–771.

Devore, E.E., Grodstein, F., & Schemhammer, E.S. (2016). Sleep duration in relation to cognitive function among older adults: A systematic review of observational studies. *Neuroepidemiology, 46,* 57–78.

DeZolt, D.M., & Hull, S.H. (2001). Classroom and school climate. In J. Worell (Ed.), *Encyclopedia of women and gender.* San Diego: Academic Press.

Di Florio, A., & others (2014). Mood disorders and parity—a clue to the etiology of the postpartum trigger. *Journal of Affective Disorders, 152,* 334–349.

Di Gessa, G., Glaser, K., & Tinker, A. (2016). The impact of caring for grandchildren on the health of grandparents in Europe: A life-course perspective. *Social Science and Medicine, 152,* 166–172.

Di Giuseppe, D., Bottai, M., Askling, J., & Wolk, A. (2016, in press). Physical activity and risk of rheumatoid arthritis in women: A population-based prospective study. *Arthritis Research and Therapy.*

Di Marco, L.Y., & others (2015). Vascular dysfunction in the pathogenesis of Alzheimer's disease—A review of endothelium-mediated mechanisms and ensuing vicious circles. *Neurobiology of Diseases, 82,* 593–606.

Diamond, A. (1985). Development of the ability to use recall to guide action, as indicated by infants' performance on A-not-B. *Child Development, 56,* 866–883.

Diamond, A. (2013). Executive functions. *Annual Review of Psychology* (Vol. 64). Palo Alto, CA: Annual Reviews.

Diamond, A., Barnett, W.S., Thomas, J., & Munro, S. (2007). Preschool program improves cognitive control. *Science, 318,* 1387–1388.

Diamond, A., & Lee, K. (2011). Interventions shown to aid executive function development in children 4 to 12 years old. *Science, 333,* 959–964.

Diamond, L.M., & Savin-Williams, R.C. (2015). Same-sex activity in adolescence: Multiple meanings and implications. In R.F. Fassinger & S.L. Morrow (Eds.), *Sex in the margins.* Washington, DC: American Psychological Association.

DiBennardo, R., & Gates, G.J. (2014). Research note: U.S. Census same-sex couple data: Adjustments to reduce measurement error and empirical implications. *Population Research and Policy Review, 33,* 603–614.

Dickinson, W.J., & others (2011). Change in stress and social support as predictors of cognitive decline in older adults with and without depression. *International Journal of Geriatric Psychiatry, 26,* 1267–1274.

Diego, M.A., Field, T., & Hernandez-Reif, M. (2008). Temperature increases in preterm infants during massage therapy. *Infant Behavior and Development, 31,* 149–152.

Diego, M.A., Field, T., & Hernandez-Reif, M. (2014). Preterm infant weight gain is increased by massage therapy and exercise via different underlying mechanisms. *Early Human Development, 90,* 137–140.

Diener, E. (2016). *Subjective well-being.* Retrieved January 6, 2016, from http://internal.psychology.illinois.edu/~ediener/SWLS.html

Diener, E., Emmons, R.A., Larson, R.J., & Griffin, S. (1985). The Satisfaction with Life Scale. *Journal of Personality Assessment, 49,* 71–75.

Dietary Guidelines Advisory Committee (2015, February). *Scientific report of the Dietary Guidelines Advisory Committee.* Washington, DC: Department of Health and Human Services.

Dimitrova, N., Moro, C., & Mohr, C. (2015). Caregivers interpret infants' early gestures based on shared knowledge about referents. *Infant Behavior and Development, 39,* 98–106.

Dimmitt, C., & McCormick, C.B. (2012). Metacognition in education. In K.R. Harris, S. Graham, &

T. Urdan (Eds.), *Handbook of educational psychology.* Washington, DC: American Psychological Association.

Dionne, G., & others (2011). Associations between sleep-wake consolidation and language development: A developmental twin study. *Sleep, 34,* 987–995.

Dirk, J., & Schmiedek, F. (2012). Processing speed. In S.K. Whitbourne & M. Sliwinski (Eds.), *Wiley-Blackwell handbook of adult development and aging.* New York: Wiley.

Dishion, T.J., & Patterson, G.R. (2016). The development and ecology of antisocial behavior. In D. Cicchetti (Ed.), *Developmental psychopathology* (3rd ed.). New York: Wiley.

Dishion, T.J., & Piehler, T.F. (2009). Deviant by design: Peer contagion in development, interventions, and schools. In K.H. Rubin, W.M. Bukowski, & B. Laursen (Eds.), *Handbook of peer interactions, relationships, and groups.* New York: Guilford.

Dittus, P.J., & others (2015). Parental monitoring and its associations with adolescent sexual risk behavior: A meta-analysis. *Pediatrics, 136,* e1587–e1599.

Diwadkar, V.A., & others (2012). Differences in cortico-striatal-cerebellar activation during working memory in syndromal and nonsyndromal children with prenatal exposure to alcohol. *Human Brain Mapping, 34,* 1931–1945.

Djukanovic, I., Carlsson, J., & Peterson, U. (2016). Group discussions with structured reminiscence and a problem-based method as an intervention to prevent depressive symptoms in older people. *Journal of Clinical Nursing, 25,* 992–1000.

Doane, L.D., & Thurston, E.C. (2014). Associations among sleep, daily experiences, and loneliness in adolescence: Evidence of moderating and bidirectional pathways. *Journal of Adolescence, 37,* 145–154.

Dodge, K.A. (1983). Behavioral antecedents of peer social status. *Child Development, 54,* 1386–1399.

Dodge, K.A. (2011). Social information processing models of aggressive behavior. In M. Mikulincer & P.R. Shaver (Eds.), *Understanding and reducing aggression, violence, and their consequences.* Washington, DC: American Psychological Association.

Dodson, L.J., & Davies, A.P.C. (2014). Different challenges, different well-being: A comparison of psychological well-being across stepmothers and biological mothers and across four categories of stepmothers. *Journal of Divorce & Remarriage, 55,* 49–63.

Domenjoz, I., Kayser, B., & Boulvain, M. (2014). Effect of physical activity during pregnancy on mode of delivery. *American Journal of Obstetrics and Gynecology, 211,* e.1–e.11.

Donaldson, C.D., Handren, L.M., & Crano, W.D. (2016). The enduring impact of parents' monitoring, warmth, expectancies, and alcohol use on their children's future binge drinking and arrests: A longitudinal analysis. *Prevention Science, 17,* 606–614.

Donatelle, R.J. (2015). *Health* (11th ed.). Upper Saddle River, NJ: Pearson.

Donatelle, R.J. (2016). *My health* (2nd ed.). Upper Saddle River, NJ: Pearson.

Donatelle, R.J. (2017). *Health: The basics* (12th ed.). Upper Saddle River, NJ: Pearson.

Donatelle, R.J., & Ketcham, P. (2016). *Access to health* (14th ed.). Upper Saddle River, NJ: Pearson.

Dondi, M., Simion, F., & Caltran, G. (1999). Can newborns discriminate between their own cry and the cry of another newborn infant? *Developmental Psychology, 35*(2), 418–426.

Dong, B., & Krohn, M.D. (2016, in press). Dual trajectories of gang affiliation and delinquent peer association during adolescence: An examination of long-term offending outcomes. *Journal of Youth and Adolescence.*

Dong, B., Wang, Z., Wang, H.J., & Ma, J. (2015). Population attributable risk of overweight and obesity for high blood pressure in Chinese children. *Blood Pressure, 24*, 230–236.

Dong, M., & others (2015). Multiple genetic variants associated with primary biliary cirrhosis in a Han Chinese population. *Clinical Reviews in Allergy and Immunology, 48*, 316–332.

Donnellan, M.B., Hill, P.L., & Roberts, B.W. (2015). Personality development across the life span: Current findings and future directions. In L. Cooper & M. Mikulincer (Eds.), *Handbook of personality and social psychology.* Washington, DC: American Psychological Association.

Donnellan, M.B., Larsen-Rife, D., & Conger, R.D. (2005). Personality, family history, and competence in early adult romantic relationships. *Journal of Personality and Social Psychology, 88*, 562–576.

Donnelly, N., & Storchova, Z. (2015). Causes and consequence of protein folding stress in aneuploid cells. *Cell Cycle, 14*, 495–501.

Doty, R.L., & Shah, M. (2008). Taste and smell. In M.M. Haith & J.B. Benson (Eds.), *Encyclopedia of infant and early childhood development.* Oxford, UK: Elsevier.

Dougherty, C.C., & others (2016). A comparison of structural brain imaging findings in autism spectrum disorder and attention deficit hyperactivity disorder. *Neuropsychology Review, 26*, 25–43.

Dovis, S., Van der Oord, S., Wiers, R.W., & Prins, P.J. (2015). Improving executive functioning in children with ADHD: Training multiple executive functions within the context of a computer game. A randomized double-blind placebo controlled trial. *PLoS One, 10*(4), e0121651.

Dozier, M., Stovall-McClough, K.C., & Albus, K.E. (2009). Attachment and psychopathology in adulthood. In J. Cassidy & P.R. Shaver (Eds.), *Handbook of attachment* (2nd ed.). New York: Guilford.

Drollette, E.S., & others (2014). Acute exercise facilitates brain function and cognition in children who need it most: An ERP study of individual differences in inhibitory control capacity. *Developmental Cognitive Neuroscience, 7*, 53–64.

Dryfoos, J.G. (1990). *Adolescents at risk: Prevalence or prevention.* New York: Oxford University Press.

Dryfoos, J.G., & Barkin, C. (2006). *Growing up in America today.* New York: Oxford University Press.

Du Roscoat, E., & others (2016). Risk factors for suicide attempts and hospitalizations in a sample of 39,542 French adolescents. *Journal of Affective Disorders, 190*, 517–521.

Dubois, J., & others (2016). Exploring the early organization and maturation of linguistic pathways in the human infant brain. *Cerebral Cortex, 26*, 2283–2298.

Dudovitz, R.N., McCoy, K., & Chung, P.J. (2015). At-school substance use as a marker for serious health risks. *Academic Pediatrics, 15*, 41–56.

Duff, F.J., Reen, G., Plunkett, K., & Nation, K. (2015). Do infant vocabulary skills predict school-age language and literacy outcomes? *Journal of Child Psychology and Psychiatry, 56*, 848–856.

Duggan, K.A., & Friedman, H.S. (2014). Lifetime biopsychosocial trajectories of the Terman gifted children: Health, well-being, and longevity. In D.K. Simonton (Ed.), *Wiley-Blackwell handbook of genius.* New York: Oxford University Press.

Duke, S.A., Balzer, B.W., & Steinbeck, K.S. (2014). Testosterone and its effects on human male adolescent mood and behavior: A systematic review. *Journal of Adolescent Health, 55*, 315–322.

Dulin, P.L., Gavala, J., Stephens, C., Kostick, M., & McDonald, J. (2012). Volunteering predicts happiness among Maori and non-Maori in the New Zealand Health, Work, and Retirement Study. *Aging and Mental Health, 16*, 617–624.

Dumitrache, C.G., Rubio, L., & Rubio-Herrera, R. (2016, in press). Perceived health status and life satisfaction in old age, and the moderating role of social support. *Aging and Mental Health.*

Duncan, G.J., Magnuson, K., & Votruba-Drzal, E. (2015). Children and socioeconomic status. In M.H. Bornstein & T. Leventhal (Eds.), *Handbook of child psychology and developmental science* (7th ed., Vol. 4). New York: Wiley.

Dunn, E.C., McLaughlin, K.A., Slopen, N., Rosand, J., & Smoller, J.W. (2013). Developmental timing of child maltreatment and symptoms of depression and suicidal ideation in young adulthood: Results from the National Longitudinal Study of Adolescent Health. *Depression and Anxiety, 30*, 955–964.

Dunn, J. (1984). Sibling studies and the developmental impact of critical incidents. In P.B. Baltes & O.G. Brim (Eds.), *Life-span development and behavior* (Vol. 6). Orlando, FL: Academic Press.

Dunn, J. (2007). Siblings and socialization. In J.E. Grusec & P.D. Hastings (eds.), *Handbook of socialization.* New York: Guilford.

Dunn, J. (2015). Siblings. In J.E. Grusec & P.D. Hastings (Eds.), *Handbook of socialization* (2nd ed.). New York: Guilford.

Dunn, J., & Kendrick, C. (1982). *Siblings.* Cambridge, MA: Harvard University Press.

Dunsmore, J.C., Booker, J.A., & Ollendick, T.H. (2013). Parental emotion coaching and child emotion regulation as protective factors for children with oppositional defiant disorder. *Social Development, 22*(3), 444–466.

Dupere, V., & others (2015). Stressors and turning points in high school and dropout: A stress process, life course framework. *Review of Educational Research, 85*, 591–629.

Dupre, M.E., George, L.K., Liu, G., & Peterson, E.D. (2015). Association between divorce and risks for acute myocardial infarction. *Circulation: Cardiovascular Quality and Outcomes, 8*, 244–251.

Durham, R., & Chapman, L. (2014). *Maternal-newborn nursing* (2nd ed.). Philadelphia: F.A. Davis.

Durlak, J.A., Domitrovich, C.E., & Gullotta, T.P. (Eds.) (2015). *Handbook of social and emotional learning.* New York: Guilford.

Durson, A., & others (2016). Maternal risk factors associated with lead, mercury, and cadmium levels in umbilical cord blood, breast milk, and newborn hair. *Journal of Maternal-Fetal and Neonatal Medicine, 29*, 954–961.

Durston, S., & others (2006). A shift from diffuse to focal cortical activity with development. *Developmental Science, 9*, 1–8.

Dvornyk, V., & Waqar-ul-Haq, H. (2012). Genetics of age at menarche: A systematic review. *Human Reproduction Update, 18*, 198–210.

Dweck, C.S. (2006). *Mindset.* New York: Random House.

Dweck, C.S. (2012). Mindsets and social nature: Promoting change in the Middle East, the schoolyard, the racial divide, and willpower. *American Psychologist, 67*, 614–622.

Dweck, C.S. (2015, September 23). Carol Dweck revisits the 'growth mindset'. *Education Week, 35*(5), 24–26.

Dweck, C.S. (2016, March 11). *Growth mindset, revisited.* Invited address at Leaders to Learn From. Washington, DC: Education Week.

Dweck, C.S., & Master, A. (2009). Self-theories and motivation: Students' beliefs about intelligence. In K.R. Wentzel & A. Wigfield (Eds.), *Handbook of motivation at school.* New York: Routledge.

Dworkin, S.L., & Santelli, J. (2007). Do abstinence-plus interventions reduce sexual risk behavior among youth? *PLoS Medicine, 4*, 1437–1439.

Dwyer, J.W., & Coward, R.T. (1991). A multivariate comparison of the involvement of adult sons versus daughters in the care of impaired parents. *Journals of Gerontology B: Psychological Sciences and Social Sciences, 46*, S259–S269.

E

Eagly, A.H. (2001). Social role theory of sex differences and similarities. In J. Worrell (Ed.), *Encyclopedia of women and gender.* San Diego: Academic Press.

Eagly, A.H. (2010). Gender roles. In J. Levine & M. Hogg (Eds.), *Encyclopedia of group process and intergroup relations.* Thousand Oaks, CA: Sage.

Eagly, A.H. (2012). Science, feminism, and the investigation of gender. In R.W. Proctor & E.J. Capaldi (Eds.), *Psychology of science: Implicit and explicit reasoning.* New York: Oxford University Press.

Eagly, A.H., & Crowley, M. (1986). Gender and helping: A meta-analytic review of the social psychological literature. *Psychological Bulletin, 108*, 233–256.

Eagly, A.H., & Steffen, V.J. (1986). Gender and aggressive behavior: A meta-analytic review of the social psychological literature. *Psychological Bulletin, 100*, 309–330.

Eagly, A.H., & Wood, W. (2016, in press). Social role theory of sex differences and similarities. In N. Naples & others (Eds.), *Wiley-Blackwell encyclopedia of gender and sexuality studies.* New York: Wiley-Blackwell.

East, P. (2009). Adolescent relationships with siblings. In R.M. Lerner & L. Steinberg (Eds.), *Handbook of adolescent psychology* (3rd ed.). New York: Wiley.

Easterbrooks, M.A., Bartlett, J.D., Beeghly, M., & Thompson, R.A. (2013). Social and emotional development in infancy. In I.B. Weiner & others (Eds.), *Handbook of psychology* (2nd ed., Vol. 6). New York: Wiley.

Ebbert, M.T., & others (2016). Interaction between variants in CLU and MS4A4E modulates Alzheimer's disease risk. *Alzheimer's and Dementia, 12*, 121–129.

Eccles, J.S. (2007). Families, schools, and developing achievement-related motivations and engagement. In J.E. Grusec & P.D. Hastings (Eds.), *Handbook of socialization.* New York: Guilford.

Eccles, J.S., & Roeser, R.W. (2016). School and community influences on human development. In M.H. Bornstein & M.E. Lamb (Eds.), *Developmental science* (7th ed.). New York: Psychology Press.

Echevarria, J.J., Vogt, M.J., & Short, D.J. (2017). *Making content comprehensible for English learners: The SIOP model* (5th ed.). Upper Saddle River, NJ: Pearson.

Eckerman, C., & Whitehead, H. (1999). How toddler peers generate coordinated action: A cross-cultural exploration. *Early Education & Development, 10,* 241–266.

Educational Testing Service (1992, February). *Cross-national comparisons of 9- to 13-year-olds' science and math achievement.* Princeton, NJ: Educational Testing Service.

Eggenberger, P., & others (2015). Does multi-component physical exercise with simultaneous cognitive training boost cognitive performance in older adults? A 6-month randomized controlled trial with a 1-year follow-up. *Clinical Interventions in Aging, 10,* 1335–1349.

Ehninger, D., Neff, F., & Xie, K. (2014). Longevity, aging, and rapamycin. *Cellular and Molecular Life Sciences, 71,* 4325–4346.

Eichorn, D.H., Clausen, J.A., Haan, N., Honzik, M.P., & Mussen, P.H. (Eds.). (1981). *Present and past in middle life.* New York: Academic Press.

Eiferman, R.R. (1971). Social play in childhood. In R. Herron & B. Sutton-Smith (Eds.), *Child's play.* New York: Wiley.

Eisenberg, N., Fabes, R.A., & Spinrad, T.L. (2006). Prosocial development. In W. Damon & R. Lerner (Eds.), *Handbook of child psychology* (6th ed.). New York: Wiley.

Eisenberg, N., Smith, C.L., & Spinrad, T.L. (2016). Effortful control: Relations with emotion regulation, adjustment, and socialization in childhood. In K.D. Vohs & R.F. Baumeister (Eds.), *Handbook of self-regulation* (3rd ed.). New York: Guilford.

Eisenberg, N., & Spinrad, T.L. (2016). Multidimensionality of prosocial behavior: Rethinking the conceptualization and development of prosocial behavior. In L. Padilla-Walker & G. Carlo (Eds.), *Prosocial behavior.* New York: Oxford University Press.

Eisenberg, N., Spinrad, T.L., & Knafo-Noam, A. (2015). Prosocial development. In R.M. Lerner (Ed.), *Handbook of child psychology and developmental science* (7th ed.). New York: Wiley.

Eisenberg, N., Spinrad, T.L., & Valiente, C. (2016). Emotion-related self-regulation and children's social, psychological, and academic functioning. In L. Balter & C.S. Tamis-LeMonda (Eds.), *Child psychology* (3rd ed.). New York: Routledge.

Eisner, B., Pfeifer, C., Parker, C., & Hauf, P. (2013). Infants' perception of actions and situational constraints. *Journal of Experimental Child Psychology, 116,* 428–442.

Ejlerskov, K.T., & others (2015). The impact of early growth patterns and infant feeding on body composition at 3 years of age. *British Journal of Nutrition, 114,* 316–327.

Ekblad, A., & others (2015). Amniotic fluid—a source for clinical therapeutics in the newborn. *Stem Cells and Development, 24,* 1405–1424.

Ekblad, M., Korkeila, J., & Lehtonen, L. (2015). Smoking during pregnancy affects foetal brain development. *Acta Poediatrica, 104,* 12–18.

Ekelin, M., Kvist, L.J., & Persson, E.K. (2016). Midwifery competence: Content in midwifery students' daily written reflections on clinical practice. *Midwifery, 32,* 7–13.

Eklund, K., Tanner, N., Stoll, K., & Anway, L. (2015). Identifying emotional and behavioral risk among gifted and nongifted children: A multi-gate, multi-informant approach. *School Psychology Quarterly, 30,* 197–211.

Elam, K.K., Sandler, I., Wolchik, S., & Tein, J.Y. (2016). Non-residential father involvement, interparental conflict, and mental health of children following divorce: A person-focused approach. *Journal of Youth and Adolescence, 45,* 581–593.

Elder, D. (2015). Reducing the risk of sudden infant death syndrome—a steady gain but still room for improvement. *New Zealand Medical Journal, 128,* 13–14.

Eliasieh, K., Liets, L.C., & Chalupa, L.M. (2007). Cellular reorganization in the human retina during normal aging. *Investigative Ophthalmology and Visual Science, 48,* 2824–2830.

Elkind, D. (1976). *Child development and education: A Piagetian perspective.* New York: Oxford University Press.

Elliott, E.M., & others (2011). Working memory in the oldest-old: Evidence from output serial position curves. *Memory and Cognition, 10,* 20–27.

Elsabbagh, M., & Johnson, M.H. (2016, in press). Autism and the social brain: The first-year puzzle. *Biological Psychiatry.*

El-Sheikh, M., Keiley, M., Erath, S.A., & Dyer, W.J. (2013). Marital conflict and growth in children's internalizing behavior: The role of autonomic nervous system activity. *Developmental Psychology, 49*(1), 92–108.

Eltonsy, S., Martin, B., Ferreira, E., & Blais, L. (2016). Systematic procedure for the classification of proven and potential teratogens for use in research. *Birth Defects Research A: Clinical and Molecular Teratology, 106,* 285–297.

Emanuel, L., Bennett, K., & Richardson, V.E. (2007). The dying role. *Journal of Palliative Medicine, 10,* 159–168.

Ember, M.R., Ember, C.R., & Peregrine, P.N. (2015). *Cultural anthropology* (14th ed.). Upper Saddle River, NJ: Pearson.

Emde, R.N., Gaensbauer, T.G., & Harmon, R.J. (1976). Emotional expression in infancy: A biobehavioral study. *Psychological Issues: Monograph Series, 10*(37).

Endes, S., & others (2016). Physical activity is associated with lower arterial stiffness in older adults: Results of the SAPALDIA 3 Cohort Study. *European Journal of Epidemiology, 45,* 110–115.

Engels, A.C., & others (2016, in press). Sonographic detection of central nervous system in the first trimester of pregnancy. *Prenatal Diagnosis.*

English, T., & Carstensen, L.L. (2014). Selective narrowing of social networks across adulthood is associated with improved emotional experience in life. *International Journal of Behavioral Development, 38,* 195–202.

Ensor, R., Spencer, D., & Hughes, C. (2011). You feel sad? Emotional understanding mediates effects of verbal ability and mother-child mutuality on prosocial behaviors: Findings from 2 to 4 years. *Social Development, 20,* 93–110.

Erickson, K.I., Hillman, C.H., & Kramer, A.F. (2015). Physical activity, brain, and cognition. *Current Opinion in the Behavioral Sciences, 4,* 27–32.

Erickson, K.I., & Liu-Ambrose, T. (2016). Exercise, cognition, and health. In K.W. Schaie & S. Willis (Eds.), *Handbook of the psychology of aging* (8th ed.). New York: Elsevier.

Erickson, K.I., & others (2011). Exercise training increases the size of the hippocampus and improves memory. *Proceedings of the National Academy of Sciences U.S.A., 108,* 3017–3022.

Ericsson, K.A., Krampe, R., & Tesch-Romer, C. (1993). The role of deliberate practice in the acquisition of expert performance. *Psychological Review, 100,* 363–406.

Ericsson, K.A., & others (Eds.) (2016, in press). *Cambridge handbook of expertise and expert performance.* New York: Cambridge University Press.

Erikson, E.H. (1950). *Childhood and society.* New York: W.W. Norton.

Erikson, E.H. (1968). *Identity: Youth and crisis.* New York. W.W. Norton.

Eriksson Sorman, D., Sunderstrom, A., Ronnlund, M., Adolfsson, R., & Nilsson, L.G. (2014). Leisure activity in old age and risk of dementia: A 15-year prospective study. *Journals of Gerontology B: Psychological Sciences and Social Sciences, 69,* 493–501.

Eriksson, U.J. (2009). Congenital malformations in diabetic pregnancy. *Seminar in Fetal and Neonatal Medicine, 14,* 85–93.

Erkut, S., & others (2013). Can sex education delay early sexual debut? *Journal of Early Adolescence, 33,* 482–497.

Espelage, D.L., & Colbert, C.L. (2016). School-based interventions to prevent bullying and promote prosocial behaviors. In K.R. Wentzel & G.B. Ramani (Eds.), *Handbook of social influences in school contexts.* New York: Routledge.

Espeland, M.A., & others (2016, in press). Brain and white matter hyperintensity volumes after ten years of random assignment to lifestyle intervention. *Diabetes Care.*

Espie, J., & Eisler, I. (2015). Focus on anorexia nervosa: Modern psychological treatment and guidelines for the adolescent patient. *Adolescent Health, Medicine, and Therapeutics, 29,* 9–16.

Etaugh, C., & Bridges, J.S. (2010). *Women's lives* (2nd ed.). Boston: Allyn & Bacon.

Evans, G.W., & English, G.W. (2002). The environment of poverty. *Child Development, 73,* 1238–1248.

Evans, G.W., Li, D., & Sepanski Whipple, S. (2013). Cumulative risk and child development. *Psychological Bulletin, 139,* 1342–1396.

Evans, S.Z., Simons, L.G., & Simons, R.L. (2016). Factors that influence trajectories of delinquency throughout adolescence. *Journal of Youth and Adolescence, 45,* 156–171.

Evans, W.J. (2010). Skeletal muscle loss: Cachexia, sarcopenia, and inactivity. *American Journal of Clinical Nutrition, 91,* S1123–S1127.

Ezkurida, L., & others (2014). The shrinking human protein coding complement: Are there fewer than 20,000 genes? *bioRxiv,* doi:10.1101/001909.

F

Fabiano, G.A., & others (2009). A meta-analysis of behavioral treatments for attention deficit/hyperactivity disorder. *Clinical Psychology Review, 29,* 129–140.

Fabricius, W.V., Braver, S.L., Diaz, P., & Schenck, C. (2010). Custody and parenting time: Links to family relationships and well-being after divorce. In M.E. Lamb (Ed.), *The role of the father in child development* (5th ed.). New York: Wiley.

Fagot, B.I., Rodgers, C.S., & Leinbach, M.D. (2000). Theories of gender socialization. In T. Eckes & H.M. Trautner (Eds.), *The developmental social psychology of gender.* Mahwah, NJ: Erlbaum.

Fagundes, C.P., Gillie, B.L., Derry, H.M., Bennett, J.M., & Kiecolt-Glaser, J.K. (2016). Resilience and immune function in older adults. In G.C. Smith and B. Hayslip (Eds.), *Annual Review of Gerontology and Geriatrics.* New York: Springer.

Faguy, K. (2016). Obesity in children and adolescents: Health effects and imaging implications. *Radiologic Technology, 87,* 279–298.

Fahey, T., Insel, P., & Roth, W. (2017). *Fit & well* (12th ed.). New York: McGraw-Hill.

Fairlie, A.M., Maggs, J.L., & Lanza, S.T. (2016). Profiles of college drinkers defined by alcohol behaviors at the week level: Replication across semesters and prospective associations with hazardous drinking and dependence-related symptoms. *Journal of Studies on Alcohol and Drugs, 77,* 38–50.

Fakhoury, J., Nimmo, G.A., & Autexier, C. (2007). Harnessing telomerase in cancer therapeutics. *Anti-Cancer Agents in Medicinal Chemistry, 7,* 475–483.

Fakhoury, M. (2015). Autistic spectrum disorders: A review of clinical features, theories, and diagnosis. *International Journal of Neuroscience, 43,* 70–77.

Falbo, T., & Poston, D.L. (1993). The academic, personality, and physical outcomes of only children in China. *Child Development, 64,* 18–35.

Falconier, M.K., & others (2015). Stress from daily hassles in couples: Its effects on intradyadic relationship satisfaction and physical and psychological well-being. *Journal of Marital and Family Therapy, 41,* 221–235.

Fall, A.M., & Roberts, G. (2012). High school dropouts: Interactions between social context, self perceptions, school engagement, and student dropout. *Journal of Adolescence, 35*(4), 787–798.

Fan, F., & others (2016). Effects of maternal anxiety and depression during pregnancy in Chinese women on children's heart rate and blood pressure response to stress. *Journal of Human Hypertension, 30,* 171–176.

Fang, L., Wang, Y., & He, X. (2013). Theoretical analysis of wavefront aberration caused by treatment decentration and transition zone after custom myopic laser refractive surgery. *Journal of Cataract and Refractive Surgery, 39,* 1336–1347.

Fantz, R.L. (1963). Pattern vision in newborn infants. *Science, 140,* 286–297.

Farajinia, S., & others (2014). Aging of the suprachiasmatic clock. *Neuroscientist, 21,* 44–55.

Farr, R.H., & Patterson, C.J. (2013). Coparenting among lesbian, gay, and heterosexual couples: Associations with adopted children's outcomes. *Child Development, 84,* 1226–1240.

Farrell, M.J. (2012). Age-related changes in the structure and function of brain regions involved in pain processing. *Pain Medicine, 13*(Suppl. 2), S37–S43.

Fasig, L. (2000). Toddlers' understanding of ownership: Implications for self-concept development. *Social Development, 9,* 370–382.

Fatusi, A.O., & Hindin, M.J. (2010). Adolescents and youths in developing countries: Health and development issues in context. *Journal of Adolescence, 33,* 499–508.

Fava, N.M., & Bay-Cheng, L.Y. (2012). Young women's adolescent experiences of oral sex: Relation of age of initiation to sexual motivation, sexual coercion, and psychological functioning. *Journal of Adolescence, 35*(5), 1191–1201.

Faye, P.M., & others (2016). Kangaroo care for low birth weight infants at Albert-Royer National Children Hospital Center of Dakar. *Archives of Pediatrics, 23,* 268–274.

Federal Drug Administration (FDA) (2016). *Fish: What pregnant women and parents should know.* Retrieved April 30, 2016, from www.fda.gov/Food/FoodbornIllnessContaminants/Metals/uc...

Fedewa, A.L. (2015). How food as a reward is detrimental to children's health, learning, and behavior. *Journal of School Health, 85,* 648–658.

Feeney, S., Moravcik, E., & Nolte, S. (2016). *Who am I in the lives of children?* (10th ed.). Upper Saddle River, NJ: Pearson.

Feijen-de Jong, E.L., & others (2015a). Determinants of use of care provided by complementary and alternative health care practitioners to pregnant women in primary midwifery care: A prospective cohort study. *BMC Pregnancy and Child Care, 15,* 140.

Feijen-de Jong, E.L., & others (2015b). Determinants of prenatal health care utilization by low-risk women: A prospective cohort study. *Women and Birth, 28,* 87–94.

Feldman, H.D. (2001, April). *Contemporary developmental theories and the concept of talent.* Paper presented at the meeting of the Society for Research in Child Development, Minneapolis.

Feldman, R., Rosenthal, Z., & Eidelman, A.I. (2014). Maternal-preterm skin-to-skin contact enhances child physiologic organization and cognitive control across the first 10 years of life. *Biological Psychiatry, 75,* 56–64.

Feldman, S.S., Turner, R., & Araujo, K. (1999). Interpersonal context as an influence on sexual timetables of youths: Gender and ethnic effects. *Journal of Research on Adolescence, 9,* 25–52.

Feldstein Ewing, S.W., & others (2016). Developmental cognitive neuroscience of adolescent sexual risk and alcohol use. *AIDS Behavior, 20*(Suppl. 1), S97–S108.

Ferguson, C.J. (2013). Spanking, corporal punishment, and negative long-term outcomes: A meta-analytic review of longitudinal studies. *Clinical Psychology Review, 33,* 196–208.

Ferguson, D.M., Harwood, L.J., & Shannon, F.T. (1987). Breastfeeding and subsequent social adjustment in 6- to 8-year-old children. *Journal of Child Psychology and Psychiatry, 28,* 378–386.

Fernald, A., Marchman, V.A., & Weisleder, A. (2013). SES differences in language processing skill and vocabulary are evident at 18 months. *Developmental Science, 16,* 234–248.

Fernandez, M.A., & others (2015). Drastic increases in overweight and obesity from 1981 to 2010 and related risk factors: Results from the Barbados Children's Health and Nutrition Study. *Public Health Nutrition, 18,* 3070–3077.

Fernandez-Jaen, A., & others (2015). Cortical thickness differences in the prefrontal cortex in children and adolescents with ADHD in relation to dopamine transporter (DAT1) genotype. *Psychiatry Research, 233,* 409–417.

Ferrari, M., & Weststrate, N. (Eds.) (2013). *Personal wisdom.* New York: Springer.

Ferreira, D., & others (2015). Cognitive decline before the age of 50 can be detected with sensitive cognitive measures. *Psychothema, 27,* 216–222.

Ferriby, M., Kotila, L., Kamp Dush, G.K., & Schoppe-Sullivan, S. (2015). Dimensions of attachment and commitment across the transition to parenthood. *Journal of Family Psychology, 29,* 938–944.

Field, D. (1999). A cross-cultural perspective on continuity and change in social relations in old age: Introduction to a special issue. *International Journal of Aging and Human Development, 48,* 257–262.

Field, N., & others (2013). Associations between health and sexual lifestyles in Britain: Findings from the third National Survey of Sexual Attitudes and Lifestyles (Natsal-3). *Lancet, 382,* 1830–1844.

Field, T.M. (2001). Massage therapy facilitates weight gain in preterm infants. *Current Directions in Psychological Science, 10,* 51–55.

Field, T.M. (2007). *The amazing infant.* Malden, MA: Blackwell.

Field, T.M. (2010a). Pregnancy and labor massage. *European Review of Obstetrics and Gynecology, 5,* 177–181.

Field, T.M. (2010b). Postpartum depression effects on early interactions, parenting, and safety practices: A review. *Infant Behavior and Development, 33,* 1–6.

Field, T.M., Delgado, J., Diego, M., & Medina, L. (2013). Tai chi/yoga reduces prenatal depression, anxiety, and sleep disturbances. *Complementary Therapies in Clinical Practice, 19,* 6–10.

Field, T.M., Diego, M., & Hernandez-Reif, M. (2008). Prematurity and potential predictors. *International Journal of Neuroscience, 118,* 277–289.

Field, T.M., Diego, M., & Hernandez-Reif, M. (2011). Preterm infant massage therapy research: A review. *Infant Behavior and Development, 34,* 383–389.

Field, T.M., Grizzle, N., Scafidi, F., & Schanberg, S. (1996). Massage and relaxation therapies' effects on depressed adolescent mothers. *Adolescence, 31,* 903–911.

Field, T.M., Hernandez-Reif, M., Diego, M., Feijo, L., Vera, Y., & Gil, K. (2004). Massage therapy by parents improves early growth and development. *Infant Behavior & Development, 27,* 435–442.

Field, T.M., & others (1986). Tactile/kinesthetic stimulation effects on preterm neonates. *Pediatrics, 77,* 654–658.

Fielder, R.L., Walsh, J.L., Carey, K.B., & Carey, M.P. (2013). Predictors of sexual hookups: A theory-based, prospective study of first-year college women. *Archives of Sexual Behavior, 42,* 1425–1441.

Finch, C.E. (2009). The neurobiology of middle-age has arrived. *Neurobiology of Aging, 30,* 503–520.

Fine, A., Steinberg, L., Frick, P.J., & Cauffman, E. (2016, in press). Self-control assessments and implications for predicting adolescent offending. *Journal of Youth and Adolescence.*

Fingerhut, A.W., & Peplau, L.A. (2013). Same-sex romantic relationships. In C.J. Patterson & A.R. D'Augelli (Eds.), *Handbook of psychology and sexual orientation.* New York: Oxford University Press.

Fingerman, K.L., & Baker, B. (2006). Socioemotional aspects of aging. In J. Wilmouth &

K. Ferraro (Eds.), *Perspectives in gerontology* (3rd ed.). New York: Springer.

Fingerman, K.L., Birditt, K.S., Nussbaum, J., & Schroeder, D. (2014). Generational juggling: Midlife. In A.L. Vangelisti (Ed.), *Handbook of family communication* (2nd ed.). New York: Elsevier.

Fingerman, K.L., Cheng, Y.P., Tighe, L., Birditt, K.S., & Zarit, S. (2011b). Parent-child relationships in young adulthood. In A. Booth & others (Eds.), *Early adulthood in a family context.* New York: Springer.

Fingerman, K.L., Pillemer, K.A., Silverstein, M., & Suitor, J.J. (2012). The Baby Boomers' intergenerational relationships. *Gerontologist, 52,* 199–209.

Fingerman, K.L., Sechrist, J., & Birditt, K. (2013). Changing views on intergenerational ties. *Gerontology, 59,* 64–70.

Fingerman, K.L., & others (2011a). Who gets what and why: Help middle-aged adults provide to parents and grown children. *Journal of Gerontology B: Psychological Sciences and Social Sciences, 66,* 87–98.

Finistrella, V., & others (2015). Eating disorders and psychopathological traits in obese preadolescents and adolescents. *Journal of the American College of Nutrition, 34,* 142–149.

Finkelstein, E.A., & others (2012). Obesity and severe obesity forecasts through 2030. *American Journal of Preventive Medicine, 42,* 563–570.

Fischhoff, B., Bruine de Bruin, W., Parker, A.M., Millstein, S.G., & Halpern-Felsher, B.L. (2010). Adolescents' perceived risk of dying. *Journal of Adolescent Health, 46,* 265–269.

Fisher, G.G., & others (2014). Mental work demands, retirement, and longitudinal trajectories of cognitive functioning. *Journal of Occupational Health Psychology, 19,* 231–242.

Fisher, K.R., Hirsh-Pasek, K., Newcombe, N., & Golinkoff, R.M. (2013). Taking shape: Supporting preschoolers' acquisition of geometric knowledge through guided play. *Child Development, 84,* 1872–1878.

Fitzpatrick, K.K. (2012). Developmental considerations when treating anorexia nervosa in adolescents and young adults. In J. Lock (Ed.), *Oxford handbook of child and adolescent eating disorders: Developmental perspectives.* New York: Oxford University Press.

Fivush, R. (2011). The development of autobiographical memory. *Annual Review of Psychology* (Vol. 62). Palo Alto, CA: Annual Reviews.

Fivush, R., & Haden, C.A. (1997). Narrating and representing experience: Preschoolers' developing autobiographical accounts. In P. van den Broek, P.J. Bauer, & T. Bourg (Eds.), *Developmental spans in event representations and comprehension: Bridging fictional and actual events.* Mahwah, NJ: Erlbaum.

Fizke, E., Barthel, D., Peters, T., & Rakoczy, H. (2014). Executive function plays a role in coordinating different perspectives, particularly when one's own perspective is involved. *Cognition, 130,* 315–334.

Fjell, A.M., & Walhovd, K.B. (2010). Structural brain changes in aging: Courses, causes, and consequences. *Reviews in the Neurosciences, 21,* 187–222.

Fjell, A.M., & others (2016). Brain events underlying episodic memory changes in aging: A longitudinal investigation of structural and functional connectivity. *Cerebral Cortex, 26,* 1272–1286.

Flam, K.K., Sandler, I., Wolchik, S., & Tein, J.Y. (2016). Non-residential father-child involvement, interparental conflict, and mental health of children

following divorce: A person-focused approach. *Journal of Youth and Adolescence, 45,* 581–593.

Flavell, J.H. (2004). Theory-of-mind development: Retrospect and prospect. *Merrill-Palmer Quarterly, 50,* 274–290.

Flavell, J.H., Friedrichs, A., & Hoyt, J. (1970). Developmental changes in memorization processes. *Cognitive Psychology, 1,* 324–340.

Flavell, J.H., Green, F.L., & Flavell, E.R. (1995). The development of children's knowledge about attentional focus: *Developmental Psychology, 31,* 706–712.

Flavell, J.H., Green, F.L., & Flavell, E.R. (2000). Development of children's awareness of their own thoughts. *Journal of Cognition and Development, 7,* 97–112.

Fleischmann, F., & Verkuyten, M. (2016). Dual identity among immigrants: Comparing different conceptualizations, their measurement, and implications. *Cultural Diversity and Ethnic Minority Psychology, 22,* 151–155.

Fletcher-Watson, S., McConnell, F., Manola, E., & McConachie, H. (2014). Interventions based on the theory of mind cognitive model for autism spectrum disorder. *Cochrane Database of Systematic Reviews, 3,* CD008785.

Flicek, P., & others (2013). Ensembl 2013. *Nucleic Acids Research, 41,* D48–D55.

Flint, M.S., Baum, A., Chambers, W.H., & Jenkins, F.J. (2007). Induction of DNA damage, alteration of DNA repair, and transcriptional activation by stress hormones. *Psychoneuroendocrinology, 32,* 470–479.

Flom, R., & Pick, A.D. (2003). Verbal encouragement and joint attention in 18-month-old infants. *Infant Behavior and Development, 26,* 121–134.

Flood, S.M., & Genadek, K.R. (2016). Time for each other: Work and family constraints among couples. *Journal of Marriage and the Family, 78,* 142–164.

Florsheim, P. (2014). *The young parenthood program.* New York: Oxford University Press.

Florsheim, P., Moore, D., & Edgington, C. (2003). Romantic relationships among pregnant and parenting adolescents. In P. Florsheim (Ed.), *Adolescent romantic relations and sexual behavior.* Mahwah, NJ: Erlbaum.

Flouri, E., & Buchanan, A. (2004). Early father's and mother's involvement and child's later educational outcomes. *British Journal of Educational Psychology, 74,* 141–153.

Flouri, E., Midouhas, E., & Joshi, H. (2014). Family poverty and trajectories of children's emotional and behavioral problems: The moderating role of self-regulation and verbal cognitive ability. *Journal of Abnormal Child Psychology, 42,* 1043–1056.

Flynn, J.R. (1999). Searching for justice: The discovery of IQ gains over time. *American Psychologist, 54,* 5–20.

Flynn, J.R. (2007). The history of the American mind in the 20th century: A scenario to explain IQ gains over time and a case for the relevance of g. In P.C. Kyllonen, R.D. Roberts, & L. Stankov (Eds.), *Extending intelligence.* Mahwah, NJ: Erlbaum.

Flynn, J.R. (2011). Secular changes in intelligence. In R.J. Sternberg & S.B. Kaufman (Eds.), *Cambridge handbook of intelligence.* New York: Cambridge University Press.

Flynn, J.R. (2013). *Are we getting smarter?* New York: Cambridge University Press.

Flynn, J.R., & Blair, C. (2013). The history of intelligence: New spectacles for developmental psychology. In P.D. Zelazo (Ed.), *Oxford handbook of developmental psychology.* New York: Oxford University Press.

Follari, L. (2015). *Foundations and best practices in early childhood education* (3rd ed.). Upper Saddle River, NJ: Pearson.

Foltynie, T. (2015). Can Parkinson's disease be cured by stimulating neurogenesis? *Journal of Clinical Investigation, 125,* 978–980.

Fonseca-Machado Mde, O., & others (2015). Depressive disorder in Latin women: Does intimate partner violence matter? *Journal of Clinical Nursing, 24,* 1289–1299.

Ford, D.Y. (2012). Gifted and talented education: History, issues, and recommendations. In K.R. Harris, S. Graham, & T. Urdan (Eds.), *APA handbook of educational psychology.* Washington, DC: American Psychological Association.

Ford, D.Y. (2015a). Multicultural issues: Recruiting and retaining Black and Hispanic students in gifted education: Equality versus equity in schools. *Gifted Child Today, 38,* 187–191.

Ford, D.Y. (2015b). Culturally responsive gifted classrooms for culturally different students: A focus on invitational learning. *Gifted Child Today, 38,* 67–69.

Ford, D.Y. (2016). Black and Hispanic students. In L. Corno & E.M. Anderman (Eds.), *Handbook of educational psychology* (3rd ed.). New York: Routledge.

Forrester, S.N., Gallo, J.J., Smith, G.S., & Leoutsakos, J.M. (2016). Patterns of neuropsychiatric symptoms in mild cognitive impairment and risk of dementia. *American Journal of Geriatric Psychiatry, 24,* 117–125.

Fosco, G.M., Stormshak, E.A., Dishion, T.J., & Winter, C.E. (2012). Family relationships and parental monitoring during middle school as predictors of early adolescent problem behavior. *Journal of Clinical Child and Adolescent Psychology, 41,* 202–213.

Fowler, M.G., & others (2014). Efficacy and safety of an extended nevirapine regimen in infants of breastfeeding mothers with HIV-1 infection for prevention of HIV-1 transmission (HPTN 046): 18-month results of a randomized, double-blind, placebo-controlled trial. *Journal of Acquired Immune Deficiency Syndromes, 65,* 366–374.

Fox, M.K., Pac, S., Devaney, B., & Jankowski, L. (2004). Feeding infants and toddlers study: What foods are infants and toddlers eating? *American Dietetic Association Journal, 104,* (Suppl.), S22–S30.

Fox, M.K., & others (2010). Food consumption patterns of young preschoolers: Are they starting off on the right path? *Journal of the American Dietetic Association, 110*(Suppl. 12), S52–S59.

Fozard, J.L. (1992, December 6). Commentary in "We can age successfully." *Parade Magazine,* pp. 14–15.

Fraiberg, S. (1959). *The magic years.* New York: Scribner's.

Fraley, R.C., Roisman, G.I., Booth-LaForce, C., Owen, M.T., & Holland, A.S. (2013). Intrapersonal and genetic origins of adult attachment styles: A longitudinal study from infancy to early adulthood. *Journal of Personality and Social Psychology, 104,* 817–838.

Fraley, R.C., & Shaver, P.R. (2016). Attachment, loss, and grief: Bowlby's views, new developments, and current controversies. In J. Cassidy & P.R. Shaver (Eds.), *Handbook of attachment* (3rd ed.). New York: Guilford.

Franchak, J.M., Heeger, D.J., Hasson, U., & Adolph, K.E. (2016). Free viewing gaze behavior in infants and adults. *Infancy, 21*, 262–287.

Francis, J., Fraser, G., & Marcia, J.E. (1989). *Cognitive and experimental factors in moratorium-achievement (MAMA) cycles.* Unpublished manuscript, Department of Psychology, Simon Fraser University, Burnaby, British Columbia.

Frankl, V. (1984). *Man's search for meaning.* New York: Basic Books.

Fransson, M., & others (2016). Is middle childhood attachment related to social functioning in young adulthood? *Scandinavian Journal of Psychology, 57*, 108–116.

Frasquilho, D., & others (2016, in press). Distress and unemployment: The related economic and non-economic factors in a sample of unemployed adults. *International Journal of Public Health.*

Frawley, J.M., & others (2016, in press). Complementary and alternative medicine practitioner use prior to pregnancy predicts use during pregnancy. *Women's Health.*

Frazier, P.A., & Scharf, R.J. (2015). Parent-infant attachment. *Pediatrics in Review, 36*, 36–41.

Frederikse, M., & others (2000). Sex differences in inferior lobule volume in schizophrenia. *American Journal of Psychiatry, 157*, 422–427.

Freeman, S., & others (2017). *Biological science* (6th ed.). Upper Saddle River, NJ: Pearson.

Frenkel, T.I., & Fox, N.A. (2015). Caregiver socialization factors influencing socioemotional development in infancy and childhood: A neuroscience perspective. In J.E. Grusec & P.D. Hastings (Eds.), *Handbook of socialization* (2nd ed.). New York: Guilford.

Freud, S. (1917). *A general introduction to psychoanalysis.* New York: Washington Square Press.

Freund, A.M., & Blanchard-Fields, F. (2014). Age-related differences in altruism across adulthood: Making personal financial gain versus contributing to the public good. *Developmental Psychology, 50*(4), 1125–1136.

Freund, A.M., & Hennecke, M. (2015). On means and end: The role of goal focus in successful goal pursuit. *Current Directions in Psychological Science, 24*, 149–153.

Freund, A.M., Nikitin, J., & Riediger, M. (2013). Successful aging. In I.B. Weiner & others (Eds.), *Handbook of psychology* (2nd ed., Vol. 6). New York: Wiley.

Frey, B.S. (2011). Happy people live longer. *Science, 331*, 542–543.

Friedman, S.L., Melhuish, E., & Hill, C. (2010). Childcare research at the dawn of a new millennium: An update. In G. Bremner & T. Wachs (Eds.), *Wiley-Blackwell handbook of infant development* (2nd ed.). Oxford, UK: Wiley-Blackwell.

Friend, M., & Bursuck, W.D. (2015). *Including students with special needs* (7th ed.). Upper Saddle River, NJ: Pearson.

Frisen, A., & Holmqvist, K. (2010). What characterizes early adolescents with a positive body image? A qualitative investigation of Swedish boys and girls. *Body Image, 7*, 205–212.

Frost, D.M. (2011). Stigma and intimacy in same-sex relationships: A narrative approach. *Journal of Family Psychology, 25*, 1–10.

Fuchs, L.S., & others (2016, in press). Supported self-explaining during fraction intervention. *Journal of Educational Psychology.*

Fuglset, T.S., Endestad, T., Landro, N.I., & Ro, O. (2015). Brain structure alterations associated with weight changes in young females with anorexia nervosa: A case series. *Neurocase, 21*, 169–177.

Fuhs, M.W., Nesbitt, K.T., Farran, D.C., & Dong, N. (2014). Longitudinal associations between executive functioning and academic skills across content areas. *Developmental Psychology, 50*, 1698–1709.

Fuligni, A.J. (2012). Gaps, conflicts, and arguments between adolescents and their parents. *New Directions for Child and Adolescent Development, 135*, 105–110.

Fuligni, A.J., & Tsai, K.M. (2015). Developmental flexibility in the age of globalization: Autonomy and identity development among immigrant adolescents. *Annual Review of Psychology* (Vol. 66). Palo Alto, CA: Annual Reviews.

Fuligni, A.J., Tsai, K.M., Krull, J.L., & Gonzales, N.A. (2015). Daily concordance between parent and adolescent sleep habits. *Journal of Adolescent Health, 56*, 244–260.

Funk, C.M., & others (2016, in press). Local slow waves in superficial layers of primary cortical areas during REM sleep. *Current Biology.*

Furman, E. (2005). *Boomerang nation.* New York: Fireside.

Furman, W., Low, S., & Ho, M.J. (2009). Romantic experience and psychosocial adjustment in middle adolescence. *Journal of Clinical Child and Adolescent Psychology, 38*, 75–90.

Furman, W., & Rose, A.J. (2015). Friendships, romantic relationships, and other dyadic peer relationships in childhood and adolescence: A unified relational perspective. In R.M. Lerner (Ed.), *Handbook of child psychology and developmental science* (7th ed.). New York: Wiley.

Furstenberg, F.F. (2007). The future of marriage. In A.S. Skolnick & J.H. Skolnick (Eds.), *Family in transition* (14th ed.). Boston: Allyn & Bacon.

Furth, H.G., & Wachs, H. (1975). *Thinking goes to school.* New York: Oxford University Press.

Furukawa, S., Sameshima, H., & Ikenoue, T. (2014). The impact of cesarean section on neonatal outcome of infants born at 23 weeks gestation. *Early Human Development, 90*, 113–118.

G

Gabe, T. (2015, January 29). *Poverty in the United States: 2013.* Retrieved September 14, 2015, from Congressional Research Service, www.crs.gov

Gabor, M. (2014, March). New college degree in hand: Now what? *Monthly Labor Review.* Washington, DC: U.S. Department of Labor.

Gaias, L.M., & others (2012). Cross-cultural temperamental differences in infants, children, and adults in the United States of America and Finland, *53*, 119–128.

Gaillard, A., & others (2014). Predictors of postpartum depression: Prospective study of 264 women followed during pregnancy and postpartum. *Psychiatry Research, 215*, 341–346.

Galambos, N.L., Howard, A.L., & Maggs, J.L. (2011). Rise and fall of sleep quality with student experiences across the first year of the university. *Journal of Research on Adolescence, 21*, 342–349.

Galdiolo, S., & Roskam, I. (2016). From me to us: The construction of family alliance. *Infant Mental Health, 37*, 29–44.

Gale, C.R., Booth, T., Mottus, R., Kuh, D., & Deary, J.J. (2013). Neuroticism and extraversion in youth predict mental wellbeing and life satisfaction 40 years later. *Journal of Research in Personality, 47*, 687–697.

Galinsky, E. (2010). *Mind in the making.* New York: Harper Collins.

Galland, B.C., Taylor, B.J., Edler, D.E., & Herbison, P. (2012). Normal sleep patterns in infants and children: A systematic review of observational studies. *Sleep Medicine Review, 16*, 213–222.

Gallant, S.N. (2016). Mindfulness meditation practice and executive functioning: Breaking down the benefit. *Consciousness and Cognition, 40*, 116–130.

Galloway, J.C., & Thelen, E. (2004). Feet first: Object exploration in young infants. *Infant Behavior & Development, 27*, 107–112.

Gallup (2013). *No major change in Americans' exercise habits in 2011.* Washington, DC: Gallup.

Gallup (2015). *Fewer young people say I do—to any relationship.* Princeton, NJ: Gallup.

Galvan, A., & Tottenham, N. (2016). Adolescent brain development. In D. Cicchetti (Ed.), *Developmental psychopathology* (3rd ed.). New York: Wiley.

Gambacciani, M., & Levancini, M. (2015). Hormone replacement therapy: Who should be treated? *Minerva Ginecologica, 67*, 249–255.

Gander, M., & Buchheim, A. (2015). Attachment classification, psychophysiology, and frontal EEG asymmetry across the lifespan: A review. *Frontiers in Human Neuroscience, 19*, 79.

Ganong, L., & Coleman, M. (2006). Obligations to stepparents acquired in later life: Relationship quality and acuity of needs. *Journals of Gerontology B: Psychological Sciences and Social Sciences, 61*, S80–S88.

Ganong, L., Coleman, M., & Russell, L. (2015). Children in diverse families. In R.M. Lerner (Ed.), *Handbook of child psychology and developmental science* (7th ed.). New York: Wiley.

Gao, W., Lin, W., Grewen, K., & Gilmore, J.H. (2016, in press). Functional connectivity of the infant human brain: Plastic and modifiable. *Neuroscientist.*

Garcia Coll, C., & others (2012). Understanding the immigrant paradox in youth: Developmental and contextual considerations. In A.S. Masten (Ed.), *Realizing the potential of immigrant youth.* New York: Cambridge University Press.

Garcia-Hermoso, A., Saavedra, J.M., & Escalante, Y. (2013). Effects of exercise on resting blood pressure in obese children: A meta-analysis of randomized controlled trials. *Obesity Reviews, 14*(11), 919–928.

Garcia-Mesa, Y., & others (2016). Oxidative stress is a central target for physical exercise neuroprotection against pathological brain aging. *Journals of Gerontology A: Biological Sciences and Medical Sciences, 71*, 40–49.

Garcia-Toro, M., & others (2016). Obesity, metabolic syndrome, and Mediterranean diet: Impact on depression outcome. *Journal of Affective Disorders, 194*, 105–108.

Gardner, H. (1983). *Frames of mind.* New York: Basic Books.

Gardner, H. (1993). *Multiple intelligences.* New York: Basic Books.

Gardner, H. (2002). The pursuit of excellence through education. In M. Ferrari (Ed.), *Learning from extraordinary minds.* Mahwah, NJ: Erlbaum.

Gardner, M., Brooks-Gunn, J., & Chase-Lansdale, P.L. (2016, in press). The two-generation approach to building human capital: Past, present, and future. In E. Votruba-Drzal & E. Dearing (Eds.), *Handbook of early childhood development programs, practices, and policies.* New York: Wiley.

Gardner, M.K. (2014). Theories of intelligence. In M.A. Bray & T.J. Kehle (Eds.), *Oxford handbook of school psychology.* New York: Oxford University Press.

Gardosi, J., & others (2013). Maternal and fetal risk factors for stillbirth: Population-based study. *British Medical Journal, 346,* f108.

Gareau, S., & others (2016, in press). Group prenatal care results in Medicaid savings with better outcomes: A propensity score analysis of CenteringPregnancy participation in South Carolina. *Maternal and Child Health.*

Garmertsfelder, E.M., & others (2016). Prevalence of advance directives among older adults admitted to intensive care units and requiring mechanical ventilation. *Journal of Gerontological Nursing, 42,* 34–41.

Garthe, A., Roeder, I., & Kempermann, G. (2016). Mice in an enriched environment learn more flexibly because of adult hippocampal neurogenesis. *Hippocampus, 26,* 261–271.

Gartland, N., O'Connor, D.B., Lawton, R., & Ferguson, R. (2014). Investigating the effects of conscientiousness on daily stress, affect, and physical symptom processes: A daily diary study. *British Journal of Health Psychology, 19,* 311–328.

Gartner, J., Larson, D.B., & Allen, G.D. (1991). Religious commitment and mental health: A review of the empirical literature. *Journal of Psychology and Theology, 19,* 6–25.

Gartstein, M.A., Putnam, S., & Kliewer, R. (2016). Do infant temperament characteristics predict core academic abilities in preschool-aged children? *Learning and Individual Differences, 45,* 299–306.

Garvey, C. (2000). *Play* (Enlarged Ed.). Cambridge, MA: Harvard University Press.

Gaskins, S. (2016). Childhood practices across cultures: Play and household work. In L.J. Arnett (Ed.), *Oxford handbook of human development and culture.* New York: Oxford University Press.

Gat, I., & others (2016). Fetal brain MRI: Novel classification and contribution to sonography. *Ultraschell Medicine, 37,* 175–184.

Gates, C.J. (2011). *How many people are lesbian, gay, bisexual, and transgender?* Los Angeles: Williams Institute, UCLA.

Gates, W. (1998, July 20). Charity begins when I'm ready (interview). *Fortune magazine.*

Gaugler, J.E. (2016). Innovations in long-term care. In L.K. George & K.F. Ferraro (Eds.), *Handbook of aging and the social sciences* (8th ed.). New York: Elsevier.

Gauvain, M. (2013). Sociocultural contexts of development. In P.D. Zelazo (Ed.), *Oxford handbook of developmental psychology.* New York: Oxford University Press.

Gauvain, M. (2016). Peer contributions to cognitive development. In K. Wentzel & G.B. Ramani (Eds.), *Handbook of social influences in school contexts.* New York: Routledge.

Gauvain, M., & Perez, S. (2015). Cognitive development in the context of culture. In R.M. Lerner (Ed.), *Handbook of child psychology and developmental science* (7th ed.). New York: Wiley.

Gawlik, S., & others (2014). Prevalence of paternal perinatal depressiveness and its link to partnership satisfaction and birth concerns. *Archives of Women's Mental Health, 17,* 49–56.

Gelman, R. (1969). Conservation acquisition: A problem of learning to attend to relevant attributes. *Journal of Experimental Child Psychology, 7,* 67–87.

Gelman, S.A. (2013). Concepts in development. In P. Zelazo (Ed.), *Oxford handbook of developmental psychology.* New York: Oxford University Press.

Gelman, S.A., & Kalish, C.W. (2006). Conceptual development. In W. Damon & R. Lerner (Eds.), *Handbook of child psychology* (6th ed.). New York: Wiley.

Genesee, F., & Lindholm-Leary, K. (2012). The education of English language learners. In K. Harris, S. Graham, & T. Urdan (Eds.), *APA educational psychology handbook.* Washington, DC: American Psychological Association.

Gennetian, L.A., & Miller, C. (2002). Children and welfare reform: A view from an experimental welfare reform program in Minnesota. *Child Development, 73,* 601–620.

Gentile, D.A., & others (2014). Protective effects of parental monitoring of children's media use: A prospective study. *JAMA Pediatrics, 168,* 479–484.

George, L.K., & Ferraro, K.F. (2016). Aging and the social sciences: Progress and prospects. In L.K. George & K.F. Ferraro (Eds.), *Handbook of aging and the social sciences* (8th ed.). New York: Elsevier.

Gershoff, E.T. (2013). Spanking and development: We know enough now to stop hitting our children. *Child Development Perspectives, 7,* 133–137.

Gershoff, E.T., & Benner, A.D. (2014). Neighborhood and school contexts in the lives of children. In E.T. Gershoff, R.S. Mistry, & D.A. Crosby (Eds.), *The societal contexts of child development.* New York: Oxford University Press.

Gershoff, E.T., Lansford, J.E., Sexton, H.R., Davis-Kean, P., & Sameroff, A. (2012). Longitudinal links between spanking and children's externalizing behaviors in a national sample of White, Black, Hispanic, and Asian American families. *Child Development, 83,* 838–843.

Gerson, S.A., & others (2015). Shifting goals: Effects of active and observational experience on infants' understanding of higher order goals. *Frontiers in Psychology, 6,* 310.

Gerst, E.H., Dirino, P.T., Fletcher, J.M., & Yoshida, H. (2016, in press). Cognitive and behavioral rating measures of executive function predictors of academic outcomes in children. *Child Neuropsychology.*

Gerstorf, D., & others (2015). Secular changes in late-life cognition and well-being: Towards a long bright future with a short brisk ending. *Psychology and Aging, 30,* 301–310.

Gertosio, C., Meazza, C., Pagani, S., & Bozzzoia, M. (2017, in press). Breast feeding: Gamut of benefits. *Minerva Pediatrica.*

Gesell, A. (1934). An atlas of infant behavior. New Haven, CT: Yale University Press.

Geva, R., Yaron, H., & Kuint, J. (2016). Neonatal sleep predicts attention orienting and distractibility. *Journal of Attention Disorders, 20,* 138–150.

Ghetti, S., & Alexander, K.W. (2004). "If it happened, I would remember it": Strategic use of event memorability in the rejection of false autobiographical events. *Child Development, 75,* 542–561.

Ghosh, S., Feingold, E., Chakaborty, S., & Dey, S.K. (2010). Telomere length is associated with types of chromosome 21 nondisjunction: A new insight into the maternal age effect on Down syndrome birth. *Human Genetics, 9,* 3834–3835.

Gialamas, A., & others (2014). Quality of childcare influences children's attentiveness and emotional regulation at school entry. *Journal of Pediatrics, 165,* 813–819.

Giallo, R., & others (2015). The emotional-behavioral functioning of children exposed to maternal depressive symptoms across pregnancy and early childhood: A prospective Australian pregnancy cohort study. *European Child and Adolescent Psychiatry, 24,* 1233–1244.

Gibbons, L., & others (2012). Inequities in the use of cesarean section deliveries in the world. *American Journal of Obstetrics and Gynecology, 206*(4), 331.e1–331.e19.

Gibbs, J.C. (2014). *Moral development and reality: Beyond the theories of Kohlberg and Hoffman* (3rd ed.). New York: Oxford University Press.

Gibbs, J.C., Basinger, K.S., Grime, R.L., & Snarey, J.R. (2007). Moral judgment development across cultures: Revisiting Kohlberg's universality claims. *Developmental Review, 27,* 443–500.

Giblin, W., & Lombard, D.B. (2016). Sirtuins, healthspan, and longevity. In M. Kaeberlein & G.W. Martin (Eds.), *Handbook of the biology of aging* (8th ed.). New York: Elsevier.

Gibson, E.J. (1969). *Principles of perceptual learning and development.* New York: Appleton-Century-Crofts.

Gibson, E.J. (1989). Exploratory behavior in the development of perceiving, acting, and the acquiring of knowledge. *Annual Review of Psychology* (Vol. 39). Palo Alto, CA: Annual Reviews.

Gibson, E.J. (2001). *Perceiving the affordances.* Mahwah, NJ: Erlbaum.

Gibson, E.J., & Walk, R.D. (1960). The "visual cliff." *Scientific American, 202,* 64–71.

Gibson, H.J. (2009). Leisure and travel, adulthood. In D. Carr (Ed.), *Encyclopedia of the life course and human development.* Boston: Gale Cengage.

Gibson, J.J. (1966). *The senses considered as perceptual systems.* Boston: Houghton Mifflin.

Gibson, J.J. (1979). *The ecological approach to visual perception.* Boston: Houghton Mifflin.

Gibson-Davis, C., & Rackin, H. (2014). Marriage or carriage? Trends in union context and birth type by education. *Journal of Marriage and the Family, 76,* 506–519.

Giedd, J.N. (2012). The digital revolution and the adolescent brain. *Journal of Adolescent Health, 51,* 101–105.

Giles, E.D., & others (2016). Exercise decreases lipogenic gene expression in adipose tissue and alters adipocyte cellularity during weight regain after weight loss. *Frontiers in Physiology, 7,* 32.

Gill, D.P., & others (2016). The healthy mind, healthy mobility trial: A novel exercise program for older adults. *Medicine and Science in Sports and Exercise, 48,* 297–306.

Gillen-O'Neel, C., Huynh, V.W., & Fuligni, A.J. (2013). To study or to sleep? The academic costs of extra studying at the expense of sleep. *Child Development, 84*(1), 133–142.

Gilligan, C. (1982). *In a different voice.* Cambridge, MA: Harvard University Press.

Gilligan, C. (1996). The centrality of relationships in psychological development: A puzzle, some evidence, and a theory. In G.G. Noam & K.W. Fischer (Eds.), *Development and vulnerability in close relationships.* Hillsdale, NJ: Erlbaum.

Gillum, R.F., & Ingram, D.D. (2007). Frequency of attendance at religious services, hypertension, and blood pressure: The third National Health and Nutrition Examination Survey. *Psychosomatic Medicine, 68,* 382–385.

Girls, Inc. (1991). *Truth, trusting, and technology: New research on preventing adolescent pregnancy.* Indianapolis: Author.

Giudetti, A.M., Romano, A., Lavecchia, A.M., & Gaetani, S. (2016). The role of brain cholesterol and its oxidized products in Alzheimer's disease. *Current Alzheimer Research, 13,* 198–205.

Glei, D.A. (1999). Measuring contraceptive use patterns among teenage and adult women. *Family Planning Perspectives, 31,* 73–80.

Glickman, K., Shear, M.K., & Wall, M. (2016). Exploring outcomes related to anxiety and depression in completers of a randomized controlled trial of complicated grief treatment. *Clinical Psychology and Psychotherapy, 23,* 118–124.

Gliga, T., & others (2016, in press). Early visual foraging in relationship to familial risk for autism and hyperactivity/inattention. *Journal of Attention Disorders.*

Glover, V. (2014). Maternal depression, anxiety, and stress during pregnancy and child outcome: What needs to be done. *Best Practice and Research: Clinical Obstetrics and Gynecology, 28,* 25–35.

Goad, H. (2016). Phonological processes in children's production: Convergence and divergence from adult grammars. In J. Lidz, W. Snyder, & J. Pater (Eds.), *Oxford handbook of developmental linguistics.* New York: Oxford University Press.

Gockley, A.A., & others (2016). The effect of adolescence and advanced maternal age on the incidence of partial molar pregnancy. *Gynecology and Oncology, 140,* 470–473.

Godyn, J., Jonczyk, J., Panek, D., & Malawska, B. (2016). Therapeutic strategies for Alzheimer's disease in clinical trials. *Pharmacological Reports, 68,* 127–138.

Gogtay, N., & Thompson, P.M. (2010). Mapping gray matter development: Implications for typical development and vulnerability to psychopathology. *Brain and Cognition, 72,* 6–15.

Goh, R., Darvall, J., Wynne, R., & Tatoulis, J. (2016). Obesity prevalence and associated outcomes in cardiothoracic patients: A single-center experience. *Anesthesia and Intensive Care Medicine, 44,* 7784.

Goh, S.N., & others (2016). Sociodemographic, home environment, and parental influences on total and device-specific screen viewing in children aged 2 years and below: An observational study. *BMJ Open, 6*(1), e009113.

Gold, M.S., Blum K., Oscar-Berman, M., & Braverman, E.R. (2014). Low dopamine function in attention deficit/hyperactivity disorder: Should genotyping signify early diagnosis in children? *Postgraduate Medicine, 126,* 153–177.

Goldberg, J.S., & Carlson, M.J. (2015). Patterns and predictors of coparenting after unmarried parents part. *Journal of Family Psychology, 29,* 416–426.

Goldberg, W.A., & Lucas-Thompson, R. (2008). Maternal and paternal employment, effects of. In M.M. Haith & J.B. Benson (Eds.), *Encyclopedia of infant and early childhood development.* Oxford, UK: Elsevier.

Goldenberg, R.L., & Culhane, J.F. (2007). Low birth weight in the United States. *American Journal of Clinical Nutrition, 85*(Suppl.), S584–S590.

Golding, J., & others (2016). Associations between prenatal mercury exposure and early child development in the ALSPAC study. *Neurotoxicology, 53,* 215–222.

Goldin-Meadow, S. (2015). Nonverbal communication: The hand's role in talking and thinking. In R.M. Lerner (Ed.), *Handbook of child psychology and developmental science* (7th ed.). New York: Wiley.

Goldin-Meadow, S. (2017, in press). Using our hands to change our minds. *Cognitive Science.*

Goldschmidt, L., Richardson, G.A., Willford, J., & Day, N.L. (2008) Prenatal marijuana exposure and intelligence test performance at age 6. *Journal of the American Academy of Child and Adolescent Psychiatry, 47,* 254–263.

Goldstein, K.M., & others (2016). Nonpharmacologic, nonherbal management of menopause-associated visuomotor symptoms: An umbrella systematic review. *Systematic Reviews, 5*(1), 56.

Goldstone, E., & Reynolds, A. (2014). Child development and behavior. In W. Hay, M. Levin, & M. Abzug (Eds.), *Pediatrics* (22nd ed.). New York: McGraw-Hill.

Golinkoff, R.M., Can, D., Soderstrom, M., & Hirsh-Pasek, K. (2015). (Baby) talk to me: The social context of infant-directed speech and its effect on early language development. *Current Directions in Psychological Science, 24,* 339–344.

Golnick, D.M., & Chinn, P.C. (2017). *Multicultural education in a pluralistic society* (10th ed.). Upper Saddle River, NJ: Pearson.

Golombok, S. (2011a). Children in new family forms. In R. Gross (Ed.), *Psychology* (6th ed.). London: Hodder.

Golombok, S. (2011b). Why I study lesbian families. In S. Ellis, V. Clarke, E. Peel, & D. Riggs (Eds.), *LGBTQ psychologies.* New York: Cambridge University Press.

Golombok, S., & others (2014). Adoptive gay father families: Parent-child relationships and children's psychological adjustment. *Child Development, 85,* 456–468.

Gomes, R.S., & others (2011). Primary versus secondary hypertension in children followed up at an outpatient tertiary unit. *Pediatric Nephrology, 26,* 441–447.

Goncalves, L.F. (2016). Three-dimensional ultrasound of the fetus: How does it help? *Pediatric Radiology, 46,* 177–189.

Gong, Y., Ericsson, K.A., & Moxley, J.H. (2015). A refined technique for identifying chunk characteristics during recall of briefly presented chess positions and their relations to chess skill. *PLoS One, 10,* e0118756.

Gonzales, N.A., & others (2016). Cultural adapted preventive interventions for children and adolescents. In D. Cicchetti (Ed.), *Developmental psychopathology* (3rd ed.). New York: Wiley.

Gonzalez, J., & others (2015). Reminiscence and dementia: A therapeutic intervention. *International Psychogeriatrics, 27,* 1731–1737.

Gonzalez-Bracken, M.A., Bamaca-Colbert, M., & Allen, K. (2016). Ethnic identity trajectories among Mexican-origin girls during early and middle adolescence: Predicting future psychosocial adjustment. *Developmental Psychology, 52,* 790–797.

Gonzalez-Echavarri, C., & others (2015). Prevalence and significance of persistently positive antiphospholipid antibodies in women with preeclampsia. *Journal of Rheumatology, 42,* 2010–2013.

Gonzalez-Freire, M., & others (2015). Reconsidering the role of mitochondria in aging. *Journals of Gerontology A: Biological Sciences and Medical Sciences, 70,* 1334–1342.

Goodenough, J., & McGuire, B.A. (2017). *Biology of humans* (6th ed.). Upper Saddle River, NJ: Pearson.

Goodkind, S. (2013). Single-sex public education for low-income youth of color: A critical theoretical review. *Sex Roles, 69,* 393–402.

Goodnow, J.J., & Lawrence, J.A. (2015). Children and cultural context. In R.M. Lerner (Ed.), *Handbook of child psychology and developmental science* (7th ed.). New York: Wiley.

Goodvin, R., Thompson, R.A., & Winer, A.C. (2015). The individual child: Temperament, emotion, self, and personality. In M. Bornstein & M.E. Lamb (Eds.), *Developmental science* (7th ed.). New York: Psychology Press.

Gopinath, B., McMahon, C.M., Burlutsky, G., Mitchell, P. (2016, in press). Hearing and vision impairment and the 5-year incidence of falls in older adults. *Age and Aging.*

Gopnik, A. (2010). Commentary. In E. Galinsky (2010). *Mind in the making.* New York: Harper Collins.

Gorby, H.E., Brownawell, A.M., & Falk, M.C. (2010). Do specific dietary constituents and supplements affect mental energy? Review of the evidence. *Nutrition Reviews, 68,* 697–718.

Gorchoff, S.M., John, O.P., & Helson, R. (2008). Contextualizing change in marital satisfaction during middle age: An 18-year longitudinal study. *Psychological Science, 19,* 1194–1200.

Gottlieb, G. (2007) Probabilistic epigenesis. *Developmental Science, 10,* 1–11.

Gottman, J.M. (1994). *What predicts divorce?* Mahwah, NJ: Erlbaum.

Gottman, J.M. (2006, April, 29). Secrets of long term love. *New Scientist, 2549,* 40.

Gottman, J.M. (2011). *The science of trust.* New York: Norton.

Gottman, J.M. (2016). *Bringing home baby.* Retrieved January 7, 2016, from www.bbhonline.org/

Gottman, J.M. (2016). *Research on parenting.* Retrieved January 6, 2016, from www.gottman.com/parenting/research.

Gottman, J.M., & Gottman, J.S. (2009). Gottman method of couple therapy. In A.S. Gurman (Ed.), *Clinical handbook of couple therapy* (4th ed.). New York: Guilford.

Gottman, J., Gottman, J., & Shapiro, A. (2009). A new couples approach to interventions for the transition to parenthood. In M.S. Schulz, P.K. Kerig, M.K. Pruett, & R.D. Parke (Eds.), *Feathering the nest.* Washington, DC: American Psychological Association.

Gottman, J.M., & Parker, J.G. (Eds.). (1987). *Conversations of friends.* New York: Cambridge University Press.

Gottman, J.M., & Silver, N. (2000). *The seven principles for making marriages work.* New York: Crown.

Gouin, K., & others (2011). Effects of cocaine use during pregnancy on low birthweight and preterm birth: Systematic and metanalyses. *American Journal of Obstetrics and Gynecology, 204*(4), e1–e12.

Gould, S.J. (1981). *The mismeasure of man.* New York: W.W. Norton.

Gouldner, H., & Strong, M.M. (1987). *Speaking of friendship.* New York: Greenwood Press.

Gove, W.R., Style, C.B., & Hughes, M. (1990). The effect of marriage on the well-being of adults. *Journal of Marriage and the Family, 11,* 4–35.

Grabenhenrich, L.B., & others (2014). Early-life determinants of asthma from birth to age 20 years: A German birth cohort study. *Journal off Allergy and Clinical Immunology, 133,* 979–988.

Graber, J.A. (2013). Pubertal timing and the development of psychopathology in adolescence and beyond. *Hormones and Behavior, 64,* 262–269.

Graber, J.A., Brooks-Gunn, J., & Warren, M.P. (2006). Pubertal effects on adjustment in girls: Moving from demonstrating effects to identifying pathways. *Journal of Youth and Adolescence, 35,* 391–401.

Graber, J.A., & Sontag, L.M. (2009). Internalizing problems during adolescence. In R.M. Lerner & L. Steinberg (Eds.), *Handbook of adolescent psychology* (3rd ed.). New York: Wiley.

Graber, R., Turner, R., & Madill, A. (2016). Best friends and better coping: Facilitating psychological resilience through boys' and girls' closest friendships. *British Journal of Psychology, 107,* 338–358.

Grace, F.M., & others (2016, in press). Age-related vascular endothelial function following lifelong sedentariness: Positive impact of cardiovascular conditioning without further improvement following low-frequency, high-intensity interval training. *Physiological Reports.*

Grady, C.L., Springer, M.V., Hongwanishkul, D., McIntosh, A.R., & Winocur, G. (2006). Age-related changes in brain activity across the adult lifespan. *Journal of Cognitive Neuroscience, 18,* 227–241.

Grafenhain, M., Behne, T., Carpenter, M., & Tomasello, M. (2009). Young children's understanding of joint commitments. *Developmental Psychology, 45,* 1430–1443.

Graham, E.K., & Lachman, M.E. (2014, in preparation). *The associations between facet level personality and cognitive performance: What underlying characteristics drive trait-level predictors across the adult lifespan?* Unpublished manuscript, Department of Psychology, Brandeis University, Waltham, MA.

Grant, J. (1993). *The state of the world's children.* New York: UNICEF and Oxford University Press.

Grant, N., Wardle, J., & Steptoe, A. (2009). The relationship between life satisfaction and health behavior: A cross-cultural analysis of young adults. *International Journal of Behavioral Medicine, 16,* 259–268.

Graven, S. (2006). Sleep and brain development. *Clinical Perinatology, 33,* 693–706.

Gravetter, R.J., & Forzano, L.B. (2016). *Research methods for the behavioral sciences* (5th ed.). Boston: Cengage.

Gray, P.B., & Garcia, J.R. (2012). *Aging and human sexual behavior: Biocultural perspectives—a mini-review, 58*(5), 446–452.

Green, M.J., Espie, C.A., Hunt, K., & Benzeval, M. (2012). The longitudinal course of insomnia symptoms: Inequalities by sex and occupational class among two different age cohorts followed for 20 years in the west of Scotland. *Sleep, 35,* 815–823.

Greenhaus, J.H. (2013). Career dynamics. In I.B. Weiner & others (Eds.), *Handbook of psychology* (2nd ed., Vol. 12). New York: Wiley.

Greer, D.M., & others (2016). Variability of brain death policies in the United States. *JAMA Neurology, 73,* 213–218.

Gregorson, M., Kaufman, J.C., & Snyder, H. (Eds.) (2013). *Teaching creatively and teaching creativity.* New York: Springer.

Gregory, R.J. (2014). *Psychological testing* (7th ed.). Boston: Cengage.

Greif, M.L., & Needham, A. (2012). The development of tool use early in life. In T. McCormack, C. Hoerl, & S. Butterfill (Eds.), *Tool use and causal cognition.* New York: Oxford University Press.

Grewal, D.S., Schultz, T., Basti, S., & Dick, H.B. (2016). Fetosecond laser-assisted cataract surgery—current status and future directions. *Survey of Ophthalmology, 61,* 103–131.

Griesler, P.C., Hu, M.C., & Kandel, D.B. (2016, in press). Nicotine dependence in adolescence and physical health symptoms in early adulthood. *Nicotine and Tobacco Research.*

Griffin, I.J., Lee, H.C., Profit, J., & Tancedi, D.J. (2015). The smallest of the small: Short-term outcomes of profoundly growth restricted and profoundly low birth weight preterm infants. *Journal of Perinatology, 35,* 503–510.

Griffin, J.A., Freund, L.S., & McCardle, P. (Eds.) (2015). *Executive function in preschool age children.* Washington, DC: American Psychological Association.

Grigorenko, E. (2000). Heritability and intelligence. In R.J. Sternberg (Ed.). *Handbook of intelligence.* New York: Cambridge U. Press.

Grigorenko, E.L., & others (2016). The trilogy of G × E genes, environments, and their interactions: Conceptualization, operationalization, and application. In D. Cicchetti (Ed.), *Developmental psychopathology* (3rd ed.). New York: Wiley.

Grindal, M., & Nieri, T. (2016). The relationship between ethnic-racial socialization and adolescent substance abuse: An examination of social learning as a causal mechanism. *Journal of Ethnicity in Substance Abuse, 15,* 3–24.

Grinde, B. (2016). Evolution and well-being. In M. Pluess (Ed.), *Genetics of psychological well-being.* New York: Oxford University Press.

Groh, A.M., & others (2014). The significance of attachment security for children's social competence with peers: A meta-analytic study. *Attachment and Human Development, 16,* 103–136.

Groh, A.M., & others (2016, in press). Mothers' electrophysiological, subjective, and observed emotional responding to infant crying: The role of secure base script knowledge. *Development and Psychopathology.*

Groppe, K., & Elsner, B. (2016, in press). Executive function and weight status in children: A one-year prospective investigation. *Child Neuropsychology.*

Gruenewald, T.L., Karlamangia, A.S., Greendale, G.A., Singer, B.H., & Seeman, T.E. (2009). Increased mortality risk in older adults with persistently low or declining feelings of usefulness to others. *Journal of Aging and Health, 21,* 398–425.

Grusec, J.E., Chaparro, M.P., Johnston, M., & Sherman, A. (2013). Social development and social relationships in middle childhood. In I.B. Weiner & others (Eds.), *Handbook of psychology* (2nd ed., Vol. 6). New York: Wiley.

Grusec, J.E., Chaparro, M.P., Johnston, M., & Sherman, A. (2014). The development of moral behavior from a socialization perspective. In M. Killen & J.G. Smetana (Eds.), *Handbook of moral development* (2nd ed.). New York: Psychology Press.

Grusec, J.E., & Davidov, M. (2015). Analyzing socialization from a domain-specific perspective. In J.E. Grusec & P.D. Hastings (Eds.), *Handbook of socialization* (2nd ed.). New York: Guilford.

Grusec, J.E., & Hastings, P.D. (Eds.) (2015). *Handbook of socialization* (2nd ed.). New York: Guilford.

Guilford, J.P. (1967). *The structure of intellect.* New York: McGraw-Hill.

Guimaraes, E.L., & Trudellia, E. (2015). Immediate effect of training at the onset of reaching in preterm infants: Randomized clinical trial. *Journal of Motor Behavior, 47,* 535–549.

Gulsahi, A. (2015). Osteoporosis and jawbones in women. *Journal of the International Society of Preventive and Community Dentistry, 5,* 263–267.

Gunderson, E.A., Ramirez, G., Beilock, S.L., & Levine, S.C. (2012). The role of parents and teachers in the development of gender-related attitudes. *Sex Roles, 66,* 153–166.

Gunn, J.K., & others (2016). Prenatal exposure to cannabis and maternal and child health outcomes: A systematic review and meta-analysis. *BMJ Open, 6*(4), e009986.

Gunnar, M.R., Malone, S., & Fisch, R.O. (1987). The psychobiology of stress and coping in the human neonate: Studies of the adrenocortical activity in response to stress in the first week of life. In T. Field, P. McCabe, & N. Scheiderman (Eds.). *Stress and coping.* Hillsdale, NJ: Erlbaum.

Gur, R.C., & others (1995). Sex differences in regional cerebral glucose metabolism during a resting state. *Science, 267,* 528–531.

Gurwitch, R.H., Silovksy, J.F., Schultz, S., Kees, M., & Burlingame, S. (2001). *Reactions and guidelines for children following trauma/disaster.* Norman, OK: Department of Pediatrics, University of Oklahoma Health Sciences Center.

Gustafsson, J-E. (2007). Schooling and intelligence. Effects of track of study on level and profile of cognitive abilities. In P.C. Kyllonen, R.D. Roberts, & L. Stankov (Eds.), *Extending intelligence.* Mahwah, NJ: Erlbaum.

Gutchess, A.H., & others (2005). Aging and the neural correlates of successful picture encoding: Frontal activations compensate for decreased medial-temporal activity. *Journal of Cognitive Neuroscience, 17,* 84–96.

Guttmannova, K., & others (2012). Examining explanatory mechanisms of the effects of early alcohol use on young adult alcohol competence. *Journal of Studies of Alcohol and Drugs, 73,* 379–390.

H

Ha, H.H., & Ingersoll-Dayton, B. (2011). Moderators in the relationship between social contact and psychological distress among widowed adults. *Aging and Mental Health, 15,* 354–363.

Hadfield, J.C. (2014). The health of grandparents raising grandchildren: A literature review. *Journal of Gerontological Nursing, 40,* 37–40.

Hadland, S.E., & others (2015). Suicide attempts and childhood maltreatment among street youth: A prospective cohort study. *Pediatrics, 136,* 440–449.

Haftenberger, M., & others (2016). Changes in body weight and obesity status in German adults: Results of seven population-based prospective studies. *European Journal of Clinical Nutrition, 70,* 300–305.

Hagen, J.W., & Lamb-Parker, F.G. (2008). Head Start. In M.M. Haith & J.B. Benson (Eds.), *Encyclopedia of infant and early childhood development.* Oxford, UK: Elsevier.

Hagenaars, S.P., & others (2016, in press). Polygenic risk for coronary artery disease is associated with cognitive ability in older adults. *International Journal of Epidemiology.*

Hagestad, G.O., & Uhlenberg, P. (2007). The impact of demographic changes on relations between age groups and generations: A comparative perspective. In K.W. Schaie & P. Uhlenberg (Eds.), *Demographic changes and the well-being of older persons.* New York: Springer.

Hahn, E.A., & Lachman, M.E. (2015). Everyday experience of memory problems and control: The adaptive role of selective optimization with compensation in the context of memory decline. *Aging, Neuropsychology, and Cognition, 22,* 25–41.

Hahn, K.A., & others (2015). Caffeine and caffeinated beverage consumption and risk of spontaneous abortion. *Human Reproduction, 30,* 1246–1255.

Hahn, W.K. (1987). Cerebral lateralization of function: From infancy through childhood. *Psychological Bulletin, 101,* 376–392.

Haidt, J. (2006). *The happiness hypothesis.* New York: Basic Books.

Haidt, J. (2013). *The righteous mind.* New York: Random House.

Hair, N.L., Hanson, J.L., Wolfe, B.L., & Pollack, S.D. (2015). Association of poverty, brain development, and academic achievement. *JAMA Pediatrics, 169,* 822–829.

Hakuta, K. (2001, April). *Key policy milestones and directions in the education of English language learners.* Paper prepared for the Rockefeller Symposium on Educational Equity, Washington, DC.

Hakuta, K. (2005, April). *Bilingualism at the intersection of research and public policy.* Paper presented at the meeting of the Society for Research in Child Development, Atlanta.

Hakuta, K., Butler, Y.G., & Witt, D. (2000). *How long does it take English learners to attain proficiency?* Berkeley, CA: The University of California Linguistic Minority Research Institute Policy Report 2000–1.

Halim, M.L., & others (2016). Children's dynamic gender identities: Cognition, context, and culture. In B. Balter & C.S. Tamis-LeMonda (Eds.), *Child psychology* (3rd ed.). New York: Routledge.

Hall, C.B., & others (2009). Cognitive activities delay onset of memory decline in persons who develop dementia. *Neurology, 73,* 356–361.

Hall, D.T., & Mirvis, P.H. (2013). Redefining work, work identity, and career success. In D.L. Blustein (Ed.), *Oxford handbook of the psychology of working.* New York: Oxford University Press.

Hall, G.S. (1904). *Adolescence* (Vols. 1 & 2). Englewood Cliffs, NJ: Prentice Hall.

Hall, S.S., & others (2014). Using discrete trial training to identify specific learning impairments in boys with fragile X syndrome. *Journal of Autism and Developmental Disorders, 44,* 1659–1670.

Hallahan, D.P., Kauffman, J.M., & Pullen, P.C. (2015). *Exceptional learners* (13th ed.). Upper Saddle River, NJ: Pearson.

Halonen, J., & Santrock, J.W. (2013). *Your guide to college success* (7th ed.). Boston: Cengage.

Halpern, D.F. (2012). *Sex differences in cognitive abilities* (2nd ed.). New York: Psychology Press.

Halpern, D.F., & others (2007). The science of sex differences in science and mathematics. *Psychological Science in the Public Interest, 8,* 1–51.

Halpern, D.F., & others (2011). The pseudoscience of single-sex schooling. *Science, 333,* 1706–1717.

Hamilton, E., & Klimes-Dougan, B. (2015). Gender differences in suicide prevention responses: Implications for adolescents based on an illustrative review of the literature. *International Journal of Environmental Research and Public Health, 12,* 2359–2372.

Hamilton, J.L., Stange, J.P., Abramson, L.Y., & Alloy, L.B. (2015). Stress and the development of cognitive vulnerabilities to depression explain sex differences in depressive symptoms during adolescence. *Clinical Psychological Science, 3,* 702–714.

Hamilton, J.L., & others (2014). Pubertal timing and vulnerabilities to depression in early adolescence: Differential pathways to depressive symptoms by sex. *Journal of Adolescence, 37,* 165–174.

Hamilton, L.D., & Julian, A.M. (2014). The relationship between daily hassles and sexual function in men and women. *Journal of Sex and Marital Therapy, 40,* 379–395.

Hamlin, J.K. (2013). Moral judgment and action in preverbal infants and toddlers: Evidence for an innate moral core. *Current Directions in Psychological Science, 22,* 186–193.

Hamlin, J.K. (2014). The origins of human morality: Complex socio-moral evaluations by preverbal infants. In J. Decety & Y. Christen (Eds.), *New frontiers in social neuroscience.* New York: Springer.

Hampson, S.E., & others (2015). A life-span mechanism relating childhood conscientiousness to adult clinical health. *Health Psychology, 34,* 87–95.

Han, J.Y., & others (2015). The effects of prenatal exposure to alcohol and environmental tobacco smoke on risk for ADHD: A large population-based study. *Psychiatry Research, 225,* 164–168.

Han, S.H., & others (2016, in press). Social activities, incident cardiovascular disease, and mortality: Health behaviors mediation. *Journal of Aging and Health.*

Hanc, T., & others (2016, in press). Perinatal risk factors and ADHD in children and adolescents: A hierarchical structure of disorder predictors. *Journal of Attention Disorders.*

Handrinos, J., Cooper, P., Pauletti, R., & Perry, D.G. (2012, April). *Influences on girls' aggression toward gender-atypical boys.* Paper presented at the Gender Development Research conference, San Francisco.

Hansell, N.K., & others (2012). Genetic comorbidity between neuroticism, anxiety/depression, and somatic distress in a sample of adolescent and young adult twins. *Psychological Medicine, 42,* 1249–1260.

Hanus, J., Zhao, F., & Wang, S. (2016). Current therapeutic developments in atrophic age-related macular degeneration. *British Journal of Ophthalmology, 100,* 122–127.

Hara, Y., & Naveh-Benjamin, M. (2015). The role of reduced working memory storage and processing resources in the associative memory deficit of older adults: Simulation studies with younger adults. *Neuropsychology, Development, and Cognition B. Aging, Neuropsychology, and Cognition, 22,* 129–154.

Harada, K., & others (2016). Sources of strength training information and strength training behavior among Japanese older adults. *Health Promotion International, 31,* 5–12.

Haran, C., van Driel, M., Mitchell, B.L., & Brodribb, W.E. (2014). Clinical guidelines for postpartum women and infants in primary care—a systematic review. *BMC Pregnancy and Childbirth, 14,* 51.

Harkins, S.W., Price, D.D., & Martinelli, M. (1986). Effects of age on pain perception. *Journal of Gerontology, 41,* 58–63.

Harkness, S., & Super, E.M. (1995). Culture and parenting. In M.H. Bornstein (Ed.), *Handbook of parenting* (Vol. 3). Hillsdale, NJ: Erlbaum.

Harlow, H.F. (1958). The nature of love. *American Psychologist, 13,* 673–685.

Harper, K.M., Tunc-Ozcan, E., Graf, E.N., & Redel, E.E. (2014). Intergenerational effects of prenatal ethanol on glucose tolerance and insulin responses. *Physiological Genomics, 46,* 159–168.

Harrington, B.C., Jimerson, M., Haxton, C., & Jimerson, D.C. (2015). Initial evaluation, diagnosis, and treatment of anorexia nervosa and bulimia nervosa. *American Family Physician, 91,* 46–52.

Harris, G., Thomas, A., & Booth, D.A. (1990). Development of salt taste in infancy. *Developmental Psychology, 26,* 534–538.

Harris, J., Golinkoff, R.M., & Hirsh-Pasek, K. (2011). Lessons from the crib for the classroom: How children really learn vocabulary. In S.B. Neuman & D.K. Dickinson (Eds.), *Handbook of early literacy research.* New York: Guilford.

Harris, K.M., Gorden-Larsen, P., Chantala, K., & Udry, J.R. (2006). Longitudinal trends in race/ethnic disparities in leading health indicators from adolescence to young adulthood. *Archives of Pediatric and Adolescent Medicine, 160,* 74–81.

Harris, P.L. (2000). *The work of the imagination.* Oxford University Press.

Harris, P.L. (2006). Social cognition. In W. Damon & R. Lerner (Eds.), *Handbook of child psychology* (6th ed.). New York: Wiley.

Harrison, C. (2012). Aging: Telomerase gene therapy increases longevity. *Nature Reviews/Drug Discovery, 11,* 518.

Harrison, T.M., & Bookheimer, S. (2016). Neuroimaging genetic risk for Alzheimer's disease in preclinical individuals: From candidate genes to polygenic approaches. *Biological Psychiatry: Cognitive Neuroscience and Neuroimaging, 1,* 14–23.

Hart, B., & Risley, T.R. (1995). *Meaningful differences.* Baltimore, MD: Paul Brookes.

Hart, C.H., Yang, C., Charlesworth, R., & Burts, D.C. (2003, April). *Early childhood teachers'* curriculum beliefs, classroom practices, and children's outcomes: What are the connections?* Paper presented at the biennial meeting of the Society for Research in Child Development, Tampa, FL.

Hart, D., & Karmel, M.P. (1996). Self-awareness and self-knowledge in humans, great apes, and monkeys. In A. Russori, K. Bard, & S. Parker (Eds.), *Reaching into thought.* New York: Cambridge University Press.

Hart, D., Matsuba, M.K., & Atkins, R. (2008). The moral and civic effects of learning to serve. In L. Nucci & D. Narváez (Eds.), *Handbook of moral and character education.* Clinton, NJ: Psychology Press.

Hart, W., Adams, J., & Tullett, A. (2016). "It's complicated"—Sex differences in perceptions of cross-aged friendships. *Journal of Social Psychology, 156,* 190–201.

Harter, S. (2006). The self. In W. Damon & R. Lerner (Eds.), *Handbook of child psychology* (6th ed.). New York: Wiley.

Harter, S. (2012). *The construction of the self* (2nd ed.). New York: Wiley.

Harter, S. (2013). The development of self-esteem. In M.H. Kermis (Ed.), *Self-esteem: Issues and answers.* New York: Psychology Press.

Harter, S. (2016). I-self and me-self processes affecting developmental psychopathology and mental health. In D. Cicchetti (Ed.), *Developmental psychopathology* (3rd ed.). New York: Wiley.

Hartescu, I., Morgan, K., & Stevinson, C.D. (2016). Sleep quality and recommended levels of physical activity in older adults. *Journal of Aging and Physical Activity, 24,* 201–206.

Hartshorne, H., & May, M.S. (1928–1930). *Moral studies in the nature of character: Studies in the nature of character.* New York: Macmillan.

Hartup, W.W. (1983). The peer system. In P.H. Mussen (Ed.), *Handbook of child psychology* (4th ed., Vol. 4). New York: Wiley.

Hartup, W.W. (1996). The company they keep: Friendships and their developmental significance. *Child Development, 67,* 1–13.

Hartup, W.W. (2009). Critical issues and theoretical viewpoints. In K.H. Rubin, W.M. Bukowski, & B. Laursen (Eds.), *Handbook of peer interactions, relationships, and groups.* New York: Guilford.

Hasbrouck, S.L., & Pianta, R. (2016). Understanding child care quality and implications for dual language learners. In K.E. Sanders & Guerra, A.W. (Eds.), *The culture of child care.* New York: Oxford University Press.

Hasmanova Marhankova, M.J. (2016). Women's attitudes toward forming new partnerships in widowhood: The search for "your own someone" and for freedom. *Journal of Women and Aging, 28,* 34–45.

Hassan, A., & others (2016). Association of Parkinson disease age with DRD2, DRD3, and GRIN2B polymorphisms. *Parkinsonism and Related Disorders, 22,* 102–105.

Hassan, J., & Barkin, J. (2016). Testosterone deficiency syndrome: Benefits, risks, and realities associated with testosterone replacement therapy. *Canadian Journal of Urology, 23*(1, Suppl. 1), 20–30.

Hastings, P.D., Miller, J.G., & Troxel, N.R. (2015). Making good: The socialization of children's prosocial development. In J.E. Grusec & P.D. Hastings (Eds.), *Handbook of socialization* (2nd ed.). New York: Guilford.

Hasvold, P., & others (2016). Association between paradoxical HDL cholesterol decrease and risk of major adverse cardiovascular events in patients initiated on statin treatment in a primary care setting. *Clinical Drug Investigation, 36,* 225–233.

Hatemi, P.K., McDermott, R., & Eaves, L. (2015). Genetic and environmental contributions to relationships and divorce attitudes. *Personality and Individual Differences, 72,* 135–140.

Hawk, S.T., Becht, A., & Branje, S. (2016, in press). "Snooping" as a distinct monitoring strategy: Comparison with overt solicitation and control. *Journal of Research on Adolescence.*

Hawkes, C. (2006). Olfaction in neurogenerative disorder. *Advances in Otorhinolaryngology, 63,* 133–151.

Hay, P. (2013). A systematic review of evidence for psychological treatments in eating disorders: 2005–2012. *International Journal of Eating Disorders, 46,* 462–469.

Hayatbakhsh, R., & others (2013). Early childhood predictors of early onset of smoking: A birth prospective study. *Addictive Behaviors, 38,* 2513–2519.

Haydon, A.A., Herring, A.H., Prinstein, M.J., & Halpern, C.T. (2012). Beyond age at first sex: Patterns of emerging sexual behavior in adolescence and young adulthood. *Journal of Adolescent Health, 50,* 456–463.

Hayflick, L. (1977). The cellular basis for biological aging. In C.E. Finch & L. Hayflick (Eds.), *Handbook of the biology of aging.* New York: Van Nostrand.

Hayslip, B., Pruett, J.H., & Caballero, D.M. (2015). The "how" and "when" of parental loss in adulthood: Effects on grief and adjustment. *Omega, 71,* 3–18.

Hayutin, A., Beals, M., & Broges, E. (2013). *The aging laborforce.* Palo Alto, CA: Stanford Center on Longevity.

Hazan, C., & Shaver, P.R. (1987). Romantic love conceptualized as an attachment process. *Journal of Personality and Social Psychology, 52,* 522–524.

He, M., Walle, E.A., & Campos, J.J. (2015). A cross-national investigation between infant walking and language development. *Infancy, 20,* 283–305.

Heard, E., & others (2011). Mediating effects of social support on the relationship between perceived stress, depression, and hypertension in African Americans. *Journal of the American Medical Association, 103,* 116–122.

Heberlein, E.C., & others (2016). The comparative effects of group prenatal care on psychosocial outcomes. *Archives of Women and Mental Health, 19,* 259–269.

Hedayat, K. (2006). When the spirit leaves: Childhood death, grieving, and bereavement in Islam. *Journal of Palliative Medicine, 9,* 1282–1291.

Hedden, T., & others (2016). Multiple brain markers are linked to age-related variation in cognition. *Cerebral Cortex, 26,* 1388–1400.

Heiman, G.W. (2014). *Basic statistics for the behavioral sciences* (7th ed.). Boston: Cengage.

Heiman, G.W. (2015). *Behavioral sciences STAT* (2nd ed.). Boston: Cengage.

Heimann, M., & others (2006). Exploring the relation between memory, gestural communication, and the emergence of language in infancy: A longitudinal study. *Infant and Child Development, 15,* 233–249.

Heinonen, M.T., & others (2015). GIMAP GTPase family genes: Potential modifiers in autoimmune diabetes, asthma, and allergy. *Journal of Immunology, 194,* 5885–5894.

Helgeson, V.S. (2012). *Psychology of gender* (4th ed.). Upper Saddle River, NJ: Pearson.

Helgeson, V.S. (2017). *Psychology of gender* (5th ed.). New York: Routledge.

Helles, A., Gillberg, C.L., Gillberg, C., & Bilistedt, E. (2015). Asperger syndrome in males over two decades: Stability and predictors of diagnosis. *Journal of Child Psychology and Psychiatry, 56,* 711–718.

Helman, R., Copeland, C., & VanDerhei, J. (2012). The 2012 Retirement Confidence Survey: Job insecurity, debt weigh on retirement confidence, savings. *EBRI Issue Brief, 369,* 5–32.

Henderson, J., & others (2014). Laboring women who used a birthing pool in obstetric units in Italy: Prospective observational study. *BMC Pregnancy and Childbirth, 14*(1), 17.

Henderson, V.W. (2011). Gonadal hormones and cognitive aging: A midlife perspective. *Women's Health, 7,* 81–93.

Hendricks-Munoz, K.D., & others (2013). Maternal and neonatal nurse perceived value of kangaroo mother care and maternal care partnership in the Neonatal Intensive Care Unit. *American Journal of Perinatology, 30,* 875–880.

Henretta, J.C. (2010). Lifetime marital history and mortality after age 50. *Journal of Aging and Health, 22*(8), 1198–1212.

Henricks, T.S. (2015a). Classical theories of play. In J.E. Johnson & others (Eds.), *Handbook of the study of play.* Blue Ridge Summit, PA: Rowman & Littlefield.

Henricks, T.S. (2015b). Modern theories of play. In J.E. Johnson & others (Eds.), *Handbook of the study of play.* Blue Ridge Summit, PA: Rowman & Littlefield.

Henriksen, T.B., & others (2004). Alcohol consumption at the time of conception and spontaneous abortion. *American Journal of Epidemiology, 160,* 661–667.

Hensch, T.K. (2016). The power of the infant brain. *Scientific American, 314,* 64–69.

Herbers, J.E., & others (2011). Direct and indirect effects of parenting on academic functioning of young homeless children. *Early Education and Development, 22,* 77–104.

Herman-Giddens, M.E. (2007). The decline in the age of menarche in the United States: Should we be concerned? *Journal of Adolescent Health, 40,* 201–203.

Hernandez, L.F., Redgrave, P., & Obeso, J.A. (2015). Habitual behavior and dopamine cell vulnerability in Parkinson disease. *Frontiers in Neuroanatomy, 9,* 99.

Heron, M. (2016). Deaths: Leading causes for 2013. *National Vital Statistics Reports, 65*(2), 1–95.

Hershner, S.D., & Chervin, R.D. (2015). Causes and consequences of sleepiness among college students. *Nature and Science of Sleep, 6,* 73–84.

Herting, M.M., Colby, J.B., Sowell, E.R., & Nagel, B.J. (2014). White matter connectivity and aerobic fitness in male adolescents. *Developmental Cognitive Neuroscience, 7,* 65–75.

Hetherington, E.M. (1989). Coping with family transitions: Winners, losers, and survivors. *Child Development, 60,* 1–14.

Hetherington, E.M. (2006). The influence of conflict, marital problem solving, and parenting on children's adjustment in nondivorced, divorced, and remarried families. In A. Clarke-Stewart & J. Dunn (Eds.), *Families count.* New York: Oxford University Press.

Hetherington, E.M., & Kelly, J. (2002). *For better or for worse: Divorce reconsidered.* New York: Norton.

Hetherington, E.M., & Stanley-Hagan, M. (2002). Parenting in divorced and remarried families. In M.H. Bornstein (Ed.), *Handbook of parenting* (2nd ed., Vol. 3). Mahwah, NJ: Erlbaum.

Heward, W.L., Alber-Morgan, S., & Konrad, M. (2017). *REVEL for exceptional children* (11th ed.). Upper Saddle River, NJ: Pearson.

Hewko, S.J., & others (2015). Invisible no more: A scoping review of the health care aide workforce literature. *BMC Nursing, 14,* 38.

Hewlett, B.S. (1991). *Intimate fathers: The nature and context of Aka Pygmy.* Ann Arbor: University of Michigan Press.

Hewlett, B.S. (2000). Culture, history and sex: Anthropological perspectives on father involvement. *Marriage and Family Review, 29,* 324–340.

Hewlett, B.S., & MacFarlan, S.J. (2010). Fathers, roles in hunter-gatherer and other small-scale cultures. In M.E. Lamb (Ed.) *The role of the father in child development* (5th ed.). New York: Wiley.

Heyman, G.D., Fu, G., & Lee, K. (2013). Selective skepticism: American and Chinese children's reasoning about evaluative feedback. *Developmental Psychology, 49,* 543–553.

Hiekel, N., Liefbroer, A.C., & Poortman, A.R. (2015). Marriage and separation risks among German cohabitors: Differences between types of cohabitor. *Population Studies, 69,* 237–251.

High/Scope Resource (2005, Spring). The High/Scope Perry Preschool Study and the man who began it. *High/Scope Resource 9.* Ypsilanti, MI: High/Scope Press.

Highfield, R. (2008, April 30). *Harvard's baby brain research lab.* Retrieved January 24, 2009, from http://www.telegraph.co.uk/science/science-news/3341166/Harvards-baby-brain-research-lab.html

Higo, M., & Williamson, J.B. (2009). Retirement. In D. Carr (Ed.), *Encyclopedia of the life course and human development.* Boston: Gale Cengage.

Hill, C.R., & Stafford, E.P. (1980). Parental care of children: Time diary estimate of quantity, predictability, and variety. *Journal of Human Resources, 15,* 219–239.

Hill, E.M. (2016, in press). The role of narcissism in health-risk and health-protective behaviors. *Journal of Health Psychology.*

Hill, K., & Roth, T.L. (2016). Epigenetic mechanisms in the development of behavior. In D. Cicchetti (Ed.), *Developmental psychopathology* (3rd ed.). New York: Wiley.

Hill, P.C., & Pargament, K.I. (2003). Advances in conceptualization and measurement of religion and spirituality: Implications for physical and mental health research. *American Psychologist, 58,* 64–74.

Hill, P.L., Allemand, M., & Roberts, B.W. (2014). Stability of behavior: Implications for research. In R. Zinbarg (Ed.), *Encyclopedia of clinical psychology.* New York: Springer.

Hill, P.L., & Roberts, B.W. (2016). Personality and health: Reviewing recent research and setting a directive for the future. In K.W. Schaie & S. Willis (Eds.), *Handbook of the psychology of aging* (8th ed.). New York: Elsevier.

Hill, P.L., & others (2011). Conscientiousness and longevity: An examination of possible mediators. *Health Psychology, 30,* 536–541.

Hill, P.L., & others (2014). Perceived social support predicts increased conscientiousness during older adulthood. *Journals of Gerontology B: Psychological Sciences and Social Sciences, 69,* 543–547.

Hill, P.L., & others (2016). Purpose in life in emerging adulthood: Development and validation of a new brief measure. *Journal of Positive Psychology, 11,* 237–245.

Hill, T.D., Angel, J.L., Ellison, C.G., & Angel, R.J. (2005). Religious attendance and mortality: An 8-year follow-up of older Mexican Americans. *Journals of Gerontology B: Psychological Sciences and Social Sciences, 60,* S102–S109.

Hillemeier, M.M., Morgan, P.L., Farkas, G., & Maczuga, S.A. (2013). Quality disparities in child care for at-risk children: Comparing Head Start and non-Head Start settings. *Journal of Maternal and Child Health, 17*(1), 180–188.

Hillman, C.H., & others (2014). Effects of the FIT-Kids randomized controlled trial on executive control and brain function. *Pediatrics, 134,* e1063–e1071.

Himes, C.L. (2009). Age structure. In D. Carr (Ed.), *Encyclopedia of the life course and human development.* Boston: Gale Cengage.

Hines, M. (2015). Gendered development. In R.M. Lerner (Ed.), *Handbook of child psychology and developmental science* (7th ed.). New York: Wiley.

Hinze, S.W., Lin, J., & Andersson, T.E. (2012). Can we capture the intersections? Older Black women, education, and health. *Women's Health Issues, 22,* e91–e98.

Hirsch, B.J., & Rapkin, B.D. (1987). The transition to junior high school: A longitudinal study of self-esteem, psychological symptomatology, school life, and social support. *Child Development, 58,* 1235–1243.

Hirsch, J.K., & Sirois, F.M. (2016). Hope and fatigue in chronic illness: The role of perceived stress. *Journal of Health Psychology, 21,* 451–456.

Hirsh-Pasek, K., & Golinkoff, R.M. (2014). Early language and literacy: Six principles. In S. Gilford (Ed.), *Head Start teacher's guide.* New York: Teacher's College Press.

Hirsh-Pasek, K., Golinkoff, R.M., Singer, D., & Berk, L. (2009). *A mandate for playful learning in preschool: Presenting the evidence.* New York: Oxford University Press.

Hirsh-Pasek, K., & others (2015). Putting education in "educational" apps: Lessons from the science of learning. *Psychological Science in the Public Interest, 16,* 3–34.

Hisasue, S.I. (2015). Contemporary perspective and management of testosterone deficiency: Modifiable factors and variable management. *International Journal of Urology, 22,* 1084–1095.

Hochberg, C., & others (2012). Association of vision loss in glaucoma and age-related macular degeneration with IADL disability. *Investigative Ophthalmology and Visual Science, 53,* 3201–3206.

Hodge, S.E., Hager, V.R., & Greenberg, D.A. (2016). Using linkage analysis to detect gene-gene interactions. *PLoS One, 11,* e0146240.

Hoehl, S., & Striano, T. (2015). The development of brain mechanisms of joint attention. In S.D. Calkins (Ed.), *Handbook of biopsychosocial development.* New York: Guilford.

Hoeijmakers, L., Lucassen, P.J., & Korosi, A. (2015). The interplay of early-life stress, nutrition, and immune activation programs adults hippocampal structure and function. *Frontiers in Molecular Neuroscience, 7,* 103.

Hoelter, L. (2009). Divorce and separation. In D. Carr (Ed.), *Encyclopedia of the life course and human development.* Boston: Gale Cengage.

Hoeve, M., & others (2012). A meta-analysis of attachment to parents and delinquency. *Journal of Abnormal Child and Adolescent Psychology, 40*(5), 771–785.

Hofer, A., & others (2007). Sex differences in brain activation patterns during processing of positively and negatively balanced emotional stimuli. *Psychological Medicine, 37,* 109–119.

Hofer, J., & others (2016). Generativity does not necessarily satisfy all of your needs: Associations among cultural demand for generativity, generative concern, generative action, and need satisfaction in the elderly in four cultures. *Developmental Psychology, 52,* 509–519.

Hoff, E. (2014). *Language development* (5th ed.). Boston: Cengage.

Hoff, E. (2015). Language development. In M.H. Bornstein & M.E. Lamb (Eds.), *Developmental science* (7th ed.). New York: Psychology Press.

Hoff, E., Laursen, B., & Tardif, T. (2002). Socioeconomic status and parenting. In M.H. Bornstein (Ed.), *Handbook of parenting* (2nd ed.). Mahwah, NJ: Erlbaum.

Hoff, E., & others (2014). Expressive vocabulary development in children from bilingual homes: A longitudinal study from two to four years. *Early Childhood Research Quarterly, 29,* 433–444.

Hogan, C.L., Mata, J., & Carstensen, L.L. (2013). Exercise holds immediate benefits for affect and cognition in younger and older adults. *Psychology and Aging, 28,* 587–594.

Hognas, R.S., & Thomas, J.R. (2016). Birds of a feather have babies together? Family structure homogamy and union stability among cohabiting parents. *Journal of Family Issues, 37,* 29–52.

Hohman, T.J., & others (2016). Discovery of gene-gene interactions across multiple independent data sets of late onset Alzheimer disease from the Alzheimer Disease Genetics Consortium, 38, 141–150.

Holden, G.W., Vittrup, B., & Rosen, L.H. (2011). Families, parenting, and discipline. In M.K. Underwood & L.H. Rosen (Eds.), *Social development.* New York: Guilford.

Hollams, E.M., de Klerk, N.H., Holt, P.G., & Sly, P.D. (2014). Persistent effects of maternal smoking during pregnancy on lung function and asthma in adolescents. *American Journal of Respiratory and Critical Care Medicine, 189,* 401–407.

Holland, J.M., Graves, S., Klinsport, K.L., & Rozalski, V. (2016). Prolonged grief symptoms related to loss of physical functioning: Examining unique associations with medical service utilization. *Disability and Rehabilitation, 38,* 205–210.

Holland, J.M., & others (2014). The unique impact of late-life bereavement and prolonged grief on diurnal cortisol. *Journals of Gerontology B: Psychological Sciences and Social Sciences, 69,* 4–11.

Hollister, M. (2011). Employment stability in the U.S. labor market: Rhetoric versus reality. *Annual Review of Sociology* (Vol. 37). Palo Alto, CA: Annual Reviews.

Holme, A.M., & others (2015). Placental glucose transfer: A human in vivo study. *PLoS One, 10*(2), e117084.

Holmes, C.J., Kim-Spoon, J., & Deater-Deckard, K. (2016). Linking executive function and peer problems from early childhood through middle adolescence. *Journal of Abnormal Child Psychology, 44,* 31–42.

Holmes, L.B. (2011). Human teratogens: Update 2010. *Birth Defects Research A: Clinical and Molecular Teratology, 91,* 1–7.

Holmes, T.H., & Rahe, R.H. (1967). The social readjustment rating scale. *Journal of Psychosomatic Research, 11,* 213–218.

Holsen, I., Carlson Jones, D., & Skogbrott Birkeland, M. (2012). Body image satisfaction among Norwegian adolescents and young adults: A longitudinal study of the influence of interpersonal relationships and BMI. *Body Image, 9,* 201–208.

Holway, G.V. (2015). Vaginal and oral sex initiation timing: A focus on gender and race/ethnicity. *International Journal of Sexual Health, 27,* 351–367.

Holzman, L. (2016). *Vygotsky at work and play* (2nd ed.). New York: Routledge.

Hong, X., & others (2015). Normal aging selectivity diminishes alpha lateralization in visual spatial attention. *Neuroimage, 106,* 353–363.

Hong, Z., & others (2015). Differential age-dependent associations of gray matter volume and white matter integrity with processing speed in healthy older adults. *Neuroimage, 123,* 42–50.

Hooyman, N., Kiyak, H.A., & Kawamoto, K. (2015). *Aging matters.* Upper Saddle River, NJ: Pearson.

Hope, D.A. (2009). Contemporary perspectives on lesbian, gay, and bisexual identities: Introduction. *Nebraska Symposium on Motivation, 54,* 1–4.

Hoppmann, C.A., Infuma, F.J., Ram, N., & Gerstorf, D. (2016, in press). Associations among individuals' perceptions of future time, individual resources, and subjective well-being in old age. *Journals of Gerontology B: Psychological Sciences and Social Sciences.*

Horgusluoglu, E., Nudelman, K., Nho, K., & Saykin, A.J. (2016, in press). Adult neurogenesis and neurodegenerative diseases: A systems biology perspective. *American Journal of Medical Genetics B: Neuropsychiatric Genetics.*

Horn, J.L., & Donaldson, G. (1980). Cognitive development II: Adulthood development of human abilities. In O.G. Brim & J. Kagan (Eds.), *Constancy and change in human development.* Cambridge, MA: Harvard University Press.

Hosny, K.M., El-Say, K.M., & Ahmed, O.A. (2016). Optimized sildenafil citrate fast orodissolvable film: A promising formula for overcoming the barriers hindering erectile dysfunction treatment. *Drug Delivery, 23,* 355–361.

Hospital for Sick Children & others (2010). *The Hospital for Sick Children's handbook of pediatrics* (11th ed.). London: Elsevier.

Hostinar, C., Cicchetti, D., & Rogosch, F.A. (2014). Oxytocin receptor gene (OXTR) polymorphism, perceived social support, and psychological symptoms in maltreated adolescents. *Development and Psychopathology, 26,* 465–467.

Hou, L., & others (2016). Systems approaches to understanding aging. In M.R. Kaeberlein & G.M. Martin (Eds.), *Handbook of the biology of aging* (8th ed.). New York: Elsevier.

Hou, Y., Kim, S.Y., & Wang, Y. (2016, in press). Parental acculturative stressors and adolescent adjustment through interparental and parent-child relationships in Chinese American families. *Journal of Youth and Adolescence.*

Houston, D., Golinkoff, R., Ma, W., & Hirsh-Pasek, I. (2016, in press). Word learning in infant- and adult-directed speech. *Language Learning and Development.*

Howe, G.W., Homberger, A.P., Weihs, K., Moreno, F., & Neiderhiser, J.M. (2012). Higher-order structure in the trajectories of depression and anxiety following sudden involuntary unemployment. *Journal of Abnormal Psychology, 121,* 325–338.

Howe, M.J.A., Davidson, J.W., Moore, D.G., & Sloboda, J.A. (1995). Are there early childhood signs of musical ability? *Psychology of Music, 23,* 162–176.

Howe, M.L. (2015). An adaptive view of memory development. In R.M. Lerner (Ed.), *Handbook of child psychology and developmental science* (7th ed.). New York: Wiley.

Howes, C. (2016). Children and child care: A theory of relationships within cultural communities. In K. Sanders & A.W. Guerra (Eds.), *The culture of child care.* New York: Oxford University Press.

Hoyer, W.J. (2015). Brain aging: Behavioral, cognitive, and personality consequences. In J.D. Wright (Ed.), *International encyclopedia of the social and behavioral sciences* (2nd ed.). New York: Elsevier.

Hoyer, W.J., & Roodin, P.A. (2009). *Adult development and aging* (6th ed.). New York: McGraw-Hill.

HSBC Insurance (2007). *The future of retirement: The new old age global report.* London: HSBC.

Hsin, A., & Xie, Y. (2014). Explaining Asian Americans' academic advantage over whites. *Proceedings of the National Academy of Sciences U.S.A., 111,* 8416–8421.

Hsu, H.C. (2015). Trajectories of multimorbidity and impacts on successful aging. *Experimental Gerontology, 66,* 32–38.

Hu, W., Lin, X., & Chen, K. (2015). Integrated analysis of differential gene expression profiles in hippocampi to identify candidate genes involved in Alzheimer's disease. *Molecular Medicine Reports, 12,* 6679–6687.

Hua, L., & others (2016). Four-locus gene interaction between IL13, IL4, FCER1B, and ADRB2 for asthma in Chinese Han children. *Pediatric Pulmonology, 51,* 364–371.

Huang, J-H., DeJong, W., Towvim, L.G., & Schneider, S.K. (2009). Sociodemographic and psychobehavioral characteristics of U.S. college students who abstain from alcohol. *Journal of American College Health, 57,* 395–410.

Huang, Y., & Spelke, E. (2015). Core knowledge and the emergence of symbols: The case of maps. *Journal of Cognition and Development, 16,* 81–96.

Hudson, A., & Jacques, S. (2014). Put on a happy face! Inhibitory control and socioemotional knowledge predict emotion regulation in 5- to 7-year-olds. *Journal of Experimental Child Psychology, 123,* 36–52.

Hudson, N.W., Fraley, R.C., Chopik, W.J., & Hefferman, M.E. (2016, in press). Not all attachment relationships change alike: Normative cross-sectional age trajectories in attachment to romantic partners, friends, and parents across the lifespan. *Journal of Research in Personality.*

Hudson, P., & others (2016). Toward a systematic approach to assessment and care planning in palliative care: A practical review of clinical tools. *Palliative and Supportive Care, 14,* 161–173.

Hudson, R.B. (2016). Politics and policies of aging in the United States. In L.K. George & K.F. Ferraro (Eds.), *Handbook of aging and the social sciences* (8th ed.). New York: Elsevier.

Huesmann, L.R., Dubow, E.F., Eron, L.D., & Boxer, P. (2006). Middle childhood family-contextual and personal factors as predictors of adult outcomes. In A.G. Huston & M.N. Ripke (Eds.), *Developmental contexts in middle childhood: Bridges to adolescence and adulthood.* New York: Cambridge University Press.

Huffman, J.C., & others (2016). Effects of optimism and gratitude on physical activity, biomarkers, and readmissions after an acute coronary syndrome: The Gratitude Research in Acute Coronary Events Study. *Circulation. Cardiovascular Quality and Outcomes, 9,* 55–63.

Hughes, C., & Devine, R.T. (2015). Individual differences in theory of mind: A social perspective. In R.M. Lerner (Ed.), *Handbook of child psychology and developmental science* (7th ed.). New York: Wiley.

Hughes, C., Marks, A., Ensor, R., & Lecce, S. (2010). A longitudinal study of conflict and inner state talk in children's conversations with mothers and younger siblings. *Social Development, 19,* 822–837.

Hughes, M.E., Waite, L.J., LaPierre, T.A., & Luo, Y. (2007). All in the family: The impact of caring for grandchildren on grandparents' health. *Journals of Gerontology B: Psychological Sciences and Social Sciences, 62,* S108–S119.

Huhtaniemi, I.T. (2014). Andropause—lessons from the European Male Aging Study. *Annals of Endocrinology, 75,* 128–131.

Hulsegge, G., & others (2016, in press). Lifestyle changes in young adulthood and middle age and risk of cardiovascular disease and all-cause mortality: The Doetinchem Cohort Study. *Journal of the American Heart Association.*

Hunt, S.R., Corazzini, K., & Anderson, R.A. (2014). Top nurse-management staffing and care quality in nursing homes. *Journal of Applied Gerontology, 33,* 51–74.

Hur, K., Liang, J., & Lin, S.Y. (2014). The role of secondhand smoke in allergic rhinitis: A systematic review. *International Forum of Allergy and Rhinology, 4,* 110–116.

Hurt, H., Brodsky, N.L., Roth, H., Malmud, R., & Giannetta, J.M. (2005). School performance of children with gestational cocaine exposure. *Neurotoxicology and Teratology, 27,* 203–211.

Huseth-Zosel, A.L., & others (2016, in press). Health care provider mobility counseling provision to older adults: A rural/urban comparison. *Journal of Community Health.*

Hustedt, J.T., Friedman, A.H., & Barnett, W.S. (2012). Investments in early education: Resources at the federal and state levels. In R.C. Pianta (Ed.), *Handbook of early childhood education.* New York: Guilford.

Huston, A.C., & Ripke, N.N. (2006). Experiences in middle and late childhood and children's development. In A.C. Huston & M.N. Ripke (Eds.), *Developmental contexts in middle childhood.* New York: Cambridge University Press.

Huston, T.L., & Holmes, E.K. (2004). Becoming parents. In A.L. Vangelisti (Ed.), *Handbook of family communication*. Mahwah, NJ: Erlbaum.

Hutchinson, J., Emerick, J., & Saxena, H. (2016, in press). The future of pediatric obesity. *Primary Care*.

Huttenlocher, P.R., & Dabholkar, A.S. (1997). Regional differences in synaptogenesis in human cerebral cortex. *Journal of Comparative Neurology, 37*(2), 167–178.

Huxhold, O., Miche, M., & Schuz, B. (2014). Benefits of having friends in older ages: Differential effects of informal social activities on well-being in middle-aged and older adults. *Journals of Gerontology B: Psychological Sciences and Social Sciences, 69*, 366–375.

Hyde, J.S. (2014). Gender similarities and differences. *Annual Review of Psychology* (Vol. 66). Palo Alto, CA: Annual Reviews.

Hyde, J.S., & DeLamater, J.D. (2014). *Understanding human sexuality* (12th ed.). New York: McGraw-Hill.

Hyde, J.S., & Else-Quest, N. (2013). *Half the human experience* (8th ed.). Boston: Cengage.

Hyde, J.S., Lindberg, S.M., Linn, M.C., Ellis, A.B., & Williams, C.C. (2008). Gender similarities characterize math performance. *Science, 321*, 494–495.

Hysing, M., & others (2015). Sleep and school attendance in adolescence: Results from a large population-based study. *Scandinavian Journal of Public Health, 43*, 2–9.

Hysing, M., & others (2016, in press). Sleep and academic performance in later adolescence: Results from a large population-based study. *Journal of Sleep Research*.

Hyson, M.C., Copple, C., & Jones, J. (2006). Early childhood development and education. In W. Damon & R. Lerner (Eds.), *Handbook of child psychology* (6th ed.). New York: Wiley.

I

Ibrahim, J.E., MacPhail, A., Winbolt, M., & Grano, P. (2016). Limitation of care orders in patients with a diagnosis of dementia. *Resuscitation, 98*, 118–124.

Igarashi, H., Hooker, K., Coehlo, D.P., & Manoogian, M.M. (2013). "My nest is full": Intergenerational relationships at midlife. *Journal of Aging Studies, 27*, 102–112.

Igualada, A., Bosch, L., & Prieto, P. (2015). Language development at 18 months is related to multimodal communicative strategies at 12 months. *Infant Behavior and Development, 39*, 42–52.

Ihle, A., & others (2015). The association of leisure activities in middle adulthood with cognitive performance in old age: The moderating role of educational level. *Gerontology, 61*, 543–550.

Ikram, U.Z., & others (2016). Perceived ethnic discrimination and depressive symptoms: The buffering effects of ethnic identity, religion, and ethnic social network. *Social Psychiatry and Psychiatric Epidemiology, 51*, 679–688.

Ingul, C.B., & others (2016, in press). Maternal obesity affects fetal myocardial function already in first trimester. *Ultrasound in Obstetrics and Gynecology, 47*, 433–442.

Innella, N., & others (2016, in press). Determinants of obesity in the Hispanic preschool population: An integrative review. *Public Health Nursing*.

Insel, P., & Roth, W. (2016). *Connect core concepts in health* (14th ed.). New York: McGraw-Hill.

International Montessori Council (2006). Larry Page and Sergey Brin, founders of Google.com, credit their Montessori education for much of their success on prime-time television. Retrieved June 24, 2006, from www.Montessori.org/enews/barbara_walters.html

Isaacs, B. (2012). *Understanding the Montessori approach: Early years education practice*. New York: Routledge.

Ishak, S., Franchak, J.M., & Adolph, K.E. (2014). Fear of height in infants. *Current Directions in Psychological Science, 23*, 60–66.

Ishikawa, N., & others (2016). Changes of telomere status with aging: An update. *Geriatrics and Gerontology International, 16*(Suppl. 1), S30–S42.

Isidori, A.M., & others (2014). A critical analysis of the role of testosterone in erectile function: From pathophysiology to treatment—a systematic analysis. *European Urology, 65*(1), 99–112.

Isla, A.G., Vazquez-Cuevas, F.G., & Pena-Ortega, J.F. (2016, in press). Exercise prevents amyloid-*b*-induced hippocampal network disruption by inhibiting GSK3*b* activation. *Journal of Alzheimer's Disease*.

Issel, L.M., & others (2011). A review of prenatal home-visiting effectiveness for improving birth outcomes. *Journal of Obstetrics, Gynecologic, and Neonatal Nursing, 40*, 157–165.

Iwata, S., & others (2012). Qualitative brain MRI at term and cognitive outcomes at 9 years after very preterm birth. *Pediatrics, 129*, e1138–1147.

J

Jaber, L., Kirsh, D., Diamond, G., & Shuper, A. (2015). Long-term functional outcomes in Israeli adults diagnosed in childhood with attention deficit hyperactivity disorder. *Israeli Medical Association, 17*, 481–485.

Jackson, A.M., & Deve, K. (2015). Aspects of abuse: Consequences of childhood victimization. *Current Problems in Pediatric and Adolescent Health Care, 45*, 86–93.

Jackson, A.M., Kissoon, N., & Greene, C. (2015). Aspects of abuse: Recognizing and responding to child maltreatment. *Current Problems in Pediatric and Adolescent Health Care, 45*, 58–70.

Jackson, J.J., & Roberts, B.W. (2016). Conscientiousness. In T.A. Widiger (Ed.), *Oxford handbook of the five factor model*. New York: Oxford University Press.

Jackson, J.J., & others (2009). Not all conscientiousness scales change alike: A multimethod, multisample study of age differences in the facets of conscientiousness. *Journal of Personality and Social Psychology, 96*, 446–459.

Jackson, J.S., Govia, I.O., & Sellers, S.L. (2011). Racial and ethnic influences over the life course. In R.H. Binstock & L.K. George (Eds.), *Handbook of aging and the social sciences* (7th ed.). New York: Elsevier.

Jackson, M.I. (2015). Early childhood WIC participation, cognitive development, and academic achievement. *Social Science and Medicine, 126*, 145–153.

Jackson, P.A., & others (2016, in press). Promoting brain health through exercise and diet in older adults: A physiological perspective. *Journal of Applied Psychology*.

Jackson, S.L. (2016). *Research methods* (5th ed.). Boston: Cengage.

Jacobs, J.M., Hammerman-Rozenberg, R., Cohen, A., & Stressman, J. (2008). Reading daily predicts reduced mortality among men from a cohort of community dwelling 70-year-olds. *Journals of Gerontology B: Psychological Sciences and Social Sciences, 63*, S73–S80.

Jacoby, N., Overfeld, J., Brinder, E.B., & Heim, C.M. (2016). Stress neurobiology and developmental psychopathology. In D. Cicchetti (Ed.), *Developmental psychopathology* (3rd ed.). New York: Wiley.

Jaffee, S., & Hyde, J.S. (2000). Gender differences in moral orientation: A meta-analysis. *Psychological Bulletin, 126*, 703–726.

Jaffee, S.R. (2016). Quantitative and molecular genetic studies of gene-environmental correlation. In D. Cicchetti (Ed.), *Developmental psychopathology* (3rd ed.). New York: Wiley.

Jakobsen, K.V., Umstead, L., & Simpson, E.A. (2016). Efficient human face detection in infancy. *Developmental Psychobiology, 58*, 129–136.

Jalles, J.T., & Andresen, M.A. (2014). Suicide and unemployment: A panel analysis of Canadian provinces. *Archives of Suicide Research, 18*, 14–27.

James, J., Ellis, B.J., Scholmer, G.L., & Garber, J. (2012). Sex-specific pathways to early puberty, sexual debut, and sexual risk taking: Tests of an integrated evolutionary-developmental model. *Developmental Psychology, 48*, 687–702.

James, W. (1890/1950). *The principles of psychology*. New York: Dover.

Jansen, A.G., & others (2015). What twin studies tell us about the heritability of brain development, morphology, and function: A review. *Neuropsychology Review, 25*, 27–46.

Jansen, J., & others (2015). Systematic review of clinical practice guidelines recommendations about primary cardiovascular disease prevention for older adults. *BMC Family Practice, 16*(1), 104.

Jansen, J., de Weerth, C., & Riksen-Walraven, J.M. (2008). Breastfeeding and the mother-infant relationship—A review. *Developmental Review, 28*, 503–521.

Jansen, S.W., & others (2016). Physiological responding to stress in middle-aged males enriched for longevity: A social stress study. *Stress, 19*, 28–36.

Janssen, I. (2014). Active play: An important physical activity strategy in the fight against childhood obesity. *Canadian Journal of Public Health, 105*, e22–e27.

Janssen, I., & others (2005). Comparison of overweight and obesity prevalence in school-aged youth from 34 countries and their relationships with physical activity and dietary patterns. *Obesity Reviews, 6*, 123–132.

Jardri, R., & others (2012). Assessing fetal response to maternal speech using a noninvasive functional brain imaging technique. *International Journal of Developmental Neuroscience, 30*, 159–161.

Jaremka, L.M., Derry, H., & Kiecolt-Glaser, J.K. (2016). Psychoneuroimmunology of interpersonal relationships: Both the presence/absence of social ties and relationship quality matter. In D.I. Mostofsky (Ed.), *Handbook of behavioral medicine*. New York: Wiley.

Jarman, M., & others (2015). How do mothers manage their preschool children's eating habits and does this change as children grow older? A longitudinal analysis. *Appetite, 95,* 466–474.

Jarosinka, D., Polanska, K., Woityniak, B., & Hanke, W. (2014). Towards estimating the burden of disease attributable to second-hand smoke exposure in Polish children. *International Journal of Occupational Medicine and Environmental Health, 27,* 38–49.

Jelding-Dannemand, E., Malby Schoos, A.M., & Bisgaard, H. (2015). Breast-feeding does not protect against allergic sensitization in early childhood and allergy-associated disease at age 7 years. *Journal of Allergy and Clinical Immunology, 136,* 1302–1308.

Jenni, O.G., and Carskadon, M.A. (2007). Sleep behavior and sleep regulation from infancy through adolescence: Normative aspects. In O.G. Jenni and M.A. Carskadon (Eds.), *Sleep medicine clinics: Sleep in children and adolescents.* Philadelphia: W.B. Saunders.

Jensen, M.M., & others (2015). Prostate stem cell antigen interacts with nicotinic acetylcholine receptors and is affected in Alzheimer's disease. *Neurobiology of Aging, 36,* 1629–1638.

Jeon, H., & Lubben, J. (2016). The influence of social networks and supports on depressive symptoms: Differential pathways for older Korean immigrants and non-Hispanic White Americans. *Care Management, 17,* 13–23.

Ji, B.T., & others (1997). Paternal cigarette smoking and the risk of childhood cancer among offspring of nonsmoking mothers. *Journal of the National Cancer Institute, 89,* 238–244.

Jia, R., & Schoppe-Sullivan, S.J. (2011). Relations between coparenting and father involvement in families with preschool-age children. *Developmental Psychology, 47,* 106–118.

Jiao, S., Ji, G., & Jing, Q. (1996). Cognitive development of Chinese urban only children and children with siblings. *Child Development, 67,* 387–395.

Job, V., Dweck, C.S., & Walton, G.M. (2010). Ego-depletion—Is it all in your head? Implicit theories about willpower affect self-regulation. *Psychological Science, 21,* 1686–1693.

Job, V., Walton, G.M., Bernecker, K., & Dweck, C.S. (2015). Implicit theories about willpower predict self-regulation and grades in everyday life. *Journal of Personality and Social Psychology, 108,* 637–647.

Johns Hopkins University (2006, February 17). *Undergraduate honored for launching health program in India.* Baltimore: Johns Hopkins University News Releases.

Johnson, D.C., & others (2016, in press). Genome-wide association study identifies variation at 6Q25.1 associated with survival in multiple myeloma. *Nature Communications.*

Johnson, J.E., Eberle, S.G., Henricks, T.S., & Kuschner, D. (Eds.) (2015). *Handbook of the study of play.* Blue Ridge Summit, PA: Rowman & Littlefield.

Johnson, J.S., & Newport, E.L. (1991). Critical period effects on universal properties of language: The status of subjacency in the acquisition of a second language. *Cognition, 39,* 215–258.

Johnson, L.G., & others (2016, in press). An acute bout of exercise improves the cognitive performance of older adults. *Journal of Aging and Physical Activity.*

Johnson, M.B., & Chen, J. (2015). Blame it on alcohol: The influence of alcohol consumption during adolescence, the transition to adulthood, and young adulthood on one-time sexual hookups. *Journal of Sex Research, 52,* 570–579.

Johnson, M.D. (2017). *Human biology* (8th ed.). Upper Saddle River, NJ: Pearson.

Johnson, M.H. (2008, April 30). Commentary in R. Highfield, *Harvard's baby brain research lab.* Retrieved January 24, 2008, from http://www.telegraph.co.uk/science/science-news/3341166/Harvards-baby-brain-research-lab.html

Johnson, M.H. (2015). Developmental neuroscience, psychophysiology, and genetics. In M.H. Bornstein & M.E. Lamb (Eds.), *Developmental science* (7th ed.). New York: Psychology Press.

Johnson, M.H., Grossmann, T., & Cohen-Kadosh, K. (2009). Mapping functional brain development: Building a social brain through interactive specialization. *Developmental Psychology, 45,* 151–159.

Johnson, S.P. (2010). How infants learn about the visual world. *Cognitive Science, 34,* 1158–1184.

Johnson, S.P. (2011). A constructivist view of object perception in infancy. In L.M. Oakes & others (Eds.), *Infant perception and cognition.* New York: Oxford University Press.

Johnson, S.P. (2013). Object perception. In P.D. Zelazo (Ed.), *Handbook of developmental psychology.* New York: Oxford University Press.

Johnson, S.P., & Hannon, E.E. (2015). Perceptual development. In R.M. Lerner (Ed.), *Handbook of child psychology and developmental science* (7th ed.). New York: Wiley.

Johnson, W., & Bouchard, T.J. (2014). Genetics of intellectual and personality traits associated with creative genius: Could geniuses be cosmobian dragon kings? In D.K. Simonton (Ed.), *Wiley-Blackwell handbook of genius.* New York: Wiley.

Johnston, L.D., O'Malley, P.M., Bachman, J.G., & Schulenberg, J.E. (2011). *Monitoring the Future national survey results on drug use, 1975–2010 (Vol. 2: College students and adults ages 19–50).* Bethesda, MD: National Institute on Drug Abuse.

Johnston, L.D., & others (2015). *Monitoring the future: National survey results on drug use, 1974–2014. Vol 2: College students and adults ages 19–55.* Ann Arbor: University of Michigan Institute for Social Research.

Johnston, L.D., & others (2016). *Monitoring the future: National survey results on drug use, 1975–2015.* Ann Arbor, MI: Institute for Social Research, U. of Michigan.

Jolly, C.A. (2005). Diet manipulation and prevention of aging, cancer, and autoimmune disease. *Current Opinions in Clinical Nutrition and Metabolic Care, 8,* 382–387.

Jones, B.F., Reedy, E.J., & Weinberg, B.A. (2014). Age and scientific genius. In D.K. Simonton (Ed.), *Wiley-Blackwell handbook of genius.* New York: Wiley.

Jones, E., & Reynolds, G. (2011). *The play's the thing: Teachers' roles in children's play.* New York: Columbia University Press.

Jones, L., & others (2012). Pain management for women in labor: An overview of systematic reviews. *Cochrane Database of Systematic Reviews, 14*(3), CD009234.

Jones, M.C. (1965). Psychological correlates of somatic development. *Child Development, 36,* 899–911.

Jones, N.A. (2012). Delayed reactive cries demonstrate emotional and physiological dysregulation in newborns of depressed mothers. *Biological Psychiatry, 89,* 374–381.

Jones, P.S., & others (2011). Development of a caregiver empowerment model to promote positive outcomes. *Journal of Family Nursing, 17,* 11–28.

Jones, S.A., Wen, F., Herring, A.H., & Evenson, K.R. (2016, in press). Correlates of U.S. adult physical activity and sedentary behavior patterns. *Journal of Science and Medicine in Sport.*

Jonson-Reid, M., Kohl, P.L., & Drake, B. (2012). Child and adolescent outcomes of chronic child maltreatment. *Pediatrics, 129,* 839–845.

Jopp, D., & Rott, C. (2006). Adaptation in very old age: Exploring the role of resources and attitudes for centenarians' happiness. *Psychology and Aging, 21,* 266–280.

Jorgensen, M.J., & others (2015). Sexual behavior among young Danes aged 15–29 years: A cross-sectional study of core indicators. *Sexually Transmitted Infections, 91,* 171–177.

Jose, A., O'Leary, K.D., & Moyer, A. (2010). Does premarital cohabitation predict subsequent marital stability and marital quality? A meta-analysis. *Journal of Marriage and the Family, 72,* 105–116.

Joseph, J. (2006). *The missing gene.* New York: Algora.

Jouriles, E.N., McDonald, R., & Kouros, C.D. (2016). Interparental conflict and child adjustment. In D. Cicchetti (Ed.), *Developmental psychopathology* (3rd ed.). New York: Wiley.

Juang, L.P., & Umana-Taylor, A.J. (2012). Family conflict among Chinese- and Mexican-origin adolescents and their parents in the U.S.: An introduction. *New Directions in Child and Adolescent Development, 135,* 1–12.

Judd, F.K., Hickey, M., & Bryant, C. (2012). Depression and midlife: Are we overpathologizing the menopause? *Journal of Affective Disorders, 136,* 199–211.

Julvez, J., & others (2016). Maternal consumption of seafood in pregnancy and child neuropsychological development: A longitudinal study based on a population with high consumption levels. *American Journal of Epidemiology, 183,* 169–182.

Jung, C. (1933). *Modern man in search of a soul.* New York: Harcourt Brace.

Jung, S., & others (2016). Obesity and muscle weakness as risk factors of mobility limitation in community-dwelling older Japanese women: A two-year follow-up investigation. *Journal of Nutrition, Health, and Aging, 20,* 28–34.

Juster, R-P., & others (2016). Social inequalities and the road to allostatic load. In D. Cicchetti (Ed.), *Developmental psychopathology* (3rd ed.). New York: Wiley.

K

Kackar-Cam, H., & Schimdt, J.A. (2014). Community-based service-learning as a context for youth autonomy, competence, and relatedness. *High School Journal, 98,* 83–108.

Kadlecova, P., & others (2015). Alcohol consumption at midlife and risk of stroke during 43 years of follow-up: Cohort and twin analysis. *Stroke, 46,* 627–633.

Kaeberlein, M.R., & Martin, G.M. (Eds.) (2016). *Handbook of the biology of aging* (8th ed.). New York: Elsevier.

Kaffashi, F., Scher, M.S., Ludington-Hoe, S.M., & Loparo, K.A. (2013). An analysis of kangaroo care intervention using neonatal EEG complexity: A preliminary study. *Clinical Neurophysiology, 124,* 238–246.

Kagan, J. (1987). Perspectives on infancy. In J.D. Osofsky (Ed.), *Handbook on infant development* (2nd ed.). New York: Wiley.

Kagan, J. (2002). Behavioral inhibition as a temperamental category. In R.J. Davidson, K.R. Scherer, & H.H. Goldsmith (Eds.), *Handbook of affective sciences.* New York: Oxford University Press.

Kagan, J. (2010). Emotions and temperament. In M.H. Bornstein (Ed.), *Handbook of cultural developmental science.* New York: Psychology Press.

Kagan, J. (2013). Temperamental contributions to inhibited and uninhibited profiles. In P.D. Zelazo (Ed.), *Oxford handbook of developmental psychology.* New York: Oxford University Press.

Kagan, J.J., Kearsley, R.B., & Zelazo, P.R. (1978). *Infancy: Its place in human development.* Cambridge, MA: Harvard University Press.

Kagan, S.H. (2008). Faculty profile, University of Pennsylvania School of Nursing. Retrieved January 5, 2008, from www.nursing.upenn.edu/faculty/profile.asp

Kahrs, B.A., Jung, W.P., & Lockman, J.J. (2013). Motor origins of tool use. *Child Development, 84*(3), 810–818.

Kakinami, L., Barnett, T.A., Sequin, L., & Paradis, G. (2015). Parenting style and obesity risk in children. *Preventive Medicine, 75,* 18–22.

Kalanithi, P. (2016). *When breath becomes air.* New York: Random House.

Kalish, R.A. (1981). *Death, grief, and caring relationships,* Monterey, CA: Brooks/Cole.

Kalsi, D.S. (2015). What is the effect of fasting on the lifespan of neurons? *Aging Research Reviews, 24,* 160–165.

Kamat, P.K., & others (2016). Mechanism of oxidative stress and synapse dysfunction in the pathogenesis of Alzheimer's diseae: Understanding the therapeutics strategy. *Molecular Neurobiology, 53,* 648–661.

Kamiya, M., Sakurai, T., Ogama, N., Maki, Y., & Toba, K. (2014). Factors associated with increased caregivers' burden in several cognitive stages of Alzheimer's disease. *Geriatrics and Gerontology International, 14*(Suppl. 2), S45–S55.

Kan, P.F. (2014). Novel word retention in sequential bilingual children. *Journal of Child Language, 41,* 416–438.

Kanazawa, S. (2015). Breastfeeding is positively associated with child intelligence even net of parental IQ. *Developmental Psychology, 51,* 1683–1689.

Kandler, C., & others (2016, in press). The nature of creativity: The roles of genetic factors, personality traits, cognitive abilities, and environmental sources. *Journal of Personality and Social Psychology.*

Kane, J.C., & others (2016). The impact of intergenerational cultural dissonance on alcohol use among Vietnamese and Cambodian adolescents in the United States. *Journal of Adolescent Health, 58,* 174–180.

Kann, L., & others (2014). Youth Risk Behavior Surveillance—United States, 2013. *MMWR Surveillance Summaries, 63*(4), 1–169.

Kantowitz, B.H., Roediger, H.L., & Elmes, D.G. (2015). *Experimental psychology* (10th ed.). Boston: Cengage.

Kantrowitz, B., & Namuth, T. (1991, Summer). The good, the bad, and the difference. *Newsweek, 117,* 48–50.

Kao, T.A., & Huang, B. (2015). Bicultural straddling among immigrant adolescents: A concept analysis. *Journal of Holistic Nursing, 33,* 269–281.

Karantzas, G.C., Evans, L., & Foddy, M. (2010). The role of attachment in current and future parent caregiving. *Journals of Gerontology B: Psychological Sciences and Social Sciences, 65,* 573–580.

Karlamangia, A.S., & others (2013). Biological correlates of adult cognition: Midlife in the United States (MIDUS). *Neurobiology of Aging, 35*(2), 387–394.

Karmiloff-Smith, A., Doherty, B., Cornish, K., & Scerif, G. (2016). Fragile X syndrome as a multi-level model for understanding behaviorally-defined disorders. In D. Cicchetti (Ed.), *Developmental psychopathology* (3rd ed.). New York: Wiley.

Karniol, R., Grosz, E., & Schorr, I. (2003). Caring, gender-role orientation, and volunteering. *Sex Roles, 49,* 11–19.

Karoly, L.A., & Bigelow, J.H. (2005). *The economics of investing in universal preschool education in California.* Santa Monica, CA: RAND Corporation.

Karreman, A., van Tuijl, C., van Aken, M.A., & Dekovic, M. (2008). Parenting, coparenting, and effortful control in preschoolers. *Journal of Family Psychology, 22,* 30–40.

Karstad, S.B., & others (2015). What enhances the development of emotion understanding in young children? A longitudinal study of interpersonal predictors. *British Journal of Developmental Psychology, 33,* 340–354.

Kask, K., & others (2015). Deletion of RIC8A in neural precursor cells leads to altered neurogenesis and neonatal lethality of mouse. *Developmental Neurobiology, 75,* 984–1002.

Kastbom, A.A., & others (2015). Sexual debut before the age of 14 leads to poorer psychosocial health and risky behavior in later life. *Acta Pediatrica, 104,* 91–100.

Kastenbaum, R.J. (2009). *Death, society, and human experience* (10th ed.). Boston: Allyn & Bacon.

Kastenbaum, R.J. (2012). *Death, society, and human experience* (11th ed.). Boston: Allyn & Bacon.

Kato, T., & others (2016). Extremely preterm infants small for gestational age are at risk for motor impairment at 3 years corrected age. *Brain Development, 38,* 188–195.

Katsiaficas, D., Suarez-Orozco, C., Sirin, S.R., & Gupta, T. (2013). Mediators of the relationship between acculturative stress and internalizing symptoms for immigrant origin youth. *Cultural Diversity and Ethnic Minority Psychology, 19,* 27–37.

Katz, L. (1999). Curriculum disputes in early childhood education. *ERIC Clearinghouse on Elementary and Early Childhood Education,* Document EDO-PS-99-13.

Kauffman, J.M., McGee, K., & Brigham, M. (2004). Enabling or disabling? Observations on changes in special education. *Phi Delta Kappan, 85,* 613–620.

Kaufman, S.B., & others (2016). Openness to experience and intellect differentially predict creative achievement in the arts and sciences. *Journal of Personality, 84,* 248–258.

Kaushik, G., & others (2016, in press). Maternal exposure to carbamazepine at environmental concentrations can cross intestinal and placental barriers. *Biochemical and Biophysical Research Communications.*

Kavanaugh, R.D. (2006). Pretend play and theory of mind. In L.L. Balter & C.S. Tamis-LeMonda (Eds.), *Child psychology* (2nd ed.). New York: Psychology Press.

Kavosi, Z., & others (2015). A comparison of mothers' quality of life after normal vaginal, cesarean, and water birth deliveries. *International Journal of Community Based Nursing and Midwifery, 3,* 198–204.

Kavsek, M. (2013). The comparator model of infant visual habituation and dishabituation: Recent insights. *Developmental Psychobiology, 55,* 793–808.

Kawagoe, T., & Sekiyama, K. (2014). Visually encoded working memory is closely associated with mobility in older adults. *Experimental Brain Research, 232,* 2035–2043.

Kawakami, R., & others (2015). Dynapenic obesity and prevalence of type 2 diabetes in middle-aged Japanese men. *Journal of Epidemiology, 25,* 656–662.

Kawakita, T., & others (2016). Adverse maternal and neonatal outcomes in adolescent pregnancy. *Journal of Pediatric and Adolescent Gynecology, 29,* 130–136.

Keating, D.P. (1990). Adolescent thinking. In S.S. Feldman & G.R. Elliott (Eds.), *At the threshold: The developing adolescent.* Cambridge, MA: Harvard University Press.

Keen, R. (2011). The development of problem solving in young children: A critical cognitive skill. *Annual Review of Psychology* (Vol. 62). Palo Alto, CA: Annual Reviews.

Keen, R., Lee, M-H., & Adolph, K.E. (2014). Planning an action: A developmental progression for tool use. *Ecological Psychology, 26,* 98–108.

Keles, S., & others (2016). Depression among unaccompanied minor refugees: The relative contribution of general and acculturation-specific daily hassles. *Ethnicity and Health, 21,* 300–317.

Kell, H.J., & Lubinski, D. (2014). The study of mathematically precocious youth at maturity: Insights into elements of genius. In D.K. Simonton (Ed.), *Wiley-Blackwell handbook of genius.* New York: Wiley.

Keller, A., Ford, L., & Meacham, J. (1978). Dimensions of self-concept in preschool children. *Developmental Psychology, 14,* 483–489.

Kelley, G.A., & Kelley, K.S. (2013). Effects of exercise in the treatment of overweight and obese children and adolescents: A systematic review and analysis. *Journal of Obesity, 2013,* 783103.

Kelley-Moore, J. (2009). Chronic illness, adulthood and later life. In D. Carr (Ed.), *Encyclopedia of the life course and human development.* Boston: Gale Cengage.

Kelly, A.B., & others (2016, in press). Depressed mood during early to middle adolescence: A binational longitudinal study of the unique impact of family conflict. *Journal of Youth and Adolescence.*

Kelly, J.P., Borchert, J., & Teller, D.Y. (1997). The development of chromatic and achromatic sensitivity in infancy as tested with the sweep VEP. *Vision Research, 37,* 2057–2072.

Kelly, Y., & others (2013). Light drinking versus abstinence in pregnancy—behavioral and cognitive outcomes in 7-year-old children: A longitudinal cohort study. *BJOG, 120,* 1340–1347.

Keltner, K.W. (2013). *Tiger babies strike back.* New York: William Morrow.

Kemmler, W., Engelke, K., & von Stengel, S. (2016). Long-term exercise and bone mineral density changes in postmenopausal women—are there periods of reduced effectiveness? *Journal of Bone and Mineral Research, 31,* 215–222.

Kemp, J., Despres, O., Pebayle, T., & Dufour, A. (2014). Age-related decrease in sensitivity to electrical stimulation is unrelated to skin conductance: An evoked potentials study. *Clinical Neurophysiology, 125,* 602–607.

Kempermann, G., Song, H., & Gage, F.H. (2015). Neurogenesis in the adult hippocampus. *Cold Spring Harbor Perspectives in Biology, 7*(9), a018812.

Kendler, K.S., Ohlsson, H., Sundquist, K., & Sundquist, J. (2016, in press). The rearing environment and risk for drug use: A Swedish national high-risk adopted and not adopted co-sibling control study. *Psychological Medicine.*

Kendrick, K., Jutengren, G., & Stattin, H. (2012). The protective role of supportive friends against bullying perpetration and victimization. *Journal of Adolescence, 35*(4), 1069–1080.

Kennedy, E., & Guthrie, J.F. (2016). Nutrition assistance programs: Cause or solution to obesity. *Current Obesity Reports, 5,* 175–183.

Kennedy, K.M., & others (2015). Lifespan age trajectory differences in functional brain activation under conditions of low and high processing demands. *Neuroimage, 104,* 31–34.

Kennell, J.H. (2006). Randomized controlled trial of skin-to-skin contact from birth versus conventional incubator for physiological stabilization in 1200 g to 2199 g newborns. *Acta Paediatica (Sweden), 95,* 15–16.

Kennell, J.H., & McGrath, S.K. (1999). Commentary: Practical and humanistic lessons from the third world for perinatal caregivers everywhere. *Birth, 26,* 9–10.

Kerig, P. (2016). Family systems from a developmental psychopathology perspective. In D. Cicchetti (Ed.), *Developmental psychopathology* (3rd ed.). New York: Wiley.

Kerns, K.A., & Brumariu, L.E. (2016). Attachment in middle childhood. In J. Cassidy & P. Shaver (Eds.), *Handbook of attachment* (3rd ed.). New York: Guilford.

Kerns, K.A., & Seibert, A.C. (2012). Finding your way through the thicket: Promising approaches to assessing attachment in middle childhood. In E. Waters & B. Vaughn (Eds.), *Measuring attachment.* New York: Guilford.

Kershaw, K.N., & others (2014). Associations of stressful life events and social strain with incident cardiovascular disease in the Women's Health Initiative. *Journal of the American Heart Association, 3*(3), e000687.

Kerstis, B., & others (2016). Association between parental depressive symptoms and impaired bonding with the infant. *Archives of Women's Mental Health, 19,* 87–94.

Kesten, J.M., & others (2016, in press). Understanding the accuracy of parental perceptions of child physical activity: A mixed methods analysis. *Journal of Physical Activity and Health.*

Kettrey, H.H. (2016, in press). What's gender got to do with it? Sexual double standards and power in heterosexual hookups. *Journal of Sex Research.*

Kettunen, O., Vuorimaa, T., & Vasankari, T. (2015). A 12-month exercise intervention decreased stress symptoms and increased mental resources among working adults—results perceived after a 12-month follow-up. *International Journal of Occupational Medicine and Environmental Health, 28,* 157–168.

Keyes, K.M., Maslowsky, J., Hamilton, A., & Schulenberg, J. (2015). The great sleep recession: Changes in sleep duration among U.S. adolescents, 1991–2012. *Pediatrics, 135,* 460–468.

Khan, K.S., & Chaudry, S. (2015). An evidence-based approach to an ancient pursuit: Systematic review on converting online contact into a first date. *Evidence Based Medicine, 20,* 48–56.

Khanzada, F.J., Soomro, N., & Khan, S.Z. (2015). Association of physical exercise on anxiety and depression amongst adults. *Journal of the College of Physicians and Surgeons—Pakistan, 25,* 546–548.

Kharitonova, M., Winter, W., & Sheridan, M.A. (2015). As working memory grows: A developmental account of neural bases of working memory capacity in 5- to 8-year-old children and adults. *Journal of Cognitive Neuroscience, 27,* 1775–1788.

Khashan, A.S., Baker, P.N., & Kenny, L.C. (2010). Preterm birth and reduced birthweight in first and second teenage pregnancies: A register-based cohort study. *BMC Pregnancy and Childbirth, 10,* 36.

Kherada, N., Heimowitz, T., & Rosendorff, C. (2015). Antihypertensive therapies and cognitive function: A review. *Current Hypertension Reports, 17,* 79.

Khoury, J.E., & Milligan, K. (2016, in press). Comparing executive functioning in children and adolescents with fetal alcohol spectrum disorders and ADHD: A meta-analysis. *Journal of Attention Disorders.*

Kida, Y., & Goligorsky, M.S. (2016). Sirtuins, cell senescence, and vascular aging. *Canadian Journal of Cardiology, 32,* 634–641.

Kidd, C., Piantadosi, S.T., & Aslin, R.N. (2012). The Goldilocks effect: Human infants allocate attention to visual sequences that are neither too simple nor too complex. *PLoS One, 7*(5), e36399.

Kiecolt-Glaser, J.K., & others (2014). Yoga's impact on inflammation, mood, and fatigue in breast cancer survivors: A randomized controlled trial. *Journal of Clinical Oncology, 32,* 1040–1049.

Kielsmeier, J. (2011). The time is now. *Prevention Researcher, 18,* 3–7.

Kilic, A., Sayali, Z.C., & Oztekin, I. (2016, in press). Aging slows access to temporal information from working memory. *Journals of Gerontology B: Psychological Sciences and Social Sciences.*

Kilic, S., & others (2012). Environmental tobacco smoke exposure during intrauterine period promotes granulosa cell apoptosis: A prospective, randomized study. *Journal Maternal-Fetal and Neonatal Medicine, 25*(10), 1904–1908.

Killen, M., & Smetana, J.G. (2015). Morality: Origins and development. In R.M. Lerner (Ed.), *Handbook of child psychology and developmental science* (7th ed.). New York: Wiley.

Kilpi, F., Konttinen, H., Silventoinen, K., & Martikainen, P. (2015). Living arrangements as key determinants of myocardial infarction incidence and survival: A prospective register study of over 300,000 Finnish men and women. *Social Science and Medicine, 133,* 93–100.

Kim, A.S. (2016). Nursing home report card and performance gap. *Health Care Management Review, 25,* 1326–1335.

Kim, E.S., Chopik, W.J., & Smith, J. (2014). Are people healthier if their partners are more optimistic? The dyadic effect of optimism on health among older adults. *Journal of Psychosomatic Research, 76,* 447–453.

Kim, E.S., & Konrath, S.H. (2016). Volunteering is prospectively associated with health care use among older adults. *Social Science and Medicine, 149,* 122–129.

Kim, H.J., Yang, J., & Lee, M.S. (2015). Changes in heart rate variability during methylphenidate treatment in attention deficit hyperactivity disorder children: A 12-week prospective study. *Yonsei Medical Journal, 56,* 1365–1371.

Kim, K.H. (2010, May). Unpublished data. School of Education, College of William & Mary, Williamsburg, VA.

Kim, S.Y., Wang, Y., Chen, Q., Shen, Y., & Hou, Y. (2015). Parent-child acculturation profiles as predictors of Chinese American adolescents' academic trajectories. *Journal of Youth and Adolescence, 44,* 1263–1274.

Kim-Fuchs, C., & others (2014). Chronic stress accelerates pancreatic cancer growth and invasion: A critical role for beta-adrenergic signaling in the pancreatic microenvironment. *Brain, Behavior, and Immunity, 40,* 40–47.

Kindermann, T.A. (2016). Peer group influences on students' academic achievement and social behavior. In K. Wentzel & G. Ramani (Eds.), *Handbook of social influences in school contexts.* New York: Psychology Press.

King, C.T., Chase-Lansdale, P.L., & Small, M. (Eds.) (2015). *Two generations, one future: An anthology from the Ascend Fellowship.* Washington, DC: Ascend at the Aspen Institute.

King, L.A. (2016). *Experience psychology* (3rd ed.). New York: McGraw-Hill.

King, L.A. (2017). *Psychology: An appreciative experience* (4th ed.). New York: McGraw-Hill.

King, L.A., & Hicks, J.A. (2007). Whatever happened to "What might have been?" Regrets, happiness, and maturity. *American Psychologist, 62,* 625–636.

King, V., & Scott, M.E. (2005). A comparison of cohabiting relationships among older and younger adults. *Journal of Marriage and the Family, 67,* 271–285.

Kingdon, D., Cardoso, C., & McGrath, J.J. (2016). Research review: Executive function deficits in fetal alcohol spectrum disorders and attention-deficit/hyperactivity disorder—a meta-analysis. *Journal of Child Psychology and Psychiatry, 57,* 116–131.

Kingo, O.S., & Krojgaard, P. (2015). Eighteen-month-olds' memory for short movies of simple shots. *Scandinavian Journal of Psychology, 56,* 151–156.

Kins, E., & Beyers, W. (2010). Failure to launch, failure to achieve criteria for adulthood? *Journal of Adolescent Research, 25,* 743–777.

Kiray, H., Lindsay, S.L., Hosseinzadeh, S., & Barnett, S.C. (2016, in press). The multifaced role of astrocytes in regulating myelination. *Experimental Neurology.*

Kirk, S.A., Gallagher, J.J., & Coleman, M.R. (2015). *Educating exceptional children* (14th ed.). Boston: Cengage.

Kirk, S.M., & Kirk, E.P. (2016). Sixty minutes of physical activity per day included within preschool academic lessons improves early literacy. *Journal of School Health, 86,* 155–163.

Kirkham, N.Z., Wagner, J.B., Swan, K.A., & Johnson, S.P. (2012). Sound support: Intermodal information facilitates infants' perception of an occluded trajectory. *Infant Behavior and Development, 35,* 174–178.

Kirkorian, H.L., Anderson, D.R., & Keen, R. (2012). Age differences in online processing of video: An eye movement study. *Child Development, 83,* 497–507.

Kisilevsky, B.S., & others (2009). Fetal sensitivity to properties of maternal speech and language. *Infant Behavior and Development, 32,* 59–71.

Kit, B.K., Simon, A.E., Brody, D.J., & Akinbami, L.J. (2013). U.S. prevalence and trends in tobacco smoke exposure among children and adolescents with asthma. *Pediatrics, 131,* 407–414.

Kitaoka, M., & others (2016, in press). The relationship between hypertension and health-related quality of life: Adjusted by chronic pain, chronic diseases, and life habits in the general middle-aged population in Japan. *Environmental Health and Preventive Medicine.*

Kitsantas, A., & Cleary, T.J. (2016). The development of self-regulated learning in secondary school years: A social cognitive instructional perspective. In K.R. Wentzel & D.B. Miele (Eds.), *Handbook of motivation at school* (2nd ed.). New York: Routledge.

Kitsantas, P., & others (2016). Nature and nurture in the development of childhood obesity: Early infant feeding practices of overweight/obese mothers compared to mothers of normal body size. *Journal of Maternal-Fetal and Neonatal Medicine, 29,* 290–293.

Klahr, A.M., & Burt, S.A. (2014). Elucidating the etiology of individual differences in parenting: A meta-analysis of behavioral genetic research. *Psychological Bulletin, 140,* 544–586.

Klassen, H. (2016). Stem cells in clinical trials for treatment of retinal degeneration. *Expert Opinion on Biological Therapy, 16,* 7–14.

Klaus, M., & Kennell, H.H. (1976). *Maternal-infant bonding.* St. Louis: Mosby.

Kliegman, R.M., Stanton, B., St. Geme, J., & Schor, N. (2016). *Nelson textbook of pediatrics* (20th ed.). New York: Elsevier.

Klinedinst, N.J., & Resnick, B. (2014). Volunteering and depressive symptoms among residents in a continuing care retirement community. *Journal of Gerontological Social Work, 57,* 52–71.

Klinenberg, E. (2013). *Going solo: The extraordinary rise and surprising appeal of living alone.* New York: Penguin.

Klingman, A. (2006). Children and war trauma. In W. Damon & R. Lerner (Eds.), *Handbook of child psychology* (6th ed.). New York: Wiley.

Klotz, L.O., & others (2015). Redox regulation of FoxO transcription factors. *Redox Biology, 6,* 51–72.

Klug, J., & others (2016). Secondary school students LLL competencies and their relation with classroom structure and achievement. *Frontiers in Psychology, 7,* 680.

Klug, W.S., & others (2016). *Essentials of genetics* (9th ed.). Upper Saddle River, NJ: Pearson.

Kmietowicz, Z. (2015). Ingredients for successful online dating are outlined in evidence based study. *British Medical Journal, 350,* h794.

Knight, B.G., Rastegar, S., & Kim, S. (2016). Age differences in the connection of mood and cognition: Evidence from mood congruent effects. In K.W. Schaie & S.L. Willis (Eds.), *Handbook of the psychology of aging* (8th ed.). New York: Elsevier.

Knight, L.F., & Hope, D.A.M. (2012). Correlates of same-sex attractions and behaviors among self-identified heterosexual university students. *Archives of Sexual Behavior, 41,* 1199–1208.

Knopik, V.S., & others (2016, in press). Smoking during pregnancy and ADHD risk: A genetically informed, multi-rater approach. *American Journal of Medical Genetics B: Neuropsychiatric Genetics.*

Knowles, E.E., & others (2016). Genome-wide linkage on chromosome 10q26 for a dimensional scale of major depression. *Journal of Affective Disorders, 191,* 123–131.

Ko, Y.L., Yang, C.L., Fang, C.L., Lee, M.Y., & Lin, P.C. (2013). Community-based postpartum exercise program. *Journal of Clinical Nursing, 22*(15–16), 2122–2131.

Koba, S., & others (2016, in press). Beneficial effects of exercise-based cardiac rehabilitation on high-density lipoprotein-mediated cholesterol efflux capacity in patients with acute coronary syndrome. *Journal of Atherosclerosis and Thrombosis.*

Kobak, R.R., & Kerig, P.K. (2015). Introduction to the special issue: Attachment-based treatments for adolescents. *Attachment and Human Development, 17,* 111–118.

Kochanek, K.D., & others (2011). Deaths: Preliminary data 2009. *National Vital Statistics Reports, 59*(4), 1–51.

Kochanska, G., & Kim, S. (2013). Early attachment organization with both parents and future behavior problems: From infancy to middle childhood. *Child Development, 84,* 283–296.

Koh, H. (2014). The Teen Pregnancy Prevention Program: An evidence-based public health program model. *Journal of Adolescent Health, 54*(Suppl. 1), S1–S2.

Kohan-Ghadr, H.R., & others (2016, in press). Potential role of epigenetic mechanisms in regulation of trophoblast differentiation, migration, and invasion in the human placenta. *Cell Adhesion and Migration.*

Kohen, D.E., Lerenthal, T., Dahinten, V.S., & McIntosh, C.N. (2008). Neighborhood disadvantage: Pathways of effects for young children. *Child Development, 79,* 156–169.

Kohlberg, L. (1958). *The development of modes of moral thinking and choice in the years 10 to 16.* Unpublished doctoral dissertation, University of Chicago.

Kohlberg, L. (1986). A current statement of some theoretical issues. In S. Modgil & C. Modgil (Eds.), *Lawrence Kohlberg.* Philadelphia: Falmer.

Kojola, E., & Moen, P. (2016). No more lock-step retirement: Boomers' shifting meanings of work and retirement. *Journal of Aging Studies, 36,* 59–70.

Kok, R., & others (2015). Normal variation in early parental sensitivity predicts child structural brain development. *Journal of the American Academy of Child and Adolescent Psychiatry, 54,* 824–831.

Kollins, S.H., & Adcock, R.A. (2014). ADHD, altered dopamine neurotransmission, and disrupted reinforcement processes: Implications for smoking and nicotine dependence. *Progress in Neuro-Psychopharmacology and Biological Psychiatry, 52,* 70–78.

Kominiarek, M.A., & Chauhan, S.P. (2016). Obesity before, during, and after pregnancy: A review and comparison of five national guidelines. *American Journal of Perinatology, 33,* 433–441.

Kondo, A., & others (2015). Awareness of folic acid use increases its consumption and reduces the risk of spina bifida. *British Journal of Nursing, 114,* 84–90.

Konrath, S.H., Chopik, W.J., Hsing, C.K., & O'Brien, E. (2014). Changes in adult attachment styles in American college students over time: A meta-analysis. *Personality and Social Psychology Bulletin, 18,* 326–348.

Koo, Y.J., & others (2012). Pregnancy outcomes according to increasing maternal age. *Taiwan Journal of Obstetrics and Gynecology, 51,* 60–65.

Koolschijn, P.C., Peper, J.S., & Crone, E.A. (2014). The influence of sex steroids on structural brain maturation in adolescence. *PLoS One, 9*(1), e83929.

Koorevaar, A.M., & others (2013). Big Five personality factors and depression diagnosis, severity, and age of onset in older adults. *Journal of Affective Disorders, 151,* 178–185.

Koren, C., Simhi, S., Lipman-Schiby, S., & Fogel, S. (2016, in press). The partner in late-life repartnering: Caregiving expectations from an intergenerational perspective. *International Psychogeriatrics.*

Koropeckyj-Cox, T. (2009). Loneliness, later life. In D. Carr (Ed.), *Encyclopedia of the life course and human development.* Boston: Gale Cengage.

Korte, J., Dorssaert, C.H., Westerhof, G.J., & Bohlmeijer, E.T. (2014). Life review in groups? An explorative analysis of social processes that facilitate or hinder the effectiveness of life review. *Aging and Mental Health, 18,* 376–384.

Korten, N.C., & others (2014). Heterogeneity of late-life depression: Relationship with cognitive functioning. *International Psychogeriatrics, 26,* 953–963.

Koss, C.S., & Baker, T.A. (2016, in press). Race differences in advance directive completion: The narrowing gap between White and African American older adults. *Journal of Aging and Health.*

Koss, K.J., & others (2014). Asymmetry in children's salivary cortisol and alpha-amylase in the context of marital conflict: Links to children's emotional security and adjustment. *Developmental Psychobiology, 56,* 836–849.

Kostanyan, T., & others (2016). Glaucoma structural and functional progression in American and Korean cohorts. *Ophthalmology, 123,* 783–788.

Kostelnik, M.J., Soderman, A.K., Whiren, A.P., & Rupiper, M. (2015). *Developmentally appropriate curriculum* (6th ed.). Upper Saddle River, NJ: Pearson.

Kostovic, I., Judas, M., & Sedmak, G. (2011). Developmental history of the subplate zone, subplate neurons, and interstitial white matter neurons: Relevance for schizophrenia. *International Journal of Developmental Neuroscience, 29,* 193–205.

Kotre, J. (1984). *Outliving the self: Generativity and the interpretation of lives.* Baltimore: Johns Hopkins University Press.

Kotter-Gruhn, D., & Smith, J. (2011). When time is running out: Changes in positive future perception and their relationships to changes in well-being in old age. *Psychology and Aging, 26,* 381–387.

Koumbaris, G., & others (2016, in press). Cell-free DNA analysis of targeted genomic regions in maternal plasma for non-invasive prenatal testing of trisomy 21, trisomy 18, trisomy 13, and fetal sex. *Clinical Chemistry.*

Kouros, C.D., Morris, M.C., & Garber, J. (2016). Within-person changes in individual symptoms of depression predict subsequent depressive episodes in adolescents: A prospective study. *Journal of Abnormal Child Psychology, 44,* 483–494.

Kowalski, R.M., Giumetti, G.W., Schroeder, A.N., & Lattanner, M.R. (2014). Bullying in the digital age: A critical review and meta-analysis of cyberbullying research on youth. *Psychological Bulletin, 140,* 1073–1137.

Kozhimmanil, K.B., & others (2013). Doula care, birth outcomes, and costs among Medicaid beneficiaries. *American Journal of Public Health, 103*(4), e113–e121.

Kozhimmanil, K.B., & others (2016, in press). Modeling the cost-effectiveness of doula care associated with reductions in preterm birth and cesarean delivery. *Birth.*

Kozol, J. (2005). *The shame of the nation.* New York: Crown.

Kraft, E. (2012). Cognitive function, physical activity, and aging: Possible biological links and implications for multimodal interventions. *Neuropsychology, Development, and Cognition B: Aging, Neuropsychology, and Cognition, 19,* 248–263.

Krafft, C.E., & others (2014). An eight-month randomized controlled exercise trial alters brain activation during cognitive tasks in overweight children. *Obesity, 22,* 232–242.

Kramer, C.K. (2015). Weight loss is a useful therapeutic objective. *Canadian Journal of Cardiology, 31,* 211–215.

Kramer, L. (2006, July 10). Commentary in "How your siblings make you who you are" by J. Kluger. *Time,* 46–55.

Kramer, L., & Perozynski, L. (1999). Parental beliefs about managing sibling conflict. *Developmental Psychology, 35,* 489–499.

Kramer, L., & Radey, C. (1997). Improving sibling relationships among young children: A social skills training model. *Family Relations, 46,* 237–246.

Krans, E.E., & others (2016, in press). Factors associated with buprenorphine versus methadone use in pregnancy. *Substance Abuse.*

Krause, N. (2008). The social foundations of religious meaning in life. *Research on Aging, 30*(4), 395–427.

Krause, N. (2009). Deriving a sense of meaning in late life. In V.L. Bengtson, D. Gans, N.M. Putney, & M. Silverstein (Eds.), *Handbook of theories of aging.* New York: Springer.

Krause, N., & Hayward, R.D. (2016). Religion, health, and aging. In L.K. George & G.M. Martin (Eds.), *Handbook of aging and the social sciences* (8th ed.). New York: Elsevier.

Krause, N., Ingersoll-Dayton, B., Liang, J., & Sugisawa, H. (1999). Religion, social support, and health among the Japanese elderly. *Journal of Health and Social Behavior, 40,* 405–421.

Kretch, K.S., & Adolph, K.E. (2016, in press). Active vision in passive locomotion: Real-world free viewing in infants and adults. *Developmental Science.*

Kretch, K.S., Franchak, J.M., & Adolph, K.E. (2014). Crawling and walking infants see the world differently. *Child Development, 85,* 1503–1518.

Kreutzer, M., Leonard, C., & Flavell, J.H. (1975). An interview study of children's knowledge about memory. *Monographs of the Society for Research in Child Development, 40* (Serial No. 159).

Kriemler, S., & others (2010). Effect of school-based physical activity program (KISS) on fitness and adiposity in primary schoolchildren: Cluster randomized controlled trial. *British Medical Journal, 45,* 923–930.

Kring, A.M. (2000). Gender and anger. In A.H. Fischer (Ed.), *Gender and emotion: Social psychological perspectives.* New York: Cambridge University Press.

Kroger, J. (2015). Identity development through adulthood: The move toward "wholeness." In K.C. McLean & M. Syed (Eds.), *Oxford handbook of identity development.* New York: Oxford University Press.

Kroll-Desrosiers, A.R., & others (2016). Improving pregnancy outcomes through maternity care coordination: A systematic review. *Women's Health Issues, 26,* 87–99.

Krueger, J.I., Vohs, K.D., & Baumeister, R.F. (2008). Is the allure of self-esteem a mirage after all? *American Psychologist, 63,* 64.

Krueger, P.M., & Chang, V.W. (2008). Being poor and coping with stress: Health behaviors and the risk of death. *American Journal of Public Health, 98,* 889–896.

Kruger, J., Blanck, H.M., & Gillespie, C. (2006). Dietary and physical activity behaviors among adults successful at weight loss management. *International Journal of Behavioral Nutrition and Physical Activity, 3,* 17.

Kübler-Ross, E. (1969). *On death and dying.* New York: Macmillan.

Kucian, K., & von Aster, M. (2015). Developmental dyscalculia. *European Journal of Pediatrics, 174,* 1–13.

Kuebli, J. (1994, March). Young children's understanding of everyday emotions. *Young Children,* 36–48.

Kuhl, P.K. (2000). A new view of language acquisition. *Proceedings of the National Academy of Science. 97*(22), 11850–11857.

Kuhl, P.K. (2007). Is speech learning "gated" by the social brain? *Developmental Science, 10,* 110–120.

Kuhl, P.K. (2009). Linking infant speech perception to language acquisition: Phonetic learning predicts language growth. In J. Colombo, P. McCardle, & L. Freund (Eds.), *Infant pathways to language.* New York: Psychology Press.

Kuhl, P.K. (2011). Social mechanisms in early language acquisition: Understanding integrated brain systems and supporting language. In J. Decety & J. Cacioppo (Eds.), *Handbook of social neuroscience.* New York: Oxford University Press.

Kuhl, P.K. (2012). Language learning and the developing brain: Cross-cultural studies unravel the effects of biology and culture. *Journal of the Acoustical Society of America, 131*(4).

Kuhl, P.K. (2015). Baby talk. *Scientific American, 313,* 64–69.

Kuhl, P.K., & Damasio, A. (2012). Language. In E.R. Kandel & others (Eds.), *Principles of neural science* (5th ed.). New York: McGraw-Hill.

Kuhn, D. (1998). Afterword to Vol. 2: Cognition, perception, and language. In W. Damon (Ed.), *Handbook of child psychology* (5th ed., Vol. 2). New York: Wiley.

Kuhn, D. (2009). Adolescent thinking. In R.M. Lerner & L. Steinberg (Eds.), *Handbook of adolescent psychology* (3rd ed.). New York: Wiley.

Kuhn, D. (2013). Reasoning. In P.D. Zelazo (Ed.), *Handbook of developmental psychology.* New York: Oxford University Press.

Kuhn, S., & Lindenberger, U. (2016). Research on human plasticity in adulthood: A lifespan agenda. In K.W. Schaie & S.L. Willis (Eds.), *Handbook of the psychology of aging* (8th ed.). New York: Elsevier.

Kuhn-Popp, N., & others (2016). Left hemisphere EEG coherence in infancy predicts infant declarative pointing and preschool language. *Social Neuroscience, 11,* 49–59.

Kulmala, J., & others (2013). Perceived stress symptoms in midlife predict disability in old age: A 28-year prospective study. *Journals of Gerontology A: Biological Sciences and Medical Sciences, 68,* 984–991.

Kulu, H. (2014). Marriage duration and divorce: The seven-year itch or a lifelong itch? *Demography, 51,* 881–893.

Kuntsche, S., & Kuntsche, E. (2016). Parent-based interventions for preventing or reducing adolescent substance use: A systematic literature review. *Clinical Psychology Review, 45,* 89–101.

Kuo, L.J., & Anderson, R.C. (2012). Effects of early bilingualism on learning phonological regularities in a new language. *Journal of Experimental Child Psychology, 111,* 455–467.

Kuperberg, A. (2014). Age at coresidence, premarital cohabitation, and marriage dissolution: 1985–2009. *Journal of Marriage and Family, 76,* 352–369.

Kusaka, M., Matsuzaki, M., Shiraishi, M., & Haruna, M. (2016, in press). Immediate stress reduction effects of yoga during pregnancy: One group pre-post test. *Women and Birth.*

Kymre, I.G. (2014). NICU nurses' ambivalent attitudes in skin-to-skin care practice. *International Journal of Qualitative Studies on Health and Well-Being, 9,* 23297.

L

Labouvie-Vief, G. (1986, August). *Modes of knowing and life-span cognition.* Paper presented at the meeting of the American Psychological Association, Washington, DC.

Labouvie-Vief, G. (2009). Cognition and equilibrium regulation in development and aging. In V. Bengtson & others (Eds.), *Handbook of theories of aging.* New York: Springer.

Labouvie-Vief, G., Gruhn, D., & Studer, J. (2010). Dynamic integration of emotion and cognition: Equilibrium regulation in development and aging. In M.E. Lamb, A. Freund, & R.M. Lerner (Eds.), *Handbook of life-span development* (Vol. 2). New York: Wiley.

Lacelle, C., Hebert, M., Lavoie, F., Vitaro, F., & Tremblay, R.E. (2012). Sexual health in women reporting a history of child sexual abuse. *Child Abuse and Neglect, 36,* 247–259.

Lachman, M.E. (2004). Development in midlife. *Annual Review of Psychology* (Vol. 55). Palo Alto, CA: Annual Reviews.

Lachman, M.E. (2006). Perceived control over aging-related declines. *Current Directions in Psychological Science, 15,* 282–286.

Lachman, M.E., Agrigoroaei, S., & Hahn, E.A. (2016). Making sense of control: Change and consequences. In R. Scott & S. Kosslyn (Eds.), *Emerging trends in the social and behavioral sciences.* New York: Wiley.

Lachman, M.E., & Firth, K.M.P. (2004). The adaptive value of feeling in control during midlife. In O.G. Brim, C.D. Ruff, & R.C. Kessler (Eds.), *How healthy are we?* Chicago: University of Chicago Press.

Lachman, M.E., Maier, H., & Budner, R. (2000). *A portrait of midlife.* Unpublished manuscript, Brandeis University, Waltham, MA.

Lachman, M.E., Neupert, S.D., & Agrigoroaei, S. (2011). The relevance of control beliefs for health and aging. In K.W. Schaie & S.L. Willis (Eds.), *Handbook of the psychology of aging* (7th ed.). New York: Elsevier.

Lachman, M.E., Teshale, S., & Agrigoroaei, S. (2015). Midlife as a pivotal period in the life course: Balancing growth and decline at the crossroads of youth and old age. *International Journal of Behavioral Development, 39,* 20–31.

Lacombe, J., & others (2015). Neural changes associated with semantic processing in healthy aging despite intact behavioral performance. *Brain and Language, 149,* 118–127.

Laflin, M.T., Wang, J., & Barry, M. (2008). A longitudinal study of adolescent transition from virgin to nonvirgin status. *Journal of Adolescent Health, 42,* 228–236.

Lafreniere, D., & Mann, N. (2009). Anosmia: Loss of smell in the elderly. *Otolaryngologic Clinics of North America, 42,* 123–131.

Lagattuta, K.H. (2014a). *Children and emotion. New insights into developmental affective science.* Basel, Switzerland: Karger.

Lagattuta, K.H. (2014b). Linking past, present, and future: Children's ability to connect mental states and emotions across time. *Child Development Perspectives, 8,* 90–95.

Lagattuta, K.H., & others (2015). Beyond Sally's missing marble: Further development in children's understanding of mind and emotion in middle childhood. *Advances in Child Development and Behavior, 48,* 185–217.

Lagraauw, H.M., Kuiper, J., & Bot, I. (2015). Acute and chronic psychological stress as risk factors for cardiovascular disease: Insights gained from epidemiological, clinical, and experimental studies. *Brain, Behavior, and Immunity, 50,* 18–30.

Lahat, A., & others (2014). Early behavioral inhibition and increased error monitoring predict later social phobia symptoms in childhood. *Journal of the American Academy of Child and Adolescent Psychiatry, 53,* 447–455.

Laible, D.J., & Karahuta, E. (2016). Prosocial behaviors in early childhood: Helping others, responding to the distress of others, and working with others. In L. Padilla-Walker & G. Carlo (Eds.), *Prosocial behavior.* New York: Oxford University Press.

Laible, D.J., Thompson, R.A., & Froimson, J. (2015). Early socialization: The influence of close relationships. In J.E. Grusec & P.D. Hastings (Eds.), *Handbook of socialization* (2nd ed.). New York: Guilford.

Lakoski, S., & others (2013, June 2). *Exercise lowers cancer risk in middle-aged men.* Paper presented at the American Society of Clinical Oncology meeting, Chicago, IL.

Lalley, P.M. (2013). The aging respiratory system—pulmonary structure, function, and neural control. *Respiratory Physiology and Neurology, 187,* 199–210.

LaMantia, M.A., & others (2015). The aging brain care medical home: Preliminary data. *Journal of the American Geriatrics Society, 63,* 1209–1213.

Lamb, M.E. (1994). Infant care practices and the application of knowledge. In C.B. Fisher & R.M. Lerner (Eds.), *Applied developmental psychology.* New York: McGraw-Hill.

Lamb, M.E. (2013). Non-parental care and emotional development. In S. Pauen & M. Bornstein (Eds.), *Early childhood development and later outcomes.* New York: Cambridge University Press.

Lamb, M.E., Bornstein, M.H., & Teti, D.M. (2002). *Development in infancy* (4th ed.). Mahwah, NJ: Erlbaum.

Lamb, M.E., & Lewis, C. (2015). The role of parent-child relationships in child development. In M.H. Bornstein & M.E. Lamb (Eds.), *Developmental science* (7th ed.). New York: Psychology Press.

Lamb, M.E., Malloy, L.C., Hershkowitz, I., & La Rooy, D. (2015). Children and the law. In R.E. Lerner (Ed.), *Handbook of child psychology and developmental science* (7th ed.). New York: Wiley.

Lamb, S., & Kwok, K.C. (2016). A longitudinal investigation of work environmental stressors on the performance and well-being of office workers. *Applied Ergonomics, 52,* 104–111.

Lamela, D., & Figueiredo, B. (2016, in press). Co-parenting after marital dissolution and children's mental health: A systematic review. *Journal de Pediatria (Rio J.).*

Lampard, A.M., Byrne, S.M., McLean, N., & Fursland, A. (2012). The Eating Disorder Inventory-2 perfectionism scale: Factor structure and associations with dietary restraint and weight and shape concern in eating disorders. *Eating Behaviors, 13,* 49–53.

Lampit, A., & others (2015). Cognitive training-induced short-term functional and long-term structural plastic change is related to gains in global cognition in healthy older adults: A pilot study. *Frontiers in Aging Neuroscience, 7,* 14.

Lamy, S., & others (2014). Psychosocial and organizational work factors and incidence of arterial hypertension among female healthcare workers: Results of the Organisation des soins et santé des soignants cohort. *Journal of Hypertension, 32,* 1229–1236.

Landes, S.D., Ardelt, M., Vaillant, G.E., & Waldinger, R.J. (2014). Childhood adversity, midlife generativity, and later life well-being. *Journals of Gerontology B: Psychological Sciences and Social Sciences, 69,* 942–952.

Landrum, A.R., Mills, C.M., & Johnston, A.M. (2013). When do children trust the expert? Benevolence information influences children's trust more than expertise. *Developmental Science, 16,* 622–638.

Lane, A., Harrison, M., & Murphy, N. (2014). Screen time increases risk of overweight and obesity in active and inactive 9-year-old Irish children: A cross sectional analysis. *Journal of Physical Activity and Health, 11,* 985–991.

Lane, H. (1976). *The wild boy of Aveyron.* Cambridge, MA: Harvard University Press.

Lane, J.D., Evans, E.M., Brink, K.A., & Wellman, H.M. (2016). Developing concepts of ordinary and extraordinary communication. *Developmental Psychology, 52,* 19–30.

Langille, D.B., Asbridge, M., Cragg, A., & Rasic, D. (2015). Associations of school connectedness with adolescent suicidality: Gender differences and the role of risk of depression. *Canadian Journal of Psychiatry, 60,* 258–267.

Langstrom, N., Rahman, Q., Carlstrom, E., & Lichtenstein, P. (2010). Genetic and environmental effects on same-sex sexual behaviour: A population study of twins in Sweden. *Archives of Sexual Behavior, 39,* 75–80.

Lankford, L., & others (2015). Early gestation chorionic villi-derived stromal cells for fetal tissue engineering. *World Journal of Stem Cells, 7,* 195–207.

Lansford, J.E. (2009). Parental divorce and children's adjustment. *Perspectives on Psychological Science, 4,* 140–152.

Lansford, J.E. (2012). Divorce. In R.J.R. Levesque (Ed.), *Encyclopedia of adolescence.* New York: Springer.

Lansford, J.E. (2013). Single- and two-parent families. In J. Hattie & E. Anderman (Eds.), *International guide to student achievement.* New York: Routledge.

Lansford, J.E., Wager, L.B., Bates, J.E., Pettit, G.S., & Dodge, K.A. (2012). Forms of spanking and children's externalizing problems. *Family Relations, 61*(2), 224–236.

Lansford, J.E., & others (2005). Cultural normativeness as a moderator of the link between physical discipline and children's adjustment: A comparison of China, India, Italy, Kenya, Philippines, and Thailand. *Child Development, 76,* 1234–1246.

Lansford, J.E., & others (2010). Developmental precursors of number of sexual partners from ages 16 to 22. *Journal of Research on Adolescence, 20,* 651–677.

Lansford, J.E., & others (2014). Corporal punishment, maternal warmth, and child adjustment: A longitudinal study in eight countries. *Journal of Clinical Child and Adolescent Psychology, 43,* 670–685.

Laranjo, J., Bernier, A., Meins, E., & Carlson, S.M. (2010). Early manifestations of theory of mind: The roles of maternal mind-mindedness and infant security of attachment. *Infancy, 15,* 300–323.

Larson, R.W., & Dawes, N.P. (2015). How to cultivate adolescents' motivation: Effective strategies employed by the professional staff of American youth programs. In S. Joseph (Ed.), *Positive psychology in practice.* New York: Wiley.

Larson, R.W., Wilson, S., & Rickman, A. (2009). Globalization, societal change, and adolescence across the world. In R.M. Lerner & L. Steinberg (Eds.), *Handbook of adolescent psychology* (3rd ed.). New York: Wiley.

Larzelere, R.E., & Kuhn, B.R. (2005). Comparing child outcomes of physical punishment and alternative disciplinary tactics: a meta-analysis. *Clinical Child and Family Psychology Review, 8,* 1–37.

Latt, E., & others (2015). Vigorous physical activity rather than sedentary behavior predicts overweight and obesity in pubertal boys: A 2-year follow-up study. *Scandinavian Journal of Public Health, 43,* 276–282.

Lau, J.S., Adams, S.H., Irwin, C.E., & Ozer, E.M. (2013). Receipt of preventive health services in young adults. *Journal of Adolescent Health, 52,* 42–49.

Lau, M., Lin, H., & Flores, G. (2015). Clusters of factors identify a high prevalence of pregnancy involvement among U.S. adolescent males. *Maternal and Child Health Journal, 19,* 1713–1723.

Laumann, E.O., Glasser, D.B., Neves, R.C., & Moreira, E.D. (2009). A population-based survey of sexual activity, sexual problems, and associated help-seeking behavior patterns in mature adults in the United States of America. *International Journal of Impotence Research, 21,* 171–178.

Lavender, J.M., & others (2014). Dimensions of emotion dysregulation in bulimia nervosa. *European Eating Disorders Review, 22,* 212–216.

Lavner, J.A., & Bradbury, T.N. (2013). Newly-weds' optimistic forecasts of their marriage: For better or for worse? *Journal of Family Psychology, 27,* 531–540.

Lavner, J.A., & others (2016). Narcissism and new-lywed marriage: Partner characteristics and marital trajectories. *Personality Disorders, 7,* 169–179.

Lawler, M., Selby, P., Aapro, M.S., & Duffy, S. (2014). Ageism in cancer care. *British Medical Journal, 348,* g1614.

Le Doare, K., & Kampmann, B. (2014). Breast milk and Group B streptococcal infection: Vector of transmission or vehicle for protection? *Vaccine, 32,* 3128–3132.

Leaper, C. (2015). Gender development from a social-cognitive perspective. In R.M. Lerner (Ed.), *Handbook of child psychology and developmental science* (7th ed.). New York: Wiley.

Leaper, C., & Farkas, T. (2015). The socialization of gender during childhood and adolescence. In J.E. Grusec & P.D. Hastings (Eds.), *Handbook of socialization* (2nd ed.). New York: Guilford.

LeBlanc, A.G., & others (2015). Correlates of to-tal sedentary time and screen time in 9- to 11-year-old children around the world: The International Study of Child Obesity, Lifestyle, and the Environment. *PLoS One, 10*(6), e0129622.

Lecarpentier, E., & others (2016). Computational fluid dynamic simulations of maternal circulation: Wall shear stress in the human placenta and its biological implications. *PLoS One, 11,* e0147262.

Lee, G.R. (2014). Current research on widowhood: Devastation and human resilience. *Journals of Gerontology B: Psychological Sciences and Social Sciences, 69,* 2–3.

Lee, I.M., & Skerrett, P.J. (2001). Physical activity and all-cause mortality: What is the dose-response relation? *Medical Science and Sports Exercise, 33* (6 Suppl.), S459–S471.

Lee, J., Hong, Y.P., Shin, H.J., & Lee, W. (2016). Associations of sarcopenia and sarcopenic obesity with metabolic syndrome considering muscle mass and muscle strength. *Journal of Preventive Medicine and Public Health, 49,* 35–44.

Lee, J.E., Kahana, B., & Kahana, E. (2016). Social support and cognitive functioning as resources for elderly persons with chronic arthritis pain. *Aging and Mental Health, 20,* 370–379.

Lee, J.H., & others (2014). Five-factor model personality traits as predictors of incident coronary heart disease in the community. *Psychosomatics, 55,* 352–361.

Lee, K., Cameron, C.A., Doucette, J., & Talwar, V. (2002). Phantoms and fabrications: Young children's detection of implausible lies. *Child Development, 73,* 1688–1702.

Lee, K., Quinn, P.C., Pascalis, O., & Slater, A. (2013). Development of face-processing ability in children. In P.D. Zelazo (Ed.), *Handbook of developmental psychology.* New York; Oxford University Press.

Lee, K.Y., & others (2011). Effects of combined radiofrequency radiation exposure on the cell cycle and its regulatory proteins. *Bioelectromagnetics, 32,* 169–178.

Lee, R., Zhai, F., Brooks-Gunn, J., Han, W.J., & Waldfogel, J. (2014). Head Start participation and school readiness: Evidence from the Early Child-hood Longitudinal Study–Birth Cohort. *Developmental Psychology, 50,* 202–215.

Lee, Y.H., & Song, G.G. (2014). Genome-wide pathway analysis in attention-deficit/hyperactivity disorder. *Neurological Sciences, 35,* 1189–1196.

Leedy, P.D., & Ormrod, J.E. (2016). *Practical research* (11th ed.). Upper Saddle River, NJ: Pearson.

Leerkes, E.M., Parade, S.H., & Gudmundson, J.A. (2011). Mothers' emotional reactions to crying pose risk for subsequent attachment insecurity. *Journal of Family Psychology, 25,* 635–643.

Lefkowitz, E.S., & Gillen, M.M. (2006). "Sex is just a normal part of life": Sexuality in emerging adulthood. In J.J. Arnett & J.L. Tanner (Eds.), *Emerging adults in America.* Washington, DC: American Psychological Association.

Leger, K.A., & others (2016, in press). Personality and stressor-related affect. *Journal of Personality and Social Psychology.*

Leggett, A., Burgard, S., & Zivin, K. (2016). The impact of sleep disturbance on the association between stressful life events and depressive symptoms. *Journals of Gerontology B: Psychological Sciences and Social Sciences, 71,* 118–128.

Lehman, E.B., & others (2010). Long-term stability of young children's eyewitness accuracy, suggestibility, and resistance to misinformation. *Journal of Applied Developmental Psychology, 31,* 145–154.

Lehman, H.C. (1960). The age decrement in out-standing scientific creativity. *American Psychologist, 15,* 128–134.

Lehmann, L.S. (2016, in press). How can we improve amniocentesis decision-making? *Israeli Journal of Health Policy Research.*

Lehr, C.A., Hanson, A., Sinclair, M.F., & Christenson, S.I. (2003). Moving beyond dropout prevention towards school completion. *School Psychology Review, 32,* 342–364.

Leiser, S.F., Miller, H.A., & Kaeberlein, M. (2016). The hypoxic response and aging. In M. Kaeberlein & G.M. Martin (Eds.), *Handbook of the biology of aging* (8th ed.). New York: Elsevier.

Lenhart, A. (2012). Teens, smartphones, and texting: Texting volume is up while the frequency of voice calling is down. Retrieved May 2, 2013, from http://pewinternet.org/~/medai/Files/Reorts/2012/PIP_Teens_Smartphones_and-Texting.pdf.

Lenhart, A. (2015a, April 9). *Teens, social media, and technology: Overview 2015.* Washington, DC: Pew Research Center.

Lenhart, A. (2015b, August 6). *Teens, technology, and friendship.* Washington, DC: Pew Research Center.

Leon, J., & others (2015). A combination of physical and cognitive exercise improves reaction time in persons 61-84 years old. *Journal of Aging and Physical Activity, 23,* 72–77.

Leone, J.E., Mullin, E.M., Maurer-Starks, S.S., & Rovito, M.J. (2014). The Adolescent Body Image Satisfaction Scale (ABISS) for males: Exploratory factor analysis and implications for strength and conditioning professionals. *Journal of Strength and Conditioning Research, 28,* 2657–2668.

Lepage, J.F., & others (2014). Brain morphology in children with 47, XYY syndrome: A voxel- and surface-based morphometric study. *Genes, Brain, and Behavior, 13,* 127–134.

Lerner, H.G. (1989). *The dance of intimacy.* New York: Harper & Row.

Lerner, R.M., Boyd, M., & Du, D. (2008). Adolescent development. In I.B. Weiner & C.B. Craighead (Eds.). *Encyclopedia of psychology* (4th ed). Hoboken, NJ: Wiley.

Lerner, R.M., Lerner, J.V., Bowers, E., & Geldhof, J. (2015). Positive youth development: A relational developmental systems model. In R.M. Lerner (Ed.), *Handbook of child psychology and developmental science* (7th ed.). New York: Wiley.

Lesaux, N.K., & Siegel, L.S. (2003). The development of reading in children who speak English as a second language. *Developmental Psychology, 39,* 1005–1019.

Leslie, S.J., Cimpian, A., Meyer, M., & Freeland, E. (2015). Expectations of brilliance underlie gender distributions across academic disciplines. *Science, 347,* 262–265.

Lethin, C., & others (2016). Formal support for informal caregivers to older persons with dementia through the course of the disease: An exploratory, cross-sectional study. *BMC Geriatrics, 16*(1), 32.

Leung, J.Y., Lam, H.S., Leung, G.M., & Schooling, C.M. (2016). Gestational age, birth-weight for gestational age, and childhood hospitalizations for asthma and other wheezing disorders. *Pediatric and Perinatal Epidemiology, 30,* 149–159.

Leung, R.C., & others (2016). The role of executive functions in social impairment in autism spectrum disorder. *Child Neuropsychology, 22,* 336–344.

Levelt, W.J.M. (1989). *Speaking: From intention to articulation.* Cambridge, MA: MIT Press.

Leventhal, T., Dupere, V., & Shuey, E. (2015). Children in neighborhoods. In R.M. Lerner (Ed.), *Handbook of child psychology and developmental science* (7th ed.). New York: Wiley.

Lever-Duffy, J., & McDonald, J. (2015). *Teaching and learning with technology* (5th ed.). Upper Saddle River, NJ: Pearson.

Levine, T.P., & others (2008). Effects of prenatal cocaine exposure on special education in school-aged children. *Pediatrics, 122,* e83–e91.

Levinson, D.J. (1978). *The seasons of a man's life.* New York: Knopf.

Levinson, D.J. (1996). *The seasons of a woman's life.* New York: Alfred Knopf.

Levy, M., & others (2016). Palliative care version 1.2016. *Journal of the National Comprehensive Cancer Network, 14,* 82–113.

Lewanda, A.F., & others (2016, in press). Preoperative evaluation and comprehensive risk assessment for children with Down syndrome. *Pediatric Anesthesia.*

Lewin, A., & others (2015). Strengthening positive coparenting in teen parents: A cultural adaptation of an evidence-based intervention. *Journal of Primary Prevention, 36,* 139–154.

Lewis, A.C. (2007). Looking beyond NCLB. *Phi Delta Kappan, 88,* 483–484.

Lewis, C., Hill, M., Skirton, H., & Chitty, L.S. (2012). Non-invasive prenatal diagnosis for fetal sex determination: Benefits and disadvantages from the service users' perspective. *European Journal of Genetics, 20*(11), 1127–1133.

Lewis, M. (2005). Selfhood. In B. Hopkins (Ed.), *The Cambridge encyclopedia of child development.* Cambridge, UK: Cambridge University Press.

Lewis, M. (2007). Early emotional development. In A. Slater & M. Lewis (Eds.), *Introduction to infant development.* Malden, MA: Blackwell.

Lewis, M. (2010). The emergence of consciousness and its role in human development. In W.F. Overton & R.M. Lerner (Eds.), *Handbook of life-span development.* New York: Wiley.

Lewis, M. (2014). *The rise of consciousness and the development of emotional life.* New York: Guilford.

Lewis, M. (2015). Emotional development and consciousness. In R.M. Lerner (Ed.), *Handbook of child psychology and developmental science* (7th ed.). New York: Wiley.

Lewis, M. (2016). Self-conscious emotions: Embarrassment, pride, shame, guilt, and hubris. In L.F. Barrett, M. Lewis, & J.M. Haviland-Jones (Eds.), *Handbook of emotion* (4th ed.). New York: Guilford.

Lewis, M., & Brooks-Gunn, J. (1979). *Social cognition and the acquisition of the self.* New York: Plenum.

Lewis, M., Feiring, C., & Rosenthal, S. (2000). Attachment over time. *Child Development, 71,* 707–720.

Lewis, R.B., Wheeler, J.J., & Carter, S.L. (2017). *REVEL for teaching students with special needs in general education* (9th ed.). Upper Saddle River, NJ: Pearson.

Lewis, T.L., & Maurer, D. (2005). Multiple sensitive periods in human visual development: Evidence from visually deprived children. *Developmental Psychobiology, 46,* 163–183.

Lewis, T.L., & Maurer, D. (2009). Effects of early pattern deprivation on visual development. *Optometry and Vision Science, 86,* 640–646.

Lewis-Morrarty, E., & others (2015). Infant attachment security and early childhood behavioral inhibition interact to predict adolescent social anxiety symptoms. *Child Development, 86,* 598–613.

Leyton, M., & Vezina, P. (2014). Dopamine ups and downs in vulnerability to addictions: A neurodevelopmental model. *Trends in Pharmacological Sciences, 35,* 268–276.

Li, J., & Prigerson, H.G. (2016). Assessment and associated features of prolonged grief disorder among Chinese bereaved individuals. *Comprehensive Psychiatry, 66,* 9–16.

Li, T., & Zhang, Y. (2015). Social network types and the health of older adults: Exploring reciprocal associations. *Social Science & Medicine, 130,* 59–68.

Li, W., Farkas, G., Duncan, G.J., Burchinal, M.R., & Vandell, D.L. (2013). Timing of high-quality child care and cognitive, language, and preacademic development. *Developmental Psychology, 49,* 1440–1451.

Li, X., & others (2015). Sonographic markers of fetal a-thalassemia major. *Journal of Ultrasound Medicine, 34,* 197–206.

Li, Y., & others (2015). Decreased resting-state connections within the visuospatial attention-related network in advanced aging. *Neuroscience Letters, 597,* 13–18.

Li, Z., Zhang, L., Li, H., Ye, R., Liu, J., & Ren, A. (2013). Maternal severe life events and risk of neural tube defects among rural Chinese. *Birth Defects Research A: Clinical and Molecular Teratology, 97,* 109–114.

Liang, W., & Chikritzhs, T. (2015). Age at first use of alcohol predicts the risk of heavy alcohol use in early adulthood: A longitudinal study in the United States. *International Journal on Drug Policy, 26,* 131–134.

Liang, Y.J., Xi, B., Song, A.Q., Liu, J.X., & Mi, J. (2012). Trends in general and abdominal obesity among Chinese children and adolescents, 1993–2009. *Pediatric Obesity, 7,* 355–364.

Liben, L.S. (1995). Psychology meets geography: Exploring the gender gap on the national geography bee. *Psychological Science Agenda, 8,* 8–9.

Liben, L.S., Bigler, R.S., & Hilliard, L.J. (2014). Gender development: From universality to individuality. In E.T. Gershoff, R.S. Mistry, & D.A. Crosby (Eds.), *Societal contexts of child development.* New York: Oxford University Press.

Libertus, K., & Needham, A. (2010). Teach to reach: The effects of active versus passive reading experiences on action and perception. *Vision Research, 50,* 2750–2757.

Lickliter, R., & Honeycutt, H. (2015). Biology, development, and human systems. In R.M. Lerner (Ed.), *Handbook of child psychology and developmental science* (7th ed.). New York: Wiley.

Liddon, N., & others (2016). Withdrawal as pregnancy prevention and associated risk factors among U.S. high school students: Findings from the 2011 National Youth Behavior Risk Survey. *Contraception, 93,* 126–132.

Lieberman, A.F., & Chu, A.T. (2016). Childhood exposure to interpersonal trauma. In D. Cicchetti (Ed.), *Developmental psychopathology* (3rd ed.). New York: Wiley.

Lieberman, P. (2016, in press). The evolution of language and thought. *Journal of Anthropological Studies.*

Lillard, A. (2006). Pretend play in toddlers. In C.A. Brownell & C.B. Kopp (Eds.), *Socioemotional development in the toddler year.* New York: Oxford University Press.

Lillard, A. (2015). The development of play. In R.M. Lerner (Ed.), *Handbook of child psychology and developmental science* (7th ed.). New York: Wiley.

Lillard, A.S., & Kavanaugh, R.D. (2014). The contribution of symbolic skills to the development of explicit theory of mind. *Child Development, 85,* 1535–1551.

Lim, K.T., & Yu, R. (2015). Aging and wisdom: Age-related changes in economic and social decision making. *Frontiers in Aging Neuroscience, 7,* 120.

Lin, F.R. (2011). Hearing loss and cognition among older adults in the United States. *Journals of Gerontology A: Biological Sciences and Medical Sciences, 66,* 1131–1136.

Lin, F.R., Thorpe, R., Gordon-Salant, S., & Ferrucci, L. (2011). Hearing loss prevalence and risk factors among older adults in the United States. *Journals of Gerontology A: Biological Sciences and Medical Sciences.* doi: 10.1093/gerona/glr002

Lin, H.W., Hsu, H.C., & Chang, M.C. (2011). Gender differences in the association between stress trajectories and depressive symptoms among middle aged and older adults in Taiwan. *Journal of Women and Aging, 23,* 233–245.

Lin, L.Y., & others (2015). Effects of television exposure on developmental skills of young children. *Infant Behavior and Development, 38,* 20–26.

Lindau, S.T., & others (2007). A study of sexuality and health among older adults in the United States. *New England Journal of Medicine, 357,* 162–174.

Lindberg, S.M., Hyde, J.S., Petersen, J.L., & Lin, M.C. (2010). New trends in gender and mathematics performance: A meta-analysis. *Psychological Bulletin, 136,* 1123–1135.

Lindblad, F., & Hjern, A. (2010). ADHD after fetal exposure to maternal smoking. *Nicotine and Tobacco Research, 12,* 408–415.

Lindholm, M.E., & others (2014). An integrative analysis reveals coordinated reprogramming of the epigenome and the transcriptome in human skeletal muscle after training. *Epigenetics, 9,* 1557–1569.

Lindsay, M.K., & Burnett, E. (2013). The use of narcotics and street drugs during pregnancy. *Clinical Obstetrics and Gynecology, 56,* 133–141.

Lindvall, O. (2016). Clinical translation of stem cell transplantation in Parkinson's disease. *Journal of Internal Medicine, 279,* 30–40.

Lindwall, M., & others (2012). Dynamic associations of change in physical activity and change in cognitive function: Coordinated analyses across four studies with up to 21 years of longitudinal data. *Journal of Aging Research, 493598.*

Ling, J., Robbins, L.B., & Wen, F. (2016). Interventions to prevent and manage overweight or obesity in preschool children; A systematic review. *International Journal of Nursing Studies, 53,* 270–289.

Lipowski, M., Lipowska, M., Jochimek, M., & Krokosz, D. (2016). Resilience as a factor protecting youths from risky behavior: Moderating effects of gender and sport. *European Journal of Sport Science, 16,* 246–255.

Lippa, R.A. (2013). Men and women with bisexual identities show bisexual patterns of sexual attraction to male and female "swimsuit models." *Archives of Sexual Behavior, 42,* 187–196.

Lisha, N.E., & others (2012). Evaluation of the psychometric properties of the Revised Inventory of the Dimensions of Emerging Adulthood (IDEA-R) in a sample of continuation high school students. *Evaluation & the Health Professions, 37,* 156–177.

List, J., Ott, S., Bukowski, M., Lindenberg, R., & Floel, A. (2015). Cognitive function and brain structure after recurrent mild traumatic brain injuries in young-to-middle-aged adults. *Frontiers in Human Neuroscience, 9,* 228.

Litz, J., Snyder, W., & Pater, J. (Eds.) (2016). *Oxford handbook of developmental linguistics.* New York: Oxford University Press.

Liu, H., & others (2016, in press). A voxel-based morphometric study of age- and sex-related changes in white matter volume in the normal aging brain. *Neuropsychiatric Disease and Treatment.*

Liu, R., Chao, M.T., Jostad-Laswell, A., & Duncan, L.G. (2016, in press). Does CenteringPregnancy group prenatal care affect the birth experience of underserved women? A mixed methods analysis. *Journal of Immigrant and Minority Health.*

Liu, X., & others (2015). Folic acid supplementation, dietary folate intake, and risk of preterm birth in China. *European Journal of Nutrition, 103,* 501–508.

Lively, W., & Bromley, D. (1973). *Person perception in childhood and adolescence.* New York: Wiley.

Livingston, G. (2014, June 5). *Growing number of dads home with the kids.* Washington, DC: Pew Research Center.

Llewellyn, C.H., & others (2014). Satiety mechanisms in genetic risk for obesity. *JAMA Pediatrics, 168,* 338–344.

Lloyd, J.W., & others (2015). *Evidence-based reading instruction for ALL learners.* Upper Saddle River, NJ: Pearson.

Lo, C.C., Cheng, T.C., & Simpson, G.M. (2016). Marital status and work-related health limitation: A longitudinal study of young adult and middle-aged Americans. *International Journal of Public Health, 61,* 91–100.

Lo, J.C., & others (2016). Self-reported sleep duration and cognitive performance in older adults: A systematic review and meta-analysis. *Sleep Medicine, 17,* 87–98.

Locher, J.L., & others (2016, in press). Caloric restriction in overweight older adults: Do benefits exceed potential risks? *Experimental Gerontology.*

Lock, M. (1998). Menopause: Lessons from anthropology. *Psychosomatic Medicine, 60,* 410–419.

Lojko, D., & others (2015). Atypical features in depression: Association with obesity and biopolar disorder. *Journal of Affective Disorders, 185,* 75–80.

Lonigan, C.J. (2015). Early literacy. In R.M. Lerner (Ed.), *Handbook of child psychology and developmental science* (7th ed.). New York: Wiley.

Loprinzi, P.D. (2015a). Dose-response association of moderate-to-vigorous physical activity with cardiovascular biomarkers and all-cause mortality: Considerations of individual sports, exercise, and recreational physical activities. *Preventive Medicine, 81,* 73–77.

Loprinzi, P.D. (2015b). Leisure-time screen-based sedentary behavior and leukocyte telomere length: Implications for a new leisure-time screen-based sedentary behavior mechanism. *Mayo Clinic Proceedings, 90,* 786–790.

Loprinzi, P.D., & Loenneke, J.P. (2016). Lower extremity muscular strength and leukocyte telomere length: Implications of muscular strength in attenuating age-related chronic disease. *Journal of Physical Activity and Health, 13,* 454–457.

Lorenz, K.Z. (1965). *Evolution and the modification of behavior.* The University of Chicago Press.

Loucks, J., & Sommerville, J.A. (2012). The role of motor experience in understanding action function: The case of precision grip. *Child Development, 83,* 801–809.

Love, J.M., Chazan-Cohen, R., Raikes, H., & Brooks-Gunn, J. (2013). What makes a difference: Early Head Start evaluation findings in a developmental context. *Monographs of the Society for Research in Child Development, 78,* 1–173.

Low, S., & Shortt, J.W. (2016, in press). Family, peer, and pubertal determinants of dating involvement in adolescence. *Journal of Research in Adolescence.*

Lowe, K., & Dotterer, A.M. (2013). Parental monitoring, parental warmth, and minority youths' academic outcomes: Exploring the integrative model of parenting. *Journal of Youth and Adolescence, 42,* 1413–1425.

Lowson, K., Offer, C., Watson, J., McGuire, B., & Renfrew, M.J. (2016, in press). The economic benefits of increasing kangaroo skin-to-skin care and breastfeeding in neonatal units: Analysis of a pragmatic intervention in clinical practice. *International Journal of Breastfeeding.*

Lu, P.H., & others (2011). Age-related slowing in cognitive processing speed is associated with myelin integrity in a very healthy elderly sample. *Journal of Clinical and Experimental Neuropsychology, 33,* 1059–1068.

Lucas, R.E., Clark, A.E., Yannis, G., & Diener, E. (2004). Unemployment alters the setpoint for life satisfaction. *Psychological Science, 15,* 8–13.

Lucassen, P., & others (2015). Regulation of adult neurogenesis and plasticity by (early) stress, glucocorticoids, and inflammation. *Cold Spring Harbor Perspectives in Biology, 7*(9), a021303.

Lucchetti, G., Lucchetti, A.L., & Koenig, H.G. (2011). Impact of spirituality/religiosity on mortality: Comparison with other health interventions. *Explore, 7,* 234–238.

Luchetti, M., Terracciano, A., Stephan, Y., & Sutin, A.R. (2016, in press). Personality and cognitive decline in older adults: Data from a longitudinal sample and meta-analysis. *Journals of Gerontology B: Psychological Sciences and Social Sciences.*

Luders, E., & others (2004). Gender differences in cortical complexity. *Nature Neuroscience, 1,* 799–800.

Luecken, L.J., & others (2016). A longitudinal study of the effects of child-reported warmth on cortisol stress response 15 years after parental divorce. *Psychosomatic Medicine, 78,* 163–170.

Luiselli, J.K. (Ed.) (2014). *Children and youth with autism spectrum disorder (ASD).* New York: Oxford University Press.

Lukowski, A.F., & Bauer, P. (2014). Long-term memory in infancy and early childhood. In P. Bauer & R. Fivush (Eds.), *Wiley-Blackwell handbook of children's memory.* New York: Wiley.

Lum, H.D., Sudore, R.L., & Bekelman, D.B. (2015). Advance care planning in the elderly. *Medical Clinics of North America, 99,* 391–403.

Lumpkin, A. (2014). *Introduction to physical education, exercise science, and sport studies* (9th ed.). New York: McGraw-Hill.

Luna, B., & others (2015). An integrative model of the maturation of cognitive control. *Annual Review of Neuroscience, 38,* 151–170.

Lund, H.G., Reider, B.D., Whiting, A.B., & Prichard, J.R. (2010). Sleep patterns and predictors of disturbed sleep in a large population of college students. *Journal of Adolescent Health, 46,* 124–132.

Lundin, A., Falkstedt, D., Lundberg, I., & Hemmingsson, T. (2014). Unemployment and coronary heart disease among middle-aged men in Sweden: 39,243 men followed for 8 years. *Occupational and Environmental Medicine, 71,* 183–188.

Lunenfeld, B., & others (2015). Recommendations on the diagnosis, treatment, and monitoring of hypogonadism in men. *Aging Male, 18,* 5–15.

Luo, L., & Craik, F.I.M. (2008). Aging and memory: A cognitive approach. *Canadian Journal of Psychology, 53,* 346–353.

Luo, Y., Hawkley, L.C., Waite, L.J., & Caccioppo, J.T. (2012). Loneliness, health, and mortality in old age: A national longitudinal study. *Social Science and Medicine, 74,* 907–914.

Luong, G., Rauers, A., & Fingerman, K.L. (2015). The multi-faceted nature of late-life socialization: Older adults as agents and targets of socialization. In J.E. Grusec & P.D. Hastings (Eds.), *Handbook of socialization* (2nd ed.). New York: Guilford.

Lupsa, B.C., & Insogna, K. (2015). Bone health and osteoporosis. *Endocrinology and Metabolism Clinics of North America, 44,* 517–530.

Luria, A., & Herzog, E. (1985, April). *Gender segregation across and within settings.* Paper presented at the biennial meeting of the Society for Research in Child Development, Toronto.

Lushington, K., Pamula, Y., Martin, A.J., & Kennedy, J.D. (2014). Developmental changes in sleep. In A.R. Wolfson & H.E. Montgomery-Downs (Eds.), *Oxford handbook of infant, child, and adolescent sleep and behavior.* New York: Oxford University Press.

Lustig, C., & Lin, Z. (2016). Memory: Behavior and neural basis. In K.W. Schaie & S.L. Willis (Eds.), *Handbook of the psychology of aging* (8th ed.). New York: Elsevier.

Luszcz, M. (2011). Executive functioning and cognitive aging. In K.W. Schaie & S.L. Willis (Eds.), *Handbook of the psychology of aging* (7th ed.). New York: Elsevier.

Luyster, F.S., & others (2012). Sleep: A health imperative. *Sleep, 35,* 727–734.

Lynch, M. (2015). *Call to teach.* Upper Saddle River, NJ: Pearson.

Lyon, T.D., & Flavell, J.H. (1993). Young children's understanding of forgetting over time. *Child Development, 64,* 789–800.

Lyons, D.M., & others (2010). Stress coping stimulates hippocampal neurogenesis in adult monkeys. *Proceedings of the National Academy of Sciences U.S.A., 107,* 14823–14827.

Lyons, H., Manning, W.D., Longmore, M.A., & Giordano, P.C. (2015). Gender and casual sexual activity from adolescence to emerging adulthood: Social and life course correlates. *Journal of Sex Research, 52,* 543–557.

M

Ma, J., & others (2016). Mid-adulthood cardio-metabolic risk factor profiles of sarcopenic obesity. *Obesity, 24,* 526–534.

Ma, Y., & others (2015). Genetic variants modify the effect of age on APOE methylation in the Genetics of Lipid Lowering Drugs and Diet Network Study, *14,* 49–59.

Maalouf, F.T., & Brent, D.A. (2012). Child and adolescent depression intervention overview: What works for whom and how well? *Child and Adolescent Psychiatry Clinics of North America, 21,* 299–312.

Maccallum, F., & Bryant, R.A. (2013). A cognitive attachment model of prolonged grief: Integrating attachments, memory, and identity. *Clinical Psychology Review, 33,* 713–727.

Maccalum, F., Sawday, S., Rinck, M., & Bryant, R.A. (2015). The push and pull of grief: Approach and avoidance in bereavement. *Journal of Behavior Therapy and Experimental Psychiatry, 48,*105–109.

Maccoby, E.E. (1984). Middle childhood in the context of the family. In *Development during middle childhood.* Washington, DC: National Academy Press.

Maccoby, E.E. (1998). *The two sexes: Growing up apart, coming together.* Cambridge, MA: Harvard University Press.

Maccoby, E.E. (2002). Gender and group processes. *Current Directions in Psychological Science, 11,* 54–58.

Maccoby, E.E. (2015). Historical overview of socialization research and theory. In J.E. Grusec & P.D. Hastings (Eds.), *Handbook of socialization* (2nd ed.). New York: Guilford.

Maccoby, E.E., & Martin, J.A. (1983). Socialization in the context of the family: Parent-child interaction. In P.H. Mussen (Ed.), *Handbook of child psychology* (4th ed., Vol. 4). New York: Wiley.

MacDonald, S.W., DeCarlo, C.A., & Dixon, R.A. (2011). Linking biological and cognitive aging: Toward improving characterizations of developmental time. *Journals of Gerontology B: Psychological Sciences and Social Sciences, 66B*(Suppl. 1), i59–i70.

MacDonald, S.W.S., Hultch, D., Strauss, E., & Dixon, R. (2003). Age-related slowing of digit symbol substitution revisited: What do longitudinal age changes reflect? *Journals of Gerontology B: Psychological Sciences and Social Sciences, 58B,* P187–P184.

MacDonald, S.W.S., & Stawski, R.S. (2015). Intraindividual variability—an indicator of vulnerability or resilience in adult development and aging? In M. Diehl, I. Hooker, & M. Sliwinski (Eds.), *Handbook of intraindividual variability across the life span.* New York: Routledge.

MacDonald, S.W.S., & Stawski, R.S. (2016). Methodological perspectives for the psychology of aging in a lifespan context. In K.W. Schaie & S.L. Willis (Eds.), *Handbook of the psychology of aging* (8th ed.). New York: Elsevier.

MacDougall, B.J., Robinson, J.D., Kappus, L., Sudikoff, S.N., & Greer, D.M. (2014). Simulation-based training in brain death determination. *Neurocritical Care, 21,* 383–391.

Mace, S.E. (2016). Global threats to child safety. *Pediatric Clinics of North America, 63,* 19–35.

MacFarlane, J.A. (1975). Olfaction in the development of social preferences in the human neonate. In *Parent-infant interaction.* Ciba Foundation Symposium No. 33. Amsterdam: Elsevier.

MacGeorge, E.L. (2003). Gender differences in attributions and emotions in helping contexts. *Sex Roles, 48,* 175–182.

Machado, B., & others (2014). Risk factors and antecedent life events in the development of anorexia nervosa: A Portuguese case-control study. *European Eating Disorders Review, 22,* 243–251.

Machielse, A. (2015). The heterogeneity of socially isolated older adults: A social isolation typology. *Journal of Gerontological Social Work, 58,* 338–356.

Mackin, R.S., & others (2014). Association of age at depression onset with cognitive functioning in individuals with late-life depression and executive dysfunction. *American Journal of Geriatric Psychiatry, 22,* 1633–1641.

Macleod, A.D. (2015). Euthanasia and physician-assisted dying: Editorial comment and reply to the Waikato GP survey findings by Dr. Havill. *New Zealand Medical Journal, 128,* 9–11.

MacWhinney, B. (2015). Language development. In R.M. Lerner (Ed.), *Handbook of child psychology and developmental science* (7th ed.). New York: Wiley.

Madden, D.J., & others (1999). Aging and recognition memory: Changes in regional cerebral blood flow associated with components of reaction time distributions. *Journal of Cognitive Neuroscience, II,* 511–520.

Mader, S.S., & Windelspecht, M. (2016). *Human biology* (14th ed.). New York: McGraw-Hill.

Madill, A. (2012). Interviews and interviewing techniques. In H. Cooper (Ed.), *APA handbook of research methods in psychology.* Washington, DC: American Psychological Association.

Maercker, A., & Lalor, J. (2012). Diagnostic and clinical considerations in prolonged grief disorder. *Dialogues in Clinical Neuroscience, 14,* 167–176.

Maher, J.P., & others (2013). A daily analysis of physical activity and satisfaction with life in emerging adults. *Health Psychology, 32,* 647–656.

Maher, J.P., Pincus, A.L., Ram, N., & Conroy, D.E. (2015). Daily physical activity and life satisfaction across adulthood. *Developmental Psychology, 51,* 1407–1419.

Maiese, K. (2015). Stem cell guidance through the mechanistic target of rapamycin. *World Journal of Stem Cells, 26,* 999–1009.

Maillard, P., & others (2012). Effects of systolic blood pressure on white-matter integrity in young adults in the Framington Heart Study: A cross-sectional study. *Lancet Neurology, 11,* 1039–1047.

Malamitsi-Puchner, A., & Boutsikou, T. (2006). Adolescent pregnancy and perinatal outcome. *Pediatric Endocrinology Review, 3*(1, Suppl.), S170–S171.

Malinger, G., & Lerman-Sagie, T. (2015). Re: Additional value of fetal magnetic resonance imaging in the prenatal diagnosis of central nervous system anomalies: A systematic review of the literature. *Ultrasound in Obstetrics and Gynecology, 45,* 236–237.

Malmberg, L.E., & others (2016, in press). The influence of mothers' and fathers' sensitivity in the first year of life on children's cognitive outcomes at 18 and 36 months. *Child Care, Health, and Development.*

Maloy, R.W., Verock, R-E., Edwards, S.A., & Woolf, B.P. (2017). *Transforming learning with new technologies* (3rd ed.). Upper Saddle River, NJ: Pearson.

Mandara, J. (2006). The impact of family functioning on African American males' academic achievement: A review and clarification of the empirical literature. *Teachers College Record, 108,* 206–233.

Mandelbrot, L., Duro, D., Belissa, E., & Peytavin, G. (2015). Placental transfer or rilpivirine in an ex vivo human cotyledon perfusion model. *Antimicrobiological Agents and Chemotherapy, 59,* 2901–2903.

Mandler, J. (2000). Unpublished review of J.W. Santrock's *Life-Span Development,* 8th ed. (New York: McGraw-Hill).

Mandler, J.M. (2004). *The foundations of mind.* New York: Oxford University Press.

Mandler, J.M. (2009). Conceptual categorization. In D.H. Rakison & L.M. Oakes (Eds.), *Early category and concept development.* New York: Oxford University Press.

Mandler, J.M., & DeLoache, J. (2012). The beginnings of conceptual development. In S. Pauen & M. Bornstein (Eds.), *Early child development and later outcome.* New York: Cambridge University Press.

Mandler, J.M., & McDonough, L. (1993). Concept formation in infancy. *Cognitive Development, 8,* 291–318.

Manenti, R., Cotelli, M., & Miniussi, C. (2011). Successful physiological aging and episodic memory: A brain stimulation study. *Behavioral Brain Research, 216,* 153–158.

Manlove, J., Fish, H., & Moore, K.A. (2015). Programs to improve adolescent sexual and reproductive health in the U.S.: A review of the evidence. *Adolescent Health, Medicine, and Therapeutics, 6,* 47–79.

Mann, F.D., & others (2015). Person × environment interactions on adolescent delinquency:

Sensation seeking, peer deviance, and parental monitoring. *Personality and Individual Differences, 76,* 129–134.

Mansikkamaki, K., & others (2016). Hot flashes among aging women: A 4-year follow-up study to a randomized controlled exercise trial. *Maturitas, 88,* 84–89.

Mantua, J., Baran, B., & Spencer, R.M. (2016). Sleep benefits consolidation of visuo-motor adaptation learning in older adults. *Experimental Brain Research, 234,* 587–595.

Manuck, S.B., & McCaffery, J.M. (2014). Gene-environment interaction. *Annual Review of Psychology* (Vol. 65). Palo Alto, CA: Annual Reviews.

Manzanares, S., & others (2016, in press). Accuracy of fetal sex determination on ultrasound examination in the first trimester of pregnancy. *Journal of Clinical Ultrasound.*

Marcdante, K., & Kliegman, R.M. (2015). *Nelson essentials of pediatrics* (7th ed.). New York: Elsevier.

Marcell, J.J. (2003). Sarcopenia: Causes, consequences, and preventions. *Journals of Gerontology A: Biological Sciences and Medical Sciences,* M911–M916.

March of Dimes (2016). *Multiple pregnancy and birth: Considering fertility treatments.* White Plains, NY: Author.

Marcia, J.E. (1980). Ego identity development. In J. Adelson (Ed.), *Handbook of adolescent psychology.* New York: Wiley.

Marcia, J.E. (1994). The empirical study of ego identity. In H.A. Bosma, T.L.G. Graafsma, H.D. Grotevant, & D.J. De Levita (Eds.), *Identity and development.* Newbury Park, CA: Sage.

Marcia, J.E. (2002). Identity and psychosocial development in adulthood. *Identity: An International Journal of Theory and Research, 2,* 7–28.

Marcovitch, S., & others (2015). A longitudinal assessment of the relation between executive function and theory of mind at 3, 4, and 5 years. *Cognitive Development, 33,* 40–55.

Mares, M-L., & Pan, Z. (2013). Effects of *Sesame Street*: A meta-analysis of children's learning in 15 countries. *Journal of Applied Developmental Psychology, 34,* 140–151.

Marino, E.N., & Fromme, K. (2016). Early onset drinking predicts greater level but not growth of alcohol-induced blackouts beyond the effect of binge drinking during emerging adulthood. *Alcoholism, Clinical and Experimental Research, 40,* 599–605.

Mark, K.S., & others (2015). Knowledge, attitudes, and practice of electronic cigarette use among pregnant women. *Journal of Addiction Medicine, 9,* 266–272.

Markant, J.C., & Thomas, K.M. (2013). Postnatal brain development. In P.D. Zelazo (Ed.), *Handbook of developmental psychology.* New York: Wiley.

Markert, L., & others (2016). Renaissance of criticism on the concept of brain death—the role of legal medicine in the context of interdisciplinary discussion. *International Journal of Legal Medicine, 130,* 587–595.

Markham, C.M., & others (2010). Connectedness as a predictor of sexual and reproductive health outcomes for youth. *Journal of Adolescent Health, 46*(3, Suppl.), S23–S41.

Markovic, G., Sarabon, N., Greblo, Z., & Krizanic, V. (2015). Effects of feedback-based balance and core resistance training vs. Pilates training on balance and muscle function in older women:

A randomized-controlled task. *Archives of Gerontology and Geriatrics, 61,* 117–123.

Marks, A.K., Ejesi, K., McCullough, M.B., & Garcia Coll, C. (2015). The implications for discrimination in child and adolescent development. In R.M. Lerner (Ed.), *Handbook of child psychology and developmental science* (7th ed.). New York; Wiley.

Marques, A.H., Biorke-Monsen, A.L., Teixeira, A.L., & Silverman, M.N. (2015). Maternal stress, nutrition, and physical activity: Impact on immune function, CNS development, and psychopathology. *Brain Research, 1617,* 28–46.

Marra, K.V., & others (2016). Care of older adults: Role of primary care physicians in the treatment of cataracts and macular degeneration. *Journal of American Geriatrics Society, 64,* 369–377.

Marsh, H., Ellis, L., & Craven, R. (2002). How do preschool children feel about themselves? Unraveling measurement and multidimensional self-concept structure. *Developmental Psychology, 38,* 376–393.

Marsh, H.W., Martin, A.J., & Xu, M. (2012). Self-concept: Synergy of theory, mind, and application. In K.R. Harris, S. Graham, & T. Urdan (Eds.), *APA educational psychology handbook.* Washington, DC: American Psychological Association.

Marshall, S.L., Parker, P.D., Ciarrochi, J., & Heaven, P.C.L. (2014). Is self-esteem a cause or consequence of social support? A 4-year longitudinal study. *Child Development, 85,* 1275–1291.

Martin, A.J., & others (2016). Personal best (PB) goal structure, individual PB goals, engagement, and achievement: A study of Chinese- and English-speaking students in Australian schools. *British Journal of Educational Psychology, 86,* 75–91.

Martin, C.L., & Ruble, D.N. (2010). Patterns of gender development. *Annual Review of Psychology* (Vol. 61). Palo Alto, CA: Annual Reviews.

Martin, C.L., & others (2013). The role of sex of peers and gender-typed activities in young children's peer affiliative networks: A longitudinal analysis of selection and influence. *Child Development, 84,* 921–937.

Martin, J.A., & others (2015). Births: Final data for 2013. *National Vital Statistics Reports, 54, 1,* 1–65.

Martin, L.R., Friedman, H.S., & Schwartz, J.E. (2007). Personality and mortality risk across the life span: The importance of conscientiousness as a biopsychosocial attribute. *Health Psychology, 26,* 428–436.

Marvin, R.S., Britner, P.A., & Russell, B.S. (2016). Normative development: The ontogeny of attachment in childhood. In J. Cassidy & P.R. Shaver (Eds.), *Handbook of attachment* (3rd ed.). New York: Guilford.

Mary, A., & others (2016). Executive and attentional contributions to theory of mind deficit in attention deficit/hyperactivity disorder (ADHD). *Child Neuropsychology, 22,* 345–365.

Masapollo, M., Polka, L., & Menard, L. (2016). When infants talk, infants listen: Pre-babbling infants prefer listening to speech with infant vocal properties. *Developmental Science, 19,* 318–328.

Mascolo, M.F., & Fischer, K. (2007). The co-development of self and socio-moral emotions during the toddler years. In C.A. Brownell & C.B. Kopp (Eds.), *Transitions in early development.* New York: Guilford.

Mascalo, M.F., & Fischer, K.W. (2010). The dynamic development of thinking, feeling, and acting over the life span. In W.F. Overton & R.M. Lerner (Eds.), *Handbook of life-span development* (Vol. 1). New York: Wiley.

Mason, J., Wheeler, W., & Brown, M.J. (2015). The economic burden of exposure to secondhand smoke for child and adult never smokers residing in U.S. public housing. *Public Health Reports, 130,* 230–244.

Masten, A.S. (2006). Developmental psychopathology: Pathways to the future. *International Journal of Behavioral Development, 31,* 46–53.

Masten, A.S. (2012). Faculty profile: Ann Masten. *The Institute of Child Development, further developments.* Minneapolis: School of Education.

Masten, A.S. (2013). Risk and resilience in development. In P.D. Zelazo (Ed.), *Oxford handbook of developmental psychology.* New York: Oxford University Press.

Masten, A.S. (2014). *Ordinary magic.* New York: Guilford.

Masten, A.S. (2015). Pathways to integrated resilience science. *Psychological Inquiry, 27,* 187–196.

Masten, A.S., Burt, K., & Coatsworth, J.D. (2006). Competence and psychopathology in development. In D. Cicchetti & D. Cohen (Eds.), *Developmental psychopathology: Risk, disorder, and psychopathology* (2nd ed., Vol. 3). New York: Wiley.

Masten, A.S., & Cicchetti, D. (2016). Resilience in development: Progress and transformation. In D. Cicchetti (Ed.), *Developmental psychopathology* (3rd ed.). New York: Wiley.

Masten, A.S., Fiat, A.E., Labella, M.H., & Strack, R. (2016, in press). Educating homeless and highly mobile students: Implications of research on risk and resilience. *School Psychology Review.*

Masten, A.S., & Monn, A.R. (2015). Child and family resilience: A call for integrated science, practice, and professional training. *Family Relations, 64,* 5–21.

Masten, A.S., Narayan, A.J., Silverman, W.K., & Osofsky, J.D. (2015). Children in war and disaster. In R.M. Lerner (Ed.), *Handbook of child psychology and developmental science* (7th ed.). New York: Wiley.

Masten, A.S., & others (2008). School success in motion: Protective factors for academic achievement in homeless and highly mobile children in Minneapolis. *Center for Urban and Regional Affairs Reporter, 38,* 3–12.

Mastin, J.D., & Vogt, P. (2016, in press). Infant engagement and early vocabulary development: A naturalistic observation study of Mozambican infants from 1;1 to 2;1. *Journal of Child Language.*

Mastroeni, D., & others (2015). Novel antioxidants protect mitochondria from the effects of oligomeric amyloid beta and contribute to the maintenance of epigenome function. *ACS Chemical Neuroscience, 6,* 588–598.

Masumoto, D., & Juang, L. (2017). *Culture and psychology* (6th ed.). Boston: Cengage.

Mather, M. (2012). The emotion paradox in the human brain. *Annals of the New York Academy of Sciences, 1251,* 33–49.

Mathews, B., Lee, X., & Norman, R.E. (2016). Impact of a new mandatory reporting law on reporting and identification of child abuse: A seven-year time trend analysis. *Child Abuse and Neglect, 56,* 62–79.

Matias, M., & Fontaine, M. (2015). Coping with work and family: How do dual-earners interact? *Scandinavian Journal of Psychology, 56,* 212–222.

Matlin, M.W. (2012). *The psychology of women* (7th ed.). Boston: Cengage.

Matlow, J.N., Jubetsky, A., Aleksa, K., Berger, H., & Koren, G. (2013). The transfer of ethyl glucuronide across the dually perfused human placenta. *Placenta, 34*(4), 369–373.

Matos, K. (2015). *Modern families: Same- and different-sex couples negotiating at home.* New York: Families and Work Institute.

Matsushima, S., & Sadoshima, J. (2015). The role of sirtuins in heart disease. *American Journal of Physiology: Heart and Circulatory Physiology, 309,* H1375–H1389.

Maurer, D., & Lewis, T.L. (2013). Sensitive periods in visual development. In P.D. Zelazo (Ed.), *Oxford handbook of developmental psychology.* New York: Oxford University Press.

Maurer, D., Lewis, T.L., Brent, H.P., & Levin, A.V. (1999). Rapid improvement in the acuity of infants after visual input. *Science, 286,* 108–110.

Maurer, D., Mondloch, C.J., & Leis, T.L. (2007). Effects of early visual deprivation on perceptual and cognitive development. In C. von Hofsten & K. Rosander (Eds.), *Progress in Brain Research, 164,* 87–104.

Mayas, J., Parmentier, F.B., Andres, P., & Ballesteros, S. (2014). Plasticity of attentional functions in older adults after non-action video game training: A randomized controlled trial. *PLoS One, 9,* e92269.

Mayer, K.D., & Zhang, L. (2009). Short-and long-term effects of cocaine abuse during pregnancy on heart development. *Therapeutic Advances in Cardiovascular Disease, 3,* 7–16.

Mayo Clinic (2016). *Male hypogonadism.* Rochester, MN: Mayo Clinic.

Mayo Clinic (2016). Pregnancy and fish: *What's safe to eat?* Retrieved January 10, 2016, from www.mayoclinic.com/health/pregnancy-and-fish/PR00158

Mazul, M.C., Salm Ward, T.C., & Ngui, E.M. (2016, in press). Anatomy of good prenatal care: Perspectives of low income African-American women on barriers and facilitators to prenatal care. *Journal of Racial and Ethnic Health Disparities.*

Mbulo, L., & others (2016, in press). Secondhand smoke exposure at home among one billion children in 21 countries: Findings from the Global Adult Tobacco Survey (GATS). *Tobacco Control.*

McAdams, D.P., Josselson, R., & Lieblich, A. (2006). *Identity and story: Creating self in narrative.* Washington, DC: American Psychological Association.

McAdams, D.P., & Olson, B.D. (2010). Personality development: Continuity and change over the life course. *Annual Review of Psychology* (Vol. 61). Palo Alto, CA: Annual Reviews.

McAdams, D.P., & Zapata-Gietl, C. (2015). Three strands of identity development across the human life cource: Reading Erik Erikson in full. In K.C. McLean & M. Syed (Eds.), *Oxford handbook of identity development.* New York: Oxford University Press.

McAdams, T.A., & others (2015). The relationship between parental depressive symptoms and offspring psychopathology: Evidence from a children-of-twins study and an adoption study. *Psychological Medicine, 45,* 2383–2394.

McBride Murry, V., Hill, N.E., Witherspoon, D., Berkel, C., & Bartz, D. (2015). Children in diverse social contexts. In R.M. Lerner (Ed.), *Handbook of* child psychology and developmental science (7th ed.). New York: Wiley.

McCabe, K.O., & Fleeson, W. (2016). Are traits useful? Explaining trait manifestations as tools in the pursuit of goals. *Journal of Personality and Social Psychology, 110,* 287–301.

McCartney, K. (2003, July 16). Interview with Kathleen McCartney in A. Bucuvalas, "Child care and behavior." *HGSE News,* pp. 1–4. Cambridge, MA: Harvard Graduate School of Education.

McCartney, K., Dearing, E., Taylor, B.A., & Bub, K.L. (2007). Quality child care supports the achievement of low-income children: Direct and indirect pathways through caregiving and the home environment. *Journal of Applied Developmental Psychology, 28,* 411–426.

McCartney, K., & Yoshikawa, H. (Eds.) (2015). *Framing the future for America's children: In honor of 40 years of the Children's Defense Fund.* Cambridge, MA: Harvard University Press.

McClellan, M.D. (2004, February 9). Captain Fantastic: The interview. *Celtic Nation,* pp. 1–9.

McClelland, M.M., Acock, A.C., Piccinin, A., Rhea, S.A., & Stallings, M.C. (2013). Relations between preschool attention span persistence and age 25 educational outcomes. *Early Childhood Research Quarterly, 28,* 314–324.

McCormack, L.A., & others (2011). Weight-related teasing in a racially diverse sample of sixth-grade children. *Journal of the American Dietetic Association, 111,* 431–436.

McCormack, T., Hoerl, C., & Butterfill, C. (2012). *Tool use and causal cognition.* New York: Oxford University Press.

McCormick, C.B., Dimmitt, C., & Sullivan, F.R. (2013). Metacognition, learning, and instruction. In I.B. Weiner & others (Eds.), *Handbook of psychology* (2nd ed., Vol. 7). New York: Wiley.

McCoy, D.C., & Raver, C.C. (2011). Caregiver emotional expressiveness, child emotion regulation, and child behavior problems among Head Start families. *Social Development, 20,* 741–761.

McCoy, K.P., George, M.R., Cummings, E.M., & Davies, P.T. (2013). Constructive and destructive marital conflict, parenting, and children's school and social adjustment. *Social Development, 20,* 641–662.

McCrae, R.R., & Costa, P.T. (2006). Cross-cultural perspectives on adult personality trait development. In D.K. Mroczek & T.D. Little (Eds.). *Handbook of personality development.* Mahwah, NJ: Erlbaum.

McCrae, R.R., Gaines, J.F., & Wellington, M.A. (2013). The five-factor model in fact and fiction. In I.B. Weiner & others (Eds.), *Handbook of psychology* (2nd ed., Vol. 5). New York: Wiley.

McDonald, J.A., Argotsinger, B., Mojarro, O., Rochar, R., & Amalya, A. (2015). First trimester initiation of prenatal care in the U.S.–Mexico border. *Medical Care, 53,* 700–707.

McDuffie, A., Thurman, A.J., Hagerman, R.J., & Abbeduto, L. (2015). Symptoms of autism in males with fragile X syndrome: A comparison to nonsyndromic ASD using current ADI-R scores. *Journal of Autism and Developmental Disorders, 45,* 1925–1937.

McElhaney, K.B., & Allen, J.P. (2012). Sociocultural perspectives on adolescent autonomy. In P.K. Kreig, M.S. Schulz, & S.T. Hauser (Eds.), *Adolescence and beyond.* New York: Oxford University Press.

McElvaney, R., Greene, S., & Hogan, D. (2014). To tell or not to tell? Factors influencing young people's informal disclosures of child sexual abuse. *Journal of Interpersonal Violence, 29,* 928–947.

McGarry, J., Kim, H., Sheng, X., Egger, M., & Baksh, L. (2009). Postpartum depression and help-seeking behavior. *Journal of Midwifery and Women's Health, 54,* 50–56.

McGhee, L.M., & Richgels, D.J. (2012). *Literacy's beginnings* (6th ed.). Boston: Allyn & Bacon.

McHale, S.M., Salman-Engin, S., & Coovert, M.D. (2015). Improvements in unmarried African American parents' rapport, communication, and problem-solving following a prenatal parenting intervention. *Family Process, 54,* 619–629.

McHale, S.M., Updegraff, K.A., & Whiteman, S.D. (2013). Sibling relationships. In G.W. Peterson & K.R. Bush (Eds.), *Handbook of marriage and family* (3rd ed.). New York: Springer.

McHugh, J.E., & Lawlor, B.A. (2016). Executive function independently predicts self-rated health and improvement in self-rated health over time among community-dwelling older adults. *Aging and Mental Health, 20,* 415–422.

McInerney, K., & Suhr, J. (2016). Neuropsychological correlates of hazard perception in older adults. *Journal of the International Neuropsychological Society, 22,* 332–340.

McInnis, C.M., & others (2015). Response and habituation of pro- and anti-inflammatory gene expression to repeated acute stress. *Brain, Behavior, and Immunity, 46,* 237–248.

McIntosh, E., Gillanders, D., & Rodgers, S. (2010). Rumination, goal linking, daily hassles, and life events in major depression. *Clinical Psychology and Psychotherapy, 17,* 33–43.

McKain, W.C. (1972). A new look at older marriages. *The Family Coordinator, 21,* 61–69.

McKay, A.S., & Kaufman, J.C. (2014). Literary geniuses: Their life, work, and death. In D.K. Simonton (Ed.), *Wiley-Blackwell handbook of genius.* New York: Wiley.

McLaughlin, K. (2003, December 30). Commentary in K. Painter, "Nurse dispenses dignity for dying." *USA Today,* Section D, pp. 1–2.

McLean, K.C., & Syed, M. (2015). The field of identity development needs and identity: An introduction to the *Handbook of identity development.* In K.C. McLean & M. Syed (Eds.), *Oxford handbook of identity development.* New York: Oxford University Press.

McLean, K.C., Syed, M., Yoder, A., & Greenhoot, A. (2016, in press). The role of domain content in understanding identity development processes. *Journal of Research on Adolescence, 26,* 60–75.

McLoyd, V.C., Purtell, K.M., & Hardaway, C.R. (2015). Race, class, and ethnicity as they affect emerging adulthood. In R.M. Lerner (Ed.), *Handbook of child psychology and developmental science* (7th ed.). New York: Wiley.

McMahon, D.M., Liu, J., Zhang, H., Torres, M.E., & Best, R.G. (2013). Maternal obesity, folate intake, and neural tube defects in offspring. *Birth Defects A: Clinical and Molecular Teratology, 97,* 115–122.

McMahon, E.M., Reulbach, U., Keeley, H., Perry, I.J., & Arensman, E. (2012). Reprint of: Bullying victimization, self-harm, and associated factors in Irish boys. *Social Science and Medicine, 74,* 490–497.

McMillan, J.H. (2014). *Classroom assessment* (6th ed.). Upper Saddle River, NJ: Pearson.

McMurray, B. (2016). Language at three time-scales: The role of real-time processes in language development and evolution. *Topics in Cognitive Science, 8,* 393–407.

McNicholas, F., & others (2014). Medical, cognitive, and academic outcomes of very low birth weight infants at 10–14 years in Ireland. *Irish Journal of Medical Science, 183,* 525–532.

McRae, C., Petrov, M.E., Dautovich, N., & Lichstein, K.L. (2016). Late-life sleep and sleep disorders. In K.W. Schaie & S.L. Willis (Eds.), *Handbook of the psychology of aging* (8th ed.). New York: Elsevier.

Meade, C.S., Kershaw, T.S., & Ickovics, J.R. (2008). The intergenerational cycle of teenage motherhood: An ecological approach. *Health Psychology, 27,* 419–429.

Meerlo, P., Sgoifo, A., & Suchecki, D. (2008). Restricted and disrupted sleep: Effects on autonomic function, neuroendocrine stress systems, and stress responsivity. *Sleep Medicine Review, 12,* 197–210.

Meert, K.L., & others (2015). Meaning making during parent-physician bereavement meetings after a child's death. *Health Psychology, 34,* 453–461.

Meffert, C., Stobel, U., Korner, M., & Becker, G. (2015). Perceptions of a good death among German medical students. *Death Studies, 39,* 307–315.

Meier, E.A., & others (2016). Defining a good death (successful dying): Literature review and a call for research and public dialogue. *American Journal of Geriatric Psychiatry, 24,* 261–271.

Meins, E., & others (2013). Mind-mindedness and theory of mind: Mediating processes of language and perspectival symbolic play. *Child Development, 84,* 1777–1790.

Melancon, M.O., Lorrain, D., & Dionne, I.J. (2015). Sleep depth and continuity before and after chronic exercise in older men: Electrophysiological evidence. *Physiology and Behavior, 140,* 203–208.

Meltzoff, A.N. (1988). Infant imitation and memory: Nine-month-old infants in immediate and deferred tests. *Child Development, 59,* 217–225.

Meltzoff, A.N. (2004). Imitation as a mechanism of social cognition: Origins of empathy, theory of mind, and the representation of action. In U. Goswami (Ed.), *Blackwell handbook of childhood cognitive development.* Malden, MA: Blackwell.

Meltzoff, A.N. (2005). Imitation. In B. Hopkins (Ed.), *Cambridge encyclopedia of child development.* Cambridge: Cambridge University Press.

Meltzoff, A.N. (2007). Infants' causal learning. In A. Gopnik & L. Schulz (Eds.), *Causal learning.* New York: Oxford University Press.

Meltzoff, A.N. (2011). Social cognition and the origins of imitation, empathy, and theory of mind. In U. Goswami (Ed.), *Wiley-Blackwell handbook of childhood cognitive development* (2nd ed.). New York: Wiley.

Meltzoff, A.N., & Brooks, R. (2009). Social cognition: The role of gaze following in early word learning. In J. Colombo, P. McCardle, & L. Freund (Eds). *Infant pathways to language.* Clifton, NJ: Psychology Press.

Meltzoff, A.N., & Williamson, R.A. (2013). Imitation: Social, cognitive, and theoretical perspectives. In P.D. Zelazo (Ed.), *Oxford handbook of developmental psychology.* New York: Oxford University Press.

Memari, A., Ziaee, V., Mirfaxeli, F., & Kordi, R. (2012). Investigation of autism comorbidities and associations in a school-based community sample. *Journal of Child and Adolescent Psychiatric Nursing, 25,* 84–90.

Mendelson, M., & others (2016). Sleep quality, sleep duration, and physical activity in obese adolescents: Effects of exercise training. *Pediatric Obesity, 11,* 26–32.

Mendes, A. (2016). Nursing care to facilitate and support 'good' grieving. *British Journal of Nursing, 24,* 95.

Mendez-Sanz, R., de la Torre-Diez, I., & Lopez-Coronado, M. (2016, in press). What is your risk of contracting Alzheimer's Disease? A telematics tool helps you to predict it. *Journal of Molecular Systems.*

Menesini, E., Palladino, B.E., & Nocentini, A. (2016). Let's not fall into the trap: Online and school based program to prevent cyberbullying among adolescents. In T. Vollink, F. DeHue, & C. McGuckin (Eds.), *Cyberbullying.* New York: Psychology Press.

Meng, H., Dobbs, D., Wang, S., & Hyer, K. (2013). Hospice use and public expenditures at the end of life in assisted living residents in a Florida Medicaid waiver program. *Journal of the American Geriatrics Society, 61,* 1777–1781.

Meng, X., & D'Arcy, C. (2014). Successful aging in Canada: Prevalence and predictors from a population-based sample of older adults. *Gerontology, 60,* 65–72.

Menn, L., & Stoel-Gammon, C. (2009). Phonological development: Learning sounds and patterns. In J. Berko Gleason & N. Ratner (Eds.), *The development of language* (7th ed.). Boston: Allyn & Bacon.

Menon, R., & others (2011). Cigarette smoking induces oxidative stress and atopsis in normal fetal membranes. *Placenta, 32,* 317–322.

Menotti, A., Puddu, P.E., Maiani, G., & Catasta, G. (2015). Lifestyle behavior and lifetime incidence of heart diseases. *International Journal of Cardiology, 401,* 293–299.

Mercer, N., & others (2016, in press). Childhood predictors and adult life success of adolescent delinquency abstainers. *Journal of Abnormal Child Psychology.*

Meredith, N.V. (1978). Research between 1960 and 1970 on the standing height of young children in different parts of the world. In H.W. Reece & L.P. Lipsitt (Eds.), *Advances in child development and behavior* (Vol. 12). New York: Academic Press.

Merrill, D.M. (2009). Parent-child relationships: Later-life. In D. Carr (Ed.), *Encyclopedia of the life course and human development.* Boston: Gale Cengage.

Mesman, J., van IJzendoorn, M.H., & Sagi-Schwartz, A. (2016). Cross-cultural patterns of attachment: Universal and contextual dimensions. In J. Cassidy & P.R. Shaver (Eds.), *Handbook of attachment* (3rd ed.). New York: Guilford.

Messiah, S.E., Miller, T.L., Lipshultz, S.E., & Bandstra, E.S. (2011). Potential latent effects of prenatal cocaine exposure on growth and the risk of cardiovascular and metabolic disease in childhood. *Progress in Pediatric Cardiology, 31,* 59–65.

Metcalf, C.J., & Jones, J.H. (2015). The evolutionary dynamics of timing of maternal immunity: Evaluating the role of age-specific mortality. *Journal of Evolutionary Biology, 28,* 493–502.

Meuwissen, A.S., & Carlson, S.M. (2016, in press). Fathers matter: The role of father parenting in preschool children's executive function. *Journal of Experimental Child Psychology.*

Meyer, A., & others (2015). Self-reported and observed punitive parenting prospectively predicts increased error-related activity in six-year-old children. *Journal of Abnormal Child Psychology, 43,* 821–829.

Mian, M., & others (2015). Shaken baby syndrome: A review. *Fetal and Pediatric Pathology, 34,* 168–175.

Micali, N., Rask, C.U., Olsen, E.M., & Skovgaard, A.M. (2016). Early predictors of childhood restrictive eating: A population-based study. *Journal of Developmental and Behavioral Pediatrics, 37,* 314–321.

Michael, R.T., Gagnon, J.H., Laumann, E.O., & Kolata, G. (1994). *Sex in America.* Boston: Little, Brown.

Mick, P., & Pichora-Fuller, M.K. (2016, in press). Is hearing loss associated with poorer health in older adults who might benefit from hearing screening? *Ear and Hearing.*

Miguel-Neto, J., & others (2016). New approach to phenotypic variability and karyotype-phenotype correlation in Turner syndrome. *Journal of Pediatric Endocrinology and Metabolism, 29,* 475–479.

Mike, A., Harris, K., Roberts, B.W., & Jackson, J.J. (2015). Conscientiousness: Lower-order structure, life course consequences, and development. In J. Wright (Ed.), *International encyclopedia of social and behavioral sciences* (2nd ed.). New York: Elsevier.

Mikkola, T.M., & others (2016). Self-reported hearing is associated with time spent out-of-home and withdrawal from leisure activities in older community-dwelling adults. *Aging: Clinical and Experimental Research, 28,* 297–302.

Mikulincer, M., & Shaver, P.R. (2016). *Attachment in adulthood* (2nd ed.). New York: Guilford.

Milani, H.J., & others (2015). Fetal brain tumors: Prenatal diagnosis by ultrasound and magnetic resonance imaging. *World Journal of Radiology, 28,* 17–21.

Mileva-Seitz, V.R., Bakermans-Kranenburg, M.J., & van IJzendoorn, M.H. (2016). Genetic mechanisms of parenting. *Hormones and Behavior, 77,* 211–223.

Miller, A.C. (2016). Opinions on the legitimacy of brain death among Sunni and Shi'a scholars. *Journal of Religion and Health, 55,* 394–402.

Miller, C., & Price, J. (2013). *The number of children being raised by gay or lesbian parents.* Unpublished manuscript, Department of Economics, Brigham Young University, Provo, UT.

Miller, E.B., Farkas, G., & Duncan, G.J. (2016, in press). Does Head Start differentially benefit children with risks targeted by the program's service model? *Early Childhood Research Quarterly.*

Miller, E.M., & others (2012). Theories of willpower affect sustained learning. *PLoS One, 7*(6), e38680.

Miller, J.D., & others (2015). Narcissism and the United States culture: The view from home and around the world. *Journal of Personality and Social Psychology, 109,* 1068–1089.

Miller, L.M., & Bell, R.A. (2012). Online health information seeking: The influence of age, information trustworthiness, and search challenges. *Journal of Aging and Health, 24,* 525–541.

Miller, M., Loya, F., & Hinshaw, S.P. (2013). Executive functions in girls with and without ADHD: Developmental trajectories and associations with symptom change. *Journal of Child Psychology and Psychiatry, 54*(9), 1005–1015.

Miller, P.H. (2011). Piaget's theory: Past, present, and future. In U. Goswami (Ed.), *Wiley-Blackwell handbook of childhood cognitive development* (2nd ed.). New York: Wiley.

Miller, P.H. (2015). *Theories of developmental psychology* (6th ed.). New York: Worth.

Miller, R., Wankerl, M., Stalder, T., Kirschbaum, C., & Alexander, N. (2013). The serotonin transporter gene-linked polymorphic region (5-HTTLPR) and cortisol stress reactivity: A meta-analysis. *Molecular Psychiatry, 18,* 1018–1024.

Miller, S., McCulloch, S., & Jarrold, C. (2015). The development of memory maintenance strategies: Training cumulative rehearsal and integrative imagery in children aged between 5 and 9. *Frontiers in Psychology, 6,* 524.

Miller, S.E., & Marcovitch, S. (2015). Examining executive function in the second year of life: Coherence, stability, and relations to joint attention and language. *Developmental Psychology, 51,* 101–114.

Miller, S.L., Huppi, P.S., & Mallard, C. (2016). The consequences of fetal growth restriction on brain structure and neurodevelopmental outcome. *Journal of Physiology, 594,* 807–823.

Miller-Perrin, C.L., Perrin, R.D., & Kocur, J.L. (2009). Parental, physical, and psychological aggression: Psychological symptoms in young adults. *Child Abuse and Neglect, 33,* 1–11.

Mills, C.M. (2013). Knowing when to doubt: Developing a critical stance when learning from others. *Developmental Psychology, 114,* 63–76.

Mills, C.M., & Elashi, F.B. (2014). Children's skepticism: Developmental and individual differences in children's ability to detect and explain distorted claims. *Journal of Experimental Child Psychology, 124C,* 1–17.

Mills-Koonce, W.R., Propper, C.B., & Barnett, M. (2012). Poor infant soothability and later insecure-ambivalent attachment: Developmental change in phenotypic markers of risk or two measures of the same construct? *Infant Behavior and Development, 35,* 215–235.

Milne, E., & others (2012). Parental prenatal smoking and risk of childhood acute lymphoblastic leukemia. *American Journal of Epidemiology, 175,* 43–53.

Milner, A., & others (2014). The effects of involuntary job loss on suicide and suicide attempts among young adults: Evidence from a matched case-control study. *Australian and New Zealand Journal of Psychiatry, 48,* 333–340.

Minkler, M., & Fuller-Thompson, E. (2005). African American grandparents raising grandchildren: A national study using the Census 2000 American Community Survey. *Journals of Gerontology B: Psychological Sciences and Social Sciences, 60,* S82–S92.

Minnes, S., & others (2010). The effects of prenatal cocaine exposure on problem behavior in children 4–10 years. *Neurotoxicology and Teratology, 32,* 443–451.

Minnesota Family Investment Program (2009). *Longitudinal study of early MFIP recipients.* Retrieved January 12, 2009, from www.dhs.state.mn.us/main/idcplg?IdcService=GET_DYNAMIC_CONVERSION&RevisionSelectionMethod=LatestReleased&dDocName=id_004113

Minsart, A.F., Buekens, P., Spiegelaere, M., & Englert, Y. (2013). Neonatal outcomes in obese mothers: A population-based analysis. *BMC Pregnancy and Childbirth, 13,* 36.

Min-Wen, J.C., Jun-Hao, E.T., & Shyh-Chang, N. (2016). Stem cell mitochondria during aging. *Seminars in Cell and Developmental Biology, 52,* 110–118.

Mirachi, F.L., & others (2015). TRIAD VII: Do prehospital providers understand Physician Orders for Life-Sustaining Treatment documents? *Journal of Patient Safety, 11,* 9–17.

Mirkovic, B., & others (2015). Coping skills among adolescent suicide attempters: Results of a multisite study. *Canandian Journal of Psychiatry, 60*(2, Suppl. 1), S37–S45.

Mischel, W. (2004). Toward an integrative science of the person. *Annual Review of Psychology* (Vol. 55). Palo Alto, CA: Annual Reviews.

Mischel, W. (2014). *The marshmallow test; Mastering self-control.* New York: Little Brown.

Mischel, W., Cantor, N., & Feldman, S. (1996). Principles of self-regulation: The nature of will power and self-control. In E.T. Higgins & A.W. Kruglanski (Eds.), *Social psychology.* New York: Guilford.

Mischel, W., & Moore, B.S. (1980). The role of ideation in voluntary delay for symbolically presented rewards. *Cognitive Therapy and Research, 4,* 211–221.

Mischel, W., & others (2011). "Willpower" over the life span: Decomposing self-regulation. *Social Cognitive and Affective Neuroscience, 6,* 252–256.

Mishra, G.D., Cooper, R., Tom, S.E., & Kuh, D. (2009). Early life circumstances and their impact on menarche and menopause. *Women's Health, 5,* 175–190.

Mistry, J., Contreras, M., & Dutta, R. (2013). Culture and child development. In I.B. Weiner & others (Eds.), *Handbook of psychology* (2nd ed., Vol. 6). New York: Wiley.

Mistry, J., & Dutta, R. (2015). Human development and culture: Conceptual and methodological issues. In R.M. Lerner (Ed.), *Handbook of child psychology and developmental science* (7th ed.). New York: Wiley.

Mitanchez, D., & others (2015). The offspring of the diabetic mother—short- and long-term implications. *Best Practice and Research: Clinical Obstetrics and Gynecology, 29,* 256–269.

Mitchell, A.B., & Stewart, J.B. (2013). The efficacy of all-male academies: Insights from critical race theory (CRT). *Sex Roles, 69,* 382.

Mitchell, E.A., & Krous, H.F. (2015). Sudden unexpected death in infancy: A historical perspective. *Journal of Pediatrics and Child Health, 5,* 108–112.

Mitchell, E.S., & Woods, N.F. (2015). Hot flush severity during the menopausal transition and early postmenopause: Beyond hormones. *Climacteric, 18,* 536–544.

Mitchell, M.B., & others (2012). Cognitively stimulating activities: Effects on cognition across four studies with up to 21 years of longitudinal data. *Journal of Aging Research,* Article ID 461592.

Mitchell, S., & Dale, J. (2015). Advance care planning in palliative care: A qualitative investigation into the perspective of Pediatric Intensive Care Unit staff. *Palliative Medicine, 29,* 371–379.

Miyakoshi, K., & others (2013). Perinatal outcomes: Intravenous patient-controlled fentanyl versus no analgesia in labor. *Journal of Obstetrics and Gynecology Research, 39*(4), 783–789.

Miyawaki, S., & others (2016). Facial pigmentation as a biomarker of carotid atherosclerosis in middle-aged to elderly healthy Japanese subjects. *Skin Research and Technology, 22,* 20–24.

Miyazaki, K., Song, J.W., & Takahashi, E. (2016). Asymmetry of radial and symmetry of tangential neuronal migration pathways in developing human fetal brains. *Frontiers in Neuroanatomy, 10,* 2.

Mobley, A.S., Rodriquez-Gil, D.J., Imamura, F., & Greer, C.A. (2014). Aging in the olfactory system. *Trends in Neuroscience, 37,* 37–44.

Moed, A., & others (2015). Parent-adolescent conflict as sequences of reciprocal negative emotion: Links with conflict resolution and adolescents' behavior problems. *Journal of Youth and Adolescence, 44,* 1607–1622.

Moen, P. (2007). Unpublished review of J.W. Santrock's *Life-span development* (12th ed.). New York: McGraw-Hill.

Moen, P. (2009a). Careers. In D. Carr (Ed.), *Encyclopedia of the life course and human development.* Boston: Gale Cengage.

Moen, P. (2009b). Dual-career couples. In D. Carr (Ed.), *Encyclopedia of the life course and human development.* Boston: Gale Cengage.

Moilanen, J.M., & others (2012). Effect of aerobic training on menopausal symptoms—a randomized controlled trial. *Menopause, 19,* 691–696.

Moise, K.J., & others (2013). Circulating cell-free DNA for the detection of RHD status and sex using reflex fetal identifiers. *Prenatal Diagnosis.*

Mola, J.R. (2015). Erectile dysfunction in the older adult male. *Urological Nursing, 35,* 87–93.

Moleti, C.A. (2009). Trends and controversies in labor induction. *MCN: The American Journal of Maternal and Child Nursing, 34,* 40–47.

Molina, R.C., Roca, C.G., Zamorano, J.S., & Araya, E.G. (2010). Family planning and adolescent pregnancy. *Best Practices and Research: Clinical Obstetrics and Gynecology, 24,* 209–222.

Moline, H.R., & Smith, J.F. (2016, in press). The continuing threat of syphilis in pregnancy. *Current Opinion in Obstetrics and Gynecology.*

Mollborg, P., Wennergren, G., Almqvist, P., & Alm, B. (2015). Bed sharing is more common in sudden infant death syndrome than in explained sudden unexpected deaths in infancy. *Acta Pediatrica, 104,* 777–783.

Molton, I.R., & Terrill, A.L. (2014). Overview of persistent pain in older adults. *American Psychologist, 69,* 197–207.

Molyneaux, E., Trevillion, K., & Howard, L.M. (2015). Antidepressant treatment for postnatal depression. *JAMA, 313,* 1965–1966.

Monahan, K.C., & others (2016). Integration of developmental neuroscience and contextual approaches to the study of adolescent psychopathology. In D. Cicchetti (Ed.), *Developmental psychopathology* (3rd ed.). New York: Wiley.

Monni, G., & others (2016). How to perform transabdominal chorionic villus sampling: A practical guideline. *Journal of Maternal-Fetal and Neonatal Medicine, 29,* 1499–1505.

Monserud, M.A. (2008). Intergenerational relationships and affectual solidarity between grandparents and young adults. *Journal of Marriage and the Family, 70,* 182–195.

Monserud, M.A. (2011). Changes in grandchildren's adult role statuses and their relationships to grandparents. *Journal of Family Issues, 32,* 425–451.

Monserud, M.A., & Markides, K.S. (2016, in press). Changes in depressive symptoms during widowhood among older Mexican Americans: The role of financial strain, social support, and religious attendance. *Aging and Mental Health.*

Montano, Z., & others (2015). Longitudinal relations between observed parenting behaviors and dietary quality of meals from ages 2 to 5. *Appetite, 87,* 324–329.

Montirosso, R., & others (2015). A categorical approach to infants' individual differences during the still-face paradigm. *Infant Behavior and Development, 38,* 67–76.

Moon, M. (2016a). Aging and society. In L.K. George & K.F. Ferraro (Eds.), *Handbook of aging and the social sciences* (8th ed.). New York: Elsevier.

Moon, M. (2016b). Organization and financing of health care. In L.K. George & K.F. Ferraro (Eds.), *Handbook of aging and the social sciences* (8th ed.). New York: Elsevier.

Moon, M., & others (2015). Serving older adults with complex care needs: A new benefit option for Medicare. *Issue Brief, 23,* 1–11.

Moon, R.Y., Hauck, F.R., & Colson, E.R. (2016). Safe infant sleep interventions: What is the evidence for successful behavior change? *Current Pediatric Reviews, 12,* 67–75.

Moore, D. (2001). *The dependent gene.* New York: W.H. Freeman.

Moore, D.S. (2013). Behavioral genetics, genetics, and epigenetics. In P.D. Zelazo (Ed.), *Handbook of developmental psychology.* New York: Oxford University Press.

Moore, D.S. (2015). *The developing genome.* New York: Oxford University Press.

Moore, M.W., Brendel, P.C., & Fiez, J.A. (2014). Reading faces: Investigating the use of a novel face-based orthography in acquired alexia. *Brain and Language, 129C,* 7–13.

Moore, R.M. (2015). Appreciating cultural dimensions and connections in hospice care. *Journal of Social Work in End-of-Life and Palliative Care, 11,* 6–10.

Moore, S.J., & Murphy, G.G. (2016). Age-related alterations in neural plasticity. In M. Kaeberlein & G.M. Martin (Eds.), *Handbook of the biology of aging* (8th ed.). New York: Elsevier.

Moore, S.R., Harden, K.P., & Mendle, J. (2014). Pubertal timing and adolescent sexual behavior in girls. *Developmental Psychology, 50,* 1734–1745.

Moosmann, D.A., & Roosa, M.W. (2015). Exploring Mexican American adolescent romantic relationship profiles and adjustment. *Journal of Adolescence, 43,* 181–192.

Moran, S., & Gardner, H. (2007). Hill, skill, and will: Executive function from a multiple intelligences perspective. In L. Meltzer (Ed.), *Executive function in education.* New York: Guilford.

Moriguchi, Y., Chevalier, N., & Zelazo, P.D. (2016). Editorial: Development of executive function during childhood. *Frontiers in Psychology, 7,* 6.

Morra, S., Gobbo, C., Marini, Z., & Sheese, R. (2008). *Cognitive development: Neo-Piagetian perspectives.* Mahwah, NJ: Erlbaum.

Morrill, M.I., Hawrilenko, M., & Cordova, J.V. (2016). A longitudinal examination of positive parenting following an acceptance-based couple intervention. *Journal of Family Psychology, 30,* 104–113.

Morris, A.S., & others (2013). Effortful control, behavior problems, and peer relations: What predicts academic adjustment in kindergartners from low-income families. *Early Education Development, 24,* 813–828.

Morris, B.J., & others (2012). A 'snip' in time: What is the best age to circumcise? *BMC Pediatrics, 12,* 20.

Morrison, G.S. (2015). *Early childhood education today* (13th ed.). Upper Saddle River, NJ: Pearson.

Morrison, G.S. (2017). *Fundamentals of early childhood education* (8th ed.). Upper Saddle River, NJ: Pearson.

Morrison, R.S. (2013). Models of palliative care delivery in the United States. *Current Opinion in Supportive and Palliative Care, 7,* 201–206.

Morrison-Beedy, D., & others (2013). Reducing sexual risk behavior in adolescent girls: Results from a randomized trial. *Journal of Adolescent Health, 52,* 314–322.

Morrissey, T.W. (2009). Multiple child-care arrangements and young children's behavioral outcomes. *Child Development, 80,* 59–76.

Morrow-Howell, N. (2010). Volunteering in later life: Research frontiers. *Journals of Gerontology B: Psychological Sciences and Social Sciences, 65B,* 461–469.

Morrow-Howell, N., & Greenfield, E.A. (2016). Productive engagement in later life. In L.K. George & K.F. Ferraro (Eds.), *Handbook of aging and the social sciences* (8th ed.). New York: Elsevier.

Mortimer, J.T. (2012). The evolution, contributions, and prospects of the Youth Development Study: An investigation in life course social psychology. *Social Psychology Quarterly, 75,* 5–27.

Mosing, M.A., & others (2012). Genetic influences on life span and its relationship to personality: A 16-year follow-up study of a sample of aging twins. *Psychosomatic Medicine, 74,* 16–22.

Motorwala, Z.S., & others (2016). Effects of Yogasanas on osteoporosis in postmenopausal women. *International Journal of Yoga, 9,* 44–48.

Mparmpakas, D., & others (2013). Immune system function, stress, exercise, and nutrition profile can affect pregnancy outcome: Lessons from a Mediterranean cohort. *Experimental and Therapeutic Medicine, 5,* 411–418.

Mrkva, K., & Narváez, D. (2015). Moral psychology and the "cultural other": Cultivating openness to experience and the new. In B. Zizek & A. Escher (eds.), *Ways of approaching the strange.* Dornach, Switzerland: Steiner Verlag.

Mroczek, D.K., Spiro, A., & Griffin, P.W. (2006). Personality and aging. In J.E. Birren & K.W. Schale (Eds.). *Handbook of the psychology of aging* (6th ed.). San Diego: Academic Press.

Mroczek, D.K., & others (2015). Emotional reactivity and mortality: Longitudinal findings from the VA Normative Aging Study. *Journals of Gerontology B: Psychological Sciences and Social Sciences, 70*(3), 398–406.

Muller Mirza, N. (2016, in press). Emotions, development, and materiality at school: A cultural-historical approach. *Integrative Psychological and Behavioral Science.*

Muller, L., & Pawelec, G. (2015, Feb. 9). As we age: Does slippage of quality control in the immune

system lead to collateral damage? *Aging Research Reviews,* S1568–S1637.

Muller, L., & Pawelec, G. (2016). The aging immune system: Dysregulation, compensatory mechanisms, and prospects for intervention. In M. Kaeberlein & G.W. Martin (Eds.), *Handbook of the biology of aging* (8th ed.). New York: Elsevier.

Muller, U., & Kerns, K. (2015). Development of executive function. In R.M. Lerner (Ed.), *Handbook of child psychology and developmental science* (7th ed.). New York: Wiley.

Mun, M.J., Kim, J.H., Choi, J.Y., & Jang, W.C. (2016). Genetic polymorphisms of interleukin genes and the risk of Alzheimer's disease: An update meta-analysis. *Meta Gene, 8,* 1–10.

Mundy, P., & others (2007). Individual differences and the development of joint attention in infancy. *Child Development, 78,* 938–954.

Murphy, R.A., & others (2014). Associations of BMI and adipose tissue area and density with incident mobility limitation and poor performance in older adults. *American Journal of Clinical Nutrition, 99,* 1059–1065.

Murphy-Hoefer, R., Alder, S., & Higbee, C. (2004). Perceptions about cigarette smoking and risks among college students. *Nicotine and Tobacco Research, 6*(Suppl. 3), S371–S374.

Musameh, M.D., & others (2015). Analysis of gene-gene interactions among common variants in candidate cardiovascular genes in coronary artery disease. *PLoS One, 10*(2), e117684.

Mussen, P.H., Honzik, M., & Eichorn, D. (1982). Early adult antecedents of life satisfaction at age 70. *Journal of Gerontology, 37,* 316–332.

Mutreja, R., Craig, C., & O'Boyle, M.W. (2016, in press). Attentional network deficits in children with autism spectrum disorder. *Developmental Neurorehabilitation.*

Mychasiuk, R., Muhammad, A., & Kolb, B. (2016). Chronic stress induces persistent changes in global DNA methylation and gene expression in the medial frontal cortex, orbitofrontal cortex, and hippocampus. *Neuroscience, 322,* 489–499.

Myers, D.G. (2010). *Psychology* (9th ed.). New York: Worth.

Myerson, J., Rank, M.R., Raines, F.Q., & Schnitzler, M.A. (1998). Race and general cognitive ability: The myth of diminishing returns in education. *Psychology Science, 9.*

N

Nabe-Nielsen, K., & others (2014). Demand-specific work ability, poor health, and working conditions in middle-aged full-time employees. *Applied Ergonomics, 45,* 1174–1180.

Nadimpalli, S.B., & others (2015). The association between discrimination and depressive symptoms among older African Americans: The role of psychological and social factors. *Experimental Aging Research, 41,* 1–24.

Nadon, N.L., Miller, R.A., Strong, R., & Harrison, D.E. (2016). NIA interventions testing program: A collaborative approach for investigating interventions to promote healthy aging. In M.R. Kaeberlein & G.M. Martin (Eds.), *Handbook of the biology of aging* (8th ed.). New York: Elsevier.

NAEYC (2009). *Developmentally appropriate practice in early childhood programs serving*

children from birth through age 8. Washington, DC: NAEYC.

Nagamatsu, L.S., & others (2016, in press). Exercise mode moderates the relationship between mobility and basal ganglia volume in healthy older adults. *Journal of the American Geriatrics Society.*

Nagel, B.J., & others (2011). Altered white matter microstructure in children with attention-deficit/hyperactivity disorder. *Journal of the American Academy of Child and Adolescent Psychiatry, 50,* 283–292.

Naicker, K., Galambos, N.L., Zeng, Y., Senthilselvan, A., & Colman, I. (2013). Social, demographic, and health outcomes in the 10 years following adolescent depression. *Journal of Adolescent Health, 52,* 533–538.

Najman, J.M., & others (2009). The impact of episodic and chronic poverty on child cognitive development. *Journal of Pediatrics, 154,* 284–289.

Najman, J.M., & others (2010). Timing and chronicity of family poverty and development of unhealthy behaviors in children: A longitudinal study. *Journal of Adolescent Health, 46,* 538–544.

Nakajima, S., Masaya, I., Akemi, S., & Takako, K. (2012). Complicated grief in those bereaved by violent death: The effects of post-traumatic stress disorder on complicated grief. *Dialogues in Clinical Neuroscience, 14,* 210–214.

Nakawaki, B., & Crano, W. (2015). Patterns of substance use, delinquency, and risk factors among adolescent inhalant users. *Substance Use and Misuse, 50,* 114–122.

Nansel, T.R., & others (2001). Bullying behaviors among U.S. youth. *Journal of the American Medical Association, 285,* 2094–2100.

Napper, L.E., Montes, K.S., Kenney, S.R., & LaBrie, J.W. (2016, in press). Assessing the personal negative impacts of hooking up experienced by college students: Gender differences in mental health. *Journal of Sex Research.*

Narváez, D. (2015). The neurobiology of moral sensitivity: Evolution, epigenetics, and early experience. In D. Mowrer & P. Vanderberg (Eds.), *The art of morality.* New York: Routledge.

Narváez, D. (2016a, in press). The ontogenesis of moral becoming. In A. Fuentes & A. Visala (Eds.). *Verbs, bones, and brains.* Notre Dame, IN: University of Notre Dame Press.

Narváez, D. (2016b, in press). *Embodied morality.* New York: Palgrave-McMillan.

Narváez, D. (2016c, in press). Ethogenesis: Evolution, early experience, and moral becoming. In J. Graham & K. Gray (Eds.), *The atlas of moral psychology.* New York: Guilford.

Nasiri, S. (2015). Severity of menopausal symptoms and related factors among 40- to 60-year-old women. *Nursing and Midwifery Studies 4*(1), e22882.

NASSPE (2012). *Single-sex schools/schools with single-sex classrooms/what's the difference.* Retrieved from www.singlesexschools.org/schools-schools.com

National Alliance for Caregiving (2009). *Caregiving in the United States 2009.* Retrieved June 29, 2012, from www.caregiving.org/pdf/research/Caregiving

National Assessment of Educational Progress (2012). *The nation's report card: 2012.* Washington, DC: U.S. Department of Education.

National Association for Gifted Children (2009). *State of the states in gifted education: 2008–2009.* Washington, DC: Author.

National Association for Sport and Physical Education (2002). *Active start: A statement of physical activity guidelines for children birth to five years.* Reston, VA: National Association for Sport and Physical Education Publications.

National Cancer Institute (2016). *Childhood cancer.* Rockville, MD: Author.

National Center for Education Statistics (2002). *Work during college.* Washington, DC: U.S. Office of Education.

National Center for Education Statistics (2009). *Comparative indicators of education in the United States and other G-8 countries: 2009.* Washington, DC: U.S. Department of Education.

National Center for Education Statistics (2013, May). *Characteristics of postsecondary students.* Washington: U.S. Department of Education.

National Center for Education Statistics (2014). Status dropout rates. *Digest of Education Statistics.* Washington, DC: U.S. Department of Education.

National Center for Education Statistics (2015). *The condition of education, 2015.* Washington, DC: U.S. Department of Education.

National Center for Health Statistics (2000). *Health United States, 2000, with adolescent health chartbook.* Bethesda, MD: U.S. Department of Health and Human Services.

National Center for Health Statistics (2002). *Sexual behavior and selected health measures: Men and women 15–44 years of age, United States, 2002,* PHS 2003-1250. Atlanta: Centers for Disease Control and Prevention.

National Center for Health Statistics (2014). *Death statistics.* Atlanta: Centers for Disease Control and Prevention.

National Center for Health Statistics (2014). *HIV/AIDS.* Atlanta: Centers for Disease Control and Prevention.

National Center for Health Statistics (2015). *Deaths.* Atlanta: Centers for Disease Control and Prevention.

National Center for Health Statistics (2016). *Accidents and deaths.* Atlanta: Centers for Disease Control and Prevention.

National Center for Health Statistics (2016). *Death statistics.* Atlanta: Centers for Disease Control and Prevention.

National Center for Health Statistics (2016). *Sexually transmitted diseases.* Atlanta: Centers for Disease Control and Prevention.

National Center for Vital Statistics (2013). *Births, marriages, divorces, deaths: 2011.* Washington, DC: Author.

National Center on Shaken Baby Syndrome (2012). *Shaken baby syndrome.* Retrieved April, 20, 2011, from www.dontshake.org/

National Clearinghouse on Child Abuse and Neglect (2013, July). *What is child abuse and neglect?* Washington, DC: U.S. Department of Health and Human Services.

National Council on Aging (2000, March). *Myths and realities survey results.* Washington, DC: Author.

National Institute of Mental Health (2016). *Autism spectrum disorder (ASD).* Retrieved January 7, 2016, from http://www.nimh.nih.gov/health/topics/autism-spectrum-disorders-asd/index.shtml

National Marriage Project (2011). *Unmarried cohabitation.* Retrieved June 9, 2012, from www.stateofourunions.org/2011/social_indicators.php.

National Sleep Foundation (2006). *Sleep in America poll 2006.* Washington, DC: Author.

National Sleep Foundation (2007). *Sleep in America poll 2007.* Washington, DC: Author.

Naumova, O.Y., & others (2016). Epigenetic patterns modulate the connection between developmental dynamics of parenting and offspring psychosocial adjustment. *Child Development, 87,* 98–110.

Naxerova, K., & Elledge, S.J. (2016, in press). Taking the brakes off telomerase. *Elife.*

Nechuta, S.J., & others (2015). Adolescent exercise in the association with mortality from all causes, cardiovascular disease, and cancer among middle-aged and older Chinese women. *Cancer Epidemiology, Biomarkers, and Prevention, 24,* 1270–1276.

Needham, A.W. (2016). *Learning about objects in infancy.* New York: Psychology Press.

Needham, A., Barrett, T., & Peterman, K. (2002) A pick-me-up for infants' exploratory skills: early simulated experiences reaching for objects using "sticky mittens" enhances young infants' object exploration skills. *Infant Behavior and Development, 25,* 279–295.

Negriff, S., Susman, E.J., & Trickett, P.K. (2011). The development pathway from pubertal timing to delinquency and sexual activity from early to late adolescence. *Journal of Youth and Adolescence, 40,* 1343–1356.

Nelson, C.A. (2003). Neural development and life-long plasticity. In R.M. Lerner, F. Jacobs, & D. Wertlieb (Eds.), *Handbook of applied developmental science* (Vol. 1). Thousand Oaks, CA: Sage.

Nelson, C.A. (2008). Unpublished review of J.W. Santrock's *Topical approach to life-span development,* 5th ed. New York: McGraw-Hill.

Nelson, C.A. (2011). Brain development and behavior. In A.M. Rudolph, C. Rudolph, L. First, G. Lister, & A.A. Gershon (Eds.), *Rudolph's pediatrics* (22nd ed.). New York: McGraw-Hill.

Nelson, C.A., Fox, N.A., & Zeanah, C.H. (2014). *Romania's abandoned children.* Cambridge, MA : Harvard University Press.

Nelson, J.A., Leerkes, E.M., O'Brien, M., Calkins, S.D., & Maracovitch, S. (2012). African American and European American mothers' beliefs about negative emotions and emotion socialization practices. *Parenting, 12,* 22–41.

Nelson, L.J., & others (2007). "If you want me to treat you like an adult, start acting like one!" Comparing the criteria that emerging adults and their parents have for adulthood. *Journal of Family Psychology, 21,* 665–674.

Nelson, S.E., Van Ryzin, M.J., & Dishion, T.J. (2015). Alcohol, marijuana, and tobacco use trajectories from ages 12 to 24 years: Demographic correlates and young adult substance use problems. *Development and Psychopathology, 27,* 253–277.

Nelson, S.K., Kushlev, K., English, T., Dunn, E.W., & Lyubomirsky, S. (2013). In defense of parenthood: Children associated with more joy than misery. *Psychological Science, 24,* 3–10.

Nelson, S.K., Kushley, K., & Lyubomirsky, S. (2014). The pains and pleasures of parenting: When, why, and how is parenthood associated with more or less well-being? *Psychological Bulletin., 140,* 846–895.

Nemet, D. (2016). Childhood obesity, physical activity, and exercise. *Pediatric Exercise Science, 28,* 48–51.

Nes, R., & Roysamb, E. (2016). The heritability of subjective well-being: Review and meta-analysis. In M. Pluess (Ed.), *Genetics of psychological well-being.* New York: Oxford University Press.

Neugarten, B.L., Havighurst, R.J., & Tobin, S.S. (1968). Personality and patterns of aging. In B.L. Neugarten (Ed.), *Middle age and aging.* Chicago: University of Chicago Press.

Neville, H.J. (2006). Different profiles of plasticity within human cognition. In Y. Munakata & M.H. Johnson (Eds.), *Attention and Performance XXI: Processes of change in brain and cognitive development.* Oxford, UK: Oxford University Press.

Newton, N.J., & Stewart, A.J. (2012). Personality development in adulthood. In S.K. Whitbourne & M. Sliwinski (Eds.), *Wiley-Blackwell handbook of adult development and aging.* New York: Wiley.

Ng, F.F., Pomerantz, E.M., & Deng, C. (2014). Why are Chinese parents more psychologically controlling than American parents? "My child is my report card." *Child Development, 85,* 355–369.

Ng, F.F., Pomerantz, E.M., & Lam, S. (2013). Mothers' beliefs about children's learning in Hong Kong and the United States: Implications for mothers' child-based worth. *International Journal of Behavioral Development, 37,* 387–394.

Nguyen, P.V., Hong, T.K., Nguyen, D.T., & Robert, A.R. (2016). Excessive screen viewing time by adolescents and body fatness in a developing country: Vietnam. *Asia Pacific Journal of Clinical Nutrition, 25,* 174–183.

Nho, K., & others (2015). Comprehensive gene- and pathway-based analysis of depressive symptoms in older adults. *Journal of Alzheimer's Disease, 45,* 1197–1206.

NICHD (2016). *SIDS facts.* Retrieved January 6, 2016. www.nichd.nih/gov/sids

NICHD Early Child Care Research Network (2001). Nonmaternal care and family factors in early development: An overview of the NICHD study of Early Child Care. *Journal of Applied Developmental Psychology, 22,* 457–492.

NICHD Early Child Care Research Network (2002). Structure→Process→Outcome: Direct and indirect effects of child care quality on young children's development. *Psychological Science, 13,* 199–206.

NICHD Early Child Care Research Network (2003). Does amount of time spent in child care predict socioemotional adjustment during the transition to kindergarten? *Child Development, 74,* 976–1005.

NICHD Early Child Care Research Network (2004). Type of child care and children's development at 54 months. *Early Childhood Research Quarterly, 19,* 203–230.

NICHD Early Child Care Research Network (2005). *Child care and development.* New York: Guilford.

NICHD Early Child Care Research Network (2005). Predicting individual differences in attention, memory, and planning in first graders from experiences at home, child care, and school. *Developmental Psychology, 41,* 99–114.

NICHD Early Child Care Research Network (2006). Infant-mother attachment classification: Risk and protection in relation to changing maternal caregiving quality. *Developmental Psychology, 42,* 38–58.

NICHD Early Child Care Research Network (2009). Family-peer linkages: The mediational role of attentional processes. *Social Development, 18*(4), 875–895.

NICHD Early Child Care Research Network (2010). Testing a series of causal propositions relating time spent in child care to children's externalizing behavior. *Developmental Psychology, 46*(1), 1–17.

Nicolaisen, M., & Thorsen, K. (2014). Loneliness among men and women—a five-year follow-up study. *Aging and Mental Health, 18,* 194–206.

Nicoteri, J.A., & Miskovsky, M.J. (2014). Revisiting the freshman "15": Assessing body mass index in the first college year and beyond. *Journal of the American Association of Nurse Practitioners, 26,* 220–224.

Ning, L.F., & others (2015). Meta-analysis of differentially expressed genes in autism based on gene expression data. *Genetics and Molecular Research, 14,* 2146–2155.

Nisbett, R. (2003). *The geography of thought.* New York: Free Press.

Nisbett, R.E., & others (2012). Intelligence: New findings and theoretical developments. *American Psychologist, 67*(2), 130–159.

Nishamura, Y., Kanakogi, Y., & Myowa-Yamakoshi, M. (2016). Infants' emotional states influence maternal behaviors during holding. *Infant Behavior and Development, 43,* 66–74.

Nishimura, A., & others (2015). Paternal postnatal depression in Japan: An investigation of correlated factors including relationship with a partner. *BMC Pregnancy and Childbirth, 15,* 128.

Niu, K., & others (2016). The traditional Japanese dietary pattern and longitudinal changes in cardiovascular disease risk factors in apparently healthy Japanese adults. *European Journal of Nutrition, 55,* 267–279.

Nixon, S.A., Rubincam, C., Casale, M., & Flicker, S. (2011). Is 80% a passing grade? Meanings attached to condom use in an abstinence-plus HIV prevention programme in South Africa. *AIDS Care, 23,* 213–220.

Noel-Miller, C.M. (2011). Partner caregiving in older cohabiting couples. *Journals of Gerontology B: Psychological Sciences and Social Sciences, 66B,* 341–353.

Noguchi, H., & others (2015). Expression of DNMT1 in neural stem/precursor cells is critical for survival of newly generated neurons in the adult hippocampus. *Neuroscience Research, 95,* 1–11.

Nomoto, M., & others (2009). Inter- and intra-individual variation in L-dopa pharmacokinetics in the treatment of Parkinson's disease. *Parkinsonism and Related Disorders, 15*(Suppl. 1), S21–S24.

Norman, J.F., Holmin, J.S., & Bartholomew, A.N. (2011). Visual memories for perceived length are well preserved in older adults. *Vision Research, 51,* 2057–2062.

Norouzieh, K. (2005). Case management of the dying child. *Case Manager, 16,* 54–57.

Nosraty, L., Jylha, M., Raittila, T., & Lumme-Sandt, K. (2015). Perceptions by the oldest old of successful aging, vitality 90+ study. *Journal of Aging Studies, 32,* 50–58.

Nottelmann, E.D., & others (1987). Gonadal and adrenal hormone correlates of adjustment in early adolescence. In R.M. Lerner & T.T. Foch (Eds.), *Biological-psychological interactions in early adolescence.* Hillsdale, NJ: Erlbaum.

Notzon, D.P., & others (2016, in press). ADHD is highly prevalent in patients seeking treatment for cannabis use disorders. *Journal of Attention Disorders.*

Notzon, S., & others (2016). Attachment style and oxytocin receptor gene variation interact in influencing social anxiety. *World Journal of Biological Psychiatry, 17,* 76–83.

Novick, G., & others (2013). Group prenatal care: Model fidelity and outcomes. *American Journal of Obstetrics and Gynecology, 209*(2), 112.e1–112.e6.

Nucci, L. (2006). Education for moral development. In M. Killen & J. Smetana (Eds.), *Handbook of moral development.* Mahwah, NJ: Erlbaum.

Nutter, E., Meyer, S., Shaw-Battista, J., & Marowitz, A. (2014). Waterbirth: An integrative analysis of peer-reviewed literature. *Journal of Midwifery and Women's Health, 59,* 286–319.

Nye, C., Allemand, M., Gosling, S., Potter, J., & Roberts, B.W. (2016, in press). Personality trait differences between young and middle-aged adults: Measurement artifacts or actual trends? *Journal of Personality.*

Nygard, C-H. (2013). *The ability to work peaks in middle age.* Interview. Retrieved September 15, 2013, from http://researchandstudy.uta.fi/2013/094/12/the-ability-to-work-peaks-in-middle-age/

O

O'Brien, J.L., & others (2013). Cognitive training and selective attention in the aging brain: An electrophysiological study. *Clinical Neurophysiology, 124,* 2198–2208.

O'Brien, M., & Moss, P. (2010). Fathers, work, and family policies in Europe. In M.E. Lamb (Ed.), *The role of the father in child development* (5th ed.). New York: Wiley.

O'Brien, M., & others (2014). Women's work and child care: Perspectives and prospects. In E.T. Gershoff, R.S. Mistry, & D.A. Crosby (Eds.), *Societal contexts of child development.* New York: Oxford University Press.

O'Caoimh, R., Timmons, S., & Molloy, D.W. (2016). Screening for mild cognitive impairment: Comparison of "MCI specific" screening instruments. *Journal of Alzheimer's Disease, 51,* 619–629.

O'Connor, D.B., & others (2011). The relationships between sex hormones and sexual function in middle-aged and older European men. *Journal of Clinical Endocrinology and Metabolism, 96,* E1577–E1587.

O'Connor, T.G. (2016). Development of models and mechanisms for understanding the effects of early experiences on psychological development. In D. Cicchetti (Ed.), *Developmental psychopathology* (3rd ed.). New York: Wiley.

O'Halloran, A.M., & others (2011). Falls and fall efficacy: The role of sustained attention in older adults. *BMC Geriatrics, 11,* 85.

O'Hara, M.W., & McCabe, F. (2013). Postpartum depression: Current status and future directions. *Annual Review of Clinical Psychology* (Vol. 9). Palo Alto, CA: Annual Reviews.

O'Hara, M., & others (2016, in press). Children neglected: Where cumulative risk theory fails. *Child Abuse and Neglect.*

O'Hara, R.E., Gibbons, F.X., Weng, C.Y., Gerrard, M., & Simons, R.L. (2012). Perceived racial discrimination as a barrier to college enrollment for African Americans. *Personality and Social Psychology Bulletin, 38,* 77–89.

O'Keeffe, L.M., Greene, R.A., & Kearney, P.M. (2014). The effect of moderate gestational alcohol consumption during pregnancy on speech and language outcomes in children: A systematic review. *Systematic Reviews, 3,* 1.

Obel, C., & others (2016). The risk of attention deficit hyperactivity disorder in children exposed to smoking during pregnancy—a re-examination using a sibling design. *Journal of Child Psychology and Psychiatry, 57,* 532–537.

Occupational Outlook Handbook (2016/2017). Washington, DC: U.S. Department of Labor, Bureau of Labor Statistics.

Odejide, O.O. (2016). A policy prescription for hospice care. *JAMA, 315,* 257–258.

OECD (2010). *Obesity and the economics of prevention—Fit or fat.* Paris: OECD.

OECD (2014). Life satisfaction. *Society at a glance 2014: OECD social indicators.* Paris: OECD Publishing.

Oesen, S., & others (2015). Effects of elastic band resistance training and nutritional supplementation on physical performance of institutionalized elderly—a randomized controlled trial. *Experimental Gerontology, 72,* 99–108.

Offer, D., Ostrov, E., Howard, K.I., & Atkinson, R. (1988). *The teenage world: Adolescents' self-image in ten countries.* New York: Plenum.

Ogawa, E.F., You, T., & Leveille, S.G. (2016). Potential benefits of exergaming for cognition and dual-task function in older adults: A systematic review. *Journal of Aging and Physical Activity, 24,* 332–336.

Ogbuanu, I.U., & others (2014). Maternal, fetal, and neonatal outcomes associated with measles during pregnancy: Namibia, 2009–2010. *Clinical Infectious Diseases, 58,* 1086–1092.

Ogden, C.L., Carroll, M.D., Kit, B.K., & Flegal, K.M. (2012, January). Prevalence of obesity in the United States, 2009–2010. *NCHS Data Brief,* 1–9.

Ogden, C.L., Carroll, M.D., Kit, B.K., & Flegal, K.M. (2013, October). Prevalence of obesity among adults: United States, 2011–2012. *NCHS Data Brief, 131.*

Ogden, C.L., Carroll, M.D., Kit, B.K., & Flegal, K.M. (2014). Prevalence of childhood and adult obesity in the United States, 2011–2012. *Journal of the American Medical Association, 311,* 308–314.

Ogden, C.L., Carroll, M.D., Kit, B.K., & Flegal, K.M. (2014). Prevalence of childhood obesity in the United States, 2011–2012. *Journal of the American Medical Association, 311,* 806–814.

Ohlin, A., & others (2015). Sepsis as a risk factor for neonatal morbidity in extremely preterm infants. *Acta Pediatrica, 104,* 1070–1076.

Ojha, S., & others (2015). Maternal health and eating habits: Metabolic consequences and impact on child health. *Trends in Molecular Medicine, 21,* 126–133.

Okada, H.C., Alleyne, B., Varghai, K., Kinder, K., & Guyuron, B. (2013). Facial changes caused by smoking: A comparison between smoking and non-smoking identical twins. *Plastic and Reconstructive Surgery, 132*(5), 1085–1092.

Okada, M., & others (2016). Abrogation of age-induced microRNA-195 rejuvenates the senescent mesenchymal stem cells by reactivating telomerase. *Stem Cells, 34,* 148–159.

Okubo, Y., & others (2016, in press). Walking can be more effective than balance in fall prevention among community-dwelling older adults. *Geriatrics and Gerontology International.*

Okun, M.A., Yeung, E.W., & Brown, S. (2013). Volunteering by older adults and risk of mortality: A meta-analysis. *Psychology and Aging, 28,* 564–577.

Olds, D.L., & others (2004). Effects of home visits by paraprofessionals and nurses: Age four follow-up of a randomized trial. *Pediatrics, 114,* 1560–1568.

Olds, D.L., & others (2007). Effects of nurse home visiting on maternal and child functioning: Age nine follow-up of a randomized trial. *Pediatrics, 120,* e832–e845.

Olds, D.L., & others (2014). Effects of home visits by paraprofessionals and by nurses on children: Follow-up of a randomized trial age 6 and 9 years. *JAMA Pediatrics, 168,* 114–121.

Olesen, K., Rugulies, R., Rod, N.H., & Bonde, J.P. (2014). Does retirement reduce the risk of myocardial infarction? *A prospective registry linkage study of 617,511 Danish workers. International Journal of Epidemiology, 43,* 160–167.

Olino, T.M., & others (2016). Maternal depression, parenting, and youth depressive symptoms: Mediation and moderation in short-term longitudinal study. *Journal of Clinical Child and Adolescent Psychology, 45,* 279–290.

Olsen, D.P. (2016). Ethically relevant differences in advance directives for psychiatric and end-of-life care. *Journal of the American Psychiatric Nurses Association, 22,* 52–59.

Olshansky, S.J., & others (2012). Differences in life expectancy due to race and educational differences are widening, and many may not catch up. *Health Affairs, 31,* 1803–1813.

Olszewski-Kubilius, P., & Thomson, D. (2013). Gifted education programs and procedures. In I.B. Weiner & others (Eds.), *Handbook of psychology* (2nd ed., Vol. 7). New York: Wiley.

Olweus, D. (2003). Prevalence estimation of school bullying with the Olweus bully/victim questionnaire. *Aggressive Behavior, 29*(3), 239–269.

Olweus, D. (2013). School bullying: Development and some important challenges. *Annual Review of Clinical Psychology* (Vol. 9). Palo Alto, CA: Annual Reviews.

Ong, J., Brennsteiner, A., Chow, E., & Herbert, R.S. (2016). Correlates of family satisfaction with hospice care: General inpatient hospice care versus routine home hospice care. *Journal of Palliative Medicine, 19,* 97–100.

Ornoy, A., Weinstein-Fudim, L., & Ergaz, Z. (2015). Prenatal factors associated with autism spectrum disorder (ASD). *Reproductive Toxicology, 56,* 155–169.

Ornstein, K., & others (2014). The differential impact of unique behavioral and psychological symptoms for the dementia caregiver: How and why do patients' individual symptom clusters impact caregiver depressive symptoms? *American Journal of Geriatric Psychiatry, 21,* 1277–1286.

Orosz, G., & others (2015). Elevated romantic love and jealousy if relationship is declared on Facebook. *Frontiers in Psychology, 6,* 214.

Orpinas, P., McNicholas, C., & Nahapetyan, L. (2015). Gender differences in trajectories of relational aggression perpetration and victimization from middle to high school. *Aggressive Behavior, 41,* 401–412.

Orsi, C.M., Hale, D.E., & Lynch, J.L. (2011). Pediatric obesity epidemiology. *Current Opinion in Endocrinology, Diabetes, and Obesity, 18,* 14–22.

Orth, U., Robins, R.W., Meier, L.L., & Conger, R.D. (2016). Refining the vulnerability model of low self-esteem and depression: Disentangling the effects of genuine self-esteem and narcissism. *Journal of Personality and Social Psychology, 110,* 133–149.

Ossenkoppele, R., & others (2016, in press). Tau PET patterns mirror clinical and neuroanatomical variability in Alzheimer's disease. *Brain.*

Osterberg, E.C., Bernie, A.M., & Ramasamy, R. (2014). Risk of replacement testosterone therapy in men. *Indian Journal of Urology, 30,* 2–7.

Otte, R.A., Donkers, F.C., Braeken, M.A., & Van den Bergh, B.R. (2015). Multimodal processing of emotional information in 9-month-old infants I: Emotional faces and voices. *Brain and Cognition, 95,* 99–106.

Oveisgharan, S., & Hachinski, V. (2015). Executive dysfunction is a strong stroke predictor. *Journal of Neural Science, 349,* 161–167.

Owen, J., Fincham, F.D., & Manthos, M. (2013). Friendship after a friends with benefits relationship: Deception, psychological function, and social connectedness. *Archives of Sexual Behavior, 42,* 1443–1449.

Owens, J.A., Belon, K., & Moss, P. (2010). Impact of delaying school start time on adolescent sleep, mood, and behavior. *Archives of Pediatric and Adolescent Medicine, 164,* 608–614.

Owsley, C., & others (2016). Comparison of visual function in older eyes in the earliest stages of age-related macular degeneration to those in normal macular health. *Current Eye Research, 41,* 266–272.

Ozturk, S. (2015). Telomerase activity and telomere length in male germ cells. *Biology of Reproduction, 92,* 53.

P

Pabisiak, K. (2016, in press). Brain death criteria formulated for transplantation purposes: fact or myth? *Anesthesiology Intensive Care.*

Pace, A., & others (2016, in press). The story of language acquisition: From words to world and back again. In L. Alter & C. Tamis-LeMonda (Eds.), *Child psychology: A handbook of contemporary issues* (3rd ed.). New York: Psychology Press.

Pageon, H., & others (2014). Skin aging by glycation: Lessons from the reconstructed skin model. *Clinical Chemistry and Laboratory Medicine, 52*(1), 169–174.

Pakhomov, S.V., & Hemmy, L.S. (2014). A computational linguistic measure of clustering behavior on semantic verbal fluency task predicts risk of future dementia in the Nun Study. *Cortex, 55,* 97–106.

Palmer, R.H., & others (2016, in press). Effects of maternal smoking during pregnancy on offspring externalizing problems: Contextual effects in a sample of female twins. *Behavior Genetics.*

Palmore, E.B. (2004). Research note: Ageism in Canada and the United States. *Journal of Cross Cultural Gerontology, 19,* 41–46.

Pan, B.A., & Uccelli, P. (2009). Semantic development. In J. Berko Gleason & N.B. Ratner (Eds.) (2009). *The development of language* (7th ed.). Boston: Allyn & Bacon.

Pan, C.Y., & others (2016, in press). Effects of physical exercise intervention on motor skills and executive functions with ADHD: A pilot study. *Journal of Attention Disorders.*

Pan, Z., & Chang, C. (2012). Gender and the regulation of longevity: Implications for autoimmunity. *Autoimmunity Reviews, 11,* A393–A403.

Paneque, M., Sequeiros, J., & Skirton, H. (2015). Quality issues concerning genetic counseling for presymptomatic testing: A European Delphi study. *European Journal of Human Genetics, 23,* 1468–1472.

Papastavrou, E., Charlalambous, A., Tsangari, H., & Karayiannis, G. (2012). The burdensome and depressive experience of caring: What cancer, schizophrenia, and Alzheimer's disease caregivers have in common. *Cancer Nursing, 35,* 187–194.

Parens, E., & Johnston, J. (2009). Facts, values, and attention-deficit hyperactivity disorder (ADHD): An update on the controversies. *Child and Adolescent Psychiatry and Mental Health, 3,* 1.

Parent, J., & others (2016). Mindfulness in parenting and coparenting. *Mindfulness, 7,* 504–513.

Parfitt, Y., Pike, A., & Ayers, S. (2014). Infant developmental outcomes: A family systems perspective. *Infant and Child Development, 23,* 353–373.

Parish-Morris, J., Golinkoff, R.M., & Hirsh-Pasek, K. (2013). From coo to code: A brief story of language development. In P.D. Zelazo (Ed.), *Handbook of developmental psychology.* New York: Oxford University Press.

Park, B.Y., & others (2016). Connectivity analysis and feature classification in attention deficit hyperactivity disorder sub-types: A task functional magnetic resonance imaging study. *Brain Topography, 29,* 429–439.

Park, C.H., Elavsky, S., & Koo, K.M. (2014). Factors influencing physical activity in older adults. *Journal of Exercise Rehabilitation, 10,* 45–52.

Park, C.L. (2010). Making sense out of the meaning literature: An integrative review of meaning making and its effect on adjustment to stressful life events. *Psychological Bulletin, 136,* 257–301.

Park, C.L. (2012). Meaning, spirituality, and growth: Protective and resilience factors in health and illness. In A.S. Baum, T.A. Revenson, & J.E. Singer (Eds.), *Handbook of health psychology* (2nd ed.). New York: Sage.

Park, C.L. (2013). Meaning making in cancer survivorship. In P.T.P. Wong (Ed.), *Handbook of meaning* (2nd ed.). Thousand Oaks, CA: Sage.

Park, D. (2001). Commentary in R. Restak, *The secret life of the brain.* Washington, DC: Joseph Henry Press.

Park, D.C., & Farrell, M.E. (2016). The aging mind in transition: Amyloid deposition and progression toward Alzheimer's disease. In K.W. Schaie & S.L. Willis (Eds.), *Handbook of the psychology of aging* (8th ed.). New York: Elsevier.

Park, D.C., & others (2014). The impact of sustained engagement on cognitive function in older adults: The Synapse Project. *Psychological Science, 25,* 103–112.

Park, E.M., Meltzer-Brody, S., & Stickgold, R. (2013). Poor sleep maintenance and subjective sleep quality are associated with postpartum depression symptom severity. *Archives of Women's Mental Health, 16*(6), 539–547.

Park, H.K., & others (2014). Practical application of kangaroo mother care in preterm infants:

Clinical characteristics and safety of kangaroo mother care. *Journal of Perinatal Medicine, 42,* 239–245.

Park, K.M., & Park, H. (2015). Effects of self-esteem improvement program on self-esteem and peer attachment in elementary school children with observed problematic behaviors. *Asian Nursing Research, 9,* 53–59.

Park, M.J., Paul Mulye, T., Adams, S.H., Brindis, C.D., & Irwin, C.E. (2006). The health status of young adults in the United States. *Journal of Adolescent Health, 39,* 305–317.

Park, S., Mori, R., & Shimokawa, I. (2013). Do sirtuins promote mammalian longevity? A critical review on its relevance to the longevity effect induced by calorie restriction. *Molecules and Cells, 35,* 474–480.

Parkay, F.W. (2016). *Becoming a teacher* (10th ed.). Upper Saddle River, NJ: Pearson.

Parker, C.B. (2016, February 11, 2016). Stanford project suggests longer, healthier lives possible. *Stanford Report,* 1–4.

Parker, S.K. (2014). Work design for our times: Going beyond intrinsic motivation. *Annual Review of Psychology* (Vol. 65). Palo Alto, CA: Annual Reviews.

Parkes, A., Sweeting, H., Young, R., & Wight, D. (2016, in press). Does parenting help to explain socioeconomic inequalities in children's body mass index trajectories? Longitudinal analysis using the Growing Up in Scotland study. *Journal of Epidemiology and Community Health.*

Parkes, K.R. (2006). Physical activity and self-rated health: Interactive effects of activity in work and leisure domains. *British Journal of Health Psychology, 11,* 533–550.

Parra-Cardona, J.R., & others (2016, in press). A balancing act: Integrating evidence-based knowledge and cultural relevance in a program of prevention parenting research with Latino immigrants. *Family Process.*

Parrott, A.C., & others (2014). MDMA and heightened cortisol: A neurohormonal perspective on the pregnancy outcomes of mothers who used 'Ecstasy' during pregnancy. *Human Psychopharmacology, 29,* 1–7.

Pasco-Fearon, R.M., & Belsky, J. (2016). Precursors of attachment security. In J. Cassidy & P.R. Shaver (Eds.), *Handbook of attachment* (3rd ed.). New York: Guilford.

Pasco-Fearon, R.M., & others (2016). Attachment and developmental psychopathology. In D. Cicchetti (Ed.), *Developmental psychopathology* (3rd ed.). New York: Wiley.

Pasley, K., & Moorefield, B.S. (2004). Stepfamilies. In M. Coleman & L. Ganong (Eds.), *Handbook of contemporary families.* Thousand Oaks, CA: Sage.

Pate, R.R., & others (2015). Prevalence of compliance with a new physical activity guideline for preschool-aged children. *Childhood Obesity, 11,* 45–70.

Patel, S., & others (2016). Association of maternal diabetes/glycosuria and pre-pregnancy body mass index with offspring indicators of non-alcoholic fatty liver disease. *BMC Pediatrics, 16,* 47.

Pathman, T., Doydum, A., & Bauer, P.J. (2013). Bringing order to life events: Memory for the temporal order of autobiographical events over an extended period in school-aged children and adults. *Journal of Experimental Child Psychology, 115,* 309–325.

Patrick, M.E., & Schulenberg, J.E. (2010). Alcohol use and heavy episodic drinking prevalence among national samples of American eighth- and tenth-grade students. *Journal of Studies on Alcohol and Drugs, 71,* 41–45.

Patterson, C.J. (2013). Family lives of gay and lesbian adults. In G.W. Peterson & K.R. Bush (Eds.), *Handbook of marriage and the family* (3rd ed.). New York: Springer.

Patterson, C.J. (2014). Sexual minority youth and youth with sexual minority parents. In A. Ben Areah & others (Eds.), *Handbook of child research.* Thousand Oaks, CA: Sage.

Patterson, C.J., & Farr, R.H. (2014). Children of lesbian and gay parents: Reflections on the research-policy interface. In H.R. Schaffer & K. Durkin (Eds.), *Blackwell handbook of developmental psychology in action.* New York: Wiley.

Patterson, C.J., Farr, R.H., & Hastings, P.D. (2015). Socialization in the context of family diversity. In J.E. Grusec & P.D. Hastings (Eds.), *Handbook of socialization* (2nd ed.). New York: Guilford.

Patton, G.C., & others (2011). Overweight and obesity between adolescence and early adulthood: A 10-year prospective study. *Journal of Adolescent Health, 45,* 275–280.

Paulhus, D.L. (2008). Birth order. In M.M. Haith & J.B. Benson (Eds.), *Encyclopedia of infant and early childhood development.* Oxford, UK: Elsevier.

Pauliks, L.B. (2015). The effect of pregestational diabetes on fetal heart function. *Expert Review of Cardiovascular Therapy, 13,* 67–74.

Paulson, J.F., Bazemore, S.D., Goodman, J.H., & Leiferman, J.A. (2016, in press). The course and interrelationship of maternal and paternal perinatal depression. *Archives of Women's Mental Health.*

Paunesku, D., & others (2015). Mind-set interventions are a scaleable treatment for academic underachievement. *Psychological Science, 26,* 784–793.

Paus, T., & others (2007). Morphological properties of the action-observation cortical network in adolescents with low and high resistance to peer influence. *Social Neuroscience 3*(3), 303–316.

Payer, L. (1991). The menopause in various cultures. In H. Burger & M. Boulet (Eds.), *A portrait of the menopause.* Park Ridge, NJ: Parthenon.

Payne, K. (2015). *The remarriage rate.* Bowling Green, Ohio: Bowling Green State University, National Center for Family and Marriage Research.

Pea, R., & others (2012). Media use, face-to-face communication, media multitasking, and social well-being among 8- to 12-year-old girls. *Developmental Psychology, 48,* 327–336.

Pearlstein, T. (2015). Depression during pregnancy. *Best Practices in Research: Clinical Obstetrics and Gynecology, 29,* 754–764.

Peck, T., Scharf, R.J., Conaway, M.R., & De-Boer, M.D. (2015). Viewing as little as 1 hour of TV daily is associated with higher change in BMI between kindergarten and first grade. *Obesity, 23,* 1680–1686.

Pedersen, L.R., & others (2016, in press). Risk factors for myocardial infarction in women and men: A review of the current literature. *Current Pharmaceutical Design.*

Peek, M.K. (2009). Marriage in later life. In D. Carr (Ed.), *Encyclopedia of the life course and human development.* Boston: Gale Cengage.

Peets, K., Hodges, E.V.E., & Salmivalli, C. (2011). Actualization of social cognitions into aggressive behavior toward disliked targets. *Social Development, 20,* 233–250.

Pelaez, M., Virues-Ortega, J., & Gewirtz, J.L. (2012). Acquisition of social referencing via discrimination training in infants. *Journal of Applied Behavior Analysis, 45,* 23–36.

Peltz, C.B., Gratton, G., & Fabiani, M. (2011). Age-related changes in electrophysiological and neuropsychological indices of working memory, attention control, and cognitive flexibility. *Frontiers in Psychology, 2,* 190.

Penazzi, L., Bakota, L., & Brandt, R. (2016). Microtuble dynamics in neuronal development, plasticity, and neurodegeneration. *International Review of Cell and Molecular Biology, 321,* 89–169.

Peng, F., & others (2016). A cross-sectional voxel-based morphometric study of age- and sex-related changes in gray matter volume in the normal aging brain. *Journal of Computer Assisted Tomography, 40,* 307–315.

Peng, P., & Fuchs, D. (2016a). A meta-analysis of working memory deficits in children with learning difficulties: Is there a difference between the verbal domain and numerical domain? *Journal of Learning Disabilities, 49,* 3–20.

Penn, S. (2015). Overcoming the barriers to use of kangaroo care in neonatal settings. *Nursing Children and Young People, 27,* 22–27.

Pennell, A., Salo-Coombs, V., Hering, A., Spielman, F., & Fecho, K. (2011). Anesthesia and analgesia-related preferences and outcomes of women who have birth plans. *Journal of Midwifery and Women's Health, 56,* 376–381.

Perales, M., & others (2016). Benefits of aerobic or resistance training during pregnancy on maternal health and perinatal outcomes: A systematic review. *Early Human Development, 94,* 43–48.

Peregoy, S.F., & Boyle, O.F. (2017). *Reading, writing, and learning ESL* (7th ed.). Upper Saddle River, NJ: Pearson.

Perez, E.M., & others (2015). Massage therapy improves the development of HIV-exposed infants living in a low socioeconomic, peri-urban community of South Africa. *Infant Behavior and Development, 38,* 135–146.

Perez-Edgar, K.E., & Guyer, A.E. (2014). Behavioral inhibition: Temperament or prodrome? *Current Behavioral Neuroscience Reports, 1,* 182–190.

Perry, N.B., Swingler, M.M., Calkins, S.D., & Bell, M.A. (2016). Neurophysiological correlates of attention behavior in early infancy: Implications for emotion regulation during early childhood. *Journal of Experimental Child Psychology, 142,* 245–261.

Peskin, H. (1967). Pubertal onset and ego functioning. *Journal of Abnormal Psychology, 72,* 1–15.

Petersen, I.T., & others (2012). Interaction between serotonin transporter polymorphism (5-HTTLPR) and stressful life events in adolescents' trajectories of anxious/depressed symptoms. *Developmental Psychology, 48*(5), 1463–1475.

Petersen, J.L., & Hyde, J.S. (2010). A meta-analytic review of research on gender differences in sexuality, 1973–2007. *Psychological Bulletin, 136,* 21–38.

Pew Research Center (2010). *Millennials: Confident, connected, open to change.* Washington, DC: Pew Research Center.

Pew Research Center (2010). *The decline of marriage and rise of new families.* Washington, DC: Author.

Pew Research Center (2011, December). *Barely half of U.S. adults are married—a record low*. Washington, DC: Pew Research Center.

Pew Research Center (2012). *Religion & Public Life Project*. Washington, DC: Pew Research Center.

Pew Research Center (2015a). *Five facts about online dating*. Washington, DC: Author.

Pew Research Center (2015b). *For most highly educated women, motherhood doesn't start until the 30s*. Washington, DC: Pew Research Center.

Pfefferbaum, B., Newman, E., & Nelson, S.D. (2014). Mental health interventions for children exposed to disasters and terrorism. *Journal of Child and Adolescent Psychopharmacology, 24,* 24–31.

Pfeifer, C., & Bunders, M.J. (2016, in press). Maternal HIV infection alters the immune balance in the mother and fetus: Implications for pregnancy outcome and infant health. *Current Opinion in HIV and AIDS.*

Phaniendra, A., Jestadi, D.B., & Periyasamy, L. (2015). Free radicals: Sources, targets, and their implication for various diseases. *Indian Journal of Clinical Biochemistry, 30,* 11–26.

Phinney, J.S. (2008). Bridging identities and disciplines: Advances and challenges in understanding multiple identities. In M. Azmitia, M. Syed, & K. Radmacher (Eds.), *The intersections of personal and social identities. New Directions for Child and Adolescent Development, 120,* 97–109.

Phinney, J.S., & Vedder, P. (2013). Family relationship values of adolescents and parents: Intergenerational discrepancies and adaptation. In J.W. Berry & others (Eds.), *Immigrant youth in cultural transmission*. New York: Psychology Press.

Piaget, J. (1932). *The moral judgment of the child*. New York: Harcourt Brace Jovanovich.

Piaget, J. (1952). *The origins of intelligence in children* (M. Cook, Trans.). New York: International Universities Press.

Piaget, J. (1954). *The construction of reality in the child*. New York: Basic Books.

Piaget, J. (1962). *Play, dreams, and imitation*. New York. W.W. Norton.

Piaget, J., & Inhelder, B. (1969). *The child's conception of space* (F.J. Langdon & J.L. Lunger, Trans.). New York: W.W. Norton.

Pianta, R.C. (2016). Classroom processes and teacher-student interaction: Integrations with a developmental psychopathology perspective. In D. Cicchetti (Ed.), *Developmental psychopathology* (3rd ed.). New York: Wiley.

Piazza, J.R., & Charles, S.T. (2012). Affective disorders and age: The view through a developmental lens. In S.K. Whitbourne & M.J. Sliwinski (Eds.), *Wiley-Blackwell handbook of adult development and aging*. New York: Wiley.

Piazza, J.R., Charles, S.T., Sliwinski, M.J., Mogle, J., & Almeida, D.M. (2013). Affective reactivity to daily stressors and long-term risk of reporting chronic physical health condition. *Annals of Behavior Medicine, 45,* 110–120.

Piko, B.F., & Balazs, M.A. (2012). Authoritative parenting style and adolescent smoking and drinking. *Addictive Behaviors, 37,* 353–356.

Pinker, S. (2015). *Language, cognition, and human nature*. New York: Oxford University Press.

Pinninti, S.G., & Kimberlin, D.W. (2013). Neonatal herpes simplex virus infections. *Pediatric Clinics of North America, 60,* 351–365.

Pinquart, M., Feubner, C., & Ahnert, L. (2013). Meta-analytic evidence for stability of attachments from infancy to early adulthood. *Attachment and Human Development, 15,* 189–218.

Pinto, M., & Moraes, C.T. (2015). Mechanisms linking mtDNA damage and aging. *Free Radical Biology and Medicine, 85,* 250–258.

Pinto Pereira, S.M., van Veldhoven, K., Li, L., & Power, C. (2016). Combined early and adult life risk factor associations for mid-life obesity in a prospective birth cohort: Assessing potential public health impact. *BMJ Open, 6*(4), e011044.

Pipp, S.L., Fischer, K.W., & Jennings, S.L. (1987). The acquisition of self and mother knowledge in infancy. *Developmental Psychology, 23,* 86–96.

Pitkänen, T., Lyrra, A.L., & Pulkkinen, L. (2005). Age of onset of drinking and the use of alcohol in adulthood: A follow-up study from age 8–42 for females and males. *Addiction, 100,* 652–661.

Pitzer, L.M., Fingerman, K.L., & Lefkowitz, E.S. (2014). Support and negativity in the adult parent tie: Development of the Parent Adult Relationship Questionnaire (PARQ). *International Journal of Aging and Human Development, 58,* 127–146.

Platt, B., Kadosh, K.C., & Lau, J.Y. (2013). The role of peer rejection in adolescent depression. *Depression and Anxiety, 30,* 809–821.

Plomin, R., DeFries, J.C., McClearn, G.E., & McGuffin, P. (2009). *Behavioral genetics* (5th ed.). New York: W.H. Freeman.

Plucker, J. (2010, July 19). Commentary in P. Bronson & A. Merryman, The creativity crisis. *Newsweek,* pp. 45–46.

Pluess, M., & Belsky, J. (2009). Differential susceptibility to rearing experience: The case of child care. *Journal of Child Psychology and Psychiatry, 50,* 396–404.

Pluess, M., & Meaney, M. (2016). Genes, environment, and well-being. In M. Pluess (Ed.), *Genetics of psychological well-being*. New York: Oxford University Press.

Podgurski, M.J. (2016). Theorists and techniques: Connecting education theories to Lamaze teaching techniques. *Journal of Perinatal Education, 25,* 9–17.

Poehlmann-Tynan, J., & others (2016, in press). A pilot study of contemplative practices with economically disadvantaged preschoolers: Children's empathic and self-regulatory behaviors. *Mindfulness.*

Polat, U., & others (2012). Training the brain to overcome the effect of aging on the human eye. *Scientific Reports, 2,* 278.

Pollack, W. (1999). *Real boys*. New York: Owl Books.

Polo-Kantola, P. (2011). Sleep problems in midlife and beyond. *Maturitas, 68,* 224–232.

Pomerantz, E.M. (2016). *Center for Parent-Child Studies*. Retrieved January 6, 2016, from http://labs.psychology.illinois.edu/cpcs/

Pomerantz, E.M., Cheung, C.S., & Qin, L. (2012). Relatedness between children and parents: Implications for motivation. In R. Ryan (Ed.), *Oxford handbook of motivation*. New York: Oxford University Press.

Pomerantz, E.M., & Kempner, S.G. (2013). Mothers' daily person and process praise: Implications for children's intelligence and motivation. *Developmental Psychology, 49,* 2040–2046.

Pomerantz, E.M., Kim, E.M., & Cheung, C.S. (2012). Parents' involvement in children's learning.

In K.R. Harris & others (Eds.), *APA educational psychology handbook*. Washington, DC: American Psychological Association.

Pong, S., & Landale, N.S. (2012). Academic achievement of legal immigrants' children: The roles of parents' pre- and post-immigration characteristics in origin-group differences. *Child Development, 83,* 1543–1559.

Pope, T.M., & Okinski, M.E. (2016, in press). Legal standards for brain death and undue influence in euthanasia laws. *Journal of Bioethical Inquiry.*

Popenoe, D. (2009). *The state of our unions 2008. Updates of social indicators: Tables and charts*. Piscataway, NJ: The National Marriage Project.

Popham, W.J. (2017). *Classroom assessment* (8th ed.). Upper Saddle River, NJ: Pearson.

Porcelli, B., & others (2016). Association between stressful life events and autoimmune diseases: A systematic review and and meta-analysis of retrospective case-control studies. *Autoimmunity Reviews, 15,* 325–334.

Posner, M.I., & Rothbart, M.K. (2007). *Educating the human brain*. Washington, DC: American Psychological Association.

Posner, M.I., Rothbart, M.K., Sheese, B.E., & Voelker, P. (2014). Developing attention: Behavioral and brain mechanisms. *Advances in Neuroscience, 2014,* 405094.

Powell, B., Cooper, G., Hoffman, K., & Marvin, B. (2014). *The circle of security intervention*. New York: Guilford.

Powell, S.D. (2015). *Your introduction to education* (3rd ed.). Upper Saddle River, NJ: Pearson.

Powers, K.E., Chavez, R.S., & Heatherton, T.F. (2016). Individual differences in response of dorsomedial prefrontal cortex predict daily social behavior. *Social Cognitive and Affective Neuroscience, 11,* 121–126.

Powers, S.K., & Dodd, S.L. (2017). *Total fitness and wellness* (7th ed.). Upper Saddle River, NJ: Pearson.

Prager, K.J. (2013). *The dilemmas of intimacy*. New York: Taylor & Francis.

Prairie, B.A., & others (2015). Symptoms of depressed mood, disturbed sleep, and sexual problems in midlife women: Cross-sectional data from the Study of Women's Health Across the Nation. *Journal of Women's Health, 24,* 119–126.

Prakash, R.S., Voss, M.W., Erickson, K.I., & Kramer, A.F. (2015). Moving toward a healthier brain and mind. *Annual Review of Psychology* (Vol. 66). Palo Alto, CA: Annual Reviews.

Prameela, K.K. (2011). Breastfeeding—anti-viral potential and relevance to the influenza virus pandemic. *Medical Journal of Malaysia, 66,* 166–169.

Pratt, M.W., Norris, J.E., Hebblethwaite, S., & Arnold, M.O. (2008). International transmission of values: Family generality and adolescents' narratives of parent and grandparent value teaching. *Journal of Personality, 76,* 171–198.

Pressley, M. (2007). An interview with Michael Pressley by Terri Flowerday and Michael Shaughnessy. *Educational Psychology Review, 19,* 1–12.

Prigerson, H.G., & Maciejewski, P.K. (2014). Predicting prolonged grief disorder: Caregiver prodrome turns bereaved survivor syndrome. Commentary on Thomas et al. *Journal of Pain and Symptom Management, 47,* 516–517.

Prinstein, M.J., & Giletta, M. (2016). Peer relations and developmental psychopathology.

In D. Cicchetti (Ed.), *Developmental psychopathology* (3rd ed.). New York: Wiley.

Propst, M., & others (2015). Diabetes and prediabetes significantly higher in morbidly obese children compared to obese children. *Endocrine Practice, 21,* 1046–1053.

Puccini, D., & Liszkowski, U. (2012). 15-month-old infants fast map words but not representational gestures of multimodal labels. *Frontiers in Psychology, 3,* 101.

Pudrovska, T. (2009). Midlife crises and transitions. In D. Carr (Ed.), *Encyclopedia of the life course and human development.* Boston: Gale Cengage.

Pufal, M.A., & others (2012). Prevalence of overweight in children of obese patients: A dietary overview. *Obesity Surgery, 22*(8), 1220–1224.

Puma, M., & others (2010). *Head Start impact study. Final report.* Washington, DC: Administration for Children & Families.

Putallaz, M., & others (2007). Overt and relational aggression and victimization: Multiple perspectives within the school setting. *Journal of School Psychology, 45,* 523–547.

Puzzanchera, C., & Robson, C. (2014, February). Delinquency cases in juvenile court, 2010. *Juvenile offenders and victims: National Report Series.* Washington, DC: U.S. Department of Justice.

Puzzanchera, C., & Sickmund, M. (2008, July). *Juvenile court statistics 2005.* Pittsburgh: National Center for Juvenile Justice.

Q

Qin, J., & others (2015). Impact of arthritis and multiple chronic conditions on selected life domains—United States, 1913. *MMWR Morbity and Mortality Weekly Report, 64,* 578–582.

Qin, L., & others (2016, in press). Aging of immune system: Immune signature from peripheral blood lymphocyte subsets in 1068 healthy adults. *Aging.*

Qu, Y., & Pomerantz, E.M. (2015). Divergent school trajectories in early adolescence in the United States and China: An examination of underlying mechanisms. *Journal of Youth and Adolescence, 44,* 2095–2109.

Qu, Y., & others (2016). Conceptions of adolescence: Implications for differences in engagement in school over early adolescence in the United States and China. *Journal of Research on Adolescence, 26,* 126–141.

Quesnel-Vallée, A., Willson, A., & Reiter-Campeau, S. (2016). Health inequalities among older adults in developed countries: Reconciling theories and policy approaches. In L.K. George & K.F. Ferraro (Eds.), *Handbook of aging and the social sciences* (8th ed.). New York: Elsevier.

Quigley, C., & Muller, M.M. (2014). Feature-selective attention in healthy old age: A selective decline in selective attention. *Journal of Neuroscience, 34,* 2471–2476.

Quinn, P.C. (2016). What do infants know about cats, dogs, and people? Development of a "like-people" representation for non-human animals. In L. Freund & others (Eds.), *Social neuroscience and human-animal interaction.* Washington, DC: American Psychological Association.

Quinn, P.C., & Bhatt, R.S. (2015). Development of perceptual organization in infancy. In J. Wagemans (Ed.), *Oxford handbook of perceptual organization.* New York: Oxford University Press.

Quinn, P.C., & others (2013). On the developmental origins of differential responding to social category information. In M.R. Banaji & S.A. Gelman (Eds.), *Navigating the social world.* New York: Oxford University Press.

R

Raby, K.L., Roisman, G.I., & Booth-LaForce, C. (2016, in press). Genetic moderation of stability in attachment security from early childhood to age 18 years: A replication study. *Developmental Psychology.*

Rachwani, J., Santamaria, V., Saavedra, S.L., & Woollacott, M.H. (2015). The development of trunk control and its relation to reaching in infancy: A longitudinal study. *Frontiers in Human Neuroscience, 9,* 94.

Radbruch, L., & others (2016). Euthanasia and physican-assisted suicide: A white paper from the European Association for Palliative Care. *Palliative Medicine, 30,* 104–116.

Raglan, G.B., Lannon, S.M., Jones, K.M., & Schulkin, J. (2016). Racial and ethnic disparities in preterm birth among American Indian and Alaska Native women. *Maternal and Child Health Journal, 20,* 16–24.

Raikes, H., & others (2006). Mother-child bookreading in low-income families: Correlates and outcomes during the first three years of life. *Child Development, 77,* 924–953.

Rajaraman, P., & others (2011). Early life exposure to diagnostic radiation and ultrasound scans and risk of childhood cancer: Case-control study. *British Medical Journal, 342,* d472.

Raji, C.A., & others (2016, in press). Longitudinal relationships between caloric expenditure and gray matter in the Cardiovascular Health Study. *Journal of Alzheimer's Disease.*

Rakison, D.H., & Lawson, C.A. (2013). Categorization. In P.D. Zelazo (Ed.), *Oxford handbook of developmental psychology.* New York: Oxford University Press.

Rakoczy, H. (2012). Do infants have a theory of mind? *British Journal of Developmental Psychology, 30,* 59–74.

Ramchandani, P.G., & others (2013). Do early father-infant interactions predict the onset of externalizing behaviors in young children? Findings from a longitudinal cohort study. *Journal of Child Psychology and Psychiatry, 54,* 56–64.

Ramirez-Esparza, N., Garcia-Sierra, A., & Kuhl, P.K. (2014). Look who's talking: Speech style and social context in language input to infants are linked to concurrent and future speech development. *Developmental Science, 17,* 880–891.

Ramos Dos Santos, L., & others (2016). Association study of the BIN1 and IL-6 genes on Alzheimer's disease. *Neuroscience Letters, 614,* 65–69.

Randall, W.L. (2013). The importance of being ironic: Narrative openness and personal resilience in later life. *Gerontologist, 53*(1), 9–16.

Rangey, P.S., & Sheth, M. (2014). Comparative effect of massage therapy versus kangaroo mother care on body weight and length of hospital stay in low birth weight infants. *International Journal of Pediatrics, 2014,* 434060.

Rapee, R.M. (2014). Preschool environment and temperament as predictors of social and nonsocial anxiety disorders in middle adolescence. *Journal of the American Academy of Child and Adolescent Psychiatry, 53,* 320–328.

Rapp, S.R., & others (2013). Educational attainment, MRI changes, and cognitive function in older postmenopausal women from the Women's Health Initiative Memory Study. *International Journal of Psychiatry in Medicine, 46,* 121–143.

Rasulo, D., Christensen, K., & Tomassini, C. (2005). The influence of social relations on mortality in later life: A study on elderly Danish twins. *Gerontologist, 45,* 601–608.

Rathunde, K., & Csikszentmihalyi, M. (2006). The developing person: An experiential perspective. In W. Damon & R. Lerner (Eds.), *Handbook of child psychology* (6th ed.). New York: Wiley.

Ratner, N.B. (2013). Why talk with children matters: Clinical implications of infant- and child-directed speech research. *Seminars in Speech and Language, 34,* 203–214.

Raver, C.C., & others (2011). CSRP's impact on low-income preschoolers' preacademic skills: Self-regulation as a mediating mechanism. *Child Development, 82,* 362–378.

Raver, C.C., & others (2012). Testing models of children's self-regulation within educational contexts: Implications for measurement. *Advances in Child Development and Behavior, 42,* 245–270.

Raver, C.C., & others (2013). Predicting individual differences in low-income children's executive control from early to middle childhood. *Developmental Science, 16,* 394–408.

Ravicz, M.M., & others (2015). Infants' neural responses to facial emotion in the prefrontal cortex are correlated with temperament: A functional near-infrared spectroscopy study. *Frontiers in Psychology, 6,* 922.

Razaz, N., & others (2016). Five-minute Apgar score as a marker for developmental vulnerability at 5 years of age. *Archives of Disease in Childhood: Fetal and Neonatal Edition, 101,* F114–F120.

Razza, R.A., Martin, A., & Brooks-Gunn, J. (2012). The implications of early attentional regulation for school success among low-income children. *Journal of Applied Developmental Psychology, 33,* 311–319.

Reale, M.A., & others (2014). Selective acetyl- and butyrylcholinesterase inhibitors reduce amyloid-B ex vivo activation of peripheral chemo-cytokines from Alzheimer's disease subjects: Exploring the cholinergic anti-inflammatory pathway. *Current Alzheimer Research, 11,* 608–622.

Reat, A.M., Crixell, S.H., Friedman, B.J., & Von Bank, J.A. (2015). Comparison of food intake among infants and toddlers participating in a South Central Texas WIC Program reveals some improvements after WIC package changes. *Maternal and Child Health Journal, 19,* 1834–1841.

Rebok, G.W., & others (2014). Ten-year effects of the Advanced Cognitive Training for Independent and Vital Elderly Cognitive Training Trial on cognition and everyday functioning in older adults. *Journal of the American Geriatrics Society, 62*(1), 16–24.

Redlinger-Grosse, K., & others (2016). Defining our clinical practice: The identification of genetic counseling outcomes utilizing the reciprocal engagement model. *Journal of Genetic Counseling, 25,* 239–257.

Reed, A.E., & Carstensen, L.L. (2015). Age-related positivity effect and its implications for social and health gerontology. In N.A. Pachana (Ed.), *Encyclopedia of geropsychology*. New York: Springer.

Reed, L.A., Tolman, R.M., & Ward, L.M. (2016, in press). Snooping and sexting: Digital media as a context for dating aggression and abuse among college students. *Violence Against Women.*

Reed, R., Rowe, J., & Barnes, M. (2016, in press). Midwifery practice during birth: Ritual companionship. *Women and Birth.*

Reed, S.D., & others (2014). Menopausal quality of life: RCT of yoga, exercise, and omega-3 supplements. *American Journal of Obstetrics and Gynecology, 210,* 244.e1–244.e14.

Reese, B.M., Haydon, A.A., Herring, A.H., & Halpern, C.T. (2013). The association between sequences of sexual initiation and the likelihood of teenage pregnancy. *Journal of Adolescent Health, 52,* 228–233.

Reeve, C.L., & Charles, J.E. (2008). Survey of opinions on the primacy of g and social consequences of ability testing: A comparison of expert and non-expert views. *Intelligence, 36,* 681–688.

Regalado, M., Sareen, H., Inkelas, M., Wissow, L.S., & Halfon, N. (2004). Parents' discipline of young children: Results from the National Survey of Early Childhood Health. *Pediatrics, 113,* 1952–1958.

Regev, R.H., & others (2003). Excess mortality and morbidity among small-for-gestational-age premature infants: A population based study. *Journal of Pediatrics, 143,* 186–191.

Reichstadt, L., Depp, C.A., Palinkas, L.A., Folsom, D.P., & Jeste, D.V. (2007). Building blocks of successful aging: A focus group study of older adults' perceived contributors to successful aging. *American Journal of Geriatric Psychiatry, 15,* 194–201.

Reilly, D. (2012). Gender, culture, and sex-typed cognitive abilities. *PLoS One, 7*(7), e39904.

Reiner, I., & others (2016). Adult attachment representation moderates psychotherapy treatment efficacy in clinically depressed inpatients. *Journal of Affective Disorders, 195,* 163–171.

Reis, S.M., & Renzulli, J.S. (2014). Challenging gifted and talented learners with a continuum of research-based intervention strategies. In M.A. Bray & T.J. Kehle (Eds.), *Oxford handbook of school psychology.* New York: Oxford University Press.

Reiss, D. (2016). Genetics and family systems articulation and disarticulation. In D. Cicchetti (Ed.), *Developmental psychopathology* (3rd ed.). New York: Wiley.

Renzetti, C.M., & Kennedy-Bergen, R.M. (2015). *Understanding diversity.* Upper Saddle River, NJ: Pearson.

Repetti, R., Flook, L., & Sperling, J. (2011). Family influences in development across the life span. In K.L. Fingerman, C.A. Berg, J. Smith, & T.C. Antonucci (Eds.), *Handbook of life-span development.* New York: Springer.

Reproductive Endocrinology and Infertility Committee & others (2012). Advanced reproductive age and fertility. *Journal of Obstetrics and Gynecology Canada.*

Reuter-Lorenz, P.A., Festini, S.B., & Jantz, T.K. (2016). Executive functions and neurocognitive aging. In K.W. Schaie & S.L. Willis (Eds.), *Handbook of the psychology of aging* (8th ed.). New York: Elsevier.

Reutzel, D.R., & Cooter, R.B. (2015). *Teaching children to read* (7th ed.). Upper Saddle River, NJ: Pearson.

Reville, M.C., O'Connor, L., & Frampton, I. (2016, in press). Literature review of cognitive neuroscience and anorexia nervosa. *Current Psychiatric Reports.*

Reyna, V.F., & Rivers, S.E. (2008). Current theories of risk and rational decision making. *Developmental Review, 28,* 1–11.

Reyna, V.F., Wilhelms, E.A., McCormick, M.J., & Weldon, R.B. (2015). Development of risky decision making: Fuzzy-trace theory and neurobiological perspectives. *Child Development Perspectives, 9,* 122–127.

Reyna, V.F., & Zayas, V. (Eds.) (2014). *Neuroscience of risky decision making.* Washington, DC: American Psychological Association.

Reynolds, C.A., & Finkel, D.G. (2016). Cognitive and physical aging: Genetic influences and gene-environment interplay. In K.W. Schaie & S.L. Willis (Eds.), *Handbook of the psychology of aging* (8th ed.). New York: Elsevier.

Reynolds, G.D., & Romano, A.C. (2016). The development of attention systems and memory in infancy. *Frontiers in Systems Neuroscience, 10,* 15.

Rhodes, M., & Brandone, A.C. (2014). Three-year olds' theories of mind in actions and words. *Frontiers in Psychology, 5,* 263.

Rhodes, M., Hetherington, C., Brink, K., & Wellman, H.M. (2015). Infants' use of social partnerships to predict behavior. *Developmental Science, 18,* 909–916.

Rhyner, K.T., & Watts, A. (2016). Exercise and depressive symptoms in older adults: A systematic meta-analytic review. *Journal of Aging and Physical Activity, 24,* 234–246.

Ricco, R.B. (2015). Development of reasoning. In R.M. Lerner (Ed.), *Handbook of child psychology and developmental science* (7th ed.). New York: Wiley.

Richard, A.E., & Lajiness-O'Neill, R. (2015). Visual attention shifting in autism spectrum disorders. *Journal of Clinical and Experimental Neuropsychology, 37,* 671–687.

Richards, J.E., Boswell, C., Stevens, M., & Vendemia, J.M. (2015). Evaluating methods for constructing average high-density electrode positions. *Brain Topography, 28,* 70–86.

Richardson, G.A., Goldschmidt, L., & Willford, J. (2008). The effects of prenatal cocaine use on infant development. *Neurotoxicology and Teratology, 30,* 96–106.

Richardson, G.A., Goldschmidt, L., Leech, S., & Willford, J. (2011). Prenatal cocaine exposure: Effects on mother- and teacher-rated behavior problems and growth in school-age children. *Neurotoxicology and Teratology, 33,* 69–77.

Richardson, M.A., & others (2016). Psychological distress among school-aged children with and without intrauterine cocaine exposure: Perinatal versus contextual effects. *Journal of Abnormal Child Psychology, 44,* 547–560.

Richmond, J.L., Zhao, J.L., & Burns, M.A. (2015). What goes where? Eye tracking reveals spatial relational memory during infancy. *Journal of Experimental Child Psychology, 130,* 79–91.

Rideout, V., Foehr, U.G., & Roberts, D.P. (2010). *Generation M: Media in the lives of 8- to 18-year-olds.* Menlo Park, CA: Kaiser Family Foundation.

Riedel, B.C., Thompson, P.M., & Brinton, R.D. (2016, in press). Age, APOE, and sex: Triad of risk of Alzheimer's disease. *Journal of Steroid Biochemistry and Molecular Biology.*

Rieger, S., Gollner, R., Trautwein, U., & Roberts, B.W. (2016). Low self-esteem prospectively predicts depression in the transition to young adulthood: A replication of Orth, Robins, & Roberts (2008). *Journal of Personality and Social Psychology, 110,* e16–e22.

Ries, S.K., Dronkers, N.F., & Knight, R.T. (2016, in press). Choosing words: Left hemisphere, right hemisphere, or both? Perspective on the lateralization of word retrieval. *Annals of the New York Academy of Sciences.*

Riggins, T. (2012). Building blocks of recollection. In S. Ghetti & P.J. Bauer (Eds.), *Origins and development of recollection.* New York: Oxford University Press.

Rimsza, M.E., & Kirk, G.M. (2005). Common medical problems of the college student. *Pediatric Clinics of North America, 52,* 9–24.

Ringman, J.M., & others (2016, in press). Neuropathology of autosomal dominant Alzheimer disease in the National Alzheimer Coordinating Center Database. *Journal of Neuropathology and Experimental Neurology.*

Rink, B.D., & Norton, M.E. (2016). Screening for fetal aneuploidy. *Seminars in Perinatology, 40,* 35–43.

Ristic, J., & Enns, J.T. (2015). Attentional development: The past, the present, and the future. In R.M. Lerner (Ed.), *Handbook of child psychology and developmental science* (7th ed.). New York: Wiley.

Rix, S. (2011). Employment and aging. In R.H. Binstock & L.K. George (Eds.), *Handbook of aging and the social sciences* (7th ed.). New York: Elsevier.

Rizvi, S.J., & others (2015). Depression and employment status in primary and tertiary care settings. *Canadian Journal of Psychiatry, 60,* 14–22.

Rizzo, M.S. (1999, May 8). Genetic counseling combines science with a human touch. *Kansas City Star,* p. 3.

Roberson, P.N., Olmstead, S.B., & Fincham, F.D. (2015). Hooking up during the college years: Is there a pattern? *Culture, Health, & Sexuality, 17,* 576–591.

Roberts, B.W., Donnellan, M.B., & Hill, P.L. (2013). Personality trait development in adulthood: Findings and implications. In I.B. Weiner & others (Eds.), *Handbook of psychology* (2nd ed., Vol. 5). New York: Wiley.

Roberts, B.W., & Mroczek, D. (2008). Personality trait change in adulthood. *Current Directions in Psychological Science, 17,* 31–35.

Roberts, B.W., & Wood, D. (2006). Personality development in the context of the neo-socioanalytic model of personality. In D. Mroczek & T. Little (Eds.), *Handbook of personality development.* Mahwah, NJ: Erlbaum.

Roberts, B.W., & others (2014). What is conscientiousness and how can it be assessed? *Developmental Psychology, 50,* 1315–1330.

Roberts, D.F., & Foehr, U.G. (2008). Trends in media use. *The Future of Children, 18,* 11–18.

Robinson, S., & Lachman, M. (2017, in press). Perceived control and behavior change: A personalized approach. In F. Infurna & J. Reich (Eds.), *Perceived control: Theory, research, and practice in the first 50 years.* New York: Oxford University Press.

Robinson, S.A., Rickenbach, E.H., & Lachman, M.E. (2016). Self-regulatory strategies in daily life: Selection, optimization, and compensation and everyday memory problems. *International Journal of Behavioral Development, 40,* 126–136.

Robinson, S.M. (2015). Infant nutrition and lifelong health: Current perspectives and future challenges. *Journal of Developmental Origins of Health and Disease, 6,* 384–389.

Robinson-Zanartu, C., Doerr, P., & Portman, J. (2015). *Teaching 21 thinking skills for the 21st century.* Upper Saddle River, NJ: Pearson.

Roblyer, M.D. (2016). *Integrating technology into teaching* (7th ed.). Upper Saddle River, NJ: Pearson.

Rocca, M.S., & others (2016, in press). The Klinefelter syndrome is associated with high recurrence of copy number variations on the X chromosome with a potential role in the clinical phenotype. *Andrology.*

Rochlen, A.B., McKelley, R.A., Suizzo, M.-A., & Scaringi, V. (2008). Predictors of relationship satisfaction, psychological well-being, and life-satisfaction among stay-at-home fathers. *Psychology of Men and Masculinity, 9,* 17–28.

Rode, S.S., Chang, P., Fisch, R.O., & Sroufe, L.A. (1981). Attachment patterns of infants separated at birth. *Developmental Psychology, 17,* 188–191.

Rodin, J., & Langer, E.J. (1977). Long-term effects of a control-relevant intervention with the institutionalized aged. *Journal of Personality and Social Psychology, 35,* 397–402.

Rodrique, K.M., & Kennedy, K.M. (2011). The cognitive consequences of structural changes to the aging brain. In K.W. Schaie & S.L.Willis (Eds.), *Handbook of the psychology of aging* (7th ed.). New York: Elsevier.

Roehrich-Gascon, D., Small, S.L., & Tremblay, P. (2015). Structural correlates of spoken language abilities: A surface-based region-of-interest morphometry study. *Brain and Language, 149,* 46–54.

Roelfs, D.J., Shor, E., Davidson, K.W., & Schwartz, J.E. (2011). Losing life and livelihood: A systematic review and meta-analysis of unemployment and all-cause mortality. *Social Science & Medicine, 72,* 840–854.

Roese, N.J., & Summerville, A. (2005). What we regret most … and why. *Personality and Social Psychology Bulletin, 31,* 1273–1285.

Roeser, R.W. (2016). Beyond all splits: Mindfulness in students' motivation, learning, and self-identity at school. In K.R. Wentzel & D.B. Miele (Eds.), *Handbook of motivation at school.* New York: Routledge.

Roeser, R.W., & Eccles, J.S. (2015). Mindfulness and compassion in human development: Introduction to the special section. *Developmental Psychology, 51,* 1–6.

Roeser, R.W., & Zelazo, P.D. (2012). Contemplative science, education and child development. *Child Development Perspectives,6,* 143–145.

Roeser, R.W., & others (2014). Contemplative education. In L. Nucci & others (Eds.), *Handbook of moral and character education.* New York: Routledge.

Rogers, M.L., & others (2016). Maternal emotion socialization differentially predicts third-grade children's emotion regulation and lability. *Emotion, 16,* 280–291.

Roggman, L.A., & others (2016). Home visit quality variations in two early Head Start programs in relation to parenting and child vocabulary outcomes. *Infant Mental Health Journal, 37,* 193–207.

Rognum, I.J., & others (2014). Serotonin metabolites in the cerebrospinal fluid in sudden infant

death syndrome. *Journal of Neuropathology and Experimental Neurology, 73,* 115–122.

Rogoff, B., Moore, L.C., Correa-Dhavez, M., & Dexter, A.L. (2015). Children develop cultural repertoires through engaging in everyday routines and practices. In J.E. Grusec & P.D. Hastings (Eds.), *Handbook of socialization* (2nd ed.). New York: Guilford.

Roh, J., Rhee, J., Chaudhari, V., & Rosenzeig, A. (2016). The role of exercise in cardiac aging: From physiology to molecular mechanisms. *Circulation Research, 1118,* 279–295.

Rohde, C., & others (2014). Unrestricted fruits and vegetables in the PKU diet: A 1-year follow-up. *European Journal of Clinical Nutrition, 68,* 401–403.

Roisman, G.I., & Fraley, R.C. (2013). Developmental mechanisms underlying the legacy of childhood experiences. *Child Development Perspectives, 7,* 149–154.

Roisman, G.I., & Groh, A.M. (2011). Attachment theory and research in developmental psychology: An overview and appreciative critique. In M.K. Underwood & L.H. Rosen (Eds.), *Social development.* New York: Wiley.

Roisman, G.I., & others (2016, in press). Strategic considerations in the search for transactional processes. *Development and Psychopathology.*

Rolland, B., & others (2016). Pharmacotherapy for alcohol dependence: The 2015 recommendations of the French Alcohol Society, issued in partnership with the European Federation of Addiction Societies. *CNS Neuroscience and Therapeutics, 22,* 25–37.

Rollins, B.Y., Savage, J.S., Fisher, J.O., & Birch, L.L. (2016, in press). Alternatives to restrictive feeding practices to promote self-regulation in childhood: A developmental perspective. *Pediatric Obesity.*

Romo, L.F., Mireles-Rios, R., & Lopez-Tello, G. (2014). Latina mothers' and daughters' expectations for autonomy at age 15 (La Quinceañera). *Journal of Adolescent Research, 29*(2), 279–294.

Roozen, S., & others (2016). Worldwide prevalence of fetal alcohol spectrum disorders: A systematic literature review including meta-analysis. *Alcoholism: Clinical and Experimental Research, 40,* 18–32.

Roring, R.W., Hines, F.G., & Charness, N. (2007). Age differences in identifying words in synthetic speech. *Human Factors, 49,* 25–31.

Ros, L., & others (2016, in press). Reminiscence function scale: Factorial structure and its relation with mental health in a sample of Spanish older adults. *International Psychogeriatrics.*

Rosano, C., & others (2012). Slower gait, slower information processing, and smaller prefrontal area in older adults. *Age and Aging, 41,* 58–64.

Rose, A.J., & others (2012). How girls and boys expect disclosure about problems will make them feel: Implications for friendship. *Child Development, 83,* 844–863.

Rose, S.A., Feldman, J.F., & Jankowski, J.J. (2015). Pathways from toddler information processing to adolescent lexical proficiency. *Child Development, 86,* 1935–1947.

Roseberry, S., Hirsh-Pasek, K., & Golinkoff R. (2014). Skype me! Socially contingent interactions help toddlers learn language. *Child Development, 85,* 956–970.

Roseberry, S., Hirsh-Pasek, K., Parish-Morris, J., & Golinkoff, R. (2009). Live action: Can young children learn verbs from video? *Child Development, 80,* 1360–1375.

Rosengard, C. (2009). Confronting the intendedness of adolescent rapid repeat pregnancy. *Journal of Adolescent Health, 44,* 5–6.

Rosenstein, D., & Oster, H. (1988). Differential facial responses to four basic tastes in newborns. *Child Development, 59,* 1555–1568.

Ross, L.A., & others (2016). The transfer of cognitive speed of processing training to older adults' driving mobility across 5 years. *Journals of Gerontology B: Psychological Sciences and Social Sciences, 71,* 87–97.

Rossi, A.S. (1989). A life-course approach to gender, aging, and intergenerational relations. In K.W. Schaie & C. Schooler (Eds.), *Social structure and aging.* Hillsdale, NJ: Erlbaum.

Rostamian, S., & others (2015). Executive function, but not memory, associates with incident coronary heart disease and stroke. *Neurology, 85,* 783–789.

Roth, B., & others (2015). Intelligence and school grades: A meta-analysis. *Intelligence, 53,* 118–137.

Roth, J., Brooks-Gunn, J., Murray, L., & Foster, W. (1998). Promoting healthy adolescents: Synthesis of youth development program evaluations. *Journal of Research on Adolescence, 8,* 423–459.

Roth, W.N. (2016). The primacy of the social and sociogenesis. *Integrative Psychological and Behavioral Science, 50,* 122–141.

Rothbart, M.K. (2011). *Becoming who we are.* New York: Guilford.

Rothbart, M.K., & Bates, J.E. (2006). Temperament. In W. Damon & R. Lerner (Eds.), *Handbook of child psychology* (6th ed.). New York: Wiley.

Rothbart, M.K., & Posner, M. (2015). The developing brain in a multitasking world. *Developmental Review, 35,* 42–63.

Rothbaum, F., Poll, M., Azuma, H., Miyake, K., & Welsz, J. (2000). The development of close relationships in Japan and the United States: Paths of symbiotic harmony and generative tension. *Child Development, 71,* 1121–1142.

Rothman, M.S., Miller, P.D., Lewiecki, E.M., & Bilezikian, J.P. (2014). Bone density testing: Science, the media, and patient care. *Current Osteoporosis Reports, 12,* 227–229.

Rothman, R. (2016). Accountability for what matters. *State Education Standard, 16,* 10–13.

Rovee-Collier, C. (1987). Learning and memory in children. In J.D. Osofsky (Ed.), *Handbook of infant development* (2nd ed.). New York: Wiley.

Rovee-Collier, C. (2008). The development of infant memory. In N. Cowan & M. Courage (Eds.), *The development of memory in infancy and childhood.* Philadelphia: Psychology Press.

Rovee-Collier, C., & Barr, R. (2010). Infant learning and memory. In U.J.G. Bremner & T.D. Wachs (Ed.), *Wiley-Blackwell handbook of infant development* (2nd ed.). New York: Wiley.

Rowe, J.W., & Kahn, R.L. (2015). Successful aging 2.0: Conceptual expansions for the 21st century. *Journals of Gerontology B: Psychological Sciences and Social Sciences, 70,* 593–596.

Rowland, T. (2016). Pediatric exercise science: A brief overview. *Pediatric Exercise Science, 28,* 167–170.

Roza, S.J., & others (2010). Maternal folic acid supplement use in early pregnancy and child behavioral problems: The Generation R study. *British Journal of Nutrition, 103,* 445–452.

Rubin, K.H., Bukowski, W.M., & Bowker, J. (2015). Children in peer groups. In R.M. Lerner (Ed.), *Handbook of child psychology and developmental science* (7th ed.). New York: McGraw-Hill.

Rubin, K.H., Bukowski, W.M, & Parker, J.G. (2006). Peer interactions, relationships, and groups. In W. Damon & R. Lerner (Eds.), *Handbook of child psychology* (6th ed.). New York: Wiley.

Rubin, K.H., & others (2016). Peer relationships. In M.H. Bornstein & M.E. Lamb (Eds.), *Developmental science* (7th ed.). New York: Psychology Press.

Ruble, D. (1983). The development of social comparison processes and their role in achievement-related self-socialization. In E. Higgins, D. Ruble, & W. Hartup (Eds.), *Social cognitive development: A social-cultural perspective.* New York: Cambridge University Press.

Rudolph, K.D., Troop-Gordon, W., Lambert, S.F., & Natsuaki, M.N. (2014). Long-term consequences of pubertal timing for youth depression: Identifying personal and contextual pathways of risk. *Development and Psychopathology, 26,* 1423–1444.

Rueda, M.R., Posner, M.I., & Rothbart, M.K. (2005). The development of executive attention: Contributions to the emergence of self-regulation. *Developmental Neuropsychology, 28,* 573–594.

Ruffman, T., Slade, L., & Crowe, E. (2002). The relation between children's and mothers' mental state language and theory-of-mind understanding. *Child Development, 73,* 734–751.

Ruitenberg, M.F., & others (2015). Sequential movement skill in Parkinson's disease: A state-of-the-art. *Cortex, 65C,* 102–112.

Ruiter, M., & others (2012, June 11). *Short sleep predicts stroke symptoms in persons of normal weight.* Paper presented at the annual meeting of the Associated Professional Sleep Societies (APSS), Boston.

Rumberger, R.W. (1983). Dropping out of high school: The influence of race, sex, and family background. *American Educational Research Journal, 20,* 199–220.

Rumi Kataguiri, M., & others (2014). Influence of second-trimester ultrasound markers for Down syndrome in pregnant women of advanced maternal age. *Journal of Pregnancy, 2014,* 785730.

Runquist, J. (2007). Persevering through postpartum fatigue. *Journal of Obstetric, Gynecologic, and Neonatal Nursing, 36,* 28–37.

Rupp, D.E., Vodanovich, S.J., & Crede, M. (2005). The multidimensional nature of ageism: Construct validity and group differences. *Journal of Social Psychology, 145,* 335–362.

Ryan, A.S., & others (2014). Aerobic exercise and weight loss reduce vascular markers of inflammation and improve insulin sensitivity in obese women. *Journal of the American Geriatrics Society, 62,* 607–614.

Ryff, C.D. (1984). Personality development from the inside: The subjective experience of change in adulthood and aging. In P.B. Baltes & O.G. Brim (Eds.), *Life-span development and behavior.* New York: Academic Press.

S

Saarni, C. (1999). *The development of emotional competence.* New York: Guilford.

Saarni, C., Campos, J., Camras, L.A., & Witherington, D. (2006). Emotional development.

In W. Damon & R. Lerner (Eds.), *Handbook of child psychology* (6th ed.). New York: Wiley.

Sabir, M., Henderson, C.R., Kang, S.Y., & Pillemer, K. (2016). Attachment-focused integrative reminiscence with older African Americans: A randomized controlled intervention study. *Aging and Mental Health, 20,* 517–528.

Sabol, T.J., & others (2016, in press). Parents' persistence and certification in a two-generation education and training program. *Children and Youth Services Review.*

Sacrey, L.A., Germani, T., Bryson, S.E., & Zwaigenbaum, L. (2014). Reaching and grasping in autism spectrum disorder: A review of recent literature. *Frontiers in Neurology, 5,* 6.

Sadeghi, B., & others (2016). A hospital-based advance care planning intervention for patients with heart failure: A feasibility study. *Journal of Palliative Medicine, 19,* 451–455.

Sadeh, A. (2007). Consequences of sleep loss or sleep disruption in children. *Sleep Medicine, 2,* 513–520.

Sadeh, A. (2008). Sleep. In M.M. Haith & J.B. Benson (Eds.), *Encyclopedia of infant and early childhood development.* Oxford, UK: Elsevier.

Sadeh, A., & others (2015). Infant sleep predicts attention regulation and behavior problems at 3-4 years of age. *Developmental Neuropsychology, 40,* 122–137.

Sadker, D.M., & Zittleman, K. (2012). *Teachers, schools, and society* (3rd ed.). New York: McGraw-Hill.

Sadker, D.M., & Zittleman, K. (2016). *Teachers, schools, and society* (4th ed.). New York: McGraw-Hill.

Saffran, J.R., Werker, J.F., & Werner, L.A. (2006). The infant's auditory world: Hearing, speech, and the beginnings of language. In W. Damon & R. Lerner (Eds.), *Handbook of child psychology* (6th ed.). New York: Wiley.

Sahoo, K., & others (2015). Childhood obesity: Causes and consequences. *Journal of Family Medicine and Primary Care, 4,* 187–192.

Saifer, S. (2007, August 29). *Tools of the Mind—A Vygotskian-inspired early childhood curriculum.* Paper presented at the 17th Annual Conference of the European Early Childhood Education Research Association, Prague.

Saint-Onge, J.M. (2009). Mortality. In D. Carr (Ed.), *Encyclopedia of the life course and human development.* Boston: Gale Cengage.

Saito, S., & Ihara, M. (2016). Interaction between cardiovascular disease and Alzheimer pathology. *Current Opinion in Psychiatry, 29,* 168–173.

Sajber, D., & others (2016, in press). Alcohol drinking among Kosovar adolescents: An examination of gender-specific sociodemographic, sport, and family factors associated with harmful drinking. *Substance Use and Misuse.*

Salama, R.H., & others (2013). Clinical and biochemical effects of environmental tobacco smoking on pregnancy outcome. *Indian Journal of Clinical Biochemistry, 28,* 368–373.

Salkind, N.J. (2017). *Exploring research* (9th ed.). Upper Saddle River, NJ: Pearson.

Sallam, N., & Laher, I. (2016). Exercise modulates oxidative stress and inflammation in aging and cardiovascular diseases. *Oxidative Medicine and Cellular Longevity, 2016,* 7239639.

Salm Ward, T.C., & Balfour, G.M. (2016). Infant safe sleep interventions, 1990–2015: A review. *Journal of Community Health, 41,* 180–196.

Salmivalli, C., Peets, K., & Hodges, E.V.E. (2011). Bullying. In P.K. Smith & C.H. Hart (Eds.), *Wiley-Blackwell handbook of childhood social development* (2nd ed.). New York: Wiley.

Salthouse, T.A. (2009). When does age-related cognitive decline begin? *Neurobiology of Aging, 30,* 507–514.

Salthouse, T.A. (2012). Consequences of age-related cognitive declines. *Annual Review of Psychology* (Vol. 63). Palo Alto, CA: Annual Reviews.

Salthouse, T.A. (2013). Executive functioning. In D.C. Park & N. Schwartz (Eds.), *Cognitive aging* (2nd ed.). New York: Psychology Press.

Salthouse, T.A. (2014). Why are there different age relations in cross-sectional and longitudinal comparisons of cognitive functioning? *Current Directions in Psychological Science, 23,* 252–256.

Salthouse, T.A. (2016). Aging cognition unconfounded by prior test experiences. *Journals of Gerontology B: Psychological Sciences and Social Sciences, 71,* 49–58.

Salthouse, T.A., & Skovronek, E. (1992). Within-context assessment of working memory. *Journals of Gerontology, 47,* P110–P117.

Salvatore, J.E., Kuo, S.I., Steele, R.D., Simpson, J.A., & Collins, W.A. (2011). Recovering from conflict in romantic relationships: A developmental perspective. *Psychological Science, 22,* 376–383.

Sameroff, A.J. (2009). *The transactional model of development: How children and contexts shape each other.* Washington, DC: American Psychological Association.

Sameroff, A.J. (2012). Conceptual issues in studying the development of self-regulation. In S.L. Olson & A.J. Sameroff (Eds.), *Biopsychosocial regulatory processes in the development of childhood behavioral problems.* New York: Cambridge University Press.

Samjoo, I.A., & others (2013). The effect of endurance exercise on both skeletal muscle and systemic oxidative stress in previously sedentary obese men. *Nutrition and Diabetes, 3,* e88.

Sampath, A., Maduro, G., & Schillinger, J.A. (2016, in press). Infant deaths due to herpes simplex virus, congenital syphilis, and HIV in New York City. *Pediatrics.*

Sanders, K.E., & Guerra, A.W. (Eds.) (2016). *The culture of child care.* New York: Oxford University Press.

Sanders, R.H., Han, A., Baker, J.S., & Cobley, S. (2015). Childhood obesity and its physical and psychological co-morbidities: A systematic review of Australian children and adolescents. *European Journal of Pediatrics, 174,* 715–746.

Sandrini, M., & others (2016). Older adults get episodic memory boosting from noninvasive stimulation of prefrontal cortex during learning. *Neurobiology of Aging, 39,* 210–216.

Sangree, W.H. (1989). Age and power: Life-course trajectories and age structuring of power relations in East and West Africa. In D.I. Kertzer & K.W. Schaie (Eds.), *Age structuring in comparative perspective.* Hillsdale, NJ: Erlbaum.

Sanson, A., & Rothbart, M.K. (1995). Child temperament and parenting. In M.H. Bornstein (Ed.), *Handbook of parenting* (Vol. 4). Hillsdale, NJ: Erlbaum.

Santangeli, L., Satter, N., & Huda, S.S. (2015). Impact of maternal obesity on perinatal and child outcomes. *Best Practices and Research: Clinical Obstetrics and Gynecology, 29*, 438–448.

Santos, L.M., & others (2016). Prevention of neural tube defects by fortification of flour with folic acid: A population-based retrospective study in Brazil. *Bulletin of the World Health Organization, 94*, 22–29.

Santrock, J.W., Sitterle, K.A., & Warshak, R.A. (1988). Parent-child relationships in stepfather families. In P. Bronstein & C.P. Cowan (Eds.), *Fatherhood today: Men's changing roles in the family.* New York: Wiley.

Sanz-Cortez, M., & others (2015). Association of brain metabolism with sulcation and corpus callosum development assessed by MRI in late-onset small fetuses. *American Journal of Obstetrics and Gynecology, 2012*(804), e1–e8.

Sarchiapone, M., & others (2014). Hours of sleep in adolescents and its association with anxiety, emotional concerns, and suicidal ideation. *Sleep Medicine, 15*, 248–254.

Sarlak, G., & Vincent, B. (2016). The roles of the stem cell-controlling Sox2 transcription factor: From neuroectoderm development to Alzheimer's disease? *Molecular Neurobiology, 53*, 1679–1698.

Sarquella-Brugada, G., & others (2016). Sudden infant death syndrome caused by cardiac arrhythmias: Only a matter of genes encoding ion channels? *International Journal of Legal Medicine, 130*, 415–420.

Sauter, D., McDonald, N.M., Grangi, D., & Messinger, D.S. (2014). Nonverbal expressions of positive emotions. In M. Tugade & others (Eds.), *Handbook of positive emotions.* New York: Guilford.

Savin-Williams, R.C. (2015). The new sexual-minority teenager. In D.A. Powell & J.S. Kaufman (Eds.), *The meaning of sexual identity in the 21st century.* New York: Cambridge.

Savin-Williams, R.C., & Cohen, K. (2015). Gay, lesbian, and bisexual youth. In J.D. Wright (Ed.), *International encyclopedia of the social and behavioral sciences* (2nd ed.). New York: Oxford University Press.

Sbarra, D.A. (2015). Divorce and health: Current trends and future directions. *Psychosomatic Medicine, 77*, 227–236.

Sbarra, D.A., Hasselmo, K., & Bourassa, K.J. (2015). Divorce and health: Beyond individual differences. *Current Directions in Psychological Science, 24*, 109113.

Scarr, S. (1993). Biological and cultural diversity: The legacy of Darwin for development. *Child Development, 64*, 1333–1353.

Scelfo, J. (2015, February 3). A university recognizes a third gender: neutral. *New York Times.* Retrieved on June 18, 2016, from www.nytimes.com/2015/02/08/education/edlife/a-university-re...

Schaefer, R.T. (2015). *Racial and ethnic groups* (14th ed.). Upper Saddle River, NJ: Pearson.

Schafer, A. (2013). Physician assisted suicide: The great Canadian euthanasia debate. *International Journal of Law and Psychiatry, 36*, 522–531.

Schafer, M.J., & others (2015). Calorie restriction suppresses age-dependent hippocampal transcriptional signatures. *PLoS One, 10*(7), e0133923.

Schaffer, H.R. (1996). *Social development.* Cambridge, MA: Blackwell.

Schaffer, M.A., Goodhue, A., Stennes, K., & Lanigan, C. (2012). Evaluation of a public health nurse visiting program for pregnant and parenting teens. *Public Health Nursing, 29*, 218–231.

Schaie, K.W. (1994). The life course of adult intellectual abilities. *American Psychologist, 49*, 304–313.

Schaie, K.W. (1996). *Intellectual development in adulthood: The Seattle Longitudinal Study.* New York: Cambridge University Press.

Schaie, K.W. (2005). *Developmental influences on adult intelligence: The Seattle Longitudinal Study.* New York: Oxford University Press.

Schaie, K.W. (2009). When does age-related cognitive decline begin? Salthouse again reifies the "cross-sectional fallacy." *Neurobiology of Aging, 30*, 528–529.

Schaie, K.W. (2010). Adult intellectual abilities. *Corsini encyclopedia of psychology.* New York: Wiley.

Schaie, K.W. (2011). Historical influences on aging and behavior. In K.W. Schaie & S.L. Willis (Eds.), *Handbook of the psychology of aging* (7th ed.). New York: Elsevier.

Schaie, K.W. (2013). *Developmental influences on adult intelligence: The Seattle Longitudinal Study* (2nd ed.). New York: Oxford University Press.

Schaie, K.W. (2016). Theoretical perspectives for the psychology of aging in a lifespan context. In K.W. Schaie & S.L. Willis (Eds.), *Handbook of psychology of aging* (8th ed.). New York: Elsevier.

Schaie, K.W., & Willis, S.L. (Eds.) (2016). *Handbook of the psychology of aging* (8th ed.). New York: Elsevier.

Scheeringa, M.S., Cobham, V.E., & McDermott, B. (2014). Policy and administrative issues for large-scale clinical interventions following disasters. *Journal of Child and Adolescent Psychopharmacology, 24*, 39–46.

Schick, U.M., & others (2016). Genome-wide association study of platelet count identifies ancestry-specific loci in Hispanic/Latino Americans. *American Journal of Human Genetics, 98*, 229–242.

Schieber, F. (2006). Vision and aging. In J.E. Birren & K.W. Schaie (Eds.), *Handbook of the psychology of aging* (6th ed.). San Diego: Academic Press.

Schieve, L.A., & others (2016). Population impact of preterm birth and low birth weight on developmental disabilities in U.S. children. *Annals of Epidemiology, 26*, 267–274.

Schiff, W.J. (2015). *Nutrition essentials.* New York: McGraw-Hill.

Schiff, W.J. (2016). *Nutrition for healthy living* (4th ed.). New York: McGraw-Hill.

Schiffman, S.S. (2007). Smell and taste. In J.E. Birren (Ed.), *Encyclopedia of gerontology* (2nd ed.). San Diego: Academic Press.

Schilling, E.A., Aseltine, R.H., Glanovsky, J.L., James, A., & Jacobs, D. (2009). Adolescent alcohol use, suicidal ideation, and suicide attempts. *Journal of Adolescent Health, 44*, 335–341.

Schlam, T.R., Wilson, N.L., Shoda, Y., Mischel, W., & Ayduk, O. (2013). Preschoolers' delay of gratification predicts their body mass 30 years later. *Journal of Pediatrics, 162*, 90–93.

Schlegel, M. (2000). All work and all play: Developmental psychologist finds a niche in a "smart toy" world. *Monitor on Psychology 31*(11), 50–51.

Schmidt, E.L., Burge, W., Visscher, K.M., & Ross, L.A. (2016). Cortical thickness in frontoparietal and cingulo-opercular networks predicts executive function performance in older adults. *Neuropsychology, 30*, 322–331.

Schmidt, S.M., Chari, R., & Davenport, M.H. (2016). Exercise during pregnancy: Current recommendations by Canadian maternity health care providers. *Journal of Obstetrics and Gynecology Canada, 38*, 177–178.

Schmitow, C., & Stenberg, G. (2015). What aspects of others' behaviors do infants attend to in live situations? *Infant Behavior and Development, 40*, 173–182.

Schneider, B. (2016). *Childhood friendship and peer relations.* New York: Routledge.

Schneider, W. (2011). Memory development in childhood. In U. Goswami (Ed.), *Wiley-Blackwell handbook of childhood cognitive development* (2nd ed.). New York: Wiley.

Schnittker, J. (2007). Look (closely) at all the lonely people: Age and social psychology of social support. *Journal of Aging and Health, 19*, 659–682.

Schnohr, P., & others (2015). Dose of jogging and long-term mortality: The Copenhagen Heart Study. *Journal of the American College of Cardiology, 65*, 411–419.

Schoeneberger, J. (2012). Longitudinal attendance patterns: Developing high school dropouts. *Clearinghouse, 85*, 7–14.

Schoenmaker, C., & others (2015). From maternal sensitivity in infancy to adult attachment representations: A longitudinal adoption study with secure base scripts. *Attachment and Human Development, 17*, 241–256.

Schoffstall, C.L., & Cohen, R. (2011). Cyber aggression: The relation of online offenders and offline social competence. *Social Development, 20*(3), 587–604.

Schonert-Reichl, K.A., & others (2015). Enhancing cognitive and socio-emotional development through a simple-to-administer mindfulness-based school program for elementary school children: A randomized controlled trial. *Developmental Psychology, 51*, 52–56.

Schooler, C., Mulatu, S., & Oates, G. (1999). The continuing effects of substantively complex work on the intellectual functioning of older workers. *Psychology and Aging, 14*, 483–506.

Schooreel, T., & Verbruggen, M. (2016). Use of family-friendly work arrangements and work-family conflict: Cross-over effects in dual-earner couples. *Journal of Occupational Health Psychology, 21*, 119–132.

Schreiber, K.H., O'Leary, M., & Kennedy, B.K. (2016). The mTOR pathway and aging. In M. Kaeberlein & G.M. Martin (Eds.), *Handbook of the psychology of aging* (8th ed.). New York: Elsevier.

Schuch, F.B., & others (2016a, in press). Neurobiological effects of exercise on major depressive disorder: A systematic review. *Neuroscience and Biobehavioral Reviews.*

Schuch, F.B., & others (2016b). Exercise as a treatment for depression: A meta-analysis adjusting for publication bias. *Journal of Psychiatric Research, 77*, 42–51.

Schunk, D.H. (2008). *Learning theories: An educational perspective* (5th ed.). Upper Saddle River, NJ: Prentice Hall.

Schunk, D.H. (2012). *Learning theories: An educational perspective* (6th ed.). Upper Saddle River, NJ: Prentice Hall.

Schunk, D.H. (2016). *Learning theories: An educational perspective* (7th ed.). Upper Saddle River, NJ: Prentice Hall.

Schwalbe, C.S., Gearing, R.E., MacKenzie, M.J., Brewer, K.B., & Ibrahim, R. (2012). A meta-analysis of experimental studies of diversion programs for juvenile defenders. *Clinical Psychology Review, 32,* 26–33.

Schwartz, D., & others (2015). Peer victimization during middle childhood as a lead indicator of internalizing problems and diagnostic outcomes in late adolescence. *Journal of Clinical Child and Adolescent Psychology, 44,* 393–404.

Schwartz, S.J., Donnellan, M.B., Ravert, R.D., Luyckx, K., & Zamboanga, B.L. (2013). Identity development, personality, and well-being in adolescence and emerging adulthood: Theory, research, and recent advances. In I.B. Weiner & others (Eds.), *Handbook of psychology* (2nd ed., Vol. 6). New York: Wiley.

Schwartz, S.J., & others (2015a). Identity. In J.J. Arnett (Ed.), *Oxford handbook of emerging adulthood.* New York: Oxford University Press.

Schwartz, S.J., & others (2015b). What have we learned since Schwartz (2001)? A reappraisal of the field. In K. McLean & M. Syed (Eds.), *Oxford handbook of identity development.* New York: Oxford University Press.

Schwartz, S.J., & others (2015c). The identity dynamics of acculturation and multiculturalism: Situating acculturation in context. In V. Benet-Martinez & Y.Y. Hong (Eds.), *Oxford handbook of multicultural identity.* New York: Oxford University Press.

Schwarzer, R., & Luszczynska, A. (2013). Stressful life events. In I.B. Weiner & others (Eds.), *Handbook of psychology* (2nd ed., Vol. 9). New York: Wiley.

Schweinhart, L.J., & others (2005). *Lifetime effects: The High/Scope Perry Preschool Study through age 40.* Ypsilanti, MI: High/Scope Press.

Scialfa, C.T., & Kline, D.W. (2007). Vision. In J.E. Birren (ed.), *Encyclopedia of gerontology* (2nd ed.). San Diego: Academic Press.

Sclar, D.A., & others (2012). Attention deficit/hyperactivity disorder among children and adolescents in the United States: Trends in diagnosis and use of pharmacotherapy by gender. *Clinical Pediatrics, 51,* 584.

Scotti, S. (2016, in press). Physician orders for life-sustaining treatment. *NCSL Legisbrief.*

Scourfield, J., Van den Bree, M., Martin, N., & McGuffin, P. (2004). Conduct problems in children and adolescents: A twin study. *Archives of General Psychiatry, 61,* 489–496.

Seay, G. (2011). Euthanasia and common sense: A reply to Garcia. *Journal of Medical Philosophy, 36,* 321–327.

Sebastiani, P., & Perls, T.T. (2012). The genetics of extreme longevity: Lessons from the New England Centenarian study. *Frontiers in Genetics, 30*(3), 277.

Sebastiani, P., & others (2013). Meta-analysis of genetic variants associated with human exceptional longevity. *Aging, 5,* 653–661.

Seccombe, K.T. (2015). *Exploring marriages and families* (2nd ed.). Upper Saddle River, NJ: Pearson.

Sedgh, G., & others (2015). Adolescent pregnancy, birth, and abortion rates across countries: Levels and recent trends. *Journal of Adolescent Health, 56,* 223–230.

Seftel, A.D., Kathrins, M., & Niederberger, C. (2015). Critical update of the 2010 Endocrine Society clinical practice guidelines for male hypogonadism: A systematic analysis. *Mayo Clinic Proceedings, 90,* 1104–1115.

Seidman, G., & others (2015). Barriers and enablers of kangaroo mother care practice: A systematic review. *PLoS One, 10*(5), e0125643.

Seiter, L.N., & Nelson, L.J. (2010). An examination of emerging adulthood in college students and nonstudents in India. *Journal of Adolescent Research, 26,* 506–536.

Selemon, L.D. (2016). Frontal lobe synaptic plasticity in development and disease: Modulation by the dopamine D1 receptor. *Current Pharmaceutical Design, 20,* 5194–5201.

Selim, A.J., & others (2005). Comprehensive health status assessment of centenarians: Results from the 1999 Large Health Survey of Veteran Enrollees. *Journals of Gerontology A: Biological Sciences and Medical Sciences, 60,* 515–519.

Sen, B. (2010). The relationship between frequency of family dinner and adolescent problem behaviors after adjusting for other characteristics. *Journal of Adolescence, 33,* 187–196.

Sengpiel, V., & others (2013). Maternal caffeine intake during pregnancy is associated with birth weight but not gestational length: Results from a large prospective observational cohort study. *BMC Medicine, 11,* 42.

Seo, Y.S., Lee, J., & Ahn, H.Y. (2016, in press). Effects of kangaroo care on neonatal pain in South Korea. *Journal of Tropical Pediatrics.*

Serini, S., & Calviello, G. (2016). Reduction of oxidative/itrosative stress in the brain and its involvement in the neuroprotective effects of n-3 PUFA in Alzheimer's disease. *Current Alzheimer Research, 13,* 123–134.

Sesker, A.A., Suilleabhain, P.O., Howard, S., & Hughes, B.M. (2016). Conscientiousness and mindfulness in midlife coping: An assessment based on MIDUS II. *Personality and Mental Health, 10,* 28–42.

Sethna, V., Murray, L., & Ramchandani, P.G. (2012). Depressed fathers' speech to their 3-month-old infants: A study of cognitive and mentalizing features in paternal speech. *Psychological Medicine, 42,* 2361–2371.

Setterson, R.A. (2009). Neugarten, Bernice. In D. Carr (Ed.), *Encyclopedia of the life course and human development.* Boston: Gale Cengage.

Setterson, R.A., & Trauten, M.E. (2009). The new terrain of old age: Hallmarks, freedoms, and risks. In V.L. Bengtson, D. Gans, N.M. Putney, & M. Silverstein (Eds.), *Handbook of theories of aging.* New York: Springer.

Shah, M.K., & Austin, K.R. (2014). Do home visiting services received during pregnancy improve birth outcomes? Findings from Virginia PRAMS 2007–2008. *Public Health Nursing, 31,* 405–413.

Shah, R., Sobotka, S.A., Chen, Y.F., & Msall, M.E. (2015). Positive parenting practices, health disparities, and developmental progress. *Pediatrics, 136,* 318–326.

Shahrokni, A., Mahmoudzadeh, S., Saeedi, R., & Ghasemzadeh, H. (2015). Older people with access to hand-held devices: Who are they? *Telemedicine Journal and E-Health, 21,* 550–556.

Shang, L., & others (2015). Screen time is associated with dietary intake in overweight Canadian children. *Preventive Medicine Reports, 2,* 265–269.

Shankar, A., Hamer, M., McMunn, A., & Steptoe, A. (2013). Social isolation and loneliness: Relationships with cognitive function during 4 years of follow-up in the English Longitudinal Study of Aging. *Psychosomatic Aging, 75,* 161–170.

Sharma, R., & others (2015). Effects of increased paternal age on sperm quality, reproductive outcome, and associated epigenetic risks to offspring. *Reproductive Biology and Endocrinology, 13,* 35.

Sharma, R., & others (2015). Normalization of testosterone level is associated with reduced incidence of myocardial infarction and mortality in men. *European Heart Journal, 36,* 2706–2715.

Sharma, S., & Ford-Jones, E. (2015). Child poverty. Ways forward for the pediatrician: A comprehensive overview of poverty reduction strategies requiring pediatric support. *Pediatrics and Child Health, 20,* 203–207.

Shatz, M., & Gelman, R. (1973). The development of communication skills: Modifications in the speech of young children as a function of the listener. *Monographs of the Society for Research in Child Development, 38*(Serial No. 152).

Shaver, P. (1986, August). *Being lonely, falling in love: Perspectives from attachment theory.* Paper presented at the meeting of the American Psychological Association, Washington, DC.

Shaw, P., & others (2007). Attention-deficit/hyperactivity disorder is characterized by a delay in cortical maturation. *Proceedings of the National Academy of Sciences, 104*(49), 19649–19654.

Shaywitz, B.A., Lyon, G.R., & Shaywitz, S.E. (2006). The role of functional magnetic resonance imaging in understanding reading and dyslexia. *Developmental Neuropsychology, 30,* 613–632.

Shaywitz, S.E., Gruen, J.R., & Shaywitz, B.A. (2007). Management of dyslexia, its rationale and underlying neurobiology. *Pediatric Clinics of North America, 54,* 609–623.

Shear, M.K. (2015). Clinical practice. Complicated grief. *New England Journal of Medicine, 372,* 153–160.

Shebloski, B., Conger, K.J., & Widaman, K.F. (2005). Reciprocal links among differential parenting, perceived partiality, and self worth: A three-wave longitudinal study. *Journal of Family Psychology, 19,* 633–642.

Sheehan, M.J., & Watson, M.W. (2015). Reciprocal influences between maternal discipline and techniques and aggression in children and adolescents. *Aggressive Behavior, 34,* 245–255.

Sheehan, W.J., & Phipatanakul, W. (2015). Difficult-to-control asthma: Epidemiology and its link with environmental factors. *Current Opinion in Allergy and Clinical Immunology, 15,* 397–401.

Sheinbaum, T., & others (2015). Attachment style predicts affect, cognitive appraisals, and social functioning in daily life. *Frontiers in Psychology, 6,* 296.

Sherman, C.W., Webster, N.J., & Antonucci, T.C. (2016). Dementia caregiving in the context of late life remarriage: Support networks, relationship quality, and well-being. In K.W. Schaie & S.L. Willis (Eds.), *Handbook of the psychology of aging* (8th ed.). New York: Elsevier.

Sherwood, C.C., & others (2011). Aging of the cerebral cortex differs between humans and chimpanzees. *Proceedings of the National Academy of Sciences U.S.A., 108,* 13029–13034.

Sheu, M.T., & others (2016, in press). Rapid-onset sildenafil sublingual drug delivery systems: In vitro evaluation and in vivo pharmacokinetic studies in rabbits. *Journal of Pharmaceutical Services.*

Shin, D.W., & others (2016). End-of-life communication in Korean older adults: With focus on advance care planning and advance directives. *Geriatrics and Gerontology International, 16,* 407–415.

Shin, S.H., Lee, S., Jeon, S.M., & Wills, T.A. (2015). Childhood emotional abuse, negative emotion-driven impulsivity, and alcohol use in young adulthood. *Child Abuse and Neglect, 50,* 94–103.

Shiner, S., Many, A., & Maslovitz, S. (2016). Questioning the role of pituitary oxytocin in parturition: Spontaneous onset of labor in women with panhypopituitarism—a case series. *European Journal of Obstetrics and Gynecology and Reproductive Medicine, 197,* 83–85.

Shirazian, T., & others (2016). The life style modification project: Limiting pregnancy weight gain in obese women. *Journal of Maternal-Fetal and Neonatal Medicine, 29,* 80–84.

Shivers, E., & Farago, F. (2016). Where the children are: Exploring quality, community, and support for family, friend, and neighbor care. In K.E. Sanders & A.W. Guerra (Eds.), *The culture of child care.* New York: Oxford University Press.

Shors, T.J. (2009). Saving new brain cells. *Scientific American, 300,* 46–52.

Short, D. (2015, April 7). *Demographic trends in the 50-and-older work force.* Retrieved April 19, 2015, from www.advisorperspectives.com/commentaries/dshort_011314.php

Short, D. (2015, August 11). *Another look at long-term trends in employment by age group.* Lexington, MA: Advisor Perspectives.

Shulman, E.P., & others (2016). The dual systems model: Review, reappraisal, and reaffirmation. *Developmental Cognitive Neuroscience, 17,* 103–117.

Shuman, V., & Scherer, K. (2014). Concepts and structure of emotions. In R. Pekrun & L. Linnenbrink-Garcia (Eds.), *International handbook of emotions in education.* New York: Routledge.

Siegel, R.S., & Brandon, A.R. (2014). Adolescents, pregnancy, and mental health. *Journal of Pediatric and Adolescent Gynecology, 27*(3), 138–150.

Siegler, R.S. (2006). Microgenetic analysis of learning. In W. Damon & R. Lerner (Eds.), *Handbook of child psychology* (6th ed.). New York: Wiley.

Siegler, R.S. (2013). From theory to application and back: Following in the giant footsteps of David Klahr. In S.M. Carver & J. Shrager (Ed.), *The journey from child to scientist.* Thousand Oaks, CA: Sage.

Siegler, R.S. (2016a). Continuity and change in the field of cognitive development and in the perspective of one cognitive developmentalist. *Child Development Perspectives, 10,* 128–133.

Siegler, R.S. (2016b, in press). How does change occur? In R. Sternberg, S. Fiske, & D. Foss (Eds.), *Scientists make a difference: One hundred eminent behavioral and brain scientists talk about their most important contributions.* Cambridge, UK: Cambridge University Press.

Siegler, R.S., & others (2015). The Center for Improving Learning of Fractions: A progress report. In S. Chinn (Ed.), *Routledge international handbook of dyscalculia and mathematical learning difficulties.* New York: Routledge.

Sierra, T.A. (2015). *Working with remarried couples.* Unpublished manuscript, MMATE Center. Virginia Beach, VA: Regent University.

Sievert, L.L. (2014). Menopause across cultures: Clinical considerations. *Menopause, 21,* 421–423.

Silva, C. (2005, October 31). When teen dynamo talks, city listens. *Boston Globe,* pp. B1, B4.

Silva, K., Chein, J., & Steinberg, L. (2016, in press). Adolescents in peer groups make more prudent decisions when a slightly older adult is present. *Psychological Science.*

Silva, L.C., & others (2016). Moderate and intense exercise lifestyles attenuate the effects of aging on telomere length and the survival and composition of T cell subpopulations. *Age, 38,* 24.

Silva Garcia, K., & others (2016). Latina mothers' influence on child appetite regulation. *Appetite, 103,* 200–207.

Silverstein, M. (2009). Caregiving. In D. Carr (Ed.), *Encyclopedia of the life course and human development.* Boston: Gale Cengage.

Simic, G., & others (2016, in press). Tau protein hyperphosphorylation and aggregation in Alzheimer's disease and other taupathies, and possible neuroprotective strategies. *Biomolecules.*

Simm, A., & others (2008). Potential biomarkers of aging. *Biological Chemistry, 389,* 257–265.

Simmons, E.S., Lanter, E., & Lyons, M. (2014). Supporting mainstream educational success. In F.R. Volkmer & others (Eds.), *Handbook of autism and pervasive developmental disorders.* New York: Wiley.

Simms, S.L., Huettner, D.P., & Kortagere, S. (2016). In vivo characterization of a novel dopamine D3 receptor agonist to treat motor symptoms of Parkinson's disease. *Neuropharmacology, 100,* 106–115.

Simon, E.J. (2017). *Biology* (2nd ed.). Upper Saddle River, NJ: Pearson.

Simon, E.J., Dickey, J.L., Reece, J.B., & Hogan, K.A. (2016). *Campbell essential biology* (5th ed.). Upper Saddle River, NJ: Pearson.

Simons, L.G., & others (2016). Mechanisms that link parenting practices to adolescents' risky sexual behavior: A test of six competing theories. *Journal of Youth and Adolescence, 45,* 255–270.

Simons, R.L., & others (2016). Economic hardship and biological weathering: The epigenetics of aging in a U.S. sample of black women. *Social Science and Medicine, 150,* 192–200.

Simpkins, S.D., Fredricks, J.A., Davis-Kean, P.E., & Eccles, J.S. (2006). Healthy mind, healthy habits: The influence of activity involvement in middle childhood. In A.C. Huston & M.N. Ripke (Eds.), *Developmental contexts in middle childhood.* New York: Cambridge University Press.

Simpkins, S.D., Fredricks, J.A., & Eccles, J.S. (2015). Families, schools, and developing achievement-related motivations. In J.E. Grusec & P.D. Hastings (Eds.), *Handbook of socialization* (2nd ed.). New York: Guilford.

Simpson, H.B., & others (2013). Treatment of obsessive-compulsive disorder complicated by comorbid eating disorders. *Cognitive Behavior Therapy, 42,* 64–76.

Simpson, J., & Belsky, J. (2016). Attachment theory within a modern evolutionary framework. In J. Cassidy & P. Shaver (Eds.), *Handbook of attachment theory and research* (3rd ed.). New York: Guilford.

Simpson, J.A., Collins, W.A., Tran, S., & Haydon, K.C. (2007). Attachment and the experience and expression of emotions in romantic relationships: A developmental perspective. *Journal of Personality and Social Psychology, 92,* 355–367.

Sims, J. (2016). Ageism: The next big 'ism' to address? *Australasian Journal of Aging, 35*(1),8.

Sims, T., Hogan, C., & Carstensen, L.L. (2015). Selectivity as an emotion regulation strategy: Lessons from older adults. *Current Opinion in Psychology, 3,* 80–84.

Sin, N.L., Graham-Engeland, J.E., Ong, A.D., & Almeida, D.M. (2015). Affective reactivity to daily stressors is associated with elevated inflammation. *Health Psychology, 34,* 1154–1165.

Sin, N.L., Sloan, R.P., McKinley, P.S., & Almeida, D.M. (2016, in press). Linking daily stress processes and laboratory-based heart rate variability in a national sample of midlife and older adults. *Psychosomatic Medicine.*

Singer, A.E., & others (2015). Symptom trends in the last year of life from 1998 to 2010: A cohort study. *Annals of Internal Medicine, 162,* 175–183.

Singer, D., Golinkoff, R.M., & Hirsh-Pasek, K. (Eds.) (2006). *Play = learning: How play motivates and enhances children's cognitive and social-emotional growth.* New York: Oxford University Press.

Singer, J.A., & Kasmark, A.M. (2015). A translational approach to narrative identity in psychotherapy. In K.C. McLean & M. Syed (Eds.), *Oxford handbook of identity development.* New York: Oxford University Press.

Singer, M.A. (2016). The origins of aging: Evidence that aging is an adaptive phenotype. *Current Aging Science, 9,* 95–115.

Singh, N.N., & others (2016, in press). Effects of Samatha meditation on active academic engagement and math performance of students with attention/deficit/hyperactivity disorder. *Mindfulness.*

Sinnott, J.D. (2003). Postformal thought and adult development: Living in balance. In J. Demick & C. Andreoletti (Eds.), *Handbook of adult development.* New York: Kluwer.

Sirard, J.R., & others (2013). Physical activity and screen time in adolescents and their friends. *American Journal of Preventive Medicine, 44,* 48–55.

Sirsch, U., Dreher, E., Mayr, E., & Willinger, U. (2009). What does it take to be an adult in Australia? Views of adulthood in Australian adolescents, emerging adults and adults. *Journal of Adolescent Research, 24,* 275–292.

Skingley, A. (2013). Older people, isolation, and loneliness: Implications for community nursing. *British Journal of Community Nursing, 18,* 84–90.

Skinner, B.F. (1938). *The behavior of organisms: An experimental analysis.* New York: Appleton-Century-Crofts.

Skinner, B.F. (1957). *Verbal behavior.* New York: Appleton-Century-Crofts.

Skinner, O.D., & McHale, S.M. (2016, in press). Parent-adolescent conflict in African American families. *Journal of Youth and Adolescence.*

Skinner, S.R., & others (2015). Childhood behavior problems and age at first sexual intercourse: A prospective birth cohort study. *Pediatrics, 135,* 255–263.

Slater, A., Field, T., & Hernandez-Reif, M. (2007). The development of the senses. In A. Slater & M. Lewis (Eds.), *Introduction to infant development* (2nd ed.). New York: Oxford University Press.

Slater, A.M., Bremner, J.G., Johnson, S.P., & Hayes, R. (2011). The role of perceptual processes in infant addition/subtraction events. In L.M. Oakes, C.H. Cashon, M. Casasola, & D.H. Rakison (Eds.), *Early perceptual and cognitive development*. New York: Oxford University Press.

Sleet, D.A., & Mercy, J.A. (2003). Promotion of safety, security, and well-being. In M.H. Bornstein, L. Davidson, C.L.M. Keyes, & K.A. Moore (Eds.), *Well-being*. Mahwah, NJ: Erlbaum.

Slobin, D. (1972, July). Children and language: They learn the same way around the world. *Psychology Today,* 71–76.

Slopen, N., & others (2016). Racial disparities in child adversity in the U.S.: Interactions with family immigration history and income. *American Journal of Preventive Medicine, 50,* 47–56.

Sloutsky, V. (2015). Conceptual development. In R.M. Lerner (Ed.), *Handbook of child psychology and developmental science* (7th ed.). New York: Wiley.

Smaldino, S.E., Lowther, D.L., Russell, J.W., & Mims, C. (2015). *Instructional technology and media for learning* (11th ed.). Upper Saddle River, NJ: Pearson.

Small, B.J., Dixon, R.A., McArdle, J.J., & Grimm, K.J. (2012). Do changes in lifestyle engagement moderate cognitive decline in normal aging? Evidence from the Victoria Longitudinal Study. *Neuropsychology, 26,* 144–155.

Small, H. (2011). *Why not? My seventy year plan for a college degree.* Franklin, TN: Carpenter's Son Publishing.

Small, L., & Aplasca, A. (2016). Child obesity and mental health: A complex interaction. *Child and Adolescent Psychiatry Clinics of North America, 25,* 269–282.

Smetana, J.G., & Rote, W.M. (2015). What do mothers want to know about teens' activities? Levels, trajectories, and correlates. *Journal of Adolescence, 38,* 5–15.

Smetana, J.G., Robinson, J., & Rote, W.M. (2015). Socialization in adolescence. In J.E. Grusec & P.D. Hastings (Eds.), *Handbook of socialization* (2nd ed.). New York: Guilford.

Smith, A. (2014, April 3). *Older adults and technology use.* Washington, DC: Pew Research Center.

Smith, A.D. (1996). Memory. In J.E. Birren (Ed.), *Encyclopedia of gerontology* (Vol. 2). San Diego: Academic Press.

Smith, A.J., Abeyta, A.A., Hughes, M., & Jones, R.T. (2015). Persistent grief in the aftermath of mass violence: The predictive roles of posttraumatic stress symptoms, self-efficacy, and disrupted worldview. *Psychological Trauma, 7,* 179–186.

Smith, C.A., Armour, M., & Ee, C. (2016). Complementary therapies and medicines and reproductive medicine. *Seminars in Reproductive Medicine, 34,* 67–73.

Smith, C.A., Collins, C.T., Crowther, C.A., & Levett, K.M. (2011). Acupuncture or acupressure for pain management of labor. *Cochrane Database of Systematic Reviews, 7,* July 6. CD009232.

Smith, C.A., Levett, K.M., Collins, C.T., & Jones, L. (2012). Massage, reflexology, and other manual methods for pain management. *Cochrane Database of Systematic Reviews, 15*(2), CD009290.

Smith, C.L., Diaz, A., Day, K.L., & Bell, M.A. (2016). Infant frontal electroencephalogram asymmetry and negative emotional reactivity as predictors of toddlerhood effortful control. *Journal of Experimental Child Psychology, 142,* 262–273.

Smith, L.E., & Howard, K.S. (2008). Continuity of paternal social support and depressive symptoms among new mothers. *Journal of Family Psychology, 22,* 763–773.

Smith, R.A., & Davis, S.F. (2016). *The psychologist as detective* (7th ed.). Upper Saddle River, NJ: Prentice Hall.

Smith, R.L., Rose, A.J., & Schwartz-Mette, R.A. (2010). Relational and overt aggression in childhood and adolescence: Clarifying mean-level gender differences and associations with peer acceptance. *Social Development, 19,* 243–269.

Smith, T.E., & others (2016). *Teaching students with special needs in inclusive settings* (7th ed.). Upper Saddle River, NJ: Pearson.

Smock, P.J., & Gupta, S. (2013). Cohabitation in contemporary North America. In A. Booth, A.C. Crouter, & N.S. Lansdale (Eds.), *Just living together.* New York: Psychology Press.

Smokowski, P.R., Bacallao, M.L., Cotter, K.L., & Evans, C.B. (2015). The effects of positive and negative parenting practices on adolescent mental health outcomes in a multicultural sample of rural youth. *Child Psychiatry and Human Development, 46,* 333–345.

Smokowski, P.R., Guo, S., Cotter, K.L., Evans, C.B., & Rose, R.A. (2016). Multi-level risk factors and developmental assets associated with aggressive behavior in disadvantaged adolescents. *Aggressive Behavior, 42,* 222–238.

Snarey, J. (1987, June). A question of morality. *Psychology Today,* pp. 6–8.

Snow, C.E., & Kang, J.Y. (2006). Becoming bilingual, biliterate, and bicultural. In W. Damon & R. Lerner (Eds.), *Handbook of child psychology* (6th ed.). New York: Wiley.

Snowdon, D.A. (2003). Healthy aging and dementia: Findings from the Nun Study. *Annals of Internal Medicine, 139,* 450–454.

Snyder, P.J., & others (2016). Effects of testosterone in older men. *New England Journal of Medicine, 374,* 611–624.

Snyder, W. (2016). Compound word formation. In J. Lidz, W. Snyder, & J. Pater (Eds.), *Oxford handbook of developmental linguistics.* New York: Oxford University Press.

So, H.K., & others (2016). Association between waist circumference and childhood-masked hypertension: A community-based study. *Journal of Pediatrics and Child Health, 52,* 385–390.

Soares-Miranda, L., & others (2016). Physical activity and risk of coronary heart disease and stroke in older adults: The Cardiovascular Health Study. *Circulation, 133,* 147–155.

Sockol, L.E. (2015). A systematic review of the efficacy of cognitive behavioral therapy for treating and preventing perinatal depression. *Journal of Affective Disorders,177,* 7–21.

Sodian, B., & others (2016, in press). Understanding of goals, beliefs, and desires predicts morally relevant theory of mind: A longitudinal investigation. *Child Development.*

Sokolowski, M., Wasserman, J., & Wasserman, D. (2016, in press). Polygenic associations of neurodevelopmental genes in suicide attempt. *Molecular Psychiatry.*

Solish, N., & others (2016). Efficacy and safety of onabotulinumtoxin A of forehead lines: A multicenter, randomized, dose-ranging controlled trial. *Dermatologic Surgery, 42,* 410–419.

Soller, B. (2014). Caught in a bad romance: Adolescent romantic relationships and mental health. *Journal of Health and Social Behavior, 55,* 56–72.

Solomon, E., Martin, C., Martin, D.W., & Berg, L.R. (2015). *Biology* (10th ed.). Boston: Cengage.

Solomon, J., & George, C. (2016). The measurement of attachment security and related concepts. In J. Cassidy & P.R. Shaver (Eds.), *Handbook of attachment* (3rd ed.). New York: Guilford.

Somerville, L.H. (2016). Emotional development in adolescence. In L.F. Barrett, M. Lewis, & J.M. Haveland-Jones (Eds.), *Handbook of emotions* (4th ed.). New York: Guilford.

Sommer, T., & others (2016). Two-generation education programs for parents and children. In S. Jones & N. Lesauz (Eds.), *The leading edge of early childhood education.* Cambridge, MA: Harvard Education Press.

Song, F., & others (2015). Alzheimer's disease: Genomics and beyond. *International Review of Neurobiology, 121,* 1–24.

Sophian, C. (1985). Perseveration and infants' search: A comparison of two-and three-location tasks. *Developmental Psychology, 21,* 187–194.

Sorbye, I.K., Wanigaratne, S., & Urgula, M.L. (2016). Variations in gestational length and preterm delivery by race, ethnicity, and migration. *Best Practices in Research: Clinical Obstetrics and Gynecology, 32,* 60–68.

Sorte, J., Daeschel, I., & Amador, C. (2017). *Nutrition, health, and safety for young children* (3rd ed.). Upper Saddle River, NJ: Pearson.

Soska, K.C., & Adolph, K.E. (2014). Perception-action development from infants to adults: Perceiving affordances for reaching through openings. *Journal of Experimental Child Psychology, 117,* 92–105.

Soto, C.J. (2015). Is happiness good for your personality? Concurrent and prospective relations of the Big Five with subjective well-being. *Journal of Personality, 83,* 45–55.

South, S.C., & Jarnecke, A. (2016). Behavior genetics: Introduction to methodology. In M. Pluess (Ed.), *Genetics of psychological well-being.* New York: Oxford University Press.

Spangler, G., Johann, M., Ronai, Z., & Zimmermann, P. (2009). Genetic and environmental influence on attachment disorganization. *Journal of Child Psychology and Psychiatry, 50,* 952–961.

Specht, J., Egloff, B., & Schukle, S.C. (2011). Stability and change of personality across the life course: The impact of age and major life events on mean-level and rank-order stability of the Big Five. *Journal of Personality and Social Psychology, 101*(4), 862–882.

Spelke, E.S. (2004). Core knowledge. In N. Kanwisher & J. Duncan (Eds.), *Attention and Performance: Functional neuroimaging of visual cognition* (Vol. 20, pp. 29–56). Oxford, UK: Oxford University Press.

Spelke, E.S. (2011). Natural number and natural geometry. In E. Brannon & S. Dehaene (Eds.), *Space, time, and number in the brain.* New York: Oxford University Press.

Spelke, E.S. (2013). Developmental sources of social divisions. *Neurosciences and the human person: New perspectives on human activities.* Unpublished manuscript, Department of Psychology, Harvard University, Cambridge, MA.

Spelke, E.S., & Owsley, C.J. (1979). Intermodal exploration and knowledge in infancy. *Infant Behavior and Development, 2,* 13–28.

Spelke, E.S., Bernier, E.P., & Snedeker, J. (2013). Core social cognition. In M.R. Banaji & S.A. Gelman (Eds.), *Navigating the social world: What infants, children, and other species can teach us.* New York: Oxford University Press.

Spence, A.P. (1989). *Biology of human aging.* Englewood Cliffs, NJ: Prentice Hall.

Spence, J.T., & Helmreich, R. (1978). *Masculinity and femininity: Their psychological dimensions.* Austin: University of Texas Press.

Spencer, M.B., & Swanson, D.P. (2016). Vulnerability and resilience in African American youth. In D. Cicchetti (Ed.), *Developmental psychopathology* (3rd ed.). New York: Wiley.

Spiegler, M.D. (2016). *Contemporary behavior therapy* (6th ed.). Boston: Cengage.

Spieker, S.J., & others (2012). Relational aggression in middle childhood: Predictors and adolescent outcomes. *Social Development, 21,* 354–375.

Spindel, E.R., & McEvoy, C.T. (2016). The role of nicotine in the effects of maternal smoking during pregnancy and lung development and childhood respiratory disease. Implications for dangers of e-cigarettes. *American Journal of Respiratory and Critical Care Medicine, 193,* 486–494.

Spira, D., & others (2015). Association of low lean body mass with frailty and physical performance: A comparison between two operational definitions of sarcopenia–data from the Berlin Aging Study II (BASE-II). *Journals of Gerontology A: Biological Sciences and Medical Sciences, 70,* 779–784.

Sprecher, S., Treger, S., & Sakaluk, J.K. (2013). Premarital sexual standards and sociosexuality: Gender, ethnicity, and cohort differences. *Archives of Sexual Behavior, 42,* 1395–1405.

Sroufe, L.A. (2016). The place of attachment in development. In J. Cassidy & P.R. Shaver (Eds.), *Handbook of attachment* (3rd ed.). New York: Guilford.

Sroufe, L.A., Egeland, B., Carlson, E., & Collins, W.A. (2005). The place of early attachment in developmental context. In K.E. Grossman, K. Krossman, & E. Waters (Eds.), *The power of longitudinal attachment research: From infancy and childhood to adulthood.* New York: Guilford.

Sroufe, L.A., Waters, E., & Matas, L. (1974). Contextual determinants of infant affectional response. In M. Lewis & L. Rosenblum (Eds.), *Origins of fear.* New York: Wiley.

Staff, J., Mont'Alvao, A., & Mortimer, J.T. (2015). Children at work. In R.M. Lerner (Ed.), *Handbook of child psychology and developmental psychology* (7th ed.). New York: Wiley.

Stahl, A., Romberg, A., Roseberry, S., Golinkoff, R.M., & Hirsh-Pasek, K. (2014). Infants segment continuous events using transitional probabilities. *Child Development, 85,* 1821–1826.

Stancil, S.L., & others (2016, in press). Contraceptive provision to adolescent females prescribed teratogenic medicines. *Pediatrics.*

Stanford Center for Longevity (2011). *Experts' consensus on brain health.* Retrieved April 30, 2011, from http://longevity.stanford.edu/my mind/cognitiveagingstatement

Stanford Center for Longevity and Max Planck Institute for Human Development (2014). *A consensus on the brain training industry from the scientific community.* Retrieved

September 16, 2015, from http://longevity3.stanford.edu.blog/2014/10/15

Stang, J., & Huffman, L.G. (2016). Position of the American Academy of Nutrition and Dietetics: Obesity, reproduction, and pregnancy outcomes. *Journal of the Academy of Nutrition and Dietetics, 116,* 667–691.

Stangor, C. (2015). *Research methods for the behavioral sciences* (5th ed.). Boston: Cengage.

Starr, L.R., & others (2012). Love hurts (in more ways than one): Specificity of psychological symptoms as predictors and consequences of romantic activity among early adolescent girls. *Journal of Clinical Psychology, 68*(4), 373–381.

Staszewski, J. (Ed.) (2013). *Expertise and skill acquisition: The impact of William C. Chase.* New York: Taylor & Francis.

Staudinger, U.M. (1996). Psychologische Produktivitat und Selbstenfaltung im Alter. In M.M. Baltes & L. Montada (Eds.), *Produktives Leben im Alter.* Frankfurt: Campus.

Stawski, R.S., Sliwinski, M.J., & Hofer, S.M. (2013). Between-person and within-person associations among processing speed, attention switching, and working memory in younger and older adults. *Experimental Aging Research, 39,* 194–214.

Steck, N., & others (2013). Euthanasia and assisted suicide in selected European countries and U.S. states: Systematic literature review. *Medical Care, 51,* 938–944.

Steckler, C.M., & Hamlin, J.K. (2016, in press). Theories of moral development. In H. Miller (Ed.), *Encyclopedia of theory in psychology.* Thousand Oaks, CA: Sage.

Steele, J., Waters, E., Crowell, J., & Treboux, D. (1998, June). *Self-report measures of attachment: Secure bonds to other attachment measures and attachment theory.* Paper presented at the meeting of the International Society for the Study of Personal Relationships, Saratoga Springs, NY.

Steffener, J., Barulli, D., Habeck, C., & Stern, Y. (2014). Neuroimaging explanations of age-related differences in task performance. *Frontiers in Aging Neuroscience, 6,* 46.

Steiger, A.E., Allemand, M., Robins, R.W., & Fend, H.A. (2014). Low and decreasing self-esteem during adolescence predict adult depression two decades later. *Journal of Personality and Social Psychology, 106,* 325–338.

Stein, P.K., & others (2012). Caloric restriction may reverse age-related autonomic decline in humans. *Aging Cell, 11*(4), 644–650.

Steinberg, L. (2014). *Age of opportunity.* Boston: Houghton Mifflin Harcourt.

Steinberg, L. (2015a). How should the science of adolescent brain pathology inform legal policy? In J. Bhabba (Ed.), *Coming of age.* Philadelphia: University of Pennsylvania Press.

Steinberg, L. (2015b). The neural underpinnings of adolescent risk-taking: The roles of reward-seeking, impulse control, and peers. In G. Oettigen & P. Gollwitzer (Eds.), *Self-regulation in adolescence.* New York: Cambridge University Press.

Steiner, J.E. (1979). Human facial expressions in response to taste and smell stimulation. In H. Reese & L. Lipsitt (Eds.), *Advances in child development and behavior, 13,* 257–295.

Steinsbekk, S., Belsky, J., & Wichstrom, L. (2016, in press). Parental feeding and child eating: An investigation of reciprocal effects. *Child Development.*

Stella, F., & others (2015). Anti-dementia medications: Current prescriptions in clinical practice and new agents in progress. *Therapeutic Advances in Drug Safety, 6,* 151–165.

Stenholm, S., & others (2014). Age-related trajectories of physical functioning in work and retirement: The role of sociodemographic factors, lifestyles, and disease. *Journal of Epidemiology and Community Health, 68,* 503–509.

Stephanie, D., & Julie, F. (2015). Exploring links between language and cognition in autism spectrum disorders: Complementary sentences, false belief, and executive functioning. *Journal of Communication Disorders, 54,* 15–31.

Stephenson, T., & Schiff, W. (2016). *Human nutrition.* New York: McGraw-Hill.

Steptoe, A., & Kivimaki, M. (2012). Stress and cardiovascular disease. *Nature Reviews. Cardiology, 9,* 360–370.

Steptoe, A., Deaton, A., & Stone, A.A. (2015). Subjective well being, health, and aging. *Lancet, 385,* 640–648.

Steptoe, A., Shankar, A., Demakakos, P., & Wardle, J. (2013). Social isolation, loneliness, and all-cause mortality in older men and women. *Proceedings of the National Academy of Sciences, 110,* 5797–5801.

Steri, A., & de Hevia, M.D. (2015). Manual lateralization in infancy. *Frontiers in Psychology, 5,* 1575.

Steric, M., & others (2015). The outcome and course of pregnancies complicated with fetal neural tube defects. *Clinical and Experimental Obstetrics and Gynecology, 42,* 57–61.

Sternberg, K., & Sternberg, R.J. (2013). Love. In H. Pashler (Ed.), *Encyclopedia of the mind.* Thousand Oaks, CA: Sage.

Sternberg, R.J. (1986). *Intelligence applied.* San Diego: Harcourt Brace Jovanovich.

Sternberg, R.J. (1988). *The triangle of love.* New York: Basic Books.

Sternberg, R.J. (2004). Individual differences in cognitive development. In U. Goswami (Ed.), *Blackwell handbook of childhood cognitive development.* Malden, MA: Blackwell.

Sternberg, R.J. (2010). Componential models of creativity. In M. Runco & S. Spritzker (Eds.), *Encyclopedia of creativity.* New York: Elsevier.

Sternberg, R.J. (2012). Human intelligence. In V.S. Ramachandran (Ed.), *Encyclopedia of human behavior* (2nd ed.). New York: Elsevier.

Sternberg, R.J. (2013). Contemporary theories of intelligence. In I.B. Weiner & others (Eds.), *Handbook of psychology* (2nd ed., Vol. 7). New York: Wiley.

Sternberg, R.J. (2015a). Human intelligence: Historical and conceptual perspectives. In J. Wright (Ed.), *Encyclopedia of social and behavioral sciences* (2nd ed.). New York: Elsevier.

Sternberg, R.J. (2015b). Competence versus performance models of people and tests. *Applied Developmental Science, 19,* 170–175.

Sternberg, R.J. (2016a). Multiple intelligences in the new age of thinking. In S. Goldstein, D. Princiotta, & J. Naglieri (Eds.), *Handbook of intelligence.* New York: Springer.

Sternberg, R.J. (2016b, in press). Theories of intelligence. In S. Pfeiffer (Ed.), *APA handbook of giftedness and talent.* Washington, DC: American Psychological Association.

Sternberg, R.J. (2016c, in press). What does it mean to be intelligent? In R.J. Sternberg & others (Eds.), *Scientists making a difference*. New York: Cambridge University Press.

Sternberg, R.J., & Bridges, S.L. (2014). Varieties of genius. In D.K. Simonton (Ed.), *Wiley-Blackwell handbook of genius*. New York: Wiley.

Sternberg, R.J., & Sternberg, K. (2016). *Cognitive psychology* (7th ed.). Boston: Cengage.

Sterns, H., & Huyck, M.H. (2001). The role of work in midlife. In M. Lachman (Ed.), *Handbook of midlife development*. New York: Wiley.

Stessman, J., & others (2014). Loneliness, health, and longevity. *Journals of Gerontology B: Psychological Sciences and Social Sciences, 69,* 744–750.

Stevens, C., & Bavelier, D. (2012). The role of selective attention on academic foundations: A cognitive neuroscience perspective. *Developmental Cognitive Neuroscience, 15* (Suppl. 1), S30–S48.

Stevenson, H.W. (1995). Mathematics achievements of American students: First in the world by the year 2000: In C.A. Nelson (Ed.), *Basic and applied perspectives on learning, cognition, and development*. Minneapolis: University of Minnesota Press.

Stevenson, H.W. (2000). Middle childhood: Education and schooling. In A. Kazdin (Ed.), *Encyclopedia of psychology*. Washington, DC, & New York: American Psychological Association and Oxford University Press.

Stevenson, H.W., Hofer, B.K., & Randel, B. (1999). *Middle childhood: Education and schooling*. Unpublished manuscript, Dept. of Psychology, University of Michigan, Ann Arbor.

Stevenson, H.W., Lee, S., & Stigler, J.W. (1986). Mathematics achievement of Chinese, Japanese, and American children. *Science, 231,* 693–699.

Stevenson, H.W., & Zusho, A. (2002) Adolescence in China and Japan: Adapting to a changing environment. In B.B. Brown, R.W. Larson, & T.S. Saraswathi (Eds.), *The world's youth*. New York: Cambridge University Press.

Stevenson, H.W., & others (1990). Contexts of achievement. *Monograph of the Society for Research in Child Development, 55* (Serial No. 221).

Stevenson, M., & others (2016, in press). Understanding how bereaved parents cope with their grief to inform the services provided to them. *Qualitative Health Research.*

Stewart, A.J., Ostrove, J.M., & Helson, R. (2001). Middle aging in women: Patterns of personality change from the 30s to the 50s. *Journal of Adult Development, 8,* 23–37.

Stifter, C., & Dollar, J. (2016). Temperament and developmental psychopathology. In D. Cicchetti (Ed.), *Developmental psychology* (3rd ed.). New York: Wiley.

Stiggins, R. (2008). *Introduction to student involved assessment for learning* (5th ed.). Upper Saddle River, NJ: Prentice Hall.

Stiles, J., Brown, T.T., Haist, F., & Jernigan, T.L. (2015). Brain and cognitive development. In R.M. Lerner (Ed.), *Handbook of child psychology and developmental science* (7th ed.). New York: Wiley.

Stilwell, D. (2016). Helping couples fulfill the "highest of life's goals": Mate selection, marriage counseling, and genetic counseling in the United States. *Journal of Genetic Counseling, 25,* 157–165.

Stipek, D. (2005, February 16). Commentary in *USA Today*, p. 10.

Stokes, C.E., & Raley, R.K. (2009). Cohabitation. In D. Carr (Ed.), *Encyclopedia of the life course and human development*. Boston: Gale Cengage.

Stolp, H.B., & Molnar, Z. (2015). Neurogenic niches in the brain: Help and hindrance of the barrier systems. *Frontiers in Neuroscience, 9,* 20.

Stone, A.A., Schwartz, J.E., Broderick, J.E., & Deaton, A. (2010). A snapshot of the age distribution of psychological well-being in the United States. *Proceedings of the National Academy of Sciences USA, 107,* 9985–9990.

Straker, L.M., & Howie, E.K. (2016, in press). Young children's screen time: It is time to consider healthy bodies as well as healthy minds. *Journal of Developmental and Behavioral Pediatrics.*

Street, S.J., Wells, J.C., & Hills, A.P. (2015). Windows of opportunity for physical activity in the prevention of obesity. *Obesity Reviews, 16,* 857–870.

Strenze, T. (2007). Intelligence and socioeconomic success: A meta-analytic review of longitudinal research. *Intelligence, 35,* 401–426.

Strookappe, B., & others (2015). Benefits of physical training in sarcoidosis. *Lung, 193,* 701–708.

Stroope, S., McFarland, M.J., & Uecker, J.E. (2015). Marital characteristics and the sexual relationships of U.S. older adults: An analysis of national social life, health, and aging project data. *Archives of Sexual Behavior, 44,* 233–247.

Strough, J., & others (2016, in press). Hour glass half full or half empty? Future time perspective and preoccupation with negative events across the life span. *Psychology and Aging.*

Stubbs, B., Brefka, S., & Denkinger, M.D. (2015). What works to prevent falls in community-dwelling older adults? An umbrella review of meta-analyses of randomized controlled trials. *Physical Therapy, 95,* 1095–1110.

Stubbs, B., Schofield, P., & Patchay, S. (2016). Mobility limitations and fall-related factors contribute to the reduced health-related quality of life in older adults with chronic musculoskeletal pain. *Pain Practice, 16,* 80–89.

Stuebe, A.M., & Schwartz, E.G. (2010). The risks and benefits of infant feeding practices for women and their children. *Journal of Perinatology, 30,* 155–162.

Su, D., Stimpson, J.P., & Wilson, F.A. (2015). Racial disparities in mortality among middle-aged and older men: Does marriage matter? *American Journal of Men's Health, 9,* 289–300.

Suarez-Orozco, M.M., & Suarez-Orozco, C. (2015/2016). Children of immigration. *Phi Delta Kappan, 97*(4), 8–14.

Subramaniam, P., & Woods, B. (2012). The impact of individual reminiscence therapy for people with dementia: Systematic review. *Expert Review of Neurotherapeutics, 12,* 545–555.

Sue, D., Sue, D.W., Sue, S., & Sue, D.M. (2015). *Understanding abnormal behavior* (11th ed.). Boston: Cengage.

Sugiura, M. (2016, in press). Functional neuroimaging of normal aging: Declining brain, adapting brain. *Aging Research Reviews.*

Suitor, J.J., Gilligan, M., & Pillemer, K. (2016). Stability, change, and complexity in later life families. In L.K. George & K.F. Ferraro (Eds.), *Handbook of aging and the social sciences* (8th ed.). New York: Elsevier.

Sullivan, A.R., & Fenelon, A. (2014). Patterns of widowhood mortality. *Journals of Gerontology B: Psychological Sciences and Social Sciences, 69,* 53–62.

Sullivan, H.S. (1953). *The interpersonal theory of psychiatry*. New York: W.W. Norton.

Sullivan, K., & Sullivan, A. (1980). Adolescent-parent separation. *Developmental Psychology, 16,* 93–99.

Sullivan, M.D., & others (2014). Early stage second-language learning improves executive control: Evidence from ERP. *Brain and Language, 139,* 84–98.

Sun, R., & others (2016, in press). Congenital heart disease: Causes, diagnosis, symptoms, and treatment. *Cellular Biochemistry and Biophysics.*

Sun, Y., Tao, F., Hao, J., & Wan, Y. (2010). The mediating effects of stress and coping on depression among adolescents in China. *Journal of Child and Adolescent Psychiatric Nursing, 23,* 173–180.

Sun, Y., & others (2012). National estimates of the pubertal milestones among urban and rural Chinese girls. *Journal of Adolescent Health, 51,* 279–284.

Sung, G., & Greer, D. (2011). The case for simplifying brain death criteria. *Neurology, 76,* 113–114.

Suo, C., & others (2016, in press). Therapeutically relevant structural and functional mechanisms triggered by physical and cognitive exercise. *Molecular Psychiatry.*

Suri, G., & Gross, J.J. (2012). Emotion regulation and successful aging. *Trends in Cognitive Science, 16,* 409–410.

Susman, E.J., & Dorn, L.D. (2013). Puberty: Its role in development. In I.B. Weiner & others (Eds.), *Handbook of psychology* (3rd ed., Vol. 6). New York: Wiley.

Sutcliffe, K., & others (2012). Comparing midwife-led and doctor-led maternity care: A systematic review of reviews. *Journal of Advanced Nursing, 68*(11), 2376–2386.

Suter, M.A., Mastrobattista, J., Sachs, M., & Aagaard, K. (2015). Is there evidence for potential harm of electronic cigarette use in pregnancy? *Birth Defects Research A: Clinical and Molecular Technology, 103,* 186–195.

Sutphin, G.L., & Korstanje, R. (2016). Longevity as a complex genetic trait. In M.R. Kaeberlein & G.M. Martin (Eds.), *Handbook of the biology of aging* (8th ed.). New York: Elsevier.

Svendsboe, E., & others (2016, in press). Caregiver burden in family carers of people with dementia with Lewy bodies and Alzheimer's disease. *International Journal of Geriatric Psychiatry.*

Sviri, S., & others (2009). Contraindications in end-of-life decisions for self and others, expressed by relatives of chronically ventilated persons. *Journal of Critical Care, 24,* 293–301.

Swanson, H.L. (2016). Cognition and cognitive disabilities. In L. Corno & E.M. Anderman (Eds.), *Handbook of educational psychology* (3rd ed.). New York: Routledge.

Swartzendruber, A., Sales, J.M., Rose, E.S., & DiClemente, R.J. (2016). Alcohol use problems and sexual risk among young adult African American mothers. *AIDS Behavior, 20*(Suppl. 1), S74–S83.

Sweeney, M.M. (2009). Remarriage. In D. Carr (Ed.), *Encyclopedia of the life course and human development*. Boston: Gale Cengage.

Sweeney, M.M. (2010). Remarriage and stepfamilies: Strategic sites for family scholarship in the 21st century. *Journal of Marriage and the Family, 72,* 667–684.

Swing, E.L., Gentile, D.A., Anderson, C.A., & Walsh, D.A. (2010). Television and video game exposure and the development of attention problems. *Pediatrics, 126,* 214–221.

Syed, M., & Juang, L.P. (2014). Ethnic identity, ethnic coherence, and psychological functioning: Testing basic assumptions of the developmental model. *Cultural Diversity and Ethnic Minority Psychology, 20,* 176–190.

Sykes, C.J. (1995). *Dumbing down our kids: Why America's children feel good about themselves but can't read, write, or add.* New York: St. Martin's Press.

Szyf, M., & Pluess, M. (2016). Epigenetics and well-being: Optimal adaptation to the environment. In M. Pluess (Ed.), *Genetics of psychological well-being.* New York: Oxford University Press.

T

Tabuchi, M., Nakagawa, T., Miura, A., & Gondo, Y. (2015). Generativity and interaction between the old and young: The role of perceived respect and perceived rejection. *Gerontologist, 55,* 537–547.

Tach, L.M., & Eads, A. (2015). Trends in the economic consequences of marital and cohabitation dissolution in the United States. *Demography, 52,* 401–432.

Tai, L.M., & others (2015). APOE-modulated A*B*-induced neuroinflammation in Alzheimer's disease: Current landscape, novel data, and future perspective. *Journal of Neurochemistry, 133,* 465–488.

Taige, N.M., & others (2007). Antenatal maternal stress and long-term effects on child neurodevelopment: How and why? *Journal of Child Psychology and Psychiatry, 48,* 245–261.

Takasaki, N., & others (2014). A heterozygous mutation of GALNTL5 affects male infertility with impairment of sperm motility. *Proceedings of the National Academy of Sciences USA, 11,* 1120–1125.

Tamis-LeMonda, C.S., & Bornstein, M.H. (2015). Infant word learning in biopsychosocial perspective. In S.D. Calkins (Ed.), *Handbook of biopsychosocial development.* New York: Guilford.

Tan, C.C., & Holub, S.C. (2015). Emotion regulation feeding practices link parents' emotional eating to children's emotional eating: A moderated mediation study. *Journal of Pediatric Psychology, 40,* 657–663.

Tan, P.Z., Armstrong, L.M., & Cole, P.M. (2013). Relations between temperament and anger regulation over early childhood. *Social Development, 22,* 755–772.

Tan, Q., Christiansen, L., Bornemann Hjelmborg, J., & Christiansen, K. (2015). Twin methodology in epigenetic studies. *Journal of Experimental Biology, 18,* 134–139.

Tang, S. (2015). Social capital and determinants of immigrant family educational involvement. *Journal of Educational Research, 108,* 22–34.

Tang, S., Davis-Kean, P.E., Chen, M., & Sexton, H.R. (2016, in press). Adolescent pregnancy's intergenerational effects: Does an adolescent mother's education have consequences for children's achievement? *Journal of Research on Adolescence.*

Tang, S., McLoyd, V.C., & Hallman, S.K. (2016). Racial socialization, racial identity, and academic attitudes among African American adolescents:

Examining the moderating influence of parent-adolescent communication. *Journal of Youth and Adolescence, 45,* 1141–1155.

Tarokh, L., & Carskadon, M.A. (2010). Developmental changes in the human sleep EEG during early adolescence. *Sleep, 33,* 801–809.

Taverno Ross, S., Dowda, M., Saunders, R., & Pate, R. (2013). Double dose: The cumulative effect of TV viewing at home and in preschool on children's activity patterns and weight status. *Pediatric Exercise Science, 25,* 262–272.

Tay, A.K., & others (2016). Factorial structure of complicated grief: Associations with loss-related traumatic events and psychosocial impacts of mass conflict amongst West Papuan refugees. *Social Psychiatry and Psychiatric Epidemiology, 51,* 395–406.

Taylor, C., & others (2016, in press). Ways that a mindfulness-based training program reduces stress in public school teachers: A mixed-methods approach. *Mindfulness.*

Taylor, C.A., Manganello, J.A., Lee, S.J., & Rice, J.C. (2010). Mothers' spanking of 3-year-old children and subsequent risk of children's aggressive behavior. *Pediatrics, 125,* e1057–e1065.

Taylor, H., & others (2016, in press). Neonatal outcomes of waterbirth: A systematic review and meta-analysis. *Archives of Disease in Childhood: Fetal and Neonatal Edition.*

Taylor, S.E. (2011a). Affiliation and stress. In S.S. Folkman (Ed.), *Oxford handbook of stress, health, and coping.* New York: Oxford University Press.

Taylor, S.E. (2011b). *Health psychology* (8th ed.). New York: McGraw-Hill.

Taylor, S.E. (2011c). Tend and befriend theory. In A.M. van Lange, A.W. Kruglanski, & E.T. Higgins (Eds.), *Handbook of theories of social psychology.* Thousand Oaks, CA: Sage.

Taylor, S.E. (2015). *Health psychology* (9th ed.). New York: McGraw-Hill.

Tchamo, M.E., Prista, A., & Leandro, C.G. (2016, in press). Low birth weight, very low birth weight, and extremely low birth weight in African children aged between 0 and 5 years old: A systematic review. *Journal of the Developmental Origins of Health and Disease.*

Tearne, J.E., & others (2016, in press). Older maternal age is associated with depression, anxiety, and stress symptoms in young adult female offspring. *Journal of Abnormal Psychology.*

Tee, L.M., Kan, E.Y., Cheung, J.C., & Leung, W.C. (2016, in press). Magnetic resonance imaging of the fetal brain. *Hong Kong Medical Journal.*

ten Hoope-Bender, P., & others (2016, in press). Midwifery 2030: A woman's pathway to health. What does this mean? *Midwifery.*

Ten Hoor, G.A., & others (2016). A new direction in psychology and health: Resistance exercise training for obese children and adolescents. *Psychology & Health, 31,* 1–8.

Tenenbaum, H., & May, D. (2014). Gender in parent-child relationships. In P. Leman & H. Tenenbaum (Eds.), *Gender and development.* New York: Psychology Press.

Terali, K., & Yilmazer, A. (2016). New surprises from an old favorite: The emergence of telomerase as a key player in the regulation of cancer stemness. *Biochimie, 121,* 170–178.

Teri, O., McKenzie, G., & Coulter, C.A. (2016). Psychosocial interventions for older adults and

dementia and their caregivers. In K.W. Schaie & S.L. Willis (Eds.), *Handbook of the psychology of aging* (8th ed.). New York: Elsevier.

Terman, L. (1925). *Genetic studies of genius. Vol. 1: Mental and physical traits of a thousand gifted children.* Stanford, CA: Stanford University Press.

Terry, D.F., Nolan, V.G., Andersen, S.L., Perls, T.T., & Cawthon, R. (2008). Association of longer telomeres with better health in centenarians. *Journals of Gerontology A: Biological Sciences and Medical Sciences, 63,* 809–812.

Thanh, N.X., & Jonsson, E. (2016). Life expectancy of people with fetal alcohol syndrome. *Journal of Population Therapeutics and Clinical Pharmacology, 23,* e53–e59.

The, N.S., & others (2010). Association of adolescent obesity with risk of severe obesity in adulthood. *JAMA, 304,* 2042–2047.

Theendakara, V., & others (2016). Direct transcriptional effects of apolipoprotein E. *Journal of Neuroscience, 36,* 685–700.

Thelen, E., & Smith, L.B. (1998). Dynamic systems theory. In W. Damon & R. Lerner (Eds.), *Handbook of child psychology* (5th ed., Vol. 1.). New York: Wiley.

Thelen, E., & Smith, L.B. (2006). Dynamic development of action and thought. In W. Damon & R. Lerner (Eds.), *Handbook of child psychology* (6th ed.). New York: Wiley.

Theunissen, M.H., Vogels, A.G., & Reijneveld, S.A. (2015). Punishment and reward in parental discipline for children aged 5 to 6 years: Prevalence and groups at risk. *Academic Pediatrics, 15,* 96–102.

Thomas, A., & Chess, S. (1991). Temperament in adolescence and its functional significance. In R.M. Lerner, A.C. Petersen, & J. Brooks-Gunn (Eds.), *Encyclopedia of adolescence* (Vol. 2). New York: Garland.

Thomas, H.N., Hess, R., & Thurston, R.C. (2015). Correlates of sexual activity and satisfaction in midlife and older women. *Annals of Family Medicine, 13,* 336–342.

Thomas, J.R., & Hognas, R.S. (2015). The effect of parental divorce on the health of adult children. *Longitudinal and Life Course Studies, 6,* 279–302.

Thomas, K., & others (2014). Risk factors for developing prolonged grief during bereavement in family carers of cancer patients in palliative care: A longitudinal study. *Journal of Pain and Symptom Management, 47,* 531–541.

Thomas, K.A., & Spieker, S. (2016). Sleep, depression, and fatigue in late postpartum. *MCN American Journal of Maternal and Child Nursing, 41,* 104–109.

Thomas, M.S.C., & Johnson, M.H. (2008). New advances in understanding sensitive periods in brain development. *Current Directions in Psychological Science, 17,* 1–5.

Thomas, P.A. (2010). Is it better to give or to receive? Social support and the well-being of older adults. *Journals of Gerontology B: Psychological Sciences and Social Sciences, 65B,* 351–357.

Thompson, A.E., & Voyer, D. (2014). Sex differences in the ability to recognize non-verbal displays of emotion: A meta-analysis. *Cognition and Emotion, 28,* 1164–1195.

Thompson, J., & Manore, M. (2016). *Nutrition for life* (4th ed.). Upper Saddle River, NJ: Pearson.

Thompson, J., Manore, M., & Vaughan, L. (2017). *The science of nutrition* (4th ed.). Upper Saddle River, NJ: Pearson.

Thompson, P.A., & others (2015). Developmental dyslexia: Predicting individual risk. *Journal of Child Psychology and Psychiatry, 56,* 976–987.

Thompson, R.A. (2006). The development of the person. In W. Damon & R. Lerner (Eds.), *Handbook of child psychology* (6th ed.). New York: Wiley.

Thompson, R.A. (2011). The emotionate child. In D. Cicchetti & G.I. Roissman (Eds.), *The origins and organization of adaptation and maladaptation. Minnesota Symposium on Child Psychology* (Vol. 36). Minneapolis: University of Minnesota Press.

Thompson, R.A. (2012). Whither the preoperational child? Toward a life-span moral development theory. *Child Development Perspectives, 6,* 423–429.

Thompson, R.A. (2014). Why are relationships important to children's well-being? In A. Ben-Arieh, I. Frones, F. Cases, & J. Korbin (Eds.), *Handbook of child well-being.* New York: Springer.

Thompson, R.A. (2015). Relationships, regulation, and development. In R.M. Lerner (Ed.), *Handbook of child psychology* (7th ed.). New York: Wiley.

Thompson, R.A. (2016). Early attachment and later development: New questions. In J. Cassidy & P.R. Shaver (Eds.), *Handbook of attachment* (3rd ed.). New York: Guilford.

Thompson, R.A., & Goodvin, R. (2016). Social support and developmental psychopathology. In D. Cicchetti (Ed.), *Developmental psychopathology* (3rd ed.). New York: Wiley.

Thomsen, M.S., Andreasen, J.T., Arvaniti, M., & Kohlmeier, K.A. (2016, in press). Nicotinic acetylcholine receptors in the pathophysiology of Alzheimer's disease: The role of protein interactions in current and future treatment. *Current Pharmaceutical Design.*

Thorgrimsdottir, S.H., & Bjornsdottir, K. (2016). Reminiscence work with older people: The development of a historical reminiscence tool. *International Journal of Older People Nursing, 11,* 70–79.

Thorley, J. (2016, in press). HRT for menopause: A delicate balance. *The Lancet: Diabetes and Endocrinology.*

Thornton, A., & Camburn, D. (1989). Religious participation and sexual behavior and attitudes. *Journal of Marriage and the Family, 49,* 117–128.

Thornton, R. (2016). The acquisition of syntax. In J. Lidz, W. Snyder, & Pater, J. (Eds.), *Oxford handbook of developmental linguistics.* New York: Oxford University Press.

Thorup, E., & others (2016). Altered gaze following during live interaction in infants at risk for autism: An eye tracking study. *Molecular Autism, 7,* 12.

Tian, S., & Xu, Y. (2016). Association of sarcopenic obesity with the risk of all-cause mortality: A meta-analysis of prospective cohort studies. *Geriatrics and Gerontology International, 16,* 155–166.

Tikotzky, L., & Shaashua, L. (2012). Infant sleep and early parental sleep-related cognitions predict sleep in pre-school children. *Sleep Medicine, 13,* 185–192.

Tilton-Weaver, L.C., Burk, W.J., Kerr, M., & Stattin, H. (2013). Can parental monitoring and peer management reduce the selection or influence of delinquent peers? Testing the question using a dynamic social network approach. *Developmental Psychology, 49,* 2057–2070.

Tincoff, R., & Jusczyk, P.W. (2012). Six-month-olds comprehend words that refer to parts of the body. *Infancy, 17*(4), 432–444.

Todd, A.S., & others (2015). Overweight and obese adolescent girls: The importance of promoting sensible eating and activity behaviors from the start of the adolescent period. *International Journal of Environmental Research and Public Health, 12,* 2306–2329.

Tolani, N., & Brooks-Gunn, J. (2008). Family support, international trends. In M.M. Haith & J.B. Benson (Eds.), *Encyclopedia of infant and early childhood development.* Oxford, UK: Elsevier.

Tolppanen, A.M., & others (2015). Leisure-time physical activity from mid- to late life, body mass index, and risk of dementia. *Alzheimer's and Dementia, 11,* 434–443.

Tomasello, M. (2003). *Constructing a language: A usage-based theory of language acquisition.* Harvard University Press.

Tomasello, M. (2006). Acquiring linguistic constructions. In W. Damon & R. Lerner (Eds.), *Handbook of child psychology* (6th ed.). New York: Wiley.

Tomasello, M. (2011). Language development. In U. Goswami (Ed.), *Wiley-Blackwell handbook of childhood cognitive development* (2nd ed.). New York: Wiley.

Tomasello, M. (2014). *A natural history of human thinking.* Cambridge, MA: Harvard University Press.

Tomassay, G.S., Dershowitz, L.B., & Ariotta, P. (2016). Diversity matters: A revised guide to myelination. *Trends in Cellular Biology, 26,* 135–147.

Tomizawa, D. (2015). Recent progress in the treatment of infant acute lymphoblastic leukemia. *Pediatrics International, 57,* 811–819.

Tompkins, G.E. (2015). *Literacy in the early grades* (4th ed.). Upper Saddle River, NJ: Pearson.

Tomporowski, P.D. (2016). Exercise and cognition. *Pediatric Exercise Science, 28,* 23–27.

Tong, X., Deacon, S.H., & Cain, K. (2014). Morphological and syntactic awareness in poor comprehenders: Another piece of the puzzle. *Journal of Learning Disabilities, 47,* 22–33.

Toth, S.L., & others (2016). Advances in prevention science: A developmental psychopathology perspective. In D. Cicchetti (Eds.), *Developmental psychopathology* (3rd ed.). New York: Wiley.

Toy, W., Nai, Z.L., & Lee, H.W. (2016). Extraversion and agreeableness: Divergent routes to daily satisfaction with social relationships. *Journal of Personality, 84,* 121–134.

Trainor, L.J., & He, C. (2013). Auditory and musical development. In P.D. Zelazo (Ed.), *Handbook of developmental psychology.* New York: Oxford University Press.

Traisrisilp, K., & Tongsong, T. (2015). Pregnancy outcomes of mothers with very advanced age (40 years and more). *Journal of the Medical Association of Thailand, 98,* 117–122.

Traskowski, M., Yang, J., Visscher, P.M., & Plomin, R. (2014). DNA evidence for strong genetic stability and increasing heritability of intelligence from age 7 to 12. *Molecular Psychiatry, 19*(3), 380–384.

Treas, J., & Gurbernskaya, Z. (2016). Immigration, aging, and the life course. In L.K. George & K.F. Ferraro (Eds.), *Handbook of aging and the social sciences* (8th ed.). New York: Elsevier.

Trehub, S.E., Schneider, B.A., Thorpe, L.A., & Judge, P. (1991). Observational measures of auditory sensitivity in early infancy. *Developmental Psychology, 27,* 40–49.

Tremblay, M.S., & others (2012). Canadian sedentary behavior guidelines for the early years (0–4 years). *Applied Physiology, Nutrition, and Metabolism, 37,* 370–380.

Trickett, P.K., Negriff, S., Ji, J., & Peckins, M. (2011). Child maltreatment and adolescent development. *Journal of Research on Adolescence, 21,* 3–20.

Trivedi, A.N. (2016). Understanding seniors' choices in Medicare Advantage. *Journal of General Internal Medicine, 31,* 151–152.

Trivedi, A.N., Wilson, I.B., Charlton, M.E., & Kizer, K.W. (2016, in press). Agreement between HEDIS performance assessments in the VA and Medicare Advantage: Is quality in the eye of the beholder? *Inquiry.*

Trochim, W., Donnelly, J.P., & Arora, K. (2016). *Research methods: The essential knowledge base* (2nd ed.). Boston: Cengage.

Tromp, D., & others (2015). Episodic memory in normal aging and Alzheimer disease: Insights from imaging and behavior studies. *Aging Research Review, 24,* 232–262.

Troop-Gordon, W., & Ladd, G.W. (2015). Teachers' victimization-related beliefs and strategies: Associations with students' aggressive behavior and peer victimization. *Journal of Abnormal Child Psychology, 43,* 45–60.

Trost, S.G., Fees, B., & Dzewaltowski, D. (2008). Feasibility and efficacy of "move and learn" physical activity curriculum in preschool children. *Journal of Physical Activity and Health, 5,* 88–103.

Trotman, G., & others (2015). The effect of CenteringPregnancy versus traditional prenatal care models on improved adolescent health behaviors in the prenatal period. *Journal of Pediatric and Adolescent Gynecology, 28,* 395–401.

Trucco, E.M., & others (2014). Early adolescent alcohol use in context: How neighborhoods, parents, and peers impact youth. *Development and Psychopathology, 26,* 425–436.

Tsang, A., & others (2008). Common persistent pain conditions in developed and developing countries: Gender and age differences and comorbidity with depression-anxiety disorders. *Journal of Pain, 9,* 883–891.

Tsang, T.W., & others (2016, in press). Prenatal alcohol exposure, FASD, and child behavior: A meta-analysis. *Pediatrics.*

Tse, M., & others (2014). Health supplement consumption behavior in the older population: An exploratory study. *Frontiers in Public Health, 2,* 11.

Tun, P.A., & Lachman, M.E. (2010). The association between computer use and cognition across adulthood: Use it so you won't lose it? *Psychology and Aging, 25*(3), 560–568.

Turecki, G., & Meaney, M.J. (2016). Effects of the social environment and stress on glucocorticoid receptor gene methylation: A systematic review. *Biological Psychiatry, 79,* 87–96.

Turiel, E. (2015). Moral development. In R.M. Lerner (Ed.), *Handbook of child psychology and developmental science* (7th ed.). New York: Wiley.

Turkeltaub, P.E., Gareau, L., Flowers, D.L., Zeffiro, T.A., & Eden, G.F. (2003). Development of neural mechanisms for reading. *Nature Neuroscience, 6,* 767–773.

Turnbull, A., Rutherford-Turnbull, H., Wehmeyer, M.L., & Shogren, K.A. (2016). *Exceptional lives* (8th ed.). Upper Saddle River, NJ: Pearson.

Tweed, E.J., & others (2016). Five-minute Apgar scores and educational outcomes: Retrospective cohort study for 751,369 children. *Archives of Disease in Child, Fetal, and Neonatal Medicine, 101,* F121–F126.

Tyas, S.L., & others (2007). Transitions to mild cognitive impairments, dementia, and death: Findings from the Nun Study. *American Journal of Epidemiology, 165,* 1231–1238.

Tyrell, F.A., & others (2016). Family influences on Mexican American adolescents' romantic relationships: Moderation by gender and culture. *Journal of Research on Adolescence, 26,* 142–158.

U

U.S. Bureau of Labor Statistics (2008). *Employment of older workers.* Washington, DC: Author.

U.S. Bureau of Labor Statistics (2013). *Volunteering in the United States: 2013.* Washington, DC: Author.

U.S. Census Bureau (2011). *Births, deaths, marriages, divorces: Life expectancy.* Table 102. Washington, DC: Author.

U.S. Census Bureau (2012). *Age and sex composition in the United States: 2012.* Washington, DC: Author.

U.S. Census Bureau (2012). *Births, deaths, marriages, divorces: Life expectancy.* Table 102. Washington, DC: Author.

U.S. Census Bureau (2012). *Families and living arrangements: 2012.* Washington, DC: Author.

U.S. Census Bureau (2013). *Marriages, births, and deaths.* Washington, DC: Author.

U.S. Census Bureau (2015). *Births, deaths, marriages, divorces.* Washington, DC: Author.

U.S. Census Bureau (2015). *Current population survey: Marriages and divorces.* Washington, DC: Author.

U.S. Census Bureau (2015). *People.* Washington, DC: Author.

U.S. Census Bureau (2015, February 20). *Children.* Retrieved November 21, 2015, from www.census.gov/newroom/press-releases2015/cb15-16.html

U.S. Census Bureau (2015, May 8). *Older Americans month: May 2015.* Washington, DC: Author.

U.S. Census Bureau (2015a). *Unmarried and single Americans.* Washington, DC: Author.

U.S. Census Bureau (2015b). *Population statistics.* Washington, DC: Author.

U.S. Department of Energy (2001). *The human genome project.* Washington, DC: Author.

U.S. Department of Health and Human Services (2015). *Child maltreatment: 2013.* Washington, DC: Author.

U.S. Department of Health and Human Services (2016). *Folic acid.* Retrieved January 9, 2016, from www.cdc.gov/ncbddd/folicacid/

UNAIDS (2011). *AIDS at 30: Nations at a crossroads.* Geneva, Switzerland: United Nations.

UNAIDS (2015). *UNAIDS fact sheet: 2015.* Geneva, Switzerland: United Nations.

Ungar, M. (2015). Practitioner review: Diagnosing childhood resilience: A systematic diagnosis of adaption in diverse social ecologies. *Journal of Child Psychology and Psychiatry, 56,* 4–17.

UNICEF (2007). *The state of the world's children: 2007.* Geneva, Switzerland: UNICEF.

UNICEF (2016). *The state of the world's children: 2016.* Geneva, Switzerland: UNICEF.

UNSTAT (2011). *Marriages and crude marriage rates.* Retrieved September 4, 2013, from http://unstats.un.org/unsd/demographic/products/dyb/dyb2011/Table23.pdf.

Updegraff, K.A., & Umana-Taylor, A. (2015). What can we learn from the study of Mexican-origin families in the United States? *Family Process, 54,* 205–216.

Ursache, A., Blair, C., & Raver, C.C. (2012). The promotion of self-regulation as a means of enhancing school readiness and early achievement in children at risk for school failure. *Child Development Perspectives, 6,* 122–128.

V

Vaillant, G.E. (1977). *Adaptation to life.* Boston: Little, Brown.

Vaillant, G.E. (2002). *Aging well.* Boston: Little, Brown.

Vaish, A., Carpenter, M., & Tomasello, M. (2010). Young children selectively avoid helping people with harmful intentions. *Child Development, 81,* 1661–1669.

Valentino, K., & others (2014). Mother-child reminiscing and autobiographical memory specificity among preschool-age children. *Developmental Psychology, 50,* 1197–1207.

Valenzuela, C.F., Medina, A.E., Wozniak, J.R., & Klintsova, A.Y. (2016). Proceedings of the annual meeting of the Fetal Alcohol Spectrum Disorders Study Group. *Alcohol, 50,* 37–42.

Valenzuela, C.F., Morton, R.A., Diaz, M.R., & Topper, L. (2012). Does moderate drinking harm the fetal brain? Insights from animal models. *Trends in Neuroscience, 35*(5), 284–292.

Valera, M.C., Gourdy, P., Tremollieres, F., & Arnal, J.F. (2015). From the Women's Health Initiative to the combination of estrogen and selective estrogen receptor modulators to avoid progestin addition. *Maturitas, 82,* 274–277.

Valero, S., & others (2014). Neuroticism and impulsivity: Their hierarchical organization in the personality characterization of drug-dependent patients from a decision tree learning perspective. *Comprehensive Psychiatry, 55,* 1227–1233.

Valiathan, R., Ashman, M., & Asthana, D. (2016, in press). Effects of aging on the immune system: Infants to elderly. *Scandinavian Journal of Immunology.*

Valimaki, T.H., & others (2016). Impact of Alzheimer's disease on the family caregiver's long-term quality of life: Results from the ALSOVA follow-up study. *Quality of Life Research, 25,* 687–697.

Van Assche, L., & others (2013). Attachment in old age: Theoretical assumptions, empirical findings, and implications for clinical practice. *Clinical Psychology Review, 33,* 67–81.

Van de Vondervoort, J., & Hamlin, J.K. (2016a, in press). Evidence for intuitive morality: Preverbal infants make sociomoral evaluations. *Child Development Perspectives.*

Van de Vondervoort, J., & Hamlin, J.K. (2016b, in press). The infantile roots of sociomoral evaluations. In K. Gray & J. Graham (Eds.), *The atlas of moral psychology.* New York: Guilford.

Van der Star, A., & Branstrom, R. (2015). Acceptance of sexual minorities, discrimination, social capital, and health and well-being: A cross-European study among members of same-sex and opposite-sex couples. *BMC Public Health, 15*(1), 812.

Van Elderen, S.S., & others (2016). Brain volume as an integrated marker for the risk of death in a community-based sample: Age gene/environment susceptibility–Reykjavik study. *Journals of Gerontology A: Biological Sciences and Medical Sciences, 71,* 131–137.

van Geel, M., Vedder, P., & Tanilon, J. (2014). Relationship between peer victimization, cyberbullying, and suicide in children and adolescents: A meta-analysis. *JAMA Pediatrics, 168,* 435–442.

Van Hecke, V., & others (2012). Infant responding to joint attention, executive processes, and self-regulation in preschool children. *Infant Development and Behavior, 35,* 303–311.

Van Hedel, K., & others (2015). Marital status, labor force activity, and mortality: A study in the USA and six European countries. *Scandinavian Journal of Public Health, 43,* 469–480.

van Hooft, E.A. (2014). Motivating and hindering factors during the reemployment process: The added value of employment counselors' assessment. *Journal of Occupational Health Psychology, 19,* 1–17.

Van Lissa, C.J., & others (2015). Divergence between adolescent and parent perceptions of conflict in relationship to adolescent empathy development. *Journal of Youth and Adolescence, 44,* 48–51.

Van Ryzin, M.J., Carlson, E.A., & Sroufe, L.A. (2011). Attachment discontinuity in a high-risk sample. *Attachment and Human Development, 13,* 381–401.

Vandell, D.L., & others. (2010). Do effects of early childcare extend to age 15 years? From the NICHD Study of Early Child Care and Youth Development. *Child Development, 81,* 737–756.

Vanhaelen, Q. (2015). Aging as an optimization between cellular maintenance requirements and evolutionary constraints. *Current Aging Science, 8,* 110–119.

Vanhalst, J., Luyckx, K., Raes, F., & Goossens, L. (2012). Loneliness and depression symptoms: The mediating and moderating role of uncontrollable ruminative thoughts. *Journal of Psychology, 146,* 259–276.

Vardavas, C.I., & others (2016, in press). The independent role of prenatal and postnatal exposure to active and passive smoking on the development of early wheeze in children. *European Respiratory Journal.*

Vargens, O.M., Silva, A.C., & Progianti, J.M. (2013). Non-invasive nursing technologies for pain relief during childbirth—the Brazilian nurses midwives' view. *Midwifery, 29,* e99–e106.

Varner, M.W., & others (2014). Association between stillbirth and illicit drug use and smoking during pregnancy. *Obstetrics and Gynecology, 123,* 113–125.

Vart, P., & others (2015). Mediators of the association between low socioeconomic status and chronic kidney disease in the United States. *American Journal of Epidemiology, 181,* 385–396.

Vatalaro, A., Szente, J., & Levin, J. (2015). Transformative learning of pre-service teachers during study abroad in Reggio Emilia, Italy: A case study. *Journal of the Scholarship of Teaching and Learning, 15,* 42–55.

Vaughn, B.E., & Bost, K.K. (2016). Attachment and temperament as intersecting developmental products and interacting developmental contexts throughout infancy and childhood. In J. Cassidy & P.R. Shaver (Eds.), *Handbook of attachment* (3rd ed.). New York: Guilford.

Vaughn, S.R., & Bos, C.S. (2015). *Strategies for teaching students with learning and behavior problems* (9th ed.). Upper Saddle River, NJ: Pearson.

Velayudhan, L., & others (2014). Review of brief cognitive tests for patients with suspected dementia. *International Psychogeriatrics, 26,* 1247–1262.

Velez, C.E., Wolchik, S.A., Tein, J.Y., & Sandler, I. (2011). Protecting children from the consequences of divorce: A longitudinal study of the effects of parenting on children's coping responses. *Child Development, 82,* 244–257.

Veness, C., Prior, M., Eadie, P., Bavin, E., & Reilly, S. (2014). Predicting autism diagnosis by 7 years of age using parent report of infant social communication skills. *Journal of Pediatrics and Child Health, 50,* 693–700.

Venners, S.A., & others (2005). Paternal smoking and pregnancy loss: A prospective study using a biomarker of pregnancy. *American Journal of Epidemiology, 159,* 993–1001.

Vespa, J., Lewis, J.M., & Kreider, R.M. (2013, August). *America's families and living arrangements: 2012.* Washington, DC: U.S. Census Bureau.

Vieira, J.M., Matias, M., Ferreira, T., Lopez, F.G., & Matos, P.M. (2016, in press). Parents' work-family experiences and children's problem behaviors: The mediating role of the parent-child relationship. *Journal of Family Psychology.*

Villamor, E., & Jansen, E.C. (2016). Nutritional determinants of the timing of puberty. *Annual Review of Public Health, 37,* 33–46.

Villemagne, V.L., Fodero-Tavoletti, M.T., Masters, C.L., & Rowe, C.C. (2015). Tau imaging: Early progress and future directions. *Lancet Neurology, 14,* 114–124.

Villodas, M.T., Litrownik, A.J., Newton, R.R., & Davis, I.P. (2016). Long-term placement trajectories of children who were maltreated and entered the child welfare system at an early age: Consequences for physical and behavioral well-being. *Journal of Pediatric Psychology, 41,* 46–54.

Vinik, J., Almas, A., & Grusec, J. (2011). Mothers' knowledge of what distresses and comforts their children predicts children's coping, empathy, and prosocial behavior. *Parenting: Science and Practice, 11,* 56–71.

Virta, J.J., & others (2013). Midlife cardiovascular risk factors and late cognitive development. *European Journal of Epidemiology, 28,* 405–416.

Virudachalam, S., & others (2016, in press). Mothers' and clinicians' priorities for obesity prevention among black, high-risk infants. *American Journal of Preventive Medicine.*

Vittrup, B., Holden, G.W., & Buck, M. (2006). Attitudes predict the use of physical punishment: A prospective study of the emergence of disciplinary practices. *Pediatrics, 117,* 2055–2064.

Vlatkovic, I.B., & others (2014). Prenatal diagnosis of sex chromosome aneuploidies and disorders of sex development—a retrospective analysis of 11-year data. *Journal of Perinatal Medicine, 42,* 529–534.

Voelker, D.K., Reel, J.J., & Greenleaf, C. (2015). Weight status and body image perceptions in adolescents: Current perspectives. *Adolescent Health, Medicine, and Therapeutics, 6,* 149–158.

Vollink, T., Dehue, F., & McGuckin, C. (Eds.) (2016). *Cyberbullying.* New York: Psychology Press.

von Bonsdorff, M.B., & others (2011). Work ability in midlife as a predictor of mortality and disability in later life: A 28-year prospective follow-up study. *Canadian Medical Association Journal, 183,* E235–E242.

von Bonsdorff, M.B., & others (2012). Work ability as a determinant of old age disability severity: Evidence from the 28-year Finnish longitudinal study on municipal employees. *Aging: Clinical and Experimental Research, 24,* 354–360.

Voorpostel, M., & Blieszner, R. (2008). Intergenerational solidarity and support between adult siblings. *Journal of Marriage and the Family, 70,* 157–167.

Vorona, R.D., & others (2014). Adolescent crash rates and school start times in two Central Virginia counties, 2009–2011: A follow-up study to a Southeastern Virginia study, 2007–2008. *Journal of Clinical Sleep Medicine, 10,* 1169–1177.

Votavova, H., & others (2012). Deregulation of gene expression induced by environmental tobacco smoke exposure in pregnancy. *Nicotine and Tobacco Research, 14*(9), 1073–1082.

Votruba-Drzal, E., Coley, R.L., & Chase-Lansdale, P.L. (2004). Child care and low-income children's development: Direct and moderated effects. *Child Development, 75,* 296–312.

Vozzola, E.C. (2014). *Moral development: Theory and applications.* New York: Psychology Press.

Vrangalova, Z. (2015a). Does casual sex harm college students' well-being? A longitudinal investigation of the role of motivation. *Archives of Sexual Behavior, 44,* 945–949.

Vrangalova, Z. (2015b). Hooking up and psychological well-being in college students: Short-term prospective links across different hookup definitions. *Journal of Sex Research, 52,* 485–498.

Vreeman, R.C., & Carroll, A.E. (2007). A systematic review of school-based interventions to prevent bullying. *Archives of Pediatric and Adolescent Medicine, 161,* 78–88.

Vu, J.A. (2016). The fourth 'R': Relationships, shifting from risk to resilience. In K.E. Sanders & A.W. Guerra (Eds.), *The culture of child care.* New York: Oxford University Press.

Vukelich, C., Christie, J., Enz, B.J., & Roskos, K.A. (2016). *Helping children learn language and literacy* (4th ed.). Upper Saddle River, NJ: Pearson.

Vuolo, M., Staff, J., & Mortimer, J.T. (2012). Weathering the great recession: Psychological and behavioral trajectories in the transition from school to work. *Developmental Psychology, 48,* 1759–1773.

Vurpillot, E. (1968). The development of scanning strategies and their relation to visual differentiation. *Journal of Experimental Child Psychology, 6,* 632–650.

Vygotsky, L.S. (1962). *Thought and language.* Cambridge, MA: MIT Press.

Vysniauske, R., Verburgh, L., Oosteriaan, J., & Molendijk, M.L. (2016, in press). The effects of physical exercise on functional outcomes in the treatment of ADHD. *Journal of Attention Disorders.*

W

Wachs, T.D., & Bates, J.E. (2010). Temperament. In J.G. Bremner & T.D. Wachs (Eds.), *Wiley-Blackwell handbook of infant development* (2nd ed.). New York: Wiley.

Wadsworth, M.E., & others (2016). Poverty and the development of psychopathology. In D. Cicchetti (Ed.), *Developmental psychopathology* (3rd ed.). New York: Wiley.

Waldenstrom, U., Cnattingius, S., Norman, M., & Schytt, E. (2015). Advanced maternal age and stillbirth risk in nulliparous and parous women. *Obstetrics and Gynecology, 126,* 355–362.

Waldenstrom, U., & others (2014). Adverse pregnancy outcomes related to advanced maternal age compared with smoking and being overweight. *Obstetrics and Gynecology, 123,* 104–112.

Waldinger, R.J., & Schulz, M.C. (2010). What's love got to do with it? Social functioning, perceived health, and daily happiness in married octogenarians. *Psychology and Aging, 25,* 422–431.

Waldinger, R.J., Vaillant, G.E., & Orav, E.J. (2007). Childhood sibling relationships as a predictor of major depression in adulthood: A 30-year prospective study. *American Journal of Psychiatry, 164,* 949–954.

Waldron, J.J., & Dieser, R.B. (2010). Perspectives of fitness and health in college men and women. *Journal of College Student Development, 51,* 65–78.

Walker, L. (1982). The sequentiality of Kohlberg's stages of moral development. *Child Development, 53,* 1130–1136.

Walker, L.J. (2004). Progress and prospects in the psychology of moral development. *Merrill-Palmer Quarterly, 50,* 546–557.

Walker, L.J., & Frimer, J.A. (2011). The science of moral development. In M.K. Underwood & L. Rosen (Eds.), *Social development.* New York: Guilford.

Walker, R., & others (2013). Marital satisfaction in older couples: The role of satisfaction with social networks and psychological well-being. *International Journal of Aging and Human Development, 76,* 123–139.

Waller, A., & others (2016). Assisting the bereaved: A systematic review of the evidence for grief counseling. *Palliative Medicine, 30,* 132–148.

Waller, E.M., & Rose, A.J. (2010). Adjustment trade-offs of co-rumination in mother-adolescent relationships. *Journal of Adolescence, 33,* 487–497.

Waller, K.L., & others (2016). Subjective sleep quality and daytime sleepiness in late midlife and their association with age-related changes in cognition. *Sleep Medicine, 17,* 165–176.

Walsh, R. (2011). Lifestyle and mental health. *American Psychologist, 66*(7), 579–592.

Wang, B., & Jin, K. (2015). Current perspectives on the link between neuroinflammation and neurogenesis. *Metabolic Brain Disease, 30,* 355–365.

Wang, B., & others (2014). The impact of youth, family, peer, and neighborhood risk factors on developmental trajectories of risk involvement from early through middle adolescence. *Social Science Medicine, 106,* 43–52.

Wang, B., & others (2016). The influence of sensation-seeking and parental and peer influences in early adolescence on risk involvement through middle adolescence: A structural equation modeling analysis. *Youth and Society, 48,* 220–241.

Wang, C., & others (2016). Coevolution of adolescent friendship networks and smoking and drinking behaviors with consideration of parental influence. *Psychology of Addictive Behaviors, 30,* 312–324.

Wang, H., & Cai, T. (2016, in press). Parental involvement, adolescents' self-determined learning, and academic achievement in urban China. *International Journal of Psychology.*

Wang, H., Lin, S.L., Leung, G.M., & Schooling, C.M. (2016, in press). Age at onset of puberty and adolescent depression: "Children of 1997" birth cohort. *Pediatrics.*

Wang, H.J., & others (2016). Association of common variants identified by recent genome-wide association studies with obesity in Chinese children: A case-control study. *BMC Medical Genetics, 17,* 7.

Wang, M., Monticone, R.E., & Lakatta, E. (2016). The arterial wall. In M. Kaeberlein & G.M. Martin (Eds.), *Handbook of the biology of aging* (8th ed.). New York: Elsevier.

Wang, M., & Shi, J. (2016). Work, retirement, and aging. In K.W. Schaie & S. Willis (Eds.), *Handbook of the psychology of aging* (8th ed.). New York: Elsevier.

Wang, M., & others (2016). Body mass index trajectories among middle-aged and elderly Canadians and associated health outcomes. *Journal of Environmental Public Health, 2016,* 7014857.

Wang, W. (2014). *Record shares of Americans have never been married.* Washington, DC: Pew Research Center.

Wang, W.Y., & others (2016, in press). Impacts of CD33 genetic variations on the atrophy rates of hippocampus and parahippocampal gyrus in normal aging and mild cognitive impairment. *Molecular Neurobiology.*

Wang, Z., Tang, B., He, Y., & Jin, P. (2016). DNA methylation dynamics in neurogenesis. *Epigenomics, 8,* 401–414.

Wang, Z.W., Hua, J., & Xu, Y.H. (2015). The relationship between gentle tactile stimulation on the fetus and its temperament 3 months after birth. *Behavioral Neuroscience, 2015,* 371906.

Wardlaw, G.M., & Smith, A.M. (2015). *Contemporary nutrition* (4th ed.). New York: McGraw-Hill.

Wardlaw, G.M., Smith, A.M., & Collene, A.L. (2015). *Contemporary nutrition* (4th ed.). New York: McGraw-Hill.

Warr, P. (2004). Work, well-being, and mental health. In J. Baring, E. K. Kelloway, & M.R. Frone (Eds.), *Handbook of work stress.* Thousand Oaks, CA: Sage.

Warshak, R.A. (2014). Social science and parenting plans for young children: A consensus report. *Psychology, Public Policy, and the Law, 20,* 46–67.

Wataganara, T., & others (2016, in press). Fetal magnetic resonance imaging and ultrasound. *Journal of Perinatal Medicine.*

Watamura, S.E., Phillips, D.A., Morrissey, D.A., McCartney, T.W., & Bub, K. (2011). Double jeopardy: Poorer social-emotional outcomes for children in the NICHD SECCYD who experience home and child-care environments that convey risk. *Child Development, 82,* 48–65.

Waterman, A.S. (1985). Identity in the context of adolescent psychology. In A.S. Waterman (Ed.), *Identity in adolescence: Processes and contents.* San Francisco: Jossey-Bass.

Waterman, A.S. (1992). Identity as an aspect of optimal psychological functioning. In G.R. Adams,

T.P. Gullotta, & R. Montemayor (Eds.), *Adolescent identity formation.* Newbury Park, CA: Sage.

Waterman, A.S. (2015). Identity as internal processes: How the "I" comes to define the "me." In K.C. McLean & M. Syed (Eds.), *Oxford handbook of identity development.* New York: Oxford University Press.

Waters, S.F., West, T.V., & Mendes, W.B. (2014). Stress contagion: Physiological covariation between mothers and infants. *Psychological Science, 25,* 934–942.

Watson, G.L., Arcona, A.P., Antonuccio, D.O., & Healy, D. (2014). Shooting the messenger: The case of ADHD. *Journal of Contemporary Psychotherapy, 44,* 43–52.

Watson, J.A., Randolph, S.M., & Lyons, J.L. (2005). African-American grandmothers as health educators in the family. *International Journal of Aging and Human Development, 60,* 343–356.

Waxman, S. (2013). Building a better bridge. In M. Banaji, S. Gelman, & S. Lehr (Eds.), *Navigating the social world: The early years.* New York: Oxford University Press.

Waxman, S., & Goswami, U. (2012). Acquiring language: Learning the spoken and the written word. In S. Pauen & M. Bornstein (Eds.), *Early childhood development and later outcome.* New York: Cambridge University Press.

Wayne, A. (2011). Commentary in interview: Childhood cancers in transition. Retrieved April 12, 2011, from http://home.ccr.cancer.gov/connections/2010/Vol4_No2/clinic2.asp

Weaver, J.M., & Schofield, T.J. (2015). Mediation and moderation of divorce effects on children's behavior problems. *Journal of Family Psychology, 29,* 39–48.

Webb, M.S., Passmore, D., Cline, G., & Maguire, D. (2014). Ethical issues related to caring for low birth weight infants. *Nursing Ethics, 21,* 731–741.

Webster, N.S., & Worrell, F.C. (2008). Academically talented students' attitudes toward service in the community. *Gifted Child Quarterly, 52,* 170–179.

Wechsler, H., Davenport, A., Sowdall, G., Moetykens, B., & Castillo, S. (1994). Health and behavioral consequences of binge drinking in college. *Journal of the American Medical Association, 272,* 1672–1677.

Weersing, V.R., & others (2016). Prevention of depression in at-risk adolescents: Predictors and moderators of acute effects. *Journal of the American Academy of Child and Adolescent Psychiatry, 55,* 219–226.

Weikert, D.P. (1993). [Long-term positive effects in the Perry Preschool Head Start Program.] Unpublished data, High Scope Foundation, Ypsilanti, MI.

Weinraub, M., & others (2012). Patterns of developmental change in infants' nighttime sleep awakenings from 6 through 36 months of age. *Developmental Psychology, 48*(6), 1511–1528.

Weisleder, A., & Fernald, A. (2013). Talking to children matters: Early language experience strengthens processing and builds vocabulary. *Psychological Science, 24,* 2143–2152.

Welch, K.J. (2015). *Family life now* (2nd ed.). Upper Saddle River, NJ: Pearson.

Wellman, H.M. (2011). Developing a theory of mind. In U. Goswami (Ed.), *Wiley-Blackwell handbook of childhood cognitive development* (2nd ed.). New York: Wiley.

Wellman, H.M. (2015). *Making minds.* New York: Oxford University Press.

Wellman, H.M., Cross, D., & Watson, J. (2001). Meta-analysis of theory-of-mind development: The truth about false belief. *Child Development, 72,* 655–684.

Wells, E.M., & others (2011). Body burdens of mercury, lead, selenium, and copper among Baltimore newborns. *Environmental Research, 111,* 411–417.

Wendelken, C., Gerrer, E., Whitaker, K.J., & Bunge, S.A. (2016). Fronto-parietal network reconfiguration supports the development of reasoning ability. *Cerebral Cortex, 26,* 2178–2190.

Wenger, N.K., & others (2014). Prevention of cardiovascular diseases: Highlights for the clinician of the 2013 American College of Cardiology/American Heart Association guidelines. *Clinical Cardiology, 37,* 239–251.

Wenger, N.S., & others (2003). The quality of medical care provided to vulnerable community-dwelling older patients. *Annals of Internal Medicine, 139,* 740–747.

Wennergren, G., & others (2015). Updated Swedish advice on reducing the risk of sudden infant death syndrome. *Acta Pediatrica, 104,* 444–448.

Wentzel, K.R. (2015). Socialization in school settings. In J.E. Grusec & P.D. Hastings (Eds.), *Handbook of socialization* (2nd ed.). New York: Guilford.

Wentzel, K.R., Barry, C.M., & Caldwell, K.A. (2004). Friendships in middle schools: Influences on motivation and school adjustment. *Journal of Educational Psychology, 96,* 195–203.

Wentzel, K.R., & Miele, D.B. (Eds.) (2016). *Handbook of motivation at school.* New York: Routledge.

Wentzel, K.R., & Muenks, K. (2016). Peer influence on students' motivation, academic achievement, and social behavior. In K.R. Wentzel & G. Ramani (Eds.), *Handbook of social influences in school contexts.* New York: Routledge.

Wentzel, K.R., & Ramani, G. (2016). *Social influences on social-emotional, motivational, and cognitive outcomes in school contexts.* New York: Taylor & Francis.

Werner, N.E., & others (2014). Maternal social coaching quality interrupts the development of relational aggression during early childhood. *Social Development, 23,* 470–486.

West, E., & others (2016). Hospice care in the Netherlands: Who applies and who is admitted to inpatient care? *BMC Health Services Research, 16,* 33.

West, S.K., & others (2010). Older drivers and failure to stop at red lights. *Journals of Gerontology A: Biological Sciences and Medical Sciences, 65A,* 179–183.

Westerhof, G.J. (2009). Age identity. In D. Carr (Ed.), *Encyclopedia of the life course and human development.* Boston: Gale Cengage.

Westermann, G., Thomas, M.S.C., & Karmiloff-Smith, A. (2011). Neuroconstructivism. In U. Goswami (Ed.), *Wiley-Blackwell handbook of childhood cognitive development* (2nd ed.). New York: Wiley.

Westmoreland, P., Krantz, M.J., & Mehler, P.S. (2016). Medical complications of anorexia nervosa and bulimia. *American Journal of Medicine, 129,* 30–37.

Whaley, S.E., Jiang, L., Gomez, J., & Jenks, E. (2011). Literacy promotion for families participating in the Women, Infants, and Children program. *Pediatrics, 127,* 454–461.

Wheeler, J.J., Mayton, M.R., & Carter, S.L. (2015). *Methods of teaching students with autism spectrum disorders.* Upper Saddle River, NJ: Pearson.

White, D.K., & others (2015). Can an intensive diet and exercise program prevent knee pain among overweight adults at high risk? *Arthritis Care and Research, 67,* 965–971.

White, L. (1994). Stepfamilies over the life course: Social support. In A. Booth and J. Dunne (Eds.), *Stepfamilies: Who benefits and who does not.* Hillsdale, NJ: Erlbaum.

Whitehead, B.D., & Popenoe, D. (2003). *The state of our unions.* Piscataway, NJ: The National Marriage Project, Rutgers University.

Whiteman, S.D., McHale, S.M., & Soli, A. (2011). Theoretical perspectives on sibling relationships. *Journal of Family Theory and Review, 3,* 124–139.

Whitley, E., Popham, F., & Benzeval, M. (2016, in press). Comparison of the Rowe-Kahn model of successful aging with self-rated health and life satisfaction: The West of Scotland Twenty-07 Prospective Cohort Study. *Gerontologist.*

Whitton, S.W., Stanley, S.M., Markman, H.W., & Johnson, C.A. (2013). Attitudes toward divorce, commitment, and divorce proneness in first marriages and remarriages, *75,* 276–287.

Widman, L., Choukas-Bradley, S., Helms, S.W., & Prinstein, M.J. (2016). Adolescent susceptibility to peer influences in sexual situations. *Journal of Adolescent Health, 58,* 323–329.

Widom, C.S., Czaja, S.J., Bentley, T., & Johnson, M.S. (2012). A prospective investigation of physical health outcomes in abused and neglected children: New findings from a 30-year follow-up. *American Journal of Public Health, 102*(6), 1135–1144.

Widom, C.S., Czaja, S.J., & DuMont, K.A. (2015). Intergenerational transmission of child abuse and neglect: Real or detection bias? *Science, 347,* 1480–1485.

Wigfield, A., Tonks, S.M., & Klauda, S.L. (2016). Expectancy-value theory. In K.R. Wentzel & D.B. Miele (Eds.), *Handbook of motivation at school.* New York: Routledge.

Wigfield, A., & others (2015). Development of achievement motivation and engagement. In R.M. Lerner (Ed.), *Handbook of child psychology and developmental science* (7th ed.). New York: Wiley.

Wikman, A., Wardle, J., & Steptoe, A. (2011). Quality of life and affective well-being in middle-aged and older people with chronic medical illnesses: A cross-sectional population based study. *PLoS One, 7,* e18952.

Wilder-Smith, A., Mustafa, F.B., Earnest, A., Gen, L., & Macary, P.A. (2013). Impact of partial sleep deprivation on immune markers. *Sleep Medicine, 14*(10), 1031–1034.

Willcox, D.C., Scapagnini, G., & Willcox, B.J. (2014). Healthy aging diets other than Mediterranean: A focus on the Okinawan diet. *Mechanisms of Aging and Development, 136–137,* 148–162.

Willette, A.A., & others (2012). Calorie restriction reduces the influence of glucoregulatory dysfunction on regional brain volume in aged rhesus monkeys. *Diabetes, 61,* 1036–1042.

Williams, A.M., & others (2016). Breastfeeding and complementary feeding practices among HIV-exposed infants in coastal Tanzania. *Journal of Human Lactation, 32,* 112–122.

Williams, J.L., Aiyer, S.M., Durkee, M.I., & Tolan, P.H. (2014). The protective role of ethnic identity for urban adolescent males facing multiple stressors. *Journal of Youth and Adolescence, 43,* 1728–1741.

Williams, K.E., & Sciberras, E. (2016, in press). Sleep and self-regulation from birth to 7 years: A retrospective study of children with and without attention-deficit/hyperactivity disorder at 8 to 9 years. *Journal of Developmental and Behavioral Pediatrics.*

Williams, S.R., & others (2016). Shared genetic susceptibility of vascular-related biomarkers with ischemic and recurrent stroke. *Neurology, 86,* 351–359.

Williamson, D. (2013). Of years of love, and a long goodbye. Retrieved from www.telegram.com/article/20130929/COLUMN01/309299933

Williamson, J.B., & Beland, D. (2016). The future of retirement security in comparative perspective. In L.K. George & K.F. Ferraro (Eds.), *Handbook of aging and the social sciences* (8th ed.). New York: Elsevier.

Willis, S.L., & Belleville, S. (2016). Cognitive training in later adulthood. In K.W. Schaie & S.L. Willis (Eds.), *Handbook of the psychology of aging* (8th ed.). New York: Elsevier.

Willoughby, B.J., & Belt, D. (2016). Marital orientation and relationship well-being among cohabiting couples. *Journal of Family Psychology, 30,* 181–192.

Willoughby, M.T., & others (2016, in press). Developmental delays in executive function from 3 to 5 years of age predict kindergarten academic readiness. *Journal of Learning Disabilities.*

Wilson, D.M., & others (2013). The preferred place of last days: Results of a representative population-based survey. *Journal of Palliative Medicine, 16,* 502–508.

Wilson, K.R., Havighurst, S.S., & Harley, A.E. (2012). Tuning in to kids: An effectiveness trial of a parenting program targeting emotion socialization of preschoolers. *Journal of Family Psychology, 26,* 56–65.

Wilson, R.S., & others (2015). Conscientiousness, dementia-related pathology, and trajectories of cognitive aging. *Psychology and Aging, 30,* 74–82.

Windle, W.F. (1940). *Physiology of the humantus.* Philadelphia: W.B. Saunders.

Windsor, T.D., & others (2016). Structural and functional social network attributes moderate the association of self-rated health with mental health in midlife and older adults. *International Psychogeriatrics, 28,* 49–61.

Winett, R.A., & others (2014). Develoment of a new treatment paradigm for disease prevention and healthy aging. *Translational Behavior Medicine, 4,* 117–123.

Wingfield, A., & Lash, A. (2016). Audition and language comprehension in adult aging: Stability in the face of change. In K.W. Schaie & S.L. Willis (Eds.), *Handbook of the psychology of aging* (8th ed.). New York: Elsevier.

Wink, P., & Dillon, M. (2002). Spiritual development across the adult life course: Findings from a longitudinal study. *Journal of Adult Development, 9,* 79–94.

Winner, E. (1996). *Gifted children: Myths and realities.* New York: Basic Books.

Winner, E. (2009). Toward broadening our understanding of giftedness: The spatial domain. In F.D. Horowitz, R.F. Subotnik, & D.J. Matthews (Eds.), *The development of giftedness and talent across the life span.* Washington, DC: American Psychological Association.

Winsler, A., Carlton, M.P., & Barry, M.J. (2000). Age-related changes in preschool children's systematic use of private speech in a natural setting. *Journal of Child Language, 27,* 665–687.

Winsper, C., Lereya, T., Zanarini, M., & Wolke, D. (2012). Involvement in bullying and suicide-related behavior at 11 years: A prospective birth cohort study. *Journal of the Academy of Child and Adolescent Psychiatry, 51,* 271–282.

Wise, P.M. (2006). Aging of the female reproductive system. In E.J. Masoro & S.N. Austad (Eds.), *Handbook of the biology of aging* (6th ed.). San Diego: Academic Press.

Witard, O.C., McGlory, C., Hamilton, D.L., & Phillips, S.M. (2016, in press). Growing older with health and vitality: A nexus of physical activity, exercise, and nutrition. *Biogerontology.*

Witherington, D.C., Campos, J.J., Harriger, J.A., Bryan, C., & Margett, T.E. (2010). Emotion and its development in infancy. In J.G. Bremner & T.D. Wachs (Eds.), *Wiley-Blackwell handbook of infant development* (2nd ed.). New York: Wiley.

Witkin, H.A., & others (1976). Criminality in XYY and XXY men. *Science, 193,* 547–555.

Witt, N., Coynor, S., Edwards, C., & Bradshaw, H. (2016, in press). A guide to pain assessment and management in the neonate. *Current Emergency and Hospital Medicine Reports.*

Witt, W.P., & others (2014). Maternal stressful life events prior to conception and the impact on infant birth in the United States. *American Journal of Public Health, 104*(Suppl. 1), S81–S89.

Witte, A.V., & others (2014). Long-chain omega-3 fatty acids improve brain function and structure in older adults. *Cerebral Cortex, 24,* 3059–3068.

Wittig, S.L., & Spatz, D.L. (2008). Induced lactation: Gaining a better understanding. *MCN. The Journal of Maternal Child Nursing, 33,* 76–81.

Woelders, L.C.S., Larsen, J.K., Scholte, R., Cillessen, T., & Engles, R.C.M.E. (2011). Friendship group influences on body dissatisfaction and dieting among adolescent girls: A prospective study. *Journal of Adolescent Health, 47,* 456–462.

Wolke, D., & Lereya, S.T. (2015). Long-term effects of bullying. *Archives of Disease in Childhood, 100,* 879–885.

Wolke, D., Lereya, S.T., & Tippett, N. (2016). Individual and social determinants of bullying and cyberbullying. In T. Vollink, F. Dehue, & C. McGuckin (Eds.), *Cyberbullying.* New York: Psychology Press.

Wood, J.T. (2012). *Gendered lives* (10th ed.). Boston: Cengage.

Wood, L.R., & others (2016). Impairment-targeted exercises for older adults with knee pain: A proof-of-principle study (TargET-Knee-Pain). *BMC Musculoskeletal Disorders, 17,* 47.

Woods, D.L. (2015). Improving neonatal care in district and community health facilities in South Africa. *Pediatrics and International Child Health, 35,* 187–191.

Wu, J., & others (2016, in press). Risks and predictors of mild diastolic dysfunction among middle-aged and aged women: A population-based cohort study. *Journal of Human Hypertension.*

Wu, T., Gao, X., Chen, M., & van Dam, R.M. (2009). Long-term effectiveness of diet-plus-exercise interventions vs. diet-only interventions for weight loss: A meta-analysis. *Obesity, 10,* 313–323.

Wu, X., & others (2016). Finding gastric cancer related genes and clinical biomarkers for detection based on gene-gene interaction network. *Mathematical Biosciences, 276,* 1–7.

Wu, Z., Schimmele, C.M., & Quellet, N. (2015). Repartnering after widowhood. *Journal of Gerontology B: Psychological Sciences and Social Sciences, 70,* 496–507.

Wuest, D.A., & Fisette, J.L. (2015). *Foundations of physical education, exercise science, and sport* (18th ed.). New York: McGraw-Hill.

Wurm, S., & Benyamini, Y. (2014). Optimism buffers the detrimental effect of negative self-perceptions of aging on physical and mental health. *Psychology and Health, 29,* 832–848.

X

Xaverius, P., Alman, C., Holtz, L., & Yarber, L. (2016). Risk factors associated with very low birth weight in a large urban area, stratified by adequacy of prenatal care. *Maternal and Child Health Journal, 20,* 623–629.

Xiang, A.H., & others (2016). Association of maternal diabetes with autism in offspring. *JAMA, 313,* 1425–1434.

Xiao, N.G., & others (2015). Eye tracking reveals a crucial role for facial motion in recognition of faces by infants. *Developmental Psychology, 51,* 744–757.

Xiao, O., & others (2013). A large prospective investigation of sleep duration, weight change, and obesity in the NIH-AARP Diet and Health Study cohort. *American Journal of Epidemiology, 178,* 1600–1610.

Xie, Y., Ho, S.C., Su, X., & Liu, Z.M. (2016, in press). Changes in body weight from young adulthood to middle age and its association with blood pressure and hypertension: A cross-sectional study in Hong Kong Chinese women. *Journal of the American Heart Association.*

Xu, C., & others (2015). Calorie restriction prevents metabolic aging caused by abnormal SIRT 1 function in adipose tissues. *Diabetes, 64,* 1576–1590.

Xu, H., Wen, L.M., Hardy, L.L., & Rissel, C. (2016). Associations of outdoor play and screen time with nocturnal sleep duration and pattern among young children. *Acta Pediatrica, 105,* 297–303.

Xu, H., Wen, L.M., & Rissel, C. (2014). Associations of maternal influences with outdoor play and screen time of two-year-olds: Findings from the Healthy Beginnings trial. *Journal of Pediatrics and Child Health, 50,* 680–686.

Xu, J. (2016). Mortality among centenarians in the United States, 2000–2014. *NCHS Data Brief, 233,* 1–8.

Xu, J., & others (2016). Deaths: Final data for 2013. *National Vital Statistics Reports, 64,* 1–119.

Xu, L., & others (2011). Parental overweight/obesity, social factors, and child overweight/obesity at 7 years of age. *Pediatric International, 53,* 826–831.

Xu, M., Thomas, P.A., & Umberson, D. (2016). Marital quality and cognitive limitations in late life.

Journals of Gerontology B: Psychological Sciences and Social Sciences, 71, 165–176.

Xu, W., & others (2015). Meta-analysis of modifiable risk factors for Alzheimer's disease. *Journal of Neurology, Neurosurgery, and Psychiatry, 86,* 1299–1306.

Xue, F., Holzman, C., Rahbar, M.H., Trosko, K., & Fischer, L. (2007). Maternal fish consumption, mercury levels, and risk of preterm delivery. *Environmental Health Perspectives, 115,* 42–47.

Xue, S., & Xue, Y. (2016). Pediatric obesity: Causes, symptoms, and treatment. *Experimental and Therapeutic Medicine, 11,* 15–20.

Y

Yan, L., & others (2013). Calorie restriction can reverse, as well as prevent, aging cardiomyopathy. *Age, 35,* 2177–2182.

Yang, T.T., & others (2015). Aging and exercise affect hippocampal neurogenesis via different mechanisms. *PLoS one, 10*(7), e0132152.

Yang, T-L.B., Song, S., & Johnson, F.B. (2016). Contributions of telomere biology to human aged-related disease. In M. Kaeberlein & G.M. Martin (Eds.), *Handbook of the biology of aging* (8th ed.). New York: Elsevier.

Yang, Y. (2008). Social inequalities in happiness in the United States, 1972–2004: An age-period-cohort analysis. *American Sociological Review, 73,* 204–226.

Yang, Y., & Kozloski, M. (2011). Sex differences in age trajectories of physiological deregulation: Inflammation, metabolic syndrome, and allostatic load. *Journals of Gerontology A: Biological Sciences and Medical Sciences, 66A,* 493–500.

Yaniv-Salem, S., & others (2016). Obesity in pregnancy: What's next? Long-term cardiovascular morbidity in a follow-up period of more than a decade. *Journal of Maternal-Fetal and Neonatal Medicine, 29,* 619–623.

Yarber, W., Sayad, B., & Strong, B. (2015). *Human sexuality* (8th ed.). New York: McGraw-Hill.

Yasnitsky, A., & Van der Veer, R. (Eds.) (2016). *Revisionist revolution in Vygotsky studies.* New York: Psychology Press.

Yavorsky, J.E., Dush, C.M., & Schoppe-Sullivan, S.J. (2015). The production of inequality: The gender division of labor across the transition to parenthood. *Journal of Marriage and the Family, 77,* 662–679.

Yawn, B.P., & John-Sowah, J. (2015). Management of sickle-cell disease: Recommendations from the 2014 expert panel report. *American Family Physician, 92,* 1069–1076.

Yazdkhasti, M., Simbar, M., & Abdi, F. (2015). Empowerment and coping strategies in menopause women: A review. *Iranian Red Crescent Medical Journal, 17*(3), e18944.

Yazigi, A., & others (2016, in press). Fetal and neonatal abnormalities due to congenital rubella syndrome: A review of the literature. *Journal of Maternal-Fetal and Neonatal Medicine.*

Yen, C.F., & others (2014). Association between school bullying levels/types and mental health problems among Taiwanese adolescents. *Comprehensive Psychiatry, 55,* 405–413.

Yeung, W-J., & Mui-Teng, Y. (Eds.) (2015). *Economic stress, human capital, and families in Asia: Research and policy challenges.* New York: Springer.

Yin, R.K. (2012). Case study methods. In H. Cooper (Ed.), *APA handbook of research methods in psychology.* Washington, DC: American Psychological Association.

Yip, P.S., & others (2015). The roles of culture and gender in the relationship between divorce and suicide risk: A meta-analysis. *Social Science and Medicine, 138,* 87–94.

Yochum, C., & others (2014). Prenatal cigarette smoke exposure causes hyperactivity and aggressive behavior: Role of catecgikanubes and BDNF. *Experimental Neurology, 254C,* 145–152.

Yokoyama, A., & others (2013). Trends in gastrectomy and ADH1B and ALDH2 genotypes in Japanese alcoholic men and their gene-gastrectomy, gene-gene, and gene-age interactions. *Alcohol and Alcoholism, 48,* 146–152.

Yolton, K., & others (2010). Associations between secondhand smoke exposure and sleep patterns in children. *Pediatrics, 125,* e261–e268.

Yoo, K.B., & others (2016). Association between employment status change and depression in Korean adults. *BMJ Open, 6*(3), e008570.

Yoon, S.H., & others (2015). Correlates of self-reported sleep duration in middle-aged and elderly Koreans: From the Health Examinees Study. *PLoS One, 10*(5), e0123510.

Yoshikawa, H., & others (2016). Money, time, and peers in antipoverty programs for low-income families. In C.S. Tamis-LeMonda & L. Balter (Eds), *Child psychology: A handbook of contemporary issues* (3rd ed.). New York: Taylor & Francis.

You, W., & others (2016). Robust preprocessing for stimulus-based functional MRI of the moving fetus. *Journal of Medical Imaging, 3,* 026001.

Young, K.T. (1990). American conceptions of infant development from 1955 to 1984: What the experts are telling parents. *Child Development, 61,* 17–28.

Yu, C., & Smith, L.B. (2016, in press). The social origins of sustained attention in one-year-old humans. *Current Biology.*

Yu, C.Y., & others (2012). Prenatal predictors for father-infant attachment after childbirth. *Journal of Clinical Nursing, 49,* 127–137.

Yu, J., Cheah, C.S., & Calvin, G. (2016, in press). Acculturation, psychological adjustment, and parenting styles of Chinese immigrant mothers in the United States. *Cultural Diversity and Ethnic Minority Psychology.*

Yu, J., Wu, Y., & Yang, P. (2016, in press). High glucose-induced oxidative stress represses sirtuin deacetylase expression and increases histone acetylation leading to neural tube defects. *Journal of Neurochemistry.*

Yu, N.X., Chan, C.L., Zhang, J., & Stewart, S.M. (2016). Resilience and vulnerability: Prolonged grief in the bereaved spouses of marital partners who died of AIDS. *AIDS Care, 28,* 441–444.

Yusuf, S., & others (2016). Cholesterol lowering in intermediate-risk persons without cardiovascular disease. *New England Journal of Medicine, 374,* 2021–2031.

Z

Zachrisson, H.D., Lekhal, R., Dearing, E., & Toppelberg, C.O. (2013). Little evidence that time in child care causes externalizing problems during early childhood in Norway. *Child Development, 84*(4), 1152–1170.

Zamuner, T., Fais, L., & Werker, J.F. (2014). Infants track words in early word-object associations. *Developmental Science, 17*, 481–491.

Zandona, M.R., & others (2016, in press). Validation of obesity susceptibility loci identified by genome-wide association studies in early childhood in South Brazilian children. *Pediatric Obesity.*

Zannas, A.S., & others (2012). Stressful life events, perceived stress, and 12-month course of geriatric depression: Direct effects and moderation by the 5-HTTLPR and COMT Val158Met polymorphisms. *Stress, 15*(4), 425–434.

Zayas, V., & Hazan, C. (Eds.) (2014). *Bases of adult attachment.* New York: Springer.

Zayas, V., Merrill, S., & Hazan, C. (2015). Fooled around and fell in love: The role of sex in adult romantic attachment formation. In W.S. Rholes & J.A. Simpson (Eds.), *Attachment theory and research.* New York: Guilford.

Zeifman, D., & Hazan, C. (2008). Pair bonds as attachments: Reevaluating the evidence. In J. Cassidy & P.R. Shaver (Eds.), *Handbook of attachment* (2nd ed.). New York: Guilford.

Zeisel, S.H. (2011). The supply of choline is important for fetal progenitor cells. *Seminars in Cell and Developmental Biology, 22*, 624–628.

Zelazo, P.D. (2013). Developmental psychology: A new synthesis. In P.D. Zelazo (Ed.), *Oxford handbook of developmental psychology.* New York: Oxford University Press.

Zelazo, P.D., & Muller, U. (2011). Executive function in typical and atypical children. In U. Goswami (Ed.), *Wiley-Blackwell handbook of childhood cognitive development* (2nd ed.). New York: Wiley.

Zeskind, P.S., Klein, L., & Marshall, T.R. (1992). Adults' perceptions of experimental modifications of durations and expiratory sounds in infant crying. *Developmental Psychology, 28*, 1153–1162.

Zettel-Watson, L., & Rook, K.S. (2009). Friendship, later life. In D. Carr (Ed.). *Encyclopedia of the life course and human development.* Boston: Gale Cengage.

Zhai, F., Raver, C.C., & Jones, S. (2012). Quality of subsequent schools and impacts of early interventions: Evidence from a randomized controlled trial in Head Start settings. *Children and Youth Services Review, 34*(5), 946–954.

Zhai, L., & others (2015). Association of obesity with onset of puberty and sex hormones in Chinese girls: A 4-year longitudinal study. *PLoS One, 10*(8), e134656.

Zhang, D., & others (2016, in press). Is maternal smoking during pregnancy associated with an increased risk of congenital heart defects among offspring? A systematic review and meta-analysis of observational studies. *Journal of Maternal-Fetal and Neonatal Medicine.*

Zhang, J., & others (2016). Aging and the telomere connection: An intimate relationship with inflammation. *Aging Research Reviews, 25*, 55–69.

Zhang, L.-F., & Sternberg, R.J. (2012). Learning in cross-cultural perspective. In T. Husen & T.N. Postlethwaite (Eds.), *International encyclopedia of education* (3rd ed.). New York: Elsevier.

Zhang, M., & others (2015). Cognitive function in older adults according to current socioeconomic status. *Neuropsychology, Development, and Cognition B: Aging, Neuropsychology, and Cognition, 22*, 534–543.

Zhao, M., Kong, L., & Qu, H. (2014). A systems biology approach to identify intelligence quotient score-related genomic regions and pathways relevant to potential therapeutic targets. *Scientific Reports, 4*, 4176.

Zhong, P., Liu, W., & Yan, Z. (2016). Aberrant regulation of synchronous network activity by the attention deficit hyperactivity disorder-associated human dopamine D4 receptor variation D4.7 in the prefrontal cortex. *Journal of Physiology, 594*, 135–147.

Zhou, J., & Hearst, N. (2016, in press). Health-related quality of life among elders in rural China: The effect of widowhood. *Quality of Life Research.*

Zhou, Q. (2013). Commentary in S. Smith, "Children of 'tiger parents' develop more aggression and depression, research shows." Retrieved July 20, 2013, from http://www.cbsnews.com/news/children-of-tiger-parents-develop-more-aggression-and-depression-research-shows/

Zhou, Q., & others (2013). Asset and protective factors for Asian American children's mental health adjustment. *Child Development Perspectives, 6*, 312–319.

Zhou, X., & others (2016). A potential tool for diagnosis of male infertility: Plasma metabolics based on GC-MS. *Talanta, 147*, 82–89.

Zhu, H., & others (2016). Polymorphisms in mismatch repair genes are associated with risk and microsatellite instability of gastric cancer, and interact with life exposures. *Gene, 579*, 52–57.

Ziegler, D.V., Wiley, C.D., & Velarde, M.C. (2016, in press). Mitochondrial effectors of cellular senescence: Beyond the free radical theory of aging. *Aging Cell.*

Zielinski, R.E., Brody, M.G., & Low, L.K. (2016). The value of the maternity care team in the promotion of physiologic birth. *Journal of Obstetric, Gynecological, and Neonatal Nursing, 45*, 275–284.

Zigler, E.F., Gilliam, W.S., & Jones, S.M. (2006). *A vision for universal preschool education.* New York: Cambridge University Press.

Zigler, E., Gilliam, W.S., & Barnett, W.S. (Eds.) (2011). *The pre-K debates: Controversies and issues.* Baltimore: Brookes.

Zigler, E.F., & Styfco, S.J. (1994). Head Start: Criticisms in a constructive context. *American Psychologist, 49*, 127–132.

Zigler, E.F., & Styfco, S.J. (2010). *The hidden history of Head Start.* New York: Oxford University Press.

Zirpoli, T.J. (2016). *Behavior management* (7th ed.). Upper Saddle River, NJ: Pearson.

Zisner, A.R., & Beauchaine, T.P. (2016). Psychophysiological methods and developmental psychopathology. In D. Cicchetti (Ed.), *Developmental psychopathology* (3rd ed.). New York: Wiley.

Zosh, J.M., Hirsh-Pasek, K., & Golinkoff, R. (2015). Guided play. In D.L. Couchenour & K. Chrisman (Eds.), *Encyclopedia of contemporary early childhood education.* Thousand Oaks, CA: Sage.

Zuberer, A., Brandeis, D., & Drechsler, R. (2015). Are treatments for neurofeedback training in children with ADHD related to successful regulation of brain activity? A review on the learning of regulation of brain activity and a contribution to the discussion on specificity. *Frontiers in Human Neuroscience, 9*, 135.

Zucker, R.A., Hicks, B.M., & Heitzeg, M.M. (2016). Alcohol use and the alcohol use disorders over the life course. In D. Cicchetti (Ed.), *Developmental psychopathology* (3rd ed.). New York: Wiley.

Benson, P. L., 254
Benson, R., 410
Benyamini, Y., 361
Benzeval, M., 410
Berardi, A., 385
Berchicci, M., 411
Berenbaum, S. A., 131, 231, 233, 234, 255, 256, 309
Berens, A. E., 79, 99
Berg, A. I., 423
Berge, J. M., 264–265
Bergen, D., 188–190
Berger, I., 200
Berger, S. E., 84, 87, 96, 98, 99, 124
Bergman, J. E., 53
Bergman, L. R., 350
Berk, L. E., 148
Berko, J., 158, 164
Berko Gleason, J., 157, 217, 218
Berlyne, D. E., 189
Berman, M. G., 153
Berndt, T. J., 243
Bernie, A. M., 344
Bernier, A., 77, 81, 128, 154
Bernier, E. P., 99
Bernier, R., 201
Berninger, V., 198, 244
Berry, D. J., 175
Berry, J. W., 186
Berryman, N., 386
Bersamin, M. M., 307
Berscheid, E., 322–324
Bertenthal, B. I., 92
Bertorelle, R., 373
Bertrand, R., 339
Beste, C., 200
Betts, K. S., 61
Beuker, K. T., 101
Beyene, Y., 343
Beyers, W., 279, 300, 301
Bhatt, R. S., 102, 103
Bialystok, E., 219–220
Bian, Z., 378
Bianchi, L., 339
Bider-Canfield, Z., 59
Biehle, S. N., 130
Bielak, A. A., 399
Bigelow, J. H., 163
Bigler, R. S., 173, 233, 236
Bindler, R. C., 138, 139
Binet, A., 209
Birditt, K. S., 367, 405–407
Birkeland, M. S., 224
Birman, B. F., 245
Birnbaum, G. E., 322
Bischoff, K. E., 415
Bisgaard, H., 82
Bjorklund, D. F., 37
Bjornsdottir, K., 398
Black, D. M., 381
Black, M. M., 58, 83, 141
Blackford, J. U., 119
Blackstone, S. R., 264
Blackwell, L. S., 250, 251
Blair, C., 154, 169, 175, 208, 213, 226
Blair, M., 205
Blair, S. N., 381
Blake, J. S., 83, 140, 264, 304
Blakely-McClure, S. J., 235
Blakemore, J.E.O., 131, 231, 233, 234
Blanchard-Fields, F., 408
Blanck, H. M., 305
Blanco, C., 224
Blandthorn, J., 58–59
Blankinship, L., 263

Blazer, D. G., 392
Bleeker, F. E., 197
Bliesnzer, R., 323, 365, 405
Blonski, S. C., 357
Blood, J. D., 28
Bloodworth, M., 415
Bloodworth, N., 415
Bloom, B., 216, 217
Bloom, L., 105
Blumberg, J. H., 326
Blumberg, S. J., 326
Blumel, J. E., 343
Bluschke, A., 200
Boden, J. S., 323
Bodner, E., 406
Bodrova, E., 149, 189, 208
Boelen, P. A., 361
Bohlin, G., 116
Bol, T., 366
Bonanno, R. A., 242
Bonazzo, C., 275
Bond, V. L., 137
Bonney, C. R., 206
Booker, J. A., 169
Bookheimer, S., 394
Boot, W. R., 389, 403–404
Booth, A., 103
Booth, D. A., 94
Booth, M., 176, 290
Booth-LaForce, C., 127
Boraska, V., 268
Boraxbekk, C. J., 385
Borchert, J., 91
Borden Maier, V., 41
Borich, G. D., 149, 244
Bornick, P., 58
Bornstein, M. H., 96, 97, 105, 107, 174, 284
Bos, C. S., 198
Bosch, L., 101
Bost, K. K., 127
Bot, I., 342
Botkin, D., 178
Bouchard, T. J., 36, 216
Boulvain, M., 63
Boundy, E. O., 69
Bourassa, K. J., 330, 334, 364
Boutsikou, T., 262
Bovbjerg, M. L., 66
Bowers, M., 376
Bowker, J., 173, 188, 240, 286
Bowling, A., 411
Bowman, N. A., 301
Boyd, M., 259
Boyle, O. F., 220
Braccio, S., 59
Bradbury, T. N., 326
Bradley, R. H., 246
Brainerd, C. J., 206
Brand, J., 349
Brand, M., 374
Brandeis, D., 200
Brandon, A. R., 262
Brandone, A. C., 156
Brandt, R., 375
Branje, S., 282
Brannstrom, L., 239
Bransford, J., 244
Branstrom, R., 331
Brassen, S., 399
Braver, S. L., 183, 329, 330
Brazdova, A., 55
Brazelton, T. B., 83
Bredekamp, S., 137, 160, 161, 163
Brefka, S., 377

Brember, I., 225
Bremner, J. G., 94
Brendel, P. C., 78
Brenner, J. D., 227
Brent, D. A., 296
Brent, R. L., 59
Bretherton, I., 116, 125
Breveglieri, G., 55
Bridges, J. S., 367
Bridges, S. L., 216
Bridgett, D. J., 116
Brigadoi, S., 77
Brigham, M., 202
Bril, B., 87
Briley, D. A., 360
Brim, G., 338
Brim, O., 344, 351, 363
Brimah, P., 303
Brin, S., 161
Brinkman-Stoppelenburg, A., 414
Brinton, R. D., 394
Britner, P. A., 126, 128
Britton, W. B., 206
Broadus, I., 408
Brock, R. L., 184
Brody, G. H., 48
Brody, M. G., 65
Brody, N., 211, 214
Brody, R. M., 308
Broekhof, E., 157
Broges, E., 391
Bromley, D., 223
Bronfenbrenner, U., 23–25, 33, 143
Bronstein, P., 173
Brook, J. S., 284
Brooker, R. J., 39
Brookhart, S. M., 244, 245
Brooks, J. G., 206
Brooks, M. G., 206
Brooks, R., 100, 101
Brooks-Gunn, J., 9, 121, 133, 152, 214, 246, 256, 257
Broskey, N. T., 382
Brothers, A., 336
Brott, A. A., 112
Broughton, J., 105
Brown, B. B., 186, 188, 286, 287, 289, 290
Brown, C. L., 389
Brown, D. A., 152
Brown, H. L., 57
Brown, J. C., 382
Brown, J. V., 70
Brown, M. J., 143
Brown, R., 107, 108
Brown, S., 409
Brown, S. L., 363, 406
Brown, W. H., 142
Brownawell, A. M., 389
Browne, T. K., 55
Brownell, C. A., 113, 123, 125
Bruce, A., 418
Bruce, I., 395
Bruck, M., 152, 153
Brumariu, L. E., 238
Brummelman, J. E., 225
Brummelte, S., 71
Brunell, P. A., 59
Brunton, P. J., 61
Bryant, C., 308
Bryant, J. B., 218
Bryant, R. A., 421
Buchanan, A., 132
Buchheim, A., 126
Buchman, A. S., 382
Buck, M., 131
Budner, R., 337

Bugental, D. B., 37
Buhl, H. M., 300
Buhrmester, D., 243, 285–286
Bui, E., 421
Bukowski, R., 60
Bukowski, W. M., 173, 188, 240, 286
Bulanda, J. R., 406
Bulik, C. M., 268
Bullard, J., 7
Bullock, M., 122
Bumpus, M. F., 283
Bunders, M. J., 51
Burack, J. A., 214–215
Buratti, S., 207
Burchinal, M., 133, 160, 213
Burden, P. R., 244
Burgard, S., 357
Burgers, D. E., 188, 240, 286
Burke, J. D., 294
Burnett, E., 58
Burns, M. A., 91
Burr, J. A., 408
Burraston, B., 294
Bursuck, W. D., 199, 202
Burt, K., 10
Burt, K. B., 15
Burt, S. A., 46
Burton, E., 382
Burton, G. J., 51
Busching, R., 235
Bush, K. R., 175
Buss, D. M., 15, 37, 172
Busschaert, C., 191
Busse, E. W., 392
Bussey, K., 172
Butler, R. N., 398
Butler, Y. G., 220
Butrica, B. A., 405
Butterfill, C., 88
Buzwell, S., 259
Byers, A. L., 392
Byers, B. E., 36
Bynner, J. M., 300–301
Byrd, D. M., 244

C

Caballero, D. M., 338
Cabeza, R., 376, 390
Cacioppo, J. T., 328
Caeymaex, L., 422
Cahill, K. E., 348, 349, 391, 403
Cai, L., 375
Cai, T., 226
Cain, K., 218
Cain, M. A., 58
Cain, M. S., 292
Cairncross, M., 200
Caldwell, K. A., 243
Calkins, S. D., 77, 113, 117, 119, 168, 169, 226
Callaghan, M. E., 375
Callan, J. E., 172
Calment, J. L., 372
Caltran, G., 115
Calvert, S. L., 191, 292
Calviello, G., 394
Calvin, G., 182
Calvo-Garcia, M. A., 53
Camacho, D. E., 274
Camburn, D., 259
Campbell, B., 211
Campbell, K. L., 386, 391
Campbell, L., 211
Campione-Barr, N., 181
Campos, J., 114, 117

Goncalves, L. F., 53
Gong, Y., 205
Gonzales, E., 281
Gonzales, N. A., 8, 9, 15, 186, 187, 254, 291
Gonzalez, J., 399
Gonzalez-Bracken, M. A., 281
Gonzalez-Echavarri, C., 56
Gonzalez-Freire, M., 373
Goodenough, J., 39
Goodkind, S., 235
Goodman, J., 105
Goodnow, J. J., 204
Goodvin, R., 16, 113, 114, 117, 120, 122, 226
Goodyer, I. M., 296
Gopinath, B., 378
Gopnik, A., 103
Gorby, H. E., 389
Gorchoff, S. M., 363, 364
Goswami, U., 105
Gottlieb, G., 40, 47
Gottman, J., 129–130
Gottman, J. M., 129, 169, 243, 331–332, 335
Gottman, J. S., 331
Gouin, K., 58
Gould, E., 315
Gould, S. J., 38
Gouldner, H., 323
Gove, W. R., 329
Govia, I. O., 409
Grabenhenrich, L. B., 57
Graber, J. A., 257, 295
Graber, R., 286
Grace, F. M., 382
Grady, C. L., 390
Grafenhain, M., 167
Graham, E. K., 339, 360
Grant, J., 75
Grant, N., 304
Gratton, G., 386
Graven, S., 81
Graves, C. R., 57
Gravetter, R. J., 30
Gray, P. B., 379
Green, F. L., 156
Green, K. M., 262
Green, M. J., 341
Greenberg, D. A., 42
Greene, C., 179
Greene, R. A., 57
Greene, S., 282
Greene, S. M., 330
Greenfield, E. A., 411
Greenhaus, J. H., 315
Greenleaf, C., 257
Greenwald, A. G., 233
Greer, D., 414
Greer, D. M., 414
Greer, K. B., 181
Gregorson, M., 207
Gregory, R. J., 27
Greif, M. L., 88
Grewal, D. S., 378
Griesler, P. C., 264
Griffin, I. J., 68
Griffin, J. A., 153, 169, 208
Griffin, P. W., 362
Grigorenko, E., 212
Grigorenko, E. L., 16, 28, 47–48, 212–214
Grindal, M., 281
Grinde, B., 37
Grodstein, F., 379
Groh, A. M., 117, 125, 126, 128
Groppe, K., 153, 208

Gross, J. J., 399
Grossmann, T., 194–195
Grosz, E., 236
Gruen, J. R., 198
Gruenewald, T. L., 408
Gruhn, D., 312
Grusec, J., 169
Grusec, J. E., 128, 182, 231, 237
Gudmundson, J. A., 115
Guerra, A. W., 133
Guilford, J. P., 207
Guimaraes, E. L., 88
Gullotta, T. P., 168–169
Gulsahi, A., 340
Gunderson, E. A., 234
Gunn, J. K., 58
Gunnar, M. R., 94, 117
Gupta, S., 326
Gur, R. C., 233
Gurbernskaya, Z., 409
Gursky, O., 394
Gurwitch, R. H., 228
Gustafsson, J-E., 213
Gutchess, A. H., 391
Guthery, A. M., 200
Guthrie, J. F., 142
Guttmannova, K., 267
Guyer, A. E., 118

H

Ha, H. H., 423
Hachinski, V., 386
Hadani, H., 155
Haden, C. A., 153
Hadfield, J. C., 366
Hadland, S. E., 297
Haftenberger, M., 339
Hagekull, B., 116
Hagen, J. W., 161–162
Hagenaars, S. P., 388, 393
Hager, V. R., 42
Hagestad, G. O., 365–366
Hahn, E. A., 338, 359, 411
Hahn, K. A., 56
Hahn, W. K., 77
Haidt, J., 230–231
Hair, N. L., 139
Hakuta, K., 220
Hale, D. E., 196
Halim, M. L., 174
Hall, C. B., 388
Hall, D. T., 316
Hall, G. S., 254, 284
Hall, S. S., 44
Hallahan, D. P., 202
Hallman, S. K., 281
Halonen, J., 302
Halpern, D. F., 233–235
Hamilton, E., 296
Hamilton, J. L., 257, 295
Hamilton, L. D., 358
Hamlin, J. K., 99
Hammond, R., 294–295
Hampson, S. E., 360
Han, J. Y., 62
Han, S. H., 408, 409
Hanc, T., 67
Handren, L. M., 282
Handrinos, J., 173
Hannon, E. E., 91, 92, 95, 96, 98, 99, 270
Hansell, N. K., 296
Hansen, M. V., 384
Hanus, J., 378
Hara, Y., 385

Harada, K., 381
Haran, C., 71
Hardaway, C. R., 187
Harden, K. P., 257
Harhay, M. N., 382
Harhay, M. O., 382
Harkins, S. W., 379
Harkness, S., 128
Harley, A. E., 115
Harlow, H. F., 124
Harmon, R. J., 116
Harper, K. M., 56
Harrington, B. C., 269
Harris, G., 94
Harris, J., 158
Harris, K. M., 303
Harris, P. L., 155, 156
Harrison, C., 373
Harrison, M., 196
Harrison, T. M, 394
Hart, B., 108
Hart, C. H., 161
Hart, D., 122, 275
Hart, W., 323
Harter, S., 166–168, 223–225
Hartescu, I., 379
Hartshorne, H., 171
Hartup, W. W., 240, 243
Harwood, L. J., 82–83
Hasbrouck, S. L., 133
Hasmanova Marhankova, M. J., 423
Hassan, A., 395
Hassan, J., 343–344, 380
Hasselmo, K., 330, 334
Hastings, P. D., 182, 185, 236
Hasvold, P., 340
Hatemi, P. K., 334
Hattenschwiler, N., 205
Hauck, F. R., 81
Havighurst, R. J., 399
Havighurst, S. S., 115
Hawk, S. T., 282
Hawkes, C., 378
Hawrilenko, M., 182
Haxby, J. V., 385
Hay, P., 269
Hayatbakhsh, R., 143
Haydon, A. A., 259
Hayflick, L., 373
Hayslip, B., 338
Hayutin, A., 391
Hayward, R. D., 351, 352
Hazan, C., 320–322
He, C., 93
He, M., 87
He, X., 340
Heard, E., 407
Hearst, N., 422–423
Heatherton, T.F., 157
Heberlein, E. C., 63
Hedayat, K., 418
Hedden, T., 5
Heiman, G. W., 29
Heimann, M., 100, 124
Heimowitz, T., 388
Hein, D., 179
Heinonen, M. T., 42
Heitzeg, M. M., 267
Helgeson, V. S., 172, 173, 323
Helles, A., 201
Helman, R., 403
Helmreich, R., 236
Helson, R., 356, 363, 364
Hemmy, L. S., 376
Henderson, J., 66
Henderson, V. W., 343
Hendricks-Munoz, K. D., 69

Hendriks, A.A.J., 402
Henkens, K., 392
Hennecke, M., 401
Henretta, J. C., 328–329
Henricks, T. S., 188
Henriksen, T. B., 57
Hensch, T. K., 77
Herbers, J. E., 154
Herman-Giddens, M. E., 256
Hernandez, L. F., 395–396
Hernandez-Reif, M., 69, 70, 92
Herold, K., 159
Heron, M., 81
Herrmann, L. K., 264
Hershner, S. D., 303
Herting, M. M., 264
Hertzog, C., 386
Herzog, E., 173
Hess, R., 380
Hetherington, E. M., 24, 183, 184, 239, 330, 334
Heward, W. L., 202
Hewko, S. J., 383
Hewlett, B. S., 132
Heyman, G. D., 224
Hickey, M., 343
Hicks, B. M., 267
Hicks, J. A., 399
Hiekel, N., 325
Higbee, C., 303
Highfield, R., 99
Higo, M., 392
Hill, C., 135
Hill, C. R., 237
Hill, E. M., 224
Hill, K., 16, 47–48
Hill, P. C., 352
Hill, P. L., 315, 360, 362, 402
Hill, T. D., 409
Hillemeier, M. M., 162
Hilliard, L. J., 173, 233, 236
Hillman, C. H., 208, 382, 391
Hills, A. P., 141, 197
Himes, C. L., 337
Hindin, M. J., 303
Hines, F. G., 340
Hines, M., 172
Hinshaw, S. P., 200
Hinze, S. W., 410
Hirsch, B. J., 273
Hirsch, J. K., 380
Hirsh-Pasek, K., 105, 109, 110, 158, 189–191
Hisasue, S. I., 343
Hjern, A., 200
Ho, M. J., 288
Hochberg, C., 377
Hodge, S. E., 42
Hodges, E.V.E., 241
Hoehl, S., 100, 124
Hoeijmakers, L., 376
Hoelter, L., 329
Hoerl, C., 88
Hoeve, M., 283
Hofer, A., 233
Hofer, B. K., 248
Hofer, J., 355
Hofer, S. M., 31
Hoff, E., 104, 110, 157, 187, 219
Hogan, C., 14, 357, 400, 401
Hogan, C. L., 386
Hogan, D., 282
Hognas, R. S., 184, 325
Hohman, T. J., 42
Holden, G. W., 131
Hollams, E. M., 57
Holland, J. M., 421, 422

Hollich, G., 95
Hollister, M., 315
Holme, A. M., 51
Holmes, C. J., 154
Holmes, E. K., 333
Holmes, L. B., 56
Holmes, T. H., 357
Holmin, J. S., 385
Holmqvist, K., 257
Holsen, I., 257
Holt, N. A., 91
Holub, S. C., 141
Holway, G. V., 260
Holzman, L., 147
Honeycutt, H., 40, 46
Hong, X., 376
Honzik, M., 304
Hooyman, N., 10
Hope, D. A., 330–331
Hope, D.A.M., 309
Hoppmann, C. A., 336
Hopwood, C. J., 292
Horgusluoglu, E., 376
Horn, J., 353
Horn, J. L., 345
Horn, M. C., 358
Hosny, K. M., 344, 380
Hostinar, C., 48
Hou, L., 39, 382
Hou, Y., 285
Houston, D., 107, 108, 110
Howard, A. L., 266
Howard, K. S., 72
Howard, L. M., 72
Howarth, G. Z., 123
Howe, G. W., 317
Howe, M. L., 122, 205
Howe, M.J.A., 216
Howes, C., 133
Howie, E. K., 190–191
Hoyer, W. J., 13, 339, 348, 349, 375, 377, 379, 384
Hoyt, J., 208
Hritz, A., 152, 153
Hsin, A., 249
Hsu, H. C., 359, 411
Hu, M. C., 264
Hu, W., 394
Hua, J., 94
Hua, L., 42
Huang, B., 291
Huang, J-H., 306
Huang, Y., 98, 99
Huda, S. S., 60
Hudson, A., 168
Hudson, N. W., 127, 416
Hudson, P., 403
Hudson, R. B., 4, 8–10
Huesmann, L. R., 239
Huettner, D. P., 395–396
Huffman, J. C., 361
Huffman, L. G., 60
Hughes, C., 155–157, 168, 181
Hughes, M., 329
Hughes, M. E., 366
Huhtaniemi, I. T., 344
Hull, S. H., 234
Hulsegge, G., 340
Hunt, S. R., 383
Huppi, P. S., 53
Hur, K., 143
Hurt, H., 58
Huseth-Zosel, A. L., 377
Hustedt, J. T., 161
Huston, A. C., 237, 239
Huston, T. L., 333
Hutchinson, J., 140

Hutman, T., 101
Huttenlocher, P. R., 78, 258
Huxhold, O., 407
Huyck, M. H., 349
Huynh, V. W., 265
Hyde, J. S., 37, 173, 231, 234, 236–237, 263, 308, 325–326
Hymel, S., 242
Hysing, M., 265
Hyson, M. C., 160, 161

I

Ibrahim, J. E., 415
Ickovics, J. R., 262
Igarashi, H., 367
Igualada, A., 101
Ihara, M., 394
Ihle, A., 350
Ikenoue, T., 66–67
Ikram, U. Z., 281
Ingersoll-Dayton, B., 423
Ingram, D. D., 351
Ingul, C. B., 60
Inhelder, B., 144
Innella, N., 142, 195
Insel, P., 7, 304, 305
Insogna, K., 381, 382
Intapad, S., 56
Isaacs, B., 160
Ishak, S., 86
Ishikawa, N., 373
Ishmael, H., 45
Isidori, A. M., 380
Isla, A. G., 394
Issel, L. M., 63
Iwata, S., 69

J

Jaber, L., 200
Jackson, A. M., 179
Jackson, J. J., 402
Jackson, J. R., 63
Jackson, J. S., 409
Jackson, M. I., 142
Jackson, P. A., 375
Jackson, S. L., 26, 32
Jacobs, J. M., 388
Jacoby, N., 28
Jacques, S., 168
Jaffee, S., 231
Jaffee, S. R., 46
Jager, J., 284
Jakobsen, K. V., 91, 123
Jalles, J. T., 317
James, J., 256
James, W., 91
Jankowski, J. J., 152
Jansen, A. G., 46, 379
Jansen, E. C., 256
Jansen, J., 82
Jansen, S. W., 342
Janssen, I., 141, 142
Jantz, T. K., 4, 386, 388, 389–390
Jardri, R., 93
Jaremka, L. M., 342
Jarman, M., 141
Jarnecke, A., 46
Jarosinska, D., 81
Jarrold, C., 205
Jauniaux, E., 51
Jaworski, D., 14, 410
Jeka, J., 84
Jelding-Dannemand, E., 82
Jenni, O. G., 265

Jennings, S. L., 121
Jensen, M. M., 375
Jeon, H., 407
Jessberger, S., 376
Jestadi, D. B., 373
Ji, G., 181
Jia, R., 178
Jiao, S., 181
Jin, K., 376
Jing, Q., 181
Job, V., 251
Johansson, M., 207
John, O. P., 363, 364
Johnson, D. C., 39, 382
Johnson, D. R., 363
Johnson, F. B., 15, 373
Johnson, J. E., 188
Johnson, J. S., 219
Johnson, M. B., 307
Johnson, M. D., 36, 39, 40, 172
Johnson, M. H., 11, 28, 76, 77, 79, 91, 99, 139, 194–195, 219, 258, 259
Johnson, R. B., 26
Johnson, S. P., 91, 92, 95, 96, 98, 99, 270
Johnson, W., 216
John-Sowah, J., 45
Johnston, A. M., 167
Johnston, J., 200
Johnston, L. D., 266–267, 306
Jolly, C. A., 382
Jones, B. F., 312
Jones, E., 137
Jones, J., 160, 161
Jones, J. H., 372
Jones, L., 66
Jones, M. C., 257
Jones, N. A., 115
Jones, P. S., 407
Jones, S., 169
Jones, S. A., 399
Jonson-Reid, M., 180
Jonsson, E., 57
Jopp, D., 411
Jorgensen, M. J., 261
Jose, A., 326
Joseph, J., 36
Joshi, H., 226
Josselson, R., 280
Jouriles, E. N., 184
Juang, L., 8
Juang, L. P., 281, 285
Judas, M., 53
Judd, F. K., 343
Julian, A. M., 358
Julie, F., 157
Julvez, J., 60
Jung, C., 337
Jung, S., 377
Jung, W. P., 89
Jun-Hao, E. T., 373
Jusczyk, P. W., 93, 105
Juster, R-P., 254
Jutengren, G., 241

K

Kackar-Cam, H., 275
Kaczynski, T., 1–2, 4, 5, 10, 14, 16
Kadlecova, P., 31
Kadosh, K. C., 240
Kaeberlein, M., 372
Kaeberlein, M. R., 5
Kaffashi, F., 69
Kagan, J., 114, 116, 118, 119, 127–128, 136

Kagan, S. H., 384
Kahana, B., 407
Kahana, E., 407
Kahn, R. L., 14, 410, 411
Kahrs, B. A., 89
Kakinami, L., 175
Kalanithi, P., 422
Kalish, C. W., 158
Kalish, R. A., 420
Kalmijn, M., 366, 392
Kalsi, D. S., 373, 382–383
Kamat, P. K., 394
Kamiya, M., 395
Kampmann, B., 82
Kan, P. F., 158
Kanakogi, Y., 130
Kanazawa, S., 82
Kandel, D. B., 264
Kandler, C., 312
Kane, J. C., 291
Kang, J. Y., 220
Kann, L., 260, 261, 264, 265, 296
Kantowitz, B. H., 29
Kantrowitz, B., 165
Kao, T. A., 291
Karahuta, E., 232
Karantzas, G. C., 406
Karlamangia, A. S., 342
Karmel, M. P., 122
Karmiloff-Smith, A., 42, 44, 80
Karniol, R., 236
Karoly, L. A., 163
Karreman, A., 178
Karstad, S. B., 168
Kask, K., 375
Kasmark, A. M., 280
Kastbom, A. A., 260
Kastenbaum, R. J., 418, 419
Kathrins, M., 343–344
Kato, T., 68
Katsiaficas, D., 291
Katz, L., 163
Kauffman, J. M., 202
Kaufman, J. C., 207, 312
Kaufman, S. B., 312–313, 360
Kaushik, G., 56
Kavanaugh, R. D., 144, 157
Kavosi, Z., 66
Kavsek, M., 100
Kawakami, R., 339
Kawakita, T., 61
Kawamoto, K, 10
Kayser, B., 63
Kearney, P. M., 57
Kearsley, R. B., 116
Keating, D. P., 272
Keen, R., 88, 91
Keles, S., 358
Kell, H. J., 216
Keller, A., 167
Kelley, G. A., 142
Kelley, J., 382
Kelley, K. S., 142
Kelley-Moore, J., 342
Kelly, A. B., 296
Kelly, J., 239, 334
Kelly, J. P., 91
Kelly, K. R., 157, 158, 217
Kelly, Y., 57
Keltner, K. W., 250
Kemmler, W., 381
Kemp, J., 379
Kempermann, G., 375–376
Kempner, S. G., 249
Kendler, K. S., 46
Kendrick, C., 181
Kendrick, K., 241

McDonald, J. A., 62
McDonald, R., 184
McDonough, L., 103
McDuffie, A., 44
McElhaney, K. B., 283
McElvaney, R., 282
McEvoy, C. T., 58
McFarland, M. J., 330
McGarry, J., 72
McGee, K., 202
McGhee, L. M., 159
McGrath, J. J., 56–57
McGrath, S. K., 70
McGuckin, C., 242
McGuire, B. A., 39
McHale, S. M., 178, 181, 283, 284, 365
McHugh, J. E., 386
McInerney, K., 385
McInnis, C. M., 40
McIntosh, E., 358
McIsaac, C., 287, 288
McKain, W. C., 405
McKay, A. S., 312
McKenna, K.Y.A., 328
McKenzie, G., 393
McLaughlin, K., 417
McLean, K. C., 278
McLean, K.C., 280
McLeod, S., 197
McLoyd, V. C., 187, 281
McMahon, D. M., 53
McMahon, E.M., 297
McMillan, J. H., 244
McMurray, B., 106, 110
McNicholas, C., 235
McNicholas, F., 68
McRae, C., 379
McWhorter, R. R., 404
McWilliams, L. A., 322
Meacham, J., 167
Meade, C. S., 262
Meaney, M., 40, 47–48
Meerlo, P., 71
Meert, K. L., 422
Meffert, C., 416
Mehler, P. S., 268
Meier, E. A., 416
Meins, E., 157
Melancon, M. O., 379
Melhuish, E., 135
Meltzer-Brody, S., 71
Meltzoff, A. N., 100, 101, 233
Memari, A., 201
Menard, L., 104
Mendelson, M., 264
Mendes, A., 421
Mendes, W. B., 113
Mendez-Sanz, R., 394
Mendle, J., 257
Menesini, E., 242
Meng, H., 416
Meng, X., 410–411
Menn, L., 157
Menon, R., 51
Menotti, A., 341
Mercer, N., 294
Mercy, J. A., 143
Meredith, N. V., 138
Merrill, D. M., 364, 368
Merrill, S., 322
Mesman, J., 126
Messiah, S. E., 58
Metcalf, C. J., 372
Meuwissen, A. S., 154
Meyer, A., 139
Mian, M., 76–77

Michael, R. T., 307–309, 344
Miche, M., 407
Mick, P., 378
Mickelson, K. D., 130
Midouhas, E., 226
Miele, D. B., 234
Miga, E. M., 283–284
Miguel-Neto, J., 44
Mike, A., 360
Mikkola, T. M., 378
Mikulincer, M., 320, 322
Milani, H. J., 54–55
Mileva-Seitz, V. R., 48
Miller, A. C., 418
Miller, C., 9, 331
Miller, C. J., 200
Miller, E. B., 161, 162
Miller, E. M., 251
Miller, H. A., 372
Miller, J. D., 224
Miller, J. G., 236
Miller, L. M., 184, 404
Miller, M., 48, 200
Miller, P. H., 19, 21
Miller, P.H., 270
Miller, R. L., 56
Miller, S., 205
Miller, S. E., 101
Miller, S. L., 53
Miller-Perrin, C. L., 180
Milligan, K., 56
Mills, C. M., 167, 224
Mills-Koonce, W. R., 115
Milne, E., 62
Milner, A., 317
Miner, J. L., 133
Miniussi, C., 390
Minkler, M., 366
Minnes, S., 58
Minsart, A. F., 60
Min-Wen, J. C., 373
Mirachi, F. L., 415
Mireles-Rios, R., 283
Mirkovic, B., 296–297
Mirvis, P. H., 316
Mischel, W., 153, 154, 172
Mishra, G. D., 343
Miskovsky, M. J., 303
Mistry, J., 128, 185
Mitanchez, D., 59
Mitchell, A. B., 235
Mitchell, E. A., 81
Mitchell, E. S., 343
Mitchell, M. B., 389
Mitchell, S., 415
Mitchell, W., 134
Miyakoshi, K., 67
Miyawaki, S., 339
Miyazaki, K., 53
Mobley, A. S., 376
Moed, A., 284
Moen, P., 314, 318, 349, 392
Mohr, C., 104
Moilanen, J. M., 343
Moise, K. J., 55
Mola, J. R., 344
Moleti, C. A., 66
Molina, R.C., 262
Moline, H. R., 59
Mollborg, P., 81
Molloy, D. W., 395
Molnar, Z., 376
Molton, I. R., 379
Molyneaux, E., 72
Monahan, K. C., 11, 76, 78–80, 139, 257–259, 272
Monn, A. R., 10

Monni, G., 54
Monserud, M. A., 365, 368, 423
Mont'Alvao, A., 315–316
Montano, Z., 83
Montessori, M., 160–161, 164
Monticone, R. E., 379
Montirosso, R., 123
Moodley, D., 75
Moon, M., 10, 383
Moon, R. Y., 81
Moore, B. S., 153
Moore, D., 40, 288
Moore, D. S., 40, 42, 47, 48–49, 130, 416
Moore, K. A., 263
Moore, M. W., 78
Moore, S. J., 375, 376
Moore, S. R., 257
Moorefield, B. S., 238
Moosmann, D. A., 288
Moraes, C. T., 373
Moran, S., 211
Moravcik, E., 7, 160, 163, 189
Morgan, K., 379
Mori, R., 374
Moriguchi, Y., 153, 208
Moro, C., 104
Morra, S., 204
Morreale, M. K., 422
Morrill, M. I., 182
Morris, A. S., 118
Morris, B. J., 94
Morris, M. C., 295
Morris, P. A., 24
Morris, R. G., 241
Morrison, G. S., 138, 160, 163
Morrison, R. S., 416
Morrison-Beedy, D., 261
Morrissey, T. W., 132
Morrow-Howell, N., 408, 411
Mortimer, J. T., 315–316
Mosher, W. D., 326–327, 329
Mosing, M. A., 402
Moss, P., 131, 266
Motorwala, Z. S., 381
Moxley, J. H., 205
Moyer, A., 326
Mparmpakas, D., 62
Mrkva, K., 231
Mroczek, D., 362
Mroczek, D. K., 342, 362
Mudrazija, S., 410
Mueller, M. R., 204
Muenks, K., 286
Muhammad, A., 40
Mui-Teng, Y., 8
Mulatu, S., 387
Muller, L., 374
Muller, M. M., 384
Muller, U., 21, 153–156, 208, 226, 270, 272
Muller Mirza, N., 150
Mun, M. J., 394
Mundy, P., 109
Munholland, K. A., 125
Munoz, K. D., 83
Murphy, G. G., 375, 376
Murphy, N., 196
Murphy, P. A., 63
Murphy, R. A., 377
Murphy-Hoefer, R., 303
Murray, L., 132
Musameh, M. D., 42
Mussen, P. H., 304
Mutreja, R., 157
Mychasiuk, R., 40
Myers, D. G., 49

Myerson, J., 214
Myowa-Yamakoshi, M., 130

N

Nabe-Nielsen, K., 348
Nadimpalli, S. B., 409
Nadon, N. L., 374
Nagamatsu, L. S., 382
Nagel, B. J., 200
Nahapetyan, L., 235
Nai, Z. L., 360
Naicker, K., 295–296
Najman, J. M., 246, 294
Nakajima, S., 422
Nakawaki, B., 297
Namuth, T., 165
Nansel, J. M., 241
Napper, L. E., 307
Narayan, K. M., 141, 264
Narváez, D., 230, 231
Nasiri, S., 343
Naumova, O. Y., 48
Naveh-Benjamin, M., 385
Naxerova, K., 373
Nechita, A., 216
Nechuta, S. J., 341
Needham, A., 88
Needham, A. W., 99
Neff, F., 374
Negriff, S., 257
Neimeyer, R., 422
Nelson, C. A., 79, 99, 259, 376
Nelson, J. A., 168
Nelson, L. J., 301
Nelson, S. D., 227
Nelson, S. E., 267
Nelson, S. K., 174
Nemet, D., 195, 196
Nes, R., 46
Neugarten, B. L., 399
Neupert, S. D., 359
Neville, H. J., 219
Newman, E., 227
Newport, E. L., 219
Newton, N. J., 356
Ng, F. F., 249, 250
Ngui, E. M., 62–63
Nguyen, P. V., 196
Nho, K., 39
Nicolaisen, M., 364, 408
Nicoteri, J. A., 303
Niederberger, C., 343–344
Niehuis, S., 323
Nieri, T., 281
Nikitin, J., 401
Nimmo, G. A., 373
NIng, K., 201
Nisbett, R., 212
Nisbett, R. E., 213
Nishamura, Y., 130
Nishimura, A., 72
Nishina, A., 257
Nitko, A. J., 244, 245
Niu, K., 340–341
Nixon, S. A., 263
Nocentini, A., 242
Noel-Miller, C. M., 406
Noguchi, H., 376
Nolte, S., 7, 160, 163, 189
Nomoto, M., 396
Norman, J. F., 385
Norman, R. E., 179
Norouzieh, K., 418
Norton, M. E., 53
Nosraty, L., 411

Schorr, I., 236
Schreiber, K. H., 374, 382, 383
Schuch, F. B., 305
Schukle, S. C., 360
Schulenberg, J. E., 268
Schuler, M. S., 294
Schulz, M. C., 405
Schunk, D. H., 226
Schuz, B., 407
Schwalbe, C. S., 294
Schwartz, D., 242
Schwartz, E. G., 82
Schwartz, J. E., 402
Schwartz, S. J., 279, 280, 291, 300
Schwartz-Mette, R. A., 235
Schwarzer, R., 357
Schweinhart, L. J., 163
Scialfa, C. T., 340, 377–378
Sclar, D. A., 200
Scott, M. E., 406
Scotti, S., 415
Scourfield, J., 46
Seay, G., 415
Sebastiani, P., 372
Seccombe, K. T., 326
Sechrist, J., 406
Sedgh, G., 261
Sedmak, G., 53
Seftel, A. D., 343–344
Seibert, A. C., 238
Seidman, G., 69
Seiter, L. N., 301
Selemon, L. D., 78
Selim, A. J., 371–372
Sellers, S. L., 409
Sen, B., 267
Sengpiel, V., 56
Seo, Y. S., 94
Sepanski Whipple, S., 186
Sequeiros, J., 45
Serini, S., 394
Sesker, A. A., 360
Sethna, V., 132
Setterson, R. A., 336, 337
Sgoifo, A., 71
Shaashua, L., 80
Shah, M., 94
Shah, M. K., 63
Shah, R., 143
Shahrokni, A., 403–404
Shamsuddin, K., 317
Shang, L., 195
Shankar, A., 408
Shannon, F. T., 82–83
Shapiro, A., 129–130
Sharaf, M. F., 399
Sharland, M., 59
Sharma, R., 62, 344
Sharma, S., 143
Sharp, S., 423
Shatz, M., 159
Shaver, P., 324
Shaver, P. R., 320–322
Shaw, P., 200
Shaywitz, B. A., 198–199
Shaywitz, S. E., 198–199
Shear, M. K., 421
Shebloski, B., 181
Sheehan, M. J., 178
Sheehan, W. J., 143
Sheinbaum, T., 322
Sheridan, M. A., 204
Sherman, C. W., 407
Sherwood, C. C., 375
Sheth, M., 69
Sheu, M. T., 344, 380

Shi, J., 348, 387, 392
Shimokawa, I., 374
Shin, D. W., 415
Shin, S. H., 179
Shiner, S., 65
Shirazian, T., 63
Shivers, E., 133
Shors, T. J., 376
Short, D., 348, 391
Short, D. J., 220
Shortt, J. W., 282
Shuey, E, 246
Shuey, E., 187
Shulman, E. P., 258
Shuman, V., 113
Shyh-Chang, N., 373
Sickmund, M., 293
Siegel, L. S., 220
Siegel, R. S., 262
Siegler, R. S., 21, 150
Sierra, T. A., 330
Sievert, L. L., 343
Silva, A. C., 66
Silva, C., 277, 278
Silva, K., 272–273, 373, 374
Silva Garcia, K., 141
Silver, N., 331
Silverstein, M., 366
Simbar, M., 343
Simic, G., 393
Simion, F., 115
Simm, A., 374
Simmons, E. S., 201
Simms, S. L., 395–396
Simon, E. J., 36, 41, 42
Simon, T., 209
Simons, L. G., 260, 286, 294, 325, 339
Simons, R. L., 286, 294, 325
Simpkins, S. D., 237, 273
Simpson, E. A., 91, 123
Simpson, G. M., 328, 363
Simpson, H. B., 268
Simpson, J., 121, 127
Simpson, J. A., 285
Sims, J., 402
Sims, T., 14, 357, 400, 401
Sin, N. L., 342
Singer, A. E., 416
Singer, D., 190
Singer, J. A., 280
Singer, M. A., 372
Singh, N. N., 206
Sinnott, J. D., 312
Sirard, J.R., 265
Sirois, F. M., 380
Sirsch, U., 300
Sitterle, K. A., 239
Skerrett, P. J., 382
Skingley, A., 408
Skinner, B. F., 21–22, 33, 100, 107
Skinner, O. D., 284
Skinner, S. R., 260
Skirton, H., 45
Skogbrott Birkeland, M., 257
Skovronek, E., 347–348
Slade, L., 156
Slater, A., 92
Slater, A.M., 95, 96
Sleet, D. A., 143
Sliwinski, M. J., 31
Slobin, D., 106
Slopen, N., 291
Sloutsky, V., 271
Smaldino, S. E., 293
Small, B. J., 388
Small, H., 369–370

Small, L., 141
Small, M., 9
Small, S. L., 106–107
Smetana, J. G., 230, 231–232, 282
Smith, A. D., 385
Smith, A. J., 421
Smith, A. M., 141, 196
Smith, C. A., 66, 99, 199, 202
Smith, C. L., 226
Smith, J., 12, 336, 361
Smith, J. F., 59
Smith, K., 14, 410
Smith, K. E., 405
Smith, L. B., 84, 86, 91, 96, 100, 101, 124
Smith, L. E., 72
Smith, R. A., 16
Smith, R. L., 235
Smock, P. J., 326
Smokowksi, P. R., 296
Smokowski, P. R., 284
Snarey, J., 231
Snedeker, J., 99
Snow, C. E., 220
Snowdon, D. A., 376
Snyder, H., 207
Snyder, J., 294
Snyder, P. J., 343–344
Snyder, W., 157
So, H. K., 196
Soares-Miranda, L., 399
Sockol, L. E., 72
Sodian, B., 155
Sokolowski, M., 39
Soli, A., 365
Solish, N., 339
Soller, B., 297
Solomon, E., 41
Solomon, J., 125
Somerville, L. H., 258, 259, 272
Somerville, S. C., 205
Sommer, T., 8, 9
Sommerville, J. A., 89
Song, F., 393
Song, G. G., 199–200
Song, H., 376
Song, J. W., 53
Song, S., 15, 373
Sontag, L. M., 295
Soomro, N., 305
Sophian, C., 98
Sorbye, I. K., 68
Sorte, J., 140, 141, 196
Soska, K. C., 86
Soto, C. J., 360
South, S. C., 46
Spangler, G., 128
Spatz, D. L., 82
Specht, J., 360
Spelke, E., 98, 99
Spelke, E. S., 98, 99
Spence, A. P., 375
Spence, J. T., 236
Spence, M. J., 93
Spencer, D., 168
Spencer, M. B., 8, 254, 291
Spencer, R. M., 379
Sperling, J., 329
Spiegler, M. D., 21
Spieker, S., 71
Spieker, S. J., 296
Spindel, E. R., 58
Spinrad, T. L., 168–169, 226, 231, 232, 236
Spira, D., 339
Spiro, A., 362
Sprang, G., 366

Sprecher, S., 308
Spuhl, S. T., 148
Sroufe, L. A., 16, 116, 126–128
Staff, J., 315–316
Stafford, E. P., 237
Stahl, A., 105
Stancil, S. L., 56
Stang, J., 60
Stangor, C., 26
Stanley-Hagan, M., 183
Stannard, S. R., 340–341
Starr, L. R., 288
Staszewski, J., 205
Stattin, H., 241
Staudinger, U., 4, 338, 389, 401
Staudinger, U. M., 401
Stawski, R. S., 13, 31
Steck, N., 416
Steckler, C. M., 99
Steele, J., 321
Steffen, V. J., 235
Steffener, J., 387
Steiger, A. E., 224
Stein, P. K., 383
Steinbeck, K. S., 256
Steinberg, L., 176, 257–258, 269, 272–273, 284
Steinberg, R. J., 215
Steiner, J. E., 94
Steinsbekk, S., 141
Stella, F., 395
Stenberg, G., 91
Stenholm, S., 392
Stephanie, D., 157
Stephenson, T., 264
Steptoe, A., 14, 304, 374, 408
Steri, A., 77
Steric, M., 52
Stern, W., 209
Sternberg, K., 207, 322, 324
Sternberg, R. J., 206, 207, 210–214, 216, 221, 322, 324, 335
Sterns, H., 349
Stessman, J., 408
Stevens, C., 151
Stevenson, H. W., 176, 248–249
Stevenson, M., 422
Stevinson, C. D., 379
Stewart, A. J., 356
Stewart, J. B., 235
Stickgold, R., 71
Stifter, C., 117, 174
Stiggins, R., 245
Stigler, J. W., 249
Stiles, J., 51, 98
Stilwell, D., 45
Stimpson, J. P., 363
Stipek, D., 225
Stoel-Gammon, C., 157
Stokes, C. E., 325
Stolberg, U., 116
Stolp, H. B., 376
Stone, A. A., 14, 400–401
Storchova, Z., 40
Stovall-McClough, K. C., 180
Straker, L. M., 190–191
Street, S. J., 141, 197
Strenze, T., 212
Striano, T., 100, 124
Strickland, A. L., 420
Strong, B., 309
Strong, M. M., 323
Strookappe, B., 341
Stroope, S., 330
Strough, J., 336
Stubbs, B., 377
Studer, J., 312

Waldron, J. J., 303
Walhovd, K. B., 375
Walk, R. D., 92, 93, 110
Walker, A., 1–2, 9–10
Walker, L., 230
Walker, L. J., 230, 231
Walker, R., 405
Wall, M., 421
Walle, E. A., 87
Waller, A., 341, 421
Waller, E. M., 296
Walsh, R., 272
Walton, G. M., 251
Wang, B., 45, 196, 257, 267, 282, 339, 376
Wang, H., 226
Wang, J., 261
Wang, M., 348, 379, 387, 392
Wang, S., 378
Wang, W., 327
Wang, Y., 285, 340
Wang, Z. W., 94
Wanigaratne, S., 68
Waqar-ul-Haq, H., 256
Ward, C. E., 81
Ward, L. M., 327
Wardlaw, G. M., 141, 196
Wardle, J., 14, 304
Warr, P., 391
Warren, M. P., 256, 257
Warshak, R. A., 184, 239
Wasserman, D., 39
Wasserman, J., 39
Wataganara, T., 54, 55
Watamura, S. E., 135
Waterman, A. S., 279, 280
Waters, E., 116
Waters, S. F., 113
Watson, G. L., 199
Watson, J., 156
Watson, J. A., 366
Watson, M. W., 178
Watts, A., 381
Waxman, S., 105, 159
Wayne, A., 197
Weaver, J. M., 183, 184
Webb, M. S., 68
Webster, N. J., 407
Webster, N. S., 275
Wechsler, D., 210
Wechsler, H., 306
Weersing, V. R., 295
Weikart, D., 298
Weikert, D. P., 163
Weinberg, B. A., 312
Weinraub, M., 80
Weinstein-Fudim, L., 59
Weisleder, A., 108
Welch, K. J., 327
Wellington, M. A., 360
Wellman, H. M., 155, 156
Wells, B., 333
Wells, E. M., 61
Wells, J. C., 141, 197
Wells, M. G., 225
Wen, F., 197
Wen, L. M., 191
Wendelken, C., 194, 226
Wenger, N. K., 341

Wenger, N. S., 10
Wennergren, G., 81, 82
Wentzel, K. R., 234, 239, 243, 285, 286
Wenzel, A., 61
Werker, J. F., 93, 94, 105
Werner, L. A., 93, 94
Werner, N. E., 188
West, E., 416–417
West, S. K., 378
West, T. V., 113
Westerhof, G. J., 337
Westermann, G., 80
Westmoreland, P., 268
Weststrate, N., 387
Whaley, S. E., 142
Wheeler, J. J., 201, 202
Wheeler, W., 143
Whisman, M. A., 364
White, D. K., 380–381
White, L., 406
White, N., 181
White, R., 153, 154
Whitehead, B. D., 326
Whitehead, H., 123
Whiteman, S. D., 181, 365
Whiteman, V., 58
Whitley, E., 410
Whitton, S. W., 330
Wichstrom, L., 141
Widaman, K. F., 181
Widman, L., 261, 286
Widom, C. S., 179–180
Wigfield, A., 234, 273, 274
Wikman, A., 14
Wild Boy of Aveyron, 103, 110
Wilder-Smith, A., 341
Wiley, C. D., 373
Willcox, B. J., 371
Willcox, D. C., 371
Willette, A. A., 382
Willford, J., 58
Williams, A. M., 45, 75
Williams, D., 408
Williams, J. L., 281
Williams, K. E., 81
Williamson, D., 397
Williamson, J. B., 10, 392, 403
Williamson, R. A., 101
Willis, S. L., 3, 5, 384, 388, 389–390, 403–404, 411
Willoughby, B. J., 325
Willoughby, M. T., 154
Willson, A., 403
Wilson, A. R., 281
Wilson, D. M., 418
Wilson, F. A., 363
Wilson, K. R., 115
Wilson, R. S., 13, 402
Wilson, S., 289
Windelspecht, M., 36
Windle, W. F., 94
Windsor, T. D., 407
Winer, A. C., 113, 114, 117, 120, 122, 226
Winett, R. A., 339
Wingfield, A., 378
Wink, P., 351
Winner, E., 216, 217

Winsler, A., 148
Winsper, C., 242
Winter, W., 204
Wirth, M., 394
Wise, P. M., 343
Witard, O. C., 382
Witherington, D. C., 113, 116
Witkin, H. A., 44
Witt, D., 220
Witt, N., 94
Witt, W. P., 61
Witte, A. V., 389
Wittig, S. L., 82
Woelders, L.C.S., 268
Wolke, D., 242
Wood, D., 362
Wood, J. T., 323
Wood, L. R., 380–381
Wood, W., 172
Woods, B., 399
Woods, D. L., 75
Woods, N. F., 343
Worrell, F. C., 275
Wright, H. F., 240
Wu, J., 42, 340
Wu, N., 275
Wu, T., 305
Wu, Y., 53
Wu, Z., 406
Wuest, D. A., 140, 142, 195
Wurm, S., 361
Wyatt, T., 168–170, 226

X

Xaverius, P., 63
Xiao, N. G., 91
Xiao, O., 379
Xie, K., 374
Xie, Y., 249, 339
Xu, C., 382, 394
Xu, H., 191, 195, 371
Xu, J., 371
Xu, L., 196
Xu, M., 224, 405
Xu, Y., 340
Xu, Y. H., 94
Xue, F., 61
Xue, S., 140
Xue, Y., 140

Y

Yan, L., 382
Yan, Z., 200
Yang, J., 28
Yang, P., 53
Yang, T. T., 376
Yang, T-L. B., 15, 373
Yang, Y., 14, 371
Yaniv-Salem, S., 60
Yarber, W., 309
Yaron, H., 81
Yasnitsky, A., 146–147, 150
Yavorsky, J. E., 130
Yawn, B. P., 45
Yazdkhasti, M., 343
Yazigi, A., 59

Yen, C. F., 242
Yeung, E. W., 409
Yeung, W-J., 8
Yilmazer, A., 373
Yin, R. K., 28
Yochum, C., 200
Yokoyama, A., 42
Yolton, K., 143
Yoo, K. B., 317
Yoon, S. H., 341
Yorgason, J. B., 363
Yoshikawa, H., 9, 186, 292
You, T., 388
You, W., 54
Young, K. T., 82–83
Yu, C., 91, 100, 101, 124
Yu, C. Y., 132
Yu, J., 53, 182, 422
Yu, R., 5
Yusuf, S., 341

Z

Zachman, M., 377
Zachrisson, H. D., 135
Zamuner, T., 105
Zandona, M. R., 39
Zannas, A. S., 48
Zapata-Gietl, C., 280
Zayas, V., 270, 272, 320, 322
Zeanah, C. H., 79
Zeifman, D., 322
Zeisel, S. H., 53
Zelazo, P. D., 153, 154–155, 169, 206, 208, 258
Zelazo, P. R., 116
Zerwas, S., 123
Zeskind, P. S., 115
Zettel-Watson, L., 407
Zhai, F., 169
Zhai, L., 256
Zhang, D., 57, 373, 381
Zhang, L., 58
Zhang, L.-F., 212, 214
Zhang, M., 403
Zhang, Y., 407
Zhao, F., 378
Zhao, J. L., 91
Zhao, M., 212
Zhao, S., 120, 185
Zhong, P., 200
Zhou, J., 422–423
Zhou, Q., 250
Zhou, X., 55
Zhu, H., 339
Ziegler, D. V., 373
Zielinski, R. E., 65
Zigler, E. F., 161, 163
Zimprich, D., 402
Zinsser, K. M., 113
Zirpoli, T. J., 201
Zisner, A. R., 28
Zittleman, K., 244, 245
Zivin, K., 357
Zosh, J. M., 189
Zuberer, A., 200
Zucker, R. A., 267
Zusho, A., 176

Subject Index

Preschoolers. *See* Early childhood
Prescription drugs, 56. *See also* Medication
Pretense/symbolic play, 189–190
Preterm infants. *See also* Low birth weight infants
   explanation of, 68
   methods to nurture, 69–70
Private speech, 148
Project Head Start, 161
Prolonged grief disorder, 421
Prosocial behavior
   gender and, 235–236
   moral development and, 232
Proteins, 40
Proximodistal pattern, 76
Psychoactive drugs, during pregnancy, 56–59
Psychoanalysis, 17
Psychoanalytic theories. *See also* Erikson's psychosocial theory
   Erikson's psychosocial theory, 18–19
   evaluation of, 19
   explanation of, 17
   Freud's psychoanalytic theory, 17–18
   of gender, 172
Psychological age, 13
Psychological measures, 28
Psychologists, 7, 155
Psychosocial moratorium, 279
Psychosocial theory. *See* Erikson's psychosocial theory
Puberty. *See also* Adolescence
   body image in, 257
   early and late, 257
   explanation of, 255
   hormonal changes in, 28
   sexual maturation and, 255–256
   timing and variations in, 257
Punishment. *See also* Child maltreatment
   in early childhood, 176–178

R

Random assignment, 30
Reading
   gender and, 234
   in middle and late childhood, 218–219
Reasoning
   conventional, 229
   hypothetical-deductive, 270
   moral, 230
   postconventional, 229
   preconventional, 229
   social conventional, 232
Recasting, 108
Receptive vocabulary, 105
Recessive genes, 42
Reciprocal socialization, 130
Reflexes, 85–86
Reflexive smile, 115
Rejected children, 240
Relational aggression, 235
Religion
   health and, 351–352
   meaning of life and, 352–353
   in middle adulthood, 350–353
Remarriage
   nature of, 238–239, 330
   stepfamilies and, 238–239
   trends in, 330
Reminiscence therapy, 399
REM sleep, 80–81

Research
   correlational, 28–29
   data collection for, 26–28
   descriptive, 28
   ethics in, 32–33
   experimental, 29–30
   time span of, 30–32
Resilience, factors contributing to, 9–10
Respite care, 395
Retirement, 392
Ritalin, 200
Rite of passage, 290
Romantic love, 323–324
Romantic relationships. *See also* Love
   in adolescence, 287–288
   in early adulthood, 323–324
   friendship and, 287–288
Rooting reflex, 85
Rubella, 59

S

Safety, in early childhood, 143
Same-sex couples, parenting and, 185
Same-sex marriage, 330–331
Same-sex parents, 185, 330–331
Same-sex relationships, 330–331. *See also* Gays; Lesbians
Sarcopenia, 339
Scaffolding, 130, 147
Schemes, 96–97
School dropout rate, 274–275
School readiness, 151
Schools. *See also* Achievement; Colleges/universities; Early childhood education; Education
   accountability in, 244–245
   ethnic diversity in, 247–248
   exercise programs in, 195
   high school, 274–275
   service learning in, 275
   transition to middle or junior high, 273
   for young adolescents, 273
Science achievement, 248–249
Screen time, 190–192. *See also* Television viewing
The Seasons of a Man's Life (Levinson), 356
Seasons of a man's life theory, 356–357
Seattle Longitudinal Study, 346–347
Second-language learning, 219–220
Secure attachment, 125–126, 131, 321
Selective optimization with compensation theory, 401–402
Self
   development of sense of, 121–122
   in early childhood, 166–168
   in middle and late childhood, 223–226
Self-awareness
   in early childhood, 168
   in infancy, 122
Self-concept, 224–225
Self-conscious emotions, 168
Self-control, 208
Self-efficacy, in middle and late childhood, 225–226
Self-esteem
   achievement and, 225

friendship and, 243
   in middle and late childhood, 224–225
   overweight and, 196–197
Self-image. *See* Self-esteem
Self-recognition, 121–122
Self-regulation
   in early childhood, 148
   in infancy, 118–119
   in middle and late childhood, 226
Self-talk, 148
Self-understanding
   in early childhood, 166–168
   explanation of, 166
   in infancy, 121–122
   in middle and late childhood, 223
Self-worth. *See* Self-esteem
Semantics, 158–159. *See also* Language development
Sensation, 89
Sensorimotor play, 189
Sensorimotor stage (Piaget)
   evaluation of, 98–99
   explanation of, 19, 97
   object permanence in, 98, 99
Sensory development
   in infancy, 89–96
   in late adulthood, 377–379
Separation protest, 116
Seriation, 203
Service learning, 275
Sex education programs, 263
Sex in America Survey, 344
Sex-linked chromosomal abnormalities, 43–44
Sex-linked genes, 42
Sexual abuse, 179. *See also* Child maltreatment
Sexual activity
   in adolescence, 260–261
   in early adulthood, 307–309
   in middle adulthood, 345–346
Sexual identity, 259–260
Sexuality
   in adolescence, 259–266
   in early adulthood, 307–309
   gender differences in, 308
   in late adulthood, 379–380
   in middle adulthood, 342–345
Sexually transmitted infections (STIs). *See also* HIV/AIDS
   in adolescence, 261
   explanation of, 310
   statistics related to, 310–311
   strategies to avoid, 311
   types of, 310
Sexual maturation. *See* Puberty
Sexual orientation, 308–309. *See also* Gays; Lesbians; Same-sex relationships
Short-term memory, 152. *See also* Memory
Sibling relationships
   delinquency and, 294
   in early childhood, 180–181
   in middle adulthood, 365
Sickle-cell anemia, 44, 45
Silent Generation, 32
Single adults, 325
Single-parent families, 186
Single-sex education, 234–235
Skinner's operant conditioning theory, 22
Sleep
   in adolescence, 265–266
   in early adulthood, 266, 303–304

   in infancy, 80–81
   in late adulthood, 379
   in middle adulthood, 341
   in postpartum period, 71
   REM, 71
Small for gestational age infants, 68
Smell sense
   in infancy, 94
   in late adulthood, 378–379
Smiling, in infancy, 115–116
Smoking. *See* Tobacco/tobacco use
Social age, 13
Social cognitive theory
   explanation of, 21–22
   of gender, 172
   moral development and, 170–171
Social constructivist approach, 146
Social contract or utility and individual rights stage (Kohlberg), 229
Social conventional reasoning, 232
Social integration, 407–408
Social media, 293
Social orientation, in infancy, 123
Social play, 190
Social policy, 8–10, 132–133, 403–404
Social referencing, 116
Social role theory, 172
Social smile, 115
Social support, in late adulthood, 407–408, 423
Social systems morality (Kohlberg), 229
Social work professors and administrators, 409
Sociocultural cognitive theory. *See* Vygotsky's sociocultural cognitive theory
Socioeconomic status (SES)
   child-rearing practices in, 187
   delinquency and, 294
   divorce and, 184–185
   education and, 161–163, 246
   ethnicity and, 291–292
   explanation of, 8
   families and, 187
   intelligence tests and, 213–214
   tobacco smoke exposure and, 143
Socioemotional development. *See also* Emotional development; Emotions; Personality/ personality development
   in adolescence, 277–298
   aging and theories of, 398–399
   in early adulthood, 320
   in early childhood, 165–192
   in infancy, 113–136
   in middle and late childhood, 235–236
   theories of, 398–402
Socioemotional processes, 10–11
Socioemotional selectivity theory, 400–401
Spatial intelligence, 211
Speech. *See also* Language development
   child-directed, 108
   telegraphic, 106
Spina bifida, 44, 52–53
Spirituality, in middle adulthood, 351
Stability-change issue, 15–16
Stagnation, 355
Standardized tests, 27